Presents

*The World of*
**Professional Golf**
*Founded by*
*Mark H. McCormack*
**2006**

sports · entertainment · media

Editor: Bev Norwood
Contributors: Andy Farrell, Doug Ferguson, Donald (Doc) Giffin, Jim Nantz, Marino Parascenzo

First published 2006
© IMG Operations, Inc. 2006

Designed and produced by Davis Design

ISBN 1-878843-43-5

Printed and bound in the United States.

# Contents

# Introduction

It came as no surprise to me when I was told that Rolex had agreed to assume sponsorship of *The World of Professional Golf.* Having been associated with Rolex for many years, I know the high regard that my friends, the Heinigers, and others in the firm's executive family have always had for the great game of golf. Few companies have supported the game as extensively and in as many ways as Rolex. As do so many of us, I'm sure that Patrick Heiniger appreciates what Mark McCormack gave to golf when he came up with the idea for this one-of-a-kind annual publication four decades ago. Mark was always a visionary and he recognized that there was a void in modern golf libraries. Historians and golf buffs alike had nowhere to turn to easily find in one set of volumes the stories and statistics of professional tournaments that had been played around the world in years past. We talked about it at the time back in the middle 1960s and I encouraged him to go ahead with the project. It came into being in 1967 and has grown in content in concert with the great growth of golf throughout the world and still has no literary peer. Thus, anybody seeking details about any professional tour event anywhere over the last 40 years can find what he needs to know in one of Mark's annuals. I'm sure Mark would be pleased to know that Rolex is keeping his project going. Enjoy this 40th edition.

Arnold Palmer
Orlando, Florida
February 2006

# Foreword
## (Written in 1968)

It has long been my feeling that a sport as compelling as professional golf is deserving of a history, and by history I do not
mean an account culled years later from the adjectives and en-
thusiasms of on-the-spot reports that have then sat in newspaper
morgues for decades waiting for some patient drudge to paste
them together and call them lore. Such works can be excellent
when insight and perspective are added to the research, but this
rarely happens. What I am talking about is a running history,
a chronology written at the time, which would serve both as a
record of the sport and as a commentary upon the sport in any
given year — an annual, if you will....

When I embarked on this project two years ago (the first of these
annuals was published in Great Britain in 1967), I was repeatedly
told that such a compendium of world golf was impossible, that
it would be years out of date before it could be assembled and
published, that it would be hopelessly expensive to produce and
that only the golf fanatic would want a copy anyway. In the last
analysis, it was that final stipulation that spurred me on. There
must be a lot of golf fanatics, I decided. I can't be the only one.
And then one winter day I was sitting in Arnold Palmer's den
in Latrobe, Pennsylvania, going through the usual motions of
spreading papers around so that Arnold and I could discuss some
business project, when Arnold happened to mention that he wanted
to collect a copy of each new golf book that was published from
now on, in order to build a golf library of his own. "It's really
too bad that there isn't a book every year on the pro tour," he
said. "Ah," I thought. "Another golf fanatic. That makes two of
us." So I decided to do the book. And I have. And I hope you
like it. If so, you can join Arnold and me as golf fanatics.

Mark H. McCormack
Cleveland, Ohio
January 1968

# Mark H. McCormack
## 1930 – 2003

In 1960, Mark Hume McCormack shook hands with a young golfer named Arnold Palmer. That historic handshake established a business that would evolve into today's IMG, the world's premier sports and lifestyle marketing and management company — representing hundreds of sports figures, entertainers, television properties, artists, musicians, writers, celebrities and prestigious organizations and events around the world. With just a handshake Mark McCormack had invented a global industry.

Sean McManus, President of CBS Sports, reflects, "I don't think it's an overstatement to say that like Henry Ford and Bill Gates, Mark McCormack literally created, fostered and led an entirely new worldwide industry. There was no sports marketing before Mark McCormack. Every athlete who's ever appeared in a commercial, or every right holder who sold their rights to anyone, owes a huge debt of gratitude to Mark McCormack."

Mark McCormack's philosophy was simple. "Be the best," he said. "Learn the business and expand by applying what you already know." This philosophy served him well, not only as an entrepreneur and CEO of IMG, but also as an author, a consultant and a confidant to a host of global leaders in the world of business, politics, finance, science, sports and entertainment.

He was among the most-honored entrepreneurs of his time. *Sports Illustrated* recognized him as "The Most Powerful Man in Sports." In 1999, ESPN's Sports Century listed him as one of the century's 10 "Most Influential People in the Business of Sport."

*Golf Magazine* called McCormack "the most powerful man in golf" and honored him along with Arnold Palmer, Gerald Ford, Dwight D. Eisenhower, Bob Hope and Ben Hogan as one of the 100 all-time "American Heroes of Golf." *Tennis* magazine and *Racquet* magazine named him "the most powerful man in tennis." Tennis legend Billie Jean King believes, "Mark McCormack was the king of sports marketing. He shaped the way all sports are marketed around the world. He was the first in the marketplace, and his influence on the world of sports, particularly his ability to combine athlete representation, property development and television broadcasting, will forever be the standard of the industry."

The London *Sunday Times* listed him as one of the 1000 people who influenced the 20th century. Alastair Cooke on the BBC said simply that "McCormack was the Oracle; the creator of the talent industry, the maker of people famous in their profession famous to the rest of the world and making for them a fortune in the process … He took on as clients people already famous in their profession as golfer, opera singer, author, footballer, racing car driver, violinist — and from time to time if they needed special help, a prime minister, or even the Pope."

McCormack was honored posthumously by the Golf Writers Association of America with the 2004 William D. Richardson Award, the organization's highest honor, "Given to recognize an individual who has consistently made an outstanding contribution to golf."

Among McCormack's other honors were the 2001 PGA Distinguished Service Award, given to those who have helped perpetuate the values and ideals of the PGA of America. He was also named a Commander of the Royal Order of the Polar Star by the King of Sweden (the highest honor for a person living outside of Sweden) for his contribution to the Nobel Foundation.

Journalist Frank Deford states, "There have been what we love to call dynasties in every sport. IMG has been different. What this one brilliant man, Mark McCormack, created is the only dynasty ever over all sport."

Through IMG, Mark McCormack demonstrated the value of sports and lifestyle activities as effective corporate marketing tools, but more importantly, his lifelong dedication to his vocation — begun with just a simple handshake — brought enjoyment to millions of people worldwide who watch and cheer their heroes and heroines. That is his legacy.

# ROLEX

All truly great players share a common passion rooted in the same pursuit of perfection that has always motivated Rolex. This passion is at the heart of numerous partnerships with exceptional personalities and prestigious events.

Rolex's first venture into golf was the commercial agreement that Mark McCormack completed in 1967 on behalf of his first client, Arnold Palmer. This key moment for McCormack and Rolex marked the beginning of a close and steadfast professional partnership.

We are, therefore, very proud to be associated with *The World of Professional Golf.*

Pioneers in sports sponsoring, we are a known and recognised supporter of men's and women's golf. Partners in the strongest sense of the word, we have cultivated a very close and enduring relationship with the best-known tournaments, including the four Majors. As of this year, we are also sponsoring the Rolex Women's World Rankings.

Year after year, Rolex has been honoured to witness unforgettable moments of intense emotion. We owe this to golfers whose passion and determination are equalled only by their rigour and precision. For that, they have earned our admiration and respect.

Our unwavering commitment will allow us to ensure Rolex's presence on all golf courses where excellence is achieved through mastery of the sport and the will to succeed.

Golf is Rolex!

Patrick Heiniger
Managing Director
Chief Executive Officer
Rolex SA
February 2006

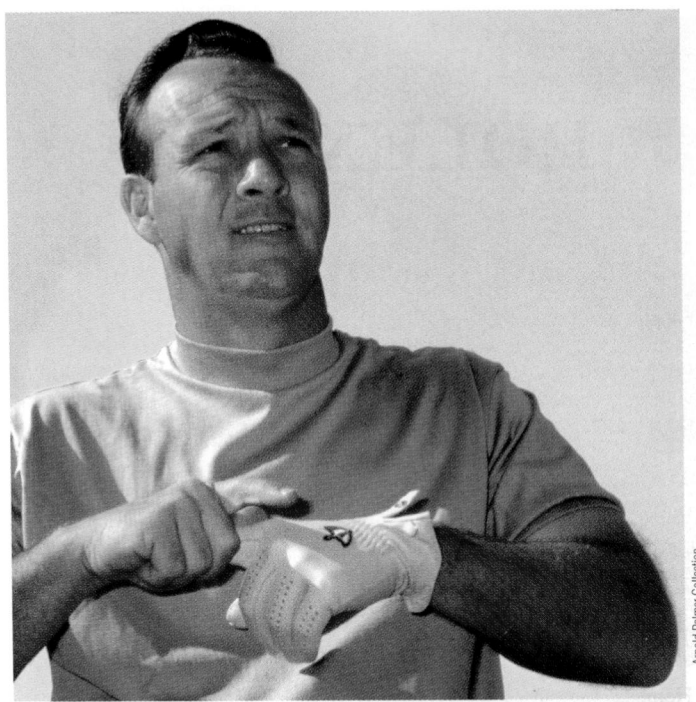

Rolex and Arnold Palmer have been partners since 1967.

Arnold Palmer, Andre Heiniger, Patrick Heiniger and Alastair Johnston of IMG (1984)

Sylvan Mason

Andre Heiniger (left), former Managing Director and Chief Executive Officer of Rolex SA, playing golf with Mark H. McCormack

Annika Sorenstam, McDonald's LPGA champion in 2005 for the third consecutive year

# Rolex Women's World Golf Rankings

Daytona Beach, Florida, February 21, 2006 – Annika Sorenstam is the No. 1 player in women's golf. Not that anyone was prepared to dispute that, but thanks to a joint unveiling by the Ladies Professional Golf Association (LPGA), Ladies European Tour (LET), Ladies Professional Golfers' Association of Japan (JLPGA), Korea Ladies Professional Golf Association (KLPGA), Australian Ladies Professional Golf (ALPG) and the Ladies' Golf Union (LGU), women's golf now has its first official rankings system, the Rolex Women's World Golf Rankings.

The Rolex Women's World Golf Rankings — which was developed at the May 2004 World Congress of Women's Golf — is the first-ever world rankings system for women's golf sanctioned by the five major women's professional golf tours: the LPGA; LET; JLPGA; KLPGA; and the ALPG, as well as the LGU, which administers the Weetabix Women's British Open. The Rolex Rankings are the only official women's world rankings that incorporate player performances from the five major tours and the Duramed Futures Tour, the official developmental tour of the LPGA.

"Rolex is delighted to become the founding sponsor of the Rolex Women's World Golf Rankings," said Jean-Noel Bioul, co-director of sponsorship at Rolex S.A. "The Rolex commitment to golf is substantial and widespread and the addition of the Rolex Women's World Golf Rankings is confirmation of the company's support for the women's game worldwide.

"The Rolex Women's World Golf Rankings create the opportunity to bring all the women's golf around the world together as one family. Golf and Rolex are perfect partners."

The five major golf tours and the LGU developed the Rolex Rankings and the protocol that governs the rankings, while R2IT, an independent software development company, was retained to develop the software for the Rolex Rankings and will continue to maintain the rankings on a weekly basis. The Rolex Rankings will be updated and released every Tuesday following the completion of the previous week's tournaments around the world.

"The Rolex Rankings make nationality, tour membership and amateur or professional status virtually invisible, providing a definitive answer to the question, 'Who are the best women golfers in the world,'" said Carolyn F. Bivens, LPGA commissioner.

The formation of the Rolex Rankings provides a unified and authoritative reference source to the relative performance of the world's leading players. Rolex Rankings shares the established men's world rankings philosophy of awarding points based on field strength and evaluates players performance over a rolling two-year period weighted in favor of the current year with even more importance placed on the most recent 13 weeks. A divisor is used to take into account the number of tournaments played by each ranked player, and players must compete in at least 15 events over the two-year rolling period in order to be ranked.

The official events from all of the world's five major tours will be taken into account and points will be awarded according to the strength of field with the exception of the four major championships on the LPGA Tour schedule and the Futures Tour events, which will have a fixed point distribution. The number of points distributed to each player is dependant upon her finish and scale of points allocated on the basis of the number and rankings of players in the field.

# Rolex and Golf

The Rolex association with golf dates to 1967 when the company presented Arnold Palmer with a gold Oyster Perpetual to honor his achievements on the golf course. This marked the beginning of a loyal and privileged relationship, not only with Arnold Palmer and afterwards two other golfing greats, Gary Player and Jack Nicklaus, but also many of the great talents who have followed them. Rolex has also established relationships with the major organizing bodies of the game.

Evian Masters

Annika Sorenstam

2006 Ryder Cup Captains Ian Woosnam and Tom Lehman

Retief Goosen

Arnold Palmer

The winning 2005 United States team at The Solheim Cup

U.S. Open Championship

Fred Couples

Lorena Ochoa

The Open Championship

2005 Presidents Cup Captains Jack
Nicklaus and Gary Player

Adam Scott

Phil Mickelson, 2005 PGA Championship winner

# 1. The Year in Retrospect

## By Jim Nantz
## ROLEX Ambassador

St. Andrews is universally known as the home of golf, and thus it seems only fitting that so many significant story lines converged on the Old Course during a glorious summer week in Scotland.

The most indelible image of 2005? Jack Nicklaus dressed in navy blue slacks, a white shirt under a red vest and hair that was thinner, shorter and not quite as golden as when he first came to St. Andrews. He strolled one last time over the Swilcan Bridge along the 18th fairway, turning to place his left foot on the stone arch and to wave goodbye to an incomparable career in the majors. He played in 164 of the Grand Slam events and won 18 of them, the record that stands as the definition of greatness in golf.

Nicklaus is never one for ceremony, but he indulged thousands who pressed their faces against shops and packed into balconies, rooftops and every nook and cranny. And he treated them one last time to a birdie on his final hole, even if it still wasn't enough to make the cut.

Two days later came another crossing of the bridge, this one marking the defiant return to the top of Tiger Woods. He had already won the Masters to end his 33-month drought without a major championship, but his second claret jug at St. Andrews answered any lingering doubts that Woods, indeed, had taken his place atop the pinnacle of golf. It gave Woods his second career Grand Slam, along with another feat that further linked him to golf's greatest champion. Woods had won all four majors that Nicklaus played for the last time.

One layer beneath those memorable occasions in 2005 were images of two other men headed in opposite directions, both finding a fork in the road at St. Andrews. The runner-up at the Open Championship was Colin Montgomerie, who had fallen as low as No. 83 in the World Ranking until a dramatic climb to No. 8 by year's end, the pivotal moments coming at St. Andrews. He no longer plodded along with eyes cast to the ground, rather he strode tall and soaked in the deafening cheers of his countrymen in his fruitless attempt to catch Woods. Confidence restored, he returned to the fabled links course 10 weeks later and won the Dunhill Links Championship for his first victory in more than a year.

The other man was Ernie Els, who was lost in the space between his ears. The Big Easy won three times, but otherwise went through the motions one year after coming so close to winning all four majors and getting shut out. St. Andrews proved to be his final competitive event of the 2005 season, as the big South African injured his knee the next week during a holiday on the Mediterranean and had surgery to repair torn ligaments. His year was over, and in many ways, the forced break was just what he needed. It gave Els time to take inventory of his career, to figure out where he was and where he was headed.

It leads to 2006, where Nicklaus won't be around, but Woods is again the dominant image in the game.

## TIGER WOODS

| EVENT | POSITION |
|---|---|
| Mercedes Championships | T-3 |
| Buick Invitational | 1 |
| Nissan Open | T-13 |
| WGC - Accenture Match Play Championship | T-17 |
| Ford Championship at Doral | 1 |
| Bay Hill Invitational | T-23 |
| The Players Championship | T-53 |
| Masters Tournament | 1 |
| Wachovia Championship | T-11 |
| EDS Byron Nelson Championship | MC |
| Memorial Tournament | T-3 |
| U.S. Open Championship | 2 |
| Cialis Western Open | 2 |
| JP McManus Pro-Am | T-6 |
| The Open Championship | 1 |
| Buick Open | T-2 |
| PGA Championship | T-4 |
| WGC - NEC Invitational | 1 |
| Deutsche Bank Championship | T-40 |
| WGC - American Express Championship | 1 |
| Funai Classic at Walt Disney World Resort | MC |
| The Tour Championship | 2 |
| HSBC Champions Tournament | 2 |
| Dunlop Phoenix | 1 |
| PGA Grand Slam of Golf | 1 |
| Target World Challenge | T-14 |

Woods turned 30 on December 30, 2005, and what he accomplished in his 20s was far more than most players could ever dream of doing for an entire career. He had won 46 times on the PGA Tour, 17 other events around the world, and in the category that trumps all others, he already had 10 major championships. That trails only Nicklaus's 18 majors, and the 11 majors won by Walter Hagen. And for those keeping score, Nicklaus only had 30 victories on the PGA Tour and seven majors in his 20s.

And Woods managed to do this with three swings — the raw power that brought him a 12-shot victory at the Masters in 1997, a revamped swing under the eye of Butch Harmon that led to Woods winning four straight majors from the 2000 U.S. Open to the 2001 Masters, and a reconfigured swing under Hank Haney designed to alleviate the stress on his knee and to attempt to match the plane of his backswing with his downswing.

He won two more majors in 2005, yet when someone asked him how close he was to figuring it all out, Woods offered an answer that indicated the best might be yet to come. "You're never there," he said.

No one was entirely foolish enough to write him off after Woods went through perhaps the worst season of his career. He won only once on the PGA Tour, in the Accenture Match Play Championship, and spent more time struggling to make the cut than contending in the majors. The only one under greater scrutiny than Woods was Haney, the Dallas-based swing coach whom Woods met through Mark O'Meara. The week after winning at La Costa, Woods knew it was time to scrap a swing that had brought him seven majors and unparalleled supremacy.

The immediate results were ugly. Woods lost his spot at No. 1 in the world for the first time in five years, replaced by Vijay Singh. There were whispers that his best golf already was behind him at age 29, and snickers that Haney had proven to be the only one capable of stopping Woods. One joke making the rounds early in the year was that players might sue Haney for loss of wages because the PGA Tour was preparing to negotiate a new television contract, and it would be a tough sell with Woods in a funk.

The jokes subsided at the Buick Invitational, his second tournament of the year. He lingered around the lead in soupy fog, starting his marathon Sunday with three straight bogeys but never falling too far behind. Woods let others make the mistakes, then got away with one of his own. With a one-shot lead playing the par-five 18th on the South Course at Torrey Pines, Woods went for the green with a two iron and hit it so badly that it turned out good, landing in a narrow strip of fairway to the right of a pond. He rapped his 18-foot birdie putt too hard, but it was on the right line and fell for a three-shot victory, his first in a stroke-play event in 16 months.

Then came perhaps the best duel of the year, in the Ford Championship, a titanic battle against Phil Mickelson on the Blue Monster at Doral, filled with bravado and power, not ending until Woods made a five-foot par putt on the final hole for a one-stroke victory. He hammered a three wood some 300 yards into 25 feet on the par-five 12th for an eagle to take the lead for the first time. And right when it appeared that Woods had let Mickelson back into the tournament by missing a short putt on the 15th, he drained a 35-footer for birdie on the next hole that proved to be the margin.

"With all the feelings I have about losing today, this was probably the best thing that could have happened to me heading into the majors," Mickelson said. "I just knew I was going to win today and when I didn't, it was a real slap in the face. Because I'm going to work my tail off to salvage a couple more shots. When I come back to The Players Championship and the Masters, I'm going to be ready."

Lefty would have to wait longer than that. Woods, meanwhile, kept right on rolling. He had won his three previous Masters by taking the lead on Saturday. Not this time, but only because rain kept the third round from finishing. In the best golf hardly anyone saw, Woods stormed into the lead Sunday morning with four straight birdies — with three from the previous day, that matched the Masters record of seven in a row — and appeared to be on the verge of a record score for the majors. No one had ever shot lower than 63, and Woods already was nine under par with five holes to play. He lost his momentum with a three-putt bogey and had to settle for a 65, but that was enough for a three-shot lead over Chris DiMarco.

The final round showed that while Woods remains the best closer in golf, this was a different cat. His chip-in for birdie on the 16th hole, a shot that became part of the rich legacy at Augusta National when it paused on the lip of the cup before dropping dramatically, was sheer magic. The next two holes were a mess, bogeys on both of them to slip into a playoff.

Facing the very real possibility of choking, Woods answered with his two best swings of the week, and what he considers his best two swings of the year — a three wood to the fairway, an eight iron that covered the flag and dropped 15 feet behind the hole for a birdie on the 18th hole to win the sudden-death playoff.

"My two best golf shots of the week," Woods said. "You can think of 16 all you want, but if 18 doesn't happen, then (the Masters is) DiMarco's."

Order restored? Not quite. It wasn't up there with death and taxes, but it was a good bet that Woods would be somewhere on the golf course when the weekend rolled around at the EDS Byron Nelson Championship. He had missed only one cut in his career, at the 1997 Bell Canadian Open at Royal Montreal, and had survived a dozen or so close calls. He broke Nelson's record on the PGA Tour by making his 114th consecutive cut at the end of 2003, and the streak was at 142 when Woods began to grind along the back nine at Cottonwood Valley.

A three-putt from 20 feet for bogey on the 13th. Another bogey from the bunker after a careless approach on the 15th. He was on the cut line playing the 18th hole, from the middle of the fairway, when his seven iron rode the right-to-left wind into a bunker. He blasted out to 15 feet, studied the putt from both sides of the hole and pulled the trigger. Then, a strange thing happened. He missed. For the first time in nearly eight years, Woods had a weekend off. Players gathered around televisions in the locker room, expecting him to pull it off as he has done so many times in his career.

"It's probably more impressive than all the tournaments he's won," Jesper Parnevik said. "Most guys out here, you have one bad day and you go home. Even on a bad day, he was able to scramble around and make cuts. He probably has the toughest heart of anyone who ever played this game. That record will never be broken again."

Woods didn't finish outside the top four over the next three months, even though his game was rarely hitting on all cylinders. His putter let him down at Pinehurst No. 2 in the U.S. Open, and he was second, two strokes behind. The infamous turtleback greens of Donald Ross left Woods tentative all week, and he finished at the bottom in putting statistics. The biggest setback was when he missed an eight-foot par putt on the 16th hole to fall two shots behind. Needing a birdie on the 17th, he rammed it six feet by the hole and three-putted for bogey.

He had no such problems at St. Andrews, where Woods went wire-to-wire for the third time in a major championship (the other two came at the 2000 and 2002 U.S. Opens). He never found a bunker when he won by eight shots at St. Andrews in 2000, and that streak came to an end on the seventh hole of the first round, when he hit a driver into the bunker. No problem. He blasted out to a few feet and made birdie, shot 66 and was only briefly challenged on Saturday by the resurgent Montgomerie.

There was nothing spectacular about this Open Championship, merely a methodical dismantling of the field. The pivotal shot was a bump-and-run up the throat of the green for birdie on the 12th. The best shots came on the practice range. While warming up, Woods's first four wedges hit the right zero on the 100-yard sign. It was such an exhibition that Haney told caddie Steve Williams, "You might want to tell him to aim away from the flag." Williams thought he was joking, and sure enough, the first time

Woods was inside 100 yards, his wedge hopped off the flag and rolled off the shelf. He had that much control of his game, winning by five shots.

It wasn't just another major, giving him 10 for his career. Counting his three U.S. Amateurs, it was his 13th, equaling the total of Bobby Jones, and just seven behind Nicklaus's 20. Most importantly, it was validation to those who questioned why he would tinker with a swing that had brought so much success. And it was vindication for Woods and Haney, who had been mocked so much during the lean times while the swing changes took hold.

"I've been criticized for the last couple of years. 'Why would I change my game?' This is why," Woods said. "First, second and first in the last three majors. That's why."

Woods left to meet with officials from the Royal & Ancient Golf Club for the traditional champagne toast, and Haney lingered behind in the press center, surrounded by reporters. There was a tear in his eye for a quiet, proud man who skin can be like onion paper when it comes to criticism, but who cared only about his pupil's progress. The questions shifted from "What have you done to him?" to "How did you do it?"

"He's not going to ever be satisfied with getting there," Haney said. "He's not looking for 'getting there.' He's looking for getting better. That's what he looks for every day."

Woods again stole the show at the PGA Championship, at least on Friday when he nearly missed the cut. He made birdie on the par-five 18th to make the cut on the number. He was 12 strokes behind Mickelson, and nearly made that up on the last two days until he ran out of time and holes. Still, he was the clubhouse leader at two under par when play was suspended by storms, then darkness.

That meant Woods had to return to Baltusrol on Monday morning to make sure either Mickelson, Thomas Bjorn, Steve Elkington, Retief Goosen and Davis Love didn't drop enough shots among them to force a playoff. Or did it? Turns out Woods did his own math, figured it was virtually impossible that all those players would make bogey over the final three holes, so he went home to Florida.

He won twice more on the PGA Tour the rest of the year, both times in the World Golf Championships. A sharp-breaking birdie on the 16th hole at Firestone South gave him a one-shot victory in the NEC Invitational in Akron, Ohio, and another stirring duel, this time with John Daly, led to victory in the American Express Championship at Harding Park in San Francisco. It was perhaps the most empty feeling of any trophy he held, as Woods thought he was doomed for second when Daly lined up a 15-foot birdie putt for the win on the second playoff hole. It went three feet by, and Daly missed that to hand the title to Woods. The victory gave Woods 10 titles in the World Golf Championship out of 19 starts.

He ended the season with six victories — eight, including the Dunlop Phoenix in Japan and the four-man, 36-hole PGA Grand Slam in Hawaii — more than $10 million to win the PGA Tour's money title ($12 million worldwide), and far fewer questions about the state of his game.

"If he keeps his desire the way it is, there are no limits for how good he can be," Bjorn said. "He was dominant from the day he came out. We were well aware we had someone special on our hands."

# PHIL MICKELSON

| EVENT | POSITION |
|---|---|
| Buick Invitational | T-56 |
| Bob Hope Chrysler Classic | T-12 |
| FBR Open | 1 |
| AT&T Pebble Beach National Pro-Am | 1 |
| WGC - Accenture Match Play Championship | T-9 |
| Ford Championship at Doral | 2 |
| The Players Championship | T-40 |
| BellSouth Classic | 1 |
| Masters Tournament | 10 |
| Wachovia Championship | T-7 |
| EDS Byron Nelson Championship | T-14 |
| Bank of America Colonial | T-26 |
| Booz Allen Classic | T-29 |
| U.S. Open Championship | T-33 |
| Barclays Scottish Open | T-44 |
| The Open Championship | T-60 |
| The International | T-10 |
| PGA Championship | 1 |
| WGC - NEC Invitational | T-51 |
| 84 Lumber Classic | T-28 |
| WGC - American Express Championship | T-29 |
| Michelin Championship at Las Vegas | MC |
| PGA Grand Slam of Golf | 2 |

Mickelson has his own set of special qualities, starting with his ability to take it low without warning. He ended his breakthrough season in 2004, when he won his first major at the Masters, by shooting a 59 in the PGA Grand Slam. And it didn't take him long to warm up for what had all the trappings of another big year. It started in the Arizona desert, when Mickelson shot a 60 in the second round of the FBR Open on the TPC at Scottsdale and won by five strokes.

Even more impressive was his opening round at the AT&T Pebble Beach National Pro-Am the following week, when he shot 62 at Spyglass Hill, considered to be the toughest track in northern California. That broke the course record by two strokes, and it got everyone's attention. Kevin Sutherland was playing Poppy Hills that day, and even he had a good idea what was going on.

"We were on the 18th tee, and it's amazing to say this, but we heard a roar," Sutherland said. "That's got to be a couple miles away. We heard it pretty easily, and I thought it can only be one person. I'm not sure it was him, but a 62 at Spyglass? I'm sure it was."

Mickelson found his groove early, and when he followed that up with a 54-hole lead at Doral, it marked 10 consecutive rounds in stroke play that his name was atop the leaderboard. He relished a chance to go head-to-head with Woods at Doral, just like everyone else. And it crushed him to see his chip from just off the 18th green lip out, leaving him one shot behind. But it was hardly the end of him.

While most players spend the week before a major practicing, Mickelson prefers to prepare by competing, even if the weather is miserable. It was on the TPC at Sugarloaf, forcing the BellSouth Classic to be extended to a Monday and held over 54 holes. Mickelson was part of a five-man playoff and hardly looked like a winner when Jose Maria Olazabal twice had putts inside five feet to win, missing them both. Mickelson won the playoff, his third victory in six starts, with the heart of the season approaching.

The only news Mickelson made at Augusta National as the defending champion was his flap with Vijay Singh over spike marks. It happened Friday when the first round was being completed. Singh was in the group behind Mickelson, noticed large spike marks and figured it had to be Lefty. He called over a rules official, who then approached Mickelson in the 13th fairway and asked to see the soles of his shoes. The spikes were within regulation, but Mickelson felt Singh was out of line for the way it was handled. They later argued in the Champions Room at Augusta National, the only fight that either of them put up the rest of the week.

Mickelson was not much of a factor the rest of the year, taking himself out of contention at Pinehurst No. 2 with a 41 on his first nine Friday in the second round on his way to a 77, his highest U.S. Open score in 11 years. He was an afterthought at St. Andrews, finishing in a tie for 60th. No one had any reason to believe that the PGA Championship at Baltusrol would be any different. Just like the other majors, Mickelson showed up a week early for three days of painstaking practice, rounds that often lasted as many as eight hours. This time, practice paid off.

"I really want to put everything I have into finishing off the year right," he said.

Adventures were not in short supply. He played the sixth hole down the adjacent 17th fairway, then hit a towering wedge from 92 yards over the trees and the spectators to about five feet, exchanging high-fives with the gallery as he ambled to the green. There was no doubt who the favorite was that week. Mickelson didn't disappoint them, either, building a three-shot lead going into the weekend, then losing some ground to be tied with Davis Love heading to Sunday.

The PGA of America tried to capture a large television audience and sent the leaders off at 3 p.m., even though the forecast was rife with thunderstorms. Sure enough, a storm delay kept a dozen players from finishing until Monday, the first time the fourth major had gone five days since Bob Tway won in 1986 at Inverness.

Mickelson's moment came on the final hole. He was tied with Bjorn and Elkington as he stood on the 18th tee, needing a birdie to win. He cracked the best drive of the week, leaving himself a three wood to the green. Mickelson spotted a plaque in the fairway to commemorate the one iron Nicklaus hit in 1967 to win the U.S. Open. He reached over and tapped it twice for good luck, not that he needed any.

His shot came up just short in the right rough, a shot Mickelson had practiced as a boy in his backyard in San Diego. He hit a flop to within two feet for a tap-in birdie and his second major title. It was just what he needed to prove he would do all he could to stop Woods's assault on the majors. Other than Woods, Mickelson became the first player since Nick Faldo (1989-90) to win majors in consecutive years.

"He's not a one-major guy, he's a 10-major guy," Bjorn said. "And it's going to be easier and easier for him to win them now."

## VIJAY SINGH

| EVENT | POSITION |
|---|---|
| Mercedes Championships | T-5 |
| Sony Open in Hawaii | 1 |
| Buick Invitational | T-24 |
| FBR Open | T-11 |
| AT&T Pebble Beach National Pro-Am | MC |
| WGC - Accenture Match Play Championship | T-17 |
| Ford Championship at Doral | T-3 |
| Honda Classic | T-2 |
| Bay Hill Invitational | T-2 |
| The Players Championship | T-12 |
| Masters Tournament | T-5 |
| Shell Houston Open | 1 |
| Zurich Classic of New Orleans | T-21 |
| Wachovia Championship | 1 |
| EDS Byron Nelson Championship | T-3 |
| Memorial Tournament | MC |
| Booz Allen Classic | T-29 |
| U.S. Open Championship | T-6 |
| Barclays Classic | T-7 |
| Cialis Western Open | T-13 |
| The Open Championship | T-5 |
| Buick Open | 1 |
| PGA Championship | T-10 |
| WGC - NEC Invitational | T-3 |
| Bell Canadian Open | T-7 |
| 84 Lumber Classic | T-13 |
| WGC - American Express Championship | T-6 |
| Funai Classic at Walt Disney World Resort | MC |
| Chrysler Championship | MC |
| The Tour Championship | T-4 |
| HSBC Champions Tournament | T-5 |
| PGA Grand Slam of Golf | 4 |

Singh remains stuck on three majors.

By almost every account, it was a successful year, and not a bad encore from a 2004 season in which the 42-year-old Fijian won nine times, became golf's first $10 million man and replaced Woods at No. 1 in the world. Singh won his second start of the year at the Sony Open with a clutch birdie on the 72nd hole, finished the year with four victories, won over $8 million to finish second on the money list and had 18 finishes in the top 10. He also joined Woods as the only players to finish in the top 10 at all four majors.

But Singh knew it would be tough to stay on top. He knew everyone was gunning for him.

"I feel like I'm in an open plain and ... all you see is just the horizon," Singh said at the end of last year. "I feel like I'm running and everybody is chasing me. How fast can I run? How long can I stay up there? Sooner or later, I'm going to get tired and guys are going to catch me. I want to keep ahead of the pack as long as possible, and that's the battle I'm going to face."

Singh won the Sony Open by making a clutch par putt on the 15th hole, and hitting a mammoth tee shot on the par-five 18th to set up a birdie for a one-shot victory. And he had a chance to win twice more before the Masters until he got in his way. At the Honda Classic, he missed a two-foot par putt in a playoff to lose to Padraig Harrington, and at the Bay Hill Invitational, Singh went after the flag on the 18th hole and put it in the water.

His victories were equally dramatic, beating Daly in a playoff at the Shell Houston Open, and outlasting Jim Furyk and Sergio Garcia two weeks later in a playoff at the Wachovia Championship. That gave him three victories in the first five months, although he lost the No. 1 ranking to Woods along the way.

"I've done away with trying to be No. 1," Singh said. "It seems like I've got to win five times to get up there. I just want to go out there and win golf tournaments."

Their biggest showdown came at the Buick Open in August, and it was a statement from Singh that while he has yielded the top ranking, he wasn't about to back down. Paired with Woods in the third round, he shot 63 to beat Woods by seven strokes and cruise to his fourth victory of the year.

Still, they seemed somewhat hollow without a major title to go with them. And while he was in the top 10 at all four majors, looks are deceiving. The only noise he made at Augusta National was his argument with Mickelson, which nearly became physical depending on who was telling the story. Only former Masters champions were present. He never broke par at Pinehurst No. 2. He finished seven shots behind Woods at St. Andrews, and while he had an outside chance at Baltusrol, he returned Monday morning and made bogey on two of his three holes.

As his season concluded, Singh failed to win any of his five matches at the Presidents Cup, earning 1½ points through three halves. On the final day, he told officials to have a cart ready to bring Couples back to the clubhouse on about the 12th hole, yet he lost to Couples on a dramatic birdie putt at the final hole.

Singh still struck the ball beautifully, and was fourth on the PGA Tour in greens in regulation. Success depended largely on his putting, and it was a sore spot most of the year. He missed the cut four times, twice when he was the defending champion (Pebble Beach and the Chrysler Championship at Tampa). And while most players would love to have the kind of season Singh had, he asked himself tough questions at year's end.

"I think I got very complacent," said Singh, reputed to be the hardest working man in golf. "I worked really hard last year, and toward the end of this year, I kind of slowed down with the way I was practicing and the way I was working out. My mind wasn't as free, where I could just go out there and play golf and not worry about anything. There was a lot more obligations to do, and it kind of got in the way."

In his eyes, he paid for his success.

# MICHAEL CAMPBELL

| EVENT | POSITION |
|---|---|
| Heineken Classic | MC |
| Holden New Zealand Open | MC |
| Carlsberg Malaysian Open | MC |
| Dubai Desert Classic | MC |
| Qatar Masters | MC |
| TCL Classic | T-12 |
| Johnnie Walker Classic | T-3 |
| BMW Asian Open | T-46 |
| Daily Telegraph Dunlop Masters | 4 |
| Nissan Irish Open | MC |
| BMW Championship | T-8 |
| Celtic Manor Wales Open | T-15 |
| U.S. Open Championship | 1 |
| Smurfit European Open | T-25 |
| JP McManus Pro-Am | T-6 |
| The Open Championship | T-5 |
| Deutsche Bank Players' Championship | T-14 |
| PGA Championship | T-6 |
| WGC - NEC Invitational | 68 |
| Volkswagen Masters China | 2 |
| Linde German Masters | T-36 |
| HSBC World Match Play | 1 |
| WGC - American Express Championship | T-46 |
| Volvo Masters | 14 |
| HSBC Champions Tournament | T-10 |
| Dunlop Phoenix | T-13 |
| PGA Grand Slam of Golf | 3 |
| Australian PGA Championship | 13 |
| Target World Challenge | T-3 |

For Michael Campbell, it was all about patience and perseverance. His potential was undeniable 10 years ago at St. Andrews when he made a miraculous escape from the Road Hole bunker in the third round to save par and led going into the final round of the Open. He stumbled to a 76, then slowly vanished through a series of injuries, shattered confidence and bad play. There were no indications this would be a breakthrough year, especially when the 36-year-old from New Zealand missed the cut in his first five tournaments.

Campbell made it to Pinehurst No. 2 through the first U.S. Open qualifier held in Europe, although his expectations could not have been terribly high. Campbell had not made a cut in the U.S. Open since 2000 at Pebble Beach. No one paid much attention to him the first three days, and he entered the final round four shots out of the lead.

But first came the quick collapse by Jason Gore, then a shocking one from Retief Goosen. Olin Browne faded, too, and suddenly Campbell found himself atop the leaderboard with Woods making a charge. Woods was eight strokes out of the lead walking up the third fairway, but was only two behind after a birdie on the 11th. Campbell kept reminding himself to focus on every shot, and he made frequent trips to the port-a-loo to do eye exercises. Whatever he was doing worked, as he made a birdie on the toughest hole, No. 12, to restore some calm, not to mention a cushion.

The greatest test came on the par-three 15th, with his ball semi-plugged in the bunker, a shot so difficult that anything struck slightly too hard or too soft likely would roll off the green. Bogey looked certain. Double bogey was not out of the question. Using a tip from Singh earlier in the week, Campbell's bunker shot stopped six feet away for a par, and he let Woods do the rest by self-destructing with bogeys on the 16th and 17th. Campbell made a meaningless bogey on the 18th, but when he tapped in for a two-shot victory, the magnitude of the moment hit him.

"I stayed patient for 10 years, and I went through some ups and downs, some injuries, missing cuts, missing tournaments," Campbell said. "But deep down inside, I knew that I had something in me to do something special."

He moved up 73 spots in the World Ranking, from No. 89 to No. 16 at the end of the year. Campbell was the first Kiwi to win a major since Bob Charles at the 1963 British Open, and he re-emerged as a threat. He lingered at St. Andrews and tied for fifth, and finished strong at the PGA Championship to tie for sixth. He cashed in later in the year at the HSBS World Match Play Championship at Wentworth, winning 2 and 1 over Paul McGinley. Those were his only two victories of the year, but he felt like a world-beater considering how far he had come.

"Twelve months ago, I sat down and wrote out a list of my thoughts for the year, and they're pretty negative things," Campbell said. "The last thing I wrote down was, 'I've had enough of this game.' I wrote down these thoughts and I said, 'This is pretty negative.' I ripped the piece of paper up and from that point on, I changed my attitude. People have said to me, 'What's gone on the last six months?' Basically, I just changed myself. Every thought I had, every step I took, it was more positive."

## COLIN MONTGOMERIE

| EVENT | POSITION |
| --- | --- |
| Caltex Masters | T-2 |
| Heineken Classic | T-11 |
| Nissan Open | T-5 |
| Dubai Desert Classic | 4 |
| TCL Classic | 6 |
| Standard Chartered Indonesia Open | T-4 |
| Johnnie Walker Classic | T-6 |
| BMW Asian Open | T-31 |
| Daily Telegraph Dunlop Masters | T-24 |
| Nissan Irish Open | T-28 |
| BMW Championship | T-11 |
| Celtic Manor Wales Open | MC |
| U.S. Open Championship | T-42 |
| Open de France | T-17 |
| Smurfit European Open | T-2 |

| | |
|---|---|
| JP McManus Pro-Am | T-34 |
| Barclays Scottish Open | T-18 |
| The Open Championship | 2 |
| Johnnie Walker Championship at Gleneagles | MC |
| PGA Championship | MC |
| WGC - NEC Invitational | T-9 |
| Linde German Masters | MC |
| HSBC World Match Play | T-9 |
| Dunhill Links Championship | 1 |
| WGC - American Express Championship | T-3 |
| Open de Madrid | T-8 |
| Volvo Masters | T-3 |
| HSBC Champions Tournament | T-40 |
| UBS Hong Kong Open | 1 |
| Target World Challenge | T-14 |

Campbell wasn't the only player who made a surge up the World Ranking, who found himself lower than he ever imagined and then brought himself back to where he always felt he belonged. Montgomerie not only was battling confidence, but a personal life that had been shattered, allegations of misconduct in Indonesia and the harsh fact he was getting older.

He struggled through a very public divorce in 2004, and he started the new season at No. 81 in the world. He was in such dire position that Montgomerie had to travel in search of World Ranking points, hopeful it would be enough to get into The Players Championship and the Masters. He failed on both accounts. The 42-year-old Scot went to the Indonesian Open during the week of The Players Championship for one last shot at getting into the Masters. Instead, it led to one of the biggest controversies of his career.

His approach shot landed in the shaggy collar of a bunker, leaving him a lie so awkward that Montgomerie shifted his feet for nearly a minute trying to figure out how to play his chip. Then, the siren sounded because of approaching storms. Montgomerie stomped off the course without marking his ball, and it was gone when he returned the next day. Under the rules, he dropped it where he thought it had been, but then had no trouble hitting the shot. He wound up in a tie for fourth, enough points that eventually helped him get into the U.S. Open.

Only a month later, when Montgomerie saw the drop on a television replay, did he realize it was wrong. Because it was not intentional, and the tournament was over, there was no change in the results. He donated his fourth-place earnings to charity, although his peers were outraged. Under this turmoil, he arrived at St. Andrews with only limited signs that his game was turning around. But oh, the magic of the old town.

Montgomerie shot 66 in the second round, putting him in the final group with Woods on Saturday. They have played together before, no occasion more notable than the third round of the Masters in 1997 when Montgomerie said his experience would pay dividends against the 21-year-old Woods. Woods shot 65, Montgomerie shot 74, and that was that. But this was a new man on the Old Course, and he was up to the challenge. He whipped the flag-waving crowd into a frenzy, and the support rattled Woods. He only shaved one shot from Woods's four-shot advantage, and he could get no closer than one shot in the final round, finishing five behind. Still, it was a brave effort, and it did wonders.

"There is no disgrace finishing second to the best player in the world," Montgomerie said.

And there was no greater joy than winning at St. Andrews. Okay, so it wasn't the Open. Montgomerie was only too glad to win the Dunhill Links Championship in October, holing a short putt on the 18th hole for a one-shot victory, his first of any kind in 19 months. From there, he went to San Francisco for the American Express Championship and again challenged Woods, finishing third. The money kept piling up until Montgomerie had enough left at the end of the year to capture his eighth Order of Merit on the PGA European Tour, and his first one since 1999. Under the circumstances, Montgomerie said No. 8 was bigger than the rest of his Order of Merit titles.

"I never questioned my golf," he said. "I can do this. This is what I do best. It's just sometimes when outside influences are affecting you, some players in the past have questioned their golf, and I was fortunate enough not to question my golf and just to be patient, if you like, and it's coming right again, which is great, especially at my age, which is getting on a bit now. It's nice to know it's still there."

## RETIEF GOOSEN

| EVENT | POSITION |
|---|---|
| Mercedes Championships | T-13 |
| Sony Open in Hawaii | T-56 |
| WGC - Accenture Match Play Championship | 3 |
| Ford Championship at Doral | T-8 |
| Bay Hill Invitational | 4 |
| The Players Championship | T-12 |
| BellSouth Classic | T-22 |
| Masters Tournament | T-3 |
| Johnnie Walker Classic | 2 |
| EDS Byron Nelson Championship | MC |
| BMW Championship | T-11 |
| Booz Allen Classic | T-59 |
| U.S. Open Championship | T-11 |
| Smurfit European Open | T-13 |
| Barclays Scottish Open | T-44 |
| The Open Championship | T-5 |
| Deutsche Bank Players' Championship | MC |
| The International | 1 |
| PGA Championship | T-6 |
| WGC - NEC Invitational | T-58 |
| Volkswagen Masters China | 1 |
| Linde German Masters | 1 |
| HSBC World Match Play | T-3 |
| Funai Classic at Walt Disney World Resort | T-58 |
| Chrysler Championship | T-44 |

| | |
|---|---|
| The Tour Championship | T-4 |
| Limpopo Classic | T-3 |
| Nelson Mandela Invitational | T-3 |
| Nedbank Golf Challenge | T-2 |
| South African Airways Open | 1 |

Goosen must be wondering what happened to his aura as front-runner. Sure, he three-putted from 12 feet at Southern Hills and had to come back the next day in a playoff to win the 2001 U.S. Open. But the image of the stoic South African is his quiet, killer demeanor. He kept his cool to beat Mickelson at Shinnecock Hills in the 2004 U.S. Open. He joined a short list of players to come from behind and beat Woods, at the 2004 Tour Championship. And everyone expected him to win his third U.S. Open when he took a three-shot lead into the final round at Pinehurst No. 2. But it fell apart in shocking fashion as Goosen stumbled to an 81. "I messed up badly," he said, with only a trace of pulse.

It was a chance for him to get credit that is so unfairly lacking. Goosen started the season at No. 4 in the world, yet he was conveniently left out of all the conversations involving the "Big Four." Most preferred to talk about Woods, Singh, Els and Mickelson. Goosen took it in stride, reasoning that if he ever did become part of the Big Four, someone would change the top to the Big Three.

He wound up with four victories — the same as Els, Mickelson and Singh — although no one could be faulted if they couldn't remember them. His only victory on the PGA Tour came at The International. He won once on the European Tour at the Linde German Masters, and on the Asian Tour in the China Masters. He ended his season by holding off a late charge from Els in the South African Open, which left him in the same position he started — at No. 4 in the World Ranking, and largely forgotten.

## ERNIE ELS

| EVENT | POSITION |
|---|---|
| Mercedes Championships | T-3 |
| Sony Open in Hawaii | 2 |
| Buick Invitational | T-6 |
| Heineken Classic | 5 |
| Dubai Desert Classic | 1 |
| Qatar Masters | 1 |
| Bay Hill Invitational | T-23 |
| The Players Championship | T-17 |
| Masters Tournament | 47 |
| Johnnie Walker Classic | T-6 |
| BMW Asian Open | 1 |
| EDS Byron Nelson Championship | T-10 |
| BMW Championship | T-39 |
| Memorial Tournament | T-45 |
| Booz Allen Classic | T-7 |
| U.S. Open Championship | T-15 |
| JP McManus Pro-Am | T-6 |

| | |
|---|---|
| Barclays Scottish Open | 11 |
| The Open Championship | T-34 |
| Nedbank Golf Challenge | 7 |
| Dunhill Championship | 1 |
| South African Airways Open | 2 |

It was easy to forget about Els. A year in which he was stuck in neutral suddenly was thrust into reverse when Els tore knee ligaments during a holiday after the British Open and had season-ending knee surgery. That knocked him out for the final four months of the season, although he returned to win the Dunhill Championship in South Africa, which counts toward the 2006 season on the European tour.

The forced break from the game could not have come at a better time.

Els was haunted by an empty feeling in 2004, when he had a chance to win all four majors and didn't get any of them. He finished one shot behind Mickelson at the Masters, one shot out of a playoff at the PGA Championship, lost in a playoff to unheralded Todd Hamilton at the British Open, and shot 80 from the final group at the U.S. Open.

Perhaps the first sign that 2005 would be a struggle came in the opening tournament, the Mercedes Championships at Kapalua. Els needed a birdie on the par-five 18th hole to force a playoff and, trying to put a little something extra into his tee shot, pushed it well to the right and out-of-bounds. A week later at the Sony Open, he put together a phenomenal charge Sunday to shoot a 62 and was poised to force a playoff until Singh birdied the last hole to win by one.

Success might have been his undoing. Els skipped the Accenture Match Play Championship for the second straight year, determined to avoid too much travel before the Masters. He won the Dubai Desert Classic in dramatic fashion, holing an 18-foot eagle putt on the final hole for a one-shot victory. But instead of taking a week off, Els was lured to the Qatar Masters, which he rallied to win.

Els flew to fabled Seminole Golf Club in south Florida for a member-guest tournament on his way to the Bay Hill Invitational, where he shot 77 in the second round while paired with Woods and Goosen. After a lackluster performance, he played in the Tavistock Cup, club matches between tour players at neighboring Isleworth and Lake Nona. And by the time he arrived at the Masters, he was run down and trying to recover from a virus. It set the tone for the rest of his short year.

Along with the desert double of Dubai and Qatar, Els won the BMW Asian Open in China. He appeared to be back on track until he got to the U.S. Open, where he failed to break par and took himself out of contention with a 76 in the second round. He left North Carolina a tired man, needing a break and threatening to take a week off during the Scottish Open at Loch Lomond. But he couldn't stay away, grinded all four rounds to finish 11th, and again was low on fuel when he got to St. Andrews. It was lackluster performance on a course he loves. Els opened with a 74, realized he already was eight shots behind Woods and never recovered. The next week, he was at sea with his family when his season ended.

"No doubt about it, it's been the strangest year of my professional career," Els said.

The lost time kept him out of the Presidents Cup and the Tour Championship, and he finished the year at No. 5, his lowest ranking since the end of the 1999 season.

## ANNIKA SORENSTAM

| EVENT | POSITION |
|---|---|
| MasterCard Classic | 1 |
| Safeway International | 1 |
| Kraft Nabisco Championship | 1 |
| Michelob Ultra Open | T-12 |
| Chick-fil-A Charity Championship | 1 |
| LPGA Corning Classic | T-2 |
| ShopRite LPGA Classic | 1 |
| McDonald's LPGA Championship | 1 |
| U.S. Women's Open | T-23 |
| HSBC Women's World Match Play | T-5 |
| Evian Masters | 12 |
| Weetabix Women's British Open | T-5 |
| Scandinavian TPC | 1 |
| Wendy's Championship for Children | T-2 |
| John Q. Hammons Hotel Classic | 1 |
| Office Depot Championship | T-9 |
| Longs Drugs Challenge | T-22 |
| Samsung World Championship | 1 |
| CJ Nine Bridges Classic | T-14 |
| Mizuno Classic | 1 |
| ADT Championship | 1 |

There is no Big Five, Big Four or Big Three in women's golf. There is only Annika Sorenstam. The 35-year-old Swede again showed herself to be the most dominant player in her sport, by a wider margin than Woods ever has been. When the LPGA Tour season ended, Sorenstam collected her 10th victory. No one else won more than twice. She captured the Vare Trophy for the lowest scoring average, a staggering 1½ strokes better than anyone else. And for the fifth consecutive year, Sorenstam swept all the major awards.

Goals are becoming harder to find, but Sorenstam is aiming for the galaxy, and her golf at the start of the year was simply out of this world. Despite filing for divorce from her husband of eight years, before the first tournament of the year, Sorenstam was more determined than ever. She won her first three tournaments, giving her five straight victories dating to the end of 2004 and tying the LPGA record set by Nancy Lopez in 1978.

That included the first major, the first step toward her primary goal of winning the LPGA Grand Slam. Sorenstam set out to do that in 2004, but crashed and burned at the Kraft Nabisco Championship. This time, she was as relentless as ever, lapping the field at Mission Hills to win by eight strokes. Next up was the LPGA Championship, which moved from DuPont Country Club in Wilmington, Delaware, to a beefy new course north of Baltimore called Bulle Rock. It featured a par-five that nearly stretched 600 yards, and rolling terrain that figured to be a strong test.

Sorenstam made it look more like a pop quiz, building a five-stroke lead going into the final round and leading by eight shots at the turn. The results show that she beat 15-year-old Michelle Wie by three strokes, and indeed, the teenage sensation from Hawaii got equal attention as she tried to make a run on the back nine. But Sorenstam was never seriously threatened, and the Grand Slam suddenly began to look like a slam dunk.

She became the first LPGA Tour player in 19 years to win the first two legs of the Grand Slam, and even a national search would have had a hard time finding someone capable of stopping her. Keeping up a playful, personal rivalry with Woods, she walked out of the clubhouse that Sunday afternoon with her cell phone and sent him a text message that said simply, "Nine." Both had nine career majors. Her next stop was Cherry Hills in Denver for the U.S. Women's Open, the toughest test in women's golf and the major that had eluded Sorenstam since she won consecutive titles in 1995-96 before anyone really knew how good she could be.

For someone who tested herself at the highest level, playing in the Colonial in 2003, and who had ruled her sport for five years, Sorenstam was caught up by the magnitude of the possibilities. In other words, she was nervous. She was two shots behind after the first round, six shots behind going into the weekend. Her bid for the Grand Slam ended early in the third round, when in a span of four holes she three-putted for bogey and four-putted for double bogey.

The enormous letdown of a dream that slipped away showed, and Sorenstam went through a small slump in the summer before she emerged anew to remind the teenagers who's the boss. First came Wie, who turned professional and signed endorsement contracts for more money than Sorenstam gets. Wie made her professional debut at the Samsung World Championship, and Sorenstam used that occasion to open with a 64 and win by eight strokes. She said she wasn't interested in sending a message, but there was no denying it.

"I'm very competitive," she said. "I want to play well when everyone is talking about someone else."

They were talking about 19-year-old rookie Paula Creamer by the end of the year, especially when she all but guaranteed victory at the Solheim Cup and then won 3½ points in her five matches. The focus in women's golf was shifting toward youth, especially with a tall blonde who dressed in pink and bled red, white and blue.

A rivalry might have taken root at the season-ending ADT Championship, when Creamer twice challenged Sorenstam on the rules and refused to budge when Sorenstam insisted her tee shot on the 18th hole of the final round crossed land. "It's her conscience," Creamer later said, a subtle suggestion that Sorenstam wasn't playing fair and square. Sorenstam said she was disappointed in Creamer's position, but the Swede quietly and efficiently spent the next three days pulling away.

That gave her 10 victories on the LPGA, and 11 worldwide with a victory in Sweden, and easily No. 1 in the LPGA's new world ranking that makes it debut next year. She had flirted with the idea of early retirement a few years ago, but with 66 career victories, she is in range of the record 88 wins by Kathy Whitworth. At this rate, Sorenstam might be able to get there in the next three years.

About the only thing Sorenstam failed to do was deliver another victory to Europe in the Solheim Cup.

This was the year of America's cup, no matter what the gender. It started in September with the Solheim Cup, played at Crooked Stick in Indiana. The U.S. team was rife was rookies, led by an emotional captain in Nancy Lopez, who could barely get through a standard welcome or a greeting without getting teary-eyed. This was an aging American team, with Hall of Famers such as Juli Inkster and Beth Daniel, multiple major winners like Meg Mallon, and the spirited Rosie Jones, who earlier in the year announced she would be retiring.

Leadership came from the kids, with no one making quite a statement as Creamer. When the U.S. team was finalized, they all stood together for a press conference when the 19-year-old rookie said of Europe, "All I can say is that they better get ready, because they're going to get beat." Even some of the U.S. veterans raised their eyebrows, but Creamer backed it up. She teamed with women old enough to be her mother — Daniel and Inkster — to help produce 2½ points from the four team matches. And when Lopez sent her out against European stalwart Laura Davies, Creamer simply smoked her. The final score was 15½-12½, and it allowed the Americans to keep their record perfect at home. Creamer had help among her kiddie brigade, with young rookies Natalie Gulbis and Christina Kim also pitching in to win big points.

The American men had a score to settle on two counts. A year ago, they were embarrassed by Europe in the Ryder Cup, losing 18½-9½ for their biggest beating in the history of the matches. The Woods-Mickelson team was a disaster, and the general feeling was that Americans don't play well together. They also were coming off a controversial tie against the International team in the Presidents Cup, and Nicklaus and Player returned as the respective captains.

This was the year the Presidents Cup grew up, with so many stars on both teams it was hard to pick a favorite. And while the emotion is not quite as intense as the Ryder Cup, it sure felt that way Sunday afternoon at Robert Trent Jones Golf Club. Woods was nursing sore ribs and gave in to Goosen, who also had a rib injury but, typical of the South African, never said a word about it. Couples, who has provided so many great moments in the Presidents Cup, added the best one yet when he made a birdie on the 18th hole to upset Singh. Love was in the middle of his match when he heard what Couples had done, and it brought a tear to his eye.

But the moment belonged to Chris DiMarco, perhaps the most unheralded player to ever be ranked in the top 10. He was the guy who couldn't finish a job, whether that was a playoff loss to Woods at the Masters, a sloppy finish at New Orleans, or the simple fact that the last of his three PGA Tour victories came in 2002. He again was losing control on the closing holes, all square with Stuart Appleby, when his drive on the 18th found a bunker and left him an awkward lie. That's where it all turned. DiMarco hit a sensational nine iron to about 15 feet right of the flag. The putt was so pure that DiMarco started walking toward the cup and screaming like a linebacker who had just made a goal-line hit in the Super Bowl. He kept walking right into the arms of Captain Nicklaus, who got a send-off that was nearly as special as he felt at St. Andrews.

"As far as being something special, I may never captain another team, I may never play another round of golf, and if I end my career this way, it's a pretty good way to end it," Nicklaus said.

It was an emotional week, not to mention an emotional year.

Nicklaus takes more pride in his 18 grandchildren than his 18 majors, and he lost one in March when Jake Nicklaus, the 17-month-old son of Steve and Krista, wandered through a gate to the backyard and fell into a hot tub, where he drowned. This was the grandson who scampered to Grandpa Jack whenever he walked into the room, and Nicklaus was devastated. He agreed to keep a scheduled press conference at a course he had refurbished, The Loxahatchee Club in south Florida. "I have absolutely zero plans as it relates to golf," he said. But he spent time with Steve on the golf course, a father and a son needing each other, and they found therapy at Augusta National.

Nicklaus played in the Masters for the last time, not telling anyone that it would be his last until he tapped in on his final hole of the second round — the ninth hole because of a two-tee start — and blew kisses to a gallery that had watched him dominate the course like no other player in winning his six green jackets. Nicklaus did not know how to retire, yet this one fell into his lap. (Who knows when to call it quits in a game that is simply ageless?) He made his major farewell at St. Andrews, and took the stage one last time as captain of the Presidents Cup. His impact might best be illustrated by the gift his 12 players gave to Nicklaus on the eve of the matches — an oil painting of his beloved Jake. Nicklaus was in tears, and his team carried that emotion and spirit onto the course for the next four days.

The Presidents Cup was without an Asian player for the first time since the matches began in 1994, with Player choosing Trevor Immelman ahead of either K.J. Choi or Shigeki Maruyama.

Choi again was the highest-ranked Asian player, using his victory in the Chrysler Classic of Greensboro to climb to No. 31 in the world, followed by Shingo Katayama at No. 39 and Shigeki Maruyama at No. 44. Katayama won the Japan PGA Tour money title with a consistent year, winning the Japan Open and ABC Championship, with 11 other finishes in the top 10. Thaworn Wiratchant won twice on the Asian PGA Tour to win that money title.

Even so, the biggest star from the Far East might have been a young woman who stood barely more than five feet tall. Ai Miyazato already was creating quite a buzz at the end of 2004, attracting attention that surpassed the men. In one case, her television ratings for a victory were double that on the men's Japanese tour — even though Woods himself won wire-to-wire that week at the Dunlop Phoenix.

Miyazato, 20, won six times on the Japan LPGA Tour in 2005. Her swing is long and slow, and she has incredible control over her irons and, perhaps more importantly, her putter. Miyazato decided to bring her game to America, and she overwhelmed a strong list of qualifiers to win by a record 12 shots.

Europe began gearing up for the 2006 Ryder Cup, and at this rate, they might look close to the Americans on paper. Montgomerie played so well that he is virtually a lock to make the team for the eighth time. Padraig

Harrington of Ireland won twice on the PGA Tour, outlasting Singh in the playoff at the Honda Classic, then holing a 65-foot eagle putt on the final hole at Westchester to beat Jim Furyk in the Barclays Classic.

Harrington's victories were bittersweet, however, as the affable Irishman learned his father, Paddy, had cancer when he got home from the Honda Classic, and his father passed away the week of the British Open. David Howell, whose six iron on the 17th hole at Oakland Hills was the defining shot for Europe in the last Ryder Cup, continued his steady march up the World Ranking and was at No. 11. Europeans still haven't won a major since Paul Lawrie at Carnoustie, although eight of them were ranked among the top 22 at the end of the year. "We're coming back," Montgomerie said.

Robert Allenby came back with a fury. The rail-thin Aussie was saddled with a mysterious hand injury that left him feeling numb at times, and he suffered through one of his worst years, falling out of the top 50 and in danger of missing out on World Golf Championships. All it took was three weeks of a history-making performance Down Under, where he became the first player to win the "Triple Crown" — the Australian Open, Australian PGA and Australian Masters.

It was a banner year for other Aussies, from Stuart Appleby to Adam Scott, from Mark Hensby to Peter Lonard. A record 22 Australians were fully exempt on the PGA Tour this year, twice as many as any other country outside the United States, and three fewer than all the European countries combined. Eight of them were eligible for the Masters.

On the Champions Tour, 60-year-old Hale Irwin showed he is simple ageless. A three-time U.S. Open champion, Irwin debunked the myth that Champions Tour players have only a two- or three-year window to win before they become too old to compete with the "rookies." Irwin won four times, twice after turning 60. The money title went to Dana Quigley, a man whose passion for golf is so strong that he never takes a day off, even when he has a day off. His streak of playing every Champions Tour event ended at 278 consecutive tournaments when he missed the Senior British Open with a sore hip.

The Charles Schwab Cup, a points race throughout the year, went to Tom Watson. He got into the hunt by winning another Senior British Open in Scotland, this one at Royal Aberdeen, and he closed out the year with a spectacular charge, shooting 64 in the final round to win the Charles Schwab Cup Championship.

The PGA Tour will have its own version of a points race in 2007, announcing the FedEx Cup. It represents a significant overhaul of the schedule, with three blockbuster events leading to the Tour Championship, and a large payoff to the winner of the Cup. Details were still to be announced, but it will give the players another way of gauging success. It was far more simple in 2005. There was Tiger Woods in a green jacket at Augusta National. There he was again, holding aloft the silver claret jug at St. Andrews. He won two of the three World Golf Championships, and won two other PGA Tour events against some of the strongest fields of the year.

Indeed, 2005 might be remembered as the year Jack Nicklaus left, and the year that Tiger Woods returned. If he even left us.

# 2. Masters Tournament

He was a man under the microscope at the 2005 Masters Tournament. He had already won twice in 2005, an excellent start to the year by most measures. But this was Tiger Woods, and he was winless in his last 10 major championships. Nearly three years without one. Worse, he'd had a dormant year (for him) in 2004, a year marked by erratic play. He was working on swing changes again, having fired Butch Harmon, whom he credited for helping get him to where he was, and hired Hank Haney, to get him even higher. Woods spent practically all of 2004 saying he had put almost all the pieces together. Still, something wasn't working quite right, and so he had won just once on the PGA Tour, the WGC - Accenture Match Play in February, but no stroke-play event until the Dunlop Phoenix in Japan in November.

Now, in the balmy spring of 2005, he was just about his old self. Coming into the Masters, he had won twice in seven starts, the Buick Invitational and the Ford Championship. But he had also shown some distant finishes, such as a tie for 23rd and a tie for 53rd in his two outings leading up to Augusta. It's not that the jury was still out on Woods. The jury was sitting right there, watching him through the microscope.

What the jury saw was a Woods that was — and yet wasn't quite — himself. He had won his first three Masters by 12, two and three strokes, respectively. This time, he stumbled late and had to go to a playoff to beat Chris DiMarco. First, he holed a miraculous roundhouse-curve chip shot at the 16th for a two-stroke lead. Then he bogeyed the 17th and 18th and was tied. Then he won on a gutsy 15-foot birdie putt on the first hole of the playoff.

"Interesting finish," Woods said. "Even though I was throwing up on myself the last couple of holes ..."

But in one incredible outburst in the second and third rounds, he made seven straight birdies, and 11 birdies in a 17-hole stretch. The jury had seen enough. Their Tiger was back.

Battered by storms, this Masters was perhaps the most disjointed in history, with play being suspended and rounds having to be carried over into successive days. It was just another victim of a storm-whipped early season on the PGA Tour. On Thursday alone, early storms dumped 1.26 inches of rain on the area, forcing the first round back from its 8:05 a.m. start off No. 1 tee, to 1:30 p.m. off the first and 10th tees.

There was also a poignant edge to this Masters. Jack Nicklaus, winner of a record six green jackets but now 65 years old and limping, had intended to pass up the Masters after his 17-month-old grandson Jake drowned in the family hot tub in March. But the entire family needed some brightness, and so he agreed to play. It would be tough for him. Hiking across Augusta's hills with that artificial hip would be tough enough. Then there was the back surgery in November. "I can't even stand up straight anymore," Nicklaus said. The fans didn't care, someone said. They just want to see you. "I think they'd all like to see me play," Nicklaus said, "but they're not living in this body."

The Masters opened on stormy Thursday, but only 24 of the 93 in the field could complete the first round. Australia's Mark Hensby, a Masters rookie, the only finisher able to break par, was the leader in the clubhouse with his three-under-par 69. Would he still be there when the round was completed Friday morning? Not likely. Chris DiMarco, who started on the second nine, was four under through his 14th hole when play was suspended. Someone asked him whether he was encouraged by his start. DiMarco was polite at the silly question.

"This is a marathon," DiMarco said. "We've got a long way to go."

Interestingly enough, it wasn't a low score but a high one that stopped the show on opening day. Billy Casper, the 1970 champion, age 73, limping on an artificial hip, was playing in his 45th and last Masters. He shot 106, with a 14 at the par-three 16th, where he put five balls into the water. Both the 106 and the 14 would have been records, but Casper withdrew. He kept the card to frame it. Said the gentle Casper: "I wanted to play just one more time, just to walk the fairways during tournament time."

Casper's dream was over, but Tiger Woods's was just beginning, and it started out as something like a nightmare for the three-time champion. Woods, who started on the second nine, had to be muttering to himself when he left the par-five 13th green (his fourth hole). How can you putt for an eagle and make a bogey? Simple. Woods put a four-iron shot over the ditch and stream and onto the green, 30 feet past the hole. He had an eagle in his sights. His putt rolled off the front of the green and down and into the little run, settling in about two inches of water. Woods had three options. He could play out of the water, or go back to the fairway, across the creek, and play from there under a one-stroke penalty, or return to his original spot on the green, taking a penalty stroke. He elected to putt it again, but carefully. He left the first five feet short, and missed that one, too.

Woods birdied the par-five 15th to turn in one over par. Then he bogeyed No. 1 (his 10th) when his approach hit the flagstick and caromed into a bunker. He blasted out and two-putted for the five, and was two over through 12 holes when darkness stopped play.

It was in this stretch that one of those historic blips appears on the radar screen that can determine the outcome of things. Woods had tapped in for par at the 14th (his fifth hole), and the question was raised on whether he had violated Rule 16(e), which says a player cannot straddle or have either foot touching the line of his putt. The matter was referred to Will F. Nicholson Jr., chairman of the competition and rules committee, who said the video tape was inconclusive. There would be no penalty. That could have been a fatal little storm. Woods had weathered it.

Woods returned Friday morning and played his last six holes in an erratic even par. Resuming at No. 5 (his 14th), he went birdie-bogey-birdie-bogey for a 74 that tied him for 33rd place, seven strokes off the lead. Of course, anyone thinking he was out of it had to be reminded that in 1997 he was seven strokes behind after nine holes and went on to win by 12.

DiMarco had returned to Augusta remembered both as the guy who shot 76, head-to-head against Phil Mickelson in the final round of the 2004 Masters, and also as the one bright spot in the United States' embarrassing loss to Europe in the Ryder Cup in September. It was the DiMarco of the

Ryder Cup who teed it up Thursday afternoon. He bogeyed his first hole, the 10th, then rang up five birdies — three of them in a row — before getting stranded by darkness.

DiMarco's three-birdie burst started with a great break at No. 1, his 10th hole. His tee shot hit a tree and caromed back into the fairway. From there, he hit a seven iron to 25 feet. An average hitter, DiMarco needed three shots to reach the par-five No. 2, the third an elegant sand wedge from 90 yards to four feet. And at No. 3, he birdied from eight feet. It was his wedge again. He came back out Friday morning and tapped in after a near ace at the par-three No. 6, the hole he did ace in 2004. He parred in for a 67, the first-round lead and another strong Masters start. He'd opened with a 65, 70 and 69 in three of his first four Masters. What is it about you and the first round, a writer asked.

"This media room," DiMarco cracked at his interview. "I like this media room."

By the time the first round was finally completed, some fresh faces were working their way into the fraternity. Freshest of all was that of Luke Donald, the English golfer, a one-time winner in his four years on the PGA Tour and a rookie in the Masters. Donald, who started on the 10th, birdied four holes in a five-hole stretch, three of them in a row from No. 2 on Thursday, then No. 6 on Friday. His 68 left him a stroke behind DiMarco's lead, and tied for second with Vijay Singh, who bogeyed the 11th, three-putting from 100 feet just before dark. Singh tormented himself over whether he might have done better holding off until Friday morning. "Maybe I should have waited," he said. "Or maybe even [waited] on the second putt from five feet. But who knows — I may have missed it tomorrow." But he bounced back on Friday and birdied the 13th and 14th to tie Donald.

Mickelson, who finally broke through for his first major victory in the 2004 Masters, was having as hot a year as Woods. He won three times — the FBR Open and the AT&T Pebble Beach National Pro-Am, then the BellSouth Classic the week before the Masters. He opened with a 70 this time, three strokes off the lead, but it seemed traces of his former erratic game had seeped back in. Said his playing companion, amateur Ryan Moore, "He's not hitting the ball as close as he wants, but he's making 25- and 30-footers, so he's not too worried about it."

Moore was the only one of four amateurs in the field to break par in the first round, wrapping up a two-birdie, one-bogey 71 Friday, and noted, "I go play with what I've got. I'm hitting it well, and I wish I could have kept going." Moore, a senior at the University of Nevada at Las Vegas, in 2004 won what some call the Grand Slam of amateur golf — U.S. Amateur, U.S. Public Links, NCAA Championship and Western Amateur. Long and accurate drives were his strength. He hit 12 of the 14 driving fairways.

Ernie Els, the big, smooth South African, a two-time Masters runner-up, had won twice on the European Tour earlier but he was still spinning his wheels in the United States. Starting on the second nine Thursday, he bogeyed his first two holes, shot 39, and finished his last seven Saturday morning with a wash — two birdies and a double-bogey five at No. 4 for a 75.

Elsewhere from around the first round:

South African Gary Player, a three-time winner, became the oldest foreign player in the Masters, at age 69. And with Arnold Palmer already gone, Jack Nicklaus in his finale, and Billy Casper declaring his exit, Player was the last of the four who dominated professional golf in the 1960s. England's David Howell, a rookie hero of the Ryder Cup in September and a rookie at the Masters, shot par and was asked what four 72s would do for him. "Well, it wouldn't win, but it wouldn't be last," he said.

And how tough was the new Augusta National soaked by rain? There was one hint. Rory Sabbatini, who shot 80, eagled No. 8 — the only eagle of the first round. Only five times previously had Augusta National given up just one eagle in the first round, the last time in 1970.

The first round leaders:

| | | | |
|---|---|---|---|
| Chris DiMarco | 67 | Thomas Bjorn | 71 |
| Luke Donald | 68 | Retief Goosen | 71 |
| Vijay Singh | 68 | Thomas Levet | 71 |
| Stuart Appleby | 69 | Ryan Moore | 71 |
| Mark Hensby | 69 | Chris Riley | 71 |
| Phil Mickelson | 70 | Adam Scott | 71 |
| Ryan Palmer | 70 | | |

At the Masters, rarely is heard a discouraging word, but there were a few this time. It was late Friday afternoon and murmurs drifting around the press building held that Vijay Singh was in a high dudgeon. He had complained that Phil Mickelson was damaging greens with over-long spikes on his golf shoes. He called on officials to check them [they were cleared]. Mickelson resented being approached by officials on the course, and he and Singh had words in the Champions Locker Room.

Before long, a Mickelson representative was circulating through the press building, handing out a release in which Mickelson politely said he was sorry if he had damaged the greens — it was clearly a pro forma apology — and he also noted that he would have appreciated it if Singh had come to him rather than talked it around. The discussion in the Champions room clearly had not been a milk-and-cookies session.

"How hot was it in there?" a golf writer wondered.

Said a man close to the episode, with a knowing grin, "Let's say that it sure wasn't tepid."

Apart from that, there wasn't much to Friday. There was "weather" again, as some like to put it, and golf was played for all of about three hours. The first round, suspended Thursday because of darkness, was completed early Friday. The second round then barely got under way, with 88 of the 91 players starting off Nos. 1 and 10 tees. The Masters was so disjointed at this point that England's David Howell had birdied five of eight holes to take a share of the lead with countryman Luke Donald and first-round leader Chris DiMarco. When the second round resumed Saturday morning, Howell had 28 holes to play, Donald 24 and DiMarco 35. Keeping track of this Masters was much like trying to follow the Indianapolis 500.

Almost lost in all the shuffling was the fact that on Friday morning, DiMarco would resume the first round by nearly acing the par-three No. 6, the hole he had aced a year ago. This time he missed by an inch. A tap-in birdie and three pars later and he had the first-round lead on a 67.

Allowing for the scrambling and overlapping from Friday, the second round worked out this way through Saturday:

DiMarco played 17 holes Saturday morning to wrap up a second 67 for a 134 total to keep the lead. He was four ahead of Thomas Bjorn, six ahead of Tiger Woods, and seven ahead of Vijay Singh and Howell. DiMarco had a remarkably steady, bogey-free round. In fact, only DiMarco and Jim Furyk came through the second round without a bogey. DiMarco had had only one for the tournament, that on his first hole in the first round, so he had come 35 holes without one.

DiMarco's run started with a save at No. 1, where he chipped to three feet, and he then rang up birdies at Nos. 2, 8, 9, 15 and 16. These were the fruits of an aggressive game. Would he stick with it? "Yeah," he said, "especially with Tiger behind me. I've got a lot of great players behind me that are trying to win, too. Going out there and trying to hold on to a lead isn't going to get it. Go out and step on it. That's what you have to do around here."

Woods roused himself from his indifferent play and turned in the best golf of the second round, a six-under 66, pulling to within six strokes of DiMarco's lead. Woods's frustration was easing. About that 74 in the first round: "I kept hitting good golf shots and I would just mess it up, or I'd get a bad break," he said. "So I said, 'Just keep hanging in there, keep hitting quality shots and it will turn,' and luckily, it turned."

Indeed. Woods had a Tiger Woods kind of day. He was a stunning 11 under par over 26 holes, going nine under for the tournament and zooming to within four strokes of DiMarco before darkness shut down Saturday's play. Woods got under way with a birdie at No. 2 and rang up six others against one bogey for the second-round 66. "It was a nice turnaround," Woods allowed. "I hit the ball better. The three-putt [the bogey at No. 14] was the only disappointing thing all day." Then came the next leg of this fragmented Masters — a three-hour wait and the start of the third round. "We've got 27 holes to go," Woods said. "As I said out there, it's a long day, and I've just got to continue being patient."

Denmark's Thomas Bjorn eagled his way into the hunt. In the second round, he accomplished the rare feat of eagling both par-fives on the second nine in the same round. At the 13th, he hit a driver and a utility club to three feet, and at the 15th, it was a driver and a four iron to about a foot en route to a 67 and a 138 total, four behind DiMarco. By the time darkness stopped the third round Saturday, Bjorn was eight under par and five off the lead. He gave himself a pep talk. "Out here, you have got to keep your head up," Bjorn said. "You know you're going to drop shots. You just have to keep steady and make the best of it."

Vijay Singh, after his opening 68, just couldn't summon that marvelous putting touch and shot 73. Mickelson and his long spikes aside, Singh blamed the greens. "We've played 18 [holes] with those greens," Singh said. "They have spike marks, heel marks. They're chewed up. They're bumpy." He had only one birdie, at No. 2. He had needed 79 putts total. "I just need to make a few more putts," he said. But at the halfway mark, he was already seven shots off the lead.

Mickelson was in no better shape, but his biggest problem was just getting to the greens. He missed eight in the second round and shot a so-so

72 for a 142, eight off the lead. "I've made a few too many mistakes," he said. "I thought I was in a pretty good rhythm, but it just never manages to hold." Oddly enough, Mickelson was making his share of birdies. He had five in the first round and three in the second. Trouble was, he was making bogeys, too — three in each round. "I've made more bogeys this week than all of last year," Mickelson said.

And as though he were writing a script for the finale of this Masters, Bjorn noted, "I can only say that if Chris plays the way he is, he's going to be difficult to beat. Tiger is Tiger, and when he gets on those kind of runs, then we never know what's going to happen. I think I have to say, actually, I think it's great for the game that he's playing the kind of golf that we are used to seeing him play."

Ryan Moore (easily) and Luke List (not as easily) were the only two of the four amateurs to make the cut. Moore, the brightest American amateur since Woods, breezed in by seven shots with 71-71–142, six off the lead. He was not all that impressed with seeing his name up on the leaderboard. "I don't feel out of place or feel in awe of myself being there," Moore said. List had opened with a 77, and rallied for a six-birdie, three-bogey 69 to make the cut by two shots at 146. List, runner-up to Moore at the 2004 U.S. Amateur, said he'd remain at Vanderbilt University for his final two years. "I want to qualify for this as an amateur again," he said.

This wasn't the Ernie Els who was runner-up to Mickelson in that breathtaker a year ago. This one was merely a fringe figure this time. A 75 in the first round left him eight strokes off the lead, and a battered second nine in the second allowed him to survive, but only just. Els stumbled to a 38 on the second nine, with two birdies and four bogeys for a 73 and 148 total that just made the cut.

Writers returned for a day-after check on what was called, of course, "Spikegate," another in an endless stream of references to Watergate. "I tried to be as careful as I could today," said Mickelson. Said a reporter to Singh: "We haven't heard your side of 'Spikegate.'"

"There's no 'side,'" Singh said. "You know it all. Let's talk about my golf game."

Meanwhile, back at the golf tournament ...

Luke Donald, the promising young English professional, was in the running with a 68 in the first round, but posted a tough 77 in the second. "I just missed a bunch of putts inside 10 feet, and stuck in the water at the 16th," Donald said. "I just need a couple good rounds at the weekend."

Kirk Triplett, after a 75 in the first round, blew his way back into contention in the second with a three-under-par start on his first four holes. He birdied the 10th, then holed a 94-yard wedge shot for an eagle at the 13th. Then he birdied the 15th and 16th, and a bogey at the 18th gave him a 68 — tying his lowest score in seven Masters — and a tie for ninth at 143.

Jim Furyk, who opened with a threatening 76, worked some magic to survive the cut. "I did a little Houdini on the last two holes," Furyk said. He closed with two birdies. He pitched in at the 17th, and at the 18th, after nearly pitching in again, tapped in for a bogey-free 67, matching his all-time low in nine Masters. At one-under 143, he made the cut for the eighth time.

The 36-hole cut, to the low 44 players and ties, came in at four-over

At the majestic par-three 16th, Woods made the shot of the tournament, and one of the great shots in Masters history. He had lofted his tee shot across the placid pond, and his ball ended up just off the back of the green, in excellent position to make bogey. He was 30 feet from the pin, but there would be a huge arc to the shot. Woods aimed maybe 20 feet left of the hole and popped an incredibly delicate chip shot.

"I wasn't necessarily thinking about making it," Woods said. "I just wanted to throw the ball up on the slope, have it feed down there, and hopefully get a makeable putt." The ball swept lazily toward the hole, paused on the edge, and dropped in. Davis Love made a putt much like that six years earlier. DiMarco was on the green, 14 feet from the hole. He missed the birdie, tapped in for par, and Woods had a two-shot lead with two holes to play.

"It's one of the best shots I've ever hit because of the turning point involved," Woods said. "If Chris makes his putt and I make bogey, all of a sudden I'm one back. Got a great break on 16. Didn't go in the bunker, didn't go in the rough, and somehow an earthquake happened and it fell in the hole."

It seemed the Masters was over. Not quite. It was just getting started.

Suddenly, Woods was hitting stray shots. At the 17th, he missed the fairway by some 30 yards and bogeyed. DiMarco holed a five-footer for par. At the 18th, a brawny, uphill dogleg-right, Woods put his eight-iron approach into a bunker and bogeyed again. DiMarco didn't want to risk a dangerous downhill putt so he hit his approach to the front of the green. But his ball rolled back down off the edge of the green. His chip for a birdie lipped out of the hole. He had come that close to winning the Masters. Woods had dodged a bullet. DiMarco holed the return putt. Woods shot 71, DiMarco 68. They were tied at 12-under 276. On to the 13th playoff in Masters history. It started at the 18th hole for the first time.

In the playoff, both drove into the fairway. DiMarco, hitting first, went carefully for the pin at the lower level again. Again his ball hit the green and rolled off the front. Woods put his second shot about 15 feet above and left of the hole. DiMarco's birdie chip just missed, and he tapped in for his par. Woods did not pass up this chance. He took his fourth Masters title, equaling Arnold Palmer's career total and two behind Jack Nicklaus.

"This would hurt if I gave it away," said DiMarco, who made just five bogeys and one double bogey. "But I didn't. I really didn't. I played him as hard as I could down the stretch, birdieing a bunch of holes and putting it on him. Twelve under is usually good enough to win," he added, "but I was playing against Tiger Woods."

And so Woods answered all the questions. "More than anything, it's the validation of all the hard work I've put into it," Woods said. "Hank [Haney] and I have put some serious hours into this, and, you know, I read some of the articles over past year of him getting ripped, and I'm getting ripped for all the changes I'm making, and to play as beautifully as I did this entire week is pretty cool."

Then Woods wanted to pay another tribute.

"Before I go, I want to say this is for my dad," Woods said. "My dad has been in some bad health lately and I know he's watching.

"Dad, I dedicate this one for you."

# 3. U.S. Open Championship

More than half of the contestants in the United States Open Championship must gain entry through one or two stages of qualifying competitions. There are local and then sectional qualifying tests, or for the more accomplished players, just sectional. Those were the routes this year for 84 of the contestants, from among the record 9,048 entrants, while 72 of that number were fully exempt from having to qualify.

Qualifying is a time-consuming and expensive process, particularly for foreign players. This year, for the first time, there were sectional qualifying sites in foreign countries. Three places in the U.S. Open were available to 17 qualifiers in Ono City, Japan, near Osaka, and nine places were available for 53 qualifiers in England, at Walton Heath, near London.

Without this innovation, Michael Campbell, a New Zealander who makes his home in England while playing the European Tour, would not have won the 2005 championship. He said after accepting the trophy that but for the qualifying at Walton Heath, he would not have entered.

Campbell shot 69 in the final round for an even-par total of 280 and won by two strokes over Tiger Woods, who also finished with 69, ending the bid of the Masters champion for the Grand Slam in 2005. But for Campbell to win, that also required Retief Goosen to lose the tournament.

The champion in 2001 and 2004, and looking to become only the fifth man to win the U.S. Open more than twice, Goosen entered the final round with a lead of three strokes. His closest challengers, Jason Gore and Olin Browne, struck no fear. Campbell was four strokes back, tied for fourth place, and Woods was six back, tied for seventh.

The game was on when Goosen took a double-bogey six on the second hole and a bogey five on the third. Three more bogeys followed before the South African made the turn in 41. He scored five bogeys in succession starting at the 12th hole, and finished with 81, tied for 11th place, eight strokes behind the winner. It was the highest score by a 54-hole U.S. Open leader since Gil Morgan's collapse, also with 81, in 1992.

Campbell, age 36, became the second New Zealander to win one of golf's major championships. Bob Charles was the first in the 1963 Open Championship, and Charles also was the first left-hander to win a major title. "To be in the same circle, the same sentence, as Bob Charles is an honor for me," Campbell said. He also became the latest of the U.S. Open's 23 foreign-born champions, responsible for a total of 29 championships.

With a brown complexion and black hair, Campbell is a Maori, a people indigenous to New Zealand. "I am very proud to be who I am," Campbell said. Emphasizing his roots on the final day, Campbell wore a shirt with a contemporary Maori design that was produced for him by a Maori-owned company, Kai Kaha, which carries a "Cambo" line. In the Maori language, the company name means inner strength.

Woods's caddie, Steve Williams, is also a New Zealander, from Wellington, Campbell's home town. Waiting behind the 18th green as Campbell finished, Williams put his arm around him and said, "You've made a lot of people back home very, very proud." Talking to reporters, Williams said,

It was no surprise that Retief Goosen advanced into a first-place tie after the second round, but those who were alongside him were not expected to be there. Goosen shot 70, two strokes higher than his score in the first round, for a total of 138, two under par. Olin Browne remained in a tie for first after posting 71, and Jason Gore joined them at 138 after his 67.

Rocco Mediate, who had a share with Browne of the first-round lead, recorded five bogeys over a stretch of seven holes, shot 74 and dropped into a tie for 10th place at 141. Among the seven others tied with Mediate was Tiger Woods, who shot 71.

David Toms had been in position to take the lead but played his last two holes in five over par and shot 72, falling into a tie for 17th place at 142. Toms finished on the eighth and ninth holes. He drove in the rough and took three shots to reach the eighth green, then three-putted for a double bogey. At the par-three ninth, Toms hit into a bunker then hit over the green. He took three putts again, for a triple bogey.

"Everyone is going to have a bad stretch here," Toms said. "Now I can't afford to have another one."

Meanwhile Chris DiMarco, who had lost a playoff at the Masters to Woods, shot 82 and missed the 36-hole cut. Phil Mickelson, only two strokes behind after the first round, shot 77 and dropped to a tie for 45th at 146. Ernie Els was a stroke further back at 147, tied for 57th, after his 76.

"That's a tough course," Mickelson said. "I don't know what else to say."

Michael Campbell was in the mix with 69 and a 140 total. Just ahead of Campbell, in fourth place at 139, were K.J. Choi and Mark Hensby. In sixth place along with Campbell were Vijay Singh, Sergio Garcia and Lee Westwood. The 10th place group at 141 included Mediate and Woods.

Although just at 145, Corey Pavin also merited attention. He wanted to attend his son's high school graduation in San Diego, also on Thursday, so starting times were arranged for 7:22 a.m. in the first round and 12:32 p.m. in the second. He hired a private airplane for the trip and returned Friday early enough for a short nap. He shot 73 and 72 and was tied for 33rd place.

The skies were overcast for the second round and the temperature fell to the low 80s, a more comfortable level. Out early with the low round of the day, and of the week — four-under-par 66 — was Peter Hedblom, a 35-year-old Swede with spiky blond hair, who had reached Pinehurst through the qualifying event with Campbell in England at Walton Heath.

Hedblom's clubs were misplaced in transit and only arrived Tuesday, two days after him. Whether that had an effect, Hedblom shot 77 in the first round, but he found his game on Friday. In the first group off at 7 a.m., Hedblom started with a birdie and ran on from there. He played an almost error-free round, hitting 10 of 14 fairways (excluding the par-threes), and although he missed seven greens, he putted like a dream.

He hit a perfect drive down the middle and pitched on to six feet for his birdie at the first hole. He got a birdie at the fourth with a shot to six feet again, this one from a greenside bunker. He birdied the eighth with a three wood, a seven iron and a 40-foot putt. On the 607-yard, par-five No. 10, Hedblom drove in the rough, hit an eight iron out and a seven iron to 40 feet, and he again holed the putt.

On the other hand, Goosen did not play as well as he had in the first round, when he hit 11 fairways and 16 greens. In the second round, he hit just five fairways and 10 greens. "It's not easy," Goosen said. "It's hard work. It works on your nerves."

Goosen began with a birdie on the 10th hole and hit five consecutive greens in regulation. He missed the green on No. 15, a very tough par-three of 203 yards, and took a bogey. He was out in 35, playing the second nine, his first, in even par. He went to two under par after four holes on the other nine, but missed the greens on the fifth and seventh holes and fell back to even par again.

"The guy is so good, so solid," Woods said of Goosen. "Come major championship time, he's always there."

Browne had surprised everyone, but the presence of Gore was almost beyond belief. The 31-year-old Californian had struggled even on the secondary Nationwide Tour. However, he had led the U.S. Open once before, when he birdied the first hole at Olympic in 1998. It didn't last, but this time it did.

Gore obviously enjoys what he does and he quickly became a gallery favorite. Even after he took four putts on the fifth green for a double-bogey six in the first round, he walked away smiling. He said, "What can you do? It's the U.S. Open. Things like that happen."

Sandy-haired, round-faced and weighing 235 pounds, Gore had played through both stages of qualifying, local and sectional, and was one of only 30 players to do so. Then on Gore's way to Pinehurst, a thief broke into his car and stole his wife's clothes, but only his underwear and his computer. To top it off, their son had an ear infection. But Gore was still smiling all the way.

Gore began the second round just before 2 p.m. on No. 10. He pitched to 10 feet and birdied his first hole, but butchered the next and had to hole from 12 feet for a bogey. He came back with a birdie on No. 12 with a sand wedge to 20 feet, and holed from 10 feet to birdie No. 13. He also bogeyed No. 15.

He scored 34 for his first nine and played his second nine in 33, with birdies at the fourth and sixth holes, the latter a rare two following a four iron to 15 feet.

Browne did not play as well as he had in the first round but still turned in a respectable 71 for a share of first place. To do so, Browne needed 10 one-putt greens, including a 20-foot putt for a double bogey on the sixth.

Starting on the 10th tee, Browne went out in 36 with a bogey on No. 14, where he holed from eight feet. He went to one under par with birdies at the second and third holes. He hit a five iron from the rough to 15 feet on the second, and he holed a putt from 20 feet on the third.

At the par-three sixth, Browne hit his tee shot into a bunker, pitched over the green into another bunker with his second shot, then hit back over the green again with his third. He played a weak chip from there and was still 20 feet from the hole. He holed that putt for five, a double bogey. "I got away with murder," he said later.

Browne completed his round with pars for his 71 and 138 total. "I've got no fingernails left today," he said. "I was just hanging on all day long."

time, none of this seemed to matter because Goosen was so far ahead.

The mood changed rapidly. Goosen's approach shot from the fairway to the second green rolled off the right side, leaving him a delicate shot to the hole. He struck the ball too hard, and it sped across the green. For a moment, it appeared his next shot would do the same, but it stayed on, and Goosen got down in two putts for his six, a double bogey. He lost another stroke at the third hole with a weak first putt and a missed second. Goosen had turned a runaway into a tense battle.

Singh ran off three consecutive birdies to close within two strokes of Goosen. Campbell had caught Goosen at even par, and Hensby had moved into third place at two over par, tied with Singh and Browne. Gore was at three over, and Woods and Toms were at four over.

Pinehurst No. 2 was taking its toll, and at the eighth, Singh dropped back. He took four putts, his first having run off the green, and made a double-bogey six. Toms went out in 40, Browne and Gore had nothing left, and Goosen collapsed. The Open was left to Campbell and Woods, although for a while there were two other unlikely challengers who were still hanging with them, Hensby and Tim Clark.

It had become apparent that Campbell was playing better shots into the greens than either Goosen or Woods. His approaches hit softly and held the greens, and theirs landed harder and some ran away.

Woods played a monstrous drive to the seventh that left nothing but a short pitch to a hole that measured just over 400 yards. He birdied, went to three over par and was three behind Campbell. Woods stumbled at the par-three ninth, when his tee shot was short of the green. He bogeyed and again was four strokes behind.

Campbell pulled his drive into the gallery at the eighth, and the ball bounced out into the rough. He took a bogey there, then saved par at the ninth with a delicate chip close to the hole. Making the turn in 35, Campbell led Woods by three.

As the tension climbed when they went into the final nine, Woods made his move. He split the fairway with a driver on the 607-yard, par-five No. 10, and was left with 265 yards to the green. Woods slashed into a four iron and reached the right greenside bunker in two. His recovery shaved the hole and he birdied. Campbell led by two.

Woods was left with only 125 yards to the green at the 11th after another long drive. His pitch hit past the hole but spun back within three feet, leaving him another birdie putt. It was Campbell by one stroke, but Woods's charge now stalled and he played through the 14th with pars.

Campbell was also playing solid golf. He hit his second shot to the right of the green on No. 10, pitched to 25 feet and holed the putt for a birdie. He saved par with a five-footer after an approach shot into a bunker on No. 11. He struck a long drive at No. 12, pitched well and holed the putt for another birdie. He was one under par, with six holes to play. He made routine pars on the next two holes.

Woods hit a beautiful six-iron shot into the green at the par-three No. 15 and holed the putt. He was one over par, trailing Campbell by two strokes. Then, when it looked like Woods might win, he let it slip away. He drove into the dense rough right of the 16th fairway, couldn't reach the green, and two-putted for a bogey five. On the par-three 17th, he three-putted from 20 feet. His birdie on the final hole was not enough, unless Campbell slipped.

Campbell bogeyed No. 16, but he sealed the victory with a 20-foot birdie putt on No. 17, right into the center of the hole. Three strokes ahead, Campbell laid up safely from the rough at No. 18, took two putts for a bogey five, and still won by two strokes.

He raised his head and arms to the overcast sky, then as he walked off the green, he pulled his cap down and buried his face in his hands to hide his tears.

At that moment, Campbell thought, "It's been a long journey, my career." Explaining later, he said, "I was thinking about people back home in New Zealand, and my wife, who is in England right now, Julie, and my two boys, Thomas and Jordan, because they couldn't be with me. And obviously Father's Day, my dad watching me back home, and the family."

After raising the U.S. Open trophy over his head, Campbell recalled the sporting heroes of his homeland. "I think for the first time I actually made the front page of the newspapers back home with the All Blacks," Campbell said, referring to New Zealand's great national rugby team, named for their all-black uniforms. "They've been champions and heroes of mine, and to knock them off the front pages for this one week means a lot to me."

# 4. The Open Championship

As Jack Nicklaus played in his final Open Championship, he was one of only four men to have won twice over the Old Course at St. Andrews, Scotland. Nicklaus had won there in 1970 and 1978, and also included in his record of 18 major professional titles, the 1967 Open at Muirfield. Others who had two Open victories at St. Andrews were Bob Martin in 1876 and 1885, J.H. Taylor in 1895 and 1900, and James Braid in 1905 and 1910.

Many others had won once on the ancient links but, interestingly, Harry Vardon never won at St. Andrews even though he held the most Open titles with six, nor had Tom Watson, despite five victories.

On the first morning of the 2005 Open Championship, Tiger Woods played the Old Course in 66 strokes to announce his intention to join Nicklaus and company with a second St. Andrews victory. There were three more rounds to play, but from the moment Woods ran off seven birdies over nine holes, from the fourth to the 12 holes, the other 155 contestants understood they could probably hope for nothing better than second place.

Five years earlier, Woods had played the four rounds at St. Andrews in 269 strokes, with all four of his 18-hole scores below 70, and had won the championship by eight strokes. He had begun with 67, and now he had bettered that score by one. After a look at the scoreboard, Colin Montgomerie described it as "Ominous. If ever a course was built for him, this is it."

And so it proved to be. Even though Woods's 72-hole total of 274, 14 under par, was five strokes below his winning score in 2000, he won by five strokes over Montgomerie, a Scot who was spurred on by passionate countrymen.

Woods demonstrated again that he was the best player of his time, 75 years after Bobby Jones concluded his career and two days after Nicklaus ended his, also as the best players of their times. Including his three U.S. Amateur victories, Woods tied Jones with his 13th major championship, with only Nicklaus and his total of 20 ahead of them. In professional majors, Woods now had 10 championships. It took Nicklaus to age 32 to win 10, while Woods would not be 30 until the end of 2005.

"It's pretty cool. I've gone one past halfway. Jack's got 18 and I've got 10," Woods said to the press. "Honestly, when I first started playing the (PGA) Tour, I didn't think I would have this many majors before age 30. There's no way. Usually, the golden years are in your 30s for a golfer. Hopefully that will be the case."

At the end of the first day, Woods held a one-stroke lead over the 67 of Mark Hensby, the surprising Australian who had tied for fifth in the Masters Tournament and tied for third in the U.S. Open Championship. There were 10 who played the Old Course in 68 strokes: Retief Goosen, Jose Maria Olazabal, Luke Donald, Fred Couples, Trevor Immelman, Peter Lonard, Scott Verplank, Chris Riley, Tino Schuster and Scottish amateur Eric Ramsay. New U.S. Open champion Michael Campbell, Vijay Singh and six others scored 69, for a total of 20 players who broke 70. That did not include Montgomerie, who started with 71.

Nicklaus and Watson played together, along with Donald. Both shot 75s. Nicklaus had reached the age of 65 determined to play his best in this, his final appearance in the Open. At 55, Watson would be eligible for the next 10 years.

Clouds covered the sky for much of the morning and a light wind ruffled the grass of the Old Course. Conditions could hardly have been better for scoring. The wind picked up once the tide turned, occasionally gusted to 20 miles an hour, and rain fell late in the afternoon.

Nevertheless, the Old Course did not play at its most severe. Since the 2000 Open, 164 yards had been added, stretching it to 7,279 yards, but the difference had little effect on the power players. With the ground dry and hard, balls rolled along and made up for the added length.

Goosen was out just after 7 a.m., and demonstrated that scores could be quite low. He began with a rush, posting birdies on five of the first 12 holes. He stumbled on the 13th, a testing par-four with a blind approach. He drove into one of the Coffins bunkers, took two more strokes to find the green, and three-putted for a double-bogey six.

He had gone out in 34, two under par. He picked up birdies on the 10th, one of the shorter par-fours, the 12th, with a drive and a 60-yard approach to 10 feet, and the 14th, a 618-yard par-five where he reached the green with his second shot. He completed his second round of 68 with a drive and two putts for birdie three at the 18th. With his record of two U.S. Open titles, Goosen appeared a legitimate contender.

Ian Poulter, ever the exhibitionist, arrived in trousers bearing a picture of the Open trophy, the claret jug, on the left leg and the names of all the Open champions on the right leg. He posted a round of 70.

Throughout the day the Old Course demonstrated that while it might bend a little, it wouldn't yield easily. Steve Webster, a 29-year-old PGA European Tour player, tore through the first nine holes in 30 strokes, but he found the second nine full of hazards. He caught six bunkers and came back in 41 for a score of 71.

Sergio Garcia played flawlessly through the first 12 holes except for a bogey on the third. He made six birdies. Then he lost control of his shots. After a series of escapes from the punishing rough, Garcia bogeyed three of the last six holes and shot a 70. It was a solid start, but Garcia was frustrated, walking away saying, "I had four three-putt greens, and you can't do that out here."

Garcia dropped his last stroke on the 17th, the notorious Road Hole, where so many dreams have ended. It begins with a drive over replicas of the old railway sheds that were torn down during the construction of the Old Course Hotel, then an approach to a narrow green set at an angle to the shot and protected on the left by the difficult Road bunker. More than once golfers escaped by playing away from the green because the bunker's face rises straight up, considerably higher than one might expect. Some players had trouble seeing over it.

Miss the green to the right and you deal with a shot off a paved road if you're lucky, or from against a stone wall if you are not. It is a frightening hole that cost more than one golfer dearly. Even a putt can be dangerous. Misplayed, a putt could roll into the bunker, as Tommy Nakajima famously discovered in 1978, when he reached the green in two and took a nine.

The 17th played by far as the most difficult hole of all. The field averaged 4.64 strokes, higher than all but two of the par-fives. It surrendered just nine birdies and only 72 pars, but it claimed 51 bogeys, two fewer than the 13th, and 16 scores of six, two more than the 13th. Seven players scored sevens and one, Zach Johnson, scored a nine. Fifth-four golfers had played through before Scott Verplank scored the first birdie three.

Montgomerie made a par from the road, running his ball across the pavement and up the slope onto the green, then holing his putt. Playing with him, David Toms needed two strokes from the road to reach the green, then two-putted for a six. Montgomerie shot 71, but Toms came in with 74. The following morning, Toms told officials he believed his ball may have moved after he addressed his second putt. Since he had not penalized himself, he had turned in a score lower than his correct score, and he should disqualify himself. His decision was accepted.

After finishing at one under par, Montgomerie said, "A 71 isn't great, but it's not a disaster."

Woods had gone through what was, for him, a frustrating period, when he failed in 10 consecutive efforts to win one of the four major championships. He ended that famine in April by winning his fourth Masters title, and followed that by placing second to Michael Campbell in the U.S. Open. He was due off the first tee at 8:20 a.m., a half-hour after the group of Nicklaus, Watson and Donald.

Grouped with Olazabal and Robert Allenby, Woods started with three pars, then began that string of birdies. The fourth hole had been lengthened to 480 yards, presumably to force shots either right or left of a group of mounds that could be carried with nothing less than 300-yard drives. Woods pulled out his driver for the first time and ripped into a shot that ran to 350 yards. He scored his first birdie with a wedge to 20 feet.

He made his next birdie at the fifth, a par-five of 568 yards, with a drive that measured 344 yards, an iron to 30 feet, and two putts. On the sixth hole, he was in the rough for the first time but still saved his par, then he played his best hole of the day.

In the Open five years earlier, Woods had not hit into a single one of the 112 bunkers of the Old Course in the 72 holes. But now, on his 79th hole, he drove with a three wood and lay short of the wide and deep Shell bunker that guards the approach to the seventh green. The ball rolled into the sand, 310 yards out. Woods played a beautiful recovery shot and holed a putt from four feet for his third birdie.

Woods drove the green on the 352-yard ninth hole and took two putts from 90 feet for the birdie three. Out in 32 strokes, he began the second nine with three consecutive birdies for a total of four in a row. He hit a pitching wedge to the green at the 10th and holed from eight feet. His two on the 11th followed a slight delay when a spectator became ill and was treated on the spot. When clear to play, Woods hit an iron to 15 feet and holed the putt. He added another birdie at the 12th with another pitch shot to eight feet.

He found sand again at the 13th, one of the Coffins bunkers that left him nothing but a saving shot out, and he bogeyed. A 335-yard drive avoided the Beardies on the 14th, but his second shot was 30 yards short of the green. As he approached his golf ball, sirens blared to signal two minutes of silence in respect of bombing victims in London earlier in the month.

Woods had been affected by the bombings more than most. His mother was staying in a hotel not far from one of the bombing sites. She had not been harmed, and was there following her son.

When a second siren sounded, Woods ran his golf ball onto the green and holed the putt for a par five. He lost a chance for a birdie when he missed a short putt on the 15th, and misplayed his approach to the 16th into a bunker — his third of the round — and bogeyed. He played the 17th with a five iron onto the green and two putts for his par, then drove onto the 18th green and putted through the Valley of Sin for a final birdie three. Back in 34, he had a score of 66 to hold first place.

In his first Open Championship, Mark Hensby hung close with a 67. He teed off at 2:20 p.m., six hours after Woods, who had finished by then. He had no experience at links golf yet played the Old Course like a veteran. He considers his short game to be his strength, saying, "I don't hit a lot of greens when I play regular events, so I get to chip a lot." He hit 12 greens in the first round, however, and went out in 34 and back in 33.

Hensby began by holing from 15 feet on the first hole. He lost a stroke after driving into the rough on the second, but saved his par from off the green at the seventh. On the ninth, he drove the green and holed for an eagle two from 20 feet. He holed for a birdie from 10 feet on the 10th. He played a driver on the 12th and had only a chip shot to 13 feet for another birdie. He made his last birdie on the 15th with a wedge to 13 feet again.

Asked about his expectations, Hensby responded, "I don't have any. I'll just go out and play tomorrow and hopefully have a chance on Sunday."

The first-round leaders:

| | | | |
|---|---|---|---|
| Tiger Woods | 66 | Scott Verplank | 68 |
| Mark Hensby | 67 | Chris Riley | 68 |
| Retief Goosen | 68 | (a)Eric Ramsay | 68 |
| Luke Donald | 68 | Tino Schuster | 68 |
| Peter Lonard | 68 | Trevor Immelman | 68 |
| Jose Maria Olazabal | 68 | Fred Couples | 68 |

The second day belong to Jack Nicklaus. It was an extraordinary time, when Tiger Woods, on the brink of dominating the Open, played second fiddle to Nicklaus, who was about to miss the 36-hole cut in his last appearance in the championship. As Nicklaus battled to make this more than a ceremonial occasion, Woods was posting a round of 67 to take a four-stroke lead.

Nicklaus had played in 38 Opens. His first was in 1962 and he did not miss a championship through 1996, a total of 36 years in succession. He returned to St. Andrews in 2000 and again this year. He had won three Opens, including those at St. Andrews in 1970 and 1978, and he had placed second seven times. One of the seven was in 1977 at Turnberry, when he and Tom Watson played one of the most dramatic Opens ever.

He struggled and failed over the closing holes to make the 36-hole cut. He thought he had a chance until he took a bogey on the 17th hole, and he knew then his competitive days were over.

None of that mattered to the galleries. They applauded on every hole, and when he came up the final hole, the grandstands were overflowing, the crowds lined the street along the right and hung from the open windows of the buildings along the way. It was appropriate that Nicklaus should hole his final putt, from 14 feet for a birdie, and he did. He finished with 72, even par, but his 36-hole total of 147 missed the cut by two strokes.

Woods recorded a total of 133, 11 under par. Colin Montgomerie moved into second place at 137 after a stirring round of 66. Seven others tied at 138, a group that included Brad Faxon, who also shot 66. Vijay Singh posted a second 69 and lost ground, along with Robert Allenby, with 68, and Trevor Immelman, Peter Lonard, Jose Maria Olazabal, and Scott Verplank, all with 70s.

Mark Hensby, who had trailed by one stroke, posted a 77 and dropped from second place to a tie for 55th. Retief Goosen, who had shot 68 in the first round, followed with 73 and dropped to a tie for 25th along with Luke Donald, who had played alongside Nicklaus and Watson. Donald shot 73.

Former Open champion Sandy Lyle birdied six holes and shot 67, advancing from a tie for 74th to a tie for 25th place. David Frost had an even greater move. His 65 took him 89 places up to a tie for 39th. That 65 would remain the lowest score of the week.

The 36-hole cut came at one over par, 145. In addition to Nicklaus, these other past Open champions were sent away: Mark O'Meara, Nick Price, Ben Curtis, Todd Hamilton, Tony Jacklin and David Duval. Ian Woosnam also bowed out, along with Thomas Bjorn, who tied for second behind Woods in 2000 and was second again in 2003. Other notables who were gone included 2003 U.S. Open winner Jim Furyk, 2005 Players champion Fred Funk, Davis Love and Shigeki Maruyama. Joe Durant shot 67 in the second round but missed by one stroke.

The weather was pleasant again, there was little wind, and the scores were low. Thirty of the 155 players scored in the 60s. Playing early in the day, Trevor Immelman shot 70 and caught Woods at six under par. But Woods hadn't started yet. At the end of the round, Immelman was in a tie for third place at 138.

Also tied for third, Vijay Singh struggled with his driver through the first two rounds. His iron play in the second round was wonderful. He hit every green except the 10th, and he missed that one because his approach shot ran off the back. He drove the ninth hole and made birdie with two putts from 50 feet.

Singh's long game was not his problem. His putting was. He started the second round with a birdie, then over the next five holes, he missed putts from 10, 12, 20, six and 12 feet. Singh said, "It wasn't that I wasn't stroking it well, it was just not going in." With 69 for his 138 total, he added, "You make some, you miss some. Hopefully over the weekend I can make some."

Brad Faxon played the first round in even-par 72 and bettered that score by six strokes in the second round. It was unusual that Faxon was in the Open, because he held no exemption and he had not played in America in the International Final Qualifying because of a scheduling conflict. He flew to Scotland early and earned his place in the Local Final Qualifying.

Faxon played outstanding golf, breezing through the first nine in 31 strokes with five birdies, and playing the second nine in 35 with a birdie on the last hole. He did not have a single bogey in his round of 66.

Ernie Els and Phil Mickelson sprang back after lackluster 74s in the first round. Both shot 67s, but that did them little good. They jumped from a tie for 74th into a tie for 25th place.

Mark Hensby had his hopes wrecked by playing the first four holes in 22 strokes, six over par, including a triple-bogey seven on the second hole. He birdied the third hole, then took another triple bogey with a seven on the fourth. He played the remaining 14 hole in one under par, courtesy of a birdie on the last hole. Although falling from 67 to 77, Hensby made the cut.

Montgomerie did better than that. With his 66, he vaulted into second place at 137, four strokes behind Woods and one stroke ahead of the seven players tied for third place.

In the first round, Montgomerie had pulled his tee shot on the first hole into the Swilcan Burn and lost a stroke right way. This time, he drove with an iron, pitched to eight feet, and holed for a birdie three. After a saved par four on the second, he picked up another stroke on the third, holing from four feet. Then he made his biggest move on the fifth, the easier of the two par-five holes. He struck a solid drive, then a three iron that bounded onto the green within 12 feet of the hole. He made that putt for an eagle three.

Four under par for the day, Montgomerie gave back one stroke by missing the eighth green. He drove the green at the ninth and got down in two putts from 60 feet. He was four under par for the outward nine. He birdied the 10th hole as well, but lost strokes on the 12th and 13th. He closed with three birdies on the last five holes and came home in 34.

Because David Toms had disqualified himself, Montgomerie and Paul Lawrie had played as a twosome. They started four groups ahead of Woods, and when they finished, it seemed likely that Montgomerie would be paired with Woods in the third round. Asked if that would be fun, he said no, just the opposite of what probably most players and spectators would think.

"This isn't fun," Montgomerie contended. "This is a major championship. It's a lot of work, and it's very much a business. All I can say is I look forward to the whole atmosphere of the day."

Woods went around the Old Course in 67 strokes for his halfway score of 133, which matched his 36-hole total five years earlier. Then he went on to win the Open by eight strokes. He again wasted no time in putting pressure on the rest of the field.

After two pars, he pitched to six feet and holed the putt for a birdie at the third. He reached the green of the par-five fifth hole with a six iron for his second shot to 25 feet. Two putts gave him another birdie. Three more pars followed, then he reached the ninth hole. He drove the green in the first round, but not this time. Instead, he putted from about 50 yards and still got down in two for the birdie, his third of the day.

There was a change in the wind as Woods stepped to the 10th tee. He had intended to lay up with an iron, but he pulled out his driver and struck a blast that was estimated to have traveled 380 yards to about 70 feet from the hole. He got down in two again for a birdie.

He made his last birdie of the round on the 14th with a drive, a three iron, and two putts from 60 feet.

Once again, Woods had shown there was more to his game than just power.

The second-round leaders:

| | | | | |
|---|---|---|---|---|
| Tiger Woods | 67 - 133 | | Robert Allenby | 68 - 138 |
| Colin Montgomerie | 66 - 137 | | Scott Verplank | 70 - 138 |
| Trevor Immelman | 70 - 138 | | Sergio Garcia | 69 - 139 |
| Vijay Singh | 69 - 138 | | Fred Couples | 71 - 139 |
| Brad Faxon | 66 - 138 | | Bo Van Pelt | 67 - 139 |
| Peter Lonard | 70 - 138 | | Bart Bryant | 70 - 139 |
| Jose Maria Olazabal | 70 - 138 | | Simon Khan | 70 - 139 |

When Tiger Woods won the Open in 2000, his four scores were 67, 66, 67 and 69. When Woods started with 66 and 67, it seemed unlikely that he would play a round on the Old Course in 70 or more strokes this time either. But Woods lost some of his precision overnight and posted a third-round score of 71, still under par, and still good enough to hold onto his lead, but his margin had been reduced to two strokes over Jose Maria Olazabal and three over Colin Montgomerie and Retief Goosen.

Woods led with a 54-hole score of 204. Olazabal, with 68, followed at 206. Montgomerie, with 70, and Goosen, matching Woods's opening 66, were three strokes behind at 207. Behind them were Sergio Garcia and Brad Faxon at 208, then Michael Campbell and Vijay Singh at 209. Eleven players were tied for ninth place at 210.

In the final tee time just after 3 p.m., Montgomerie played alongside Woods and had the vocal Scottish crowd much in his favor. Montgomerie picked up a stroke when Woods bogeyed the second hole. He missed the fairway then three-putted from 50 feet. He made pars on the third and fourth, where he missed another green yet ran the ball close with his putter.

Then Woods stepped onto the fifth tee. Holes such as this — a 568-yard par-five — have become easy for many professionals, and certainly for Woods. He hit a drive, a four iron into the green, and a putt from 30 feet that almost dropped for an eagle. Montgomerie matched him with a three-iron second shot and two putts for a birdie.

Over the past few years, when Woods has struggled it has usually been because of his driver. Occasionally he seemed to have swung so hard he threw himself off balance, and the ball flew off line, most often to the right. This year Woods had kept better control of his driver and had played superbly in winning the Masters and coming close in the U.S. Open. He didn't win there because of his putting.

On the sixth tee, Woods's drive drifted right and ran into a gorse bush. The ball was easily found, but it couldn't be played. He took a drop, pitched on, and, with two putts and a penalty stroke, he bogeyed. Montgomerie played the sixth flawlessly, and with his par four, had gained two strokes on the leader with 12 holes still ahead of them. He had begun the day four strokes behind and now he had moved within two.

Woods birdied the seventh hole with a three wood and a sand wedge to 18 feet. With the ninth hole coming up, another birdie appeared likely for Woods. Instead, Montgomerie drove the green and holed in two from a great distance. Meanwhile, Woods lost another battle with the gorse. His golf ball was just far enough into the branches that he had to take a penalty stroke. He made his par nevertheless, but Montgomerie was back to that two-stroke deficit by going out in 34 while Woods scored 36.

On the 10th, Woods made his par four, but Montgomerie played a six iron to five feet, holed the putt, and stepped onto the 11th tee within one stroke of the lead. He would climb no closer. He overshot the 11th green with a six iron and bogeyed. Woods got a par, and followed that with a drive to the front of the 12th green and birdied again. Woods lost another stroke on the 16th, but he ripped into a three wood on the final hole, two putted from 50 yards, and birdied again. Montgomerie had dropped one stroke at the 17th, but he birdied the 18th as well.

Looking back, Woods said it had been a difficult day.

"The wind started to pick up in the middle of the round," Woods said. "I hit one loose shot on 10; otherwise I hit it decently. But the greens got so hard, and the fairways had gotten harder. Shots on the fairway were sometimes running 80 yards. It's really hard to judge just how much it's going to roll. It became very difficult."

Among others who were expected to contend, Singh had opened with a pair of 69s, but followed with a loose 71 in the third round. He hit more fairways in the third round than in either of his first two rounds, and he reached 13 greens in regulation, which was not bad. But he bogeyed as many holes (three) as he birdied on the first nine, and had one more birdie (three) than bogeys on the second nine. He parred only seven holes in the erratic round.

Singh had complained of his putting, which was understandable when he three-putted the first hole for a bogey. But, after losing another stroke on the third hole, missing both the fairway and the green, Singh ran off four consecutive one-putt greens, three for birdies and one to save par on the fourth.

As a measure of his inconsistency, Singh birdied the 12th, bogeyed the 13th, birdied the 14th, and bogeyed the 17th. He did birdie the 18th, which in this company amounted to very little. Over the four rounds, the 18th surrendered 452 scores of par or better, and only 19 scores above par. But Singh simply shrugged it all off and headed, as usual, for the practice range.

This was an interesting day, first with Woods committing a few mistakes that cost him strokes, backed up by Goosen recovering from his 73 in the second round, Faxon holding on with a solid 70, and outstanding golf from some of the lesser-known players in the field.

Earlier in the day, Soren Hansen, a Dane, played with Peter Hanson, a Swede, a pair which already had everyone confused. The Dane shot 66 and soared from a 55th-place tie to a share of ninth. Hansen shared his position with, among others, Darren Clarke, who shot a 67; Sandy Lyle, the 1985 champion, with 69; Bernhard Langer and John Daly, the 1995 champion, who both shot 70; and Maarten Lafeber, who shot 67 as well.

Meanwhile, Ernie Els, who had shown some spark with his 67 the previous day, slumped to 75 and, with 216, fell completely away. Phil Mickelson lost all hope as well. His 72 left him nine strokes behind Woods, at 213, along with Nick Faldo, Greg Norman, and Mark Hensby, who had recovered from his second-round 77 with 69.

Once again, the weather was pleasant, although the wind did kick up at times. It was strong enough to put doubts in the minds of men deciding their club selections. It also had to be considered when putting. Garcia posted a 69 through the wind and said he was happy to have done so well. "I played pretty decently again today," Garcia said. "I was striking the ball nicely, I hit a lot of good drives, and I made some key putts when the wind was blowing, which was hard to do."

Garcia had some disappointments as well. "I bogeyed the 11th, didn't birdie the 12th, and then I three-putted the 16th. Other than that I was happy. I have a chance tomorrow," he said. "The course was tougher today and people were struggling. It was nice to see it that way. It made people play their best."

Goosen teed off just after noon, nearly three hours ahead of Woods. When Goosen birdied the 16th, he had moved to nine under par, within a stroke of Woods, who by then had bogeyed the second and fallen to 10 under par. It didn't last, of course, but Goosen had at least regained his confidence. After his bogey on the fifth, he had said to his caddie, "We're a little bit out of this now."

He had birdied the first, and so he stood even par for the round, but just three under par overall. Quickly, Goosen ran off three birdies from the seventh through the ninth. He played a three wood off the seventh tee to stay short of the Shell bunker, pitched to 12 feet with his sand wedge, and holed the putt. He was one under for the round, four under overall.

Goosen hit an eight iron to the eighth, and holed a 20-footer. His drive missed the ninth green to the right, but he chipped to seven feet for another birdie. Out in 33, he started back with four pars, then began his run. A chip to 15 feet at the 14th set up a birdie. Then he struck a wedge to three feet on the 15th for another birdie.

There was an unorthodox tactic on the 16th. A cluster of three bunkers called the Principal's Nose sits in the center of the fairway, about 275 yards from the tee, and beyond that is the widest part of the fairway. Goosen drove into safe ground with his five iron, then played a seven iron to 20 feet, and once again holed his putt. He had climbed to nine under par and had Woods within sight.

That was how Goosen finished. He three-putted the 17th and lost a stroke, then birdied the 18th to come back in 33 for his 66. He still needed another round such as this to challenge the leaders.

Olazabal moved up the ranks with his second 68. He scored 70 in the second round, giving him 206 for the 54 holes, two strokes behind Woods, and one ahead of Montgomerie and Goosen. Olazabal began the day slowly but soundly, playing the opening four holes in pars, then he went to work.

A drive and a five wood brought Olazabal close to the fifth green, but his pitch shot missed the hole by 30 feet. With new confidence in his putter, Olazabal made the putt for his first birdie of the day. His play was steady through the eighth. When his drive didn't reach the ninth green, he played a running shot with his nine iron that stopped within three feet of the hole, and he had another birdie.

He played a superb drive to the 12th fairway and holed for an eagle two from what he estimated was 20 yards. He had climbed to four under par, but he wasn't finished yet. His three wood on the 13th found a bunker, and he needed two more strokes to reach the green, setting up his only bogey. He ended with a drive left of the home hole and a 15-foot putt that fell in for a birdie.

Olazabal had played the first two rounds alongside Woods, and now he would again.

The third-round leaders:

| | | | |
|---|---|---|---|
| Tiger Woods | 71 - 204 | Darren Clarke | 67 - 210 |
| Jose Maria Olazabal | 68 - 206 | Kenny Perry | 68 - 210 |
| Retief Goosen | 66 - 207 | Sandy Lyle | 69 - 210 |
| Colin Montgomerie | 70 - 207 | Sean O'Hair | 70 - 210 |
| Sergio Garcia | 69 - 208 | Bernhard Langer | 70 - 210 |
| Brad Faxon | 70 - 208 | Tim Clark | 70 - 210 |
| Michael Campbell | 68 - 209 | John Daly | 70 - 210 |
| Vijay Singh | 71 - 209 | Bart Bryant | 71 - 210 |
| Soren Hansen | 66 - 210 | Scott Verplank | 72 - 210 |
| Maarten Lafeber | 67 - 210 | | |

Tiger Woods did not break any records as he did in 2000 when he won at St. Andrews with 269, the lowest winning aggregate ever in relation to par (19 under), and with an eight-stroke victory margin, the largest in 87 years.

He did what he needed to do, and that was more than enough. He had a round of 70 and a total score of 274 that increased his final margin from two strokes after 54 holes to five strokes at the end, as one after another of his closest challengers tried but could not catch up.

While five strokes was not remarkable by his standards, only five times since Arnold Palmer revived this old championship by his presence in 1960 had a player other than Woods won by five strokes or more: Palmer by six in 1962, Tony Lema by five in 1964, Johnny Miller by six in 1976, Greg Norman by five in 1986, and Nick Faldo by five in 1990.

Colin Montgomerie shot 72 for his final round and took second place with 279. Jose Maria Olazabal closed with 74 and dropped into a tie for third with the surprising Fred Couples. Age 45, Couples had come within sight with a final round of 68 and caught Olazabal, who stumbled through the final nine holes in 39 strokes.

Despite an outcome that had been anticipated, this was an interesting day, as first one player made a move and then another. Spiced by an eagle three on the fifth hole and a birdie three on the ninth, Bernhard Langer played the first nine in 33 strokes and moved to nine under par.

The surge ended for Langer on the 15th hole, the tough par-four of 456 yards. Langer's drive caught the rough and his second shot settled behind a bunker, short of the green. Then Langer hit a shot with an eight iron that he said was "one of the worst shots I've ever hit." He dumped it into the bunker. With no other option, he played out sideways and walked off with a six. He finished with 72 and, at 281, tied with five others in fifth place.

Then there was Nick Faldo. He played the last two holes in a total of five strokes — a rare birdie three on the 17th and an eagle two on the 18th. He posted a 69 for a total of 282 and tied for 11th place.

Four amateurs, including two Scots, shared in the glory. Lloyd Saltman, age 19, played the Old Course in 71 for a total of 283, tied for 15th place, and was the low amateur among a field of four. He scored one stroke better than Eric Ramsay, another Scot. The young Italian Edoardo Molinari, who would win the U.S. Amateur title later in the summer, tied for 60th place with 289, and Matthew Richardson, an Englishman, was last at 297. Still, he had played all 72 holes, an accomplishment for an amateur.

The road to Woods's 10th professional major championship had not been without bumps. When 2005 began, he had not won a major title since the U.S. Open in 2002, and he had won just one PGA Tour event in 2004. But Woods persisted and was seeing the results. He had already won the 2005 Masters and two other tournaments. When he teed off alongside Olazabal for the fourth round, he had led the Open's last six rounds over the Old Course. Ernie Els edged him by one stroke in the first round in 2000, then Woods had taken command.

Woods began with a drive to the center of the wide fairway, a tactic which essentially took the Swilcan Burn out of play. From where his ball lay, Woods approached the green from an angle, played short of the hole onto the left edge of the green, where, from this position, his putt would run parallel to the water, not towards it or possibly into it. His ball slipped past the hole, and he began with a routine par.

Goosen was up ahead. A marginal contender at the beginning, Goosen pitched well past the hole on the first and three-putted. Then he pulled his approach shot to the second into a greenside bunker and bogeyed once again, ending what faint hope he might have had. He finished with 74.

Brad Faxon dumped his approach to the first hole into the Swilcan Burn and dropped two strokes, starting with a six. He slipped to a closing 76 and tied for 23rd place at 284.

Vijay Singh birdied the first hole but missed birdie putts on the ninth and 10th, scored four fives over a stretch of five holes on the second nine, only one for a par, scored 72, yet climbed two places into a tie for fifth at 281.

In the end, the championship would be settled among Woods, Olazabal, who was paired with him, and Montgomerie, playing one hole ahead with Goosen.

Montgomerie began with two pars, then after a drive perhaps 75 yards short of the third green, he pitched on and holed a putt for a birdie three. Ten under par, he had moved within two strokes of Woods. Two holes later he cut the margin to one. His drive on the fifth ran for some distance before stopping in the shortest rough. He played his iron shot from about 215 yards onto the green. His putt for an eagle skimmed past the hole, but he birdied to advance to 11 under.

Woods meanwhile was playing safe, conservative golf and avoiding the risks. Alongside him, Olazabal played the first three holes in pars. He picked up a stroke at the fourth with a pitch and a good putt for a birdie three. Now 11 under, Olazabal had tied Montgomerie, and both were just one stroke behind.

Woods had thrived on the par-five holes. He had played the fifth in three under par and the 14th in one under par. He was four under in six holes played. He birdied the fifth again. Pulling out his driver, he ripped it so far he had only a seven-iron shot left. His first putt ran five feet past the hole, but he made that for his first birdie of the day. Olazabal was short of the green with his second, putted his ball on within eight feet and missed. He scored a par five and lost a stroke to both Woods and Montgomerie.

All three were receiving support from the crowd swarming around them, many of course urging on Montgomerie, the fellow Scot, but some pulling for Olazabal, and many for Woods.

In his first Open at St. Andrews five years earlier, Woods had bogeyed just three holes, the second hole in the third round, and the 17th in both the third and fourth rounds, an incredible record. By now, Woods had lost strokes on five holes, none on the 17th, as one might expect, but two on the 16th, a record not as remarkable as 2000, but certainly impressive.

Montgomerie could use the crowd support as he tried to win his first major championship. He had placed second in two U.S. Opens, in 1994 and 1997, both won by Ernie Els, the first in a playoff also involving Loren Roberts. He also lost in a playoff to Steve Elkington in the 1995 PGA Championship.

Montgomerie had a routine par on the sixth and a good drive short of the Shell bunker on the seventh, but an awful second shot that missed the green. Still, he saved his par, added another at the eighth, the first of the two par-threes, then stepped onto the ninth tee. He tore into his shot and drove the green. He barely missed his eagle putt, and holed from three feet for a birdie three. He had gone out in 33, three under par, and at that stage had gained two strokes on Woods.

Olazabal had not kept up. Eleven under par following his birdie on the fourth, he had failed to birdie the fifth, then made a major mistake on the sixth, not a strong hole. Olazabal pulled his drive left into one of the Coffins bunkers that lie between the sixth and 13th fairways. Less than 150 yards from the sixth green, and with his ball in a good lie, he hit his shot heavy. It pulled up short, his pitch fell short as well, and he bogeyed.

Over the next three holes, he could have birdied both the seventh and eighth, but did not. His drive stopped short of the ninth green, but a master of the short game, he ran the ball on, made his birdie, and turned for home with a first-nine score of 35, one under par, and 11 under for the championship.

Woods played a very long drive on the sixth, then his pitch shot hit the flagstick and bounded 40 or 50 feet off the green. When Woods was practicing before the round, he peppered the first '0' of the 100-yard sign with wedge shots. His coach, Hank Haney, advised Steve Williams, his caddie, to tell Woods to aim a bit wide of the flagsticks. Williams had not done that. He thought Haney was joking. Woods made his par on the sixth, but it might easily have been a birdie.

He missed a birdie putt on the seventh and another on the eighth, where his tee shot almost caught the hole for a hole-in-one. He two-putted for a birdie on the ninth and went out in 34. He had gained one stroke on Olazabal and lost one to Montgomerie. Within the next three holes the championship changed.

Montgomerie parred the 10th, then once again overshot the 11th, that difficult par-three, and bogeyed. The error cost him, because just then Woods had dropped a stroke on the 10th, a hole he practically owned. He had played the 10th in two under par, now he gave a stroke away.

Moving on to the 11th tee, Woods played an eighth iron inside 20 feet and got down in two for his par, then stepped onto the 12th tee. The next few minutes settled the Open. Woods drove into the left rough close to the green, chipped to within eight feet, and holed the putt for a birdie three. He stood 14 under par. Olazabal bogeyed and fell four behind.

Montgomerie, meanwhile, two behind as he stood on the 13th tee, drove with an iron. With his next shot he went for the green with a six iron. His ball hung up in the wind and fell short. He played a shot to five feet but missed the putt for a bogey five and a two-stroke swing. Montgomerie had fallen four strokes behind Woods as well.

It was over. Neither Montgomerie nor Olazabal could hope to catch Woods now, and they did not. Woods needed to do nothing more than run up the pars, avoid careless mistakes, and claim the trophy. On and on he went. A big drive on the 14th led to another birdie and now he led by five strokes. That is how it ended.

Woods played the 17th cautiously for a bogey five rather than risk something worse. One more hole, and he could tuck away his 10th professional major championship. He played the 18th with caution, despite a crescendo of a reception from the crowd almost like that for Nicklaus on the second day. Dismissing any chance of driving out of bounds or having an awkward approach, he drove with an iron well short of the green, ran his approach shot short, rolled the ball on with his third, and holed safely for a par four.

When asked about Nicklaus and his record, Woods reminded the press that this was a career opportunity. "It's not going to happen overnight," Woods said. "Jack took 25 years I believe to win all 18 of his. It's going to take a long time to win 18 major championships. More importantly, what did he finish (56 times) in the top five and 19 seconds? There's no other player who has been that consistent in the biggest events.

"To have the opportunity to get to 10 already this soon in my career, it's very exciting to hopefully look forward to some good years in my 30s and hopefully into my 40s."

# 5. PGA Championship

Considering sports history, it was appropriate that it took a squabble involving Boston for metropolitan New York area sports fans to renew their romance with Phil Mickelson.

This PGA Championship was originally scheduled for Brookline, Massachusetts, but there was a bitter split between The Country Club and the PGA of America in February of 2002. Neither side would discuss it publicly, but the word was that the hosts wanted to scale back on the corporate tents and commercialism that restricted crowd movement and resulted in huge repair work after the Ryder Cup there in 1999. The PGA wanted more of what made that event so financially successful, with $65 million in revenues.

The PGA also seemed to have rubbed the members wrong at The Country Club, which had close ties to the United States Golf Association.

Enter another USGA-oriented venue, the Baltusrol Golf Club in Springfield, New Jersey, which had been host to seven U.S. Open Championships over a span of 91 years, including two won by Jack Nicklaus in 1967 and 1980. Designed by the renowned A.W. Tillinghast, Baltusrol's Lower Course was last used for a championship in 1993, when Lee Janzen won.

Mickelson won with a total of 276, four under par, which was four strokes more than Janzen scored.

While technology had changed over the 12 years since, Baltusrol held up well, having been lengthened 237 yards to 7,392 yards, with nines of par 34 and 36, for a par-70 course having par-fives for the last two holes. The scoring average for 1993 was 72.109, which was 0.345 of a stroke lower than this year's 72.454. Perhaps more telling figures were that three players averaged 300 yards or more off the tees in 1993, while 26 of the 79 players who made the 36-hole cut this year did so. Mickelson was not one, his 274-yard average drives ranking him next-to-last (Darrell Kestner had a 271.5 average).

Before this week, Mickelson had abandoned the fade that won the Masters Tournament for him in 2004 and returned to a power game that was proving less successful as the year wore on. He won three times early in 2005, the FBR Open in Phoenix, the AT&T Pebble Beach National Pro-Am, and the BellSouth Classic in Atlanta. After that, Mickelson had just three top-10 finishes and his best was a tie for seventh at the Wachovia Championship in Charlotte in May.

For the PGA, Mickelson went to a high, soft cut shot that he would use to trade off yards in distance to find the Baltusrol fairways. It was a move that earned his second major championship, by one stroke over Steve Elkington and Thomas Bjorn. Mickelson held or shared the lead at the end of every day.

To win, Mickelson had to come back on Monday morning for 57 minutes of play. Lightning forced a suspension late on Sunday with 12 players still on the golf course and with Tiger Woods the leader among those who had finished, at 278, two under par. Woods, the winner of this year's Masters and Open Championship, had started the tournament with a 75 that put him in a tie for 113th place.

The leaderboard looked like this on Monday as they set out at 10:05 a.m.

|                 | Status       | Holes Played |
| --------------- | ------------ | ------------ |
| Phil Mickelson  | 4 under par  | 13           |
| Thomas Bjorn    | 3 under par  | 14           |
| Steve Elkington | 3 under par  | 15           |
| Davis Love      | 2 under par  | 13           |
| Vijay Singh     | 2 under par  | 15           |
| Tiger Woods     | 2 under par  | 18           |

No one realized better than Woods that all tied with or in front of him were major champions except Bjorn, who had come close and also had won other important tournaments. Elkington, Davis Love and Vijay Singh were past PGA Championship winners, in addition to Woods.

Mickelson holed an uphill, left-to-right, three-foot putt for par with his first stroke of the morning. Alongside Mickelson, Love also parred No. 14, and would par the next four holes, never threatening to lead. Elkington, too, held steady and finished with three consecutive pars. Bjorn dropped a shot on No. 15 to fall to two under, after hitting through the green from the rough, chipping back and missing the putt from five feet. Singh also fell back and finished at even par.

Trouble for Mickelson came on the 230-yard, par-three No. 16. His four-iron tee shot buried in a bunker and he could only hit out 18 feet right of the hole. He missed that putt and was tied with Elkington at three under. Then Bjorn holed from 25 feet for a birdie on the 650-yard, par-five No. 17, and the three of them shared first place.

Elkington had a good chance for birdie on the 17th and missed. He was in trouble off the tee on the 554-yard, par-five No. 18. He hooked his drive into the trees, but his golf ball rebounded out, and he hit a three wood from there. For his third shot, 96 yards away and with his ball in a divot, Elkington managed to hit eight feet below the hole. His putt stayed just out to the left.

While Mickelson played No. 17, taking a par with a driver, three wood, pitching wedge, and his 15-foot birdie effort that skimmed the hole, Bjorn was ahead on No. 18 with a perfect drive in the fairway. Bjorn came over the top of his three-wood second shot and found a tough lie in the back-left bunker. He exploded out to 20 feet but missed the putt, over the right edge.

"I think Phil was in the best position, playing last," Elkington said. "It would have been nice to be able to make four on 18 to put pressure on him, rather than him having a free shot at a birdie. He led the tournament all week. It's a hard course to hold the lead on, and I knew if I could keep the pressure on him, he would have to keep hitting good shots. But the same could be said for Thomas Bjorn, as well, I suppose. Either one of us could be at four."

"I got a good break on 18 that Steve and Thomas did not birdie it," Mickelson said. "It was kind of an emotional boost because now I felt as though it was my tournament to win."

So Mickelson stepped to the No. 18 tee, tied with Elkington and Bjorn, and needing a birdie for victory. The stage was his. His tee shot landed in the fairway, about five yards behind a plaque on the spot from which Nicklaus hit a one iron onto the green to win the 1967 U.S. Open. Mickelson knew the story and, as someone phrased it, let his three wood touch a piece of history before making his own.

"I just wanted some good karma, some good positive thoughts," Mickelson said. "Hey, Jack Nicklaus hit a one iron on the green from here. It can be done."

Mickelson hit the three-wood shot into the rough just right of the green. Then, with a lob wedge, he floated the ball onto the green and watched it roll to about two feet from the hole. Bjorn said, "I saw where he hit it on the last, and if there's anybody you'll bank on to get it up and down from there in the world, it's Phil Mickelson."

"It was a chip shot that I had hit tens of thousands of times in my backyard," Mickelson said.

Although obviously elated, Mickelson calmly shook hands with Love. Then Mickelson's wife, Amy, and their three children, age six and under, bounded on the green to celebrate with him. And the uproarious crowd, surprisingly large for a Monday morning, couldn't have been happier to witness the scene. "You're one of ours now," one spectator yelled. "We need a new governor, Phil," another shouted.

"It's an amazing feeling to be the winner and to be able to hold this trophy," the 35-year-old Mickelson said. "But it was a very stressful week. Having the lead after each night just added to the stress and the difficulty and the challenge of it, which is why I think it feels so good right now."

Mickelson finished with a 72, two over par, for his 276 total. Elkington (71) and Bjorn (72) tied at 277, then Love (74) shared fourth place at 278 with Woods. There were four tied for sixth place at 279: Geoff Ogilvy (69), Michael Campbell (69), Retief Goosen (72) and Pat Perez (73). Ted Purdy finished with 66 to tie for 10th place at 280 with Singh (74), David Toms (68), Steve Flesch (70) and Dudley Hart (71).

When informed that Tiger Woods had shot 75 in the first round, Phil Mickelson said, "If you are looking for me to shed a tear, it's not going to happen. But I believe, as we all do, that come Sunday his name will find his way on top there."

Tied for first place with Mickelson at 67, three under par, were another American, Ben Curtis, winner of the Open Championship in Britain in 2003 but nothing before or since, and four recognizable names from other countries who were all searching for their first major victories: Trevor Immelman and Rory Sabbatini of South Africa, Stuart Appleby of Australia, and Stephen Ames of Canada by way of Trinidad and Tobago.

Thirty-nine players shot even-par 70 or better, including defending champion Vijay Singh, who birdied his last two holes for a 70. The 11 players with 68s included two-time U.S. Open champion Retief Goosen, 1997 PGA champion Davis Love, 1995 PGA champion Steve Elkington, and past European Ryder Cup captain Bernhard Langer.

The New York area spectators adopted Mickelson when he was second to Woods at the 2002 U.S. Open at Bethpage Black, over on Long Island, in a way they had never fallen for other famous golfers over the years. Mickelson was loving it. "I just think the people here are awesome to play in front of, and they support so many great championships, that I really enjoy coming here and playing," he said. "That was kind of cool there, going through the gallery after hitting right over them."

On the 482-yard, par-four sixth hole, Mickelson's drive struck a tree on the right and fell straight down. Instead of going for the green, he played down the No. 17 fairway to within 92 yards of the hole position.

"The tree was really not going to affect the shot any, because I left myself far enough back," Mickelson said. "It was just a good full wedge and I was able to fly it on and spin it back to about five feet."

Mickelson missed the putt there to go one over par. He had bogeyed the third hole when he drove far left and could only chip out, but birdied the fifth with a three-wood tee shot and a nine iron to three feet. He birdied No. 9 and No. 10, then No. 14 — all three on putts of over 30 feet — and No. 18, where he two-putted from 35 feet as Doug Steffen, the Baltusrol club professional, was watching.

Mickelson had played a practice round with Steffen at Baltusrol about two weeks earlier. "I just tried to pick up some tidbits on some of the greens," Mickelson said. "How some greens break more than it looks."

Steffen said, "With his ball flight and his game around the greens, this course is perfect for him. He can hit that little cut right-to-left shot." During their practice round, Steffen had told Mickelson that the firmer the greens become, the more difficult they are to putt, because then the little subtleties are more likely to throw putts off line. He said that Mickelson was the only one of the high-ranking players to ask him about Baltusrol's intricacies.

"It obviously felt great to make those putts," Mickelson said. "If you give yourself enough chances here, the greens are rolling so well that you will make a couple. You just have to be patient. The one at No. 9 was nice because I was able to turn at even par and that gave me a little bit of momentum."

After holing a long putt for birdie on the par-four No. 10, Mickelson parred his next three holes — including a clutch 10-foot par save from the edge of the green at the par-four 11th — before sinking a 35-footer for birdie on the par-four No. 14. He also had a nice par-saving putt on the par-five No. 17.

Woods's bid for a third major championship in 2005 was in trouble from the start as he took bogey five on his first hole of the opening day and proceeded to a 75. Meant to reward length and precision, Baltusrol punished his inaccuracy. "It was just every hole you could say there's something that I did wrong not to make birdie," Woods said. His only birdie was on the eighth hole, a par-four of 380 yards. He posted four bogeys and a double bogey on the seventh. "That was frustrating."

At No. 18, his ninth hole of the day, Woods hit a low hook that struck a tree and nearly landed in a gully bordering the left rough. Woods and his caddie, Steve Williams, could not find the golf ball, so Woods asked the gallery across the creek for help. "No one saw it splash?" he said. The response was negative.

Williams found the golf ball, inside the hazard line, buried in mud about a foot from the water. Woods appealed to rules officials that the ball was so embedded, someone must have stepped on it accidentally. The officials, having no evidence of that, ruled that the ball remained in play.

Then Woods declared the ball unplayable and took a one-stroke penalty. He made a drop and hit his third shot into the rough in front of the green. From there he hit a pitch that came up 20 feet short of the hole, and he missed that putt, taking a bogey on a hole where 67 players that day made birdies and seven made eagles.

"There were marshals and camera crews looking for my golf ball and they were walking on the hazard line," Woods said. "We don't know if they actually stepped on my golf ball or not. We couldn't get any confirmation, so I had to play it as it was."

As Damon Hack observed in *The New York Times*, it was "just one more aspect of a day that conspired against Woods." He was in the 8:25 a.m. group starting at No. 10, with two contestants who outplayed him as they had months before, Michael Campbell (73) and Kevin Sutherland (74).

It was Campbell who denied Woods a possible shot at the Grand Slam this year by defeating him in the U.S. Open. It was Sutherland who was in the group with Woods in the EDS Byron Nelson Championship in May when he missed the 36-hole cut to end his record streak of 142 consecutive tournaments.

The 75 was his worst score in relation to par in a major championship in his career. He opened with a four-over-par 76 in the 2003 Masters Tournament. But Woods could not be considered out of contention. Four months earlier when he won the Masters, he had started with a 74. He had 10 scores of 74 or higher in the first rounds of majors in his career, but had never missed the 36-hole cut, never even finished out of the top 40, and out of the top 20 only three times.

"I'm still in the tournament, no doubt about that," said Woods, who missed eight of 14 fairways and needed 35 putts. "There's a long way to go. And as you all know, the golf course is only going to get harder. There won't be too many guys under par by the end of the week, and hopefully I can get myself over there in the next three days."

The first-round leaders:

| | | | |
|---|---|---|---|
| Trevor Immelman | 67 | Greg Owen | 68 |
| Ben Curtis | 67 | Davis Love | 68 |
| Stuart Appleby | 67 | Lee Westwood | 68 |
| Phil Mickelson | 67 | Retief Goosen | 68 |
| Rory Sabbatini | 67 | Jesper Parnevik | 68 |
| Stephen Ames | 67 | Pat Perez | 68 |
| Steve Elkington | 68 | Ben Crane | 68 |
| Bernhard Langer | 68 | John Rollins | 68 |
| Heath Slocum | 68 | | |

Tiger Woods awoke to controversy when an article in *The Star-Ledger* of Newark strongly suggested that Steve Williams stepped on Woods's golf ball in the first round beside the 18th fairway. The newspaper said, "Williams was the only person near the spot where he eventually found the ball, embedded in the ground.

"And, during the search, just before he found the ball, Williams was walking along the creek's bank when he made a step and quickly appeared to pull back his foot — perhaps as if he had stepped on something."

If Williams had stepped on Woods's ball, that would have incurred a one-stroke penalty. And if that were not reported, Woods would have signed an incorrect scorecard, which would now cause him to be disqualified. Woods said he and Williams discussed it briefly. "We saw each other this morning and I told him what I saw on TV this morning, and that was about it," Woods said. "I saw the videotape, just like all of you guys saw, and if you look at it, he walks three steps closer to actually point out the golf ball, so he wasn't even near it. The ball was embedded in there somehow. We don't know if it was a marshal who did it five minutes ago or some photographer. We don't know."

Kerry Haigh, the tournament director for the PGA of America, said he was convinced that if anyone stepped on the golf ball, it was not Williams.

When Woods defeated Phil Mickelson head-to-head in the Ford Championship at Doral back in March, that was a sign of what was to come for the next four months until their fates took turns at the PGA Championship. Mickelson shot a five-under-par 65 in the second round for a two-day total of eight-under 132 and a three-stroke lead over Jerry Kelly, who also posted a 65. Kelly was a two-time PGA Tour winner, but his best this year was a tie for eighth.

Meanwhile, Woods shot a 69 and made the 36-hole right on the number, at four-over 144, to trail Mickelson by 12 strokes.

Kelly's 65 included five birdies and no bogeys. In his last outing before the PGA, Kelly tied for 14th in the U.S. Bank Championship, but he traced his confidence, strangely, to a missed cut in the Open Championship at St. Andrews.

"Forget about my golf game and what I've done this year," Kelly said. "I feel great playing golf. So I've tried not to beat myself up, and I hope this mindset continues."

Other than Kelly, those closest to Mickelson were Davis Love (68), Lee Westwood (68) and Rory Sabbatini (69), all trailing by four strokes. Vijay Singh (67) trailed by five. In addition to Mickelson and Sabbatini, the second-round scores of the other Thursday co-leaders were Stuart Appleby (70), Stephen Ames (72), Trevor Immelman (72) and Ben Curtis (73).

"There were some birdies out there this morning, for sure," Love said. "I'm not surprised. I would be surprised if that keeps up."

Among the others, Retief Goosen (70) was at 138, Michael Campbell (68) was at 141, Sergio Garcia (70) was at 142, Adam Scott (69) was at 143, Masters runner-up Chris DiMarco (71) missed the cut at 146, and so did Open Championship runner-up Colin Montgomerie (71) at 148.

Error-prone in his three previous majors of the year — 10th in the Masters, tied for 33rd in the U.S. Open, and tied for 60th in the Open Championship — Mickelson said, "I want to put everything I've got into this one event. There's a lot of golf left, but I'm entering the final two rounds with a lot more confidence than I've had in a while."

After beginning the second round tied with five others at 67, Mickelson posted seven birdies, an eagle, two bogeys and a double bogey. By the time Woods teed off for the second round, he was 13 strokes behind Mickelson. The play of Mickelson and Woods, though hours apart, could be summarized by the fourth hole, a par-three of 194 yards.

With a morning tee time, Mickelson hit a routine iron shot and two putts for a par, leaving the green to rousing cheers. In the afternoon, Woods hit a tee shot that fell short, into the water, and stilled the gallery. After Woods pitched his third shot onto the green from the drop area, a large tree limb to the left of the green collapsed, injuring three men. Woods and his playing companions waited about 10 minutes for the paramedics to treat the injured. Woods then rolled in a 15-foot putt for bogey and resumed a round that flirted with the cut line until the very end.

On the 650-yard, par-five 17th hole, playing downwind, Woods hit a drive and a three wood that had the distance to reach the green in two, which no one had done this week. But Woods's golf ball hit the lip of a greenside bunker and shot across the sand to the other lip, and he made a bogey after punching out backward — his best escape route — and failing to get up and down from the rough.

Needing a birdie to make the cut on the 554-yard, par-five final hole, Woods obliged, stroking a seven iron to 15 feet and two-putting to go to four over par for 36 holes. He and Williams smiled and shook hands. "Here I was, back at five over par, even for the day," Woods recalled the situation on the 18th tee. "Now you've got to suck it up and hit two good golf shots. And that's what I'm really proud of."

Ever the optimist, Woods was still trying to figure out how he could win. "I need to shoot something that gets me into the red figures [under par] for the tournament tomorrow," he said. "And then see the number I'm going to have to shoot Sunday, but I need to get into red figures."

Things looked promising when Woods birdied the first hole, and another birdie seemed likely at the second when his wedge from the right rough, 50 yards out, stopped eight feet past the hole. But his putt went three feet past, he missed the comeback putt, and tapped in for a bogey.

At the third, Woods hit his tee shot into the rough to the right. His approach reached the green but ran off into the right rough. His chip rolled six feet past the hole, then he two-putted for another bogey.

Then, at the par-three fourth hole, Woods splashed his tee shot into a pond. His wedge shot from the drop area was spinning back towards the hole when there came the crackling sound of that tree limb breaking and falling.

It might have been a good time for Woods to relax. When play resumed, Woods holed the putt for a bogey, his third straight, but then got himself going with four birdies in the next 10 holes — at the par-four No. 11, the par-three No. 12 and par-four No. 15. The finish kept Woods there for the weekend, but left him far behind Mickelson, who had come to Baltusrol with a game plan that he was executing.

Mickelson began on No. 10 and birded four of his first eight holes. A nine iron to 10 feet provided the first birdie on the 11th hole. On No. 13, Mickelson struck a nine iron to three feet. He went to three under par for the day on No. 14, where he hit a wedge shot to 12 feet.

A bogey resulted at the par-three No. 16 after he hit into a greenside bunker and missed a five-foot putt. That stroke was recovered on the next hole, the 650-yard par-five, with a wedge for his third shot to 15 feet.

At No. 18, Mickelson struck a four iron from 222 yards that settled 20 feet from the hole. When he rolled in the eagle putt, the crowd rejoiced and Mickelson tipped his cap.

Mickelson gave two strokes back at the par-four first hole. He needed three shots out of the rough and two putts to make a double-bogey six. But Mickelson responded with three more birdies against one bogey. "That's the way Phil's playing," Woods said. "It's going to be hard for myself or anyone else to catch him."

On the par-four third hole, Mickelson left a four-iron shot 40 feet from the cup but holed that putt for a birdie. His birdie at the fifth was from six feet after an eight-iron shot into that 423-yard, par-four hole. Then on the sixth, Mickelson drove into the right rough, hit a six iron short of the green, chipped poorly to 25 feet and missed that putt, taking a bogey. He recovered that stroke with a wedge for another 25-footer that he holed at the 380-yard, par-four eighth.

Mickelson was playing those right-to-left fades off the tee, safer shots for him that sacrificed some distance, about 20 to 25 yards, for accuracy. Asked why he did not use the same fade at the other majors this year, Mickelson said, "That's probably a question I should answer after the week is over. Right now, I just want to hit that cut shot, which I think is most effective here because the fairway is drying out. I want the ball to come in softer."

The second-round leaders:

| | | | | | |
|---|---|---|---|---|---|
| Phil Mickelson | 65 | - 132 | Greg Owen | 69 | - 137 |
| Jerry Kelly | 65 | - 135 | Stuart Appleby | 70 | - 137 |
| Rory Sabbatini | 69 | - 136 | Vijay Singh | 67 | - 137 |
| Davis Love | 68 | - 136 | Jesper Parnevik | 69 | - 137 |
| Lee Westwood | 68 | - 136 | Shingo Katayama | 66 | - 137 |

It had been hot all week but the third round's temperature was sizzling, the hottest day at a major championship since that second week of June in 1994 at Oakmont, Pennsylvania, in the U.S. Open, the tournament that shared headlines with former football star O.J. Simpson's murder charges.

The temperature at Baltusrol at 3 p.m. Saturday was 102 degrees, with a "heat index" of 106. Heat index is a term used to describe the apparent temperature, or what it feels like, and this was a level that the weather services labeled as "hazardous." The actual temperatures had been 95 degrees on Thursday and 92 degrees on Friday at that hour, and the forecast for Sunday was for 91 degrees, windy and with rain and lightning likely.

Phil Mickelson, who has been called "Hefty" instead of "Lefty" on occasion, wilted on this steamy afternoon, shooting a two-over-par 72 after starting with a three-stroke lead. With his final putt after trudging up the 18th fairway, Mickelson had fallen into a tie for first place. Davis Love posted a 68 to join Mickelson at 204, six under par.

Thomas Bjorn tied a major championship record by shooting 63 to stand one stroke behind at 205, while four players including two past PGA champions were tied for fourth place at 206: Vijay Singh (69), Steve Elkington (68), Pat Perez (67) and Stuart Appleby (69).

Retief Goosen (69) and Ben Curtis (67) headlined the group at 207, three strokes behind the leaders. Tied with them were Lee Westwood (71), Greg Owen (70) and a little-known American, Jason Bohn (68).

Mickelson had let several golfers back into contention, but still possibly not Tiger Woods, who was six strokes (and 19 players) behind despite recording a 66. "After the start I had, I thought for me to fight and still be in the lead is a huge boost," Mickelson said. "Guys were out there making birdies, and I was going the other way."

In the final group of the day at 3 p.m., with Jerry Kelly (74), Mickelson was off when the temperature was at the highest point. For all who played in the afternoon, the greens picked up speed and the course became more difficult, and Mickelson did not play with the precision he had shown on the first two days. (Bjorn's tee time was at 11:20 a.m., and Woods was off at 8:20 a.m.)

Mickelson's lead was quickly in jeopardy. He drove into the right fairway bunker on the second hole, then knocked his approach shot over the green. After hitting his chip shot 40 feet past the hole, he missed the putt and recorded a bogey.

"I can't control the way the ball reacts on some of the greens," Mickelson said. "I thought I hit some good shots that weren't rewarded. We expect that at major championships. I didn't let it bother me. I thought the course was very difficult but very fair."

Mickelson made back-to-back bogeys on the fifth and sixth holes, both par-fours. On the fifth, Mickelson hit an eight iron to 35 feet then blew the putt eight feet past the hole and missed on the return. On the sixth, his approach shot from the left rough was up against the lip of a greenside bunker. He shot the ball out 30 feet from the hole and missed that putt.

The only birdie by Mickelson came at the par-three No. 12, where he hit a six-iron shot to 18 feet.

Love had not won a tournament since 2003, when he recorded four of his 18 career victories on the PGA Tour, including The Players Championship. But his greatest moment in golf had come in this area, that 1997 PGA Championship at Winged Foot Golf Club in Mamaroneck, New York.

On Saturday, Love's round included four bogeys but he made four birdies on the second nine to chase down Mickelson. It started well for Love, with birdies on the first two holes, with a pitching wedge to 10 feet on the first, and a seven iron to 25 feet on the second. He gave back both strokes when he missed the fairways and took bogeys on both the sixth and seventh. He missed a 20-foot putt for par on the sixth and a 15-footer on the seventh.

Love slipped over par for the round at No. 10, when he drove in the rough, hit a nine iron over the green, and missed a 12-foot putt. There was another bogey on three putts at the par-three No. 16, but there also was the flurry of four birdies on Nos. 11, 13, 15 and 17.

On No. 11, Love hit a six iron to 10 feet, and he holed the putt. Two holes later, he made a 20-footer, and on No. 15 it was a 30-footer. He had two putts for the final birdie on No. 17.

Love, age 41, had fought through neck and back problems in recent years but has found a workout regimen that he says has helped him during the difficult conditions of this championship. "I'm digging balls out of the rough that I wasn't able to and I'm hitting drives powerfully at the end of a round like I couldn't last year," Love said. "I've been remarkably calm.

"I'm confident and excited about the way I'm playing, and I'm looking forward to the next round. As far as my golf game, I feel good about it. I'm hitting the ball more solidly than I have in a long time."

The 34-year old Bjorn found himself in contention at a major championship again. He was the second-place finisher to Woods in the Open at St. Andrews in 2000 — although trailing by eight strokes — and had his best chance three years later at Royal St. George's. He led by three strokes with four holes remaining, then bogeys at Nos. 15 and 17 and a double bogey at No. 16 enabled Curtis to slip past him.

"You've got to go away from championships like that and say, 'The one thing I can take away from this is that I am capable of putting myself in good position,'" said Bjorn, who defeated Woods head-to-head at the 2001 Dubai Desert Classic. "My golf game is good enough."

Some might have been surprised that a golfer from Denmark would play so well under hot conditions. But Bjorn, who also has a home in Dubai, said, "I've done well in warm weather. We get a lot of practice on the European Tour in the early part of the year when we play in Asia and Australia. I've gone to the four corners of the world to play golf, so this is nothing new to me."

Bjorn's round of 63 tied the lowest score ever in a major championship, a record he now shared with 19 others, including Jack Nicklaus and Tom Weiskopf here on the first day of the 1980 U.S. Open.

He recorded 10 birdies and one bogey, which came on the 505-yard, par-four No. 7, where Bjorn drove into the left rough and could only chop his second shot out. On the green in three, he missed a 25-foot putt for par. The birdies came on approach shots and putts as follows: No. 4 – six iron to 12 feet; No. 5 – six iron to eight feet; No. 10 – nine iron to 25 feet; No. 11 – seven iron to 12 feet; No. 14 – nine iron to eight feet; No. 15 – nine iron to eight feet; No. 18 – five iron to 50 feet, two putts.

Bjorn had done what Woods wanted to do, although Tiger finished three strokes higher and slapped a small sign in frustration as he left the 18th hole. He had closed from 12 to six strokes behind Mickelson and Love, the leaders, but missed his chance for a truly special round.

"I thought if I shot 63 today it would be a pretty good number," Woods said. "I had four more opportunities out there, short putts that I missed or three-putted or pulled a three wood on 17."

Woods began the round with a bogey, but responded by making birdies at Nos. 5, 9 and also 10, when he chipped in from off the green. Another birdie seemed almost assured when he hit an iron shot to six feet on No. 12, but the putt slid past the hole. Woods missed a 10-footer on No. 13, then recovered for birdies on Nos. 14 and 15.

His most critical misses came on the last two holes.

On No. 17, the 650-yard par-five, Woods ripped a drive of about 360 yards, leaving him about 290 yards to the hole. He went for the green in two, and for the second straight day, left with a score other than an eagle or a birdie. His three-wood shot had the distance but hooked into the gallery, beneath a chair. After the chair was removed, Woods chipped to about 25 feet, and missed that putt, taking a par. In the second round, he had a bogey there.

On No. 18, another par-five, Woods split the middle of the fairway with his drive and hit a seven iron to 30 feet. He ran the eagle putt 10 feet past the hole, and missed the next putt as well. It was another unexpected par.

"Bad putt, the wrong time," Woods said. "Welcome to golf. I wish we could say we could putt well every day, but it doesn't happen. This week, my speed has been erratic, as you saw on 18, a couple of holes where I left it short or ran it by."

When asked his chances, Woods referred to Paul Lawrie's 10-stroke comeback in the 1999 Open at Carnoustie, the largest ever in a major championship. "Guys have come back and won before," Woods said. "It's out there. If I play like I did today and make some putts, I can shoot a low one."

The third-round leaders:

| | | | | | |
|---|---|---|---|---|---|
| Davis Love | 68 | - 204 | Vijay Singh | 69 | - 206 |
| Phil Mickelson | 72 | - 204 | Ben Curtis | 67 | - 207 |
| Thomas Bjorn | 63 | - 205 | Jason Bohn | 68 | - 207 |
| Pat Perez | 67 | - 206 | Retief Goosen | 69 | - 207 |
| Steve Elkington | 68 | - 206 | Lee Westwood | 71 | - 207 |
| Stuart Appleby | 69 | - 206 | Greg Owen | 70 | - 207 |

Phil Mickelson had slept on the lead for three nights in a row and now he would sleep on it for a fourth. He had fallen behind and rallied to regain the lead on Sunday when lightning forced officials at 6:35 p.m. to suspend fourth-round play until Monday morning.

He was standing over a three-foot putt for par at No. 14 as lightning struck nearby and a horn soon blared to bring an end to the day's competition, providing for the first Monday finish in this championship since 1986, the year Bob Tway holed out from a greenside bunker on No. 18 to stun Greg Norman at the Inverness Club in Toledo, Ohio.

Twelve players were left to complete the final round. With four-plus holes to play, Mickelson was four under par for the championship. He was one stroke ahead of Steve Elkington, who had three holes to play, and Thomas Bjorn, who had four holes left. At two under par, still on the golf course, were Vijay Singh, with three holes remaining, and Davis Love, who was walking with Mickelson with four-plus holes to go.

Tiger Woods was also at two under par and was the leader among those who had completed the fourth round. He posted a two-under-par 68 for a 278 total, and had what most probably felt was still a glimmer of hope. Behind Woods, Geoff Ogilvy and Michael Campbell both shot 69s for 279 totals.

Others who still had to return to finish on Monday were Retief Goosen (one under on 17th fairway), Pat Perez (even par on 15th green), Stuart Appleby (one over on 16th tee), Lee Westwood (three over on 18th green), Ben Curtis (four over on 17th tee), Jason Bohn (five over on 17th fairway), and Greg Owen (seven over on 18th green).

After building a three-stroke lead through four holes, including a birdie on the par-three fourth, Mickelson bogeyed Nos. 6, 7, 9 and 10 to fall behind, but he birdied No. 13 and regained the lead.

"I don't feel like today was a slide like yesterday," Mickelson said. "I thought the course was playing tremendously harder. Every bogey I made, I put myself in the proper spot to get up and down. Whether it was No. 6, leaving it right in the bunker, I had a good chance at getting up and down.

Whether it was No. 7, leaving it short right to get up and down. Whether it was No. 9, leaving it right of the pin to get up and down. And I just didn't get up and down on those holes. But I gave myself chances to do that.

"So I don't feel like there were any spots where I wasted a shot or where I couldn't save par. And I hit a couple of good shots on No. 13 to make birdie, and I hit a good shot on No. 14 and just missed that putt. I'm starting to hit some good shots and we've got some birdie holes coming in."

Elkington took the lead with a bogey-free first nine holes and birdie on No. 9. He made his first bogey at No. 10 but got the stroke back on the next hole, and held a two-stroke lead on Mickelson after the 12th. Then came two more bogeys on Nos. 13 and 15.

"It's a shame obviously that we didn't get to finish, but I didn't really want to play those last three holes into the wind either," said Elkington, whose dark polka-dot shirt that he bought while in New Jersey was similar to that he wore in the final round when he won the 1995 PGA Championship at Riviera Country Club, near Los Angeles.

Bjorn and Love were two players who had reason to feel especially good about their games entering the final round and found little but trouble that afternoon. Bjorn was coming off that 63 on Saturday and Love had posted three 68s, the only player in the field with three rounds in the 60s.

When play was suspended, Bjorn was two over par for the day and Love was four over. Bjorn had three bogeys in the first 10 holes before recording his first birdie of the day at No. 13. "It turned into some hell of a golf course today, I'll have to say," Bjorn commented. "It was a completely different golf course to what we've seen the other three days."

After starting with a share of the lead, Love bogeyed four holes out of five starting at No. 3. He pushed his drive at No. 3 so far into the trees that he needed a wedge just to punch out sideways to the fairway. He three-putted No. 4, missing a six-footer, then missed the green at No. 5 and failed to get up and down for par. At No. 7 he was in the rough for three consecutive shots and did well to make an eight-foot putt for a bogey.

"You arrogantly think if you win one that the rest of them are easy," said Love, eight years removed from his 1997 PGA title. "The second one is just as hard. That's why when you see a guy who has three or four or five of them, he's looked upon a little bit differently than the rest of the players. One major puts you in the club, but it's just in the club. Four or five of them puts you in superstar status."

Or 10 of them, in the case of Woods, who reached that figure in the Open Championship at St. Andrews.

Woods appeared out of the running when he bogeyed the first and third holes, but he made four birdies after that, including Nos. 17 and 18, par-fives where he needed eagles instead, but couldn't produce the required second shots. But his main problem in this PGA Championship — as in the U.S. Open — was putting. It wasn't as bad as at Pinehurst, where he tied for 80th. Here, he tied for 27th. "I didn't have my speed all week," he said.

He contended that "my putting is as good (as in 2000), but it's been sporadic this year, which is interesting. I normally don't putt that way. I've usually been a very consistent putter over the years. This year is one of those weird years where I either putt great or don't putt well at all."

Summing up his major performances, Woods said, "I've had a wonderful four tournaments. I won two, I was close in one, and I don't know about the other one yet."

While talking with the press after his round, Woods still thought he had a chance to win this championship under the heavy damp and windy conditions that the players remaining on the course would face — and then the round was suspended. And Woods knew that rain was forecast overnight, that clear and calm weather would return in the morning, and the course would be softer and play much easier.

Several days later when Woods arrived in Akron, Ohio, for the WGC - NEC Invitational, he revealed in a press conference that he had gone home to Orlando, Florida, on Sunday night. He was asked if there had been a risk in doing that. "Yeah it was, but also it really wasn't either," Woods said. "These are the best players in the world. Look who's on that board. It wasn't like guys who have never been there before. If you have guys who had never been there before, then it might have been a different story."

Still, probably many or most people were surprised.

"Yeah, I'm surprised, very surprised," Michael Campbell said. "The last two holes, anything could have happened, especially in that rough. I would have hung around for a playoff."

Stewart Cink said, "I thought he'd be hitting balls Monday morning at the golf course because it's a tough course to finish on and it's a major championship. It would have been totally sportsmanlike for him to come out there and be prepared for whatever happened. ... Just him being there in the clubhouse and being seen might have affected how they played on Monday."

Fortunately for Woods, it was not a question that would haunt him.

# 6. The Players Championship

There's the old saw that holds — those who can, do, and those who can't, teach. Well, then, what are scholars to make of bouncy Fred Funk, former golf coach at the University of Maryland and, as of late March 2005, winner of the prestigious and very demanding Players Championship, an exercise against a full field of PGA Tour players. He obviously could teach. He spent 1982-1988 as the Maryland golf coach. And he obviously could play a bit, because when you win the Players, you're beating everybody who is anybody.

Funk — a diminutive 5-feet-8 and 165 pounds, gregarious, energetic — was merely the most unlikely to succeed in the field. He was 48 years old, one of the shortest hitters, and he had won six times, the previous being the Southern Farm Bureau Classic in 2004. By every measure, including his first prize of $1.44 million, this was his most impressive by far. For openers, this was the day of power golf, and he was barely getting 250 yards off the tee, meaning that he was giving up 30, 40, 50 yards per drive to most of his competitors. This was especially true after the Stadium Course at the TPC at Sawgrass, par-72 and over 7,000 yards long, was drenched with rain, which meant soft fairways, meaning less roll. In a word, a horror to short hitters.

"I felt kind of like Herbie the Volkswagen, the Love Bug," Funk said, "because I'm out there just hitting my little peashooters, and the bombers are going 40 by me — everybody I was playing with."

Other problems: With the foul weather most of the weekend, it also meant frustrating delays, and a 32-hole grind on Monday. And in addition, he was starting the final round four strokes off the lead. All in all, it didn't figure to be the most promising of prospects to a 48-year-old. And he won by a stroke.

So the first and principal question was, how did a player like Funk manage to win the prestigious Players Championship, against most of the best players in the world, on the long, tough Stadium Course? Funny — Funk was discussing that very point after he tore up the course in the first round. "It's actually set up pretty good in these conditions, with these fairways, for the long hitters," he said. "But fortunately it's a golf course — and they're getting fewer and fewer — where a guy with my lack of power can still score well. Even though I can't overpower anything, I can go from Point A to Point B and give myself enough chances for birdies."

And that was as good an answer as any — the right man in the right place at the right time.

If Funk was a work in progress, Steve Jones was a case of resurrection. Jones, the much injured 1996 U.S. Open champion, came to The Players Championship after a 22-month sabbatical following elbow surgery. The elbow was still weak, but in the first round he managed to shoot an amazing 64, eight-under-par at the tournament's home, the rain-soaked TPC Stadium Course at Ponte Vedra Beach, Florida. That gave him a one-stroke lead over Zach Johnson, England's Lee Westwood and Funk. "Steve Jones?" cracked Funk. "Where did he come from?"

Jones was wondering himself. "I'm surprised," he said. "But I knew I was close. I had that feeling that something is going to happen. I don't know what's going to happen over the next three days, but I felt like I had a good one in me. I was due."

Still soggy and receptive, the course played at about its easiest, an average of 71.87, with 87 players shooting par or better, and 29 shooting in the 60s. "It was a strange day," said Padraig Harrington, who was at five-under 67 in a group along with world No. 1, Vijay Singh. "It's going to get tougher. It looks like they used up all the easy pins today. Can only see tough ones left for 54 holes."

Singh matched his career best at the Stadium Course, a 67, which was more than an encouraging sign. The last time he opened at five under, he finished second. "It was nice to start off ... in contention for a change," Singh said. "Normally, I'm always chasing."

Jones took the stage from what he called "The Fab Four" — Singh, Tiger Woods, Ernie Els and Phil Mickelson, Nos. 1 through 4, respectively, in the World Ranking, and they opened with 67, 70, 71 and 70, respectively.

Els figured to be in great shape coming in. He'd already won twice on the European Tour and had three top-six finishes on the PGA Tour this season. "I made some silly mistakes and that's why I'm one under and not three or four under," Els said.

Mickelson logged seven birdies, three bogeys and a double bogey. "I wasn't thinking about a score," Mickelson said, mystifying everyone. "It's hard to go all 18 holes without missing any shots."

Tiger Woods, who could have regained the No. 1 spot from Singh in the tournament, also shot 70, but was somewhat steadier with four birdies and two bogeys. He finished on a high note, with a birdie from eight feet on his final hole of the day. He praised the greens, although he needed 29 putts. "They were so perfect," Woods said. "It's just that somehow, mine didn't go in."

There would be some such story for all four of the Big Four. All told, they had started 42 times at the Players. Woods was the only one who ever won. They had only nine top-10 finishes but missed the cut eight times. And in this one, Singh had the best finish, a tie for 12th. Els tied for 17th, Mickelson for 40th and Woods for 53rd.

Jones had himself quite a day in his opening 64. The key was accuracy. He hit 12 of 14 driving fairways and 15 greens in regulation, and needed just 26 putts. It was quite a reversal from the depressing days after his surgery in August 2003. But the performance didn't elevate him to favorite. Not yet.

Funk wasn't up there, either. Given the power of the field, and his lack of it, Funk could forgive anyone who didn't count him among the favorites. So he was something of a pleasant surprise when he posted that opening 65, tied for second with Zach Johnson and Lee Westwood, a stroke behind Jones.

Funk's 65 was impressive beyond the sheer low number. He was playing the course as though he owned it. He suffered no bogeys and racked up seven birdies. He salvaged a birdie at the par-five 11th, hitting a bunker shot to a foot. He holed a 20-foot putt at the 12th, and at the nasty par-three 17th, remembering the seven he took there in 2004, he lobbed an eight iron to three and a half feet. Then he hit a six iron to eight feet at the 18th. Coming in, he holed a 12-footer at No. 2, hit a bunker shot to 10 feet at No. 6, and holed a three-footer at No. 9.

This Players Championship was weather-whipped into a frazzle, and nobody knew it better or was hurt more than Steve Jones. The frustration of waiting, to begin with. He had to wait nearly 51 hours from the end of his first round on Thursday to the start of his second on Saturday afternoon. Then he played the second nine of his second round Sunday and shot 43. "I made some poor club selections," Jones said. He shot 77, made the cut, but finished tied for 77th.

Funk might have been the first player to be disqualified for napping during a rain delay. Funk slipped home, just three miles from the course, to take a nap during the nearly three-hour rain delay in the second round Saturday, and he was still in his pajamas when his caddie, Mark Long, called. "I thought we were done for the day," Funk said. "I was dead asleep. My caddie told me, you'd better get out here." Funk made it in plenty of time — and not in his jammies.

Singh was making something of a move in the second round and was two off the lead coming to the 18th. There, he put two shots into the water and took a quadruple-bogey eight for a 74.

The end of the second round — apart from the fact that it finally did end — was marked by the news that Tiger Woods had just made his 140th consecutive cut, and right on the number — 143, with 70-73. And Tim Herron tied the tournament record with six straight birdies, starting from No. 8. "I teed off at 7:30 and was still asleep," Herron said. "That probably helped."

On Monday, it was the wind. It blew at a steady 20 mph and gusted to 35, lifting scores to a whopping average of 76.512. Of the classy field, 16 couldn't break 80, including first-round leader Steve Jones, who closed with an 84. The field was completing the third round Monday morning, ranging from some having six holes to play, to 14 for Funk and some others. Then they would play the fourth round.

"Today was more a survival test than anything," said Joe Durant. "It took us over five hours to play 14 holes this morning."

The wind made the little island 17th, in particular, a monster trap for many, none more so than Bob Tway. Completing his third round Monday morning, he was in contention, tied for 10th, coming to the 17th. He proceeded to hit four balls into the water and make 12, thereby getting Robert Gamez off the hook. Gamez was the previous record-holder at 11, that in 1990. "I didn't think anybody would break it," Gamez said.

Said Tway: "You're playing great in the tournament, and all of a sudden, in one hole, you might as well be finishing last." The 12 gave him an 80, and with a 76 in the wind in the afternoon, he tied for 56th. Scott Verplank, his good friend and playing partner, could only watch in horror, knowing that the hole was a crapshoot. "With the wind blowing like that — well, you can't out-think it," he said, "because you could hit the same shot twice, and one of them is going to be perfect and one is going in the water."

There were other prominent victims. Phil Mickelson watered two shots in the morning and one in the afternoon, and played it in seven and five.

Sergio Garcia hit his first over the green, his second short, and made six.

Defending champion Adam Scott had figured he was out of it, then birdied three of the only four holes left to his third round for a 73, in the hunt at 10 under. But another 73 left him tied for eighth.

When the fourth round began later Monday, Luke Donald was leading at 12 under, with Joe Durant a stroke behind. Funk didn't seem to have much of a chance, not from four shots off the lead. Then things began to break his way, thanks in part to the miseries of others.

Donald had a brutal front nine — a double-bogey six at the fourth, where a gust brought his ball down short, and three bogeys and only one birdie. That was a 40 going out, and two birdies and two bogeys brought him home in par for a 76. The final injury came at the demanding 18th. He had 188 yards to the hole. "The breeze was off to my left," he said, "and I really hit a four iron, pitched pin-high, maybe four feet to the right of the hole. I hit a great shot. Unfortunately, it just caught that runoff." Someone thought he smiled after that shot. "I think it was a grimace," Donald said. "I hit a good shot. You could tell from the crowd it had gone off the edge." Indeed — 25 feet away. And he had needed a birdie there to tie for the lead. He made par for a 76–280 and a tie for second place.

Tom Lehman, playing well ahead of the leaders, made the big run at it. He birdied four of five holes starting at No. 2, and he just missed on a 15-foot birdie try at the 18th that would have tied him with Funk. But he zoomed from a tie for 23rd in the third round to almost picking it off before settling for a tie for second with a 68. It was one of only four rounds in the 60s that windy Sunday. Steve Lowery, Ernie Els and Brett Quigley all shot 69.

Scott Verplank, who played 30 holes on Sunday, also made a strong move, from a tie for 10th to join the tie for second with a closing 70. He still had a chance at the 18th, but he missed the green with a five iron and two-putted from eight feet.

Durant led briefly, but his chances slipped away. "I hadn't been in that position in a while, and I really felt good," he said. "I wasn't nervous. I was just trying hard to hit the proper golf shots, and I didn't quite pull them off. But I hung in there. I didn't play particularly well down the stretch, but I could have given up a long time ago and I didn't, so I was proud of myself." He was 12 under through No. 2, but played the rest of the way in five over and closed with a 76–281 for fifth place alone.

Funk closed with a one-under 71 and a nine-under 279 total, ducking just under the bar by a stroke in heavy winds. It was his career seventh victory in 523 starts on the tour, and he was the oldest ever to win The Players Championship, at 48 years, nine months and 14 days. He had been looking forward to joining the Champions Tour, that mulligan for the over-50 set, but the five-year exemption that goes with winning the Players would inspire him to rethink that possibility. Maybe not. "My wife really doesn't want me to go to the Champions Tour," he said. ("Not yet," Sharon Funk interjected.)

The final round spun out the appropriate drama. Funk bogeyed No. 3 but rebounded with birdies at Nos. 7 and 8 to make the turn at one under par. That was when, he said, "I actually thought I could win this thing." He also birdied the 12th and 13th. "And then ... I thought for sure I could definitely win this thing," he said. And when he reached the 14th and glanced at the scoreboard — "mistakenly," he said — he found himself leading by two strokes.

But not for long. Three-putt bogeys at the 14th and 15th hauled him back into a tie at nine under, and this time with Verplank. Then came the critical shot at the par-five 16th. He was hitting his new three iron, a club he had praised for its height and accuracy. The shot flirted with the water for a moment, then cleared a mound beside the green and rolled on. "That," he said, "was probably the best shot I hit all week. With my new three iron. I love that thing."

Funk two-putted for a birdie and was back in the lead. He anguished at the island 17th. "Because it can just ruin a whole week," he said. (He had witnessed Tway's 12 in the morning.)

At the 18th, Verplank ran afoul of the mounds at the green and couldn't get up and down. Funk had the edge, but still had to swallow hard. His approach flirted with the water down the left side of the hole and ended up in a bunker. "I hit it on the toe," Funk said. "I didn't know whether I hit it solid enough to carry that bulkhead just short of that bunker. But I didn't see it splash. I was happy about that."

Funk blasted out to about five feet, and knocked in the winning putt.

The beauty of Herbie the Volkswagen's play emerged from the statistics. True, he averaged just 253.4 yards off the tee, a distant 80th in the driving rankings. But length isn't always the key. "With the rough as thick as it was this week ... there's a premium on hitting the fairway here," Funk said. "That's what you need to do to score."

He could document that statement. He ranked tied for first in driving accuracy, having hit 85.7 percent of the fairways, and he was No. 1 in hitting greens in regulation, at 80.6 percent. In this way, he'd won the biggest tournament of his career against one of the strongest fields he could ever face.

"That's what really feels good," Funk said. "Not only the Big Four, but the Big 140-something who started this thing. It feels really great to come out on top in as strong a field as this is, with all these great players. As strong as the tour is, from top to bottom, I can't comprehend how big this really is for me."

# 7. HSBC World Match Play

Michael Campbell had a mantra he kept repeating to himself: "I'm the U.S. Open champion. I'm good enough to win this match." In the grueling marathon that is the HSBC World Match Play Championship, Campbell proved certainly he was good enough, just as he had in holding off Tiger Woods at Pinehurst. By winning at Wentworth, in Virginia Water, England, he became only the fourth player to win both the U.S. Open and the World Match Play, arguably two of the most arduous events of any season, in the same year. The others were Gary Player in 1965, Hale Irwin in 1974 and Ernie Els in 1994.

The only time Els, the record six-time champion, was seen on the West course was when he was walking his dog, but the absence of the winner for the previous three years, due to a knee injury, at least ensured someone else would get a crack at the £1 million first prize. As the only reigning major champion in the field, Campbell deservedly took the crown and the cash, but only after seeing off the challenges of Geoff Ogilvy, Steve Elkington, Retief Goosen and then Paul McGinley, 2 and 1 in the final.

Campbell had made only one other appearance in the World Match Play and that came in 2002 when he defeated Nick Faldo and Ian Woosnam before losing to Sergio Garcia in the semi-finals. This time his semi-final clash with Goosen, the top seed, provided his best golf and most convincing victory. Otherwise there was plenty of grit and determination as he progressed through 138 holes in four days. A new fitness and well-being routine that includes yoga, hot baths, headstands and stretching as well as more traditional workouts, seemed to serve the 36-year-old New Zealander well.

McGinley was the last player to qualify for the championship and at age 38 was making his debut in the event. He was attempting to become only the fifth player to win who was not also a major champion after Graham Marsh, Isao Aoki, Colin Montgomerie and Lee Westwood. But ultimately the Irishman, reared on match play golf as an amateur in Ireland and who has distinguished himself in two Ryder Cups, had to settle for a second runner-up finish over the West course. In May he had lost out to Angel Cabrera in the BMW Championship, but for a player who admits to being a slow developer, those results, along with a third place at the WGC-NEC Invitational, represented valuable experiences.

Happy to be the underdog throughout the championship, McGinley relished taking part in the 41st playing of the traditional autumn tournament. "At the champions' dinner I was looking at the menu with all the champions and it's unbelievable," he said. "There is not a tournament in the world which would not want the quality of the champions you've had here. The winners are magnificent."

McGinley could not quite add his name to the list but it meant much to Campbell to be able to do so, more than even receiving the huge winner's check. "Obviously, I'm financially quite set for my family and for myself, but competing and winning tournaments around the world is the mojo," he said. "That's why we play the game. Winning is great. I'm trying to prove to the world that I am part of golfing history.

"I'm a big Ben Hogan fan and I recall seeing Ben holding the U.S. Open trophy in his books, you know, and then here I am with the same trophy. I'm sure all of the past winners of this trophy here have had the same feeling. We play for prestige; we play for the honor of being part of history.

"My big buzz is to have some sort of influence on the junior golf back home in New Zealand. All I can do right now, in my prime, is win trophies like this and it's going to encourage a lot of kids back home to play the sport. After my U.S. Open win and winning this now, hopefully even more so."

Campbell knew he was in for a long week right from the start when he was taken the full distance in the first round by the Australian Ogilvy. This had not looked likely when Campbell opened a commanding lead. Birdies at the 17th and 18th put him 3 up after the morning round, and by the fifth in the afternoon the Kiwi had doubled that advantage. When Ogilvy birdied the sixth and even when he won the seventh with a bogey five, the U.S. Open champion appeared still to be in control.

But Ogilvy's run continued with another birdie at the eighth and then three in a row came from the 10th to the 12th and suddenly the 28-year-old was even. Campbell regained the lead immediately when his opponent got into trouble at the 13th, but bogeyed the 15th himself. It was Ogilvy's dropped shot at the 16th, where he was bunkered, that decided the outcome with the 17th halved in pars and the 18th in birdie fours. "It was a tough battle," Campbell said. "Geoff had a great stretch with five birdies in seven holes and there was not much I could do against that. I never thought I had it in the bag and I just managed to fall over the finish line."

It was another Australian who caused the biggest upset of the first round when Mark Hensby defeated former winner Colin Montgomerie, 2 and 1. With the Scot's success around the West course, where he has also been the PGA champion, Hensby started as the underdog, but the seeding system suggested it was more of a level contest; Montgomerie was seeded eighth and Hensby, ninth. The Australian had qualified with consistent play in the major championships and a few weeks earlier had won the Scandinavian Masters. Montgomerie's form during the season was far better than in recent years, but since the Open Championship, where he was runner-up to Woods at St Andrews, he was in a bit of a lull.

This was Hensby's first appearance at Wentworth and a visit to the clubhouse, as well as the words of his caddie, Fanny Sunesson, let him know what he was in for. "When I got here and found out I was playing Colin, I didn't think much of it until I went to dinner and saw his name on every board in the clubhouse," he said. "I sat down and said to Fanny, 'Does he like this course?' She said, 'Oh yeah, we're going to have a hard match.' I had never played with him or against him, but you can see why he's done so well around here."

Montgomerie led from the first hole, was 4 up after 13 and 3 up at lunch. But then a strange thing happened. The Scot did not win a single hole in the afternoon. Worse, his bogeys handed the first, third and fifth holes to the Australian. Ten of the next 12 holes were halved but the ninth should not have been. With Hensby dropping a shot, Montgomerie missed from three feet for his par and the tide was turning. Hensby won the 10th with a six iron to five feet for a two at the par-three and then the 16th where his sand-iron approach finished four feet away. Montgomerie knew he would in all likelihood have to hole his 15-footer for a half but, as so often in the afternoon, the effort lipped out. "That happened a lot and the 16th was just the most dramatic," Monty said. "I didn't score well enough to win."

"I played so poorly this morning, but this afternoon I just hung in there," said the Australian. "I made some nice putts at the right times. Once I got ahead, I didn't give him a break."

Hensby was due to meet Goosen in the second round. The top seed dismissed Kenneth Ferrie, 8 and 7. Ferrie, the winner of the European Open, won the first hole and, apart from an eagle at the fourth, that was his lot as the South African collected eight birdies in a morning 66. "That can happen when you are playing one of the best players in the world," said the 26-year-old Englishman, who was ranked 104 places below his opponent. "He was just holing everything and that's what you have to do to be one of the best in the world. It continued in the afternoon. He holed from 20 feet at the first and that was the tone of the day." Birdies at the 10th and 11th from Goosen brought the game to a premature end.

In the remaining match in the top half of the draw, Elkington, the 12th seed, defeated Tim Clark, the fifth seed, 6 and 5. Elkington, who qualified from his runner-up finish at the U.S. PGA Championship, was 2 up at lunch and won three holes in a row from the third hole in the afternoon to take a stranglehold on the contest. The run included an eagle at the fourth where he hit a two iron to six feet. A birdie at the par-five 12th left the end only one hole away. "Retief is deservedly the No. 1 seed, but I think all the rest have much the same chance," said the Australian. "All the matches could go either way."

McGinley opened his campaign against Denmark's Thomas Bjorn, the runner-up to Els in 2003. It was a close contest between close friends. Both players led during the morning round but only Bjorn got to 2 up, at the 16th, and then he lost the next. The first four holes in the afternoon were halved, McGinley getting up and down for his birdie at the par-five fourth, but then the Irishman won seven of the next eight holes. Suddenly, it was a different match. Bjorn bogeyed the short fifth and the seventh; McGinley birdied the sixth and the eighth and he was 3 up. The ninth was halved scrappily in bogeys, but then McGinley won the 10th with a par, the 11th with an eagle two and the 12th with a birdie.

McGinley holed out from the fairway from 85 yards at the 11th for only the second two at the hole, the first by Peter Oosterhuis in 1977. "Thomas had hit a decent shot in to 15 feet and I just wanted to get it close and give myself a chance of a birdie. The last thing I wanted to do was hand him a hole," McGinley said. "Nobody is more surprised than me that I won 6 and 5 after being 1 down after 18 holes. I played really well this afternoon, but then I needed to. The half at the fourth this afternoon was probably the key, because if Thomas had gone 2 up at that point it would have been a big momentum boost for him."

The only major champion to depart in the first round was Bernhard Langer, who was shown little gratitude by Luke Donald. As captain of the 2004 European Ryder Cup team, Langer had selected the young Englishman as one of his two wild cards. Donald showed he was worthy of the pick at Oakland Hills, and Langer got another demonstration here. It did not help bogeying three of the first six holes, by which time Donald was 4 up. Langer perked up to come home in three under, and from 5 down after 11 he got back to 3 down after 18, but then promptly lost the first two holes in the afternoon. Donald ran out a winner by 7 and 6.

Armed with a new putter and putting with left hand below right for the first time in competition, Donald was as consistent as ever, only making one bogey in 30 holes. In many ways, the 27-year-old plays a similar game to the two-time Masters champion. "He's obviously someone I watched growing up and have a lot of respect for," Donald said of Langer. "We have similar games and I have learnt a lot from Bernhard. He's very meticulous in his game; he gets the most out of it; he's very good at course management; he never forces a shot and plays within himself. I think some of those traits I've taken on myself."

Cabrera, the second seed, almost suffered as much as Campbell after establishing a 5-up lead on Trevor Immelman. But then, at the 10th in the afternoon, the South African hit a seven iron to a foot for a winning two, holed from 18 feet at the 11th for another birdie, and eagled the 12th with a five iron to 11 feet. Cabrera's lead was back to two holes, but with the next five holes all halved, he claimed a 2-and-1 victory. "I had to fight hard today against Trevor, especially after he went birdie, birdie, eagle. It was great golf," he said.

Perhaps the tightest match of all was that between David Howell, the seventh seed, and Jose Maria Olazabal, the 10th seed and playing for the first time since 1999. The Spaniard never trailed during a morning 68 and took lunch at 2 up, although his advantage was cut by Howell's eagle at the 18th, where he hit a five wood to 10 feet. Olazabal opened up with three bogeys in a row in the afternoon to put Howell ahead for the first time. But Howell could not extend his lead at the fourth when he missed from six feet for eagle. The sixth was halved in birdies, then Howell bogeyed the seventh, so they were back to level.

The Englishman missed the chance to go ahead at the short 10th when his birdie effort from eight feet missed, and instead he went behind at the next, where Olazabal improbably holed from 40 feet. But he failed to birdie the par-five 12th, so Howell was even again only to lose the 14th, where Olazabal hit a six iron up the hill to four feet for a two. Both struggled at the 15th, but Howell holed from 13 feet for his par, only for Olazabal to follow him in from 12 for the half.

But Howell was even again when he birdied the 16th from nine feet, and after the 17th was halved in birdies, they were back at the 18th. This time it was Olazabal's turn to make an eagle, his five-wood approach finishing eight feet away and the Spaniard ruthlessly holed the putt for a one-hole win. "I don't know where that shot came from at the last," admitted Ollie. "I hit a wonderful five wood and it saved the day because I was struggling with my driving. David is so straight and so solid and only one good shot in 36 holes beat him."

For Friday's second round the weather was better, sunny but with an unexpectedly biting breeze for mid-September. There was again some fine golf but, with one exception, the matches did not boil up quite as might be hoped. In the battle of the Spanish-speakers, Cabrera defeated Olazabal 4 and 3. Despite his heroics the evening before, Olazabal could never get in the lead. Ollie had said he would have to get his binoculars out to see where the big-hitting Argentinean's drives finished, and Cabrera's power dominated the West course.

Two up at lunch after a morning 67, Cabrera eagled the fourth in the afternoon, where he dispatched a five wood and then a six iron which finished four feet from the hole to put him 3 up. The six iron was working well as he used it on the short fifth and finished a foot away to go 4 up. Olazabal won the ninth and the 10th, but his double bogey at the 13th, followed by a birdie two at the 14th — the six iron again, this time to six feet — put Cabrera through. "It is a great day for me to beat one of the great match-players in Chema," Cabrera said. "I played fantastic in the morning, but made the mistake of playing the man in the second round."

McGinley set up a re-match from May with Cabrera by disposing of his Ryder Cup teammate, Donald, with surprising ease. A 9-and-8 score was the last thing anyone expected from an eagerly anticipated contest. But McGinley's 66 in the morning was a superb round of golf, and after four birdies in a row he was 4 up after just six holes. Donald's best moment came when he chipped in for an eagle at the 12th, but the Irishman was 6 up at lunch and went seven ahead at the third in the afternoon.

At the fifth he made his second birdie of the day at the par-three, this time by holing from fully 45 feet. He looked just a tiny bit sheepish and admitted he had just been trying to putt close. "Perhaps I should try that more often," he said. Two bogeys from Donald at the seventh and eighth holes and then two more halves and the match was over. "I don't take anything for granted in this game," said McGinley. "Even when I was 6 up at lunch I realized that match play is so fickle and momentum is massive. I was aware I had to keep my foot down as hard as I could."

Goosen had his foot down even firmer against Montgomerie's conqueror, Hensby. The 12-and-11 winning margin equaled his own record for the championship from his defeat of Jeff Maggert in 2004. The South African's eight-hole advantage after the first 11 holes was a new best of the tournament and he was 9 up at lunch; it would have been 10 but for a fluffed putt on the 18th green. Hensby struggled in the conditions and only two birdies at the last two holes gave him an approximate 77; Goosen was round in 66. Goosen won three holes in a row from the fourth in the afternoon and sealed it on the seventh green. "I'll hit some balls, go to the physio truck and then go home and play with the kids," Goosen said of his plans for the rest of the afternoon. No one before had managed to get through two rounds of the championship playing a full 18 holes less than the regulation distance.

For Campbell, it was a very different story. By the time the Kiwi had defeated Elkington at the first extra hole, he had completed 73 holes in two long days. "It was pretty ugly out there," Campbell sighed. "It's an intense seven-and-a-half hour day and you are going to see some great shots and some poor ones. You lose concentration. I thought I was packing my bags a couple of times."

Campbell, with two birdies and an eagle in the first four holes, went ahead first, but the Australian got even at the eighth and on the back nine won four holes in a row. Campbell's birdie at the 18th got him back to 4 down, but he reduced the deficit in the afternoon before Elkington won the seventh and eighth, where he chipped in, to go back four in front. Campbell birdied the ninth from 11 feet, but then Elkington, the runner-up to Ernie Els in 1995, saw his game collapse on the inward half. Time and again he struggled to get up and down, although he did at the 18th for a half in birdies to stay alive. The contest only went one more hole, with Campbell chipping close while Elkington bogeyed again.

Campbell knew he had to play better the following day against Goosen, and after more of the hot baths, yoga and the like, he did just that. A four iron to eight feet at the fourth set up an eagle and he birdied the next three holes to go 4 up. The reigning U.S. Open champion realized there was something not quite right with the double former U.S. Open champion when Goosen could not mount a recovery on the back nine. The South African had won in China and Germany in the preceding two weeks and had cruised through the first two rounds at Wentworth.

But no part of his game seemed to be quite on song on this Saturday morning and Campbell grew in confidence simply from looking at his opponent's body language. The approximate morning scores were a 64 for Campbell and a 71 for Goosen, which was enough to put the New Zealander 5 up.

Again, after the break, there was no comeback from Goosen, and a double bogey at the third let Campbell slip further ahead. Campbell birdied the sixth and the eighth to go 8 up, and though the 10th was halved in twos and Goosen won the 11th with a birdie, Campbell clinched a commanding 7-and-6 victory. "I played great today," Campbell said. "I knew I had to play a lot better and to do that against one of the best players in the world makes me very proud."

With the top seed out of the competition, the No. 2 was soon to follow. Urged on by strong support in the gallery, with a number of Irish voices to be heard, McGinley defeated Cabrera 4 and 3. It was a terrific battle. Both men led briefly before McGinley made the first move, spurred on by holing a huge putt at the ninth. He then chipped in at the 10th, hit a seven iron to four feet at the 11th, and got up and down at the 12th for his fourth birdie in a row, none of which Cabrera could match.

McGinley bogeyed the 13th but holed a good eight-footer for par at the next to avoid losing two holes in a row. He did lose the 16th with a birdie, but then won both the 17th and 18th, despite Cabrera having a huge power advantage at the two par-fives. McGinley holed from 15 feet for a birdie at the 17th and then hit a five wood to 14 feet to eagle the last. "That was a key for me," said the Irishman. "It was a big difference going into lunch 3 up rather than 1 up." In the afternoon it was a tense affair. McGinley lost the third with a bogey but won the fifth with a birdie. The next three holes were halved, but then Cabrera bogeyed the ninth and 10th and that gave McGinley some breathing space at 5 up. Cabrera responded with birdies at the next two holes but could only pick up one hole. A bogey from the Argentinean at the 15th brought the match to a close.

So two likeable and popular players teed off in the final on Sunday. There was never more than a hole either way in the morning. Campbell bogeyed the first but got back to even when McGinley bunkered himself at the short fifth. McGinley led again at the eighth but drove into trees at the next. Campbell got even again and then holed from 20 feet for a birdie at the 10th to go ahead for the first time. McGinley got the hole back at the 16th, but Campbell's birdie at the 18th put the New Zealander 1 up at lunch.

Campbell immediately increased his lead at the first hole in the afternoon and then went 3 up at the third. But then the momentum began to swing. McGinley got back into the match with birdies at the sixth and seventh and he won the ninth, where Campbell drove into the trees, to make it all-square with nine to play. By now the pair were getting to the end of a very long week, and given the tension, it was understandable that the errors increased.

They halved the 10th in bogeys but managed not to be distracted by a streaker at the next. At the 12th, Campbell flirted with the out of bounds but made his birdie to go 1 up, only to give the hole back at the 13th. Campbell took the 15th with a par and then drove into sand at the 16th. But McGinley was in the trees and the error led to the Kiwi going 2 up. A delicate chip at the 17th closed the door on McGinley.

"I'm bitterly disappointed, particularly having fought so hard to finish as poorly as I did on 15 and 16," McGinley said. "You know, I felt the ball never ran for me all day. Sure, I'm fatigued, but then again, I'm sure Mike felt the same. He didn't hit as many destructive shots as I did over the two rounds and he kept the ball in play better than I did. He didn't really hand me any holes at all. I had to earn every hole that I won and I handed him two or three holes, and that's disappointing."

"I think we both found it hard to read the greens for some reason," Campbell said. "It wasn't great golf out there today, I admit. It wasn't fantastic, but it was good enough. I mean, you're not playing against par; you're playing against the player, and I was playing against Paul today. I was in the mode of just trying to be ahead of him on every single shot or every single hole.

"But, look, it was very tense and a great tussle today with Paul. He's a wonderful iron player and a great putter. He had lots of chances and opportunities for birdies out there today, lots of times out there, and fortunately enough it went my way and that's the bottom line. It could have gone Paul's way, easily. It was like a knife edge, really; could have gone either way."

Campbell's victory gave him a chance of winning the European Order of Merit. It was not to be as he was overtaken by Montgomerie. But for McGinley there was a happy ending a month later at Valderrama when he won the Volvo Masters.

# 8. American Tours

It was a pretty great season while it lasted. Vijay Singh won the Sony Open, the second stop on the PGA Tour, and Tiger Woods answered in the Buick Invitational the next week. Phil Mickelson dealt himself a hand in the Big 4 (or 5) Derby with back-to-back wins in the FBR Open and the AT&T Pebble Beach National Pro-Am. But Woods pulled away in due time. First, he won his fourth Masters in April, his second Open Championship in July, and then turned 2005 into the Year of the Tiger, Part VI. (He had won his first five Player of the Year awards beginning in 1999, and after Singh interrupted his reign in 2004, he resumed in 2005.)

Woods's season on a thumbnail: He won six times on the PGA Tour, he won his sixth Vardon Trophy with a stroke average of 68.66, and with the Masters and Open Championship, he rose to third in career majors as a professional with 10 (behind Jack Nicklaus's 18 and Walter Hagen's 11), and rose to seventh in all-time tour wins with 46. And his streak of consecutive cuts made ended at 142 when he missed at the EDS Byron Nelson Championship. He had shot one-over-par 141 and missed by a stroke.

Woods had been fond of saying through most of 2004 that he was remaking his swing, and that he'd just about got all the pieces together. It seemed he finished the job. Woods opened 2005 with four rounds in the 60s at the Mercedes Championships and finished third. Then he won the Buick Invitational in mid-January, his first stroke-play victory in 15 months. Woods returned to No. 1 in the world at the Ford Championship at Doral early in March (he'd been second to Singh since the previous September), and as showdowns go, this one did fine. Woods and Mickelson went head-to-head down the stretch. Woods finished with 66 for a one-stroke win over Mickelson (69), and Singh (66) tied for third.

Woods took the Masters in a gripping duel with Chris DiMarco, who seemed to have choked it away with a 41 on the back nine of the third round. But he rebounded and Woods bogeyed the final two holes to fall into a tie. On the first playoff hole (No. 18), DiMarco just missed the front of the green, and Woods rolled in a 15-foot putt for the win. In contrast, Woods just strolled around the Old Course at St. Andrews to pick up the Open Championship. The Grand Slam was safe for another year when New Zealand's Michael Campbell beat Woods by two shots in the U.S. Open, and a "triple crown" was out of reach, with Mickelson outlasting Thomas Bjorn and Steve Elkington by one in the PGA Championship. Woods finished two strokes off the lead.

The unofficial Big Four were Woods, Mickelson, Singh and Ernie Els. Throw in the taciturn Retief Goosen, as some do, and that makes five. At all events, 2005 was promising to be the year for the great showdown. But the number dropped by one in July when Els suffered a knee ligament injury in a sailing accident. His season, with five top-10 finishes in 11 events, was over. He underwent surgery July 28 in England, and returned to action in South Africa in December, and finished ninth out of 12 in the Nedbank Golf Challenge in South Africa, then won the Dunhill Championship.

Woods's other two wins came in his favorite events, the WGC-NEC

Invitational and the WGC-American Express Championship. He has won them four times each. Mickelson also won the BellSouth Classic, and Singh made it four with the Shell Houston Open, the Wachovia Championship and the Buick Open.

Four others won two tournaments each, and none more unlikely than Bart Bryant, who at age 42, with only one other victory behind him, won both the Memorial and the season-ending, winners-only Tour Championship. He not only won The Tour Championship, he led wire-to-wire and beat Tiger Woods by six shots. "I'm as surprised as you are," Bryant said.

Kenny Perry won the Bay Hill Classic in a face-down against Singh, and in the Bank of America Colonial, he double-bogeyed the 17th in the final round and still won by seven. Joe Ogilvie seemed set to end his six winless seasons in the Bob Hope Chrysler Classic, but after four strong rounds, he needed the fifth. He didn't get it, and there was Justin Leonard saying, "I've been sitting on eight wins for almost two years — it's nice to get a ninth." He got the 10th at the FedEx St. Jude Classic, but the hard way. He started the final round with an eight-stroke lead, bogeyed the final hole, and won by only one over hard-closing David Toms. Leonard had shot 62-65-66 in the first three rounds, then closed with a 73. Against that, Toms shot 63.

Padraig Harrington figured he'd got a gift from Singh in the Honda Classic. Mr. No. 2 — Harrington had finished second 26 times worldwide — shot 63 in the final round, erased a seven-shot deficit to tie Singh and Joe Ogilvie, and on the second hole, Singh needed a 30-inch putt to stay alive. He missed it. "I thought it was a gimme," Harrington said. Harrington's win in the Barclays Classic was even stranger. Harrington had missed the cut in his previous two events and he was worried about his father, ill back home in Ireland, and on the final hole he rolled in a 65-foot putt for his second eagle of the day and a one-stroke victory over Jim Furyk. "You know," said Harrington, "I'm a strange person."

The 2005 season was notable in other ways:

David Toms collapsed in the first round of the 84 Lumber Classic and was rushed to a hospital. What was feared to be a heart attack turned out to be a very rapid heartbeat. A medical procedure corrected the problem later in the year.

The most engaging first-time winner was Jason Gore, who played in the 84 Lumber Classic on a sponsor's exemption, and rolled a 90-foot putt to tap-in distance on the final hole for the win. Gore also charmed the country as the poor man who threatened to win the U.S. Open, and who later won three straight starts on the Nationwide Tour to gain his PGA Tour card.

A record 78 players earned $1 million or more in 2005, and a record 30 earned $2 million or more.

Seven rookies finished in the top 125 — Sean O'Hair, Greg Owen, Joey Snyder, James Driscoll, Brian Davis, D.J. Trahan and Ryuji Imada.

O'Hair became only the third rookie ever to win $2 million or more, joining Todd Hamilton and Zach Johnson, who did it in 2004.

O'Hair was the youngest winner (John Deere Classic) at 22 years, 11 months and 29 days, and the oldest winner was Fred Funk at The Players Championship — 48 years, nine months, 14 days.

Tournament winners hailed from nine countries, and 17 countries were represented among the top 125 players.

# U.S. PGA Tour

### Mercedes Championships—$5,300,000
Winner: Stuart Appleby

There were a couple good reasons why Stuart Appleby shouldn't have returned to defend his title at the season-opening Mercedes Championships. For one thing, there was the painful sciatic nerve problem in his hip, and for another, his wife Ashley was back in Australia expecting their first child. But he did go to Hawaii for the 31-player winners-only tournament (only Masters champion Phil Mickelson was missing). Maybe he checked the stars first. He might have had a sign that good things would happen because after that 74 in the first round, he needed some terrific breaks. And he got them, as though the stars had lined up for him.

Appleby's biggest worry came one day when he had two telephone messages waiting — one on his hotel room telephone and the other on his cell phone. He didn't know which emergency to deal with first. Happily, there were none. "Ashley told me to go have some fun," he said. And he did. On a windy, rainy Sunday, he won his second straight Mercedes Championship. But only after some of the best golfers in the world conveniently got themselves out of his way.

Casualty No. 1 was Vijay Singh, the No. 1 player in the world and author of nine victories the year before, who came to the final round with a great chance to pick up where he left off. He was tied for the lead coming down the final stretch. But at the 13th hole he hooked his drive into tangled vegetation, and eventually two-putted for a triple bogey.

The Mercedes Championship was played in the second week of January 2005. But for three rounds it looked more like 2004, with Singh leading all the way. "I'm here," he had said, smiling. "You want to start the year off strong." Then came his stumble in the final round, leaving him only one thing to say: "Can't win 'em all." He closed with a 74 and tied for fifth place, three strokes behind Appleby.

Casualty No. 2 was Ernie Els, who rushed up the leaderboard with a 65 in the second round, led briefly in the third round until he bogeyed out of a bunker, and was two behind starting the final round. Els came to the 18th needing a birdie to force a playoff. He aimed his tee shot to the right but overdid it. His ball bounced off the cart path and into trees and rough. That cost him a two-stroke penalty and a 71. He tied for third, two strokes back.

Casualty No. 3 was Jonathan Kaye, not a marquee name like Els and Singh, but he was right there with them with rounds of 68-67-66, and trailing Singh by only a stroke going into the final round. Then he was lying two just in front of the 18th green and needing to get up and down to tie Appleby. But his pitch was much too easy, saddling him with a 30-footer for birdie to tie, and he didn't get it. He closed with a 71 and was second by a stroke.

Meanwhile, after that 74 in the first round, Appleby bounced back with a 64 in the second to get into the running. A 66 in the third left him four strokes off the lead. Then in the fourth, Appleby began his move at No. 6, a 398-yard, par-four, playing downwind, with a big tee shot that caught the long hill and rolled onto the green and stopped 12 feet from the cup. He got the eagle. "With Vijay and Ernie and so many others playing well," Appleby said, "I knew I had to shoot a low score Sunday. Then the weather came in." Appleby made four birdies to go with the eagle to close with a 67, wrapping up a card of 21-under 271 to win by one over Kaye (71), by two over Els (71) and Tiger Woods (68), and by three over Singh (74), Stewart Cink (71) and Adam Scott (65).

As a subplot, the 2005 Tiger Woods Watch began. Did the swing changes he fiddled with for all 2004 really take? The jury was still out, except on the putting. It was poor. Said Woods: "I probably had more opportunities within 15 feet than I've had in a long time. I don't feel like I got anything out of my rounds."

## Sony Open in Hawaii—$4,800,000
Winner: Vijay Singh

With the coming of the Sony Open in Hawaii in mid-January, it was clear this week there were two No. 1 players in the world. One was Vijay Singh, who goes around winning golf tournaments — this one, for example — and the other was Michelle Wie, the 15-year-old schoolgirl and golf prodigy, who goes around outdrawing Singh and everyone else in attention when she shows up at tournaments. She again got a sponsor's invitation to the tournament in her home state, and the media recorded her every shot and smile. Wie was trying to become the first female to make the cut on the PGA Tour in 60 years, since Babe Zaharias in the 1945 Tucson Open. She missed again, but the media carnival rolled on, still giving her high billing even against an electrifying final in which Ernie Els charged to a 62 but Singh picked off the tournament on the final hole.

Wie struggled along with everyone else in the winds at Waialae Country Club at Honolulu. She shot a five-over-par 75 in the first round, tying for 120th. "At least I'm not in last place," she said. In the second round, she triple-bogeyed her sixth hole, three-putting from eight feet, and went on to shoot 74 and miss the cut again, this time by seven strokes instead of the one in 2004. She tied for 128th out of the 144 starters. "I want another chance because I know I can do better," Wie said.

Meanwhile, Hank Kuehne, Brett Quigley, Tom Byrum and Stewart Cink amazed everyone by getting 66s when only 29 could break par in the winds. Ernie Els, going for his third straight Sony title, had to birdie his last hole for a 71. Retief Goosen, the reigning U.S. Open champion, made nine on his first hole and shot 72. While everyone was watching Wie miss the cut on Friday, Japan's Shigeki Maruyama nailed four birdies and an eagle for a 65 and a one-stroke lead at 132 at the halfway point. He opened the third round with a double bogey, aced the 202-yard par-three No. 4, and shot 68 to hold a one-stroke lead on Brett Quigley, winless in 220 starts.

Where was No. 1 Vijay Singh through all this? Largely ignored and tooling along to 69-68-67 and rising to a tie for sixth going into the final round. Els put his finger on the situation when he said, "I always felt like it was going to be just a little shy. But I had a great day." This was after he tied the course record with a 62, rocketing from nowhere to close birdie-birdie-eagle on a 10-foot putt at the 16th, a three-footer at the 17th, and an 18-footer at the 18th. He was right. Right, he was shy — by a stroke.

The fates cleared away some obstacles for Singh. Maruyama was still leading until he bogeyed the 12th from the rough, then bogeyed the 14th. Quigley also bogeyed the 14th, then sealed his own fate by missing a four-foot par putt at the 17th.

Singh, four strokes out of the lead when the final round started, birdied through the turn — No. 9 on two putts, No. 10 after a bunker shot around a tree to 18 feet, and No. 11 with a seven iron to 10 feet. At the 14th, his birdie try from 60 feet went eight feet past, but he saved par coming back. Els still had a chance. Singh still had to play the par-five 18th.

"The 18th owed me," Singh said. He hadn't birdied it in three rounds. This time, he slugged a 300-yard drive, put his approach on the edge of the green, and two-putted for the birdie and the victory. And No. 1 Singh, who had missed a chance to win the season-opening Mercedes Championships the week before, had a 65, an 11-under 269, his first win of 2005 and his 25th in his career on the PGA Tour.

## Buick Invitational—$4,800,000
Winner: Tiger Woods

Reflecting briefly on his heady success in the Buick Invitational, Tiger Woods explained it by citing one of golf's axioms. He worded it differently, though: "I hit it great at Mercedes and lost. I didn't hit it well here and won. It comes down to making putts."

Woods didn't even come close to "driving for show." He hit only 25 of 56 fairways at Torrey Pines. But "putting for dough"? That was a different matter. He was second in putts per round, averaging 26.5. It all added up to his third victory in the Buick Invitational, but more to the point for the man remaking his swing, it was his first PGA Tour stroke-play victory since the WGC-American Express Championship in October 2003, and his first PGA Tour victory since the WGC-Accenture Match Play in February 2004, the latter almost a full year ago.

And Woods denied a man who deserved better. Tom Lehman, age 45, the 2006 U.S. Ryder Cup captain, who hadn't won since the 2000 Phoenix Open, started with a 62 (at the easier Torrey Pines North) and was winning this tournament for 70 holes. He led outright for the first two rounds (he shot 67 at the tougher South Course in the second round), and was tied for the lead with Luke Donald through the third. Woods trailed until those final two holes. When Lehman erred, Woods jumped in.

First off, it was a confused, disjointed tournament, thanks to stubborn fogs that caused delays to the point where the third round was forced over into Sunday morning. This, in turn, forced some players into marathon golf.

"For 30 holes today, I really held my own," Lehman said. "Until the end, I felt I had a chance. I mis-hit an eight iron, and that kind of took the wind out of my sails." Lehman was like the thoroughbred stumbling just a few steps from the finish line. Coming down the final nine, he hit every fairway. But at the 17th, his eight-iron approach plugged in a bunker, and at the 18th, his wedge was short of the green. He bogeyed both. Against an oncoming Tiger Woods, the errors were fatal.

Woods parred the 17th and coolly rolled in an 18-footer for a birdie at the 18th to lock up the win. Woods closed with a four-under 68 for a 16-under 272 total, and a three-stroke win over Lehman (73), Luke Donald (73) and Charles Howell (72). Howell also deserved better. He would have been no worse that solo second except for a crazy bounce. His sand wedge approach to the 18th slammed into the cup, then bounced back out some 25 feet into the pond. It was an eagle for an instant, then turned into a bogey. "I didn't know whether to laugh or cry," Howell said. Donald was making a move, but he double-bogeyed the 14th when his six iron went over the green, and he bogeyed the 17th after a tee shot into the bushes. When the tournament was over, two men had proved something to themselves.

"I didn't hit it my best," said Woods. "My mechanics are sound enough now that I could place my misses. Now I know what to do, what to fix and how to fix it out there."

Lehman found himself in the interesting position of possibly playing his way onto his own Ryder Cup team. "I'd like to be able to play well to be on the team," Lehman said. "It would be an upset if I made the team at this point. But if my game keeps progressing, you never know."

## Bob Hope Chrysler Classic—$4,700,000
Winner: Justin Leonard

Pity Joe Ogilvie. Winless in his six seasons on the PGA Tour, he finally put four excellent winning rounds together. But it was a five-round tournament.

And so in the tale of two miseries, Justin Leonard's ended and Ogilvie's rolled on in the Bob Hope Chrysler Classic at La Quinta, California. Ogilvie suffered that little lapse early in the final round, and Leonard, the 1997 Open Championship winner who had been painfully searching for his game, jumped on his opportunity and rode it to a three-stroke victory over Ogilvie, who closed with a 73, and South Africa's Tim Clark, who shot a 69. Ogilvie was empty for six years. His best finish was a tie for second in the 2004 Zurich Classic of New Orleans. He was leading with nine to play, then Vijay Singh shot 29 for a 63 to beat him by one. For Leonard, it had been only about two years of frustration, and he was coming off his worst year since joining the tour full time in 1995. Maybe what hurt most was when he stumbled over the last few holes and lost a chance to win the 2004 PGA Championship.

"I've been sitting on eight wins for almost two years," Leonard said. "It's nice to get a ninth."

Said a disappointed Ogilvie: "I certainly didn't play the way I would have liked today, but I got a pretty good front row seat for a great round of golf." Leonard's, that is.

The tournament rotated over four courses for the first four rounds — PGA West-Palmer, Bermuda Dunes, Tamarisk and La Quinta — and finished at

La Quinta. They're of differing difficulty, but it was hard to tell that first day. Of the 128 players in the field, only 13 were over par. For the first time in the 35 years of the tournament, five players were tied for the lead at the end of a round — in this case, the first, all at eight-under 64: Duffy Waldorf, Robert Damron, Ted Purdy, Fred Funk and Joe Ogilvie. Leonard had a seven-birdie, one-bogey 66 and was in a group tied for 11th, along with defending champion Phil Mickelson.

Ogilvie broke out in the second round with a 63 and a 17-under 127 total, for a three-stroke lead over Mickelson, who shot 64. Ogilvie wasn't impressed with his play. "You look at the history of golf, I don't think I'm going to be in any encyclopedia of golf," he insisted. After a 66 in the third round, he waved off the admirers. "I got lucky, basically," he said. "The way I played, 66 was a gift." But the gift got him a two-shot lead over Australia's Peter Lonard going into the fourth round.

Leonard was on the fringes for the first three rounds, tied for 11th, 12th and 13th on rounds of 66-67-68. He finally entered the chase in the fourth with a 64 that included six birdies over the back nine, and four of them in a row from the 10th. He had moved to within three of Ogilvie, who was driving more accurately but leaving his irons short of the pin. But he still handled the par-fives. He eagled the 512-yard 11th with a 12-foot putt, and birdied Nos. 6 and 13 against one bogey for a 69–262.

So Ogilvie started the final round two ahead of Peter Lonard and three ahead of Leonard, and that changed almost immediately. Leonard started the final round birdie-birdie-par, and when Ogilvie started bogey-par, they were tied. And when Ogilvie bogeyed No. 3, Leonard parred and was ahead to stay. He birdied No. 4, bogeyed No. 5, then birdied three of the next five holes, and was on his way to the three-stroke win.

Said a disappointed Ogilvie: "The rain dance didn't work. I was trying for a rainout today, but that didn't happen."

Leonard was reminded that the last two winners here went on to win the Masters — Mike Weir in 2003 and Mickelson in 2004. "I certainly hope to keep that streak alive," Leonard said. "I may write that in my yardage book to give me a little boost of confidence."

## FBR Open—$5,200,000
Winner: Phil Mickelson

Phil Mickelson started the FBR Open — nee Phoenix Open — with a weak two-over-par 73, six strokes out of the lead. He needed to get back into the race in a hurry. And so he put on a sprint in the second round. How much of a sprint was it? "I would have taken 65 and been ecstatic," he said. Instead, he took a little ol' 60.

More than just getting back into the race, Mickelson had zoomed from a tie for 40th to a tie for the halfway lead with Kevin Na, at age 21 the youngest player on the PGA Tour. Then Mickelson ran away from the field, closing with 66-68 for a 17-under 267 total at the TPC at Scottsdale. He won by five strokes, the largest winning margin of his career.

It was his 24th career win, but more important, it also was at least a partial vindication for the Ryder Cup debacle when he switched to new woods just two weeks before the event. He failed miserably and got roasted from all sides. But a few weeks later, he shot 59 in the PGA Grand Slam of Golf — exciting but unofficial. And now a flawless 60, his lowest round on the PGA Tour, for his first victory since the 2004 Masters. Here's how he did it (starting on the second nine):

No. 13, par 5, birdie: Driver, five iron left of the green, chip to five feet, one putt.

No. 14, par 4, birdie: Driver, seven iron to 30 feet, one putt.

No. 16, par 3, birdie: Eight-iron tee shot to 30 feet, one putt.

No. 17, par 4, eagle: Driver to left fringe, 95 feet, one putt.

No. 3, par 5, birdie: Driver, four iron to 30 feet, two putts.

No, 5, par 4, birdie: Driver, sand wedge to a foot, one putt.

No. 6, par 4, birdie: Three wood, sand wedge to five feet, one putt.

No. 7, par 3, birdie: Eight-iron tee shot to six feet, one putt.

No. 8, par 4, birdie: Driver, nine iron to 10 feet, one putt.

No. 9, par 4, birdie: Driver, six iron to three feet, one putt.

The 60 was all the more interesting because on that Friday morning he had to complete his first round, which was forced over by strong winds. He hit the ground running with a birdie-eagle finish for his 73. Then in the second round, he raced past first-round leader Dudley Hart (67-73) and tied with Kevin Na (68-65), a Mickelson fan. "I was rooting for him when he won the Masters," Na said.

Na met a whole bunch of Mickelson rooters. The FBR Open draws some of the biggest crowds on the tour. It was home cooking for Mickelson, with thousands remembering him as a hometown hero from his days at Arizona State. They crossed their fingers when Na took the lead with a birdie at the 11th. But he bogeyed the 12th and they were tied again. At the par-three 16th, Mickelson bunkered his tee shot, and Na hit the green, but a long way from the pin. Na three-putted for a bogey, and Mickelson got up and down with a 12-footer for a par and the lead. He birdied the 17th and 18th as well and was on his way.

Na had a moral victory. "I was right up there putting pressure on Phil," he said. "A great round tomorrow can do it."

Unfortunately, Na didn't have one. Mickelson did, considering that he managed a three-under 68 while hitting tee shots into the desert and water. Na got as close as three shots with a birdie at the 11th. But Mickelson pulled out of reach with a remarkable birdie at the par-five 13th. His tee shot ended up amid cactus and rocks, but he fired a magnificent five-iron escape 230 yards almost to the green. His eagle chip narrowly missed, and he tapped in for a birdie. Then he hit into the water at the 15th, but saved par. There was no catching him.

"It was such an unlikely win, given the first nine holes, that I was fighting to make the cut," he said. "Then to shoot 60 in the second round was an incredible experience."

# AT&T Pebble Beach National Pro-Am—$5,300,000
Winner: Phil Mickelson

Somewhere up there, the ol' Crooner — Bing Crosby — must have been pushing his hat back, taking his pipe out of his mouth, and saying, "Hey, what are you trying to do to my Clambake?"

Crosby would be addressing Phil Mickelson, he of the rejuvenated swing and refreshed attitude, who spent four days trying to demolish the AT&T Pebble Beach National Pro-Am. This was the old Crosby Clambake played at a rotation of three courses on the Monterey Peninsula in California. Mickelson, who set records in the first three rounds, was the first in the tournament's 68-year history to go wire-to-wire over 72 holes. He won by four strokes (after leading by nine in the fourth round). And it was his second straight victory, after the five-shot victory in the FBR Open the previous week.

"It was weird," Mickelson said. "I didn't feel the normal intensity, the normal stress. It was a very enjoyable round."

And why not? Three strokes was the closest anyone could get to him, and that was in the first round. It all went this way:

First round: Mickelson, who posted a 60 in the FBR Open the week before, shot 62 at Spyglass Hill, the toughest of the three courses. He got one birdie out of one of those stubborn, rubbery ice plants. He set up another with a six iron off a cart path. At the 325-yard 17th, his drive was just eight yards short of the green, and he ended up with a top-in birdie. He holed a 15-foot putt for the final one at the last hole. "A 62 is good at Bermuda Dunes," said Kevin Sutherland. "A 62 at Spyglass is a whole different story. That's an amazing round." Mickelson led Sutherland and four others by three.

Second round: Mickelson shot a 67 at Poppy Hills for a 129 total, breaking the halfway record by two strokes despite some erratic play. He pulled his opening tee shot (at No. 10) into an unplayable lie, and scrambled to save par on a 30-footer. He birdied the 12th after hooking a lucky bounce off a tree. Then there was the eight iron out of the woods for another birdie. "I just cut it around a tree," he said. "It wasn't that big of a deal." He led Mike Weir by four.

Third round: Mickelson played Pebble Beach, the host course, in five-under 67, and extended his lead. He birdied the 106-yard No. 7 with a sand wedge to 15 feet, and got another at No. 8 with a five iron across the chasm to 12 feet. Said Billy Andrade, after a 63: "He won last week, so he's on a high. And when you're on a high, the game is pretty easy." Said Mickelson: "I don't want to do anything stupid, but I don't want to play defensive, either." It was Mickelson's third tournament record: 20-under 196 for three rounds. He led Greg Owen by seven.

Fourth round: Enjoying a big lead and facing a light rain and brisk winds at Pebble Beach, Mickelson opted to rein in his aggressive game. Even so, he went after some tough flags. He led by nine until Weir rallied when Mickelson bogeyed against the wind at Nos. 9 and 10. Weir shot 67, the only round in the 60s for the day, and finished second, his third straight top four in this event. Mickelson didn't set any records this time. "I don't really think about records," he says. "I just wanted to win the tournament." He closed with a 73 and 19-under 269 total, and won by four.

"It's been fun," Mickelson said. "I've been playing well the last couple of weeks. I'm excited to get the year started with a couple of wins."

## Nissan Open—$4,800,000
Winner: Adam Scott

The Nissan Open ended with the kind of question professors like to hit freshmen with: "When is a victory not a victory?" Adam Scott, 24-year-old Australian of rich promise, found the answer: Right now, that's when.

Scott got the Nissan Open trophy with his name on it, got the $864,000 first prize in official money, got a lift from 12th to seventh in the World Ranking, but he didn't get credit for his fourth victory. That was because maddening rains, saturating Riviera Country Club in Los Angeles, forced the tournament to be cut to two rounds, the first time since the former Buick Challenge in 1996. Under PGA Tour rules, a tournament has to be of at least 54 holes to be official. So when Scott beat Chad Campbell, second-round co-leader, on the first extra hole Monday morning, he had everything but an official victory.

It was a strange finish. Campbell opened with a 68, then shot 65 in the second round, finishing on Friday with the lead at nine-under-par 133. Rain washed out play Saturday. Then Scott ended his second round on Sunday, holing a 20-foot birdie putt on his final hole for a 66 and 133 total to tie Campbell. The second round was completed early Sunday afternoon, and officials then tried to start the third, but rains hit again. Officials had planned to resume the third round Monday morning, but two more inches of rain had already fallen, and that was it.

Except for Scott and Campbell and their playoff, the tournament was over. This really stung a number of golfers. England's Brian Davis, the first-round leader with a 65, and Northern Ireland's Darren Clarke, who aced the par-three No. 6 in the first round, were only a stroke out of the lead after the second round. Colin Montgomerie, still looking for his first PGA Tour victory, was only two off the lead after 36 holes. Tiger Woods missed a chance to take over No. 1 in the World Ranking from Vijay Singh. Woods, who had to finish fourth to do it, had shot 67 in the first round ("I putted like a fool," he said, after three three-putt bogeys). With a 70 in the second, he tied for 13th.

The other golfers were leaving Monday when Campbell and Scott headed for the 18th tee for the playoff. Campbell drove down the middle, but put his five wood to the right of the green. After getting relief from a puddle, he chipped five feet past the hole. Scott hooked his tee shot into the left rough and had 218 yards to the green. His three-wood approach came down 80 feet short of the hole, and he chipped to four feet. Campbell's par putt hit the left edge and stayed out. Scott holed his four-footer for the more-or-less victory. And thus ended a weird week of golf.

"I don't feel like I played much golf this week," Scott said. "I don't feel tired and drained like you normally do when you've been battling."

It was only fitting that this strange Nissan Open had a strange start. Retief

Goosen found a new way to get disqualified before he'd even teed it up. He didn't make his 6:40 starting time for the pro-am Wednesday morning. The penalty for missing a pro-am: DQ.

## WGC - Accenture Match Play Championship—$7,500,000
Winner: David Toms

After cruising through his bracket, and capping the run with a 6-and-5 whipping of Chris DiMarco for the WGC-Accenture Match Play Championship, David Toms — though he may not have realized it — gave a perfect working definition of "the zone," that magical nirvana golfers sometimes find themselves in and are loathe to leave.

"I can't explain why I felt like I did all week," Toms said. "I just felt very, very comfortable with myself and the golf in front of me. I just felt very calm, no matter what the match was. I don't know that I've ever felt like that in an event."

Consider that in 116 holes playing at the rain-whipped LaCosta Resort in California, he had only four bogeys.

The Accenture Match Play, to the surprise of many, developed this way:

Of the four No. 1 seeds, only Retief Goosen made it as far as the semi-finals. DiMarco ousted him there, 2 and 1. Phil Mickelson was stopped in the third round by Toms, 4 and 2. And Tiger Woods and Vijay Singh were bounced out in the second round on Friday morning. Woods, seeking his third straight championship, lost to the slender Australian, Nick O'Hern, 3 and 1. "I'm going home to get warm," Woods said, and then complained, "I can't wait to putt on some good greens." Jay Haas, 51, the oldest player in the tournament, erased Singh, 3 and 2. "I knocked me down a big, old sequoia today," Haas said. Singh was unhappy. "The course is ... soft and with so many forward tees that it takes the advantage away from the longer hitters," he said. Then he added: "I have no excuses. Good for Jay."

Toms had only a few uneasy moments. In the first round, he was extended — comparatively speaking — in beating Richard Green, 1 up. In the quarter-finals Saturday morning, Adam Scott, the young Australian whiz, came back from two down to go all-square at the 13th hole. Toms solved that one, winning the 14th with a par and the 16th with a birdie to win, 2 and 1. And then trailing Ian Poulter in the Saturday afternoon semi-finals, he blistered his way through the turn, birdie-eagle-eagle from No. 9, and won, 3 and 2.

DiMarco, the No. 4 seed in Singh's bracket, beat Tim Herron in the first round, 1 up, then beat John Daly, 4 and 3. Next went Haas, the sequoia-killer, 2 and 1. He beat Stewart Cink in 20 holes, and against Goosen in the semi-final, he lost the first three holes then came charging back for a 2-and-1 victory. This put two No. 4 seeds in the final, and neither was a power-hitter. The closest either had come before was Toms, 2-and-1 runner-up to Woods in 2003.

This was a 36-hole final, but it was over long before that. Toms was hitting some demonic irons. On the back nine in the morning, he won seven of eight holes, taking five of them with birdies inside eight feet, and getting the other two on DiMarco's bogeys, and was six up at the break. He ran that to nine up in a hurry in the afternoon, with birdies at Nos. 6 and 7 and DiMarco's bogey at No. 8. And then Toms surrendered to the inevitable.

"I was walking up the eighth hole, and all of a sudden it came into my head — what was I going to say at the trophy presentation?" Toms said. DiMarco got his attention, winning four of the next five holes, including a string of three straight birdies. And at the 13th, DiMarco put his approach inside Toms's, at a little over seven feet. Toms was about a foot farther out. He rolled it in, and went over and shook DiMarco's hand. Then it was off to the trophy ceremony, complete with ready acceptance speech. But he'd already given a more revealing talk earlier, though a much shorter one.

After the morning 18, an amazed DiMarco, finding himself already six down, turned to Toms and asked, "Have you been hitting your irons like that all week?"

The answer was yes. To which five other guys could have testified.

## Chrysler Classic of Tucson—$3,000,000
Winner: Geoff Ogilvy

Geoff Ogilvy, an Australian, had spent a lot of time explaining that he wasn't Joe Ogilvie, an American. This matter of identity figured to get easier now that he could be introduced as the Chrysler Classic of Tucson champion, his first title in five years on the PGA Tour.

It was fitting that Ogilvy should win his first here. He started his tour career in the Tucson in 2001, finishing third. Then he finished second in the next three years. And now he was the champion. But he had to survive a final-round battle and then a playoff against two guys as hungry as he was — Mark Calcavecchia, age 44, an 11-win veteran trying to regenerate his career, and Kevin Na, 21, the youngest player on the PGA Tour, winless and trying to start his.

It didn't take long. Calcavecchia exited with a double bogey on the first extra hole when he needed two shots to get out of a bunker.

The decision came at the second playoff hole, the par-five 10th. Na and Ogilvy both missed the fairway. Ogilvy punched his second shot back into the fairway, then put his approach 18 feet above the hole. Na carried the trees with his second shot and ended up just off the back fringe, and chipped eight feet past. Ogilvy made his birdie, Na missed, and Ogilvy had his first victory.

The tournament ended the way it started, in a mad scramble, thanks to a 7,109-yard, par-72 Omni Tucson National golf course that was pushed around like a nerd at day camp. "No rough, no wind — it's pretty defenseless," said Calcavecchia. In the first round, for example, 102 of the 144 starters broke par. The cut came in at five-under-par 139, lowest so far in the season, and 68 of the 70 finishers broke the par of 288 for the four rounds.

The assault began with an unlikely duo. Billy Mayfair, 16-year veteran of the PGA Tour, and Mario Tiziani, a 35-year-old rookie, finally making it after 12 cracks at the qualifying tournament, shared the first-round lead with 63s. Calcavecchia was at 64, Ogilvy 65 and Na 67. Calcavecchia went one ahead of Mayfair with a 65–129 in the second round, and was two up on Ogilvy (66) and four on Na (66).

In the third round, Brett Wetterich, a third-year player, turned in the most amazing round of the tournament. He had an eagle and six birdies in the first eight holes, had nine birdies overall and was working on a 61. The catch was, he also had two double bogeys and a bogey. He shot 66 and was no threat to Ogilvy (67) and Na (65), who tied for the third-round lead at 198, two ahead of Calcavecchia.

The fourth round was a game of tag and leapfrog. Calcavecchia, playing in the twosome ahead of Ogilvy and Na, struck fast, with birdies at Nos. 2, 3, 5 and 6. Two bogeys and a birdie the rest of the way gave him a 69. Na took the lead at No. 1 with a par against Ogilvy's bogey, birdied the next two, bogeyed the par-three No. 4 when he overshot the green, bogeyed the 15th, then holed a 28-foot uphill putt for a birdie at the 18th for a 71. After his opening bogey, Ogilvy birdied Nos. 2, 3, 5 and 6, getting to 21 under par. But he bogeyed the 11th and 15th for a 71.

Then the playoff: Calcavecchia ran afoul of the bunker and bowed out on the first hole. And at the second, when Na missed his eight-footer, Ogilvy, for the first time in his five years, cut loose. "I have never really got too revved up on a golf course," Ogilvy said. But when it hit him that he'd won, he let out a yell, raced across the green and hugged his wife Juli.

## Ford Championship at Doral—$5,500,000
Winner: Tiger Woods

"What a day," Tiger Woods was saying, in a sense mopping his brow. "If you're not nervous on a day like this, you're not alive."

Or, in the case of Phil Mickelson, maybe wishing you weren't. In a manner of speaking, of course.

This was at the Ford Championship at Doral, at Miami early in March, where Mickelson played outstanding golf for four days, but where Woods picked his pocket in the last round for a one-stroke victory. It was Woods's second victory of the year, and it returned him to No. 1 in the Official World Golf Ranking ahead of Vijay Singh, who had been No. 1 since September.

It a dramatic stretch drive, Woods finished with a six-under-par 66 and a tournament-record 24-under 264 total for a one-stroke win over Mickelson, who closed with a 69. Singh (66) and Zach Johnson (67) tied for third place, five strokes behind.

The field was unusually strong, with 11 of the world's top 12 players, thanks to vigorous recruiting.

"Four or five under isn't going to cut it with those guys," said Mickelson, after his 64 tied for the first-round lead. "I find myself pushing to go even lower." Which explains the mammoth drives he risked down the stretch. At the 465-yard 18th hole, for example, he caught the left rough, but he had only an eight iron left and he put it to six feet and birdied.

Woods stayed close with a 65. He birdied three straight before the turn, and added the 18th on a 15-footer. The class of the field was showing.

U.S. Open champion Retief Goosen shot 67, and Singh birdied three of his last four holes for a 68.

Woods was backing up after an erratic second round that included a stretch of five birdies in six holes, four in a row, then three straight bogeys for a 70 and 135 total. He was five strokes behind Mickelson, whose bogey-free 66 included a huge break at the par-five No. 8. His tee shot was headed for big trouble, but hit a spectator and bounced back in. "Just another fairway hit," Mickelson said. He was at 130 and leading by two over Billy Andrade (66).

Then it became a Woods-Mickelson battle in the third round, and the tournament organizers couldn't have asked for more. Mickelson turned in another 66, and Woods came charging with a 63. Mickelson went for distance over accuracy off the tee, and depended on his wedge from there. He hit only four fairways, but set up six birdies with his wedge. Woods turned on the power on the second nine. At the par-five 10th, he hit a three-wood second shot from 270 yards just over the green and birdied. Then he reached the 603-yard 12th green in two shots, hitting a three wood from 262 yards into a breeze, and birdied again. And finally, he birdied the 18th from eight feet to get within one stroke of the lead. But Mickelson lofted another wedge from the rough at the 16th and birdied from six feet, and at 20-under 196, led by two, setting up a great shootout in the final round.

"I want to go head-to-head against him," Mickelson said. "If I'm able to turn things around from the past and come out on top, it will make for a very special week." Said Woods: "We're going to have a bunch of fun tomorrow."

The real fun began at the par-five 12th. Woods bombed a three wood 290 yards to the green, and holed a 25-foot putt for an eagle to take the lead for the first time. Mickelson fired back with birdies at the 13th and 14th holes to regain a share of the lead, then missed two great chances — a 10-foot birdie putt at the 15th and a five-foot par putt at the 16th. When Woods also bogeyed the 16th, it was the first time in a combined 67 holes that either had made a bogey.

Woods then inched ahead with a birdie from 30 feet at the 17th, and it held up when Mickelson's 30-foot birdie chip shot at the 18th lipped out. Woods then holed his six-footer for par, to win by a stroke with 66 and a 264 total, 24 under par, to Mickelson's 69–265. That gave Woods a 3-0 record head-to-head against Mickelson.

"I'm a little ticked off at myself for not getting it done," Mickelson said. Said Woods, "What a day..."

## Honda Classic—$5,500,000
Winner: Padraig Harrington

Padraig Harrington would have loved to join the boys in the pubs back in Dublin. Trouble was, he was the reason they were celebrating. He was at the Honda Classic at the Country Club of Mirasol, in Florida, becoming — to the best of anyone's knowledge — the first Irishman to win on the PGA Tour.

And what a show Mr. No. 2 put on. (What else would you call a guy who had finished second 26 times worldwide?) In the final round, he shot 63 to wipe out a seven-stroke deficit, tie Vijay Singh (64) and Joe Ogilvie (68), and beat them in a playoff. Ogilvie exited on a bogey on the first hole. At the second, Singh needed a 30-inch par putt to stay with Harrington.

"I thought it was a gimme," Harrington said.

"I shouldn't have missed," Singh said.

And Harrington had the Honda Classic as his 10th career victory, his first in the United States, and a telephone call from Mary McAleese in Ireland.

"There you go," Harrington said. "President of the country congratulates you. Not too bad."

During that final-round rampage, Harrington wasn't thinking about winning. He had birdied 10 of the first 13 holes. He was thinking about a 59. "I birdied six in a row," he said, "and 'I'm 10 under.' I'm thinking, 'Make three more birdies.'" That was a more realistic ambition. After all, Harrington had started seven behind co-leaders Geoff Ogilvy, who had won his first at the Chrysler Classic of Tucson two weeks earlier, and Brett Wetterich, still looking for his first. Singh was only a little better off, six behind.

It wasn't as simple as it looked. When the final round began, 20 players were within six strokes of the lead, and five of them shared the lead at one time or another. Ogilvy and Wetterich slipped to 73s and tied for sixth. Wetterich triple-bogeyed the par-four 13th from a hazard, and Ogilvy bogeyed the 11th and 12th and double-bogeyed the 18th.

Gone from the scene was Chad Campbell, who led the first round with a 64, slipped in the second round, then sank in the third round with an 80. Wetterich shot a second bogey-free 66 to take his first lead on the PGA Tour at the halfway point. Two headliners were still quiet. Singh (69) was eight shots back, and Harrington (69) 10 back. Ogilvy, needing just 24 putts, shot 64 and tied for the third-round lead with Wetterich, who struggled for a 72 that included a bunker shot from 100 feet to six inches for a birdie at the 17th. In the third round, Singh shot 70–210, six off the lead, and Harrington, 69–211, seven back.

Then came Harrington, chasing a 59 in the final round. All of his birdies were from under 13 feet except for the 33-footer at the 13th for the lead at 15 under. Then he missed two consecutive greens and bogeyed both, and birdied the 17th from six feet for the 63 to tie Singh. On the first playoff hole, when Ogilvie departed on the bogey, Singh missed a 15-foot birdie putt for the win. At the second, Harrington rolled in a six-footer for his par. Then Singh blew the 30-incher to tie him.

"It was a shock," said Harrington. "It's nice when somebody does that, considering how many times I've been close and it has been taken away from me."

Then he thought about the boys back home.

"I'm sure I kept a few pubs open tonight," he said.

## Bay Hill Invitational—$5,000,000
Winner: Kenny Perry

Arnold Palmer's Bay Hill Invitational in mid-March figured to be the next leg on the Who's No. 1 Derby, with Tiger Woods and Vijay Singh, Ernie Els and Retief Goosen on hand. But only Singh made a run at it, and then he tripped at the last hole, and there stood the unflappable Kenny Perry with his first victory since his three in 2003.

Perry, shooting 70-68-68-70–276, eight under par, took the lead in the second round and stayed there for his eighth career victory, and this by two strokes over Singh. But first — the weather report. This was the sixth of the 12 tournaments of the young season to have stop-and-go play, and rounds carried over into the next day.

Woods, the world's No. 1 player and grouped with Els and Goosen, started like a weekender. He caught more turf than ball with his opening tee shot. The ball traveled only 198 yards. Woods could only grin. "I've never done that before," he said. He would recover. But he wasn't a factor.

Perry trailed only once. His 70 tied for fourth place behind Joe Ogilvie's 66 in the first round. Perry was the sole leader at the end of the other three rounds, but along the way he was in some uncomfortable positions in the carryover play. On Saturday morning, he found himself trailing by three strokes with 29 holes that day, and at the end he had the lead by one over Stephen Ames. He also had a weary body. Said Perry, age 44: "I'm definitely not a spring chicken out here anymore."

In the final analysis, it was Perry's accuracy that got him around the toughened Bay Hill, with its narrowed fairways and deeper rough. All told, Perry hit 79 percent of the greens, tops for the week, and 84 percent of the fairways, tied for fourth. Perry had gone 21 holes without a bogey, and the streak ended at a bad time — at No. 1 in the fourth round. Singh, playing with Perry, could smell blood. But not for long. Perry birdied No. 4 and three straight from No. 9 to hold off Singh, who birdied three in a span of seven from No. 6. This one came down to the stretch drive.

Perry birdied the 11th, and after both birdied the 12th, he led by three heading into the final stretch. Singh gained a stroke with a birdie at the 15th, then another when he birdied the reachable par-five 16th, which Perry could only par. And when Perry missed a par putt from eight feet and bogeyed the 17th, it was a tie game with one hole to play. And then the unthinkable happened.

At the tough par-four 18th, Singh was fatally short with his approach from 174 yards, ending up in the lake in front of the green. He took a double bogey. "It was a good shot," Singh said. "I just hit the wrong club. The wind switched on me."

"It stunned me," Perry said. "It was a big break for me. I just aimed left and played it safe. I knew I could three-putt." Perry lagged to within two feet and holed the next for a 70 and a two-shot victory.

It was Singh's second bitter pill in two weeks. In the Honda Classic a week earlier, he lipped out a 30-inch par putt on the second playoff hole and lost to Padraig Harrington. And he wasn't the only one of the elite with troubles. Els, nursing a sore hip, blew to a 77 in the second round. Woods shot 71-70 in the first two rounds, then a 74 and he was out of it. They finished tied for 23rd place. Goosen was set to withdraw after a crushing 78 in the first round, but he made an inspired comeback to finish fourth. There was one redeeming aspect for Singh. In the computations of the World Rankings, he had returned to No. 1 ahead of Woods.

"Big deal," Singh said. "I lost the tournament."

## The Players Championship—$8,000,000
Winner: Fred Funk

See Chapter 6.

## BellSouth Classic—$5,000,000
Winner: Phil Mickelson

The BellSouth Classic was played at the TPC at Sugarloaf, outside Atlanta, in April. It was more like the Aleutian Open. Wind, rain, sleet, chill — they were all there. Thursday and Friday were washed out, the tournament was shortened to 54 holes, and it ended on Monday, with Phil Mickelson plucking his third victory of the season out of a five-way playoff.

"There were probably six to 10 people who could have won this tournament," Mickelson said. "I don't know how I was fortunate to dodge the bullets and ultimately win, but I'll take it."

Actually, there were five who could have won it, all tied at eight-under-par 208 for the three rounds. Mickelson and Jose Maria Olazabal closed with 69s, former PGA champion Rich Beem a 68, Brandt Jobe a 67, and India's Arjun Atwal, an Asian Tour star in his second year on the PGA Tour, a tournament-low 64.

This was the week before the Masters, and Mickelson was the object of some debate — shouldn't he be practicing at Augusta National to defend his 2004 green jacket? But Mickelson didn't hurt himself, picking up some hot competition plus $900,000. He won on the fourth extra hole, the 455-yard, par-four 17th. Earlier, he couldn't find a fairway. But he drove it perfectly this time, then hit his second to about 15 feet and holed the birdie putt to beat Rich Beem, the only other guy left from the five-man tie. Beem, who hadn't won since the 2002 PGA Championship, caught a fairway bunker, was short with his approach, and pitched to two feet. Mickelson's 15-footer spared him the trouble of tapping in.

Mickelson addressed the big question. "I love playing the week before a major," he said, "and I love how this tournament has set up the course as close as Augusta as possible." But he didn't look like a winner at first. He opened with a 74, six shots behind first-round co-leaders Billy Mayfair and Jason Allred, who started Saturday and who, once scores were all in by 10:36 Sunday morning, had shot 68s. Mickelson jumped into the chase with a 65 in the second round Sunday to move within a stroke of leader Scott McCarron (69), who was gone on a 76 in the third round.

Mickelson's 65 included one bogey, six birdies and an eagle on a 26-yard pitch-in at the 310-yard, par-four 13th. Despite Mickelson's fireworks, this turned into Jose Maria Olazabal's tournament to lose, and he did.

Olazabal had lost his PGA Tour card, and — playing on a sponsor's exemption — he would have regained it by winning. But a careless error in the second round cost him the victory. His blast out of a bunker at the par-three No. 8 came trickling back down into the bunker, and in disgust, he slapped the sand with his club — a two-stroke penalty. Then at the final hole in regulation, he missed a five-foot birdie putt for the win.

On the first extra hole, the 18th, Jobe and Atwal departed with watery bogeys. Olazabal missed a three-footer for birdie to win. And then on the third extra hole, again the 18th, he put two balls into the water. He shrugged and walked in. It was over. Mickelson and Beem were already on the green in two. They weren't likely to make a seven.

Mickelson and Beem tied with birdies, and Mickelson untied it all with that 15-footer at the fourth playoff hole. Now it was on to the Masters.

## Masters Tournament—$7,000,000
Winner: Tiger Woods

See Chapter 3.

## MCI Heritage—$5,200,000
Winner: Peter Lonard

This was the tale of the 2005 MCI Heritage in a nutshell: There was Northern Ireland's Darren Clarke, birdieing four of the first five holes of the final round, leading by four strokes over Australia's Peter Lonard, getting to 14 under par for the tournament, and then going into a terrific freefall, dropping 11 shots. As for Lonard, a man who could flirt with a 59 deserves something, and in this case it was, at age 37, his first PGA Tour victory. But only just. Clarke had blown to a 76. Lonard, not exactly dazzling, shot 75. It was a clumsy moment that called for insightful statements.

Said Clarke: "Honest, I can't believe I've done what I've done. I played like a 36-handicapper."

Said Lonard: "My mother is having her 80th birthday back in Sydney. I hope she didn't have a heart attack watching this."

There were a few interesting footnotes at the famed Harbour Town Golf Links on Hilton Head Island, South Carolina. The veteran Tom Kite, 33 years a professional, signed an incorrect scorecard and was disqualified. Alex Cejka used a non-conforming ball and was disqualified. And David Frost needed only 92 putts, a PGA Tour record that got him a tie for 38th place. But all in all, this was Lonard's tournament from the start, except he had trouble keeping it that way. This tournament was an exercise in bi-polar golf.

Lonard froze the golf course in the first round with his march toward a historic 59. He came to the par-three 17th at 10 under par on the par-71 course. He would have to birdie the last two holes. "Up until 17, I didn't really think about it," he said. But there, he left his five-foot birdie putt a foot short, then bogeyed the 18th for a 62. No history, but a two-stroke lead over France's Thomas Levet, who birdied six of his last eight holes for a 64. Clarke was in at 65. Then a kind of carnival was on.

Clarke shot his second straight 65 in the second round for a 12-under 130 and a six-stroke lead on Lonard, who blew to a 74. Lonard was looking strong at 10 under with six holes to play, then bogeyed four of the next five holes. "That didn't do me any favors," he said. Then came the next twist. In the third round, Lonard bounced back with a 66 to regain the lead, going one up on Clarke, who shot 73. Lonard birdied three of his first five holes, including a 40-foot chip-in at the par-three No. 4. Clarke bogeyed four of the first seven holes. Then at the par-five 15th, Lonard rolled in a 55-foot putt for a birdie, and Clarke ran his 50-footer six feet by and missed the return. Lonard had gone from trailing by six to leading by one.

Came the final act. Lonard started the last round leading Clarke by one, but five holes later he was four behind. Clarke had run off four birdies in the first five holes, against Lonard's two bogeys and a birdie. Clarke's edge disappeared in a flash. He bogeyed the sixth and seventh, and double-bogeyed the par-four No. 8 after driving into water. Clarke went back up by two with a birdie at the 12th, then double-bogeyed the 13th from a bunker, and bogeyed the next two. He ended this wild ride with a double bogey at the par-four 18th. And against this, Lonard sprinkled four bogeys and not one birdie over the final 10 holes. It was just enough. It was a 75 and a seven-under 277 total. He won by two. Clarke's 76 dropped him to a tie for second with Jim Furyk (69), Billy Andrade (68) and Davis Love (71). Said a relieved Lonard: "It's something I'll never forget."

## Shell Houston Open—$5,000,000
Winner: Vijay Singh

It must be something in the water. Vijay Singh, beating a surging John Daly in a playoff, took his second straight Shell Houston Open — the first ever to do so back-to-back — and his third in four years. Singh had no explanation for this success, but the only possible one is that the big Fijian can win anytime, anywhere. It's the kind of thing that gets a guy elected to the World Golf Hall of Fame, which Singh was earlier in the week. And this one ended up with the two protagonists being quite proud of themselves.

"I'm really pleased with the way I hung in there and never gave up," Singh said. "Fortunately for me, nobody came out of the pack except for John and made a run at it. It was a good way to finish."

Said Daly, "I'm proud of myself for coming back like that and hitting some shots when I needed to. I wish I could have done better in the playoff."

Daly birdied the last two holes for a five-under-par 67 to catch Singh at 13-under 275 at the par-72 Redstone Golf Club. Singh, who made only two birdies in his closing 70, won on the first extra hole with a par when Daly hit his three-wood tee shot into the water, took a drop and hit his third over the green. It was Singh's second win of the year and the 26th of his career. Daly may have been the only one to make a run, but Singh had plenty of company along the way.

Singh opened with an eight-under 64 and led by a stroke over little-known Australians Gavin Coles and Brendan Jones. Jones blew to an 80 in the second round and missed the cut, and Coles (69) and Brett Quigley (67) tied for the halfway lead at 10-under 134, a stroke ahead of an imposing foursome — Singh (71), Daly (67), Joe Ogilvie (67) and Jeff Maggert (68).

Singh still couldn't break loose in the third round. In a wry twist, Singh, ranked No. 2 in the world, shot 70, and was tied by Coles, No. 388, who shot 71. "It's awesome, mate," Coles said, shrugging off a mismatch that went one step further — Singh is a gangly 6-foot-2, Coles 5-foot-4. "I can't imagine too many guys that wouldn't want to be in my shoes tomorrow ... that's for sure," Coles added. "What better could it be, playing with the No. 2 player in the world?" Coles stuck with Singh until the 11th, where he doubled-bogeyed out of woods and bunker. Maggert, three-time Houston runner-up, and Greg Owen were tied for the lead with Singh through the 15th, but both faded. Jose Maria Olazabal and Darren Clarke made late moves and fell short. Daly hung on like a bulldog.

Singh was thwarted by his putting. He missed a four-footer at No. 2, ground out 13 straight pars, then missed again at No. 12, where a bunker shot left him 10 feet from the hole. Finally, at the 14th, he dropped a six-footer and retook the lead.

"The lines were just really difficult to read," Singh said. "I was under-reading and over-reading. But that's where you have to have patience."

Daly, often the soul of impatience, this time posted three birdies and two bogeys on the first nine, then notched three birdies on the back. He dropped a five-footer at the 12th. He grabbed a share of the lead at the par-five 15th when he scrambled out of the woods and fired his third to four feet, and dropped the putt for his first share of the lead. Daly saved par at the 16th after hitting over the green, and he tied Singh again at the 17th, firing his approach to four feet and dropping the putt.

Singh, three groups behind, birdied the 15th. Then Daly birdied the par-four 18th, firing his approach to nine feet and holing the birdie putt. "I take it that under pressure, maybe I've still got it," Daly said. Singh just missed winning in regulation when his eight-foot birdie putt at the 18th slid by. He and Daly were tied. The playoff was decided when Daly hit his tee shot into the water. Singh then made a routine par for a far-from-routine win.

## Zurich Classic of New Orleans—$5,500,000
Winner: Tim Petrovic

They say when you start hearing voices, you're in trouble. And when you answer, well ...

Tim Petrovic — former pizza maker, floor scrubber and dishwasher — who languished for years on the fringes of professional golf, heard a voice in the Zurich Classic of New Orleans. It was at the par-three 17th hole in the final round, just after he bogeyed that he heard someone say, "Well, there's one more down — two to go." Petrovic was a goner, the voice was saying, and it was now up to Chris DiMarco and James Driscoll, the final group behind him. Petrovic seethed for a while, then answered, but only to himself, and thereby hangs the tale of his victory. "That kind of got me fired up," Petrovic said. "I said, 'Well, we've still got one hole left.'" It was a slim chance, but a chance.

Chris DiMarco, making his first start since the playoff loss to Tiger Woods in the Masters three weeks earlier, posted his season's best, a seven-under-par 65, to tie India's Arjun Atwal for the first-round lead. DiMarco went bogey-free on a windy day at the TPC of Louisiana at Avondale, in its first year after the tournament spent 16 years at English Turn. Said Atwal: "I just tried to make pars because it was so windy." Vijay Singh, defending champion, was two behind with a confusing 67. "I had a lot of long putts that I couldn't judge," Singh said. "I three-putted four times."

Atwal solved the winds in the second round for a 68 and a halfway 133 total and a one-stroke lead over J.J. Henry (67). DiMarco had a chance to tie him but hit his tee shot in the water at the 18th and suffered a double-bogey seven. "A lack of knowledge of the golf course," he said. "I thought it was going to fly into the bunker, and it didn't even get close." The double bogey nullified his eagle at the par-five No. 7, and he settled for a 71–136, three strokes behind Atwal. Petrovic, who opened with a 72, shot 69 and was eight behind.

Then came a storm Saturday, the delay forcing 69 players to complete their third rounds on Sunday morning. DiMarco played 10 holes on Saturday, and came back Sunday morning and finished up a 68 for a 204 total and a one-stroke lead over James Driscoll. Atwal (73) was two back, and Petrovic (66) and Lucas Glover (70) three behind.

DiMarco was halfway home in the final round. He had saved par at No. 1 with a 24-foot putt, and made three birdies to get to 15 under through the turn, two ahead of Petrovic. But coming home, he hit five bunkers and made three bogeys, the last at the 18th, where a lip-out cost him a spot in the playoff. He had come home in 39, shot 72, and tied Glover (69) for third.

Petrovic was in the group ahead, and came to the par-five 18th irked at being written off by a spectator. But he held himself in check and rolled in a 20-foot putt for the birdie and a 68 and 275 total. James Driscoll, coming along behind him with DiMarco, missed an outright victory when he lipped out a four-foot birdie putt at the 18th. The playoff, at the 18th, was short and simple. Driscoll left his wedge third on the front of the green, 30 feet short. His first putt, a roller coaster, went 12 feet past. Petrovic, also on in three, lagged his first putt to four feet, then dropped the next for his first PGA Tour victory.

And so Petrovic had finally made it. Twelve years earlier, after two fruitless years, he went broke, gave up golf and turned to making pizzas and washing and scrubbing. In 1998, an angel of a backer helped him return.

"That last putt," Petrovic said, "seemed to take about 12 minutes to fall in."

Funny he should say 12 minutes. One minute for each year?

## Wachovia Championship—$6,000,000
Winner: Vijay Singh

The old saying says, "Youth will be served." But not as far as Vijay Singh, age 42, is concerned. Not unless the serving is a dose of bitter medicine. The youth in this case was Spain's Sergio Garcia, a former whiz kid, now age 25, who led until he lost a six-shot lead going into the final round. He got caught by Singh and Jim Furyk, and Singh proceeded to beat them both in a playoff.

"I'm just playing golf," Singh insisted. "I said after Houston, I'm playing better golf this year than I did last year. It's just that I won more times last year." True. He won nine in 2004. This was No. 3 by mid-May.

Despite the quality field at the Quail Hollow Club in Charlotte, North Carolina, no one else could work up a threat. Phil Mickelson closed with a 66 and climbed to a tie for seventh, and Tiger Woods, whose best was a 70 in the first round, tied for 11th.

Garcia was having a high time in the first three rounds. He opened the first round in a fog, with bogeys at the first two holes, then caught fire at No. 5, birdieing six of eight holes, and overall played the last 14 holes in eight under par for a six-under 66 and a two-stroke lead. Blustery winds cooled him and everybody else off in the second round. He managed a three-birdie, one-bogey 71 and kept his two-shot lead, with Singh heading the small group tied for second. The third was a rampage. Garcia birdied eight of the first 15 holes, and only a double bogey at the fourth and a bogey at the 12th, both from trees, kept him from a runaway. His 67 gave him a six-shot lead over Singh, Furyk and D.J. Trahan.

Squandering a six-shot lead sounds like a collapse, but that wasn't entirely true in Garcia's case. "He didn't shoot a high number or anything," Singh said. "We won it." Garcia closed with a par-72, Singh and Furyk with 66s.

Wasting that six-shot lead put Garcia into exclusive but unwanted company with only four others: Bobby Cruickshank in 1928, Gay Brewer in 1969, Hal Sutton in 1983, and most noted of all, Greg Norman closing with a 78 and losing the 1996 Masters.

Garcia's closing 72 was ragged. He bogeyed No. 1, birdied Nos. 7 and 8, then double-bogeyed No. 9 after a tee shot into the trees. He saved par out of the trees at the 10th, and Singh tied him for the first time with a birdie at the 11th on a four-foot putt. Garcia bogeyed out of a bunker at the 13th and was trailing by two. He wasted a big chance at the par-five 15th, where an amazing two iron from 248 yards put him six feet from the hole. He missed the eagle, but he got the birdie and regained the lead, a stroke up on Singh, three up on Furyk. But he watered his seven-iron tee shot at the par-three 17th and bogeyed to fall back into the tie.

Singh put on a brilliant burst, going six under in a seven-hole stretch — an eagle at the par-five No. 7, and four birdies from No. 10. He lost his edge at the par-five 15th, knocking his second over the green, then failing on a flop shot coming back. He bogeyed, then parred in for his 66. Furyk made four straight birdies from No. 5, bogeyed No. 9, and birdied three holes coming home, including the tough 18th for a 66 to tie for the lead.

All three started the playoff with good drives at the 18th. And all three missed the green with their seconds — Singh wide right, Garcia short right, and Furyk long. All three hit so-so chips. Garcia, from six feet, putted first and missed. Then he was out when Singh holed from five feet and Furyk from four. Singh and Furyk tied at the 16th and 17th, then it was back to the 18th. Furyk hit his tee shot left, into the creek. He dropped and ended up in a bad lie. He wedged up the fairway, and then from 88 yards hit the flagstick with his approach. But the ball glanced off the green. Singh wrapped it up neatly. After a good drive and a second into a bunker, he blasted out to a foot and tapped in for a par and the win.

Said a sobered Garcia: "They say you learn more from your losses than your wins. And I've got a lot from this week to learn."

## EDS Byron Nelson Championship—$6,200,000
Winner: Ted Purdy

The EDS Byron Nelson Championship, with the venerable Hall-of-Fame namesake in attendance, was hit by something of an identity problem. The Fab Five were all on hand — "fab" being short for fabulous, referring to the top players of the day. So the question became, who's Ted Purdy? For that matter, who were Sean O'Hair, Brett Wetterich, Doug Barron and assorted others who occupied a leaderboard once thought to be the exclusive domain of the Fab Five.

Well, the answer was: Ted Purdy, 31, who toiled for six years on the Asian Tour, was the obscure individual who won this tournament, his first victory on the PGA Tour. He shot 65-67-68-65—265, 15 under par, and won by a stroke over the equally obscure O'Hair, 22, a rookie who was also seeking his first victory.

The satisfying thing was that Purdy did it with all the Fabs on hand at Cottonwood Valley and the TPC at Las Colinas, near Dallas. This included Tiger Woods, but only for the first two rounds. He missed the cut for the first time in 142 tournaments, a stretch of seven years. His 69-72—141 missed by a stroke. "I just had a tough day," Woods said. "Things I don't normally do, I did today." He'd had close calls, but he always pulled through. This time, he needed a par at the 18th at Cottonwood. He bogeyed.

Vijay Singh rallied in the final round — an ace at the par-three 17th and a birdie at the 18th for a 65 to tie for third, four behind Purdy. Ernie Els faded after a strong start, and birdied four of his last five holes to tie for 10th. Goosen (70-71) also missed the cut after making 24 in a row, worldwide, and Phil Mickelson just never got hot and tied for 14th.

Not that Purdy had never won. He'd won the Indian Open on the Asian Tour and the First Tee Arkansas Classic on the Nationwide Tour. But the PGA Tour was what he was aiming for, and he'd had two bitter disappointments in 2004, faltering and finishing second at the MCI Heritage and the B.C. Open. Those were still sticking in his throat.

"I don't think I would have been able to pull it off today without those previous failures," Purdy said. He trailed by two strokes in the first round, and by one in the second and third. And in the fourth, he was bogey-free and nearly perfect. He birdied No. 6 from 25 feet and No. 8 from 30 feet, overtaking and passing O'Hair, who started the day leading by one. O'Hair was within a stroke of Purdy until he hit into a bunker at the 14th and bogeyed. Purdy two-putted the 16th for another birdie for a three-shot lead that held up when O'Hair birdied two of the last three holes.

"I played my guts out today," said O'Hair, who turned pro at 17 and who was in a dispute with his dad, trying to get un-stuck from a contract. "Now that I've got a taste of this … I'm just going to work my butt off and, hopefully, I'll be in this situation a lot more."

Purdy was a man liberated. "The Fab Five were here, and No. 177 in the world won," he said.

## Bank of America Colonial—$5,600,000
Winner: Kenny Perry

Kenny Perry double-bogeyed the 17th in the final round without a groan. What was there to groan about? After all, he still had enough of a lead to win by seven strokes.

Perry took the lead in the second round and simply ran off and left everyone, turning the Bank of America Colonial into a pure runaway. It's something about him and Colonial Country Club at Fort Worth, Texas. It's the course known as "Hogan's Alley," where Ben Hogan won five times.

Without intending to, Perry may have tipped off what was coming after he opened with a 65, three shots off the lead. "The rhythm of my golf swing feels like it did in '03," Perry said. "It was very relaxing, a very enjoyable round … When I get here, something clicks."

Indeed. Here's Perry's juggernaut card at the par-70 course: 65-63-64-69, a 19-under-par 261, and a seven-stroke win over Billy Mayfair. The opening 65 was, at that time, his best round of the year. With the 63–128, he broke the tournament 36-hole record, and then broke the 54-hole record with the 64–192. The 19-under total matched the course record he set in 2003, though hardly anyone noticed. That was the year Annika Sorenstam became the first woman in 58 years to play on the PGA Tour.

Considering all the fireworks, it falls under the heading of "Amazing" that Perry was hampered by vision problems. He had a tough time reading greens, and seeing clearly from a distance and in shady areas.

"I know the greens," said Perry, who was playing Colonial for the 16th time. "I don't really have to see that well. I know what's uphill, what's downhill. I know the breaks. I pretty much know where the pin placements are going to be."

Perry wasn't perfect. But darn good. When he got into trouble, he got out of it. At the par-five No. 1 in the third round, for example, he drove into nasty rough, hit his second into more rough, pitched to 18 feet and got down in two for his par. At No. 5, he put his approach into a deep front bunker, blasted to three feet and saved par. At No. 6, he drove into rough, but got his second to 12 feet and birdied. In the final round, he missed the first fairway again, but eventually birdied from three feet. And at the par-four No. 5, he was on track to break his course record. He dropped an 11-footer for a birdie that put him at 20 under. He just missed going even lower. At No. 6, his short pitch burned the hole and he missed a birdie coming back from six feet. At the 13th, his 39-footer singed the edge.

All told, Perry had 22 birdies, and went 53 straight holes between his only two errors, from the bogey at his 17th hole (No. 8) in the first round to the double bogey at the 17th in the fourth, where he missed the green and three-putted from 40 feet. "Things have gone my way," Perry said. "I understand how to play here. I just feel very relaxed and very comfortable when I play here."

## FedEx St. Jude Classic—$4,900,000

Winner: Justin Leonard

If the FedEx St. Jude Classic had been an auto race, Justin Leonard would have just managed to cross the finish line with a wheeze, a gasp and a splat of oil. He got there just ahead of the record book. He bogeyed the last hole, and when he pulled the ball out of the cup, he fell over on his back in sheer relief.

"It's a good thing I had an eight-shot cushion," said Leonard, who won the Bob Hope Chrysler Classic in January, "because I was able to stay just enough in front of a great round by David."

But only just. Leonard started with an eight-stroke lead, and he came to the final hole with one left. If he had lost that one last stroke, he would have gone into the record book for blowing the biggest final-round lead in PGA Tour history. But he holed that four-footer at the 18th for a bogey and a three-over-par 73. It wasn't a really ugly score, but it was unsightly compared to his 62-65-66 start, and it was downright scary against David Toms's closing 63. But it was enough for a 14-under 266 total and a one-stroke win at the TPC at Southwind in Memphis, Tennessee.

Toms, who won the previous two tournaments here — last year's by six shots — turned Leonard's cakewalk into a nightmare with a back nine that included an eagle and four birdies and a bogey. "It made it interesting, at least," Toms said.

Leonard, on his way to his first wire-to-wire win, opened with a 62 in what he called "benign" conditions. "I feel like I played my way into the round," he said. "Certainly shooting 62 is a surprise." He hit 11 fairways and 16 greens and had only 26 putts, including some longish ones for birdies — 47 feet at No. 7, 28 at No. 15 and 20 at No. 17. He led Kirk Triplett by two in the first round, and with a 65 in the second, he was up by five, this time over Fredrik Jacobson (64–132). Then came what looked like the clincher. In the third round, Leonard shot a bogey-free 66, and at 193 was up by eight strokes. The man in second was Heath Slocum. Toms was 11 strokes behind and tied for seventh place.

The way Leonard got into trouble was this: In the final round, whether he had turned conservative or just didn't get the opportunities, he started making pars. He bogeyed No. 7 and made the turn in one-over 36. Toms birdied the third and fourth and turned in 33. Toms had picked up three strokes — insignificant. Leonard still led by five with nine to play. Then the game was on.

With Leonard still running pars, Toms birdied the 10th but gave the stroke back when his tee shot bounced off the 11th green and into the water, costing him a bogey. Next, Toms birdied the 13th and 14th, then eagled the par-five 16th with a seven-foot putt, and chipped in for a birdie from 60 feet at the 17th. A par at the 18th gave him the 63. Leonard bogeyed the 15th, and all he wanted, as he put it, was to "get it in the house." He saved par at the par-four 17th on a seven-foot putt, and came to the 18th wanting only to avoid the water lining the left side. He drove into a fairway bunker and left his second 44 yards short of the green in front of the grandstands. He took a drop, chipped over a bunker to 34 feet, and putted out for a bogey and the awkward victory

"It wasn't going to be a pretty win no matter what I did on 18," Leonard said. "At that point, I didn't care. I just wanted to get it in."

## Memorial Tournament—$5,500,000
Winner: Bart Bryant

Bart Bryant will never forget the 2005 Memorial Tournament. At age 42 and after 20 years of toiling in the game, injuries, and after sleepless nights of doubt, he had finally won a big one. It doesn't demean the Valero Texas Open, which he won in 2004, to note that this was Jack Nicklaus's tournament. Unfortunately for Bryant — despite a remarkable shot at the final hole — the rest of golf probably would remember it as the final tournament for Nicklaus.

Nicklaus, founder and builder of both the Memorial Tournament and the Muirfield Village Golf Club near Columbus, Ohio, was 65, hurting and embarrassed by his un-Nicklaus-like game. So he would play one last time in his own tournament, for the sake of the home folks. He shot 75-77–152, missing the cut by six strokes. As he left the final green, he pressed both hands to his lips and wafted a farewell kiss to the cheering crowd.

"It will probably close out my golf in the United States in regular tournament golf, more than likely," said Nicklaus. But leaving one tiny crack, just in case, he added, "I may come back here, but I certainly wouldn't plan on it."

The first thing to remember about Bart Bryant is that he's not his better-known big brother Brad, now a rookie on the Champions Tour. The confusion didn't materialize until the third round, when Bryant tied for the lead with Jeff Sluman, Fred Couples and David Toms.

Sluman, 47, who had had just one top-10 finish so far, led by a stroke in the first round with a seven-under-par 65. He kept the one-stroke lead (71–136) in the second round on a flop-shot birdie at the 17th. Tiger Woods (68) led a group tied for second, and Bryant, after another 69, was two behind.

Bryant (66) finally drew attention when he tied three others for the third-round lead at 204. Sluman (68) would have kept the solo lead if that 40-footer at the 18th hadn't slid by. Couples (66) was a surprise contender considering he had to wear a knee-to-back brace to help a bad back that had kept him out of the past eight tournaments. Toms (64), hitting a five iron, aced the 201-yard No. 4. Bryant bounced back from a double bogey at No. 2 and played the last 11 holes in seven under for his 66.

In the fourth round, on-off play dropped three guys into a tie for third.

Sluman (72) had four birdies and four bogeys, and Bo Van Pelt (68) three and three down the final nine holes. Woods (68) double-bogeyed the par-three No. 8. Toms (74) doubled-bogeyed the par-four 14th and tied for eighth.

It was a Bryant-Couples battle down the stretch. Couples birdied the 11th from two feet and the 12th from 10 feet to take the lead for the first time Sunday. Then a nine iron to six feet at the 14th paid off, and at the par-five 15th, he converted a four iron to six feet into a two-putt birdie. But he bogeyed the 16th out of a bunker. It would prove fatal.

Bryant, after a birdie at the 11th, holed a testy 20-footer at the 14th, and birdied the 15th out of a bunker for a two-shot swing that gave him the lead. The clincher came at the 18th. Bryant's tee shot ended up to the left, hanging on the bank of a little stream. The bank was too steep to stand on, the water too deep to stand in, and he needed a par four to force Couples, just behind him, to birdie to tie. Bryant took a penalty drop, then smacked a six iron up the hill to 15 feet and holed the putt for a terrific four and a 68. Couples hit the fairway but missed the green and parred. Bryant had won by a shot.

"For me," Bryant said, "this year was kind of about validation for myself. I don't think anybody else really cared one way or another, but for me, I needed to show myself that I belonged in the winner's circle, and I could compete with Tiger Woods and Vijay Singh and these guys."

## Booz Allen Classic—$5,000,000
Winner: Sergio Garcia

The PGA Tour returned to Congressional Country Club after an absence of eight years when the Booz Allen Classic — successor to the Kemper Open — teed it up early in June, bringing some of the names in the game back to the famous Bethesda, Maryland, course.

And in case anyone was wondering whatever became of Sergio Garcia after he blew a six-stroke lead to lose the Wachovia Championship five weeks earlier, you had only to watch the last round of the Booz Allen Classic. It was a simple reversal of form, that's all — Garcia rushing out of the pack to chalk up his sixth PGA Tour victory. It was a good tune-up for the U.S. Open, coming the next week.

Even with a bogey at the last hole, Garcia turned back his friend and fellow youth-movement member, Adam Scott, the defending champion, along with Davis Love and Ben Crane, beating the bunch of them by two strokes. Garcia played the somewhat friendlier, par-71 Congressional in 71-68-66-65, tying the course record of 14-under-par 270. But he wasn't without his nervous moments. For example, what he called his "Wachovia Ghost" when he missed the green at the par-three final hole.

"I could see the guys just flying around, saying 'Ooo-oooh, what's going on?'" Garcia said. Meaning, was he about to crash again, as he did in the Wachovia. But he held the damage to a bogey this time, and won comfortably. With his opening 71, Garcia was in 60th place, and a waver in the second round might well have cost him the cut, which came in at one-under 141. But he made his way up the leaderboard to a tie for 30th, then a tie for eighth, two strokes off the lead. Then he raced through the field in the final round, shooting the front in 30 and leading by as many as four strokes.

The tournament had opened pretty much without him. Matt Gogel, ranked 170th in the world, showed the top-heavy field a thing or two by birdieing eight of his last 13 holes for a course-record 63 in the first round. "It's kind of my time," said Gogel, who had slipped badly since his only PGA Tour victory in the 2002 AT&T Pebble Beach National Pro-Am. Australian Robert Allenby, suffering from a mysterious and painful hand ailment, took the second-round lead with a 65, but he faded from there to a tie for 13th. "I've had no feel, no touch around the greens at all," said Allenby, hoping that doctors would soon find the cure. Came the third round, and this time it was Tom Kite, age 55, trying to become the Tour's oldest winner ever. A 66 for a 203 total gave him a one-stroke edge on a crowd led by Ernie Els.

And so the final round opened up like a mad dash, with 16 players within two strokes of the lead. But not for long. Kite was betrayed by his putter and shot 74. Els, despite an unruly driver, got to 13 under par but bogeyed three straight and shot himself out of the race with a 72. Phil Mickelson lipped out a two-foot par putt at No. 1 and shot 74, and Steve Elkington got to 12 under but self-destructed with a bogey-double bogey making the turn and shot 73. Vijay Singh tied for 29th, tossing the No. 1 world ranking back to Tiger Woods, who wasn't playing. And in one of the strangest episodes ever, Rory Sabbatini grew impatient with the slow-playing Ben Crane, putted out of turn on the 17th and went to the 18th tee before Crane had finished.

Meanwhile, Garcia was motoring along in his own world. He was putting like a machine, thanks to a tip from, of all people, Adam Scott. "I was standing over a lot of putts thinking, 'This is going in,'" Garcia said. "It didn't matter the length or the difficulty of the putt. I could see the putt going in." Said Scott: "Maybe I should charge him."

## U.S. Open Championship—$6,250,000
Winner: Michael Campbell

See Chapter 4.

## Barclays Classic—$5,750,000
Winner: Padraig Harrington

"You know, I'm a strange person," Padraig Harrington was saying. "My emotions dictate how I play."

Harrington must be really strange, because playing under a heavy burden, he scored his second PGA Tour victory, the Barclays Classic — the former Westchester Classic — beating Jim Furyk by a stroke at par-71 Westchester Country Club, near New York City, in late June heat. By all accounts, Harrington should have been depressed and playing badly. For one thing, he had missed the cut in his last two events, the Booz Allen Classic and the

U.S. Open. But his real pain lay in his father Patrick being seriously ill with cancer back home in Ireland. He had withdrawn from two tournaments to visit him. And he opened this tournament with no bright prospects, not sitting in a tie for 28th in the first round behind a hot Jim Furyk.

But nothing is hotter than a huge breaking putt with eyes of its own, and that's what Harrington rolled in from 65 feet on the final hole for an eagle, his second of the day, for a one-stroke victory over Furyk.

"I was just trying to two-putt, trying to get it down there close," Harrington said. "If you'd offered me three or four feet, I probably would have said, 'All right, I'll take that.'" But the ball did drop, giving him a one-under-par 70 and a 10-under 274 total.

Furyk, his playing companion, then had to set about his own business. All he had left was a 10-footer for a birdie, although this wouldn't catch Harrington. But Furyk got the birdie to lock up second place with 71 and a 275 total. It was a two-man show at the end. Tying for third, five shots off the lead, were Brad Faxon (73), Kenny Perry (71) and Brian Gay (73).

"He just hit a fabulous putt," Furyk said. "There's nothing you can really do. I opened the door a little bit with a bogey on 16, and then missing the short one on 17 … I make that putt 99 percent of the time."

Furyk failed to get up-and-down for par at the 16th, and then missed a four-footer for par at the 17th for another bogey. "On 16, that was the first big break of the day — something I didn't expect," said Harrington, who overcame a three-stroke deficit with five holes to play.

Big break, indeed. Harrington had bogeyed the 11th and 12th to fall three strokes behind. But he birdied the 14th from five feet to let Furyk know he was still there. Then, while Furyk was bogeying the 16th and 17th, Harrington made up two strokes, saving par from the rough at the par-three 16th, and two-putting for par at the 17th.

Second place was worth $621,000 to Furyk, but that didn't soothe the disappointment. He had led most of the way. In the first round, he shot 65 for a three-stroke lead over Vijay Singh, Hidemichi Tanaka, John Rollins, Kenny Perry, Brian Bateman and Ian Leggatt. In the second round, Furyk holed out from 153 yards for an eagle two at No. 8 (his 17th hole) for a 69–134 total to lead Brian Gay (66) by one. And in the third round, he shot 70 and got tied for the lead by Harrington and his 68. In the final round, Furyk fell behind on a three-putt bogey at No. 1, but went three ahead with a birdie against Harrington's three-putt double bogey at No. 3. Harrington's heroics included his first eagle on a 10-foot putt at the par-five No. 9. He gave the strokes back with bogeys at the 11th and 12th.

Furyk hadn't won since the 2003 Buick Open, a stretch of 39 tournaments, and now he was runner-up for the third time this season. "There's no consolation," Furyk said. "Finishing second really stinks."

And then there was this possible signpost for the future: Ryan Moore, former amateur whiz kid, picked up his first professional check. He shot 71-74-73-73–290, tied for 51st place and won $13,532.

## Cialis Western Open—$5,000,000
Winner: Jim Furyk

If finishing second has a disagreeable odor, how must winning be? Especially if you beat Tiger Woods.

It took Jim Furyk one week to find out. Just a week earlier, he led the Barclays Classic most of the way, only to be overtaken and beaten down the final few holes by Padraig Harrington, after which he proclaimed: "Finishing second really stinks." When he got to Cog Hill, outside Chicago, he was to say, "I knew I would be asked about it, and I realized I had to get over it to play again."

And he did that in spades in the Cialis Western Open, playing the par-71 Cog Hill course in 64-70-67-69–270, 14 under par, tied for the lead in the first and third rounds and only one behind in the second, and then holding off a charging Woods in the fourth round for a two-stroke victory. Woods, a three-time Western Open winner, started with a two-over 73 and said, "If I shoot 64, 65, I'll be right back in this thing where I could win it." He didn't shoot 64 but he scored well enough to tie Furyk with a stunning eagle at the 11th.

"I had half a dozen people telling me Tiger's coming to get me," Furyk said. "It was funny more than anything else because I wanted to say, 'Yeah, I know. I can read the scoreboards, too.'"

If Furyk was a surprise in the first round, rebounding from an ego wounded in the Barclays Classic, Ben Curtis was at least a co-surprise. Curtis was also co-leader with a 64, a huge relief after struggling since winning the Open Championship in 2003. "I'm still a long ways from playing really good golf," said Curtis, who would finish alone in third, five behind Furyk. Vijay Singh, in the No. 1 race with Woods, got within six strokes of the lead with a 65 in the third round and that was it. He tied for 13th place, 10 strokes behind.

Woods was flirting with missing the cut, but hauled himself to safety with a 66, sparked by an eagle on his sixth hole (No. 15).

Furyk, a stroke behind Chad Campbell in the second round, shot 67 in the third to return to a share of the lead with Curtis (66). Furyk's big move came at the par-five 15th, where he dropped a 30-foot putt for an eagle. Curtis tied him with a three-foot birdie at the 18th. Then came Furyk's real test — standing up to the pressure of Woods in the final round.

It looked grim from the start. Furyk bogeyed the second and third holes, and fell four shots behind Curtis. "I was thrown for a little loop early, being four down so quick," Furyk said. He scrambled back into a tie by No. 6. But now Woods came roaring up. Five behind starting the last round, Woods raced into a tie with Furyk at 13 under par on a birdie-birdie-eagle stretch from No. 9. Furyk more than withstood the heat. He holed birdie putts of 15, 17 and 11 feet, while up ahead Woods started to waver. He bogeyed two in a row, three-putting the 13th and needing two shots to get out of a bunker at the 14th. Furyk, hearing the galleries groan ahead of him, figured Woods was having problems.

"I thought I was two up, maybe three," Furyk said. "I asked my caddie where I stood. He said, 'Four up.' And that's a good feeling with four to go."

# John Deere Classic—$4,000,000
Winner: Sean O'Hair

It was the neatest bit of traveling since the invention of the science fiction time machine. Sean O'Hair, a winless PGA Tour rookie, stepped into the John Deere Classic in Silvis, Illinois, and could step out in the Open Championship at St. Andrews, Scotland.

Under the exemption criteria, a spot in the Open awaited the highest John Deere Classic finisher not otherwise exempt. For a while, the golf world wondered if it would be Michelle Wie, age 15, again playing on a sponsor's invitation.

The other question was, would she become the first female since Babe Didrickson Zaharias in 1945 to make the cut in a PGA Tour event? Both answers came up "No" in the second round when she went double bogey-bogey down the stretch. She shot 70-71–141 at the par-71 TPC at Deere Run, tied for 88th place, and missed the cut by two strokes.

"Geez, she's great," said J.L. Lewis, who led the middle two rounds. "I was hoping she'd make the cut."

"I'm disappointed that I was shooting so well, and then the two holes just kind of screwed me over," said Wie, an 11th-grader-to-be from Honolulu. She was four under par with three holes to play, then three-putted her 15th (No. 6) from 21 feet for a double bogey. She also missed the green and bogeyed her 16th. "She played so well, and then you realize she's a 15-year-old girl," said rookie Nick Watney. "That's mind-boggling." There was speculation she would turn professional when she turned 16 in October. "We haven't decided yet," said her father, B.J. Wie.

Some performance statistics on Wie: She averaged 271 yards off the tee, hit 23 greens in regulation, played the second nine in five under par, and broke par in two of the six rounds she played on the PGA Tour.

O'Hair at first didn't look like the man headed for Scotland. Shooting 66-69-68, he tied for eighth place, 14th place, then seventh through the first three rounds. He started the final round five strokes behind Lewis, and built up steam fast, getting into contention with three birdies on the first nine. With Lewis and Hank Kuehne two groups behind him, he took the lead at the 14th, holing a 14-foot birdie putt. Then it seemed he'd locked up the victory at the 17th when he blasted out of a bunker to two feet and birdied again. Then he had to sweat out the final hole, literally.

"On No. 18, especially a guy in my situation, who never won before," he said, "you're definitely almost puking. My hands were so sweaty. I was more concerned about keeping my hands dry than anything."

He nearly hit his second shot into the water, and from an awkward lie on the hazard line, he had to swing his eight iron like a baseball bat, and chipped to 10 feet. He got the par, ending a remarkable performance. O'Hair hadn't made a bogey over his last 60 holes. He closed with a 65 and a 16-under 268 total. Now he had to sweat out Lewis and Kuehne, both 15 under coming to the 18th. If either birdied — or both — he would be in a playoff.

Not Lewis. He hit his second shot into the water, shot 72 and tied for fourth. Not Kuehne. A huge drive left him only 94 yards to the green, but he hit his second 25 feet past the pin and two-putted for par and a 68, and fell a stroke short, tying for second with Robert Damron (67). So O'Hair had a berth in the Open. He had only a few days to get to Scotland. There was one final problem. "I have no passport," O'Hair said, chuckling. "I just thought about that." But he was able to overcome that problem, too.


## The Open Championship — €5,607,600
Winner: Tiger Woods

See Chapter 4.


## B.C. Open — $3,000,000
Winner: Jason Bohn

In terms of efficiency, Jason Bohn did a lot better in a hole-in-one contest. He was 19 and a freshman at the University of Alabama when he made the ace and won $1 million with one swing. Now age 32, he won $540,000 for 264 swings in taking the B.C. Open title. That's $2,045 per swing. But never mind efficiency. In terms of value, Bohn did much better at the B.C. Open. It was his first PGA Tour victory, conferring on him not only the first prize but all the rights and privileges of a winner, and also ending six years of doubt, struggle and frustration.

Bohn, in his second year on the PGA Tour, finally found a bright spot in a gloomy year and sluggish career, closing with a second straight six-under-par 66 for his 264 total and a one-stroke win over Australian rookie Brendan Jones (68), J.P. Hayes (66), John Rollins (66) and Ryan Palmer (67). "You don't really expect when your first win is going to come," Bohn said. "I hadn't played that well this year. I missed a lot of cuts, and I haven't seen that many great things come out of my game. And this week I kind of got turned around."

Bohn, shooting rounds of 64-68-66-66, set a course record with the 264 at the par-72 En-Joie Golf Club, a municipal course in Endicott, New York. He trailed all the way. He was a stroke behind the 63s posted by co-leaders Glen Day and Matt Hendrix in the first round. Hendrix, 24, a rookie on a sponsor's exemption, got his 63 the hard way. He started with a double-bogey six on No. 1. "From there … I was just trying to stop the bleeding," Hendrix said. He did better than that. He eagled two of the three par-fives on the first nine.

A name from the past popped up in the second round — David Edwards, now age 49, with a 63 to lead Hendrix by one. "It's nice to be competitive again," Edwards said. It wouldn't last totally. He would tie for 20th place. Bohn, with a 68, was three behind Edwards, and then with a 66 in the third round, closed to within one of Brendan Jones, who posted a 66 of his own. "If I play the way I've been playing," Jones said, "then hopefully, guys only two or three back have got a chance." The bad news was, Bohn was only one behind.

In the final round, Bohn had taken over, but wasn't home free yet. Jones rallied for three straight birdies at the end, but three earlier bogeys ruined his chances. Ryan Palmer, Bohn's good friend and now playing companion, who charged into the picture with four straight birdies from the 14th, drove into the trees on the right at the 18th. And Bohn, who logged the last two of his six birdies at the 16th and 17th for a one-stroke lead, promptly followed him into the trees. Palmer's ball had caromed back to the edge of the fairway, leaving him a good shot at the green. Bohn's ball was under the trees, but he had a shot to the green. Palmer hit his second to the green, 16 feet from the hole. Bohn's tougher approach came down just short, and he chipped on to seven feet and waited.

Palmer looked at the 16-footer. "I thought, 'This putt could mean me winning the tournament,'" Palmer said. "If I make that, he has to make his to stay in it." But Palmer missed the birdie, and Bohn rolled home his seven-footer for the win. And therein lay an interesting statistic. For the tournament, Bohn made 63 out of 67 putts inside 10 feet.

## U.S. Bank Championship in Milwaukee—$3,800,000
Winner: Ben Crane

When Ben Crane last came to national attention, he was the tortoise in a tortoise-and-hare tale. Rory Sabbatini, the hare, grew exasperated at Crane's extremely slow play and went on ahead over the final two holes at the Booz Allan Classic early in June. This time, in the U.S. Bank Championship in mid-July, it was just the tortoise story, and the result was the same as in the fable. Crane led the hares all the way around Brown Deer Park in Milwaukee, wire-to-wire.

Crane stayed the course solidly, despite the rains that delayed play and split rounds into the next day. This was the 14th tournament out of 31 to be affected by bad weather this season. Crane never had the luxury of a big cushion. It was pressure all the way. Crane played the hot, soggy par-70 course in 62-65-64-69 and led by one over Kenny Perry (63) in the first round, by one over Jeff Sluman (64) in the second round, and by two over Scott Verplank (64) going into the final round. His 20-under-par 260 total beat Verplank by four strokes. It was his second PGA Tour victory, after the 2003 BellSouth Classic.

Perhaps it took a golfer of patience and resilience to handle the U S. Bank Championship, and that was Crane. In the first round, he was four under par when the horn sounded for a rain delay just as he was making the turn about 10 a.m. The delay lasted some five hours. "I just went back to the hotel, laid down, and relaxed," Crane said. "I came back and went through my regular routine. It worked out well. I was able to continue the momentum." Crane shot a career-best eight-under 62, just ahead of Perry.

The tournament was an exercise in make-do in the rain delays. Sluman was waiting to play his final hole Friday when play was called because of darkness, so he had to get up at 5 a.m. to finish his round. And after playing one hole, he had to wait nearly five hours to begin the third round. He rejected the notion of returning to his hotel. "It doesn't make sense to go back and forth," Sluman said. "I'll just fire up my computer."

All told, 55 golfers had to return early Saturday morning to finish their second rounds before getting on with the third. But Crane wasn't among them. He and his group were on the 18th Friday night when play was suspended. So they were allowed to finish, and they had the luxury of sleeping in. The rest of the field finished the second round at almost 9:30, with 77 making the cut at two-under 138. Ryan Moore, the U.S. Amateur champion, shot 71-66–137, making his second cut in four starts as a professional.

In the final round, Crane's 69, his fourth consecutive score in the 60s, was an adventure. He birdied No. 2, and went two ahead when Verplank bogeyed No. 1. Then Crane went bogey-eagle-bogey from No. 4. The eagle came at No. 6 on a chip-in from the first cut of rough. It got him to 21 under par. He bogeyed No. 7 but still made the turn leading by four strokes over Verplank. Crane went on to bogey the 13th, then birdied the 17th for the stroke that held up for the win and stretched Verplank's winless streak to 96 tournaments, since the 2001 Bell Canadian Open.

"I just didn't play well enough," he said. "I never found the rhythm. The wind and the playing conditions made it that way, and certain challenges of playing in the last group made it tough, too." Some observers thought that last comment might have been an oblique reference to Crane's slow play.

## Buick Open—$4,600,000
Winner: Vijay Singh

It was the third round. A monumental showdown was about to take place in the Buick Open. Tiger Woods and Vijay Singh stepped out on the first tee, like two heavyweights climbing into the ring. Singh was leading by one stroke, but all he got was a polite reception from the gallery. Woods got a roar. "It was noisy out there," Singh said, with no little satisfaction, "but they kind of quieted after two, three holes."

Singh birdied the first three holes. Woods bogeyed the second, third and fourth. In a span of four holes, Singh's lead had rocketed from one to seven strokes. Racking up his 28th career victory, Singh played the Warwick Hills course in Grand Blanc, Michigan, in rounds of 65-66-63-70 for a 24-under-par 264 total, and beat Woods and Zach Johnson by four strokes.

Woods provided some early thrills. He opened with 71, a repeat of which would put him in danger of missing the cut. He saw to it that he didn't with a tournament-record 61 in the second round. The 61 was hardly routine. He had to scramble for pars after spraying his tee shots on the first two holes. Then he birdied four out of five holes and turned in 31. Coming home, he eagled twice and went six under par from the 13th through the 16th holes. "We were watching the best golf anyone is going to play," said Fred Funk.

Singh shot 66 to lead by one at the halfway mark, 131-132. Was this a dream rivalry?

"Tiger Woods and I are cordial," Singh said. "He's one of the best players ever, but I can't worry about what his ball does. I worry about my ball. He has his clique, I have my friends. I don't go to dinner with him, he'll never go to dinner with me. But this thing about our rivalry, it comes from the outside. Inside the ropes, I want to play my best when I play anybody. It doesn't matter who."

Said Woods: "We're not out there to talk. I respect him, and he respects me."

Singh shrugged off the rousing welcome for Woods and shot a 63, tying the tournament record of 22-under-par 194 for 54 holes. He led by five over Johnson (65), and by eight over Woods, who settled down after that shaky start and shot a 70. Singh now looked like a shoo-in to become the first three-time winner of the tournament and the first to repeat since Tony Lema in 1965. And if he were to finish with 67 or better, he would break the tournament record of 26 under.

"If I break the record, that would be great," Singh said. "If I don't, I don't care. I just want to win the golf tournament."

Singh went two-for-three on the possibilities. His only miss was the record. He shot an almost leisurely 70 for a 264 total, 24 under par, and won by four over Woods (66) and Johnson (69). Singh might have done better if he had realized that Woods was on a rampage. "Tiger was never really within five shots of me all day," Singh said. In fact, Woods was almost breathing down his neck. He'd got within two, charging with six birdies and an eagle in a nine-hole stretch. But Singh rendered it all academic.

"I'm playing better this year than I did last year," Singh said. "I just hope I can follow what I did last year. It's going to be almost impossible, but I'm going to give it a shot."

## The International—$5,000,000
Winner: Retief Goosen

No matter how you score it, Brandt Jobe was sitting pretty down the final stretch at The International, all set to notch his first victory. But Retief Goosen, the quiet South African, wasn't going to be denied. Breaking out of a season-long malaise, Goosen took advantage of Jobe's meltdown, wiped out a big deficit, and slipped by for his first victory of the year.

Before that, although Goosen had won three times on the European Tour, he was best known for two celebrated collapses. He was leading the U.S. Open by three strokes going into the final round, and shot 81. He was just three off the lead in the Open Championship, and killed his chances with a 74. "I wouldn't say I lost confidence," Goosen said. "But I was disappointed in the way I played. At some stage, you figure the tide is going to turn."

And it did, but under unusual circumstances. The first round was washed out and played on Friday, the second round was played on Saturday, and the last two rounds were crammed into Sunday. Meaning that in the thin air some 6,300 feet up in the Rockies near Denver, at the hilly, 7,619-yard Castle Pines course, the golfers would be trudging nearly nine miles in August temperatures in the mid-90s. The chase might not go to the swiftest, but the strongest.

"We're not out here hitting people and tackling people," Charles Howell noted, "but walking 36 holes on this golf course is not easy."

It was no surprise that Billy Mayfair broke from the gate fast. The International is played under a modified-Stableford system that awards two points for birdies, five for eagles, eight for double eagles, none for pars, and deducts one for bogeys and three for double bogeys or worse. And Mayfair was second only to Vijay Singh in making birdies and eagles. He took a two-point lead with 15 points on five birdies and a thrilling eagle. "It was just one of those 40-footers," Mayfair said. Someone noted that it was actually a 70-footer. "Oh, okay — 70 feet," Mayfair said.

Cameron Beckman, looking for his second career victory, edged into the second-round lead with five birdies and an eagle for 23 points, one ahead of Mayfair, Howell and Jobe. Then came the 36-hole endurance test on Sunday.

Jobe seemed to have a good grip on the tournament in the third round Sunday morning. He took the lead with an eagle from 190 yards at the 18th. Finishing on the first nine, he ran off three straight birdies, two four-footers and a 20-footer. He led with 34 points, nine ahead of Goosen and Kevin Stadler. Jobe birdied his first hole of the final round Sunday afternoon. But he bogeyed No. 2, double-bogeyed No. 4, and bogeyed the seventh and eighth. He lost the lead at the par-five 14th, where he bogeyed to fall a point behind Goosen.

"I did play some great golf," Jobe said, "but I played nine terrible holes in the afternoon."

Goosen scored seven points on the first nine, but went scoreless on the second nine. Despite driving into the rough on four of the last nine holes, he managed six pars and two bogeys canceling out one birdie. His last three holes were crucial. At the par-three 16th, he missed the green by a whopping 40 yards, but pitched out of heavy rough to four feet and saved par. At the uphill, par-five 17th, he hit his second onto the green and two-putted for a birdie. At the 18th, he hit his second to the fringe, then two-putted for the par. Goosen racked up 15 points over the last two rounds for a total of 32 to beat Jobe by one. It was a huge relief.

"I was sort of wondering where my golf was going," Goosen said. "I started practicing more than I used to. I started working harder on my putting. And that started paying off."

## PGA Championship—$6,500,000
Winner: Phil Mickelson

See Chapter 5.

## WGC - NEC Invitational—$7,500,000
Winner: Tiger Woods

This was one of those "last man standing" tournaments, and to no one's surprise, Tiger Woods was that man because, first, this was Tiger Woods, and second, this was the WGC-NEC Invitational on the South Course at Firestone Country Club in Akron, Ohio — Woods's tournament at his course. He owned them both.

Woods wobbled through the final round, but he came from behind for his fifth victory of the season, and his fourth win here. (It was also his last under the NEC banner. The tournament returns for the next five years with Bridgestone as the sponsor.) It was also Woods's ninth win in the 18 World Golf Championships he has played.

Woods recovered from the early wobbles to nip Chris DiMarco by a stroke. His putting was shaky in the final round, but he made the one he needed most. At the monstrous par-five 16th, he faced an 18-footer for a birdie, and it bothered him. "I've had that putt for three or four years, and I miss it low every time," Woods said. "I made sure I threw the ball out there a little more, and I thought it was going to lip out ... But it lipped in, which was sweet."

Then Woods recovered from the trees at the 18th and parred for a one-over-par 71, a six-under 274 total, and a one-stroke victory over DiMarco. He covered Firestone in rounds of 66-70-67-71, tied for the lead through the first three rounds, but he didn't lock it up until the end.

Vijay Singh and Sweden's Henrik Stenson tied Woods for the first-round lead at 66, when 49 of the world's top 50 players — only the injured Ernie Els was absent — averaged 71.930 strokes, the highest at Firestone since the series began in 1999. Only 12 players broke par, and DiMarco, Nick Dougherty and Davis Love were a stroke off the lead at 67.

Woods, needing just 25 putts, birdied from 12, 20, two and 15 feet. Singh, nursing a sore back, needed just 24, but he three-putted his ninth hole from 18 feet for a bogey. Stenson ranked fourth in hitting fairways and first in hitting greens in regulation, and had quite a ride. Among his seven birdies was the one at No. 5 on a 65-foot putt.

Luke Donald made a move in the second round, his 67 tying him with Woods for the halfway lead at 136. Donald bogeyed the 11th, then ran off three straight birdies on a 25-foot putt at No. 13 and six-footers at the next two. "It was a nice little run for me," said Donald, whose control and creativity offset his lack of sheer length on the 7,360-yard course.

Kenny Perry came out of the pack to catch Woods through the third. He carded a six-under 64, but he didn't get it wrapped up until Sunday morning. He was stranded on the 18th green when play was suspended because of lightning in the area. He returned Sunday morning and completed the 64 to tie Woods at 203.

In the final round, Perry moved past a stumbling Woods, and it looked next like a duel with DiMarco, who was coming out of the pack four groups ahead. But that was only until Perry reached the turn. Then he bogeyed five of six holes and slumped home with a 74, and finished tied for sixth. "There is not much to say, except I played lousy," Perry said.

Woods won this one in style, adding that last dramatic touch. He had regained the lead with the birdie at the 16th, and then at the 18th found himself in the rough, 103 yards from the green, and with just enough room between two trees to get through. He punched a nine iron to the fringe, and two-putted from 25 feet for the one-stroke win.

DiMarco had waited in the clubhouse, holding himself ready in case of a playoff, and watched Woods finish. "Once he hit the second shot on 18," DiMarco said, "I went up and took a shower."

## Reno-Tahoe Open—$3,000,000
Winner: Vaughn Taylor

The Reno-Tahoe Open can be summed up in two statements:

"A six-shot lead is definitely a lot. I'm just going to go out there tomorrow and keep to my game plan and just play golf."

"Today was a pretty boring, uneventful round of golf, but I'm thrilled."

The first was from Vaughn Taylor, after shooting 64 for a six-stroke lead in the third round. The second was also Taylor, after closing with a par 72 to win by three strokes. It was Taylor's second career victory, the first having been as a rookie in the 2004 Reno-Tahoe Open. In truth, if Taylor was bored, he had only himself to blame. He simply ran away with it, wire-to-wire.

Taylor, age 29, grew up in Augusta, Georgia, graduated in business administration from Augusta State University, played on the Nationwide Tour, and was a $1 million winner as a PGA Tour rookie in 2004.

The Reno-Tahoe Open was held in August, opposite the WGC-NEC Invitational, and it may have been the last. A club official said that members were divided on whether to let the tournament return for its final contract year in 2006.

Taylor showed no such uncertainty as he played his way through the 7,472-yard, par-72 course. Taylor rang up 10 birdies and two bogeys, and birdied six of his last eight holes for an eight-under 64 and a one-stroke lead over Sweden's Fredrik Jacobson and Reno's own Todd Fischer. Said Taylor, thinking of his win in 2004: "I had some good feelings, some good memories, and I think it rubbed off a little." Fischer saw his chance for a 64 disappear into the water with his gamble to reach the 619-yard ninth in two. "I walked away there a little angry," said Fischer. He let off steam with four straight birdies.

Taylor hung on to the one-shot lead with a 67 and 131 total in the second round, but while he was one ahead of Fischer (67), it was the veteran Bill Glasson who stole the show. Glasson, who'd had some 20 surgeries, blistered Montreux for a 10-under, course-record 62 to close within three of Taylor. He had six birdies and two eagles. "For a minute there, I thought this was the way I used to play," Glasson said. Said Taylor: "I've been hitting it well and doing everything pretty well. I've had quite a few tapins and three- or four-footers."

Taylor all but wrapped up the victory in the third round. He birdied four of his first five holes en route to another 64 for a 21-under 195 total and a six-shot lead on Fischer. Taylor's irons set him up with six of his eight birdies from within five feet. These included a seven-inch tap-in at No. 4 and a three-incher at No. 11. The other two birdies were from about nine feet. "I can't remember a tournament, tapping in and knocking in two- or three-footers for birdie as often as I have here," Taylor said. Now came a problem — how to avoid becoming complacent with a six-stroke lead.

The final round left Taylor almost apologizing for boring and uneventful golf. He saved par with a five-foot putt at No. 1, and saved bogey at No. 6 with a four-footer. He made his only birdie of the day with two putts from 50 feet at No. 9. Jonathan Kaye closed with a 67 to take second, but was no real threat. Taylor won by three, and set three tournament records

— 131 for two rounds, 195 for three, and the 21-under 267. Now he could allow himself to dream of playing in the Masters.

"I'm sure I'm not there yet, but close," he said. "This week was huge."

## Buick Championship—$4,300,000
Winner: Brad Faxon

When it comes to homecooking, things were considerably underdone for Brad Faxon at the Buick Championship. Faxon, a native son of New England out of Rhode Island, was on the verge of an early drive home. But he did make the cut, right on the number, and got to hang around for the weekend. And then he shot a tidy 61 in the final round to tie for the lead, and then beat South Africa's Tjaart van der Walt on the first hole of a playoff.

"This was really kind of out of the blue," Faxon said. "The first two days I played okay. Then something happened where all the putts started going in." Of course, it helps if you're simply one of the finest putters on the PGA Tour to begin with. First Faxon played the par-70 TPC at River Highlands near Hartford, Connecticut, in 69-71–140, and just made it under the wire. When the "something" happened, he moved up from the cellar to a tie for 10th with a 65, and then finally to a tie for the lead with a career-low 61 that also tied the course record. This was the eighth victory of his career and his first in 22 trips to this tournament.

Faxon spoiled a couple of good Cinderella stories, two of them with roots in the British Open, in Justin Rose, who nearly won it as a teenager in 1998, and in Ohioan Ben Curtis, who did win it as a rookie in 2003. Both had been sputtering ever since.

Curtis shared the first-round lead with J.L. Lewis at six-under 64. Curtis birdied his first two holes and made his last on a 16-foot putt at the par-three 17th. "It's just fun to go and play again," he said. Lewis would sink from there, but Curtis would challenge the rest of the way.

Rose, after an opening 65, led through the middle rounds. He took a four-stroke lead in the second with 63, wrapping up two bogey-free rounds. He thwarted the course on the back nine, driving with his three wood or five wood to stay out of the rough as fairways were firming up. Curtis (68) and Kevin Sutherland (67) tied for second, four behind. Could he win? Said Rose: "I've learned it's a million miles from winning the tournament." And he felt much the same the next day when he shot 70–198 to hold on to a one-stroke lead on Curtis (67), his friend and playing partner. "We've both worked hard on our games this year, and it's starting to pay off," Rose said.

Faxon didn't play badly in the first two rounds, but just not well enough to keep pace. In the first round he made one birdie and 17 pars for his 69, and in the second, he had one birdie and two bogeys for a 71 to just make the cut. In his third-round 65, he had six birdies and an eagle, and also one bogey and a double bogey. Then came his skyrocket 61 in the fourth round — nine birdies, no bogeys. The heart of it was a cluster of five birdies in a stretch of six holes from No. 7, including four straight from No. 9. The 61 forced the playoff with van der Walt. They went to No. 18, a 434-yard par-four.

In the playoff, both hit excellent second shots. Faxon had driven into a fairway bunker 169 yards from the hole. He fired a seven iron to three feet. Van der Walt was down the middle and had 134 left. His approach was too good. It glanced off the flagstick and stopped nine feet away. Van der Walt missed, and Faxon didn't, and that was it.

Then Faxon had a problem. He had planned to have surgery to repair ligament damage in his right knee. But this victory qualified him for the 2006 PGA Tour opener in Hawaii in January. The recovery would keep him from going. The solution? Simple. "My wife says if we don't go to Kapalua, 'I'm going to kill you,'" Faxon said. "So what do you think?"

Michael Putnam, a Pepperdine University star and Walker Cupper, made his professional debut here on a sponsor's exemption, closed with a 63, tied for fourth place and won $177,733. And Jason Gore, a hero in the U.S. Open, played his first PGA Tour event as a full member after getting a battlefield promotion with three victories on the Nationwide Tour. Gore tied for 73rd and won $8,299.

## Deutsche Bank Championship—$5,500,000
Winner: Olin Browne

It was hard to tell which was the bigger story at the Deutsche Bank Championship — that Olin Browne, age 46, a long-time laborer in golf's vineyards, had won, or that Tiger Woods, the world's No. 1 golfer, was a distant also-ran. Woods opened with a six-under-par 65 for the first-round lead, saying, "I don't feel like I'm on a roll at all. I feel like this is the way I should play every day." Then came a 73, and he was on his way to a tie for 40th place. "To be honest with you, I really don't care right now," he said. "I'm done. I've had a very long summer."

Browne, on the other hand, fought his way to the top of the leaderboard in the second round and stayed there to take the third victory of his career. He shot 68-65-70-67 for a 14-under-par 270 total at the TPC of Boston to win by a stroke over Jason Bohn, who had scored his breakthrough victory in the B.C. Open in July. "This validates a year and a half of busting my tail," Browne said. It was in February 2004 that he was ready to give up the game. Then he met with an instructor, Jim Hardy, who helped retool his swing. It took 18 months, but Browne finally got there.

With a one-bogey 65 in the second round, Browne tied for the lead at nine-under 133 with Jeff Brehaut (66), another struggler. Browne made five straight birdies at one point, and through his first 11 holes he had only one birdie try longer than 15 feet. The tournament still hadn't firmed up. Going into the third round, only eight strokes separated first place from last.

The third round ended like a fire drill. Five players had tied for the lead at 10-under 203 — Browne, with a 70, John Rollins (63), Jason Bohn (67), Carl Pettersson (68) and Billy Andrade (69). The situation brought out some pithy comments. "I'm going to have a blast," said Andrade, who hadn't won for five years. "I haven't been in that position in a long time." Said Rollins, "I joked with my caddie at the turn, told him he was going to see the best 29 on the back nine." In fact, Rollins shot a 28. And said Browne: "We just have to wait until the last few holes to see the way things shake out."

In the final round, the challengers fell away, one by one. The irrepressible Andrade double-bogeyed No. 6 and shot 41 on the first nine, and Rollins shot 40. Pettersson just had no zip. It came down to Browne and Bohn.

At No. 9, Bohn pushed his tee shot to the right and saved bogey. He hit over the 10th green, chipped long and bogeyed again. He never caught up. Browne saved par at the 11th with a delicate chip to five feet, and birdied the 17th off a seven iron to 15 feet to lead by two. Bohn needed an eagle at the par-five 18th to force a playoff. But he drove into the rough, missed the green, and his chip for the eagle wasn't close, and he birdied. Browne had closed with a 67 for 270, and Bohn 68 for 271. Browne felt a sense of deliverance.

Browne won the 1998 Canon Greater Hartford Open and the 1999 MasterCard Colonial, but had fallen on hard times and had been reduced to asking for sponsor's exemptions to get into tournaments, and sponsors were becoming reluctant to grant them. Now those days were over. For two years, at least, with the exalted exempt status that goes with winning. "I couldn't be happier about the way I played," Browne said.

## Bell Canadian Open—$5,000,000
Winner: Mark Calcavecchia

Mark Calcavecchia, age 45 and four years removed from his last victory, was somewhat distressed over not making any birdies in the third round. Always so eloquent in his own way, he sought comfort in his own version of the law of probabilities. "The good thing about making no birdies," he said, "is it can't possibly happen two days in a row."

Calcavecchia was right. He did not go two days in a row without a birdie. But almost. He had one birdie in the final round — at the par-four No. 5 — and it was precisely enough to win the Bell Canadian Open. "Thank God we ran out of holes," Calcavecchia said. "I saved my best drive and my best iron for the last hole, and I knew I could two-putt from six feet. How embarrassing to lag from six feet."

The two-putt gave him a one-over-par 71 and a one-stroke victory over Ben Crane (66), winner of the U.S. Bank Championship in July, and Ryan Moore (70), the 2004 U.S. Amateur champion, having his best finish since turning professional after the U.S. Open in June.

Calcavecchia, whose last victory came in the 2001 Phoenix Open, opened the tournament in a tie for the lead with Lucas Glover, seeking his first win, at five-under 65 at the par 70 Shaughnessy Golf and Country Club at Vancouver. Glover, who had six top-10 finishes and 11 missed cuts so far, was the solo leader until he bogeyed the 15th. Then he missed eight-foot birdie putts at the 16th and 18th. Calcavecchia was precision personified on the tight, tree-lined course. He hit 13 of the 14 fairways, and had six birdies against one bogey. "That gave me a lot of enthusiasm," he said, "because if you don't drive it well here, you're cooked." Vijay Singh, defending champion and No. 1 player in the world, shot a no-birdie, three-over 73.

Calcavecchia was even better in the second round. He hit 10 fairways and 11 greens. Three of his five birdies came in a row from No. 7 on putts of 20, six and 20 feet. His 67 gave him a five-stroke lead on Glover (72) that looked huge on the demanding course. Singh, seven behind, wasn't impressed. "Seven shots around here is not much at all," he said after a 66 carried him from a tie for 71st to a tie for eighth.

Singh turned out to be more right than he knew. Calcavecchia's five-shot lead wasn't insurmountable, but in his renewed hands it would seem a lock. Then he did an about-face in the final two rounds. In the third, the no-birdie 72 cut his lead to one. "The good news is I hung in there and only shot two over without making a birdie," Calcavecchia said. "The bad news is I was in position to get to nine or 10 under and put some space between me and the rest of the guys." The reverse happened. Craig Barlow, an eight-year veteran looking for his first win, went five under on three late holes — an eagle at the 14th, a birdie at the 15th, an ace at the 17th — for a 65 to tie Jesper Parnevik (67) for second, one behind Calcavecchia. Singh (68) tied for fifth and noted, "I like my chances right now, I just need the putter to get hot."

But Singh's entire game turned erratic and he closed with a 72 and tied for seventh. Barlow blew to a 77. Crane, who had opened with a dangerous 74, finished with a 66, tying for second with Moore.

Calcavecchia got that one birdie at No. 5, but saved his own neck the rest of the way. He got up and down for par three times on the front nine. He missed short birdie putts four times, including a five-footer at the 315-yard 14th, where he had driven into a greenside bunker. "One birdie on the weekend and I win the tournament," said Calcavecchia, the third straight winner in his 40s. "I bet that's never happened. But only seven bogeys all week. A lot of guys probably made seven bogeys today."

## 84 Lumber Classic—$4,400,000
Winner: Jason Gore

Back in May, Jason Gore, a nobody, was wondering how he was going to make a house payment or buy formula for his child. Then in some miraculous way, he came through in the clutch at the 84 Lumber Classic. "And now, look," Gore said. "They just handed me a check for $729,000."

Gore, age 31, had just undergone one of the great transformations in golf. In June, he was a nonentity off the Nationwide Tour, and he was considering giving up the game. Then at the U.S. Open in June, he became a hero, challenging until the nerves got to him and he shot 84 in the final round. He returned to the Nationwide Tour and won three tournaments — in a row — and got a "battlefield promotion" to the PGA Tour. He was practically a storybook figure by the time he arrived at Nemacolin Woodlands Resort and its Mystic Rock course in western Pennsylvania. Even so, he was hardly expected to challenge the likes of Phil Mickelson, John Daly, Justin Leonard, Chris DiMarco and defending champion Vijay Singh. And he'd needed a sponsor's exemption just to get into the tournament. He not only challenged, he was among the leaders all the way. But he faced his stiffest test at the last hole.

Gore shot 65-72-67-70–274, 14 under par. He tied with Charlie Wi, Shaun Micheel and Mark O'Meara at 65 in the first round. He tied for seventh in the second round, after Stuart Appleby vaulted into the lead with a 66, then took the solo lead by two in the third, and spent the back nine of the fourth trying to hold on. He never trailed, but Carlos Franco, in the group ahead, tied him with a birdie on the par-five No. 8.

America was in love with Gore, and now he had to prove he had the guts. He answered Franco's birdie at No. 8 with an eagle from 12 feet for a two-stroke lead. Gore birdied the par-five 11th with a wedge to 12 feet and the par-four 13th on a wedge to about 16 inches. He was 16 under par and four strokes ahead of Franco. Then came trouble. He bogeyed the 14th from the rough and missed the green at the 17th and bogeyed again, and Franco, who had birdied the 16th, was just one behind.

"He wasn't nervous because he's won three times on the Nationwide Tour," Franco said. Wrong — Gore said he was feeling the pressure. "It was pretty brutal," Gore said. "It was a lot more than I expected. I never really played well in a PGA Tour event. Before, I never really had anything to lose. And now I had something to prove."

And he had to prove it at the par-four 18th. Gore hit his drive into heavy rough, then slashed his ball to the front of the green, some 90 feet from the pin. From there, he had to get down in two to win. "It looked like six miles," Gore said. "That was the most nervous I've ever been in my life. Sometimes you have to bear down and just say you're not going to go down like that." Now the putt across those last 90 feet. "I had to go up and down two elephants and through the windmill," he said. The ball rolled dead about 14 inches from the hole. "The longest 14 inches I've ever seen in my life," Gore said. And he tapped it in.

"Just five, six months ago, I was thinking of hanging it up," Gore said. "Instead, I get to hang up this nice, red jacket, right in the closet. It's amazing what a little perseverance and grit — and maybe a little ignorance — can do."

David Toms collapsed in the first round on leaving the tee at No. 1 (his 10th hole) and was rushed to a Pittsburgh hospital, where he was diagnosed as having supraventricular tachycardia, a rapid heartbeat. Toms returned to the course Saturday morning and insisted he would play in the Presidents Cup the following week. His condition would be controlled by medication until he could undergo surgical correction.

## The Presidents Cup
Winner: United States

See Special Events section.

## Valero Texas Open—$3,500,000
Winner: Robert Gamez

It seemed Robert Gamez was doomed to be remembered — if at all — as merely one of the guys who harpooned the Shark. Gamez joined Robert Tway, David Frost and Larry Mize among the players who beat Greg Norman with a dramatic shot on a final hole. Gamez, then a rookie, did it in the 1990 Nestle Invitational (now the Bay Hill Invitational), holing out a seven iron from 176 yards at the 72nd hole. He had won the Tucson Open two months earlier and was the 21-year-old sensation of the year. Then the lights went dim on his career. And, except for a win in Japan in 1994, they stayed dim for 15½ years — the longest time between wins in PGA Tour history.

"It has been a long time — a long time coming," said Gamez, who had gone 394 tournaments between wins in that stretch. "I knew it would happen. I just didn't know when."

The "when" was mid-September, in the Valero Texas Open at LaCantera Golf Club at San Antonio. Gamez was no longer the whiz kid of the tour, not at age 37, but he played like it, playing the par-70 golf course in 62-68-68-64—262, 18 under par. He led the first round, then rallied in the last to beat Olin Browne by a comfortable three strokes.

"I sure wish I made a couple more putts and at least made him stress a little more," said Browne, who himself had broken a long drought in the Deutsche Bank Open three weeks earlier. "He's obviously immensely talented and he's playing like he knows how again."

Not that Gamez had been without stress. True, that bogey-free 62 in the first round had a cakewalk air to it. He birdied eight of the first 16 holes, among them No. 8 on a 30-foot putt, No. 9 on an 80-foot chip and No. 11 on a 38-foot putt. At that, he led Jeff Maggert and John Senden by only a stroke. Then things got tight. Gamez tied for fourth in the second round when Dean Wilson took the lead with a 62, and he was tied for second when Woody Austin took over in the third with a 67 in 30 mile-an-hour winds and 100-degree heat from Hurricane Rita 150 miles to the east.

There was no reason to think Gamez was on the verge of storming back in the final round — not until he birdied the first three holes for a three-stroke lead. Browne caught up with him at the par-five 14th, holing a six-footer for a birdie. Gamez, four holes behind, went back in front off an 11-footer for birdie at the 11th. Then he birdied the 13th and 14th, matched Browne's 64, and had his victory.

"To come all the way back — I'm so proud of myself," Gamez said. "I've worked so hard."

Gamez wasn't the only one to break out of a long slump. For David Duval, former No. 1, it was a lesser breakout but just as big a relief, and maybe more so. Duval finally made the halfway cut after 18 misses, dating to the Michelin Championship in October 2004. And it was a modest finish, but a finish nonetheless. He shot 69-68-70-74 for a 281 total and won $7,630. "I've been No. 1 and No. 1,000," Duval said. "I've hit bottom and I'm coming back up."

## Chrysler Classic of Greensboro—$5,000,000
Winner: K.J. Choi

The South Korean women were throwing a world golf party. Birdie Kim won the U.S. Women's Open in June and Jeong Jang took the Weetabix Women's British Open in July. Then there was Jimin Kang, Meena Lee and Soo-Yun Kang — all with victories on the LPGA Tour. It was quite a bash. K.J. Choi decided to crash it.

Choi would do this in the Chrysler Classic of Greensboro, but prospects were a bit dim at first. Choi opened with a 64 — and found himself in second place. Charles Warren, a hopeful with a year on the PGA Tour and some time on the Nationwide Tour, played the Forest Oaks Country Club course in 10-under-par 62. The challengers piled close behind. D.J. Trahan, a rookie, was at 65, and Tim Clark, John Huston, J.J. Henry and Hidemichi Tanaka at 66.

How does a hopeful feel about a 62? "I'm not going to tell you I could have shot 59," Warren said. "But if I was ever going to shoot 59, today would have been the chance. It was nice to get off to a good start."

Only the cast changed in the second round. Warren shot 74, but Huston took over the lead with a 66. Choi, with a 69, found himself still alone in second, but this time only a stroke behind. Huston, the winner of seven tournaments but none since 2003, was encouraged. He was 127th on the money list and had to crack the top 125 to regain his exempt status. But October was at hand. His time was running out, but he was trying hard. "I guess I decided I wasn't ready to give up on the game yet," he said. Justin Rose shot 65 and tied with Trahan (69) for third at 134.

For Choi, the secret was in the wrists. He explained his slump. "It's been about my putting," he said, through an interpreter. "Prior to this week, I was very wristy with my short putts." Some hard practice keeping his wrists firm did the trick, and it showed in the 67 in the third round, tying at 16-under 200 with Trahan, who punctuated his 66 with a 165-yard eight iron from the fairway for an eagle at the par-four 16th. Choi, who started the day a stroke off the lead, slipped three behind, then birdied the 12th, 13th and 16th.

He still had the touch in the final round. Choi broke from the gate in a hurry. His putter still under control, he birdied No. 1 on a 17-footer, the first of four straight, and was four ahead of Shigeki Maruyama, who had taken up the chase. Choi three-putted the 10th for a bogey, then holed out a bunker shot for a birdie at the par-three 12th, and came home safely from there for a 66 and a two-stroke win at 22-under 266.

Maruyama finished second with 67–268. Warren, who sank after the 62 in the first round, pulled himself back up and closed with a 65 to tie for third with Jason Bohn (70) and Brandt Jobe (67). For Choi, the victory was a tribute to the friend who had told him, just before the tournament started, that he'd gotten wristy with his putter. And now if felt like old times — three years ago, to be exact. He immediately went to the firm wrists.

"This feel came back to me, like in 2002," Choi said. "That same feeling came back to me. I was able to carry that throughout the tournament."

## WGC - American Express Championship—$7,500,000
Winner: Tiger Woods

It was the grandest irony that the duel between two siege guns, Tiger Woods and John Daly, would come down to a gentle three-foot putt. John Daly needed it to stay alive in the playoff with Woods. But he missed. And Woods put his hand to his eyes.

"I feel so bad for J.D.," Woods said. "You never, ever want to win a golf tournament like that." Said Daly: "I know Tiger didn't want to win that way. I didn't want to lose that way. It's very disappointing."

And so Woods had won the WGC-American Express Championship, his sixth victory of the year, his second of the four WGC events and his 10th out of 19. Daly's costly error overshadowed a week of inspired play at San Francisco's Harding Park, a municipal course with a $16 million facelift.

It was a four-way battle in the final round, with a rejuvenated Colin Montgomerie, age 42, and Sergio Garcia scrambling along with Woods and Daly. Monty opened with a 64 and had fully 11 players jammed behind him at 67, including Woods, Daly, Garcia and Vijay Singh. Montgomerie shot 69 in the second round and still was the solo leader, and thus, after 108 events, that elusive first win in the United States was on the horizon.

"Whether that happens or not, it won't change my life either way, right?" Monty said.

Montgomerie slid to second place with a 69 in the third round, a stroke behind Daly, who had an interesting 67 for a 201 total. Daly started bogey, par, then double-bogeyed the third hole when he flew both the green and the gallery with a seven iron. Then he eagled the 10th, on a 378-yard drive (with the wind at his back) and an eight iron to 20 feet. "It's a lot of fun, but it's stressful," Daly said. Woods had a free-swinging 68. He hit only five fairways, and at the 14th ended up under a vehicle. "Pretty much saw most of Harding Park," said Woods.

It was a four-way struggle in the fourth round, with No. 7 the focal point. Woods somehow got his tee shot out of bad rough to inches for a tap-in birdie. Garcia hit an iron off the tee and holed out a 110-yard wedge for an eagle. Montgomerie missed putts of six and 10 feet down the stretch, and there went the chance for his first U.S. win. Monty shot 70 and tied for third with Garcia (69) and Henrik Stenson (68), two off the lead.

Daly and Woods made it a two-man race. Woods, trailing by three, birdied the 10th, 11th and 12th and tied Daly at 10 under par. Daly chipped in from 55 feet at the 13th for a birdie. Up ahead, Woods bogeyed the 14th from the rough, then made up two shots over the last three holes for a 68. He birdied the 16th off a wedge to four feet, and Daly three-putted for a bogey at the 17th, missing a par putt of five feet. Daly had one last chance to win in regulation at the 18th, but missed the 16-foot putt for birdie and closed with 69, Woods with 67, to tie at 10-under 270.

The first playoff hole, at the par-four 18th, was sheer drama. Woods hit first and slugged the ball over the dogleg and into the first cut of rough, 346 yards. Daly hit it 10 yards past him. They tied with pars.

The second was the par-four 16th. Woods caught the light rough on the left off the tee, and Daly hit a tree and ended up in the right rough. Woods hit his second to the front edge, and Daly put his on the green, 15 feet from the pin. Woods's birdie try ended up an inch short, and he tapped in for his par. Daly's birdie try grazed the hole and slid three feet past. Then, fatally, he missed that one coming back.

"I'm longer, but he's better," said Daly. "I'd rather be better."

## Michelin Championship at Las Vegas—$4,000,000
Winner: Wes Short, Jr.

With the PGA Tour stopping at gambler's paradise — the Michelin Championship at Las Vegas — it's not inappropriate to ask: What are the odds of having one golfer summon the ghost of Paul Revere, another getting disqualified for carrying a damaged club, another seeing his hopes die when, with two holes to play, his tee shot caromed off a sprinkler head into the water, and another scoring an accidental hole-in-one? Only at Las Vegas.

It was Kevin Stadler, son of Craig Stadler, who had the offending club. Stadler, tied for fifth going into the final round, discovered a bent wedge — an illegal club — in his bag. Under the rules, he was disqualified. How did it get bent? Said Stadler: "I have no idea."

Worse for Ted Purdy. He was the third-round leader, and in the final round he'd pulled within a stroke of Jim Furyk, the leader, when his tee shot at the par-three 17th hit a sprinkler head and bounced into the water. He triple-bogeyed.

The accidental hole-in-one — more accidental than others — was authored by Briny Baird in the second round. It came at the 145-yard 12th at the TPC at the Canyons, one of two courses in the tournament (the other being the TPC at Summerlin). "I hit a nine iron and pulled it," Baird said. "I didn't mean to hit it all the way over there. You hit it to the right and everything kind of funnels to the hole. I pulled it, and it went in. Simple. Lucky." But it helped him to a two-stroke lead at the halfway point.

And with apologies to Paul Revere, the war cry at Las Vegas was not "One if by land," but "Three if by land." That was Wes Short, Jr. talking to himself before the second playoff hole against Jim Furyk.

"I knew if I kept it on land, I was going to have a chance to win the tournament," said Short, who joined the tour last year as a 40-year-old rookie. This was in the playoff against Jim Furyk, who had won the tournament three times. They came to the second extra hole, the par-three 17th. Furyk watered his tee shot. Short kept his tee shot on land, but in a bunker. He blasted out to within a foot, and tapped in for his par three and his first victory. And Furyk was now one-for-six in playoffs.

The event opened on a far different note, and people did need a scorecard to keep track. The tournament is played on the two courses, Summerlin, a par-72, and the Canyons, a par-71. Baird opened with a 10-under-par 62 at Summerlin, and Ryan Palmer a nine-under 62 at the Canyons. Baird led the first round by a stroke and the second by two, and then the tournament moved to Summerlin for the third round. Baird hit a wall, of sorts. The biggest damage was a quadruple-bogey eight at the 12th and a 78 that blew him out of the picture. Moore was bounced at the par-five 16th, and hit water and rocks and made nine.

Purdy, who scored his only victory in the EDS Byron Nelson Championship earlier in the year, birdied his first four holes and held on in strong winds for a 65 and an 18-under 197 to lead by two. Short (66) was three back, and Furyk (69) four back.

Things were reversed in the final round. Short and Furyk were on something of a roll. Purdy, who had slipped behind, got back to within a stroke, then bounced the shot off the sprinkler head at the 17th. Furyk was homing in on his fourth Las Vegas victory until he three-putted the 18th for a bogey in regulation. Short birdied the hole and tied him at 21-under 266. "It was my tournament to win again, and I didn't get it done on the last hole," Furyk said.

Furyk and Short tied on the first playoff hole. At the second, Fury watered his tee shot, and Short stayed on dry land — sand, that is — then blasted to a foot and won.

"Right now, I don't have any emotions," Short said. "I thought when I first won, I'd be jumping to the moon. But it's like it hasn't sunk in yet."

## Funai Classic at the Walt Disney World Resort—$4,400,000
Winner: Lucas Glover

Lucas Glover recalls the time someone told him he'd win when he least expected it. It's safe to say that when he was standing in a greenside bunker at the 18th and final hole of the Funai Classic at the Walt Disney World Resort, 35 yards from the cup, winning never even popped into his head.

"It wasn't a bunker shot I walked up to and said, 'Hey, let's make this one,'" Glover said. "It was one of those, 'Let's get it close and get out of here.'" So he took a nice, comfortable swing, and darned if "close" in this case didn't turn out to mean right in the hole. Couple that with the 40-foot birdie putt he'd holed back at the 17th, and Glover, 25, from Greenville, South Carolina — Nationwide Tour winner and former Walker Cupper — had his first PGA Tour victory. And he got it just in time to lift a load off Tour rules official Slugger White. White was busy getting slips of paper ready for a draw for a crowded playoff. He was figuring on perhaps five tying for the lead. That was an improvement. A little earlier, at least 10 guys were battling for the lead down the final nine holes.

Glover, with his start of 68-66-66, trailed by five strokes in each of the first two rounds, and by three going into the final. Those stunning birdies at the last two holes gave him a seven-under-par 65, a 23-under 265 at Disney's Magnolia Course, and a one-stroke victory over Tom Pernice, who closed with 69. The wild finish left five tied for third, two strokes behind — Rich Beem (70), Harrison Frazar (68), Geoff Ogilvy (69), Ryan Palmer (64) and Justin Rose (68).

Glover had already finished and was on the practice range, staying loose for what almost certainly would be a playoff. Rose, still seeking his first tour win, took the lead with a birdie at the 15th off a six iron to eight feet. But he caught the rough at the 16th and bogeyed, then bogeyed the 18th out of a hazard, and there went his bid. Ogilvy birdied the 17th on an eight-footer and was tied for the lead going to the par-four 18th. Ogilvy put his six-iron approach into the back bunker, and he also bogeyed.

Pernice was the last man with a chance to catch Glover. At the 18th, Pernice put his drive into the fairway and hit a six iron to the green, 15 feet right of the hole. He needed the birdie to tie Glover, but his first putt pulled up short. The par gave him solo second, a stroke behind. "I had my opportunities," Pernice said. "Lucas shot 65 and birdied the last two holes. He did everything he could to win a golf tournament. My hat's off to him."

At the 18th, a par-four of 492 yards, Glover drove into the left rough and near some trees, then had to punch a shot out that ended up in the bunker 35 yards from the green. At this point, Ogilvy stepped into the story.

"I knew I was tied when I made that putt," Ogilvy said of his birdie at the 17th. And then he could see Glover in the distance, spraying sand, then lifting his arm in triumph. "And I knew," said Ogilvy, "I was one behind before I hit my next tee shot."

Said Glover: "I was trying to make par. It was a lucky shot, and everyone can say that because it's true."

## Chrysler Championship—$5,300,000
Winner: Carl Pettersson

How do you say "champion" in Swedish? In the case of Carl Pettersson, it doesn't matter. He's a Swede, all right, but he can say it in excellent English, maybe with a touch of North Carolina. And now other people can call him champion. Pettersson came from behind in the last two rounds of the Chrysler Championship and walked a tightrope down the final stretch to pick off his first PGA Tour title.

"It was a little easier in the dreams," Pettersson said. It had to be. Pettersson was up against it when Chad Campbell raced home with five birdies on the back nine at Innisbrook's tough par-71 Copperhead Course, and was in with a 67–276.

Pettersson's adventure actually began back at the par-three eighth, when his tee shot ended on an uphill lie in the front bunker and his best bunker shot left him 30 feet short of the pin. But he rolled it in and saved par. Then he was trying to nurse his lead home. He saved par with a scary chip at the 15th, and made a clutch 10-foot par putt at the 16th. At the 17th, he chipped from heavy rough to within three feet of a close-cut pin. ("I would have been happy with 10 feet," he said.) And at the 18th his touch saved him again when he lagged a dangerous downhill 20-footer and tapped in for his par, a par 71, and a one-stroke win at nine-under-par 275.

Pettersson, age 28, was 14 when his dad, an executive with the Volvo Trucks Division, was transferred to Raleigh, North Carolina. Pettersson, a former North Carolina State golfer, won nearly $1 million in 2003, his first year on the tour, and then $1.3 million in 2004.

"I'm not happy with second," Campbell said, "but I'm happy the result got me in The Tour Championship."

Steve Lowery, who missed eight straight cuts and 11 in the first 12 tournaments, was the biggest victim of Copperhead. He led at the halfway point and was tied for the lead with Pettersson going into the final round. The par-three No. 8, where Pettersson made his saving putt, did Lowery in. He fired a bunker shot across the green, and his ball ended up in pine straw but with a branch behind it. It took him two chips to get to the green and two putts to get down. The triple-bogey six knocked him out of the running. He tied for third.

While the tournament was a breakthrough for Pettersson, it was the Tour Championship Derby for players on the margin, scrambling to get into the top-30 field for the rich season-ender the following week. Charles Howell finished with 10 straight pars and a par 71 and had to wait two hours to see whether he'd made it. To his relief, he did. "It's a whole lot better slipping in than slipping out," he said. Tim Herron missed a 10-foot birdie putt on the 18th hole and figured he was out, but got in when Tom Pernice, Jr. double-bogeyed the 17th hole and Lowery missed a 25-foot birdie putt on the 18th.

Even more relieved was Tag Ridings. He shot 67 and tied for third, and moved from 125th to 101st on the money list, locking up his playing card for 2006. "It will be nice," Ridings said, "playing golf without any heat on me."

## The Tour Championship—$6,500,000
Winner: Bart Bryant

Simple arithmetic says that in a 29-man field, each guy has a 1-in-29 chance of winning. But this was The Tour Championship, the season finale for the cream of the PGA Tour, which meant Tiger Woods, Vijay Singh, Retief Goosen and the boys. So for a guy named Bart Bryant, a late-bloomer, age 42, maybe the odds weren't 1-in-29, but 1-in-astronomical. But on that final Sunday at East Lake Golf Club in Atlanta, there was Bart Bryant, standing tall and six shots clear of Tiger Woods. So much for odds.

"I'm as surprised as you are," Bryant said. The Tour Championship marked the end of a great 15 months. Bryant had struggled for years, overcoming injuries, bashing his head against the wall with a half-dozen cracks at the Tour's qualifying tournament. Then sweet reward: He won the Valero Texas Open in 2004, and then he took the Memorial Tournament in the spring of 2005. And now The Tour Championship, the rich season-ending, no-cut, ultra-exclusive romp at Eastlake Golf Club in the mild November days in Atlanta.

A profiler might not believe it. In the exclusive field, who was most likely to: Shoot a course-record 62, rank first in fairways hit (45), first in greens hit in regulation (58), seventh in putting. Tiger Woods? Retief Goosen? Vijay Singh? Chris DiMarco? In fact, Bryant hit 45 fairways, and that was more than Woods and Goosen put together (43).

Bryant did shoot that 62 in the first round for a two-stroke lead on Goosen, the defending champion, including a chip from an awkward stance that stopped a tap-in away. "I almost felt like apologizing for that one," Bryant said. That's about the way he felt for the entire tournament — almost apologetic, as though he didn't belong among the tour's elite. His scores suggested otherwise: 62-68-66-67—263, 17 under par and a light year ahead of Tiger Woods. The closest anyone came to him was Goosen, with a tie at 10-under 130 in the second round. Then he led Goosen by three going into the final round.

It was a bright finish, but not spotless. Bryant birdied the first hole off an approach to six feet, and the par-three second from four feet. He bogeyed the par-four fifth, East Lake's hardest hole, and then showed it was his week with a superb bogey at the par-three sixth. He caught the water short of the green, flipped a 50-yard wedge over the water to eight feet, and held the damage to a bogey. The magic touch stayed with him coming in. He birdied the 11th from 25 feet and the 12th from 30. Up ahead at the 16th, Woods's tee shot ended up in the bushes to the right. He took a penalty drop, punched a shot through the trees to the green, and three-putted for a double bogey. It was over, and Woods knew it.

And thus went the story of Bryant, the man who felt unworthy just to be there. He'd spent most of his 18 years on the PGA Tour in doubt and frustration. He had rotator cuff surgery in 1992, played the mini-tours, tried to qualify six times, and had surgery on both elbows. He analyzed himself: He said it took him this long to succeed because he was afraid to fail. And now there would be old ghosts that would not leave willingly.

Someone noted that shooting 62 in the first round of The Tour Championship proved that he belonged in this fast company.

"I don't think I'll ever believe it in my head," Bryant said. "People try to pound it in my head — 'You belong, you belong.' If I go out and shoot three more 62s, maybe I'll believe it." It turned out he didn't need anything that extreme. It remained to be seen, however, whether a six-shot win over Tiger Woods would convince him.

## Southern Farm Bureau Classic—$3,000,000
Winner: Heath Slocum

Heath Slocum remembered that piece of fatherly advice. In fact, it was more than fatherly advice. It was a caddie's advice, too.

"Hearing that same voice that I've heard all my life — 'Commit to this, stay still,' — it was nice," Slocum said. It wasn't just the echo from childhood days. He was hearing it right over his shoulder. His dad, Jack Slocum, a former Mississippi club professional, was also his caddie in the Southern Farm Bureau Classic, and it was dad's steadying reminder that he credited for getting him through to his second PGA Tour victory. His other was in the 2004 Chrysler Classic of Tucson.

Dad's advice was especially important this time. Slocum and Loren Roberts, the "Boss of the Moss," were tied at 20 under par coming to the par-four 17th. Slocum fired his second shot to within nine feet of the flag, then rolled in the putt for a birdie. At the 18th, he tapped in a two-footer for his par, wrapping up a bogey-free, six-under-par 66 for a 21-under 267 and a two-stroke victory at Annandale Golf Club at Annandale, Mississippi. Then there was the big victory hug for dad, who played in the event nine times, but never finishing higher than a tie for 26th in 1983.

"It was special just to have him on the bag, and with us being from around this area, it was just a special week," said Slocum, 31, who grew up nearby and who won at Annandale for the first time in five tries. As to following the advice from dad at the 17th: "I picked a target, I committed to that target, and I made a good swing."

The advice was particularly important at that point because Roberts had hit his drive into the water. The birdie gave Slocum a two-stroke lead. "Really, the only bad shot I hit all week was the tee shot at 17," Roberts said. He closed with a 68 to share second with Carl Pettersson (67), two strokes behind Slocum.

The big surprise was that the tournament was held at all. It had been scheduled for October 3-9, but Hurricane Katrina, which devastated New Orleans and much of the Gulf Coast, also did great damage 200 miles inland. Annandale was in no shape for a tournament. It was postponed to this week of November, opposite The Tour Championship, so that the course could be ready for play.

The tournament opened with Bob Tway setting the pace by tying the course record with a 64 for a one-stroke lead. Tway, seeking his first win since the 2003 Bell Canadian Open, was still in the lead in the second round, but he had lots of company. Thanks to a couple of errors, he shot a two-under 70 and found himself in a six-way jam at 10-under 134 with John Cook, who birdied his last four holes for a 65, and Kevin Na (68), Tag Ridings (66), Tom Pernice, Jr. (68) and Jonathan Byrd (69). Tway, who started the round at eight under, double-bogeyed the 14th after driving into the water, but was 11 under at the 18th, then hit his second shot into water. "Hitting two shots like that is ridiculous," Tway said.

Slocum moved in with a 64 in the third round, birdieing his last four holes. "I don't want to think ahead, but it would be great to win it here," he said. "It would mean so much to my father." Slocum and Roberts (66) were within a stroke of rookie Joey Snyder, who shot a seven-under 65. Roberts, age 50, was the old vet of the group. "I'll have to be at my best to keep up with these young guys," he said.

The final round was a scramble. Snyder slipped back with bogeys at the 14th and 18th and finished fourth. Pettersson, seeking his second straight win (after the Chrysler Championship), bogeyed the 16th, shot 67, and tied for second at 19-under 269 with Roberts, who suffered the watered tee shot. It came down to the Slocum father-son combination, unbeatable in this case.

"He trusts me enough," Heath Slocum said. "All he was there for was the support."

# Special Events

## Tavistock Cup—$1,400,000
Winners: Isleworth/Lake Nona

The Tavistock Cup, a throwback to a much earlier day in golf, was for bragging rights and turf. In this case, Isleworth and Lake Nona, two clubs near Orlando, Florida. The membership is a tad different, however. For example, Tiger Woods captained the Isleworth team, and Ernie Els the Lake Nona (the host this time). It could have been a heck of a finish, but the two teams — 18 players each — settled for a tie when the two-round event was cut to one when The Players Championship did not finish until Monday because of rain delays. And then that one round itself ended in a tie when darkness fell after three extra holes between Woods and Els.

"It seems like we're making a habit of this — finishing in the dark and ties all the time," said Els. The reference was to the 2003 Presidents Cup in South Africa, when the matches ended in a tie and Woods and Els were picked for a playoff. They battled for three holes before darkness shut it down in a tie between the United States and International teams.

In the Tavistock Cup — Woods and Lee Janzen for Isleworth and Els and Retief Goosen for Nona — Woods forced the playoff with a 31 on the back nine in the better-ball format. Els extended the playoffs with an adventurous par out of the trees, finishing it with a 12-foot putt. They went back to the 18th, and it seemed Goosen won it for Lake Nona when he dropped a 30-foot birdie putt. But Woods, not to be outdone, followed him in from 18 feet to halve the hole. On the third extra hole, Goosen and Els both missed 15-foot birdie putts that would have won it. Woods shot the low score of the event, a 66.

Isleworth was the defending champion. But with the tie, each club will hold the trophy for six months, and the match returns to Isleworth in 2006.

## CVS Charity Classic—$1,300,000
Winners: Fred Funk and Chris DiMarco

If Fred Funk and Chris DiMarco had proved nothing else, they proved they could come through pressure. Funk did it in The Players Championship, plucking that prestigious plum in the final round, and DiMarco, hero of the 2004 Ryder Cup, fought Woods into a playoff before falling in the Masters. This was the CVS Charity Classic at Rhode Island Country Club, and while it didn't rank with the Players or the Masters, it was still not a cakewalk in the 10-team field made up of tour professionals.

It was the lively Funk who wrapped it up in the second and final round, rolling in a 25-foot putt at the 17th for a birdie that spurred them to a better-ball 62, and a total of 19-under-par 123. They won by two over

Dana and Brett Quigley, and Brad Faxon and Sergio Garcia, both teams at 17-under 125.

"After I bogeyed on 17, Fred's putt for bird was the key putt today," DiMarco said. They had been giving a putting clinic. They birdied the 11th and 12th, then cooled to four straight pars from the 13th. Then they resumed the clinic.

If Funk's putt at the 17th was the key, DiMarco's at the 18th was the clincher. He dropped a 22-footer for birdie on the final hole to lock up the win. Faxon and Garcia closed with a rush, with birdies on three of the last four holes to take a share of second.

In the first round, Faxon, co-founder of the tournament with fellow Rhode Islander Billy Andrade, holed a six-footer for birdie on the 18th to give himself and Garcia a share of the lead with DiMarco and Funk at 10-under 61. Five teams tied behind them at seven-under 64, including two father-son combinations — Craig and Kevin Stadler, and 2004 champions Jay and Billy Haas.

"We did a very good job of complementing each other," Faxon said, after he accounted for six of their birdies, including those at the 12th, 13th and 18th. Garcia had birdied four holes, including the 14th and 16th. Funk racked up eight of his and DiMarco's 10 birdies, including those at the 10th, 12th, 13th and 16th.

"We were relaxed," Funk said. "I was in trouble on No. 9 and Chris made a great putt to keep the momentum going. On No. 17, I pushed a putt a hair. That was the only putt we should have made that we missed."

## The Presidents Cup
Winner: United States

As if the pressure wasn't already stifling as an afternoon in the tropics. Chris DiMarco was on the final hole of the final singles match, tied with Stuart Appleby. He could now win The Presidents Cup for the United States. All he needed was a birdie. But he was facing an immensely missable 15-foot putt. And on top of this, as the reality of it all was descending full on him, there came the voice of his caddie, Pat O'Bryan, saying to him simply: "This is the moment you've been waiting for all your life." Right. Thanks for the reminder.

"I was so nervous, I thought I was going to whiff," DiMarco said. "Every piece of my body was shaking."

DiMarco lined up that 15-footer, and under the pressure and with his caddie's soft words echoing in his ears, he stroked the putt. And he began charging after it before it even reached the hole.

"I knew it wasn't going to miss," DiMarco said. It dropped, and then he charged over to Jack Nicklaus, the U.S. captain, and hugged him. The United States Team had won, 18½-15½.

"All I thought about," DiMarco said, "was to get him a win."

Long before the teams arrived at the Robert Trent Jones Golf Club at Gainesville, Virginia, Nicklaus was only too aware of what happens when you mix oil and water, as Hal Sutton discovered when he paired Tiger Woods and Phil Mickelson at the 2004 Ryder Cup. Nicklaus didn't want the silent indifference of Woods and the awkward discomfort of Mickelson. He'd intended to pair Mickelson and David Toms, but Mickelson and DiMarco, friends from their college days, talked him out of it. Something clicked wonderfully. They went undefeated, 3-0-1, as a pair. Then Mickelson halved his singles match, and DiMarco won his — and The Presidents Cup with it.

It was the amazing story of DiMarco again. He was winless on the PGA Tour since the 2002 Phoenix Open, but a fire-breather in team play. He was the driving force for the Americans in a losing cause at the 2004 Ryder Cup, and now The Presidents Cup.

The Internationals may have been limited by the absence of the injured Ernie Els. And it didn't help that Vijay Singh was having a bad time, going 0-2-3.

### First Day

In the opening alternate shot, Retief Goosen and Adam Scott got the International team off and running with a 4-and-3 win over Tiger Woods and Fred Couples. Goosen set the tone at No. 3, rolling a 60-foot putt to within 16 inches for a conceded birdie. Then Woods chipped poorly at the fourth and Couples missed a four-foot putt and lost the sixth. Mike Weir and Trevor Immelman came along in the sixth and last match of the day, ran off four birdies in the first five holes, and dispatched Steward Cink and David Toms, 6 and 5. Mickelson and DiMarco salvaged a point with a 1-up win over Nick O'Hern and Tim Clark.

"It's like a mile race, and you're 50 yards ahead," Captain Gary Player cautioned his team.

Internationals lead, 3½-2½.

### Second Day

This was a classic 3-3 standoff in the better-ball. Mickelson and DiMarco led off, halving with Angel Cabrera and Michael Campbell, and Woods, paired now and the rest of the way with Jim Furyk — both hurting — beat Stuart Appleby and Mark Hensby, 2 up. Furyk had sore ribs and Woods a sore back. Both needed treatment on the course. Just as Appleby and Hensby were making a move with consecutive birdies, Furyk holed an eight-footer for birdie to close them out at the 16th.

Internationals lead, 6½-5½.

### Third Day

Mickelson and DiMarco were on a rampage. In the morning alternate shot, they walloped Campbell and Cabrera, 5 and 3, then crushed Peter Lonard and Nick O'Hern, 6 and 5, in the afternoon better-ball. The day included DiMarco's ace at No. 7 in the morning and a 15-foot birdie putt in the afternoon.

Said Mickelson: "We really jell well as a team, and it's hard not to ... when you have somebody here rolling in every single putt and hitting the ball fabulously." Fred Funk ventured a deeper analysis: "Chris is such a fired-up guy. He gets up in the moment no matter what. And I think he deflects some of the attention away from Phil. He lets Phil relax more. Phil would be the focus if it wasn't for a guy like DiMarco." Whatever the reason, the U.S. won the morning, 3-2, and halved the afternoon at 2½, and The Presidents Cup was tied going into Sunday's singles.

Teams tied, 11-11.

Fourth Day

The first crusher in the singles for the U.S. came when Goosen beat Woods, 2 and 1. Couples answered by beating Singh, 1 up. Kenny Perry, age 45, winless so far, made eight birdies in 15 holes to dismiss Mark Hensby, 4 and 3. Davis Love routed O'Hern, 4 and 3, and then, while Mickelson and Cabrera were battling into extra holes, it came down to DiMarco and Appleby, all-square at the 18th. DiMarco's 15-footer was almost identical to the one Couples had holed to beat Singh earlier. Nicklaus asked Couples how much the putt would break. "I don't know," Couples said. "I just closed my eyes and hit it." DiMarco didn't close his eyes.

The last word belonged to Nicklaus. "I may never captain another team, I may never play another round of golf," he said, "but if I end my career this way, it's a pretty darn good way to end it."

## Franklin Templeton Shootout—$2,600,000

Winners: Kenny Perry and John Huston

Kenny Perry had it all figured out. "'We're going to turn it around and win this thing' — that's what I was thinking to myself the whole time," Perry said. Good thinking. Doing it was something else. All he and John Huston — two "old" warhorses — had to do was overhaul Fred Couples, age 46, and Adam Scott, 25, an excellent mix of veteran savvy and youthful exuberance, down the final nine.

"Sure enough," Perry said, "we birdied two holes, they let two get away, we caught them and ended up taking the lead on them and kind of cruised to victory."

And thus ended the Franklin Templeton Shootout at Tiburon Golf Club at Naples, Florida, a team fixture in post-season golf. Perry and Huston combined for a 13-under 59 in the scramble format in the final round for a 30-under 186 total and a one-stroke victory over Couples and Scott, who closed with a 62 and a 29-under total.

In the first round, Fred Funk with his accuracy and Jason Gore with his power combined for a nine-under 63 and a one-stroke lead in the alternate-shot format. "I've never really been paired with a guy who's as long as he is," Funk said. "The game's a lot easier from where he plays it."

Couples and Scott took the lead in the second round in better-ball, running off six consecutive birdies for an 11-under 61 and a two-stroke lead at 19 under. "We're two guys who can make a lot of birdies, and we did today," Scott said. "We did a pretty good job of picking up the slack for one another." Perry and Huston broke out of a traffic jam with a birdie-eagle-par-birdie burst for a 63, going 17 under.

The third and final round was played as a scramble, and it was here that Perry and Huston came from behind on the back nine. They birdied the 11th and 12th to tie Couples and Scott, then took the lead with a birdie at the 14th. Another birdie at the 15th moved them two strokes ahead, but Scott got a stroke back at the 16th, holing a sensational 60-footer for a birdie. The Perry-Huston one-stroke lead held up when both duos birdied the 17th and parred the 18th.

Mark O'Meara and Nick Price (60) were third at 27 under. Greg Norman, the tournament founder and host, playing a month after minor knee surgery, and Steve Elkington teamed for 15 birdies and an eagle for a closing 17-under 55 to finish fourth at 26 under.

Perry, who was nursing a pinched nerve, credited Huston for their success. "I don't know what it was, even though my shoulder's killing me, my elbow, and my thumb's completely numb," Perry said. "I just kind of hung on to him and he drug me around this place." The language was flawed, but the sentiment was clear.

## PGA Grand Slam of Golf—$1,000,000
Winner: Tiger Woods

The good news is that Tiger Woods was ailing in the first round. No telling how much he would have won by if he'd been feeling well.

This was the PGA Grand Slam of Golf, the late-November slugfest for the winners of the four majors. Woods was in as the winner of the Masters and the Open Championship, Michael Campbell from the U.S. Open, Phil Mickelson from the PGA Championship, and Vijay Singh taking the spot left by Woods having won two. As slugfests go, Woods turned this one into a few days in balmy trade winds at Poipu Bay in Hawaii. Woods was the only one throwing the KO punches. In the first round, despite a bout of stomach flu, he shot a five-under-par 67 and led Mickelson (70) by three. Campbell was back at 73, Singh at 75. So much for Woods playing golf with a case of the miseries.

The next day Woods announced, "My stomach's good. I got a great night's rest." That was the bad news for the others. In the second and final round, Woods shot a 64. He beat Mickelson (68) by seven, Campbell (70) by 12 and Singh (69) by 13.

"Tiger was so far ahead, you couldn't stop him," Campbell said. "He's a great challenge and a great player."

Woods started the runaway at the 573-yard, par-five No. 6. He bombed a drive 344 yards and hit a five iron to the green, 55 feet from the pin. It was an uphill putt that bent to the left. He dropped it for an eagle. At the par-five 14th, he slugged a drive 293 yards into the breezes, then smashed a three wood 244 yards to the green. "Oh, baby," Woods said. "That was pretty cool."

It was cooler still when he dropped the 12-foot putt for another eagle. And he just missed another eagle at the 18th, when his 65-footer stayed out. "It's more luck than anything else," Woods said. "It really is."

The tournament wasn't without its spirited moments, such as they were. In the second round, Mickelson birdied Nos. 5, 6 and 8 to get within three of Woods at the final turn. Then he watered his tee shot at the par-three 11th, and so there went that threat.

"I'm surprised there weren't more of those," Mickelson said. "I felt very rusty. I didn't feel like I was on top of my game. But I was able to keep it in play, with the exception of that shot."

Mickelson said he wasn't too disappointed, since he hadn't touched a club in five weeks. "It was kind of a friendly round of golf," he said. "There wasn't much of a competition going on, so we just enjoyed the day."

But nobody enjoyed it more than Tiger Woods. "I feel very comfortable here," Woods said. "Most of the holes really suit my eye, and for some reason, I just kind of put it together every time I've come here."

## MBNA WorldPoints Father-Son Challenge—$1,085,000
Winners: Bernhard and Stefan Langer

Bernhard Langer and son Stefan, age 15, were more like a 1-2 punch than a golf team in the MBNA WorldPoints Father-Son Challenge. First they posted an elegant 59 in the first round for a one-stroke lead. Then in the second round, they took turns landing the telling blows that delivered a one-stroke victory over Raymond and Robert Floyd.

Bernhard holed a long putt for a birdie on the 11th, then a four-footer for another on the 12th to tie for the lead at 20 under par. Then they combined to two-putt for a birdie at the 18th, an 11-under 61 at the Champions Gate Golf Resort near Orlando, Florida, and the championship. The 61 gave them a two-round total of 24-under 120 and the one-stroke victory over the frustrated Floyds.

"We just tried to stay in front all day," Bernhard said. "I didn't want to have to do my heroics to win. We knew we needed to make a birdie on the final hole. Stefan hit the best three wood he's hit all week. I was very proud of him."

Five teams, including Vijay and Qass Singh, tied for third at 22 under.

In the first round, both Langers holed 40-foot putts for birdies, Stefan at the 11th and dad at the 17th. It was clear then that the combination was going to be tough to beat.

Gretchen Zoeller, playing out of the College of Charlotte, became the first female ever to play in the event when she teamed with dad Fuzzy. They combined for a seven-under 137.

The star pairing was Saturday's final — Jack Nicklaus and son Jackie, and Arnold Palmer and grandson Sam Saunders. Saunders, heading for Clemson University in the fall, smashed a drive far, far down the fairway.

Said grandpap Arnie: "Do I have to hit?"

Said Nicklaus, with a grin: "Nope."

Said Palmer: "He always tends to agree with me on things like this."

## Target World Challenge—$5,500,000
Winner: Luke Donald

Luke Donald, English golfing artist, couldn't have been more of a surprise if he'd worn a mask at the Target World Challenge, the rich plum in what used to be called the "silly season." But there's nothing silly about a $5.5 million purse and a $1.3 million first prize for a 16-man field, and so it's called the "Challenge Season."

The Target World Challenge, played in early December at Sherwood Country Club at Thousand Oaks, California, was something of a private party for the first three rounds. U.S. Open champion Michael Campbell (63) led Darren Clarke (65) by two in the first round, then led Clarke and

Padraig Harrington by three in the second, and then in the third, Clarke reversed the field, taking a one-stroke lead on Campbell and Harrington. It was a nice, neat little package shaping up as a grudge match down the stretch. But not for long.

The boyish-looking Donald, who turned 28 during the week, came riding up. He was trailing Clarke by six heading into the final round, but he shot an eight-under-par 64 for a 272 total, 16 under. He beat Clarke by two, Campbell and Harrington by four, and as he rode off, maybe he heard the question, "Who was that guy in the white hat?"

"Luckily, I played great today," Donald said. "Fortunately for me, the guys in the top two groups didn't play their best and let me have this one a little bit. This has been a year of 'nearlys.' Luckily, I got the last one. It will make Christmas a little better."

Hardly anyone was paying any real attention to Donald until he bolted to five birdies in a seven-hole stretch on the back nine. He hauled himself into a tie for the lead at the par-five 16th, dropping an eight-foot birdie putt.

Clarke, who spent the year troubled over his wife's battle with cancer, was 16 under on the par-fives going into the final nine. His domination ended on the par-five 16th. He drove into the fairway, but pulled his second into deep rough, and he wound up three-putting for a bogey and a 72. Then he needed a birdie at the 18th to force a playoff. But he pulled his approach, and three-putted for a bogey and a 72–274.

Tiger Woods, the tournament host, was playing in his sixth event in six weeks and never was a factor. He finished 15th out of the 16 with a two-under 286. He'd had a sensational season, but he was more than happy to see it come to an end. At the 18th, after driving into the fairway, he noted: "One more iron, three more putts and I'm done for the year."

# Nationwide Tour

The Jason Gore Story lacked that one little part necessary to make it truly heroic and immortal. It should have had an introduction that began, "Once upon a time …" Failing that, Jason Gore will go into the history books as one of the most enriching and inspiring tales in golf, and it was spawned by a little pathos, an exciting and improbable pass at the U.S. Open, an explosive three-victory outburst on the Nationwide Tour, and then a win on the "big" tour, the PGA Tour. Gore's story was such that it left unanswered the question of, who is Troy Matteson? Matteson, it turns out, was merely the leading money winner on the Nationwide Tour in 2005. And this proves that money isn't everything.

Gore became the unlikeliest of folk heroes. Hardly the John Wayne type, he is big and beefy, looking more like a linebacker than a golfer, and he smiles and jokes, his good nature warming everything around him. It had to be this good nature that saw him through in 2005. He will be remembered as the struggling Nationwide Tour golfer who could hardly win a buck, who refused to give up his dream, and then, when circumstances finally had driven him to the point where it might be wise for him to bail out and try some other line of work, his career flowered like Fourth of July fireworks.

The pathos: Gore was so far down on his luck that he almost literally didn't know where his baby's next meal was coming from. He went to the store one day wondering whether he could afford to buy baby formula. On his way to the U.S. Open at Pinehurst with wife and child, he was robbed of almost everything he owned. Even his underwear. When he was threatening to win the Open, under a case of nerves in the final round, he shot 84 and tied for 49th. His assessment: "That's golf."

This was golf, too, for Gore. In the second round of the Cox Classic, he was 10 under par facing the 315-yard, par-four No. 9, his final hole of the day. He needed an eagle for 59. He drove the green, to within 20 feet of the cup, and dropped the putt for the 59. He had just improved by 12 strokes over his even-par first round. He had just become the third player, after Notah Begay and Doug Dunakey, to shoot 59 on the Nationwide Tour. His round included nine birdies, two eagles and one bogey. "It was a good day," Gore allowed. "I was trying to get a decent round in after playing so shabby yesterday. That was pretty cool, wasn't it?"

It was time for Gore to get his foot into the glass slipper, and this he did by following up the U.S. Open by winning three straight starts — the "battlefield promotion" that elevated him to the PGA Tour. He won the National Mining Association Pete Dye Classic the first week of July, the Scholarship America Showdown a week later, and a few weeks after that, in his third straight start, the Cox Classic. The 59 was great, but he had to go through a playoff against Roger Tambellini to win the tournament, and this he did on a five-foot putt on the second extra hole. "It's pretty cool, pretty cool," Gore said.

And then Gore polished off the year at the 84 Lumber Classic in September with more theatrics. He needed a sponsor's exemption to get in the field, and he won on the final hole when he rolled an incredible putt some 90 feet to tap-in range.

Just four months earlier, he was a nobody in anguish, wondering whether he could afford baby formula. "And now, look," he said. "They just handed me a check for $729,000."

Through it all, obscured by the glare of Gore's rocket ride, Troy Matteson labored in relative obscurity to become the Nationwide's leading money winner with a record $495,009, topping Zach Johnson's $494,882 in 2003. That would have made Matteson the Player of the Year, except for Jason Gore's rise. Matteson won the Virginia Beach Open in April and the Mark Christopher Charity Classic in September, and had six other top-five finishes and four other top 10s.

Chris Couch was the only other player to win twice, taking the Rheem Classic in May and the LaSalle Bank Open in June. Couch won the Rheem with a flash. He was five behind starting the final round, then shot a 10-under-par 60. He took third place on the money list with $337,205, but he finished weakly, either missing the cut or withdrawing in his final five events.

Australian Steven Bowditch, age 22, the Rookie of the Year, stamped himself a man to watch by finishing fourth on the money list with $333,329. He scored his career-first victory in the Jacob's Creek Open in February, becoming the second youngest to win on the Nationwide Tour, at 21 years, eight months and 12 days. Bowditch had a wild ride in the ING New Zealand PGA Championship the following week. He led the first round, sagged in the third, then closed with a 63, tying the course record, and also tying Peter O'Malley. He lost on the fourth extra hole, but his $64,800 check made him the fastest in Nationwide history to top $200,000.

Fireworks won left-hander Eric Axley his PGA Tour card. He was 27th on the money list coming into the Nationwide Tour Championship, and he promptly shot 77 in the first round. Dead? Not quite. He followed that up with a pair of 66s, then closed with a 69 to finish second to David Branshaw. The feat carried him to 16th on the money list.

Jerry Smith also ducked through the closing door in the last three tournaments to take his 2006 PGA Tour card. He finished third in the Gila River Golf Classic, tied for second in the Permian Basic Charity Golf Classic and third in the Nationwide Tour Championship. The critical bottom line for Smith was this: He finished sixth on the money list with $267,756, and he'd won $110,267 of that in his last three tournaments.

# Canadian Tour

Life was varied, fast and intriguing on the Canadian Tour, meaning break-throughs, comebacks and odd circumstances. Consider: You had your average hungry, ambitious professional, namely Michael Harris, who waited a long time for that first win, and then wasted no time to get his second. You had David Mathis winning on a broken ankle, and Jamie Gomez coming back from a three-year break to win. And the tour was also the House of Dreams. In the 12 tournaments on the schedule, there were nine first-time winners.

Harris, age 27, a former University of Michigan standout, was getting restless. He figured five runner-up finishes over two years were plenty. Now where was that win? It turned out it was in the tour's final full-field tournament of the season, the Bay Mills Open Players Championship at Wild Bluff Golf Club at Brimley, Michigan, late in August. Harris did it, and appropriately with sufficient drama — a come-from-behind playoff win over Sweden's Anders Hultman. Harris shot a final-round six-under-par 66 to tie Hultman (66) at 13-under 275.

Halfway through the last round, things didn't look good for Harris. Hult-man birdied the last three holes on the first nine and led by three at the turn. The comeback started modestly enough. Harris chipped in for a birdie at the 11th. He was short of the green at the par-three 13th, but chipped in from the rough. Then he birdied the 14th to tie. Hultman retook the lead when Harris misread a tap-in for par. But incredibly enough, at the par-five 17th, Harris pitched in from the rough for an eagle three for the lead. That was three pitch-ins in eight holes. Hultman birdied to tie him again. At the par-four 18th, Hultman hit his approach to 12 feet, but Harris put his, a wedge from 104 yards, to six inches. Hultman dropped his for a birdie to tie and force a playoff. On the first extra hole, Hultman's 16-foot birdie putt hung on the lip, and Harris knocked in his 10-footer for the victory.

"I've had to answer those questions [of finishing runner-up] for the past two years," Harris said. "Now I can put that behind me. I call it divine intervention."

That being the case, he then went from the divine to the sublime the very next week, in the Niagara Fallsview Casino Resort Pro-Am Classic at Niagara Falls, Ontario. No playoff this time, but there were plenty of fireworks and drama at Thundering Waters Golf Course. Harris, fresh from his first win, came from five strokes behind in the final day and had his second victory in back-to-back weeks. And he had to play 32 holes on Sunday to do it, thanks to rain delays.

Four players were tied at eight under par as the final group was playing the 17th. Harris rolled in a 25-footer for birdie, and at the last hole, after driving behind a tree, he laid up, then nearly holed a wedge from 88 yards. He had an eight-inch putt left for a birdie, a three-under 69 for a 10-under 278 total, and a two-stroke victory. The C$18,000 first prize gave him the Order of Merit title as well, at over C$95,000 for the season.

"I honestly thought it was over. I didn't think I could come back," Harris said. "It turned out to be a sprint to the finish. I guess that's the way I operate."

They teach a lot of things on the practice tee — grip, takeaway, weight shift, and the like. One thing they don't teach is how to play on a broken ankle. Enter David Mathis, of Raleigh, North Carolina, in the Michelin Morelia Classic in Morelia, Mexico. He had stepped into a hole in the second round and twisted his right ankle. The pain almost drove him out before the third round. But he soldiered on, hobbling the rest of the way. He overcame both the pain and a seven-shot deficit to win his first Canadian Tour title. He birdied his final hole for an eight-under-par 64 and a 17-under 271 total.

"I really couldn't put any weight on it over the last few days," Mathis said. "It wasn't really a problem during my swing, but on impact I just couldn't put any weight on it. On Friday, Derek and Stuart [playing partners Gillespie and Anderson] were trying to keep straight faces. I think I had the worst follow-through in the history of this game."

Texan Jaime Gomez, 37, hadn't played for nearly three years. A shoulder injury had knocked him off the tour and into teaching. And now, six years after his lone tour victory in 1999, he took the Corona Mazatlan Classic, at Mazatlan, Mexico. He toured El Cid in 67-68-66-69, an 18-under 270 and a three-stroke win in just his third tournament since 2002. The realization finally took him as he was standing in the 18th fairway on the last day. He began to cry. And he fired his approach to three feet anyway. "To make birdie on the final hole, with tears in my eyes — man, it's just crazy," Gomez said.

Harris's adventures were the fireworks at the end of the season. The season wasn't exactly dull before that. Start with the opening tournament, the Barton Creek Austin Pro-Am Classic. Californian Scott Gibson had been looking for that first win, and he got it in spades — a nine-stroke victory, the biggest since Arron Oberholser's 11-stroke win in 1999. Gibson led Erik Compton by three heading into the final round. Gibson shot a two-under 70, and won by the nine over Compton, who skied to a 76, and Brian Guetz and Blaine McCallister. "I'm just ecstatic," Gibson said. "What better feeling can you have than that?"

Peter Tomasulo, 23, from Long Beach, California, was possibly the most closely watched rookie after an outstanding college career at the University of California. He didn't wait long to start living up to expectations. After a handful of close calls this season, he took the Montreal Open at Club de golf de I'lle de Montreal. He closed with a one-over-par 71 on a windy August afternoon for a three-shot win over Michael Harris. "That was the toughest day by far today," said Tomasulo, who won C$24,000. "For a while, it wasn't looking too good, but I bounced back. This was my first time with the lead going into the final round, so I'm glad I was able to close it."

The other first-time winners: Jim Seki in the Northern California Classic; Stuart Anderson, Foster Farms California Classic; Craig Taylor, Times Colonist Open; Matt McQuillan, Telus Edmonton Open, and Lee Williamson, MTS Classic.

Only three of the 12 tournaments were won by players who had already won — Gomez, Omar Uresti, a veteran of the PGA Tour, and of course, Michael Harris.

# Tour de las Americas (South America)

Argentina's Daniel Barbetti was a few days early, but he gave himself a blowout of a present for his 24th birthday, the 2005 Tour de las Americas' Order of Merit title, with a total of US$41,514 in winnings in the nine (of 16) TLA tournaments he played.

His breakthrough year began with his first tour victory, the American Express Puerto Rico Open at Costa Caribe Golf & Country Club in May, when he holed a delicate putt at the first playoff hole to beat countryman Eduardo Argiro. Argiro just missed the green at the 181-yard par-three and chipped to two feet. Barbetti had put his seven iron 10 feet above the hole on the fast, tricky green. "I saw the putting line very clear and said to myself, 'Just touch it and it will go in,' and it did," he said, and he had picked up the bulk of his season's winnings, $22,500, by mid-May.

Barbetti followed up his Puerto Rico win the next week with a fourth place in the Players Championship Acafest, and was fifth in the Mexican Open in December.

Barbetti, however, came within a whisker of not winning the Order of Merit. Fellow Argentinean Rafael Gomez, the winner in 2004, was hot on his heels. When Barbetti missed the cut in the Visa Argentine Open, the final event in early December, Gomez needed just a half-decent finish to beat him out. But Gomez tied for 53rd and won only $1,100, falling a mere $921 short of taking the title.

Barbetti led the Argentinean domination of the tour. In all, Argentineans won eight of the 16 tournaments, and they took 14 of the top 20 spots on the Order of Merit, taking a big piece of the $1.5 million in purses. In fact, Argentineans swept the top five places. Cesar Monasterio, who won the Telefonica de Guatemala, took third; Miguel Rodriguez, winner of the Siemens Venezuela Open, was fourth, and Eduardo Argiro, who piled up enough good finishes without winning, was fifth.

The season opened and closed with American winners.

In the Costa Rica Open in mid-February, Kyle Dobbs beat Argentina's Sebastian Fernandez on the first extra hole. Dobbs closed with a 67, Fernandez with 68 to tie at four-under-par 280. Dobbs started the final round a stroke off the lead, then got four ahead before running into trouble. "I was fortunate I putted well today," he said. "I feel lucky to be here." Dobbs won it with a six-foot birdie while Fernandez two-putted from 20 feet.

Kevin Haefner took the Panama Masters the following week, surviving the high winds that whipped the Summit Golf & Resort in the final round for his first professional win. Haefner, who joined the tour in October 2003, had four bogeys and a birdie on the front nine but finished with a 72 for an eight-under 276 and a two-stroke win over England's James Hepworth. "I didn't play well on the front nine, but I've been playing well all week so I just stayed patient, waiting for the good shots to come," Haefner said.

The Telefonica de Guatemala at Hacienda Nueva was a time of close calls. Argentina's Monasterio came to the final hole needing a birdie for a fourth straight 67 and a one-stroke win. "I still can't explain how that ball didn't go in," he said, after his 15-footer just missed. He shot 68. Ireland's David Higgins came to the 18th with the lead at 20 under, but he caught some trees off the tee and had to chip out, and bogeyed for a 65. They tied at 19-under 269.

There might have been another in the mix, but Argentina's Daniel Vancsik, the defending champion, cost himself the chance by misreading the situation. "I thought Higgins had finished at 20 under and I decided to attack," Vancsik said. "If I had known the way things stood, I would've hit the center of the green for two putts." But he missed the green, bogeyed, and finished third.

Back at the par-four 18th for the playoff, both missed the green to the left. Higgins chipped to six feet, and Monasterio to a foot. Higgins missed, and Monasterio tapped in for his par and his first tour win. "That's golf," Higgins said. "It was Cesar's day."

A more serious error, and a strange one, figured in the American Express Brazil Classic at Sao Fernando Golf Club. Argentina's Fernandez would go on to win in a playoff over Brazil's Alex Rocha, but it was Brazilian Philippe Gasnier who shut himself out of any chance at the title. Gasnier was in contention most of the day, then all but slammed the door on himself at the 10th when he raked a bunker that was in his line to the green. The two-stroke penalty knocked him back, and he finished with a 71 and solo third place, three out of the playoff.

Fernandez led Gasnier by three and Rocha by four starting the final round and thought a two-under finish ought to be enough. "But I didn't play the putt effectively," he said. In particular, a three-putt at the 13th hurt him. He finished with a 71 and Rocha a 67 to tie at nine-under 275. At the first playoff hole, Fernandez saved par from five feet, and Rocha missed from three, losing for the fifth or sixth time — he wasn't sure which — in playoffs. "This is obviously something I have to deal with," Rocha said.

The season ended in early December with the Visa Argentine Open at the Jockey Club, and with a familiar name atop the leader board — Stadler. But this wasn't Craig, "The Walrus." This was his son, the impressively sized Kevin, age 25, and there was a wonderful irony here. His dad won the tournament in 1992, defeating Argentina's Eduardo Romero in a playoff. Thus they became the only father-son duo to win the tournament.

Stadler stood off all comers, including Argentina's Angel Cabrera, with rounds of 69-66-67-72, a six-under-par 274. He won by two over Cabrera, who closed with a 71.

Stadler entered the final round leading Cabrera by three. Kevin birdied the third hole but bogeyed the fourth, while Cabrera caught him with birdies at three of the first six holes. Both bogeyed the ninth and made the turn tied. Then the tough 10th, a par-four of 470 yards, proved to be decisive. Cabrera missed with his second shot and double-bogeyed, while Stadler survived it with a bogey and moved back into the lead. Both birdied the 11th, but Cabrera then staggered to a bogey at the 12th and a double bogey at the 14th.

Cabrera had won the BMW Championship on the European Tour earlier, but that didn't ease his disappointment here. "This was a great year, but I wanted to close it with a victory at this event," he said. "The second place only means that I lost."

# 9. European Tours

Romance and redemption seemed to be everywhere in European golf in 2005, although, as ever, hard luck stories and even controversy could also be found. Pride of place went to Michael Campbell, who started the year with five missed cuts in a row but went on to win the U.S. Open at Pinehurst. More strong finishes in the Open Championship and the U.S. PGA Championship, plus another victory at the HSBC World Match Play deservedly meant Campbell was voted the PGA European Tour Golfer of the Year.

About the only thing Campbell did not win was the Order of Merit, which went — for an astonishing eighth time — to Colin Montgomerie. Other big breakthroughs were achieved by Angel Cabrera, David Howell and Paul McGinley. Then, there were the 13 first-time winners. Some had been waiting for ages, like Stephen Dodd, who won his first title at the end of 2004 in China at the start of the "2005" season and then followed it up by winning the Nissan Irish Open and the World Cup for Wales with Bradley Dredge. Steve Webster, John Bickerton and Emanuele Canonica could all celebrate at last, while Raphael Jacquelin put behind him a string of near-misses, and talented youngsters like Nick Dougherty and Charl Schwartzel started their tally.

Tiger Woods collected the most titles on the PGA European Tour, and got back to major domination at the Masters and the Open Championship as well as winning two of the World Golf Championships. Ernie Els won three titles, including back-to-back wins in Dubai and Qatar, but then injured a knee in a sailing accident in the summer. The rehabilitation took much effort, but by the end of the year Els was back playing, and winning, in South Africa.

Woods's return to major-winning form helped extend the drought of European-born players not having won a major championship since 1999. There were some fine performances — Luke Donald third at the Masters, Sergio Garcia third at the U.S. Open, Montgomerie runner-up to Woods in the Open, and Thomas Bjorn tied for second behind Phil Mickelson at the U.S. PGA Championship — but the win continues to prove elusive.

But Campbell's triumph over Woods at the U.S. Open could genuinely be enjoyed by everyone on the European Tour, not least for restating the case that it is possible to win the game's biggest titles from a base on the east of the Atlantic. Campbell had tried his hand on the PGA Tour in America in the past, but decided to return with his family to their home in Brighton, on the south coast of England. The New Zealander admits to being inconsistent, but when he gets on a roll, watch out. His win at Pinehurst would not have been possible without the United States Golf Association holding a pre-qualifying event for the first time in Europe. Campbell qualified at Walton Heath and changed the course of his season, and career.

Campbell rose 73 places on the World Ranking over the year, from 89th place to 16th, the same rise as Montgomerie, who went from 81st to eighth. The Scot's form had dipped during the break-up of his marriage in 2004, but buoyed by making the winning putt at the Ryder Cup at Oakland Hills, Montgomerie set out determined to regain his place at the top of the game. He could not do so quickly enough to play in The Players Championship or the Masters, but one of his promising results, a fourth place in the Indonesian Open, caused a controversy that would rumble for much of the season.

When play was suspended one evening due to a thunderstorm, Montgomerie faced a tricky chip from the bank at the side of a bunker. He left the course without marking his ball, but the following morning appeared, from television pictures, to have played the shot with a less awkward stance. His playing partners had agreed with the drop at the time and he was also cleared by the tournament director. But a few weeks later, having seen the television footage, Montgomerie donated his prize to charity, although he retained World Ranking and Order of Merit points.

Despite being discussed by the tournament committee of the Tour, with no further action taken, the matter was not quickly forgotten by many of the players. Montgomerie, however, continued to play ever more consistent golf, his rallying from the cut-line to second place at the Smurfit European Open being a timely boost. But his play on Sundays was not proving quite so good, and at St. Andrews he could not catch Woods. At the same venue a few months later, however, he won for the first time in a year and a half.

At the Volvo Masters, Montgomerie needed to stay ahead of Campbell to add another money title to his incredible run of seven in a row from 1993-99. "Winning this is very important. I didn't need this — I wanted it," he said. "It was a tall order, but after the third place in the American Express, I believed I could do it. There were times in the past when it was half expected of me to win this, which is unfair in many ways, so this is very special to me. It was skill and self belief — lots and lots of self belief and commitment in what I was trying to do. I never backed off."

Montgomerie had 13 top-10 finishes in the season, two more than Howell, whose wait for a second victory after six years was ended at the BMW International. He went on to win the HSBC Champions Tournament in China, where he defeated Woods, for the biggest win of his career. Cabrera, at the BMW Championship at Wentworth, achieved the same feat, as did McGinley at the Volvo Masters after a number of close calls, including to Cabrera and Campbell at Wentworth. Patience and hard work were well rewarded this year.

# PGA European Tour

### South African Airways Open—£500,000
Winner: Tim Clark

See African Tours chapter.

### Caltex Masters—US$1,000,000
Winner: Nick Dougherty

See Asia/Japan Tours chapter.

### Heineken Classic—A$2,000,000
Winner: Craig Parry

See Australasian Tour chapter.

### Holden New Zealand Open—NZ$1,500,000
Winner: Niclas Fasth

See Australasian Tour chapter.

### Carlsberg Malaysian Open—US$1,210,000
Winner: Thongchai Jaidee

See Asia/Japan Tours chapter.

### Dubai Desert Classic—€1,692,170
Winner: Ernie Els

Only one eagle was achieved on the par-five finishing hole of the Majlis course at the Emirates Golf Club on the final day of the Dubai Desert Classic. But when it finally came, in the last group of the day, the rare bird gave victory to Ernie Els. The South African teed off on the 18th one behind his playing partner, Miguel Angel Jimenez, and Stephen Dodd, whose birdie ahead of the final pairing took the Welshman into a tie with Jimenez at 18 under par.

Els launched a huge drive that left him with 178 yards over the water to the green. His six-iron shot finished 22 feet away and then the big man rolled in the putt for a magnificent finale. Jimenez was also on the green in two, but his long approach putt came up six feet short, and the Spaniard missed the chance to join Els in a playoff. This was Els's third victory in the tournament, after triumphs in 1994 and 2002, and he became the first man to achieve that feat.

From the first day he found himself in a duel with Jimenez, who also finished runner-up in the event to Colin Montgomerie in 1996. Els opened with a 66 to lead Jimenez and David Howell by a stroke. Jimenez responded with a 65 on Friday to go two ahead of Els, who followed his 68 with a 67 on Saturday to leave himself just one behind Jimenez. An early bogey left the South African two adrift of Jimenez and he never caught up until the drama at the last.

Els closed with 68 for a 19-under-par total of 269, while Jimenez finished with a 70. Dodd was the man to make a strong charge on the final day. After a 65 on the second day, he added a closing 66, the second-best score of the final round. He birdied three times on the front nine, including a monster putt at the seventh, and continued his momentum after the turn. The Welshman made vital par putts of seven feet at the 16th and 12 feet at the 17th before holing another seven-footer for a birdie at the last.

But it was Els who sealed the victory with his stunning eagle at the last. "That putt was right up there with my best," said Els, who won €277,877 for his 19th title on the European Tour.

Jimenez was philosophical in defeat. "It was hard to lose," he said. "It was a nice comeback from Ernie the last two days. But that's the game of golf. Someone has to finish first, second, third and fourth." It was Montgomerie who finished fourth, two behind Jimenez and Dodd after a closing 69.

## Qatar Masters — €1,141,050
Winner: Ernie Els

Ernie Els again made a brilliant comeback to win for the second week in a row and claim the Qatar Masters. Els started the final round five strokes behind Henrik Stenson, but he produced the best score of the week, a 65, just at the right time to win by one stroke.

After his last-ditch eagle to win in Dubai, Els started his week at Doha in leisurely fashion with rounds of 73, 69 and 69. He was at five under par after 54 holes and tied for ninth place, while Stenson topped the leaderboard at 10 under after a 66 in the third round.

With the Shamaal wind increasing throughout the final afternoon, Els made six birdies in the first 12 holes to bear down on the leaders. When he added another birdie at the short par-four 16th, Els suddenly found himself two strokes ahead after Stenson had dropped three strokes in two holes with a bogey at the 13th and a double bogey at the 14th.

With Els in the clubhouse at 12 under par and a total of 276, Stenson rallied with a birdie at the 16th, but his 25-foot effort at the next amazingly stopped on the lip. The tall Swede still needed an eagle at the last to tie, and his chip for a three only just missed, but he had to settle for a 71. "One hundredth of an inch at the 17th cost me the chance of a play-off," Stenson said. "I was certain that putt had to go in." Pierre Fulke and Richard Green tied for third place, three behind Els, while Barry Lane, Robert Karlsson and James Kingston were one further back.

"I wanted to give myself a lower score and as it turned out I shot low, which doesn't normally happen," Els said. "The three birdies on the bounce on the front nine were really big as the wind was beginning to blow at the time. I suppose I got lucky and got the win, but I feel really good. I feel like my game is right there and I can't wait to get to America. The way things are going, I look forward to playing golf."

## TCL Classic—US$1,000,000
Winner: Paul Casey

See Asia/Japan Tours chapter.

## Enjoy Jakarta Standard Chartered Indonesia Open—US$1,000,000
Winner: Thaworn Wiratchant

See Asia/Japan Tours chapter.

## Estoril Open de Portugal Caixa Geral de Depositos—€1,250,000
Winner: Paul Broadhurst

When Paul Broadhurst drove into a bush on the 18th hole at Oitavos, it appeared his late bid to win the Estoril Open de Portugal Caixa Geral de Depositos was at an end. He certainly thought so after he recorded a bogey and reached the clubhouse at 13 under par.

But an extraordinary finale to the tournament had only just begun. Four players had started the final round with a chance of winning. Paul Lawrie led at 11 under par, Barry Lane and Jose-Felipe Lima were at 10 under, and Broadhurst was at nine under. Lima had led at the halfway stage and was the darling of the gallery. Although born and raised in Versailles, near Paris in France, over the winter he had adopted the nationality of his Portuguese parents. He was never quite in contention on the final day, although his chip-in for a birdie three at the last secured him third place.

Broadhurst looked to have dropped out of the race early by dropping two strokes in the first six holes. But from the seventh he played some terrific golf with seven birdies in 11 holes before dropping a shot at the last. After rounds of 68, 66 and 70, his closing 67 left him with a total of 271.

Both Lawrie and Lane went to the turn in 33 and were out in front on their own, the Scot having maintained a one-stroke lead at 14 under par. Then the fun began. The 1999 Open champion dropped a shot at the 12th and then Lane eagled the 13th to go two ahead. But the next hole produced a two-shot swing back again as Lawrie birdied and Lane three-putted. At the 15th Lane pulled away again with a birdie two, but Lawrie's birdie at the par-five 16th saw him draw even again.

But the closing two holes are the hardest on the course and Lawrie was the first to suffer as he ran up a triple-bogey seven at the 17th. Lane also dropped a shot, which left him just one ahead of Broadhurst, before his nightmare came at the 18th. The 44-year-old drove into a bush on the left, squeezed his second across into the bushes on the right, hit his third into some roots and out of bounds, dropped for his fourth, took an unplayable for his fifth, put his sixth in front of the green, after which he chipped and two-putted for a nine.

The quintuple bogey left Lane in fifth place, behind Lima and Richard Sterne, who closed with a 66 for fourth place. Lawrie could still catch Broadhurst, but although he hit his approach at the 18th to eight feet, the birdie putt did not drop. Lawrie closed with 70 for 12 under par.

The incredible afternoon left the 39-year-old Broadhurst with his fifth European Tour title but his first for 10 years. "I was marking my card when we heard that Paul had taken seven and then we saw Barry's ball in the bush at the last," said Broadhurst. "But you still expect Barry to make five, and then I was thinking playoff, but we all saw what happened.

"Early on I was too far back, but then I got a good run going from the seventh, which just about kept me on the verges of the tournament. Obviously, I was relying on Barry or Paul to mess up a hole somewhere along the line. This is probably one of the most surprising days of my career. I feel a lot of sympathy for Barry — you don't wish that on anybody, because I've done it enough myself."

## Madeira Island Open Caixa Geral de Depositos—€600,000
Winner: Robert-Jan Derksen

In 2003 Robert-Jan Derksen held off the challenge of Ernie Els to win the Dubai Desert Classic. The 31-year-old became the first Dutchman to record multiple wins on the European Tour when he added his second title at the Madeira Island Open Caixa Geral de Depositos. Derksen scored rounds of 67, 70, 71 and another 67 to finish with a total of 275.

He began the final round a stroke behind Andrew McLardy and Kyron Sullivan and even with Gary Orr. With Orr playing with the leaders, Derksen was a hole ahead, and on the 18th tee found himself tied for the lead with Orr.

Derksen knew he needed a birdie to put the pressure on and hit his approach to 15 feet before holing the putt to get to the clubhouse at 13 under par. Orr now needed a birdie to tie, but his second shot, having found himself between clubs, came up short and the Scot took three to get down. The bogey meant McLardy shared second place with Orr, while David Higgins and Tom Whitehouse were fourth and fifth respectively. Sullivan finished in a tie for seventh in an event that was co-sanctioned by the European Challenge Tour.

"Obviously I am delighted to have won," said Derksen. "My birdie on the 18th was excellent and really won the tournament for me, because when I was playing the hole I was level with Gary and didn't think he would finish with a bogey, so it was a great birdie.

"I have been coming to Madeira the past eight years and I really like the place. I felt confident and comfortable coming here. I really enjoy the place, so this win means a lot to me. When I was going out for the final round today, I thought that a 68 would be good enough to do it and I shot 67 to win by two, so it seems my prediction was right."

## Jazztel Open de Espana en Andalucia—€1,650,000
Winner: Peter Hanson

Seven years after turning professional Peter Hanson won his first title at the Jazztel Open de Espana en Andalucia. It was a winter practicing on the Costa del Sol in Spain that helped the 27-year-old Swede to victory at San Roque. His first duty as a new champion was to buy dinner for his friend and compatriot Peter Gustafsson, who was defeated in a playoff.

Hanson shared the lead on the opening day after a 70 and then took sole possession with a 68 on Friday. Two 71s on the weekend meant an eight-under-par total of 280, but he was joined at the top by Gustafsson's stunning 66 after starting the final day five strokes behind.

Gustafsson had six birdies on the front nine in equaling the best round of the week to catch Hanson. In the playoff at the 18th hole, both missed the green on the left, hardly surprising with the wind from the left and water waiting on the right. But while Hanson chipped virtually stone-dead, Gustafsson's chip ran 15 feet past and he missed the putt back.

"I was hoping to come out and get a good start and that's what happened," said Gustafsson. "The weather was good at the beginning and I thought I had a chance to win it with eight under in the clubhouse. But Peter played fantastic yesterday and today. I guess he deserves it. At least he will be buying dinner tonight."

Hanson, whose promise as a top amateur took time to show once he turned professional, said: "I am really happy with the way I played today under that pressure, coming out with the lead. I don't think I missed any shots the whole way round. A couple of bad clubs, on the first and fifth, but apart from that it was really good golf.

"This means a lot to me. It is always hard to get your first win and I haven't been in this position of being able to win many times, so to pull it off on my first time feels great."

Hennie Otto was Hanson's nearest challenger overnight and drew even with the Swede thanks to an eagle at the ninth. But the South African dropped out of contention with double bogeys at the 10th and 15th. Otto finished tied with Ireland's Peter Lawrie in third place, three strokes outside the playoff.

## Johnnie Walker Classic—US$2,350,000
Winner: Adam Scott

See Asia/Japan Tours chapter.

## BMW Asian Open—US$1,500,000
Winner: Ernie Els

See Asia/Japan Tours chapter.

## Telecom Italia Open—€1,300,000
Winner: Steve Webster

At the 1995 Open Championship at St. Andrews there were more high-profile non-professionals in the field — Tiger Woods, for one — but it was Steve Webster who took the silver medal as the low amateur. But it took 10 years as a professional for the Englishman to claim his maiden title at the Telecom Italia Open.

There had been some near-misses along the way, with no less than five runner-up finishes, but Webster, helped by a pep talk from none other than Seve Ballesteros, finally found the winning formula with a three-stroke victory at Castello di Tolcinasco in Milan.

After rounds of 68, 68 and 66, Webster had a one-stroke lead over Richard Finch with a round to play, but a closing 68, including four birdies on the second nine, saw the 30-year-old in with an 18-under-par total of 270.

"It is a real tough driving course and I have driven it great for four days," said Webster, "especially on the back nine today when it really mattered. This is like a dream come true. I was concentrating really hard. My mind was racing ahead. I always thought I could win and with nine holes to go I was telling myself you are going to win this. But to make the winning putt with a couple of shots in hand was a great feeling.

"I saw Seve at San Roque last week and he said time was running out for me. Seve has always taken a big interest in my career, he's my hero, still is, and that clicked a bit with me. It was another kick to get me into the winner's circle."

Going into the back nine, Webster was being challenged strongly by Anders Hansen. The Dane closed with 66, but could only share second place with Finch and Bradley Dredge, whose bogey at the 18th further eased the pressure on Webster. Emanuele Canonica scored a final-round 67 to the delight of the local fans to finish in fifth place.

Webster also credited a psychologist, Jamil Qureshi, another of whose clients, Nick Dougherty, won his maiden title earlier in the season. "Jamil and I have had some great sessions this week, an hour every night. It really got me focused and it proved its worth today," Webster said. As well as a check for €216,660, Webster took home his weight in Grana Padano cheese.

## Daily Telegraph Dunlop Masters — €2,532,800
Winner: Thomas Bjorn

From 1996 until 2002, Thomas Bjorn won every year on the European Tour bar one. But his regular visits to the winner's enclosure stopped after his BMW International win in 2002, and although he took the Dunlop Phoenix title in Japan the following year, it was a season marred by his late collapse at the Open Championship at Royal St George's. In 2004, his form dipped so much due to injury and illness that he was only at the Ryder Cup at Oakland Hills as one of European captain Bernhard Langer's helpers.

So it was not surprisingly a delighted and relieved Dane who won the Daily Telegraph Dunlop Masters at the Forest of Arden. But the victory was only secured after two holes of a playoff in which he saw off the challenges of two Englishmen, David Howell and Brian Davis.

With overnight leader Michael Campbell fading with a final round of 73 to finish one stroke outside the playoff, it was Bjorn who set the clubhouse target at six under par. After starting four behind Campbell, an eagle at the 17th hole gave the 34-year-old a closing 68 — after earlier rounds of 73, 68 and 73 — for a total of 282. Davis, tied for second along with Howell and Steve Webster, three behind Campbell overnight, closed with a 69, as did Howell.

But Howell had actually taken the lead with an eagle at the 17th, where he chipped in from off the green, before bunkering himself at the par-three 18th and failing to get up and down for the victory.

In the playoff, the threesome went back to the 18th and this time Howell holed from eight feet after missing the green to match Bjorn's three. Davis, however, also missed the green but was forced out with a bogey four. Once again playing the long par-three for the second extra hole, this time Howell could not get up and down after missing the green for the third time, and Bjorn's three secured the title.

"It's been a long time coming," said Bjorn. "I kept perfectly cool over the whole weekend, and in the end it paid off. I don't think I've been as relaxed as I was over those two playoff holes. It has been a long time and hard work and there have been some tough times since I last won on the European Tour. This was important for me and it is nice to have that feeling again."

For Howell, it was a disappointing end to the week. "All the stuff I have been working on with my swing just didn't stand up to the pressure there at the end," he said. "Simple as that. I got lucky there at the 17th. Poor swing with my second shot and managed to chip it in. Just needed one good swing on the last and just couldn't do it." Webster, in front of his home fans a week after winning his first title, shared fifth place with Simon Khan and Soren Hansen, while Oliver Wilson won a £33,000 Jaguar XJS for being the nearest to the pin on the 18th. His four-iron shot finished a mere one foot, nine inches away from the hole.

## Nissan Irish Open — €2,000,000
Winner: Stephen Dodd

It took Stephen Dodd 10 trips to the qualifying tournament, 11 years and 166 events to win his first PGA European Tour title. It came on the 2005 schedule, but in November 2004, at the Volvo China Open. Eight events later the 38-year-old former British Amateur champion had his second victory. For David Howell, it was a second week of playoff misery in a row.

Dodd won the Nissan Irish Open at the first extra hole after tying with Howell on the new Carton House course designed by Colin Montgomerie. It all came down to the par-five 18th, where, given the identity of the architect, driving was crucial. Even more so as play went on late into the evening after a 90-minute delay for a hailstorm in the afternoon.

In regulation play, Dodd found the green safely and two-putted for a birdie. Howell, however, drove into the rough. But he laid up with his second and hit his third to 14 feet before holing the putt to make the playoff. At the first extra hole, Dodd played the 18th in an identical manner, only for Howell to find the rough with his second shot. He failed to get up and down for one of his more exasperating near-misses since winning his only European Tour title in 1999.

But Dodd had found the magic ingredient for success, even if he was not sure what it was. "I don't really know how it's happened," said Dodd, who won €333,330. "I can't explain it, but after winning I developed more confidence and belief in what I'm doing. I never believed I wasn't good enough — if I didn't think that, I would have stopped a long time ago. As time goes on you're not sure it's going to happen."

Nick Dougherty was the third-round leader by two strokes over Howell and Oliver Wilson. But Dougherty dropped four strokes in four holes after four-putting from the edge of the fifth green for a double bogey. Dodd closed with 68, his birdie at the 15th then putting him two ahead of Dougherty, but a bogey at the 17th dropping him back to a tie with Howell. He set the target at nine under par with a total of 279, which Howell matched with a 70, having eagled the 15th.

Dougherty, after a 74, tied with Angel Cabrera for third place, with Padraig Harrington, Lee Westwood and Nick O'Hern in fifth. There was no repeat success for defending champion Brett Rumford, but the Australian won the use of a private jet for 10,000 miles after winning a side competition for the best aggregate score over the final five holes.

## BMW Championship — €4,000,000
Winner: Angel Cabrera

Angel Cabrera's liking for the West course at Wentworth was already evident when he finished runner-up in the PGA Championship in 2001 and 2004. Still the old PGA and the European Tour's flagship event, but under the new name of the BMW Championship, Cabrera proved himself a worthy champion in 2005.

Cabrera, the 35-year-old from Argentina whose first few seasons in Europe were sponsored by his mentor, Eduardo Romero, claimed his third European Tour victory and the biggest title of his career with a two-stroke victory over Ireland's Paul McGinley. Cabrera is very much the gentle giant, except when he is smashing his drives miles down the fairway. After two opening rounds of 70, Cabrera showed what his power can achieve by waltzing around the West course with scores of 66 and 67 over the weekend.

Cabrera finished with a 15-under-par total of 273 and collected the first prize of €666,660. But it was only late on the final afternoon that he could shake off the determined challenge of McGinley, who matched the winner's closing 67, but fell just short despite edging in front in the middle of the round.

"It was a very tough day and I knew I had to concentrate and did that," said Cabrera. "I played very well and this is a huge victory for me. It's really the best moment of my life, winning the biggest event in Europe after the Open Championship. I was twice very close, and fortunately, this time when I had my chance, I was able to take it."

Cabrera began the day tied for the lead at 10 under par with Sweden's Peter Hedblom, with McGinley and David Howell two strokes behind. In fine conditions, good scoring was possible and Australian Nick O'Hern equaled the course record with a 64 to eventually finish in third place. Howell, the runner-up in playoffs the previous two weeks, had a frustrating day on the greens and a 71 left him in fourth place. Hedblom slipped back to a tie for fifth with Peter Hanson and Marten Olander.

But it was McGinley who made a superb charge with four birdies in a row from the third hole. Cabrera demonstrated his power with an eagle at the fourth, but was soon tied at the top with the Irishman. McGinley added another birdie at the eighth to go in front, but Cabrera drew even at the 11th and they remained tied heading down the closing stretch.

But at the 16th, McGinley, hitting a four iron from the tee, found a fairway bunker and took a bogey. The error, his first dropped shot of the round, was compounded as Cabrera holed from 20 feet to go two ahead. With two par-fives to finish, McGinley was up against it considering the Argentinean's power, and at the 17th it all went wrong when the Dubliner found a nasty lie in the right rough off the tee. He could only pitch back to the fairway, and another bogey took the pressure off his opponent.

One consolation for McGinley was moving into the world's top 50 and earning a place in the U.S. Open at Pinehurst. Colin Montgomerie, who finished tied for 11th, did likewise, but it was a week of distractions for the Scot, as unrest among his fellow professionals over his controversial drop at the Indonesian Open earlier in the year continued to rumble, with one player lambasting him in the press.

But McGinley's mind was on other matters after Darren Clarke's wife Heather, who has been battling cancer, was admitted to the hospital during the week. Clarke withdrew from the tournament, but close friend McGinley became only more determined to succeed. "I wanted to win this for her today," he said in an emotional interview afterwards. "It just wasn't meant to be. I played well, but Angel played better and it was his week. I gave it my best shot, but at the end of the day, it wasn't good enough. All credit to Angel."

## Celtic Manor Wales Open — €2,207,900
Winner: Miguel Angel Jimenez

Miguel Angel Jimenez continued his magnificent winning streak at the Celtic Manor Wales Open. It was his seventh victory in 39 tournaments and came in dramatic fashion as he swept to a course record-equaling 62 on the Roman Road to win by four strokes.

Jimenez's victory, his 13th European Tour title, might have appeared comfortable at the finish, but with nine holes to play more than half a dozen players remained in contention. Italy's Alessandro Tadini led at eight under par with a round to play, but Jimenez was one of four players a stroke behind, along with Jean-Francois Lucquin, Jose Manuel Lara and local hero Ian Woosnam. David Lynn was two behind and five others were a shot further back.

Woosnam chipped in at the first to get the gallery excited, but became frustrated with his putter after missing from four feet and 14 inches in the next few holes. Martin Erlandsson, a Swede without a top-10 finish on the European Tour, made the first move of the day, as Jimenez went to the turn in 33.

But it was the 41-year-old Spaniard's inward half of 29 that swept away the opposition. Birdies at the 13th and 14th holes put him one ahead of Erlandsson, but it was at the 16th that the decisive blow came. Jimenez had 253 yards left for his second shot at the par-five and he hit a three wood onto the green and then holed the putt from 45 feet for an eagle.

A birdie at the last gave him the lowest final-round winning score of the season. "The key was the putting," said Jimenez, who finished with a total of 262, 14 under par. "I hit it very well and only made one mistake when I bogeyed the second. But I hit it very well all day and the birdies came. I'm delighted."

Erlandsson closed with a 63 to tie for second place with Lara, who had a 66. Lucquin finished in fourth place, with Woosnam tied for fifth with Tadini and Joakim Haeggman.

## KLM Open — €1,500,000
Winner: Gonzalo Fernandez-Castano

Like all young players in Spain, Seve Ballesteros was an inspiration for Gonzalo Fernandez-Castano. And like Seve, Fernandez-Castano achieved his first professional victory in the Netherlands. The former business student from Madrid won the KLM Open at Hilversumsche in only his 16th start.

The 24-year-old enjoyed a dramatic opening nine to overtake 54-hole leader Gary Emerson and eventually won by two strokes over the Englishman. Emerson's 63 in the second round had put him on top of the leaderboard, and after rounds of 66, 70 and 66, Fernandez-Castano was one stroke behind alongside Paul Broadhurst.

Fernandez-Castano went into the lead in amazing fashion when he holed a seven iron from 161 yards for an eagle at the third hole. Then he closed out the front nine by holing putts of 40 feet and 25 feet at the eighth and ninth holes to go three ahead. He was four ahead when Emerson chipped in for an eagle himself at the 12th, but a bogey on the 16th from the Englishman signaled the end of his challenge.

Fernandez-Castano closed with a 67 for an 11-under-par total of 269, with Emerson's 70 leaving him at nine under. Broadhurst also had a 70 to finish third, while the home country's Maarten Lafeber tied with Markus Brier for fourth place.

"Just a year ago I was not sure about turning professional," said Fernandez-Castano, a former Spanish Amateur champion who finished eighth at the 2004 qualifying tournament. "I was studying for my degree in business studies and playing amateur golf and I was not sure my game was good enough, but at the end of last year I decided to give it a go. But this win has come quickly, quicker than I thought it would. Today I felt the pressure because there is a big difference to the amateur game, but I stayed focused and I had some good up-and-downs and sank a lot of big putts."

## Aa St. Omer Open — €400,000
Winner: Joakim Backstrom

Joakim Backstrom became the second qualifying school graduate to win on the European Tour in successive weeks at the Aa St. Omer Open. The 27-year-old Swede beat Englishman Paul Dwyer at the first extra playoff hole in an event co-sanctioned by the Challenge Tour and played in the same week as the U.S. Open.

Backstrom, a tall man with a history of spinal problems, earned €66,660 and a one-year exemption on the PGA European Tour. He won with a par in the playoff when Dwyer three-putted. Dwyer hit his approach to 30 feet and then putted up to three feet from the hole. Backstrom had a 20-footer for his birdie, but left the attempt beside the hole for a secure par. Dwyer then pushed his par effort wide.

Dwyer had set the clubhouse target at four under par after a final round of 68. His total of 280 was matched by Backstrom, who responded to a bogey at the 17th with a birdie at the last from 12 feet to tie. Michael Jonzon, Steven Jeppesen and James Heath all shared third place, just a shot outside the playoff, while overnight leaders Ross Fisher and Carl Suneson tied for sixth along with Ben Mason, James Hepworth and Alvaro Salto, all only one more stroke back.

"This means the world to me," Backstrom said. "I have guaranteed starts until the end of 2006 and I can start to plan and play in the really big events. I have been playing the last eight and nine weeks straight, but for a lot of those I have been waiting by the phone to see if I would get into these events because I had a low category. Now I can prepare properly for every event, and I think that's massive in this sport, because you have to use everything you can to your advantage."

## Open de France—€3,500,000
Winner: Jean-Francois Remesy

Having become the first Frenchman to win the Open de France for 35 years in 2004, Jean-Francois Remesy successfully defended the title, but only after a dramatic battle with his compatriot Jean Van de Velde that ended in a playoff. After three years of dealing with knee injuries that could have cut short his career, Van de Velde showed he was back when he shot a 64 in the first round at Le Golf National.

With a round to play, Van de Velde found himself tied for the lead with Remesy and Eduardo Romero, whose early bogeys on the final day took him out of contention and left the stage for a magnificent duel between the French heroes. Even a three-and-a-half-hour delay due to thunderstorms was worth enduring for the gallery before being able to watch their men in action.

Van de Velde started the better, birdieing the first and holing a bunker shot at the second. But Remesy holed from 35 feet at the same hole to stay only one back and drew even with a 25-footer at the sixth. Van de Velde bogeyed the next and Remesy went into the back nine one in front.

But this was a contest in which the momentum kept switching, and Van de Velde birdied the 12th and set up another with two huge blows at the par-five 14th to nose ahead again. At the short 16th, however, he pulled his tee shot, and although he played a great chip, his bogey meant they were even again.

Immediately, though, Remesy dropped a shot at the 17th, so Van de Velde was one ahead at the 18th, a par-five where water runs down the left-hand side and encircles the green. Van de Velde will never escape the images of the Frenchman in the Barry Burn at Carnoustie when he lost the Open Championship and everyone waited nervously for what was to happen next.

While Remesy made a safe par, Van de Velde was in trouble again. He pulled his drive into the water, and although he hit a terrific long iron for his third shot, he made bogey. Both players had scored 69 to finish at 11 under par. At the same hole in the playoff, both players found the fairway before the problems started.

Van de Velde's second shot was pulled long and it went over the green into the water, only for Remesy to come up short in the water with his approach. However, although Remesy was able to hit his next to seven feet, Van de Velde was playing from an awkward spot and could only get into a greenside bunker, leaving Remesy to lift the trophy again.

"This is completely different to last year," said the 41-year-old Remesy, who won €583,330. "It is a shame for Jean, as he also deserved the title, but I am very pleased to win it. Two times in a row is incredible. By the playoff we were both exhausted and it was difficult to really finish that. But I am very happy it was me who won, and it is difficult to realize what has happened."

Van de Velde's only consolation was that he had secured his card after so many years of struggling with injury. "What a day, what a week," he said. "It was fun playing against Jean-Francois. He is a tough competitor. He played really well. Kept the pressure going. He made a little mistake on 17, but I equally made one on 18. Then there was no playoff, we were both done for.

"But the crowd was delighted and so happy, and that is what matters at the end of the day. When was the last time two French guys were playing head to head? It is great for French golf. I am delighted for Jean-Francois. I had a good chance and couldn't close it out, but I am pretty tough with myself. I have to look at it a different way. I haven't been in any position like this in the last three years and haven't been able to play golf the last two, so at least I am playing well, put myself up there, and all I can hope is to have another chance pretty soon. I have a job now."

Soren Hansen took third place with a closing 71, three shots outside the playoff, while Peter O'Malley, Richard Finch and Frenchmen Gregory Havret and Francois Delamontagne tied for fourth.

## Smurfit European Open—€3,482,520
Winner: Kenneth Ferrie

Kenneth Ferrie was the benefactor of an extraordinary series of collapses to win the Smurfit European Open on the Palmer course at The K Club. Ferrie claimed the biggest victory of his career and only his second European Tour title by maintaining his composure while disaster struck all around. Thomas Bjorn was the man most tormented, as his hold on the trophy was ripped away with an 11 on the 17th hole.

Bjorn, who let the 2003 Open slip at Sandwich, walked off the course after only six holes of this tournament in 2004, with his form and confidence at an all-time low, but now appeared set for redemption. In 30 mph winds in the third round, his 69 put the Dane four strokes ahead of the field. It was lashing rain on the last day that made it a miserable experience for some, but water of another kind that sunk Bjorn's hopes.

With four holes to play, Bjorn was at four under par and still a stroke ahead of his playing partner, Raphael Jacquelin. But Bjorn played the last four holes in 10 over par, while Jacquelin went bogey, bogey, double bogey, double bogey. Even after two bogeys at the 15th and 16th, Bjorn was still tied for the lead with Ferrie and Andrew Coltart, whose challenge ended when he four-putted from 12 feet at the 17th for a triple bogey.

Up ahead, Ferrie birdied the par-five 18th to record a closing 70 and set the clubhouse target at three under par with a total of 285. Bjorn may have wasted one of the finishing par-fives when he went in the water at the 16th, but no one could have predicted what was about to happen on the 17th. The River Liffey runs up the left-hand side of the fairway and Bjorn proceeded to put three successive drives into the water. He eventually took a five with his fourth ball to be seven over par on that one hole.

Another bogey followed at the last as the final pairing limped in. "That was the worst day of my golfing life," Bjorn admitted. "I tried to keep it together but it just didn't work out. This was my golf tournament and I had to take it on at the 16th. It was only a four iron and I thought it was the right thing to do. It was a tough day."

Bjorn signed for an 86 and finished tied for 33rd place at six over par. Jacquelin tied for 19th at three over after a 79. Instead, Ferrie won by two strokes over Graeme Storm and Colin Montgomerie, the only other two players to finish under par. Rounds of 70 and 69 had taken Montgomerie from the cut-line to runner-up. Storm closed with a 73. Darren Clarke, whose approach at the last ran over the green but hit a rock and bounced back onto the putting surface, finished as the leading Irishman, in fourth place with Peter Hanson.

But Ferrie, the 26-year-old from the northeast of England, was delighted with his victory. It was his second following his win at the Spanish Open in 2003 and came after he had lost 50 pounds in an effort to trim down his bulky physique.

"I'm really, really pleased," said Ferrie, who earned €577,816. "To win the Spanish Open as your first event on Tour was obviously an achievement, but then to win again and take a step up by winning one of the more prestigious tournaments is fantastic. To beat the quality of guys who were here today and to see the names on the trophy who have won this tournament before, it feels pretty good."

## JP McManus Pro-Am
Winner: Padraig Harrington

Having won twice on the PGA Tour in America, Padraig Harrington added another victory on home soil, albeit an unofficial one in the 36-hole JP McManus Pro-Am at Adare Manor. But Harrington swept away one of the strongest fields ever assembled for such an event with rounds of 63 and 67 for a 14-under-par total of 130. He won by six shots over South African Tim Clark, with Englishmen Luke Donald and Paul Casey in third place.

Richard Green was fifth with Tiger Woods, Ernie Els, Michael Campbell and Angel Cabrera among those sharing sixth place at three under. The event raised over €30 million for local charities in the midwest of Ireland.

## Barclays Scottish Open — €3,564,990
Winner: Tim Clark

Tim Clark followed in the footsteps of his distinguished countrymen Ernie Els and Retief Goosen to become the third South African to win the Barclays Scottish Open at the majesty Loch Lomond course on the banks of the famous loch. Clark had already had two top-five finishes on the course and sealed a two-stroke victory over Darren Clarke and Maarten Lafeber with a birdie at the last.

The 29-year-old from Durban, who received €592,388, had already won the South African Open for a second time earlier in the year and this was his third European Tour title. Clark produced some superb scoring with rounds of 67, 66, 65 and 67 for a 19-under-par total of 265.

Clark began the final round in a tie for the lead with Lafeber, with Angel Cabrera and Alastair Forsyth a shot behind. Irishman Clarke was three back but was four under for the first four holes, including an eagle two at the fourth when he holed out with a wedge from 130 yards. But Clarke was destined to fall short despite a closing 66, as Lafeber pushed Clark in the final group.

The Dutchman made two early birdies to take the lead, but three birdies in an outward 33 put Clark back in front. But the lead switched back and forth over the early part of the back nine with Clark bogeying the 11th and then Lafeber birdieing the 12th. Clark responded with another birdie at the 13th, and when Lafeber three-putted the 15th, his challenge faltered and Clark holed from 25 feet at the last for a grandstand finish.

"I am extremely honored to win the Scottish Open title," Clark said. "I have a couple of South African Opens to my name, but this is right up there with them. I've been third and fifth here and always felt I could play well on this course. My game is as good as it's been for a long time, so I hoped to play well. It's always great to win your home Open, but this is bigger in terms of the quality of the field. I respect this tournament and all the great winners from the past."

Lafeber, who closed with a 69, at least had the consolation of collecting a free pass into the Open Championship as the highest finisher not already exempt. Ian Poulter's 65 took him up into fourth place, while Cabrera shared fifth place with Luke Donald and Nick Dougherty.

## The Open Championship — €5,607,600
Winner: Tiger Woods

See Chapter 4.

# Deutsche Bank Players' Championship of Europe—€3,300,000
Winner: Niclas Fasth

Niclas Fasth, of Sweden, won his second playoff of the year when he beat Angel Cabrera at the third extra hole to win the Deutsche Bank Players' Championship of Europe. At the end of a long final day when 36 holes were required to complete the regulation 72, the pair went on for another three before Fasth birdied the 18th. Such was the difficulty of the closing hole at Gut Kaden that only one birdie had been made there in the entire final round.

No less than 14 players were within two strokes of the lead with nine holes to play, including American John Daly and Germany's hero, Bernhard Langer. But it was Cabrera, already winner of the BMW Championship at Wentworth, who broke free from the crowd with five birdies in eight holes from the 10th. Only a bogey at the 18th put the result in doubt again after the Argentinean had set the clubhouse target at 14 under par.

When Fasth birdied the 13th he was still three behind, but birdies at the 15th and 17th, combined with Cabrera's dropped shot at the last, brought the Swede even. However, he only squeezed into the playoff when he played an exquisite bunker shot at the 18th, allowing him to tap in for a par when a bogey looked likely. Fasth, the halfway leader who had slipped three behind Bradley Dredge with a round to play, closed with a 68 to Cabrera's 67 to tie at 274.

Daly, with a closing 65, along with his 64 in the second round, left himself in third place with Stephen Gallacher, two shots outside the playoff, while Dredge finished one further back with Langer, Graeme Storm and Peter Lawrie.

Fasth and Cabrera halved the first two playoff holes in pars, but playing the 18th once again, they both produced terrific approaches to around 12 feet. But after Cabrera missed his chance, Fasth rolled in his to secure his second title of the year after taking the New Zealand Open.

"It is by far the biggest win of my career," said Fasth, who won €550,000 for his third European Tour title. "I thrive on the pressure like I did in the Ryder Cup — it seems to bring out the best in me. I knew I had to pick up some shots in the closing holes, but there are chances there and I managed to hole a few putts. We both played very well in the playoff and I just managed to win it third time around. The putt was a downhill left to right, and I said to my caddie it was exactly the same putt as I holed to win in New Zealand. It was perfect.

"It feels fantastic, of course. This is one of the big ones, and to get this is worth a lot to me. It's the first really big tournament I've won, and you do feel like you have to prove yourself. I won a couple of smaller events. A win is a win, it's great, but this is really, really big. It feels great."

# Scandinavian Masters—€1,600,000
Winner: Mark Hensby

On his first visit to continental Europe, Mark Hensby survived a thrilling duel with a young Swede playing on home turf to win the Scandinavian

Masters at Kungsangen. Hensby won in a playoff and knew exactly the task before him after playing with Stenson for the first three days. But he at least had one local on his side after securing the services of Nick Faldo's caddie, Fanny Sunesson, for the week. "As we were walking back for the playoff she said to me: 'We're either going to make a lot of Swedes happy or I'm going to be the only happy Swede in the place!'" Hensby revealed.

It was the second victory of Hensby's career after he won the John Deere Classic on the PGA Tour in 2004. After staying on after the Open Championship to play on an invitation in Stockholm, Hensby was in impressive form with rounds of 65, 68, 64 and 65 for a 22-under-par total of 262. But Stenson, the runner-up to Luke Donald the year before, matched the Australian over the weekend. Both had started the final round two strokes behind the overnight leaders, Bradley Dredge and Barry Lane. But Dredge finished tied for third, three strokes outside the playoff, along with Marc Cayeux, who came home in 28 strokes, while Lane dropped back to seventh.

Stenson went to the top of the leaderboard when he played the front nine in three under. But it was his eagle at the 17th that looked decisive when he holed from 25 feet. Hensby had other ideas, however, and he holed from 30 feet for a birdie at the last to keep the pressure on Stenson, who required a stunning bunker shot at the 18th to make the playoff.

After the first extra hole was halved, Stenson was the one to submit as he three-putted on the next, missing his par effort from six feet to stay alive. "Obviously it was his day and not mine," said Stenson. "I was tied second and now second on my own, so at least I'm moving in the right direction."

Getting in the playoff was the key to the winner. "When you know you've got a putt for a playoff, you've kind of got a free shot, and I hit a great putt, but you need a bit of luck for it to go in," said the 34-year-old from Melbourne. "I played with Henrik for the first three days and I knew what a great player he was, so I knew I needed something special."

## Johnnie Walker Championship at Gleneagles—€2,076,061
Winner: Emanuele Canonica

Emanuele Canonica has always been able to hit the ball a long way despite his frame of five feet, four inches. At the Catalan Open one year in Spain he hit a drive measured at 475 yards, albeit downwind and downhill. But by 2004, without a victory, he was thinking of giving up the game but was talked out of it by family and friends, including a number of leading Italian football players.

His decision to carry on was rewarded at Gleneagles when he won the Johnnie Walker Championship by two strokes over Bradley Dredge, David Lynn, Barry Lane and Nicolas Colsaerts. The triumph ended a 14-year wait for a win on the European Tour and earned the 34-year-old from Turin a check for €338,442. "It feels great," said Canonica. "I waited a long time, over 10 years, and came close a couple of times, but now I have reached my dream."

For once, Canonica did not need his driver around the tight PGA Centenary Course, but he produced a superb display with his long irons. Rounds of 70, 71, 69 and 71 gave him a seven-under total of 281. Colsaerts, a 22-year-old from Belgium, was the third-round leader, with Canonica two behind, but his challenge faded with three consecutive bogeys from the 13th.

Canonica only just cleared the water with his second shot at the par-five 16th, but having done so, a birdie there put him two clear. "The key was to stay calm and play the normal game," said the Italian. "I played great and putted so-so. I missed a couple, but made a very good birdie on the 16th, and this gave me confidence. Two shots ahead with two to play and one of them is a par-five. I thought maybe I had a chance to win."

## Cadillac Russian Open — €405,615
Winner: Mikael Lundberg

With the Cadillac Russian Open co-sanctioned with the Challenge Tour, Mikael Lundberg took the opportunity to get back on the main circuit with a four-hole playoff victory over England's Andrew Butterfield. Lundberg lost his card for the PGA European Tour after three years in 2003 after struggling with a pull-hook ever since 2001. The problem persisted until the eve of the Scandinavian Masters when he suddenly solved the problem in a "Eureka moment," as the 32-year-old Swede described it.

A few weeks later everything came right at Le Meridien Moscow Country Club. Lundberg took the lead after rounds of 67, 68 and 69, but on the final day he was put under pressure by a magnificent charge from Butterfield, another Challenge Tour player. Starting three strokes off the lead, Butterfield came home in 30 to set the target at 15 under par.

Lundberg came to the 18th needing a birdie to win, but drove into a bunker. However, a great second shot gave him a chance from five feet but he missed the putt. A final round of 69, compared to Butterfield's 66, gave the Swede a total of 273. The pair finished three clear of David Drysdale and Jarrod Moseley in third place, with Fredrik Widmark finishing in fifth.

For the first three extra holes, the pair played the 18th, and it was Butterfield who missed the best chance to win on the second occasion when he missed from three feet to match Lundberg's bogey. For the fourth extra hole they moved to the par-five 17th and here a terrific three-wood shot from Lundberg put him on the green, 30 feet from the hole. Butterfield missed the green on the left and chipped awkwardly, the ball rolling 40 feet past the hole. Although he very nearly sank the birdie putt, his par meant Lundberg had two for the title, and he lagged up his first putt so that he only needed to tap in for victory.

"This is incredible, a dream come true," said Lundberg. "I came out today and tried to stick to my game plan, which I did. I played quite safe, especially after 12 holes when I had a couple of shots advantage, but then Andrew played some great golf to catch up with me. But I am just very happy to have come through the playoff. Having my European Tour card is a great feeling — not only for me, but for my whole family. It feels fantastic."

## BMW International Open — €2,000,000
Winner: David Howell

After losing two playoffs in consecutive weeks, David Howell's season got worse when he picked up Vijay Singh's heavy practice club on the driving range during the U.S. Open. Howell took a few swings and then had to pull out of the event, having torn abdominal muscles. It was almost two months before the 30-year-old Englishman could return to tournament action, but in only his third week back he won the BMW International at Munchen Nord-Eichenried.

It was a sweet victory for Howell, not just because of what had been a disappointing season to date, but because it ended a wait of over six years for his second win following his maiden triumph at the Dubai Desert Classic in 1999. "I've become very, very consistent in Europe, but I had a very bare trophy cabinet, so it's nice I've finally got a bit of silverware to put in it," said Howell, part of Europe's winning Ryder Cup team in 2004 at Oakland Hills. "The next 10 years of my life are going to be the best 10 years, and this has made me look forward to bigger and better things."

Howell began the final round a stroke behind Luke Donald, his playing partner, who slipped back outside the top 10. Howell suffered an early bogey but then compiled eight birdies for a closing 65. Following rounds of 66, 68 and 66, he posted a 23-under-par total of 265. It was a superb putting display as he holed a 45-footer on the 10th to go ahead for the first time, a 30-footer on the 14th to maintain his advantage and a vital par-save at the 16th, which gave him a heart murmur by looping around the entire lip of the cup.

At the last he only needed two putts to win and managed it safely. "I just told myself I was the best putter in the world and went for it on the greens," Howell said. He won by one stroke over John Daly and Brett Rumford, who closed with rounds of 64 and 65 respectively.

Daly, the winner of the tournament in 2001, almost pulled off a repeat victory, but missed a birdie putt from six feet at the 18th which would have put Howell under more pressure. "I misread the putt at the end," Daly said. "But after not firing on Thursday and Friday, my weekend has been phenomenal, a bit like four years ago."

## Omega European Masters — €1,700,000
Winner: Sergio Garcia

Ever since Sergio Garcia bought a home in the beautiful mountain village of Crans-sur-Sierre in Switzerland, he became keen to win the European Tour event that is an annual visitor to the town. In 2004 he was denied only by the man he was putting up as a house guest for the week, Luke Donald. Donald's victory did not mean he had to alter his accommodation plans for the week — although he was not sure if winning again would do his chances of being invited back once more any good — but it did provide Garcia with extra motivation.

Garcia duly went on to win the Omega European Masters for the first time by one stroke over Sweden's Peter Gustafsson. Donald was involved again, but whatever he did, Garcia trumped it. In the third round, Donald holed a wedge shot from the fairway for an eagle at the 17th. Garcia then holed his own wedge shot at the 18th from 111 yards for an eagle two, which vaulted him from one behind Welshman Garry Houston to one in front.

Garcia was otherwise untidy on Saturday, but on Sunday he remained in control after an outward half of 32. A closing 68, following rounds of 66, 65 and 71, gave him a total of 270, 14 under par, and the check for €283,330. Gustafsson made a terrific charge with a round of 64, but came up one short. Paul Casey also came into contention with a closing 66 to finish in third place, two behind Garcia, while Houston and Donald tied for fourth with scores of 70 and 69 respectively.

Garcia chipped in from 22 feet for a birdie two at the 16th and parred the last two holes to seal his second win of the year. He also won the Booz Allen Classic in America. "I am very pleased to have my second win of the season and to start the Ryder Cup qualifying this way," said the 25-year-old Spaniard. "I couldn't have done any better. My game wasn't as sharp as usual on the back nine, but I hung in well and came through."

It was an emotional weekend for Garcia after the death of a close friend, and amateur golfer, Maria Garcia Estrada, from cancer. "I guess Maria was watching me from the sky," he said. "She has been fighting cancer for about eight months and unfortunately she couldn't handle it any more. She was a lovely, caring person and it's such a shame that she's gone."

## Linde German Masters — €3,000,000
Winner: Retief Goosen

Retief Goosen gave himself a quite a fright when he found water on the final hole, but steeled his nerve to complete a one-stroke victory in the Linde German Masters at Gut Larchenhof. Goosen was two ahead standing on the 18th tee, but pulled his three-wood shot into the hazard that runs along the left-hand side of the fairway.

His ball was just about playable on the edge of the lake, but he decided to take a penalty drop and proceeded to hit a marvelous nine-iron shot to six feet. He missed the par putt, but by limiting the damage to a bogey, he claimed victory ahead of David Lynn, Nick Dougherty, Jose Maria Olazabal and Henrik Stenson. Olazabal and Lynn had already set the clubhouse target at 19 under par, after rounds of 66 and 67 respectively, while Stenson and Dougherty, in the group behind Goosen, had the chance to tie but could not make the birdies they required.

Goosen's rounds of 67, 68, 66 and 67 for a total of 268 gave the South African his second victory in two weeks, as he had just won the Volks-wagen Masters in China. It was his 12th European Tour title and was also his third win of the year after taking The International title in the United States. He began the final round in a four-way tie for the lead with Stenson, Dougherty and Anthony Wall. Stenson and Dougherty both closed with 68s, while Wall had a 70.

Three birdies in the first five holes from Lynn put the Englishman briefly in front, while Goosen's round did not get off to the most positive start when he took a double-bogey six at the second hole. But he responded with eight birdies in the next 13 holes and appeared to be cruising to victory, and the €500,000 first prize, until the hiccup at the last.

"The breeze was a little bit off the right, but not too much, and I just felt like hitting a solid three wood down the left side, which was the right club, but I just pulled it," Goosen said. "As soon as I saw it flying through the air I knew it was in the water. There was a slight chance that I could have played it, but where I had to drop it, the rough wasn't very thick and I knew I could get onto the green in three shots. I dropped it perfectly and hit a perfect nine iron.

"I have come to Germany so many years now and not done any good. To finally win one here is great. I have never done well in the past around this golf course either, but this week the weather was great and my putter got hot and I holed a lot of putts."

## HSBC World Match Play—£2,440,000
Winner: Michael Campbell

See Chapter 7.

## Seve Trophy—€2,000,000
Winner: Great Britain and Ireland

Colin Montgomerie led Great Britain and Ireland to their successive third victory in the Seve Trophy with a stunning comeback at the Wynyard Club in the northeast of England. A winning margin of 16½-11½ looked extremely unlikely after Continental Europe won the first session, 4-1.

With five fourballs played on each of the first two days, Jose Maria Olazabal, standing in for the injured Seve Ballesteros as the Continental team captain, was delighted to take such an advantage on the first day. But the home team won each of the remaining four sessions. They took the second-day fourballs 3-1, won the greensomes on day three by the same score to draw even overall, and edged ahead by a point with a 2½-1½ win in the foursomes on Saturday afternoon.

But it was in the singles that Great Britain and Ireland dominated, taking the session 7-3. Their only losers were Montgomerie, to opposing captain Olazabal in a repeat of their 1984 Amateur Championship final, and Padraig Harrington to Emanuele Canonica. David Howell set the tone with a convincing 6-and-5 win over Thomas Bjorn, while Paul Casey defeated Niclas Fasth 4 and 3.

Both Howell and Casey finished with the event's best records with four wins and one defeat, while Henrik Stenson impressed with three wins and two halves for Europe. Graeme McDowell defeated Maarten Lafeber 6 and 5, but it was two Welshmen who sealed the triumph, with Stephen Dodd beating Jean-Francois Remesy 2 and 1 and Bradley Dredge defeating Thomas Levet by the same score.

Europe won the first Seve Trophy at Sunningdale in 2000, but Great Britain and Ireland have won ever since, in 2002 and 2003 as well as in 2005. "I'm delighted, especially coming back the way we did," said Montgomerie. "To win the singles 7-3 was a real team effort.

"Everyone got at least a point and contributed to a wonderful victory. The matches were very close and we did very well, very well indeed, and I'm very, very proud of the team." Montgomerie believed the experience will be repeated for some of his players by stepping up to the Ryder Cup against the United States in Ireland next year. "I expect many of this team can look forward to playing at The K Club," he said.

Olazabal's defeat of Montgomerie in the first match, 2 and 1, was his only consolation. "I'm proud of the team," said Olazabal. "The Britain and Ireland team made a lot of putts. I expected each match to be much closer, but next time the boys are going to work their socks off and the rookies have learned a lot from this week."

## Dunhill Links Championship—€3,974,490
Winner: Colin Montgomerie

Ever since the break-up of his marriage in 2004, Colin Montgomerie kept telling himself that his next victory would be the most important of his career. It did not quite happen at St. Andrews during the Open Championship when the Scot could not overhaul Tiger Woods, but on another Sunday on the Old Course, three months later, Montgomerie achieved his much-desired win.

It came in the Dunhill Links Championship and after an enthralling, if not always perfect, final round in cold, blustery conditions. Eventually, Montgomerie holed a three-foot putt for birdie at the 18th for a one-stroke victory over Kenneth Ferrie. Monty made up a five-stroke deficit with a closing 71, for a nine-under-par total of 279, while Ferrie struggled home with a 77. Padraig Harrington, Henrik Stenson, Robert Karlsson and Anders Hansen shared third place a stroke further back.

It was Montgomerie's second victory in Scotland after his win at Loch Lomond in 1999, and the 36th of his career. He won a huge prize of €662,415, putting the Scot in the running for a record eighth Order of Merit title, but this win was all about the accomplishment, not the accoutrements, for the 42-year-old.

"I said the next win would be the most important of my career, and it is, so this is the most important win of my career," said Montgomerie. "The seven Orders of Merit just kept rolling along. It wasn't, I wouldn't say it was easy, but it was expected. And then it stops. And then my life changed dramatically a couple of years ago, and I always said to myself, the next win would be the most influential and the most important of my career, and this is it. And especially being here at St. Andrews."

After opening the tournament with scores of 70 at Carnoustie, 65 at St. Andrews and 73 at Kingsbarns, Montgomerie was still five strokes behind Ferrie, in second place with Stenson and Ricardo Gonzalez. But he was playing alongside Ferrie, who had been disappointed not to make Montgomerie's Great Britain and Ireland team for the Seve Trophy that was played near Ferrie's home in northeast England. Monty birdied the second hole, the fifth and the ninth to be out in 33, and this was enough to draw even with Ferrie after the leader dropped three strokes at the sixth and seventh.

But Monty himself dropped three strokes in two holes at the 11th and 12th, the area of the course where his challenge faltered in the Open. Here he was helped by Ferrie bogeying the 13th, 15th and 16th holes. Even again, both parred the Road Hole, where Montgomerie hit a terrific eight-iron shot from the left rough over the famous bunker onto the green, allowing him to steal victory at the last.

Ferrie, the European Open winner, said: "To have been five in front and then Colin to just shoot 71 to win is pretty poor. Colin did play pretty poor, but I needed to shoot 75 to win basically, and to not do that after playing so well all week... All the little breaks that I have been getting all week and that had gone my way seemed to go against me today, so it's just one of those days that is very disappointing.

"I feel that I let him win. I could have put more pressure on him when I had a chance. I got back to three ahead after 13, but then made silly bogeys all the way in. It's my own fault — I have got nobody to blame but myself."

## Abama Open de Canarias — €450,000
Winner: John Bickerton

After five second-place finishes and 287 events, England's John Bickerton finally made his winning breakthrough on the PGA European Tour with a superb five-stroke victory in the Abama Open de Canarias. Bickerton extended his narrow one-stroke overnight lead with a final round of 68 over the spectacular Abama course in Tenerife to finish at 10-under-par 274, five clear of fellow Englishman Stuart Little and South African Michael Kirk.

It was a timely win for the 35-year-old, who had been on tour since 1995, because he went into the week in 118th place on the Order of Merit, with only the top 116 retaining their cards. Instead of a struggle in the remaining events of the season, Bickerton could relax after receiving an exemption for 2006 thanks to his win in the co-sponsored Challenge Tour and main circuit event.

Bickerton soon pulled clear of the field with three birdies in his first 10 holes. He dropped a shot on the 12th, but made sure of victory with a fourth birdie on the 13th before parring in. "Finally," he sighed afterwards. "It feels fantastic, awesome. It's been a long time coming and I've been very worried about my place on tour. It's your career, your future lies on this game and a few quid makes such a difference. I moved down five spots last week, but it made me more determined and it's nice to pull it off under pressure."

Playing in his 500th event, Mark Roe also secured his card for 2006 by finishing tied for fourth with Marc Warren and Johan Axgren, his best finish for four years. "That was hard work," he said. "It's pleasant on reflection, but not when you are doing it. It does not get any easier the older you get."

## Open de Madrid — €1,000,000
Winner: Raphael Jacquelin

Raphael Jacquelin finally found out what it is like to be sprayed with champagne on the 18th green after achieving his maiden victory in the Open de Madrid. The traditional salute from his fellow French players came after a three-stroke victory over Paul Lawrie at Club de Campo. It was a well-deserved victory for the 31-year-old from Lyon and came in his 238th event and after four runner-up finishes. He was also the 13th first-time winner of the season.

The victory was set up by his magnificent play in the earlier rounds when he recorded three 64s. The first left him one stroke off the lead; the second put him three shots ahead; and the third meant he took a seven-stroke advantage over Darren Clarke and Jose-Filipe Lima into the final day.

Lawrie, the 1999 Open champion, began the day eight strokes behind and made a charge at the Frenchmen with a brilliant 64. But he could never get closer than three strokes to Jacquelin, whose closing 69 meant he finished with a total of 261, 23 under par.

"It's just fantastic," said Jacquelin, who won €166,660. "I have waited so long for this. It was tough when Paul started to get close, but I knew if could get some birdies on the back nine I could hang on." Two birdies coming home were enough, and it turned out there was more to celebrate. "My wife Fanny and I are expecting our second baby very soon, so this is a good present," he said.

Lawrie said: "Someone had to have a go, but Raphael had to make a few mistakes for me to have any chance, so good luck to him. He was so far ahead, second place seems like winning."

## Mallorca Classic — €1,500,000
Winner: Jose Maria Olazabal

Jose Maria Olazabal had a definite advantage at the Mallorca Classic because he is currently working on a three-year redesign of the Pula course. But it is one thing to have an intimate knowledge of a layout, and another to produce winning golf upon it, but that is exactly what Olazabal did. The 39-year-old Spaniard won by five strokes over Sergio Garcia, the 2004 winner, Jose Manuel Lara and Paul Broadhurst.

Winning made up for his late collapse in 2003 when he handed the title to Miguel Angel Jimenez. It also meant the third Spanish winner in the three years of the event. Olazabal was only one ahead of the field with a round to play, but played a superb front nine of 31 to go ahead by four strokes. Two holes later he was six in front and cruising to victory.

"It is a very special victory and the last three holes were very emotional," said Olazabal. "I am very happy because it happened on a course I've been involved with. I've been climbing the world rankings again by working hard and this is the result. I'm moving in the right direction. It would be nice to get back into the Ryder Cup team."

Olazabal missed out on playing in the match in 2002 and 2004, but his victory was reward for his hard work on his driving over the season. It was his first win since the 2002 Buick Invitational, while his 23rd European Tour title was his first for almost four years. He recorded rounds of 69, 65, 70 and 66 for a 10-under-par total of 270.

The other order of business in the last full-field event of the season was who would secure their cards for 2006 from finishing in the top 116 on the Order of Merit. Spain's Miguel Angel Martin moved up from 117th to 112th by finishing with a 68 for 27th place, while England's Sam Little snuck into 116th place by saving par from a bunker at the last hole.

## Volvo Masters — €3,928,500
Winner: Paul McGinley

Colin Montgomerie and Paul McGinley both got what they wanted at the Volvo Masters. Montgomerie appeared ready to seal his eighth Order of Merit title in the grand manner by winning at Valderrama, but for once he was less concerned with not claiming the tournament title, as McGinley completed a brilliant comeback to capture the biggest victory of his career.

McGinley's season was littered with chances to win some of the season's more impressive titles. He was second at both the BMW Championship and the HSBC World Match Play, a loss at Wentworth he described as "devastating," and third at the NEC Invitational. His redemption came at the last time of asking, but only after a slow start to the tournament.

The 38-year-old Irishman had a double bogey and triple bogey in his first seven holes before rallying for a 74 on the first day. When he bogeyed the first hole in the second round, he was four over par, but from that moment onwards he did not drop a shot over 53 holes of the demanding Valderrama layout. At the halfway stage, however, he was still nine strokes behind Montgomerie, who was determined to lead from the front in his battle with Michael Campbell for the Order of Merit title.

Montgomerie opened with a 67 to Campbell's 72, which always left the U.S. Open champion with too much to do to overtake the Scot. Monty added a 66 on Friday and at one point on Saturday was six strokes ahead of the field. But three birdies over the closing holes from Sergio Garcia and three dropped shots from Montgomerie, including a double bogey at the notorious 17th hole, meant that Garcia and Montgomerie would share the 54-hole lead.

McGinley, with rounds of 68 and 65 on Friday and Saturday, had hauled himself up to a tie for third place, four strokes behind, with Lee Westwood, Paul Broadhurst and defending champion Ian Poulter. Playing in the last group together, Montgomerie and Garcia simply did not fire on Sunday. Montgomerie double-bogeyed the seventh to be out in three over, while Garcia went to the turn in two over.

Birdies at the fourth, seventh and 10th holes put McGinley into the lead, and he kept a steely nerve to stay in front over the back nine. Coming to the par-five 17th he was two ahead, but knew he needed to get past the potential disasters that lurk at the infamous hole. Instead of going for the green in two, McGinley laid up short of the water and left himself a pitch from 112 yards. It still needed to be played precisely to avoid spinning back into the water or going into the back bunker. He did neither, leaving himself a 10-footer for a birdie that he duly sank to secure victory.

A closing 67 gave him a total of 274, 10 under par and equal to Montgomerie's tournament record. He won by two strokes over Garcia, the runner-up for the second year running, after a 73. Montgomerie finished with 74 to tie for third place with Jose Maria Olazabal and Luke Donald. With Campbell finishing in 14th place, Montgomerie could celebrate his own triumph. "I didn't need this, I just wanted it," said Montgomerie on being presented with the Harry Vardon Trophy.

McGinley won €666,660 to finish third on the Order of Merit after waiting four years for his fourth European Tour win. It was also four years since he had lost a narrow battle with Padraig Harrington for the Volvo Masters title at Montecastillo. "I was very close to winning three huge titles this year and it didn't happen for one reason or another," McGinley said. "This one means a huge, huge amount to me. I am proud to have won here, competing against the top 60 players on the European Tour.

"Those losses really, really hurt me, but I learned from them. I felt I would win a big one because of the quality of my golf. The difference is mental. I had to move up mentally to the level my game is at."

## HSBC Champions Tournament—US$5,000,000
Winner: David Howell

See Asia/Japan Tours chapter.

## WGC - Algarve World Cup in Portugal—US$4,000,000
Winners: Stephen Dodd and Bradley Dredge

Stephen Dodd and Bradley Dredge followed in the footsteps of Ian Woosnam and David Llewellyn from 1987 by winning the World Cup for Wales at the Victoria club in Vilamoura on the Portuguese Algarve. Torrential rain and thunderstorms washed out the final round, so the Welsh pair owed their triumph to their second fourball round of 61 on the third day. They had also completed a foursomes score of 67 on Friday to give them a 27-under-par total of 189 for the three rounds.

"It was the best rain I've ever watched," joked Dodd as he sheltered in the clubhouse. "It would have been nice to have won over four days, but we'll take winning over three days." Wales won by two strokes over England's David Howell and Luke Donald and the Swedish pairing of Henrik Stenson and Niclas Fasth. France's Raphael Jacquelin and Thomas Levet finished in fourth place.

"This means the world to us," said Dredge. "Wales haven't won it since 1987, so for Stephen and I to repeat what Ian Woosnam and David Llewellyn did, is obviously huge for us and for golf in Wales. It's fantastic. We had a picture of Ian and David with the World Cup in our clubhouse at Bryn Meadows, where I played golf as a young man, and I've always said one day that might be me."

Dredge's only previous victory came at the Madeira Island Open in 2003, but for the 39-year-old Dodd, it was his third title in the season of his career, having won at the Volvo China Open and the Nissan Irish Open. They went in front at the short par-four 15th in the third, and what turned out to be the final, round when Dredge drove the green and holed the putt from 35 feet.

But Dredge found water at both the last two holes, so Dodd was on his own. He was up to the task as he hit a superb three wood over the water to set up a birdie at the par-five 17th and then parred the last. "It was a great team effort," said the 32-year-old Dredge. "Stephen had a lot of pressure on him and came through."

Donald, who had won the title with Paul Casey the year before in Seville, compiled a 59 in the first of the fourball rounds, but slipped back with a 69 in foursomes before a 63 on Saturday. "Obviously, it's disappointing not to get a chance today, but that's the way the cookie crumbles," said Donald. "I've benefited from the weather in the past and you just have to accept what happens."

Sweden had rounds of 61 and 63 in the fourballs and 67 in foursomes, while Argentina's Ricardo Gonzalez and Angel Cabrera, who finished tied for sixth, shot a 61 in the foursomes but relatively disappointing rounds of 68 and 67 in the fourballs.


## Volvo China Open—US$1,300,000
Winner: Paul Casey

See Asia/Japan Tours chapter.


## UBS Hong Kong Open—US$1,200,000
Winner: Colin Montgomerie

See Asia/Japan Tours chapter.


## Dunhill Championship—€1,000,000
Winner: Ernie Els

See African Tours chapter.


## South African Airways Open—€1,000,000
Winner: Retief Goosen

See African Tours chapter.

# Challenge Tour

Marc Warren holed the winning putt for Great Britain and Ireland at the Walker Cup at Sea Island in 2001. After turning professional, the Scot took his time to come through the ranks, but after getting onto the Challenge Tour in 2005, he never looked back. Warren, 24, won the Ireland Ryder Cup Challenge and, a few weeks later, the Rolex Trophy in Geneva. With three other top-four finishes, Warren deservedly finished top of the Order of Merit with €103,576.

But he only did so by a mere €448 over Spain's Carl Suneson, who won the season-ending Apulia San Domenico Grand Final in Italy. "It's an amazing feeling to be the best player on the Challenge Tour considering the amount of good players there are out here. It's a tremendous feeling and I didn't think it was possible six months ago," he smiled.

Suneson had not won since his three victories on the Challenge Tour in 1999, when he topped the Order of Merit. He had not been on the main circuit since 2002, so was delighted to get his card back. A four-foot par putt at the last hole gave him victory by one stroke over Warren and Argentina's Daniel Vancsik, who finished ninth on the money list.

"I can't describe what this feels like or means to me," said Suneson. "I wouldn't wish that final putt I had on anyone, but I made it, and it's awesome to be going back to the European Tour, because it has been a long hard battle for me to get back up to that level and hopefully I can stay there for years to come."

Other than Warren, three other players won twice. The unluckiest was American Brad Sutterfield, who won the TIM Peru Open in December 2004 and the Open de Toulouse. But in the Grand Final, despite four birdies in the last six holes, he was edged out of the top 20 on the Order of Merit by Stephen Browne and Finland's Toni Karajalainen, dropping from 19th to 21st place. Only the top 20 players earned cards for the main PGA European Tour. Browne, from Ireland, made history by winning the first event ever played in Kazakhstan.

Sweden's Fredrik Widmark won the Rui Tikida Hotels Moroccan Classic and the Texbond Open in Italy to finish third on the money list to qualify from the Challenge Tour as he did in 2002. The other two-time winner was Rafael Gomez, who won the Albierto Mexicano de Golf and the Tessali-Metaponto Open titles. The 38-year-old Argentinean only started playing the game at the age of 22, having previously just caddied at his local club, but twice won the Tour de las Americas Order of Merit.

Two Swedes, Joakim Backstrom and Mikael Lundberg, both won immediate exemptions for the main tour with their victories in the Aa St. Omer Open and the Cadillac Russian Open respectively.

England's Tom Whitehouse, who finished 17th on the Order of Merit, went on to win the qualifying tournament with a 13-under-par score and by two strokes over countryman Robert Rock. Those finishing 16th-20th on the Challenge Tour are ranked below the leading qualifying spots, so Whitehouse's outstanding effort meant he improved his exemption category.

# 10. Asia/Japan Tours

Without overwhelming fanfare, Shingo Katayama has established himself as Japan's leading player of the 21st century. The dashing Katayama, he of the unique cowboy hats, added another layer of gloss to his growing reputation on the Japan Tour when, despite some nagging back aches that limited him to playing in 21 of the 2005 season's 29 events, he became the circuit's No. 1 player as leading money winner for the third time since the turn of the century. Significantly, the 32-year-old joined the hallowed Isao Aoki, Masashi (Jumbo) Ozaki and Tsuneyuki (Tommy) Nakajima as the fourth man in modern times to have led the tour at least three times.

Notably, too, he finished second (2001), third (2002) and fourth (2003) at the end of the seasons that he didn't wind up on top of the list and now has 18 titles on his record. Just as in 2004, Katayama acquired the No. 1 position even though winning just twice — his first Japan Open Championship and the ABC Championship — in a season during which six other players scored two victories apiece but, as in 2004, nobody won more often.

Another 32-year-old wound up the season in the runner-up position on the money list. Yasuhiro Imano, who had won just four times during his first nine seasons on the Japan Tour, took over the No. 2 spot when he won his second tournament of the year in the Nippon Series finale. Double winners occupied the next three positions — Keiichiro Fukabori (Sun Chlorella and ANA), South Korea's S.K. Ho (Japan PGA Championship, a repeat, and JCB Classic Sendai) and New Zealand's David Smail (Acom International and Bridgestone Open). The veteran Naomichi (Joe) Ozaki resurrected memories of his earlier glory days when he won two of the season's first three tournaments — Tsuruya Open and Chunichi Crowns — but did little after that, played in just 19 events and finished 18th on the money list.

Tadahiro Takayama was the other dual victor, but the second one was in the Okinawa Open event that is officially the opening event on the 2006 Japan and Asia Tours. Takayama also was one of eight first-timers among the 22 different winners of 2005. Two of the others — Chang Ik-je (South Korea) and Chris Campbell (Australia) — were rookies among the seven non-Japanese winners of the year.

The most notable of the wins by overseas players were the back-to-back victories in Japan's rich and prestigious fall events. Darren Clarke and Tiger Woods both repeated 2004 triumphs in the Taiheiyo Masters and the Dunlop Phoenix. It was Clarke's only victory of the season, but for Woods it was the seventh of his eight during the year. Lin Keng-chi joined Chang and Ho as South Korea winners.

The story on the Asian Tour for 2005 was the story of Thailand's Thaworn Wiratchant, age 39, winning an unprecedented four tournaments to take his first Asian Tour Order of Merit title and the Johnnie Walker Asian Golfer of the Year award. He also set the single-season money record, winning US$510,122. England's Paul Casey was named the Johnnie Walker Young Player of the Year, winning the TCL Classic in China and then the Volvo China Open.

Thaworn stamped himself as a golfer for all nations in Asia, taking on all comers everywhere, and he also took three national opens. He won the Standard Chartered Indonesian Open, Taiwan Open, Hero Honda Indian Open and the Carlsberg Masters Vietnam. He opened the season modestly, winning the Indonesian Open late in March. Then he raced through the late schedule, winning three of the last 11 tournaments from mid-September through mid-November. The tale of Thaworn:

• Standard Chartered Indonesian Open — Thaworn held the lead easily despite a final-round 60 by Colin Montgomerie in the Asian-European Tour co-sponsored event. Thaworn closed with a 63 for a hefty 25-under 255 total and beat France's Raphael Jacquelin by five strokes, becoming only the second Thai — with Thongchai Jaidee — to win a European Tour event. That closing 60 was a great sign for Monty, who had been struggling for a few years. "I'm trying my hardest here to get back to where I feel I should be," he said, and so he did. He ended the 2005 season winning his eighth European Tour Order of Merit title.

• Taiwan Open — Thaworn might have scratched this one off his list at the start. He was eight behind in the first round, then four, and then still found himself in a tough spot going into the final round. "I thought that three shots back were a bit too much for me," he said. But his putter started sizzling, and he shot 64 and overran fellow Thai Chapchai Nirat by a stroke, leaping back to the top of the Order of Merit, ahead of another fellow Thai, Thongchai Jaidee, who wasn't in the field.

• Hero Honda Indian Open — Thaworn made the Indian Open his third national championship of the season, leading some to believe his secret lay in a lack of confidence. "At the beginning of the week, I did not think I could win the tournament," he said, a sentiment he'd expressed in various ways through the season thus far. Even a 66 in the second round didn't improve his outlook. "This is not really my kind of course," he said, pointing to his lack of accuracy. He left his driver in the bag and missed only two fairways, and hit 16 greens in regulation. "I've missed cuts here on this course," Thaworn was insisting, this after he logged a two-shot victory over India's Gaurav Ghei. And what does a new champion say to that? "Fortunately," Thaworn said, "I did not lose a ball this week."

• Carlsberg Masters Vietnam — For the moment, Thaworn was fresh out of national championships to win, so he settled for a kind of grand slam of geography, this time winning a title in his fourth different country, Vietnam. This one was a running battle down the final round with Malaysia's Danny Chia and England's Chris Rodgers. Chia crashed early, and Rodgers late, and Thaworn birdied the 18th to beat Rodgers by two. Thus with only three tournaments left, the Order of Merit crown was just at Thaworn's fingertips. The message to come out of this victory? "Anything can still happen," the cautious Thaworn said. "I should not let my guard down as the season comes to a close."

A little while later, Thaworn could let his guard down and pick up his crown.

# Asian Tour

## Caltex Masters—US$1,000,000
Winner: Nick Dougherty

England's Nick Dougherty was age 22 and a professional for four years, but he must have been older and more seasoned, judging from the way he calmly downplayed his first victory. Also judging from the way he won it.

This was the Caltex Masters co-sponsored by both the Asian and European tours and the 2005 season-opener for both late in January. It had drawn some heavy hitters to the Laguna National Golf Club in Singapore, including Colin Montgomerie, the defending champion, and Thomas Bjorn.

"All in all," said Dougherty, after standing up to both of them, "I think I just about played good enough golf today."

All in all, what Dougherty did was take the lead from Montgomerie in the second round, lead the rest of the way, and hold up down the final stretch to win by a deceptive five strokes over him and the Netherlands' Maarten Lefeber, and by seven over Bjorn.

Dougherty shot 68-67-68-67–270, 18 under par. The first turning point came in the second round. Dougherty started three behind Monty and shot a marginal 37 over his first nine holes (the course's second nine). But coming in, he played the first seven holes in seven under, including an eagle at No. 7, off a three wood from 288 yards to within a foot. He shot 67 and was leading by one.

If Dougherty were to crack, it should have been in the third round, during a running battle with Montgomerie and Bjorn, surely intimidating to a 22-year-old. "The guys I grew up watching on television, doing great things," Dougherty said. He closed with three birdies for a two-stroke lead.

But Dougherty's five-shot win was anything but luxurious. He played the final round with Bjorn and Montgomerie. Bjorn double-bogeyed No. 7, battled back with three birdies in four holes, then was done in by a watery double bogey at the par-three 17th. Montgomerie closed to within a shot with a birdie at the 15th. And then Dougherty got a huge break at the 16th. He pulled his tee shot badly, apparently against the wooden sleepers in the face of a fairway bunker. But the ball had gone through and stopped in grass in front of the sleepers. Under a local rule, he was allowed a free drop on top, out of the bunker, and from there he belted his approach to three feet. Monty had a perfect drive, hit the green, then three-putted for a bogey, and Dougherty dropped his three-footer for a birdie. At the 18th, Montgomerie's tee shot landed in a divot hole, and he bogeyed from there.

"The ruling [at the 16th] was the turning point," said Montgomerie, who finished with 70–275. "I was one behind and in the middle of the fairway and he is in the bunker, up the face of the bunker. Next minute you know, he's three feet away."

Said Dougherty, "I'm still a little shell-shocked. But it was picture-perfect, I suppose."

## Carlsberg Malaysian Open—US$1,210,000
Winner: Thongchai Jaidee

Sweet 16 means something else to Thailand's Thongchai Jaidee. It means the par-three 16th at Kuala Lumpur's Saujana Golf and Country Club. He won the 2004 Carlsberg Malaysian Open with an ace at the hole. And then he won the 2005 Malaysian Open there, this time with a birdie.

Well, he didn't exactly win it. He was running away with the tournament, but when things turned dicey down the home stretch, he birdied the 16th and pretty much locked up the wire-to-wire victory. He rolled on from there to a two-under-par 70 — his highest round of the tournament — for a 21-under 267 total and a three-stroke margin that established a number of personal landmarks. It was his career-seventh victory, his first successful defense of a title, and it made him the third player to win back-to-back Malaysian Opens since the tournament started in 1962. And it earned him a return trip to the WGC-NEC Invitational, in which he tied for 32nd in 2004.

The Malaysian Open, co-sanctioned by the Asian and PGA European Tours, was slipping away from the former Thai paratrooper. He had opened the final round with a whopping six-shot lead, but ran into trouble. He bogeyed No. 9 from a greenside bunker, and then faced the threat of a big score.

At the 11th, he had hooked his tee shot out of bounds, but then got to the green and faced a tricky putt that would hold the damage to a bogey. "I told myself I needed to make it, because it was getting close," Thongchai said. Then he shook off the pressure and made the putt, and just in time. With India's Jyoti Randhawa and Sweden's Henrik Stenson in hot pursuit, his six-stroke lead had shrunk to two.

Next, Thongchai came to his old pal, the 16th, a par-three of 188 yards. He had aced it with a six iron in the final round a year ago and became the first Thai to win on the European Tour. He nearly aced again this time, in the second round — with a six iron again. His tee shot hit the flagstick and stopped a foot from the cup. And in the final round, leading by three, he put his tee shot 12 feet from the cup, dropped the birdie putt, and the rest was a formality, leaving Randhawa second, Stenson third.

Thongchai reached that point with strong golf. In the first round, he logged six birdies and an eagle for a 64 and a three-stroke lead. In the second, he birdied the last three holes for a 66 and a two-stroke lead. And his third-round 67 carried him to a 19-under 197 and the six-shot lead.

Thongchai's victory was all the more convincing considering that some European stars were far back in his wake. Paul McGinley was nine behind, Miguel Angel Jimenez 10 and Padraig Harrington, ranked No. 8 in the world, 11.

## Myanmar Open—US$200,000
Winner: Scott Strange

It started out with a Thai veteran chasing a dream. It ended up as the tale of a little-known Australian and the caddie who could track birdies like a bird dog.

And so went the Myanmar Open. Thailand's Thongchai Jaidee, who won the Malaysian Open the week before, was favored to take his second consecutive victory. He was also aiming for a berth in the Masters, needing to jump from 58th to the magic top 50 in the World Ranking. Scott Strange's dream was more modest. Strange, 27, was in his third year on the Asian Tour, and all he wanted was his first victory.

For three rounds, it looked as though Thongchai would get his wish. Then Thongchai and Strange proved again that the chase often belongs to the quick down the back nine on the final day. Strange, no threat earlier, was the quick this time, closing with a flurry of long putts and birdies for a two-stroke victory over Canada's surging Rick Gibson. Thongchai, in or near the lead for the first three rounds, faded and tied for third, three back.

Strange played the par-72 Yangon Golf Club in 69-72-69-67–277, 11 under par. He trailed by two in the first round, five in the second and four in the third. But he made up ground in a hurry. His secret lay in his local caddie, Zaw Moe. "I thought 67 might have a chance and I came out strong on the back nine," Strange said. "You have to play this course in a certain way. Zaw read some great lines all week. He picked everything out there."

Strange, of course, still had to make the putts, and he wasn't good at first. He three-putted No. 1 for a bogey. Then the chase was on. He birdied Nos. 3 and 7, and coming home, tracking on Zaw's reads, he holed 30-footers at the 12th and 13th, and he birdied the 15th and 17th as well to lock up his first win.

Thongchai was looking great for a while. An eight-birdie 67 tied England's Matthew Cort for the first-round lead. Then it shaped up like a battle between two old Thai pals when Boonchu Ruangkit shot 68 and took a one-stroke lead over Thongchai (70) in the second. Thongchai (69) then retook the lead by two over India's Ashok Kumar in the third, and Strange was four down. Then, following the reads of his radar-eyed caddie, Strange had his first win. "It's nice, isn't it?" he said.

## Thai Airways International Thailand Open—US$500,000
Winner: Richard Lee

Anyone looking for Richard Lee's credentials early in March would have to be contented with these two facts: Lee, a New Zealander, beat Michael Campbell to win the 1992 New Zealand amateur championship, and coming into this Thai Airways International Thailand Open, he was ranked 574th in the world. Obscurity doesn't get much deeper than that. So it was no surprise that when Lee won the Thai Open, many observers at the Blue Canyon Country Club on the resort island of Phuket said, "Who?" It was, after all, his first win in 11 years of trying. Not bad for a guy who, just a week earlier, hated golf.

"I wasn't really expecting to get the title," said Lee. "I've been playing a long time and it's nice to finally get a win."

Lee, 31, who tagged along for most of the four rounds, closed with a two-under-par 70 for a nine-under 279 total to tie Australia's Scott Barr, then beat him on the first hole of a playoff. Barr led or shared the lead all the way, and was bogey-free in his 65-68 start. The 74-72 finish did him in.

In the playoff, Barr pulled his drive into a flower bed. He got a free drop, but overshot the green. Then a tough downhill chip left him a long putt from the edge of the green. Lee hit a good drive, hit the green with his second, and when Barr missed his long putt, Lee two-putted for a par and the win.

Lee made his way through a clutch of contenders. Barr and India's Jeev Milkha Singh tied for the first-round lead with 65s. India's Harmeet Kahlon shot 67 in wind and weather to tie Barr for the third-round lead. Australia's Scott Strange, who won the Myanmar Open the week before, took the lead in the final round, then missed the playoff by a shot after calling a moving-ball penalty on himself.

It's almost as though this first win was scripted for Lee. It was, to begin with, a terrific reversal. He missed the cut in his past two tournaments, and was particularly miffed at his performance the week before.

"Last week at the Myanmar Open, I really hated the game," Lee said. He'd shot 80-75. Then came the turnaround. "In the last nine holes of my second round here, I started to tinker with my swing and I found something," he said. He did, indeed: his first win.

## Qatar Masters—€1,141,050
Winner: Ernie Els

See European Tours chapter.

## TCL Classic—US$1,000,000
Winner: Paul Casey

In a way, the TCL Classic was a little like home cooking for England's Paul Casey. He likes the work of golf course architect Robert Trent Jones Jr. His home course in England is a Jones design, and so he said he felt right at home at Jones's Yalong Bay Golf Club on Hainan Island, China. "This is a lot like what I play every day of the week when I am not on tour," Casey said. "I can figure my way around his courses." Which he did at Yalong Bay, hanging in or near the lead all week, then beating Ireland's Paul McGinley in a playoff to take the TCL Classic, co-sponsored by the Asian and European tours.

Apparently Casey wasn't the only person who felt comfortable on the 7,097-yard, par-72 course. When Casey shot an eight-under-par 64 in the first round, he shared the lead with three others. Out of 160 starters, 109 opened with 70 or better. And the 36-hole cut came in at six-under 138, setting the record on the Asian Tour and tying it on the European Tour. Casey slipped two strokes out of the lead in the second round, and was tied again at the third. Then the fourth round turned into a sprint.

Thomas Bjorn was in the running but got destroyed by a quadruple bogey at the par-three No. 3. He bounced back with a wild eight birdies and an eagle, but at 66–267, he had fallen one stroke short of the playoff.

McGinley, starting the final round three off the lead, put on a mad dash with five consecutive birdies from the 13th to tie the course record with a 63. At the 18th, his try for a sixth straight birdie and a record 62 — and the win — burned the hole and stayed out. Casey ducked in under the wire with a clutch up-and-down for birdie at the 16th to tie McGinley. He had a 12-footer for the outright win at the 18th, left the ball well short, but got down for a 66 and a tie with a 22-under 266 total.

They tied on the first playoff hole. Then Casey dropped a 20-foot birdie putt at the second, and had his fourth European title, but his first victory since 2003. There were those who said maybe there was more than just course familiarity at work here for Casey. The tip-off was a comment he made. He said he felt at home, and added: "The place is fantastic and the people so friendly."

## Enjoy Jakarta Standard Chartered Indonesia Open—US$1,000,000
Winner: Thaworn Wiratchant

Time was when all Colin Montgomerie had to do to get into the Masters Tournament was say yes to that coveted invitation. Now the Enjoy Jakarta Standard Chartered Indonesia Open would be his ticket. All he had to do was win it. Montgomerie, a seven-time No. 1 player in Europe, hadn't missed a Masters since his first in 1992. But now, late in March, he would have to leap from 54th in the World Ranking into the top 50 to get invited. He found out in a hurry just what his prospects were. He opened with a three-under-par 67 and found himself five strokes off the lead.

Alas, Monty wouldn't make it. But he did put on a sizzling finish — a 10-under 60 in the final round. He made 10 birdies, and just missed an 11th at the final hole for a 59.

While Montgomerie and his quest were the center of attention all week, Thailand veteran Thaworn Wiratchant came up from the outside to run off with the European Tour-Asian Tour co-sponsored tournament by five strokes. The victory made Thaworn the second Thai — with Thongchai Jaidee — to win on the European Tour.

India's Arjun Atwal and Northern Ireland's Michael Hoey set the early pace at eight-under 62 at the par-70 Cengkareng Golf Club in Jakarta. They were in the second round when rain halted play. About this time, Thaworn, who was a stroke off the lead in the first round with a 63, eagled the par-five No. 9 in the second for another 63, a 14-under 126 total and a one-stroke lead over Belgium's Nicolas Colsaerts at the halfway point. The weather-disrupted tournament found Thaworn was still clinging to that lead in the third round through nine holes when play was suspended because of darkness. This meant the leaders would have to play 27 rounds on Sunday. Filipino veteran Frankie Minoza, flashing a hot putter, went eight under par on 14 holes to move within a stroke of the lead when play was stopped.

Thaworn wrapped up his third round Sunday with a four-under 66, then wouldn't be denied in the fourth. He posted eight birdies and suffered only one bogey for his third 63 of the tournament to finish with a 25-under 255 total and the five-stroke win over France's Raphael Jacquelin.

## Visa Dynasty Cup
Winner: Asia

The weakest links in team matches generally are the rookies, the first-timers who haven't been under that kind of pressure before. Not so in the Visa Dynasty Cup. Asia was led by China's Zhang Lian-wei and his perfect record, but take a bow, Mardan Mamat and Angelo Que.

They were making their debuts in the Asia vs. Japan Dynasty Cup matches, and all they did was lock it up in the final day's singles. Singapore's Mamat ensured that Asia would keep the cup with a 3-and-1 win over Toru Suzuki. Then the Philippines' Angelo Que, at 27 the "baby" of the team, dropped a 15-foot putt for par at the final hole to beat Hideki Kase to win it again. What had been a two-day struggle ended up in an Asian romp, 14½ points to 9½.

"Japan brought out a good team this time after losing in 2003, but we showed we are strong," said Asian captain Hsieh Min-nan.

"Obviously, the Asian team was better," said Isao Aoki, the Japanese captain, on the losing side again. "My players have to get used to the condition of the course more. This is a difficult golf course, especially the greens."

The matches, played at Mission Hills in Shenzhen, China, didn't start with great promise for Asia, judging from a couple of heavy-handed Japanese victories in the opening foursomes (alternate shot). Take Hideki Kase and Ryoken Kawagishi breezing over the Asian veterans, Thaworn Wiratchant and Thammanoon Srirot, 5 and 4. And then Tomohiro Kondo and Takuya Taniguchi beating Mamat and the redoubtable Thongchai Jaidee, 5 and 3. But Asia rallied and Japan came out with a narrow 3½-2½ lead. Asia took the four-ball (better-ball) the next day, with Mamat teaming with Thongchai for a 3-and-1 win over Toru Suzuki and Tetsuji Hiratsuka. Asia won the better-ball 4-2, and went into the singles with a one-point lead, 6½ to 5½.

Asia wrapped it up with an 8-to-4 runaway in the singles. Mamat, dangerously three down over the first three holes, regrouped and beat Toru Suzuki, 3 and 1, for the point that kept the cup. Then Que, a late replacement for South Korea's Charlie Wi, brought the cup back with the 1-up win over Kase. Overall in the singles, Asia won five, Japan two, and four were halved. China's Zhang Lian-wei, beating Shigeki Maruyama, 3 and 2, kept his record perfect. He went 3-0-0, running his record to 6-0-0 in the two Dynasty Cups. Que went unbeaten in his debut, going 1-0-2, and Mamat went 2-1-0.

"Winning for the second time proves that Asian golf has a high standard," said Hsieh. "We kept fighting and never gave up. That was the key to victory."

## Johnnie Walker Classic—US$2,350,000
Winner: Adam Scott

The scoreboard groaned with the usual suspects. Colin Montgomerie was up there, and Retief Goosen, Ernie Els, Nick Faldo, Michael Campbell, and also the youth, Sergio Garcia and Adam Scott. But also some names not usually associated with those, such as Chawalit Plaphol and Chen Yuan-chi. And the dateline on the news reports was odd for a group like this — Beijing, China.

Just another week in the growth of the game. This was the Johnnie Walker Classic, co-sanctioned by the European, Asian and Australasian Tours, played at the Jack Nicklaus-designed Pine Valley course.

And that being the case, it was only fitting that a fresh face should emerge. Scott, the 24-year-old Australian, showed why he had been tagged for star status. He opened the storm-interrupted tournament with a course-record, nine-under-par 63, and wouldn't be budged, adding 66-69-72 for an 18-under 270 total and a three-stroke win over Goosen.

Said Scott, ranked No. 10 in the world, "Things were just going my way."

Enjoying the lead, Scott provided his own comfort zone with that opening 63, spread over two days by storms. He started from No. 10 on Thursday, birdied the 13th and 16th, both par-fives, and then the 18th before strong winds stopped play. In the second round, he birdied his first two holes, then added a birdie-eagle-birdie streak for the 63, breaking the course record by two. Thailand's Chawalit Plaphol was second with a 66, while more youth, Spain's Garcia, joined Australia's Adam Fraser and Taiwan's Chen Yuan-chi tied at 67. Strung out behind — Goosen and Montgomerie at 68, defending champion Els at 71, and Faldo, suffering six bogeys on the second nine, with 75.

"Two different days, but my game stayed the same," Scott said. "I played great yesterday, and this morning I kept swinging in the rhythm." Scott didn't hit a really sour note until the third round, when he double-bogeyed the final hole for a 69. All that did was knock a shot off his lead. He went into the final round with a five-shot cushion, and then he stumbled, but still left a frustrated Goosen behind him.

"The chances were there to catch him, but I didn't take them," said Goosen. Losing his rhythm, Scott bogeyed Nos. 3, 7, 9 and 10, and there, Goosen had closed to within a stroke. But Goosen was running pars — 10 straight from No. 6. And Scott straightened out and birdied the par-three 12th, and was on his way to a 72 and a three-stroke margin. "I like playing with a lead, I definitely do," said Scott. "I've never won a tournament coming from behind."

Goosen had put it well earlier: "I think I'm too far behind. Just fight for second place now." He was right.

## BMW Asian Open—US$1,500,000
Winner: Ernie Els

Ernie Els shot five-under par 67 in the first round of the BMW Asian Open, and was joined by six others in the lead. That's a seven-way tie, and that's as close as anyone got to him. Beginning with the next round, the Big Easy turned the championship into something out of the Theater of the Absurd.

"My confidence is back," Els said. "I'm looking forward to carrying this momentum into the next few months." With the tournament co-sanctioned by the Asian and European tours, the victory was his third of the season on the European Tour, and it was only early May. It's worth remembering who finished second because England's Simon Wakefield shot a credible 13 under par and finished 13 strokes behind.

Els shot 67-62-68-65 for a 26-under-par 262 total at Tomson Shanghai Pudong Golf Club. And it wasn't even a European-Asian record. Els had already set that at 29 under par in the 2003 Johnnie Walker Classic.

For the record, the six who tied Els for the first-round lead were Wakefield, Ireland's Peter Lawrie, Australia's Larry Austin, New Zealand's Eddie Lee, and France's Raphael Jacquelin and Jean Van de Velde. Els didn't see much of them after the first round. Some observers might have thought Els had no pressure because the field lacked the heavy hitters, and also because the course wasn't so tough. It has to be noted also that, true to one of golf's axioms, Els played the course, not the man, and the same course as everyone else, including such notables as Thomas Bjorn, Luke Donald, Miguel Angel Jimenez and Colin Montgomerie who added some spice but no friction to the field.

Els credited some recent work on his swing for his performance. "I know when I'm doing it right," he said. "The ball feels right off the clubface, and goes in the right direction." So he pulled away in the second round, getting four birdies on the front nine, and four more coming in along with an eagle at the par-five No. 9, his last hole. The 10-under 62 wasn't a course record because of the lift-clean-place rule after storms hit, but it put him four ahead. Then he went up by five after a 68 in the third round, and then eight ahead through six holes of the final round, when play was suspended because of rain and darkness. He wrapped up the rest of it Monday morning. The win eased the disappointment of his poor start on the PGA Tour, which had him running for help to get his swing back. "I'm surprised it came so fast," Els said. "Obviously the 62 was the key, but you still have to hit the shots when it counts."

## SK Telecom Open—US$500,000
Winner: K.J. Choi

K.J. Choi had a comfortable homecoming, five strokes being as cozy as anyone might dream of. So much so, in fact, that a double bogey down the back stretch barely raised his eyebrows, even with the great Fred Couples bearing down on him.

Choi, a two-time winner on the U.S. PGA Tour, came home to South Korea early in May for the SK Telecom Open, which he'd won two years earlier. After sparring for three rounds, he pulled away for the five-stroke win over Couples and Australia's Andrew Buckle at Il Dong Lakes Golf Club near Seoul.

"I was having some problems with my swing a couple of months ago and had no power in my shots," Choi said. The problem: He was getting too quick. The discovery paid off fast. In the first round, Choi shared the lead briefly on a birdie at his 14th hole, No. 5. He bogeyed the 15th, then wedged from an old divot hole to 10 feet and birdied his final hole for a five-under-par 67, tying for the lead with Japan's Koji Katoh and Australia's Terry Pilkadaris.

Buckle, shaking off the rain and the cold in the second round, was two over after No. 7, then carded four birdies and an eagle at the 15th for a 68 and a 136 total, and a two-stroke lead on Choi, Katoh and Pilkadaris, who all shot 71. Buckle's surge was sparked by an up-and-down for birdie at No. 8. "Got me back on track," Buckle said. Choi posted five birdies and four bogeys in his 71, frustrated by the change to cold and rain. The uphill putts were slower, downhill putts faster. "It was complicated out there," Choi said. He uncomplicated things in the third round and shot a 68 to tie Buckle for the lead at 10 under going into the final round. Buckle's game plan was simple. "I'm sure that Choi is going to want to win here in Korea," he said, "so I'll be out there just trying to have fun." Couples had an erratic 71 and was five behind them.

The fun ended fast. Buckle shot a 74, and Couples had rung up five birdies but slowed to a 69, and they tied for second at 280. Choi never broke stride. He made five birdies, went birdie-birdie-double bogey from the 12th, then sank a 16-foot putt for a birdie at the 18th for a 69 and a 13-under 275 total. "I think I played well because of so many fans," said Choi, the native son.

## Macau Open—US$275,000
Winner: Wang Ter-chang

Taiwan's Wang Ter-chang hadn't enjoyed this feeling for a golfer's lifetime. "At my age, it feels great to win again," Wang said. "It's not often that golfers can win when they are 42. I hope it won't be another six years before I win again."

Not likely, the way he opened the final round with a surge and then pulled himself together after two shaky holes down the final stretch to take the Macau Open by one stroke with a 14-under-par 270 total. Wang, never more than three off the lead, played the par-71 Macau Golf and Country Club in 66-69-67-68, nosing out two Australians, Marcus Both (66) and Jarrod Lyle (67). Lyle was the one kicking himself the most. "I was very aggressive," Lyle said, "but it probably didn't pay off on 12 when I made double bogey."

Both, winner of the 2003 Sanya Open, shared the first-round lead at 65 with China's Zheng Wen-gen, whose best finish on the Asian Tour was a 23rd. Errors cost the two the outright lead. Both carded eight birdies and a double bogey, and Zheng seven birdies and a bogey on the second nine.

At the halfway point, Wang was three off the lead — his farthest back — with his 69–135, trailing Taiwan's Lu Wei-lan, who solved the changing winds for a six-birdie 66–132 and a one-shot lead over Both (68). "It was a little tougher today," Both said. "The breeze was coming from a different direction and made it difficult to judge the distance."

Wang moved into position to win in the third, with a 67–202, chased by American Ed Loar, who posted an eight-birdie 66 and trailed by one. Now came the big question: After going winless for six years, could Wang stand up under such unfamiliar pressure in the final round? He answered with four birdies over the front nine, and again after bogeys at the 12th and 13th, pulling himself together and parring home for the 68 and the one-stroke victory.

PGA Tour star Fred Couples, playing his second straight Asian event, finished nine shots off the lead but never threatened. A crash in his second-round 72 saw to that. "It's like high school," Couples said. "I don't know when was the last time I made an eight."

## Philippine Open—US$200,000
Winner: Adam Le Vesconte

When a player is 119th on the Order of Merit, nobody notices him, much less expects anything from him. So Adam Le Vesconte startled everyone, including himself, by coming from behind to score his first victory by four strokes in the 89th Philippine Open, Asia's oldest national championship. Other things people suddenly found out about him: He's Australian, age 34, turned professional in 1996, joined the Asian Tour three years earlier after two cracks at the qualifying tournament, and his best previous finish was a tie for 25th.

"It's a wonderful feeling," said Vesconte, using the first words to come to mind. He shot 71-70-67 in the first three rounds, and after starting the final round two off the lead, he racked up a seven-under-par 64 for a 12-under total of 272 at Mt. Malayarat Golf and Country Club near Manila. Local hero Gerald Rosales, who had his sister, LPGA Tour star Jennifer, rooting for him, finished with 67–276.

Vesconte was not without unsettling moments. Angelo Que, another homeland favorite, and big-hitting Australian Andrew Buckle tied for the first-round lead on 66s. Filipino amateur star Juvic Pagunsan, 26, shot 68, bidding to become the first amateur to win the title since 1967. (His bid died on a 72 in the second round and a closing 74.) Jason Dawes shot a course-record 62 for the third-round lead, but bogeyed No. 1 on Sunday, shot 72 and finished third. Thai veteran Boonchu Ruangkit, who led the second round, knocked himself off the perch with a double-bogey six at the 16th in the third round when his birdie putt rolled off the green. Then he slammed the door on himself in the fourth with a 76 that included double bogeys at Nos. 4 and 17, both par-threes. He tied for sixth with Pagunsan, Buckle, Malaysia's Danny Chia and Canada's Darren Griff.

Vesconte was even more of a surprise when one considers that he started the final round with a bogey. Suddenly, he caught fire and made eight birdies the rest of the way. Getting the fifth, seventh and eighth put him two under through the turn. Then he logged five more birdies coming home.

Then he revealed that, apart from the money and the prestige, there were other fruits of victory.

"Last night, I had a feeling that I could win this championship, and doing it today will give me the opportunity to play in the bigger events," Vesconte said. "The Asian Tour is growing so fast and I can now pick the events that I want to play in."

## KT&G Maekyung Open—US$500,000
Winner: Choi Sang-ho

South Korea's Choi Sang-ho not only won the KT&G Maekyung Open with a wire-to-wire dash, he added a new twist to an old saying: Life — for a golfer — begins at 50. When the final putt dropped, it gave Choi a three-stroke victory over Thailand's Thaworn Wiratchant, and left him, at 50, the oldest player to win on the Asian Tour.

It may have looked easy. He led by at least three strokes after each round. But the mere thought of holding the lead in front of the home crowd on his home course, Nam Seoul Country Club, was tough on his constitution. "I was very anxious and couldn't eat or sleep well this week," Choi said,

Choi started his sprint with a six-under-par 66 and a three-stroke lead in the first round over Cho Chul-sang. Choi opened his lead to four with a four-birdie 70 for a 136 at the halfway point. But he got a scare from Australia's Marcus Both and from his own shaky spell. Choi slipped back to par twice but birdied two of the last three holes for his 70. Meanwhile, Both, runner-up at the Macau Open earlier in May, had a rocky road to his 70–141. He birdied three holes on the first nine, made a bogey and a double bogey coming home, then birdied the last two holes.

Choi was happy with his start to the third round. "But that mistake on 10 set me back a little bit," he said. After a three-birdie first nine, he stumbled to a double bogey at the 10th, then suffered two single bogeys coming home. But a final birdie kept Thaworn (69) at bay, three strokes behind going into the final round. "I'm still looking good," Choi said, "and I'm confident I can win the title."

Choi justified that confidence, but it took some doing. Thaworn closed to within a stroke with three birdies on the first nine. But a bogey at the 11th set him back, and Choi locked up the title with birdies at the 13th and 17th. Thaworn had to birdie the 18th to finish three behind, and South Korea's Sung Si-woo was a shot further back.

"I was very nervous as Thaworn and Sung were catching up on me," said Choi, who finished at 10-under 278. "After finding the fairway on the 18th hole, only then was I confident of winning."

## Brunei Open—US$300,000
Winner: Terry Pilkadaris

Australian Terry Pilkadaris had a very important reason to win a golf tournament. He and Monique had been married for nine months and she was still waiting for that honeymoon. His golf schedule had kept him from that ceremonial introduction to marital bliss, and the new Mrs. — she was also his caddie — was getting impatient.

"I'll leave on my honeymoon tonight," said Pilkadaris, 31, after plucking the inaugural Brunei Open late in June by five shots at the par-71 Empire Hotel and Country Club. Married life clearly agreed with him. This was his third career victory in eight months. He won back-to-back titles just after getting married the previous September.

Brunei Tourism staged the tournament in hopes of spurring tourism and golf in the tiny oil-rich sultanate on the northern tip of Borneo. The honor of hitting the first tee shot went to rookie Thai professional Siripong Maitreeyeunyong.

Pilkadaris opened with 67-63 and trailed Malaysia's Danny Chia by four strokes in the first round and by one at the halfway point. He closed with 68-67 for a 19-under-par 265 total, pulling five strokes clear of fellow Aussie Jarrod Lyle.

Chia, 32, who in a few weeks would become the first Malaysian to play in the Open Championship, highlighted his opening 63 with an eagle at the 12th, with a three wood from 253 yards to eight feet. "I'm looking forward to the British Open," Chia said, "but I'm looking to do something here this week." His two-shot lead shrank in the second round to one over Pilkadaris and Lyle, both with 63s.

Pilkadaris started his move in the third round with birdies at Nos. 2, 9, 12 and 15, then bogeyed the 18th for a 68–198, a stroke ahead of Lyle. Lyle turned hot in the humid weather, birdieing four of five holes from No. 4. "That was a good run, but it all dried up on the back nine," he said, after his 69. Chia slipped to third with a 72.

Pilkadaris made short work of the rest of it when his challengers couldn't get moving. Lyle birdied the 18th from 15 feet and locked up a solo second by a stroke over Canadian Rick Gibson and Aussie Matt Keegan. Chia, who got within two shots of Pilkadaris on the first nine, finished with a 71 for fifth place. Pilkadaris, meantime, had stretched his overnight one-shot lead to seven after 12 holes. He birdied Nos. 3, 4 and 6 on the front, then the 10th and 12th, then bogeyed the next two. Still, he had a huge cushion but wasn't content to rest on it. At the 18th, he fired a five iron to two feet and closed with a birdie and a 67. It was a nifty finish to Brunei's first pro tournament and a terrific start to the Pilkadaris' honeymoon.

## Volkswagen Masters China—US$300,000
Winner: Retief Goosen

Whatever it was Retief Goosen told himself after that choppy third round, he should have made a tape of it.

It was billed as the Volkswagen Masters China, but it was the Retief Goosen-Michael Campbell Show. From the second round on they battled. New Zealand's Campbell, the surprise winner of the U.S. Open back in June, couldn't pull ahead, but South Africa's Goosen, a two-time U.S. Open champion, couldn't pull away. Goosen led him by two in the first round, then one in the second and third. But after that ragged third, Goosen was baffled.

"I kept pulling my irons left," he said. "I tried everything, but it didn't want to go straight. I've got some work to do tomorrow."

Goosen found something in contemplation that night, and the next day he sprinted past an amazed Campbell to a six-stroke victory. It was sweet success. Goosen had been having a shaky year, what with the final-round meltdowns in the U.S. Open and Open Championship, and generally discouraging play. And then came the victory in The International in August, and now another win early in September.

True, this wasn't a U.S. Open kind of field. And the Jinghua Golf Club at Beijing wasn't a U.S. Open course. But starting with a course-record 64 and closing with 64, with 67-71 in between for a 22-under-par 266 total and a runaway victory would lift the spirits.

Goosen started the first round par-bogey, then had two birdies and an eagle over the next five holes. He closed with a rush from the 14th — birdie-birdie-eagle-birdie for the record 64 and a two-stroke lead. Campbell was at 67, and responded in the second with an eight-birdie 65 to pull within one after 36 holes. Both were erratic in the third round. Campbell led briefly with birdies at the 11th, 13th and 14th. Then he two-putted from two feet for bogey at the 15th and saved bogey from six feet at the 17th. Goosen faltered early. After a birdie at No. 3, he bogeyed the seventh and eighth, and at the par-three 17th, he hooked his tee shot into a bunker and bogeyed again. Both shot 71. Goosen still led by one going into the final round.

Then Goosen's overnight lecture kicked in. After saving par at No. 1, he raced off to seven birdies over the next eight holes, birdied two more on the second nine, and a bogey at the 18th stopped him from breaking his own course record. But he matched the 64 for the six-stroke win.

"I was on the back foot with nine holes to play," Campbell said. "He played awesomely."

"I'd won in a lot of countries, except in China," Goosen said. "It's great to win all around the world."

## Singapore Open—US$2,000,000
Winner: Adam Scott

"I was smart and I had a game plan," said Adam Scott, the young Australian star. "I seemed to execute just how I wanted to — only one bogey, on 16." And that was pretty much the story of the Singapore Open, the richest national championship on the Asian Tour, returned to the schedule after a three-year absence.

Scott didn't elaborate on his game plan, but clearly it included avoiding bogeys, which he did. How many bogeys can you have when you close with a runaway six-under-par 65? Scott also avoided the grasping rough at the par-71 Sentosa Golf Club at Beijing, shooting 70-69-67-65, for a 13-under 271 total, winning by seven over Britain's Lee Westwood (68–278), and by eight over Australia's Andrew Buckle (71–279). So Scott, who won the Johnnie Walker Classic in April, had his second Asian victory of the year and his third overall, with the Nissan Open on the PGA Tour in February.

The tournament was hit by bad weather, meaning delays. Scott wrapped up his third round on Sunday morning, and led by a stroke over American Edward Michaels. Then he put his game plan, such as it was, into effect. "I got off to a bit of a flyer," Scott said. "It was the perfect start, and it was going to make it hard for anyone to come up and challenge." Scott parred No. 1, birdied the next two, and eagled the 589-yard No. 4, putting his second shot to six feet. Michaels, hampered by a bad shoulder, broke down at No. 4, and there went the challenge. No one else was close. England's

Lee Westwood was the only other golfer with the remotest chance to catch him, but he knew better.

"When I got to No. 9, I saw he was 11 under and I was six behind," Westwood said. "It was going to be difficult from then." Westwood, given that polite understatement, closed with a solid three-under 68 to finish second by seven.

The Singapore Open began with high hopes for two golfers in particular. Chapchai Nirat, a 22-year-old Thai in his seventh Asian Tour event, tied for the first-round lead at 67 with Thai veteran Thongchai Jaidee. "It's good to lead," Chapchai said, "as Thongchai is my hero."

Thongchai made five birdies in seven holes after the turn for that opening 67, and he had two goals. He wanted to top the Asian Order of Merit for the third time in five years, he was also honing his game for another crack at the U.S. PGA Tour qualifying tournament. "I have three more Asian Tour events to play this year," he said, after finishing fifth, "and I have the US PGA Tour School [second stage] to go to. If I ... have a chance to be No. 1 in Asia again, then I might have to change my schedule a bit."

## Taiwan Open—US$300,000
Winner: Thaworn Wiratchant

Coming into the Taiwan Open, Thaworn Wiratchant — then No. 2 on the Asian Tour Order of Merit — was looking for his second victory of the year. But from his point of view, it was out of sight. "I thought that three shots back were a bit too much for me," said the Thai star, who won the Indonesian Open in March. To his delight, he had badly underestimated himself. Thaworn, who trailed through the first three rounds, came charging out of the pack, riding a hot putter to an eight-under-par 64 and a one-stroke win over fellow Thai Chapchai Nirat.

Things didn't look so cheery at the start. Thaworn had reason to believe that Chung Kung Golf Club in Taipei just wasn't meant for him. He was eight strokes behind. While he was laboring to a one-over 73, a pair of Australians, Adam Blyth, a rookie, and Pat Giles, posted 65s to share the first-round lead. Blyth racked up seven birdies in the morning and was sitting pretty until Giles came along in the afternoon and crowned his round by holing a 40-foot putt for an eagle at the par-five 12th. "It's probably the first time I'm in the lead on the tour," said Giles, who regained his card in the qualifying school in January. They were one up on another Aussie, Brad Kennedy.

Thaworn cut his deficit in half with a 65 in the second round, moving within four of Taiwan's Chang Tse-peng, who took the lead with a 67 for a 10-under 134 total. And then Scott Strange, another Aussie and also seeking his second title of the year, took the lead with a 64 for a 203 total. Thaworn inched up with a 68 and was three behind at 206. Those were the three strokes he didn't think he could make up.

Then came the hot putter. In the final round, Thaworn birdied Nos. 3, 4, 7 and 8, and tied for the lead with a chip-in birdie at the 10th. "When I started to putt well and caught the leaders," he said, "I knew I had a good chance to win." So he went ahead and birdied the 11th, 12th and 14th for the 64 and the win that put him back atop the Order of Merit, ahead of fellow Thai Thongchai Jaidee, who wasn't in the field.

## Mercuries Taiwan Masters—US$400,000
Winner: Lu Wei-chih

Lu Wei-chih was dropping shots all over the place in the final round. The good news was that it was a tough scoring day at the Mercuries Taiwan Masters, and everyone was making bogeys or worse at the Taiwan Golf and Country Club in Taipei. It's not often that a golfer can shoot two over par in the last round and win, but Lu Wei-chih did. A first victory never felt so good. And the pressure could not have been greater.

He had set the tone for himself in the third round, when he realized that he had gotten himself into both the lead and a quandary. At the prospect of his first win, he was experiencing both the thrill and the fear that go with it. "I want to win, but I must try to not get ahead of myself," Lu said, after that two-under 70 in the third round gave him a one-stroke lead. "It's the first time that I'm leading into the last day of an Asian Tour event, and I will try to treat tomorrow as another day."

Lu Wei-chih, age 27, who turned professional in 2002, had opened quietly with a 71, three behind Hsu Mong-nan's leading 68, carved out of strong winds. It was bigger news that Thailand's Thaworn Wiratchant — defending champion, No. 1 on the Asian Order of Merit and pre-tournament favorite — opened with a 74. (He would close worse, with an 81 to tie for 35th place.) Lu Wei-chih shot 69 in the second round to move within a stroke of the halfway lead taken by Lu Wen-tang (69) after Hsu blew to a 78.

So Lu Wei-chih led by one going into the final round, but the victory was much in doubt when he bogeyed the second, fourth and eighth on a disagreeable day. It was even more in doubt with Australian rookie Kurt Barnes leaping into the lead with an outward 34. But a pair of bogeys and a double bogey coming in stuck him with a 76. Taiwan's Lin Wen-tang made an early move, but dropped three shots in a three-hole stretch, and when a pair of late birdies gave him hope, a bogey at the 17th left him the runner-up by two.

Lu Wei-chih bounced back from the tough first nine, saving par beautifully from bunkers at the 10th and 11th, and holing an 18-foot putt at the 12th for his only birdie of the day. It worked out to a two-over 74 and a four-under total of 284, and his first victory, by two strokes. "I was very nervous," Lu said. "After a poor start, I just didn't know how to swing the club, but my caddie helped calm me down. I'm so happy. It's a real pleasure to win on my own course."

## Crowne Plaza Open—US$200,000
Winner: Prayad Marksaeng

As the season headed toward its end, Thai rookie Chapchai Nirat, age 22, the runner-up in the recent Taiwan Open, had to believe his time was just around the corner. Here it was, late September, and he was threatening once again, this time in the Crowne Plaza Open in Beijing. He played the Grand Epoch City Golf Club in a six-under-par 66 in the second round for a four-under 140 total, tying for the halfway lead with India's Digvijay Singh. Chapchai's round included a veteran-like six birdies and a chip-in eagle. "I guess I've gained a lot of experience and confidence over the weeks," he said. But a 78 in the third round stuck him with another disappointment and cleared the way, ultimately, for one of his heroes, Thai veteran Prayad Marksaeng.

"I'm really happy to win this title," said Prayad, age 39. "It's been a long time since I last won on the Asian Tour." Since the 2000 Casino Filipino Open, in fact. And it didn't come easy. Prayad, dogging the leaders all the way, finally caught up in the last round with a 68 that tied him for the lead with Australia's Marcus Both (68) at eight-under 280, a stroke ahead of Australia's Alistair Presnell (68–281), India's Shiv Kapur and third-round co-leader Singh (70). The disappointment wasn't limited to Chapchai Nirat, who tied for 20th with a 73–291. Lu Wen-teh, who with Singh led by a stroke coming into the final round, exploded to a 78 and tied for 10th at 289.

Prayad notched five birdies against one bogey in his closing 68, and Both, winner of the 2003 Sanya Open, also shot 68, but with six birdies and two bogeys. It was over in a flash. On the first playoff hole, Prayad dropped a 16-foot putt for a birdie. Marcus Both put his finger on it. "I did the right thing down the stretch with four birdies," he said, "but Prayad did the right thing in the playoff."

## Bangkok Airways Open—US$200,000
Winner: Lu Wen-teh

The Bangkok Airways Open, at Santiburi Samui Country Club on the Thai island of Samui, was shaping up into a Thai family feud, with cousins Thammanoon Srirot and Chawalit Plaphol tossing the lead back and forth. And while fans were watching this fascinating episode, Taiwan veteran Lu Wen-teh, 42, worked his way up the leaderboard and picked off the title, his first in seven years.

The cousins made a neat exchange of the lead. Chawalit shot 65 for the first-round lead, two ahead of Thammanoon. Then Thammanoon shot a 65 in the second round to Chawalit's 68 to take a one-stroke lead after two rounds, 132-133. It looked like the cousin show. The closest pursuers were Lu and Filipino Frankie Minoza, six behind.

"It'll be fun to play with Chawalit tomorrow," Thammanoon said. "We grew up learning golf together." Thammanoon, a five-time winner in Asia, chalked up a stunning burst heading into the turn. He eagled the par-four seventh with a sand wedge from 39 yards. He birdied the eighth from 16 feet, then eagled the par-five ninth after a six iron to 25 feet. He also birdied the 12th and 15th, then bogeyed the 18th for the 65.

Chawalit, a five-time winner in Japan, saved his round with a birdie at the 18th after a bogey at the 16th and a double bogey at the 17th knocked him out of the lead. "There are two more rounds, and you never know on this course," Chawalit said.

How true. Lu, who had enjoyed five top-10 finishes in his last six tournaments, took the lead by one through the rain-interrupted third round. Then he lost it with three bogeys against just one birdie in the first five holes and fell two behind with a bogey at the 11th. But he rallied for birdies at the 15th and 17th to tie Thammanoon at seven-under 277.

In the playoff, Thammanoon hit first and ended up in a bunker. He blasted out 10 feet past the pin and double-bogeyed. Lu chipped to two feet and made his winning par. "I'm very happy," Lu said. "It was a long day, and I was feeling very tired at the end."

## Hero Honda Indian Open—US$300,000
Winner: Thaworn Wiratchant

"At the beginning of the week, I did not think I could win the tournament," Thailand's Thaworn Wiratchant was saying. That was an odd bit of self-doubt, coming from the Asian Tour's Order of Merit leader. But by the final round, he'd reversed himself in play if not in thinking, wrapping up a tidy two-stroke victory in the Hero Honda Indian Open.

"I've missed cuts here on this course," Thaworn explained. Not this time. He shot the par-72 Delhi Golf Club in a 16-under-par 272 (68-66-68-70), taking not only his third victory of the year but his third national championship. His other two wins were in the Indonesian and Taiwan Opens.

Thaworn was four strokes back after his opening 68, with a small crowd between him and first-round leader Anura Rohana, the Sri Lanka star, who had the opposite opinion of the course. "I like this course," he said. "I've played well here in the past." He tied the course record with a 63 earlier in the year, and this time took a one-stroke lead with an eight-under-par 64. But a 75 in the second round took him out of the chase.

Thaworn took the lead in the second round with a six-under 66, but still hadn't warmed to the course. "This is not really my kind of course," he said. "You need to hit it very straight off the tee, and that is not something I do very well." He left his driver in the bag and missed only two fairways and hit 16 greens in regulation, taking a one-stroke lead over the Philippines' Gerald Rosales (67) and India's Harmett Kahlon (64). Said Rosales, "Don't even bother looking for your ball if you go in the bushes. I haven't lost a ball for two days, so I am doing a good job."

The wind came up in the third round, complicating things for Thaworn. "I was just trying to keep my ball on the fairway," he said. He bogeyed the 13th and 15th, but birdied the 18th, hitting his third shot from a cart path to 20 feet. That gave him six birdies as against two bogeys for a 68 for a three-stroke lead over South Africa's Hendrik Buhrmann (69) and Thailand's Prom Meesawat (69).

Next up as a challenger came Indian veteran Gaurav Ghei with a day's-best 66 after narrowly missing birdie putts at the 14th, 15th and 16th. "After that miss at the 14th, I knew my chances were slim," Ghei said, "because Thaworn was not going to give it away from there on."

And Thaworn didn't. He finished with a 70, a 16-under 272, the two-stroke win, and all the golf balls he started with. "Fortunately," Thaworn said, "I did not lose a ball this week."

## Double A International Open—US$300,000
Winner: Chinarat Phadungsil

Asian golf has been coming so fast that no one was surprised to find Thai amateur Nakarintra Ratanakul among the early leaders when the inaugural Double A International Open got under way, and no one would really be surprised to see him win it. Well, an amateur won it, all right, but it was a different one. This was Thailand's Chinarat Phadungsil, who came out of the pack to become the youngest winner ever on the Asian Tour when he beat Indian professional Shiv Kapur with a birdie on the second hole of a playoff.

Chinarat, the reigning World Junior Champion, was age 17 years and five days, 78 days younger than Korea's Kim Dae-sub at the 1998 Korean Open. Chinarat also was only the third amateur to win on the tour. He shot 73-68-70-67, a 14-under-par 278 total on the par-73 St. Andrews Hill course at Rayong, Thailand. But he talked like a veteran. "After the first round, I wanted to break my putter," said Chinarat, who played on a sponsor's exemption. But he felt better after three hours on the practice green.

The loss stung Kapur, himself just 23 and a rookie poised to take his first victory. He tied for the first-round lead and was the solo leader through the second and third, and went into the final round with Thai star Thongchai Jaidee just a stroke behind.

Chinarat started the final round seven shots off the lead. He made eight birdies, and he got a lot of help from Kapur, who triple-bogeyed the third hole, bounced back for five birdies, but bogeyed the 14th and 18th for a 72. Chinarat closed with a great run. He birdied the 13th, bogeyed the 14th, then birdied the 16th, 17th and 18th. "The 17th was the key because it was the hardest hole on the course," Chinarat said. "I hit a five wood and it stopped two feet from the cup."

Both players birdied the first playoff hole from about six feet. On the second, Chinarat nearly chipped in for an eagle. When Kapur missed his birdie try from 12 feet, Chinarat tapped in for his birdie and the victory.

"Of course I am disappointed," Kapur said. "But Chinarat was fantastic. He held his nerve so well for a youngster."

"I am so happy, and felt so lucky to win," said Chinarat. "I did not feel any pressure in the playoff. "

## HSBC Champions Tournament—US$5,000,000
Winner: David Howell

The $5 million HSBC Champions Tournament, Asia's richest event, which drew a sparkling international field to Shanghai's Sheshan International Golf Club, was just a wearisome exercise of lost chances for Tiger Woods. Every time he grabbed for it, it slipped away.

And there aren't many golfers who can say they beat Woods head-to-head, but now count David Howell among them. As the retiring Howell proved as a rookie star of Europe's 2004 Ryder Cup victory, he can manage under pressure. He led Woods by only a stroke going into the final round and won by three.

"I didn't want to beat him too badly," said Howell, not so retiring that he couldn't come up with a little poke in the ribs. But it was a well-earned poke, considering that many golfers have withered in the heat of going against Woods in the final round. He turned the scenario around this time. He birdied three of the first five holes, stretched his lead from one stroke to four, and easily stayed in front. Howell shot 65-67-68-68, a 20-under-par 268. Woods shot 65-69-67-70. They were tied in the first round, a stroke off the lead. Then Howell led Woods by two in the second and one through the third, and won by three.

The missed chances: In the first round, Woods racked up 10 birdies, but also three bogeys, including one at his final hole, No. 9, after he buried his tee shot in a fairway bunker. The 65 tied him with Howell, a stroke behind Paul Lawrie, Peter O'Malley and Nick Dougherty. In the second round, Woods charged with three straight birdies from the 13th, but he chipped into a bunker at the 16th and bogeyed, and watered his second at the par-five 18th and could only par, falling two behind. In the third, Woods had four birdies and an eagle in the first 14 holes, but also some big errors. Among them, he bogeyed the ninth on three putts from 15 feet, bogeyed the 15th from the rough, and missed a three-foot birdie putt at the 17th.

"I know what I can do, and it's frustrating when I know I didn't do it," Woods said.

In a tournament co-sanctioned by the European, Asian, Australasian and Sunshine tours and the China Golf Association, Woods was the only one in the strong field to make a real run at Howell. In the final round, Woods made two birdies on the front nine, but also a weak bogey at No. 5, where he three-putted from 15 feet, missing his par from two feet. Howell dropped an 18-footer for birdie to go up by four at No. 7, but bogeyed the next two holes to let Woods get within two at the final turn. Howell pulled away again on the back with birdies at the 10th and 12th, and he finished with six straight pars. Woods made two birdies and a bogey coming in, cutting Howell's final margin to three.

Howell was paired with Woods in the third round of the Masters back in April, and shot 76. He might have been intimidated. But not this time.

"It's a great opportunity," Howell said, "for me to take on the world's best player, with a one-stroke lead, and win a massive tournament."

## Carlsberg Masters Vietnam — US$200,000
Winner: Thaworn Wiratchant

It was mid-November and only three tournaments remained on the schedule. The Asian Order of Merit title race was all over but the celebrating — almost. Uh, don't chill the champagne just yet, the man was saying.

This was Thailand's Thaworn Wiratchant, preaching caution and patience even through he'd just picked off his fourth win of the year in the Carlsberg Masters Vietnam, and even though he had the Order of Merit title all but locked up. "Anything can still happen," Thaworn said. "I should not let my guard down as the season comes to a close."

Still, he was in a comfortable position. The victory, worth $31,500, pushed his total to a tour-record $483,420, nearly $100,000 better than his closest competition, countryman Thongchai Jaidee.

Thaworn would win by two strokes, but he needed some help. Going into the final round, he was tied with Malaysia's Danny Chia and England's Chris Rodgers, and while he held his own, they obligingly cleared the path for him with some loose play. Chia left the chase with a 76 at the par-72 Chi Linh Star Golf and Country Club.

It was a battle for a while. Thaworn birdied the fourth and sixth holes but bogeyed the ninth, and he and Rodgers were tied for the lead at the final turn. But not for long. Rodgers reeled to four straight bogeys and finally righted himself in time to birdie the 16th and 18th. Thaworn, who had bogeyed the 14th, locked up the win with a birdie at the par-five 18th for a 71 and a seven-under-par 281 to Rodgers' 73–283.

The Philippines' Frankie Minoza birdied three of the last five holes for a 70 and finished third, while Chia, who dropped four strokes over the first three holes, birdied the 18th to tie for fourth. Amateur Huynh Van Son, the only Vietnamese to make the cut, closed with a 76 for a 16-over 304 and a tie for 59th.

"I am very happy to win here, as this is a tough course, not very forgiving," said Thaworn, who had just completed a kind of grand slam of geography for 2005. He had won in Indonesia, Taiwan, India and now Vietnam.

## Volvo China Open—US$1,300,000
Winner: Paul Casey

For England's Paul Casey, it was a day of one wasted chance after another — an eagle here, a birdie there, a near-gimme somewhere else. All he missed was the course record and an outright win. Then he got one last chance. The reprieve got him into a playoff, and this time he cashed in, taking the Volvo China Open on the first extra hole.

"I was a little bit frustrated with the putts that didn't go in today," Casey said. "But I gave myself so many chances that I didn't feel like I was under that much pressure."

Casey shot a final-round 65, tying the newly set course record at the par-72 Shenzhen Golf Club at Jiangsu. Then he was tied by England's Oliver Wilson, who also blew some chances in shooting 69 to tie Casey at 13-under 275. Casey then birdied the first extra hole for his fifth European Tour championship and his second playoff victory in China, after beating Paul McGinley in the TCL Classic in March.

England's Barry Lane finished third with a closing 68, one stroke off the lead. And Ross Fisher, another Englishman, who led going into the final round, closed with a 72 and tied for fourth, two off the lead, with Thailand's Chawalit Plaphol (71). Plaphol had begun his bid to become the third Thai golfer to win an Asian and European Tour co-sanctioned event with a course-record 65 in the first round. He led or shared the lead for the first two rounds, then in the third slipped back with a 74 to joint second with Wilson, who logged a birdie and 17 pars for a 71. Fisher, playing in just his 11th European Tour tournament, moved up to a one-stroke lead after the third round on a 68.

Victory made those lost chances a lot easier to digest for Casey. Take the par-five 12th, where he missed an eagle putt; then the seven-foot birdie putt at the 15th, which went wide; then possibly worst of all, the three-footer at the 18th in regulation that would have given him a birdie, a course-record 64 and the win. Even so, he ended a superb round with a par and the 65. In at 13 under, Casey had to wait out Wilson for an hour to see whether he would win, lose or tie.

First, Wilson actually passed him. He ran off four straight birdies from the 12th and was 14 under and leading by one. He scrambled to a par at the 16th, but missed a 12-footer at the 17th to drop back to a tie at 13 under. His last chance was at the 18th, but he hit his approach over the green and his return chip killed any chance for a birdie, and the playoff was on.

They returned to the 539-yard, par-five 18th. Casey drove into the first cut of rough but fired an iron to the middle of the green. Wilson drove into the fairway, but hit a fairway wood into a greenside bunker. Then a nightmare: Wilson popped his sand shot into another bunker. He had to hole his next for any chance to win, but left it short on the fringe. Casey only had to two-putt for the victory, and he did.

"I thought maybe I'd blown it at the last," Casey said. "I played a wonderful round of golf today, so I can't complain. I didn't make the putts in regulation, but it was nice to get the chance in a playoff. I didn't think I'd have it, and I capitalized."

## UBS Hong Kong Open—US$1,200,000
Winner: Colin Montgomerie

To paraphrase an old saying, one man's curse is another man's blessing, and that certainly was the case in the UBS Hong Kong Open. The curse: South Africa's James Kingston, age 40, was about to score his first European Tour win, but he double-bogeyed the final hole. The blessing: The rejuvenated Colin Montgomerie, age 42, who had finished and who thought his chances died when he missed birdies on the last two holes, ended up with the victory in the Asian and European Tour co-sponsored tournament.

It was great icing to go with the eighth European Order of Merit title Montgomerie had recently won. And he shared Kingston's anguish. "We all feel for him," Monty said. "Every golfer ... feels for someone who doubles the last to lose. That should have been a playoff at worst ... and then we would have had more drama coming down that last hole."

Alas, this was old hat for Kingston. In the 2004 tournament, he bogeyed the last and handed the win to Miguel Angel Jimenez. This time he bogeyed the 16th, but still was in command when Montgomerie blew the two closing birdies. Then the crisis. At the 18th, Kingston blasted his tee shot into the trees, then needed a 10-foot putt to force a playoff with Monty. He missed.

"Obviously I'm disappointed," Kingston said. "Obviously I was aware of the situation. I was just so nervous."

Montgomerie admitted he was tired after his stunning comeback season. He opened with a one-under-par 69 and was five behind surprise leader

Kang Wook-soon of South Korea. Monty opened birdie-bogey-double bogey, but played the last 15 holes in three under. "There was nothing really wrong," Monty said. "Three decent 65s, and you never know." It wasn't a 65 in the second round, but he did post a 66, including two birdies over his last three holes. "That should have been a very, very low round if I had taken the putts that I should normally take," said Monty, at 135 four behind Rick Gibson's 66–131 lead.

Just when Montgomerie thought he might be making some headway, along came Scotland's Simon Yates with a course-record 61 for a two-stroke lead on Monty (66) and the doomed Kingston (64), both at 201 through the third round. This was another shoulda-been round for Monty until he bogeyed the 15th and 16th. But he birdied the 17th on an approach to two feet, and parred the 18th.

The signs for Yates were hard to read. He'd birdied three straight from No. 2 and then all four of his last four holes. But the day before, his tee shot at the par-three 12th plunged into the cup, only to jump back out. The answer: The signs were bad. He shot 75 in the final round — a curse for Yates, a blessing for Monty.


## Volvo Masters of Asia—US$600,000
Winner: Shiv Kapur

It was starting to sound like a line of succession in Indian golf. First Jyoti Randhawa, then Arjun Atwal (and he went off to the U.S. PGA Tour), and now Shiv Kapur, age 23, a rookie but also a champion, thanks to a clutch wire-to-wire performance in his last chance of 2005, against a 43-man field in the Asian Tour's season-ending Volvo Masters of Asia.

Kapur might have been known as the upstart rookie with four straight top-10 finishes recently, a playoff loss in the Double A International a month earlier, and also a contender in the Volvo China Open before fading in the last round. Was he a rookie flash, or a rookie with a victory waiting to happen? Bet on the latter. The tipoff: Kapur swept into a tie for the first-round lead with birdies on four of his last five holes, dropping putts of 15, three, 15 and 10 feet.

Kapur shot the Thai Country Club course in a five-under-par 67 in the final round for a tournament-record 20-under 268 and a two-stroke win over — fittingly — Randhawa himself, the defending champion, in a head-to-head battle in the final round. If it doesn't get any better than that, it doesn't get any tougher, either.

"It will be nice," Kapur had said after the third round, looking ahead to the coming final-round battle with one of the giants on the Asian Tour, and in fact, paired with him. "As far as stature or anything goes, I am not one to pay much attention to that. I have played with Thongchai Jaidee in Thailand and it does not get any more difficult than that."

"Shiv just played great," said Randhawa, Asia's No. 1 in 2002. "I lost to a great champion."

Kapur had to play great. Randhawa, the crusty veteran, turned up the heat down the final stretch, but Kapur refused to crack. Kapur opened with a bogey at No. 1, but brushed it off and birdied No. 4 and No. 7. Then he counterpunched Randhawa all the way home. Randhawa birdied the 10th, and Kapur matched him with a 15-footer. Randhawa birdied the 11th, and Kapur shot back at the 12th, and then birdied the 15th as well. Undiscouraged, Randhawa birdied the 17th. Unflappable, Kapur answered in grand and final style, rolling in a 20-footer from off the green for a birdie at the 18th, wrapping up a card of 66-67-68-67.

Since Kapur was a surprise as a rookie, it might be well to watch two other "babies" as the Asian Tour continues to grow. Both were age 23. Australia's Andrew Buckle tied Kapur for the first-round lead at 66 and finished sixth, and Thailand's Prom Meesawat was third at 67 and finished tied for 11th.

Kapur's breakthrough was matched by that of Thaworn Wiratchant. He finished an unimpressive 14th in the tournament, but wrapped up his Asian Order of Merit title with records for the year — four victories and $510,122 in winnings.

But the week belonged to Shiv Kapur. "I thought I had the game to win, but I never thought I would win the most important one, our tour championship," Kapur said. "Three months ago, I was 85th on the Order of Merit and struggling to keep my card. I have to say I'm more than pleased."

## Asia/Japan Okinawa Open—¥100,000,000
Winner: Tadahiro Takayama

See Japan Tour section.

# Japan Tour

### Token Homemate Cup—¥100,000,000
Winner: Tadahiro Takayama

It wasn't exactly the way Japan Tour officials would have liked to have launched the 2005 season. They certainly prefer their tournaments to go the full 72 holes, but right off the bat at the Token Homemate Cup they had to settle for a 54-hole tournament. March is always a bit of a gamble for golf in much of Japan, but the schedule-makers have continued to slate that traditional opener at the end of that month. This time the weather tripped them up as temperatures hovered around the freezing mark through the weekend and a snow storm wiped out the second round.

Probably the only person pleased about that turn of events was Tadahiro Takayama, who picked up his first career victory at chilly Token Tado Country Club, Mie Prefecture, defeating Nozomi Kawahara on the third hole of a playoff after the two men completed their rounds with identical 205 totals. Takayama had finished second in the Token Homemate tournament two years earlier in his first season of full-time action on the circuit.

Takayama had entered the final round two strokes behind pace-setters Toru Taniguchi, Hideto Tanihara and Kawahara, tied at 137. That trio had supplanted first-round leaders Hiroyuki Fujita and Tatsuhiko Takahashi, who led Takayama and three others with their 66s. Takayama came out firing Sunday, shooting 31 on the front nine to take the lead. Only Kawahara could stay with him on the incoming holes and he needed a two-stroke swing at the 17th hole to make up a two-stroke deficit and force the play-off by matching his par on the 18th. Takayama shot 66 and Kawahara 68 for 205s. A 10-foot birdie putt brought victory to Takayama at the 18th moments later when it was played as the third overtime hole. Australia's Steven Conran (206) and Craig Jones (207) took the next two spots in the final standings.

### Tsuruya Open—¥100,000,000
Winner: Naomichi Ozaki

A touch of déjà vu visited the Tsuruya Open when the Japan Tour resumed action after a month's hiatus following its March opener. Naomichi (Joe) Ozaki, whose last victory had come 18 months earlier in a Bridgestone playoff against Australian Paul Sheehan, found himself once more battling Sheehan through much of the final round of the Tsuruya before emerging again as the winner. This time, though, Ozaki maintained a narrow margin over the Aussie throughout the final nine holes and pulled away to a three-stroke victory, shooting 68 for his 13-under-par 271.

Although distant from the phenomenal success of older brother Masashi (Jumbo) Ozaki, Naomichi's record is still one of the best in Japanese golf annals. Consider that his 31 victories were achieved even though he spent the bulk of eight seasons playing on the rugged U.S. PGA Tour.

The 48-year-old Ozaki and Sheehan pretty much dominated the tournament from the start. Sheehan, a two-time winner in his three seasons in Japan and the No. 4 finisher on the 2004 money list, got off to a flying start Thursday with eight birdies and an eight-under-par 63 at Yamanohara Golf Club, Hyogo Prefecture. That staked him to a three-stroke lead over Makoto Inoue and four over Ozaki and four others. Sheehan gutted out two late birdies to salvage a 73 in the second round and hold onto a share of the lead with Ozaki, who birdied the 18th hole for 69 and his 136.

Once again Sheehan needed a late surge to hang onto his position Saturday. He birdied the last two holes for 67 to match Ozaki's card and remain tied at 203. They stood three strokes ahead of Craig Jones and Toyokazu Fujishima, their closest pursuers, and turned the final round into a duel. Ozaki moved ahead with two early birdies, and Sheehan never caught up. He shot 71 and had to share the runner-up spot at 274 when Ryoken (Ricky) Kawagishi closed with 66 despite two bogeys on the front nine.

## Chunichi Crowns—¥120,000,000
Winner: Naomichi Ozaki

A week later, a different Australian challenged Naomichi (Joe) Ozaki in the Chunichi Crowns tournament, the oldest of the non-major championships on the Japan Tour, but the outcome was the same. Ozaki, winning for the first time the tournament that his brother, Masashi (Jumbo) Ozaki, won five times, had a little tougher time of it with Steven Conran than he had defeating Paul Sheehan in the Tsuruya Open, going two extra holes in a steady rain before landing his 32nd career title at Nagoya Golf Club's Wago course.

Both players tooled along behind other leaders for three rounds before moving in front and battling to a 72-hole deadlock at 11-under-par 269 and into the playoff, which ended when both players missed the green on the second extra hole and Ozaki converted a three-foot par putt. They were far behind after the first round when South Korean Y.E. Yang set a tournament and course record with a 61, keyed by a 29 on the front nine. Yang, a two-time winner in 2004, led Yusaku Miyazato by two and the rest of the field by four as Ozaki began with 68 and Conran with 71.

Yang and Miyazato came back to the field Friday with 71s and Kiyoshi Maita slipped a stroke in front of Yang with 65-66–131. Ozaki and Conran were four back, Naomichi after a 67 and Steven after a 64. After 54 holes, they were right on the heels of leader Daisuke Maruyama (69-64-68–201). Ozaki (67) was at 202 and Conran (68) was at 203 with Yang (71) and Ozaki's other brother, Tateo (70). In the Sunday rain, Conran had the upper hand until they reached the 16th, where Naomichi's birdie and Steven's bogey swung them into the tie that carried through the 18th to the decisive second playoff hole. Yang, with 67, missed the overtime session by a stroke.

# Japan PGA Championship—¥110,000,000
Winner: S.K. Ho

It had been more than 20 years since a winner of the Japan PGA Champion-ship repeated the victory as South Korea's S.K. Ho did in the Japan Tour's fourth event of the season in mid-May. It last happened when Tsuneyuki (Tommy) Nakajima, then at the pinnacle of his outstanding career, scored back-to-back wins in 1983 and 1984. Ho had to go one more round than he did in 2004 when heavy rains wiped out play the first day. He played four solid rounds, never posting a score out of the 60s at Tamana Country Club in Kumamoto Prefecture, and posted a two-stroke victory over Hideto Tanihara. It was the fourth win in Japan for the 31-year-old.

Hiroyuki Fujita opened his bid for his first major title with a 66, requir-ing just 23 putts as he led five players — Toru Taniguchi, David Smail, Tetsuji Hiratsuka, Toshinori Muto and Hiroo Okamo — by a stroke. Ho and Tanihara were among four who had 68s. Tanihara, who returned from campaigning on the U.S. PGA Tour for the championship, slipped into the lead, one ahead of Fujita (71) and Ho (68), when he shot 67 Friday for 135.

The South Korean came up blazing Saturday and surged two strokes in front at day's end. He birdied three of the first five holes and went on to 67–203 as Fujita (69) and Tanihara (70) settled into second place with 205s. Ryoken (Ricky) Kawagishi jumped into contention with 65 for 206. Ho never trailed Sunday after another fast start — three birdies on the first seven holes. He built his lead to four strokes at one point, but Tanihara never quit and closed the gap back to two on the back nine and missed several short birdie putts on the final holes as Ho scrambled a string of pars for 69 and his 16-under-par 272. Tanihara matched the 69 and finished a shot ahead of Yasuharu Imano, who fired a closing 65 for 275.

# Munsingwear Open KSB Cup—¥100,000,000
Winner: Hiroyuki Fujita

Deprived of a major title when he faded from contention on the closing holes of the PGA Championship, Hiroyuki Fujita bounced back immediately and racked up a convincing, wire-to-wire victory in the Munsingwear Open KSB Cup the following week. For the 35-year-old Fujita, it was the fifth title he has acquired in his 14 seasons on the Japan Tour and his first since the opening event of the 2004 tour. It jumped him into second place on the circuit money list behind two-time winner Naomichi Ozaki.

Fujita repeated himself in the opening round, taking the lead for the sec-ond straight week. This time he built himself a three-stroke cushion with a 10-birdie 63 at Tojigaoka Marine Hills Golf Club, Okayama Prefecture, and only three other players were closer than five strokes — Craig Jones at 66 and Jun Kikuchi and ageless Masashi (Jumbo) Ozaki at 67. The lead went to five strokes Friday when Fujita sank three birdie putts on the first six holes and tacked on a 66 for 129. Australia's Steven Conran, who was to hold a runner-up position the rest of the way, also shot 66 for 134, and Ozaki remained a threat with 68–135.

The opposition whittled away at Fujita's margin Saturday as he struggled on the back nine and shot 72 to remain 15 under par at 201. Conran shot 69 for 203 and was joined there by Tadahiro Takayama, the Token winner in March, who shot a fiery 64. Takayama and Australian Craig Jones caught Fujita early in the final round, but Hiroyuki quickly pulled away from them with three consecutive birdies, and another at the 13th steered him to a 69 finish and 270 total. He won by three over Takayama and Conran, who posted his second runner-up finish of the season. Both had 70s for 273.

## Mitsubishi Diamond Cup—¥110,000,000
Winner: Chang Ik-je

The Japan Tour got its second first-time and initial circuit rookie winner when South Korea's Chang Ik-je captured the Mitsubishi Diamond Cup, but he was not a stranger to victory or fanfare. Chang came to Japan for the first time as the leading money winner on South Korea's domestic tour in 2004 and the man whose victory in a 2003 event was overshadowed by Se Ri Pak, the country's world-class woman star, who stole the headlines when she made the cut, a female feat that hadn't happened in 60 years anywhere in the world.

No doubt those experiences in his homeland helped Chang, who carried a three-stroke lead into the final round on the difficult Higashi Hirono Golf Club course, Hyogo Prefecture, and finished that way. He shot 69 for a five-under-par 275, fending off the challenges of Shingo Katayama and Ryoken Kawagishi, two of Japan's strongest players. The pressure had been expected to come from Toshimitsu Izawa, the tour's leading money winner in 2001 and 2003, who was the runner-up to Chang going into the final round, but stumbled early and took a one-over-par 71.

Chang hardly looked like a potential winner Thursday when he opened with 74, six strokes behind a five-player logjam in first place. Australian Paul Sheehan and American Peter Teravainen, both former winners in Japan, shared the 68 slot with Yutaka Horinouchi, Azuma Yano and Sushi Ishigaki. Sheehan, a two-time winner in Japan in 2004, found a par 70 good enough to move him into sole possession of the lead Friday with his 138. That gave him a two-shot lead over Yano, Kawagishi and Daisuke Maruyama, whose 69 was one of only nine sub-70 scores that day. Teravainen plummeted from contention with 75.

Chang, who began the third round five shots off the pace, spurted in front with a dazzling 64 for 207, and Izawa moved into second place at 210 with a 67. The South Korean picked up six birdies in his birdie-free round. A strategy of playing to the middle of Higashi Hirono's tough greens paid off for Chang Sunday. He had four birdies and two bogeys for 68–275. Katayama, the reigning money leader, blazed home with 65 and tied Kawagishi (67) for second place at 278. Maruyama, at 279, was the only other player to break par for the distance.

## JCB Classic Sendai—¥100,000,000
Winner: S.K. Ho

S.K. Ho became the second double winner of the 2005 season, joining Naomichi Ozaki in that department and edging past him into the top spot on the circuit's money list with his victory in the JCB Classic Sendai the first week of June. Ho, winning on the heels of South Korea countryman Chang Ik-je's victory in the Diamond Cup, was never out of the lead as a sizeable segment of the field manhandled the Omotezao Kokusai Golf Club course at Shibata in Miyagi Prefecture.

The scoring, led by Ho's 265, was so low that each of the leading 19 finishers all hammered out four sub-par rounds. That this would happen shouldn't be surprising, since the winner started the week with a sizzling, eight-under-par 63 and didn't even have the lead to himself. Ryuichi Oda matched it and two other players — Kazuhiro Takami and Jin Murakami — shot 64s Thursday. Ho, who repeated as PGA Champion three weeks earlier, took control of first place Friday. With an eagle, four birdies and two bogeys, Ho shot 67 for 130 and established a two-stroke lead over Oda (69), Tomohiro Kondo (66) and Katsumune Imai (64), then maintained the margin with a stout five-birdie 66 for 196. Toshimitsu Izawa, twice the No. 1 player on the tour but without a victory since 2003, set himself up for a final-round bid with a 64 that jumped him into second place, two ahead of Shinichi Yokota and Australian rookie Chris Campbell.

However, Ho was equal to the threat of Izawa and, as it turned out, Yokota, Sunday and scored his fifth victory in Japan. Ho carved out a work-man-like 69 with two birdies and 16 pars to finish at 265, a shot ahead of Yokota, who picked up three strokes on the last four holes in shooting 66 and finishing second. Izawa managed only a 70 but placed third, a stroke in front of five others.

## Mandom Lucido Yomiuri Open—¥100,000,000
Winner: Satoru Hirota

Satoru Hirota had been making slow progress since coming onto the Japan Tour full-time in 1999 and had not missed a cut in his six starts in 2005, but there was little to indicate he was about to land his first victory when the circuit arrived outside of Osaka for the Mandom Lucido Yomiuri Open. One thing about it, though. Hirota had done well at Yomiuri Country Club in the past — 13th one year, seventh another and runner-up to Toru Taniguchi in 2002. Whether or not Yomiuri was in his comfort zone, the 32-year-old Hirota staged a final-round rally with a 67 to pluck a one-stroke victory away from Tetsuji Hiratsuka and Shinichi Akiba with his 18-under-par 270.

Hirota kept himself within range all week at Yomiuri. He was two back after the first round, when Hiratsuka opened with 64, a shot in front of Ryoken (Ricky) Kawagishi, once again a contender on the circuit in 2005. Kawagishi, who had finished second twice in earlier 2005 events, roared four strokes into the lead Friday when he shot a sensational 63 for 128, the season's lowest midway score. His start: birdie, birdie, hole-in-one. In all, he had nine birdies as he raced four ahead of Shigeru Nonaka, who had a pair of 66s. Hirota was another two back after a 68.

The 38-year-old Kawagishi came back to the field Saturday when he could muster only a par round and dropped into a tie for the lead with Shinichi Akiba (65) and Hiratsuka, who bounced back from a 70 Friday with a 66 for his 200. Hirota was tied for fifth with S.K. Ho and Hiroyuki Fujita at 203. Hirota went out in 33 Sunday afternoon and climbed into a five-way tie for the lead at 16 under par. When he finished a steady back nine with a birdie at the par-five 18th, he had the lead with two groups yet to finish. The score stood up and he became the season's third first-time winner, joining South Korea's Chang Ik-je (Diamond Cup) and Tadahiro Takayama (Token Homemate Cup). The result was particularly disappointing to Kawagishi, a six-time career winner but without a victory on tour in six years. He shot 72 and tied for fourth with Takayama.

A sidelight: Masashi (Jumbo) Ozaki teed off in his 1,000th tournament as a professional, but shot 76 and withdrew.

## Mizuno Open—¥100,000,000
Winner: Chris Campbell

Chris Campbell beat his sister to the punch. Only several months into his first season on the Japan Tour, the 29-year-old Australian achieved what his sister Nikki has been unable to accomplish despite very respectable performances at times in her first three seasons on the Japan LPGA circuit — a victory. Campbell, who honed his game in American collegiate golf in the late 1990s and earned playing privileges in the Japan Tour qualifier at the end of 2004, battled from behind in the final round of the Mizuno Open and prevailed in a three-man playoff to become the fourth first-time winner of the season.

Campbell had given an inkling that he could be joining the lengthy list of Australian players who have enjoyed success in Japan when he made a strong showing two weeks earlier in the JCB Sendai. He pulled it off at Setonaikai Golf Club at Kasaoka in Okayama Prefecture, keeping himself in the thick of things all week. After three lightly regarded Japanese players — Hiroaki Iijima (65) and Toshinori Muto and Shintaro Iizuka (66s) — led the first day, Campbell scored his second successive 68 and climbed into a four-way tie for the lead at 136 with Yeh Wei-tze of Taiwan (71-65), Tsukasa Watanabe (69-67) and Iizuka (70).

Tadahiro Takayama, seeking his second win of the season, fired a brilliant eight-under-par 64 on a windy Saturday and soared from 19th place into a two-stroke lead. He had eight birdies, four on the first six holes and three on the final four. Campbell and Iizuka shot 71s and shared second place, a stroke in front of David Smail, Hiroyuki Fujita and Watanabe, who had a par round. Takayama added a stroke to his lead on the front nine Sunday, but Campbell chipped away coming in and slipped in front when he birdied the 17th. Smail double-bogeyed the 16th hole, but his birdie at the 18th put him in the three-way tie with Campbell and Takayama when Chris bogeyed the 72nd hole.

A birdie at the second playoff hole brought Campbell the title, the first-place money (¥20 million) and a berth in the British Open later in the summer. Smail and Takayama also received Open invitations along with fourth-place finisher Thammanoon Srirot of Thailand.

## Japan Golf Tour Championship—¥120,000,000
Winner: Kazuhiko Hosokawa

Kazuhiko Hosokawa broke two distasteful streaks when he won the Japan Golf Tour Championship in the circuit's second consecutive three-way playoff. A winner seven times in his first seven seasons, the 34-year-old Hosokawa hadn't added a title since the 2001 Acom International and he had gone 0 for 4 in playoffs before the Tour Championship at Shishido Hills Country Club at Tomobe in Ibaragi Prefecture.

While the victory was delightful for Hosokawa, it was particularly unpleasant for David Smail, one of the playoff victims with Yasuharu Imano. Smail was coming off another playoff loss the week before in the Mizuno Open and had led from the first round to a bogey at the 71st hole that brought about two extra holes and Hosokawa's triumph.

New Zealander Smail, 35, who had three Japan Tour victories on his record, started his bid at the Tour Championship with a four-under-par 66 that gave him a two-stroke advantage over nine players, including S.K. Ho, the defending champion. Thunderstorms interrupted play Friday, but Smail got his round in — another 66 for 132 that maintained his two-shot margin when the full field had finished Saturday morning. Smail's 70 later that day once more left him two strokes in front with his 202 for 54 holes. Hosokawa, who had trailed by five after 36 holes, shot 67 and seized second place with 204, a stroke ahead of Imano, Jun Kikuchi and Liang Wen-chong.

Hosokawa took the lead early in the final round, but Smail regained the advantage with a birdie at the eighth hole and held it until his bogey at the 17th. Imano, playing ahead of Smail and Hosokawa, birdied the 18th hole, forcing the other two to par the last hole for the deadlock. A six-foot par putt at the second extra hole — the par-four 18th — decided the tournament.

## Woodone Open Hiroshima—¥100,000,000
Winner: Takao Nogami

Takao Nogami gave himself as a birthday present a bauble that had eluded him for his near decade on the Japan Tour. Nogami toughed out a one-stroke victory in the Woodone Open Hiroshima on his 34th birthday to finally put his name on the winners' list after campaigning for that first win since 1998. He was the third first-time winner in the last four tournaments and fifth new victor of the 2005 season.

Nogami established his position in the second round at the par-71 Hiroshima Country Club when he shot 67 and moved into a three-way tie at 135 with Yutaka Horinouchi, another little-known non-winner, and Katsumasa Miyamoto, the first-round leader who was seeking his sixth career victory and first in two years. Miyamoto, who had opened with 66 to lead by a stroke over eight others, shot 69 Friday, and Horinouchi had rounds of 68-67. Nogami had a five-birdie run early in his round.

Takao broke in front Saturday, firing another 67 for 202 to take a two-stroke lead over Nobuhito Sato, who also shot 67. Nogami had another birdie run, running off three in a row on the back nine after an erratic front nine that consisted of three birdies, three bogeys and three pars. Nogami's challenger Sunday came from far off the pace. Fiji's Dinesh Chand, a three-time winner in Japan, began the final round six strokes off the lead, cut that to four on the front, then roared home with a 31 to put a 13-under-par 271 on the scoreboard long before Nogami reached the final holes. But Takao responded to the pressure with three finishing pars for the winning 68–270. Sato shot 70 and placed third, a stroke ahead of Miyamoto.

## Sega Sammy Cup—¥120,000,000
Winner: Lin Keng-chi

The Sega Sammy Cup stop on the Japan Tour in late July had age and international overtones. Players from Australia, India and Taiwan intermingled with the Japanese core of contestants through the early rounds of the tournament at North Country Golf Club at Chitose in Hokkaido before the issue came down to the 39-year-old winner and his most serious older challenger. The junior of the two — Taiwan's Lin Keng-chi, a two-time winner in Japan in 2002 — held on at the end of the final round for a one-stroke victory over Kiyoshi Maita, at 45 one of the oldest players in the field.

Australia's Scott Laycock, back in Japan after a spell on the U.S. PGA Tour, attracted the attention the first two days. He shared the first-round lead with Takashi Kanemoto and Shinichi Yokota at 66, then moved in front alone with 70–136 Friday. Dinesh Chand, who made a strong run at the Woodone Open title the previous Sunday, and Lin shot 69s and shared second place at 138.

The leadership shuffled Saturday. Shingo Katayama, the defending No. 1, and India's Jeev Milkha Singh carded 68s and tied for first with the Taiwanese veteran (69) at 207 as Chand slipped back with 71. Maita became the unlikely strongest pursuer Sunday as Lin struggled on the final holes behind him. Maita came up with an unexpected 66 and finished 20 minutes before Lin with his 276. Lin had six birdies, including a holed bunker shot at the second hole, but he bogeyed the 14th and 16th holes to make his situation a bit dicey. However, he parred the last two holes for 68 and the winning 275.

## Aiful Cup—¥120,000,000
Winner: Tatsuhiko Takahashi

The 2005 gallery of new winners on the Japan Tour continued to grow at the Aiful Cup tournament as Tatsuhiko Takahashi held off strong final-round bids to post his initial victory in his 10th season on the circuit. The

31-year-old Takahashi recorded a 16-under-par 268 at Daisen Ark Country Club, Tottori Prefecture, and joined five others who broke the victory ice earlier in the season.

The course yielded more than the usual number of 64s during the tournament. Daisuke Maruyama, another winless veteran, had the first one Thursday as he took a one-stroke lead over Tadahisa Inoue and two over Yasuharu Imano and Jun Kikuchi. Lightning and darkness prevented 15 players from finishing their rounds until Friday morning, but it had no bearing at the top of the standings. Takahashi shot 64 Friday and so did Keiichiro Fukabori, the 2003 Japan Open champion, who moved into a piece of the lead at 132 with Kikuchi, who matched his opening 66. Takahashi was one stroke back with Masayuki Kawamura, yet another 64 shooter, and Maruyama, who had a 69 before plunging from contention on the weekend.

Takahashi took charge Saturday, producing a 66 for 199 to jump two strokes in front of Soshi Tajima (66) and 55-year-old Katsunari Takahashi, the king of the Japan Senior Tour with 11 victories. However, it was Yasuaki Takashima who gave the winner the most trouble Sunday. Takashima came up with a 66, but Takahashi, with four birdies and two bogeys for 69, held on for the one-shot triumph.

## Sun Chlorella Classic—¥150,000,000
Winner: Keiichiro Fukabori

Keiichiro Fukabori, who kicked away a sizeable amount of money and pride with a poor finish to a fast start the week before in the Aiful Cup, more than made up for the transgressions in the Sun Chlorella Classic, one of the richest events on the Japan Tour. Surviving a three-way battle over the final holes, Fukabori captured his seventh career title and a healthy ¥30 million first prize. It was the first win since the 2003 Japan Open for the 36-year-old, who boosted himself into third place on the money list behind S.K. Ho and Naomichi Ozaki.

Hidemasa Hoshino, another player without a win since 2003 (Chunichi Crowns), dominated the early going at Otaru Country Club in the Hokkaido city of the same name. With nine birdies and a bogey for 64, Hoshino established a three-stroke lead over Fukabori, Satoru Hirota and Kaname Yokoo. He maintained that margin Friday with a 69 for 133 as Shingo Katayama joined the fray with 66–136. Fukabori shot 70 and shared third place with Toshimitsu Izawa (69).

Another country was heard from Saturday as Australian Paul Sheehan surged into a first-place tie with Hoshino, who slipped to 73 for his 206. Sheehan shot 66. Fukabori trailed by a stroke after another 70, joined in third place by Tetsuji Hiratsuka and Kiyoshi Miyazato. He was still behind as the leaders played the back nine Sunday. Hoshino and Sheehan shared the lead at 15 under par through 13 holes, then both men self-destructed en route to the clubhouse. Sheehan bogeyed the 15th, 16th and 17th and Hoshino two of the last three holes. Fukabori, making several clutch putts along with the seven birdies and bogey that created the winning 66–273, finished a shot in front of Hoshino and three ahead of Sheehan.

## Under Armour KBC Augusta—¥100,000,000
Winner: Toshimitsu Izawa

It had been a frustrating couple of years for Toshimitsu Izawa, long considered one of Japan's finest players. The fifth all-time money winner on the Japan Tour with 14 titles on his sparkling record, Izawa had finished 10th or better 11 times since his last two wins in 2003 but had failed to take home a victory in that span. The 37-year-old international player brought that negative run to an abrupt and resounding halt when the circuit resumed action after a three-week hiatus with the Under Armour KBC Augusta tournament. Izawa grabbed the lead the second day at Keya Golf Club at Shima in Fukuoka Prefecture and rolled to a five-stroke victory.

First, he had to settle for a position three strokes off the lead as Kazuhiko Hosokawa, the winner of the Tour Championship in early July, began with a front-nine 30 powered by an eagle at the par-five sixth hole and posted a 64, leading Tadahiro Takayama and Thailand's Thammanoon Srirot by a stroke. Izawa, twice the tour's leading money winner, began the drive to his 15th title Friday. He birdied five of his last seven holes for 65–132. That put him two strokes ahead of runner-up Ryuichi Oda. Then he doubled his margin over Oda and three others to four strokes Saturday when he shot 67 for 199, 14 under par. Katsumasa Miyamoto (63), Gregory Meyer (67) and Hosokawa (68) were at 203 with Oda (69).

By the turn Sunday, Izawa had things pretty well wrapped up. He went out in 31 and gathered seven birdies and a harmless late bogey into a 65 for his winning, 20-under-par 264. Five back in second place were Oda (66) and Thailand's Prayad Marksaeng (65).


## Fujisankei Classic—¥150,000,000
Winner: Daisuke Maruyama

Maybe something rubbed off on Daisuke Maruyama at the Aiful Cup tournament a month or so earlier in the Japan Tour season. Although he once again couldn't convert a strong start — 64 in the first round — into a victory there, he saw Tatsuhiko Takahashi end 10 years of frustration with his first victory. For Maruyama, the run of futility had been just as long, encompassing 123 tournaments. Finally, it ended with a crescendo at the Fujizakura Country Club at Kawaguchiko, the new venue of the Fujisankei Classic. Maruyama waltzed away to a seven-stroke victory with a 13-under-par 271.

Maruyama was in synch from the opening tee shot. He shot a four-under-par 67 Thursday and was the joint leader with Yusaku Miyazato and Shigeru Nonaka. All three did it despite each having two bogeys on their cards. South Korea's Chang Ik-je used an unorthodox hole-in-one as a springboard into the lead Friday. The Diamond Cup winner shot 64 despite a first-hole bogey and with 134 slipped a stroke in front of Maruyama (68) and Thailand's Prayad Marksaeng (65). His ace came when he mis-hit a five iron at the par-three 16th but it still landed 15 feet from the cup and rolled in.

While everybody else was shooting 69 or higher Saturday, Maruyama was carving out a 65 with a run of birdies on the back nine and pulling away to a seven-stroke lead at 200. Chang was closest and the trio of Shingo Katayama, Craig Jones of Australia and Takuya Taniguchi were at 208. Maruyama then rolled through a conservative 71 that was an unimpeded walk in the park to the long-sought victory. Katayama had a 70 and finished second. Maruyama was the seventh first-time winner of the year's first 16 tournaments.

## Suntory Open—¥100,000,000
Winner: Yasuharu Imano

Another week, another different winner. The Japan Tour continued that pattern at the Suntory Open in early September when Yasuharu Imano scored a modified wire-to-wire victory, the fifth of his career. He was the 13th different player in a row to secure a victory since Hiroyuki Fujita won the Munsingwear Open in May and he did it in a tough duel at the end with Mamoru Osanai, who also was seeking his first win of 2005.

On day one at the par-70 Suntory Country Club course at Inzai, Chiba Prefecture, Imano shot a bogey-free 65 and tied for the lead with veteran Hiroshi Goda, a stroke in front of Kiyoshi Miyazato, Shigeru Nonaka and Yudai Maeda. He went one better Friday and his 64–129 sprung him four strokes ahead of Miyazato, five ahead of Shingo Katayama, Hidemasa Hoshino and Yoshinobu Tsukada.

An eight-stroke swing hoisted Osanai into a deadlock with Imano at 199 Saturday. Yasuharu shot a respectable 70, but found himself with a first-place companion when Mamoru came up with a career-best 62 for his 199. Steven Conran, Katayama and S.K. Ho followed a stroke apart at 201, 202 and 203. Osanai got off to the faster start Sunday and led early before dropping a couple of shots midway through the round. By the 12th hole, Imano had built a three-shot lead and went smoothly on to victory, his first since back-to-back wins in mid-season 2002. With his 68 for 267, he finished two strokes ahead of Osanai (70) and three in front of Katayama (69).

## ANA Open—¥100,000,000
Winner: Keiichiro Fukabori

In a season in which titles have been spread around in unusually large numbers, the Japan Tour got just its third multiple winner of 2005 when Keiichiro Fukabori scored a playoff victory in mid-September in the ANA Open. In winning via a one-hole playoff over Yasuharu Imano, Fukabori parlayed the two victories (the other was the Sun Chlorella a month earlier) and six top-10 finishes into a move into first place on the money list, supplanting S.K. Ho, who had held that position since winning his second in mid-May.

Fukabori, who also won the ANA Open in 1998, needed a course-record 62 in the second round to get where he did on the Wattsu course of Sapporo Golf Club in Hokkaido. He had shot a par 72 in the first round and rested six shots behind leader Hidemasa Hoshino in a tie for 62nd place. In the complete turnaround Friday, Fukabori ran off an eagle and eight birdies for the 62 that vaulted him into a one-stroke lead over South Korea's Chang Ik-je with the 134. It was his first-ever 10-under-par round.

Imano entered the picture Saturday when his 70–206 thrust him into a three-way tie for the lead with Thailand's Chawalit Plaphol (68) and Fukabori, who shot another par round. Right behind at 207 were Y.E. Yang, Tomohiro Kondo, Jeev Milkha Singh and Hoshino. Things didn't begin well for Fukabori Sunday when he bogeyed the first hole, but he fought back with six birdies for 68–274, and Imano retained his chances for two in a row with a matching score, thanks to an eagle at the 17th hole. Fukabori birdied the first playoff hole, the 18th, to seal his eighth victory.

## Acom International—¥120,000,000
Winner: David Smail

It was a nice position to be in. Even a double bogey on the 72nd hole only reduced the margin of victory as David Smail recorded his fourth victory on the Japan Tour in the Acom International. It brought about a 73 and his 13-under-par 271 gave him a two-stroke victory over Taichi Teshima, three over Shingo Katayama, the reigning No. 1 champion who had been in frequent contention but had not won in 2005. It was a bit of retribution for Smail, who had been a loser in three-man playoffs on consecutive Sundays earlier in the season.

Smail, who did not take a bogey during the first three rounds, got off to a fast start in his wire-to-wire performance at Ishioka Golf Club in Ogawa, Ibaragi Prefecture. He opened with a seven-birdie 64 despite an aching back that had been bothering him since the British Open in July and led by one over Yeh Wei-tze of Taiwan, Yoshikazu Haku and Mamoru Osanai. The 35-year-old Anzac, who has campaigned in Japan for nine seasons, widened his advantage to two strokes with a 65 for 129. Scott Laycock with 63 and Takuya Taniguchi with 64 were at 131.

Katayama leaped into contention Saturday. He fired a 65 for 199, advancing within a stroke of Smail, who had two back-nine birdies and 16 pars for 69 and 198. Laycock, with 69–200, and another Australian, Paul Sheehan, with 65–202, were next in the standings. Smail, whose most recent win was in the 2004 Casio World Open, nailed an early birdie and gradually stretched his lead despite his first bogeys of the week until the anticlimactic double bogey on the last hole that put him back to 73 and the winning score of 271. Katayama faded to 75 and Teshima, the 2001 Japan Open champion, recorded his best finish of the season with 68 for 273.

## Coca-Cola Tokai Classic—¥120,000,000
Winner: Y.E. Yang

Other than a third-place finish in the early-season Chunichi Crowns tournament, little had been heard in 2005 from Y.E. Yang, the South Korean who burst into prominence on the 2004 Japan Tour with two victories and a third-place finish on the final money list. He made his presence known and felt, though, when the circuit went to Miyoshi in Aichi Prefecture for the Coca-Cola Tokai Classic. Yang staged a 65-67 finish at Miyoshi Country Club for a victory that didn't come easily in the final round.

Yang got off to a good start Thursday, shooting a six-under-par 66 that put him in a three-way tie for second place with Toru and Takuya Taniguchi, a stroke behind India's Jeev Milkha Singh, who had an eagle and five birdies on Miyoshi's West course. Yang suffered his poorest round of the tournament Friday. His 72 dropped him three behind Yeh Wei-tze, who took over first place with 67–135, a shot ahead of Singh (71) and Sushi Ishigaki (69).

Then came Yang's 65, which carried him two strokes in front at 203. Two eagles on par-fives highlighted the round, which also included four birdies and a bogey. Takuya Taniguchi shot 68 for 205 and Taichi Teshima (66), Daisuke Maruyama and Katsumasa Miyamoto (67s) were at 206. Taniguchi climbed into a tie in the early going Sunday with an eagle at the second and birdie at the fourth holes, but Yang responded with an eagle-birdie combination of his own and carried a three-stroke lead onto the back nine. Taniguchi fell quickly out of contention and Teshima followed, giving the South Korean an easy run to the victory with his 67–270. Teshima steadied, finished with 68 and took the runner-up slot.

## Japan Open—¥120,000,000
Winner: Shingo Katayama

It was just a matter of time — and Shingo Katayama's timing was right. Eleven times during the first seven months of the 2005 Japan Tour season, Katayama finished in the top 10 among his 17 starts, but with nary a victory among them. Then the Japan Open Championship appeared on the schedule with Hirono Golf Club, one of Japan's most highly regarded courses in international circles, as the venue. The prospect of making his first win of the season his first Japan Open title on a prestigious course excited Katayama and, after a brilliant final-round rally, he put the championship in his pocket.

The lead bounced around through the first three rounds with Katayama on the outer fringe of contention. Dinesh Chand, the Fijian, stepped out the first day with 67, holding a one-shot lead over Lin Keng-chi of Taiwan and Kenichi Kuboya, but none of the three held up Friday. First place went instead to Ryoken (Ricky) Kawagishi, whose 66 was the lowest round of the tournament. It gave him a 138 and a two-stroke lead over Tatsunori Nukaga, David Smail, Tadahiro Takayama and Steven Conran. Katayama was then six shots back after rounds of 71-73.

Kawagishi had to settle for a par round on a rainy Saturday, but he retained a portion of the lead with Toshimitsu Izawa, the 1995 Open champion, who shot 67 for his 210. Katayama mustered 70 for 214 and had seven players between him and the top, among them Australian Craig Parry, the 1997 winner of the year's most prized title. Katayama swept past them all Sunday with a near-flawless round of 68 and won by two strokes with his 282 score. Kawagishi and Izawa went in the opposite direction, Ryoken shooting 74 and Toshi 75. Parry had the best chance of stopping Katayama, who had taken the lead with four birdies through 14 holes, then faltered with a bogey at the 16th. However, Parry bogeyed the last two holes for 72 and dropped into a tie for second at 284 with Kawagishi (74).

The victory, Katayama's 17th since 1998, elevated him in the No. 1 position on the money list, a familiar spot for a man who has led the tour twice and never finished worse than fourth since 2000.

## Bridgestone Open—¥110,000,000
Winner: David Smail

New Zealand's David Smail embellished his most successful of nine seasons on the Japan Tour with his second victory, prevailing by two strokes at the end of a tight final round. The winner's check of ¥22 million elevated Smail to the third spot on the money list, his highest position ever as he became the fourth player of the year to win twice in a season of spread the wealth. And what if the two playoffs he lost early in the season had gone the other way?

Smail started with a 66 that put him in second place behind South Korean veteran Kim Jong-duck, 44, a three-time winner in Japan who had just picked up a victory on his home country's circuit. Smail's only glitch during the tournament was a second-round 72 that dropped him three strokes behind a three-man tie for the lead held by Makoto Inoue, Kaname Yokoo and American Gregory Meyer at 135.

Bouncing back Saturday, Smail shot 67 at Sodegaura Country Club, Chiba, and climbed into a share of the lead with Yusaku Miyazato, Ai Miyazato's oldest brother, whose eagle two at the sixth hole sparked him to 68 and his 205. Smail seized control Sunday with birdies on the first two holes and made another at the seventh. He got his only scare at the end of the round. Toru Suzuki was in with a 66, the day's best round, when Smail took his only bogey at the 17th, reducing his lead to a stroke. But David finished with a flourish, firing his approach to the final green six feet from the cup and rolling in the birdie putt for 67–272 and the two-shot triumph, his career fifth in Japan.

## ABC Championship—¥120,000,000
Winner: Shingo Katayama

Shingo Katayama wasn't about to let anything, not even an embarrassing disqualification, sidetrack his charge toward his third seasonal championship in six years. In fact, he couldn't have rebounded any higher than he did the next week when, after being ousted from the Bridgestone Open after two rounds, Katayama turned around and captured the ABC Championship just two weeks after he won his first Japan Open. With those two victories on top of a strong run of high finishes, Katayama solidified his grasp on the money list lead, moving more than ¥40 million ahead of runner-up Keiichiro Fukabori with only five events left to the 2005 Japan Tour season.

Katayama polished off his 18th tour victory in the ABC Championship in style, racking up three birdies on the final six holes at ABC Golf Club at Tojo in Hyogo Prefecture for 69–274 and a two-stroke victory over fast-finishing Dinesh Chand, who took sole possession of the runner-up position when he eagled the 72nd hole.

Katayama had held at least a share of the lead since shooting a bogey-free 65 in the second round. That brought him even at 135 with Taiwan's Lin Keng-chi, the Sega Sammy Cup winner in July, who had jointly held the first-round lead at 66 with Katsunori Kuwabara. Katayama edged a stroke in front Saturday when he shot his second 70 for 205. Lin remained close with 71–206, tied there with Toru Taniguchi, the leading money winner in 2002, who was winless so far in 2005. Neither man could keep up with Katayama Sunday, although Lin shot 71 and finished in a four-way tie for third at 277 with Daisuke Maruyama, Jun Kikuchi and Chang Ik-je.

## Asahiryokuken Yomiuri Asoiizuka Memorial—¥100,000,000
Winner: Azuma Yano

It was hard to say which outcome at the Asahiryokuken Yomiuri Asoiizuka Memorial tournament was more surprising — Azuma Yano's victory or Shingo Katayama's failure to win. Yano, winless on the Japan Tour, had collected just ¥18 million in 22 starts earlier in the 2005 season and stood 51st on the money list before squeezing out a one-stroke victory at Asoi-izuka Golf Club at Keisen, Fukuoka Prefecture. Certainly an unexpected development. Just as shocking was Katayama's inability to close out with a win after leading the tournament for three rounds amid his hottest streak of the season.

Even though Yano lurked just off the lead after the end of the second and third rounds, few expected him to hold up as he did Sunday. He birdied three of the last four holes for his third consecutive five-under-par 67 and made off with the title with 270, a shot ahead of Taichi Teshima (67), Dinesh Chand (68) and Nozomi Kawahara.

It had appeared to be money leader Katayama's tournament until Sunday as he maintained the fast pace that he taken him to victory in two of the three most recent tournaments. Katayama got away fast Thursday with 65, ripping off eight birdies and taking a lone bogey, to grab the first-round lead by a stroke over China's Liang Wen-chong and Yoshinobu Tsukada. He had a 69 Friday and still was a stroke in front, then over Satoru Hirota and Kawahara, who both had rounds of 69-66–135.

Those two, with 67s for 202, forged a three-way tie with Katayama (68) in the third round, as Yano (67) joined Liang and Chand at 203. Yano showed great patience when he won Sunday. He didn't make a birdie until the 10th hole, made another at the 12th and three in a row from the 15th that wrapped up his maiden victory on the circuit. He was the eighth and last first-time winner of 2005. Meanwhile, Katayama was shooting 70 and dropping to sixth place in the final standings.

# Mitsui Sumitomo Visa Taiheiyo Masters—¥150,000,000
Winner: Darren Clarke

It had been a trying year for Darren Clarke when he arrived in Japan to defend his title in the Mitsui Sumitomo Visa Taiheiyo Masters. Clarke, the 37-year-old Northern Ireland star of European Tour and Ryder Cup competition, had gone without a victory through the first 10 months of 2005, attributable in large measure to his deep concern and time spent with his seriously ill wife back home. Japan appeared to be a tonic for him. A regular visitor to the country over the previous seven years, Clarke had the 2001 Chunichi Crowns title on his record along with the previous year's Taiheiyo Masters and he staged a powerful weekend finish to repeat the triumph, winning by two strokes over Mitsuhiro Tateyama thanks to a 40-foot eagle putt on the final hole. It gave him a four-under-par 68 for 270.

"I tried to get it as close as I could and, fortunately, it went in," observed Clarke. "It's the first time I successfully defended a title. I was pleased to do it here (the Taiheiyo Club's Gotemba course), one of my favorite golf courses."

Clarke's strongest opposition during the tournament came from the veteran Hideki Kase, who was never out of the lead through the first three rounds. Kase, 45, a four-time winner over his 15 seasons on the Japan Tour, shot his two lowest rounds of the year with a pair of 66s the first two days. The first one put him in a three-way tie for the lead with Clarke and Christian Pena, an American with a single Japanese victory on his record. The second one boosted him three strokes in front of the field Friday. Clarke fell five behind with a 71 and Pena dropped to 73 en route to a 43rd-place finish. Katsumune Imai was second with 68-67–135, but he, too, fell by the wayside Saturday as Clarke charged back with a seven-birdie 65 to rejoin Kase (70) in first place.

As it turned out Sunday, Clarke's most serious challenge came from Tateyama, who hadn't had a top-10 finish all season. He was just a stroke behind the Ulsterman before the decisive eagle on the last hole. Kase managed just a par 72, but held onto third place, four strokes behind the winner. Besides his three wins in Japan and one in South Africa, Clarke has eight in regular European Tour events and two in World Championship events, most notably the 2000 Accenture Match Play, in which he defeated David Duval in the semi-finals and Tiger Woods in the championship match.

# Dunlop Phoenix—¥200,000,000
Winner: Tiger Woods

Tiger Woods had more prestigious victories in 2005 than the one he scored near the end of the season in the Dunlop Phoenix, but none of the eight came with more difficulty and suspense. Kaname Yokoo was the unlikely antagonist who forced the game's current greatest player to duel with him through four playoff holes before yielding Woods's second consecutive victory in the Japan Tour's richest tournament.

Although he had spruced up his game with three seasons on the U.S. PGA Tour, Yokoo had little more than a mediocre 2005 campaign when he returned to full-time play in Japan. He ranked just 30th on the money list when he teed off in the Dunlop Phoenix at Phoenix Country Club at Miyazaki. Still, he deserved attention because he had won there in 2002.

Surprises abounded at the tournament, beginning with David Duval's start in the opening round. Duval, whose victory in the Dunlop Phoenix in 2001 was his most recent one, had made only one cut all year in America as his shocking slump continued into its fourth season. But he put together eight birdies and a pair of bogeys for 64 and the first-round lead, a stroke ahead of Woods, three in front of Jim Furyk, the 2003 U.S. Open champion, Shinichi Yokota and Tomohiro Kondo.

Woods remained one off the lead after Furyk matched Duval's starting 64 and moved ahead at 131. Tiger, with 67, was at 132 with Duval, who had a 68, despite being two over par for the round after 10 holes. "To be only one back is pretty good," Woods admitted. "I missed a lot of putts and didn't drive as well as yesterday."

Yokoo moved into contention Saturday when Woods took over first place with 68–200, a stroke ahead of Furyk (70). The Japanese challenger had rounds of 68-67-68 for 203 and was tied for third with Duval, who took 71 on a windy day during which the scores were less than spectacular. Sunday's action came down to the final holes when Woods and Yokoo were at the top of the leaderboard. Yokoo birdied the 18th hole for 69–272, and Woods could only match that total with a 72 after he drove into a bad bunker lie on the par-five finishing hole and had to settle for a par there and a par round.

They used only the 18th hole in the playoff and Woods, limping on a bad ankle that he aggravated on his first tee shot of the overtime, ultimately won there the fourth time around with his third straight birdie. He reached the green in two shots and two-putted for the victory after Yokoo missed a 12-foot birdie putt. Furyk finished third at 274 with a closing 73, and Duval slipped into a seventh-place tie after a 75 final round.

## Casio World Open—¥140,000,000
Winner: Toru Taniguchi

For the first two rounds of the Casio World Open, the 101 males in the field jockeyed virtually unnoticed for position in the standings while the eyes of the golfing public were on the other golfer in the field — 16-year-old Michelle Wie and her attempt to make a cut for the first time in her sixth try in a men's tournament. The young phenom came close, but fell one stroke shy when she bogeyed the 35th and 36th holes.

When she exited the scene, the attention turned to the business at hand — the winning of the rich tournament — and Toru Taniguchi took care of that matter to salvage some glory from what had been his least successful season in recent years. Taniguchi, the Japan Tour's leading money winner in 2002 and runner-up in 2000 and 2004, had gone all season without a victory until he pulled off the two-shot triumph in the Casio World the last weekend of November at its new venue — Kochi Kuroshio Golf Club, Kochi Prefecture, on the island of Shikoku.

For the record, amid the Wie whirlwind Thursday and Friday, Toshimitsu

Izawa and Yoshiaki Kimura took the first-round lead with 68s, and the second round ended with Izawa in a four-way tie for first place with Mamoru Osanai (67), Toru Suzuki (68) and Taichi Teshima (69). Taniguchi was just two off the pace after posting a pair of 70s in the first two rounds, then took the lead for good Saturday when the Wie fury subsided. His 68 for 208 put him a shot ahead of South Korean veteran Kim Jong-duck, with 13 other players within four shots of the top.

Taniguchi, age 37, had a shaky spell at mid-round Sunday, taking a pair of bogeys, but he birdied three of the last six holes for his winning 69–277. It was his 10th victory. Kim shot 70 for 279, taking second ahead of Yasuharu Imano, the Suntory champion, who closed with 68–280.

## Golf Nippon Series JT Cup—¥100,000,000
Winner: Yasuhiro Imano

With Shingo Katayama on the sidelines, his third Japan Tour money-winning title already in hand, the question at the season-ending Golf Nippon Series JT Cup became who would finish second. Katayama, bothered again by an aching back that gave him problems from time to time toward the end of the year, had withdrawn after his 74-72 start in the event in which 27 of the season's winners and others high on the money list played. At that point, Toru Taniguchi was making a run at two in a row, but the season's runner-up spot was out of reach for him.

Not for Yasuharu Imano, though. The Suntory winner, coming off a third-place finish in the previous week's Casio World and enjoying the finest of his 10 seasons on the tour, soared into the lead with a seven-under-par 63 at Tokyo's Yomiuri Country Club Saturday and held on for a two-stroke victory at 11-under 269. The ¥30,000,000 first prize carried him past South Korea's S.K. Ho and Keiichiro Fukabori into second place at ¥118,543,753, well behind Katayama's ¥134,075,280.

Taniguchi's momentum from the Casio triumph carried over to Thursday's opening round of the Nippon Series. He opened with a 64, getting a three-stroke jump on the field as Naomichi (Joe) Ozaki, Shinichi Yokota and Satoru Hirota started with 67s. Taniguchi's lead narrowed to one Friday when he shot 70–134. Yokota had 68 for 135 and Australia's Chris Campbell posted 69-67–136. Imano was five back after rounds of 72-67–139.

With the 63 Saturday, though, Imano wound up a stroke in the lead ahead of Kiyoshi Miyazato (67) and Yokota (68) and offset a pair of bogeys with five birdies Sunday for the winning 67. Yokota shot his third straight 68 for 271, finishing a stroke in front of Taichi Teshima (65) and Taniguchi, who rebounded from a third-round 72 with a 66.

## Asia/Japan Okinawa Open—¥100,000,000
Winner: Tadahiro Takayama

Tadahiro Takayama book-ended 2005 when he won the Asia/Japan Okinawa Open, the final event of the year in Japan but the first tournament of the 2006 seasons of the Japan and Asia Tours in mid-December, to go with his maiden career victory in the first tournament of the year, the Token Homemate Cup in March.

As much as it was a thrill for Takayama, though, the outcome was disappointing for the Miyazato family and their home island followers and supporters. Takayama scored the victory in a playoff against Okinawa's Kiyoshi Miyazato, the defending champion, two days after Kiyoshi's younger sister, Ai, the sensation of Japanese women's golf in 2005 and the first female to play in a Japan Tour tournament, finished at the bottom of the standings (80-78) and missed the cut.

The Japan Tour players dominated the joint event. One of them — Fiji's Dinesh Chand — and Kaname Yokoo, the playoff loser to Tiger Woods in the Dunlop Phoenix a month earlier, opened with 65s and led Hiroyuki Fujita by a stroke, Kenichi Kubota by two. As his sister was bowing out, Kiyoshi Miyazato established his position Friday, shooting 67 and moving into a first-place tie at 135 with Yokoo (70) and Yasuharu Imano, the 2005 season runner-up on the Japan Tour, who erupted into contention with a seven-under-par 64 at the Naha Golf Club.

Despite gusty weather, Tetsuji Hiratsuka matched Imano's 64 Saturday and jumped into a one-shot lead at 203 over Yokoo (69), two ahead of Miyazato (70) and Toru Taniguchi (67). Takayama was another stroke back after his second consecutive 68 for 206. Only four players broke par on a windy Sunday and Takayama was one of them. It gave him a 276 total that Miyazato equaled with his 71. When Hiratsuka finished behind them a stroke higher with 74–277 to tie Kuboya for third, Takayama and Miyazato proceeded with the playoff. After pars at the first extra hole, Takayama holed a 17-foot birdie putt on the next one to nail the victory after Miyazato two-putted for par.

# 11. Australasian Tour

Interrupting a government cabinet meeting, since a late Sunday afternoon in America is already the start of the working week on a Monday morning in New Zealand, and later a tickertape parade through Wellington. Not bad for a golfer. Only a very special performance could make these things happen and Michael Campbell produced it with his victory at the U.S. Open at Pinehurst. Campbell not only became the second New Zealander to win a major championship, after Bob Charles at the 1963 Open Championship, but did it in style by holding off the challenge of the world No. 1, Tiger Woods, who otherwise would have taken the first three majors of the year.

It was a stunning achievement from the 36-year-old Kiwi and not least because he only made a late decision to play in the new USGA qualifier at Walton Heath in England. Then, of course, there was also the matter of missing five cuts in a row at the start of the season. He has never done consistency. But ever since he finished third at the Open at St Andrews in 1995, his talent was obvious. "I'm either missing cuts or winning golf tournaments," he said. "It's just a bizarre thing. I'm probably the most inconsistent player on tour. I'll be the first to admit that. Why, I have no idea. But when I get into a groove, you see what can happen."

Once he had it, this time Campbell did not want to lose his groove any time soon. He finished fifth in the Open and sixth at the U.S. PGA Championship before winning the HSBC World Match Play at Wentworth with a run that included wins over Retief Goosen and Paul McGinley. He went on to finish runner-up to Colin Montgomerie in the European Order of Merit, but was voted the European Tour Golfer of the Year, the NZ Maori Sportsperson of the Year and won the Best Overseas Performance Award on the Australasian Tour.

"I think the last nine holes at Pinehurst gave me a true test," Campbell said. "It was either make or break as a player for me. If I had a three-shot lead playing the last nine holes and lost the tournament that week, I would have been devastated and probably not recovered for a long time. But to actually go out there and have the best player on the planet shooting all guns blazing toward you, and I responded with birdies on 10 and 12 and up and down on 15 and birdie on 17, that was probably the toughest situation that I've ever, ever been in. Last nine holes, you're leading by three shots, Tiger is right behind you, making all these birdies in a major championship, and I won. I know that I can cope with any situation now."

Robert Allenby also produced a moment of history, but his was three weeks in the creating. Although Peter Lonard had come close the previous year after winning the Australian Open and the Australian PGA Championship, Allenby became the first player to collect the "triple crown" by adding the MasterCard Masters title. Allenby returned to Australia after a frustrating season on the PGA Tour in America when he was affected by chronic inflammation in his hands. The injury flared up again during the Australian Open, but Allenby hung to win at Moonah Links by a single shot.

He won by the same margin the following week at the PGA and then won the Masters after a playoff. So it was always tense, but the 34-year-old seems the man for such occasions: He has won nine playoffs out of nine. He said: "Going down to the Australian Open I said to my caddie, 'Lonard nearly won all three last year, I reckon if I could just win the Australian Open I could get it.' I didn't think the Australian Open would be the one I could win, but it is amazing what you can do when you put your mind to it."

Having only played in three events Allenby was not eligible for the Australasian Tour Order of Merit, so Adam Scott took the title. Scott won the Johnnie Walker Classic, a co-sanctioned event with the European and Asian Tours, as well as adding overseas wins at the Singapore Open on the Asian Tour and the Nissan Open in America. As the Nissan was cut to 36 holes due to rain, it did not count as an official victory according to the PGA Tour, much to Scott's frustration.

Other winners in America were Stuart Appleby at the Mercedes Championships and first-timers Geoff Ogilvy and Peter Lonard. In Europe, Mark Hensby won the Scandinavian Masters following impressive performances in the majors where he was third in the U.S. Open, fifth at the Masters and 15th at the Open Championship. Steven Bowditch proved himself one of the next young Australians to watch by winning the Jacob's Creek Open at Royal Adelaide, and he qualified for the 2006 PGA Tour from the Nationwide Tour along with Greg Chalmers, Nathan Green, Mathew Goggin and David McKenzie. Nick O'Hern could not get the victory his consistent play around the globe deserves, but he did line up with four other Aussies in the International team that narrowly lost the Presidents Cup to America. He was joined by Appleby, Scott, Hensby and Lonard, and with New Zealand's Campbell they made up half the team.

## Heineken Classic—A$2,000,000
Winner: Craig Parry

Craig Parry realized a childhood dream by putting like his 10-year-old son Ryan. Time and again Parry was saved by his brilliant work on the greens as he finally beat Nick O'Hern at the fourth extra hole of a playoff to win the Heineken Classic at the revered Royal Melbourne course.

"This is fantastic. This ranks right up there with my wins," said Parry. "I came here as a five-year-old and I sat over the back of the 18th green with my grandparents," he said. "I played my first round around here when I was 13 and it's just a hell of a golf course. It's one of the best in the world and it just means a real lot."

On an unpredictable final afternoon, Parry started one stroke behind O'Hern but was leading with eight holes to play. It was then that his run of holes without a bogey ended at 30 as he dropped three shots in four holes. A birdie at the 17th, however, meant he posted the target at 14 under par after a closing 70. O'Hern, with a 71, joined him after pars at each of the last four holes.

In the playoff, O'Hern appeared to be on the verge on winning several times but, unlike Parry, he could get no joy out of the greens. At the 18th for the first extra hole, O'Hern hit his approach to seven feet while Parry bunkered himself. But Parry came out to 15 feet and holed the par putt, while the left-hander missed his chance for victory. At the 18th again, both parred, O'Hern missing from 10 feet. For the third extra hole they went to the 17th and Parry got up and down, chipping to 10 feet and holing the putt, while O'Hern missed again, this time from five feet. Back at the 18th for the third time in the playoff, both men had chances from 10 feet, and while Parry holed his, O'Hern missed yet again.

"Each time I thought I was going to lose," Parry said. "Nick could have easily finished it at the first hole and he hit a great shot in there. Every time we played the 18th hole he hit a good shot in. When you're under pressure, that's tough work. I was fortunate, he was unlucky."

Parry, 39, won for the fifth time on the European Tour and the 13th time on the Australasian Tour in the co-sanctioned event. His putter, an old faithful, had only just gone back in the bag after a "rest." "It had a holiday about midway through last year and obviously it has come back, it's learned its lesson," Parry said. "It might be in the bag for a little bit longer."

Parry also said he had learned a lot from his 10-year-old son's approach to putting. "I've been playing with my son Ryan and he's such a good putter. When I had my putts to save par I thought just do what Ryan would do, right speed and in the middle of the hole. There's no thought of missing it because he's so new to the game," he said.

In many ways the story of the tournament belonged to Jarrod Lyle, a 23-year-old Victorian in his rookie season. Lyle suffered from leukemia as a teenager but recovered to pursue his dream of becoming a professional golfer. A birdie on the 11th hole put him into the lead, but poor drives at the 15th and 18th holes cost him bogeys. There was an emotional reaction from family and friends, but his unique perspective helped deal with the disappointment of missing out on the playoff by one stroke.

Lyle shared third place with England's Simon Dyson, who was five behind after eight holes, but three birdies around the turn as the leaders struggled put him into contention. But Dyson missed a chance to take the lead at the 17th and then bogeyed the last, as did Ernie Els, the winner for the previous three years, who finished in fifth place, two strokes outside the playoff.

## Holden New Zealand Open—NZ$1,500,000
Winner: Niclas Fasth

Two rounds of 63 in three days at the Gulf Harbour club in Auckland were not quite good enough for Niclas Fasth to win the Holden New Zealand Open, but a birdie at the second extra hole, after being taken to a playoff by England's Miles Tunnicliff, certainly was. With the tournament co-sanctioned by the European Tour for the first time, Fasth was able to lift his second title after winning the Madeira Island Open in 2000. The 32-year-old Swede made seven birdies and an eagle in his closing round after the former Ryder Cup player had given the rest of the field a chance to keep up with a 75 in the third round.

Fasth moved two shots clear when he birdied the par-three 13th, but

Tunnicliff rallied immediately by holing his bunker shot for an eagle two at the 12th. After Fasth birdied the 17th to go one clear, Tunnicliff, playing two groups behind, squandered what seemed to be an ideal chance to match him, with a birdie putt of less than six feet. But the 36-year-old wasn't about to concede and rolled in a much tougher birdie putt of around 20 feet on the 72nd hole to complete a six-under round of 66 and force extra holes.

The players then returned to the 18th to start the playoff, and although the first extra hole was not decisive, it was unfortunately dramatic. Tunnicliff's approach overshot the green and struck a 12-year-old girl in the gallery on the head. The Englishman's concentration was momentarily broken as the young spectator was taken away for medical treatment, but she was conscious when Tunnicliff apologized to her. "It wasn't nice seeing her put on a stretcher, but they told me she was okay," Tunnicliff said.

Tunnicliff then had to re-group and managed to get up and down from the rough for a par as Fasth missed from 18 feet for birdie. Both players found the green the second time around, and after Tunnicliff had missed from long range, Fasth holed from 12 feet for a birdie to seal the victory. He admitted, "It was a good performance to come from behind like that."

Australians Richard Green and Simon Nash shared third place at 18 under. Nash finished with a birdie, his sixth of the day, to complete a five-under 67, while Green had five birdies and one bogey in a 68. Englishman Oliver Wilson, the leader going into the final round, had a day to forget, managing only two birdies and four bogeys to follow his excellent first three rounds of 66, 65 and 68 with a disappointing 74 to finished tied for seventh place. But compatriot Steve Webster leapt from last place to mid-table thanks to a brilliant course-record round of 10-under 62, having been the first player out following an 80 on Saturday.

## Jacob's Creek Open—A$1,000,000
Winner: Steven Bowditch

Queenslander Steven Bowditch continued a memorable Australian summer with a convincing five-shot victory in the Jacob's Creek Open at Royal Adelaide. Bowditch once worked as a cement mixer and the win proved he was laying solid foundations for a successful career. Earlier in the Australian summer, at the end of 2004, Bowditch was third in the Australian Open and fourth in the MasterCard Masters.

But this victory, for which Bowditch collected A$180,000, had more worldwide implications as the co-sanctioned event was the season-opening tournament for the U.S.-based Nationwide Tour. At 21 years, eight months and 12 days, Bowditch became the second youngest winner on that circuit.

Starting the final round three strokes ahead of the field, Bowditch was never seriously challenged on the final day. His closing 71 saw him finish at 11 under par, while American Ryan Armour and Australian Nathan Green shared runner-up honors at six under. Greg Chalmers and Craig Jones tied for fourth at five under after rounds of 71, while Brandt Snedeker and Wayne Grady finished tied for sixth.

Armour was the only player to put any pressure on the eventual winner, but his score of 69 was never enough. He made five birdies on the front nine, but a double bogey at the 12th was where his challenge faltered. Bowditch went out in three under par, but then three bogeys at the 10th, 12th and 13th holes suddenly gave the rest a glimmer of hope.

But, in fact, the 13th proved the turning point as Bowditch was thrilled not to have taken a double bogey. His tee shot went into the trees and he took three more shots to reach the green before holing an unlikely long putt for a five and not the six that looked inevitable. Bowditch punched the air after maintaining his lead at three, and when Armour bogeyed the 16th, the Australian was four clear again.

It was a shaky start to the third round, when as leader he had five bogeys in the first eight holes, that ironically helped him on the final day. "I just learnt so much from yesterday," Bowditch said. "I was so nervous yesterday I didn't know how to take it. I didn't know what to do and I just learnt so much from those first six holes out there. I really felt what I took in yesterday was a massive impact and it really got me through today early."

## ING New Zealand PGA Championship—A$762,000
Winner: Peter O'Malley

Steven Bowditch's attempt to win in successive weeks was only prevented by Peter O'Malley at the fourth extra hole of a playoff. O'Malley won the ING New Zealand PGA Championship at the Clearwater resort in Christchurch in style by holing from almost 30 feet for the victory on the 18th green.

It was the fifth time in rapid succession that the pair had played the hole. O'Malley could have won without the need for extra holes except for missing a putt conservatively estimated at 15 inches. Instead, O'Malley had to settle for a round of 69 and fell back into a tie with Bowditch at 14 under par. Bowditch had come from six strokes behind starting the last round with a course record-equaling nine-under-par 63.

Bowditch had opened the event with a 64, but an inward half of 42 in the third round had dropped him back with a 76. The young Queenslander scorched the course the next day with nine birdies in the first 14 holes, six coming in seven holes from the eighth. After 14 holes, where his eagle putt only just missed, Bowditch had edged one stroke in front of O'Malley.

But Bowditch could only par in and then had to wait for O'Malley to respond. Birdies at the 10th and 11th put the 39-year-old Australian in front again, only he then bogeyed the 12th. He went ahead with a birdie three at the 15th only to struggle at the last, where he almost chipped in with a driver before missing the tiny putt. Nevertheless, O'Malley eventually secured his fourth Australasian Tour title and his first since winning at the same venue three years earlier. Bowditch had the consolation of again performing well in another Nationwide Tour event, and he would go on to secure his card for the 2006 PGA Tour from the circuit.

Americans Johnson Wagner and Jerry Smith shared third place at 11 under, Wagner after an even-par round of 72 and Smith thanks to a closing 70.

New South Welshman Steven Jeffress and American Troy Matteson both came home with 70s, while Brandt Snedeker carded a 71 to finish at 10 under, tied for fifth.

## Johnnie Walker Classic—US$2,350,000
Winner: Adam Scott

See Asia/Japan Tours chapter.

## HSBC Champions Tournament—US$5,000,000
Winner: David Howell

See Asia/Japan Tours chapter.

## MFS Australian Open—A$1,250,000
Winner: Robert Allenby

Battling a hand condition that had affected him all year and increasingly difficult weather conditions at the Moonah Links, Robert Allenby hung on to win the MFS Australian Open for the second time. On a fine morning on the first day, Allenby set a course record of 63. On the next two days he added par rounds of 72, and then he closed with a 77 for a four-under-par total of 284.

Suffering from chronic inflammation in his hands, the condition flared up late in the third round and the blustery weather over the weekend did not help. His five-stroke advantage with a round to play was soon trimmed as the 34-year-old Allenby dropped four shots in the first six holes.

Allenby steadied the ship after that, but two late bogeys, at the 16th and 17th holes, suddenly made for a tight finish. Paul Sheehan, Allenby's playing partner, went out in 38 to Allenby's 39, but a birdie at the 17th put him within one of the leader. But he could not make the birdie he needed at the last, and Allenby used all his experience in making sure of his par and the victory.

"I needed every shot, that is for sure," Allenby said. "I thought I was going to even need one more in the end. Friday was tough, yesterday was tougher, today was even tougher. Obviously with my hand, that sort of let me down. Over the first five or six holes, I was scared that it wasn't going to hold up for the day and I was just too scared to commit to shots."

Sheehan shared second place with John Senden, who closed with a 70 after bogeying the 16th and the 17th like Allenby, and Nick O'Hern, who shot a 72. Matthew Goggin scored 70 to move to two under and a share of fifth place alongside Aaron Baddeley, who eagled the last, also for a round of 70.

Allenby won the Australian Open for the first time in 1994 and was mighty relieved to hang on to his 17th career victory. "I started with a five-shot lead, but it was just one of those days when you could just lose two or three shots in one hole," he said. "I was making bogeys but I was making good bogeys. I was stopping myself from making doubles, which is what I needed to do out there. It was just one of those days where I really had to grind it out.

"It's your national title though," he added. "It's like the U.S. Open and that's the way it's meant to play. You can't say it's too tough. I read the papers this morning and the comments from a lot of players about the course. It's the same for everyone, we all have to play it. So why whine about it? Why not just get on with it and play? I was happy to see everyone whining about it, because I knew that they weren't going to win."

## Cadbury Schweppes Australian PGA Championship—A$1,200,000
Winner: Robert Allenby

Robert Allenby made it two wins in a row with a one-stroke victory at the Cadbury Schweppes Australian PGA Championship at Hyatt Regency Coolum. Allenby birdied the last hole with a putt of six feet to leave Matthew Goggin in second place. It was the third time Allenby had won the title after his victories in 2000 and 2001. His closing 67 left him at 18 under par and just ahead of the charging Goggin.

After going to the turn in 31, the 31-year-old Tasmanian made four more birdies coming home to equal the course record of 63. But Allenby hit a brilliant approach at the last to avoid a playoff. After his win the week before and rain interruptions on the first two days, Allenby was not surprisingly weary.

"Believe it or not, I could go more holes, but coming down those last couple I'd had enough," an elated Allenby said. "At the last I hit it absolutely perfect, I couldn't have hit it any better. It's been a long week, I haven't had too many wake-up calls at 3:30 a.m. before, but I had one this week. But I think the Tour and the PGA have done an unbelievable job to get 72 holes in there. At the start of the week I didn't think we'd even get 54 holes in. The golf course was just perfect today."

Goggin said, "I'm certainly not super-disappointed or anything like that. Shooting 63 on the last day, it's pretty hard to get upset about anything. To be honest, I really didn't miss any putts I should have made, and I made a couple of bonus ones. It was one of those days where I got absolutely everything out of it."

Rod Pampling, Nick O'Hern and Nathan Green shared third place at 13 under par, while John Senden and Wade Ormsby were a shot further back. Green had been on top for most of the tournament and had entered the final round as co-leader with Allenby, but the New South Welshman stumbled coming down the stretch, with bogeys at the 10th, 11th and 16th holes dropping him out of contention after a 72.

## MasterCard Masters—A$1,250,000
Winner: Robert Allenby

Robert Allenby made history by maintaining his 100 percent record in the nerve-racking form of the game — the playoff. Allenby became the first person to win the Australian Open, PGA Championship and MasterCard Masters triple with victory at the first extra hole against American Bubba Watson at Huntingdale.

It was Allenby's ninth playoff and the ninth he has won. The 24-year-old from Victoria also won the Masters in a playoff in 2003, and his second title at Huntingdale was his 19th in all. But claiming the "triple crown" of Australian golf was a sweet moment.

"I can't imagine ever playing three weeks of unbelievable golf," said Allenby. "When I came down to Australia, I never expected to win. I was nervous on every single shot this week. That's the absolute truth. I kept telling myself, 'You've got to be strong, it's a long way from Thursday morning to Sunday afternoon. It's a marathon.' It was just a matter of hanging in there."

Watson, a 27-year-old from Florida, had just graduated from the Nationwide Tour to earn his PGA Tour card for 2006. A huge hitter, the left-hander was less than 100 yards from the green with his drive at the playoff hole. Allenby put his approach to 20 feet and two-putted for a par. But Watson, despite putting his short approach shot close to the hole, ended up three-putting.

"Nerves got to me, I just pulled it," Watson said of his par putt. "I wanted to make it and end it right then. It was hard to get back up after sitting around before the playoff. This is the biggest tournament of my life. It's great and at the same time it's sad. It's a hard way to end it."

Allenby and Watson finished the regulation 72 holes at 17 under after tussling with Nick O'Hern for the lead throughout the day. Allenby recorded his third 68 of the week, following an opening 67, after Watson's closing 67 posted the target at 271. O'Hern, who had led from the opening round, had a disappointing end to his event with a 73 that included two pairs of bogeys on the back nine that cost him the title. He finished two strokes outside the playoff, with John Senden taking fourth place and England's Paul Casey fifth.

O'Hern started the day three shots ahead, but dropped shots on the 11th and 12th allowed Allenby and Watson to pull even, and another pair of bogeys on the 16th and 17th saw the West Australian fall away. Watson's seven birdies in 11 holes looked as if they would give him the gold jacket that goes with the trophy, but he could not force an extra birdie at the last.

Allenby kept himself in contention with an eagle at the 14th and came to the 18th needing a birdie to overtake Watson. He missed the 18-footer, but safely made par to force the playoff. But it was almost a hole too far after an intense three weeks of competition. "I can't explain the fatigue that I had," he said. "I got back from Coolum after the PGA late on Sunday night. I was up at five o'clock for my charity day, which I would never miss in the world. I was fatigued. Even from Thursday I was telling myself, you've just got to be strong.

"It was just a matter of hanging in there and making birdies when I could and trying to make some pars. There were a lot of times when I was 20, 30 feet away and I'd just knock it up to a foot and tap it in for par and go to the next. I knew it would come down to the end, so I wasn't trying to force it. I knew if I tried to force it, I would make mistakes," he said.

# 12. African Tours

Perhaps the most heartening aspect of the year came right at the end when Ernie Els returned to action with such success. Els damaged anterior cruciate ligaments in his left knee during a sailing holiday in the Mediterranean in July. The injury required two operations and not too long ago might have been a career-ending one. But his rehabilitation went so well that Els was back on the course less than five months later. After a slow start at the Nedbank Golf Challenge, Els won the Dunhill Championship and then finished runner-up to Retief Goosen in the South African Airways Open.

"Those were probably the three most important weeks of my golfing life," Els said. "Before I resumed, I had been genuinely apprehensive as to whether I would ever be the same player I was. Thankfully, I got the answer I needed at the Dunhill. It was so important for me to know that my game hadn't changed."

In many ways the enforced break was good for the 36-year-old. Although he had won three times around the globe before the injury, Els's lackluster performances in the three major championships in which he played suggested he was still suffering a hangover from all the disappointments of the previous season when he contended at all the majors but failed to win any. Mainly, Els was able to enjoy a break from his hectic, globe schedule. "The layoff wasn't all bad," he said. "It gave me a chance to spend lots of time with the family and basically get to know my kids again. I loved that. And being able to wake up in my own bed every morning and lead a pretty normal life ... well, that made a nice change for me. Although I think Liezl was pretty desperate to get me out of the house by the end of it."

Els won four times during the year. He won back-to-back at the Dubai Desert Classic and the Qatar Masters and then claimed the BMW Asian Open in China before adding the Dunhill late in the year.

The following week Goosen took his fourth title of the year. His victory at Fancourt followed wins at The International in America, the Volkswagen China Masters and the Linde German Masters. The only disappointing aspect of Goosen's year was his attempt to win a second successive U.S. Open and third in all. He led by three with a round to play, but crashed to an 81 on the final day as Michael Campbell claimed the title.

Moving the South African Open from the start of the year to the end worked a treat with three big weeks starting with the Nedbank Golf Challenge, won dramatically by Jim Furyk when the American chipped in at the second extra hole. Then Els gave a master class to some of his talented younger compatriots at Leopard Creek before the brilliant duel with Goosen for the national championship. Els birdied four of the last five holes but still came up one shy when Goosen birdied the last two.

Tim Clark won the first South African Open of the year when it was played in January, repeating his triumph on home turf at Durban Country Club from 2002. Third place in the U.S. Open was the highlight of his campaign in the United States, and he joined Goosen and Trevor Immelman in the International team at the Presidents Cup. Immelman missed out on a victory but claimed fifth place at the Masters at Augusta.

On the domestic scene, Zimbabwean Marc Cayeux won the Vodacom Tour Championship, but Charl Schwartzel had tied up the 2004-05 Order of Merit with his victory at the Dunhill Championship in December 2004. On the winter circuit, there were two wins apiece for Desvonde Botes and Thomas Aiken, who won the winter Order of Merit for the second year running. Good young prospects abound, but it was Anton Haig who created history by becoming the youngest-ever winner on the Sunshine Tour. Haig won the Seekers Travel Pro-Am at the age of 19 years and four months, breaking Dale Hayes's 34-year-old record by a month.

## South African Airways Open—£500,000
Winner: Tim Clark

Tim Clark continued his love affair with Durban Country Club by winning the South African Airways Open for the second time at his favorite course. The 28-year-old was born and raised not far from the layout and won three Natal junior titles there before making history by becoming the first player to make it through pre-qualifying and go on to win the South African Open in 2002. With the championship returning to Durban for the first time since then, Clark repeated his triumph with a highly impressive performance.

Starting the final round in a four-way tie for the lead, Clark cruised to a six-stroke victory thanks to a closing round of six-under-par 66. Along with earlier rounds of 68, 71 and 68, Clark finished with a 15-under-par total of 273. The victory was sealed with birdies at the last two holes, but the most pertinent aspect of his disciplined performance was that he did not drop a shot in the last 45 holes of the championship.

"I felt a lot of pressure to play well this week," said Clark. "A lot of people expected me to play well and I hadn't played much golf, so I'm extremely pleased. It means a great deal to me to win here at Durban Country Club, I have a lot of good memories here. I think my next goal should be to win it somewhere else!"

Clark banked R894,635 for the perfect start to a season which would see him make a second appearance for the International team at the Presidents Cup. Titch Moore, Hendrik Buhrmann and Tjaart van der Walt, who stood alongside Clark with a round to go, fell from contention with rounds of 74, 74 and 75 respectively, while those who did mount a charge did so from too far back in the field. Charl Schwartzel and Gregory Havret both birdied the last hole for rounds of 68 and 69 to finish in a share of second place at nine under par. Darren Clarke scored a second successive 67 over the weekend to share fourth place with James Kingston, Graeme Storm and Nick Dougherty.

Schwartzel, who broke through to win his first title at the Dunhill Championship a few weeks earlier at the end of 2004, earned R521,776 as co-runner-up to take an unassailable lead on the Southern Africa PGA Tour Order of Merit. "I'm playing well, so we'll see where it takes me," said Schwartzel. "Maybe I can go on and win the European Order of Merit now."

## Dimension Data Pro-Am—R1,000,000
Winner: Simon Wakefield

A comment on television about Colin Montgomerie helped England's Simon Wakefield to victory at the Dimension Data Pro-Am at the Gary Player Country Club at Sun City. "I was watching the Singapore Open on television and the commentators mentioned that Colin Montgomerie played the course for the first three rounds and then on the final day, if he finds himself in a match play situation, plays his opponent," said Wakefield.

Rounds of 72, 70 and 68 over the first three days gave the 30-year-old from Newcastle-under-Lyme a one-stroke lead over Nic Henning, and the final day indeed turned into a match play battle between the two. Wakefield closed with a 69 for a total of 279, nine under par, and a three-stroke victory over Henning, who finished with 71. Tjaart van der Walt was four back, and Louis Oosthuizen was the only other player to finish the tournament below par. Defending champion Darren Fichardt had a disappointing 76 on Sunday, which saw him end the event at even par, along with Englishmen Andrew Butterfield and Phillip Archer.

Wakefield had an extraordinary start to his round. At the par-five first hole, his second shot hit a woman spectator on the back of the shoulder. "When I knew the ball hit somebody, it was the worst feeling," said Wakefield. "She was a bit tearful and still in shock but she was otherwise okay. I wrote 'sorry' on the ball and put a smile on it and gave it to her after the hole as I was going to the second tee." But while Wakefield was checking on the spectator, a photographer in a cart unwittingly ran over his ball and left it imbedded in the rough. He was allowed a free drop and then went on to birdie the hole. But, shaken after all those events, he drive poorly at the second, had to take a penalty drop and took a double bogey. "After that I had to work hard to get my score back on track," he said.

He did just that with birdies at the fifth and sixth, and although Henning made three birdies early on the back nine, Wakefield birdied the 11th and the 16th, where his tee shot at the par-three finished two feet away, and clinched his second professional victory. The first came at the Tessali Open on the European Challenge Tour in 2002. Having had to go back to the qualifying tournament and regain his card at the end of the previous season, Wakefield was aiming to return home for a successful season on the European Tour. "I want to take this week's experience on to the European Tour and hopefully I can win a tournament there so I don't have to qualify again," he said.

## Nashua Masters—R1,000,000
Winner: Richard Sterne

Richard Sterne won for the first time as a professional in South Africa with his victory at the Nashua Masters at Wild Coast Sun Country Club. As a playoff loomed, Sterne, the leader after rounds two and three, held firm on the final green. A even-par round of 70 gave the former South African Amateur champion a one-shot win over Titch Moore and Grant Muller.

But it was the collapse of James Kingston, who finished fourth two strokes behind, which provided the dramatic conclusion to the event. Kingston, who had leapt into contention with a 61 in the third round, was tied for the lead playing the 18th with Sterne. Kingston drove into a fairway bunker and his second shot came up short of the green. A difficult chip left him seven feet away, and when the putt missed, and his chance of a playoff with it, he distractedly missed the tap-in to finish with an ugly double bogey.

Sterne, who won the 2004 Madrid Open on the European Tour, began the game at the age of four playing with his grandmother and comes from a sporting family; his father was involved in motor racing, his mother was an ice skater and his sister is a top squash player in South Africa. When Sterne bogeyed the 13th and 15th holes he dropped one behind the charging Moore, but then Moore bogeyed the 16th and Sterne birdied. He finished at 11 under par and won R158,500, while Moore closed with a 66 and Muller a 68, as did Kingston, despite the poor finish.

"I didn't think it was over at that point after the 15th, but I certainly thought I'd need a couple of shots over the last three holes," a relieved Sterne said. "The putt on 16 was definitely my turning point today. It feels great to win at home. I had a solid start, and felt comfortable after the early nerves of leading. I knew today would be a great experience no matter what happened, and having to fight will stand me in good stead in the future. I'll have a lot more confidence now this season — leading for two rounds and then winning takes a lot out of you, but I'm just really happy to get this win."

### Telkom PGA Championship—R1,750,000
Winner: Warren Abery

Warren Abery won his third title on the Sunshine Tour, but by far his biggest, when he took the Telkom PGA Championship at the Woodhill Golf Estate with a calm three-foot par putt at the last hole. Abery won by one stroke over Charl Schwartzel and overnight leader Jaco Van Zyl. Scotsmen Alan McLean and Doug McGuigan shared fourth place, while Nic Henning ended alone in sixth place.

Abery had three rounds of 68 and then closed with a 69 for a 15-under-par total of 273 to claim the R277,375 first prize. The 31-year-old was delighted to have won his biggest title yet. "The lesson here is to never stop believing in yourself," he said. "With this game you never know what's around the corner."

Abery started the final round two behind Van Zyl. Louis Oosthuizen hit the front at the turn and looked to be going further ahead when his tee shot at the par-three 12th landed two feet from the pin. But once he missed that birdie putt, Oosthuizen's game fell apart. Instead it was Abery who took the lead with birdies on the 10th, 11th and 12th. He dropped a shot on the 13th when he three-putted, but then made up for it courtesy of a 40-foot birdie putt on the 14th. "That was definitely the turning point," he said. "Once I had that putt, I felt I was in control."

Van Zyl birdied the 11th and the 18th, but it was too little too late after a poor start. Schwartzel made a late charge with an eagle at the 15th and a birdie on the last, but it still meant that Abery had to come back to the field. "I kept thinking that Louis was my main threat, because he had a lot of support and I could hear all the cheers coming from him. I didn't realize Charl was 14 under until I was on the 18th," said Abery. "I knew I just had to make a par to win, so I aimed for the middle of the green and looked for a two-putt."

## Vodacom Tour Championship—R2,000,000
Winner: Marc Cayeux

A magnificent course-record 11-under-par 61 from Zimbabwean Marc Cayeux saw him run away with the season-ending Vodacom Tour Championship at Woodmead Country Club. Cayeux became the first non-South African to capture this title, although it was his seventh victory on the Sunshine Tour. A six-stroke victory earned him a check for R317,000 and fifth place on the Sunshine Tour Order of Merit, which had already been won by Charl Schwartzel.

Cayeux was due to play the rest of the season on the European Tour after qualifying from the Challenge Tour in 2004. "I have to admit that I have been stressed out financially," said Cayeux. "I didn't know how I was going to afford to travel on the European Tour. Now that problem is solved." Cayeux admitted he had been hoping to produce a wonder round for some time. "I've been waiting for a round like this for at least a year because I've been hitting the ball so well. But I suppose it's all about self-belief and confidence. Right now I am honored to hold the course record on a course like this."

His round comprised nine birdies on holes one, three, six, nine, 10, 12, 13, 15 and 16, all of which he followed in the grand manner with an eagle at the 18th. The final hole perhaps best summed up Cayeux's remarkable round. "I teed off with a five-shot lead and the tournament all but over. Keith Horne said to me that if I was going to mis-hit the shot, mis-hit it straight." Bizarrely, this was exactly what happened. Cayeux took one hand off the club as he came down on the ball, saw it go straight and walked off the tee with a big smile on his face. He still reached the green in two and was left with a 25-footer for his eagle.

Cayeux finished with a total of 268, which was 20 under par. Horne, one of the overnight leaders, took second place with a 69, which had started with a double bogey. Defending champion Andrew McLardy, with 67, and Nic Henning, after 68, shared third place at 12 under, while Ulrich van den Berg, Justin Walters, Richard Sterne and Hendrik Buhrmann ended tied for fifth at 11 under. Buhrmann had been the co-leader with Horne after three rounds, but dropped shots at the first two holes and could only manage a 72.

The only time Cayeux looked challenged in the final round was at the turn when van den Berg moved within one shot of him. But his birdies on the 12th and 14th, coupled with a drop by van den Berg on the 15th, soon left him clear of the field again.

## Hassan II Trophy—US$621,000
Winner: Erik Compton

American Erik Compton won the 33rd Hassan II Trophy at Royal Dar-es-Salam in Rabat. Compton won the traditional unofficial event, named after the former king of Morocco, by five strokes in rainy conditions on the Red course. The 25-year-old from Miami, who took up the game as rehabilitation following a heart transplant in 1992, produced rounds of 71, 69, 69 and 68 for a 15-under-par total of 277. The former Walker Cup player made six birdies in the final round, including three on the back nine at the 12th, 16th and 18th holes. Portugal's Jose-Filipe Lima posted four birdies in the last eight holes for a 71 to finish as runner-up at 10 under. Santiago Luna, a three-time winner of the event, was third at seven under, along with Frenchmen Gregory Havret and Gregory Bourdy, while Moroccan golfer Younes El-Hassani was eighth at five under.

## FNB Botswana Open—R250,000
Winner: Nico van Rensburg

Nico van Rensburg achieved his first victory in over four years with a breathtaking finish at the FNB Botswana Open at Phakalane. Warren Abery had set the clubhouse target at 14 under par after a final round of 65 and van Rensburg was one behind heading to the 18th tee. An eagle at the last then gave van Rensburg his first win since the 2000 Vodacom Series Gauteng event. A closing 67 gave him a 54-hole total of 201, his 10th professional title and secured a check for R39,250.

After hitting a three wood off the tee at the 18th, van Rensburg was between clubs but hit a soft cut with his three wood again. The ball hit the flag and came to rest 12 feet away and the Pretoria professional holed the putt to leapfrog over Abery. "I can't tell you what I'm feeling right now," said van Rensburg. "This has taken me four long years. I started off feeling a little more confident than yesterday and I hit a lot of good shots. I mean, my putter was just unbelievable this week. Every putt I could make, I probably made. When I got to the 18th green and saw the distance and the line of the putt, I knew I could make it if I didn't leave it too short. Once I hit it, I knew it was on the line, but it felt short. I couldn't believe it when it actually rolled in, center of the hole."

Ross Wellington produced a 69 to finish third at 11 under, while Des Terblanche carded a 68 to tie Brazil's Adilson da Silva at 10 under. Da Silva, who got within one shot of the leaders at one point, signed for a 71.

## Parmalat Classic—R300,000
Winner: Ulrich van den Berg

Ulrich van den Berg captured the Parmalat Classic by one stroke to deny hopefuls Lindani Ndwandwe and Peter Karmis their day of glory at Paarl. Van den Berg marched to his fourth Sunshine Tour victory with a final-round, three-under-par 69 and a total score of 15-under-par 201, ahead of

Ndwandwe and Karmis at 14 under and waiting in the wings hoping for a playoff.

Ndwandwe and Karmis destroyed the course, shooting 62 and 63 respectively on a day when scoring was otherwise higher than the first two days. Ndwandwe's 10-under effort could not count as a new course record since preferred lies were allowed. But van den Berg stayed calm to overtake overnight leader Bradford Vaughan with three birdies early on the back nine and then saved par with two putts from 60 feet at the 17th to keep a one-stroke cushion up the last. Chris Williams claimed fourth place at 13 under, while Michiel Bothma was fifth, with Vaughan slipping back to sixth place with Sammy Daniels and Keith Horne.

"I'm over the moon," said van den Berg, who won R47,100. "I've been in this position often in the last few months, and I'm really glad I could nail it again. Today I played the best final round of a tournament, ever. Coming in over the last nine holes, I really felt like a seasoned professional — clinical, measured, thinking about the best way to play each shot. This is by far my best win ever."

## Capital Alliance Royal Swazi Sun Open — R500,000
Winner: Hendrik Buhrmann

Hendrik Buhrmann came from behind to win the Capital Alliance Royal Swazi Sun Open, his eighth title on the Sunshine Tour, by a single point over overnight leader Ross Wellington. Under the modified-Stableford scoring system, Buhrmann produced a six-under-par 66 for 14 points on the final day and a winning score of 42 points, while Wellington added just six to finish one point short. Brett Liddle was third with 39 points after he produced a blistering nine-under-par 63 that earned him 21 points, the richest haul of the tournament.

The 41-year-old Buhrmann, who made five consecutive birdies from the sixth hole, negotiated a nervy closing stretch with Liddle's imposing score already on the board and Wellington chasing hard. Under pressure to find points over the closing holes, Wellington effectively ruined his chances by finding the water with his approach shot at the par-five 17th hole, although he went on to save par.

With his birdie on the same hole, Buhrmann needed no more than a bogey on the 18th hole, as Wellington, who had to make a birdie to force a playoff, holed from 17 feet for par and second place on his own. "Ross never went away, and Brett came out of nowhere, so I couldn't relax on the back nine at all," said Buhrmann. "Only on the 18th green, when I had two putts to win, I knew it was mine."

## Vodacom Origins of Golf Tour at Pretoria — R330,000
Winner: Desvonde Botes

Desvonde Botes claimed a controversial victory in the Vodacom Origins of Golf Tour in Pretoria after one of his playing partners claimed he had breached a rule during a tense final round. Botes beat Jean Hugo with a birdie on the first extra hole after both players finished regulation play at 14-under-par 202 with respective final rounds of 71 and 70. But Botes had to endure a lengthy discussion with his playing partners and tournament director Theo Manyama during and after his round.

According to Manyama, Botes's playing partner, Michiel Bothma, queried how Botes had marked his ball on the opening few holes, claiming that he was placing his ball a good deal in front of his marker. Bothma confronted Botes on the issue and it continued to fester, causing tension between the two players. Both their games suffered as a result. Botes, after an eagle at the fourth, bogeyed holes five and six, while Bothma dropped a string of shots to fall right off the pace and was eventually disqualified for signing an incorrect scorecard.

But Botes denied any wrongdoing. "There is no way it happened and I don't know what he saw," he said. "On the first hole I didn't even mark my ball because I was left with a tap-in putt. Then he brought it up while I was putting on the fifth, which you just don't do, and I bogeyed the hole. It really bothered me, but I just tried to block it out of my mind."

After the back-to-back bogeys, Botes found his rhythm again and birdied holes seven, eight and 10 to streak away from the field. On the 12th tee, Manyama spoke to the players about the earlier incident. The third player in the leading group, Hugo, said he did not see the issue Bothma was referring to, and it was left as such with no penalties imposed.

Botes regained his composure and was four clear of Hugo through 16 holes. But he dropped a shot at the 17th while Hugo birdied for a two-shot swing that closed the gap to two strokes with the par-five 18th to come. Botes parred a hole he had eagled the previous two days after finding the greenside bunker with his approach, while Hugo forced the playoff with a brilliant approach to six feet, from where he holed the eagle putt.

## Vodacom Origins of Golf Tour at Pezula—R330,000
Winner: Desvonde Botes

Desvonde Botes blazed away from the field to record his second victory in three weeks in the Vodacom Origins of Golf Tour at Pezula. Botes closed with a brilliant seven-under-par 65 to seal a wire-to-wire win at 18 under par and a total of 198. It was his 14th win on the Sunshine Tour. Ian Hutchings produced an impressive 69 to take second place at 12 under, while Nico van Rensburg overcame a mid-round wobble to end the day in third place at 10 under after carding a 68.

Botes led by two strokes going into the final round and quickly extended his advantage to six after four holes. By the turn he was eight ahead and cruising to victory. Botes credited pregnant wife Cisna and sports psychologist Maretha Claassens with setting him back on the winning track. "I struggled with injury last year and just couldn't get my game together, with the result that I lost my exemption," said Botes. "Maretha helped me with some focus techniques that are really working well for me, and Cisna has been a constant source of support through the tough times.

"I'm delighted with this win. It feels great to know the first one wasn't just a flash-in-the-pan victory, that I could pull it through for the second time, even better than the first. I believe right now I am playing the best golf of my career."

## Vodacom Origins of Golf Tour at Wild Coast Sun—R330,000
Winner: Dean Lambert

As amateurs, Dean Lambert and Richard Sterne were South Africa's best and enjoyed a fierce rivalry on the golf course. But just as Lambert was beginning to give up hope of making it as a professional, a word of encouragement from Sterne provided the spark that saw him claim his maiden victory on the Vodacom Origins of Golf Tour at the Wild Coast Sun Country Club. Lambert closed with a 67 to win by a single stroke at five-under-par 205, his first victory since turning professional three years ago. Lindani Ndwandwe and Grant Muller shared second place at four under par.

Lambert came close to giving up the game when his professional career failed to mirror the phenomenal success he achieved as an amateur. But while caddieing for Sterne on his way to victory in the 2004 Madrid Open on the European Tour, Sterne encouraged Lambert to start playing competitively again. "What he said got me excited again," said Lambert.

"I came back to South Africa after Richard's win and picked up my clubs again. It's been a long road to this point. There were days when I thought that maybe this was not for me. I think you get to a point where the only person who believes in you is you. But I've always been a slow learner. Even as an amateur it took me a long time to win."

Lambert had to pre-qualify for this event, having not made it into any of the summer Sunshine Tour events and then missing several cuts once the winter season started up. During a windy final round, Lambert kept his composure, especially during a tough stretch around the turn. A birdie at the 16th took him into a tie for the lead, and after a crucial par save from 25 feet at the 17th, he hit a huge drive at the last to just short of the green and made the birdie he needed for victory.

## Vodacom Origins of Golf Tour at Bloemfontein—R330,000
Winner: Nic Henning

Helped out with some multi-vitamins for his ailing back from his roommate for the week, Nic Henning did not exactly return the favor as he birdied the last two holes to win the Vodacom Origins of Golf Tour at Bloemfontein. The 36-year-old won his fourth Sunshine Tour title after a final round of 67 for an 11-under total of 205, which left 54-hole leader Doug McGuigan one back after a 71.

Tied for the lead through 16 holes, Henning moved one stroke clear of the Scot when he hit a nine iron to three feet for birdie at the 17th. At the 18th, Henning overshot the green but chipped to 10 feet and holed the putt to go two clear. McGuigan, playing in the group behind and needing an eagle at the last to force a playoff, hit a superb three iron to 15 feet, but just missed the eagle putt.

"I wasn't going to blow it. I just had the feeling that I would win. I was playing well and I was confident I wasn't going to make a mistake," said Henning, whose last victory came in the 2004 Royal Swazi Sun Classic on the same day his father passed away. "I remember speaking to him half an hour before he died. The funny thing is, I never practiced for a month before that win because my father was so ill. Coming into this tournament I also couldn't practice because my back was acting up again. I roomed with Doug (McGuigan) this week and he gave me these multi-vitamins every day, except on the final day. I think he did that on purpose."

## Telkom PGA Pro-Am—R300,000
Winner: Thomas Aiken

Thomas Aiken recovered the form that brought him three titles the previous winter to win the inaugural Telkom PGA Pro-Am at Centurion Country Club. The 22-year-old also recovered from a wrist injury that had affected him for six months. Aiken recorded rounds of 68, 66 and 67 for a 15-under total of 201 and a six-stroke win over Henk Alberts. Omar Sandys gave a polished performance that included eight pars on the back nine to finish tied for third with Andre Cruse at seven under par.

"I took the strapping off my wrist at the start of the week and, for the first time in months, I could play with no pain. From that moment, I wanted this win," said Aiken. "I was nervous as hell this morning, but it's healthy. It got me through that awkward moment on the first; from there on, I just kept my nose in front."

Aiken picked up early birdies in quick succession at the first and third holes and turned in 34 to maintain his handy advantage. More birdies followed on the back nine as he cruised in. "I felt a lot of pressure to play well this week," he said. "A lot of people expected me to play well and I hadn't played much golf, so I'm extremely pleased. It means a great deal to me to win here after the struggle over the last six months to get myself into the form I hit when I was winning last year. This win is really good for my confidence. I'm very, very happy to win again before I leave for Europe and the U.S. Hopefully I can take this form over there and come back with a card."

## Vodacom Origins of Golf Tour at Erinvale—R330,000
Winner: Hennie Otto

Hennie Otto took advantage of Jean Hugo's dramatic collapse on the 16th hole of the final round to end a two-year victory drought with a win in the Vodacom Origins of Golf Tour at Erinvale. Otto and Hugo were tied for the lead at 13 under par with three holes to go. But on the par-five 16th, Hugo pulled his drive out of bounds and went on to make a double bogey that essentially handed the title to Otto.

It was an exact duplicate of the error Hugo made in the final round of the 2003 South African Open on the same course, and which also cost him a title that instead went to Trevor Immelman. "You'd think I would've learned from last time," sighed Hugo. But Otto still had to stave off a strong challenge by Thomas Aiken before clinching a one-stroke victory at 14 under par with a final round of 68. Aiken took second place at 13 under with a closing 69, while Hugo shared third with Nico Le Grange at 11 under.

Otto birdied the first hole to negate Hugo's one-shot overnight lead. Hugo responded with birdies at the second and third hole, but Otto kept up the pressure, and with his birdie at the eighth and Hugo's dropped shot at the ninth the pair were tied again. "It's funny because I was thinking about what happened to Jean on the 16th during the 2003 SA Open, and then it happens again. I felt really sorry for him, but after that I knew the gap was open," Otto said of Hugo's crucial mistake.

Otto birdied the hole for a three-shot swing, but so did Aiken, who also birdied the brutal 17th to be one behind coming down the last. "I started feeling the tension on the 17th because that's not an easy hole," Otto said. "Thomas made birdie there and I thought, 'Here we go. It's down the stretch now.' But I've been in that position before and decided to just try and make my par at the last and let Thomas try and come at me. Fortunately it worked out."

## Seekers Travel Pro-Am—R300,000
Winner: Anton Haig

With his victory in the Seekers Travel Pro-Am, Anton Haig broke a 34-year record set by Dale Hayes to become the youngest winner on the Sunshine Tour. At the age of 19 years and four months, Haig was one month younger than Hayes when he captured his maiden professional title at the Dainfern Country Club after a thrilling final-day tussle with Nic Henning.

Haig, first in the clubhouse at 12-under-par 204, was forced into a playoff when Henning birdied the final hole in regulation play. The teenager held his nerve to defeat Henning at the first playoff hole to win just inside of 12 months since he made his professional debut.

Haig, who won the 2003 South African Amateur at the age of 16, had almost withdrawn from the event due to injury. "I went to Theo Manyama (Sunshine Tour tournament director) on Thursday before I was due to tee off because my neck was really stiff and the tablets I took didn't seem to be working," said Haig. "He told me to give it a few minutes and reconsider. I thought I might as well try and give it a go. What a decision it turned out to be! It was unbelievable to win. I really believe in myself, but it is such a great feeling to prove yourself to the people around you who support you all the time."

## Bearingman Highveld Classic—R400,000
Winner: Bradford Vaughan

Bradford Vaughan got revenge for being disqualified at the same venue the previous year by winning the Bearingman Highveld Classic in front of an adoring crowd at Witbank. The 25-year old Vanderbijlpark professional produced a flawless final-round 66 for a stunning 15-under-par total of 201 to take the R62,800 first prize and finish two shots clear of Peter Karmis and Thomas Aiken.

It was Vaughan's sixth victory and came after he was in contention the year before but was disqualified after a mix-up at the 17th where he played a provisional after his first drive went out of bounds. "This is a great moment for me," said Vaughan. "To win here in Witbank in front of such a great crowd, wearing the logo of my new sponsor and the tournament sponsor, and getting a little revenge for last year's disqualification, gives me a really special feeling. I have won six tournaments now and I would love to be able to make the next step for my career to win the winter swing Order of Merit."

Vaughan's first birdie of the day came when he drove the green at the par-four third hole. Two more followed at the fifth and seventh, while another at the 11th put him three clear of the field. He also birdied the 15th and 17th, but his two-footer for another at the last lipped out, not that it then mattered.

## MTC Namibia PGA Championship—R500,000
Winner: Thomas Aiken

Thomas Aiken won his second title of the season at the MTC Namibia PGA Championship at Windhoek despite struggling with a groin injury. It was a wrist problem when Aiken won his first title of the season a few months earlier. Rounds of 64, 67 and 67 gave him a 15-under-par total of 198 and four-stroke win over Michiel Bothma, Sean Farrell, Keith Horne and Werner Geyer. Andre Cruse and Peter Karmis finished in a tie for sixth at 10 under.

"Some weeks you just feel great and that's how I felt this week," said the 22-year-old Aiken. "I felt I could win and I was in contention from the start. That makes a difference, to be in amongst it from the first day. It's beyond my dreams this week to have won a PGA."

On a final day of many interruptions for hail and lightning, Aiken came from one behind Bothma with three birdies in the first six holes and an eagle at the seventh giving him a three-stroke lead. "I got very nervous because with each interruption you lose the momentum, your concentration goes and you get cold. When we went out to finish I knew I had a three-shot lead and I knew at that point that I just had to keep it steady from there."

## Vodacom Origins of Golf Tour Championship—R400,000
Winner: Steve Basson

Steve Basson claimed his first professional victory in the Vodacom Origins of Golf Tour Championship at The Links at Fancourt, finishing the tournament as the only player below par. Basson recovered from a brutal day in the second round when he shot 79, by no means the worst of the day, to post a three-under-par 70 for a total of one-under-par 218 and a four-stroke win over Chris Williams and six ahead of Brazil's Adilson da Silva and reigning Telkom PGA champion Warren Abery.

Starting out the day at two over par, Basson never relinquished the lead throughout the entire round. The key moment came when he chipped in for an eagle at the 13th which put him four ahead. He then birdied the 14th, 15th and 16th, and although Williams eagled the 17th, Basson could afford to three-putt the 18th where he had attempted, but failed, to end in style by holing a 30-footer for birdie.

"I thought it would be great to finish with a flourish, but my putter just wouldn't stand still. I guess I finally let the nerves get the better of me," said Basson. The 26-year-old dedicated his win to his wife Daphne, who has supported him since he turned professional in 1998. "Daphne has been amazing, sticking with me through highs and lows, especially the lows. She is the one who deserves this most."

## Platinum Classic—R500,000
Winner: Jaco Van Zyl

Jaco Van Zyl holed a mammoth 30-foot putt at the first playoff hole to snatch victory from Grant Muller in the Platinum Classic at Mooi Nooi. Van Zyl started the final round one behind Muller, but a 66, after rounds of 67 and 65, gave the 26-year-old an 18-under-par total of 198. And it could have been better but for a bogey at the last, although even then Van Zyl played a miracle recovery.

In trees over the green, behind a mound, a bench and the gallery and around 60 feet from the hole, he played an amazing shot with a three wood to eight feet. But he missed the putt and Muller had the chance to tie with a birdie and did so by holing from eight feet. In the playoff it was Muller who tangled with the trees, and Van Zyl ended his agony by holing from long range for his first victory.

"It's my first win and it couldn't come at a better time," said Van Zyl, who won R79,250. "I feel like Phil Mickelson must have felt when he won his first major. I've been knocking for so long; it's great to finally get that first victory under the belt."

Wallie Coetsee and Warren Abery finished two strokes outside the playoff in third place. The event saw the conclusion of the winter swing on the Sunshine Tour with two-time winner Thomas Aiken winning the Order of Merit for the second successive year. Aiken won a trip to the HSBC Champions tournament in Shanghai.

## HSBC Champions Tournament—US$5,000,000
Winner: David Howell

See Asia/Japan Tours chapter.

## Limpopo Classic—R1,000,000
Winner: Bradford Vaughan

Retief Goosen was the star attraction at the Limpopo Classic, but it was Bradford Vaughan who claimed his seventh career victory. A closing round of 69 for Vaughan, who had led since the second round, gave him a 19-under-par total of 265 and a three-stroke win over Titch Moore. Goosen struggled with his swing for much of the tournament, but a closing 67 put the former U.S. Open champion into a share of third place with Richard Sterne and Darren Fichardt, one behind Moore, whose birdie at the last had broken the tie for second.

Vaughan started shakily with a bogey eating into his commanding overnight lead, but he settled with birdies at the fourth and sixth holes, and by not dropping a shot on the back nine, he was able to enjoy a victory parade. "It was a bit of a wake-up call at the first and I knew I had to knuckle down and get on with the job," Vaughan said after his second win of the year. "I was a bit worried, a five-stroke lead sounds like a lot, but if the guys behind you are hot and you go cold, you're in trouble."

Vaughan collected a winner's check of R158,500 as reward for three scintillating rounds of 65, 67 and 64 before he ground out the win on the last day. "I tried not to play too conservatively, but my swing wasn't there like it was in the previous three days," said Vaughan. "It gives me confidence for the upcoming summer. To beat Goose makes it even better; he was the man to beat from the word go."


## Nelson Mandela Invitational—R250,000
Winners: Tim Clark and Vincent Tshabalala

Vincent Tshabalala became the first player to win the Nelson Mandela Invitational in successive years, but only thanks to the help of Tim Clark. The year before Tshabalala had virtually carried his then-partner Ernie Els to victory, but this time it was Clark who did the work in the second of the two rounds as the pair compiled an inward 30 at Arabella. Their score of 64 gave them a 17-under-par total, and after leading by two shots on the opening day ahead of Gary Player and Trevor Immelman, they were never threatened.

Clark donated his R125,000 winner's check to a pupil at the Carel du Toit School for the hearing impaired in Cape Town who needs a cochlear implant. "Siobhan has been my inspiration for the weekend," Clark said. "I think it kind of took the pressure off me, because standing over some of those putts I just thought of the kids at the school and it seemed to make the putts less meaningful. This means a lot to me because I'd played here four times before and never managed to win, so this was great. It really means a lot."

"I carried Ernie last year, but I needed somebody to carry me this year," Tshabalala said. "I couldn't have asked for anyone better than Tim because he hits the ball straight."

# Nedbank Golf Challenge—US$4,060,000
Winner: Jim Furyk

Jim Furyk won for the first time since a wrist injury struck the former U.S. Open champion in 2004 at the Western Open in America. But otherwise his 2005 season was full of near-misses. Four times he finished as runner-up and twice was only beaten in playoffs. The American got his revenge by winning the Nedbank Golf Challenge in dramatic fashion. Furyk chipped in from the back of the green to win at the second extra hole and collect the $1.2 million first prize at the Gary Player Country Club at Sun City. Retief Goosen, Darren Clarke and Adam Scott were his vanquished opponents.

Goosen, the defending champion, was the first to depart the playoff at the first extra hole. Playing the 18th, the South African three-putted to leave the other three returning to the 18th tee. Clarke had made a fine up-and-down to stay alive, and Scott a tricky putt, but they were not so fortunate the second time around. Scott finished on the lower plateau, misjudged the slope and three-putted. Clarke had a birdie putt, but it came up just short. Furyk's approach sailed right over the pin and finished on the fringe, but a brilliant chip ended the contest.

"I've had six opportunities to win here and I was starting to think I've been here the longest without winning," Furyk said. "It's a quite amazing tournament and purse, so it's nice to finally win. Plus it's been a year of close calls for me. I lost in two playoffs and was leading by two with a couple of holes to play in another tournament, but Padraig Harrington sunk a 70-footer to beat me by one. It looked like being like that again, but I was fortunate enough to get into a playoff and things went my way, which hasn't really happened this year. It's good reason to come back here."

Furyk has kept coming back to Sun City despite disqualifying himself during the 2001 event. Realizing too late that he had made a mistake while placing his ball during the round, the American turned himself in. What further impressed the locals was his decision to stay on and act as a marker for the rest of the event.

Furyk posted rounds of 68, 70, 72 and 72 to finish at six under par. He started the final day one behind Scott, Tim Clark and Angel Cabrera and had his nose in front before bogeying the 15th and 18th holes. Even so, the 35-year-old's determination and scrambling skills were in evidence as he conjured pars at the 14th and 16th to stay in the contest. Goosen, in spite of never being fully comfortable with his swing during the week, also returned a 72.

Scott made the playoff despite a 73, but his co-leaders, Clark and Cabrera, fell out of contention completely with rounds of 75 and 80 respectively. Irishman Clarke came home in 32, including birdies at the 16th and the 17th, where he holed out from just over 100 yards, and closed with a 69 to force his way into the playoff.

It was the eighth time in 25 years that extra time was necessary to declare a winner, but the first time more than two players had been involved. Luke Donald, after a 70, finished one stroke outside the playoff at five under. Former champion Ernie Els, playing in his first event since damaging his knee during the middle of the year, finished at two over par in ninth place out of the 12-man field.

## Dunhill Championship—€1,000,000
Winner: Ernie Els

In only his second tournament following a five-month injury break, Ernie Els returned to the winner's enclosure at the Dunhill Championship at Leopard Creek. The South African's experience told on the final day as others wilted. Els compiled a solid four-under-par 68 for a 14-under-par total of 274. That gave him a three-shot cushion over 2004 winner Charl Schwartzel and Louis Oosthuizen. Overnight leader Ulrich van den Berg had a dire finish to his tournament, dropping eight shots in the final 10 holes after holding a three-shot lead through the eighth.

"I think it was my experience that helped me pull this one off, but I really feel for Ulrich," said Els. "He was so relaxed and putting so well that after eight holes I turned to my caddie said I didn't know how we were going to catch him. But then the wheels came off a little bit and that opened the door for me. But he is a great golfer and a true gentleman and I really admire the way he kept his composure. I'm not sure that I could have behaved that way under the circumstances."

Els took away a check for R1,180,825 for his third victory at the event, having captured the title in 1995 at Wanderers and in 1999 at Houghton. It was also his fourth win of the year, following victories in Dubai, Qatar and China, all of which, as this one, also count on the PGA European Tour.

Els injured his left knee in July, immediately after the Open Championship, while on a sailing holiday in the Mediterranean. He required surgery on a ruptured anterior cruciate ligament and only returned to action at the Nedbank Golf Challenge the previous week. The knee required ice treatment and anti-inflammatories every day, but the 36-year-old was relieved to rediscover the winning touch so quickly after returning to the game. "It might come across a bit cocky if you say you are going to win, considering my circumstances," Els said. "But I was hitting the ball well enough to have a chance."

Van den Berg's troubles started at the 11th where he drove into the rough and took a triple bogey. That brought Els even, and when van den Berg bogeyed the 12th and Els birdied the 13th, the three-time major champion was two clear. Els also birdied the 15th, and then van den Berg put his tee shot in the water at the 16th, and the contest was over. "I just melted down," said van den Berg. "I hit a bad tee shot on 11 and lost a lot of confidence after that."

## South African Airways Open—€1,000,000
Winner: Retief Goosen

In a dramatic final-round battle between South Africa's twin two-time U.S. Open champions, Retief Goosen birdied the final two holes to beat Ernie Els at the South African Airways Open at The Links at Fancourt. Tied for the lead with Els at eight under par with two holes to play, Goosen chipped in for birdie on the 17th and then birdied the last as well, after getting up and down from over the green, to win by a single stroke at 10 under par with a final round of 70.

Els missed a five-foot putt, the ball lipping out, for eagle at the last for a possible victory or a playoff at worst, and took second place at nine under with a closing 68 in which he birdied four of the final five holes. Darren Fichardt and Frenchman Gregory Bourdy shared third place at two under par.

This was the second time Goosen had won his national Open, following his triumph in 1995 at Randpark Golf Club in Johannesburg where he also beat Els for the title, winning by five strokes on that occasion. "It's been 10 years since I've last won it and it's great to have the trophy in my hands again," said Goosen after his fourth victory of the season. "It's been a great year for me. I've won in America, Asia and now South Africa."

Goosen enjoyed a three-stroke lead over Els going into the final round. But Els chipped away at it and drew even with a birdie at the eighth. Goosen responded with a 25-foot birdie putt at the ninth to take a one-stroke lead into the back nine. The championship seemed certain to go Goosen's way when Els double-bogeyed the 12th after pitching into the hazard left of the green, forcing him to take a penalty drop. That gave Goosen a three-stroke lead. But Els surged back into contention with three successive birdies from the 14th to again draw even with Goosen, who had parred every hole since the 12th.

# 13. Senior Tours

Newcomers such as Jay Haas, Loren Roberts and Peter Jacobsen made their presences felt, but the 2005 Champions Tour season was pretty much held in the hands of the veteran seniors on the circuit. Dana Quigley, Tom Watson and the ever-present Hale Irwin in particular.

The 58-year-old Quigley, better known for his iron-man role during his previous eight years on the Champions Tour even though he was an eight-time winner, emerged as a top gun in 2005 and came very close to a totally overwhelming season. As it was, he led the money winners with $2,170,258, the only player to top the $2 million mark, and was chosen Player of the Year. He missed the other big prize when Tom Watson staged a spectacular finish to win the season-ending Charles Schwab Cup Championship and grab the $1 million annuity, nosing out Quigley, who had led the season-long Schwab points race through the previous 17 tournaments.

Quigley won only two events in 2005 — the opening MasterCard Championship, where, ironically, he defeated Watson in a playoff, and the Bayer Advantage Classic in Kansas City, but he was in almost constant contention. He lost two playoffs in senior majors, had five seconds in all and was in the top 10 in 15 tournaments. His iron-man run ended at 278 consecutive tournaments for which he was eligible (264 in a row) when he skipped the overseas trip for the Senior British Open in Scotland because of an ailing hip and travel problems.

Watson, in his 56th year, also had just two wins, but they were important events — the Schwab and the Senior British Open, one of the year's majors. He finished fifth on the money list with $1,532,482 to go with the $1 million annuity. His eight Champions Tour victories include two Senior British Opens, a Senior PGA, a Tradition and two Tour Championships to go with the Schwab.

Irwin continued his incredible winning pace, the only man to win more than twice with his four victories. The runner-up to Quigley on the money list with $1,983,596, Irwin won the Outback Steakhouse Pro-Am, Wal-Mart First Tee Open, SAS Championship and set a new tour record when he won the Turtle Bay Championship in Hawaii for the fifth straight time in its various reincarnations. The 60-year-old Hall-of-Famer now has 44 Champions Tour titles, 15 more than runner-up Lee Trevino.

Haas, like several others in their early 50s still competing on the regular PGA Tour, played in just 10 events on the Champions Tour, but easily captured Rookie of the Year honors with a sensational run at the end of the season. He won twice in the last four tournaments (Greater Hickory Classic and SBC Championship), was fifth in between and lost the Schwab when Watson overcame Haas's six-stroke, final-round lead with his tournament-record 64.

The only other double winners in 2005 were England's Des Smyth (SBC Classic, Legends of Golf), Mark McNulty (Bank of America, Administaff) and Jim Thorpe, who won the FedEx Kinko's and Blue Angels events back to back. In stunning fashion much like Watson's at the Schwab, Allen Doyle won the U.S. Senior Open at Dayton's NCR with a dazzling, final-round

63, and Jacobsen picked off the Senior Players Championship to put on his record with the 2004 Senior Open, his only two Champions Tour wins in his limited number of starts while still playing the PGA Tour.

Mike Reid was one of five other first-time winners, bagging the Senior PGA Championship at Laurel Valley via the overtime route. The others were Roberts, who won the other major, the Tradition; little-known Mark Johnson (Toshiba), Ron Streck (Long Island), and Smyth. Roberts, another pro remaining active on the junior circuit, won the Tradition in his third Champions Tour start in a playoff against Quigley. Craig Stadler, the leading money winner in 2004 with five victories, failed to land a title in 2005 and finished ninth in the standings.

Carl Mason, the Order of Merit winner in 2003 and 2004, won twice on the 2005 European Seniors Tour, even though plagued through much of the season with back trouble, and yielded the leadership mantle to Sam Torrance. Torrance, the former Ryder Cup player and captain who decided during the previous year to spend his time on the European circuit rather than in America, made that decision look very good by racking up three victories — the De Vere PGA Seniors Championship, the Jersey Classic and the Bendinat London Masters. Mason's back-to-back victories in the De Vere Northumberland Classic and the Ryder Cup Wales Open ran his career seniors total to 11 in less than three full seasons on the European Seniors Tour.

Torrance and Mason were the only multiple winners in a 21-tournament season that saw six men score their first victories on the circuit. Two of them were Mark James (Bovis Lend Lease European Senior Masters) and Smyth (Arcapita Seniors Tour Championship), who already had Champions Tour wins on their records. The others were Frenchman Gery Watine (Italian Seniors Open), Italian Guiseppe Cali (Mobile Cup), Argentine Eduardo Romero (Travis Perkins Masters) and American Bob Boyd (Castellon Costa Azahar Open de Espana).

Takashi Miyoshi landed three of the eight titles on the Japan Senior Tour in a season spotted between mid-May and the end of November. However, the year's two major events went to two players of winning vintage on the regular Japan Tour. Tsuneyuki (Tommy) Nakajima, 51, one of Japan's all-time golfing greats, won the Japan Senior Open, and Kiyoshi Murota, a four-time winner in his younger days, copped the Japan PGA Senior Championship. Katsunari Takahashi won the Philanthropy Rebornest Open, his 11th victory on the senior circuit, tying him with Fujio Kobayashi atop the tour's career title list.

# Champions Tour

## MasterCard Championship—$1,600,000

Winner: Dana Quigley

Dana Quigley has his own way for getting ready for each new golf season. He never takes a break from the game, never stops playing, even if it's just casual rounds with family and friends. You will never find any rust on his clubs or his game. "Golf is a lot of fun for me," says the 57-year-old native New Englander, who won the season-opening MasterCard Championship in his record 249th consecutive start on the Champions Tour. "It's not only my job, but it's my enjoyment and it's my passion."

It was not just that, of course, when he defeated Tom Watson in a play-off at Hualalai Golf Club at Ka'upulehu-Kona on Hawaii's "Big Island." Quigley practically owns the host course where they play the tournament that brings together the circuit's winners of the previous two seasons, the winners of the majors the previous five years and a few Hall of Fame guests. Besides capturing the championship in 2003, Quigley has finished second twice and fourth once in the new century. He has won almost $1 million in the MasterCard Championship.

Watson seemed well on his way to victory after the first two rounds, although Quigley, who lost by a stroke to Fuzzy Zoeller in 2004, was among a handful of players close behind after 36 holes. Employing a flippy putting stroke he had just adopted earlier in the week, Watson fired back-to-back, eight-under-par 64s and took a three-stroke lead over Wayne Levi into the final round. He had eight birdies on a fairly windy opening day, one with a 45-foot putt on the par-three fifth hole that "was like stealing." That 64 gave him a two-stroke lead over Levi and three over Craig Stadler, Morris Hatalsky, John Jacobs and Quigley, who posted his ninth straight round in the 60s at Hualalai.

Watson widened the margin to three with the second 64 on a benign day when all except two of the 37 players broke par and Hale Irwin said "this place was a sitting duck." Levi's 65 put him at 131, a shot ahead of Gil Morgan, who also shot 64, and Quigley, with his 67-65. Watson's iron game was deadly, six of his eight birdies coming with virtual tap-in putts. He made four in a row from the 13th to fend off Quigley, who caught him for a moment when he eagled the 14th.

Quigley made up his four-stroke deficit over the first 13 holes Sunday and had a one-stroke lead at the 18th hole when Watson overshot the 17th green into the lava and took a bogey. However, Quigley three-putted from the fringe at the last hole and the two men went into overtime when Watson couldn't convert a nine-foot birdie putt at the 18th. Irwin (65) and Morgan (67) finished with 199s and missed the playoff by a shot. Quigley shot 66 and Watson 70 Sunday.

They parred the first two extra holes before Quigley's three-foot par putt at the third gave him the victory, his ninth in his eight years on the Champions Tour. Watson, who has won six times on the senior circuit and

39 times on the regular tour, has prevailed in just one of eight playoffs he has faced on the Champions Tour.

## Turtle Bay Championship—$1,500,000
Winner: Hale Irwin

Talk about players' affinities for particular courses. Two impressive examples emerged at the start of the Champions Tour season in Hawaii. Right out of the box, Dana Quigley polished off his second victory in three years to go with two second-place finishes and a fourth in the last five years in the MasterCard Championship at Hualalai Golf Club at Kona. A week later, Hale Irwin outdid that performance when he won the Turtle Bay Championship for the fifth straight time, a first in men's tournament golf history. The last four were registered on the Palmer course at the Turtle Bay Resort; the first at Kaanapali on Maui in 2000 before the tournament was island-hopped to Oahu's north shore. Irwin also won at Kaanapali in 1997 among eight victories in the Aloha State.

Showing no signs of slowing down even though just a few months short of his 60th birthday, the Champions Tour's most dominant player ever followed up his third-place finish in the MasterCard, one shot out of the title playoff, with a commanding wire-to-wire victory at Turtle Bay. Irwin has now won at least one tournament in each of his 11 seasons on the Champions Tour, a record achievement. It was his 41st title on the senior circuit, 12 more than Lee Trevino, the runner-up in that category.

Launching his title defense 15 months after the tournament's last staging in October 2003, Irwin took a share of the first-round lead with a five-under-par 67 on a rare benign day when two-thirds of the field managed par or better. Keith Fergus, Gil Morgan and Allen Doyle matched the 67, and five men, including MasterCard champion Quigley, had 68s. Irwin actually was disappointed with the results because he had birdied five of his first six holes, then didn't make a birdie putt the rest of the way.

Irwin took command of the tournament Saturday as his putter came alive. He took just 23 putts, made six birdies, shot 66 for 133 and moved into a two-stroke lead over Doyle (68) and three ahead of Quigley (68) and Fergus and Morgan (69s).

Irwin left nothing in doubt with a fast start Sunday. He ran off five birdies on the front nine for 31, establishing a six-stroke cushion. He coasted home with a 67 and his 200 total shattered the tournament record by five strokes. Quigley shot 69–205 to put a second-place finish behind his MasterCard victory, but had no illusions about catching Irwin that day. "Hale was just on another planet. No one could've beaten him today."

## ACE Group Classic—$1,600,000
Winner: Mark James

Mark James felt as though he had proved a point when he spurted to the wire and won the ACE Group Classic when the Champions Tour resumed action in late February in Naples, Florida. "It's very satisfying to win again," said the Englishman who captained the European team in the 2002 Ryder Cup Matches. "You feel, well, you might just have gotten lucky once, but to get lucky twice is stretching the imagination a bit."

James, who won the major Ford Senior Players Championship in his rookie 2003 season on the senior circuit, posted a strong, six-under-par 66 in the final round to take the title away from journeyman Mike McCullough, who had been in first place the first two rounds at The Club at TwinEagles.

McCullough, making his best victory bid since the 2001 season when he captured the Mexico and Emerald Coast Classics, shared the first-round lead with R.W. Eaks at 66, but they achieved that score in two different ways. McCullough had a solid, bogey-free round while Eaks, playing in the day's final group, sank his 24th putt for a birdie on his final hole in a round in which he hit just six of 14 fairways. Hale Irwin, coming off his Turtle Bay victory, shot 67, one better than the scores of Ron Streck, Wayne Levi, Jim Thorpe, Jerry Pate and Leonard Thompson.

McCullough followed with a 69 for 135 Saturday and jumped two strokes in front of Irwin (70) and James (68) as he moved closer to erasing memories of his poorest season on the Champions Tour in 2004. McCullough produced four back-nine birdies after going one over par on the front side.

As McCullough headed for a 71 and a tie-for-fourth finish despite a birdie-eagle-birdie-birdie stretch late in the round Sunday, the battle for the title developed between James and Irwin. The Englishman took a two-stroke lead to the par-five 17th hole, birdied there, but lost a shot to Irwin's eagle. Irwin was long at the 18th and missed his birdie try from the fringe before James dropped a 23-footer for a closing birdie and, with 203, the two-stroke margin over Irwin and Tom Wargo, who had finished earlier with 66 for his 205.

## Outback Steakhouse Pro-Am—$1,600,000
Winner: Hale Irwin

Weather made a shambles of the Outback Steakhouse Pro-Am. Repeated heavy rains stretched 36 holes of the Tampa tournament to an unusual Monday finish. But there was nothing unusual about the winner as Hale Irwin nosed in front by a stroke that day and picked off his 42nd victory on the Champions Tour, a new record every time he wins.

Irwin's victory, his seventh as a senior in Florida, came at the expense of Morris Hatalsky, who sat on the lead for two days after completing his 36 holes in possession of first place with his 135 total. Irwin, who had 12 holes to go when play resumed at the TPC of Tampa Bay course, got in with 68 for 134 and a one-stroke victory over Hatalsky and defending champion Mark McNulty, who also shot 68.

Rain plagued the tournament from the start as only 40 players and their amateur partners even got off the first tee Friday and no one finished. Hatalsky, an early starter in the field, completed his first round with 68 and was one of only 22 players to finish his second round Saturday before yet another downpour halted play. He posted his 67 for the clubhouse lead. Then all he could do was wait for two days as Sunday's round was washed out.

Irwin, who finished his first round Saturday with 66, relied on his experience Monday. "It wasn't spectacularly played golf. I didn't drive the ball well and I certainly didn't putt all that well, but I did what I had to do when I had to do it," he observed afterward. Irwin took the lead with six holes left and parred in, uncertain of his status until he finished.

With his second victory of the young season, Irwin made it 11 straight years on the Champions Tour during which he has won at least two tournaments.

## SBC Classic—$1,550,000
Winner: Des Smyth

Age doesn't seem to be a deterrent to the golf game of Irishman Des Smyth. At a time when most tournament players are well past their competitive peak on the regular circuits of the golf world, Smyth became, at age 48, the oldest winner in PGA European Tour history with his victory in the 2001 Madeira Island Open.

He resumed his winning ways in his third season on the Champions Tour with his victory in mid-March in the SBC Classic in Santa Clarita, California, on what was probably the most celebrated day in Irish golf. Just hours after countryman Padraig Harrington won his first tournament in America at the Honda Classic in Florida, Smyth landed his initial title in America, coming from six strokes off the lead at Valencia Country Club to snatch a one-stroke victory from D.A. Weibring and winless Keith Fergus, the second-round leader.

The 52-year-old Smyth had survived a rugged opening round in which Japan's 62-year-old Isao Aoki flashed the game that put him in the World Golf Hall of Fame in 2004. Amid strong winds, heavy rough and slick greens, Aoki shot 69 to lead the field. Smyth shot 71, one of just seven players to break par that day.

Fergus posted a 72 Friday, then followed with a 65, the best round of the week, to slip into a one-stroke lead over Mark McNulty, who shot 66 for 138 and two over Gary McCord (66) and Weibring (69). The former golf coach at the University of Houston, his alma mater, and a three-time winner on the PGA Tour accumulated eight birdies and a bogey and said of the round: "It was fun out there. I love this course. You have to be precise to score well." As for Smyth, he slipped back in the standings with a 72.

Sunday was a different story for the Irishman. He played the front nine in 32, then ran off birdies at the 12th, 13th and 15th, bogeyed the 16th and parred in for 68 to post his five-under-par 211 as the clubhouse lead. It held up, although he was holding his breath watching McNulty stroke a 20-foot putt on the 18th green for a birdie that would have sent them out in a playoff. "I'm certainly happy I didn't have to go into a playoff with him," remarked Smyth, the season's initial first-time winner. "I really feel like I kind of stole it." Fergus finished with a 74 and Weibring with 72.

## Toshiba Senior Classic—$1,650,000
Winner: Mark Johnson

Every so often, somebody follows an unconventional route to a victory on the Champions Tour. Not the usual career professionals coming off years of experience on the major tours of the world, who, as they should, win the vast majority of the tournaments. Occasionally, the winner hails from the club pro ranks or, as in the case of Mark Johnson at the Toshiba Senior Classic, turned pro later in life after compiling impressive credentials as an amateur.

In Johnson's case, the one-time California Amateur champion was 44 when he left the driver's seat of a beer truck in Southern California after 18 years and foraged among the secondary Nationwide and Canadian Tours for six years, tuning up for a shot at the Champions Tour when he turned 50.

Medalist at its National Qualifying Tournament for 2005, he brewed an impressive four-stroke victory in his home area at Newport Beach Country Club in mid-March. With his winning total of 13-under-par 200, he became the second straight first-time winner on the circuit, following Des Smyth's victory the week before in the SBC Classic.

The burly Johnson played himself into a contending position in Friday's opening round, shooting a 67 that put him in a nine-man group two strokes behind the leader, Gil Morgan, the 23-time winner on the Champions Tour. Morgan, coming off a dismal showing in the SBC Classic (tie 53rd), shot a bogey-free 65 that was highlighted by an eagle at the par-five 15th, where he holed a 49-foot putt.

Johnson took over Saturday with a dazzling, eight-under-par 63 that propelled him into the lead, three strokes in front of Fergus (66). Johnson ran off an eagle, seven birdies and a bogey, putting himself in the same position as he was going into the final round of the national qualifier. "I felt confident and good about everything that happened today," he said. "But I'll be nervous tomorrow. I was nervous at Q-School with the lead, too."

He showed those signs through much of Sunday's one-under-par 70, but never surrendered his lead despite three bogeys and an early out-of-bounds double bogey. He moved himself out of reach in the stretch when he eagled both the 15th and the 18th, the latter when he holed his 89-yard wedge shot to double his victory margin over Fergus (71) and Wayne Levi (70).

"You know, $247,500 is a lot of money for a beer truck driver," Johnson observed when he received the first-place check. "It would take seven or eight years for me to make that delivering beer."


## Liberty Mutual Legends of Golf—$2,400,000
Winner: Des Smyth

Although he conceded that "I wouldn't play on a day like this back home unless I was in a tournament," Des Smyth felt that the foul weather that visited Savannah, Georgia, for the final round of the Liberty Mutual Legends of Golf probably worked in his favor. "I suppose I had some small advantage. This type of day back home is fairly regular for us," said Irishman Smyth after coming from two strokes off the pace to score his second victory of the Champions Tour season.

Shooting the day's only sub-par round, a one-under 71 in winds that gusted up to 30 miles an hour amid temperatures in the low 50s, Smyth finished with an eight-under 208 and a two-shot win over Tom Jenkins at The Club at Savannah Harbor, an island course in the middle of the Savannah River. With his second victory in three events on the circuit, Smyth joined Hale Irwin as the only multiple winners of 2005 at that point of the season.

Smyth, a 19-tournament winner during his earlier career on the European Tour, took charge of the tournament with back-to-back birdies in the stretch Sunday. He drove the green on the downwind, 324-yard 14th and two-putted for the first one, then drew his tee shot within two feet of the cup at the par-three 15th to establish a three-stroke lead over second-round leader Wayne Levi, first-round pacesetter Tom Purtzer and Jenkins. Purtzer shot 75 and Levi 76 to tie for third at 211. Jenkins had a 73.

Purtzer, coming off a busman's-holiday win in the Australian PGA Seniors earlier in the month while visiting his college-student daughter in Sydney, got off to a fast start in the Legends, tying the course record with a seven-under-par 65 for a one-stroke lead over Smyth. Purtzer, who had wins in each of the last two seasons on the Champions Tour, started weakly with a three-putt bogey at the second hole, then ran off eight birdies for the 65. Four players — Jay Haas, Andy Bean, Morris Hatalsky and Levi — had 67s.

That was the last the field saw of benign weather conditions. Saturday turned up windy and chilly, the gusts particularly telling on the relatively barren island course. Levi got the best of it, though, shooting 68 to take a one-shot lead over Purtzer, who shot 71, and two over Smyth (71) and Jenkins (67). Levi led by three before taking bogeys on the last two holes, making a hard save for the bogey at the 18th out of a plugged bunker lie.

## FedEx Kinko's Classic—$1,650,000
Winner: Jim Thorpe

Jim Thorpe had a divine plan for the money he was trying to win in the FedEx Kinko's Classic. Whether or not there was heavenly intervention in support of his quest, Thorpe achieved his goal when he won his 10th title on the Champions Tour in the Austin, Texas, tournament and turned over the entire $247,500 purse to help the building fund for his church's new 500-seat sanctuary in a community near Orlando, Florida.

He won the tournament in rather spectacular fashion, breaking from a four-way tie with four birdies on the last five holes for 68 and a four-stroke victory over Dana Quigley with his 10-under-par 206 final score. Quigley, with a win and a runner-up finish already under his belt, had just a string of pars over those same final holes.

The 56-year-old Thorpe scored the victory despite unreliable putting. Instead, he was solid off the tee, ranking fourth in the field in driving accuracy, and the leader in greens hit in regulation — 44 of 54, with 15 of 18 in Sunday's shootout. His longest birdie putt in the stretch run was an 11-footer at the par-three 16th.

Thorpe was two strokes off the lead with his opening-round 69 as Curtis Strange led a Champions Tour round for the first time with 67. Making his sixth start on the circuit, the two-time U.S. Open champion and three-time leading money winner took a one-shot lead over Brad Bryant and Mark Johnson, the surprise winner of the Toshiba Classic the previous month.

A morning thunderstorm forced a delay of the start of the second round for nearly three hours and Wayne Levi brewed up a storm of his own at the end of his round. Levi, who has two senior victories on his record, holed a 182-yard approach for an eagle at his 17th hole and birdied the 18th for 67–138. With that, he jumped into a tie for the lead with Thorpe, who birdied the last two holes for another 69. He holed a 35-foot putt at the 18th, verifying his opinion of his putting. "I'm a streaky putter. Sometimes I can go all day. Other times, I can't hit it from six inches."

## Blue Angels Classic—$1,500,000
Winner: Jim Thorpe

Jim Thorpe made it two victories in a row when he captured the Blue Angels Classic two weeks after his win in the FedEx Kinko's, but it took an extra day in Pensacola, Florida, to accomplish the feat. He and Morris Hatalsky ran out of daylight after winding up the regulation 54 holes tied at 194, having time for just the one playoff hole they parred in the deepening dusk. Two holes later on Monday morning, Thorpe dropped a six-foot birdie putt for the title after Hatalsky bunkered his approach.

The two men were in the thick of contention all three days at The Moors Golf Club. Along with Vicente Fernandez, Thorpe and Hatalsky opened the tournament with seven-under-par 63s as two-thirds of the field broke par. They had just a one-stroke lead over Dick Mast, Bruce Lietzke and Hajime Meshiai, and 16 other players were within three of the top. Overall, the field averaged 68.346, the lowest figure in Champions Tour history, surpassing the 68.885 posted in a 1997 round at Pensacola.

Another record fell Saturday when Thorpe took the lead with 64. His 127 total was the lowest 36-hole score in tournament history. Thorpe had 15 birdies in the first two rounds as he took a one-stroke lead over Hatalsky, who shot 65. However, the big noise was made by Craig Stadler, who became the sixth player to shoot 60 in circuit history and missed by inches a birdie putt on his last hole to set a new tour record. He had 11 birdies and a bogey as he jumped into third place at 129.

Rain plagued the Sunday round, causing two delays totaling more than four hours and barely leaving time for the single extra hole when Thorpe and Hatalsky wound up in the deadlock. Hatalsky, a top-10 finisher in his three previous starts, forged a two-stroke lead over Thorpe after 14 holes. A Thorpe birdie at No. 15 and a Hatalsky bogey at No. 16 squared the count. Hatalsky birdied the 17th to regain the lead, but Thorpe dropped a 10-footer on the 18th green to force the playoff and just missed another on the lone extra hole, keeping the two men in the Florida Panhandle for another night.

SENIOR TOURS / 255

## Bruno's Memorial Classic—$1,500,000
Winner: D.A. Weibring

The Bruno's Memorial Classic has spread its championships around. D.A. Weibring became the 14th consecutive different winner since its inception in 1992 when he outplayed Tom Jenkins and Tom Kite down the stretch and survived a ruling involving his final putt of the tournament.

What at first appeared to be a comfortable two-stroke victory became a nail-biter for the good-natured Midwesterner at the end when his ball moved as he was about to tap in the final four-inch putt. However, a review of videotapes confirmed that Weibring had not soled his putter behind the ball before it moved. Had he done so, he would have been assessed a two-stroke penalty and would have faced a playoff with Jenkins and Kite, who tied for second behind his winning 15-under-par 201. Weibring shot 69 Sunday to win his third Champions Tour title, one a year since he joined the circuit in 2003.

The ever-present Dana Quigley led with a sensational 65 in the rain-delayed opening round at Greystone Golf and Country Club in suburban Birmingham, Alabama, that wasn't completed until Saturday morning. Weibring and Jenkins were two back with Curtis Strange and Mark Johnson, one behind Tom Wargo. Quigley was one over par when he made a four-foot par putt at the ninth hole. He then went on to tie the longest birdie streak in circuit history with eight in a row on the next eight holes and failed to set a new record when he three-putted the par-five 18th hole.

Weibring seized the lead in the regular round Saturday, slipping a shot in front of Quigley and Kite with a 65 of his own for 132. Weibring birdied five of the last seven holes to forge that edge over Quigley, who shot 68, and Kite, who tied the tournament record with a 63 on top of his first-round 70. "It was a great day for scoring," said Kite, who was playing mostly on the regular tour through the first months of 2005. "The leaderboard is bleeding."

"I'll try to be reasonably aggressive," said Weibring of his strategy for the final round. He was steady, the only one of the contenders who didn't make a bogey Sunday. Quigley fell from contention early with a bogey and double bogey. Jenkins, the 2003 Bruno's winner, who started the round five back, was six under on the first 14 holes, aided hugely when he holed from 125 yards for eagle at the 12th, but ran out of gas in the stretch. Kite could manage only a 70, his chances hurt when he missed a tap-in putt at the 13th for bogey.

## Senior PGA Championship—$2,000,000
Winner: Mike Reid

A lone pot bunker and a questionable decision set the door ajar and the unassuming Mike Reid slipped through the opening to score an improbable victory in the Senior PGA Championship, his first on the Champions Tour and his first anywhere in 15 years. In little more than the blink of an eye, Reid went from likely third-place finisher to winner of a title that had appeared headed for either Dana Quigley or Jerry Pate.

Reid trailed Quigley, then the leader, by six strokes at the turn Sunday, but recalled how he had lost the 1989 PGA Championship when Payne Stewart birdied four of the last five holes for 32 on the final nine while he was giving back three shots to par. "You hear all the time in this sport about not quitting because you never know what might happen," Reid remarked. "As I walked up the hill to the 10th tee, I said to myself that a 32 today might not win, but it sure would look good on the scorecard."

When he rolled in a 20-foot eagle putt at the challenging, water-guarded 18th hole at the picturesque Laurel Valley Golf Club in the Laurel Highlands of Western Pennsylvania, he had the 32, but it appeared that it would merely tie him with Quigley, who had easily reached the green at the last hole only to watch his ball bound into the course's only pot bunker on the far side of the green. Quigley was just able to get his next shot onto the putting surface and two-putted for 72. That enabled Pate, seeking his first win since 1982 after which a series of injuries shelved his career, to reclaim the lead, which he had held with his 36-hole 138. A spectacular tee shot finished a foot from the cup at the 17th and he was in front by one.

Both Reid and Pate, together in the final threesome, were safely in the fairway at the 18th. After Reid nestled his approach safely across the water on the green, Pate made the fateful decision to lay up and play a wedge shot, as suggested by his caddie, rather than risk a five iron over the water. That move was heavily second-guessed, even afterward by Pate himself, who ironically scored the greatest win of his career with a five-iron shot across water to set up a short birdie putt in the 1976 U.S. Open. He put his wedge shot well above the hole, left his first putt three feet short, and missed the second to create a three-way tie at eight-under-par 280. Both he and Reid had 70s. Quigley, who took a two-stroke lead when he finished up a 66 in the rain-delayed third round that morning, had 72.

The playoff at the 18th ended quickly. Pate drove into the rough and laid up. This time he had no choice. Reid and Quigley both hit the fairway and Reid again found the green safely, but Quigley mis-hit his iron shot enough that it ricocheted off the rocks in front of the green into the water. Reid rolled his eagle putt to tap-in range and claimed the victory when Pate missed his birdie putt.

For the record: Australia's Graham Marsh led after the opening round with 68, a shot ahead of Hale Irwin, the defending champion; R.W. Eaks, Tom McKnight and Dave Barr. Arnold Palmer, playing perhaps his final Senior PGA Championship and the only man who played at Laurel Valley in the 1965 PGA Championship shot 82-86.

## Allianz Championship—$1,500,000
Winner: Tom Jenkins

Tom Jenkins turned the tables on D.A. Weibring at the Allianz Championship. Runner-up to winner Weibring in the 2004 tournament at the Tournament Club of Iowa, Jenkins scored the victory he had been verging on for more than a month by beating D.A. on the second hole of a playoff in the 2005 event in early June. In his previous five starts since the Masters break, Jenkins had finished in the top five four times, two of them in second place.

The 57-year-old Jenkins, who already had five Champions Tour wins in the bag, launched his bid early in Polk City. He shot 65 and shared the lead with rookie Mike Sullivan, a three-time winner in his earlier years on the PGA Tour. "I've had several chances to win and I'm certainly disappointed I haven't been able to do that," Jenkins noted.

First, though, he had to contend with Mike Reid, who remained hot coming off his stunning victory the previous Sunday in the Senior PGA Championship at Laurel Valley. Reid, who opened comfortably with 69, produced a 66 Saturday and vaulted two strokes ahead of Jenkins, Morris Hatalsky and Bruce Fleisher with his 135. Just as he had done at the decisive hole at Laurel Valley, the short-hitting Reid capitalized on the par-five holes at the Tournament Club, racking up three birdies and an eagle on the long holes. (His eagle at the par-five 18th at Laurel got him into the playoff that he won.) Jenkins shot 72, Fleisher 70 and Hatalsky 67 on Saturday.

Reid retained his bid for back-to-back victories through the first 14 holes before missing a short putt at the 15th. He finished with 71, two shots out of the playoff in third place. Jenkins rallied on the back nine. Down three after 10 holes, Jenkins birdied four of the next six holes, including both par-threes, to take the lead. But Weibring, who didn't have a bogey in his final 40 holes, caught him with a birdie at the 17th. Both missed birdie tries at the 18th to close with nine-under-par 204, Jenkins with a 67 and Weibring with a 66.

In the playoff, both parred the 18th, but Jenkins wedged to five feet at the 17th, the next hole, and sank the putt after Weibring missed his birdie from 10 feet.

## Bayer Advantage Classic—$1,650,000
Winner: Dana Quigley

Dana Quigley seems to have Tom Watson's number, particularly in Watson's hometown. Five years earlier, when the tournament in Kansas City was called the TD Waterhouse Championship, Quigley rolled in a 12-foot birdie putt on the final hole to nip Watson by a stroke. In the MasterCard Championship that opened the 2005 season, Quigley nipped Watson in the playoff. Then, in a rather bizarre finish to the Bayer Advantage Classic in the Midwestern city, Quigley did it again to the Hall-of-Famer in another playoff, prompting Watson to comment: "I've got to do something about that boy."

Actually, it was a three-man playoff, also involving Gil Morgan, and the circumstances were unusual to say the least. Quigley and Morgan had finished rounds of 66 and 68 respectively for 133 before another downpour on a rainy weekend washed out play Sunday afternoon. So, Quigley and Morgan waited Monday as Watson, with six holes to play, was shooting a 66 for a matching 133, leaving a winning birdie putt on the lip at the last hole.

It then took Quigley only one hole to pick up his second victory of 2005 and 10th of his nine-season career on the Champions Tour. He knocked his six-iron approach 11 feet from the pin on the playoff 18th hole and dropped the putt after Morgan and Watson missed their birdie tries from longer range. The victory capped a hot, but disappointing, streak for Quigley, who had finished no worse than seventh in his previous five starts, but (with Jerry Pate) lost to Mike Reid in the Senior PGA Championship playoff two weeks earlier. It came in his 261st straight Champions Tour start.

Weather was a major factor all week at the Nicklaus Golf Club at Lions-Gate. Wind and rain forced an 85-minute delay during Friday's first round, but R.W. Eaks, undaunted by a shanked wedge shot, and Morgan shared the lead with seven-under-par 65s, a shot ahead of Jim Ahern and two in front of a horde of nine men, including Watson and Quigley.

A heavy overnight drenching and a stationary morning storm wiped out Saturday's play entirely and, for the third time in four years, the tournament was reduced to 36 holes. Things weren't much better Sunday. Amid three rain delays and a 6 p.m. suspension, the morning half of the field, which included Quigley and Morgan, completed their rounds. Watson, starting at eight under Monday, played his final 12 holes solidly with three birdies, but it was all for naught, as it turned out.

Nicklaus, the course designer, who may have played his final non-major Champions Tour event, strung together three 73s.

## Bank of America Championship—$1,600,000
Winner: Mark McNulty

The contenders continued to work overtime on the Champions Tour when Mark McNulty joined the long parade of 2005 winners with his victory in the Bank of America Championship in suburban Boston in late June. He won a disjointed playoff on the second extra hole at Nashawtuc Country Club. It was the fourth consecutive overtime event on the Champions Tour, a never-before occurrence on the circuit.

McNulty, the 51-year-old Zimbabwe native who had three previous victories on the Champions Tour, finished the regulation round in a three-way tie at 204 with Tom Purtzer, the second-round leader with his 71-64–135, and Don Pooley, who closed with a 65. Purtzer, who also led after 36 holes in 2004, opened the door for McNulty and Pooley when he bogeyed the 17th hole and dropped back to 11 under. Both he and McNulty, playing in the final group, birdied the par-five 18th, McNulty from a bunker and Purtzer after leaving his winning eagle putt three feet short of the cup.

Pooley was eliminated on the first extra hole when he bogeyed the 18th before threatening weather forced the other two men to shelter for an hour. Nothing happened, though, and when play resumed on the par-three 17th, McNulty nailed the title with a 15-foot birdie putt. He became the 10th different winner in the first 14 events of the season.

Broiling heat plagued players and spectators alike the first two days. In fact, the tour relaxed its no-carts rule in the blistering weather Saturday. Leonard Thompson came up with his best round of the season Friday and his 66 gave him solo possession of the first-round lead for the first time ever on the Champions Tour. It established a one-stroke advantage over McNulty, Walter Hall, John Harris and Tom McKnight.

Purtzer, who opened with 71, roared into the lead Saturday. When he holed out a nine iron from 147 yards for an eagle at the seventh, "that shot definitely jump-started me." He birdied the next two holes, made six in all for 64–135 and moved a stroke in front of McNulty (69) and R.W. Eaks (65). Thompson slipped to 71 and shared fourth place at 137 with Jerry Pate and John Bland.

Purtzer didn't surrender the lead Sunday until the 17th-hole bogey that led to the record-setting playoff.

## Commerce Bank Championship—$1,500,000
Winner: Ron Streck

Ron Streck arrived on the Champions Tour in the summer of 2004 without fanfare and barely made a stir over the next 12 months. In fact, he worked out his best showing in 17 starts the week before the Commerce Bank Championship with an unimpressive tie for 21st place in Boston. How things changed on Long Island!

It started Friday when the Oklahoman exploded a 62 on the field and took a two-stroke lead that he never relinquished. The first winner of the year to go wire to wire, Streck went on to post a 16-under-par 197 on the Red Course at Eisenhower Park and pick up his first victory as a senior. In so doing, he became the first player ever to score wins on the Champions, PGA and Nationwide Tours.

Interestingly, Streck shot 62s in the process of winning titles in Houston and San Antonio during his 22 years on the PGA Tour. His Nationwide victory came in the 1993 Yuma Open in a playoff against Chris DiMarco, then 24 years old. He set another precedent in 1981, too. He was the first player to use a metal "wood" in a PGA Tour event.

Streck's opening round was a masterpiece. He missed only one green and made five of his nine birdies from within three feet, including the final two of the day. Craig Stadler had eight birdies as he took second place with 64, a stroke ahead of Dave Eichelberger, Wayne Levi, Gary McCord and Darrell Kestner.

Streck maintained his two-shot margin with a 68 Saturday, citing the obvious: "I didn't hit it as close as I did yesterday." In front going into a final round for the first time in his career, he led Tom Jenkins, who shot 63; Stadler (68) and Eichelberger (67). Jim Ahern staged the only challenge Sunday, matching Streck at 14 under with a birdie at the 15th hole. However, he gave a stroke back in the stretch and Streck pulled away to a three-stroke final margin with his 67–197, becoming the circuit's fourth first-time winner of the season, joining Mark Johnson, Des Smyth and Mike Reid.

# Ford Senior Players Championship—$2,500,000
Winner: Peter Jacobsen

No victories in routine, run-of-the-mill tournaments for Peter Jacobsen on the Champions Tour. The personable Jacobsen, in his second season playing on both that circuit and the regular PGA Tour, scored his second win on the senior circuit when he edged Hale Irwin in the Ford Senior Players Championship, just like his first one a Champions Tour major. Jacobsen picked up his initial victory in the 2004 U.S. Senior Open, ironically by the same one-stroke margin over Irwin.

Jacobsen, who began the final round at the TPC of Michigan in Dearborn three strokes behind Irwin, the leader, birdied two of the last three holes for 66–273, then waited as Irwin, three groups back, tried in vain to catch him in the stretch. His putting failed him and his two-under-par 70 left him one stroke short at 274. He left a 13-footer short at the 17th and just missed a 12-footer at the 18th.

Jacobsen, on the other hand, won with his putter, making a birdie from 14 feet deep in a collection area at the 16th and two-putting from 80 feet for the winning birdie at the par-five 17th, capping a six-under stretch over the last 12 holes. The nearest other challengers were Tom Watson (68) and Tom McKnight (71) at 276.

The early-round leaders fell by the wayside. Australian Graham Marsh, who numbers two majors among his six Champions Tour titles, tied the opening-day record Thursday with an eight-under-par 64. In fact, the entire field averaged 70.96, the best start ever at the TPC of Michigan. Marsh disappeared Friday when he shot 76 and money leader Dana Quigley took over the lead with 66 for 133 as he played in his 278th consecutive tournament for which he was eligible, a record streak that ended there when he didn't go to Scotland for the Senior British Open the following week. Quigley led McKnight and Japan's Isao Aoki by two and Jacobsen, Irwin and Ron Streck, the previous week's winner on Long Island, by three.

Irwin, the 1999 Senior Players champion, inched in front Saturday with a 68 for 204 as he took aim on his 43rd Champions Tour victory. Quigley (72) stayed one behind with McKnight (70) and Gil Morgan (67) despite a round that included three bogeys and a double bogey. Irwin had two bogeys in his round.

When he won Sunday, Jacobsen was playing in just his 19th event on the senior circuit and his feat of getting his first two wins in majors put him in distinguished company. The only others to have accomplished that in the tour's history were Arnold Palmer (1980 Senior PGA, 1981 U.S. Senior Open) and Nicklaus (1990 Tradition and Senior Players.)

# Senior British Open—€1,457,507
Winner: Tom Watson

See European Seniors Tour section.

## U.S. Senior Open—$2,600,000
Winner: Allen Doyle

The leaders hadn't even gone to the practice range when Allen Doyle teed off in the final round of the U.S. Senior Open Championship. Virtually unnoticed, Doyle started Sunday's concluding 18 holes nine strokes off the lead. "No one thought I had a chance," said the New Englander after he ripped the South course of NCR Country Club with a Senior Open record-tying, eight-under-par 63 and snatched the title away from Loren Roberts and D.A. Weibring by a stroke. "I fooled them again," chortled the long-time amateur with the unconventional, hockey-influenced style.

He posted his 10-under-par 274, then waited more than an hour to see if anybody could catch him. Nobody did, and Doyle's victory, his third Champions Tour major and 10th on the circuit, went into the books as the greatest come-from-behind final-round win in a major championship in the circuit's 26-year history. The 63, an NCR course record, bettered by four strokes the lowest final-round score ever shot by a Senior Open winner. Nobody made up more than four strokes to win any previous senior major.

By the time Doyle reached the turn Sunday, he had everybody's attention. He had birdied six of the first eight holes and was out in 30. He followed with 15-foot birdie putts at the 10th and 14th and mustered some tough pars finishing up the 63.

The course was littered with crashes behind him. Craig Stadler and Roberts, in the thick of things from the opening round, had led after 54 holes with 11-under-par 202s, three strokes in front of Weibring and 63-year-old Raymond Floyd, who won the 1969 PGA Championship at NCR. Stadler had started the week with a smart 64, then shared the lead after Friday's second round at 133 with Tom Watson and Roberts. Watson was four back entering the last round and Greg Norman, like Roberts making his second senior start, was not out of it at 207.

Floyd fell back early and neither Watson nor Norman could get anything going on the back nine. Stadler, winless in 2005, had a three-shot lead after eight holes, but double-bogeyed the ninth when he drove into the face of a fairway bunker and skied to a 76. Roberts took over first place with birdies at the ninth and 10th, but turned it over to Weibring when he left a bunker shot in the sand and double-bogeyed the next hole. Weibring, who had birdied the 10th hole, parred the next six and led by one before driving into the rough and bogeying the last two holes, giving Doyle the choice title.

## 3M Championship—$1,750,000
Winner: Tom Purtzer

For one who believes in omens, there was something in Tom Purtzer's past on the Champions Tour that foretold his victory in the 3M Championship in early August. Among Purtzer's three previous victories on the circuit was the one in the 2003 SBC Classic in which he made a hole-in-one in the first round. So, the next time he posted an ace on the Champions Tour — on opening day of the 3M Championship — he did it again. Aided by the hole-in-one, Purtzer shot a nine-under-par 63 at the Tournament Players Club of the Twin Cities to take the first-round lead and never trailed in posting a one-stroke victory.

It was just the second wire-to-wire triumph of the season, pairing with Ron Streck's like performance in the Commerce Bank Championship, and the only one among Purtzer's eight career wins. The victory, Purtzer's first in 17 months, was particularly satisfying, considering that he had led the 3M after 36 holes each of the previous two years, shot 74 the last day both years and failed to win. This time, he shot 69 in the final round and barely avoided the same fate. He dropped a seven-foot par putt on the 18th green to edge Craig Stadler and Lonnie Nielsen by a shot with his 201.

"I tried to stay positive and not think about what happened here the last two years," Purtzer said. "I just didn't want to beat myself (again)." With the opening 63 — seven birdies to go with the ace — and a 69 Saturday — four birdies and a three-putt bogey — Purtzer built a three-stroke lead to carry into the Sunday finale. Three back at 135 were Nielsen and David Eger (68s), Stadler (67), Hajime Meshiai (66) and Bruce Lietzke, who followed his opening 64 with 71.

Never holing a par longer than 10 feet, Purtzer saw his margin diminish to a single stroke by the time he reached the 18th green. There he left his birdie try seven feet short. Though putting has always been his weak suit, Purtzer rolled that decisive one into the cup to avoid a playoff and become the 11th consecutive different winner on the Champions Tour.

## Boeing Greater Seattle Classic—$1,600,000
Winner: David Eger

David Eger seems to have an affinity for winning performances in new events on new golf courses on the Champions Tour. The one-time PGA Tour official, who used to set up golf courses for its tournaments, rolled to a three-stroke victory in the Boeing Greater Seattle Classic as the Champions Tour returned to the state of Washington for the first time since the demise of the GTE Northwest Classic in 1995. It was the 53-year-old Eger's second victory, the first coming in the inaugural MasterCard Classic at a new venue in Mexico City in 2003, the third year that the tour went to Mexico.

Fully aware from his previous occupation of the caliber of play on the Champions Tour, Eger, who first earned playing privileges through the 2002 qualifying school, put his victory in this perspective: "I've always said there are a handful of stars out here, but there are also 70 or so very good players who could always win. If you're good enough to play out here, you're good enough to win."

In the process of extending the Champions Tour's string of different winners to 12 tournaments running, Eger established his challenge in the Saturday round, when he shot an eight-under-par 64 and jumped into a three-way tie for the lead at 132 with Craig Stadler and Morris Hatalsky. Eger, who built his golfing reputation with an amateur record that included three appearances in the Walker Cup Matches and two advances to the semi-finals in the U.S. Amateur, had opened with 66, two off the pace of leaders Hatalsky, Brad Bryant, Jim Thorpe and Tom Kite.

Eger broke from the 36-hole deadlock at the TPC course at Snoqualmie Ridge with a strong start Sunday. He picked off birdies at the third, fourth, sixth and eighth holes to establish a commanding lead and went five strokes in front when he birdied again at the 11th. He made only a couple of harmless errors coming in and "had the luxury of playing 18 as a pure, three-shot par-five."

He finished with a bogey-free 67 and 199, three strokes ahead of Tom Kite, who matched his 67. It was another disappointing Sunday for Stadler, who was in the final group for the fourth consecutive time in quest of his first 2005 victory but shot 73 and finished sixth.

## JELD-WEN Tradition—$2,500,000
Winner: Loren Roberts

Loren Roberts wasted little time on the Champions Tour in accomplishing something he failed to do during his exemplary career on the regular PGA Tour. In just his third start on the senior circuit after turning 50, Roberts laid claim to a major championship, though in a rather bizarre way. Roberts, whose best shot at a major during his earlier days was in the 1994 U.S. Open at Oakmont when he lost to Ernie Els in a playoff, picked off the JELD-WEN Tradition title with a bogey on the second hole of a playoff against Dana Quigley, who was trying to embellish his outstanding season by winning his first major title.

Both players came from behind to forge the final-round deadlock in the season's final major in late August at the Reserve Vineyards and Golf Club outside of Portland, Oregon. Roberts, who had finished second in the U.S. Senior Open and fifth in the Senior British Open in his first two Champions Tour starts, birdied the last two holes for 67–273 to match the 68 of Quigley, who was a two-time 2005 winner and then-current money leader. Quigley appeared to have the title in hand when he eagled the par-five 16th hole, but he bogeyed the 17th and parred the 18th to put himself into his fourth playoff of the season, two of which gave him his two wins.

After they matched birdies on the par-five 18th to start the playoff, they both misplayed the second one. Roberts's approach was long beyond the mid-green bunker on the par-four 17th and Quigley wound up on the edge of a greenside bunker. Both missed long par putts and Quigley failed to drop his three-and-a-half-footer for bogey. Roberts holed his and remarked afterward that "I'm sorry I won with a bogey, but that's the way it goes." Quigley was philosophic, as he was after losing in a playoff in the Senior PGA at Laurel Valley: "It's just not my turn yet."

Roberts and Quigley were in contention from the start. Quigley holed a 45-foot eagle putt on the 18th hole following three birdies for 67 and shared the first-round lead with Roberts, John Harris and D.A. Weibring. Gil Morgan, who won the Tradition twice when it was played at Desert Mountain in Arizona, jumped into first place Friday with a 64 for 133. He ran off an eagle and six birdies before pulling out a par without touching the fairway at the 18th. Roberts shot 69 to trail by three and Quigley 72 to fall six strokes off the pace.

Doug Tewell celebrated his 56th birthday with a 66 and moved into a first-place tie with Morgan (70) at 13-under-par 203 after 54 holes. Quigley shot 66 to climb within two and Roberts remained three shots back with 70–206. Morgan took a 71 and finished a stroke out of the playoff Sunday as Tewell faded to a fifth-place tie with 73–276.

## Wal-Mart First Tee Open at Pebble Beach—$2,000,000
Winner: Hale Irwin

Nothing else has slowed down Hale Irwin on the Champions Tour, so why should advancing years? The circuit's most dominant player hadn't won since turning 60 in June after posting two wins and a second in the year's first four tournaments, but he jumped back into the battle for year-end honors when the seniors went to Pebble Beach in early September for the second staging of the Wal-Mart First Tee Open. Never out of the lead at the storied venue where he won the old Crosby Pro-Am 21 years earlier, Irwin birdied Pebble Beach's demanding par-three 17th hole Sunday and salted away a one-stroke victory with his 68 and 13-under-par 203.

He was the first man to win three times in 2005 as he stretched his massive lead in career Champions Tour victories to 14 over Lee Trevino with his 43rd triumph. Among regularly competitive players, Irwin has a 20-win margin on Gil Morgan, who, by the way, finished second in the First Tee with Morris Hatalsky and defending champion Craig Stadler. It was the seventh season in his 10 full years on the circuit that Irwin has won at least three events.

Irwin and Dana Quigley, the man Hale and a couple of others were trying to overtake for top 2005 honors, opened with leading 66s at Del Monte, a 6,257-yard layout that replaced Bayonet as the second course in the unique tournament that is a major fundraiser for the First Tee program that promotes golf and good citizenship among the nation's young people. Quigley, coming off a playoff loss to Loren Roberts in the JELD-WEN Tradition, fired a bogey-free round in his first look at Del Monte. Irwin had a bogey in his round as the two men started a stroke ahead of Walter Hall, Bob Gilder and Doug Tewell, all of whom played at Pebble Beach.

Morgan, still without a 2005 victory in his quest to extend his unbroken string of 10 seasons with at least one title among his 23, caught up to Irwin with a 65 at Del Monte, while Irwin was shooting 69 with birdies at the last two holes at Pebble Beach for his 135. They led four others, including Stadler and Hatalsky, by two going into the final round at Pebble Beach.

At the end, Stadler and Hatalsky missed birdie putts at the par-five 18th hole before Irwin sank his 10-footer at the 17th to establish the one-shot margin of victory.

## Constellation Energy Classic—$1,700,000
Winner: Bob Gilder

Bob Gilder ended his two-year winning drought in decisive style when the Champions Tour made its final stop of the season in the East with the Constellation Energy Classic outside of Baltimore. The 54-year-old Gilder, a seven-time winner during his first 28 months of senior competition but without a victory since April of 2003, led from a resounding, eight-under-par 64 start to a four-stroke victory in the Constellation Energy Classic with a score that matched the lowest total of the 2005 season.

Despite a blooper early in the final round at Hayfields Country Club, Gilder finished with a 67 for an 18-under-par 198, matching Dana Quigley's year's-best winning score in the MasterCard Championship, which opened the season, and finishing with the biggest margin since Hale Irwin won by five in the year's second tournament. He was the 15th consecutive different victor and the third to go wire-to-wire, joining Ron Streck (Commerce Bank) and Tom Purtzer (3M Championship) in that category.

Gilder, whose best finish earlier in the season was a tie for fourth, putted just eight times on the front nine en route to his opening 64, which tied the tournament and course record and gave him a two-stroke lead over Tom Watson and Dan Pohl. He was eight under through his first 14 holes and had birdie putts that didn't drop on the last four holes. "Shoot, I didn't know it was going to be a course record. They should have told me. Maybe I'd have made one," he kidded.

A 67 in Saturday's second round kept Gilder two strokes in front of the field. His 131 matched the season's lowest 36-hole score against par (minus 13) shot by Jim Thorpe on his way to victory in the Blue Angels Classic. D.A. Weibring (67-66) and Morris Hatalsky (69-64) shared second place, a stroke ahead of Curtis Strange (68-66) and Watson (66-68). Hatalsky birdied the last four holes to equal the record 64, while Weibring led briefly with an eagle at the par-four 15th but dropped back with a bogey at the final hole.

Gilder built his lead quickly to four Sunday, then dunked a seven-iron shot in the water at the third hole and found his margin suddenly reduced to a single stroke. But that was the only flaw in his final round. By the turn, he had his lead back up to three and never looked back. When he chipped in for par at the 18th for the 198, he matched the tournament record set by Christy O'Connor, Jr., when he won in 1999. Hatalsky finished in the runner-up spot for the second week in a row with his closing 69. Strange also shot 69 to finish third, his best showing of the year.

## SAS Championship—$1,900,000
Winner: Hale Irwin

Hale Irwin continued his hot pursuit of annual honors on the Champions Tour when he won his second consecutive late-season tournament in the SAS Championship at Raleigh, North Carolina, and his fourth of the season. With that title in the bag, Irwin was dogging the heels of Dana Quigley in the runs for the Charles Schwab Cup and the No. 1 position on the money list as well as a fourth Player of the Year designation as the season neared its end. He made a major move on Quigley as Dana had his worst showing of the year, finishing 64th at Prestonwood Country Club.

Irwin stormed from four strokes off the pace in scoring his second victory since turning 60 in June and 44th of his domineering career on the Champions Tour. While Irwin kept within range with rounds of 69 and

68 the first two days, the stage was held by Bruce Summerhays and R.W. Eaks. Summerhays, 61, opened with a six-under-par 66 in his quest for his fourth tour title and first in more than a year.

Eaks, who birdied five of his last eight holes for 67 and the runner-up position Friday, slipped into the lead Saturday with a 66, again with a torrid finish — four birdies on the final eight holes. Winless in his four years and 50 starts on the Champions Tour, the 53-year-old Eaks took a one-stroke lead over Bob Gilder, trying for two wins in a row on the circuit. Gilder also shot 66 for 134, with Tom Jenkins (135) and Rodger Davis (136) just ahead of Irwin and four others.

Irwin was idling along Sunday in the early going. "I didn't play that well on the front nine, but I played No. 10 very well and got a birdie that opened the floodgates." He proceeded to shoot 31 on the back nine for the week's popular score of 66 for 13-under-par 203 that bested second-place Gilder (71) and Jenkins (70) by two strokes. The clincher was the difficult 25-foot eagle putt that he made with his ball resting against the collar of the green at the par-five 17th hole. Eaks dashed his hopes with a 77 Sunday.

## Greater Hickory Classic at Rock Barn—$1,600,000
Winner: Jay Haas

The only thing surprising about the victory of Jay Haas in the Greater Hickory Classic at Rock Barn was that it had been so long since the last one. Here was a man who had been a prominent player with nine wins and 142 finishes in the top 10 in his quarter century on the PGA Tour, yet had not picked up all the marbles in a tournament in nearly 12 years, none since his victory in the 1993 Texas Open. He had 59 top-10s between those victories.

Splitting his time between the PGA Tour and the Champions Tour since turning 50 in December of 2003, Haas finally broke the ice in his 10th start on the senior circuit, coming from three strokes off the pace in the final round of the rain-interrupted tournament in the tour's early October visit to the mountains of western North Carolina for a two-shot victory. He was the 19th different winner in the season's initial 25 events and the sixth first-timer.

Only nine men completed the first round Friday before steady, heavy rains made the Jones course of the Rock Barn Golf and Spa unplayable. Doug Tewell, the defending champion, posted a 70, but he only led until the full round was completed Saturday and Wayne Levi entered a 65 onto the record.

The second round immediately followed on Saturday and Dana Quigley made a strong move to enhance his No. 1 position on the Champions Tour. Shooting darts at the soft greens, Quigley ran off eight birdies for 64–132, with a 70-footer throw in with a batch of short putts, and took a one-stroke lead over Loren Roberts. "I just stuffed a lot of shots close that normally would run 10-15 feet past the pin," explained Quigley. Haas, meanwhile, had posted rounds of 68-67–135 and was tied for third with Tom McKnight and Jim Ahern.

Haas ran off eight birdies, five on the back nine, as he shot 65 Sunday for 200 and scooted past two-time-winner Quigley, who could manage just 70 and had to settle for second place for the fourth time in the season. Roberts also shot 70 to finish third, his fourth top-five finish in his first five Champions Tour starts.

Haas took the lead for good with a birdie at the 16th hole and secured the victory with two more on the last two holes. "Each day I felt like I left a few out there," he observed. "But today I made the putts I needed to make, both the short ones and the ones that really made the round complete."

## Administaff Small Business Classic—$1,600,000
Winner: Mark McNulty

Mark McNulty joined the meager ranks of multiple winners on the 2005 Champions Tour when he picked off the Administaff Small Business Classic in mid-October at Houston, Texas. Emerging from a bunched group of contenders in the stretch run Sunday at Augusta Pines Golf Club, McNulty added that title to his earlier victory in the Bank of America Championship at Boston to become just the fifth player with more than a single win during the season. Among the others — Hale Irwin, Dana Quigley, Jim Thorpe and Des Smyth — only Irwin with four had more than a pair of wins on their 2005 records.

McNulty's victory, the fifth in his two seasons on the Champions Tour, did not come easily. He needed every stroke of his closing, six-under-par 66 to edge Gil Morgan by a shot after Brad Bryant, the second-round leader, frittered away his bid for his first senior victory with a mid-round triple bogey. McNulty's winning total was 200.

Bryant found himself on virgin ground after Saturday's second round. His pair of 66s the first two days staked him to his first 36-hole lead in his Champions Tour career. He was two strokes in front of six players with potent credentials — Jay Haas and Morris Hatalsky, who with Des Smyth led the first day with 65s; Irwin, Morgan, Dave Barr and McNulty. Bryant had the solution for his rather tenuous position: "Pray for a rainout, which I don't think we'll get."

He handled the situation well early, running off birdies on the first three holes to go 15 under par, before disaster struck at No. 10, where he put a shot in the lake. The triple bogey there took him out of contention and he finished fourth at 203. McNulty, the highly successful player from Zimbabwe with 55 international victories on his pre-Seniors record, went in front with a birdie at the 16th and two-putted from 43 feet on the par-five 18th for the 66.

Irwin and Morgan had chances to force a playoff at the last hole, but they needed eagles to do so. Irwin bunkered his approach and parred for 68–202, while Morgan, trying to extend to 10 successive seasons his record of winning at least once a year, reached the green in two but missed the tying putt from 31 feet. Haas, going after two in a row, shot 70 and tied for fifth with Bruce Lietzke.

## SBC Championship—$1,550,000
Winner: Jay Haas

Golf has its share of clever sayings. One of the most familiar certainly applied when Jay Haas scored his second victory on the Champions Tour in three weeks in the SBC Championship, the final regular event of the season, and ensured his spot in the season-ending Charles Schwab Cup Championship: Horses for courses.

Haas went to San Antonio's venerable Oak Hills Country Club to play a course on which he won the Texas Open twice among his nine victories on the PGA Tour and did it again. As he did two weeks earlier in winning the Greater Hickory Classic, Haas came from behind in the final round, this time shooting a five-under-par 66 for 199 and a two-stroke victory over Tom Purtzer, who soared into second place with a closing 63.

"I just feel like I'm going to shoot a good round when I come here," said Haas, who won at Oak Hill in 1982 and 1993, the latter his last tour victory until he won at Hickory.

John Harris, the long-time amateur standout playing his fourth season of senior golf, shot his career round in Friday's opening round. Even with two bogeys, Harris shot the tournament's best-ever first-day score — 62 — with a run of four birdies and an eagle on Nos. 6 through 10. On a day of low scoring, Gil Morgan shot 64 and Jerry Pate, Dan Pohl and Lonnie Nielsen had 65s.

Dana Quigley, working to secure his places atop the money list and Charles Schwab standings, surged into the lead Saturday. He shot 64 for 131, nailing six birdies in a seven-hole stretch in the middle of the round. Harris was right there with him until his approach at the par-four 17th flew the green and bounced out of bounds, costing him a triple bogey. Mark James, who won the ACE Group Classic in Florida in February, shot 66 for 132, and Haas, also with 66, moved into third place, two off the lead.

Sunday turned into a duel between Haas and Quigley before Quigley's putter deserted him at the end. Haas birdied four of the last five holes on the front nine to overtake Quigley at 13 under par. It was still that way after 14 holes, then Haas took charge. He pitched to two feet and birdied the 15th, and Quigley bogeyed the final three holes as Haas parred in. "I wasn't flawless out there," Haas said. "I was just fortunate that Dana made a couple of mistakes."

Quigley, who always seems able to cope with setbacks, responded philosophically: "Winners capitalize and losers shake their heads and wait for next week."

## Charles Schwab Cup Championship—$2,500,000
Winner: Tom Watson

The season-ending Charles Schwab Championship (nee the Tour Championship) had all the drama that the Champions Tour hoped for with its big-purse, points-competition format when the seniors wrapped things up in Northern California at the end of October.

Dana Quigley had the season's money race and the Arnold Palmer Award virtually clinched when the selective field of the top 30 players of the year teed off at the Sonoma Golf Club just north of San Francisco and had close to a lock on the $1 million annuity that goes to the No. 1 man on the Schwab point standings. Things looked even better for Quigley after the first three rounds as Jay Haas, the circuit's hottest player during its final month, soared to a six-stroke lead over the five closest pursuers. That margin seemed golden, considering the fact that Haas had won two of the previous three events.

Unfortunately for Quigley and Haas, Tom Watson was one of those five players at 208, a man used to winning the big ones — 12 majors — throughout his marvelous career. Watson, who won the Tour Championship in 2000 and 2002 and the Senior British Open earlier in the season, came up with a splendid 64, the best finishing round by a winner in the tournament's history, to edge a stunned Haas by a stroke with his 16-under-par 272. Furthermore, the triple points Watson earned brought him from 686 behind to a 247 margin of victory over Quigley, who had to settle for the comfortable second prize of $500,000.

Both Quigley and Haas were philosophical about it. "There's nothing you can do," Quigley said. "I mean, Watson arguably is one of the five best players to ever play golf." Added the disappointed Haas, who managed just a 71 Sunday, "It [his game] didn't look any different than it did 20 years ago, except he drives it straighter now."

Watson, who thought Haas "would probably run away with it" after 54 holes, closed the gap fast on the front nine Sunday, moving within two of the leader. He caught Haas at 15 under on the back nine and rolled in a 20-footer on the 18th green for his 10th birdie of the afternoon and the victory. Quigley, with 70, tied for fifth with Loren Roberts at 278 behind Tom Kite (275) and defending champion Mark McNulty (277) and ran his prize winnings for the season to $2,170,258.

Lonnie Nielsen was an early factor at Sonoma. He led the first day with 66 and shared the top spot after 36 holes at 138 with Roberts and Gil Morgan, both with 69-69s. Bunched just a stroke back were six players, including Watson (69-70) and Haas (70-69). The picture changed drastically Saturday when Haas spurted away from the field with a dazzling 63, the best score of the week. "It was one of those days when things felt right from the start," he said as he birdied four of the first five holes and never looked back.

Prophetically, though, he cautioned after the round: "If I could shoot this round today, obviously someone could tomorrow."

# European Seniors Tour

## DGM Barbados Open—€189,465
Winner: Denis O'Sullivan

A fresh start in a new season on the European Seniors Tour worked wonders for Denis O'Sullivan. Winless since 2002, O'Sullivan acquired his sixth seniors title when the circuit opened shop with its traditional start in the Caribbean in early March. He broke from a first-place tie after 36 holes to post a three-stroke victory in the DGM Barbados Open at Royal Westmoreland Golf Club. He closed with a two-under-par 70 for a final 206.

"I put in a good performance," said the "delighted" Irishman, adding: "I was due one when you consider the fact that I was rubbish for most of last year."

His play at Royal Westmoreland was anything but rubbish. O'Sullivan opened with a 68 and trailed leaders Carl Mason and Hank Woodrome by a stroke. Mason, the No. 1 player on the European Seniors Tour in his first two seasons on the circuit, launched his bid for a third straight Order of Merit crown with a bogey-free round that included an eagle and three birdies. The Englishman was runner-up to Gavan Levenson in 2004 at Barbados. Woodrome, who reshaped his game and worked with a belly putter during the off-season at home in Yorba Linda, California, had five birdies for his 67.

Although a bit inconsistent with three bogeys, the 56-year-old O'Sullivan repeated his 68 Saturday and joined American John Grace (70-66) at the top with 136s. The six-birdie 66 surprised Grace, who has been without a win since his three-victory season in 2000, when he finished second to Noel Ratcliffe on the final Order of Merit. "We had a pretty poor winter back home in Texas (Fort Worth) and I didn't really get the chance to prepare for the season," remarked Grace. Sam Torrance also shot 66 Saturday and moved within a shot of the leaders.

O'Sullivan established his victory bid early Sunday with birdies on two of the first three holes and shook off a double bogey at the sixth hole en route to his 70. Nobody materialized as a challenger, particularly Grace, who managed just a 73 but took second place with his 209, and Torrance, who slumped to a shocking 79 and fell to 10th. Spaniard Emilio Rodriguez Pareja, who earned his playing privileges at the fall qualifying school, finished third at 210, and Mason, who followed his 67 with a pair of 72s, was another shot behind.

## Tobago Plantations Seniors Classic—€188,764
Winner: Luis Carbonetti

The stage was set for Carl Mason to repeat his 2004 victory in the Tobago Plantations Seniors Classic, but one of the Carbonetti brothers from Argentina upset his plans. Luis made off with a two-stroke victory when Mason and two 36-hole co-leaders failed to break par in the final round of the European Seniors Tour's second and last stop in the Caribbean in March.

Eying the 10th victory of his brief seniors career, Mason shared the top position in the standings after Saturday's round with Scotland's Bill Longmuir and Jamaica's Delroy Cambridge and felt he had a psychological edge for Sunday's finale. "Knowing that the guys are aware of me really gets me going," he said. "I'm always trying to show people that the wins I have already had were no flukes."

His 73 in the last round didn't scare anybody, particularly Luis Carbonetti and Longmuir, who battled down the stretch for the title. Longmuir, a four-time winner in his first two years on the circuit, took a two-stroke lead early in the round. Then Carbonetti mounted a charge with a four-birdie run starting at the seventh hole. His break came when Longmuir bogeyed two of the last four holes and 51-year-old Luis finished off the two-shot win with a birdie at the 18th for 68–208, eight under par at the Tobago Plantations Beach and Golf Resort course. It was his third win in his second season on the tour.

His older brother, Horacio, 57, shot 70 to share second place at 210 with the disappointed Longmuir, who "got a few bad breaks on the way home and lost my concentration." Mason finished in a five-way tie for fourth place. Lost in the shuffle was the first-round leader, Bob Cameron, who shot 65, the week's lowest score, but followed with a pair of 74s. Cameron, the tour's record-holder for lowest score with 61, had nine birdies, but gave two strokes back with a double bogey. He tied for 11th place.

## Jolie Ville Sharm El Sheikh Seniors Open—€197,245
Winner: Bob Lendzion

He'll probably never be called a desert rat, but Bob Lendzion felt that his years of playing around his hometown contributed to the victory he posted when the European Seniors Tour made its first-ever stop in Egypt during the two-month gap between its opening in the Caribbean and the start of the main body of the schedule in Europe itself in late May.

Lendzion, who came from three shots back to claim his second victory on the circuit, observed of his strong finish: "I think the fact that I'm from Las Vegas and use to desert courses like this one helped me this week in terms of the heat and humidity that a lot of the guys found tough to play in." After a bogey-bogey start in the final round, the American, who had gone seven years since posting his initial European Seniors victory in the Beko Classic in Turkey, bounced back to shoot 66 for an 18-under-par 198 and edge England's David J. Russell and South Africa's John Mashego by a stroke at the Jolie Ville Golf and Resort.

Russell, who gained encouragement after a disappointing rookie season on the senior tour with a victory the preceding week in a Callaway event in Scotland, kept the momentum going in Egypt. He put up a brilliant 63 in the opening round, but led by only a stroke over American John Benda and two over Lendzion. Russell set a 36-hole tour record Saturday when he followed with a 66 for 129 and opened a three-stroke lead over Benda (68) and Lendzion (67).

Those three players all remained in the title fight Sunday, particularly after Lendzion rallied from his feeble start with two birdies and an eagle on the next four holes. Challenges came, though, from Bob Cameron, who ultimately double-bogeyed the last hole, where Mashego, his playing partner, capped a brilliant 64 with a chip-in eagle for a back-nine 29 and a 17-under-par 199, the leader in the clubhouse.

However, Lendzion was six under for the day and 18 under as he went to the final hole. Wisely laying up short of the water hazard guarding the green on the par-five hole, Lendzion pitched on and two-putted for the victory. Russell, who had said Saturday that he needed to shoot a round of three under or better to win, had a 70 to tie Mashego. Benda finished fourth at 200 with a 68.

## Nokia 9300 Italian Seniors Open — €170,000
Winner: Gery Watine

The European Seniors Tour got its first new champion of 2005 and went to its first playoff of the season when the schedule resumed in late May in Venice, Italy. Frenchman Gery Watine, who made runs at titles in his first full season in 2004, rolled in an 18-foot birdie putt on the first extra hole in the Nokia 9300 Italian Seniors Open to pick up his first victory ever on the European and European Seniors Tours at the expense of Eamonn Darcy.

Watine, who was born and raised in Morocco, had dropped out of competitive golf for 10 years before qualifying for the over-50 circuit in late 2003, spending much of the interim time designing 15 courses in France. He posted two third-place showings as he finished 25th on the 2004 Order of Merit.

Watine started the tournament at Circolo Golf Venezia with a bang, matching the course record of 67 set by Arnold Palmer, the Venezia designer, and matched by David J. Russell in 2004, taking a one-stroke lead over Argentina's Adan Sowa and two over Irishman Darcy, South African Gavan Levenson and Englishman Nick Job. That his solid 67 — six birdies and a bogey — matched the course record of Palmer both surprised and pleased Watine, who said Palmer wrote the first golf book he ever read, at age 13.

The race remained tight Saturday. His putting less effective, Watine shot 70 for 137 and was joined in first place by Levenson, who had a second bogey-free round and birdied the 36th hole from 25 feet for the tying 68. Darcy had a second 69 for 138 and Luis Carbonetti, the winner in Tobago in March, was another stroke back with 70-69.

The focus all day Sunday was on the final threesome of Watine, Darcy and Levenson. When they reached the 18th tee, Watine and Darcy were 10 under par and Levenson was a shot behind. Both leaders then birdied the closing hole, Darcy first from 12 feet for 67 and Watine from six feet for 68 as Levenson settled for third place at 207 with a par, two shots out of the playoff. The final decision came quickly as Watine sank the 18-footer on the first playoff hole after Darcy missed from longer range.

## AIB Irish Seniors Open — €400,000
Winner: Noel Ratcliffe

"I don't know what makes me play so well here in Ireland," pondered Noel Ratcliffe. "It must be something in the water." Hardly, but still the Australian seems to be in his best form in recent years when he tees it up somewhere on the Emerald Isle. A seven-time winner on the European Seniors Tour, the 60-year-old Ratcliffe scored six of those victories before 2002. The seventh came in the 2003 AIB Irish Seniors Open and, after a third-place finish in 2004, he took the Irish Open title again the first week of June at The Heritage at Killenard.

"This is a fantastic moment for me," enthused Ratcliffe, who is in his 11th season of senior golf. "I have great memories of winning at Adare Manor (in 2003), and this is even better because I hadn't won since then."

Ratcliffe carved out a dogged one-under-par 71 in the final round to claim the title by two strokes over Luis Carbonetti, who closed with a 73 in his failed bid for a second 2005 title to go with his victory in the Tobago Plantations Classic.

Ratcliffe had some ground to make up after Friday's first round. He shot 71 for starters and trailed leader Jim Rhodes by four strokes. Englishman Rhodes had an exciting ride to his 67. He drove the front edge of the green at the 305-yard 11th hole and sank the putt for an eagle deuce and capped the day when he holed from a greenside trap for birdie at the 18th. Rhodes led long-hitting American Lee Carter and Scotsman Sam Torrance by a stroke.

Ratcliffe made his move impressively in blustery conditions Saturday. He shot the day's best score — 68 for 139 — and tied for the lead with Carbonetti, who had rounds of 70-69. Rhodes faded with a 77 as John Chillas of Scotland and Japan's Seiji Ebihara, the two-time Irish Seniors Open champion, jointly took over third place at 141. Torrance shot 75 and dropped into a tie with Alan Mew and Kevin Spurgeon two shots further back.

Only two players broke 70 in tough conditions Sunday and they were too far back for it to matter. So, Ratcliffe faced no serious challenges and his 71 was all he needed as his 210 gave him his eighth win on the senior circuit. John Chillas had a par round and finished third at 213, a shot ahead of Torrance (71–214).

## Irvine Whitlock Seniors Classic — €177,826
Winner: Sam Torrance

Sam Torrance was making his decision late in the 2004 season to quit the senior circuit in America and concentrate his efforts on the European Seniors Tour look quite good. After campaigning without particular success on the Champions Tour in the U.S., Torrance switched allegiance to the European Seniors Tour after the Senior British Open at Royal Portrush and two starts later won the Travis Perkins Senior Masters. Though playing in only two more events, Torrance finished 18th on the 2004 Order of Merit.

Skipping the long-range events in the Caribbean and Egypt at the start of the 2005 season, Torrance made his presence felt with fourth-place finishes in Italy and Ireland, then racked up a four-stroke victory in the Irvine Whitlock Seniors Classic in mid-June. Although he managed just a par-72 round Sunday for 205 at La Moye on the Isle of Jersey, Torrance was never threatened as his closest pursuer, David J. Russell, could muster only a 73, finishing second for the fourth time in his brief career on the senior circuit.

The first wire-to-wire winner of the 2005 season, Torrance staked himself to a one-stroke lead with a sparkling seven-under-par 65 in the opening round. Pronouncing his play "beautiful," he made two eagles and five birdies as he edged in front of French rookie Jean Pierre Sallat. Russell was two back with a 67. The eagles continued to fly Saturday. Torrance made two more as he shot 68 and widened his margin to three strokes despite two bogeys. Russell, who like Torrance bogeyed the last hole, moved into second place with 69–136, as Sallat slipped to third with a 73 and trailed the leader by six shots going into the final round.

Torrance got away fast Sunday with birdies at the fourth and fifth holes. He faltered slightly with "a bad patch on the eighth and ninth (bogeys off errant drives) which put me under a bit of pressure, but in the end I did what I had to do." He steadied with five consecutive pars, then virtually insured the win with a final birdie at the 15th hole. Sallat finished in a four-way tie for third, two behind Russell. John Morgan, John Mashego and Bruce Heuchan also shot 211.

"It's always great to come here and win again," said Torrance afterward, referring to his victory 14 years earlier at La Moye in the Jersey European Airways Open on the regular European Tour.

## The Mobile Cup—€186,856
Winner: Guiseppe Cali

Guiseppe Cali gave further indication that he is one of those players with undistinguished careers in their prime who prosper in their golden years when he climaxed an impressive number of strong performances in his two seasons on the European Seniors Tour with victory in The Mobile Cup. The 52-year-old Italian became the second first-time winner on the 2005 circuit with his one-stroke victory in the mid-June tournament, joining countrymen Renato Campagnoli and Alberto Croce, previous titlists on the senior tour.

Cali had never made any sort of splash in his years on the regular circuit, but had essayed 18 top-10 finishes in his first 18 months as a senior player. The breakthrough came under strong pressure but with a flourish. Locked in a tie for the lead with playing partner Martin Gray of Scotland as they went to the final tee, Cali produced two excellent shots on the par-five 18th, which he had double-bogeyed the day before, and two-putted for birdie and the winning 72–208.

Gray praised Cali's finish — "his drive and second shot ... two fantastic shots under pressure to win a title" — and accepted his second-place showing with his 70–209 without complaint, explaining: "I wasn't going to play because my game was in such bad shape, but John Chillas, who travels with me, persuaded me to play." American Alan Tapie was the other man in the contention mix all week and he picked off third place when he holed a 45-foot eagle putt at the 54th for 73–210.

Cali never trailed at Collingtree Park Golf Club in Northampton, but had to share the lead after Friday's round when Gordon Townhill, the last man into the field, matched his 66. Townhill, who ultimately tied for fourth, was summoned from his club post at Brough Golf Club in North Humberside Monday when withdrawals opened up a spot. Gray shot a solid 67, and Tapie, who won his lone title in the 1999 Elf Open, had 68.

Cali squandered the opportunity to carry a three-stroke lead into the final round with a costly miscue at the last hole of Saturday's second round. He was 10 under par before his tee shot at the 18th bounced wildly off a cart path and could not be found. The double bogey resulted in a 70–136 and cut his lead over runner-up Tapie (68-69) to a shot. Gray slipped three strokes behind with 72–139.

Although the narrowed margin made the job more testing, Cali battled Gray stoutly through Sunday's competition, putting the finishing touches on the one-shot win with a mammoth drive and a six-iron approach to 20 feet at the final hole to settle up the deciding birdie.


## De Vere Northumberland Seniors Classic — €223,847
Winner: Carl Mason

One has to wonder how much more Carl Mason would have accomplished in his already impressive first two seasons on the European Seniors Tour if his back weren't so troublesome. Mason, the Order of Merit winner in 2003 and 2004, wasn't even through a full 24 months on the circuit when he registered his 10th victory in the De Vere Northumberland Seniors Classic. Over that period, he was sidelined on three different occasions for several tournaments when his cranky back acted up, once during a tournament in which he had the first-round lead.

In fact, Mason had missed the last two events with a recurrence of the ailment and was not in top shape until he got help from a local physio-therapist after arriving for the De Vere event. He responded with a dazzling 63 in the second round on Slaley Hall's Priestman course and rolled to a unchallenged three-stroke victory with his 16-under-par 200.

Mason was just a stroke off the lead after the opening round, bunched with nine others behind Noel Ratcliffe, who shot 67. Saturday was Mason's 52nd birthday and he gave himself a most useful gift — the 63 that spurted him five strokes into the lead. He banged out four birdies and an eagle on the first six holes, took his only bogey when he three-putted the seventh and made two more birdies at the eighth and ninth to turn in 29. His seventh and eighth birdies completed the course-record round that gave him the five-shot margin over Ireland's Eamonn Darcy and Manuel Pinero of Spain.

"I can't remember the last time I played as well as this," said Mason, who then cited a 61 he shot in 1994 in winning the Scottish Open. "It's a great way to celebrate your birthday."

Even with a bogey at the second hole, the Englishman was never in trouble Sunday. He followed with five birdies over the next 15 holes before three-putting the final green for 69 and the 200 as Darcy shot 67 to bag the fifth second-place finish of his winless four years on the European Seniors Tour.

Summed up Mason: "I played great. Eamonn played superbly but I never really gave him much of a chance. It's amazing how much more freely you can swing when you are not suffering from backache."


## Ryder Cup Wales Seniors Open — €753,679
Winner: Carl Mason

The player most likely to be the first on the European Seniors Tour to double up on seasonal victories was the one who did. Who else but the reigning Order of Merit champion, a fit Carl Mason, would be expected to score back-to-back wins and become the first two-time winner in the initial nine games of 2005?

Just as the week before when a hot round powered the victory, Mason produced a tournament-low score that brought about his five-stroke victory in early July in the Ryder Cup Wales Seniors Open, by far the richest event of the regular season. Mason churned up a seven-under-par 65 in blustery weather in Sunday's final round at Royal St. David's Golf Club for his winning 202 total and 11th seniors title.

"It has been a tough week," Mason remarked of the victory that put him back in his familiar position atop the Order of Merit. "Royal St. David's is a difficult golf course at the best of times, but when the wind blows like this, all you can do is try to grind out pars and hope nobody gets ahead of you."

Despite his impressive performance, Mason had to share attention with the remarkable Bob Charles all weekend. On the verge of becoming the oldest winner on all of the world tours, the 69-year-old left-hander, who won the British Open Championship 42 years ago, was never worse than second at the end of any of the rounds. He finished in a runner-up tie with Barbados winner Denis O'Sullivan. (Neil Coles holds the "oldest winner" distinction — 67 years, 276 days.)

The New Zealander was deadlocked with Mason through the first two rounds as both shot 68s on a rainy Friday, sharing second place with Bob Cameron a stroke behind leaders Nick Job and John Chillas. Interestingly, Coles, now 70, and Tommy Horton, 64, were among seven players in contention with 70s. Charles made three late bogeys that cost him the lead.

Strong winds and steady rain plagued the tournament again Saturday as Job posted a 69 for 136 to retain the lead as Chillas dropped back with 71 and Mason and Charles remained second with 69s for 137. "It was brutal out there today," remarked Job, who was gunning for his first win on the circuit since 2001 (Lawrence Batley). "But I battened down the hatches and just tried to grind out pars."

Job shot 72 Sunday, no match for Mason, who birdied the first two holes to get going and countered two bogeys with four more birdies as he rolled to victory in yet another day of foul weather at the links course in Wales and picked up the €113,052 first-place check that propelled him to the top of the Order of Merit. Charles mustered a 70 and O'Sullivan joined him at 207 with a closing 68.

## Nigel Mansell Sunseeker International Classic — €222,118
Winner: Jim Rhodes

With the focus on Carl Mason and his bid to become just the second player in European Seniors Tour history to win three successive tournaments, Jim Rhodes was cruising toward his first victory in more than a year on the circuit. Mason put his chances behind the eight ball with a poor opening round in the Nigel Mansell Sunseeker International Classic and Rhodes never let him get close as he rolled to a three-stroke triumph that was more decisive than the final margin indicated.

The 59-year-old Englishman and five others began the tournament at Mansell's Woodbury Park Hotel Golf and Country Club with 69s, six strokes better than Mason's opening round. Among the leaders, most of the attention was paid to Tommy Horton, the tour's all-time leader with 23 titles, who was in his 64th year. The others were Englishmen Tony Charnley and Martin Foster, Northern Ireland's Eddie Polland and South African Gavan Levenson.

Mason didn't give up his victory quest without a fight. He bounced back with a 66 Saturday for 141 and at the end of the day was four strokes behind Rhodes, who continued his solid play with 68 — five birdies and a three-putt bogey — for 137 and a two-shot lead over Guiseppe Cali, the Italian winner of The Mobile Cup the week before Mason launched his run. Levenson was at 69-71–140, alone and a shot in front of Mason and four others.

Wielding the same 40-year-old putter that brought him his two earlier victories on the senior circuit, Rhodes jumped off to a fast start Sunday with four birdies and a bogey on the front nine. By then, he was clear enough of all pursuers that he could afford four bogeys on the back nine, including three-putts on the last two greens, and still, in the vernacular of the tournament namesake, take the checkered flag by three with his 71–208. "I did it all on the front nine," Rhodes noted. "It was disappointing to three-putt the last two, but by then it didn't really matter."

"I needed to make a fast start and put some pressure on," said Mason, "but I never got going." He shot 71 for 212, tying for third with Delroy Cambridge, a shot behind runner-up Charnley, who closed with 70–211.

## Senior British Open — €1,457,507
Winner: Tom Watson

What better place and occasion for Tom Watson to get off his rather extended victory drought on the Champions Tour? Here he was in Aberdeen, Scotland, to compete in the Senior British Open, a championship he had won down the road at Turnberry in 2003. There and elsewhere in Scotland, Watson also captured four of his five regular British Opens. He is a much-loved golfing icon in the country and he added even more admirers in the northern city that was hosting the championship, a joint major on the Champions and European Seniors Tours, for the first time when he squeezed out an overtime victory at Royal Aberdeen.

Watson, who had gone winless on his home Champions Tour since taking the JELD-WEN Tradition in August of 2003, went head to head with Irishman Des Smyth through three playoff holes before landing the title, his seventh in senior golf and fourth senior major. The Hall-of-Famer, who won 37 times in his pre-50 days, carried a two-stroke lead into the final round, shot 70 and was caught by Smyth, who surged to the top with a four-under-par 67 for his 280 and forced the playoff. The Irishman's showing was no surprise. He played the early season in America and was one of just four players with twin victories during the first seven months.

Typical British Open weather hammered the field in the opening round. With gusty winds howling over the par-71 Balgownie course all day Thursday, not a single player even matched par and the 144-man field averaged 80.119 strokes, the highest ever in a Champions Tour event. Loren Roberts, making his first start in senior golf, emerged as the leader with his one-over 72, a rare mix of six birdies, five bogeys and a double bogey. He had a shot on seven players, including Smyth, who was at even par until he double-bogeyed the final hole. Watson started with 75, not that bad under the circumstances.

The weather moderated slightly Friday, although still just four players broke par and the cut fell at 15-over-par 157. Craig Stadler had the day's second best score with 68 and took over first place with 141, two strokes in front of Greg Norman, who followed an opening 76 with a 67 in his debut senior tournament. Smyth was two shots further back (73-72) and Watson managed a par 71 and moved up into a quartet at 146 that included Roberts, who took a 74.

Watson welcomed a break in the weather Saturday with a scintillating 64 that spurted him a stroke in front of Stadler (70). On the suddenly benign afternoon, Watson rang up two birdies and an eagle on the first six holes on his way to the round which matched the Balgownie course record that had been set hours earlier by Derrick Cooper. Smyth (68) and Norman (70) remained close at 213 as the field's scoring average dropped to 73.431.

"Today it was somewhat of a struggle," Watson observed about the 70 he shot Sunday as Smyth caught him with 67 for his 280. Neither player could muster a birdie over the final five holes. Stadler fell back to fourth place with 72–283 as Norman birdied the last hole for 68–281 and missed the playoff by a stroke. Watson and Smyth both parred the 18th hole twice, then went to the par-three 17th, where Smyth bunkered his tee shot and failed to save par as Watson two-putted for the victory from the back of the green.

## De Vere PGA Seniors Championship— €290,098
Winner: Sam Torrance

The ability to shake off adversity saved the day — and the tournament — for Sam Torrance at the De Vere PGA Seniors Championship, the European Seniors Tour's second major of the season. Undaunted after having a healthy 54-hole lead virtually disappear early in the final round, Torrance righted the ship and sailed to a four-stroke victory at De Vere Carden Park in Cheshire. With the win, Torrance joined Carl Mason as the only multiple victors of the season with two wins apiece and, as he observed, "It sets me up nicely to have a go at knocking Mace (Mason) off the top of the Order of Merit. That's one of my goals this year."

Taking a triple bogey as Torrance did on the second hole of the Sunday round would have unnerved most players. His four-stroke lead suddenly reduced to one, thanks to a "quick hook" into rhododendron bushes on the second hole, Torrance firmed up his strategy for the rest of the round. "When you've got a four-shot lead, you don't know whether to attack or defend, but that doubt disappeared as soon as I dropped those shots," he explained.

The attack paid off over the next several holes. He birdied the fifth and eagled the eighth when he holed a nine-iron shot from 160 yards, added four more birdies on the back nine, rebuilding his margin to four as he finished with a three-under-par 69. In a remarkable coincidence, David J. Russell closed with 68 to take second place, just as he did three months earlier in the Irvine Whitlock Classic when Torrance beat him by four in scoring his earlier victory on the circuit.

The Scotsman, who skipped the previous week's U.S. Senior Open in Dayton, Ohio, to rest an aching back, came out strong at Carden Park and never fell out of the lead all week. He opened with a 66 that included another eagle deuce and shared the lead with Mason, the defending champion, and South Africa's John Bland, who had spent most of his senior career in America. They had just a stroke on five others on the bunched-up leaderboard.

Wind and rain Friday "made it two or three shots tougher out there" in Torrance's opinion as he shot a struggling 70, which was matched by Mason and kept the two men in first place with Nick Job (67) and Bill Longmuir (68) at 136. Torrance then distanced himself from the field in the Saturday round, racking up eight birdies en route to another 66 and the four-stroke lead, capping the day with a 25-foot birdie putt on the 18th green. His chronic back trouble cropped up on Mason and he was able to muster just another 70, as did Job and Russell, who trailed those two by a stroke at 207 at day's end. Mason and Job repeated 70s Sunday to finish a stroke behind Russell.

## Bad Ragaz PGA Seniors Open—€210,000
Winner: Terry Gale

Terry Gale had some apprehensions this year as he passed his 59th birthday, but put them to rest at the Bad Ragaz PGA Seniors Open. "It's nice to know that when I have a chance, I can still do it," said the Australian after his victory in the Switzerland stop on the European Seniors Tour. With three consistent low rounds at Golf Club Bad Ragaz, Gale took a two-stroke victory and extended his streak of winning at least once a year to four seasons, the circuit's current best mark. The win was his seventh over his nearly 10 seasons of senior play.

Little had been heard from the Americans on the circuit since Bob Lendzion's triumph in Egypt in April until Jerry Bruner made a big splash in the opening round at Bad Ragaz. The powerful little man from California emerged from a season-long dry spell with a course-record-tying, eight-under-par 62, giving a stroke back with a bogey at the last hole after running up an eagle and seven birdies, five of them producing a front-nine 30. That staked him to a three-stroke lead over Frenchman Gerry Watine, the Italian Seniors Open winner, and four over five others.

Bruner was well on the way to padding his lead Saturday before he came a-cropper late in the round and dropped into a deadlock for first place with South Africans John Bland and John Mashego and Australian Noel Ratcliffe, the Irish Seniors Open winner. Bruner double-bogeyed the par-five 16th and bogeyed the 18th around a birdie at the 17th, finishing with 70 for his 132 and one-fourth share of the lead. Bland nearly matched Bruner's first-day performance, carrying an eight-under-par round to the 17th tee then going bogey-bogey. Ratcliffe and Mashego had their second 66s on the short 6,130-yard course.

Meanwhile, Gale put himself in a strong position going into the final round with 67-66–133 and handled easily the rains that came Sunday. Three birdies on the first seven holes put him in a commanding position. He birdied the par-three 11th, took his second bogey of the round at the 15th, then birdied two of the last three holes for his second straight 66 and a final 199.

Watine, who wrapped his second 65 around a Saturday 71, tied for second place at 201 with Tobago Plantation winner Luis Carbonetti of Argentina. Bland slipped to 71 and tied for fourth at 203 with American David Oakley as Bruner finished with a 72 and slipped into a tie for sixth place.

## Travis Perkins Senior Masters — €328,556
Winner: Eduardo Romero

Fairly often, successful pros on America's PGA Tour have continued to play on that circuit after reaching their 50th birthdays and picked and chosen a handful of prime events on the senior Champions Tour for the next year or two. Such has not been the case very often in Europe, one exception being Argentina's Eduardo Romero, who, although he turned 50 in July of 2004, remained full-time on the European Tour. He played only in the Senior British Open that season and in 2005 on the European Seniors Tour before teeing it up at Wentworth in the Travis Perkins Senior Masters in late August and producing a resounding victory.

"I have a little advantage as I am playing on the regular European Tour where we play long golf courses," conceded Romero after certifying his eight-stroke victory with a closing 68 and an 11-under-par 205 on Wentworth's Edinburgh course. "I am hitting the ball fantastic — longer than 10 years ago," he added.

Romero, who won eight tournaments during his 17 years as a regular on the European Tour, including the 2002 Scottish Open when he was 48, took control of the Travis Perkins in Saturday's second round after starting the tournament with a 70 on a miserable rainy day on which only Jeff Hawkes and John Mashego of South Africa, with 68s, did any better.

On the drying course Saturday, the long-hitting Romero overpowered the par-fives, racking up two eagles at the long third and 10th holes, and added five birdies and two bogeys for a 67–137 that shot him six strokes in front of the field. At 143, the only other players under par, were Englishmen Gordon J. Brand (69), Bob Cameron (70) and Nick Job (67); Frenchman Gery Watine (70) and Mashego, who slipped to 75. Hawkes had 76.

The only challenge to Romero Sunday came from countryman Luis Carbonetti. With five birdies on the first 12 holes, the Tobago winner closed to within three strokes of Romero, but didn't get too excited. "Maybe if he had started very badly, then maybe I might have caught him, but not at that stage," Carbonetti reflected. Romero didn't exactly light things up on the front nine, but after a bogey at the seventh, he "made an eagle and a couple of birdies and I was relaxed after that." He was five under on the back nine on his way to the winning 68–205. Carbonetti (68) and Job (70) tied for second place at 213 as Romero completed the most decisive victory of the 2005 season, three shots better than the previous best margin, established by Carl Mason in the Ryder Cup Wales Open.

## Charles Church Scottish Seniors Open—€221,660
Winner: Nick Job

"I can't help feel that another win is a little overdue. I've been playing well for quite a while but each time someone seems to edge up and creep past me." This was Nick Job expressing his hope for a turn in fortunes as he took a one-stroke lead into the final round of the Charles Church Scottish Seniors Open at the end of August. A second-place performance the previous Sunday and five other top-10 finishes earlier in the season gave the 56-year-old Job cause for optimism and he got the job done in the final round at The Roxburghe Hotel and Golf Course at Kelso, ending a victory drought extending back to the 2001 Lawrence Batley Seniors.

As it turned out, he only had one man and the weather to beat that Sunday and he held onto the fragile one-shot margin. Battling Jean Pierre Sallat, a 50-year-old European Seniors Tour rookie, and winds gusting at times to 40 miles an hour, Job posted a one-under-par 71 for 206. Sallat, the only other player with a chance, battled Job stroke for stroke until falling a shot behind when he bunkered his approach and bogeyed the 16th hole.

Job finished with two solid pars, insuring the latter one with a brilliant 210-yard four-iron shot to the middle of the 18th green. With his 71–207, Sallat, a former professional football player in France, finished six strokes ahead of third-placed Terry Gale.

Job and Sallat set up their duel in the second round. Both had started with 69s, two shots behind surprise leader Martin Poxon, another first-year player who was selling flowers in Sheffield until reaching his 50th birthday in June. John Mashego of South Africa had the lone 68 and Bob Cameron, Brian Jones and Kevin Spurgeon joined Job and Sallat in joint third place.

Job strung six birdies across a bogey-free round for 66–135 Saturday and

Sallat nearly followed suit, carding a 67 by holing a 50-foot birdie putt on the final green for his 136 total. Next were Mashego (72) and countryman Bobby Lincoln (67), but they trailed Sallat by four strokes.

Job was the 14th different winner in the first 16 tournaments on the 2005 schedule that included the U.S. Senior Open.

## Bovis Lend Lease European Senior Masters—€329,832
Winner: Mark James

Followers of senior golf in Europe had not seen much of Mark James, their 1999 Ryder Cup captain, since he turned 50 in October of 2003. They weren't on hand when James scored two victories during the next two seasons because they came on America's Champions Tour, which he decided was his place to play full-time. He thought about changing things, though, when he came home to England from the United States and won the Bovis Lend Lease European Senior Masters in a nerve-rattling finish and playoff against two-time winner Sam Torrance on the Dukes course at Woburn Golf Club.

"I am going to play a bit more over here next year," James remarked after his birdie on the first extra hole gave him his first win in Europe since 1997 on the regular tour. "The European Seniors Tour is getting better and better and it's great to see old friends." One of those old friends — Sam Torrance — was James's victim in the playoff. Torrance, who also began his senior career in America, was gunning for his third win of the European Seniors Tour season and command of the Order of Merit, but both he and James had ground to make up on the final Sunday.

They trailed fellow Brit Kevin Spurgeon, the surprise second-round leader who reached the circuit in April when he turned 50 after earning privileges at the fall qualifying tournament. Spurgeon shot 68 Saturday for 135 and took a three-stroke lead over American Alan Tapie. Torrance, who played with Spurgeon and another American, Bob Boyd, in the final group after shooting 68 to their leading 67s the first day, only matched par Saturday and trailed Spurgeon by five heading into Sunday's action. James was yet another stroke back after rounds of 70 and 71.

Winning experience prevailed Sunday. While Spurgeon was sputtering to a 73, James and Torrance made their moves. James raced into the lead, going seven under par on the first 11 holes and 10 under for that distance, jumping two strokes ahead of Spurgeon and four in front of Torrance. However, he gave a stroke back with a bogey at the 16th and lipped out a birdie putt at the 18th to finish with 66 and his nine-under 207. Torrance took advantage with a four-birdie finish on the back nine, holing a difficult breaking putt for the last one at the 18th for his 67–207.

Torrance pulled a miraculous recovery shot from the trees when the two replayed the 18th in the playoff, but he missed the tricky four-footer after James ran in his seven-foot birdie putt for the sixth overtime victory of his fine career.

## Scandinavian Senior Open — €250,000
Winner: Bill Longmuir

Bill Longmuir put some meat on a lean season when the European Seniors Tour made its debut appearance in Denmark for the Scandinavian Senior Open at lush Royal Copenhagen Golf Club in early September. Longmuir, who posted four victories in his first two seasons on the circuit, had struggled through most of the 2005 season after a second-place tie in the year's second event in Tobago. But he found Royal Copenhagen's heavy rough-lined fairways to his liking, since he had his tee ball, if not his putter, under control.

"If you hit a crooked drive on this course, you lose the ball," he noted. "But I'm a solid driver of the ball, so I guess the course suited me." It suited him so well that he expanded a one-stroke lead after 36 holes into a four-stroke victory with a sizzling, seven-under-par 64 in the final round. His 17-under 196 was the lowest score of the season.

Despite that, the 52-year-old Scot disparaged his prowess on the greens. "I holed a couple of crunch putts," he admitted, "but my putting has not been good this year and I need to do something about it this winter to get it in shape."

Longmuir had gone to the belly putter the previous week, but it didn't seem to help. He took a one-stroke lead Saturday with his second straight 66 despite two three-putt greens, one from seven feet. He had seven birdies as he slipped ahead of Guiseppe Cali (68-65), Horacio Carbonetti (66-67) and Gavan Levenson (65-68). He had taken the lead from Carl Mason, the Order of Merit leader, who opened the tournament with 64, a shot ahead of Levenson, and two in front of Longmuir and Carbonetti. But Mason, who had battled a bad back all season, was to be undone by the ailment again, as he shot 71 Saturday and pulled out in pain after three holes Sunday.

An 18-foot eagle putt on the fourth hole of the final round ignited Longmuir. He was four under after five holes and four back-nine birdies around his lone bogey at the par-three 12th enabled him to glide to his first win in more than a year on the circuit. Cali, the Mobile Cup winner, stayed fairly close but never seriously threatened with his 67–200 that gave him the runner-up spot, a shot in front of Bob Cameron, who stormed from far back with 63 for 201.

## Bendinat London Seniors Masters — €221,488
Winner: Sam Torrance

With the opportunities dwindling down to a precious few events in his pursuit of Carl Mason and the Order of Merit title, Sam Torrance made an impressive statement when the European Seniors Tour resumed action after an off week with the Bendinat London Seniors Masters, another new tournament on the 2005 schedule.

Torrance became the first three-time winner of the season and moved within €8,529 of the 2004 champion when he rolled to a wire-to-wire victory at The London Golf Club. He closed with a two-under-par 70 for 201. Remarkably — and surely bittersweet for him — David J. Russell finished second to Torrance in all three of Sam's victories. It gave him six runner-up showings in his winless two seasons on the circuit.

Torrance was the story from the first day. Oblivious of the engine roars from the nearby Brands Hatch race track, the former Ryder Cup captain roared off to a four-stroke lead with an eight-under-par 64 with nine birdies and a lone bogey that came when he put his second shot on the par-five fifth into the water in front of the green. Not surprisingly, he had high praise for the Jack Nicklaus-designed Heritage course, calling it "a fantastic golf course, as good as we play on the European Seniors Tour." Nick Job started with 68 and three 2005 winners — Mason, Giuseppe Cali and Terry Gale — and Russell were next at 69.

Russell shot a flawless 65 with seven birdies Saturday and picked up two strokes on Torrance (67–131), giving him a glimmer of hope of reversing things on the Scot Sunday. "Maybe I can turn the tables tomorrow," he said. "I don't think Sam is going to back off much, so I think I would need another 65." Torrance, on the other hand, thought a 68 would do it for him.

As it turned out, Torrance's 70 was easily good enough as Russell managed just the same number. In fact, Torrance was on his way to a rout, six shots in the lead after 12 holes. But he bogeyed the next two and failed to birdie the easy 15th. However, with Russell sitting two behind, he finished with a birdie off a brilliant shot from the heavy rough to five feet at the 18th. Mason, nine behind the winner, tied for 10th.

Russell took runner-up repetitions in stride. Taking note of the fact that Torrance had decided to stay in Europe after early-year time in America, Russell remarked: "I told Sam that if he wasn't here, I'd be a legend."

## Castellon Costa Azahar Open de Espana — €250,000
Winner: Bob Boyd

The wait was worth it for Bob Boyd. The American from Wilmington, North Carolina, led the field in the fall qualifier for the 2005 European Seniors Tour, but couldn't do anything with the privilege for eight months. He was only 49 years of age at the time and had to wait until the end of next July before he was old enough to tee it up in a circuit event.

Two months later, Boyd bagged the title in the Castellon Costa Azahar Open de Espana in just his eighth start, a victory that shouldn't have been as surprising as it seemed. He played the regular U.S. PGA Tour for three seasons in the middle 1980s before turning to club work and compiling a fine playing record in regional events in the Carolinas. He finished seven strokes in front of the field in the European qualifier and had five finishes of 14th or better in his first seven starts before scoring an exciting one-stroke victory at Club de Campo del Mediterraneo in early October.

Boyd positioned himself comfortably the first day, shooting a 68 that placed him in a four-way tie for seventh, two strokes behind the leading logjam of Guiseppe Cali, Terry Gale, Alan Tapie, Jim Rhodes and Delroy Cambridge. Another 68-shooter was Carl Mason, who was trying to expand his narrow Order of Merit lead over Sam Torrance, who elected to play in an event in Scotland that week with his son Daniel.

The American moved in front Saturday, going bogey-free for the second straight day. He shot 66 for 134, slipping a stroke in front of local favorite Jose Rivero (67-68), the ex-Ryder Cupper making just his second senior start, and Jim Rhodes (66-69), the Nigel Mansell winner in July. Mason fell back with 73 and eventually tied for 15th, leaving himself vulnerable in the season title race.

Boyd's victory did not come easily Sunday. Coming off the 15th green, he trailed both Rivero and Rhodes. But he turned on the juice with a birdie at the par-three 16th and an eagle at the par-five 17th to surge in front, and his par at the 18th for 71–205 gave him the victory. That wouldn't have been good enough, though, if Rhodes hadn't butchered the 16th with a double bogey. His birdie at the 17th merely brought him level with Rivero. They both also shot 71s to tie for second place. Boyd was the fifth first-time winner of the season on the European Seniors Tour.

## Algarve Seniors Open of Portugal — €300,000
Winner: Jerry Bruner

They call 5-foot-6 Jerry Bruner "Mighty Mouse" in recognition of his tee shot power, so it was a bit surprising when the genial American from California scored his third victory on the European Seniors Tour in the Algarve Seniors Open of Portugal on the strength of his putting. Two monster putts at critical points, to be exact.

The first one salvaged a share of first place with Sam Torrance at the end of the second round after he put his drive into the water at the 454-yard, par-four finishing hole at Quinta de Cima Golf Club. He sank a 35-foot putt for his four. Then he virtually duplicated the feat on the same hole Sunday, this time from 30 feet for a birdie that gave him a one-under-par 71 and a one-stroke victory over Torrance.

Although Torrance, playing with Bruner in the final grouping, lost his chance for a playoff victory when he missed the tying putt from much closer range, he inched a mere €245 ahead of Carl Mason (joint sixth) in the Order of Merit race with the second-place money he shared with Northern Ireland's Eddie Polland and Spain's Jose Rivero, who then had two seconds and a third in his first three starts on the circuit.

Bruner, whose earlier wins had come in 2001 and 2003, positioned himself nicely with a 66 in the opening round, sharing second place with fellow American John Benda and Chile's Guillermo Encina a stroke behind Nick Job. The Englishman, who still had a shot at the Order of Merit title and an automatic spot on the Champions Tour in America, had eight birdies and an eagle as he opened with 65. Torrance and Mason both had 68s.

With an eye on the weather forecast that indicated a possible washout of the final round, Torrance birdied the 16th and 18th holes Saturday for 66 and the clubhouse lead at 134, a winning score if the Sunday round was cancelled. But Bruner's spectacular four for 68 moments later gave him a share of first place. It was a disastrous day for Job, though. Not only did he plummet to an 81, but he signed for a wrong score and was disqualified.

The rains came as predicted Sunday, making playing conditions quite difficult and for a while it appeared Bruner would suffer the same fate that had overtaken him two months earlier when he blew the 36-hole lead at Bad Ragaz. He fell four strokes behind Encina after 10 holes, but rallied with birdies at the 13th, 14th and 17th before holing the spectacular 30-footer for the victory.

## Arcapita Seniors Tour Championship — €380,454
Winner: Des Smyth

Between Des Smyth and Sam Torrance, it was hard to tell which man was happier about his achievement in the Arcapita Seniors Tours Championship. Smyth won the season-ending tournament on the European Seniors Tour in early November in the Kingdom of Bahrain and Torrance capped his three-victory season there with a tie-for-third finish that brought him the tour's Order of Merit title.

"This has been a massive year," Smyth enthused. "I had two wins in America this year and this one, my first on the European Seniors Tour, is very important to me," explained the 52-year-old Irishman, who lost to Tom Watson in the Senior British Open playoff in July. His two-stroke victory at Bahrain's Riffa Golf Club came in just his third 2005 start in Europe, Smyth having elected to play full-time on America's Champions Tour when he became eligible in 2003.

On the other hand, Torrance spent less than a full season in the United States before deciding the European circuit was his cup of tea. "I gave up playing in America last year to commit to the European Seniors Tour and it has proved fruitful," the Scot observed. "It feels awesome to be Number One. It is something I have wanted all my life and I am very proud of it." Torrance came into the Tour Championship with a razor-thin lead over Carl Mason, the Order of Merit winner the previous two years who opened with a 79 and was never a factor. To win two tournaments and come that close to a third season title was a brave accomplishment for Mason, who had to miss five tournaments because of an ailing back that plagued him all season.

Smyth was never out of the lead at Riffa. He began with a four-under-par 68 and shared first place with Argentine Horacio Carbonetti on a windy Thursday. Torrance got off to a shaky start with 75, then bounced back with a 68 Friday to climb to 10th place and virtually clinch the Order of Merit crown, standing nine strokes ahead of Mason at that point. Meanwhile, Smyth was opening a three-stroke lead with another 68. Tony Allen (71-68–139) and Carbonetti (68-72) were next in line.

John Chillas, the defending champion, took a run at Smyth in Saturday's final round, in fact leading by a shot when Smyth bogeyed the 11th. But two bogeys chilled Chillas's bid. He birdied the 18th for 67–208 before Smyth staged a birdie-birdie finish for 70 and the winning 206. Torrance sweetened the taste of his Order of Merit title with a closing 66 to tie for third at 209 with Guiseppe Cali and Gordon J. Brand.

# Japan Senior Tour

## Oberst Senior Open—¥20,000,000
Winner: Takashi Miyoshi

Little did Takashi Miyoshi know when he won the inaugural Oberst Senior Open, the first event on the 2005 Japan Senior Tour, that he was destined to be the player of the year on the circuit. Miyoshi, whose only previous victory in an official event on the Senior Tour was two years earlier in the Aderans Wellness Open, came from a stroke off the lead in the final round at Karasuyamajo Country Club, Tochigi Prefecture, to score a one-stroke victory with his six-under-par 210. Miyoshi has had four other wins in lesser senior events.

Yoshitaka Yamamoto shot 69, the only round in the 60s, on Wednesday's opening day and led by a stroke over Hideto Shigenobu and Seiji Ebihara, Japan's traveled senior who has enjoyed considerable success on the European Seniors Tour. Shigenobu, making his first start in seniors golf, moved into the lead the second day with 68–138, a shot ahead of Shuichi Sano (72-67) and three in front of Miyoshi, who recovered from a first-round 73 with 68, and Ebihara (70-71). Miyoshi wrapped up the victory with a closing 69 to edge Shigenobu, who finished with 73.

## Aderans Wellness Open—¥60,000,000
Winner: Katsuyoshi Tomori

Katsuyoshi Tomori, one of Japan's international players in recent years, scored his first victory on the Japan Senior Tour in a final-round duel against Minoru Hatsumi in the Aderans Wellness Open. Tomori closed with a five-under-par 67 at Nakajo Golf Club, Niigata Prefecture, to defeat Hatsumi (68) by two strokes.

The two players exchanged the lead the first two days. Hatsumi opened with 68 and led Tomori and Teruo Nakamura by a shot, then fell a stroke behind the ultimate winner when Tomori posted 67 for 136 and he shot 69 for 137. Nakamura (70) and Tokio Kaneko (72-67) were next at 139 and were never factors in the final round. Tateo Ozaki jumped into third place with 67–209, six strokes off Tomori's 13-under-par winning score of 203.

## Fancl Senior Classic—¥60,000,000
Winner: Takashi Miyoshi

It required four extra holes for Takashi Miyoshi to land his second 2005 victory on the Japan Senior Tour. Miyoshi was in first place at the end of all three rounds of the Fancl Senior Classic on the Susono Country Club course in Shizuoka Prefecture, but at the 54-hole juncture he was tied with Dragon Taki at nine-under-par 207, forcing the playoff. Miyoshi prevailed when he birdied the fourth overtime hole. It was a far cry from his first appearance in the Fancl Classic in 2000, when he missed the cut.

Miyoshi began the tournament with 67 in Friday's starting round, sharing the lead with Katsuji Hasegawa, one of the better players in his earlier years on the regular Japan Tour. Miyoshi followed with 69 to retain his part of first place, joined there Saturday by David Ishii, the Hawaiian who had a fine record over the years on the Japan Tour and was making his Senior Tour debut. Ishii shot a pair of 68s. Taki was then in third place with Hasegawa, tied at 140, four strokes off the pace.

Taki came up with the best final-round score, a 67, to forge the tie when Miyoshi took 71 Sunday for his 207 and moved into his successful effort in the playoff.

## Arde Pro Cup—¥20,000,000
Winner: Takashi Miyoshi

Takashi Miyoshi had an easier time of it when he ran off his third victory of 2005 on the Japan Senior Tour with a back-to-back triumph in the Arde Pro Cup in late August. After enduring a four-hole playoff the previous Sunday, Miyoshi walked off the 18th green at Okanokoen Kiyosato Golf Club, Yamanashi Prefecture, after 54 holes with a three-stroke victory despite a final-round 73.

The reason: Miyoshi carried an eight-stroke lead into Sunday's round after shooting 62 the second day, a spectacular 22-putt round that followed his opening 65, giving him a startling 127 at that point. Ironically, Dragon Taki, whom he had defeated in the Fancl playoff, held second place at 135. However, Taki shot 70 Sunday and Yoshimi Niizeki, Yoshitaka Yamamoto and Kimpachi Yoshimura finished in a second-place tie at 203, three behind Miyoshi's winning 16-under-par 200. Niizeki and Yoshimura had 65s and Yamamoto 66 Sunday.

## PGA Philanthropy Rebornest Senior Open—¥30,000,000
Winner: Katsunari Takahashi

Katsunari Takahashi, one of the most successful players in the history of the Japan Senior Tour, further established his reputation with his victory the first weekend of September in the PGA Philanthropy Rebornest Senior Open. When he nailed that 11th circuit title with a six-stroke triumph, Takahashi overtook leader Fujio Kobayashi on the all-time Japan Senior Tour victory list. He shot a final-round 68 for 275 in the season's first 72-hole event at Big Risac Country Club, Miyagi Prefecture.

Kimpachi Yoshimura led the tournament through the first three rounds. He began with a four-under-par 68 and shared first place with Taiwan's Chen Tze-ming, then took sole possession of the lead in the Friday round with 73–141, a shot ahead of the foursome of Hideaki Yamashita (74-68), Koji Okuno (73-69), Akira Yabe and Takahashi, both with 72-70 scores.

# Major Champions

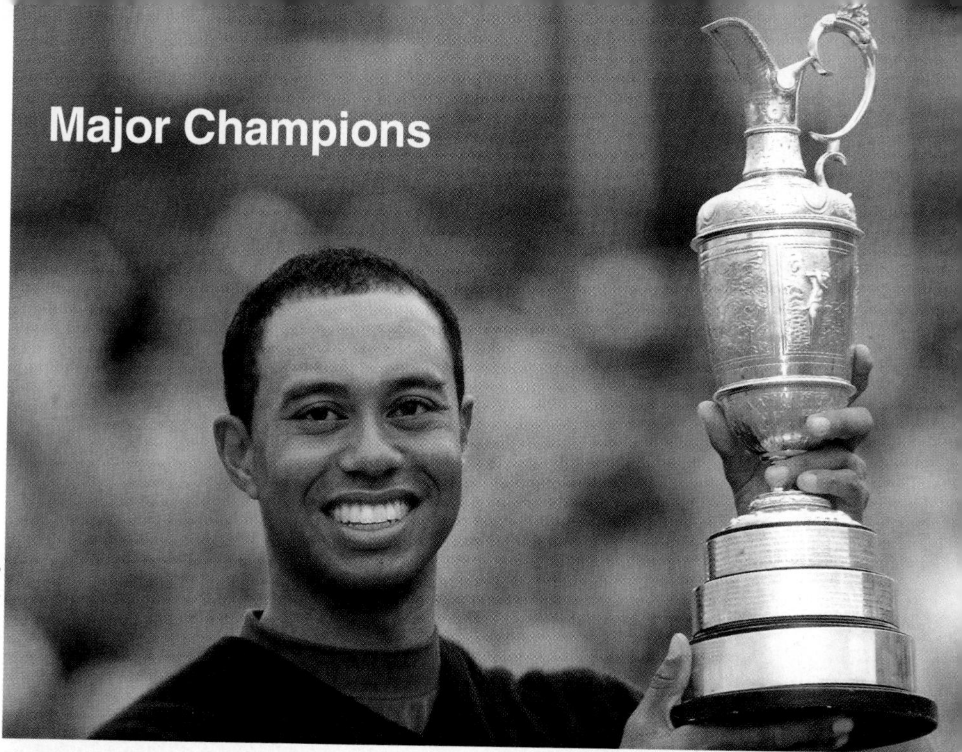

Andrew Redington/Getty Images

Tiger Woods, Masters Tournament and The Open Championship

Stuart Franklin/Getty Images

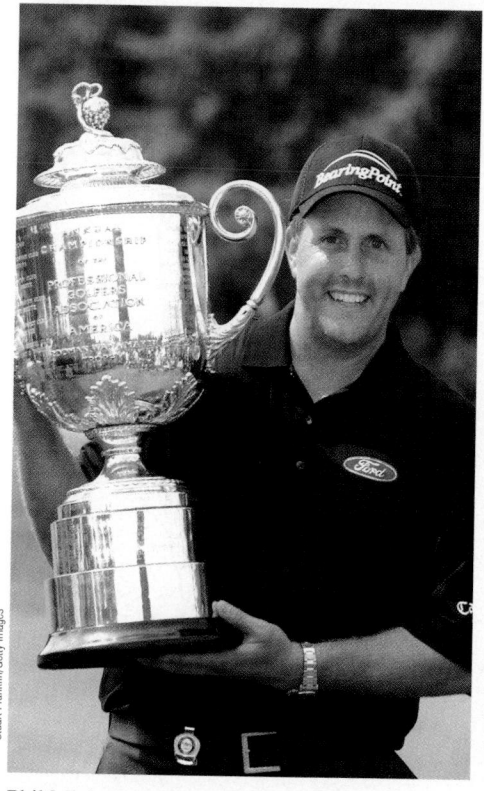

Phil Mickelson, PGA Championship

Ross Kinnaird/Getty Images

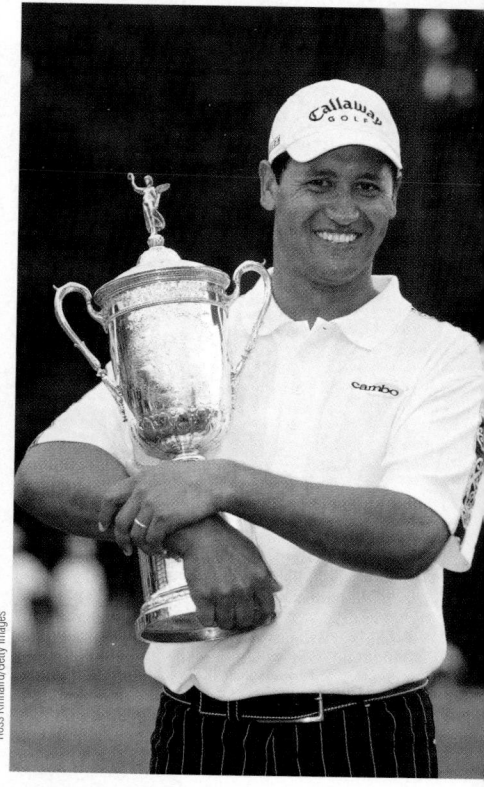

Michael Campbell, U.S. Open Championship

# Masters Tournament

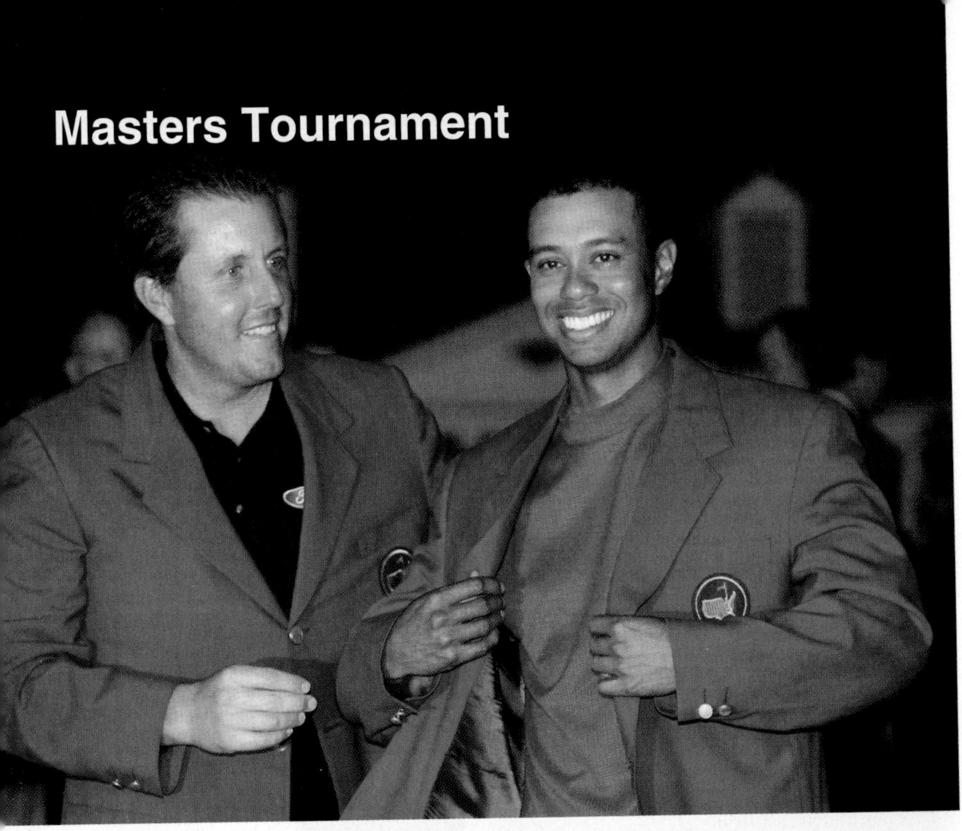

David Cannon/Getty Images

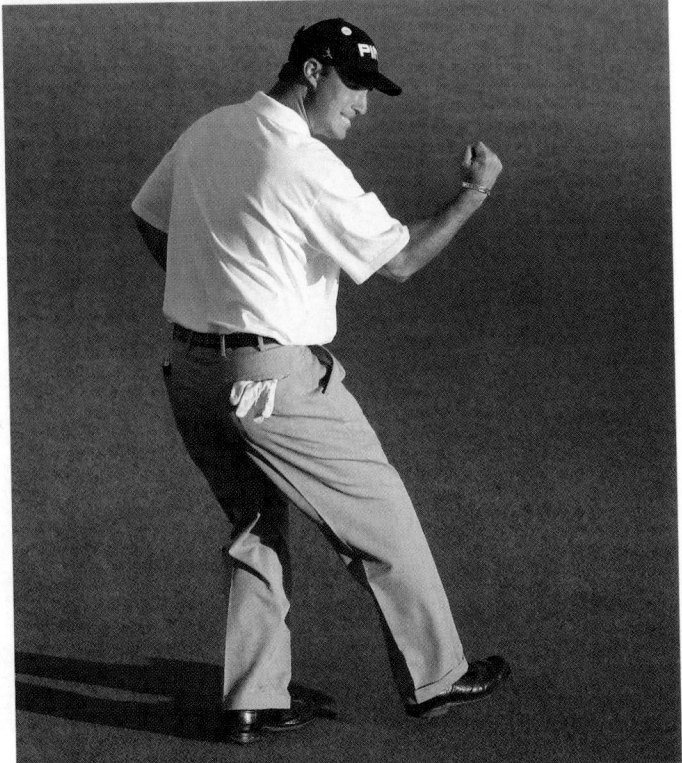

Phil Mickelson slipped the green jacket on Tiger Woods, signifying his fourth Masters title.

Chris DiMarco saved par on the 18th hole to join Woods in a playoff.

David Cannon/Getty Images

Andrew Redington/Getty Images

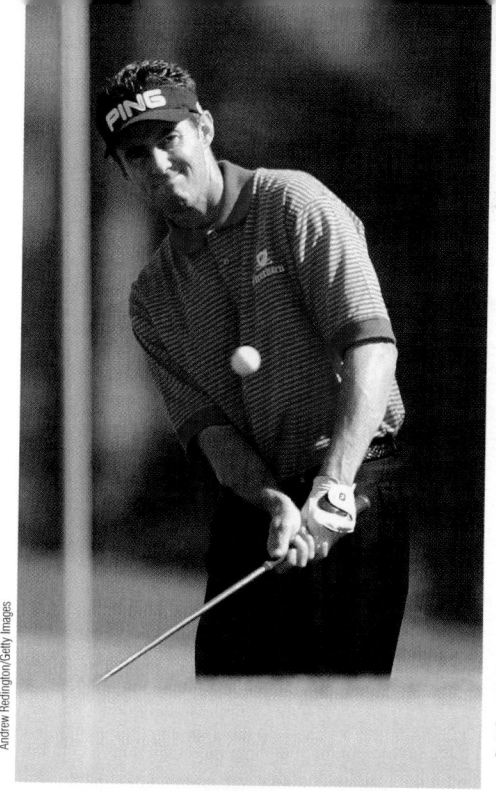

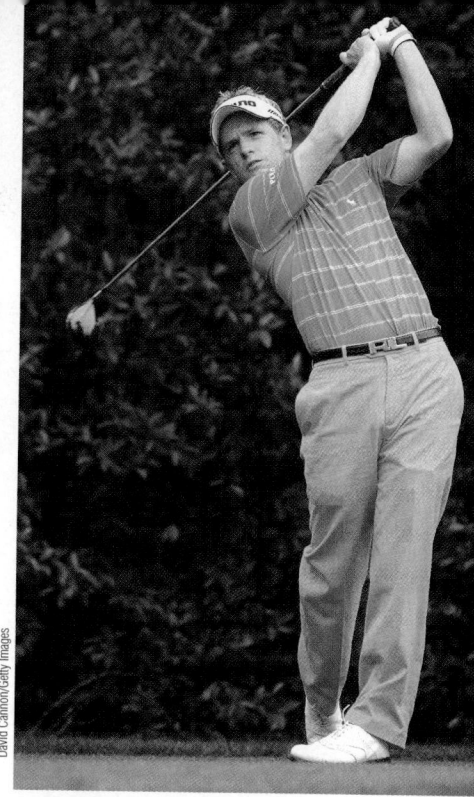

Mark Hensby tied for fifth.

David Cannon/Getty Images

Luke Donald shared third place.

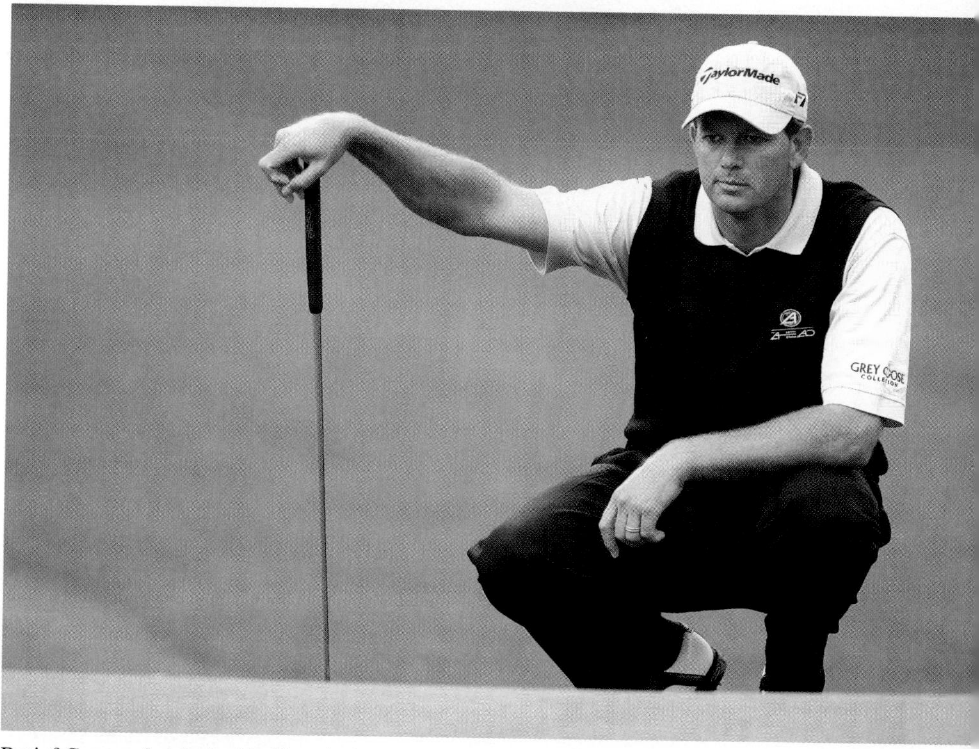
Andrew Redington/Getty Images

Retief Goosen finished with 67 to tie for third place.

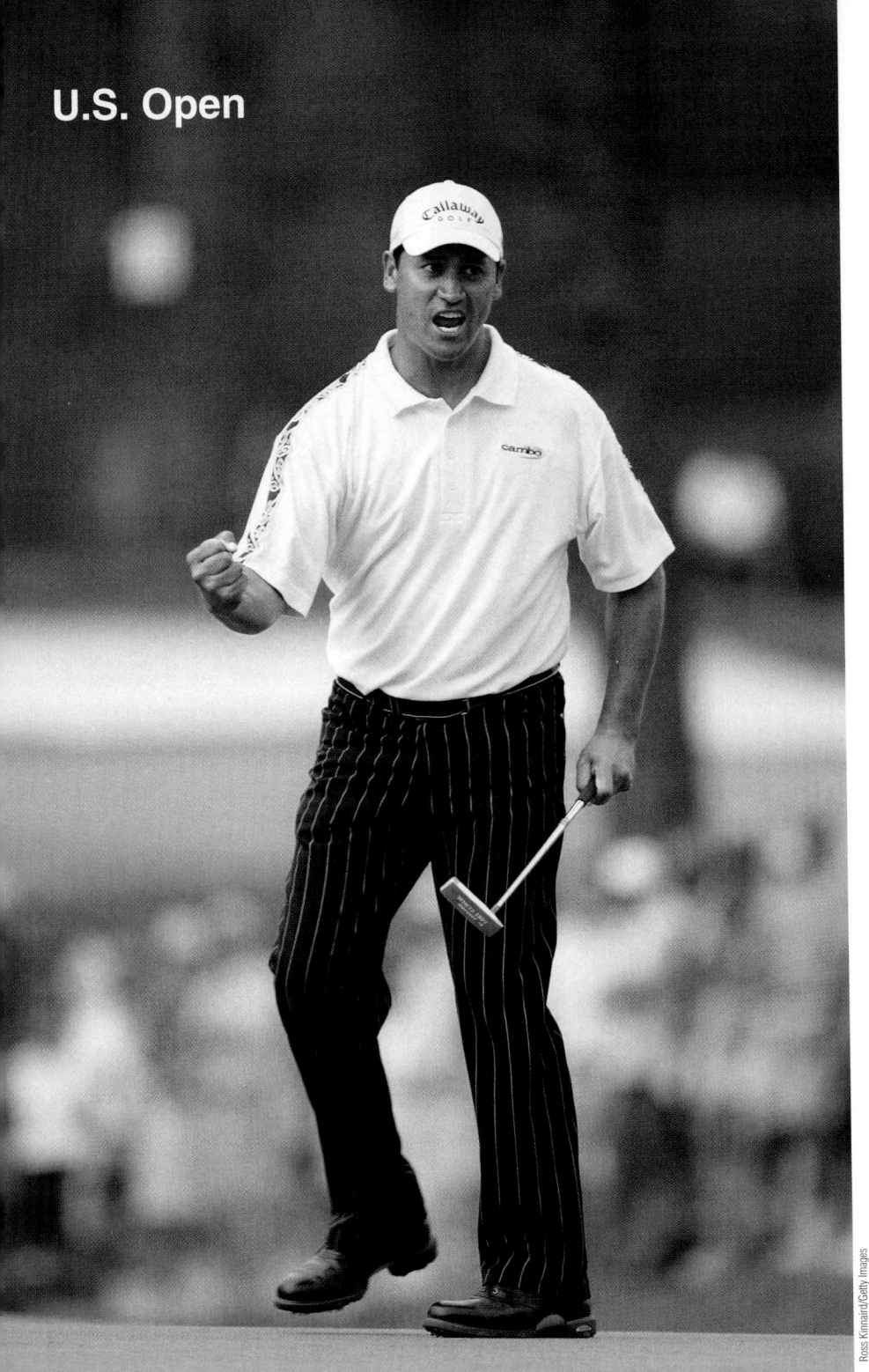

A 20-foot birdie putt on No. 17 sealed the victory for Michael Campbell in the U.S. Open.

Tiger Woods placed two strokes behind.

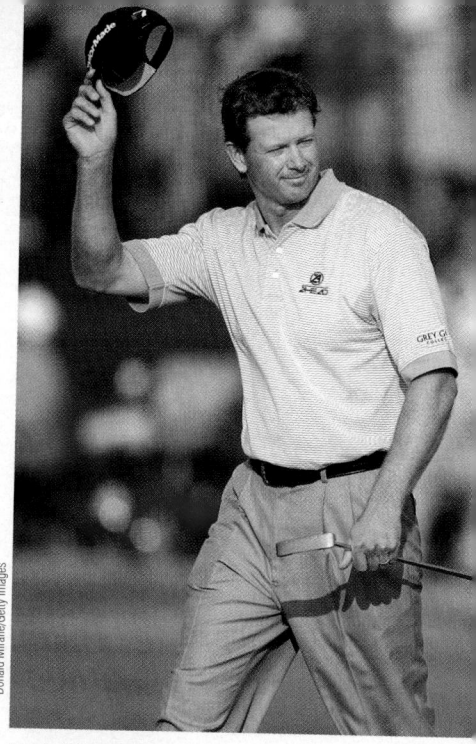

Retief Goosen fell with a closing 81.

Tim Clark finished with a pair of 70s.

Sergio Garcia shot 75 in the third round.

# The Open Championship

Tiger Woods celebrated on the 18th green at St. Andrews, having won his 10th major title.

Andrew Redington/Getty Images

Colin Montgomerie claimed second place.

Andrew Redington/Getty Images

Jose Maria Olazabal tied for third.

Jamie Squire/Getty Images

Bernhard Langer got a share of fifth place.

Andrew Redington/Getty Images

Fred Couples posted two 68s.

# PGA Championship

Phil Mickelson won the PGA Championship with a lob wedge to two feet at No. 18 for par.

Davis Love posted three 68s.

Steve Elkington tied for second place.

Thomas Bjorn shot 63 in the third round.

Geoff Ogilvy shared sixth place.

The Player of the Year in 2004, Vijay Singh followed with four wins but lost his No. 1 ranking.

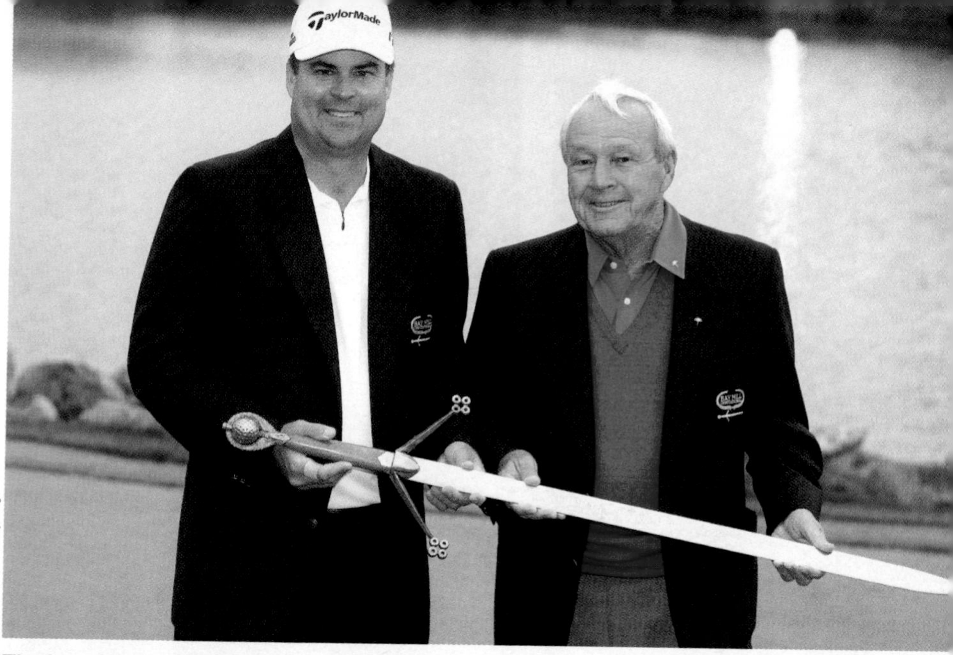


Andy Lyons/Getty Images

The first of Kenny Perry's three victories was at Bay Hill, where Arnold Palmer presented the sword.

Stuart Franklin/Getty Images

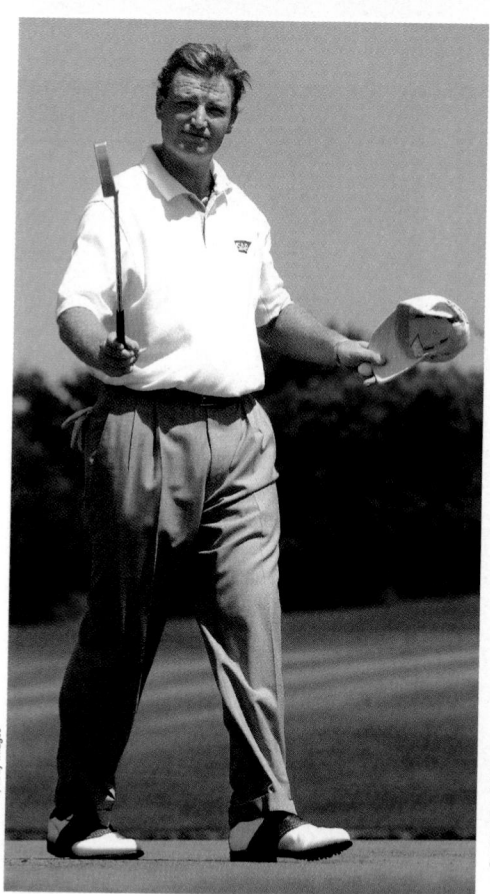

Ernie Els had four victories worldwide.

Donald Miralle/Getty Images

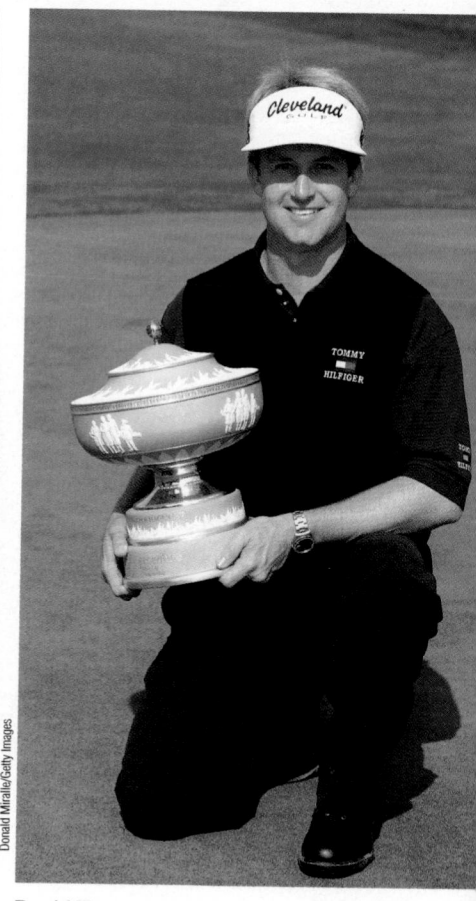

David Toms took the Accenture Match Play.

Bart Bryant recorded two wins.

Jim Furyk celebrated a Western victory.

Scott Verplank tied for second at The Players.

Stewart Cink held the No. 27 ranking.

Scott Halleran/Getty Images

Brandt Jobe rose from No. 251 to No. 42.

Donald Miralle/Getty Images

Stuart Appleby repeated at the Mercedes.

Harry How/Getty Images

John Daly climbed to the No. 29 ranking.

Stuart Franklin/Getty Images

Chad Campbell was 20th on the money list.

Jeff Gross/Getty Images

Sean O'Hair won the John Deere Classic.

Ross Kinnaird/Getty Images

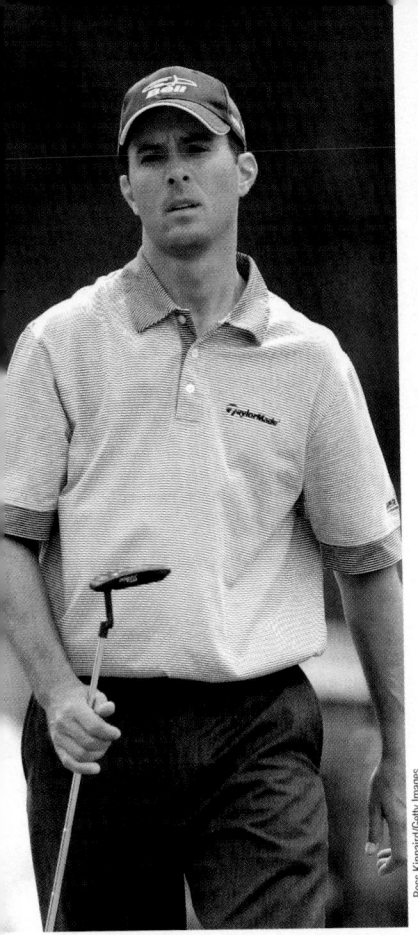

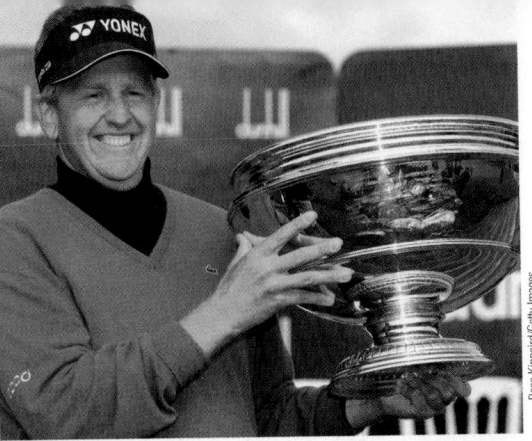

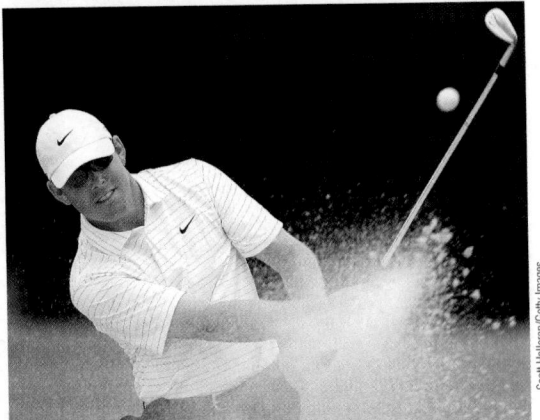

Mike Weir had a disappointing year.

Ross Kinnaird/Getty Images

Colin Montgomerie won the Dunhill Links at St. Andrews.

Scott Halleran/Getty Images

Justin Leonard posted two victories.

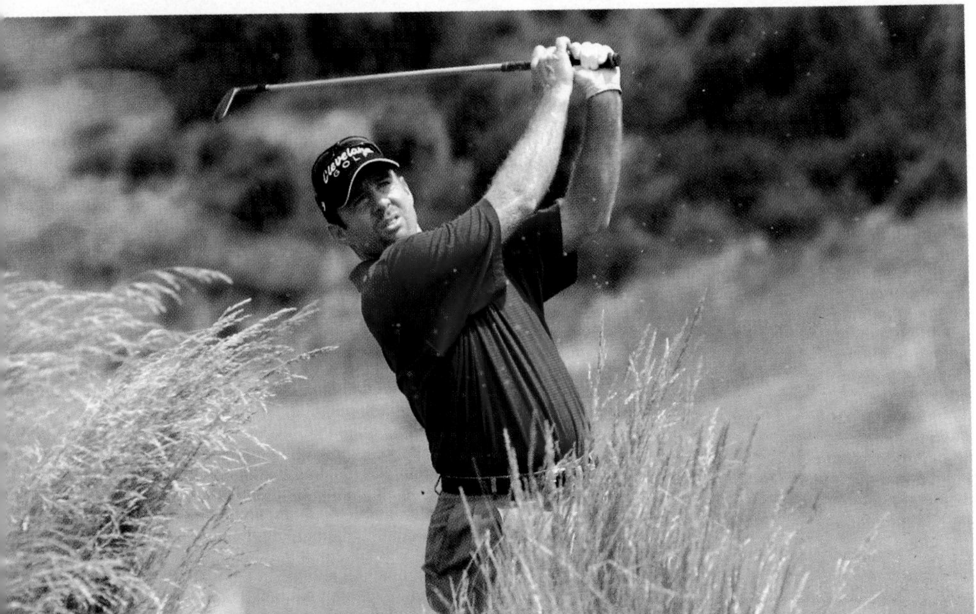

Cameron Spencer/Getty Images

Rod Pampling's season was highlighted by his tie for fifth place at the Masters Tournament.

Adam Scott had a victory in the Johnnie Walker Classic plus the Nissan Open in America.

David Howell took the HSBC Champions.

Fred Funk won The Players Championship.

Angel Cabrera won the BMW title.

Shingo Katayama had two wins in Japan.

Michael Campbell triumphed at Wentworth.

Darren Clarke held his top-20 ranking.

Padraig Harrington won three times worldwide.

Yoshimura and Takahashi took control in the third round as they both shot 65s, Kimpachi for 204 and Katsunari for 205. The next players — Yamashita and Yabe — were at 212. It was no contest Sunday as Takahashi came up with 68 and Yoshimura faltered with 75, dropping into a second-place tie at 281 with Yamashita.

## Japan PGA Senior Championship—¥50,000,000
Winner: Kiyoshi Murota

Kiyoshi Murota wasted little time making his presence felt on the Japan Senior Tour. Playing in just his second event on the over-50 circuit, Murota broke from a third-round tie with Tateo (Jet) Ozaki and raced to a six-stroke victory in the Japan PGA Senior Championship in early October. Murota had never landed a major title in his successful years on the regular Japan Tour.

Murota never trailed at Eniwa Country Club in Hokkaido after starting with an impressive 65 against the season's strongest field to date. Ozaki shot 66 and Tsuneyuki (Tommy) Nakajima, also a Senior Tour newcomer, had 67. Things barely changed at the top Friday. Ozaki overtook Murota with a 70 to Kiyoshi's 71, and Nakajima remained third with 72–139. The leadership tie remained after Saturday's round as the two men shot 69s, and Nakajima slipped three behind with 70, but stayed in third place.

Just as happened in the Rebornest, the most recent previous tournament, the competition broke wide open Sunday as Murota raced to the six-shot win with a 70 while Ozaki was absorbing a 76 and dropping into a second-place tie with Masahiro (Massy) Kuramoto at 281. Kuramoto was later to lead the qualifying competition and was set to play on the Champions Tour in the U.S. in 2006. Legendary Isao Aoki played in the Senior PGA for the first time, tying for eighth place at 286.

## Japan Senior Open—¥50,000,000
Winner: Tsuneyuki Nakajima

Victory in the Japan Senior Open meant more to Tsuneyuki (Tommy) Nakajima than the fact that his first victory in his first season on the Japan Senior Open came in such a prestigious national championship. It was particularly emotional for him because his late father had taught him to play golf and practiced with him at Ranzan Country Club, Saitama Prefecture, the site of the Open.

Nakajima was making his fourth start on the circuit when he won the championship with a final-round 70 on a rainy afternoon and posted a 282 total. Starting the day three strokes off the pace, Nakajima picked off the prized title by a stroke over Toshiaki Sudo and Katsunori Tomori, the Aderans winner earlier in the season

Australia's Terry Gale took the first-round lead with 68, two shots better than Kiyoshi Murota, the Senior PGA champion, and three ahead of Sudo, Tomori and Chen Tze-ming of Taiwan. Gale followed with 71–139, retaining a two-stroke margin, then over Tomori (71-70). Nakajima was another shot back at 142 with rounds of 74-68, tied with Murota (70-72). Tomori seized the lead Saturday, shooting 68 for 209, a stroke in front of Sudo (68) and Chen (67). Nakajima was at 212, set for his come-from-behind victory.

## Kinojyo Senior Open—¥20,000,000
Winner: Hajime Meshiai

Hajime Meshiai, who spent most of 2005 in America where he was winless but placed 50th on the Champions Tour with respectable winnings of US$311,453, found easier pickings at season's end on the Japan Senior Tour. The 51-year-old Meshiai, the leading money winner in the 1993 Japan Tour season when he won four of his 11 titles, edged Seiji Ebihara by a stroke in the concluding Kinojyo Senior Open at Kinojyo Golf Club, Okayama Prefecture, in late November.

Meshiai opened the tournament with a sparkling, seven-under-par 65, taking a one-stroke lead over Tadami Ueno, and never left first place in the standings. He produced a 70 for 135 Saturday, completing the second round a shot in front of Toru Nakamura (70-66), then held off Ebihara Sunday with his 72 and final 207 score. Ebihara, like Meshiai an international player with a money title (2002) and six victories on the European Seniors Tour to go with his three senior wins in Japan, closed with a 68, falling a stroke short with his 209.

An emotional high spot occurred on Saturday, when Masaru Amano, playing while waging a brave battle with colon cancer, scored a hole-in-one and went on to a fourth-place finish.

# 14. Women's Tours

You could say it without fear of contradiction — 2005 would go down as the most historic year of the LPGA since its founding in 1950. A statement that bold shrieks for proof. That's a reasonable request, whatever the decibel level. Consider:

• Sweden's Annika Sorenstam continued to dominate the tour, crushing all opposition.

• A shipment of huge young talent arrived, probably the greatest influx of talent at one time. The force was led by Paula Creamer, who became the Rookie of the Year. Then there was Morgan Pressel, Japan's Ai Miyazato and South Korea's Jeong Jang. Prodigy Michelle Wie, 16, turned professional and, although she may not join the tour until she reaches the minimum age of 18, she can play in up to eight LPGA Tour events each year, and will continue to play in various other events and overseas tournaments. Add to these freshest faces such tough young players as Lorena Ochoa, Christina Kim, Jennifer Rosales and Natalie Gulbis, plus a host of other South Koreans, and it's clear the LPGA won't be an easy place to earn a living.

• Commissioner Ty Votaw, after a successful six and a half years, resigned, took a post with the PGA Tour, and was succeeded by Carolyn F. Bivens, 53, the LPGA Tour's first female commissioner. She was president and CEO of Initiative Media North America, a media services company, and before that spent 18 years with *USA Today*. Where Votaw focused on competition and purses, Bivens will concentrate on "branding." "Our focus is going to be on branding, to expose the personalities of our stars to the general media," Bivens said in an early interview.

When Votaw became commissioner, the schedule had almost 40 events and only about a dozen had a purse of at least $1 million. Votaw cut the schedule to 31 events, with the average purse $1.4 million in 2005. He instituted a program for players, trying to make the tour more fan-friendly, and proposed an end-of-season playoff system for 32 women to qualify for the ADT Championship with a $1 million first prize.

Votaw agreed that it didn't hurt to be commissioner when Sorenstam was running wild. "All the media coverage, all the conjecture of how she would do or wouldn't do, it seemed like a convergence of a lot of issues in terms of what this could mean for the LPGA and women's golf," Votaw said.

It wasn't all peaches and cream for Sorenstam in the 2005 season, and no pun intended with Rookie of the Year and part-time adversary Paula Creamer. Annika started the season stating that she intended to win the Grand Slam. She won the first two majors — the Kraft Nabisco and the McDonald's LPGA Championship. She tied for 23rd in the U.S. Women's Open and tied for fifth in the Weetabix Women's British Open.

Not that the season was a bust. Sorenstam did win 11 tournaments, tied for second twice, tied for fifth twice, for ninth once, and her worst finish was the tie for 23rd. With $2,588,240 in official LPGA earnings, she topped $2 million in winnings for the fifth straight year. Her worldwide earnings were $2,756,540.

This is raw domination: She won her first three starts, four of her first five, six of her first eight. Then she won four of her last seven. Sorenstam won big, by eight and 10 strokes, and small, by one. She was an equal opportunity champion. Creamer was the only one she beat twice. The rest she scattered around, beating the youth (Wie, Ochoa) and veterans (Juli Inkster, Rosie Jones, Karrie Webb). She just overran anyone in the way.

Finishing second to Sorenstam wasn't all that bad. Creamer, 19, had a powerful rookie year, winning twice — the Sybase Classic and the Evian Masters — finishing second three times, tying for second once, and logging five other top-six finishes and winning over $1.5 million, No. 2 on the money list.

Creamer set LPGA records, becoming the youngest ever to reach $1 million in career earnings (18 years, 11 months, 18 days) and also the fastest (four months, 27 days). Creamer also starred in the U.S. Solheim Cup victory. The youngest player in Solheim history, she led the U.S. with 3½ points, and in the final-day singles, she birdied six holes on the front nine to take a 6-up lead and went on to a crushing 7-and-5 victory over European Solheim Cup legend Laura Davies.

All told, there were 20 different winners on the tour in 2005, and 10 were first-timers, including Creamer. If nothing else showed the rise of the South Koreans, this should: Six of the 10 first-timers were Korean, and two of them took the majors that Sorenstam didn't win. Birdie Kim came from obscurity to win the U.S. Women's Open by holing an improbable bunker shot on the final hole, and Jeong Jang went wire-to-wire in winning the Weetabix Women's British Open.

Then came Jimin Kang in the LPGA Corning Classic; rookie Meena Lee, the BMO Financial Group Canadian Women's Open; Soo-Yun Kang, the Safeway Classic; and Jee Young Lee, not an LPGA Tour member, in the CJ Nine Bridges Classic. The other three first-timers were Stacy Prammanasudh, in the Franklin American Mortgage; Marisa Baena, the HSBC Women's World Match Play, and Heather Bowie, the Jamie Farr Owens Corning Classic.

And what shows growth more than money? The LPGA Tour set a record of six players topping $1 million in 2005 — Sorenstam, Creamer, Cristie Kerr, Lorena Ochoa, Jeong Jang and Natalie Gulbis. Interestingly, Gulbis got her million ($1,010,154) without winning, which also was a record. She did it with 12 top-10 finishes.

For all of the records, for all of the international implications and all of that, the story of 2005 remains Annika Sorenstam. Laura Davies summed her up best. "It doesn't mean we're not good, it just means she's exceptional," Davies said. "It's almost like she's toying with us, like a mouse and a cat."

It's left for Sorenstam to look forward to the 2006 season, to pit her spirit and skill against a rising tide of talent and youth. Wherever the new season takes her, there will be one constant — her attitude. "I'm here," she said, "to reach my own goals, play my own golf."

# U.S. LPGA Tour

## Women's World Cup of Golf—$1,000,000
Winners: Ai Miyazato and Rui Kitada

See South African Women's Tour section.

## SBS Open at Turtle Bay—$1,000,000
Winner: Jennifer Rosales

It was Jennifer Rosales's victory, but it was Michelle Wie's tournament.

Wie, the precocious 15-year-old from Honolulu, who missed the cut in the PGA Tour's Sony Open in Hawaii just a few weeks earlier, now was helping launch the 2005 LPGA Tour season on the island of Oahu in the SBS Open at Turtle Bay. This was the first of eight LPGA events she had been invited to play. And once again, her presence all but obscured the tournament itself. She showed what things probably will be like when she joins the LPGA Tour. Wie started the third and final round five strokes behind Rosales, then shot her third straight 70 to finish tied for second with Cristie Kerr. She missed on her bid to become the youngest ever to win an LPGA Tour event, but she did enjoy her best finish in 18 starts.

Meanwhile, back at the tournament, Rosales opened the first round with two pars, then sprinted to four birdies on the next five holes. She hit all 18 holes in regulation and needed just 29 putts. The six-under-par 66 gave her a two-stroke lead, and she was four ahead of Wie, Kerr and 11 others at 70. "I have to say I was a little nervous," Wie said. The next day, another 70 left her at 140 and five strokes behind Rosales.

Rosales went on a wild ride of seven birdies and four bogeys for a 69 and 135 total, and a two-stroke lead over Reilly Rankin (66–137). Rosales couldn't get the feel of things. "Finally, at the end I hung in there and finished strong," she said — meaning four birdies over her last five holes.

In the final round, Rosales heard Wie more than she saw her. "I heard a lot of roars from the crowd — I knew it was her," Rosales said. The winds were brisk and the nerves high, and it was Rosales who controlled both just in time. She birdied her first two holes, then double-bogeyed the par-four No. 7 after watering her approach, then bogeyed the 13th and 15th. Kerr got within a stroke of Rosales, then erased two birdies on the back with four bogeys. Wie missed a six-foot par putt at No. 4, and three-putted No. 9 after mis-clubbing herself and overshooting the green. "I hit a three wood and it just turned out bad," she said. So Rosales, going wire-to-wire, closed with a 73 for an eight-under 208 total and the two-shot victory over Wie (70) and Kerr (72) tied at 210.

And the questions were about Wie. "She's an amazing player," Rosales said. "She's going to give us a lot of challenges and make us work harder."

## MasterCard Classic—$1,200,000
Winner: Annika Sorenstam

Annika Sorenstam, in her first tournament of the year, came to the third and final round three strokes off the lead. It didn't look good. Really? "I'm in a position," she insisted, "where I have a chance tomorrow."

A view, it should be pointed out, shared by many.

This was the MasterCard Classic at the Bosque Real Country Club high in the thin air near Mexico City, the first LPGA Tour event in Mexico since 1975. Sorenstam was trying to pick up where she left off in her eight-victory 2004 campaign. First, she had to warm up.

South Korea's Hee-Won Han, 26, the 2004 Safeway Classic winner, rang up five birdies over her first nine holes in a six-under-par 66 and led by a stroke over compatriot Young Jo. But the attention was on Lorena Ochoa, a native of Mexico, age 23, and former University of Arizona player who won twice last year to become the first Mexican-born champion in LPGA Tour history. "With all the emotions, the nerves, it was a good round," said Ochoa, relieved with her 71. Sorenstam, who caught the breezy part of the day, felt the same about her 70, even though she was trailing by four. "It was difficult to get some balls close because of the wind," she said. "But I hit 15 greens. I'm very happy with my start."

The picture changed abruptly in the second round. Han soared to a 76, and Cristie Kerr moved to the front with a 68 for a two-stroke lead over Moira Dunn (72) and South Korea's Sae-Hee Son (70). Kerr did it with some secret method for playing at the 7,400-foot altitude. She bogeyed twice, but plucked six birdies out of the thin air, and explained mysteriously, "It's like my little system. But we pretty much know what the yardages are playing and we judge accordingly." Ochoa fell eight behind with a 75. She suffered six bogeys, four of them in a crushing stretch from the 14th.

Sorenstam made a rush and was three under through the 14th. Then trouble hit. "I made a mistake on 15 that cost me a double bogey," she said, after a 71 that left her three behind going into the final round. "I've come from many more shots behind, but I have to be patient."

"The wind was gusting tremendously," Sorenstam said. She did make four bogeys that blustery Sunday, but she racked up a phenomenal eight birdies. She made five straight from No. 2, then made three straight bogeys. The wind hurt. At No. 9, she flew the green into a water hazard with a five iron and bogeyed. Then she made three birdies on the second nine for a 68 to lock up the victory by three over Karrie Webb with a seven-under 209 total. It was her 57th LPGA title.

"I wanted everybody to know," Sorenstam said, "that I'm ready to play and ready to go."

As though anyone thought otherwise.

## Safeway International—$1,400,000
Winner: Annika Sorenstam

The Safeway International went into the books as another victory by Annika Sorenstam. But it should carry an asterisk: *Lorena Ochoa's Nightmare.

You're leading by four strokes with three holes to play, and you lose? Now, that is a nightmare.

First lesson: Never count Sorenstam out. "I've learned the lesson the hard way, never to give up," Sorenstam said. "But it wasn't looking good. I saw Lorena climbing up the leaderboard with more birdies and more birdies..." Then Sorenstam got help from an unexpected source. Ochoa closed with a crash — double bogey, bogey, par, and with Sorenstam's birdie at the 18th, they were tied at 11-under-par 211. Then Sorenstam won on the first playoff hole after yet another error by Ochoa.

Until then, the tournament had gone routinely enough. Ochoa, who won twice in her sophomore year in 2004, and Malaysia's Siew-Ai Lim played Superstition Mountain, near Phoenix, in seven-under-par 65s and shared the first-round lead. Sorenstam was one behind. The tournament didn't really get perking until the final round. Ochoa started it leading by one, but was four up on Sorenstam. Then she bogeyed three of the first six holes, regained control and birdied three of the next four. Sorenstam, up ahead, bogeyed No. 6 on a weak chip, birdied the par-five No. 7, then the 11th from six feet, but couldn't make any more headway. Not until the decisive 18th.

Behind her, Ochoa birdied from 12 feet at the 15th and led Sorenstam by four with three holes to play. Then came the collapse.

At the par-four 16th, she bunkered her drive, was short with her approach, and left her chip 15 feet from the hole. She missed the par putt, and missed the return four-footer. The double bogey cut her lead to two. Then came the crusher. At the par-three 17th, she missed the green, chipped to two feet — and missed the putt. Her lead was down to one.

Sorenstam, playing the par-five 18th, jumped at her chance. Sitting 239 yards from the green, she blasted her four-wood second to 22 feet, just missed the eagle putt, and tapped in the birdie to get to 11 under. Ochoa followed, needing a birdie to win. She two-putted for a par. They were tied.

The playoff, starting at the 18th, was almost an anticlimax. Ochoa led off and hooked her tee shot into the water. All Sorenstam had to do was finish in routine order, and this she did with a drive, an approach, a chip to 15 feet, and two putts for a par, her second straight victory of the young season, and the fourth in her last four LPGA Tour starts over two years.

"I gave away the tournament," said Ochoa. "But if you are going to lose, it'd better be the best player in the world."

"Even when I was four down," Sorenstam said, "a little part of me thought I still might be holding the trophy."

## Kraft Nabisco Championship—$1,800,000
Winner: Annika Sorenstam

A sad message, almost a prayer, came out of the Kraft Nabisco Championship, the LPGA Tour's first major championship of the season. It came from a credible source — the respected veteran, Rosie Jones, age 45, who joined the LPGA Tour in 1982, and who had announced that this would be her final year. Jones had 13 wins in her career, but none of them in the majors. She tied with two others in the first round, and in the second round she was tied with one other — Annika Sorenstam, who was getting to be as scary as the shark in *Jaws*. And Jones's near-prayer was:

"I'm desperate," Jones said. "I want to win a major as bad as Annika wants to win her fifth in a row. She'll have other chances. I've got a lot more riding on it."

Rosie Jones might well have been speaking for the entire tour. It was getting to be that whenever Sorenstam surfaced at a tournament, no one else was winning anything. Sorenstam missed the SBS Open, the season-opener, but played in the next two and won them both — the MasterCard Classic and last week's Safeway International. And here, in late March, she was going for her third straight win and her fifth straight since late 2004. She had already announced that she wanted to win the Grand Slam, the four majors. The Nabisco was the first.

And so Sorenstam merely ran away with the title by eight strokes.

"I'm going to remember this Easter weekend for a long time," Sorenstam said. And the season was just getting started. She wasn't merely dominating the LPGA Tour. She was making it her own. She even had people forgetting that teen sensation Michelle Wie was in the field.

Well, at least Sorenstam didn't go wire-to-wire. But almost. In the first round, she was three under par after only four holes, with an eagle at No. 2 and a birdie at No. 4. It looked like business as usual for her. Then the Southern California winds hit Mission Hills, and Sorenstam struggled through her last 14 holes in one over, making bogey at the 18th, to finish at two-under 70 and one stroke out of the lead. "The wind made it a lot tougher, I thought," Sorenstam said. Jones, Korea's Mi Hyun Kim and England's Karen Stupples, winner of last year's Weetabix Women's British Open, tied for the first-round lead at three-under 69. And ironically, the situation was a microcosm of women's golf — past, present and future. From Jones, the veteran, to Sorenstam, the present, and then to her playing partners, the future of the tour — the amateur whizzes Michelle Wie, 15, and Morgan Pressel, 16. Wie had the early lead, then missed the green at the par-three 17th and bogeyed. Pressel parred her first nine and made two birdies on the second nine. This wrapped up the irony: Wie and Pressel tied Sorenstam at 70.

The young amateurs pretty much held their own in the second round. Pressel led briefly and was four under on the second nine until she ran into trouble and shot 73, and was at one-under 143. Wie hit it out of bounds at the 16th and suffered one of her two double bogeys. She shot 74 and was at even-par 144.

Sorenstam, playing before the winds came up, spotted the field a bogey at No. 1 — three putts from 40 feet — and hammered out a 69 for a share of the halfway lead with Rosie Jones at five-under 139. Of the three first-round leaders, only Jones kept up with Sorenstam. A clutch birdie at the 18th gave her a two-under 70 for the tie. After the opening bogey, Sorenstam broke loose with three straight birdies into the turn, including a holed-out bunker shot at No. 8. She tacked on two more birdies on the back nine, then caught a greenside bunker at the 15th and bogeyed for a 69. It was a big turnaround from a year ago, when a 76 in the second round killed her chances for a start on the Grand Slam.

"Everything is just looking really good," Sorenstam said. "So of course,

I get a little anxious, and I just have to pinch myself and say, 'Hey, this is a tournament. Play your game and go easy and hit one shot at a time.'"

It didn't take Sorenstam much longer. From that halfway tie she bolted to a five-stroke lead over Jones in the third round. She got four birdies on the first nine, and two more on the back for a six-under 66. Sorenstam was playing in the final threesome with Jones and Mi Hyun Kim, and she worked her advantages to perfection. She outdrove them consistently, often by 60 yards, and so was hitting short irons into the longer par-fours while they needed fairway woods. Object lesson: At the 387-yard 15th, Sorenstam hit a pitching wedge to three feet. Jones and Kim hit woods, one to 15 feet, the other to 18 feet. Sorenstam birdied easily. The 66 put her at 11-under 205, five up on Jones heading into the final round.

"She's the last person you want to have a five-shot lead," Jones said. "Annika executed everything just perfectly."

The final round was pretty much an anticlimax. The galleries were cheering Sorenstam as she made her way down the final nine. She underlined her victory with a grand gesture. At the 485-yard 18th, she went for the green in two, and reached it with her four wood. She did high-fives with admiring spectators as she passed the bleachers, and if she three-putted from 100 feet, who was counting? She finished with a four-under 68 and a 15-under 273 total, beating Rosie Jones by eight (Jones was under par in all four rounds), and Laura Diaz and Cristie Kerr by 10.

"She didn't show any nerves at all," said Jones, at once disappointed and admiring. "It only shows that she's that much better than the rest of us," said Grace Park, the 2004 champion, who finished 11 back.

The report from the future: Michelle Wie closed with a 71 and finished as low amateur at par 288, tied for 14th, and Morgan Pressel shot 75–290 and tied for 19th.

As for the present — Sorenstam thus had the first leg of the Grand Slam, her third straight win of the season, and her fifth straight victory, tying Nancy Lopez's record from 1978, though over two seasons. "This is a long year, and who knows what will happen," Sorenstam said. "But it's a good start. I feel like I'm starting to reach my peak — and I want to get there."

## LPGA Takefuji Classic—$1,100,000
Winner: Wendy Ward

Wendy Ward simply has got to get her husband, Nate Hair, to come out to more tournaments. "He doesn't get to come out too often," Ward said, "but he is four-for-four on wins."

With husband along — to say nothing of rounds of 65-68-67 — Ward, age 31, made it career LPGA victory No. 4 at the Takefuji Classic at Las Vegas Country Club. The three-rounder was a wire-to-wire win in which Ward displayed a new-found mindset and the ability to withstand some considerable heat. First, she had to contend with the fact that the once-formidable Karrie Webb had tied her with a 65 in the first round. Webb was still in that slump. What if she'd picked now to snap out of it? The mere thought is not easy on the nerves. Webb didn't, but that didn't make the second round any easier, not with Lorena Ochoa catching fire. That was a sizzling, career-best nine-under-par 63 that Ochoa threw at her. And then in the final round, watching Ochoa in the group ahead firing a 65, that was the worst of the heat. But Ward refused to buckle. Ward went serenely bogey-free in that 67.

"I did everything I could do," Ochoa said. "She never went down."

Ward finished at 16-under 200, winning by two strokes over Ochoa, and by three over Shi Hyun Ahn (63) and 18-year-old tour rookie Paula Creamer (65). Yet another budding talent appeared. In-Bee Park, 16, a South Korean amateur and a Las Vegas high school junior, closed with a 67 and finished fifth at 12 under.

In addition to her husband, Ward also credited her sports psychologist, Debbie Crews, for her success. Ward got some strange but interesting advice. Frustrated, she told Crews she had been trying as hard as she could. Said Crews: "I want you to quit trying and start believing." Ward took it from there.

Ochoa cut Ward's lead to one with a birdie at No. 11 that got her to 13 under. Ward, playing in the group behind, had to call on both her new mindset and her good-luck husband at the 12th. She hit her tee shot toward the out-of-bounds to the right, and feared it might have gone out. And then she gave a huge sigh of relief. Nate happened to be at the spot, and he gave her a thumbs-up. All clear. She pitched to eight feet and holed the birdie putt to go to 15 under. She was leading by two again. Finally, she arrived at the 18th, and she made the two-putt par — and her fourth win — look easy.

## Corona Morelia Championship—$1,000,000
Winner: Carin Koch

Golfers all agree that it generally takes more than just a good game to win. It also takes a little luck. Left unsaid is the fact that, sometimes, it's someone else's bad luck. And so it was at the inaugural Corona Morelia Championship in Mexico. Carin Koch and Wendy Ward were tied with seven holes to play, and Koch shot a nice but hardly devastating one-under-par 71 — and won by six strokes. It didn't take Agatha Christie to deduce that Ward had taken a mighty fall.

Koch, 34, won by six over France's Karine Icher, scoring the second win of her 11 years on the LPGA Tour, and her first after a drought of 78 tournaments and nearly four years. Ward, who won her fourth title the week before in the Takefuji Classic, plunged from a chance to win into a tie for third with Catriona Matthew, seven behind. When Koch dropped her final putt, it marked the end of a strange and erratic last round, with birdies, bogeys and worse being scattered all over the place.

"I was a little nervous," said Koch. With a card of 68-69-71-71 for a nine-under 279 total, she was the only player to break par in all four rounds at the par-72 Tres Marias Club at Morelia, Mexico.

Koch took the lead in the second round and led Ward by three strokes. Ward caught her in the third round with a 68, and they were tied at eight-under 208 and leading by five strokes going into the final round. Then the scramble was on. Koch went birdie-bogey-birdie-birdie from No. 3, the birdies on putts of 10, 15 and three feet, to regain the lead. Then Ward birdied No. 6 and got to nine under, then bogeyed No. 8. It wasn't over. Koch couldn't hold the lead. She bogeyed the 10th and 11th, and Ward made a tough par save at the 11th and they were tied.

Then came the luck Koch needed. Ward double-bogeyed the 12th. Koch then added a birdie at the 15th, recovering from a hooked tee shot with a six iron from the rough to 15 feet. Then came Ward's final crash. At the 16th, she hit into a hazard, then three-putted for a triple-bogey eight. Koch bogeyed the 17th, but closed out the tournament with a birdie from 18 feet at the par-five 18th for her 71. Icher slipped above the struggling Ward into second place with two birdies over the last three holes for a 70.

Koch defined Ward's luck. "She had that bad shot on 12," Koch said. "You just can't get in trouble here. You have to stay in play."

## Franklin American Mortgage Championship—$1,000,000
Winner: Stacy Prammanasudh

Stacy Prammanasudh had to check the calendar. Was she really in her second year on the LPGA Tour, or was she back at Tulsa University, going head-to-head against Lorena Ochoa and Arizona again? No, the calendar was right. It was the tour, the final round of the Franklin American Mortgage Championship, and Ochoa stood between her and her first championship.

It was practically match play between them. "We were three, four, five shots ahead of most of the field," Prammanasudh said. "I kind of figured Lorena was going to be my competition." Prammanasudh broke away with birdies at the 16th and 17th in the final round to become the tour's first first-time winner of the season. With a three-under-par 69 and a 14-under 274 total, she won by three over Ochoa (70), and by five over Cristie Kerr (69), Christina Kim (69) and Catriona Matthew (71).

But the tournament began as a battle of veterans, not newcomers. Kris Tschetter, an 18-year vet with one title to her credit, shot a wild 69 in a driving rain on the Vanderbilt Legends Club's Ironhorse Course in Franklin, Tennessee. She parred just one of her first seven holes and overall made six birdies and three bogeys. She led by one over Grace Park, Kerr and Prammanasudh. Liselotte Neumann, one of the first of the excellent Swedes who changed the face of the tour, shot a 67 in a rain-whipped second round which 73 players couldn't complete. Neumann, who joined the tour in 1988, birdied No. 4, chipped in for an eagle at No. 7, and later dropped a five-footer for birdie at the 16th to get to five under and tie Tschetter, who had played just six holes when play was suspended. Prammanasudh, who completed her round, birdied the 17th and 18th for a 70 to get to four under for the tournament.

Prammanasudh staked her claim against her old college foe in the third round, hitting every fairway and 17 of 18 greens in regulation. She birdied three straight holes on the first nine to tie Ochoa, playing two groups ahead, birdied the 10th and 15th, then birdied the 17th and 18th again for a 65 and a two-stroke lead. Ochoa missed a 15-foot birdie putt at the 17th, and hit the water at the par-five 18th, but scrambled to a par. In the final round, Ochoa bogeyed No. 6, then lipped out a birdie putt at No. 8, and went on to miss birdie chances at the 10th, 11th, 15th, 16th and 17th. "I always felt I had a chance on the back nine," Ochoa said. "She just didn't let me breathe."

Prammanasudh, who bogeyed just once in the final round, tightened things even more with birdies at Nos. 6 and 7, then again made late back-to-back birdies, this time at the 16th and 17th, from 10 and six feet, and finished at 14 under. Ochoa cut the margin to three with a birdie at the 18th for a 70.

Ochoa had won 12 titles in two seasons at Arizona, and Prammanasudh won 10 in four years at Tulsa. But now, gone were the burdens of college days. "Winning," said Prammanasudh, "is going to come if you play well."

## Michelob Ultra Open at Kingsmill—$2,200,000
Winner: Cristie Kerr

The Michelob Ultra Open at Kingsmill had to be the most-watched LPGA event in decades. This was Annika Sorenstam going after a tour record sixth straight victory. Not since Nancy Lopez won five in a row in her rookie year, 1978, had there been such electricity. Then Sorenstam short-circuited, clearing the way for spunky Cristie Kerr to win by five strokes.

Sorenstam hit trouble immediately. She opened with a 76, five over par at Kingsmill Resort in Williamsburg, Virginia. It was her first score over par in 43 rounds, since June 2004.

"I just needed a few birdies to get me going," Sorenstam said. She got a few, but needed a bunch more. The bigger question was whether she would make the 36-hole cut. She came back with a 67–143 and made it with three shots to spare. The next question was, could she rally and pull this one out as she had for 19 of her 59 victories? The answer was no. The hump was too big, the rally too small. The streak was over. She shot 76-67-69-74—286, tied for 12th, 10 shots behind Kerr.

This was the Cristie Kerr Show. She opened with a 68, a stroke behind co-leaders Silvia Cavalleri and Catrin Nilsmark. (Nilsmark exploded to an 84 and missed the cut, and Cavalleri went on to finish tied for 12th.) A heavy storm rolled in, forcing the second round into Saturday. Kerr took over with another 68 and led by two after 36 holes, and Sorenstam was seven back. The storm also forced a 36-hole finale on Sunday.

Kerr came through the grind with 68-72, turning back all dreamers. Twice she made birdies right after bogeys, and saved par with several clutch putts. The closest anyone came was four strokes when Jill McGill got to four under par and Kerr was eight under. But Kerr closed the door with a 20-foot putt to save par at the 16th. Kerr finished at eight-under 276, five strokes ahead of McGill.

So Kerr answered one question, but there was still the puzzle of Sorenstam's uncharacteristic play. Was it because she had taken a five-week break? Maybe it was because she was using her third set of irons this season, and it was only early May.

"I'm not going to look for excuses, other than myself," Sorenstam said. "I just have to start over. Maybe I can do another streak."

As for Kerr, maybe she exorcised a couple of demons with this win. First, in the 2003 Michelob at Kingsmill she made some late errors and tied for second, and in the 2004 edition, she led after three rounds, double-bogeyed early in the fourth and was out of the running. And then there was Sorenstam. In the 2004 ADT Championship, she battled her way into a playoff with her, then double-bogeyed and lost. And two months ago, in the MasterCard Classic, she led Sorenstam going into the final round, then shot 75 and tied for third.

So what did this victory mean to Kerr? Was it special, ending Sorenstam's streak? "Yeah, you bet it was," Kerr said. "She's the best in the world." But there were other reasons — winning for her mother, who is battling breast cancer, and for her grandmother, who recently died. "And," said Kerr, who had won only three times in nine tries when she led or shared the lead going into the final round, "it's special because I played well when I had to play well."

## Chick-fil-A Charity Championship—$1,600,000
Winner: Annika Sorenstam

It was career win No. 60 for Annika Sorenstam in the Chick-fil-A Charity Championship in Stockbridge, Georgia, and for those chasing her, there was this consolation: At least she didn't lead all the way this time.

Well, she only led from the second round on. And she won by 10 strokes. In fact, she was leading by 10 going into the final round. The only thing that changed was the name of the next nearest player — usually known as the challenger, but not this time. Emilee Klein trailed by 10 going into the fourth round, and Candie Kung, closing with a 65, was the runner-up by 10.

"We were playing a different tournament," Kung said. "She's up there in her own little world."

Said Sorenstam, from her own little world: "Here I am with 60. I have to pinch myself to believe it's real."

The 60 victories tied her with Patty Berg for third in all-time victories, 22 behind No. 2 Mickey Wright and 28 behind the all-time leader, Kathy Whitworth. Cristie Kerr stopped her from winning a record six in a row the week before, but now she has won six of her last seven tournaments, and eight of 11.

In summary, Sorenstam shot 67-64-67-67—265, 23 under par at Eagle's Landing. All the drama, such as it was, came in the first round when Sorenstam trailed by a stroke with that 67, tied with Karrie Webb. Laura Davies, a force in the mid-1990s, led with a 66. Then Sorenstam shot a 64 in the second round for a six-stroke lead, the biggest halfway lead since her own eight-shot edge in the 2001 Standard Register Ping.

"It's just two days," Sorenstam protested. "We have two more to go. It can easily swing the other way around."

That wasn't likely. Logically, the challenges would come from Davies and Webb, the two closest to her in the first round. But Davies soared to a 76 and fell 11 behind, and Webb shot a 74 and was 10 behind. Heather Bowie, with a 69, took over second place. "I haven't had a six-shot lead since I was in college," Bowie noted. "It's almost like you're playing your own tournament."

Precisely. For other highlights of Sorenstam's romp, it did relieve some that she finally made a bogey. Actually, three of them in her third-round 67. But none in the final round. This is the anatomy of a masterpiece: She hit 82 percent of the driving fairways, 76 percent of the greens in regulation, and needed only 108 putts, an average of 27 per round. And when she had finished the third round leading by 10, someone noted that she had a chance to break the record winning margin — 14 strokes.

"I just want to win the tournament," Sorenstam said. "That's all that matters to me."

## Sybase Classic—$1,250,000
Winner: Paula Creamer

Some high school kids get cars for graduation, some get vacations to spiffy places, but it's pretty safe to say that nobody ever got what Paula Creamer got — her first LPGA Tour victory. Better yet, she got it for herself, and with the kind of drama expected from a seasoned veteran. Coming down the final nine she made two clutch pars, then birdied three of the last five holes, including the last, where she dropped a 17-foot putt to win. Then she picked up a check for $187,500, and hastened back home to Bradenton, Florida, there to pick up her diploma.

"It's going to be fun, going home for graduation," Creamer said. "I can't even speak, let alone think right now. It's awesome."

It was also awesome that Creamer — at 18 years, 9 months and 17 days of age — was the youngest in LPGA history to win a tournament of more than one round. Marlene Hagge was a bit younger when she won twice in 1952, but both were one-day events. The Sybase Classic was a four-round tournament at Wykagyl Country Club at New Rochelle, New York. Creamer had won 19 national junior titles, and this was just her ninth outing as a professional.

This was Christina Kim's tournament for most of the four rounds. Except for being part of a four-way tie after 36 holes, Creamer was chasing. She got the lead when it counted most — on the very last hole. She shot the par-71 course in 69-68-71-70—278, six under par. She trailed Kim by four in the first round, and tied for the lead in the second with her and South Koreans Joo Mi Kim and Gloria Park at five-under 137. Christina retook the lead in the third, and Creamer trailed her by a stroke going into the fourth.

They began the final round under intermittent showers, and they played the final 12 holes in a cold rain, the kind of conditions that usually bring out the worst in the young and untested. And so it was with Creamer. She started to fold halfway through the round, bogeying Nos. 7, 9 and 11 to fall into a five-way tie for the lead. Said Creamer, "I told myself, 'You are not going to just give this away — you are going to fight to the end ...'"

Then crisis: At the 12th, she hit a tree, missed the green, and had a five-footer left for par. She got it. At the 13th, she had a curving nine-footer to save par. She got that, too. Then the birdies. At No. 14, she hit a seven iron to two inches, and at the par-five 15th, she chipped to four inches.

Creamer was not home free yet. Jeong Jang, playing ahead, and also looking for her first win, birdied three of her last four holes for a 67 and a five-under total, tying Creamer and Park, who were five under coming to the 18th. There, Park barely missed a 35-footer for birdie. Creamer then holed her 17-footer for the lead at six under. Christina Kim was the last one who could beat her. Kim needed an eagle from a bunker. She didn't get it, and Paula Creamer had her graduation gift.

## LPGA Corning Classic—$1,100,000
Winner: Jimin Kang

The LPGA Corning Classic was largely the story of who should have won but didn't, and who shouldn't have won but did. Those terms being used advisedly, of course.

Who should have won, first, was Annika Sorenstam. That was the price for her talent. She was expected to win any time she came to play. She was within reach of this one. But just when it seemed she would stage one of her rallies, she just couldn't put it all together. And then there was France's Karine Icher, who led after the second and third rounds. But she exploded into three double bogeys on the final nine and tied for sixth.

And then there is who shouldn't have won but did — South Korea's Jimin Kang, 25, out of both Arizona State University and the developmental Futures Tour, whose best previous finish was a tie for 19th place.

"I still can't feel it," said Kang, who trailed by three strokes in each of the first three rounds. "I just won the tournament. I look at the scoreboard, and my name is at the top." She wasn't alone in her surprise. This was one strange victory. Kang went from sure-winner to sure-loser to winner in the last five holes for a two-stroke victory over Sorenstam and rookie Meena Lee.

Take that closing stretch. Kang and Lee were tied for the lead coming to the par-five 14th. Kang put her third shot four feet from the hole, then three-putted for a bogey. Lee birdied from four feet. Kang had gone from a tie for the lead to a two-shot deficit. She reversed that immediately, after giving herself a talking-to.

"I was talking to myself," Kang said. "I said, 'Jimin, it's only golf, it's only a game, it's a three-putt. Just move on, it'll be fine. And I think that worked."

So it seemed. At the 125-yard par-three 15th, Kang's nine-iron tee shot bounced twice on the green and rolled into the hole. She was tied for the lead again. She then birdied the 16th, and Lee birdied the 17th, and they came to the 18th tied. Then Lee put her drive under a tree and double-bogeyed. Kang made a short putt for a par and a 66, and a 15-under 273 total. She won by two over Lee (67) and Sorenstam (69), who birdied the 16th and 17th.

If winning surprised Kang, her scorecards might do the same. She made 10 birdies and no bogeys on the first nine; 10 birdies, an ace and her seven bogeys on the second nine, and she of the par-fives, she couldn't handle the 14th. She parred it twice, bogeyed it twice. But she more than got even on the other three — three birdies at No. 2, three at No. 5, and four at the 12th.

## ShopRite LPGA Classic—$1,400,000
Winner: Annika Sorenstam

Annika Sorenstam, shut down the week before, opened up shop again in the ShopRite LPGA Classic. It was business as usual. This time it was a victory by four strokes over two-time U.S. Open champion Juli Inkster.

Sorenstam's sheer numbers are staggering: This was her 61st career victory, moving her ahead of Patty Berg into third place on the all-time list behind Mickey Wright (82) and Kathy Whitworth (88). And it was her fifth win in seven tournaments this year and ninth in her last 13. Her closing 64 at the par-71 Seaview Marriott at Galloway Township, New Jersey, was her 11th consecutive round in the 60s. It was the sixth consecutive time that Sorenstam won after leading or sharing the lead going into the final round. But that wasn't the number that interested her. The number she wanted next was nine — her ninth major victory. In every way, in demanding shots and heavy pressure, this was an excellent tune-up for the McDonald's LPGA Championship the next week, the next step in her quest for the LPGA Grand Slam.

"I don't know if you can really put it in perspective," Sorenstam said. "When you look at the stats, it's something I'm very proud of but not something I walk around thinking about."

Many of Sorenstam's victories are easier than the final score indicated. The reverse was true this time. She and Inkster entered the third and final round tied for the lead. Laura Davies, who had shot a tournament-record 62 in the second round, started the third with three straight birdies to take the lead briefly. Davies went on to play the rest of the way with one bogey and one birdie for a 68 and a tie for third. Sorenstam's duel with Inkster came down almost to the wire.

Sorenstam took the lead at No. 9, holing a 28-foot putt to take the lead at 12 under, then birdied the 10th from 21 feet. Inkster birdied the 10th and 12th. Then Sorenstam birdied the 13th and Inkster the 17th. The difference between them at this point was Inkster's bogey at No. 6, a three-putt from six feet. Then Sorenstam closed with a blitz. She also birdied the par-three 17th, and rolled in a 38-foot right-to-left putt for an eagle at the 18th. And there was the four-stroke victory.

Said Sorenstam: "This is when I look at my career and say, 'Hey, this is why I do this. This is why I wake up in the morning and go to practice.'"

## McDonald's LPGA Championship—$1,800,000
Winner: Annika Sorenstam

It seemed to be left to Laura Davies, fellow golfer and victim, to best define Annika Sorenstam and her place in golf. The occasion was the McDonald's LPGA Championship, where Sorenstam made her second giant step toward the first Grand Slam — winning all four major championships in the same year. Sorenstam had begun by taking the Kraft Nabisco late in March. This LPGA was next. It was not only No. 2 of her Slam conquests, but her second straight win, her sixth victory of the season (in eight outings), her 19th in the past 38 tournaments, and her ninth major. This was also her 62nd career victory. At the moment, Sorenstam was making a shambles of women's golf. The other players were looking pretty deficient. Davies, a dominant player herself on the LPGA Tour in the 1990s, put it all in perspective.

"It doesn't mean we're not good, it just means she's exceptional," Davies said. "It's almost like she's toying with us, like a mouse and a cat."

And that was as good a working definition of Sorenstam as anyone had ventured. As to the Grand Slam, observers would do well to recall that she took the Kraft Nabisco by eight strokes and that she won this one by three, and it wasn't that close. She had already announced her intention of winning the Grand Slam. Now it was two down, two to go. This was only the fifth time that a player had won the first two of the four majors, and the last time for that was 19 years ago.

"My goal was to win here and I've done that," Sorenstam said. "I worked hard for this and I want to enjoy it. I know it's going to be a lot of pressure. That's the goal I set, and if I want to achieve my goal, that's what I will have to accept. Right now, I want to absorb this."

What Sorenstam was doing was almost too much for others to absorb. Even in this win, she was on a picnic for the first 14 holes in the final round, and then only a few stray shots down the stretch cut her margin to three. What made it look like a contest is that Michelle Wie, the 15-year-old amateur marvel, closed strong to finish second, passing up veteran Laura Davies and rookie sensation Paula Creamer.

And thereby hangs one tale: An amateur in the Ladies Professional Golf Association Championship? One can only imagine the chats in the back room, but the organization changed its criteria to admit the first amateur in the 51-year history of the tournament.

Sorenstam played the par-72 Bulle Rock Golf Club at Havre de Grace, Maryland, in 68-67-69-73–277, 11 under par. Wie shot 69-71-71-69–280.

The threat to Sorenstam, such as it was, came in the first round, when she trailed by a stroke behind Davies, Natalie Gulbis and Laura Diaz, co-leaders tied at 67. If Gulbis was intimidated by Sorenstam, it didn't show. They were tied coming up their final fairway (No. 9), and Gulbis dropped an 18-foot putt at the last hole — for her fifth straight birdie. Davies, who hadn't won in four years, overpowered the par-fives. At the 596-yard 11th, thought to be the longest ever in women's golf, she hit a drive of over 300 yards and hit the driver again, trying to reach in two. She was about 30 yards short, but got an easy birdie. She had eagle putts on two other par-fives.

Paula Creamer, 18, birdied four straight holes late in her round for a 68, and Michelle Wie, who just finished 10th grade in high school and playing for the first time since tying for 14th in the Kraft Nabisco, shot a 69 looking a little queasy. "I feel really stupid saying this," Wie said. "I ate too much. Every time I breathed, it felt like I would be sick." The episode passed without incident. And Karrie Webb shot the most rewarding 74 of her career. It marked her 10th official event of the year. She had fulfilled the last requirement for entering the LPGA Hall of Fame.

Sorenstam took over the tournament in the second round with three iron shots that left her tap-in birdies — a sand wedge at the 14th, a sand wedge at the 16th and a seven iron at the 17th. "It's a great rush," Sorenstam said. "You picture something, it feels solid, and you look up and it's tap-ins." The 67 gave her a two-shot lead over Davies. Davies was still formidable. She nearly drove the 330-yard 16th, and chipped in from 30 feet for an eagle. But her putting problems cost her a 70. She three-putted for bogey three times, and she missed a birdie from five feet at the last hole. Still, she was encouraged. "If ever I was going to do well, this is the sort of course," Davies said. "It's built for a long-hitter." She didn't have to be reminded that Sorenstam again was pulling away. "She hasn't had a bogey all week," Davies said. "She's already at six [under par]. She's getting on my nerves."

It only got worse. Sorenstam expanded her lead from two to five shots in the third round, shooting a 69–204. Davies, frustrated, saw a big gamble go sour. She made four birdies on the back nine and got within three shots of Sorenstam. Then at the 330-yard 16th, where she had eagled the day before, she took her driver again. This time she ended up in waist-high grass so thick that she could only wedge the ball 30 feet. She ended up with a bogey, and Sorenstam birdied. At the par-three 17th, Davies hit into the rough and three-putted for a double bogey. Sorenstam birdied from six feet. Davies finished with a 74 and slipped to a tie for third with Wie at 211. Korea's Young Kim slipped up into second with a 68, five behind. Davies was seven back. Her bid was done for.

"I know what Laura is all about," Sorenstam said. "As a spectator, it's fun to watch. I try not to watch too much. She plays with her heart. I like to say I play with my brain."

And so she did. But not entirely without glitches in the last round. The championship was pretty much Sorenstam's. She was leading by eight through the final turn. Then she played some shaky golf down the home stretch. After a birdie-bogey exchange at the 10th and 11th, she bogeyed the 15th, 17th and 18th for a one-over 73 and the 277 total. Wie, playing in the group just ahead, made only one bogey in the final round and finished second by three strokes, but the final wasn't that close. Wie was remarkable, nonetheless. This was a 15-year-old making just seven bogeys in four rounds.

"I was trying to make it a run for her money," Wie said. "I don't want to prove anything to anyone. I was really happy to be here, and I felt like I finished really strong."

Next for Sorenstam in the chase of the Grand Slam was the U.S. Women's Open in two weeks. And if others couldn't believe Sorenstam's work, they weren't alone. "I do have to pinch myself sometimes," Sorenstam said. "I feel like I'm just a little girl from Sweden that came over here to follow my dreams and hope to win a few golf tournaments. When I look at my bio in the LPGA book, I get overwhelmed."

# Wegmans Rochester LPGA—$1,500,000
Winner: Lorena Ochoa

Lorena Ochoa knew the feeling — the pain and the helplessness as the game comes undone and victory slips away. So she could sympathize with teenage rookie sensation Paula Creamer. But only to a point. Ochoa had a tournament to win. Trailing by five strokes, Ochoa ran off six birdies over the last seven holes and raced past a faltering Creamer to take the Wegmans Rochester LPGA by four strokes.

"It's hard to believe right now, what I did," Ochoa said. "You have to just really believe, and make it real."

And so ended a battle of the tour's future. After Wales's Becky Morgan led the first round with an eight-under 64 on rainy, chilly Locust Hill Country Club, the tournament turned into a battle between two young stars. Ochoa, 23, who won twice in her second year, 2004, was a runner-up three times this year. Creamer, an 18-year-old from Florida, scored her first win in the Sybase Classic a month earlier, and went from one big ceremony to another — from the 18th green to her high school graduation.

Ochoa made the first move, vaulting into the second-round lead over Morgan on a 69 for a two-stroke edge, taking advantage of the lift-stroke-place relief from the sodden course. "But I don't know how I shot so good," she said. "Sometimes, things go your way." Creamer could say much the same. She birdied three of her first four holes, and ducked disaster at the 18th, where she got a free drop in deep rough and chipped in for a birdie from 25 yards. "Right when I hit it, I knew it was good," she said. It gave her a 68 and 139 total, three behind Ochoa.

Creamer took her turn in the third round, shooting a 67 that included three straight birdies from the 15th, on putts of 12, four and five feet. Her biggest joy was a par-saving 15-footer at the 18th. "Just making that putt makes me sleep better tonight," said Creamer, whose 10-under 206 total led Ochoa by two. Ochoa had a rocky one-under-par first nine, bogeyed the 15th and 16th, then birdied the 17th for a 72 and 208 total. "It's okay to have a so-so round today," Ochoa said. "I'm hoping tomorrow is my good day."

So Creamer took a two-stroke lead into the final round, and promptly plunged into a head-to-head duel with Ochoa. Creamer bogeyed No. 1, then birdied five of the next 10 holes. She birdied Nos. 2 and 3 from 20 feet, No. 6 from six feet, and No. 8 from four feet. She added the par-five 11th on two putts from the edge, and then trouble set in. She bogeyed the 12th after hitting into trees, and bogeyed the last two from short range. There went the second victory of her young career, and the second in a month.

Disappointed as she was, Creamer was awed by Ochoa's performance — six birdies over the last seven holes, five of them in a row. "If I was going to get beat, that's the way I wanted to get beat," Creamer said. "Just someone who lit it up."

## U.S. Women's Open—$3,100,000
Winner: Birdie Kim

There would be no Grand Slam in 2005. Annika Sorenstam didn't win the U.S. Women's Open. She would have to remain for now in the exclusive but disappointed company of those who won the first two of the LPGA's four designated major championships — the Kraft Nabisco and the McDonald's LPGA, in this case — but got no further. She was only the fifth player to go that far.

So at this U.S. Women's Open at Cherry Hills Country Club, near Denver, what didn't happen was as important as what did. What didn't happen was the Sorenstam story. What did is that a little-known 23-year-old South Korean apparently blessed with a touch of prescience, did win. She was born Ju-Yun Kim, but changed her first name to Birdie, to distinguish herself from other Koreans named Kim. She also distinguished herself by winning this U.S. Women's Open, and as fate would have it, with a birdie on the last hole.

This was Kim's first time in the U.S. Women's Open, and her first victory in her two years on the LPGA Tour. If these had the ring of destiny, so did the way she won it. She put her approach shot to the 18th green into a bunker, 30 yards from the hole. Her blast came out low and hot, as though it had been half-bladed. It barely cleared the shoulder of the bunker, and seemed headed well across the green. Kim couldn't see the hole. The jammed gallery let her know when the earth fell out from under the ball, and it dropped in for — what else? — a birdie. It was the only birdie of the day at the 18th.

"I'm not a real good bunker player," Kim said. "Also, I changed my sand wedge about two weeks ago. So I have a lot of misses this week with bunker shots. Finally, I make it."

Down the fairway in the final pairing, Morgan Pressel, the 17-year-old amateur from Florida, was set to make some history of her own. She and Kim were tied for the lead at four over par. Kim was expecting no better than par out of that bunker, and Pressel was in the fairway with a chance to make birdie and become the youngest major champion ever in golf. Then Pressel looked up and saw Kim's bunker shot race across the green, then drop out of sight.

"It was like, 'I can't believe that actually just happened,'" Pressel said. From there, she tried desperately for a tying birdie, bogeyed instead, and tied for second with Brittany Lang, 19, an amateur from Texas.

Was it an anomaly, or was it the beginning of the changing of the guard? This wasn't the U.S. Women's Open of the powerful and famous, but of the young, the little known and the unknown. Consider that 10 of the top 30 LPGA Tour money winners missed the cut, headed by No. 12, Laura Davies, shooting 84-81.

Birdie Kim was, at best, barely noticed all week and never figured to be a threat until the final hole. She shot 74-72-69-72 for a 287 total, at three over par, the first over-par winning total since Se Ri Pak, the first Korean to win the U.S. Women's Open, took it in a playoff after tying at six over par in 1998.

Sorenstam was the star of this Open, but Michelle Wie, the 15-year-old amateur whiz, had second billing of this week-long celebration of youth and the amateur. She had finished second to Sorenstam in the McDonald's LPGA just two weeks earlier, and it was taken for granted that she was going to win something big soon. When the storm-suspended first round was completed on Friday, Wie was tied for the lead at two-under-par 69 with Lang, Angela Stamford and France's Karine Icher.

At the halfway point, Wie, with a 73, tied for second with Lorena Ochoa (68) at even-par 142, two shots behind Chile's Nicole Perrot, the only player under par. Paula Creamer, 18, who won her first professional event just five weeks earlier, had the wildest round of the tournament in the second round. Playing with an upset stomach, Creamer was six over par for her first four holes and clearly heading for the door. Then she played the next nine holes in a remarkable eight under to take the lead. Then she bogeyed three straight holes and finished at 69–143, making the cut by seven strokes.

Through this all, the star of the show wasn't getting anywhere.

Sorenstam was doing some uncharacteristic things. In the second round, she bogeyed her last three holes for a 75 and fell six strokes off the lead. "Thirty-six holes of golf left," she said. "Six strokes is nothing." Early in the third round she three-putted for a bogey and four-putted for a double bogey. She held the damage to a 73 and was only five off the lead, which she was when she won her first LPGA title in 1995.

"I've got 18 more holes to play," Sorenstam said. "I'm going to give it my all." And in her last chance, she tried to drive the first green, as Arnold Palmer did when he made up seven strokes in winning the 1960 U.S. Open. But she hit a tree, her ball bounced into a creek, and she ended up with a 77 and a 12-over 296 total. "Just didn't happen," she said.

As Sorenstam's hopes were sinking, the restless young were rising. Only one amateur had ever won the U.S. Women's Open, and that was the Frenchwoman Catherine Lacoste, 38 years ago, in 1967. And now, starting the third round, two were in position to win it. Wie and Pressel were tied for the lead along with Karen Stupples, 32, winner of the Weetabix Women's British Open a year ago. Stupples crashed the picture with six straight birdies for a 69. Birdie Kim's name surfaced for the first time. She had shot 69, and this would make her an asterisk in the record book — Wie's playing partner in the final round, in the next-to-last pairing.

Dreams went crashing down everywhere in that final round. With Sorenstam pretty much out of the picture, all eyes fell on Wie — and widened when she double-bogeyed the first hole. She shot 82 and plummeted to a tie for 23rd. Creamer started tied for fourth, shot 79, and plunged to a tie for 19th. Stupples shot 78 and slid into a tie for 10th. Lorena Ochoa was coming out of the pack, and got to three under for the round, which was three over for the tournament. That might have won. Then she hit her drive into the water at the 18th and made a quadruple-bogey eight, shot 72 and tied for sixth. The tears came. "I fought so hard for 71 holes," Ochoa said. "And just the last one, you know ..."

And suddenly, it was Morgan Pressel the likely winner. She had birdied No. 2, then bogeyed three straight from No. 4, and bogeyed the 13th and was in the fairway at the 18th, at four over for the tournament. Kim had scattered five bogeys and three birdies, and she was also at four over, but in the bunker at the 18th, facing a par at best and possibly a bogey. It was Advantage — Pressel. Until Kim holed that bunker shot for a one-over 72. Pressel desperately tried to catch her. She tried to run a five iron up on the green, but came up short, in the rough. She tried to hole her pitch, but the ball ran well past the pin. She dabbed at some tears, then two-putted for a 75 and a tie for second with Lang. Kim had won by two, and was at least as surprised as anyone.

Kim was asked whether she had thought, before the Open, that she could win. "Never," she said. And it came on a shot that "not a real good bunker player" was only hoping to save par with. "I have confidence to make close to the pin," Kim said. "Maybe get close, maybe really close," and she added: "It goes in!"

## HSBC Women's World Match Play—$2,000,000
Winner: Marisa Baena

The way seeding is supposed to work, the lower seeds are there to give the tournament favorites a chance to warm up for the marquee matches. In this inaugural HSBC Women's World Match Play, the lower seeds had no respect. Of the 32 first-round matches, 17 were taken by lower seeds. Then eight of the 16 winners in the second round were lower seeds. And going into the third round, only two of the top 12 were still alive — Annika Sorenstam, No. 1, and Candie Kung, No. 8

Buried in there somewhere among the upstarts was the name Marisa Baena, age 28, a native of Colombia and former University of Arizona All-American. She couldn't get much lower. In a field of 64, she was 60th. But when the smoke cleared the final day early in July, Baena — who had all but despaired of ever making her mark on the LPGA Tour — was No. 1. She finished 132nd on the money list in 2004 and lost her tour card. And now she was a champion.

"After June of last year," Baena said, "I said I was going to give myself two more years, and that was it." To prepare for this final assault on her dreams, she switched coaches, made some swing changes, and changed her approach to the game. So she was, by her account, a different golfer when she arrived at Hamilton Farm Golf Club in Gladstone, New Jersey.

"This year, I came very relaxed," Baena said. "I said, 'You know what — I'm just going to enjoy it.'" The first installment on that enjoyment was paid in the first round by fifth-seeded Natalie Gulbis, 1 up. Then down went Grace Park (37), Jennifer Rosales (21), Karrie Webb (29), Candie Kung (8). And they were grudging battles all the way. Her wins, in order, were 19 holes, 20 holes, 2 and 1, and 2 and 1.

And finally, 1 up over South Korean rookie Meena Lee, herself the 47th seed. "My goal coming into the tournament was just to get through the first two rounds," Lee said.

Lee, who was runner-up in the Corning Classic in May, rallied to put Baena's victory very much in doubt. Lee was all but beaten, 3 down with four holes to play, when she started her comeback. She won the 15th, holing a nine-foot putt for birdie, and won the 16th, also with a birdie, this from 15 feet. Baena's lead had been cut to one. Then Lee got a half at the 17th with a stunning up-and-down from the back rough on an eight-footer.

Baena then won the 18th when Lee conceded her a par. "When I was 3 down, I kept repeating to myself, 'Try to get back one hole at a time,'" Lee said. "I was so close to winning. I am disappointed. But I gained a lot of confidence."

Said Baena: "I've been waiting for this moment since I turned pro."

## Jamie Farr Owens Corning Classic—$1,200,000
Winner: Heather Bowie

Heather Bowie had been six years trying to get that first victory, and now she came to the final round of the Jamie Farr Owens Corning Classic five strokes out of the lead and doomed — she thought — to wait yet longer.

"At the beginning of the day, I just kept telling myself I was so far out of it so I wouldn't think about it," said Bowie, and she was resigned to just trying to shoot a good final round at Highland Meadows, near Toledo, Ohio. And she did that, a four-under-par 67, but this time it got her a tie and a playoff against Gloria Park. Then she parred the third extra hole for that elusive first win.

"I'm thrilled to get the opportunity in a playoff after making bogey on 17 in regulation," said Bowie, who shot 72-66-69-67–274, 10 under par. Bowie was not really in the hunt through the first three rounds. She was five strokes back in the first round, when Becky Morgan and U.S. Women's Open champion Birdie Kim shared the lead at 65. Bowie was three behind as veteran Beth Daniel found some old magic and shot 65–135 in the second round. And in the third round, South Korea's Hee-Won Han, a three-time winner, birdied two of the last three holes for a 66 and an 11-under 202, to lead countrywoman Jeong Jang by two. Bowie, with a 69, was five back. But hope popped up fast.

Early in the final round, Han expanded her lead, but after a birdie at the 10th, she stumbled to two bogeys and a double bogey over a four-hole stretch and shot 73, dropping into a tie for third with Sung Ah Yim (68). Bowie, meanwhile, was on a roll. She posted six birdies, including five over an eight-hole stretch. At No. 6, she hit an eight iron to eight feet, and a six iron to eight feet at No. 10. Her wedges set her up from 25 feet at the seventh, seven feet at the 12th and 30 feet at the 13th. She missed the green at the 11th and 17th, and bogeyed both.

Park got to 10 under with birdies at the 15th and 17th, and when Bowie just missed a birdie at the 18th, they were in the playoff. At the first hole, the par-five 18th, Park holed a 12-foot putt for par to tie Bowie. At the second, the 17th, Park holed a 20-footer to tie Bowie again. At the third extra hole, No. 18 again, Park drove into the right rough and knocked her three-wood second shot into the water. Bowie, who had driven into the water, was in the clear. She then laid up, hit her third to 12 feet and two-putted for her winning par.

"It was a tremendous relief," Bowie said. "A huge monkey off my back — getting bigger every year."

## BMO Financial Group Canadian Women's Open—$1,300,000
Winner: Meena Lee

Meena Lee, a 23-year-old rookie, didn't cover her eyes, but she did the next best thing. She ducked behind the skyboxes and wouldn't look, and sent her caddie out to see how Janice Moodie was doing on the final hole. The BMO Financial Group Canadian Women's Open was hanging in the balance. More than that — her first career victory was hanging in the balance, and it was too much for her to bear. Moodie, an eight-year veteran, who had led all three rounds, was only a stroke behind and needed a birdie to tie her.

Then Lee's caddie came back with a grin and a thumb's-up. Moodie had double-bogeyed. Lee was the winner. Now she covered her eyes and cried. A career-first and a national championship all in one. And it was a fitting exclamation point to a season that had been a Jekyll-Hyde season. In her first eight starts, she finished in the money only twice. Her best was a tie for 69th. But in the past eight, leading up to mid-July, she finished second twice, and now posted her first win.

"I'm finally piecing it together," said Lee, after piecing together a 73-68-69-69—279 total, nine under at the par-72 Glen Arbour Golf Club in Nova Scotia. She won by one over Katherine Hull. For Moodie, it was a tough week. She was still mourning the death of her father back home in Scotland a month ago. She was solid for the first three rounds, shooting 66-69-72. Lee was never really in contention in that span, trailing Moodie by seven in the first round, then six, and then three. When none of the closer pursuers could make a move, the way was open to Lee.

She birdied No. 7 with a six iron to inches, and No. 10 with an eight iron to 20 feet. She birdied the 12th from inches and the 13th from 15 feet. She stumbled to two bogeys, hitting a shot into the water at the 14th and missing the green at the 15th. And what ultimately won for her was the birdie at the 16th, on a wedge to five feet. She joined Paula Creamer as the only rookies to win this year so far.

And while Lee was hiding behind the skybox, Moodie three-putted the 18th for a double bogey and a 75, and tied for sixth. Hull closed with a 69—280 and a career-best second place. "I feel fine at the beginning," Lee said. "In the middle, it was getting very intense." And at the end, it was great.

## Evian Masters—$2,500,000
Winner: Paula Creamer

See Ladies European Tour section.

## Weetabix Women's British Open—£1,050,000
Winner: Jeong Jang

See Ladies European Tour section.

## Safeway Classic—$1,400,000
Winner: Soo-Yun Kang

Anyone doubting the rise of women's golf in South Korea only had to check the scoreboard at the Safeway Classic. Soo-Yun Kang, scoring her first victory in her three years on the LPGA Tour, took it by a comfortable but hard-won four-stroke margin. But look again at that scoreboard. It was top heavy with Koreans: second, Jeong Jang, winner of the Weetabix Women's British Open three weeks ago; third, Gloria Park; fourth, Joo Mi Kim, and tied for fifth, Sung Ah Yim. But it was Kang's tournament all the way.

It was the third win by a South Korean in the last four tournaments and the fifth in the last 11. All five were first-time winners, and two of them won majors.

Kang opened with a 64, tying with Yim for the first-round lead. She closed with 68-69, the solo leader through both, for a 201 total, a whopping 15 under par at the par-72 Columbia Edgewater Country Club in Portland, Oregon. "I waited so long, for the past three years," said Kang, leading money winner on the Korean Tour in 2001 and 2002. "I guess I was like in a slump for three years and I worked really hard on it."

Kang played it like a veteran in the final round. She started with a three-stroke lead and made four birdies in the first seven holes. The jewel was a 60-foot putt for a birdie at the par-three No. 2. And all this was under pressure. She couldn't shake the tenacious Jang, and led her by only two at the turn. If Kang had an uneasy moment, it came at the 12th when she hit a tree with her tee shot. But she got a great break when the ball kicked back into the fairway, and she accepted the gift and turned it into a birdie and a three-shot lead.

"Before that hole, J.J. was keeping pace and trying to come after me," Kang said, through a translator. "But after that hole, I felt confident I was going to win."

## Wendy's Championship for Children—$1,100,000
Winner: Cristie Kerr

For Cristie Kerr, winning is something of an exercise in psychology, which is about as good as anything.

"Winning is a learned behavior," Kerr was saying, after tucking away the Wendy's Championship for Children. "That's what I did today. I relied on my experience and my patience and I was able to hang on."

Hanging on — that was an apt expression. In scoring her second win of the year and sixth of her career, she had to turn back Annika Sorenstam, No. 1 in the world, bright newcomer Paula Creamer, age 19, and the veteran Pat Hurst. Kerr, who didn't surface until the third round, closed with a 69 for an 18-under-par 270 total and a one-stroke victory over Creamer (71) and Sorenstam (66). Hurst fell to a tie for fourth after a freakish double-bogey six at the last hole cost her a tie for the lead. Her drop from an unplayable lie glanced off the tee she used as a distance marker and rolled into the bushes. She shot 70 and finished two behind Kerr. "I'm not going to dwell on it," Hurst said. "You can't go back."

The tournament, played at Tartan Fields, near Columbus, Ohio, began with the season's biggest first-round tie for the lead — five at six-under 66, in a United Nations mix: Heather Daly-Donofrio of the United States; Paula Marti, Spain; Soo-Yun Kang, South Korea; Marisa Baena, Colombia, and defending champion Catriona Matthew, Scotland. The next nine were at 67. Kerr (68) was tied for 15th. Things began to get sorted out in the second round. Matthew eagled No. 9, then birdied No. 18 from 10 feet for another 66, and Kang overcame a watery triple-bogey seven at the 12th and also shot another 66, and they were tied for the lead at 132. Creamer (66) was two back, Kerr (67) three, and Sorenstam (67) four.

Things changed dramatically in the third round. While Matthew blew to a 77, Creamer birdied the first three holes, then bogeyed the last two in a 66 and took a one-stroke lead on Kang (69) and Kerr (66). An erratic Sorenstam eagled the par-five No. 9 and was five under through 11 holes. At the 14th, she took her first bogey of the tournament, then made another, plus a double bogey at the 16th for a 69, and was five behind.

It was a battle down the last round, with Kerr, Creamer and Kang in the final group. Kerr tied Creamer at the second, dropping a five-foot birdie putt, then broke free with birdies at the 11th, 12th and 13th on her way to the winning 69. Sorenstam rocketed with a 66, but fell a stroke short. And Kerr didn't win without heat. Creamer, who clinched the LPGA Rookie of the Year Award with her tie for second, and Kang often walked ahead, clearly unhappy with Kerr's deliberate play.

"I wish we'd been on the clock," said Kang (72), who tied for sixth. "She is always slow. If the pace was better, I'd have had a better chance."

## State Farm Classic—$1,300,000
Winner: Pat Hurst

"Even with what happened, I brought a lot of confidence from last week," Pat Hurst was explaining after taking a three-stroke lead in the third round of the State Farm Classic at the Rail Golf Club at Springfield, Illinois. She would ride that confidence to her fourth LPGA Tour career victory the next day, but it was a success born of frustration and disappointment.

Just a week earlier, in the Wendy's Championship for Children, she was tied with Cristie Kerr going to the final hole. Her chance to win died when her penalty drop glanced off her marker tee into more trouble and cost her a double bogey. "I won't dwell on it," she had said, and clearly she didn't. No sooner had she reached the State Farm than she bounced back to a 67 in the first round, just two strokes behind Heather Bowie, who chipped in for an eagle in a bogey-free 65 for a one-stroke lead.

Sherri Turner (69) and Toni Barrett (69), both winless since 1989, tied for the halfway lead at 135. Hurst came within a stroke with a 69, but she was all over the map getting there. She had eight birdies, one bogey and two double-bogeys in a 69. No matter.

"I can't think about that," Hurst said, brushing it away. "It's over and done with. I got the birdies and will carry that into Saturday and Sunday." How right she was. She vaulted into a commanding lead with a 65 for a course-record 201 for three rounds. She was three ahead of Kim Williams

(66) and four ahead of Cristie Kerr (67), the defending champion. "I'm hitting the ball pretty good," Hurst said. "I just started making some putts."

A renewal of the Wendy's duel was shaping up. Said Kerr, who would lead the U.S. team against Europe in the Solheim Cup the next week, "I haven't been hitting the ball that great, but toward the end I started getting the feel back." And Hurst, who would be a teammate of Kerr in the Solheim, said she wouldn't sit on her lead. "I don't think that's comfortable since there are a lot of birdies out there," Hurst said. "I think if I go out and make some birdies, I'll be okay."

Right again — four birdies over the first five holes with a sizzling putter. She holed putts of 10 and 12 feet on the first two, needed two putts from 30 at the par-five No. 4, then dropped a 15-footer at No. 5. It wasn't a flawless round. She had two bogeys and a double bogey at the par-five 12th, where she hit her second shot out of bounds. She bogeyed the 13th when she missed the green, then holed a 22-footer for her sixth and final birdie at the 14th, and parred in for a 70 and a three-stroke victory. Next, it was on to the Solheim Cup.

"It's going to be a lot of fun," Hurst said, "and representing your country just feels so good."

## Solheim Cup
Winner: United States

It was a classic tale of rookie vs. veteran, of youth being served. In the singles of the 2005 Solheim Cup, it was American rookie Paula Creamer, age 19, the youngest player in the event's history, meeting the only woman to have played in all nine, the European veteran Laura Davies. This was the key singles match. The teams had battled to an 8-8 tie through two days of team matches, and now it had come down to one-on-one. Creamer and Davies were in the second match Sunday. Against all odds, and probably against all American dreams, Creamer racked up seven birdies in 13 holes and blitzed Davies, 7 and 5. This was the first point of the day, and if one match can trigger an entire team, this had to be it.

The Americans took over from there, swept the first five matches, and took the singles by 7½ to 4½ to take the cup, 15½ to 12½.

"This is a huge feat for me," Creamer said. "It was one of my goals to get here, and when I got here, I wanted to win. This is an unbelievable experience." She could have been speaking for the Americans for the entire 2005 Solheim Cup — an unbelievable experience. They sure didn't have a hint of this when the matches began.

### First Day – Alternate Shot
Just when the Americans thought they finally had this alternate shot business all sorted out — after captain Nancy Lopez sent them through drills — it was back to square one. The Americans were losing in one match but cruising along in the other three, leading by at least 2 up well into the second nine. And Europe reversed all three. The most stunning blow came from Annika Sorenstam and Suzann Pettersen, nicely paired by European captain Catrin Nilsmark. They were 4 down with six to play, and won five straight holes — four with birdies — to take the lead, and halved the last

for a 1-up victory over Laura Diaz and Michele Redman. Sorenstam set off the rally when she nearly aced the par-three 13th and won it with a birdie. Pettersen dropped a 35-footer for birdie at the par-three 17th for a 1-up lead. "You just get those moments and you want to grab them," Pettersen said. "Momentum is everything in match play," said Davies, after she and Maria Hjorth never trailed in a 2-and-1 win over Cristie Kerr and Natalie Gulbis. The Europeans won two matches and halved two.

Europe leads, 3 to 1.

### First Day – Better-Ball

The U.S. lost another two matches after leading, but won two. Davies and Pettersen trailed for the first two holes, then led from the fourth and won going away, 4 and 3, over Creamer and Juli Inkster. Pat Hurst and Wendy Ward led for five holes through No. 9, but ended up losing by 2 and 1 to Sorenstam and Catriona Matthew. Kerr and Gulbis bounced back to beat Sophie Gustafson and Karen Stupples 2 and 1, and Rosie Jones, birdieing six of the first 10 holes, teamed with Meg Mallon for a 3-and-2 win over Hjorth and Iben Tinning. With the 2-2 tie, the Americans actually lost ground because Europe was two points closer to winning.

Europe, 5 to 3.

### Second Day – Alternate Shot

Sorenstam, who slammed the door on the Americans with her rally in Friday's alternate shot, opened it this time. She missed short birdie putts at Nos. 8 and 9, missed a 10-footer at No. 17, and watered her tee shot at No. 18, and Hurst and Redman won 2 up. "All you can do is forget about it," Sorenstam said. The other two American wins came more easily. In a battle of all rookies, Gulbis and Christina Kim outdistanced the French, Gwladys Nocera and Ludivine Kreutz, 4 and 2, and Creamer and Inkster combined for six birdies against no bogeys in their 3-and-2 win over Davies and Hjorth. By taking the morning, 3-1, the U.S. squared the Solheim.

Tie, 6 to 6.

### Second Day – Better-Ball

Creamer was again the hero for the Americans. After she and Kerr went 3 down, she birdied five of nine holes to pull them into a 1-up win over Carin Koch and Matthew. Davies and Sorenstam led all the way for a 4-and-2 win over Hurst and Kim, and the other two matches were halved. The 2-2 tie left the matches deadlocked at 8-8. The only other time the Solheim was tied going into the final day was 1994, and the Americans then won decisively.

Tie, 8 to 8.

### Third Day – Singles

Three lopsided matches led to seven American victories. Creamer's 7-and-5 blitz on Davies lit the way. In the battle of the pregnants, Laura Diaz (six months) rushed past Iben Tinning (four months), 6 and 5. And the free-spirited Christina Kim beat Ludivine Kreutz, 5 and 4. Sorenstam trailed for only one hole, then raced off to a 4-and-3 win over Beth Daniel, leading Europe's four wins. With the cup decided, Rosie Jones and Suzann Pettersen halved the meaningless last match. The U.S. took the singles, 7½ to 4½.

United States, 15½ to 12½.

Interestingly enough, the United States was led by two rookies. Creamer (3-1-1) was the top point-getter, and Gulbis (3-1-0) was the only other American with three wins. Sorenstam, to no one's surprise, was the individual standout, with a 4-1-0 record, and Davies (3-2-0) was a close second.

## John Q. Hammons Hotel Classic—$1,000,000
Winner: Annika Sorenstam

It was a fine time for a golfer to pick up that first victory, and so thought, among others, Sweden's Maria Hjorth, Australia's Michelle Ellis and France's Karine Icher. And for a while, it seemed one of them might break through in the John Q. Hammons Hotel Classic at Broken Arrow, Oklahoma. Alas, who should be in the field but defending champion Annika Sorenstam. Scratch No. 1. Add No. 7 — for the year — Sorenstam.

And while others were seeing the season as just about over at this time, in mid-September, Sorenstam was saying, "The season is far from over for me … For me, it's important to play well at the end of the year. There's a lot of things that are at stake. We're talking money list … player of the year, Vare Trophy. Those are goals of mine and they mean a lot. A victory here sets me up a little closer to my goals."

That wasn't a vintage Sorenstam at Cedar Ridge Country Club. She bogeyed two of her last three holes. But it got her a one-stroke win, her first since the McDonald's LPGA Championship in June. And it was her third straight Hammons title, her seventh victory in 14 starts, one short of her harvest in 2004, plus a win on the European Tour earlier.

Sorenstam, taking the lead in the second round, shot the three-round event in 68-67-73 for a five-under 208 to beat rookie sensation Paula Creamer by one. Sorenstam opened the final round with a one-stroke lead over Hjorth (72) and Ellis (69), then ground out 15 straight pars. But not on purpose, she said. "I wasn't trying to just make pars," she said, "because I figured there's some birdies out there, and the last thing you want to do is just go out there cruising, and all of a sudden somebody catches you."

That someone was Creamer, seeking her third victory. The rookie started five strokes off the lead and birdied the 13th and 14th to get within two of Sorenstam. Then she had a ragged finish — bogeys at the 16th and 17th, then a birdie at the 18th for a 69 and a four-under total. Sorenstam was more ragged. After those 15 pars, she bogeyed the 16th and 18th for a two-over 73.

"I knew I had to play good golf," Creamer said. "She's not going to make mistakes come Sunday."

But Sorenstam did make mistakes. "Luckily, I had a little cushion … and I needed it," she said. "For me, a win is a win."

## Office Depot Championship—$1,300,000
Winner: Hee-Won Han

It was an ill wind that blew a lot of good for South Korea's Hee-Won Han. The Office Depot Championship at Trump National, near Los Angeles, was hit with so much bad early fall weather that each round had to be suspended and completed the next day. And thus did Han find herself stranded during the third and final round Sunday and have to come back and finish it Monday.

"At first, I was very unhappy about playing on Monday, but I am so much more happy now," Han said. "Actually, it was a pretty good thing, because yesterday I was just waiting for five hours on the course and played eight holes. It didn't feel very good. But this morning, I came back pretty good and started birdie-birdie. That's good for me."

It was better than good. It was great. Han went on from there to wrap up a two-stroke victory over friend and fellow Korean Soo-Yun Kang for her career fourth victory. Han was atop the leaderboard for all three rounds. A six-under-par 65 in the first round gave her a share of the lead with Wendy Ward, Nicole Perrot and Karine Icher. She shot 68 in the second for a nine-under 133 total, tying with another Korean, Jeong Jang (66), the British Women's Open champion. And then the closing 68 gave her a 12-under 201 and the two-shot win over Kang.

Han began the final round Sunday afternoon, leading Tina Barrett and Jennifer Rosales by three strokes. She bogeyed No. 3, then birdied No. 7 with a 25-foot putt. She parred No. 8 and was nine under when play was called because of darkness about 6:30. Came Monday morning and an 8 a.m. start, and she dropped an eight-footer at the ninth and a 14-footer at the 10th. The two quick birdies brightened her spirits. She got her last birdie at the 14th, on a wedge to six feet. Kang gave hot pursuit. She also came out on Monday morning and birdied the 11th and 12th, and got her final birdie at the par-five 14th.

"When there was a four-shot difference between us, I thought I might catch her," Kang said. "But then I missed many birdie putts and she did great, so I couldn't."

## Longs Drugs Challenge—$1,000,000
Winner: Nicole Perrot

In Chile, golf is almost exclusively a social recreation. So except for a sprinkling of male pros on the European Tour, Nicole Perrot is the Chilean of note on the international stage. She first drew attention by winning the U.S. Girls' Junior Championship in 2001, then joined the Futures Tour, developmental circuit to the LPGA Tour, and won twice in 2004. On the LPGA Tour, she played only five times in three years as a non-exempt player, and though only 21, when she had to she showed she could play like the crustiest veteran out there.

This was in the Longs Drug Challenge in October, where she led by three strokes going into the final round, blew it all and fell two behind with nine to play, and rallied to win by a shot with a 14-under-par 270. She was the 10th first-time winner on the tour.

"I knew it was going to be tough, but I didn't panic when I made the early bogeys," Perrot said. "I just tried to stay patient."

Perrot was seven back with her opening 69, after Cristie Kerr walloped the Ridge Golf Club near Sacramento, California, with a 62 (a 75-77 middle would end her). Perrot moved unnoticed into the picture with a 66 that left her two behind after 36 holes. Then came the seven-under 64 in the third. She three-putted the 13th for a bogey, then birdied three holes coming in, including the 18th, where she dropped a 10-foot putt for the 64 and 14-under 199 total. It put her three ahead of Sweden's Liselotte Neumann (64), veteran of 13 tour victories, and South Korea's Hee-Won Han (66), who scored her fourth win in the Office Depot Championship a week earlier. Could Perrot keep her head through one more round?

"Nicole is aggressive," said Neumann. "She's a tough player. I don't think she will be scared." (Neumann would close with a 72 and tie for third.)

Said Perrot: "Winning is always great. I'm ready for it to happen, but I'm not pushing it. I will really just try to focus on my game and what I'm feeling."

It took a little while for that determination to kick in. In the final round she bogeyed three of her first five holes — Nos. 1 and 3 on three-putts, and No. 5 after missing the green. Han bogeyed No. 3, then birdied three straight from No. 5 on near tap-ins and took a two-stroke lead. Then Han settled, unwillingly, into pars the rest of the way for a 69. "I tried hard, but my putts weren't going in," Han said.

Perrot started her comeback at the 11th, dropping a six-footer for birdie. She birdied the 15th from a foot to tie Han, then got the decisive stroke with a six-foot putt for birdie at the 16th.

"I hope this will be the first of a lot of wins out here," said Perrot, and then made a pitch for golf in Chile: "This will help get a lot of attention for golf and the LPGA. It is going to be really good for women's sport."

## Samsung World Championship—$850,000
Winner: Annika Sorenstam

There was Annika Sorenstam, No. 1 woman golfer in the world, crushing the field in the exclusive Samsung World Championship, winning by eight shots, racking up her eighth victory of the season by mid-October and topping $2 million in winnings for the fifth consecutive year. And who noticed?

Because this was the professional debut of wondergirl Michelle Wie, and there may never have been one like it. Wie, a high school prodigy of 16, after playing 24 times on the LPGA Tour and five times against men as an amateur, was now officially a professional.

"I wasn't that nervous when I put the ball down on the tee," Wie said. "I wasn't that nervous when I took my practice swings. But once I got over my tee shot, my heart was thumping. It was different."

But as a coming out party, hers turned into a dud. She finished fourth in the field of 20, and won $53,126, only to be disqualified. It developed that Wie had inadvertently taken an improper drop the day before, and therefore had signed an incorrect scorecard — minus the penalty strokes. In one of the all-time awkward moments in golf, the violation was observed by a golf writer, Michael Bamberger of *Sports Illustrated*, but he didn't report it to officials until a day later — far too late for her to correct it.

"I learned a great lesson," Wie said, fighting back tears. "From now on,

I'll call a rules official no matter where it is, whether it's three inches or 100 yards."

It happened at No. 7 in the third round. Wie took a drop from an unplayable lie near a bush, and said she didn't realize that the ball had rolled closer to the hole. Later, she said it was about three inches, and officials said it was 12 to 18 inches. Whichever it was, she saved par. Bamberger, who witnessed the drop, said he wondered whether the drop was good but didn't tell officials at the time because he was still in his "reporter's mode." The episode triggered debate all through the golf world. "I don't think she cheated," Bamberger said. "I just think she was hasty."

"I was honest out there," Wie said. "I did what I thought was right. If I did it again I'd still do that. It looked right to me."

Wie was no stranger to the rules, or to the bushes at Bighorn Golf Club at Palm Desert, California. On Friday, she invoked the "dangerous situation" rule and got a free drop from a bush around which some bees were flying.

For the record, Wie started the final round five strokes behind Sorenstam and bogeyed three of the first five holes. Wie was on the board at 70-65-71-74—280, finishing 10 behind Sorenstam before the fatal DQ came down.

The few paying attention to Sorenstam saw a good show, a 64-71-66-69—270, 18 under par, that beat 19-year-old rookie Paula Creamer by eight strokes. Sorenstam's opening 64, for example, just missed being a 62 when she missed five-footers for birdies at the last two holes. In the third round, she birdied four of the last five holes for the 66 and a four-shot lead. In the final round, she led by 10 before driving into the desert at the 18th and taking a double bogey.

There were those who thought that Sorenstam was trying to regain the spotlight in the Michele Wie Show. Not so, she had already said. "Honestly, I didn't feel like I'm here to prove anything," Sorenstam said. "I'm here to reach my own goals, play my own golf. I see this as an opportunity to win this tournament for the fifth time."

## CJ Nine Bridges Classic—$1,350,000
Winner: Jee Young Lee

It was a coin flip as to which was the bigger story at the CJ Nine Bridges Classic — Jee Young Lee, 19, a rookie on the Korean Tour, scoring her first victory, or Annika Sorenstam, the finest female golfer in the world, playing some of the worst golf she's ever played.

Sorenstam was never near the race. The figures put it bluntly. In the three-round event at the Club at Nine Bridges at Jeju, South Korea, Sorenstam shot 75-75-70, a four-over-par 220 to finish in a tie for 14th, nine strokes behind Lee. Sorenstam may have said it all in the second round. "The wind is difficult to judge," she said, "but on the other hand, I didn't make a single putt."

Lee wasn't waiting for Sorenstam's game to come around. Lee did plenty of stumbling of her own, but no one could get up enough of a challenge against her 65-73-73—211, five under, to win by three over compatriot Mi Hyun Kim and Sweden's Carin Koch.

As things developed, Lee won it with that first-round 65. Starting at No. 10, she parred the first two holes, then birdied seven of the next eight, two on huge putts — a 50-footer at the par-three 17th and a 40-footer at No. 1. "I putted very well today, and it was much better than I expected," Lee said.

But Lee flirted with disaster the rest of the way. She was leading by eight in the second round, then double-bogeyed two of her last five holes and ended up with a three-shot lead and a case of self-doubt. "I would love to win," Lee said, "but I don't know if I am qualified." Her performance in the final round would only feed that doubt, but happily for her she ran out of holes before she ran out of errors. Lee stumbled to three straight bogeys from the 15th.

"I never thought I would win this tournament until the third shot of the 18th hole," Lee said, "I didn't want to think that I won until it was over. I made a lot of mistakes yesterday, and I made a lot of mistakes today, but I held on to it."

## Mizuno Classic—¥110,000,000
Winner: Annika Sorenstam

See Japan LPGA Tour section.

## The Mitchell Company Tournament of Champions—$850,000
Winner: Christina Kim

If you're looking for a working definition of pressure, how about needing two putts from 60 feet to win? That was the burden on the effervescent Christina Kim at the final hole of The Mitchell Company Tournament of Champions. Kim, a Solheim Cup star, was short with her approach at the 18th, and Rachel Hetherington was just 20 feet away from a tying birdie. As Hetherington had observed in the second round, "it still could be anybody's tournament."

And that's what it was from the start, the way it was batted back and forth by Liselotte Neumann, Juli Inkster, defending champion Heather Daly-Donofrio, and others, and especially Hetherington and Kim. And then it came down to the 72nd hole.

Kim rolled her 60-footer to within tap-in range for a sure par. But Hetherington, an eight-time LPGA winner who last won in 2003, was only 20 feet from a tying birdie. "It was pure torture having to sit there and watch," Kim said. "She executes just about every time." But not this time. Hetherington's birdie try slid off, and Kim tapped in for the win, a hug from her father and caddie Man Kim, and a beer shower from fellow player Jennifer Rosales. Kim finished with a 15-under-par total of 273 on the Magnolia Groves Crossing Course near Mobile, Alabama. In or near the lead all the way, Kim shot the par-72 course in 67-67-72-67 to beat Hetherington by a stroke.

Neumann, 39, in the exclusive field of 43 off her 2004 Ashai Ryokuken victory, led the first and third rounds and was putting up some fireworks.

She posted six birdies in an opening 66, and birdied four of her first six holes in her third-round 67, and then birdied the tough 18th to go into the final round a shot up on Daly-Donofrio, Hetherington and Kim. Neumann led by two going into the final nine.

The par-five 13th proved pivotal. Kim, paired with Hetherington, a group ahead of Neumann and Daly-Donofrio, took a two-stroke lead with a par after Neumann drove into the trees and double-bogeyed. Kim logged a two-putt birdie at the 16th, and Hetherington dropped a 15-foot sidehiller at the 17th for a birdie to move to within one going into the 18th.

The first key was Kim's poor approach to the two-tiered green at the 18th. "There was a little bit more wind in my face than I realized," she said. "I didn't have enough club." The ball came down short and trickled back, leaving her about a 60-footer. She did well to get her first putt to tap-in range. Now she was festering while Hetherington faced the 20-footer to tie. But she missed. Kim tapped in and took her place in the front row of the LPGA.

"All of these girls here know how to win because they have done that before," Kim said. "And to know that I can beat them, it's an incredible feeling."

## ADT Championship—$1,000,000
Winner: Annika Sorenstam

Annika Sorenstam, the No. 1 female player in the world, took time in the first round to have a fabulously wild back nine, then pulled away to enjoy her 10th Annika moment of the year, in the season-ending ADT Championship at Trump International, at West Palm Beach, Florida. The challenge, as expected, came from the LPGA Tour's growing youth corps, but not the kind of challenge people expected.

A touch of friction hit the LPGA Tour in the first round. Rookie of the Year Paula Creamer contested Sorenstam's penalty drop from a plugged tee shot in the bunker at the watery 18th. Sorenstam contended she had hit a slice that curved inland, crossing the hazard line, then back out to the bunker next to the lake. Creamer, her playing partner, insisted the ball had gone straight across the water and never crossed the hazard line. Creamer said Sorenstam should have gone back to the tee to hit her third shot. But with no conclusive proof, officials favor the hitter. Under a local rule, Sorenstam was allowed to take her penalty drop in a spot outside near the bunker, leaving her a third shot of only about 190 yards.

"It's her conscience," Creamer said. The implication was clear. Said Sorenstam: "I'm disappointed she feels that way."

At all events Sorenstam double-bogeyed the 18th for a three-under-par 69, two strokes behind the leader, South Korea's Hee-Won Han (67), and one behind Creamer (68).

A great golf experience hid behind Sorenstam's innocent-looking 69. After a flawless five-under front nine, she had a breathtaking back nine — bogey-birdie-par-birdie-double bogey-eagle-bogey-par-double bogey. With that out of her system, Sorenstam led the rest of the way by narrow margins, posting a card of 69-70-74-69–282, six under in rising weather on a tough course. Her second-round 70 in light rain and strong wind was interesting. She had no birdies, but logged two eagles, both with seven-wood shots at par-five holes — to 10 feet at No. 5 and to 12 feet at No. 9. She also bogeyed twice, but still led by two over Han, who three-putted from 18 feet at the 15th and shot 74. Cristie Kerr shot 66 to share third with Michele Redman (73). Creamer suffered two double bogeys and fell back with a 75–143, four shots off. (Creamer would tie for sixth, six strokes behind.)

Sorenstam demonstrated veteran savvy in the wind-whipped third round. She was in a tough lie at the 18th, in the rough with the ball below her feet and a big water hazard next to the green. "This was too dangerous," she said. She laid up and settled for a bogey and a 74–213, and the one-stroke edge over Liselotte Neumann (71) and Marisa Baena (66). Fittingly, the end was dramatic.

Sorenstam began the final round with a one-stroke lead. Neumann ran off three straight birdies from No. 2 on putts of 10 feet and less. Sorenstam responded at the par-five third with a chip-and-putt birdie, then added another at the fifth on a 25-foot putt. Neumann watered a shot at the 10th and double-bogeyed, and then Sorenstam got a surprise. At the 13th, she was leading by two. When she got to the 15th green, her lead was zero. Neumann had tied her. Then came the final crush.

Neumann missed an 18-foot birdie putt at the 17th and looked back to find that Sorenstam had birdied the 16th on a downhill breaking putt. The 17th, a tough par-three with a waterfall behind and water left and right, was her last scary test, and it was witnessed by no less than millionaire entrepreneur Donald Trump himself. If he could have read Sorenstam's mind, he would have heard her saying (as she later revealed): "If you're going to win this championship, you have to hit this shot. You absolutely have to trust the yardage [and] the club."

Sorenstam stuck her seven-iron tee shot eight feet behind the pin, and Trump drove away saying, "That should do it." And so it did. Sorenstam, going over $2.5 million for the third time, had her 10th victory in 20 tournaments, and her career 66th, leaving her third behind all-time winner Kathy Whitworth's 88.

"I'm still 22 away, and it sounds like so much," Sorenstam said. "But then again, I'm on my way."

# Ladies European Tour

### Samsung Ladies Masters—US$200,000
Winner: Bo Bae Song

Playing in her first event sanctioned by the Ladies European Tour, Bo Bae Song won the $30,000 first prize at the Samsung Ladies Masters at Laguna National in Singapore. The victory continued a brilliant start to her professional career for the 18-year-old Korean. The previous season she won twice on the Korean LPGA circuit, not only to win the rookie of the year honors but top the money list and become the Player of the Year.

A first round of 65, seven under par, put Song at the top of the leaderboard in this event co-sanctioned by both the Korean and European circuits. She was only one stroke worse on the second day and with a round to play had established a five-stroke lead. But in the wind on the final day, it was a different matter. Her nearest challenger, Sweden's Charlotta Sorenstam, had advanced to within two strokes at the turn and appeared to be finishing the stronger of the two.

Sorenstam birdied the 16th and made sure of a par at the 17th, a par-three over a huge lake, where Song dropped a shot to leave the pair tied for the lead. But the young Korean held her nerve with an approach at the last to six feet. After Sorenstam had missed her birdie chance from 18 feet, Song made her putt for a one-stroke victory. While the Swede closed with a 71, Song's 75 was just enough at 206, 10 under par.

England's Laura Davies, starting the final round seven strokes behind, closed with a 70 to finish two strokes back in third place with New Zealand's Lynette Brooky.

### Women's World Cup of Golf—US$1,000,000
Winners: Ai Miyazato and Rui Kitada

See South African Women's Tour section.

### ANZ Ladies Masters—A$800,000
Winner: Karrie Webb

See Australian Women's Tour section.

### Princess Lalla Meriem Cup—US$72,000
Winner: Ana B. Sanchez

Spain's Ana B. Sanchez won the Princess Lalla Meriem Cup after a playoff with England's Rebecca Hudson on the Blue course at Royal Dar-es-Salam in Rabat. In difficult rainy conditions, Sanchez came from one stroke behind

Hudson before winning in extra time. Sanchez recorded rounds of 70, 75 and 78 for a four-over-par total of 223, while Hudson collapsed to a 79 in the final round after earlier efforts of 71 and 73. France's Virginie Auffret was third, four strokes back, while Laura Cabanillas Gomez and Monica Cosenza tied for fourth.

## Thailand Ladies Open—US$330,000
Winner: Shani Waugh

A decade and a half's experience of professional golf helped Shani Waugh win the Thailand Ladies Open in a playoff against Gwladys Nocera at the Alpine Golf and Sports Club in Bangkok. Waugh won for the third time on the Ladies European Tour, but after leading, or sharing the lead, for each of the first three days, it proved a nerve-racking finish for the 35-year-old Australian.

An eagle at the fifth hole gave Waugh a three-stroke lead, but she gave up her advantage with a double bogey at the eighth hole and then a triple bogey at the par-four 11th, where her second shot finished in the water. Waugh's 73 left her with a total of 282, six under par, and in a tie with Nocera, who closed with 72. The pair finished one ahead of three Koreans, Jeong Eun Lee, Ran Hong and Hee Young Park, and Japanese amateur Shinobu Moromizato.

Waugh clinched the $49,500 first prize with a par at the 18th when it was played as the first playoff hole, while Nocera, the 29-year-old French-woman, could only make a double-bogey six. "Right now I'm just feeling very relieved, because I'm very lucky to be sitting here," Waugh said. "I think Gwladys got a little bit nervous during the playoff and it was lucky for me.

"I've had two other playoffs and lost both of them. When I played against Se Ri Pak in America, it felt like she had all the experience. This time I felt I had all the experience and it was my turn to win. This is my third tournament victory in 15 years and for me it doesn't come along that much, so I'm going to cherish it."

## Tenerife Ladies Open—€242,000
Winner: Ludivine Kreutz

Consistency was the key to Ludivine Kreutz's victory in the Tenerife Ladies Open at Costa Adeje. Three successive rounds of 69 gave the 31-year-old Frenchwoman the lead, and a 70 under the pressure of the final day ensured a two-stroke winning margin over Germany's Miriam Nagl.

If Kreutz was disappointed to go to the turn in one over par, it did not affect her run for victory as she birdied the 13th and 15th holes and then the last hole for good measure. Kreutz finished at 277, 11 under par, while Nagl closed with 69. Diana Luna and Eleanor Pilgrim shared third place two more strokes behind Nagl.

Kreutz won €36,300 for her second European Tour victory. The first came in 2003 at the Italian Open, but the following season proved an up-

and-down affair. "When I won in Italy I didn't realize how I'd done it, and last year was quite hard for me because I missed a lot of cuts, so I was quite down," she said. "But I put in a lot of work last winter and it's such a good feeling to win again. At the beginning of the week it was my goal to have a win and to qualify for the Evian Masters. Now I've achieved that, I feel more relaxed, and now I know I'm in, I'm really happy as it's such a great event and all my family and friends will be there."

Kreutz was soaked in champagne by her countrywomen on the 18th green before collecting a trophy crafted from "palo santo" wood, a tree native to Tenerife, with a silver encasing at the bottom to emulate the ocean waves.

## Open de Espana Feminino — €275,000
Winner: Iben Tinning

Denmark's Iben Tinning vindicated her decision to concentrate on the European Tour in 2005 by winning the Open de Espana Feminino at Panoramica. After competing on the LPGA circuit in America in 2004, Tinning was quick to add to her tally of European wins for the first time since winning the Irish and Italian Opens in 2002.

A nine-under-par 63 in the second round put the 31-year-old Dane at the top of the leaderboard, but for the rest of the week she was a model of consistency with rounds of 70. Her total of 273 was 15 under par, and the four birdies, and two bogeys, on the final day gave Tinning a three-stroke victory over Linda Wessberg. Marine Monnet-Melocco was a further stroke back, while Lynette Brooky and Martina Eberl shared fourth place. France's Fany Schaeffer shared the 54-hole lead with Tinning but then collapsed on the final day to a 77, 10 strokes higher than both her second and third rounds.

"Patience was the key. I learned last year that you really have to be patient with golf before you get anywhere," said Tinning, who won €41,250. "You can be playing great and then you get a bad bounce and have a double bogey or something, so you can never think that you have won after 12 holes or something because anything can happen in golf.

"I tried something else last year and it didn't work out, so I'm very happy about my win, it means a lot to me. I love playing in Europe because I have good friends, good food, and it's not too far from home."

## Siemens Austrian Ladies Open — €250,000
Winner: Federica Piovano

"Impossible is nothing," was the slogan on the red tee-shirt sported by Federica Piovano, and so it proved as the 23-year-old Italian from Rome won her first professional title at the Siemens Austrian Ladies Open. Piovano broke the course record at the Fohrenwald Club with a 10-under-par 62 in the second round.

But a 72 on day three allowed Gwladys Nocera to sneak into the lead by one stroke, a lead she held for all of the final afternoon. At least until the 17th hole, where a bogey slipped her back into a tie with Piovano. Nocera birdied the par-five 18th, but Piovano was not deflected from her mission impossible and she holed from 45 feet for an eagle and a dramatic victory.

It was the second near-miss of the season for Nocera after the Frenchwoman lost a playoff to Shani Waugh in Thailand. But Piovano's closing 68 gave her a winning total of 262, 16 under par. Nocera, at 15 under, finished four strokes ahead of Laura Davies and Marta Prieto in third place.

"I saw the leaderboard on 18 and I saw the tie, but I didn't think about match play," said Piovano, who won €37,500. "Believe it or not, I had no pressure. When you get to that point, you have had pressure all day long; so when it came to the end, I thought 'this is either going to be in or it's going to be out.' It's not what you think about, it's what you do that matters."

Piovano's positive outlook was encouraged by her work with a sports psychologist, whom she had been seeing for less than a month. "I'm a great student," she joked. Another key was working with some of the other Italian players on her putting. "I'm so happy, because since I was an amateur I always had a really good game tee to green, but I couldn't score well because of my putting. Finally this year, thanks to some girls and some work I did, I got to a point where I know what I'm doing," she said. When it came to the vital putt at the last, it was all the more difficult because the green slipped away to a water hazard. "I had to imagine that the hole was a meter shorter, because I didn't want to hit it too hard and go in the water or off the green."

## BMW Ladies Italian Open — €300,000
Winner: Iben Tinning

Iben Tinning claimed her second victory in three weeks at the BMW Ladies Italian Open at Sheraton Golf Parco de' Medici. In perfect conditions, Tinning closed out the weekend with consecutive rounds of 66, but it was only just enough to win the event for the second time and claim her fourth LET title.

Tinning felt the pressure when Italian Veronica Zorzi eagled the last hole, but the Dane held her nerve to par the hole and finish one ahead at 17 under par. Zorzi matched Tinning's closing 66, a popular score also achieved by Lynette Brooky and another Italian, Sophie Sandolo, who shared third place at 15 under.

"I am so happy about this win, especially because it was so close out there," said Tinning, who won €45,000. "You had to play your best to win. I couldn't have played any better. It means quite a lot. I won the Italian Open before and I like Italy and I like Rome. I think it's a great place and I liked the back nine a lot better. After seeing Zorzi make that three on the last, that made it tougher, but then again, it's a par-five and I made my par, so I'm very delighted."

Zorzi, a 24-year-old from Verona, was urged on by the local gallery shouting "brava," and after an eagle at the 11th, she came to the 18th in the group ahead of Tinning. Facing a third shot from 80 yards with a sand wedge, Zorzi saw the ball pitch a yard short of the hole and then fly straight in for the eagle. "It was incredible and the best moment of my career," admitted Zorzi, adding, "I am very happy. It's a pity I wasn't a shot better today, but it's okay. I'll wait until another competition, next week at the French Open."

### Vediorbis Arras Open de France Dames — €300,000
Winner: Veronica Zorzi

Veronica Zorzi made good on her promise by winning the Arras Open de France Dames at Le Golf d'Arras. Where she had been one stroke short the previous week at the Italian Open, Zorzi birdied the last hole to win by one over England's Trish Johnson. The 24-year-old Italian's maiden win was achieved with the help of compatriot Federica Piovano, herself a maiden winner on the tour a few weeks earlier, who caddied for Zorzi on the final day.

Zorzi, from Verona, and Piovano have been friends for over 10 years since they started playing golf for junior national teams. Zorzi, whose father is a teaching professional in Milan, also played volleyball up to "B" national level before concentrating on golf. "I've worked very hard, but today I was very patient, and my caddie helped me to relax in between shots and keep smiling," said Zorzi.

Zorzi was one of four 54-hole leaders, along with Johnson, Ludivine Kreutz and Judith Van Hagen. Zorzi closed with a 68 to finish at 12 under par, while Johnson had a 69, missing her own birdie chance at the last. Lynette Brooky, a former two-time French champion, shot 67 to finish third, leaving Kreutz and Van Hagen to share fourth place with Gwladys Nocera.

Zorzi played brilliantly on the front nine with five birdies coming at the first, fourth, fifth, seventh and eighth holes. But the back nine was a different matter and she dropped shots at the 12th and 16th holes in the breezy conditions. But the birdie at the last saved the day. "On the last putt I just focused and hit the ball, it was like a dream," said Zorzi, in her fifth year on the LET circuit.

"I panicked on 17 when I had such a long putt, but managed to save par. When I bogeyed 16 I just thought, okay, there are another two holes left to birdie. The 12th and 16th were difficult holes because I had the wind against me. Now I'm closer to my goal to play in the Solheim Cup and I think about that a lot. I'm very happy and I feel quite emotional, because I have waited for this victory a long time."

### Algarve Ladies Open of Portugal — €300,000
Winner: Cecilia Ekelundh

After a round of 77 on the first day, Cecilia Ekelundh did not appear to have much chance of repeating her victory in the Algarve Ladies Open of Portugal. But the 27-year-old Swede made a brilliant recovery and overcame the strong winds at the Gramacho Pestana resort course with rounds of 66 and 67.

Ekelundh, who won her maiden title at Aroeira near Lisbon in 2004, completed a successful defense by finishing at six under par and three strokes ahead of Ludivine Kreutz. Cherie Byrnes and Gwladys Nocera shared third place another stroke back. Ekelundh earned €45,000 and collected her second diamond ring offered by Janico Joias of Lisbon to the winner.

At five over par after the first day, Ekelundh got back under par with a 66 in the second round. With the wind gusting up to 60 mph on the final day, Ekelundh's powerful driving and some superb iron play earned her victory. The Swede began the final round three strokes behind the co-leaders, Nina Reis and Nocera. Two birdies in the first three holes was the perfect start, but it was a 40-foot putt for birdie at the par-three 15th which virtually sealed things.

At the 18th, a par-five, her third shot from a greenside bunker came up short of the green and her chip for birdie lipped out. But she had enough in hand as Nocera closed with a 74 and Reis a 76.

"We have a saying in Sweden that goes, one win is never and twice is a habit," said Ekelundh. "To finally do this after a first round of 77 and to successfully defend my title for the first time is just an amazing feeling. I almost gave up after the first day, and I was just trying to make the cut at that point. I made a triple bogey at the third and I made two bogeys on my last two holes just because I wanted to get into the clubhouse so quickly. But I said to myself, if I hang on in there I could be okay, and here I am. Perhaps I'll buy a holiday home in Portugal for next year."

## Ladies English Open — €165,000
Winner: Maria Hjorth

Another Swedish double arrived when Maria Hjorth successfully defended her title at the Ladies English Open at Chart Hills. A year before Hjorth had run away to victory with a last round of 64. It was a different story this time, but the same result. Rounds of 68 and 69 left the 31-year-old from Falun a stroke behind four co-leaders, Becky Brewerton, Rebecca Coakley, Minea Blomqvist and former winner Laura Davies.

Hjorth, known to all as "Mimmi," outsprinted them all with a closing effort of 67 to finish with a total of 204, a 12-under-par score that earned her the €24,750 first prize. The later challengers could not catch her. Blomqvist and Brewerton both had a chance to get into a playoff with a birdie at the last, but in front of the huge gallery finished with a par and a bogey respectively.

Blomqvist's 69 gave her second place on her own, a stroke behind Hjorth, with Brewerton dropping back to a share of third place with Davies after both had rounds of 70. The ever-popular Davies could have done with a round like that of Karen Stupples, the Kent player in front of her home crowd, who closed with a 66 to finish fifth.

"At this time last year I had been through a tough 12 months, but this year, I was feeling much more relaxed and happy with my game," said Hjorth. "Coming down the last at 12 under, I thought I'd be in the playoff, and I didn't drop any shots, which was the most important thing, as it's easy to lose a tournament. I'm so happy to come back here to England, because there is so much support out here for women's golf and the weather turned out nice. I think this is one of the best tournaments we have."

## OTP Bank Ladies Central European Open — €166,000
Winner: Ludivine Kreutz

France's Ludivine Kreutz claimed her second victory of the season, and third in all, at the OTP Bank Central European Open at Old Lake, near Budapest in Hungary. Despite a seven-under-par 64 in the second round, Kreutz was still two strokes adrift of Samantha Head with a round to play. But a brilliant 66 on the final day gave her a four-stroke victory and the first prize of €24,750.

Kreutz's 14-under total of 199 left Head, after a 72, tied in second place with Minea Blomqvist, the defending champion from Finland, and Lora Fairclough, who both shot 67s. Becky Brewerton, Marta Prieto and Nina Reis tied for fifth position.

Kreutz started out slowly, but birdied the par-five fourth hole, the sixth and eighth to tie for the lead with Head. The turning point came when Kreutz birdied the ninth to move to 13 under, while Head made a double bogey to take her back to 10 under. Two more birdies at the 10th and 17th gave the Frenchwoman a five-shot lead coming down the last, but despite finding the greenside bunker at the 18th, a bogey was enough to seal the win.

"After the first nine holes, I had a two-shot lead, so I felt more confident," admitted Kreutz, 31, from Rognac. "When I made my first birdie I just tried to get on a roll." The win was the perfect preparation for the two biggest events of the season. "I'm very excited about Evian and the British, to see all those champions. But I'm going to try not to be too stressed and relax, because next to some of them I feel like a little girl!" she said.

England's Rebecca Hudson equaled the course record of 62 on the final day after a run of birdie, eagle, birdie, eagle from the 12th hole. At the 13th she chipped in for eagle and at the 15th she holed her sand wedge from a full 73 yards. Another birdie at the 17th put her on course for a possible course record as she was 10 under coming down the 18th, but she three-putted to equal the mark set by Blomqvist the year before. English amateur Henrietta Brockway, just 15 years old, became one of the youngest players to make a professional cut in an LET event.

## Evian Masters — US$2,500,000
Winner: Paula Creamer

American Paula Creamer confirmed her place as one of the most exciting young talents in women's golf by cruising to an eight-stroke victory at the Evian Masters in France. At 18 years, 11 months and 18 days, she became the youngest-ever winner on the Ladies European Tour, which co-sanctions the Evian Masters with the LPGA circuit.

Two months and a day earlier Creamer had become the youngest winner of an LPGA multi-round event with her maiden title at the Sybase Classic. The second win of her rookie season brought her the second biggest prize in women's golf, $375,000, and took her over the $1 million mark for the season. Only Karrie Webb had ever achieved that in her rookie season.

The ease of Creamer's victory was stunning given the quality of the field in the event. No one had ever won the tournament by more than four shots. Rounds of 68 and 68 had put Creamer into a share of the lead with Christina Kim at the halfway stage. But the rest of the field could not keep up with her third round of 66. Seven strokes behind were Laura Davies and Karine Icher, while Annika Sorenstam was eight adrift.

Creamer's closing round of 71, with three birdies and two bogeys, may not look as spectacular as her earlier efforts, but it did the job and gave her a 15-under-par total of 273. Icher's 74 dropped the Frenchwoman into a tie for fifth place; Sorenstam's 75 down to 12th; and Davies's 78 into a tie for 14th. Instead, runner-up honors were shared by Lorena Ochoa, who closed with a 69, and amateur Michelle Wie, whose weekend rounds of 68 made up for an opening 75. Lorie Kane took fourth place.

Even Creamer was shocked by her performance. "I can't even talk right now. I am speechless," she said. "It has been a great couple of days, that is for sure. Today was incredibly exciting. At the beginning I was very nervous because of just knowing that I had a seven-shot lead, but still it is hard to imagine that I had a seven-shot lead with the players here. They are the best players in the world."

## Weetabix Women's British Open—£1,050,000
Winner: Jeong Jang

Jeong Jang was so nervous off the course she spent all her time playing Tiger Woods Golf on her gameboy in order to relax. On the course at Royal Birkdale, the 25-year-old Korean looked as nerveless as Woods himself in claiming a wire-to-wire victory in the Weetabix Women's British Open. It made for a transatlantic double for Korea with Birdie Kim taking the U.S. Women's Open a few weeks earlier.

Jang, who turned professional in 2000, became the fourth Korean to win a major championship after Se Ri Pak, Grace Park and Kim. Everything about the performance was quietly impressive from Jang, who became the first player to win her maiden title at the Weetabix Women's British Open since Karrie Webb in 1995. She was also the first player at any major since Webb at the 2000 Nabisco Championship to win after leading on each day.

The opening day was a foul one, wet and windy, but Jang managed a four-under-par 68 that put her one ahead of Sophie Gustafson. Conditions eased the following day and it was then that Jang opened up her advantage with a 66 which put her four strokes in front of Louise Stahle, twice the British Amateur champion from Sweden who equaled the best round of the day with a 65.

No player other than Jang had managed two rounds in the 60s. Annika Sorenstam had opened with a 73, Paula Creamer, Karrie Webb and amateur

Michelle Wie all with 75s, and Grace Park a 77. Jang kept the pressure up on the third day with a 69 that put the Korean five ahead of Sorenstam and Cristie Kerr.

Sorenstam charged back into contention with a 66 in the third round, but the presence of the world No. 1 did not seem to affect Jang as they played together in the final group on the final day. At the first hole Jang hit a nine wood, her favorite club, to five feet for an opening birdie. Sorenstam rallied with birdies at the third and the sixth, but when she bogeyed the ninth, where Jang found her second birdie, the Korean was again six ahead.

Jang dropped a shot at the 11th, but made up for it with birdies at the 15th and 18th holes. Jang closed with a 69 for a total of 272, 16 under par, and a four-stroke victory over Gustafson, who produced matching rounds of 67 over the weekend. Wie, with rounds of 67, 67 and 69 from Friday onwards, produced the best result by an amateur in the championship in sharing third place with another Korean, Young Kim. Sorenstam and Kerr both closed with 71s to be tied for fifth with Liselotte Neumann.

"I'm more nervous now than I was on the golf course," admitted the diminutive Jang, who earned £160,000 for her victory. "I was really nervous before and I couldn't sleep last night, but my caddie kept me relaxed and that was really important. But I had a lot of confidence on this course, because I hit my driver low, which is good for the wind, and when I played practice rounds on this course I was very pleased, but I didn't tell anyone."

The women's game is particularly strong in Korea, but Jang was more than happy to share the spotlight with her compatriots. "We have a lot of superstars, like Se Ri, Grace and Mi-Hyun in Korea," she said. "But I just want to be J.J., I don't want to be Se Ri or Annika, I want to make my own history."

## Scandinavian TPC Hosted by Annika — €500,000
Winner: Annika Sorenstam

Annika Sorenstam made sure there was the requisite dramatic finale at the Scandinavian TPC Hosted by Annika, even if it then produced the minor problem at the prize-giving of the tournament hostess having to present herself with the trophy. "I had a great time at this party, I hope everybody else did," Sorenstam said. Perhaps not Natalie Gulbis, but then the American presumably knew what she was letting herself in for when she accepted a personal invitation from Sorenstam to play in the tournament, given the world No 1's strong record of victories in her homeland of Sweden.

A 67 in the third round at Barseback meant Sorenstam took over the lead from Liselotte Neumann, but it was to be no coronation on the final day as Gulbis made a brave fight for the crown. The American birdied the 14th, 15th and 16th holes to take a one-stroke lead. Sorenstam, playing in the group behind Gulbis, then birdied the 16th herself to draw even.

At the last hole, Gulbis had a birdie chance from 25 feet, but it just missed, so a 70 meant she posted the target at three under par. Sorenstam, urged on by thousands of fans around the green, put her approach to 35 feet and dramatically holed the putt for a winning birdie. Her closing 72 left her at four under par. Only two players broke par for the week, with Carin Koch, Patricia Meunier Lebouc and Gwladys Nocera sharing third place at even par.

"I think we had it all today," said Sorenstam, who won €75,000 for her seventh win of the season. "We had tough conditions, we had some drama coming down 18, some birdies, and to win your own tournament, it doesn't get much better than that. It really got exciting I think. I mean Natalie played some great golf down the stretch and had a good round today. She pushed me until the end."

## Wales Ladies Championship of Europe—£350,000
Winner: Kirsty Taylor

Kirsty Taylor was assured of setting history on the Ladies European Tour when she scored an 11-under-par 61 in the first round of the Wales Ladies Championship of Europe, the lowest round ever recorded on the European circuit. But she had to wait until three days later to open the champagne after clinching her first professional victory.

Taylor, 34, defeated two of the most successful British players in Laura Davies and Trish Johnson by three strokes. She led each day after adding rounds of 68, 70 and 75 to the record-breaking first-round effort for a 14-under total of 274. But at one point on the final afternoon it looked as if she might collapse completely as she dropped four strokes in a row from the ninth.

Taylor was now tied with defending champion Johnson, but with the help of her husband Alastair who was caddieing for her, she rallied with birdies at the 14th and 15th and then parred in for victory. "Fourteen was huge," she said of the 25-foot birdie putt. "I was more despondent at 13 than at 12 after I didn't hole the putt there. Alastair just gave me a good talking to and said, 'you're tied for the lead. You'd have taken that on Thursday morning. Just stick in there and keep going.'

"After that I was really relaxed until that last putt went in. It was great to play with Trish. She has been hard on my heels all week. Her and Laura were the ones I was worried about." Davies closed with a 70 and Johnson a 74 as the pair finished two shots ahead of Karen Margrethe Juul, with Rebecca Coakley finishing fifth. "I've waited 10 and a half years for this and it's been frustrating waiting for it, but thank goodness it's come," Taylor said. "It was a tough day today, but Thursday set me up for the rest of the week. A bit of champagne will be drunk tonight!"

## Ladies Finnish Masters—€200,000
Winner: Lisa Holm Sorensen

Freak weather provided a sudden and dramatic conclusion to the Ladies Finnish Masters for all the wrong reasons. A mini tornado swept through Helsinki Golf Club on the final morning of the event, following which the tournament had to be abandoned. Players and spectators were evacuated from the course at 10:20 a.m. after the storm, which had not been forecast, caused damage to the course and blew down many of the tents around the course.

Two spectators and one player, England's Kirsty Taylor, were taken to the hospital for checks on injuries caused when one of the biggest hospitality tents on the course was lifted off its moorings and blown away. Taylor was sheltering in the tent when she was struck on the back of the head by a pole. Briefly a rope fell around Taylor's neck but she managed to release herself quickly. Sweden's Linda Wessberg was struck on the arm by a flying tent pole as she rounded a corner on the fifth fairway. "Suddenly, the whole tent was coming straight at me," she said.

Local player Minea Blomqvist, who was playing the first hole at the time, said: "I'm just glad that more people weren't injured. It's not the sort of thing that ever happens in Finland." The tournament was cut back to 36 holes, and the overnight leader, Denmark's Lisa Holm Sorensen, who had yet to start the final round, was declared the winner. Due to storms on the first day, Sorensen had played 30 holes the day before in completing rounds of 70 and 70 for a two-under-par total, which had put her one stroke ahead of Suzann Pettersen, Cecilia Ekelundh, Ursula Wikstrom and amateur Caroline Westrup.

Sorensen, in her rookie season, was struggling to keep her card at 108th on the money list going into the event. She earned €30,000 and a three-year exemption for her maiden victory, but like many of the players, the 22-year-old was shaken by how the tournament ended. "I'm not really sure how to react," Sorensen said. "I'm happy to win but sorry that it had to happen this way. The most important thing is that I get to keep my card."

## Nykredit Masters—€200,000
Winner: Iben Tinning

The home gallery got the result they were wishing for when Iben Tinning won the inaugural Nykredit Masters at the Kokkedal Club near her hometown of Copenhagen. Tinning closed with an outstanding round of 65 for a 15-under-par total of 273. The 31-year-old won by two strokes over Lora Fairclough, with Cecilia Ekelundh a further stroke back in third place.

It was Tinning's third win of the season and the perfect send-off to the Solheim Cup in America. She received €30,000 for her fifth career victory and was presented with a sterling silver salver by Crown Princess Mary. "Obviously winning in your own country is an amazing feeling and the crowd was fantastic," said Tinning, who also won in Italy and Spain during the season. "I have been very happy with all my wins, but the crowd is a little more crazy here and that's fantastic."

Tinning started the day two shots behind Ekelundh, but tied for the lead at the turn after three birdies and an eagle on the front nine. Ekelundh then dropped three strokes in the next two holes, while Tinning found herself clear of the field after another birdie at the 11th. Ekelundh had the consolation of winning the Volvo Cross Country Challenge, an order of merit for the tour's Scandinavian events.

## The Solheim Cup
Winners: United States

See LPGA Tour section.

## KLM Ladies Open — €165,000
Winner: Virginie Lagoutte

France's Virginie Lagoutte claimed her first victory in the KLM Ladies Open at Kennemer after defeating Wales' Eleanor Pilgrim at the second extra hole. The 26-year-old Lagoutte came from four strokes behind Pilgrim, the 36-hole leader, but thought she had lost her chance with bogeys at the last two holes. But Pilgrim did exactly the same to fall back into the playoff.

The pair played the 18th hole twice, and on the second occasion Pilgrim drove into the rough as she had when playing the hole in regulation and bogeyed it again. Lagoutte made her charge in breathtaking fashion with four birdies on her way to the turn and then three more at the 10th, 12th and 16th holes. She posted rounds of 73, 75 and 67 for the one-under-par total which Pilgrim, who was also seeking her maiden victory, matched with efforts of 74, 70 and 71. Four players shared third place, two strokes behind, Sara Jelander, Marine Monnet-Melocco, Amanda Moltke Leth and Lora Fairclough.

"It's a huge surprise for me," said Lagoutte, who won €24,750. "I played very well today despite not such a great start to the week. I was disappointed to finish with two bogeys, as I thought that was it for me, but I concentrated in the playoff and this is a dream come true."

## Catalonia Ladies Masters — €190,000
Winner: Karine Icher

After spending most of the season as a rookie on the LPGA circuit in America, where she had eight top-10 finishes, Karine Icher returned to Europe with a successful defense of her title at the Catalonia Ladies Masters at Platja de Pais, near Gerona. It was the 26-year-old Frenchwoman's fifth European title and her third in all in Spain.

Icher clinched the victory with an eight-foot birdie putt at the last hole for a one-stroke win over Gwladys Nocera, Paula Marti and Sophie Sandolo. Icher closed with a round of 68, after efforts of 70 and 69, for a total of 207, 12 under par. Icher started the day two behind Sandolo and only drew even with the Italian, as well as Marti and Nocera, after a birdie from 20 feet at the 17th.

Marti had a chance to get to 12 under with a 25-footer at the last but it just missed. Nocera finished runner-up for the third time in the season, while Sandolo equaled her best performance on tour. Lynette Brooky took fifth place, while 15-year-old Spanish amateur Carlotta Ciganda finished tied for 11th after setting a new course record of 65 on the final day.

Icher joined Cecilia Ekelundh, Maria Hjorth and Annika Sorenstam in repeating victories during the season. "It was tough today, as Paula and Sophie both played very well," she said. "I missed so many putts out there that it was great to make those two vital putts at the last two holes. I feel more confident with my putting now under pressure. This win will give me more confidence when I return to America. It seems that Spain is very lucky for me, because I've now won here three times."

Iben Tinning became the first Danish player to win the LET Money List thanks to her three victories, but was not planning to play in another tournament until well into the 2006 season as she heads off on maternity leave. Spain's Elisa Serramia, a 21-year-old from Barcelona, was the 2005 Rookie of the Year.

# Japan LPGA Tour

## Daikin Orchid Ladies—¥80,000,000
Winner: Orie Fujino

Orie Fujino got the new Japan LPGA Tour off to a good personal start at its traditional early March opener in Okinawa. The 31-year-old, win-less since 2002 when she won twice, came from a stroke off the pace in the final round at Ryukyu Golf Club to capture the Daikin Orchid title. Fujino finished with a one-over-par 217 to edge veteran Michiko Hattori by a shot.

Fujino launched her bid with a first-round 69, leading Hattori, the only other par-breaker, by two strokes, then swapped positions the next day. Hattori shot 73 but still slipped a stroke ahead of Fujino (76) and Michie Ohba (75-70). Fujino started with a bogey Sunday, but was able to overtake Hattori when Michiko bogeyed the 12th, 13th and 16th holes, and Orie finished birdie-par for a par 72, picking up her fourth LPGA title. Hattori shot 74 for 218, two strokes ahead of Miho Koga.

## Studio-Alice Women's Open—¥50,000,000
Winner: Michiko Hattori

Michiko Hattori had a month to reflect on her near-miss in the Daikin Orchid tournament, then bounced back when the Japan LPGA Tour resumed action with the new Studio-Alice Women's Open to score the 18th victory of her illustrious career. The 36-year-old Hattori outplayed the circuit's star teenagers at Hanayashiki Golf Club and posted a three-stroke victory with her three-under-par 215. She shot 74 on a wind-blown Sunday afternoon.

Sakura Yokomine and her more noted fellow 19-year-old, Ai Miyazato, drew most of the attention in the opening round. Aided by an eagle,

Yokomine opened a bid for her first professional victory with a 69, taking a one-stroke lead over Miyazato. Hattori entered the picture Saturday, shooting a 69 herself to catch Yokomine at 141 as Yokomine settled for a par 72. Hot on their heels were Toshimi Kimura (72-71) and Miyazato, who bogeyed the last two holes for 73 and sat two strokes off the pace.

Yokomine's game deserted her Sunday. As she fell from contention, headed for 79, Hattori took charge. Despite three bogeys in strong winds on the back nine, Michiko finished with a birdie for the 74 and her three-shot margin over Miyazato, who took 75.

## Life Card Ladies—¥60,000,000
Winner: Sakura Yokomine

Sakura Yokomine wasn't about to let another one get away. The 19-year-old rookie, who suffered through a disastrous finish the previous week when sharing the lead, birdied the final hole of the Life Card Ladies tournament and salted away her first title on the Japan LPGA Tour. The birdie gave her a final, one-stroke margin over Taiwan's Julie Lu and a one-under-par 215.

Shaking off the disappointment of her closing 79 in the Studio-Alice tournament, Yokomine positioned herself well the first day with a 73, two strokes behind leaders Shinobu Moromizato and Midori Yoneyama. She wound up the second round in virtually a duplicate situation of that she faced the previous Sunday, tied for the lead with a seasoned veteran with a host of victories on her record. This time, it was South Korea's Ok-Hee Ku, a 22-tournament winner. Yokomine shot 71 and Ku a second 72 for 144s, a shot ahead of Moromizato (74), Ji-Hee Lee (71), Kaori Higo (73) and Michiko Hattori, the previous week's victor.

"I can't believe it," said the young winner Sunday evening. "I thought winning a tournament was way out of my league." Lu was in the clubhouse with her 216 well before Yokomine reached the 18th and made the deciding birdie putt.

## Fujisankei Ladies Classic—¥70,000,000
Winner: Kasumi Fujii

Kasumi Fujii successfully defended her championship in the Fujisankei Ladies Classic, but the two victories couldn't have been in greater contrast. In 2004 at the Kawana Hotel's Fuji course, Fujii led for two days, then was declared the winner when fog forced cancellation of the final round. In 2005, Fujii came from five strokes off the lead on Sunday to tie Akiko Fukushima, then won the subsequent playoff on the first extra hole.

Fukushima, the veteran internationalist, had the lead for two rounds. The first day she shared first place with Yuri Fudoh, the Japan LPGA Tour's No. 1 player for the previous five years. Both shot two-under-par 70s, Fukushima nailing birdies on her final three holes to forge the tie, a stroke ahead of Fujii and amateur Kaori Aoyama. Fukushima followed with four back-nine birdies for 68–138 Saturday, sitting a shot ahead of Kaori Higo

(73-66), as Fudoh slipped three behind with 71–141. Fujii was at 143.

Kasumi got her chance Sunday, though, when both Fukushima and Higo struggled to 75s. Fujii's 70 overtook Fukushima at 213 and set up the overtime victory, her eighth on tour.

## Katokichi Queens—¥60,000,000
Winner: Midori Yoneyama

A playoff pattern began to set in when the Japan LPGA Tour moved on to Yashima Country Club in Kagawa Prefecture for the Katokichi Queens tournament at the end of April. Play went overtime for a second straight week as Midori Yoneyama scored her first victory in nearly four years and fifth of her career on the second extra hole.

Prior to the exciting finish, the lead changed hands at the end of both of the earlier rounds. Australia's Nikki Campbell shot 68 the first day and led by one over Miho Koga, Yukari Baba and Mihoko Takahashi. Koga took over Saturday with 67–136, a shot ahead of standings-leader Michiko Hattori. Yoneyama (70-68) was two back with Campbell, and Ayako Uehara was among three players at 139.

Uehara birdied three of her last four holes Sunday for 67–206 and Yoneyama followed her in with birdies on two of the final three holes for her 68 that forged the deadlock. Two holes into the playoff, Yoneyama made the deciding birdie. Hattori continued her strong seasonal start, taking third place with 70–207, and Tamie Durdin, who had been playing with little result in America in recent years, closed with 66 to pick off fourth place.

## Salonpas World Ladies—¥60,000,000
Winner: Yuri Fudoh

Perhaps it required a 72-hole tournament to ignite Yuri Fudoh's advance toward another big season. Whatever, the Japan LPGA Tour's most established star put her 33rd career victory onto her record in the Salonpas World Ladies in the four-day tournament at Tokyo's famed Yomiuri Country Club, achieving it in the circuit's third consecutive playoff with a par on the first overtime hole.

A brilliant, eight-under-par 64 in the third round put Fudoh in position to win after she trailed leader Shiho Ohyama by seven strokes at the tournament midpoint. Ohyama, 27, who had a lone (2003) victory in her five seasons on the tour, built that margin with an opening 67 and a second-round 68 for 135. At that point, Ohyama had a five-stroke lead on runners-up Sakura Yokomine and Young-Me Lee, but when Fudoh shot the 64 she was tied with Ohyama at 206. They had three strokes on Junko Omote and five on Ai Miyazato.

Fudoh built a three-stroke lead on the front nine Sunday, but Ohyama narrowed the gap to one through 17 holes and got the playoff chance when Fudoh three-putted the 18th green and she made par.

## Vernal Ladies—¥120,000,000
Winner: Ai Miyazato

Ai Miyazato couldn't have picked a better time to start a 2005 victory run than in the Vernal Ladies, the richest tournament on the Japan LPGA Tour. Miyazato answered the challenge of her veteran protagonist, Yuri Fudoh, who had scored her first 2005 win the previous Sunday and was the defending champion, with a resounding eight-stroke triumph at Fukuoka Country Club in Fukuoka Prefecture. The ¥21.6 million first-place check from the ¥120 million purse, double the total at most of the other events on the tour, vaulted Miyazato into first place on the tour's money list.

Miyazato, who just missed unseating Fudoh from the No. 1 spot at the end of the 2004 season, set up the Vernal victory with a brilliant, eight-under-par 64, a course record, in the second round to jump six strokes ahead of the field and breezed to victory Sunday with a 70, finishing 13 under par at 203. It was the seventh tour win for the 19-year-old, who won five times in her rookie 2004 season and once before that while still an amateur. She fell one stroke shy of making it a wire-to-wire victory when she opened with 69 and trailed first-round leader Ji-Hee Lee by a stroke before the dazzling eight-birdie performance that Saturday. Akiko Fukushima occupied the distant runner-up spot Sunday when she closed with 69–211.

## Chukyo TV Bridgestone Ladies Open—¥50,000,000
Winner: Ai Miyazato

Talk about the difference between night and day. That was the sort of contrast that existed in comparing the back-to-back victories Ai Miyazato registered in mid-May on the Japan LPGA Tour. Her triumph in the rich Vernal Ladies was an eight-stroke walk in the park, but the follow-up win the next Sunday in the modest-pursed Chukyo TV Bridgestone Ladies Open couldn't have been much more difficult.

Amid a driving rain, Miyazato birdied the 54th hole for 70–209, forcing a playoff against Australian veteran Nikki Campbell, then birdied again on the first extra hole of her career to capture the title and the eighth victory of her remarkable young career. It was the tour's third playoff in four weeks.

The tournament also saw the emergence of another teenage talent with a bright future. Amateur Shinobu Moromizato, just 18, matched a long-standing tour record in the first round on the Ishino course of the Chukyo Golf Club when she made 11 birdies, shot 63 and took a two-stroke lead over Miyazato. Although she slipped to 73 Saturday, Moromizato retained the lead at 136. Campbell moved into second place with 68–137 and Miyazato slipped three shots off the pace with 74–139.

The Aussie shot 72 Sunday as she and Miyazato finished regulation play a stroke ahead of young Moromizato (74) and Hiroko Yamaguchi.

## Kosaido Ladies Golf Cup—¥60,000,000
Winner: Midori Yoneyama

Even though she had won the Katokichi Queens tournament a month earlier, Midori Yoneyama surprised herself when she triumphed again in the Kosaido Ladies event in a carbon-copy version of the previous week's finish of Ai Miyazato at Chukyo. After all, health problems had forced Yoneyama out of two of the subsequent tournaments. "I never imaged that I'd win," said Yoneyama after she birdied both the 54th and the first playoff hole to send the luckless Junko Omote to a 10th runner-up finish in her winless nine-year career. Yoneyama, in turn, posted her sixth victory.

The tournament started with a familiar face at the helm as Yuri Fudoh shot 67 and shared the lead with Omote. However, Fudoh fell from contention Saturday with 73–140 as Yoneyama surged a stroke in front of Omote (70) and two ahead of Kaori Nakamichi, Fuki Kido and Michiko Hattori with an eight-birdie 67 for 136. Omote slipped into the lead Sunday at the seventh hole when Yoneyama bogeyed and remained in front until the winner nailed the tying birdie at the last hole for 71–207. Miyazato passed up the tournament, electing not to try for three wins in a row.

## Resort Trust Ladies—¥60,000,000
Winner: Mitsuko Kawasaki

Mitsuko Kawasaki held off the more highly regarded players in a wind-blown final round of the Resort Trust Ladies tournament in early June and picked up her second career victory. The 28-year-old Kawasaki, whose only previous win came a year earlier in the Belluna Cup, struggled Sunday to a 75, but nobody was able to mount a challenge and she finished with a two-shot victory margin with her eight-under-par 208.

Akiko Fukushima came closest, shooting 72 as she absorbed her third runner-up finish of the Japan LPGA season, remaining winless for the year. Yuri Fudoh solved the tough conditions Sunday with a 68, but she had started the day 10 strokes behind and wound up in a five-way tie for third at 211 with Shiho Ohyama, Jeon Mi Jung, Sakura Yokomine and South Korean rookie Lee Eun Hye, who began the round in second place, three behind Kawasaki, and could only match her 75.

Yokomine, the 19-year-old winner of the Life Card Ladies in April, had bounced back from a missed cut in the Kosaido with an opening 66 at Grandee Nasu Shirakawa Golf Club, Fukushima Prefecture, to lead Jeon, Yukari Baba and defending champion Hiromi Mogi by a stroke, but couldn't maintain the pace.

## We Love Kobe Suntory Ladies Open—¥60,000,000
Winner: Yuri Fudoh

Another 72-hole tournament, another victory for Yuri Fudoh. The brilliant Fudoh, who had scored her first win of the season in the Salonpas World, the only earlier four-round event, needed the final 18 holes to snatch her second 2005 title in the We Love Kobe Suntory Ladies Open. Four strokes off the lead going into the fourth round at Japan Memorial Golf Club, Hyogo Prefecture, the 28-year-old capped a steadily improving series of rounds with a sizzling, eight-under-par 64 and pulled out a two-stroke victory with a 16-under-par 272.

After a first-round 72, Fudoh trailed South Korea's Ji-Hee Lee, a five-time winner in Japan, by four strokes. She followed with a 69, but slipped another shot off the pace as Michie Ohba shot 67–136 to lead by one over Yuriko Ohtsuka (71-66) and Lee, who had a 69 for her 137. Ohtsuka took over first place Saturday with 67–204. Fudoh matched that round and moved into fourth place behind Ohba (205) and Lee (207), then raced to her 34th tour victory with a 64 Sunday. Ai Miyazato, playing in her last tournament before heading for overseas competition, was never a factor and shot 283.

## Apita Circle K Sankus Ladies—¥50,000,000
Winner: Ok-Hee Ku

It was South Korea's week to shine at the Japan LPGA Tour's stop in Gifu Prefecture for the Apita Circle K Sankus Ladies tournament. One of the country's young rookies — Shin Hyun Ju — got it started and the veteran Ok-Hee Ku finished it up, posting the 23rd victory of her illustrious career on the circuit.

Ju shot a five-under-par 67 in the opening round at U Green Golf Club to take a one-stroke lead over Michiko Hattori, continuing her strong play in the early season, and Erina Hara. Ku took charge Saturday and led the rest of the way. She came from three shots back to take the 36-hole lead with 70-68–138, a stroke in front of Chieko Amanuma and Lu Ya Huei. Ku opened the gap Sunday with three early birdies and still won easily despite two late bogeys, carding 71 for 209. It was her first victory in Japan in two years, but 19th since 1993. Amanuma (72) and Ji-Hee Lee (69) placed second at 211.

## Promise Ladies—¥60,000,000
Winner: Ku Yun Hee

The Japan LPGA Tour crowned its second first-time winner of the season at the Promise Ladies tournament as Ku Yun Hee gave South Korea its second consecutive victory on the circuit. Hee outplayed Midori Yoneyama in a final round that rained birdies, shooting a 66 that gave her a one-stroke victory at Water Hills Golf Club in Hyogo Prefecture with a 15-under-par 201.

Yoneyama, seeking her third win of the season, had begun the tournament with 65 to lead Aki Nakano by a shot and seven others, including Hee, by two. Scoring in general rose Saturday as Yoneyama shot 70 and the South Korean caught her at 135 with a 68. Hee reeled off four front-nine birdies Sunday, then held on as birdie-makers behind her tried to catch her. Junko Omote, the perennial runner-up (11 times), came closest, firing a 65 for 202. Yoneyama (69) tied for third at 204 with Keiko Sasaki (67).

## Belluna Ladies Cup—¥60,000,000
Winner: Kasumi Fujii

Kasumi Fujii became the fourth double winner of the 2005 season on the Japan LPGA Tour when she made an overnight lead stand up for a two-stroke victory in the Belluna Ladies Cup. Fujii extended a one-shot edge at the end of two rounds to a two-stroke winning margin at the Obatago Golf Club in Gunma Prefecture the first weekend of July. She closed with 69 for 204.

Yukari Baba, one of the tour's young guns, started the Belluna Cup with a six-under-par 66 and led by a stroke over the experienced Kaori Higo. Nine others, including Sakura Yokomine, had 68s. When Baba could manage just a par round Saturday, Fujii climbed into the lead with 66 for 135, resting a stroke ahead of Ai Ogawa and Mika Miyazato. An eagle at the 15th hole was the deciding score for Fujii Sunday as she landed her ninth career title. Toshimi Kimura, another tour veteran, closed with 68 and claimed the runner-up spot at 206. Yokomine and Baba tied with Mayumi Murai for third at 207.

## Chateaureze Queens Cup—¥70,000,000
Winner: Junko Omote

Silver finally turned to gold for Junko Omote at the Chateaureze Queens Cup. After suffering through 11 second-place finishes and countless other near-misses, Omote finally clutched onto victory on the Japan LPGA Tour at the Chateaureze Queens Cup tournament in Sapporo, Hokkaido. She did it the hard way, too, coming from two strokes off the pace in the final round and winning a playoff against one of the season's most consistent performers.

Two strokes behind Yeo-Jin Kang, the leader after each of the first two rounds, going into the final 18 holes, Omote shot a two-under-par 70 for 214 and completed the 54 holes in a deadlock with Michiko Hattori, already a winner and a frequent contender earlier in the season. The subsequent playoff went two holes before Junko landed the long-sought-after title. Kang closed with 73, missing the extra session by a stroke with her 215, two strokes ahead of six other players. Omote was just the third first-time winner of the season.

## Stanley Ladies—¥60,000,000
Winner: Junko Omote

Junko Omote enjoyed her first career victory so much that she made it two in a row when the Japan LPGA Tour moved on to the Stanley Ladies tournament at Tomei Country Club in Shizuoka. That victory, combined with the earnings that came with the frustrating near-misses in several other 2005 events, jumped Omote into the unlikely No. 1 position on the circuit's money list with more than ¥53 million.

The Stanley triumph came in more easy fashion than her ice-breaker the week before in the Chateaureze Queens, but not without a scare. Omote shared the first-round lead in the Stanley tournament with Kasumi Fujii, a two-time 2005 winner, and Hiromi Mogi at 67, then slipped a stroke behind Fujii (71) and Miki Nakata (68-70) the second day. She appeared to have the victory in hand Sunday until South Korea's Shin Hyun Ju, playing ahead of her, came up with a rare albatross (double eagle) two at the par-five 17th hole to forge a tie on the leaderboard. But Omote nailed a birdie at the hole moments later and parred the 54th for 65–204 to edge Ju by a stroke. Fujii shot 69 and finished third, Nakata 70 and fourth.

## Crystal Geyser Ladies—¥60,000,000
Winner: Kasumi Fujii

Kasumi Fujii was the first player to reach the three-victory plateau on the year's Japan LPGA Tour when she prevailed in a three-way playoff in the Crystal Geyser Ladies tournament at Keiyo Country Club in Chiba Prefecture. She did it in spectacular fashion by rolling in a 60-foot eagle putt on the 498-yard, par-five 18th hole, the first extra hole that pitted her against the mighty Yuri Fudoh and Shiho Ohyama, who had lost an earlier playoff to Fudoh in the Salonpas World.

Fujii (69-67) and Fudoh (67-69) had entered the final round in a four-way tie at 136 with Lu Ya Huei (70-66) and Mineko Nasu (67-69), with Ohyama on their heels with two others at 137. Ohyama had started the tournament with 66, leading Fudoh, Nasu and two others by a stroke. Rounds of 68 by Fujii and Fudoh and Ohyama's 69 brought about the 12-under-par totals and the brief overtime session.

## NEC Karuizawa 72—¥60,000,000
Winner: Paula Creamer

Japanese golf fans who had been marveling over the accomplishments of their own teenaged phenoms for the last two years or so got a chance to see another talented youngster of world stature at the NEC Karuizawa 72 tournament in August, when Paula Creamer, the new American star, came, saw and conquered one of the strongest domestic fields of the Japan LPGA season in her first visit to the Orient.

Creamer, who had already won once on the U.S. LPGA Tour and again in the Evian Masters in Europe in July, put together three rounds in the 60s and assembled a 197, the lowest 54-score of the Japanese season to date. She won by three strokes, followed in order by Ai Miyazato at 200, Shiho Ohyama at 201, Yuri Fudoh at 202 and Akiko Fukushima at 203.

Creamer, only three months beyond her high school graduation, never trailed at Nagona's Karuizawa 72 Golf Club, but shared the first-round lead at 64 with Yun-Jye Wei and Rui Kitada, the defending champion struggling in 2005 after her three-win 2004 campaign. Creamer backed up the 64 with a 65 in Saturday's round to move two shots ahead as Miyazato, just back from a two-month venture overseas, made her presence known with 64 for 131. With Sunday's four-birdie 68, the new American star completed a bogey-free tournament for the three-stroke victory as the next three finishers all had 69s and Fukushima posted 67.

### New Caterpillar Mitsubishi Ladies—¥60,000,000
Winner: Ai Miyazato

Perhaps not exactly to the delight of her fellow players on the Japan LPGA Tour, Ai Miyazato put away her long-distance luggage and got back to the business of winning tournaments in her homeland in mid-August. After a runner-up finish to budding American star Paula Creamer in her first start home from a two-month international tour, Miyazato resumed her winning ways the next week in the New Caterpillar Mitsubishi Ladies tournament. She broke from a three-way tie after 36 holes with a final-round 68 for 209 and a three-stroke victory, her third of the season, ninth of her brief but sparkling career.

Miyazato, then 20 years old, held the lead from the start at Daihakone Country Club, Kanagawa Prefecture, opening with a 66 that put her a stroke in front of Akiko Fukushima, who continued to endure a frustrating run of strong but unsuccessful victory challenges. Miyazato faltered the second day, shooting 75 and enabling Shiho Ohyama (68) and Hiromi Mogi (72) to overtake her at 141, a shot ahead of Fukushima, Sakura Yokomine and Jeon Mi Jung.

Miyazato reestablished control of the tournament right off the bat Sunday with birdies on the first two holes and had three more along with a bogey en route to the three-shot win. Jung, with 70, and Mogi, with 71, tied for second at 212.

### Yonex Ladies—¥60,000,000
Winner: Shin Hyun Ju

New South Korean players continue to make inroads of success on the Japan LPGA Tour. Shin Hyun Ju joined countrywoman Yun-Hee Ku as a first-time winner on the circuit and became the third South Korean victor of the season when she captured the Yonex Ladies tournament at Yonex Country Club in Teradomari, Niigata Prefecture, at the end of August. The fourth initial winner of 2005 shot a final-round 70 and eased past Midori Yoneyama to claim a one-stroke victory with her seven-under-par 209.

Ju and several of the tour's better golfers came into play Saturday after two relative unknowns — Atomi Shiota and Mari Katayama — produced 69s and led by two after the first round. Yoneyama, already a two-time winner in 2005, shot a seven-birdie 67 for 138 and slipped a shot ahead of Ju, whose 68 put her at 139. Close behind were Ai Miyazato, the previous week's winner, at 140 and Yuri Fudoh at 141.

The 25-year-old Korean was equal to the challenge Sunday, although she trailed Midori by as much as three on the front nine. Her birdie at the 10th gave her the lead and she sealed the victory with an 18-foot birdie putt on the final green. Yoneyama wound up with 72–210, tied for second place with Yuko Saitoh. Fudoh and Miyazato were among four players at 211.

## Golf 5 Ladies—¥50,000,000
Winner: Yuri Fudoh

Yuri Fudoh has won tournaments in all sorts of ways in the course of compiling her splendid record on the Japan LPGA Tour, but few, if any, of the victories were as spectacular as the 35th, her two-stroke triumph the first week of September in her successful defense of the Golf 5 Ladies tournament. Five strokes off the lead going into the final round at Mizunami Country Club, Gifu Prefecture, she even surprised herself when she fired off a flawless 64 that brought her a two-stroke victory at 11-under-par 205.

"I was thinking at best I would be able to force a playoff or maybe lose by one stroke," said the 28-year-old star after nobody among the 11 players who began the round ahead of her could match her total, especially Akane Iijima and Ji-Hee Lee, who led the tournament after 36 holes at 136. As it turned out, Shin Hyun Ju and Yun-Jye Wei (with 68s) and Iijima (71) came closest at 207.

Fudoh was six behind after an opening-round 72 as Lee and Yukari Baba topped the standings with 66s, then shaved a stroke off her deficit the second day with 69 before her explosive finish.


## Japan LPGA Championship—¥70,000,000
Winner: Yuri Fudoh

Appropriate was the fitting word to describe the finish of the Japan LPGA Tour's first major championship of the 2005 season. What better outcome could the Japan LPGA Championship have had than Yuri Fudoh and Ai Miyazato dueling down the stretch and finishing one-two when the smoke settled? Throw in the presence of Sakura Yokomine, the circuit's other highly talented young star, who placed third (with Shiho Ohyama) in her first appearance in the championship.

The victory, achieved in much the same manner as her triumph the previous Sunday in the Golf 5 tournament, vaulted Fudoh past Miyazato on the tour's money list and in seasonal win totals. It was Fudoh's fourth of the year and 36th in her career, all since 1999.

She didn't have as much ground to make up as she did in the Golf 5 when she came from five back, but did it almost as decisively, closing with a six-under-par 66 at Meishin Yokaichi Country Club, Shiga Prefecture, to win by two strokes over Miyazato with her 10-under-par 278. Interestingly, among her four victories, three were in the only three 72-hole events played to that point in the season.

Leading up to the exciting final round, Jeong Yun-Joo led after the first round with 66, Miyazato and Toshimi Kimura, with 140s, led Fudoh and Yokomine by a stroke after 36 holes, and Ohyama spurted in front Saturday when she shot 67 for 210, jumping a shot ahead of Miyazato (71) and Yokomine (70) and two on top of Fudoh (71). Fudoh pulled off the victory Sunday when she birdied four of the last eight holes for the winning 66.

## Munsingwear Ladies Tokai Classic—¥60,000,000
Winner: Shiho Ohyama

The 2005 Japan LPGA Tour had been replete with disappointments for Shiho Ohyama, most recently the Sunday before the Munsingwear Ladies Tokai Classic when she failed to convert the third-round lead in the Japan LPGA Championship into a victory she had been seeking for more than two years.

Ohyama turned things around at the Munsingwear Tokai Classic, though, stealing a title away from veteran Kaori Higo, whom she trailed by three strokes going into the final round at Ryosen Golf Club, Mie Prefecture. Ohyama produced a flawless, six-under-par 66 and won her second career title by three strokes with her 10-under-par 206.

Yuri Fudoh, gunning for her third win in a row, got off to a strong start with a 68, a stroke behind leader Higo, whose 17th and most recent victory in her 18-season career was in the 2004 LPGA Championship. However, a 75 on Saturday took Fudoh out of contention as Higo widened her margin to three strokes with a 70–137. Ohyama, who had shared the runner-up spot Friday with Fudoh, shot 72 Saturday for 140, remaining in second place but then with Aki Nakano and Miho Koga. Although losing to Ohyama Sunday, Higo took second place with 72–209, two ahead of Midori Yoneyama and Mikiyo Nishizuka.

## Miyagi TV Cup Dunlop Ladies Open—¥60,000,000
Winner: Sakura Yokomine

Teenager Sakura Yokomine added further validity to her growing reputation as a star on the Japan LPGA Tour when she won a battle of rookies in an overtime duel in the Miyagi TV Cup Dunlop Ladies Open in late September. The 19-year-old, playing in her first full season, had scored her initial victory in the Life Card Ladies in April, but, with the impatience of youth, said of her Miyagi win: "It's been awhile since I got my first win."

Yokomine's victim was South Korea's Jeon Mi Jung, who had taken over first place from Nobuko Kizawa, a winless veteran on the circuit, who had opened with 67 and a two-stroke lead. Jung shot 71 for 140 and staked out a one-shot lead over Hiromi Takesue, Kaori Harada and Kizawa, who had a 74. Yokomine was among five players at 142. Her 71 Sunday led to the playoff when Jung shot 73 and both players finished at three-under-par 213 at Rifu Golf Club in Miyagi Prefecture.

Yokomine reached a greenside bunker in two on the par-five 18th, the second playoff hole, and made the subsequent birdie putt to grab the title when the South Korean missed her birdie chance from six feet.

## Japan Women's Open—¥70,000,000
Winner: Ai Miyazato

Already drawing universal acclaim and being ranked with the brightest stars in Japanese golfing history, Ai Miyazato took another step up that ladder when she festooned her fast-forming record of success with her first major title — the Japan Women's Open — in resounding and record fashion. Miyazato never trailed and wound up leaving the field five strokes in her wake when she finished off the victory with a five-under-par total of 283. She thus became, at 20, the youngest winner in the long history of the championship. That honor had belonged to Hisako Higuchi, who was 23 when she won the 1968 event.

The win also was a punctuation mark in the exciting duel between Miyazato, the challenger, and Yuri Fudoh, the tour champion the last five seasons, with the two now each holding one of the two most important titles on the tour. Fudoh won the LPGA Championship in September.

Miyazato had just returned to Japan from America, where she had taken the first big step toward qualifying for the 2006 U.S. LPGA Tour, when he teed off in the Women's Open at Totsuka Country Club in Yokohama. She shook off bogeys on the first two holes, shot 67 and tied for the lead with Kasumi Fujii, who already had three 2005 wins in the books. Fudoh got off to a shockingly uncharacteristic start with 78 and was never a factor.

The 20-year-old Miyazato took full control of the tournament Friday with another 69 for 138 and a four-stroke lead over Fujii (73) and Yoko Inoue (72-70). A par round Saturday inflated Miyazato's lead to six strokes over runner-up Akiko Fukushima with the 210, and she finished it off with a 73 Sunday for the five-stroke victory over Fukushima, who closed with 72 for 288. The win, Miyazato's fourth of the season, gave her 10 in her two-plus-season career.

## Sankyo Ladies Open—¥60,000,000
Winner: Ji-Hee Lee

Ji-Hee Lee further established herself as South Korea's leading performer of the new millennium in Japan when she scored her sixth victory since 2001 on the Japan LPGA Tour — a one-stroke triumph in the Sankyo Ladies Open. Lee, who won four times and finished second on the money list in 2003, took the Sankyo title despite finishing with a one-over-par 73, thanks to the back-nine collapse of leader Hikaru Kobayashi, who tumbled to a 77 and dropped into a tie for fourth.

Coming off a poor performance in the Women's Open, Yuri Fudoh, a former Sankyo winner, made a tremendous start at Akagi Country Club, Gunma Prefecture. Running off six front-nine birdies and nine in all, Fudoh rolled to a course-record 63 and took a four-stroke lead over Lee and Kobayashi. However, she followed with 73 Saturday, and Kobayashi, a non-winner on the circuit, raced into a two-stroke lead with 66–133, two ahead of Lee and three in front of Fudoh. The South Korean's 208 final score edged Fudoh (73) and Sakura Yokomine (68) by a shot.

## Fujitsu Ladies—¥60,000,000
Winner: Yuri Fudoh

For the second week in a row, Yuri Fudoh was a first-round leader. In the first case, a four-stroke lead over the field did not stand up for a victory. At the Fujitsu Ladies, she merely had a share of first place with Midori Yoneyama, but went from there to a three-stroke victory, her fifth of the season and 37th of her career on the Japan LPGA Tour.

The second round spelled out the victory. Fudoh broke from her deadlock at 68 with sparkling 65 for 133, taking a four-stroke lead over Sakura Yokomine into the final round as Yoneyama dropped back into a five-way tie for third place with her 72–140. The impressive young Yokomine was the only player within seven strokes after 36 holes and she was only able to cut a shot off Fudoh's final margin Sunday, shooting 70 as Fudoh was carding 71 for a final, 12-under-par 204. It was Yokomine's second straight runner-up finish.

## Masters Golf Club Ladies—¥120,000,000
Winner: Paula Creamer

If Paula Creamer decides in the future to play the percentages as she lays out her tournament schedule, she will pencil in a couple of annual trips to Japan. After all, she was two for two in the win column in her forays to the Land of the Rising Sun in 2005. Creamer tacked a lucrative victory in the Masters Golf Club Ladies tournament onto her August win in the NEC Karuizawa 72 when she returned to Japan and Hyogo's Masters Golf Club in late October.

She had a tougher time of it in the Masters. Instead of breezing to a three-stroke victory with the lowest total of the season as she did in the NEC event, Creamer had to go an extra hole to pry the title away from Chieko Amanuma, who was trying to land her first win since her outstanding, five-victory season in 2001 when she finished second on the money list.

Creamer started slowly at Miki, managing a 71 that left her five strokes off the lead of Australian Tamie Durdin, continuing her notable performances on the circuit. A second-round 69 pumped Creamer into first place. At 140, she led by two over six players, including Amanuma, Durdin and Yuri Fudoh, and by three over five others, leaving no room for slippage Sunday. Paula's par round Sunday allowed Amanuma to catch her with 70 for her 212, but Creamer birdied the first extra hole to wrap up the victory.

## Hisako Higuchi IDC Otsukakagu Ladies—¥70,000,000
Winner: Ai Miyazato

The back-and-forth battle for supremacy on the Japan LPGA Tour between Yuri Fudoh and her young challenger, Ai Miyazato, swung back in Miyazato's favor at the Hisako Higuchi IDC Otsukakagu tournament the last weekend of October. With Fudoh sitting out that week, Miyazato had one less worry, but it probably wouldn't have made any difference. Never headed, she rolled to a seven-stroke, wire-to-wire victory with a 14-under-par 202. It gave her a match to Fudoh's five victories for the season and a remarkable 11 career wins in little more than two years.

Miyazato jumped off fast with a five-birdie 67 in the opening round, leading the tournament by a stroke over Keiko Sasaki, who had an eagle and two birdies in her bogey-free round. The margin ballooned to four Saturday when Miyazato added 68 for 135. Kaori Higo and Julie Lu of Taiwan (both with 71-68 scores) moved into second place.

Australia's Nikki Campbell, headed for her ninth top-10 finish of the season, provided the only challenge to Miyazato Sunday. She got off to a five-under start on the front nine to pull within two strokes of the leader, but Miyazato responded with a birdie at the eighth hole and went on to shoot 67 for the 202 and the seven-shot advantage over Campbell (67), youngster Shinobu Moromizato (68) and Higo and Lu, who had 70s.

## Mizuno Classic—¥110,000,000
Winner: Annika Sorenstam

Talk about comfort zones. When Annika Sorenstam arrived in Japan in early November on her annual title-collection trip, she already had nine victories on her 2005 record and had clinched Player-of-the-Year honors. Furthermore, she had already won seven times over the years in Japan, at least once in each of the previous four seasons. Four of those victories had come in successive years in the Mizuno Classic, the joint U.S./Japan LPGA tournament, and there she was, shooting for No. 5. Little wonder that the sensational Swede carried out her mission for the week, winning the Mizuno by three strokes and thereby becoming the first player in LPGA history to win the same event five consecutive seasons.

Sorenstam perched a stroke off the lead for two days before claiming the victory with her second 64 of the tournament. South Korea's Young Kim was hot for two days as the leader. On Friday, she, like Sorenstam, shot 30 on the front nine, at one point with six straight birdies, en route to a 63, and the 25-year-old continued her quest for her first career victory with a 67 Saturday. Annika matched her 67 for 131 and Jennifer Rosales of the Philippines climbed into third place with 67-65–132.

Undaunted by a steady drizzle of rain, Sorenstam methodically carved out the second 64 Sunday, pulling away from Kim and Rosales with four birdies on the last five holes of the Seta Golf Club's Kita course at Otsu, Shiga Prefecture. Her 195 was the lowest 54-hole score of the year in Japan. Rosales shot 66 to take second place. Kim took a 70 and slipped into a third-place tie at 200 with Sophie Gustafson of Sweden (66) and Yuri Fudoh, who couldn't overcome a 71 start despite follow-up rounds of 65 and 64.

## Itoen Ladies—¥70,000,000
Winner: Yuri Fudoh

Yuri Fudoh could hardly have been in a better frame of mind when she teed off in the Itoen Ladies tournament. She was coming off rounds of 65 and 64 the previous weekend in the Mizuno Classic and was playing in a tournament and on a course (Grand Island) where she had won three of her previous 37 titles on the Japan LPGA Tour. In addition, Ai Miyazato, her strongest competitor, was sidelined with bad toe.

Fudoh rode these advantages to her 38th victory, although it required a rally from a two-stroke deficit in the final round to do so. The ¥12.6 prize elevated her back into the lead in the tight money race with Miyazato. She trailed Hiromi Mogi by two shots after the first round. Mogi, winless since late in the 2004 season, shot 69, then tumbled to 74 Saturday as Yuko Saitoh went in front with 71-69–140. Ji-Hee Lee of South Korea was at 71-70–141, and Fudoh, with another 71, joined Shin Hyun Ju, Jeong-Eun Lee, Noriko Aso and Atomi Shiota at 142.

The five-season Japan champion had a brief mid-round stumble, but was in full charge Sunday. She birdied three of the first six holes and, after bogeys at the eighth and ninth, birdied four of the next five on her way to 67–209, seven under par. Hiroko Yamaguchi also shot 67 and tied for second at 211 with Saitoh, who had a 71.

## Daioseishi Elleair Ladies Open—¥80,000,000
Winner: Ai Miyazato

Back came Ai Miyazato, doing all that she could to capture the Japan LPGA Tour's money championship by successfully defending her 2004 victory in the Daioseishi Elleair Ladies Open in the year's next-to-last tournament. Idled the previous week by a sore toe as Yuri Fudoh reclaimed the lead in her run for a sixth straight No. 1 finish, Miyazato closed with a record-tying 65 at Elleair Golf Club in Ehime Prefecture and ran away with her sixth title of the season and 12th of her career.

With Fudoh tying for sixth, Miyazato eked back into the money lead, but would not be playing in the season finale LPGA Tour Championship the following week. She would be in America, competing (and winning) the final qualifier for the 2006 LPGA Tour.

With most of the attention on those two stars, Midori Yoneyama, a two-time winner and frequent contender during the season, got off quietly with 67 and the first-round lead, one stroke better than Ji-Hee Lee and the omni-present Akiko Fukushima. Miyazato shot one of the day's seven 69s, but Fudoh had a letdown after her Itoen victory and took a 75.

Miyazato still trailed by two strokes after Saturday's round, shooting 70–139 as Yuka Irie, winless for seven years, took the lead with 70-67–137, one in front of Woo-Soon Ko, the veteran South Korean winner. Ko hung in the chase Sunday until absorbing a double bogey at the 13th hole. Miyazato, who had four birdies over the first 10 holes, broke it open with consecutive birdies at the 14th, 15th and 16th. Ko's 71 put her in a three-way tie for second with Shiho Ohyama (69) and Kasumi Fujii (70).

Miyazato completed her second full season on the Japan LPGA Tour with earnings of ¥114,377,871.

## Japan LPGA Tour Championship—¥60,000,000
Winner: Shiho Ohyama

Yuri Fudoh was in a rather different position from that which she faced at the end of the previous season when she arrived at Miyazaki Country Club for the Japan LPGA Tour Championship, the 33rd and last event of the season. In 2004, she carried a slim lead over Ai Miyazato into the Tour Championship and clinched her fifth straight title by holding her off and winning the tournament. She didn't repeat victory in 2005 — Shiho Ohyama won her second title of the season — but she finished second and collected much more than she needed to overtake the absent Miyazato, who had sacrificed her shot at the money title in her quest for playing privileges on the 2006 U.S. LPGA Tour.

After Mitsuko Kawasaki, the first-round leader with 69, yielded the lead to her the second day, Ohyama held sway the rest of the way to the delight of the gallery in her home area. Ohyama, who would finish third on the money list, roared five strokes in front Friday with a five-birdie 67–137. Kawasaki was at 73–142, and Fudoh, revved up after starting with 73, climbed into third place with 70–143.

The 28-year-old Ohyama gave the contenders, particularly Fudoh, a chance Saturday when she slipped to 75–212. Fudoh shot 72 and cut the margin in half as she took over second place, but Ohyama's solid 71–283 wrapped up the third victory of her career. Fudoh had a par round for 287 and second prize gave her the No. 1 season total of ¥122,460,908.

# Australian Women's Tour

## ABC Learning Centres & FADL Group Classic—A$100,000
Winner: Nikki Campbell

Nikki Campbell collected her first professional victory after recording a final-round two-under-par 70 in difficult windy conditions at the ABC Learning Centres & Fadl Group Classic at Lakelands Golf Club. Campbell, from Canberra, defeated Queensland's Katherine Hull by two strokes with a 12-under-par total of 204. Three strokes ahead around the turn, Campbell's lead was reduced to one with two holes to play after two birdies from Hull, but then the challenger three-putted the 17th green from 15 feet.

The 23-year-old Campbell, who had spent the previous two years playing in Japan, parred the last two holes to clinch the victory and the first prize of A$15,000. Australian Anne-Marie Knight and France's Karine Icher shared third place a further two strokes back.

Campbell, who vaulted to the top of the leaderboard with a brilliant 64 in the second round, credited her experiences overseas as preparing her for the duel. "Katherine holed a few long putts on the back nine and that made me a bit edgy" Campbell said. "But I have been trying not to think too much about my golf and I didn't start looking at leaderboards or anything like that."

## Titanium Enterprises ALPG Players Championship—A$200,000
Winner: Katherine Hull

A week after finishing as a runner-up, Katherine Hull claimed her first victory in Australia in the familiar conditions on Queensland's Sunshine Coast at the Titanium Enterprises ALPG Players Championship. Hull completed a consistent performance with a closing 70, following two rounds of 69, over the Greg Norman-designed Club Pelican course.

The 22-year-old finished at eight under par and three strokes ahead of Lynette Brooky and Frenchwomen Gwladys Nocera and Karine Icher. A shot further back were Lora Fairclough, Iben Tinning, Cecilia Ekelundh and Sara Beautell, whose 67 was the best score of the day. Anne-Marie Knight, the overnight leader, dropped down the leaderboard after shooting 76.

Hull, who had won twice on the Futures Tour in America, won A$30,000 after making three birdies and only dropping one stroke in the final round. But it was a par on the ninth that gave her most confidence. "I really scrambled well today," said Hull. "I holed a six-foot par putt on the ninth and that was a clutch putt which got me into a good attitude for the back nine, and I played the back nine well this week.

"It's a very special victory for me. I don't know how many Australian events I've played in and I've never won yet, and after coming second last week, that was bittersweet. But this week, it's very sweet, especially in front of my family and friends who came out to support me."

## ANZ Ladies Masters—A$800,000
Winner: Karrie Webb

Karrie Webb's victory in the ANZ Ladies Masters put the 30-year-old Australian alongside one of her country's most revered players. By winning the event for the fifth time, Webb became the first Australian to achieve the feat at the same tournament since Peter Thomson won the fifth of his British Opens in 1965. She won the event four times in a row from 1998-2001, but four years later she had a lot of work to do on the final day.

Ai Miyazato, the 19-year-old Japanese player, led after each of the first three rounds following an opening 63. Webb was four behind going into the final day, but her twin weekend rounds of 67 gave the local hero a one-stroke victory. She finished at 16 under par with a total of 272, while Miyazato closed with a 72. Sharing third place at 12 under par were Italian Veronica Zorzi and Sweden's Maria Hjorth in an event co-sanctioned by the Ladies European Tour.

It took only four holes of the final round for Webb to draw even with the talented Japanese teenager. She parred the first hole, but then birdied the next, holed a chip from 25 yards for an eagle at the third and then birdied the fourth. Miyazato briefly regained the lead with a birdie at the sixth, but dropped a shot two holes later. It was at the 13th that Webb struck a decisive blow. A fine six-iron approach shot set up a eight-foot birdie putt, and then her opponent three-putted the next to fall two behind. A bogey at the last from the 30-year-old Webb was of no consequence.

"It's very satisfying," said Webb, who won the A$120,000 first prize. "I guess that after the way Ai started this week and by Friday I was seven shots behind, that was a big haul to get back. Today I got off to a really hot start and eliminated four shots in the first four holes and that made it a ball game then. I feel very lucky that I've got on up on Ai already, because she is already a star and she's got huge future ahead of her now."

# South African Women's Tour

## Women's World Cup of Golf—US$1,000,000
Winners: Ai Miyazato and Rui Kitada

Japan, featuring the youngest pairing among the 20 teams, won the inaugural Women's World Cup of Golf. Ai Miyazato, the 19-year-old rising star, and 23-year-old Rui Kitada experienced contrasting fortunes on the final day but combined to collect $100,000 each as victors on the Gary Player-designed Links course at Fancourt. The diminutive pair was presented with the trophy by another giant of the game from South Africa, Ernie Els.

While there had been team competitions before in the women's game, this was the first World Cup sanctioned by all the tours. A different format was played on each of the three days. Canada's Lorie Kane and Dawn Coe-Jones and Italy's Diana Luna and Giulia Sergas had the best fourball scores of seven-under 66. Foursomes over the formidable course was not such a straightforward task, but Koreans Jeong Jang and Bo Bae Song improved on their fourball score by six shots with a 68. But after two rounds it was Scotland's Catriona Matthew and Janice Moodie, with scores of 71 and 69, and the Japanese team, after rounds of 68 and 72, who shared the lead at six under par.

On Sunday both players' singles scores counted and fortunes fluctuated wildly. Miyazato's 67 was not just the lowest round of the day and a brilliant exhibition from such a talented newcomer but was compiled while her playing partner was shooting an 82 alongside her. Miyazato went to the turn in 31 and birdied the 10th to put Japan five ahead of the field.

But then Kitada suffered a horrific run. She had a double bogey at the 11th, bogeyed the 12th and the 14th and then had another double bogey at the 15th. At the next hole, the pressure mounting, Miyazato missed a birdie chance from three feet, while Kitada dropped another shot after missing a putt of 18 inches. Japan was now tied for the lead with Korea and the Philippines but saved the day at the par-three 17th. Miyazato hit a magical tee shot next to the pin, but before she could post the birdie, Kitada holed a 20-footer, and the two twos provided the eventual two-stroke winning margin.

"The putt at the 17th was the biggest putt of my career," admitted a tearful Kitada. "It was very difficult for me out there today and I felt that I was dragging my partner back on the back nine. That putt saved me and my team."

Miyazato, who won five times in her rookie season in Japan in 2004, said: "That's probably the best front nine I have ever played under pressure. I didn't feel any pressure as Rui was not playing her best and I was trying to help her out and concentrate on my own game. When she was down, I just brought myself up. This means so much to us and to our country and we are both very happy. We came here thinking we wanted to win it, and now we have, it is a great feeling."

Japan finished at three under par, while Korea and the Philippines shared second place, the latter pairing of Jennifer Rosales and Dorothy Delasin posting the best combined singles score of 146. Scotland's Matthew and Moodie finished fourth, with Australians Rachel Hetherington and Karrie Webb fifth. Italy proved how quickly fortunes could change, as they were in second place until both Luna and Sergas suffered triple bogeys at the 15th and they eventually finished tied for 10th.

## Pam Golding Ladies International—R300,000
Winner: Ashleigh Simon

Ashleigh Simon, the 15-year-old amateur, won her second professional title when she swept through the field at the Pam Golding Ladies International at Mowbray Golf Club to win by one shot. Starting the day tied for 10th place, seven shots off the lead at five over par, Simon made five birdies and did not drop a shot in her closing 67.

On a day when none of the other leading contenders broke 70, Simon closed with even par to win by one stroke over Morgana Robbertze and Gilly Tebbutt. Robbertze, the overnight leader, was three over for the front nine and finished with a 75, while Tebbutt, like Simon an amateur, also fell short with a 73. However, a magnificent fairway wood shot to 12 feet at the 18th gave her a chance of meeting Simon in a playoff but she missed the birdie putt. As the leading professional, Robbertze collected the top check of R45,000.

Simon had started the tournament with a triple-bogey seven on the first hole, but got off on a better footing on the final day. "I knew I had to shoot low today to have a chance, and everything just clicked," she said. "When I hit it on the fairway on the first and then made birdie, I knew I had a good chance. I am very proud to have won this prestigious event and would like to thank all those who work so hard to put these tournaments together."

## Acer Women's South African Open—R300,000
Winner: Maria Boden

Sweden's Maria Boden forgot all about her boyfriend's 31st birthday, but a winner's check of R45,000 was more than enough to buy him the Playstation he was after. And she could claim she had other things on her mind, as Boden won the Acer Women's South African Open by a convincing seven shots at the Royal Johannesburg and Kensington Golf Club. Boden closed with a 69 to win her first title on the Nedbank Women's Golf Tour with a total of 204, 12 under par, her lowest 54-hole score as a professional.

Boden went into the final round with a six-shot lead that was never challenged on the final day and which saw her card three birdies and no bogeys for her first international victory. "It was nice walking up 18 with a seven-shot lead," said the 27-year-old. "This was a much-needed win. In the past I have played well for two rounds and then not in the final round, so it was good to play well for all three rounds this week. Even with a six-shot lead you never know what happens on the final day, so I didn't play conservative golf. I just went out there and played like I did the other two rounds."

South Africa's Mandy Adamson finished second at five under after a 70, while Swede Cecilia Ekelundh took third at four under with a 71. Ashleigh Simon finished as the leading amateur in fourth place at three under with a final round of 67. Simon had charged through the field on the final day the previous week to win, but starting 11 strokes back this time was too much ground to make up. Laurette Maritz finished fifth at two under.

## Telkom Women's Classic—R300,000
Winner: Laurette Maritz

Laurette Maritz birdied her final two holes for a two-stroke victory in the Telkom Women's Classic at Zwartkop Country Club. Not having looked at the leaderboards during her final round of 68, Maritz did well to have added as much insurance as possible given her slow start and a fast finish by runner-up Antonella Cvitan. The Swede closed with three birdies in a row to claim second place on her own, but could not catch Maritz, who claimed her third Nedbank Women's Golf Tour victory in two years.

Maritz started the final round in a five-way tie for the lead and immediately drove into the rough. She had to get up and down for a par and then bogeyed the third. But it was her only dropped shot of the round and she birdied the fifth and the seventh before missing a number of birdie chances around the turn. Still, her finish was superb as she emerged from the pack.

"I didn't know the situation on the leaderboard because I don't like looking at the on-course leaderboards while I'm playing," said the veteran South African. "I've always found that I tend to get ahead of myself then. So when I walked onto the 18th green, that's the first time I saw that I was ahead. When I was missing all those birdie putts, my caddie told me to just keep going because I was hitting the ball great."

Maritz finished at seven under par with a total of 209, with Cvitan two strokes back, while Mandy Adamson and Carmen Alonso shared third place at 212. Lumien Lausberg finished as the leading amateur in tied fifth place at three under par, while Ashleigh Simon finished tied for 15th place.

## Nedbank Women's Masters—R300,000
Winner: Maria Beautell

Two young Spaniards, one still in her first year as a professional and the other in her first tournament as a professional, met in a playoff for the Nedbank Women's Masters at Killarney, and it was the more experienced of the pair who prevailed. Maria Beautell, younger sister of European Tour player Sara, gained her first professional victory after leaving the amateur game less than 12 months previously.

Beautell, 24, did not enjoy playing extra holes against an opponent who was a friend from the Spanish amateur circuit, but survived when the 20-year-old Carmen Alonso hit her second shot into the water at the 18th and bogeyed the first playoff hole. Alonso had led overnight at four under par, but only birdies at the 12th and 15th holes got her back to even par for the day, and she was caught by Beautell's six birdies, offset only by a double bogey at the third hole.

Ashleigh Simon briefly tied Alonso for the lead, but finished in third place at three under par. The amateur had the distinction of finishing top of the points table ahead of Laurette Maritz, who was assured of winning the money list by finishing fourth in the Masters.

# APPENDIXES

# Official World Golf Ranking
## (As of December 31, 2005)

| Ranking | | Player | Country | Points Average | Total Points | No. of Events | 03/04 Points Lost | 2005 Points Gained |
|---|---|---|---|---|---|---|---|---|
| 1 | (2) | Tiger Woods | USA | 17.16 | 755.20 | 44 | -481.24 | 772.44 |
| 2 | (1) | Vijay Singh | Fij | 9.78 | 615.93 | 63 | -666.21 | 514.53 |
| 3 | (5) | Phil Mickelson | USA | 8.14 | 366.25 | 45 | -339.78 | 369.93 |
| 4 | (4) | Retief Goosen | SAf | 8.10 | 429.35 | 53 | -353.00 | 386.20 |
| 5 | (3) | Ernie Els | SAf | 8.03 | 377.43 | 47 | -478.78 | 274.23 |
| 6 | (7) | Sergio Garcia | Spn | 7.23 | 332.41 | 46 | -223.23 | 296.40 |
| 7 | (21) | Jim Furyk | USA | 5.80 | 237.80 | 41 | -175.18 | 272.13 |
| 8 | (81) | Colin Montgomerie | Sco | 4.78 | 267.43 | 56 | -104.62 | 282.90 |
| 9 | (11) | Adam Scott | Aus | 4.68 | 234.19 | 50 | -236.21 | 245.42 |
| 10 | (15) | Chris DiMarco | USA | 4.58 | 233.81 | 51 | -199.27 | 224.69 |
| 11 | (43) | David Howell | Eng | 4.49 | 233.53 | 52 | -121.08 | 217.40 |
| 12 | (30) | Angel Cabrera | Arg | 4.44 | 186.63 | 42 | -118.02 | 180.13 |
| 13 | (26) | Luke Donald | Eng | 4.41 | 233.93 | 53 | -163.63 | 226.91 |
| 14 | (18) | Kenny Perry | USA | 4.35 | 200.05 | 46 | -206.10 | 233.30 |
| 15 | (20) | David Toms | USA | 4.30 | 210.79 | 49 | -196.89 | 235.82 |
| 16 | (89) | Michael Campbell | NZl | 4.19 | 221.98 | 53 | -106.74 | 249.88 |
| 17 | (6) | Padraig Harrington | Ire | 4.08 | 208.06 | 51 | -239.53 | 170.32 |
| 18 | (14) | Darren Clarke | NIr | 4.03 | 201.63 | 50 | -215.76 | 177.19 |
| 19 | (9) | Davis Love | USA | 3.89 | 186.52 | 48 | -244.37 | 177.87 |
| 20 | (74) | Tim Clark | SAf | 3.69 | 213.83 | 58 | -127.00 | 241.68 |
| 21 | (68) | Paul McGinley | Ire | 3.57 | 185.61 | 52 | -96.23 | 186.26 |
| 22 | (23) | Thomas Bjorn | Den | 3.41 | 177.14 | 52 | -149.25 | 164.19 |
| 23 | (140) | Bart Bryant | USA | 3.39 | 176.50 | 52 | -59.95 | 193.07 |
| 24 | (45) | Nick O'Hern | Aus | 3.38 | 185.83 | 55 | -116.64 | 179.98 |
| 25 | (31) | Fred Couples | USA | 3.26 | 137.10 | 42 | -117.61 | 138.04 |
| 26 | (126) | Jose M. Olazabal | Spn | 3.25 | 178.92 | 55 | -80.26 | 188.66 |
| 27 | (10) | Stewart Cink | USA | 3.19 | 175.28 | 55 | -209.76 | 115.13 |
| 28 | (22) | Scott Verplank | USA | 3.14 | 153.69 | 49 | -160.14 | 144.97 |
| 29 | (41) | John Daly | USA | 3.03 | 151.73 | 50 | -102.88 | 134.07 |
| 30 | (13) | Stuart Appleby | Aus | 2.93 | 166.83 | 57 | -217.65 | 147.51 |
| 31 | (25) | K.J. Choi | Kor | 2.88 | 175.91 | 61 | -171.60 | 144.27 |
| 32 | (145) | Henrik Stenson | Swe | 2.83 | 147.04 | 52 | -62.44 | 151.33 |
| 33 | (39) | Justin Leonard | USA | 2.81 | 140.47 | 50 | -129.02 | 145.08 |
| 34 | (118) | Ben Crane | USA | 2.80 | 134.47 | 48 | -73.26 | 139.08 |
| 35 | (33) | Robert Allenby | Aus | 2.77 | 182.93 | 66 | -140.05 | 162.34 |
| 36 | (38) | Mark Hensby | Aus | 2.75 | 151.52 | 55 | -109.52 | 123.06 |
| 37 | (1155T) | Sean O'Hair | USA | 2.73 | 109.14 | 40 | -22.77 | 131.90 |
| 38 | (19) | Chad Campbell | USA | 2.66 | 146.35 | 55 | -195.40 | 145.46 |
| 39 | (54) | Shingo Katayama | Jpn | 2.66 | 138.08 | 52 | -91.25 | 115.33 |
| 40 | (12) | Miguel A. Jimenez | Spn | 2.60 | 145.42 | 56 | -167.40 | 92.54 |
| 41 | (24) | Lee Westwood | Eng | 2.57 | 136.35 | 53 | -139.67 | 93.19 |
| 42 | (251) | Brandt Jobe | USA | 2.52 | 100.87 | 40 | -36.99 | 114.74 |
| 43 | (59) | Tom Lehman | USA | 2.50 | 105.20 | 42 | -92.88 | 106.81 |
| 44 | (28) | Shigeki Maruyama | Jpn | 2.50 | 140.02 | 56 | -145.35 | 121.08 |
| 45 | (53) | Fred Funk | USA | 2.45 | 144.79 | 59 | -142.28 | 155.92 |
| 46 | (37) | Peter Lonard | Aus | 2.40 | 148.57 | 62 | -148.37 | 131.76 |
| 47 | (50) | Rod Pampling | Aus | 2.37 | 134.83 | 57 | -107.18 | 115.13 |
| 48 | (8) | Mike Weir | Can | 2.35 | 108.01 | 46 | -212.79 | 83.29 |
| 49 | (65) | Tim Herron | USA | 2.31 | 124.58 | 54 | -111.21 | 130.51 |
| 50 | (70) | Geoff Ogilvy | Aus | 2.28 | 127.73 | 56 | -100.28 | 128.96 |

(  ) Ranking in brackets indicates position as of December 31, 2004.

| Ranking | | Player | Country | Points Average | Total Points | No. of Events | 03/04 Points Lost | 2005 Points Gained |
|---|---|---|---|---|---|---|---|---|
| 51 | (17) | Stephen Ames | Can | 2.24 | 114.11 | 51 | -141.97 | 62.05 |
| 52 | (29) | Paul Casey | Eng | 2.22 | 115.23 | 52 | -126.79 | 93.60 |
| 53 | (87) | Carl Pettersson | Swe | 2.21 | 136.71 | 62 | -62.70 | 114.38 |
| 54 | (80) | Bernhard Langer | Ger | 2.18 | 89.33 | 41 | -70.37 | 86.71 |
| 55 | (57) | Charles Howell | USA | 2.16 | 127.59 | 59 | -132.41 | 132.93 |
| 56 | (55) | Graeme McDowell | NIr | 2.15 | 124.69 | 58 | -99.60 | 100.13 |
| 57 | (44) | Zach Johnson | USA | 2.14 | 128.31 | 60 | -113.73 | 115.27 |
| 58 | (386) | Steve Elkington | Aus | 2.11 | 88.45 | 42 | -28.96 | 105.43 |
| 59 | (35) | Ian Poulter | Eng | 2.06 | 123.33 | 60 | -129.48 | 93.20 |
| 60 | (156) | Niclas Fasth | Swe | 2.05 | 108.80 | 53 | -70.22 | 123.59 |
| 61 | (78) | Craig Parry | Aus | 2.01 | 92.39 | 46 | -90.65 | 103.08 |
| 62 | (49) | Trevor Immelman | SAf | 1.98 | 109.15 | 55 | -114.05 | 93.95 |
| 63 | (135) | Mark Calcavecchia | USA | 1.96 | 103.87 | 53 | -60.79 | 110.16 |
| 64 | (144) | Ted Purdy | USA | 1.93 | 133.17 | 69 | -74.67 | 134.15 |
| 65 | (274) | Lucas Glover | USA | 1.88 | 110.73 | 59 | -33.61 | 114.77 |
| 66 | (32) | Jerry Kelly | USA | 1.84 | 110.40 | 60 | -134.60 | 81.57 |
| 67 | (63) | Brad Faxon | USA | 1.80 | 91.87 | 51 | -106.24 | 89.23 |
| 68 | (230) | Kenneth Ferrie | Eng | 1.78 | 101.26 | 57 | -36.17 | 103.25 |
| 69 | (107) | Tom Pernice, Jr. | USA | 1.74 | 109.42 | 63 | -73.82 | 97.76 |
| 70 | (61) | Richard Green | Aus | 1.72 | 94.72 | 55 | -82.57 | 64.53 |
| 71 | (34) | Rory Sabbatini | SAf | 1.71 | 89.05 | 52 | -116.89 | 61.41 |
| 72 | (254) | Billy Mayfair | USA | 1.69 | 106.46 | 63 | -57.36 | 127.70 |
| 73 | (296) | Olin Browne | USA | 1.69 | 99.47 | 59 | -33.74 | 103.48 |
| 74 | (139) | Vaughn Taylor | USA | 1.67 | 99.98 | 60 | -47.62 | 98.59 |
| 75 | (360) | Nick Dougherty | Eng | 1.66 | 109.56 | 66 | -45.00 | 132.52 |
| 76 | (184) | Paul Broadhurst | Eng | 1.63 | 86.18 | 53 | -40.11 | 82.65 |
| 77 | (72) | Carlos Franco | Par | 1.62 | 89.35 | 55 | -77.75 | 63.34 |
| 78 | (122) | Joe Ogilvie | USA | 1.62 | 100.35 | 62 | -82.43 | 109.07 |
| 79 | (170) | Stephen Dodd | Wal | 1.62 | 84.04 | 52 | -52.66 | 87.49 |
| 80 | (93) | Ryan Palmer | USA | 1.61 | 109.44 | 68 | -63.81 | 82.23 |
| 81 | (638) | Wes Short, Jr. | USA | 1.61 | 67.45 | 42 | -4.59 | 67.12 |
| 82 | (109) | Bo Van Pelt | USA | 1.60 | 100.48 | 63 | -68.38 | 94.76 |
| 83 | (198) | Bradley Dredge | Wal | 1.59 | 84.35 | 53 | -45.25 | 87.83 |
| 84 | (247) | Jason Bohn | USA | 1.57 | 90.88 | 58 | -33.38 | 93.47 |
| 85 | (102) | David Smail | NZl | 1.55 | 80.59 | 52 | -55.45 | 61.91 |
| 86 | (71) | Justin Rose | Eng | 1.55 | 94.39 | 61 | -88.64 | 76.94 |
| 87 | (42) | Thomas Levet | Frn | 1.55 | 88.14 | 57 | -106.51 | 42.40 |
| 88 | (168) | Greg Owen | Eng | 1.53 | 65.62 | 43 | -53.38 | 83.03 |
| 89 | (88) | S.K. Ho | Kor | 1.53 | 74.77 | 49 | -57.07 | 65.12 |
| 90 | (666) | Jason Gore | USA | 1.51 | 69.63 | 46 | -14.16 | 78.25 |
| 91 | (114) | David Lynn | Eng | 1.51 | 78.60 | 52 | -57.87 | 63.27 |
| 92 | (62) | Toru Taniguchi | Jpn | 1.50 | 85.36 | 57 | -62.44 | 49.36 |
| 93 | (92) | Raphael Jacquelin | Frn | 1.49 | 77.48 | 52 | -72.90 | 66.60 |
| 94 | (27) | Jay Haas | USA | 1.49 | 59.41 | 40 | -119.14 | 33.58 |
| 95 | (47) | Jonathan Kaye | USA | 1.48 | 72.50 | 49 | -127.75 | 81.21 |
| 96 | (106) | Paul Sheehan | Aus | 1.47 | 80.82 | 55 | -56.00 | 62.30 |
| 97 | (16) | Todd Hamilton | USA | 1.46 | 88.90 | 61 | -134.66 | 33.92 |
| 98 | (260) | Yasuharu Imano | Jpn | 1.43 | 80.30 | 56 | -30.70 | 80.53 |
| 99 | (91) | Arron Oberholser | USA | 1.43 | 63.01 | 44 | -67.98 | 58.99 |
| 100 | (129) | Keiichiro Fukabori | Jpn | 1.41 | 79.00 | 56 | -56.94 | 69.35 |

( ) Ranking in brackets indicates position as of December 31, 2004.

| Ranking | | Player | Country | Points Average | Total Points | No. of Events | 03/04 Points Lost | 2005 Points Gained |
|---|---|---|---|---|---|---|---|---|
| 101 | (36) | Steve Flesch | USA | 1.40 | 87.01 | 62 | -142.19 | 58.45 |
| 102 | (101) | Harrison Frazar | USA | 1.38 | 77.25 | 56 | -59.70 | 62.60 |
| 103 | (182) | Maarten Lafeber | Hol | 1.38 | 74.45 | 54 | -54.57 | 82.73 |
| 104 | (79) | Loren Roberts | USA | 1.38 | 55.09 | 40 | -71.06 | 51.31 |
| 105 | (203) | Heath Slocum | USA | 1.38 | 82.54 | 60 | -49.14 | 84.51 |
| 106 | (77) | Y.E. Yang | Kor | 1.37 | 73.83 | 54 | -42.47 | 49.64 |
| 107 | (75) | Jesper Parnevik | Swe | 1.37 | 69.64 | 51 | -75.33 | 47.63 |
| 108 | (195) | Peter Hanson | Swe | 1.35 | 71.40 | 53 | -39.35 | 70.79 |
| 109 | (64) | Bob Tway | USA | 1.34 | 69.49 | 52 | -96.37 | 65.92 |
| 110 | (95) | Thongchai Jaidee | Tha | 1.33 | 70.55 | 53 | -62.66 | 70.67 |
| 111 | (104) | Tim Petrovic | USA | 1.31 | 86.78 | 66 | -91.46 | 85.23 |
| 112 | (120) | Joe Durant | USA | 1.29 | 66.04 | 51 | -68.07 | 67.73 |
| 113 | (287) | Tadahiro Takayama | Jpn | 1.29 | 64.54 | 50 | -30.19 | 70.30 |
| 114 | (76) | Bob Estes | USA | 1.28 | 64.11 | 50 | -77.37 | 56.46 |
| 115 | (197) | John Senden | Aus | 1.28 | 80.61 | 63 | -49.94 | 78.37 |
| 116 | (205) | Pat Perez | USA | 1.28 | 76.73 | 60 | -50.84 | 79.74 |
| 117 | (136) | Simon Khan | Eng | 1.27 | 60.97 | 48 | -44.27 | 50.99 |
| 118 | (138) | Dudley Hart | USA | 1.26 | 65.66 | 52 | -48.07 | 64.53 |
| 119 | (83) | Toshimitsu Izawa | Jpn | 1.26 | 60.29 | 48 | -58.07 | 51.17 |
| 120 | (52) | Kirk Triplett | USA | 1.25 | 52.68 | 42 | -89.80 | 38.11 |
| 121 | (100) | Anders Hansen | Den | 1.25 | 63.95 | 51 | -55.99 | 48.49 |
| 122 | (58) | Jeff Maggert | USA | 1.25 | 57.51 | 46 | -79.49 | 45.63 |
| 123 | (144) | Jyoti Randhawa | Ind | 1.25 | 61.20 | 49 | -59.59 | 48.17 |
| 124 | (253) | Steve Webster | Eng | 1.23 | 64.14 | 52 | -40.28 | 71.16 |
| 125 | (117) | Jeff Sluman | USA | 1.23 | 68.92 | 56 | -75.17 | 69.23 |
| 126 | (86) | Joey Sindelar | USA | 1.23 | 73.78 | 60 | -72.68 | 55.26 |
| 127 | (84) | Brian Davis | Eng | 1.22 | 73.48 | 60 | -94.62 | 77.81 |
| 128 | (221) | Thaworn Wiratchant | Tha | 1.22 | 63.66 | 52 | -29.56 | 66.45 |
| 129 | (40) | Fredrik Jacobson | Swe | 1.22 | 62.21 | 51 | -113.06 | 55.28 |
| 130 | (51) | Nick Price | Zim | 1.22 | 48.72 | 40 | -82.59 | 45.39 |
| 131 | (213) | Richard Sterne | SAf | 1.22 | 71.75 | 59 | -40.81 | 72.76 |
| 132 | (66) | Stephen Gallacher | Sco | 1.20 | 63.83 | 53 | -65.26 | 26.74 |
| 133 | (1155T) | Joey Snyder | USA | 1.19 | 47.58 | 40 | -13.17 | 60.75 |
| 134 | (150) | Ryoken Kawagishi | Jpn | 1.18 | 67.33 | 57 | -37.65 | 51.74 |
| 135 | (123) | Barry Lane | Eng | 1.18 | 62.50 | 53 | -55.38 | 49.25 |
| 136 | (119) | Steven Conran | Aus | 1.17 | 60.66 | 52 | -52.25 | 46.45 |
| 137 | (166) | Tag Ridings | USA | 1.16 | 58.22 | 50 | -24.91 | 46.62 |
| 138 | (112) | Woody Austin | USA | 1.16 | 68.45 | 59 | -74.46 | 63.01 |
| 139 | (200T) | Dinesh Chand | Fij | 1.14 | 63.64 | 56 | -30.29 | 50.46 |
| 140 | (108) | Steve Lowery | USA | 1.12 | 67.02 | 60 | -61.90 | 50.39 |
| 141 | (270) | Jeff Brehaut | USA | 1.10 | 64.80 | 59 | -33.59 | 63.56 |
| 142 | (718) | Ryan Moore | USA | 1.10 | 43.84 | 40 | -8.28 | 49.00 |
| 143 | (193) | Charl Schwartzel | SAf | 1.09 | 66.70 | 61 | -42.12 | 60.60 |
| 144 | (153) | Corey Pavin | USA | 1.04 | 51.99 | 50 | -49.14 | 46.31 |
| 145 | (128) | Jean F. Remesy | Frn | 1.04 | 52.85 | 51 | -49.41 | 40.12 |
| 146 | (125) | Scott McCarron | USA | 1.04 | 52.83 | 51 | -72.37 | 59.17 |
| 147 | (157) | Peter O'Malley | Aus | 1.00 | 50.94 | 51 | -45.40 | 44.05 |
| 148 | (563) | G. Fernandez-Castano | Spn | 0.98 | 39.16 | 40 | -11.70 | 44.99 |
| 149 | (174) | Taichi Teshima | Jpn | 0.98 | 52.84 | 54 | -39.82 | 46.22 |
| 150 | (159) | Robert Gamez | USA | 0.97 | 57.31 | 59 | -58.07 | 55.09 |

( ) Ranking in brackets indicates position as of December 31, 2004.

| Ranking | | Player | Country | Points Average | Total Points | No. of Events | 03/04 Points Lost | 2005 Points Gained |
|---|---|---|---|---|---|---|---|---|
| 151 | (162) | Brett Quigley | USA | 0.97 | 59.96 | 62 | -56.97 | 62.43 |
| 152 | (132) | J.L. Lewis | USA | 0.96 | 59.64 | 62 | -73.89 | 61.43 |
| 153 | (200T) | Jose Manuel Lara | Spn | 0.96 | 57.58 | 60 | -35.00 | 54.44 |
| 154 | (234) | Gregory Havret | Frn | 0.96 | 54.68 | 57 | -41.52 | 61.34 |
| 155 | (257) | Arjun Atwal | Ind | 0.96 | 51.70 | 54 | -33.38 | 54.38 |
| 156 | (98) | Jonathan Byrd | USA | 0.96 | 55.50 | 58 | -67.18 | 40.79 |
| 157 | (209) | Billy Andrade | USA | 0.95 | 54.20 | 57 | -47.43 | 59.16 |
| 158 | (255) | Kaname Yokoo | Jpn | 0.94 | 53.85 | 57 | -22.65 | 43.39 |
| 159 | (60) | Stephen Leaney | Aus | 0.94 | 53.59 | 57 | -84.57 | 43.09 |
| 160 | (142) | Rocco Mediate | USA | 0.94 | 40.42 | 43 | -49.45 | 43.70 |
| 161 | (299) | Graeme Storm | Eng | 0.94 | 56.34 | 60 | -22.21 | 58.40 |
| 162 | (56) | Alex Cejka | Ger | 0.94 | 57.97 | 62 | -101.68 | 29.35 |
| 163 | (152) | Brett Rumford | Aus | 0.91 | 49.39 | 54 | -41.99 | 38.47 |
| 164 | (164) | Hiroyuki Fujita | Jpn | 0.91 | 47.26 | 52 | -46.64 | 45.86 |
| 165 | (226) | Hidemasa Hoshino | Jpn | 0.91 | 48.10 | 53 | -30.91 | 44.10 |
| 166 | (288T) | Steven Bowditch | Aus | 0.90 | 36.05 | 40 | -17.82 | 34.74 |
| 167 | (218) | Peter Hedblom | Swe | 0.90 | 45.02 | 50 | -39.43 | 51.01 |
| 168 | (243) | Naomichi Ozaki | Jpn | 0.90 | 35.91 | 40 | -29.33 | 38.83 |
| 169 | (293T) | Paul Lawrie | Sco | 0.89 | 46.29 | 52 | -27.07 | 50.01 |
| 170 | (207) | Aaron Baddeley | Aus | 0.89 | 50.55 | 57 | -48.52 | 60.98 |
| 171 | (111) | Tommy Armour | USA | 0.89 | 50.45 | 57 | -60.66 | 40.33 |
| 172 | (178) | Kevin Na | USA | 0.88 | 57.38 | 65 | -50.52 | 64.79 |
| 173 | (369T) | Pierre Fulke | Swe | 0.88 | 35.14 | 40 | -18.10 | 39.93 |
| 174 | (441) | Charles Warren | USA | 0.87 | 50.58 | 58 | -19.03 | 56.56 |
| 175 | (173) | Daniel Chopra | Swe | 0.87 | 67.00 | 77 | -44.99 | 53.50 |
| 176 | (69) | Briny Baird | USA | 0.87 | 54.78 | 63 | -94.40 | 37.54 |
| 177 | (67) | Duffy Waldorf | USA | 0.87 | 46.82 | 54 | -77.53 | 29.63 |
| 178 | (177) | James Kingston | SAf | 0.87 | 52.02 | 60 | -40.15 | 47.30 |
| 179 | (121) | Tetsuji Hiratsuka | Jpn | 0.87 | 50.23 | 58 | -61.41 | 41.59 |
| 180 | (124) | John Rollins | USA | 0.86 | 51.89 | 60 | -63.10 | 45.28 |
| 181 | (190) | Terry Pilkadaris | Aus | 0.85 | 36.40 | 43 | -22.61 | 26.86 |
| 182 | (250) | Daisuke Maruyama | Jpn | 0.85 | 47.37 | 56 | -35.54 | 48.09 |
| 183 | (137) | Kevin Sutherland | USA | 0.84 | 44.68 | 53 | -61.03 | 46.65 |
| 184 | (208) | Craig Barlow | USA | 0.83 | 42.57 | 51 | -38.85 | 42.44 |
| 185 | (48) | Joakim Haeggman | Swe | 0.83 | 45.90 | 55 | -65.10 | 21.75 |
| 186 | (110) | Scott Drummond | Sco | 0.83 | 45.60 | 55 | -51.93 | 26.36 |
| 187T | (1155T) | Shiv Kapur | Ind | 0.82 | 32.85 | 40 | -0.80 | 33.65 |
| 187T | (141) | Katsumasa Miyamoto | Jpn | 0.82 | 45.16 | 55 | -44.46 | 31.14 |
| 189 | (85) | John Huston | USA | 0.82 | 41.65 | 51 | -57.31 | 33.25 |
| 190 | (206) | J.J. Henry | USA | 0.82 | 50.55 | 62 | -41.99 | 47.83 |
| 191 | (94) | Ben Curtis | USA | 0.81 | 42.19 | 52 | -70.43 | 38.07 |
| 192 | (172) | Soren Kjeldsen | Den | 0.81 | 42.83 | 53 | -39.20 | 38.99 |
| 193 | (225) | Robert-Jan Derksen | Hol | 0.81 | 43.51 | 54 | -32.74 | 41.76 |
| 194 | (258) | Liang Wen-chong | Chi | 0.79 | 38.83 | 49 | -17.27 | 33.78 |
| 195 | (163) | Hank Kuehne | USA | 0.79 | 47.35 | 60 | -44.86 | 40.36 |
| 196 | (158) | Hidemichi Tanaka | Jpn | 0.79 | 48.92 | 62 | -48.98 | 40.65 |
| 197 | (309) | Simon Dyson | Eng | 0.79 | 43.36 | 55 | -26.80 | 47.46 |
| 198 | (368) | James Driscoll | USA | 0.79 | 39.36 | 50 | -19.59 | 45.62 |
| 199 | (210) | Soren Hansen | Den | 0.79 | 41.70 | 53 | -37.20 | 41.52 |
| 200 | (180) | Prayad Marksaeng | Tha | 0.78 | 50.11 | 64 | -39.45 | 41.86 |

( ) Ranking in brackets indicates position as of December 31, 2004.

## Age Groups of Current Top 100 World Ranked Players

| Under 25 | 25-28 | 29-30 | 31-32 | 33-34 | 35-36 | 37-38 | 39-42 | Over 43 |
|---|---|---|---|---|---|---|---|---|
| | | | | | | | Singh | |
| | | | | | | | Montgomerie | |
| | | | | | | | Love | |
| | | | | | | | McGinley | |
| | | | | | | | Olazabal | |
| | Garcia | | Cink | | Mickelson | | Verplank | |
| | Scott | Woods | C.Campbell | | Goosen | | Daly | K. Perry |
| | Donald | D. Howell | Katayama | | Els | | Jimenez | B. Bryant |
| | Ogilvy | T. Clark | Westwood | Harrington | Furyk | | Jobe | Couples |
| | Casey | Stenson | Purdy | Bjorn | Cabrera | | Ames | Lehman |
| | Pettersson | Crane | Ogilvie | O'Hern | M.Campbell | | C. Parry | Funk |
| | C. Howell | Z. Johnson | Dredge | Appleby | K.J. Choi | DiMarco | Kelly | Langer |
| | McDowell | Poulter | Bohn | Leonard | Maruyama | Toms | Mayfair | Elkington |
| | Immelman | Sabbatini | S.K. Ho | Allenby | Pampling | Clarke | Broadhurst | Calcavecchia |
| | Glover | V. Taylor | Gore | Hensby | Weir | Lonard | Franco | Faxon |
| | Ferrie | R. Palmer | Lynn | Fasth | Herron | Levet | Dodd | Pernice |
| O'Hair | Rose | Van Pelt | Jacquelin | R. Green | Smail | Taniguchi | Short | Browne |
| Dougherty | Sheehan | Oberholser | Imano | Owen | Kaye | Fukabori | Hamilton | Haas |

## 2005 World Ranking Review

### Major Movements

| Upward | | | | Downward | | | |
|---|---|---|---|---|---|---|---|
| Name | Net Points Gained | Position 2004 | Position 2005 | Name | Net Points Lost | Position 2004 | Position 2005 |
| Tiger Woods | 291 | 2 | 1 | Ernie Els | 204 | 3 | 5 |
| Colin Montgomerie | 178 | 81 | 8 | Vijay Singh | 151 | 1 | 2 |
| Michael Campbell | 143 | 89 | 16 | Mike Weir | 129 | 8 | 48 |
| Bart Bryant | 133 | 140 | 23 | Todd Hamilton | 100 | 16 | 97 |
| Tim Clark | 114 | 74 | 20 | Stewart Cink | 94 | 10 | 27 |
| Sean O'Hair | 109 | – | 37 | Jay Haas | 85 | 27 | 94 |
| Jose Maria Olazabal | 108 | 126 | 26 | Chris Riley | 84 | 46 | 201 |
| Jim Furyk | 97 | 21 | 7 | Steve Flesch | 83 | 36 | 101 |
| David Howell | 96 | 43 | 11 | Stephen Ames | 80 | 17 | 51 |
| Paul McGinley | 90 | 68 | 21 | Miguel Angel Jimenez | 74 | 12 | 39 |
| Henrik Stenson | 88 | 145 | 32 | Alex Cejka | 72 | 56 | 162 |
| Nick Dougherty | 87 | 360 | 75 | Stuart Appleby | 70 | 13 | 30 |
| Lucas Glover | 81 | 274 | 65 | Padraig Harrington | 69 | 6 | 17 |
| Brandt Jobe | 77 | 251 | 42 | Davis Love | 66 | 9 | 19 |
| Steve Elkington | 76 | 386 | 58 | Thomas Levet | 64 | 42 | 87 |
| Sergio Garcia | 73 | 7 | 6 | | | | |
| Billy Mayfair | 70 | 254 | 72 | | | | |
| Olin Browne | 69 | 296 | 73 | | | | |
| Kenneth Ferrie | 67 | 230 | 68 | | | | |
| Ben Crane | 65 | 118 | 34 | | | | |
| Jason Gore | 64 | 666 | 90 | | | | |
| Nick O'Hern | 63 | 45 | 24 | | | | |
| Luke Donald | 63 | 26 | 13 | | | | |
| Wes Short, Jr. | 62 | 638 | 81 | | | | |
| Angel Cabrera | 62 | 30 | 12 | | | | |

# Highest-Rated Events of 2005

| | Event | Top 5 | Top 15 | Top 30 | Top 50 | Top 100 | World Rating Points |
|---|---|---|---|---|---|---|---|
| | | | No. of World Ranked Players Participating | | | | World Rating Points |
| 1 | PGA Championship | 4 | 13 | 28 | 48 | 93 | 793 |
| 2 | The Open Championship | 5 | 14 | 29 | 48 | 80 | 768 |
| 3 | U.S. Open Championship | 5 | 15 | 29 | 48 | 70 | 753 |
| 4 | Masters Tournament | 5 | 15 | 30 | 50 | 67 | 735 |
| 5 | The Players Championship | 5 | 15 | 30 | 50 | 82 | 810 |
| 6 | WGC - Accenture Match Play | 4 | 14 | 29 | 49 | 64 | 701 |
| 7 | WGC - NEC Invitational | 4 | 14 | 29 | 49 | 62 | 692 |
| 8 | WGC - American Express Ch. | 3 | 13 | 27 | 46 | 62 | 649 |
| 9 | Bay Hill Invitational | 4 | 9 | 20 | 34 | 62 | 590 |
| 10 | Memorial Tournament | 3 | 9 | 18 | 33 | 62 | 570 |
| 11 | Booz Allen Classic | 4 | 10 | 20 | 31 | 60 | 565 |
| 12 | Wachovia Championship | 3 | 10 | 19 | 29 | 54 | 535 |
| 13 | Ford Championship | 4 | 12 | 20 | 28 | 48 | 520 |
| 14 | EDS Byron Nelson Champ. | 5 | 9 | 17 | 28 | 50 | 505 |
| 15 | Nissan Open | 1 | 5 | 18 | 33 | 64 | 519 |
| 16 | BMW Championship | 2 | 5 | 10 | 16 | 31 | 288 |
| 17 | FBR Open | 2 | 5 | 16 | 27 | 50 | 435 |
| 18 | Sony Open | 3 | 5 | 12 | 23 | 48 | 432 |
| 19 | Chrysler Championship | 2 | 4 | 8 | 24 | 53 | 415 |
| 20 | Bank of America Colonial | 1 | 7 | 19 | 26 | 47 | 417 |
| 21 | Buick Invitational | 4 | 5 | 10 | 23 | 40 | 417 |
| 22 | The Tour Championship | 3 | 11 | 16 | 23 | 29 | 381 |
| 23 | Bob Hope Chrysler Classic | 1 | 5 | 12 | 22 | 46 | 372 |
| 24 | The International | 2 | 6 | 14 | 19 | 42 | 360 |
| 25 | Cialis Western Open | 2 | 4 | 8 | 18 | 44 | 361 |
| 26 | Mercedes Championships | 4 | 9 | 13 | 19 | 26 | 337 |
| 27 | 84 Lumber Classic | 2 | 5 | 9 | 17 | 41 | 341 |
| 28 | Funai Classic at Disney | 3 | 4 | 8 | 14 | 37 | 341 |
| 29 | Michelin Champ. at Las Vegas | 1 | 3 | 9 | 19 | 43 | 332 |
| 30 | AT&T Pebble Beach Pro-Am | 2 | 5 | 10 | 18 | 34 | 321 |
| 31 | MCI Heritage | 0 | 2 | 8 | 22 | 46 | 325 |
| 32 | Honda Classic | 1 | 4 | 8 | 16 | 38 | 307 |
| 33 | Barclays Classic | 1 | 5 | 11 | 18 | 33 | 308 |
| 34 | Barclays Scottish Open | 3 | 6 | 10 | 12 | 27 | 274 |
| 35 | Zurich Classic of New Orleans | 1 | 5 | 6 | 14 | 32 | 274 |
| 36 | HSBC Champions | 2 | 4 | 8 | 13 | 26 | 259 |
| 37 | Buick Open | 2 | 4 | 6 | 11 | 23 | 259 |
| 38 | Volvo Masters | 0 | 5 | 12 | 14 | 26 | 231 |
| 39 | Shell Houston Open | 1 | 2 | 5 | 11 | 34 | 247 |
| 40 | Johnnie Walker Classic | 2 | 5 | 6 | 9 | 16 | 194 |

# World Golf Rankings 1968-2005

| Year | No. 1 | No. 2 | No. 3 | No. 4 | No. 5 |
|------|-------|-------|-------|-------|-------|
| 1968 | Nicklaus | Palmer | Casper | Player | Charles |
| 1969 | Nicklaus | Player | Casper | Palmer | Charles |
| 1970 | Nicklaus | Player | Casper | Trevino | Charles |
| 1971 | Nicklaus | Trevino | Player | Palmer | Casper |
| 1972 | Nicklaus | Player | Trevino | Crampton | Palmer |
| 1973 | Nicklaus | Weiskopf | Trevino | Player | Crampton |
| 1974 | Nicklaus | Miller | Player | Weiskopf | Trevino |
| 1975 | Nicklaus | Miller | Weiskopf | Irwin | Player |
| 1976 | Nicklaus | Irwin | Miller | Player | Green |
| 1977 | Nicklaus | Watson | Green | Irwin | Crenshaw |
| 1978 | Watson | Nicklaus | Irwin | Green | Player |
| 1979 | Watson | Nicklaus | Irwin | Trevino | Player |
| 1980 | Watson | Trevino | Aoki | Crenshaw | Nicklaus |
| 1981 | Watson | Rogers | Aoki | Pate | Trevino |
| 1982 | Watson | Floyd | Ballesteros | Kite | Stadler |
| 1983 | Ballesteros | Watson | Floyd | Norman | Kite |
| 1984 | Ballesteros | Watson | Norman | Wadkins | Langer |
| 1985 | Ballesteros | Langer | Norman | Watson | Nakajima |
| 1986 | Norman | Langer | Ballesteros | Nakajima | Bean |
| 1987 | Norman | Ballesteros | Langer | Lyle | Strange |
| 1988 | Ballesteros | Norman | Lyle | Faldo | Strange |
| 1989 | Norman | Faldo | Ballesteros | Strange | Stewart |
| 1990 | Norman | Faldo | Olazabal | Woosnam | Stewart |
| 1991 | Woosnam | Faldo | Olazabal | Ballesteros | Norman |
| 1992 | Faldo | Couples | Woosnam | Olazabal | Norman |
| 1993 | Faldo | Norman | Langer | Price | Couples |
| 1994 | Price | Norman | Faldo | Langer | Olazabal |
| 1995 | Norman | Price | Langer | Els | Montgomerie |
| 1996 | Norman | Lehman | Montgomerie | Els | Couples |
| 1997 | Norman | Woods | Price | Els | Love |
| 1998 | Woods | O'Meara | Duval | Love | Els |
| 1999 | Woods | Duval | Montgomerie | Love | Els |
| 2000 | Woods | Els | Duval | Mickelson | Westwood |
| 2001 | Woods | Mickelson | Duval | Els | Love |
| 2002 | Woods | Mickelson | Els | Garcia | Goosen |
| 2003 | Woods | Singh | Els | Love | Furyk |
| 2004 | Singh | Woods | Els | Goosen | Mickelson |
| 2005 | Woods | Singh | Mickelson | Goosen | Els |

(The World of Professional Golf 1968-1985; World Ranking 1986-2005)

| Year | No. 6 | No. 7 | No. 8 | No. 9 | No. 10 |
|------|-------|-------|-------|-------|--------|
| 1968 | Boros | Coles | Thomson | Beard | Nagle |
| 1969 | Beard | Archer | Trevino | Barber | Sikes |
| 1970 | Devlin | Coles | Jacklin | Beard | Huggett |
| 1971 | Barber | Crampton | Charles | Devlin | Weiskopf |
| 1972 | Jacklin | Weiskopf | Oosterhuis | Heard | Devlin |
| 1973 | Miller | Oosterhuis | Wadkins | Heard | Brewer |
| 1974 | M. Ozaki | Crampton | Irwin | Green | Heard |
| 1975 | Green | Trevino | Casper | Crampton | Watson |
| 1976 | Watson | Weiskopf | Marsh | Crenshaw | Geiberger |
| 1977 | Marsh | Player | Weiskopf | Floyd | Ballesteros |
| 1978 | Crenshaw | Marsh | Ballesteros | Trevino | Aoki |
| 1979 | Aoki | Green | Crenshaw | Ballesteros | Wadkins |
| 1980 | Pate | Ballesteros | Bean | Irwin | Player |
| 1981 | Ballesteros | Graham | Crenshaw | Floyd | Lietzke |
| 1982 | Pate | Nicklaus | Rogers | Aoki | Strange |
| 1983 | Nicklaus | Nakajima | Stadler | Aoki | Wadkins |
| 1984 | Faldo | Nakajima | Stadler | Kite | Peete |
| 1985 | Wadkins | O'Meara | Strange | Pavin | Sutton |
| 1986 | Tway | Sutton | Strange | Stewart | O'Meara |
| 1987 | Woosnam | Stewart | Wadkins | McNulty | Crenshaw |
| 1988 | Crenshaw | Woosnam | Frost | Azinger | Calcavecchia |
| 1989 | Kite | Olazabal | Calcavecchia | Woosnam | Azinger |
| 1990 | Azinger | Ballesteros | Kite | McNulty | Calcavecchia |
| 1991 | Couples | Langer | Stewart | Azinger | Davis |
| 1992 | Langer | Cook | Price | Azinger | Love |
| 1993 | Azinger | Woosnam | Kite | Love | Pavin |
| 1994 | Els | Couples | Montgomerie | M. Ozaki | Pavin |
| 1995 | Pavin | Faldo | Couples | M. Ozaki | Elkington |
| 1996 | Faldo | Mickelson | M. Ozaki | Love | O'Meara |
| 1997 | Mickelson | Montgomerie | M. Ozaki | Lehman | O'Meara |
| 1998 | Price | Montgomerie | Westwood | Singh | Mickelson |
| 1999 | Westwood | Singh | Price | Mickelson | O'Meara |
| 2000 | Montgomerie | Love | Sutton | Singh | Lehman |
| 2001 | Garcia | Toms | Singh | Clarke | Goosen |
| 2002 | Toms | Harrington | Singh | Love | Montgomerie |
| 2003 | Weir | Goosen | Harrington | Toms | Perry |
| 2004 | Harrington | Garcia | Weir | Love | Cink |
| 2005 | Garcia | Furyk | Montgomerie | Scott | DiMarco |

# World's Winners of 2005

## U.S. PGA TOUR

| | |
|---|---|
| Mercedes Championships | Stuart Appleby |
| Sony Open in Hawaii | Vijay Singh |
| Buick Invitational | Tiger Woods |
| Bob Hope Chrysler Classic | Justin Leonard |
| FBR Open | Phil Mickelson |
| AT&T Pebble Beach National Pro-Am | Phil Mickelson (2) |
| Nissan Open | Adam Scott |
| WGC - Accenture Match Play Championship | David Toms |
| Chrysler Classic of Tucson | Geoff Ogilvy |
| Ford Championship at Doral | Tiger Woods (2) |
| Honda Classic | Padraig Harrington |
| Bay Hill Invitational | Kenny Perry |
| The Players Championship | Fred Funk |
| BellSouth Classic | Phil Mickelson (3) |
| Masters Tournament | Tiger Woods (3) |
| MCI Heritage | Peter Lonard |
| Shell Houston Open | Vijay Singh (2) |
| Zurich Classic of New Orleans | Tim Petrovic |
| Wachovia Championship | Vijay Singh (3) |
| EDS Byron Nelson Championship | Ted Purdy |
| Bank of America Colonial | Kenny Perry (2) |
| FedEx St. Jude Classic | Justin Leonard (2) |
| Memorial Tournament | Bart Bryant |
| Booz Allen Classic | Sergio Garcia |
| U.S. Open Championship | Michael Campbell |
| Barclays Classic | Padraig Harrington (2) |
| Cialis Western Open | Jim Furyk |
| John Deere Classic | Sean O'Hair |
| B.C. Open | Jason Bohn |
| U.S. Bank Championship in Milwaukee | Ben Crane |
| Buick Open | Vijay Singh (4) |
| The International | Retief Goosen |
| PGA Championship | Phil Mickelson (4) |
| WGC - NEC Invitational | Tiger Woods (5) |
| Reno-Tahoe Open | Vaughn Taylor |
| Buick Championship | Brad Faxon |
| Deutsche Bank Championship | Olin Browne |
| Bell Canadian Open | Mark Calcavecchia |
| 84 Lumber Classic | Jason Gore (4) |
| Valero Texas Open | Robert Gamez |
| Chrysler Classic of Greensboro | K.J. Choi (2) |
| WGC - American Express Championship | Tiger Woods (6) |
| Michelin Championship at Las Vegas | Wes Short, Jr. |
| Funai Classic at the Walt Disney World Resort | Lucas Glover |
| Chrysler Championship | Carl Pettersson |
| The Tour Championship | Bart Bryant (2) |
| Southern Farm Bureau Classic | Heath Slocum |

## SPECIAL EVENTS

| | |
|---|---|
| Tavistock Cup | Isleworth/Lake Nona |
| CVS Charity Classic | Fred Funk (2)/Chris DiMarco |
| The Presidents Cup | United States |
| Franklin Templeton Shootout | John Huston/Kenny Perry (3) |
| PGA Grand Slam of Golf | Tiger Woods (8) |

| | |
|---|---|
| MBNA WorldPoints Father-Son Challenge | Bernhard/Stefan Langer |
| Target World Challenge | Luke Donald |

## NATIONWIDE TOUR

| | |
|---|---|
| BellSouth Panama Championship | Vance Veazey |
| Chitimacha Louisiana Open | Ryan Hietala |
| Virginia Beach Open | Troy Matteson |
| BMW Charity Pro-Am at The Cliffs | Shane Bertsch |
| The Rex Hospital Open | Eric Axley |
| Rheem Classic | Chris Couch |
| Henrico County Open | Chad Collins |
| Chattanooga Classic | Jason Schultz |
| LaSalle Bank Open | Chris Couch (2) |
| Knoxville Open | Kim Felton |
| Northeast Pennsylvania Classic | Greg Kraft |
| Lake Erie Charity Classic | Esteban Toledo |
| National Mining Association Pete Dye Classic | Jason Gore |
| Scholarship America Showdown | Jason Gore (2) |
| Canadian PGA Championship | Jon Mills |
| Preferred Health Systems Wichita Open | Joe Daley |
| Cox Classic | Jason Gore (3) |
| Price Cutter Charity Championship | Roger Tambellini |
| Xerox Classic | Rick Price |
| Cleveland Open | Andrew Johnson |
| Alberta Classic | Peter Tomasulo (2) |
| Envirocare Utah Classic | Garrett Willis |
| Mark Christopher Charity Classic | Troy Matteson (2) |
| Albertsons Boise Open | Greg Chalmers |
| Oregon Classic | Jeff Gove |
| Gila River Golf Classic | David McKenzie |
| Permian Basin Charity Golf Classic | Kris Cox |
| Nationwide Tour Championship | David Branshaw |

## CANADIAN TOUR

| | |
|---|---|
| Barton Creek Austin Pro-Am Classic | Scott Gibson |
| Barton Creek Austin Challenge | Omar Uresti |
| Northern California Classic | Jim Seki |
| Foster Farms California Classic | Stuart Anderson |
| Corona Mazatlan Classic | Jaime Gomez |
| Michelin Morelia Classic | David Mathis |
| Times Colonist Open | Craig Taylor |
| Telus Edmonton Open | Matt McQuillan |
| MTS Classic | Lee Williamson |
| Montreal Open | Peter Tomasulo |
| Bay Mills Open Players Championship | Michael Harris |
| Niagara Fallsview Casino Resort Pro-Am Classic | Michael Harris (2) |

## TOUR DE LAS AMERICAS (SOUTH AMERICA)

| | |
|---|---|
| Costa Rica Open | Kyle Dobbs |
| Panama Masters | Kevin Haefner |
| Telefonica de Guatemala | Cesar Monasterio |
| Siemens Venezuela Open | Miguel Rodriguez |
| American Express Puerto Rico Open | Daniel Barbetti |
| Players Championship Acafest | Antonio Serna |
| American Express Brazil Classic | Miguel Fernando |
| MasterCard Brazil Open | Miguel Guzman |
| Torneo de Maestros Copa Personal | Angel Cabrera (2) |
| Roberto de Vicenzo Classic | Andres Romero (2) |
| Abierto Mexicano Corona | Antonio Maldonado |
| Abierto de Barranquilla | Oswaldo Villada |
| Visa Argentine Open | Kevin Stadler |

## PGA EUROPEAN TOUR

| | |
|---|---|
| Dubai Desert Classic | Ernie Els |
| Qatar Masters | Ernie Els (2) |
| Estoril Open de Portugal Caixa Geral de Depositos | Paul Broadhurst |
| Madeira Island Open Caixa Geral de Depositos | Robert-Jan Derksen |
| Jazztel Open de Espana en Andalucia | Peter Hanson |
| Telecom Italia Open | Steve Webster |
| Daily Telegraph Dunlop Masters | Thomas Bjorn |
| Nissan Irish Open | Stephen Dodd |
| BMW Championship | Angel Cabrera |
| Celtic Manor Wales Open | Miguel Angel Jimenez |
| KLM Open | Gonzalo Fernandez-Castan |
| Aa St. Omer Open | Joakim Backstrom |
| Open de France | Jean-Francois Remesy |
| Smurfit European Open | Kenneth Ferrie |
| JP McManus Pro-Am | Padraig Harrington (3) |
| Barclays Scottish Open | Tim Clark (2) |
| The Open Championship | Tiger Woods (4) |
| Deutsche Bank Players' Championship of Europe | Niclas Fasth (2) |
| Scandinavian Masters | Mark Hensby |
| Johnnie Walker Championship at Gleneagles | Emanuele Canonica |
| Cadillac Russian Open | Mikael Lundberg |
| BMW International Open | David Howell |
| Omega European Masters | Sergio Garcia (2) |
| Linde German Masters | Retief Goosen (3) |
| HSBC World Match Play | Michael Campbell (2) |
| Seve Trophy | Great Britain & Ireland |
| Dunhill Links Championship | Colin Montgomerie |
| Abama Open de Canarias | John Bickerton |
| Open de Madrid | Raphael Jacquelin |
| Mallorca Classic | Jose Maria Olazabal |
| Volvo Masters | Paul McGinley |
| WGC - Algarve World Cup in Portugal | Stephen Dodd (2)/Bradley Dredge |

## CHALLENGE TOUR

| | |
|---|---|
| Tusker Kenya Open | Daniel Vancsik |
| Peugeot Challenge R.C.G. El Prat | Tomas Jesus Munoz |
| FirstPlus Wales Challenge | Olivier David |
| XX Tessali-Metaponto Open di Puglia e Basilicata | Rafael Gomez |
| Riu Tikida Hotels Moroccan Classic | Fredrik Widmark |
| Thomas Bjorn Open | Toni Karjalainen |
| Galeria Kaufhof Pokal Challenge | Gareth Davies |
| Open Mahou de Madrid | Benn Barham |
| Open des Volcans Challenge de France | Ilya Goroneskoul |
| Texbond Open | Fredrik Widmark (2) |
| Ireland Ryder Cup Challenge | Marc Warren |
| Rolex Trophy | Marc Warren (2) |
| Skandia PGA Open | David Patrick |
| Morson International Pro-Am Challenge | Andres Romero |
| BA-CA Golf Open | Michael Hoey |
| Telia Challenge Waxholm | Morten Hagen |
| Rotterdam International Open | Per G. Nyman |
| Kazakhstan Open | Stephen Browne |
| Open de Toulouse | Brad Sutterfield |
| Apulia San Domenico Grand Final | Carl Suneson |

## ASIAN TOUR

| | |
|---|---|
| Caltex Masters | Nick Dougherty |
| Carlsberg Malaysian Open | Thongchai Jaidee |
| Myanmar Open | Scott Strange |

| | |
|---|---|
| Thai Airways International Thailand Open | Richard Lee |
| TCL Classic | Paul Casey |
| Enjoy Jakarta Standard Chartered Indonesia Open | Thaworn Wiratchant |
| Visa Dynasty Cup | Asia |
| Johnnie Walker Classic | Adam Scott (2) |
| BMW Asian Open | Ernie Els (3) |
| SK Telecom Open | K.J. Choi |
| Macau Open | Wang Ter-chang |
| Philippine Open | Adam Le Vesconte |
| KT&G Maekyung Open | Choi Sang-ho |
| Brunei Open | Terry Pilkadaris |
| Volkswagen Masters China | Retief Goosen (2) |
| Singapore Open | Adam Scott (3) |
| Taiwan Open | Thaworn Wiratchant (2) |
| Mercuries Taiwan Masters | Lu Wei-chih |
| Crowne Plaza Open | Prayad Marksaeng |
| Bangkok Airways Open | Lu Wen-teh |
| Hero Honda Indian Open | Thaworn Wiratchant (3) |
| Double A International Open | *Chinarat Phadungsil |
| HSBC Champions Tournament | David Howell (2) |
| Carlsberg Masters Vietnam | Thaworn Wiratchant (4) |
| Volvo China Open | Paul Casey (2) |
| UBS Hong Kong Open | Colin Montgomerie (2) |
| Volvo Masters of Asia | Shiv Kapur |

## JAPAN TOUR

| | |
|---|---|
| Token Homemate Cup | Tadahiro Takayama |
| Tsuruya Open | Naomichi Ozaki |
| Chunichi Crowns | Naomichi Ozaki (2) |
| Japan PGA Championship | S.K. Ho |
| Munsingwear Open KSB Cup | Hiroyuki Fujita |
| Mitsubishi Diamond Cup | Chang Ik-je |
| JCB Classic Sendai | S.K. Ho (2) |
| Mandom Lucido Yomiuri Open | Satoru Hirota |
| Mizuno Open | Chris Campbell |
| Japan Golf Tour Championship | Kazuhiko Hosokawa |
| Woodone Open Hiroshima | Takao Nogami |
| Sega Sammy Cup | Lin Keng-chi |
| Aiful Cup | Tatsuhiko Takahashi |
| Sun Chlorella Classic | Keiichiro Fukabori |
| Under Armour KBC Augusta | Toshimitsu Izawa |
| Fujisankei Classic | Daisuke Maruyama |
| Suntory Open | Yasuharu Imano |
| ANA Open | Keiichiro Fukabori (2) |
| Acom International | David Smail |
| Coca-Cola Tokai Classic | Y.E. Yang |
| Japan Open | Shingo Katayama |
| Bridgestone Open | David Smail (2) |
| ABC Championship | Shingo Katayama (2) |
| Asahiryokuken Yomiuri Asoiizuka Memorial | Azuma Yano |
| Mitsui Sumitomo Visa Taiheiyo Masters | Darren Clarke |
| Dunlop Phoenix | Tiger Woods (7) |
| Casio World Open | Toru Taniguchi |
| Golf Nippon Series JT Cup | Yasuharu Imano (2) |
| Asia/Japan Okinawa Open | Tadahiro Takayama (2) |

## AUSTRALASIAN TOUR

| | |
|---|---|
| Heineken Classic | Craig Parry |
| Holden New Zealand Open | Niclas Fasth |
| Jacob's Creek Open | Steven Bowditch |

| | |
|---|---|
| ING New Zealand PGA Championship | Peter O'Malley |
| MFS Australian Open | Robert Allenby |
| Cadbury Schweppes Australian PGA Champ. | Robert Allenby (2) |
| MasterCard Masters | Robert Allenby (3) |

## AFRICAN TOURS

| | |
|---|---|
| South African Airways Open | Tim Clark |
| Dimension Data Pro-Am | Simon Wakefield |
| Nashua Masters | Richard Sterne |
| Telkom PGA Championship | Warren Abery |
| Vodacom Tour Championship | Marc Cayeux |
| Hassan II Trophy | Erik Compton |
| FNB Botswana Open | Nico van Rensburg |
| Parmalat Classic | Ulrich van den Berg |
| Capital Alliance Royal Swazi Sun Open | Hendrik Buhrmann |
| Vodacom Origins of Golf Tour at Pretoria | Desvonde Botes |
| Vodacom Origins of Golf Tour at Pezula | Desvonde Botes (2) |
| Vodacom Origins of Golf Tour at Wild Coast Sun | Dean Lambert |
| Vodacom Origins of Golf Tour at Bloemfontein | Nic Henning |
| Telkom PGA Pro-Am | Thomas Aiken |
| Vodacom Origins of Golf Tour at Erinvale | Hennie Otto |
| Seekers Travel Pro-Am | Anton Haig |
| Bearingman Highveld Classic | Bradford Vaughan |
| MTC Namibia PGA Championship | Thomas Aiken (2) |
| Vodacom Origins of Golf Tour Championship | Steve Basson |
| Platinum Classic | Jaco Van Zyl |
| Limpopo Classic | Bradford Vaughan (2) |
| Nelson Mandela Invitational | Tim Clark (3)/Vincent Tshabalala |
| Nedbank Golf Challenge | Jim Furyk (2) |
| Dunhill Championship | Ernie Els (4) |
| South African Airways Open | Retief Goosen (4) |

## CHAMPIONS TOUR

| | |
|---|---|
| MasterCard Championship | Dana Quigley |
| Turtle Bay Championship | Hale Irwin |
| ACE Group Classic | Mark James |
| Outback Steakhouse Pro-Am | Hale Irwin (2) |
| SBC Classic | Des Smyth |
| Toshiba Senior Classic | Mark Johnson |
| Liberty Mutual Legends of Golf | Des Smyth (2) |
| FedEx Kinko's Classic | Jim Thorpe |
| Blue Angels Classic | Jim Thorpe (2) |
| Bruno's Memorial Classic | D.A. Weibring |
| Senior PGA Championship | Mike Reid |
| Allianz Championship | Tom Jenkins |
| Bayer Advantage Classic | Dana Quigley (2) |
| Bank of America Championship | Mark McNulty |
| Commerce Bank Championship | Ron Streck |
| Ford Senior Players Championship | Peter Jacobsen |
| U.S. Senior Open | Allen Doyle |
| 3M Championship | Tom Purtzer |
| Boeing Greater Seattle Classic | David Eger |
| JELD-WEN Tradition | Loren Roberts |
| Wal-Mart First Tee Open at Pebble Beach | Hale Irwin (3) |
| Constellation Energy Classic | Bob Gilder |
| SAS Championship | Hale Irwin (4) |
| Greater Hickory Classic at Rock Barn | Jay Haas |
| Administaff Small Business Classic | Mark McNulty (2) |
| SBC Championship | Jay Haas (2) |
| Charles Schwab Cup Championship | Tom Watson (2) |

## EUROPEAN SENIORS TOUR

| | |
|---|---|
| DGM Barbados Open | Denis O'Sullivan |
| Tobago Plantations Seniors Classic | Luis Carbonetti |
| Jolie Ville Sharm El Skeikh Seniors Open | Bob Lendzion |
| Nokia 9300 Italian Seniors Open | Gery Watine |
| AIB Irish Seniors Open | Noel Ratcliffe |
| Irvine Whitlock Seniors Classic | Sam Torrance |
| The Mobile Cup | Guiseppe Cali |
| De Vere Northumberland Seniors Classic | Carl Mason |
| Ryder Cup Wales Seniors Open | Carl Mason (2) |
| Nigel Mansell Sunseeker International Classic | Jim Rhodes |
| Senior British Open | Tom Watson |
| De Vere PGA Seniors Championship | Sam Torrance (2) |
| Bad Ragaz PGA Seniors Open | Terry Gale |
| Travis Perkins Senior Masters | Eduardo Romero |
| Charles Church Scottish Seniors Open | Nick Job |
| Bovis Lend Lease European Senior Masters | Mark James (2) |
| Scandinavian Senior Open | Bill Longmuir |
| Bendinat London Seniors Masters | Sam Torrance (3) |
| Castellon Costa Azahar Open de Espana | Bob Boyd |
| Algarve Seniors Open of Portugal | Jerry Bruner |
| Arcapita Seniors Tour Championship | Des Smyth (3) |

## JAPAN SENIOR TOUR

| | |
|---|---|
| Oberst Senior Open Series | Takashi Miyoshi |
| Aderans Wellness Open | Katsuyoshi Tomori |
| Fancl Senior Classic | Takashi Miyoshi (2) |
| Arde Pro Cup | Takashi Miyoshi (3) |
| PGA Philanthropy Rebornest Senior Open | Katsunari Takahashi |
| Japan PGA Senior Championship | Kiyoshi Murota |
| Japan Senior Open | Tsuneyuki Nakajima |
| Kinojyo Senior Open | Hajime Meshiai |

## U.S. LPGA TOUR

| | |
|---|---|
| SBS Open at Turtle Bay | Jennifer Rosales |
| MasterCard Classic | Annika Sorenstam |
| Safeway International | Annika Sorenstam (2) |
| Kraft Nabisco Championship | Annika Sorenstam (3) |
| LPGA Takefuji Classic | Wendy Ward |
| Corona Morelia Championship | Carin Koch |
| Franklin American Mortgage Championship | Stacy Prammanasudh |
| Michelob Ultra Open at Kingsmill | Cristie Kerr |
| Chick-fil-A Charity Championship | Annika Sorenstam (4) |
| Sybase Classic | Paula Creamer |
| LPGA Corning Classic | Jimin Kang |
| ShopRite LPGA Classic | Annika Sorenstam (5) |
| McDonald's LPGA Championship | Annika Sorenstam (6) |
| Wegmans Rochester LPGA | Lorena Ochoa |
| U.S. Women's Open | Birdie Kim |
| HSBC Women's World Match Play | Marisa Baena |
| Jamie Farr Owens Corning Classic | Heather Bowie |
| BMO Financial Group Canadian Women's Open | Meena Lee |
| Safeway Classic | Soo-Yun Kang |
| Wendy's Championship for Children | Cristie Kerr (2) |
| State Farm Classic | Pat Hurst |
| Solheim Cup | United States |
| John Q. Hammons Hotel Classic | Annika Sorenstam (8) |
| Office Depot Championship | Hee-Won Han |
| Longs Drugs Challenge | Nicole Perrot |
| Samsung World Championship | Annika Sorenstam (9) |

CJ Nine Bridges Classic — Jee Young Lee
The Mitchell Co. Tournament of Champions — Christina Kim
ADT Championship — Annika Sorenstam (11)

## LADIES EUROPEAN TOUR

Samsung Ladies Masters — Bo Bae Song
Princess Lalla Meriem Cup — Ana B. Sanchez
Thailand Ladies Open — Shani Waugh
Tenerife Ladies Open — Ludivine Kreutz
Open de Espana Femenino — Iben Tinning
Siemens Austrian Ladies Open — Federica Piovano
BMW Ladies Italian Open — Iben Tinning (2)
Vediorbis Arras Open de France Dames — Veronica Zorzi
Algarve Ladies Open of Portugal — Cecilia Ekelundh
Ladies English Open — Maria Hjorth
OTP Bank Ladies Central European Open — Ludivine Kreutz (2)
Evian Masters — Paula Creamer (2)
Weetabix Women's British Open — Jeong Jang
Scandinavian TPC Hosted by Annika — Annika Sorenstam (7)
Wales Ladies Championship of Europe — Kirsty Taylor
Ladies Finnish Masters — Lisa Holm Sorensen
Nykredit Masters — Iben Tinning (3)
KLM Ladies Open — Virginie Lagoutte
Catalonia Ladies Masters — Karine Icher

## JAPAN LPGA TOUR

Daikin Orchid Ladies — Orie Fujino
Studio-Alice Women's Open — Michiko Hattori
Life Card Ladies — Sakura Yokomine
Fujisankei Ladies Classic — Kasumi Fujii
Katokichi Queens — Midori Yoneyama
Salonpas World Ladies — Yuri Fudoh
Vernal Ladies — Ai Miyazato (2)
Chukyo TV Bridgestone Ladies Open — Ai Miyazato (3)
Kosaido Ladies Golf Cup — Midori Yoneyama (2)
Resort Trust Ladies — Mitsuko Kawasaki
We Love Kobe Suntory Ladies Open — Yuri Fudoh (2)
Apita Circle K Sankus Ladies — Ok-Hee Ku
Promise Ladies — Ku Yun Hee
Belluna Ladies Cup — Kasumi Fujii (2)
Chateaureze Queens Cup — Junko Omote
Stanley Ladies — Junko Omote (2)
Crystal Geyser Ladies — Kasumi Fujii (3)
NEC Karuizawa 72 — Paula Creamer (3)
New Caterpillar Mitsubishi Ladies — Ai Miyazato (4)
Yonex Ladies — Shin Hyun Ju
Golf 5 Ladies — Yuri Fudoh (3)
Japan LPGA Championship — Yuri Fudoh (4)
Munsingwear Ladies Tokai Classic — Shiho Ohyama
Miyagi TV Cup Dunlop Ladies Open — Sakura Yokomine (2)
Japan Women's Open — Ai Miyazato (5)
Sankyo Ladies Open — Ji-Hee Lee
Fujitsu Ladies — Yuri Fudoh (5)
Masters Golf Club Ladies — Paula Creamer (4)
Hisako Higuchi IDC Otsukakagu Ladies — Ai Miyazato (6)
Mizuno Classic — Annika Sorenstam (10)
Itoen Ladies — Yuri Fudoh (6)
Daioseishi Elleair Ladies Open — Ai Miyazato (7)
Japan LPGA Tour Championship — Shiho Ohyama (2)

## AUSTRALIAN WOMEN'S TOUR

| | |
|---|---|
| ABC Learning Centres & FADL Group Classic | Nikki Campbell |
| Titanium Enterprises ALPG Players Championship | Katherine Hull |
| ANZ Ladies Masters | Karrie Webb |

## SOUTH AFRICAN WOMEN'S TOUR

| | |
|---|---|
| Women's World Cup of Golf | Ai Miyazato/Rui Kitada |
| Pam Golding Ladies International | *Ashleigh Simon |
| Acer Women's South African Open | Maria Boden |
| Telkom Women's Classic | Laurette Maritz |
| Nedbank Women's Masters | Maria Beautell |

# Multiple Winners of 2005

| PLAYER | WINS | PLAYER | WINS |
|---|---|---|---|
| Annika Sorenstam | 11 | Fred Funk | 2 |
| Tiger Woods | 8 | Jim Furyk | 2 |
| Ai Miyazato | 7 | Sergio Garcia | 2 |
| Yuri Fudoh | 6 | Jay Haas | 2 |
| Paula Creamer | 4 | Michael Harris | 2 |
| Ernie Els | 4 | S.K. Ho | 2 |
| Retief Goosen | 4 | David Howell | 2 |
| Jason Gore | 4 | Yasuharu Imano | 2 |
| Hale Irwin | 4 | Mark James | 2 |
| Phil Mickelson | 4 | Shingo Katayama | 2 |
| Vijay Singh | 4 | Cristie Kerr | 2 |
| Thaworn Wiratchant | 4 | Ludivine Kreutz | 2 |
| Robert Allenby | 3 | Justin Leonard | 2 |
| Tim Clark | 3 | Carl Mason | 2 |
| Kasumi Fujii | 3 | Troy Matteson | 2 |
| Padraig Harrington | 3 | Mark McNulty | 2 |
| Takashi Miyoshi | 3 | Colin Montgomerie | 2 |
| Kenny Perry | 3 | Shiho Ohyama | 2 |
| Adam Scott | 3 | Junko Omote | 2 |
| Des Smyth | 3 | Naomichi Ozaki | 2 |
| Iben Tinning | 3 | Dana Quigley | 2 |
| Sam Torrance | 3 | Andres Romero | 2 |
| Thomas Aiken | 2 | David Smail | 2 |
| Desvonde Botes | 2 | Tadahiro Takayama | 2 |
| Bart Bryant | 2 | Jim Thorpe | 2 |
| Angel Cabrera | 2 | Peter Tomasulo | 2 |
| Michael Campbell | 2 | Bradford Vaughan | 2 |
| Paul Casey | 2 | Marc Warren | 2 |
| K.J. Choi | 2 | Tom Watson | 2 |
| Chris Couch | 2 | Fredrik Widmark | 2 |
| Stephen Dodd | 2 | Sakura Yokomine | 2 |
| Niclas Fasth | 2 | Midori Yoneyama | 2 |
| Keiichiro Fukabori | 2 | | |

# World Money List

This list of the 400 leading money winners in the world of professional golf in 2005 was compiled from the results of men's (excluding seniors) tournaments carried in the Appendixes of this edition. This list includes tournaments with a minimum of 36 holes and four contestants and does not include such competitions as skins games, pro-ams and shootouts.

In the 40 years during which World Money Lists have been compiled, the earnings of the player in the 200th position have risen from a total of $3,326 in 1966 to $550,634 in 2005. The top 200 players in 1966 earned a total of $4,680,287. In 2005, the comparable total was $319,303,682.

The world money list of the International Federation of PGA Tours was used for the official money list events of the U.S. PGA Tour, PGA European Tour, PGA Tour of Japan, Asian Tour, Southern Africa Tour and PGA Tour of Australasia. The conversion rates used for 2005 for other events and other tours were: Euro = US$1.23; British pound = US$1.805; Japanese yen = US$0.0091; South African rand = US$0.16; Australian dollar = US$0.76; Canadian dollar = US$0.81.

| POS. | PLAYER, COUNTRY | TOTAL MONEY |
|---|---|---|
| 1 | Tiger Woods, USA | $12,280,404 |
| 2 | Vijay Singh, Fiji | 8,420,446 |
| 3 | Phil Mickelson, USA | 5,971,710 |
| 4 | Jim Furyk, USA | 5,774,921 |
| 5 | Retief Goosen, South Africa | 5,605,264 |
| 6 | Luke Donald, England | 5,188,361 |
| 7 | Michael Campbell, New Zealand | 4,982,672 |
| 8 | Sergio Garcia, Spain | 4,636,851 |
| 9 | Kenny Perry, USA | 4,397,155 |
| 10 | David Toms, USA | 4,202,013 |
| 11 | Colin Montgomerie, Scotland | 4,175,810 |
| 12 | Adam Scott, Australia | 4,112,738 |
| 13 | Chris DiMarco, USA | 4,082,548 |
| 14 | Padraig Harrington, Ireland | 4,026,841 |
| 15 | Tim Clark, South Africa | 3,870,040 |
| 16 | Darren Clarke, N. Ireland | 3,851,891 |
| 17 | David Howell, England | 3,741,347 |
| 18 | Ernie Els, South Africa | 3,346,196 |
| 19 | Paul McGinley, Ireland | 3,306,265 |
| 20 | Bart Bryant, USA | 3,249,136 |
| 21 | Fred Funk, USA | 3,214,926 |
| 22 | Jose Maria Olazabal, Spain | 3,031,355 |
| 23 | Davis Love, USA | 2,927,242 |
| 24 | Angel Cabrera, Argentina | 2,818,249 |
| 25 | Justin Leonard, USA | 2,672,538 |
| 26 | Scott Verplank, USA | 2,580,213 |
| 27 | Sean O'Hair, USA | 2,515,482 |
| 28 | Ben Crane, USA | 2,457,329 |
| 29 | Chad Campbell, USA | 2,391,432 |
| 30 | Stuart Appleby, Australia | 2,381,228 |
| 31 | Henrik Stenson, Sweden | 2,369,474 |

| POS. | PLAYER, COUNTRY | TOTAL MONEY |
|---|---|---|
| 32 | Thomas Bjorn, Denmark | 2,330,056 |
| 33 | John Daly, USA | 2,278,620 |
| 34 | Fred Couples, USA | 2,257,381 |
| 35 | Mark Calcavecchia, USA | 2,256,560 |
| 36 | Olin Browne, USA | 2,243,178 |
| 37 | Tim Herron, USA | 2,242,300 |
| 38 | Billy Mayfair, USA | 2,236,455 |
| 39 | Ted Purdy, USA | 2,198,368 |
| 40 | K.J. Choi, Korea | 2,190,915 |
| 41 | Bradley Dredge, Wales | 2,153,494 |
| 42 | Charles Howell, USA | 2,152,107 |
| 43 | Nick O'Hern, Australia | 2,141,353 |
| 44 | Brandt Jobe, USA | 2,133,149 |
| 45 | Lucas Glover, USA | 2,110,068 |
| 46 | Peter Lonard, Australia | 2,066,018 |
| 47 | Geoff Ogilvy, Australia | 2,046,600 |
| 48 | Niclas Fasth, Sweden | 2,029,541 |
| 49 | Stephen Dodd, Wales | 2,016,994 |
| 50 | Carl Pettersson, Sweden | 1,993,851 |
| 51 | Shigeki Maruyama, Japan | 1,933,049 |
| 52 | Stewart Cink, USA | 1,911,049 |
| 53 | Jason Bohn, USA | 1,888,568 |
| 54 | Mark Hensby, Australia | 1,834,311 |
| 55 | Vaughn Taylor, USA | 1,827,574 |
| 56 | Joe Ogilvie, USA | 1,819,547 |
| 57 | Zach Johnson, USA | 1,819,441 |
| 58 | Kenneth Ferrie, England | 1,804,810 |
| 59 | Robert Allenby, Australia | 1,793,755 |
| 60 | Brad Faxon, USA | 1,779,285 |
| 61 | Nick Dougherty, England | 1,769,816 |
| 62 | Tim Petrovic, USA | 1,711,229 |
| 63 | Tom Lehman, USA | 1,705,872 |
| 64 | Rod Pampling, Australia | 1,692,799 |
| 65 | Ian Poulter, England | 1,689,140 |
| 66 | Steve Elkington, Australia | 1,651,577 |
| 67 | Tom Pernice Jr., USA | 1,608,057 |
| 68 | Heath Slocum, USA | 1,606,185 |
| 69 | Bo Van Pelt, USA | 1,606,082 |
| 70 | Graeme McDowell, N. Ireland | 1,560,228 |
| 71 | Bernhard Langer, Germany | 1,460,740 |
| 72 | Justin Rose, England | 1,456,204 |
| 73 | Greg Owen, England | 1,438,898 |
| 74 | Miguel Angel Jimenez, Spain | 1,435,484 |
| 75 | Jonathan Kaye, USA | 1,416,109 |
| 76 | Lee Westwood, England | 1,376,829 |
| 77 | Trevor Immelman, South Africa | 1,365,763 |
| 78 | Mike Weir, Canada | 1,363,467 |
| 79 | Paul Casey, England | 1,359,010 |
| 80 | Jerry Kelly, USA | 1,356,117 |
| 81 | Brian Davis, England | 1,319,194 |
| 82 | Jason Gore, USA | 1,308,964 |
| 83 | Ryan Palmer, USA | 1,284,694 |
| 84 | Jeff Brehaut, USA | 1,274,999 |
| 85 | Pat Perez, USA | 1,258,087 |

| POS. | PLAYER, COUNTRY | TOTAL MONEY |
|------|-----------------|-------------|
| 86 | Jeff Sluman, USA | 1,206,256 |
| 87 | Shingo Katayama, Japan | 1,204,597 |
| 88 | Paul Broadhurst, England | 1,191,533 |
| 89 | Peter Hanson, Sweden | 1,190,797 |
| 90 | Maarten Lafeber, Netherlands | 1,187,010 |
| 91 | Woody Austin, USA | 1,177,095 |
| 92 | Craig Parry, Australia | 1,169,468 |
| 93 | Billy Andrade, USA | 1,165,835 |
| 94 | Jean-Francois Remesy, France | 1,129,576 |
| 95 | Arjun Atwal, India | 1,120,895 |
| 96 | Scott McCarron, USA | 1,116,704 |
| 97 | Robert Gamez, USA | 1,115,364 |
| 98 | Kevin Na, Korea | 1,095,204 |
| 99 | Yasuharu Imano, Japan | 1,082,770 |
| 100 | Brett Quigley, USA | 1,076,905 |
| 101 | Bob Tway, USA | 1,072,387 |
| 102 | Wes Short, Jr., USA | 1,063,899 |
| 103 | Joey Sindelar, USA | 1,060,238 |
| 104 | Carlos Franco, Paraguay | 1,056,404 |
| 105 | Dudley Hart, USA | 1,051,339 |
| 106 | Joey Snyder, USA | 1,042,696 |
| 107 | Aaron Baddeley, Australia | 1,040,956 |
| 108 | Joe Durant, USA | 1,039,699 |
| 109 | J.L. Lewis, USA | 1,031,159 |
| 110 | Charles Warren, USA | 1,007,276 |
| 111 | Harrison Frazar, USA | 999,083 |
| 112 | John Senden, Australia | 997,595 |
| 113 | John Huston, USA | 972,970 |
| 114 | Stephen Ames, Canada | 959,665 |
| 115 | David Lynn, England | 956,647 |
| 116 | Steve Lowery, USA | 950,274 |
| 117 | J.J. Henry, USA | 942,347 |
| 118 | Steve Webster, England | 936,393 |
| 119 | Fredrik Jacobson, Sweden | 929,739 |
| 120 | Arron Oberholser, USA | 921,796 |
| 121 | Rory Sabbatini, South Africa | 920,988 |
| 122 | Daniel Chopra, Sweden | 907,143 |
| 123 | Tag Ridings, USA | 891,812 |
| 124 | Bob Estes, USA | 891,477 |
| 125 | Raphael Jacquelin, France | 880,247 |
| 126 | Steve Flesch, USA | 869,106 |
| 127 | Richard Green, Australia | 859,387 |
| 128 | John Rollins, USA | 856,540 |
| 129 | Keiichiro Fukabori, Japan | 853,939 |
| 130 | Hank Kuehne, USA | 853,067 |
| 131 | Thomas Levet, France | 851,411 |
| 132 | James Driscoll, USA | 849,891 |
| 133 | Kevin Sutherland, USA | 845,875 |
| 134 | Jesper Parnevik, Sweden | 833,211 |
| 135 | S.K. Ho, Korea | 833,200 |
| 136 | Jose Manuel Lara, Spain | 824,315 |
| 137 | Dean Wilson, USA | 821,903 |
| 138 | Anders Hansen, Denmark | 820,209 |
| 139 | Graeme Storm, England | 817,803 |

| POS. | PLAYER, COUNTRY | TOTAL MONEY |
|---|---|---|
| 140 | D.J. Trahan, USA | 806,304 |
| 141 | Thongchai Jaidee, Thailand | 805,003 |
| 142 | Emanuele Canonica, Italy | 804,476 |
| 143 | Soren Hansen, Denmark | 773,700 |
| 144 | Ryan Moore, USA | 761,250 |
| 145 | Stephen Leaney, Australia | 758,057 |
| 146 | Tadahiro Takayama, Japan | 754,209 |
| 147 | Richard Johnson, Sweden | 747,932 |
| 148 | Nick Price, Zimbabwe | 744,764 |
| 149 | Rich Beem, USA | 744,687 |
| 150 | Richard Sterne, South Africa | 744,360 |
| 151 | Jeff Maggert, USA | 743,780 |
| 152 | Robert Damron, USA | 739,836 |
| 153 | Corey Pavin, USA | 736,506 |
| 154 | Doug Barron, USA | 731,990 |
| 155 | David Smail, New Zealand | 731,307 |
| 156 | Jonathan Byrd, USA | 726,023 |
| 157 | Patrick Sheehan, USA | 723,788 |
| 158 | Craig Barlow, USA | 720,362 |
| 159 | Robert Karlsson, Sweden | 718,473 |
| 160 | Rocco Mediate, USA | 696,250 |
| 161 | Simon Khan, England | 693,411 |
| 162 | Hidemichi Tanaka, Japan | 692,515 |
| 163 | Brian Gay, USA | 689,862 |
| 164 | Gregory Havret, France | 683,536 |
| 165 | Barry Lane, England | 674,221 |
| 166 | Daisuke Maruyama, Japan | 671,230 |
| 167 | Peter Hedblom, Sweden | 668,485 |
| 168 | Paul Lawrie, Scotland | 666,373 |
| 169 | Kirk Triplett, USA | 664,395 |
| 170 | Todd Fischer, USA | 664,098 |
| 171 | Thaworn Wiratchant, Thailand | 661,017 |
| 172 | Jean Van de Velde, France | 655,602 |
| 173 | Ryuji Imada, Japan | 650,221 |
| 174 | Robert-Jan Derksen, Netherlands | 643,746 |
| 175 | Ben Curtis, USA | 643,596 |
| 176 | Tjaart van der Walt, South Africa | 643,399 |
| 177 | Peter Gustafsson, Sweden | 641,240 |
| 178 | Gonzalo Fernandez-Castano, Spain | 639,075 |
| 179 | Tommy Armour, USA | 636,643 |
| 180 | Kent Jones, USA | 629,944 |
| 181 | Toru Taniguchi, Japan | 626,645 |
| 182 | Briny Baird, USA | 624,191 |
| 183 | Charl Schwartzel, South Africa | 612,834 |
| 184 | Nick Watney, USA | 605,369 |
| 185 | Paul Sheehan, New Zealand | 604,721 |
| 186 | Y.E. Yang, Korea | 592,909 |
| 187 | Michael Allen, Ireland | 591,829 |
| 188 | Hunter Mahan, USA | 589,567 |
| 189 | Brett Wetterich, USA | 589,529 |
| 190 | Peter Lawrie, Ireland | 584,132 |
| 191 | Pierre Fulke, Sweden | 580,366 |
| 192 | Stephen Gallacher, Scotland | 576,330 |
| 193 | Lin Keng-chi, Taipei | 575,844 |

| POS. | PLAYER, COUNTRY | TOTAL MONEY |
|------|-----------------|-------------|
| 194 | Mark Wilson, USA | 573,218 |
| 195 | Peter O'Malley, Australia | 567,365 |
| 196 | Soren Kjeldsen, Denmark | 562,931 |
| 197 | Toshi Izawa, Japan | 562,410 |
| 198 | Todd Hamilton, USA | 559,495 |
| 199 | Alex Cejka, Germany | 557,582 |
| 200 | Dinesh Chand, Fiji | 550,634 |
| 201 | Omar Uresti, USA | 538,238 |
| 202 | Hidemasa Hoshino, Japan | 537,150 |
| 203 | Neal Lancaster, USA | 532,185 |
| 204 | J.P. Hayes, USA | 531,704 |
| 205 | Marco Dawson, Germany | 528,471 |
| 206 | Ryoken Kawagishi, Japan | 525,735 |
| 207 | Simon Dyson, England | 524,883 |
| 208 | Jyoti Randhawa, India | 521,591 |
| 209 | Prayad Marksaeng, Thailand | 516,018 |
| 210 | Hiroyuki Fujita, Japan | 515,291 |
| 211 | Naomichi Ozaki, Japan | 514,897 |
| 212 | Richard Finch, England | 512,251 |
| 213 | Kazuhiko Hosokawa, Japan | 511,690 |
| 214 | Damian McGrane, Ireland | 507,506 |
| 215 | Brendan Jones, Australia | 506,595 |
| 216 | Brian Bateman, USA | 505,517 |
| 217 | Shinichi Yokota, Japan | 505,003 |
| 218 | Lee Janzen, USA | 504,156 |
| 219 | Darron Stiles, USA | 502,032 |
| 220 | Shaun Micheel, USA | 501,597 |
| 221 | Jose-Filipe Lima, Portugal | 501,114 |
| 222 | Brett Rumford, Australia | 500,578 |
| 223 | Kaname Yokoo, Japan | 499,072 |
| 224 | Taichi Teshima, Japan | 496,505 |
| 225 | Troy Matteson, USA | 495,009 |
| 226 | Andrew Magee, USA | 488,779 |
| 227 | Scott Gutschewski, USA | 488,145 |
| 228 | Frank Lickliter, USA | 486,581 |
| 229 | Paul Goydos, USA | 486,362 |
| 230 | Tetsuji Hiratsuka, Japan | 482,479 |
| 231 | Chang Ik-je, Korea | 475,849 |
| 232 | Steven Conran, Australia | 475,730 |
| 233 | Cameron Beckman, USA | 474,107 |
| 234 | Duffy Waldorf, USA | 462,725 |
| 235 | Kevin Stadler, USA | 458,525 |
| 236 | John Cook, USA | 455,593 |
| 237 | Chris Smith, USA | 454,375 |
| 238 | Steven Bowditch, Australia | 452,425 |
| 239 | Anthony Wall, England | 451,003 |
| 240 | Mark O'Meara, USA | 448,078 |
| 241 | Stuart Little, England | 441,666 |
| 242 | Oliver Wilson, England | 440,069 |
| 243 | Simon Wakefield, England | 438,331 |
| 244 | Mathias Gronberg, Sweden | 436,000 |
| 245 | Chris Couch, USA | 433,872 |
| 246 | Francois Delamontagne, France | 431,728 |
| 247 | Jonathan Lomas, England | 431,209 |

| POS. | PLAYER, COUNTRY | TOTAL MONEY |
|------|-----------------|-------------|
| 248 | Wade Ormsby, Australia | 424,531 |
| 249 | Phillip Price, Wales | 422,430 |
| 250 | Martin Erlandsson, Sweden | 422,243 |
| 251 | Tom Gillis, USA | 421,050 |
| 252 | Miles Tunnicliff, England | 419,722 |
| 253 | Steve Allan, Australia | 418,428 |
| 254 | Ricardo Gonzalez, Argentina | 417,997 |
| 255 | Tatsuhiko Takahashi, Japan | 416,915 |
| 256 | Marc Cayeux, Zimbabwe | 415,198 |
| 257 | Scott Drummond, Scotland | 414,078 |
| 258 | Bill Haas, USA | 409,964 |
| 259 | Paul Gow, Australia | 405,555 |
| 260 | Mathew Goggin, Australia | 405,091 |
| 261 | Matt Kuchar, USA | 402,786 |
| 262 | Steven O'Hara, Scotland | 402,062 |
| 263 | Gary Orr, Scotland | 401,979 |
| 264 | D.A. Points, USA | 400,540 |
| 265 | Steve Stricker, USA | 397,640 |
| 266 | Takuya Taniguchi, Japan | 393,418 |
| 267 | Gary Emerson, England | 390,655 |
| 268 | Jay Williamson, USA | 382,653 |
| 269 | Chris Campbell, Australia | 382,502 |
| 270 | Franklin Langham, USA | 380,436 |
| 271 | John Bickerton, England | 379,940 |
| 272 | Azuma Yano, Japan | 377,783 |
| 273 | Hunter Haas, USA | 375,863 |
| 274 | Phil Golding, England | 374,529 |
| 275 | Satoru Hirota, Japan | 373,603 |
| 276 | Glen Day, USA | 372,428 |
| 277 | Ryuichi Oda, Japan | 371,428 |
| 278 | Paul Azinger, USA | 370,239 |
| 279 | Gary Murphy, Ireland | 367,915 |
| 280 | Gavin Coles, Australia | 364,519 |
| 281 | Liang Wen-chong, Taipei | 364,383 |
| 282 | Chawalit Plaphol, Thailand | 360,170 |
| 283 | Andrew McLardy, South Africa | 358,609 |
| 284 | Bob Heintz, USA | 358,559 |
| 285 | Scott Hend, Australia | 356,247 |
| 286 | Francesco Molinari, Italy | 355,072 |
| 287 | Tomohiro Kondo, Japan | 353,143 |
| 288 | Andrew Coltart, Scotland | 350,754 |
| 289 | James Kingston, South Africa | 349,628 |
| 290 | Joakim Haeggman, Sweden | 348,689 |
| 291 | Katsumasa Miyamoto, Japan | 347,481 |
| 292 | Matt Gogel, USA | 344,151 |
| 293 | Gregory Bourdy, France | 342,772 |
| 294 | Jamie Donaldson, Wales | 341,448 |
| 295 | Bubba Watson, USA | 338,360 |
| 296 | Alastair Forsyth, Scotland | 336,459 |
| 297 | Nozomi Kawahara, Japan | 334,024 |
| 298 | Marten Olander, Sweden | 333,534 |
| 299 | Hideto Tanihara, Japan | 329,433 |
| 300 | Roland Thatcher, USA | 326,299 |
| 301 | Jon Mills, Canada | 325,806 |

| POS. | PLAYER, COUNTRY | TOTAL MONEY |
|------|-----------------|-------------|
| 302 | Tom Byrum, USA | 323,953 |
| 303 | Kiyoshi Maita, Japan | 322,457 |
| 304 | Ian Woosnam, Wales | 316,182 |
| 305 | Camilo Villegas, Colombia | 314,660 |
| 306 | Robert Coles, England | 311,373 |
| 307 | Brent Geiberger, USA | 309,559 |
| 308 | David McKenzie, Australia | 309,145 |
| 309 | Nick Faldo, England | 302,231 |
| 310 | Jamie Spence, England | 301,629 |
| 311 | Jean-Francois Lucquin, France | 299,789 |
| 312 | Will MacKenzie, USA | 295,429 |
| 313 | D.J. Brigman, USA | 294,849 |
| 314 | Erik Compton, USA | 294,481 |
| 315 | Greg Chalmers, Australia | 293,957 |
| 316 | Marcel Siem, Germany | 290,746 |
| 317 | Kim Jong-duck, Korea | 287,274 |
| 318 | Kiyoshi Miyazato, Japan | 286,843 |
| 319 | Titch Moore, South Africa | 286,068 |
| 320 | Brenden Pappas, South Africa | 285,087 |
| 321 | Ian Garbutt, England | 283,298 |
| 322 | Nathan Green, Australia | 282,625 |
| 323 | Craig Bowden, USA | 281,924 |
| 324 | David Park, Wales | 278,846 |
| 325 | Thammanoon Srirot, Thailand | 276,875 |
| 326 | Chris Anderson, USA | 276,172 |
| 327 | Terry Pilkadaris, Australia | 275,546 |
| 328 | Nicolas Colsaerts, Belgium | 274,075 |
| 329 | Mark Brooks, USA | 273,668 |
| 330 | Garry Houston, Wales | 273,381 |
| 331 | Jose Coceres, Argentina | 269,705 |
| 332 | Paul Claxton, USA | 269,701 |
| 333 | Marcus Fraser, South Africa | 269,526 |
| 334 | Chris Riley, USA | 268,735 |
| 335 | Jerry Smith, USA | 267,757 |
| 336 | Louis Oosthuizen, South Africa | 267,589 |
| 337 | David Branshaw, USA | 266,724 |
| 338 | Peter Fowler, Australia | 266,226 |
| 339 | Toru Suzuki, Japan | 265,756 |
| 340 | Shane Bertsch, USA | 263,373 |
| 341 | Yusaku Miyazato, Japan | 261,397 |
| 342 | Kris Cox, USA | 257,352 |
| 343 | Shiv Kapur, India | 256,600 |
| 344 | Charlie Wi, Korea | 255,650 |
| 345 | Mark Roe, England | 255,522 |
| 346 | Craig Jones, Australia | 254,736 |
| 347 | Christian Cevaer, France | 253,881 |
| 348 | Peter Tomasulo, USA | 253,016 |
| 349 | Alessandro Tadini, Italy | 252,186 |
| 350 | Jeev Milkha Singh, India | 250,849 |
| 351 | David Carter, England | 250,127 |
| 352 | Markus Brier, Austria | 248,983 |
| 353 | Roger Tambellini, USA | 248,975 |
| 354 | Mitsuhiro Tateyama, Japan | 248,863 |
| 355 | Scott Dunlap, USA | 246,707 |

| POS. | PLAYER, COUNTRY | TOTAL MONEY |
|---|---|---|
| 356 | Jay Delsing, USA | 246,181 |
| 357 | Philip Archer, England | 245,991 |
| 358 | Rich Bland, England | 245,134 |
| 359 | Andrew Marshall, England | 242,243 |
| 360 | Eric Axley, USA | 239,097 |
| 361 | Andrew Buckle, Australia | 238,496 |
| 362 | Spike McRoy, USA | 238,267 |
| 363 | Mario Tiziani, USA | 237,618 |
| 364 | Kim Felton, Australia | 234,359 |
| 365 | Mark Foster, England | 232,969 |
| 366 | Joachim Backstrom, Sweden | 232,401 |
| 367 | Dennis Paulson, USA | 232,147 |
| 368 | Jason Schultz, USA | 231,658 |
| 369 | Michael Putnam, USA | 229,733 |
| 370 | Esteban Toledo, Mexico | 228,423 |
| 371 | David Peoples, USA | 228,268 |
| 372 | Vance Veazey, USA | 227,635 |
| 373 | Tom Scherrer, USA | 227,090 |
| 374 | David Hearn, Canada | 227,053 |
| 375 | Miguel Angel Martin, Spain | 226,354 |
| 376 | David Drysdale, Scotland | 225,173 |
| 377 | Mathias Eliasson, Sweden | 224,391 |
| 378 | Darren Fichardt, South Africa | 223,831 |
| 379 | Jarrod Lyle, Australia | 223,580 |
| 380 | Takao Nogami, Japan | 222,992 |
| 381 | Charley Hoffman, USA | 222,978 |
| 382 | Sam Little, England | 222,694 |
| 383 | Yeh Wei-tze, Taipei | 222,673 |
| 384 | Mamoru Osanai, Japan | 221,907 |
| 385 | Jun Kikuchi, Japan | 221,712 |
| 386 | Scott Laycock, Australia | 221,566 |
| 387 | Katsumune Imai, Japan | 219,770 |
| 388 | Terry Price, Australia | 218,560 |
| 389 | Santiago Luna, Spain | 216,961 |
| 390 | Dan Forsman, USA | 214,135 |
| 391 | Nobuhito Sato, Japan | 213,644 |
| 392 | Marcus Both, Australia | 210,954 |
| 393 | Jeff Gove, USA | 210,674 |
| 394 | Len Mattiace, USA | 209,638 |
| 395 | Justin Bolli, USA | 209,519 |
| 396 | Danny Ellis, USA | 208,826 |
| 397 | Larry Mize, USA | 206,969 |
| 398 | Greg Meyer, USA | 206,626 |
| 399 | Johan Skold, Sweden | 206,466 |
| 400 | Jaxon Brigman, USA | 204,631 |

# World Money List Leaders

| YEAR | PLAYER, COUNTRY | TOTAL MONEY |
|------|-----------------|-------------|
| 1966 | Jack Nicklaus, USA | $168,088 |
| 1967 | Jack Nicklaus, USA | 276,166 |
| 1968 | Billy Casper, USA | 222,436 |
| 1969 | Frank Beard, USA | 186,993 |
| 1970 | Jack Nicklaus, USA | 222,583 |
| 1971 | Jack Nicklaus, USA | 285,897 |
| 1972 | Jack Nicklaus, USA | 341,792 |
| 1973 | Tom Weiskopf, USA | 349,645 |
| 1974 | Johnny Miller, USA | 400,255 |
| 1975 | Jack Nicklaus, USA | 332,610 |
| 1976 | Jack Nicklaus, USA | 316,086 |
| 1977 | Tom Watson, USA | 358,034 |
| 1978 | Tom Watson, USA | 384,388 |
| 1979 | Tom Watson, USA | 506,912 |
| 1980 | Tom Watson, USA | 651,921 |
| 1981 | Johnny Miller, USA | 704,204 |
| 1982 | Raymond Floyd, USA | 738,699 |
| 1983 | Seve Ballesteros, Spain | 686,088 |
| 1984 | Seve Ballesteros, Spain | 688,047 |
| 1985 | Bernhard Langer, Germany | 860,262 |
| 1986 | Greg Norman, Australia | 1,146,584 |
| 1987 | Ian Woosnam, Wales | 1,793,268 |
| 1988 | Seve Ballesteros, Spain | 1,261,275 |
| 1989 | David Frost, South Africa | 1,650,230 |
| 1990 | Jose Maria Olazabal, Spain | 1,633,640 |
| 1991 | Bernhard Langer, Germany | 2,186,700 |
| 1992 | Nick Faldo, England | 2,748,248 |
| 1993 | Nick Faldo, England | 2,825,280 |
| 1994 | Ernie Els, South Africa | 2,862,854 |
| 1995 | Corey Pavin, USA | 2,746,340 |
| 1996 | Colin Montgomerie, Scotland | 3,071,442 |
| 1997 | Colin Montgomerie, Scotland | 3,366,900 |
| 1998 | Tiger Woods, USA | 2,927,946 |
| 1999 | Tiger Woods, USA | 7,681,625 |
| 2000 | Tiger Woods, USA | 11,034,530 |
| 2001 | Tiger Woods, USA | 7,771,562 |
| 2002 | Tiger Woods, USA | 8,292,188 |
| 2003 | Vijay Singh, Fiji | 8,499,611 |
| 2004 | Vijay Singh, Fiji | 11,638,699 |
| 2005 | Tiger Woods, USA | 12,280,404 |

# Career World Money List

Here is a list of the 50 leading money winners for their careers through the 2005 season. It includes players active on both the regular and senior tours of the world. The World Money List from this and the 39 previous editions of the annual and a table prepared for a companion book, *The Wonderful World of Professional Golf* (Atheneum, 1973) form the basis for this compilation. Additional figures were taken from official records of major golf associations, although shortcomings in records-keeping outside the United States in the 1950s and 1960s and a few exclusions from U.S. records during those years prevent these figures from being completely accurate, although the careers of virtually all of these top 50 players began after that time. Conversion of foreign currency figures to U.S. dollars is based on average values during the particular years involved.

| POS. | PLAYER, COUNTRY | TOTAL MONEY |
|------|-----------------|-------------|
| 1 | Tiger Woods, USA | $67,732,841 |
| 2 | Vijay Singh, Fiji | 54,975,158 |
| 3 | Ernie Els, South Africa | 53,168,965 |
| 4 | Davis Love, USA | 40,366,278 |
| 5 | Phil Mickelson, USA | 38,195,452 |
| 6 | Colin Montgomerie, Scotland | 33,317,108 |
| 7 | Hale Irwin, USA | 32,783,313 |
| 8 | Nick Price, Zimbabwe | 30,610,204 |
| 9 | Retief Goosen, South Africa | 29,177,898 |
| 10 | Jim Furyk, USA | 28,371,489 |
| 11 | Fred Couples, USA | 28,032,716 |
| 12 | Bernhard Langer, Germany | 27,389,025 |
| 13 | Sergio Garcia, Spain | 24,933,623 |
| 14 | David Toms, USA | 24,865,629 |
| 15 | Greg Norman, Australia | 24,274,462 |
| 16 | Darren Clarke, Northern Ireland | 24,201,085 |
| 17 | Tom Kite, USA | 23,453,024 |
| 18 | Scott Hoch, USA | 23,430,113 |
| 19 | Padraig Harrington, Ireland | 23,288,694 |
| 20 | Mark Calcavecchia, USA | 23,169,649 |
| 21 | Gil Morgan, USA | 22,580,213 |
| 22 | Tom Lehman, USA | 22,546,065 |
| 23 | Justin Leonard, USA | 22,498,874 |
| 24 | Jose Maria Olazabal, Spain | 22,061,994 |
| 25 | Masashi Ozaki, Japan | 21,794,760 |
| 26 | Kenny Perry, USA | 21,594,438 |
| 27 | Tom Watson, USA | 20,873,817 |
| 28 | Nick Faldo, England | 20,332,614 |
| 29 | Brad Faxon, USA | 20,316,586 |
| 30 | Raymond Floyd, USA | 19,874,031 |
| 31 | Mark O'Meara, USA | 19,834,760 |
| 32 | David Duval, USA | 19,805,675 |
| 33 | Fred Funk, USA | 19,751,265 |
| 34 | Chris DiMarco, USA | 19,515,241 |
| 35 | Jeff Sluman, USA | 19,400,793 |
| 36 | Larry Nelson, USA | 19,037,185 |
| 37 | Lee Westwood, England | 18,912,924 |
| 38 | Jay Haas, USA | 18,805,623 |

| POS. | PLAYER, COUNTRY | TOTAL MONEY |
|---|---|---|
| 39 | Craig Stadler, USA | 18,749,264 |
| 40 | Mike Weir, Canada | 18,466,024 |
| 41 | Ian Woosnam, Wales | 18,072,281 |
| 42 | Stuart Appleby, Australia | 17,997,740 |
| 43 | Shigeki Maruyama, Japan | 17,682,605 |
| 44 | Isao Aoki, Japan | 17,601,654 |
| 45 | Stewart Cink, USA | 17,508,057 |
| 46 | Lee Trevino, USA | 17,214,841 |
| 47 | Robert Allenby, Australia | 17,199,351 |
| 48 | Loren Roberts, USA | 16,998,804 |
| 49 | Scott Verplank, USA | 16,717,656 |
| 50 | David Frost, South Africa | 16,674,605 |

These 50 players have won $1,236,156,466 in their careers.

# Senior World Money List

This list includes official earnings from the world money list of the International Federation of PGA Tours, U.S. Senior PGA Tour, European Seniors Tour and Japan Senior Tour, along with other winnings in established unofficial events when reliable figures could be obtained.

| POS. | PLAYER, COUNTRY | TOTAL MONEY |
|---|---|---|
| 1 | Dana Quigley, USA | $2,249,008 |
| 2 | Hale Irwin, USA | 2,044,296 |
| 3 | Loren Roberts, USA | 1,905,462 |
| 4 | Mark McNulty, Zimbabwe | 1,869,230 |
| 5 | Craig Stadler, USA | 1,625,016 |
| 6 | Jay Haas, USA | 1,605,012 |
| 7 | Tom Watson, USA | 1,558,725 |
| 8 | D.A. Weibring, USA | 1,550,030 |
| 9 | Tom Jenkins, USA | 1,484,315 |
| 10 | Gil Morgan, USA | 1,364,170 |
| 11 | Morris Hatalsky, USA | 1,355,336 |
| 12 | Des Smyth, Ireland | 1,338,360 |
| 13 | Tom Purtzer, USA | 1,202,906 |
| 14 | Wayne Levi, USA | 1,081,435 |
| 15 | Jim Thorpe, USA | 1,071,084 |
| 16 | Tom Kite, USA | 1,033,881 |
| 17 | Don Pooley, USA | 1,028,289 |
| 18 | Allen Doyle, USA | 939,896 |
| 19 | Peter Jacobsen, USA | 933,116 |
| 20 | Bob Gilder, USA | 925,952 |
| 21 | Mark James, England | 920,052 |
| 22 | Jerry Pate, USA | 894,438 |
| 23 | Mike Reid, USA | 863,006 |

| POS. | PLAYER, COUNTRY | TOTAL MONEY |
|---|---|---|
| 24 | Bruce Fleisher, USA | 820,565 |
| 25 | David Eger, USA | 773,090 |
| 26 | Brad Bryant, USA | 727,438 |
| 27 | Lonnie Nielsen, USA | 693,651 |
| 28 | Bruce Lietzke, USA | 687,410 |
| 29 | Mark Johnson, USA | 650,785 |
| 30 | R.W. Eaks, USA | 550,595 |
| 31 | John Bland, South Africa | 525,310 |
| 32 | Tom McKnight, USA | 524,034 |
| 33 | Gary McCord, USA | 491,643 |
| 34 | John Harris, USA | 482,370 |
| 35 | Dan Pohl, USA | 469,345 |
| 36 | Ron Streck, USA | 467,647 |
| 37 | Keith Fergus, USA | 455,699 |
| 38 | Rodger Davis, Australia | 453,796 |
| 39 | Bruce Summerhays, USA | 419,467 |
| 40 | Tom Wargo, USA | 413,782 |
| 41 | Jim Ahern, USA | 412,389 |
| 42 | James Mason, USA | 398,428 |
| 43 | Larry Nelson, USA | 397,986 |
| 44 | Bobby Wadkins, USA | 393,082 |
| 45 | Graham Marsh, Australia | 390,796 |
| 46 | Andy Bean, USA | 386,231 |
| 47 | Sam Torrance, Scotland | 384,337 |
| 48 | Vicente Fernandez, Argentina | 382,302 |
| 49 | Curtis Strange, USA | 366,288 |
| 50 | Hajime Meshiai, Japan | 353,222 |
| 51 | Walter Hall, USA | 344,716 |
| 52 | Greg Norman, Australia | 337,380 |
| 53 | Fuzzy Zoeller, USA | 327,676 |
| 54 | Carl Mason, England | 316,250 |
| 55 | Katsuyoshi Tomori, Japan | 310,427 |
| 56 | Dave Barr, Canada | 307,385 |
| 57 | John Jacobs, USA | 298,875 |
| 58 | Mike McCullough, USA | 296,040 |
| 59 | Leonard Thompson, USA | 292,241 |
| 60 | Raymond Floyd, USA | 282,309 |
| 61 | Jay Sigel, USA | 281,414 |
| 62 | Luis Carbonetti, Argentina | 272,893 |
| 63 | Joe Inman, USA | 270,047 |
| 64 | Kiyoshi Murota, Japan | 269,703 |
| 65 | Doug Tewell, USA | 267,809 |
| 66 | Dick Mast, USA | 248,209 |
| 67 | Ed Dougherty, USA | 243,900 |
| 68 | Gary Koch, USA | 237,531 |
| 69 | Nick Job, England | 237,009 |
| 70 | Don Reese, USA | 234,144 |
| 71 | Giuseppe Cali, Italy | 226,437 |
| 72 | John Chillas, Scotland | 223,748 |
| 73 | Mike Sullivan, USA | 223,398 |
| 74 | Takashi Miyoshi, Japan | 222,222 |
| 75 | Pete Oakley, USA | 218,183 |
| 76 | Ben Crenshaw, USA | 206,795 |
| 77 | David J. Russell, England | 206,618 |

| POS. | PLAYER, COUNTRY | TOTAL MONEY |
|---|---|---|
| 78 | Tsuneyuki Nakajima, Japan | 205,525 |
| 79 | Dave Stockton, USA | 200,741 |
| 80 | Jim Colbert, USA | 199,481 |
| 81 | Terry Gale, Australia | 190,947 |
| 82 | Denis O'Sullivan, Ireland | 184,336 |
| 83 | Tateo Ozaki, Japan | 182,011 |
| 84 | Bill Longmuir, Scotland | 179,779 |
| 85 | Eduardo Romero, Argentina | 177,410 |
| 86 | Noel Ratcliffe, Australia | 176,102 |
| 87 | Mark McCumber, USA | 163,385 |
| 88 | Jose Maria Canizares, Spain | 163,060 |
| 89 | Jim Albus, USA | 162,640 |
| 90 | Bob Charles, New Zealand | 162,582 |
| 91 | Bob Cameron, England | 156,784 |
| 92 | Martin Gray, Scotland | 156,162 |
| 93 | Howard Twitty, USA | 153,819 |
| 94 | Gery Watine, France | 150,340 |
| 95 | Dave Eichelberger, USA | 148,686 |
| 96 | Bob Eastwood, USA | 145,554 |
| 97 | Eamonn Darcy, Ireland | 141,337 |
| 98 | Jim Rhodes, England | 139,785 |
| 99 | Horacio Carbonetti, Argentina | 139,455 |
| 100 | Seiji Ebihara, Japan | 134,193 |
| 101 | Isao Aoki, Japan | 130,218 |
| 102 | Lanny Wadkins, USA | 130,207 |
| 103 | Bruce Heuchan, Canada | 129,729 |
| 104 | Delroy Cambridge, Jamaica | 128,894 |
| 105 | Danny Edwards, USA | 125,073 |
| 106 | Katsunari Takahashi, Japan | 120,349 |
| 107 | Kevin Spurgeon, England | 120,032 |
| 108 | Gavan Levenson, South Africa | 117,164 |
| 109 | Jerry Bruner, USA | 117,087 |
| 110 | John Ross, USA | 112,823 |
| 111 | Scott Simpson, USA | 109,217 |
| 112 | Choi Sang-ho, Korea | 107,043 |
| 113 | Bob Murphy, USA | 106,454 |
| 114 | Ian Mosey, England | 104,589 |
| 115 | Emilio Rodriguez, Spain | 103,961 |
| 116 | Bobby Lincoln, South Africa | 103,645 |
| 117 | Arnold Palmer, USA | 102,951 |
| 118 | Gordon J. Brand, England | 100,619 |
| 119 | Alan Tapie, USA | 99,218 |
| 120 | Guillermo Encina, Chile | 99,047 |
| 121 | Rick Rhoden, USA | 97,221 |
| 122 | Norm Jarvis, Canada | 95,854 |
| 123 | Bob Boyd, USA | 94,915 |
| 124 | Tony Charnley, England | 93,903 |
| 125 | Jim Dent, USA | 93,730 |

# Women's World Money List

This list includes official earnings on the U.S. LPGA Tour, Ladies European Tour and Japan LPGA Tour, along with other winnings in established unofficial events when reliable figures could be obtained.

| POS. | PLAYER, COUNTRY | TOTAL MONEY |
|---|---|---|
| 1 | Annika Sorenstam, Sweden | $2,756,540 |
| 2 | Paula Creamer, USA | 1,835,224 |
| 3 | Cristie Kerr, USA | 1,360,941 |
| 4 | Ai Miyazato, Japan | 1,253,416 |
| 5 | Lorena Ochoa, Mexico | 1,221,786 |
| 6 | Jeong Jang, Korea | 1,193,486 |
| 7 | Yuri Fudoh, Japan | 1,144,692 |
| 8 | Natalie Gulbis, USA | 1,010,154 |
| 9 | Meena Lee, Korea | 870,182 |
| 10 | Hee-Won Han, Korea | 858,485 |
| 11 | Gloria Park, Korea | 842,349 |
| 12 | Catriona Matthew, Scotland | 829,724 |
| 13 | Shiho Ohyama, Japan | 768,062 |
| 14 | Candie Kung, Taipei | 753,959 |
| 15 | Marisa Baena, Colombia | 744,679 |
| 16 | Lorie Kane, Canada | 722,513 |
| 17 | Birdie Kim, Korea | 715,006 |
| 18 | Soo-Yun Kang, Korea | 710,710 |
| 19 | Heather Bowie, USA | 677,425 |
| 20 | Wendy Ward, USA | 675,129 |
| 21 | Carin Koch, Sweden | 647,211 |
| 22 | Pat Hurst, USA | 634,389 |
| 23 | Sakura Yokomine, Japan | 631,058 |
| 24 | Karrie Webb, Australia | 627,582 |
| 25 | Christina Kim, USA | 621,149 |
| 26 | Karine Icher, France | 620,156 |
| 27 | Liselotte Neumann, Sweden | 618,485 |
| 28 | Rosie Jones, USA | 615,499 |
| 29 | Kasumi Fujii, Japan | 610,144 |
| 30 | Mi Hyun Kim, Korea | 584,367 |
| 31 | Juli Inkster, USA | 579,240 |
| 32 | Jennifer Rosales, Philippines | 575,779 |
| 33 | Junko Omote, Japan | 574,536 |
| 34 | Laura Davies, England | 554,409 |
| 35 | Michele Redman, USA | 540,167 |
| 36 | Midori Yoneyama, Japan | 530,727 |
| 37 | Sophie Gustafson, Sweden | 524,364 |
| 38 | Ji-Hee Lee, Korea | 476,143 |
| 39 | Young Kim, Korea | 470,926 |
| 40 | Michiko Hattori, Japan | 440,951 |
| 41 | Maria Hjorth, Sweden | 438,487 |
| 42 | Shin Hyun Ju, Japan | 431,725 |
| 43 | Rachel Hetherington, Australia | 420,954 |
| 44 | Akiko Fukushima, Japan | 405,863 |
| 45 | Nicole Perrot, Chile | 386,257 |
| 46 | Grace Park, Korea | 384,855 |
| 47 | Jill McGill, USA | 364,340 |

| POS. | PLAYER, COUNTRY | TOTAL MONEY |
|------|-----------------|-------------|
| 48 | Shi Hyun Ahn, Korea | 354,219 |
| 49 | Stacy Prammanasudh, USA | 347,562 |
| 50 | Laura Diaz, USA | 339,865 |
| 51 | Karen Stupples, England | 337,899 |
| 52 | Jimin Kang, Korea | 333,661 |
| 53 | Jeon Mi Jung, Korea | 329,905 |
| 54 | Hiroko Yamaguchi, Japan | 329,398 |
| 55 | Leta Lindley, USA | 328,516 |
| 56 | Dorothy Delasin, Philippines | 321,906 |
| 57 | Hiromi Mogi, Japan | 318,900 |
| 58 | Nikki Campbell, Canada | 315,992 |
| 59 | Miho Koga, Japan | 314,132 |
| 60 | Moira Dunn, USA | 291,607 |
| 61 | Sung Ah Yim, Korea | 287,731 |
| 62 | Lee Eun Hye, Korea | 281,858 |
| 63 | Mikiyo Nishizuka, Japan | 280,941 |
| 64 | Angela Stanford, USA | 272,288 |
| 65 | Chieko Amanuma, Japan | 269,473 |
| 66 | Yun-Jye Wei, Japan | 265,225 |
| 67 | Kim Saiki, USA | 262,482 |
| 68 | Beth Daniel, USA | 260,693 |
| 69 | Young Jo, Korea | 257,777 |
| 70 | Iben Tinning, Denmark | 257,601 |
| 71 | Michie Ohba, Japan | 254,937 |
| 72 | Kaori Higo, Japan | 253,902 |
| 73 | Mitsuko Kawasaki, Japan | 253,641 |
| 74 | Tina Barrett, USA | 253,484 |
| 75 | Janice Moodie, Scotland | 252,822 |
| 76 | Tamie Durdin, Australia | 249,033 |
| 77 | Yukari Baba, Japan | 247,596 |
| 78 | Joo Mi Kim, Korea | 246,280 |
| 79 | Julie Lu, Taipei | 238,802 |
| 80 | Katherine Hull, Australia | 237,516 |
| 81 | Yun-Hee Ku, Korea | 236,987 |
| 82 | Helen Alfredsson, Sweden | 236,656 |
| 83 | Toshimi Kimura, Japan | 232,691 |
| 84 | Meg Mallon, USA | 222,732 |
| 85 | Gwladys Nocera, France | 215,898 |
| 86 | Il Mi Chung, Korea | 213,195 |
| 87 | Yuko Saitoh, Japan | 212,570 |
| 88 | Orie Fujino, Japan | 209,010 |
| 89 | Sherri Steinhauer, USA | 203,456 |
| 90 | Becky Morgan, Wales | 201,823 |
| 91 | Cecilia Ekelundh, Sweden | 200,274 |
| 92 | Emilee Klein, USA | 199,077 |
| 93 | Silvia Cavalleri, Italy | 196,636 |
| 94 | Aree Song, Korea | 195,145 |
| 95 | Keiko Sasaki, Japan | 191,747 |
| 96 | Veronica Zorzi, Italy | 191,145 |
| 97 | Noriko Aso, Japan | 185,901 |
| 98 | Wendy Doolan, Australia | 185,674 |
| 99 | Ludivine Kreutz, France | 182,568 |
| 100 | Rui Kitada, Japan | 180,229 |
| 101 | Akane Iijima, Japan | 180,205 |

| POS. | PLAYER, COUNTRY | TOTAL MONEY |
|------|-----------------|-------------|
| 102 | Fuki Kido, Japan | 174,561 |
| 103 | Ok-Hee Ku, Korea | 174,017 |
| 104 | Jeong Yun-Joo, Korea | 164,155 |
| 105 | A.J. Eathorne, Canada | 163,518 |
| 106 | Kirsty Taylor, England | 162,782 |
| 107 | Johanna Head, England | 158,687 |
| 108 | Reilley Rankin, USA | 154,783 |
| 109 | Lu Ya Huei, Korea | 154,029 |
| 110 | Beth Bader, USA | 147,720 |
| 111 | Lindsey Wright, England | 146,307 |
| 112 | Trish Johnson, England | 142,914 |
| 113 | Miriam Nagl, Germany | 139,901 |
| 114 | Nobuko Kizawa, Japan | 139,885 |
| 115 | Yuriko Ohtsuka, Japan | 139,392 |
| 116 | Heather Daly-Donofrio, USA | 138,513 |
| 117 | Lynnette Brooky, New Zealand | 135,839 |
| 118 | Minea Blomqvist, Finalnd | 135,436 |
| 119 | Woo-Soon Ko, Korea | 135,275 |
| 120 | Mineko Nasu, Japan | 134,382 |
| 121 | Mihoko Takahashi, Japan | 134,373 |
| 122 | Jamie Hullett, USA | 132,516 |
| 123 | Candy Hannemann, Brazil | 132,312 |
| 124 | Kuniko Maeda, Japan | 132,284 |
| 125 | Mie Nakata, Japan | 130,682 |
| 126 | Ayako Uehara, Japan | 129,993 |
| 127 | Linda Wessberg, Sweden | 129,347 |
| 128 | Shani Waugh, Australia | 129,274 |
| 129 | Nancy Scranton, USA | 128,808 |
| 130 | Sophie Sandolo, Italy | 128,579 |
| 131 | Yui Kawahara, Japan | 127,779 |
| 132 | Brittany Lincicome, USA | 127,452 |
| 133 | Dawn Coe-Jones, Canada | 126,168 |
| 134 | Naoko Takasaki, Japan | 123,041 |
| 135 | Suzann Pettersen, Norway | 120,613 |
| 136 | Michelle Estill, USA | 120,443 |
| 137 | Marcy Hart, USA | 116,260 |
| 138 | Patricia Meunier-Lebouc, France | 115,892 |
| 139 | Shinobu Moromizato, Japan | 114,205 |
| 140 | Joanne Morley, England | 114,097 |
| 141 | Kaori Nakamichi, Japan | 113,449 |
| 142 | Lora Fairclough, England | 112,884 |
| 143 | Bo Bae Song, Korea | 112,803 |
| 144 | Kris Tschetter, USA | 112,513 |
| 145 | Diana D'Alessio, USA | 111,028 |
| 146 | Becky Brewerton, Wales | 110,761 |
| 147 | Jean Bartholomew, USA | 109,640 |
| 148 | Giulia Sergas, Italy | 108,506 |
| 149 | Michelle Ellis, Australia | 108,445 |
| 150 | Atomi Shiota, Japan | 107,739 |

# American Tours

## Mercedes Championships

*Plantation Course at Kapalua*, Maui, Hawaii
Par 36-37–73; 7,263 yards

January 6-9
purse, $5,300,000

| | | SCORES | | | TOTAL | MONEY |
|---|---|---|---|---|---|---|
| Stuart Appleby | 74 | 64 | 66 | 67 | 271 | $1,060,000 |
| Jonathan Kaye | 68 | 67 | 66 | 71 | 272 | 600,000 |
| Ernie Els | 69 | 65 | 68 | 71 | 273 | 350,000 |
| Tiger Woods | 68 | 68 | 69 | 68 | 273 | 350,000 |
| Adam Scott | 69 | 72 | 68 | 65 | 274 | 211,333.34 |
| Stewart Cink | 68 | 68 | 67 | 71 | 274 | 211,333.33 |
| Vijay Singh | 66 | 65 | 69 | 74 | 274 | 211,333.33 |
| Vaughn Taylor | 69 | 69 | 68 | 70 | 276 | 165,000 |
| David Toms | 71 | 67 | 70 | 68 | 276 | 165,000 |
| Sergio Garcia | 68 | 67 | 73 | 70 | 278 | 145,000 |
| Craig Parry | 67 | 72 | 68 | 71 | 278 | 145,000 |
| Woody Austin | 69 | 72 | 68 | 70 | 279 | 130,000 |
| Jonathan Byrd | 72 | 70 | 71 | 67 | 280 | 110,000 |
| Retief Goosen | 71 | 67 | 69 | 73 | 280 | 110,000 |
| Mike Weir | 70 | 63 | 71 | 76 | 280 | 110,000 |
| Bart Bryant | 69 | 72 | 69 | 71 | 281 | 91,000 |
| Chad Campbell | 69 | 67 | 71 | 75 | 282 | 88,000 |
| John Daly | 70 | 69 | 70 | 73 | 282 | 88,000 |
| Stephen Ames | 73 | 72 | 67 | 71 | 283 | 83,000 |
| Mark Hensby | 70 | 73 | 71 | 69 | 283 | 83,000 |
| Rod Pampling | 70 | 72 | 69 | 72 | 283 | 83,000 |
| Andre Stolz | 73 | 71 | 71 | 70 | 285 | 79,000 |
| Zach Johnson | 72 | 70 | 71 | 73 | 286 | 75,000 |
| Joey Sindelar | 71 | 68 | 71 | 76 | 286 | 75,000 |
| Heath Slocum | 69 | 70 | 72 | 75 | 286 | 75,000 |
| Todd Hamilton | 72 | 72 | 72 | 71 | 287 | 70,000 |
| Ryan Palmer | 76 | 68 | 71 | 72 | 287 | 70,000 |
| Brent Geiberger | 72 | 73 | 71 | 72 | 288 | 68,000 |
| Steve Flesch | 69 | 73 | 72 | 75 | 289 | 67,000 |
| Fred Funk | 74 | 74 | 67 | 75 | 290 | 66,000 |
| Carlos Franco | 74 | 71 | 72 | 75 | 292 | 65,000 |

## Sony Open in Hawaii

*Waialae Country Club*, Honolulu, Hawaii
Par 35-35–70; 7,060 yards

January 13-16
purse, $4,800,000

| | | SCORES | | | TOTAL | MONEY |
|---|---|---|---|---|---|---|
| Vijay Singh | 69 | 68 | 67 | 65 | 269 | $864,000 |
| Ernie Els | 71 | 67 | 70 | 62 | 270 | 518,400 |
| Charles Howell | 70 | 70 | 64 | 67 | 271 | 278,400 |
| Shigeki Maruyama | 67 | 65 | 68 | 71 | 271 | 278,400 |
| Stewart Cink | 66 | 69 | 72 | 65 | 272 | 182,400 |
| Brett Quigley | 66 | 67 | 68 | 71 | 272 | 182,400 |
| Tommy Armour | 69 | 71 | 67 | 66 | 273 | 154,800 |

| | SCORES | | | | TOTAL | MONEY |
|---|---|---|---|---|---|---|
| Andrew Magee | 67 | 68 | 71 | 67 | 273 | 154,800 |
| Bart Bryant | 70 | 69 | 66 | 69 | 274 | 124,800 |
| Robert Gamez | 69 | 66 | 68 | 71 | 274 | 124,800 |
| Tom Lehman | 67 | 68 | 70 | 69 | 274 | 124,800 |
| Craig Stadler | 71 | 69 | 67 | 67 | 274 | 124,800 |
| Luke Donald | 74 | 67 | 65 | 69 | 275 | 90,000 |
| Jeff Maggert | 70 | 68 | 68 | 69 | 275 | 90,000 |
| Shaun Micheel | 70 | 68 | 68 | 69 | 275 | 90,000 |
| David Toms | 71 | 68 | 68 | 68 | 275 | 90,000 |
| Jason Allred | 69 | 68 | 70 | 69 | 276 | 72,000 |
| Paul Azinger | 67 | 68 | 67 | 74 | 276 | 72,000 |
| Tim Herron | 68 | 72 | 71 | 65 | 276 | 72,000 |
| Tom Byrum | 66 | 71 | 73 | 67 | 277 | 48,420 |
| Joe Durant | 69 | 72 | 69 | 67 | 277 | 48,420 |
| Jonathan Kaye | 67 | 71 | 71 | 68 | 277 | 48,420 |
| Larry Mize | 70 | 69 | 64 | 74 | 277 | 48,420 |
| Pat Perez | 71 | 70 | 66 | 70 | 277 | 48,420 |
| Loren Roberts | 70 | 70 | 69 | 68 | 277 | 48,420 |
| Justin Rose | 67 | 66 | 72 | 72 | 277 | 48,420 |
| Adam Scott | 71 | 65 | 69 | 72 | 277 | 48,420 |
| Peter Jacobsen | 72 | 68 | 70 | 68 | 278 | 32,640 |
| Arron Oberholser | 71 | 69 | 69 | 69 | 278 | 32,640 |
| Ryan Palmer | 69 | 70 | 70 | 69 | 278 | 32,640 |
| Craig Parry | 69 | 70 | 70 | 69 | 278 | 32,640 |
| Jeff Sluman | 67 | 68 | 73 | 70 | 278 | 32,640 |
| Jason Bohn | 71 | 70 | 69 | 69 | 279 | 25,920 |
| Jim Furyk | 71 | 69 | 72 | 67 | 279 | 25,920 |
| Brian Gay | 71 | 70 | 71 | 67 | 279 | 25,920 |
| Brent Geiberger | 68 | 71 | 70 | 70 | 279 | 25,920 |
| Chris Riley | 71 | 71 | 68 | 69 | 279 | 25,920 |
| Rich Beem | 70 | 69 | 74 | 67 | 280 | 21,120 |
| Franklin Langham | 71 | 68 | 70 | 71 | 280 | 21,120 |
| Sean Murphy | 70 | 72 | 70 | 68 | 280 | 21,120 |
| Heath Slocum | 72 | 70 | 69 | 69 | 280 | 21,120 |
| Briny Baird | 68 | 71 | 73 | 69 | 281 | 16,800 |
| Bob Estes | 71 | 69 | 72 | 69 | 281 | 16,800 |
| Tom Pernice, Jr. | 69 | 72 | 70 | 70 | 281 | 16,800 |
| Rory Sabbatini | 72 | 70 | 66 | 73 | 281 | 16,800 |
| D.J. Trahan | 70 | 67 | 73 | 71 | 281 | 16,800 |
| Ben Crane | 71 | 70 | 73 | 68 | 282 | 12,053.34 |
| Billy Mayfair | 71 | 71 | 71 | 69 | 282 | 12,053.34 |
| John Riegger | 72 | 68 | 73 | 69 | 282 | 12,053.34 |
| Steve Allan | 75 | 67 | 68 | 72 | 282 | 12,053.33 |
| Woody Austin | 67 | 71 | 73 | 71 | 282 | 12,053.33 |
| Chad Campbell | 67 | 71 | 73 | 71 | 282 | 12,053.33 |
| Todd Hamilton | 69 | 71 | 71 | 71 | 282 | 12,053.33 |
| Zach Johnson | 76 | 65 | 70 | 71 | 282 | 12,053.33 |
| Dick Mast | 74 | 64 | 69 | 75 | 282 | 12,053.33 |
| D.J. Brigman | 73 | 69 | 71 | 70 | 283 | 10,608 |
| Jonathan Byrd | 73 | 69 | 69 | 72 | 283 | 10,608 |
| Daniel Chopra | 73 | 69 | 69 | 72 | 283 | 10,608 |
| Steve Flesch | 73 | 69 | 69 | 72 | 283 | 10,608 |
| Retief Goosen | 72 | 70 | 72 | 69 | 283 | 10,608 |
| Steve Jones | 73 | 69 | 74 | 67 | 283 | 10,608 |
| Greg Owen | 69 | 73 | 71 | 70 | 283 | 10,608 |
| Rob Rashell | 73 | 67 | 74 | 69 | 283 | 10,608 |
| Hank Kuehne | 66 | 73 | 72 | 73 | 284 | 9,984 |
| Jesper Parnevik | 72 | 69 | 71 | 72 | 284 | 9,984 |
| D.A. Points | 71 | 70 | 71 | 72 | 284 | 9,984 |
| Omar Uresti | 70 | 72 | 70 | 72 | 284 | 9,984 |

|  | SCORES |  |  |  | TOTAL | MONEY |
|---|---|---|---|---|---|---|
| Duffy Waldorf | 74 | 68 | 75 | 67 | 284 | 9,984 |
| John Cook | 72 | 68 | 71 | 74 | 285 | 9,600 |
| Ryuji Imada | 73 | 69 | 68 | 75 | 285 | 9,600 |
| Nick Watney | 70 | 70 | 71 | 74 | 285 | 9,600 |
| Tom Kite | 71 | 71 | 69 | 75 | 286 | 9,264 |
| Sean O'Hair | 69 | 71 | 73 | 73 | 286 | 9,264 |
| Joey Snyder | 71 | 71 | 74 | 70 | 286 | 9,264 |
| Charles Warren | 74 | 68 | 76 | 68 | 286 | 9,264 |
| Dean Wilson | 69 | 70 | 72 | 77 | 288 | 9,024 |
| Greg Meyer | 71 | 70 | 74 | 74 | 289 | 8,928 |
| Paul Gow | 70 | 68 | 76 | 79 | 293 | 8,832 |

## Buick Invitational

*Torrey Pines Golf Course*, La Jolla, California
*South Course:* Par 36-36–72; 7,568 yards
*North Course:* Par 36-36–72; 6,874 yards

January 20-23
purse, $4,800,000

|  | SCORES |  |  |  | TOTAL | MONEY |
|---|---|---|---|---|---|---|
| Tiger Woods | 69 | 63 | 72 | 68 | 272 | $864,000 |
| Luke Donald | 68 | 67 | 67 | 73 | 275 | 358,400 |
| Charles Howell | 72 | 67 | 64 | 72 | 275 | 358,400 |
| Tom Lehman | 62 | 67 | 73 | 73 | 275 | 358,400 |
| Bernhard Langer | 69 | 69 | 67 | 72 | 277 | 192,000 |
| Ernie Els | 65 | 71 | 71 | 71 | 278 | 150,240 |
| Scott McCarron | 72 | 65 | 72 | 69 | 278 | 150,240 |
| Arron Oberholser | 64 | 72 | 72 | 70 | 278 | 150,240 |
| Pat Perez | 66 | 69 | 72 | 71 | 278 | 150,240 |
| Kevin Sutherland | 68 | 66 | 72 | 72 | 278 | 150,240 |
| Jason Bohn | 66 | 74 | 71 | 68 | 279 | 110,400 |
| Tom Gillis | 68 | 68 | 72 | 71 | 279 | 110,400 |
| Jerry Kelly | 68 | 71 | 73 | 67 | 279 | 110,400 |
| Robert Damron | 70 | 68 | 73 | 69 | 280 | 84,000 |
| Dudley Hart | 65 | 69 | 71 | 75 | 280 | 84,000 |
| Peter Lonard | 67 | 65 | 71 | 77 | 280 | 84,000 |
| Brett Quigley | 69 | 71 | 70 | 70 | 280 | 84,000 |
| Bill Haas | 71 | 66 | 74 | 70 | 281 | 69,600 |
| Brandt Jobe | 71 | 70 | 71 | 69 | 281 | 69,600 |
| Daniel Chopra | 73 | 66 | 73 | 70 | 282 | 55,920 |
| Bob Estes | 72 | 70 | 71 | 69 | 282 | 55,920 |
| Scott Hend | 72 | 64 | 75 | 71 | 282 | 55,920 |
| Fredrik Jacobson | 69 | 69 | 70 | 74 | 282 | 55,920 |
| Tommy Armour | 71 | 69 | 71 | 72 | 283 | 38,880 |
| Aaron Baddeley | 66 | 70 | 74 | 73 | 283 | 38,880 |
| James Driscoll | 71 | 68 | 73 | 71 | 283 | 38,880 |
| Zach Johnson | 69 | 72 | 72 | 70 | 283 | 38,880 |
| Vijay Singh | 71 | 69 | 68 | 75 | 283 | 38,880 |
| Toru Taniguchi | 74 | 66 | 72 | 71 | 283 | 38,880 |
| Craig Barlow | 68 | 71 | 71 | 74 | 284 | 28,525.72 |
| John Rollins | 69 | 71 | 71 | 73 | 284 | 28,525.72 |
| Charles Warren | 66 | 74 | 73 | 71 | 284 | 28,525.72 |
| Brian Davis | 69 | 68 | 77 | 70 | 284 | 28,525.71 |
| Joe Durant | 71 | 68 | 72 | 73 | 284 | 28,525.71 |
| Shigeki Maruyama | 69 | 72 | 71 | 72 | 284 | 28,525.71 |
| Carl Pettersson | 66 | 75 | 69 | 74 | 284 | 28,525.71 |
| Woody Austin | 70 | 72 | 74 | 69 | 285 | 21,600 |
| Jonathan Byrd | 72 | 70 | 73 | 70 | 285 | 21,600 |

| | SCORES | | | | TOTAL | MONEY |
|---|---|---|---|---|---|---|
| K.J. Choi | 67 | 73 | 72 | 73 | 285 | 21,600 |
| Fred Couples | 74 | 68 | 75 | 68 | 285 | 21,600 |
| Chris Smith | 70 | 69 | 73 | 73 | 285 | 21,600 |
| Sergio Garcia | 69 | 70 | 74 | 73 | 286 | 17,760 |
| J.J. Henry | 68 | 72 | 74 | 72 | 286 | 17,760 |
| D.J. Trahan | 67 | 72 | 75 | 72 | 286 | 17,760 |
| Jay Haas | 71 | 70 | 72 | 74 | 287 | 12,654.55 |
| Franklin Langham | 71 | 69 | 74 | 73 | 287 | 12,654.55 |
| Billy Mayfair | 71 | 70 | 71 | 75 | 287 | 12,654.55 |
| Darron Stiles | 66 | 75 | 74 | 72 | 287 | 12,654.55 |
| Mario Tiziani | 69 | 71 | 71 | 76 | 287 | 12,654.55 |
| Bob Tway | 68 | 72 | 74 | 73 | 287 | 12,654.55 |
| Danny Briggs | 74 | 68 | 73 | 72 | 287 | 12,654.54 |
| Kevin Na | 75 | 67 | 71 | 74 | 287 | 12,654.54 |
| Ted Purdy | 75 | 67 | 72 | 73 | 287 | 12,654.54 |
| Roland Thatcher | 74 | 67 | 73 | 73 | 287 | 12,654.54 |
| Mark Wilson | 73 | 66 | 73 | 75 | 287 | 12,654.54 |
| D.J. Brigman | 71 | 69 | 74 | 74 | 288 | 10,656 |
| Alex Cejka | 71 | 71 | 73 | 73 | 288 | 10,656 |
| Charley Hoffman | 71 | 69 | 72 | 76 | 288 | 10,656 |
| Phil Mickelson | 72 | 67 | 78 | 71 | 288 | 10,656 |
| Dennis Paulson | 71 | 70 | 75 | 72 | 288 | 10,656 |
| Corey Pavin | 73 | 69 | 73 | 73 | 288 | 10,656 |
| Tom Pernice, Jr. | 65 | 73 | 75 | 75 | 288 | 10,656 |
| J.L. Lewis | 71 | 71 | 74 | 73 | 289 | 10,272 |
| Len Mattiace | 73 | 66 | 74 | 77 | 290 | 10,128 |
| Phillip Price | 71 | 69 | 75 | 75 | 290 | 10,128 |
| Brendan Jones | 70 | 71 | 76 | 74 | 291 | 9,936 |
| Skip Kendall | 72 | 70 | 75 | 74 | 291 | 9,936 |
| Michael Allen | 69 | 72 | 79 | 72 | 292 | 9,744 |
| J.P. Hayes | 68 | 73 | 75 | 76 | 292 | 9,744 |
| Paul Gow | 72 | 69 | 71 | 81 | 293 | 9,552 |
| Mark O'Meara | 72 | 69 | 73 | 79 | 293 | 9,552 |
| John Daly | 72 | 70 | 77 | 75 | 294 | 9,264 |
| Michael Long | 69 | 73 | 77 | 75 | 294 | 9,264 |
| Carl Paulson | 68 | 71 | 78 | 77 | 294 | 9,264 |
| Charlie Wi | 72 | 70 | 78 | 74 | 294 | 9,264 |
| Bill Glasson | 72 | 68 | 72 | 83 | 295 | 8,976 |
| Ryuji Imada | 68 | 74 | 73 | 80 | 295 | 8,976 |
| Harrison Frazar | 68 | 74 | 76 | 78 | 296 | 8,784 |
| Scott Simpson | 69 | 71 | 81 | 75 | 296 | 8,784 |
| Will MacKenzie | 74 | 67 | 80 | 76 | 297 | 8,640 |
| Joey Sindelar | 71 | 71 | 77 | 79 | 298 | 8,544 |

## Bob Hope Chrysler Classic

*PGA West, Palmer Course:* Par 36-36–72; 6,930 yards
*Tamarisk CC:* Par 36-36–72, 7,003 yards
*Bermuda Dunes CC*: Par 36-36–72; 6,962 yards
*La Quinta CC*: Par 36-36–72; 7,060 yards
La Quinta, California

January 26-30
purse, $4,700,000

| | SCORES | | | | | TOTAL | MONEY |
|---|---|---|---|---|---|---|---|
| Justin Leonard | 66 | 67 | 68 | 64 | 67 | 332 | $846,000 |
| Tim Clark | 70 | 66 | 64 | 66 | 69 | 335 | 413,600 |
| Joe Ogilvie | 64 | 63 | 66 | 69 | 73 | 335 | 413,600 |
| Peter Lonard | 67 | 64 | 64 | 69 | 72 | 336 | 206,800 |

| | SCORES | | | | | TOTAL | MONEY |
|---|---|---|---|---|---|---|---|
| Loren Roberts | 68 | 67 | 67 | 65 | 69 | 336 | 206,800 |
| Tim Herron | 68 | 64 | 71 | 68 | 66 | 337 | 163,325 |
| John Senden | 69 | 67 | 64 | 68 | 69 | 337 | 163,325 |
| Jim Furyk | 67 | 70 | 65 | 65 | 71 | 338 | 131,600 |
| Jerry Kelly | 68 | 67 | 64 | 69 | 70 | 338 | 131,600 |
| Andrew Magee | 68 | 69 | 65 | 69 | 67 | 338 | 131,600 |
| Ian Poulter | 70 | 70 | 64 | 63 | 71 | 338 | 131,600 |
| Ryuji Imada | 66 | 69 | 64 | 69 | 71 | 339 | 103,400 |
| Phil Mickelson | 66 | 64 | 70 | 68 | 71 | 339 | 103,400 |
| Brian Davis | 68 | 66 | 69 | 68 | 69 | 340 | 82,250 |
| Fredrik Jacobson | 68 | 62 | 67 | 70 | 73 | 340 | 82,250 |
| Tom Pernice, Jr. | 67 | 69 | 67 | 69 | 68 | 340 | 82,250 |
| Craig Stadler | 68 | 67 | 65 | 71 | 69 | 340 | 82,250 |
| Todd Fischer | 67 | 69 | 69 | 65 | 71 | 341 | 61,288 |
| Davis Love | 70 | 69 | 61 | 70 | 71 | 341 | 61,288 |
| Tim Petrovic | 67 | 70 | 66 | 69 | 69 | 341 | 61,288 |
| Chris Riley | 70 | 66 | 66 | 66 | 73 | 341 | 61,288 |
| Jeff Sluman | 68 | 69 | 72 | 64 | 68 | 341 | 61,288 |
| Stewart Cink | 68 | 68 | 71 | 66 | 69 | 342 | 40,655 |
| Fred Couples | 65 | 66 | 72 | 68 | 71 | 342 | 40,655 |
| Fred Funk | 64 | 70 | 71 | 68 | 69 | 342 | 40,655 |
| Jay Haas | 70 | 68 | 68 | 67 | 69 | 342 | 40,655 |
| Bernhard Langer | 70 | 71 | 65 | 68 | 68 | 342 | 40,655 |
| Scott Verplank | 69 | 70 | 68 | 62 | 73 | 342 | 40,655 |
| Mark Calcavecchia | 70 | 68 | 68 | 65 | 72 | 343 | 30,550 |
| Ted Purdy | 64 | 68 | 71 | 67 | 73 | 343 | 30,550 |
| Justin Rose | 65 | 72 | 68 | 68 | 70 | 343 | 30,550 |
| David Toms | 69 | 69 | 67 | 66 | 72 | 343 | 30,550 |
| Nick Watney | 65 | 70 | 66 | 69 | 73 | 343 | 30,550 |
| Briny Baird | 68 | 70 | 67 | 69 | 70 | 344 | 23,231.43 |
| Bart Bryant | 68 | 69 | 66 | 69 | 72 | 344 | 23,231.43 |
| Bill Haas | 67 | 66 | 68 | 71 | 72 | 344 | 23,231.43 |
| Billy Mayfair | 67 | 64 | 69 | 74 | 70 | 344 | 23,231.43 |
| Hidemichi Tanaka | 67 | 69 | 68 | 69 | 71 | 344 | 23,231.43 |
| Duffy Waldorf | 64 | 69 | 69 | 69 | 73 | 344 | 23,231.43 |
| Neal Lancaster | 65 | 73 | 70 | 68 | 68 | 344 | 23,231.42 |
| Stephen Ames | 69 | 71 | 68 | 65 | 72 | 345 | 16,450 |
| Robert Damron | 64 | 67 | 68 | 69 | 77 | 345 | 16,450 |
| Harrison Frazar | 67 | 74 | 65 | 71 | 68 | 345 | 16,450 |
| Kent Jones | 71 | 68 | 66 | 65 | 75 | 345 | 16,450 |
| Skip Kendall | 67 | 68 | 70 | 69 | 71 | 345 | 16,450 |
| Shaun Micheel | 69 | 68 | 68 | 70 | 70 | 345 | 16,450 |
| Jesper Parnevik | 68 | 65 | 71 | 70 | 71 | 345 | 16,450 |
| Joe Durant | 66 | 66 | 72 | 68 | 74 | 346 | 11,956.80 |
| Brent Geiberger | 68 | 70 | 70 | 67 | 71 | 346 | 11,956.80 |
| Phillip Price | 69 | 67 | 68 | 68 | 74 | 346 | 11,956.80 |
| Patrick Sheehan | 69 | 70 | 69 | 66 | 72 | 346 | 11,956.80 |
| Kevin Sutherland | 68 | 69 | 67 | 67 | 75 | 346 | 11,956.80 |
| Tommy Armour | 69 | 68 | 72 | 67 | 71 | 347 | 10,828.80 |
| Olin Browne | 68 | 67 | 71 | 68 | 73 | 347 | 10,828.80 |
| Ben Crane | 73 | 66 | 68 | 68 | 72 | 347 | 10,828.80 |
| Frank Lickliter | 70 | 70 | 71 | 66 | 70 | 347 | 10,828.80 |
| Kevin Stadler | 72 | 70 | 69 | 64 | 72 | 347 | 10,828.80 |
| Brian Bateman | 67 | 67 | 75 | 67 | 72 | 348 | 10,434 |
| Joey Sindelar | 68 | 66 | 69 | 72 | 73 | 348 | 10,434 |
| Chris Smith | 70 | 67 | 67 | 66 | 78 | 348 | 10,434 |
| Billy Andrade | 69 | 66 | 72 | 69 | 73 | 349 | 9,917 |
| Aaron Baddeley | 73 | 68 | 67 | 68 | 73 | 349 | 9,917 |
| Paul Goydos | 68 | 70 | 67 | 70 | 74 | 349 | 9,917 |
| Dudley Hart | 70 | 68 | 64 | 73 | 74 | 349 | 9,917 |

| | SCORES | | | | | TOTAL | MONEY |
|---|---|---|---|---|---|---|---|
| Peter Jacobsen | 66 | 70 | 70 | 67 | 76 | 349 | 9,917 |
| Jeff Maggert | 69 | 68 | 67 | 71 | 74 | 349 | 9,917 |
| Pat Perez | 67 | 66 | 68 | 71 | 77 | 349 | 9,917 |
| Chris Starkjohann | 72 | 71 | 67 | 67 | 72 | 349 | 9,917 |
| Chris DiMarco | 69 | 74 | 67 | 67 | 73 | 350 | 9,447 |
| Robert Gamez | 70 | 70 | 70 | 67 | 73 | 350 | 9,447 |
| Craig Barlow | 68 | 68 | 66 | 70 | 79 | 351 | 9,165 |
| Ben Curtis | 72 | 70 | 66 | 69 | 74 | 351 | 9,165 |
| Steve Elkington | 70 | 69 | 67 | 69 | 76 | 351 | 9,165 |
| J.J. Henry | 70 | 68 | 70 | 69 | 74 | 351 | 9,165 |
| John Daly | 72 | 66 | 68 | 71 | 75 | 352 | 8,836 |
| Geoff Ogilvy | 75 | 68 | 67 | 67 | 75 | 352 | 8,836 |
| Jay Williamson | 72 | 67 | 67 | 71 | 75 | 352 | 8,836 |
| Jason Allred | 66 | 65 | 73 | 72 | 78 | 354 | 8,648 |

## FBR Open

*TPC of Scottsdale*, Scottsdale, Arizona
Par 35-36–71; 7,216 yards

February 3-6
purse, $5,200,000

| | SCORES | | | | TOTAL | MONEY |
|---|---|---|---|---|---|---|
| Phil Mickelson | 73 | 60 | 66 | 68 | 267 | $936,000 |
| Scott McCarron | 72 | 70 | 65 | 65 | 272 | 457,600 |
| Kevin Na | 68 | 65 | 70 | 69 | 272 | 457,600 |
| David Toms | 71 | 66 | 68 | 68 | 273 | 214,933.34 |
| Steve Flesch | 70 | 67 | 67 | 69 | 273 | 214,933.33 |
| Tim Herron | 73 | 66 | 67 | 67 | 273 | 214,933.33 |
| Kenny Perry | 70 | 67 | 67 | 70 | 274 | 174,200 |
| Charles Warren | 69 | 68 | 69 | 69 | 275 | 161,200 |
| Mark Calcavecchia | 74 | 66 | 65 | 71 | 276 | 145,600 |
| Hunter Mahan | 68 | 69 | 72 | 67 | 276 | 145,600 |
| K.J. Choi | 72 | 66 | 66 | 73 | 277 | 100,100 |
| Stewart Cink | 68 | 70 | 69 | 70 | 277 | 100,100 |
| Jesper Parnevik | 73 | 70 | 69 | 65 | 277 | 100,100 |
| Tom Pernice, Jr. | 72 | 68 | 68 | 69 | 277 | 100,100 |
| John Rollins | 70 | 74 | 66 | 67 | 277 | 100,100 |
| Patrick Sheehan | 72 | 66 | 70 | 69 | 277 | 100,100 |
| Vijay Singh | 71 | 72 | 66 | 68 | 277 | 100,100 |
| Joey Snyder | 72 | 68 | 68 | 69 | 277 | 100,100 |
| Matt Gogel | 72 | 69 | 67 | 70 | 278 | 63,024 |
| Franklin Langham | 70 | 70 | 68 | 70 | 278 | 63,024 |
| Kevin Sutherland | 72 | 68 | 69 | 69 | 278 | 63,024 |
| Scott Verplank | 73 | 66 | 68 | 71 | 278 | 63,024 |
| Duffy Waldorf | 69 | 70 | 69 | 70 | 278 | 63,024 |
| Stephen Ames | 76 | 67 | 70 | 66 | 279 | 45,760 |
| Robert Damron | 73 | 70 | 67 | 69 | 279 | 45,760 |
| Zach Johnson | 74 | 68 | 71 | 66 | 279 | 45,760 |
| Cameron Beckman | 73 | 68 | 67 | 72 | 280 | 38,480 |
| Dudley Hart | 67 | 73 | 71 | 69 | 280 | 38,480 |
| Geoff Ogilvy | 75 | 65 | 73 | 67 | 280 | 38,480 |
| Michael Allen | 70 | 66 | 73 | 72 | 281 | 31,590 |
| Tommy Armour | 74 | 66 | 69 | 72 | 281 | 31,590 |
| Bart Bryant | 69 | 71 | 71 | 70 | 281 | 31,590 |
| Bob Estes | 73 | 68 | 68 | 72 | 281 | 31,590 |
| Shaun Micheel | 70 | 67 | 70 | 74 | 281 | 31,590 |
| Bob Tway | 75 | 68 | 71 | 67 | 281 | 31,590 |
| Harrison Frazar | 73 | 65 | 66 | 78 | 282 | 25,025 |

| | SCORES | | | | TOTAL | MONEY |
|---|---|---|---|---|---|---|
| Ryuji Imada | 72 | 65 | 72 | 73 | 282 | 25,025 |
| Steve Jones | 73 | 71 | 69 | 69 | 282 | 25,025 |
| Shigeki Maruyama | 73 | 72 | 69 | 68 | 282 | 25,025 |
| Charles Howell | 74 | 69 | 69 | 71 | 283 | 20,280 |
| Jonathan Kaye | 73 | 69 | 70 | 71 | 283 | 20,280 |
| Andrew Magee | 74 | 71 | 66 | 72 | 283 | 20,280 |
| Arron Oberholser | 75 | 69 | 70 | 69 | 283 | 20,280 |
| Carl Pettersson | 77 | 68 | 69 | 69 | 283 | 20,280 |
| Robert Allenby | 73 | 67 | 74 | 70 | 284 | 15,652 |
| Jay Haas | 74 | 70 | 71 | 69 | 284 | 15,652 |
| Tom Lehman | 74 | 65 | 73 | 72 | 284 | 15,652 |
| Jay Williamson | 72 | 73 | 73 | 66 | 284 | 15,652 |
| Bernhard Langer | 70 | 66 | 74 | 75 | 285 | 12,705.34 |
| Nick Watney | 71 | 68 | 74 | 72 | 285 | 12,705.34 |
| Aaron Baddeley | 73 | 71 | 72 | 69 | 285 | 12,705.33 |
| John Elliott | 71 | 71 | 73 | 70 | 285 | 12,705.33 |
| John Huston | 74 | 69 | 75 | 67 | 285 | 12,705.33 |
| Hank Kuehne | 69 | 68 | 80 | 68 | 285 | 12,705.33 |
| J.L. Lewis | 73 | 71 | 67 | 75 | 286 | 11,700 |
| Frank Lickliter | 75 | 69 | 69 | 73 | 286 | 11,700 |
| Tim Petrovic | 74 | 70 | 70 | 72 | 286 | 11,700 |
| Brett Quigley | 70 | 71 | 67 | 78 | 286 | 11,700 |
| Joey Sindelar | 73 | 69 | 72 | 72 | 286 | 11,700 |
| Heath Slocum | 68 | 69 | 76 | 73 | 286 | 11,700 |
| Danny Briggs | 73 | 71 | 69 | 74 | 287 | 10,972 |
| Jonathan Byrd | 69 | 72 | 69 | 77 | 287 | 10,972 |
| Billy Mayfair | 76 | 67 | 73 | 71 | 287 | 10,972 |
| Jose Maria Olazabal | 72 | 69 | 68 | 78 | 287 | 10,972 |
| Craig Perks | 74 | 70 | 74 | 69 | 287 | 10,972 |
| Ted Purdy | 71 | 71 | 70 | 75 | 287 | 10,972 |
| Rory Sabbatini | 73 | 65 | 73 | 76 | 287 | 10,972 |
| Mike Weir | 74 | 71 | 71 | 71 | 287 | 10,972 |
| Daniel Chopra | 71 | 71 | 71 | 75 | 288 | 10,452 |
| Don Yrene | 74 | 71 | 70 | 73 | 288 | 10,452 |
| Robert Gamez | 72 | 68 | 73 | 76 | 289 | 10,140 |
| Brian Gay | 72 | 72 | 74 | 71 | 289 | 10,140 |
| Brent Geiberger | 76 | 69 | 70 | 74 | 289 | 10,140 |
| Kent Jones | 73 | 71 | 71 | 74 | 289 | 10,140 |
| J.J. Henry | 74 | 69 | 74 | 74 | 291 | 9,880 |
| Brian Bateman | 73 | 72 | 71 | 78 | 294 | 9,776 |
| Fredrik Jacobson | 73 | 71 | 75 | 77 | 296 | 9,672 |

## AT&T Pebble Beach National Pro-Am

*Pebble Beach GL:* Par 36-36–72; 6,816 yards
*Poppy Hills GC:* Par 36-36–72; 6,833 yards
*Spyglass Hill GC:* Par 36-36–72; 6,862 yards
Pebble Beach, California

February 10-13
purse, $5,300,000

| | SCORES | | | | TOTAL | MONEY |
|---|---|---|---|---|---|---|
| Phil Mickelson | 62 | 67 | 67 | 73 | 269 | $954,000 |
| Mike Weir | 66 | 67 | 73 | 67 | 273 | 572,400 |
| Greg Owen | 67 | 69 | 67 | 72 | 275 | 360,400 |
| Tim Clark | 67 | 71 | 67 | 71 | 276 | 233,200 |
| Paul Goydos | 67 | 68 | 70 | 71 | 276 | 233,200 |
| Darren Clarke | 70 | 66 | 70 | 71 | 277 | 184,175 |
| Arron Oberholser | 71 | 66 | 69 | 71 | 277 | 184,175 |

| | SCORES | | | | TOTAL | MONEY |
|---|---|---|---|---|---|---|
| Graeme McDowell | 68 | 69 | 70 | 71 | 278 | 164,300 |
| Davis Love | 65 | 72 | 71 | 71 | 279 | 148,400 |
| Jeff Sluman | 71 | 66 | 69 | 73 | 279 | 148,400 |
| Billy Andrade | 74 | 70 | 63 | 73 | 280 | 112,360 |
| Luke Donald | 71 | 70 | 68 | 71 | 280 | 112,360 |
| Robert Gamez | 70 | 71 | 66 | 73 | 280 | 112,360 |
| Charles Howell | 65 | 71 | 72 | 72 | 280 | 112,360 |
| Joel Kribel | 72 | 70 | 68 | 70 | 280 | 112,360 |
| Arjun Atwal | 68 | 68 | 73 | 72 | 281 | 67,310 |
| Craig Barlow | 74 | 68 | 68 | 71 | 281 | 67,310 |
| K.J. Choi | 67 | 75 | 68 | 71 | 281 | 67,310 |
| Daniel Chopra | 65 | 72 | 71 | 73 | 281 | 67,310 |
| Todd Fischer | 68 | 69 | 72 | 72 | 281 | 67,310 |
| Andrew Magee | 67 | 68 | 70 | 76 | 281 | 67,310 |
| Joe Ogilvie | 69 | 71 | 70 | 71 | 281 | 67,310 |
| Jose Maria Olazabal | 70 | 67 | 68 | 76 | 281 | 67,310 |
| Kevin Sutherland | 65 | 70 | 70 | 76 | 281 | 67,310 |
| Charles Warren | 70 | 70 | 70 | 71 | 281 | 67,310 |
| Jason Bohn | 70 | 69 | 73 | 70 | 282 | 40,015 |
| Sean O'Hair | 71 | 74 | 65 | 72 | 282 | 40,015 |
| Ted Purdy | 67 | 70 | 71 | 74 | 282 | 40,015 |
| Patrick Sheehan | 70 | 69 | 70 | 73 | 282 | 40,015 |
| Paul McGinley | 69 | 69 | 72 | 73 | 283 | 30,151.12 |
| Tom Gillis | 70 | 71 | 71 | 71 | 283 | 30,151.11 |
| Scott Gutschewski | 71 | 69 | 69 | 74 | 283 | 30,151.11 |
| Richard Johnson | 68 | 69 | 70 | 76 | 283 | 30,151.11 |
| Kent Jones | 71 | 65 | 73 | 74 | 283 | 30,151.11 |
| Dicky Pride | 66 | 71 | 72 | 74 | 283 | 30,151.11 |
| D.J. Trahan | 72 | 70 | 69 | 72 | 283 | 30,151.11 |
| Dean Wilson | 68 | 71 | 70 | 74 | 283 | 30,151.11 |
| Mark Wilson | 75 | 68 | 68 | 72 | 283 | 30,151.11 |
| Jim Furyk | 71 | 70 | 70 | 73 | 284 | 22,260 |
| Jeff Hart | 69 | 72 | 70 | 73 | 284 | 22,260 |
| Hunter Mahan | 65 | 73 | 72 | 74 | 284 | 22,260 |
| Chris Riley | 69 | 70 | 71 | 74 | 284 | 22,260 |
| Mark Brooks | 76 | 67 | 68 | 74 | 285 | 16,138.50 |
| Olin Browne | 72 | 65 | 72 | 76 | 285 | 16,138.50 |
| Matt Gogel | 73 | 69 | 70 | 73 | 285 | 16,138.50 |
| Hunter Haas | 71 | 68 | 73 | 73 | 285 | 16,138.50 |
| Matt Kuchar | 70 | 73 | 69 | 73 | 285 | 16,138.50 |
| Rocco Mediate | 76 | 70 | 66 | 73 | 285 | 16,138.50 |
| Carl Pettersson | 70 | 69 | 72 | 74 | 285 | 16,138.50 |
| Mario Tiziani | 66 | 72 | 73 | 74 | 285 | 16,138.50 |
| Fred Funk | 70 | 69 | 71 | 76 | 286 | 12,402 |
| Tim Herron | 72 | 67 | 71 | 76 | 286 | 12,402 |
| Mark O'Meara | 69 | 72 | 69 | 76 | 286 | 12,402 |
| Ryan Palmer | 68 | 71 | 70 | 77 | 286 | 12,402 |
| Steve Pate | 68 | 72 | 72 | 74 | 286 | 12,402 |
| Tim Petrovic | 71 | 70 | 71 | 74 | 286 | 12,402 |
| Peter Tomasulo | 69 | 75 | 68 | 74 | 286 | 12,402 |
| Tom Scherrer | 68 | 72 | 72 | 75 | 287 | 11,819 |
| Charlie Wi | 68 | 72 | 70 | 77 | 287 | 11,819 |
| Justin Bolli | 70 | 71 | 69 | 78 | 288 | 11,607 |
| Robert Damron | 70 | 68 | 73 | 77 | 288 | 11,607 |
| John Senden | 76 | 66 | 69 | 79 | 290 | 11,395 |
| Lee Westwood | 68 | 69 | 74 | 79 | 290 | 11,395 |
| Larry Mize | 72 | 73 | 67 | 82 | 294 | 11,236 |

# Nissan Open

*Riviera Country Club*, Pacific Palisades, California
Par 35-36–71; 7,247 yards
(Event shortened to 36 holes with playoff on Monday—rain.)

February 17-21
purse, $4,800,000

| | SCORES | | TOTAL | MONEY |
|---|---|---|---|---|
| Adam Scott | 67 | 66 | 133 | $864,000 |
| Chad Campbell | 68 | 65 | 133 | 518,400 |
| (Scott defeated Campbell on first playoff hole.) | | | | |
| Darren Clarke | 66 | 68 | 134 | 278,400 |
| Brian Davis | 65 | 69 | 134 | 278,400 |
| J.L. Lewis | 70 | 65 | 135 | 182,400 |
| Colin Montgomerie | 71 | 64 | 135 | 182,400 |
| Robert Allenby | 69 | 67 | 136 | 134,800 |
| Aaron Baddeley | 69 | 67 | 136 | 134,800 |
| Fred Funk | 69 | 67 | 136 | 134,800 |
| Billy Mayfair | 70 | 66 | 136 | 134,800 |
| Kevin Sutherland | 67 | 69 | 136 | 134,800 |
| Bob Tway | 68 | 68 | 136 | 134,800 |
| Luke Donald | 66 | 71 | 137 | 77,333.34 |
| Stephen Leaney | 70 | 67 | 137 | 77,333.34 |
| Rocco Mediate | 70 | 67 | 137 | 77,333.34 |
| Rich Beem | 69 | 68 | 137 | 77,333.33 |
| Jose Coceres | 67 | 70 | 137 | 77,333.33 |
| Lee Janzen | 70 | 67 | 137 | 77,333.33 |
| D.A. Points | 69 | 68 | 137 | 77,333.33 |
| Bo Van Pelt | 70 | 67 | 137 | 77,333.33 |
| Tiger Woods | 67 | 70 | 137 | 77,333.33 |
| Brett Quigley | 66 | 72 | 138 | 43,268.58 |
| Michael Allen | 68 | 70 | 138 | 43,268.57 |
| Mark Brooks | 70 | 68 | 138 | 43,268.57 |
| Angel Cabrera | 69 | 69 | 138 | 43,268.57 |
| Zach Johnson | 70 | 68 | 138 | 43,268.57 |
| Jerry Kelly | 68 | 70 | 138 | 43,268.57 |
| Jeff Maggert | 70 | 68 | 138 | 43,268.57 |
| K.J. Choi | 72 | 67 | 139 | 29,220 |
| Tim Clark | 70 | 69 | 139 | 29,220 |
| Brad Faxon | 71 | 68 | 139 | 29,220 |
| J.J. Henry | 72 | 67 | 139 | 29,220 |
| Brendan Jones | 71 | 68 | 139 | 29,220 |
| Rod Pampling | 68 | 71 | 139 | 29,220 |
| Corey Pavin | 71 | 68 | 139 | 29,220 |
| Tag Ridings | 70 | 69 | 139 | 29,220 |
| Alex Cejka | 70 | 70 | 140 | 19,200 |
| Fred Couples | 70 | 70 | 140 | 19,200 |
| Brandt Jobe | 69 | 71 | 140 | 19,200 |
| Justin Leonard | 68 | 72 | 140 | 19,200 |
| Jose Maria Olazabal | 68 | 72 | 140 | 19,200 |
| Kenny Perry | 74 | 66 | 140 | 19,200 |
| Chris Riley | 71 | 69 | 140 | 19,200 |
| Jeff Sluman | 69 | 71 | 140 | 19,200 |
| Duffy Waldorf | 70 | 70 | 140 | 19,200 |
| Mike Weir | 67 | 73 | 140 | 19,200 |
| Billy Andrade | 73 | 68 | 141 | 11,842.91 |
| Brian Bateman | 71 | 70 | 141 | 11,842.91 |
| John Daly | 69 | 72 | 141 | 11,842.91 |
| James Driscoll | 67 | 74 | 141 | 11,842.91 |
| Brent Geiberger | 73 | 68 | 141 | 11,842.91 |
| Charles Howell | 71 | 70 | 141 | 11,842.91 |

| | SCORES | | TOTAL | MONEY |
|---|---|---|---|---|
| Nick Price | 70 | 71 | 141 | 11,842.91 |
| Patrick Sheehan | 70 | 71 | 141 | 11,842.91 |
| Hideto Tanihara | 72 | 69 | 141 | 11,842.91 |
| Lee Westwood | 70 | 71 | 141 | 11,842.91 |
| Craig Barlow | 70 | 71 | 141 | 11,842.90 |
| Stuart Appleby | 73 | 69 | 142 | 9,936 |
| Woody Austin | 70 | 72 | 142 | 9,936 |
| Jonathan Byrd | 71 | 71 | 142 | 9,936 |
| Paul Claxton | 72 | 70 | 142 | 9,936 |
| Chris DiMarco | 70 | 72 | 142 | 9,936 |
| Steve Elkington | 68 | 74 | 142 | 9,936 |
| John Elliott | 75 | 67 | 142 | 9,936 |
| Bob Estes | 70 | 72 | 142 | 9,936 |
| Jim Furyk | 71 | 71 | 142 | 9,936 |
| Brian Gay | 73 | 69 | 142 | 9,936 |
| Tom Gillis | 73 | 69 | 142 | 9,936 |
| Jay Haas | 72 | 70 | 142 | 9,936 |
| Greg Owen | 75 | 67 | 142 | 9,936 |
| Pat Perez | 71 | 71 | 142 | 9,936 |
| Loren Roberts | 73 | 69 | 142 | 9,936 |
| Justin Rose | 74 | 68 | 142 | 9,936 |
| Omar Uresti | 67 | 75 | 142 | 9,936 |
| Scott Verplank | 73 | 69 | 142 | 9,936 |

# WGC - Accenture Match Play Championship

*La Costa Resort and Spa,* Carlsbad, California
Par 36-36–72; 7,247 yards

February 23-27
purse, $7,500,000

## FIRST ROUND

Davis Love defeated Chris Riley, 1 up.
Lee Westwood defeated Steve Flesch, 4 and 3.
Graeme McDowell defeated Darren Clarke, 1 up.
Robert Allenby defeated Todd Hamilton, 6 and 5.
Stuart Appleby defeated Joakim Haeggman, 19 holes.
Ian Poulter defeated Jim Furyk, 3 and 1.
Adam Scott defeated Trevor Immelman, 2 up.
David Howell defeated Shigeki Maruyama, 6 and 5.
Stewart Cink defeated Fred Funk, 2 up.
Tom Lehman defeated K.J. Choi, 4 and 2.
Kirk Triplett defeated Mike Weir, 1 up.
Craig Parry defeated Tim Clark, 1 up.
Padraig Harrington defeated Jeff Maggert, 1 up.
Rory Sabbatini defeated Thomas Bjorn, 6 and 5.
Sergio Garcia defeated Alex Cejka, 4 and 2.
Jerry Kelly defeated Scott Verplank, 1 up.
Chris DiMarco defeated Tim Herron, 1 up.
John Daly defeated Justin Leonard, 1 up.
Miguel Angel Jimenez defeated Rod Pampling, 3 and 2.
Chad Campbell defeated Fredrik Jacobson, 2 up.
Kenny Perry defeated Thomas Levet, 3 and 2.
Luke Donald defeated Zach Johnson, 4 and 3.
David Toms defeated Richard Green, 1 up.
Mark Hensby defeated Stephen Ames, 7 and 6.
Vijay Singh defeated Shingo Katayama, 4 and 3.
Jay Haas defeated Jonathan Kaye, 4 and 2.
Retief Goosen defeated Stephen Leaney, 1 up.

Fred Couples defeated Peter Lonard, 1 up.
Tiger Woods defeated Nick Price, 4 and 3.
Nick O'Hern defeated Charles Howell, 19 holes.
Phil Mickelson defeated Loren Roberts, 3 and 1.
Angel Cabrera defeated Paul Casey, 4 and 2.

(Each losing player received $35,000.)

## SECOND ROUND

Cink defeated Lehman, 2 and 1.
Love defeated Westwood, 7 and 6.
Sabbatini defeated Harrington, 3 and 1.
Poulter defeated Appleby, 6 and 5.
Haas defeated Singh, 3 and 2.
DiMarco defeated Daly, 4 and 3.
O'Hern defeated Woods, 3 and 1.
Donald defeated Perry, 1 up.
Triplett defeated Parry, 5 and 4.
Allenby defeated McDowell, 1 up.
Garcia defeated Kelly, 19 holes.
Scott defeated Howell, 2 and 1.
Goosen defeated Couples, 1 up.
Campbell defeated Jimenez, 24 holes.
Mickelson defeated Cabrera, 4 and 3.
Toms defeated Hensby, 2 up.

(Each losing player received $85,000.)

## THIRD ROUND

DiMarco defeated Haas, 2 and 1.
Cink defeated Love, 20 holes.
Goosen defeated Campbell, 19 holes.
Allenby defeated Triplett, 2 and 1.
O'Hern defeated Donald, 5 and 4.
Poulter defeated Sabbatini, 1 up.
Toms defeated Mickelson, 4 and 2.
Scott defeated Garcia, 4 and 3.

(Each losing player received $125,000.)

## QUARTER-FINALS

DiMarco defeated Cink, 2 and 1.
Goosen defeated Allenby, 4 and 3.
Poulter defeated O'Hern, 3 and 1.
Toms defeated Scott, 2 and 1.

(Each losing player received $240,000.)

## SEMI-FINALS

DiMarco defeated Goosen, 2 and 1.
Toms defeated Poulter, 3 and 2.

## PLAYOFF FOR THIRD-FOURTH PLACE

Goosen defeated Poulter, 20 holes.

(Goosen earned $560,000; Poulter earned $450,000.)

**FINAL**

Toms defeated DiMarco, 6 and 5.

(Toms earned $1,300,000; DiMarco earned $750,000.)

# Chrysler Classic of Tucson

*Omni Tucson National Resort,* Tucson, Arizona
Par 36-36–72; 7,109 yards

February 24-27
purse, $3,000,000

| | SCORES | | | | TOTAL | MONEY |
|---|---|---|---|---|---|---|
| Geoff Ogilvy | 65 | 66 | 67 | 71 | 269 | $540,000 |
| Mark Calcavecchia | 64 | 65 | 71 | 69 | 269 | 264,000 |
| Kevin Na | 67 | 66 | 65 | 71 | 269 | 264,000 |
| (Ogilvy defeated Calcavecchia on first and Na on second playoff hole.) | | | | | | |
| Steve Stricker | 64 | 68 | 70 | 68 | 270 | 144,000 |
| Doug Barron | 66 | 66 | 67 | 72 | 271 | 120,000 |
| Aaron Baddeley | 73 | 64 | 67 | 68 | 272 | 100,500 |
| Brent Geiberger | 67 | 66 | 68 | 71 | 272 | 100,500 |
| Billy Mayfair | 63 | 67 | 72 | 70 | 272 | 100,500 |
| Danny Briggs | 69 | 64 | 69 | 71 | 273 | 67,125 |
| Todd Fischer | 68 | 67 | 67 | 71 | 273 | 67,125 |
| Lucas Glover | 64 | 67 | 69 | 73 | 273 | 67,125 |
| Joe Ogilvie | 66 | 66 | 69 | 72 | 273 | 67,125 |
| Jose Maria Olazabal | 68 | 69 | 68 | 68 | 273 | 67,125 |
| Kevin Stadler | 67 | 68 | 69 | 69 | 273 | 67,125 |
| Darron Stiles | 64 | 70 | 67 | 72 | 273 | 67,125 |
| Kevin Sutherland | 69 | 63 | 74 | 67 | 273 | 67,125 |
| Gavin Coles | 66 | 65 | 71 | 72 | 274 | 45,000 |
| Brian Gay | 67 | 69 | 70 | 68 | 274 | 45,000 |
| Hidemichi Tanaka | 71 | 67 | 66 | 70 | 274 | 45,000 |
| Craig Bowden | 70 | 65 | 68 | 72 | 275 | 32,500 |
| Scott Gutschewski | 69 | 67 | 66 | 73 | 275 | 32,500 |
| Arron Oberholser | 66 | 69 | 67 | 73 | 275 | 32,500 |
| Corey Pavin | 68 | 69 | 68 | 70 | 275 | 32,500 |
| Ted Purdy | 69 | 70 | 65 | 71 | 275 | 32,500 |
| Brett Wetterich | 70 | 68 | 66 | 71 | 275 | 32,500 |
| Arjun Atwal | 67 | 70 | 69 | 70 | 276 | 21,300 |
| Jim Carter | 69 | 69 | 69 | 69 | 276 | 21,300 |
| Bob Estes | 68 | 67 | 72 | 69 | 276 | 21,300 |
| Kent Jones | 70 | 68 | 69 | 69 | 276 | 21,300 |
| John Rollins | 68 | 69 | 69 | 70 | 276 | 21,300 |
| D.J. Trahan | 67 | 72 | 68 | 69 | 276 | 21,300 |
| Omar Uresti | 69 | 68 | 71 | 68 | 276 | 21,300 |
| Phillip Price | 69 | 69 | 67 | 72 | 277 | 15,514.29 |
| Tom Scherrer | 67 | 67 | 71 | 72 | 277 | 15,514.29 |
| Scott Simpson | 69 | 70 | 67 | 71 | 277 | 15,514.29 |
| Roland Thatcher | 70 | 67 | 68 | 72 | 277 | 15,514.29 |
| Olin Browne | 67 | 70 | 73 | 67 | 277 | 15,514.28 |
| Carlos Franco | 65 | 72 | 68 | 72 | 277 | 15,514.28 |
| Paul Gow | 70 | 69 | 70 | 68 | 277 | 15,514.28 |
| Jason Allred | 67 | 67 | 72 | 72 | 278 | 11,400 |
| Harrison Frazar | 72 | 67 | 68 | 71 | 278 | 11,400 |
| John Huston | 66 | 72 | 65 | 75 | 278 | 11,400 |
| Ryuji Imada | 69 | 68 | 68 | 73 | 278 | 11,400 |
| Tag Ridings | 68 | 68 | 70 | 72 | 278 | 11,400 |
| Gene Sauers | 67 | 72 | 68 | 71 | 278 | 11,400 |

| | SCORES | | | | TOTAL | MONEY |
|---|---|---|---|---|---|---|
| Steve Allan | 69 | 70 | 70 | 70 | 279 | 8,316 |
| Bob Burns | 70 | 69 | 68 | 72 | 279 | 8,316 |
| David Frost | 67 | 67 | 73 | 72 | 279 | 8,316 |
| Esteban Toledo | 65 | 67 | 73 | 74 | 279 | 8,316 |
| Bob Tway | 70 | 67 | 68 | 74 | 279 | 8,316 |
| Andrew Magee | 69 | 70 | 69 | 72 | 280 | 7,290 |
| Carl Paulson | 69 | 67 | 70 | 74 | 280 | 7,290 |
| Greg Owen | 66 | 73 | 70 | 72 | 281 | 6,980 |
| Mario Tiziani | 63 | 72 | 73 | 73 | 281 | 6,980 |
| Bo Van Pelt | 73 | 66 | 68 | 74 | 281 | 6,980 |
| Ben Portie | 68 | 68 | 72 | 74 | 282 | 6,780 |
| Dicky Pride | 68 | 67 | 69 | 78 | 282 | 6,780 |
| Nick Watney | 69 | 69 | 73 | 71 | 282 | 6,780 |
| Michael Allen | 64 | 74 | 72 | 73 | 283 | 6,600 |
| Jason Bohn | 66 | 72 | 73 | 72 | 283 | 6,600 |
| Dan Forsman | 69 | 68 | 75 | 71 | 283 | 6,600 |
| Brian Davis | 72 | 67 | 68 | 77 | 284 | 6,450 |
| Brendan Jones | 71 | 67 | 70 | 76 | 284 | 6,450 |
| Notah Begay | 69 | 70 | 72 | 74 | 285 | 6,300 |
| Glen Day | 74 | 65 | 73 | 73 | 285 | 6,300 |
| Rob Rashell | 71 | 68 | 71 | 75 | 285 | 6,300 |
| Jeff Hart | 71 | 68 | 73 | 74 | 286 | 6,150 |
| Garrett Willis | 72 | 67 | 70 | 77 | 286 | 6,150 |
| Ryan Dillon | 70 | 68 | 76 | 75 | 289 | 6,060 |
| Robin Freeman | 69 | 69 | 77 | 75 | 290 | 6,000 |

## Ford Championship at Doral

*Doral Golf Resort & Spa, Blue Course,* Miami, Florida
Par 36-36–72; 7,266 yards

March 3-6
purse, $5,500,000

| | SCORES | | | | TOTAL | MONEY |
|---|---|---|---|---|---|---|
| Tiger Woods | 65 | 70 | 63 | 66 | 264 | $990,000 |
| Phil Mickelson | 64 | 66 | 66 | 69 | 265 | 594,000 |
| Zach Johnson | 68 | 70 | 64 | 67 | 269 | 319,000 |
| Vijay Singh | 68 | 67 | 68 | 66 | 269 | 319,000 |
| David Toms | 69 | 66 | 69 | 67 | 271 | 220,000 |
| Jose Maria Olazabal | 64 | 69 | 70 | 69 | 272 | 191,125 |
| Craig Parry | 69 | 66 | 67 | 70 | 272 | 191,125 |
| Jim Furyk | 70 | 66 | 67 | 70 | 273 | 165,000 |
| Retief Goosen | 67 | 69 | 73 | 64 | 273 | 165,000 |
| Angel Cabrera | 68 | 69 | 70 | 67 | 274 | 143,000 |
| Dudley Hart | 70 | 67 | 68 | 69 | 274 | 143,000 |
| Billy Andrade | 66 | 66 | 72 | 71 | 275 | 111,375 |
| Bart Bryant | 69 | 70 | 67 | 69 | 275 | 111,375 |
| Steve Elkington | 68 | 72 | 65 | 70 | 275 | 111,375 |
| Joey Snyder | 66 | 69 | 70 | 70 | 275 | 111,375 |
| Paul Casey | 66 | 70 | 69 | 71 | 276 | 69,850 |
| Tim Clark | 68 | 67 | 69 | 72 | 276 | 69,850 |
| Jose Coceres | 69 | 68 | 69 | 70 | 276 | 69,850 |
| James Driscoll | 67 | 68 | 67 | 74 | 276 | 69,850 |
| Scott Hend | 69 | 67 | 69 | 71 | 276 | 69,850 |
| Shigeki Maruyama | 69 | 67 | 70 | 70 | 276 | 69,850 |
| Billy Mayfair | 67 | 67 | 72 | 70 | 276 | 69,850 |
| Kevin Na | 70 | 68 | 69 | 69 | 276 | 69,850 |
| Greg Owen | 70 | 68 | 68 | 70 | 276 | 69,850 |
| Ryan Palmer | 70 | 69 | 66 | 71 | 276 | 69,850 |

| | SCORES | | | | TOTAL | MONEY |
|---|---|---|---|---|---|---|
| Robert Allenby | 69 | 68 | 70 | 70 | 277 | 39,875 |
| Mark Calcavecchia | 71 | 68 | 71 | 67 | 277 | 39,875 |
| Stewart Cink | 70 | 65 | 73 | 69 | 277 | 39,875 |
| Harrison Frazar | 65 | 71 | 68 | 73 | 277 | 39,875 |
| Joe Ogilvie | 68 | 70 | 66 | 73 | 277 | 39,875 |
| Jeff Sluman | 69 | 71 | 71 | 66 | 277 | 39,875 |
| Tom Gillis | 70 | 71 | 72 | 65 | 278 | 31,130 |
| Scott Hoch | 68 | 70 | 71 | 69 | 278 | 31,130 |
| Kenny Perry | 68 | 72 | 67 | 71 | 278 | 31,130 |
| John Senden | 69 | 69 | 69 | 71 | 278 | 31,130 |
| Bo Van Pelt | 70 | 67 | 69 | 72 | 278 | 31,130 |
| Daniel Chopra | 68 | 72 | 70 | 69 | 279 | 25,300 |
| Todd Hamilton | 71 | 70 | 68 | 70 | 279 | 25,300 |
| Franklin Langham | 68 | 67 | 71 | 73 | 279 | 25,300 |
| Nick Price | 73 | 67 | 69 | 70 | 279 | 25,300 |
| Doug Barron | 71 | 70 | 70 | 69 | 280 | 21,450 |
| Brian Bateman | 68 | 72 | 67 | 73 | 280 | 21,450 |
| Justin Rose | 73 | 67 | 67 | 73 | 280 | 21,450 |
| Paul Azinger | 70 | 69 | 71 | 71 | 281 | 15,895 |
| Danny Briggs | 70 | 68 | 70 | 73 | 281 | 15,895 |
| Erik Compton | 70 | 68 | 70 | 73 | 281 | 15,895 |
| Brian Davis | 64 | 71 | 76 | 70 | 281 | 15,895 |
| Chris DiMarco | 69 | 72 | 67 | 73 | 281 | 15,895 |
| D.A. Points | 70 | 69 | 71 | 71 | 281 | 15,895 |
| Kevin Stadler | 72 | 68 | 70 | 71 | 281 | 15,895 |
| Andre Stolz | 68 | 71 | 72 | 70 | 281 | 15,895 |
| Michael Allen | 71 | 68 | 72 | 71 | 282 | 12,826 |
| Padraig Harrington | 68 | 71 | 73 | 70 | 282 | 12,826 |
| Glen Hnatiuk | 70 | 68 | 74 | 70 | 282 | 12,826 |
| Hidemichi Tanaka | 74 | 66 | 69 | 73 | 282 | 12,826 |
| Mike Weir | 73 | 68 | 72 | 69 | 282 | 12,826 |
| Jason Allred | 69 | 70 | 72 | 72 | 283 | 12,100 |
| Woody Austin | 70 | 71 | 70 | 72 | 283 | 12,100 |
| Skip Kendall | 68 | 71 | 72 | 72 | 283 | 12,100 |
| Bernhard Langer | 69 | 71 | 73 | 70 | 283 | 12,100 |
| Tim Petrovic | 69 | 72 | 69 | 73 | 283 | 12,100 |
| Brett Quigley | 71 | 69 | 71 | 72 | 283 | 12,100 |
| Jay Williamson | 68 | 71 | 74 | 70 | 283 | 12,100 |
| Rich Beem | 71 | 68 | 72 | 73 | 284 | 11,275 |
| Mark Brooks | 72 | 68 | 73 | 71 | 284 | 11,275 |
| K.J. Choi | 70 | 69 | 68 | 77 | 284 | 11,275 |
| Sergio Garcia | 68 | 68 | 74 | 74 | 284 | 11,275 |
| Jay Haas | 70 | 71 | 71 | 72 | 284 | 11,275 |
| Sean O'Hair | 73 | 67 | 72 | 72 | 284 | 11,275 |
| John Riegger | 69 | 69 | 75 | 71 | 284 | 11,275 |
| Nick Watney | 70 | 70 | 72 | 72 | 284 | 11,275 |
| Hunter Mahan | 66 | 69 | 74 | 76 | 285 | 10,780 |
| Jesper Parnevik | 68 | 70 | 74 | 74 | 286 | 10,670 |
| Tom Byrum | 71 | 70 | 73 | 73 | 287 | 10,450 |
| Brendan Jones | 70 | 70 | 74 | 73 | 287 | 10,450 |
| Chris Smith | 70 | 71 | 72 | 74 | 287 | 10,450 |
| Ryuji Imada | 70 | 70 | 78 | 70 | 288 | 10,175 |
| Frank Lickliter | 70 | 71 | 73 | 74 | 288 | 10,175 |
| Gavin Coles | 70 | 71 | 74 | 76 | 291 | 9,955 |
| Marco Dawson | 64 | 77 | 78 | 72 | 291 | 9,955 |
| Rick Heath | 72 | 67 | 74 | 79 | 292 | 9,735 |
| Tag Ridings | 71 | 69 | 81 | 71 | 292 | 9,735 |

## Honda Classic

*The Country Club at Mirasol, Sunrise Course,*                  March 10-13
Palm Beach Gardens, Florida                                     purse, $5,500,000
Par 36-36–72; 7,468 yards

|  |  | SCORES |  |  | TOTAL | MONEY |
|---|---|---|---|---|---|---|
| Padraig Harrington | 73 | 69 | 69 | 63 | 274 | $990,000 |
| Joe Ogilvie | 73 | 66 | 67 | 68 | 274 | 484,000 |
| Vijay Singh | 71 | 69 | 70 | 64 | 274 | 484,000 |
| (Harrington defeated Ogilvie on first and Singh on second playoff hole.) | | | | | | |
| Pat Perez | 69 | 69 | 67 | 70 | 275 | 264,000 |
| David Toms | 71 | 71 | 67 | 67 | 276 | 220,000 |
| Brad Faxon | 69 | 71 | 72 | 65 | 277 | 184,250 |
| Geoff Ogilvy | 73 | 67 | 64 | 73 | 277 | 184,250 |
| Brett Wetterich | 66 | 66 | 72 | 73 | 277 | 184,250 |
| Jim Furyk | 71 | 69 | 70 | 68 | 278 | 154,000 |
| Lucas Glover | 70 | 71 | 74 | 63 | 278 | 154,000 |
| Billy Andrade | 69 | 69 | 75 | 66 | 279 | 126,500 |
| Aaron Baddeley | 68 | 72 | 72 | 67 | 279 | 126,500 |
| Greg Owen | 72 | 70 | 69 | 68 | 279 | 126,500 |
| Robert Allenby | 69 | 75 | 68 | 68 | 280 | 99,000 |
| Brian Bateman | 70 | 69 | 71 | 70 | 280 | 99,000 |
| Justin Rose | 69 | 72 | 71 | 68 | 280 | 99,000 |
| Lee Janzen | 69 | 64 | 72 | 76 | 281 | 77,000 |
| Neal Lancaster | 73 | 70 | 72 | 66 | 281 | 77,000 |
| Scott McCarron | 72 | 68 | 72 | 69 | 281 | 77,000 |
| Sean O'Hair | 69 | 72 | 68 | 72 | 281 | 77,000 |
| Nick Watney | 68 | 68 | 74 | 71 | 281 | 77,000 |
| Tim Clark | 73 | 66 | 71 | 72 | 282 | 43,816.67 |
| John Cook | 72 | 72 | 67 | 71 | 282 | 43,816.67 |
| Marco Dawson | 71 | 70 | 70 | 71 | 282 | 43,816.67 |
| Brian Gay | 73 | 69 | 70 | 70 | 282 | 43,816.67 |
| Billy Mayfair | 72 | 68 | 71 | 71 | 282 | 43,816.67 |
| Kevin Na | 69 | 69 | 78 | 66 | 282 | 43,816.67 |
| Tim Petrovic | 71 | 70 | 73 | 68 | 282 | 43,816.67 |
| Jay Williamson | 73 | 68 | 71 | 70 | 282 | 43,816.67 |
| Fred Couples | 73 | 69 | 66 | 74 | 282 | 43,816.66 |
| Mark Hensby | 73 | 71 | 66 | 72 | 282 | 43,816.66 |
| Kevin Stadler | 71 | 70 | 68 | 73 | 282 | 43,816.66 |
| Charlie Wi | 69 | 71 | 70 | 72 | 282 | 43,816.66 |
| Gavin Coles | 70 | 74 | 70 | 69 | 283 | 29,012.50 |
| Joe Durant | 70 | 70 | 73 | 70 | 283 | 29,012.50 |
| Todd Hamilton | 69 | 71 | 72 | 71 | 283 | 29,012.50 |
| Ryan Palmer | 70 | 69 | 72 | 72 | 283 | 29,012.50 |
| Daniel Chopra | 70 | 68 | 72 | 74 | 284 | 22,000 |
| Robert Damron | 70 | 65 | 73 | 76 | 284 | 22,000 |
| Paul Gow | 74 | 69 | 71 | 70 | 284 | 22,000 |
| Dudley Hart | 77 | 67 | 73 | 67 | 284 | 22,000 |
| Tim Herron | 71 | 69 | 70 | 74 | 284 | 22,000 |
| Justin Leonard | 71 | 69 | 71 | 73 | 284 | 22,000 |
| Jesper Parnevik | 67 | 70 | 74 | 73 | 284 | 22,000 |
| Brett Quigley | 71 | 66 | 73 | 74 | 284 | 22,000 |
| Glen Day | 73 | 70 | 72 | 70 | 285 | 14,960 |
| Glen Hnatiuk | 71 | 73 | 72 | 69 | 285 | 14,960 |
| Andrew Magee | 72 | 72 | 69 | 72 | 285 | 14,960 |
| Carl Pettersson | 72 | 72 | 72 | 69 | 285 | 14,960 |
| Tag Ridings | 70 | 70 | 73 | 72 | 285 | 14,960 |
| Hidemichi Tanaka | 73 | 69 | 70 | 73 | 285 | 14,960 |
| Doug Barron | 71 | 70 | 72 | 73 | 286 | 12,760 |

| | SCORES | | | | TOTAL | MONEY |
|---|---|---|---|---|---|---|
| Cameron Beckman | 70 | 72 | 73 | 71 | 286 | 12,760 |
| Chad Campbell | 64 | 71 | 80 | 71 | 286 | 12,760 |
| Tom Gillis | 72 | 70 | 72 | 72 | 286 | 12,760 |
| Scott Gutschewski | 74 | 69 | 72 | 71 | 286 | 12,760 |
| John Senden | 71 | 68 | 78 | 69 | 286 | 12,760 |
| Tommy Armour | 75 | 65 | 73 | 74 | 287 | 12,100 |
| James Driscoll | 69 | 74 | 73 | 71 | 287 | 12,100 |
| Bob Estes | 69 | 69 | 77 | 72 | 287 | 12,100 |
| Rob Rashell | 73 | 68 | 76 | 70 | 287 | 12,100 |
| Patrick Sheehan | 70 | 67 | 77 | 73 | 287 | 12,100 |
| Joey Snyder | 70 | 72 | 77 | 69 | 288 | 11,715 |
| Mark Wilson | 71 | 70 | 74 | 73 | 288 | 11,715 |
| Jason Bohn | 71 | 70 | 72 | 76 | 289 | 11,330 |
| Brandt Jobe | 75 | 68 | 75 | 71 | 289 | 11,330 |
| Kevin Johnson | 73 | 69 | 74 | 73 | 289 | 11,330 |
| Graeme McDowell | 70 | 73 | 71 | 75 | 289 | 11,330 |
| Vaughn Taylor | 72 | 70 | 77 | 70 | 289 | 11,330 |
| Brian Davis | 71 | 70 | 73 | 76 | 290 | 10,890 |
| Nick Faldo | 71 | 72 | 75 | 72 | 290 | 10,890 |
| Davis Love | 71 | 69 | 78 | 72 | 290 | 10,890 |
| Craig Parry | 72 | 72 | 75 | 72 | 291 | 10,505 |
| Omar Uresti | 70 | 73 | 76 | 72 | 291 | 10,505 |
| Charles Warren | 70 | 72 | 79 | 70 | 291 | 10,505 |
| Dean Wilson | 75 | 67 | 77 | 72 | 291 | 10,505 |
| Jonathan Byrd | 70 | 74 | 77 | 72 | 293 | 10,230 |
| Jeff Sluman | 75 | 69 | 76 | 74 | 294 | 10,120 |
| Jim Carter | 73 | 71 | 78 | 76 | 298 | 10,010 |

# Bay Hill Invitational

*Bay Hill Club & Lodge,* Orlando, Florida
Par 36-36–72; 7,267 yards

March 17-20
purse, $5,000,000

| | SCORES | | | | TOTAL | MONEY |
|---|---|---|---|---|---|---|
| Kenny Perry | 70 | 68 | 68 | 70 | 276 | $900,000 |
| Graeme McDowell | 69 | 73 | 70 | 66 | 278 | 440,000 |
| Vijay Singh | 72 | 68 | 69 | 69 | 278 | 440,000 |
| Retief Goosen | 78 | 67 | 68 | 70 | 283 | 240,000 |
| Aaron Baddeley | 70 | 74 | 68 | 72 | 284 | 182,500 |
| Corey Pavin | 72 | 70 | 71 | 71 | 284 | 182,500 |
| Patrick Sheehan | 71 | 71 | 75 | 67 | 284 | 182,500 |
| Bart Bryant | 72 | 73 | 71 | 69 | 285 | 109,545.46 |
| Chad Campbell | 76 | 69 | 72 | 68 | 285 | 109,545.46 |
| Charles Howell | 71 | 68 | 75 | 71 | 285 | 109,545.46 |
| Zach Johnson | 73 | 69 | 73 | 70 | 285 | 109,545.46 |
| Joe Ogilvie | 68 | 74 | 72 | 71 | 285 | 109,545.46 |
| Briny Baird | 69 | 73 | 70 | 73 | 285 | 109,545.45 |
| K.J. Choi | 70 | 70 | 70 | 75 | 285 | 109,545.45 |
| Stewart Cink | 74 | 70 | 70 | 71 | 285 | 109,545.45 |
| Darren Clarke | 76 | 71 | 70 | 68 | 285 | 109,545.45 |
| Fred Couples | 71 | 72 | 70 | 72 | 285 | 109,545.45 |
| Sergio Garcia | 70 | 70 | 73 | 72 | 285 | 109,545.45 |
| Shigeki Maruyama | 73 | 72 | 70 | 71 | 286 | 62,750 |
| Loren Roberts | 73 | 72 | 69 | 72 | 286 | 62,750 |
| Joey Snyder | 75 | 71 | 69 | 71 | 286 | 62,750 |
| Jimmy Walker | 78 | 67 | 69 | 72 | 286 | 62,750 |
| Ernie Els | 71 | 77 | 69 | 70 | 287 | 42,142.86 |

| | SCORES | | | | TOTAL | MONEY |
|---|---|---|---|---|---|---|
| Fred Funk | 73 | 72 | 70 | 72 | 287 | 42,142.86 |
| D.A. Points | 75 | 73 | 69 | 70 | 287 | 42,142.86 |
| Charles Warren | 71 | 76 | 68 | 72 | 287 | 42,142.86 |
| Tiger Woods | 71 | 70 | 74 | 72 | 287 | 42,142.86 |
| Jeff Maggert | 72 | 70 | 69 | 76 | 287 | 42,142.85 |
| Duffy Waldorf | 73 | 71 | 68 | 75 | 287 | 42,142.85 |
| Brian Davis | 71 | 74 | 70 | 73 | 288 | 30,375 |
| Jonathan Kaye | 77 | 71 | 68 | 72 | 288 | 30,375 |
| Tom Lehman | 72 | 72 | 70 | 74 | 288 | 30,375 |
| J.L. Lewis | 71 | 74 | 69 | 74 | 288 | 30,375 |
| Adam Scott | 76 | 70 | 67 | 75 | 288 | 30,375 |
| Joey Sindelar | 72 | 70 | 69 | 77 | 288 | 30,375 |
| Stuart Appleby | 74 | 73 | 70 | 72 | 289 | 24,062.50 |
| Brian Gay | 71 | 77 | 69 | 72 | 289 | 24,062.50 |
| David Howell | 73 | 70 | 70 | 76 | 289 | 24,062.50 |
| Geoff Ogilvy | 70 | 75 | 70 | 74 | 289 | 24,062.50 |
| Stephen Ames | 71 | 68 | 71 | 80 | 290 | 20,000 |
| Tommy Armour | 73 | 71 | 73 | 73 | 290 | 20,000 |
| Angel Cabrera | 72 | 75 | 73 | 70 | 290 | 20,000 |
| Nick Dougherty | 76 | 71 | 71 | 72 | 290 | 20,000 |
| Mark Calcavecchia | 70 | 73 | 71 | 77 | 291 | 15,116.67 |
| Greg Owen | 70 | 71 | 75 | 75 | 291 | 15,116.67 |
| Craig Parry | 74 | 72 | 71 | 74 | 291 | 15,116.67 |
| Jeff Sluman | 75 | 70 | 73 | 73 | 291 | 15,116.67 |
| Jerry Kelly | 73 | 69 | 77 | 72 | 291 | 15,116.66 |
| Pat Perez | 72 | 70 | 71 | 78 | 291 | 15,116.66 |
| Carlos Franco | 74 | 74 | 74 | 70 | 292 | 12,450 |
| John Senden | 74 | 71 | 72 | 75 | 292 | 12,450 |
| Woody Austin | 71 | 73 | 71 | 78 | 293 | 11,600 |
| Dan Forsman | 74 | 73 | 74 | 72 | 293 | 11,600 |
| Bernhard Langer | 70 | 74 | 75 | 74 | 293 | 11,600 |
| Frank Lickliter | 75 | 71 | 73 | 74 | 293 | 11,600 |
| Nick O'Hern | 74 | 72 | 71 | 76 | 293 | 11,600 |
| Lee Westwood | 74 | 70 | 73 | 76 | 293 | 11,600 |
| Richard Green | 71 | 73 | 73 | 77 | 294 | 11,000 |
| Todd Hamilton | 73 | 72 | 70 | 79 | 294 | 11,000 |
| Peter Lonard | 70 | 76 | 78 | 70 | 294 | 11,000 |
| Brett Quigley | 75 | 71 | 77 | 71 | 294 | 11,000 |
| Vaughn Taylor | 75 | 73 | 73 | 73 | 294 | 11,000 |
| Stephen Leaney | 74 | 72 | 70 | 79 | 295 | 10,550 |
| Craig Perks | 75 | 73 | 76 | 71 | 295 | 10,550 |
| Bo Van Pelt | 74 | 72 | 74 | 75 | 295 | 10,550 |
| Mike Weir | 71 | 73 | 74 | 77 | 295 | 10,550 |
| Billy Andrade | 74 | 74 | 74 | 74 | 296 | 10,300 |
| Justin Rose | 75 | 73 | 73 | 79 | 300 | 10,200 |
| John Daly | 72 | 75 | 75 | 80 | 302 | 10,100 |

## The Players Championship

*TPC at Sawgrass, Stadium Course,* Ponte Vedra Beach, Florida
Par 36-36–72; 7,093 yards
(Event completed on Monday—rain.)

March 24-28
purse, $8,000,000

| | SCORES | | | | TOTAL | MONEY |
|---|---|---|---|---|---|---|
| Fred Funk | 65 | 72 | 71 | 71 | 279 | $1,440,000 |
| Tom Lehman | 71 | 69 | 72 | 68 | 280 | 597,333.34 |
| Scott Verplank | 71 | 67 | 72 | 70 | 280 | 597,333.33 |

| | SCORES | | | TOTAL | MONEY |
|---|---|---|---|---|---|
| Luke Donald | 66 | 68 | 70 | 76 | 280 | 597,333.33 |
| Joe Durant | 69 | 65 | 71 | 76 | 281 | 320,000 |
| Steve Elkington | 72 | 66 | 71 | 73 | 282 | 278,000 |
| Tim Herron | 68 | 66 | 72 | 76 | 282 | 278,000 |
| J.L. Lewis | 66 | 77 | 70 | 70 | 283 | 224,000 |
| Davis Love | 72 | 66 | 74 | 71 | 283 | 224,000 |
| Zach Johnson | 65 | 70 | 72 | 76 | 283 | 224,000 |
| Adam Scott | 69 | 68 | 73 | 73 | 283 | 224,000 |
| Mark Calcavecchia | 71 | 70 | 72 | 71 | 284 | 156,800 |
| Steve Lowery | 69 | 74 | 72 | 69 | 284 | 156,800 |
| Vijay Singh | 67 | 74 | 71 | 72 | 284 | 156,800 |
| Retief Goosen | 69 | 70 | 69 | 76 | 284 | 156,800 |
| Alex Cejka | 70 | 70 | 70 | 74 | 284 | 156,800 |
| Bob Estes | 67 | 73 | 73 | 72 | 285 | 112,000 |
| Joey Sindelar | 70 | 71 | 70 | 74 | 285 | 112,000 |
| Kirk Triplett | 70 | 66 | 76 | 73 | 285 | 112,000 |
| Ernie Els | 71 | 71 | 74 | 69 | 285 | 112,000 |
| Mike Weir | 74 | 68 | 69 | 74 | 285 | 112,000 |
| Lee Westwood | 65 | 69 | 80 | 72 | 286 | 86,400 |
| John Senden | 74 | 69 | 70 | 73 | 286 | 86,400 |
| Jay Haas | 69 | 69 | 72 | 77 | 287 | 70,400 |
| Brett Quigley | 67 | 73 | 78 | 69 | 287 | 70,400 |
| Nick O'Hern | 76 | 65 | 72 | 74 | 287 | 70,400 |
| Nick Faldo | 71 | 70 | 74 | 73 | 288 | 56,800 |
| Tim Petrovic | 71 | 71 | 71 | 75 | 288 | 56,800 |
| Michael Allen | 71 | 71 | 70 | 76 | 288 | 56,800 |
| Rod Pampling | 70 | 70 | 68 | 80 | 288 | 56,800 |
| Arron Oberholser | 73 | 68 | 72 | 75 | 288 | 56,800 |
| Nick Price | 71 | 70 | 69 | 79 | 289 | 42,400 |
| Shigeki Maruyama | 70 | 68 | 76 | 75 | 289 | 42,400 |
| Stewart Cink | 70 | 68 | 73 | 78 | 289 | 42,400 |
| Sergio Garcia | 66 | 75 | 70 | 78 | 289 | 42,400 |
| Joe Ogilvie | 72 | 67 | 72 | 78 | 289 | 42,400 |
| Vaughn Taylor | 70 | 67 | 73 | 79 | 289 | 42,400 |
| Pat Perez | 70 | 70 | 72 | 77 | 289 | 42,400 |
| Jonathan Byrd | 73 | 68 | 73 | 75 | 289 | 42,400 |
| Phil Mickelson | 70 | 68 | 77 | 75 | 290 | 30,400 |
| Craig Parry | 68 | 70 | 71 | 81 | 290 | 30,400 |
| Duffy Waldorf | 72 | 69 | 72 | 77 | 290 | 30,400 |
| Daniel Chopra | 68 | 70 | 73 | 79 | 290 | 30,400 |
| Hunter Mahan | 68 | 75 | 70 | 77 | 290 | 30,400 |
| Graeme McDowell | 71 | 66 | 74 | 79 | 290 | 30,400 |
| Tom Byrum | 72 | 71 | 75 | 73 | 291 | 21,394.28 |
| Brad Faxon | 72 | 69 | 73 | 77 | 291 | 21,394.29 |
| Jeff Maggert | 70 | 71 | 71 | 79 | 291 | 21,394.29 |
| Jeff Sluman | 71 | 67 | 75 | 78 | 291 | 21,394.28 |
| Jesper Parnevik | 69 | 71 | 72 | 79 | 291 | 21,394.29 |
| Miguel Angel Jimenez | 70 | 69 | 82 | 70 | 291 | 21,394.29 |
| Richard Green | 75 | 68 | 71 | 77 | 291 | 21,394.28 |
| Tiger Woods | 70 | 73 | 75 | 75 | 293 | 18,613.33 |
| Jonathan Kaye | 72 | 69 | 77 | 75 | 293 | 18,613.34 |
| Heath Slocum | 70 | 72 | 74 | 77 | 293 | 18,613.33 |
| Tommy Armour | 70 | 73 | 74 | 77 | 294 | 17,760 |
| Robert Gamez | 68 | 75 | 69 | 82 | 294 | 17,760 |
| Bob Tway | 67 | 71 | 80 | 76 | 294 | 17,760 |
| Brian Bateman | 71 | 71 | 75 | 77 | 294 | 17,760 |
| Jay Williamson | 72 | 68 | 77 | 77 | 294 | 17,760 |
| Briny Baird | 68 | 73 | 75 | 78 | 294 | 17,760 |
| Ted Purdy | 69 | 74 | 72 | 79 | 294 | 17,760 |
| Dudley Hart | 70 | 67 | 76 | 82 | 295 | 16,800 |

| | SCORES | | | | TOTAL | MONEY |
|---|---|---|---|---|---|---|
| Craig Barlow | 73 | 70 | 73 | 79 | 295 | 16,800 |
| Darren Clarke | 73 | 70 | 73 | 79 | 295 | 16,800 |
| Robert Damron | 72 | 71 | 76 | 76 | 295 | 16,800 |
| Padraig Harrington | 67 | 73 | 77 | 78 | 295 | 16,800 |
| Lee Janzen | 73 | 69 | 74 | 80 | 296 | 16,160 |
| David Toms | 70 | 71 | 73 | 82 | 296 | 16,160 |
| Kevin Sutherland | 72 | 70 | 74 | 80 | 296 | 16,160 |
| Len Mattiace | 72 | 71 | 76 | 78 | 297 | 15,760 |
| Shaun Micheel | 68 | 74 | 72 | 83 | 297 | 15,760 |
| Cameron Beckman | 74 | 69 | 73 | 82 | 298 | 15,440 |
| Mark Hensby | 72 | 70 | 76 | 80 | 298 | 15,440 |
| Steve Jones | 64 | 77 | 74 | 84 | 299 | 15,040 |
| Kent Jones | 74 | 68 | 75 | 82 | 299 | 15,040 |
| Brian Gay | 71 | 72 | 74 | 82 | 299 | 15,040 |
| Aaron Baddeley | 73 | 69 | 80 | 78 | 300 | 14,720 |
| Steve Flesch | 72 | 71 | 78 | 81 | 302 | 14,480 |
| Frank Lickliter | 72 | 71 | 73 | 86 | 302 | 14,480 |
| Jose Coceres | 73 | 70 | 78 | 82 | 303 | 14,240 |
| Tag Ridings | 72 | 71 | 82 | 79 | 304 | 14,080 |

## BellSouth Classic

*TPC at Sugarloaf*, Duluth, Georgia　　　　　　　　　　　March 31-April 4
Par 36-36–72; 7,293 yards　　　　　　　　　　　　　　　purse, $5,000,000
(Event shortened to 54 holes and completed on Monday—rain.)

| | SCORES | | | TOTAL | MONEY |
|---|---|---|---|---|---|
| Phil Mickelson | 74 | 65 | 69 | 208 | $900,000 |
| Arjun Atwal | 77 | 67 | 64 | 208 | 330,000 |
| Rich Beem | 70 | 70 | 68 | 208 | 330,000 |
| Brandt Jobe | 72 | 69 | 67 | 208 | 330,000 |
| Jose Maria Olazabal | 70 | 69 | 69 | 208 | 330,000 |
| (Mickelson won on fourth playoff hole.) | | | | | |
| Scott Dunlap | 72 | 68 | 69 | 209 | 161,875 |
| Frank Lickliter | 71 | 70 | 68 | 209 | 161,875 |
| Arron Oberholser | 72 | 68 | 69 | 209 | 161,875 |
| Tag Ridings | 72 | 68 | 69 | 209 | 161,875 |
| Lucas Glover | 74 | 67 | 69 | 210 | 115,000 |
| Hunter Haas | 75 | 68 | 67 | 210 | 115,000 |
| Dennis Paulson | 75 | 68 | 67 | 210 | 115,000 |
| Charles Warren | 75 | 69 | 66 | 210 | 115,000 |
| Jay Williamson | 72 | 71 | 67 | 210 | 115,000 |
| Brian Bateman | 72 | 68 | 71 | 211 | 75,000 |
| Justin Bolli | 74 | 70 | 67 | 211 | 75,000 |
| Ryuji Imada | 70 | 71 | 70 | 211 | 75,000 |
| Billy Mayfair | 68 | 71 | 72 | 211 | 75,000 |
| Joey Snyder | 71 | 69 | 71 | 211 | 75,000 |
| Bob Tway | 71 | 70 | 70 | 211 | 75,000 |
| Dean Wilson | 72 | 70 | 69 | 211 | 75,000 |
| Dan Forsman | 73 | 72 | 67 | 212 | 50,000 |
| Retief Goosen | 72 | 69 | 71 | 212 | 50,000 |
| Franklin Langham | 72 | 74 | 66 | 212 | 50,000 |
| Omar Uresti | 71 | 74 | 67 | 212 | 50,000 |
| Jason Allred | 68 | 75 | 70 | 213 | 36,250 |
| J.J. Henry | 73 | 72 | 68 | 213 | 36,250 |
| Zach Johnson | 75 | 66 | 72 | 213 | 36,250 |
| Stephen Leaney | 72 | 72 | 69 | 213 | 36,250 |

| | SCORES | | | TOTAL | MONEY |
|---|---|---|---|---|---|
| Michael Long | 73 | 68 | 72 | 213 | 36,250 |
| Brett Quigley | 69 | 74 | 70 | 213 | 36,250 |
| Jonathan Byrd | 72 | 72 | 70 | 214 | 27,071.43 |
| Alex Cejka | 72 | 71 | 71 | 214 | 27,071.43 |
| Paul Claxton | 73 | 72 | 69 | 214 | 27,071.43 |
| Steve Elkington | 73 | 70 | 71 | 214 | 27,071.43 |
| Andrew Magee | 69 | 74 | 71 | 214 | 27,071.43 |
| Tom Pernice, Jr. | 73 | 71 | 70 | 214 | 27,071.43 |
| Scott McCarron | 69 | 69 | 76 | 214 | 27,071.42 |
| John Elliott | 75 | 69 | 71 | 215 | 18,500 |
| Glen Hnatiuk | 73 | 72 | 70 | 215 | 18,500 |
| John Huston | 70 | 73 | 72 | 215 | 18,500 |
| Neal Lancaster | 74 | 69 | 72 | 215 | 18,500 |
| J.L. Lewis | 69 | 72 | 74 | 215 | 18,500 |
| Len Mattiace | 75 | 69 | 71 | 215 | 18,500 |
| Sean O'Hair | 74 | 70 | 71 | 215 | 18,500 |
| Ted Purdy | 69 | 73 | 73 | 215 | 18,500 |
| Kevin Stadler | 69 | 77 | 69 | 215 | 18,500 |
| D.J. Brigman | 70 | 74 | 72 | 216 | 12,211.12 |
| Robert Allenby | 74 | 72 | 70 | 216 | 12,211.11 |
| Jason Bohn | 71 | 75 | 70 | 216 | 12,211.11 |
| Jeff Brehaut | 75 | 70 | 71 | 216 | 12,211.11 |
| Gavin Coles | 73 | 71 | 72 | 216 | 12,211.11 |
| Peter Lonard | 74 | 69 | 73 | 216 | 12,211.11 |
| D.A. Points | 74 | 71 | 71 | 216 | 12,211.11 |
| Joey Sindelar | 72 | 72 | 72 | 216 | 12,211.11 |
| Darron Stiles | 72 | 71 | 73 | 216 | 12,211.11 |
| Eric Axley | 75 | 69 | 73 | 217 | 11,100 |
| David Hearn | 70 | 73 | 74 | 217 | 11,100 |
| Brendan Jones | 73 | 72 | 72 | 217 | 11,100 |
| Hunter Mahan | 72 | 71 | 74 | 217 | 11,100 |
| Heath Slocum | 73 | 73 | 71 | 217 | 11,100 |
| Carl Pettersson | 75 | 70 | 73 | 218 | 10,750 |
| Steve Stricker | 70 | 73 | 75 | 218 | 10,750 |
| Stewart Cink | 71 | 74 | 74 | 219 | 10,450 |
| Tom Gillis | 77 | 69 | 73 | 219 | 10,450 |
| Rocco Mediate | 74 | 72 | 73 | 219 | 10,450 |
| Hideto Tanihara | 69 | 75 | 75 | 219 | 10,450 |
| Paul Goydos | 74 | 72 | 74 | 220 | 10,100 |
| Mathias Gronberg | 74 | 72 | 74 | 220 | 10,100 |
| Casey Wittenberg | 75 | 71 | 74 | 220 | 10,100 |
| Jimmy Walker | 72 | 72 | 77 | 221 | 9,900 |
| Aaron Baddeley | 72 | 74 | 76 | 222 | 9,800 |
| Nick Watney | 76 | 70 | 78 | 224 | 9,700 |
| Camilo Benedetti | 73 | 73 | 79 | 225 | 9,600 |
| Bo Van Pelt | 70 | 75 | 81 | 226 | 9,500 |

## Masters Tournament

*Augusta National Golf Club*, Augusta, Georgia
Par 36-36–72; 7,290 yards

April 7-10
purse, $7,000,000

| | SCORES | | | | TOTAL | MONEY |
|---|---|---|---|---|---|---|
| Tiger Woods | 74 | 66 | 65 | 71 | 276 | $1,260,000 |
| Chris DiMarco | 67 | 67 | 74 | 68 | 276 | 756,000 |
| (Woods defeated DiMarco on first playoff hole.) | | | | | | |
| Retief Goosen | 71 | 75 | 70 | 67 | 283 | 406,000 |

| | | SCORES | | | TOTAL | MONEY |
|---|---|---|---|---|---|---|
| Luke Donald | 68 | 77 | 69 | 69 | 283 | 406,000 |
| Vijay Singh | 68 | 73 | 71 | 72 | 284 | 237,300 |
| Mike Weir | 74 | 71 | 68 | 71 | 284 | 237,300 |
| Mark Hensby | 69 | 73 | 70 | 72 | 284 | 237,300 |
| Rod Pampling | 73 | 71 | 70 | 70 | 284 | 237,300 |
| Trevor Immelman | 73 | 73 | 65 | 73 | 284 | 237,300 |
| Phil Mickelson | 70 | 72 | 69 | 74 | 285 | 189,000 |
| Tim Herron | 76 | 68 | 70 | 72 | 286 | 168,000 |
| David Howell | 72 | 69 | 76 | 69 | 286 | 168,000 |
| Tom Lehman | 74 | 74 | 70 | 69 | 287 | 135,333 |
| Justin Leonard | 75 | 71 | 70 | 71 | 287 | 135,333 |
| Thomas Levet | 71 | 75 | 68 | 73 | 287 | 135,333 |
| *Ryan Moore | 71 | 71 | 75 | 70 | 287 | |
| Kirk Triplett | 75 | 68 | 72 | 73 | 288 | 112,000 |
| Chad Campbell | 73 | 73 | 67 | 75 | 288 | 112,000 |
| Darren Clarke | 72 | 76 | 69 | 71 | 288 | 112,000 |
| Bernhard Langer | 74 | 74 | 70 | 71 | 289 | 84,840 |
| Jeff Maggert | 74 | 74 | 72 | 69 | 289 | 84,840 |
| Scott Verplank | 72 | 75 | 69 | 73 | 289 | 84,840 |
| Jerry Kelly | 75 | 70 | 73 | 71 | 289 | 84,840 |
| Stewart Cink | 72 | 72 | 74 | 71 | 289 | 84,840 |
| Craig Parry | 72 | 75 | 69 | 74 | 290 | 61,600 |
| Thomas Bjorn | 71 | 67 | 71 | 81 | 290 | 61,600 |
| Joe Ogilvie | 74 | 73 | 73 | 70 | 290 | 61,600 |
| Jim Furyk | 76 | 67 | 74 | 74 | 291 | 53,900 |
| Kenny Perry | 76 | 68 | 71 | 77 | 292 | 50,750 |
| Steve Flesch | 76 | 70 | 70 | 76 | 292 | 50,750 |
| Mark O'Meara | 72 | 74 | 72 | 75 | 293 | 46,550 |
| Miguel Angel Jimenez | 74 | 74 | 73 | 72 | 293 | 46,550 |
| Shingo Katayama | 72 | 74 | 73 | 75 | 294 | 39,620 |
| Ian Poulter | 72 | 74 | 72 | 76 | 294 | 39,620 |
| K.J. Choi | 73 | 72 | 76 | 73 | 294 | 39,620 |
| Adam Scott | 71 | 76 | 72 | 75 | 294 | 39,620 |
| Casey Wittenberg | 72 | 72 | 74 | 76 | 294 | 39,620 |
| *Luke List | 77 | 69 | 78 | 70 | 294 | |
| Fred Couples | 75 | 71 | 77 | 72 | 295 | 32,200 |
| Todd Hamilton | 77 | 70 | 71 | 77 | 295 | 32,200 |
| Tim Clark | 74 | 74 | 72 | 75 | 295 | 32,200 |
| Ryan Palmer | 70 | 74 | 74 | 77 | 295 | 32,200 |
| Jonathan Kaye | 72 | 74 | 76 | 74 | 296 | 28,000 |
| Stuart Appleby | 69 | 76 | 72 | 79 | 296 | 28,000 |
| Stephen Ames | 73 | 74 | 75 | 75 | 297 | 25,200 |
| Nick O'Hern | 72 | 72 | 76 | 77 | 297 | 25,200 |
| Ernie Els | 75 | 73 | 78 | 72 | 298 | 23,100 |
| Jay Haas | 76 | 71 | 76 | 78 | 301 | 21,700 |
| Chris Riley | 71 | 77 | 78 | 78 | 304 | 20,300 |
| Craig Stadler | 75 | 73 | 79 | 79 | 306 | 19,180 |

**Out of Final 36 Holes**

| | | | | | | |
|---|---|---|---|---|---|---|
| Carlos Franco | 76 | 73 | | | 149 | |
| Padraig Harrington | 72 | 77 | | | 149 | |
| Sergio Garcia | 77 | 72 | | | 149 | |
| Charles Howell | 73 | 76 | | | 149 | |
| Graeme McDowell | 79 | 70 | | | 149 | |
| Fred Funk | 72 | 78 | | | 150 | |
| Robert Allenby | 77 | 73 | | | 150 | |
| Lee Westwood | 78 | 72 | | | 150 | |
| Angel Cabrera | 77 | 73 | | | 150 | |
| Davis Love | 76 | 75 | | | 151 | |

|  | SCORES |  | TOTAL |
|---|---|---|---|
| Jesper Parnevik | 77 | 74 | 151 |
| Joakim Haeggman | 79 | 72 | 151 |
| Bo Van Pelt | 76 | 75 | 151 |
| Raymond Floyd | 76 | 76 | 152 |
| Sandy Lyle | 74 | 78 | 152 |
| David Toms | 77 | 75 | 152 |
| David Duval | 75 | 77 | 152 |
| Peter Lonard | 75 | 77 | 152 |
| Fredrik Jacobson | 77 | 75 | 152 |
| Ben Curtis | 80 | 72 | 152 |
| Rich Beem | 75 | 77 | 152 |
| Rory Sabbatini | 80 | 72 | 152 |
| Zach Johnson | 81 | 71 | 152 |
| Larry Mize | 78 | 75 | 153 |
| Jack Nicklaus | 77 | 76 | 153 |
| Tom Watson | 77 | 76 | 153 |
| Jose Maria Olazabal | 77 | 76 | 153 |
| Shaun Micheel | 75 | 78 | 153 |
| John Daly | 80 | 74 | 154 |
| Nick Price | 78 | 76 | 154 |
| Ted Purdy | 77 | 78 | 155 |
| Ben Crenshaw | 76 | 80 | 156 |
| Ian Woosnam | 78 | 78 | 156 |
| Paul Casey | 79 | 78 | 157 |
| Shigeki Maruyama | 82 | 76 | 158 |
| *Austin Eaton | 81 | 77 | 158 |
| Tommy Aaron | 79 | 82 | 161 |
| Fuzzy Zoeller | 84 | 78 | 162 |
| Stuart Wilson | 82 | 82 | 164 |
| Gary Player | 88 | 79 | 167 |
| Charles Coody | 88 | 83 | 171 |
| Billy Casper | 106 |  | WD |
| Nick Faldo |  |  | WD |

(Professionals who did not complete 72 holes received $5,000.)

## MCI Heritage

*Harbour Town Golf Links,* Hilton Head Island, South Carolina　　　April 14-17
Par 35-36–71; 6,973 yards　　　purse, $5,200,000

|  | SCORES |  |  |  | TOTAL | MONEY |
|---|---|---|---|---|---|---|
| Peter Lonard | 62 | 74 | 66 | 75 | 277 | $936,000 |
| Billy Andrade | 72 | 69 | 70 | 68 | 279 | 343,200 |
| Darren Clarke | 65 | 65 | 73 | 76 | 279 | 343,200 |
| Jim Furyk | 71 | 68 | 71 | 69 | 279 | 343,200 |
| Davis Love | 69 | 70 | 69 | 71 | 279 | 343,200 |
| Stephen Ames | 71 | 69 | 69 | 71 | 280 | 174,200 |
| Thomas Levet | 64 | 74 | 73 | 69 | 280 | 174,200 |
| Rod Pampling | 70 | 69 | 68 | 73 | 280 | 174,200 |
| Nick O'Hern | 68 | 71 | 73 | 69 | 281 | 150,800 |
| Michael Allen | 71 | 70 | 71 | 70 | 282 | 130,000 |
| Matt Kuchar | 72 | 68 | 71 | 71 | 282 | 130,000 |
| Scott Verplank | 73 | 70 | 70 | 69 | 282 | 130,000 |
| Bart Bryant | 72 | 68 | 70 | 73 | 283 | 97,500 |
| Jose Maria Olazabal | 69 | 71 | 69 | 74 | 283 | 97,500 |
| Pat Perez | 72 | 70 | 71 | 70 | 283 | 97,500 |

| | SCORES | | | | TOTAL | MONEY |
|---|---|---|---|---|---|---|
| Loren Roberts | 71 | 70 | 68 | 74 | 283 | 97,500 |
| Jimmy Walker | 68 | 71 | 71 | 74 | 284 | 83,200 |
| Fred Funk | 72 | 74 | 69 | 70 | 285 | 70,200 |
| Dudley Hart | 71 | 69 | 74 | 71 | 285 | 70,200 |
| Greg Owen | 70 | 72 | 72 | 71 | 285 | 70,200 |
| Nick Price | 69 | 71 | 72 | 73 | 285 | 70,200 |
| Bob Estes | 69 | 74 | 72 | 72 | 287 | 54,080 |
| Todd Hamilton | 71 | 69 | 76 | 71 | 287 | 54,080 |
| Bob Tway | 72 | 70 | 72 | 73 | 287 | 54,080 |
| Cameron Beckman | 68 | 71 | 77 | 72 | 288 | 38,851.43 |
| Daniel Chopra | 73 | 73 | 69 | 73 | 288 | 38,851.43 |
| Brian Davis | 71 | 76 | 70 | 71 | 288 | 38,851.43 |
| Peter Jacobsen | 74 | 70 | 74 | 70 | 288 | 38,851.43 |
| Jonathan Kaye | 70 | 74 | 74 | 70 | 288 | 38,851.43 |
| Corey Pavin | 73 | 73 | 70 | 72 | 288 | 38,851.43 |
| Brad Faxon | 72 | 75 | 67 | 74 | 288 | 38,851.42 |
| Brian Bateman | 69 | 73 | 77 | 70 | 289 | 28,773.34 |
| Patrick Sheehan | 66 | 70 | 80 | 73 | 289 | 28,773.34 |
| Woody Austin | 69 | 70 | 76 | 74 | 289 | 28,773.33 |
| Brandt Jobe | 69 | 73 | 70 | 77 | 289 | 28,773.33 |
| Geoff Ogilvy | 71 | 69 | 76 | 73 | 289 | 28,773.33 |
| Joey Snyder | 74 | 67 | 69 | 79 | 289 | 28,773.33 |
| Steve Allan | 71 | 72 | 75 | 72 | 290 | 21,840 |
| Todd Fischer | 71 | 73 | 74 | 72 | 290 | 21,840 |
| David Frost | 68 | 75 | 74 | 73 | 290 | 21,840 |
| David Howell | 71 | 72 | 75 | 72 | 290 | 21,840 |
| Steve Jones | 71 | 70 | 74 | 75 | 290 | 21,840 |
| Billy Mayfair | 73 | 73 | 70 | 74 | 290 | 21,840 |
| Craig Stadler | 76 | 70 | 75 | 70 | 291 | 17,160 |
| Vaughn Taylor | 71 | 75 | 74 | 71 | 291 | 17,160 |
| Jay Williamson | 70 | 75 | 71 | 75 | 291 | 17,160 |
| Stewart Cink | 71 | 73 | 75 | 73 | 292 | 12,731.34 |
| Ben Crane | 71 | 76 | 73 | 72 | 292 | 12,731.34 |
| Jerry Kelly | 71 | 76 | 73 | 72 | 292 | 12,731.34 |
| John Senden | 71 | 73 | 77 | 71 | 292 | 12,731.34 |
| Paul Azinger | 73 | 69 | 77 | 73 | 292 | 12,731.33 |
| Tim Clark | 72 | 73 | 73 | 74 | 292 | 12,731.33 |
| Lucas Glover | 73 | 73 | 72 | 74 | 292 | 12,731.33 |
| Zach Johnson | 72 | 73 | 73 | 74 | 292 | 12,731.33 |
| Jesper Parnevik | 70 | 77 | 72 | 73 | 292 | 12,731.33 |
| Justin Rose | 73 | 73 | 72 | 74 | 292 | 12,731.33 |
| Jeff Sluman | 73 | 73 | 73 | 73 | 292 | 12,731.33 |
| Brandt Snedeker | 71 | 73 | 70 | 78 | 292 | 12,731.33 |
| Robert Damron | 70 | 73 | 78 | 72 | 293 | 11,388 |
| Marco Dawson | 68 | 78 | 74 | 73 | 293 | 11,388 |
| Joe Ogilvie | 71 | 75 | 77 | 70 | 293 | 11,388 |
| Ted Purdy | 73 | 74 | 76 | 70 | 293 | 11,388 |
| David Edwards | 73 | 71 | 77 | 73 | 294 | 11,128 |
| Mark Calcavecchia | 72 | 74 | 72 | 77 | 295 | 10,972 |
| Kent Jones | 75 | 71 | 76 | 73 | 295 | 10,972 |
| Jay Haas | 72 | 72 | 74 | 78 | 296 | 10,764 |
| John Rollins | 74 | 72 | 77 | 73 | 296 | 10,764 |
| Tommy Armour | 74 | 71 | 77 | 75 | 297 | 10,608 |
| Rocco Mediate | 72 | 72 | 79 | 75 | 298 | 10,504 |
| Franklin Langham | 77 | 69 | 75 | 78 | 299 | 10,348 |
| Graeme McDowell | 75 | 71 | 75 | 78 | 299 | 10,348 |
| Ian Poulter | 72 | 73 | 81 | 74 | 300 | 10,192 |
| Doug Tewell | 72 | 74 | 79 | 76 | 301 | 10,088 |
| Lee Westwood | 73 | 72 | 78 | 79 | 302 | 9,984 |
| Andre Stolz | 70 | 77 | 78 | 78 | 303 | 9,880 |

# Shell Houston Open

*Redstone Golf Club, Fall Creek Course*, Humble, Texas
Par 35-37–72; 7,508 yards

April 20-24
purse, $5,000,000

| | | SCORES | | | TOTAL | MONEY |
|---|---|---|---|---|---|---|
| Vijay Singh | 64 | 71 | 70 | 70 | 275 | $900,000 |
| John Daly | 68 | 67 | 73 | 67 | 275 | 540,000 |
| (Singh defeated Daly on first playoff hole.) | | | | | | |
| Jose Maria Olazabal | 70 | 67 | 70 | 70 | 277 | 340,000 |
| Darren Clarke | 71 | 69 | 71 | 67 | 278 | 220,000 |
| Greg Owen | 67 | 69 | 70 | 72 | 278 | 220,000 |
| Joe Ogilvie | 68 | 67 | 73 | 71 | 279 | 180,000 |
| Brian Davis | 71 | 69 | 70 | 70 | 280 | 140,416.67 |
| Lucas Glover | 70 | 71 | 72 | 67 | 280 | 140,416.67 |
| Jeff Maggert | 67 | 68 | 74 | 71 | 280 | 140,416.67 |
| Bo Van Pelt | 69 | 68 | 73 | 70 | 280 | 140,416.67 |
| Gavin Coles | 65 | 69 | 71 | 75 | 280 | 140,416.66 |
| Kent Jones | 70 | 71 | 68 | 71 | 280 | 140,416.66 |
| Billy Andrade | 69 | 69 | 73 | 70 | 281 | 93,750 |
| Doug Barron | 72 | 70 | 71 | 68 | 281 | 93,750 |
| Carl Paulson | 67 | 70 | 74 | 70 | 281 | 93,750 |
| Charles Warren | 73 | 68 | 71 | 69 | 281 | 93,750 |
| Charles Howell | 70 | 70 | 69 | 73 | 282 | 80,000 |
| Tom Byrum | 68 | 70 | 70 | 75 | 283 | 70,000 |
| Todd Hamilton | 71 | 69 | 71 | 72 | 283 | 70,000 |
| Rod Pampling | 69 | 74 | 71 | 69 | 283 | 70,000 |
| Stephen Ames | 70 | 73 | 72 | 69 | 284 | 48,357.15 |
| Joe Durant | 72 | 71 | 72 | 69 | 284 | 48,357.15 |
| Olin Browne | 70 | 71 | 70 | 73 | 284 | 48,357.14 |
| Mark Calcavecchia | 69 | 68 | 73 | 74 | 284 | 48,357.14 |
| Tim Herron | 67 | 76 | 69 | 72 | 284 | 48,357.14 |
| David Peoples | 73 | 68 | 70 | 73 | 284 | 48,357.14 |
| Brett Quigley | 67 | 67 | 73 | 77 | 284 | 48,357.14 |
| Brian Bateman | 68 | 73 | 68 | 76 | 285 | 33,250 |
| Harrison Frazar | 71 | 72 | 69 | 73 | 285 | 33,250 |
| Scott Gutschewski | 72 | 71 | 70 | 72 | 285 | 33,250 |
| Stephen Leaney | 71 | 68 | 70 | 76 | 285 | 33,250 |
| Billy Mayfair | 71 | 68 | 75 | 71 | 285 | 33,250 |
| Ted Purdy | 67 | 72 | 77 | 69 | 285 | 33,250 |
| Todd Fischer | 73 | 68 | 72 | 73 | 286 | 25,800 |
| Mathias Gronberg | 71 | 68 | 74 | 73 | 286 | 25,800 |
| Rory Sabbatini | 71 | 71 | 72 | 72 | 286 | 25,800 |
| John Senden | 73 | 69 | 72 | 72 | 286 | 25,800 |
| David Toms | 72 | 69 | 72 | 73 | 286 | 25,800 |
| Tommy Armour | 71 | 69 | 71 | 76 | 287 | 19,500 |
| Danny Briggs | 70 | 71 | 69 | 77 | 287 | 19,500 |
| Marco Dawson | 69 | 72 | 73 | 73 | 287 | 19,500 |
| Bob Estes | 72 | 68 | 75 | 72 | 287 | 19,500 |
| Dudley Hart | 70 | 71 | 71 | 75 | 287 | 19,500 |
| Thomas Levet | 72 | 65 | 77 | 73 | 287 | 19,500 |
| Kevin Na | 71 | 69 | 71 | 76 | 287 | 19,500 |
| Jerry Kelly | 71 | 70 | 75 | 72 | 288 | 14,566.67 |
| Blaine McCallister | 71 | 72 | 72 | 73 | 288 | 14,566.67 |
| Dean Wilson | 69 | 69 | 75 | 75 | 288 | 14,566.66 |
| Justin Bolli | 69 | 73 | 75 | 72 | 289 | 12,216.67 |
| Scott Hend | 72 | 69 | 75 | 73 | 289 | 12,216.67 |
| Neal Lancaster | 72 | 67 | 78 | 72 | 289 | 12,216.67 |
| J.L. Lewis | 70 | 71 | 79 | 69 | 289 | 12,216.67 |
| Steve Elkington | 71 | 71 | 74 | 73 | 289 | 12,216.66 |

| | SCORES | | | | TOTAL | MONEY |
|---|---|---|---|---|---|---|
| Scott McCarron | 71 | 67 | 76 | 75 | 289 | 12,216.66 |
| Arjun Atwal | 69 | 70 | 75 | 76 | 290 | 11,450 |
| Len Mattiace | 72 | 69 | 72 | 77 | 290 | 11,450 |
| Briny Baird | 74 | 66 | 76 | 75 | 291 | 11,100 |
| D.J. Brigman | 71 | 71 | 76 | 73 | 291 | 11,100 |
| Patrick Sheehan | 73 | 69 | 75 | 74 | 291 | 11,100 |
| Kevin Stadler | 72 | 69 | 77 | 73 | 291 | 11,100 |
| Charlie Wi | 69 | 70 | 76 | 76 | 291 | 11,100 |
| Jason Allred | 73 | 68 | 74 | 77 | 292 | 10,500 |
| Bob Burns | 71 | 71 | 74 | 76 | 292 | 10,500 |
| Paul Claxton | 68 | 72 | 77 | 75 | 292 | 10,500 |
| Geoff Ogilvy | 68 | 73 | 75 | 76 | 292 | 10,500 |
| Tom Pernice, Jr. | 69 | 69 | 79 | 75 | 292 | 10,500 |
| Steve Stricker | 72 | 66 | 77 | 77 | 292 | 10,500 |
| Kevin Sutherland | 76 | 67 | 74 | 75 | 292 | 10,500 |
| Cameron Beckman | 72 | 71 | 77 | 73 | 293 | 9,850 |
| Mark Brooks | 71 | 72 | 73 | 77 | 293 | 9,850 |
| David Hearn | 69 | 72 | 77 | 75 | 293 | 9,850 |
| J.J. Henry | 70 | 71 | 76 | 76 | 293 | 9,850 |
| Brandt Jobe | 70 | 72 | 76 | 75 | 293 | 9,850 |
| D.J. Trahan | 71 | 72 | 72 | 78 | 293 | 9,850 |
| Paul Azinger | 72 | 71 | 74 | 78 | 295 | 9,450 |
| Chris Smith | 67 | 72 | 78 | 78 | 295 | 9,450 |
| Sean O'Hair | 70 | 73 | 80 | 76 | 299 | 9,300 |
| Paul Gow | 72 | 69 | 77 | 83 | 301 | 9,200 |

## Zurich Classic of New Orleans

*TPC of Louisiana,* Avondale, Louisiana  
Par 36-36–72; 7,520 yards

April 28-May 1  
purse, $5,500,000

| | SCORES | | | | TOTAL | MONEY |
|---|---|---|---|---|---|---|
| Tim Petrovic | 72 | 69 | 66 | 68 | 275 | $990,000 |
| James Driscoll | 68 | 71 | 66 | 70 | 275 | 594,000 |
| (Petrovic defeated Driscoll on first playoff hole.) | | | | | | |
| Chris DiMarco | 65 | 71 | 68 | 72 | 276 | 319,000 |
| Lucas Glover | 69 | 68 | 70 | 69 | 276 | 319,000 |
| Arjun Atwal | 65 | 68 | 73 | 73 | 279 | 193,187.50 |
| Woody Austin | 71 | 70 | 71 | 67 | 279 | 193,187.50 |
| J.J. Henry | 67 | 67 | 74 | 71 | 279 | 193,187.50 |
| Bo Van Pelt | 73 | 70 | 66 | 70 | 279 | 193,187.50 |
| Chris Anderson | 70 | 70 | 69 | 71 | 280 | 137,500 |
| Daniel Chopra | 71 | 70 | 68 | 71 | 280 | 137,500 |
| Padraig Harrington | 68 | 71 | 70 | 71 | 280 | 137,500 |
| Richard Johnson | 70 | 68 | 72 | 70 | 280 | 137,500 |
| D.J. Trahan | 72 | 72 | 67 | 69 | 280 | 137,500 |
| Brendan Jones | 73 | 69 | 71 | 68 | 281 | 99,000 |
| Sean O'Hair | 68 | 71 | 73 | 69 | 281 | 99,000 |
| Jay Williamson | 71 | 71 | 68 | 71 | 281 | 99,000 |
| Brian Davis | 71 | 69 | 70 | 72 | 282 | 79,750 |
| Tom Gillis | 71 | 74 | 68 | 69 | 282 | 79,750 |
| John Rollins | 71 | 69 | 69 | 73 | 282 | 79,750 |
| Justin Rose | 71 | 71 | 71 | 69 | 282 | 79,750 |
| Paul Azinger | 70 | 73 | 72 | 68 | 283 | 53,192.86 |
| Olin Browne | 73 | 71 | 69 | 70 | 283 | 53,192.86 |
| Glen Hnatiuk | 70 | 72 | 73 | 68 | 283 | 53,192.86 |
| Hank Kuehne | 69 | 69 | 73 | 72 | 283 | 53,192.86 |

| | SCORES | | | | TOTAL | MONEY |
|---|---|---|---|---|---|---|
| Dennis Paulson | 70 | 74 | 69 | 70 | 283 | 53,192.86 |
| Tim Clark | 67 | 69 | 70 | 77 | 283 | 53,192.85 |
| Vijay Singh | 67 | 71 | 73 | 72 | 283 | 53,192.85 |
| Craig Bowden | 69 | 71 | 73 | 71 | 284 | 39,050 |
| Hunter Haas | 71 | 69 | 74 | 70 | 284 | 39,050 |
| Darron Stiles | 68 | 71 | 72 | 73 | 284 | 39,050 |
| Robert Damron | 72 | 71 | 74 | 68 | 285 | 26,871.43 |
| Marco Dawson | 70 | 71 | 71 | 73 | 285 | 26,871.43 |
| Todd Hamilton | 72 | 71 | 71 | 71 | 285 | 26,871.43 |
| Ryuji Imada | 68 | 73 | 73 | 71 | 285 | 26,871.43 |
| Jonathan Kaye | 70 | 74 | 73 | 68 | 285 | 26,871.43 |
| Davis Love | 72 | 70 | 69 | 74 | 285 | 26,871.43 |
| Brenden Pappas | 72 | 70 | 70 | 73 | 285 | 26,871.43 |
| Tom Pernice, Jr. | 67 | 77 | 71 | 70 | 285 | 26,871.43 |
| Phillip Price | 70 | 71 | 71 | 73 | 285 | 26,871.43 |
| Joey Snyder | 68 | 74 | 72 | 71 | 285 | 26,871.43 |
| Kevin Sutherland | 72 | 72 | 71 | 70 | 285 | 26,871.43 |
| Vaughn Taylor | 72 | 73 | 67 | 73 | 285 | 26,871.43 |
| Frank Lickliter | 70 | 70 | 70 | 75 | 285 | 26,871.42 |
| Hidemichi Tanaka | 69 | 70 | 70 | 76 | 285 | 26,871.42 |
| Doug Barron | 73 | 69 | 72 | 72 | 286 | 17,600 |
| Kirk Triplett | 71 | 69 | 70 | 76 | 286 | 17,600 |
| Robert Allenby | 75 | 70 | 69 | 73 | 287 | 14,542 |
| Scott Gutschewski | 72 | 71 | 71 | 73 | 287 | 14,542 |
| Bob Heintz | 71 | 74 | 72 | 70 | 287 | 14,542 |
| Scott Hend | 70 | 71 | 76 | 70 | 287 | 14,542 |
| Nick Watney | 68 | 75 | 73 | 71 | 287 | 14,542 |
| Glen Day | 73 | 68 | 73 | 74 | 288 | 12,697.15 |
| David Hearn | 71 | 72 | 71 | 74 | 288 | 12,697.15 |
| Joe Durant | 72 | 73 | 69 | 74 | 288 | 12,697.14 |
| Carlos Franco | 72 | 73 | 70 | 73 | 288 | 12,697.14 |
| Matt Gogel | 72 | 72 | 75 | 69 | 288 | 12,697.14 |
| Will MacKenzie | 71 | 71 | 71 | 75 | 288 | 12,697.14 |
| Mark O'Meara | 71 | 73 | 73 | 71 | 288 | 12,697.14 |
| Justin Bolli | 75 | 70 | 72 | 72 | 289 | 11,935 |
| Danny Ellis | 77 | 66 | 73 | 73 | 289 | 11,935 |
| Harrison Frazar | 71 | 73 | 72 | 73 | 289 | 11,935 |
| Kelly Grunewald | 73 | 71 | 74 | 71 | 289 | 11,935 |
| Jeff Hart | 74 | 71 | 72 | 72 | 289 | 11,935 |
| Charles Howell | 72 | 73 | 73 | 71 | 289 | 11,935 |
| Jerry Kelly | 70 | 73 | 72 | 75 | 290 | 11,440 |
| Greg Owen | 72 | 73 | 73 | 72 | 290 | 11,440 |
| Omar Uresti | 72 | 73 | 73 | 72 | 290 | 11,440 |
| D.J. Brigman | 73 | 71 | 76 | 71 | 291 | 10,890 |
| Bernhard Langer | 74 | 69 | 74 | 74 | 291 | 10,890 |
| Hunter Mahan | 74 | 70 | 76 | 71 | 291 | 10,890 |
| Carl Paulson | 71 | 71 | 73 | 76 | 291 | 10,890 |
| Ted Purdy | 75 | 68 | 74 | 74 | 291 | 10,890 |
| Patrick Sheehan | 72 | 70 | 74 | 75 | 291 | 10,890 |
| Charlie Wi | 70 | 72 | 75 | 74 | 291 | 10,890 |
| Jeff Brehaut | 70 | 71 | 76 | 75 | 292 | 10,340 |
| Matt Davidson | 71 | 74 | 74 | 73 | 292 | 10,340 |
| Dean Wilson | 70 | 74 | 75 | 73 | 292 | 10,340 |
| Bob Burns | 71 | 73 | 77 | 72 | 293 | 9,955 |
| Bradley Hughes | 73 | 72 | 76 | 72 | 293 | 9,955 |
| Scott McCarron | 71 | 74 | 75 | 73 | 293 | 9,955 |
| Joey Sindelar | 70 | 75 | 74 | 74 | 293 | 9,955 |
| Ahmad Bateman | 75 | 70 | 78 | 76 | 299 | 9,625 |
| Roland Thatcher | 71 | 74 | 76 | 78 | 299 | 9,625 |

# Wachovia Championship

*Quail Hollow Club,* Charlotte, North Carolina
Par 36-36–72; 7,442 yards

May 5-8
purse, $6,000,000

| | SCORES | | | | TOTAL | MONEY |
|---|---|---|---|---|---|---|
| Vijay Singh | 70 | 69 | 71 | 66 | 276 | $1,080,000 |
| Jim Furyk | 69 | 72 | 69 | 66 | 276 | 528,000 |
| Sergio Garcia | 66 | 71 | 67 | 72 | 276 | 528,000 |
| (Singh defeated Garcia on first and Furyk on fourth playoff hole.) | | | | | | |
| Chris DiMarco | 74 | 67 | 73 | 66 | 280 | 288,000 |
| Carlos Franco | 72 | 74 | 70 | 66 | 282 | 228,000 |
| Vaughn Taylor | 74 | 70 | 71 | 67 | 282 | 228,000 |
| Phil Mickelson | 71 | 73 | 73 | 66 | 283 | 193,500 |
| Greg Owen | 74 | 67 | 71 | 71 | 283 | 193,500 |
| D.J. Trahan | 72 | 67 | 71 | 74 | 284 | 174,000 |
| Billy Mayfair | 76 | 72 | 70 | 67 | 285 | 162,000 |
| Stephen Leaney | 73 | 74 | 68 | 71 | 286 | 127,200 |
| Kenny Perry | 68 | 76 | 69 | 73 | 286 | 127,200 |
| Scott Verplank | 71 | 69 | 73 | 73 | 286 | 127,200 |
| Nick Watney | 76 | 68 | 73 | 69 | 286 | 127,200 |
| Tiger Woods | 70 | 72 | 73 | 71 | 286 | 127,200 |
| Fred Funk | 70 | 75 | 70 | 72 | 287 | 87,000 |
| Mark Hensby | 73 | 71 | 72 | 71 | 287 | 87,000 |
| Per-Ulrik Johansson | 70 | 71 | 74 | 72 | 287 | 87,000 |
| Brett Quigley | 71 | 69 | 77 | 70 | 287 | 87,000 |
| Adam Scott | 76 | 69 | 69 | 73 | 287 | 87,000 |
| Jeff Sluman | 71 | 70 | 75 | 71 | 287 | 87,000 |
| Bill Haas | 74 | 71 | 74 | 69 | 288 | 55,700 |
| Charles Howell | 72 | 75 | 73 | 68 | 288 | 55,700 |
| Brandt Jobe | 74 | 68 | 75 | 71 | 288 | 55,700 |
| Geoff Ogilvy | 71 | 76 | 70 | 71 | 288 | 55,700 |
| Nick Price | 73 | 69 | 69 | 77 | 288 | 55,700 |
| John Rollins | 71 | 74 | 69 | 74 | 288 | 55,700 |
| Tommy Armour | 76 | 72 | 72 | 69 | 289 | 40,800 |
| Woody Austin | 71 | 73 | 75 | 70 | 289 | 40,800 |
| Bart Bryant | 70 | 74 | 75 | 70 | 289 | 40,800 |
| Hank Kuehne | 75 | 70 | 74 | 70 | 289 | 40,800 |
| Rod Pampling | 72 | 72 | 73 | 72 | 289 | 40,800 |
| Craig Barlow | 71 | 75 | 73 | 71 | 290 | 28,472.73 |
| Chad Campbell | 71 | 77 | 72 | 70 | 290 | 28,472.73 |
| Steve Flesch | 76 | 72 | 72 | 70 | 290 | 28,472.73 |
| Jay Haas | 73 | 74 | 71 | 72 | 290 | 28,472.73 |
| Fredrik Jacobson | 73 | 72 | 69 | 76 | 290 | 28,472.73 |
| Richard Johnson | 68 | 72 | 73 | 77 | 290 | 28,472.73 |
| Tom Pernice, Jr. | 74 | 74 | 70 | 72 | 290 | 28,472.73 |
| Kevin Sutherland | 72 | 71 | 74 | 73 | 290 | 28,472.73 |
| Patrick Sheehan | 68 | 75 | 70 | 77 | 290 | 28,472.72 |
| Joey Sindelar | 68 | 71 | 73 | 78 | 290 | 28,472.72 |
| Dean Wilson | 73 | 71 | 69 | 77 | 290 | 28,472.72 |
| Steve Allan | 74 | 73 | 72 | 72 | 291 | 18,140 |
| Marco Dawson | 73 | 73 | 72 | 73 | 291 | 18,140 |
| Brad Faxon | 72 | 76 | 73 | 70 | 291 | 18,140 |
| Brian Gay | 74 | 71 | 75 | 71 | 291 | 18,140 |
| J.L. Lewis | 73 | 75 | 72 | 71 | 291 | 18,140 |
| Justin Rose | 71 | 74 | 77 | 69 | 291 | 18,140 |
| Andrew Magee | 69 | 75 | 72 | 76 | 292 | 14,360 |
| Kevin Na | 74 | 74 | 72 | 72 | 292 | 14,360 |
| Mark O'Meara | 72 | 76 | 71 | 73 | 292 | 14,360 |
| Dennis Paulson | 73 | 74 | 76 | 69 | 292 | 14,360 |

|  | SCORES | | | | TOTAL | MONEY |
|---|---|---|---|---|---|---|
| Ted Purdy | 73 | 70 | 75 | 74 | 292 | 14,360 |
| Tag Ridings | 70 | 74 | 73 | 75 | 292 | 14,360 |
| Arjun Atwal | 75 | 73 | 75 | 70 | 293 | 13,260 |
| Paul Azinger | 72 | 75 | 74 | 72 | 293 | 13,260 |
| Tom Byrum | 74 | 73 | 76 | 70 | 293 | 13,260 |
| Ben Curtis | 71 | 72 | 75 | 75 | 293 | 13,260 |
| Shigeki Maruyama | 75 | 68 | 76 | 74 | 293 | 13,260 |
| Shaun Micheel | 74 | 71 | 73 | 75 | 293 | 13,260 |
| Jesper Parnevik | 69 | 73 | 75 | 76 | 293 | 13,260 |
| Heath Slocum | 73 | 75 | 74 | 71 | 293 | 13,260 |
| Robert Damron | 72 | 74 | 73 | 75 | 294 | 12,540 |
| Scott Hend | 74 | 74 | 71 | 75 | 294 | 12,540 |
| Sean O'Hair | 73 | 74 | 77 | 70 | 294 | 12,540 |
| Carl Pettersson | 75 | 72 | 69 | 78 | 294 | 12,540 |
| Aaron Baddeley | 72 | 76 | 76 | 71 | 295 | 12,060 |
| Hidemichi Tanaka | 74 | 72 | 77 | 72 | 295 | 12,060 |
| Duffy Waldorf | 74 | 73 | 78 | 70 | 295 | 12,060 |
| Jay Williamson | 73 | 75 | 75 | 72 | 295 | 12,060 |
| Steve Lowery | 72 | 76 | 71 | 77 | 296 | 11,760 |
| Skip Kendall | 71 | 76 | 76 | 74 | 297 | 11,640 |
| Bo Van Pelt | 72 | 74 | 74 | 78 | 298 | 11,520 |
| Robert Gamez | 75 | 71 | 74 | 79 | 299 | 11,280 |
| Todd Hamilton | 72 | 76 | 77 | 74 | 299 | 11,280 |
| Padraig Harrington | 71 | 75 | 73 | 80 | 299 | 11,280 |
| Tom Kite | 74 | 73 | 75 | 79 | 301 | 11,040 |
| Craig Perks | 76 | 70 | 79 | 78 | 303 | 10,920 |

# EDS Byron Nelson Championship

*TPC Four Seasons Resort at Las Colinas:*  May 12-15
Par 35-35–70; 7,016 yards  purse, $6,200,000
*Cottonwood Valley Course:* Par 34-36–70; 6,847 yards
Irving, Texas

|  | SCORES | | | | TOTAL | MONEY |
|---|---|---|---|---|---|---|
| Ted Purdy | 65 | 67 | 68 | 65 | 265 | $1,116,000 |
| Sean O'Hair | 66 | 65 | 67 | 68 | 266 | 669,600 |
| Doug Barron | 69 | 66 | 65 | 69 | 269 | 322,400 |
| Vijay Singh | 68 | 67 | 69 | 65 | 269 | 322,400 |
| Bob Tway | 68 | 68 | 66 | 67 | 269 | 322,400 |
| Shigeki Maruyama | 67 | 67 | 68 | 68 | 270 | 200,725 |
| Nick Price | 66 | 69 | 68 | 67 | 270 | 200,725 |
| Omar Uresti | 65 | 70 | 69 | 66 | 270 | 200,725 |
| Scott Verplank | 68 | 67 | 65 | 70 | 270 | 200,725 |
| Jaxon Brigman | 72 | 66 | 64 | 69 | 271 | 148,800 |
| Mark Brooks | 71 | 69 | 65 | 66 | 271 | 148,800 |
| Ernie Els | 64 | 72 | 69 | 66 | 271 | 148,800 |
| J.J. Henry | 67 | 69 | 67 | 68 | 271 | 148,800 |
| Skip Kendall | 70 | 68 | 68 | 66 | 272 | 108,500 |
| Phil Mickelson | 69 | 66 | 70 | 67 | 272 | 108,500 |
| John Rollins | 67 | 68 | 68 | 69 | 272 | 108,500 |
| Rory Sabbatini | 70 | 69 | 69 | 64 | 272 | 108,500 |
| Jim Furyk | 68 | 69 | 69 | 67 | 273 | 70,266.67 |
| J.P. Hayes | 69 | 65 | 72 | 67 | 273 | 70,266.67 |
| Corey Pavin | 69 | 68 | 68 | 68 | 273 | 70,266.67 |
| Heath Slocum | 69 | 66 | 69 | 69 | 273 | 70,266.67 |
| Vaughn Taylor | 67 | 71 | 69 | 66 | 273 | 70,266.67 |

| | SCORES | | | | TOTAL | MONEY |
|---|---|---|---|---|---|---|
| Brett Wetterich | 64 | 67 | 73 | 69 | 273 | 70,266.67 |
| Luke Donald | 68 | 69 | 67 | 69 | 273 | 70,266.66 |
| Todd Hamilton | 67 | 67 | 65 | 74 | 273 | 70,266.66 |
| Jesper Parnevik | 69 | 67 | 68 | 69 | 273 | 70,266.66 |
| Stuart Appleby | 63 | 73 | 68 | 70 | 274 | 41,268.75 |
| Stephen Leaney | 69 | 68 | 68 | 69 | 274 | 41,268.75 |
| Billy Mayfair | 70 | 63 | 72 | 69 | 274 | 41,268.75 |
| Mark O'Meara | 69 | 69 | 67 | 69 | 274 | 41,268.75 |
| Rod Pampling | 72 | 68 | 67 | 67 | 274 | 41,268.75 |
| John Senden | 70 | 68 | 70 | 66 | 274 | 41,268.75 |
| Kevin Sutherland | 69 | 70 | 69 | 66 | 274 | 41,268.75 |
| Jay Williamson | 67 | 70 | 66 | 71 | 274 | 41,268.75 |
| James Driscoll | 73 | 67 | 68 | 67 | 275 | 30,566 |
| Sergio Garcia | 71 | 68 | 66 | 70 | 275 | 30,566 |
| Ryuji Imada | 68 | 70 | 68 | 69 | 275 | 30,566 |
| Scott McCarron | 68 | 70 | 69 | 68 | 275 | 30,566 |
| Craig Perks | 71 | 68 | 66 | 70 | 275 | 30,566 |
| Stewart Cink | 71 | 67 | 67 | 71 | 276 | 22,320 |
| John Cook | 69 | 69 | 69 | 69 | 276 | 22,320 |
| Trevor Immelman | 67 | 72 | 70 | 67 | 276 | 22,320 |
| Jerry Kelly | 73 | 66 | 66 | 71 | 276 | 22,320 |
| Bernhard Langer | 73 | 67 | 69 | 67 | 276 | 22,320 |
| Ian Leggatt | 66 | 73 | 68 | 69 | 276 | 22,320 |
| Bo Van Pelt | 67 | 69 | 68 | 72 | 276 | 22,320 |
| Mark Wilson | 68 | 70 | 69 | 69 | 276 | 22,320 |
| Briny Baird | 68 | 72 | 68 | 69 | 277 | 15,582.67 |
| John Daly | 64 | 73 | 71 | 69 | 277 | 15,582.67 |
| Kenny Perry | 67 | 70 | 74 | 66 | 277 | 15,582.67 |
| Justin Rose | 69 | 71 | 68 | 69 | 277 | 15,582.67 |
| Cameron Beckman | 66 | 70 | 71 | 70 | 277 | 15,582.66 |
| Ben Crane | 70 | 66 | 68 | 73 | 277 | 15,582.66 |
| Jonathan Byrd | 71 | 68 | 69 | 70 | 278 | 14,322 |
| Geoff Ogilvy | 69 | 71 | 65 | 73 | 278 | 14,322 |
| Chad Campbell | 70 | 70 | 72 | 67 | 279 | 14,074 |
| Steve Elkington | 72 | 67 | 71 | 69 | 279 | 14,074 |
| Robert Allenby | 68 | 70 | 68 | 74 | 280 | 13,578 |
| Jim Carter | 72 | 68 | 71 | 69 | 280 | 13,578 |
| Tom Gillis | 69 | 70 | 68 | 73 | 280 | 13,578 |
| Paul Gow | 66 | 72 | 71 | 71 | 280 | 13,578 |
| Brandt Jobe | 69 | 69 | 68 | 74 | 280 | 13,578 |
| Justin Leonard | 72 | 68 | 72 | 68 | 280 | 13,578 |
| Todd Fischer | 66 | 69 | 71 | 75 | 281 | 12,958 |
| Harrison Frazar | 66 | 70 | 75 | 70 | 281 | 12,958 |
| Steve Lowery | 65 | 69 | 72 | 75 | 281 | 12,958 |
| Steve Stricker | 69 | 68 | 71 | 73 | 281 | 12,958 |
| Daniel Chopra | 70 | 66 | 75 | 71 | 282 | 12,648 |
| Gavin Coles | 66 | 71 | 69 | 77 | 283 | 12,524 |
| Hunter Mahan | 72 | 68 | 74 | 70 | 284 | 12,400 |
| Pat Perez | 68 | 71 | 74 | 72 | 285 | 12,276 |
| Jason Hartwick | 66 | 72 | 78 | 70 | 286 | 12,090 |
| Brendan Jones | 69 | 71 | 74 | 72 | 286 | 12,090 |
| Glen Day | 66 | 73 | 71 | 78 | 288 | 11,904 |
| Mark Hensby | 67 | 72 | 79 | 71 | 289 | 11,718 |
| Tim Petrovic | 69 | 71 | 74 | 75 | 289 | 11,718 |

# Bank of America Colonial

*Colonial Country Club,* Fort Worth, Texas
Par 35-35–70; 7,054 yards

May 19-22
purse, $5,600,000

| | SCORES | | | | TOTAL | MONEY |
|---|---|---|---|---|---|---|
| Kenny Perry | 65 | 63 | 64 | 69 | 261 | $1,008,000 |
| Billy Mayfair | 67 | 66 | 66 | 69 | 268 | 604,800 |
| Joe Durant | 71 | 63 | 69 | 66 | 269 | 291,200 |
| Peter Lonard | 69 | 66 | 65 | 69 | 269 | 291,200 |
| David Toms | 69 | 66 | 68 | 66 | 269 | 291,200 |
| Aaron Baddeley | 69 | 66 | 67 | 68 | 270 | 163,600 |
| Scott Hend | 68 | 67 | 68 | 67 | 270 | 163,600 |
| Brandt Jobe | 65 | 69 | 67 | 69 | 270 | 163,600 |
| Bernhard Langer | 68 | 69 | 66 | 67 | 270 | 163,600 |
| Rod Pampling | 66 | 67 | 68 | 69 | 270 | 163,600 |
| Tim Petrovic | 71 | 69 | 66 | 64 | 270 | 163,600 |
| Rory Sabbatini | 67 | 69 | 68 | 66 | 270 | 163,600 |
| Ted Purdy | 66 | 65 | 71 | 69 | 271 | 108,266.67 |
| Justin Rose | 68 | 68 | 71 | 64 | 271 | 108,266.67 |
| Steve Stricker | 68 | 65 | 66 | 72 | 271 | 108,266.66 |
| Fredrik Jacobson | 68 | 69 | 65 | 70 | 272 | 95,200 |
| Ben Crane | 69 | 66 | 70 | 68 | 273 | 81,200 |
| Kevin Na | 65 | 71 | 71 | 66 | 273 | 81,200 |
| Kirk Triplett | 66 | 66 | 72 | 69 | 273 | 81,200 |
| Bo Van Pelt | 70 | 67 | 68 | 68 | 273 | 81,200 |
| K.J. Choi | 69 | 66 | 70 | 69 | 274 | 58,240 |
| Tim Clark | 71 | 64 | 69 | 70 | 274 | 58,240 |
| Arron Oberholser | 68 | 67 | 70 | 69 | 274 | 58,240 |
| Tom Purtzer | 71 | 70 | 69 | 64 | 274 | 58,240 |
| Bob Tway | 67 | 69 | 69 | 69 | 274 | 58,240 |
| Stuart Appleby | 68 | 69 | 71 | 67 | 275 | 40,600 |
| Jim Furyk | 69 | 68 | 67 | 71 | 275 | 40,600 |
| Zach Johnson | 71 | 68 | 70 | 66 | 275 | 40,600 |
| Justin Leonard | 67 | 69 | 69 | 70 | 275 | 40,600 |
| Phil Mickelson | 71 | 69 | 68 | 67 | 275 | 40,600 |
| Corey Pavin | 70 | 66 | 68 | 71 | 275 | 40,600 |
| Shigeki Maruyama | 69 | 70 | 69 | 68 | 276 | 30,986.67 |
| Loren Roberts | 68 | 67 | 73 | 68 | 276 | 30,986.67 |
| Heath Slocum | 68 | 72 | 69 | 67 | 276 | 30,986.67 |
| Scott Verplank | 71 | 69 | 68 | 68 | 276 | 30,986.67 |
| Jeff Maggert | 73 | 66 | 67 | 70 | 276 | 30,986.66 |
| Jeff Sluman | 68 | 70 | 68 | 70 | 276 | 30,986.66 |
| Stephen Ames | 73 | 68 | 68 | 68 | 277 | 23,520 |
| Arjun Atwal | 70 | 65 | 69 | 73 | 277 | 23,520 |
| Brian Bateman | 64 | 72 | 74 | 67 | 277 | 23,520 |
| Geoff Ogilvy | 71 | 67 | 64 | 75 | 277 | 23,520 |
| John Senden | 70 | 68 | 66 | 73 | 277 | 23,520 |
| D.J. Trahan | 64 | 67 | 71 | 75 | 277 | 23,520 |
| Harrison Frazar | 66 | 70 | 70 | 72 | 278 | 16,528 |
| Hunter Haas | 73 | 67 | 67 | 71 | 278 | 16,528 |
| Steve Jones | 69 | 68 | 71 | 70 | 278 | 16,528 |
| Stephen Leaney | 66 | 69 | 71 | 72 | 278 | 16,528 |
| Tom Lehman | 72 | 68 | 70 | 68 | 278 | 16,528 |
| Hunter Mahan | 72 | 67 | 70 | 69 | 278 | 16,528 |
| Pat Perez | 71 | 67 | 69 | 71 | 278 | 16,528 |
| Mark Brooks | 71 | 67 | 71 | 70 | 279 | 13,178.67 |
| Jonathan Byrd | 67 | 71 | 73 | 68 | 279 | 13,178.67 |
| Joe Ogilvie | 71 | 68 | 74 | 66 | 279 | 13,178.67 |
| Jesper Parnevik | 69 | 72 | 71 | 67 | 279 | 13,178.67 |

| | SCORES | | | | TOTAL | MONEY |
|---|---|---|---|---|---|---|
| Jason Allred | 69 | 72 | 67 | 71 | 279 | 13,178.66 |
| Skip Kendall | 67 | 70 | 72 | 70 | 279 | 13,178.66 |
| Bart Bryant | 70 | 71 | 67 | 72 | 280 | 12,432 |
| Daniel Chopra | 73 | 67 | 71 | 69 | 280 | 12,432 |
| Stewart Cink | 72 | 67 | 69 | 72 | 280 | 12,432 |
| Brian Gay | 71 | 70 | 70 | 69 | 280 | 12,432 |
| Hank Kuehne | 71 | 70 | 71 | 68 | 280 | 12,432 |
| Bob Estes | 71 | 68 | 71 | 71 | 281 | 11,984 |
| Jonathan Kaye | 73 | 67 | 72 | 69 | 281 | 11,984 |
| Kevin Sutherland | 70 | 69 | 70 | 72 | 281 | 11,984 |
| Briny Baird | 69 | 65 | 75 | 73 | 282 | 11,704 |
| Craig Perks | 73 | 67 | 72 | 70 | 282 | 11,704 |
| Fred Funk | 71 | 69 | 73 | 70 | 283 | 11,480 |
| Andrew Magee | 70 | 71 | 66 | 76 | 283 | 11,480 |
| Robert Gamez | 71 | 70 | 71 | 72 | 284 | 11,256 |
| Ryan Palmer | 70 | 70 | 72 | 72 | 284 | 11,256 |
| Frank Lickliter | 70 | 70 | 73 | 72 | 285 | 11,032 |
| Patrick Sheehan | 62 | 72 | 75 | 76 | 285 | 11,032 |

# FedEx St. Jude Classic

*TPC at Southwind,* Memphis, Tennessee
Par 35-35–70; 7,244 yards

May 26-29
purse, $4,900,000

| | SCORES | | | | TOTAL | MONEY |
|---|---|---|---|---|---|---|
| Justin Leonard | 62 | 65 | 66 | 73 | 266 | $882,000 |
| David Toms | 68 | 71 | 65 | 63 | 267 | 529,200 |
| Fred Funk | 69 | 68 | 66 | 68 | 271 | 333,200 |
| Davis Love | 65 | 70 | 68 | 69 | 272 | 215,600 |
| Heath Slocum | 68 | 66 | 67 | 71 | 272 | 215,600 |
| Fredrik Jacobson | 68 | 64 | 72 | 69 | 273 | 170,275 |
| Richard Johnson | 69 | 66 | 69 | 69 | 273 | 170,275 |
| Bob Estes | 67 | 70 | 67 | 70 | 274 | 142,100 |
| Neal Lancaster | 71 | 68 | 68 | 67 | 274 | 142,100 |
| Roland Thatcher | 67 | 67 | 71 | 69 | 274 | 142,100 |
| Phillip Price | 67 | 69 | 68 | 71 | 275 | 122,500 |
| Billy Andrade | 70 | 70 | 65 | 71 | 276 | 96,040 |
| D.J. Brigman | 68 | 68 | 72 | 68 | 276 | 96,040 |
| Paul Goydos | 67 | 66 | 70 | 73 | 276 | 96,040 |
| Brenden Pappas | 69 | 68 | 72 | 67 | 276 | 96,040 |
| Tom Pernice, Jr. | 66 | 68 | 68 | 74 | 276 | 96,040 |
| Jeff Brehaut | 68 | 71 | 70 | 68 | 277 | 64,120 |
| Olin Browne | 67 | 70 | 72 | 68 | 277 | 64,120 |
| Jose Coceres | 70 | 68 | 69 | 70 | 277 | 64,120 |
| J.J. Henry | 73 | 66 | 70 | 68 | 277 | 64,120 |
| Steve Lowery | 72 | 70 | 68 | 67 | 277 | 64,120 |
| Spike McRoy | 70 | 70 | 69 | 68 | 277 | 64,120 |
| Carl Paulson | 68 | 70 | 68 | 71 | 277 | 64,120 |
| Matt Gogel | 66 | 68 | 73 | 71 | 278 | 40,670 |
| Tim Herron | 71 | 67 | 69 | 71 | 278 | 40,670 |
| Carl Pettersson | 67 | 70 | 73 | 68 | 278 | 40,670 |
| Tag Ridings | 70 | 68 | 71 | 69 | 278 | 40,670 |
| Kirk Triplett | 64 | 71 | 72 | 71 | 278 | 40,670 |
| Michael Allen | 70 | 69 | 73 | 67 | 279 | 32,585 |
| John Cook | 72 | 69 | 72 | 66 | 279 | 32,585 |
| Mathias Gronberg | 69 | 70 | 66 | 74 | 279 | 32,585 |
| Ryuji Imada | 71 | 69 | 71 | 68 | 279 | 32,585 |

| | SCORES | | | | TOTAL | MONEY |
|---|---|---|---|---|---|---|
| Hunter Haas | 67 | 69 | 74 | 70 | 280 | 25,888.34 |
| Hunter Mahan | 71 | 67 | 74 | 68 | 280 | 25,888.34 |
| Jason Bohn | 65 | 72 | 72 | 71 | 280 | 25,888.33 |
| Todd Fischer | 69 | 70 | 70 | 71 | 280 | 25,888.33 |
| Blaine McCallister | 70 | 71 | 69 | 70 | 280 | 25,888.33 |
| Hidemichi Tanaka | 73 | 67 | 70 | 70 | 280 | 25,888.33 |
| Stephen Ames | 68 | 72 | 73 | 68 | 281 | 20,090 |
| Ben Crane | 69 | 70 | 69 | 73 | 281 | 20,090 |
| Per-Ulrik Johansson | 69 | 71 | 71 | 70 | 281 | 20,090 |
| Shaun Micheel | 69 | 69 | 71 | 72 | 281 | 20,090 |
| Rob Rashell | 73 | 68 | 69 | 71 | 281 | 20,090 |
| Woody Austin | 69 | 70 | 70 | 73 | 282 | 14,161 |
| Jaxon Brigman | 70 | 70 | 73 | 69 | 282 | 14,161 |
| Stephen Gangluff | 69 | 71 | 71 | 71 | 282 | 14,161 |
| Lucas Glover | 67 | 72 | 72 | 71 | 282 | 14,161 |
| Dudley Hart | 69 | 69 | 72 | 72 | 282 | 14,161 |
| Larry Mize | 71 | 71 | 69 | 71 | 282 | 14,161 |
| Steve Stricker | 71 | 70 | 70 | 71 | 282 | 14,161 |
| Grant Waite | 72 | 66 | 70 | 74 | 282 | 14,161 |
| Arjun Atwal | 71 | 66 | 70 | 76 | 283 | 11,257.75 |
| Tom Byrum | 71 | 67 | 71 | 74 | 283 | 11,257.75 |
| Robert Damron | 73 | 68 | 70 | 72 | 283 | 11,257.75 |
| Jay Delsing | 71 | 69 | 72 | 71 | 283 | 11,257.75 |
| Brad Faxon | 69 | 70 | 73 | 71 | 283 | 11,257.75 |
| Robin Freeman | 68 | 72 | 71 | 72 | 283 | 11,257.75 |
| Scott Simpson | 70 | 71 | 70 | 72 | 283 | 11,257.75 |
| Casey Wittenberg | 72 | 70 | 68 | 73 | 283 | 11,257.75 |
| Kent Jones | 72 | 67 | 68 | 77 | 284 | 10,731 |
| Sean O'Hair | 72 | 66 | 74 | 72 | 284 | 10,731 |
| John Elliott | 71 | 69 | 71 | 74 | 285 | 10,437 |
| Bradley Hughes | 69 | 72 | 70 | 74 | 285 | 10,437 |
| John Rollins | 72 | 70 | 71 | 72 | 285 | 10,437 |
| Ted Tryba | 71 | 71 | 72 | 71 | 285 | 10,437 |
| Hank Kuehne | 67 | 71 | 76 | 73 | 287 | 10,045 |
| Will MacKenzie | 67 | 74 | 73 | 73 | 287 | 10,045 |
| Nick Price | 69 | 70 | 72 | 76 | 287 | 10,045 |
| Hideto Tanihara | 73 | 69 | 69 | 76 | 287 | 10,045 |
| Tim Clark | 74 | 67 | 75 | 72 | 288 | 9,751 |
| David Hearn | 75 | 67 | 75 | 71 | 288 | 9,751 |
| Jonathan Byrd | 72 | 69 | 76 | 72 | 289 | 9,506 |
| John Daly | 72 | 69 | 77 | 71 | 289 | 9,506 |
| Scott Gutschewski | 67 | 71 | 77 | 74 | 289 | 9,506 |

## Memorial Tournament

*Muirfield Village Golf Club,* Dublin, Ohio
Par 36-36–72; 7,265 yards

June 2-5
purse, $5,500,000

| | SCORES | | | | TOTAL | MONEY |
|---|---|---|---|---|---|---|
| Bart Bryant | 69 | 69 | 66 | 68 | 272 | $990,000 |
| Fred Couples | 71 | 67 | 66 | 69 | 273 | 594,000 |
| Jeff Sluman | 65 | 71 | 68 | 72 | 276 | 286,000 |
| Bo Van Pelt | 67 | 72 | 69 | 68 | 276 | 286,000 |
| Tiger Woods | 69 | 68 | 71 | 68 | 276 | 286,000 |
| Jonathan Kaye | 67 | 70 | 68 | 72 | 277 | 191,125 |
| Nick O'Hern | 67 | 70 | 70 | 70 | 277 | 191,125 |
| K.J. Choi | 69 | 72 | 69 | 68 | 278 | 148,500 |

| | SCORES | | | | TOTAL | MONEY |
|---|---|---|---|---|---|---|
| Jim Furyk | 73 | 73 | 64 | 68 | 278 | 148,500 |
| Lucas Glover | 67 | 70 | 73 | 68 | 278 | 148,500 |
| Richard Green | 67 | 72 | 69 | 70 | 278 | 148,500 |
| David Toms | 70 | 70 | 64 | 74 | 278 | 148,500 |
| Woody Austin | 67 | 73 | 65 | 74 | 279 | 110,000 |
| Scott Verplank | 75 | 66 | 67 | 71 | 279 | 110,000 |
| Jerry Kelly | 70 | 71 | 69 | 70 | 280 | 96,250 |
| Rory Sabbatini | 66 | 74 | 69 | 71 | 280 | 96,250 |
| Fredrik Jacobson | 71 | 73 | 65 | 73 | 282 | 79,750 |
| Peter Lonard | 71 | 68 | 67 | 76 | 282 | 79,750 |
| Geoff Ogilvy | 70 | 71 | 66 | 75 | 282 | 79,750 |
| Greg Owen | 76 | 68 | 67 | 71 | 282 | 79,750 |
| Brad Faxon | 74 | 72 | 67 | 70 | 283 | 61,600 |
| Jay Haas | 69 | 70 | 71 | 73 | 283 | 61,600 |
| Stephen Leaney | 71 | 70 | 70 | 72 | 283 | 61,600 |
| Billy Andrade | 69 | 71 | 71 | 73 | 284 | 44,550 |
| Harrison Frazar | 69 | 68 | 73 | 74 | 284 | 44,550 |
| Tom Pernice, Jr. | 72 | 72 | 72 | 68 | 284 | 44,550 |
| Kenny Perry | 69 | 72 | 71 | 72 | 284 | 44,550 |
| Vaughn Taylor | 72 | 70 | 70 | 72 | 284 | 44,550 |
| Kirk Triplett | 74 | 69 | 71 | 70 | 284 | 44,550 |
| Stephen Ames | 70 | 73 | 68 | 74 | 285 | 34,925 |
| Chad Campbell | 74 | 70 | 68 | 73 | 285 | 34,925 |
| Ian Poulter | 68 | 72 | 73 | 72 | 285 | 34,925 |
| Joey Sindelar | 72 | 70 | 71 | 72 | 285 | 34,925 |
| Steve Flesch | 69 | 69 | 73 | 75 | 286 | 28,380 |
| Zach Johnson | 73 | 68 | 75 | 70 | 286 | 28,380 |
| Billy Mayfair | 72 | 70 | 68 | 76 | 286 | 28,380 |
| Carl Pettersson | 73 | 69 | 70 | 74 | 286 | 28,380 |
| Duffy Waldorf | 72 | 70 | 73 | 71 | 286 | 28,380 |
| Briny Baird | 71 | 73 | 73 | 70 | 287 | 22,000 |
| Alex Cejka | 69 | 71 | 73 | 74 | 287 | 22,000 |
| Ryan Palmer | 69 | 72 | 74 | 72 | 287 | 22,000 |
| Jesper Parnevik | 71 | 74 | 68 | 74 | 287 | 22,000 |
| Craig Parry | 69 | 74 | 77 | 67 | 287 | 22,000 |
| Phillip Price | 70 | 72 | 72 | 73 | 287 | 22,000 |
| Ernie Els | 73 | 71 | 72 | 72 | 288 | 15,415.72 |
| Tim Herron | 68 | 70 | 79 | 71 | 288 | 15,415.72 |
| Kevin Na | 73 | 69 | 74 | 72 | 288 | 15,415.72 |
| Arjun Atwal | 71 | 72 | 71 | 74 | 288 | 15,415.71 |
| Stewart Cink | 69 | 69 | 76 | 74 | 288 | 15,415.71 |
| Sean O'Hair | 69 | 73 | 69 | 77 | 288 | 15,415.71 |
| Jose Maria Olazabal | 70 | 74 | 71 | 73 | 288 | 15,415.71 |
| Robert Allenby | 71 | 74 | 70 | 74 | 289 | 12,826 |
| Chris DiMarco | 74 | 69 | 73 | 73 | 289 | 12,826 |
| Carlos Franco | 69 | 73 | 73 | 74 | 289 | 12,826 |
| Trevor Immelman | 70 | 74 | 72 | 73 | 289 | 12,826 |
| Adam Scott | 67 | 73 | 68 | 81 | 289 | 12,826 |
| Dudley Hart | 72 | 68 | 71 | 79 | 290 | 12,265 |
| Mark Hensby | 74 | 72 | 69 | 75 | 290 | 12,265 |
| Shigeki Maruyama | 73 | 72 | 72 | 73 | 290 | 12,265 |
| Bob Tway | 72 | 73 | 71 | 74 | 290 | 12,265 |
| Charles Howell | 77 | 69 | 73 | 72 | 291 | 11,715 |
| Scott McCarron | 71 | 72 | 72 | 76 | 291 | 11,715 |
| Joe Ogilvie | 67 | 74 | 77 | 73 | 291 | 11,715 |
| Corey Pavin | 73 | 71 | 73 | 74 | 291 | 11,715 |
| Patrick Sheehan | 72 | 70 | 77 | 72 | 291 | 11,715 |
| Paul Sheehan | 73 | 71 | 73 | 74 | 291 | 11,715 |
| Stuart Appleby | 76 | 70 | 74 | 72 | 292 | 11,055 |
| Bill Haas | 70 | 76 | 66 | 80 | 292 | 11,055 |

| | SCORES | | | | TOTAL | MONEY |
|---|---|---|---|---|---|---|
| Peter Jacobsen | 73 | 69 | 74 | 76 | 292 | 11,055 |
| Brandt Jobe | 75 | 71 | 74 | 72 | 292 | 11,055 |
| Mark O'Meara | 70 | 70 | 73 | 79 | 292 | 11,055 |
| Tim Petrovic | 72 | 74 | 73 | 73 | 292 | 11,055 |
| Rod Pampling | 70 | 72 | 73 | 78 | 293 | 10,615 |
| Euan Walters | 76 | 70 | 74 | 73 | 293 | 10,615 |
| Thomas Levet | 74 | 70 | 76 | 74 | 294 | 10,395 |
| Justin Rose | 72 | 72 | 75 | 75 | 294 | 10,395 |
| Paul Azinger | 72 | 72 | 71 | 80 | 295 | 10,230 |
| Steve Lowery | 70 | 75 | 74 | 77 | 296 | 10,120 |
| Bob Sowards | 73 | 73 | 74 | 77 | 297 | 10,010 |

## Booz Allen Classic

*Congressional Country Club,* Potomac, Maryland                                      June 9-12
Par 36-35–71; 7,232 yards                                                          purse, $5,000,000

| | SCORES | | | | TOTAL | MONEY |
|---|---|---|---|---|---|---|
| Sergio Garcia | 71 | 68 | 66 | 65 | 270 | $900,000 |
| Davis Love | 69 | 68 | 69 | 66 | 272 | 373,333.34 |
| Ben Crane | 67 | 70 | 68 | 67 | 272 | 373,333.33 |
| Adam Scott | 68 | 67 | 69 | 68 | 272 | 373,333.33 |
| Ryuji Imada | 70 | 71 | 66 | 67 | 274 | 200,000 |
| Rory Sabbatini | 69 | 68 | 68 | 70 | 275 | 180,000 |
| Joe Durant | 70 | 67 | 70 | 69 | 276 | 140,416.67 |
| Matt Gogel | 63 | 72 | 70 | 71 | 276 | 140,416.67 |
| Rod Pampling | 70 | 71 | 66 | 69 | 276 | 140,416.67 |
| Joey Snyder | 69 | 72 | 67 | 68 | 276 | 140,416.67 |
| Stuart Appleby | 70 | 69 | 65 | 72 | 276 | 140,416.66 |
| Ernie Els | 69 | 67 | 68 | 72 | 276 | 140,416.66 |
| Robert Allenby | 68 | 65 | 72 | 72 | 277 | 83,125 |
| Chad Campbell | 72 | 69 | 65 | 71 | 277 | 83,125 |
| Tim Clark | 67 | 70 | 71 | 69 | 277 | 83,125 |
| Chris DiMarco | 73 | 67 | 70 | 67 | 277 | 83,125 |
| Luke Donald | 70 | 67 | 67 | 73 | 277 | 83,125 |
| Steve Elkington | 68 | 67 | 69 | 73 | 277 | 83,125 |
| Paul Goydos | 67 | 69 | 73 | 68 | 277 | 83,125 |
| Tom Kite | 68 | 69 | 66 | 74 | 277 | 83,125 |
| Steve Allan | 67 | 70 | 70 | 71 | 278 | 46,937.50 |
| Craig Barlow | 71 | 68 | 68 | 71 | 278 | 46,937.50 |
| Alex Cejka | 69 | 68 | 68 | 73 | 278 | 46,937.50 |
| Bob Estes | 69 | 72 | 67 | 70 | 278 | 46,937.50 |
| Neal Lancaster | 69 | 70 | 69 | 70 | 278 | 46,937.50 |
| Brett Quigley | 72 | 68 | 66 | 72 | 278 | 46,937.50 |
| Kirk Triplett | 69 | 69 | 69 | 71 | 278 | 46,937.50 |
| Lee Westwood | 66 | 69 | 69 | 74 | 278 | 46,937.50 |
| Jason Bohn | 70 | 69 | 68 | 72 | 279 | 30,437.50 |
| Fred Funk | 73 | 68 | 67 | 71 | 279 | 30,437.50 |
| Fredrik Jacobson | 66 | 71 | 75 | 67 | 279 | 30,437.50 |
| Shigeki Maruyama | 69 | 67 | 70 | 73 | 279 | 30,437.50 |
| Phil Mickelson | 71 | 67 | 67 | 74 | 279 | 30,437.50 |
| Geoff Ogilvy | 68 | 69 | 72 | 70 | 279 | 30,437.50 |
| Vijay Singh | 71 | 69 | 68 | 71 | 279 | 30,437.50 |
| Brett Wetterich | 66 | 74 | 65 | 74 | 279 | 30,437.50 |
| Jim Furyk | 67 | 69 | 70 | 74 | 280 | 23,000 |
| Zach Johnson | 73 | 66 | 66 | 75 | 280 | 23,000 |
| J.L. Lewis | 71 | 69 | 68 | 72 | 280 | 23,000 |

| | SCORES | | | | TOTAL | MONEY |
|---|---|---|---|---|---|---|
| Billy Mayfair | 68 | 71 | 71 | 70 | 280 | 23,000 |
| Jeff Maggert | 69 | 69 | 70 | 73 | 281 | 19,000 |
| Carl Pettersson | 69 | 71 | 70 | 71 | 281 | 19,000 |
| Kevin Stadler | 65 | 73 | 73 | 70 | 281 | 19,000 |
| Bo Van Pelt | 69 | 70 | 72 | 70 | 281 | 19,000 |
| Tommy Armour | 68 | 68 | 71 | 75 | 282 | 16,000 |
| Brandt Jobe | 70 | 70 | 73 | 69 | 282 | 16,000 |
| Tom Pernice, Jr. | 68 | 71 | 73 | 71 | 283 | 13,733.34 |
| Bill Glasson | 69 | 70 | 69 | 75 | 283 | 13,733.33 |
| Ryan Palmer | 72 | 66 | 71 | 74 | 283 | 13,733.33 |
| Tom Byrum | 68 | 71 | 69 | 76 | 284 | 11,812.50 |
| Daniel Chopra | 71 | 69 | 72 | 72 | 284 | 11,812.50 |
| Brad Faxon | 70 | 71 | 69 | 74 | 284 | 11,812.50 |
| Richard Green | 72 | 69 | 71 | 72 | 284 | 11,812.50 |
| Jonathan Kaye | 72 | 68 | 72 | 72 | 284 | 11,812.50 |
| Brenden Pappas | 72 | 68 | 74 | 70 | 284 | 11,812.50 |
| Loren Roberts | 72 | 69 | 69 | 74 | 284 | 11,812.50 |
| Joey Sindelar | 70 | 71 | 72 | 71 | 284 | 11,812.50 |
| James Driscoll | 70 | 71 | 71 | 73 | 285 | 11,200 |
| Retief Goosen | 70 | 70 | 72 | 74 | 286 | 10,950 |
| Len Mattiace | 71 | 70 | 73 | 72 | 286 | 10,950 |
| Jeff Sluman | 71 | 70 | 71 | 74 | 286 | 10,950 |
| Kevin Sutherland | 67 | 71 | 73 | 75 | 286 | 10,950 |
| Michael Allen | 67 | 74 | 75 | 71 | 287 | 10,650 |
| Olin Browne | 71 | 70 | 75 | 71 | 287 | 10,650 |
| Rocco Mediate | 70 | 68 | 76 | 74 | 288 | 10,450 |
| Ted Purdy | 71 | 68 | 73 | 76 | 288 | 10,450 |
| Jonathan Byrd | 71 | 67 | 72 | 79 | 289 | 10,250 |
| Dennis Paulson | 71 | 70 | 76 | 72 | 289 | 10,250 |
| Mark Calcavecchia | 69 | 72 | 71 | 78 | 290 | 10,050 |
| Jerry Kelly | 70 | 69 | 73 | 78 | 290 | 10,050 |

## U.S. Open Championship

*Pinehurst No. 2*, Pinehurst, North Carolina
Par 35-35–70; 7,214 yards

June 16-19
purse, $6,250,000

| | SCORES | | | | TOTAL | MONEY |
|---|---|---|---|---|---|---|
| Michael Campbell | 71 | 69 | 71 | 69 | 280 | $1,170,000 |
| Tiger Woods | 70 | 71 | 72 | 69 | 282 | 700,000 |
| Sergio Garcia | 71 | 69 | 75 | 70 | 285 | 320,039 |
| Tim Clark | 76 | 69 | 70 | 70 | 285 | 320,039 |
| Mark Hensby | 71 | 68 | 72 | 74 | 285 | 320,039 |
| Davis Love | 77 | 70 | 70 | 69 | 286 | 187,813 |
| Rocco Mediate | 67 | 74 | 74 | 71 | 286 | 187,813 |
| Vijay Singh | 70 | 70 | 74 | 72 | 286 | 187,813 |
| Nick Price | 72 | 71 | 72 | 72 | 287 | 150,834 |
| Arron Oberholser | 76 | 67 | 71 | 73 | 287 | 150,834 |
| Bob Estes | 70 | 73 | 75 | 70 | 288 | 123,857 |
| Corey Pavin | 73 | 72 | 70 | 73 | 288 | 123,857 |
| Peter Hedblom | 77 | 66 | 70 | 75 | 288 | 123,857 |
| Retief Goosen | 68 | 70 | 69 | 81 | 288 | 123,857 |
| Stewart Cink | 73 | 74 | 73 | 69 | 289 | 88,120 |
| Fred Couples | 71 | 74 | 74 | 70 | 289 | 88,120 |
| Ernie Els | 71 | 76 | 72 | 70 | 289 | 88,120 |
| Ryuji Imada | 77 | 68 | 73 | 71 | 289 | 88,120 |
| John Cook | 71 | 76 | 70 | 72 | 289 | 88,120 |

| | SCORES | | | | TOTAL | MONEY |
|---|---|---|---|---|---|---|
| Peter Jacobsen | 72 | 73 | 69 | 75 | 289 | 88,120 |
| K.J. Choi | 69 | 70 | 74 | 76 | 289 | 88,120 |
| David Toms | 70 | 72 | 70 | 77 | 289 | 88,120 |
| Fred Funk | 73 | 71 | 76 | 70 | 290 | 59,633 |
| Justin Leonard | 76 | 71 | 70 | 73 | 290 | 59,633 |
| Paul Claxton | 72 | 72 | 72 | 74 | 290 | 59,633 |
| Kenny Perry | 75 | 70 | 71 | 74 | 290 | 59,633 |
| Olin Browne | 67 | 71 | 72 | 80 | 290 | 59,633 |
| *Matt Every | 75 | 73 | 73 | 70 | 291 | |
| Geoff Ogilvy | 72 | 74 | 71 | 74 | 291 | 44,486 |
| Jim Furyk | 71 | 70 | 75 | 75 | 291 | 44,486 |
| Adam Scott | 70 | 71 | 74 | 76 | 291 | 44,486 |
| Steve Allan | 72 | 69 | 73 | 77 | 291 | 44,486 |
| Steve Elkington | 74 | 69 | 79 | 70 | 292 | 35,759 |
| Brandt Jobe | 68 | 73 | 79 | 72 | 292 | 35,759 |
| Phil Mickelson | 69 | 77 | 72 | 74 | 292 | 35,759 |
| Bernhard Langer | 74 | 73 | 71 | 74 | 292 | 35,759 |
| Angel Cabrera | 71 | 73 | 73 | 75 | 292 | 35,759 |
| Ted Purdy | 73 | 71 | 73 | 75 | 292 | 35,759 |
| Shigeki Maruyama | 71 | 74 | 72 | 75 | 292 | 35,759 |
| Tim Herron | 74 | 73 | 70 | 75 | 292 | 35,759 |
| Lee Westwood | 68 | 72 | 73 | 79 | 292 | 35,759 |
| Mike Weir | 75 | 72 | 75 | 71 | 293 | 26,223 |
| Tom Pernice | 74 | 73 | 73 | 73 | 293 | 26,223 |
| Chad Campbell | 77 | 71 | 72 | 73 | 293 | 26,223 |
| Peter Lonard | 71 | 74 | 74 | 74 | 293 | 26,223 |
| Rob Rashell | 74 | 72 | 73 | 74 | 293 | 26,223 |
| Colin Montgomerie | 72 | 75 | 72 | 74 | 293 | 26,223 |
| Paul McGinley | 76 | 72 | 71 | 74 | 293 | 26,223 |
| J.L. Lewis | 75 | 73 | 76 | 70 | 294 | 20,275 |
| Nick O'Hern | 72 | 71 | 78 | 73 | 294 | 20,275 |
| Jason Gore | 71 | 67 | 72 | 84 | 294 | 20,275 |
| Richard Green | 72 | 72 | 78 | 73 | 295 | 17,667 |
| Soren Kjeldsen | 74 | 71 | 77 | 73 | 295 | 17,667 |
| Thomas Levet | 75 | 73 | 73 | 74 | 295 | 17,667 |
| Thomas Bjorn | 71 | 74 | 75 | 75 | 295 | 17,667 |
| Nick Dougherty | 72 | 74 | 74 | 75 | 295 | 17,667 |
| Frank Lickliter | 75 | 73 | 78 | 70 | 296 | 15,223 |
| *Ryan Moore | 75 | 73 | 75 | 73 | 296 | |
| J.J. Henry | 73 | 73 | 76 | 74 | 296 | 15,223 |
| Lee Janzen | 74 | 74 | 74 | 74 | 296 | 15,223 |
| Tommy Armour | 70 | 72 | 79 | 75 | 296 | 15,223 |
| Jonathan Lomas | 72 | 74 | 75 | 75 | 296 | 15,223 |
| Ian Poulter | 77 | 69 | 74 | 76 | 296 | 15,223 |
| Steve Jones | 69 | 74 | 74 | 79 | 296 | 15,223 |
| Keiichiro Fukabori | 74 | 67 | 75 | 80 | 296 | 15,223 |
| Luke Donald | 69 | 73 | 74 | 80 | 296 | 15,223 |
| Michael Allen | 73 | 72 | 77 | 75 | 297 | 13,553 |
| Steve Flesch | 72 | 71 | 78 | 76 | 297 | 13,553 |
| John Mallinger | 74 | 72 | 73 | 78 | 297 | 13,553 |
| Bill Glasson | 74 | 73 | 71 | 79 | 297 | 13,553 |
| Stephen Ames | 71 | 75 | 76 | 76 | 298 | 12,551 |
| Rory Sabbatini | 72 | 74 | 76 | 76 | 298 | 12,551 |
| D.J. Brigman | 74 | 73 | 75 | 76 | 298 | 12,551 |
| J.P. Hayes | 77 | 71 | 74 | 76 | 298 | 12,551 |
| John Daly | 74 | 72 | 77 | 76 | 299 | 11,674 |
| Omar Uresti | 75 | 73 | 75 | 76 | 299 | 11,674 |
| Charles Howell | 77 | 68 | 73 | 81 | 299 | 11,674 |
| Bob Tway | 71 | 75 | 79 | 75 | 300 | 11,048 |
| Jeff Maggert | 72 | 75 | 75 | 78 | 300 | 11,048 |

| | SCORES | | | | TOTAL | MONEY |
|---|---|---|---|---|---|---|
| Chris Nallen | 76 | 72 | 78 | 75 | 301 | 10,547 |
| Graeme McDowell | 74 | 74 | 72 | 81 | 301 | 10,547 |
| Craig Barlow | 76 | 71 | 76 | 80 | 303 | 10,171 |
| Jerry Kelly | 76 | 71 | 78 | 80 | 305 | 9,921 |

**Out of Final 36 Holes**

| | | | |
|---|---|---|---|
| Peter Hanson | 76 | 73 | 149 |
| Shingo Katayama | 74 | 75 | 149 |
| Robert Allenby | 72 | 77 | 149 |
| Carlos Franco | 74 | 75 | 149 |
| Tom Lehman | 77 | 72 | 149 |
| Robert Karlsson | 75 | 74 | 149 |
| Zach Johnson | 74 | 75 | 149 |
| Toru Taniguchi | 70 | 79 | 149 |
| Euan Walters | 76 | 73 | 149 |
| Jerry Smith | 78 | 71 | 149 |
| Derek Brown | 75 | 74 | 149 |
| John Rollins | 75 | 74 | 149 |
| Matt Kuchar | 75 | 74 | 149 |
| Todd Hamilton | 75 | 74 | 149 |
| Eric Meichtry | 75 | 74 | 149 |
| Spencer Levin | 73 | 77 | 150 |
| *Trip Kuehne | 75 | 75 | 150 |
| Jose-Filipe Lima | 75 | 75 | 150 |
| John Merrick | 77 | 73 | 150 |
| Scott Verplank | 76 | 74 | 150 |
| Lee Rinker | 76 | 74 | 150 |
| Troy Kelly | 83 | 67 | 150 |
| Padraig Harrington | 77 | 74 | 151 |
| Stephen Gallacher | 79 | 72 | 151 |
| Ian Leggatt | 75 | 76 | 151 |
| Eric Axley | 81 | 70 | 151 |
| Nick Gilliam | 76 | 75 | 151 |
| David Oh | 74 | 77 | 151 |
| James Driscoll | 76 | 75 | 151 |
| Shaun Micheel | 78 | 74 | 152 |
| Stuart Appleby | 81 | 71 | 152 |
| David Duval | 76 | 76 | 152 |
| Craig Parry | 77 | 75 | 152 |
| Jay Haas | 82 | 70 | 152 |
| Steve Lowery | 78 | 74 | 152 |
| Steven Conran | 77 | 75 | 152 |
| Patrick Damron | 79 | 73 | 152 |
| Kyle Willmann | 75 | 77 | 152 |
| Miguel Angel Jimenez | 79 | 74 | 153 |
| Carl Pettersson | 77 | 76 | 153 |
| Bart Bryant | 79 | 74 | 153 |
| Casey Wittenberg | 75 | 78 | 153 |
| Clint Jensen | 77 | 76 | 153 |
| Y.E. Yang | 74 | 79 | 153 |
| *Luke List | 82 | 71 | 153 |
| Chris DiMarco | 71 | 82 | 153 |
| Scott Parel | 76 | 77 | 153 |
| Josh McCumber | 73 | 80 | 153 |
| Joe Ogilvie | 79 | 75 | 154 |
| Rich Beem | 78 | 76 | 154 |
| Brandt Snedeker | 79 | 75 | 154 |
| Scott McCarron | 76 | 78 | 154 |
| *David Denham | 77 | 77 | 154 |

| | SCORES | | | TOTAL |
|---|---|---|---|---|
| Robert Gamez | 77 | 78 | | 155 |
| Scott Gibson | 77 | 78 | | 155 |
| Nick Jones | 80 | 75 | | 155 |
| Len Mattiace | 76 | 79 | | 155 |
| *Michael Putnam | 76 | 79 | | 155 |
| Franklin Langham | 74 | 81 | | 155 |
| Ben Curtis | 76 | 80 | | 156 |
| Aaron Barber | 74 | 82 | | 156 |
| David Hearn | 77 | 79 | | 156 |
| Simon Dyson | 79 | 78 | | 157 |
| Michael Ruiz | 79 | 79 | | 158 |
| *Lee Williams | 79 | 79 | | 158 |
| Jim Benepe | 82 | 76 | | 158 |
| Rod Pampling | 80 | 79 | | 159 |
| *Pierre-Henri Soero | 83 | 77 | | 160 |
| Sal Spallone | 79 | 81 | | 160 |
| Wil Collins | 82 | 79 | | 161 |
| Conrad Ray | 80 | 84 | | 164 |
| David Howell | 74 | | | WD |
| Paul Casey | 85 | | | WD |

(Professionals who did not complete 72 holes received $2,000.)

## Barclays Classic

*Westchester Country Club, West Course,* Harrison, New York                June 23-26
Par 36-35–71; 6,751 yards                                        purse, $5,750,000

| | SCORES | | | | TOTAL | MONEY |
|---|---|---|---|---|---|---|
| Padraig Harrington | 71 | 65 | 68 | 70 | 274 | $1,035,000 |
| Jim Furyk | 65 | 69 | 70 | 71 | 275 | 621,000 |
| Brad Faxon | 72 | 68 | 66 | 73 | 279 | 299,000 |
| Brian Gay | 69 | 66 | 71 | 73 | 279 | 299,000 |
| Kenny Perry | 68 | 68 | 72 | 71 | 279 | 299,000 |
| Dean Wilson | 72 | 71 | 66 | 71 | 280 | 207,000 |
| Justin Leonard | 72 | 71 | 67 | 71 | 281 | 173,218.75 |
| Billy Mayfair | 72 | 68 | 75 | 66 | 281 | 173,218.75 |
| John Senden | 69 | 67 | 72 | 73 | 281 | 173,218.75 |
| Vijay Singh | 68 | 71 | 69 | 73 | 281 | 173,218.75 |
| Tom Pernice, Jr. | 70 | 69 | 72 | 71 | 282 | 143,750 |
| Jeff Brehaut | 70 | 70 | 72 | 71 | 283 | 112,700 |
| Tim Clark | 74 | 70 | 68 | 71 | 283 | 112,700 |
| Chris DiMarco | 71 | 72 | 69 | 71 | 283 | 112,700 |
| Dudley Hart | 71 | 69 | 70 | 73 | 283 | 112,700 |
| Len Mattiace | 71 | 65 | 73 | 74 | 283 | 112,700 |
| Brett Quigley | 73 | 68 | 68 | 75 | 284 | 89,125 |
| Loren Roberts | 74 | 69 | 72 | 69 | 284 | 89,125 |
| J.P. Hayes | 70 | 72 | 73 | 70 | 285 | 74,750 |
| Franklin Langham | 73 | 71 | 68 | 73 | 285 | 74,750 |
| Omar Uresti | 70 | 73 | 74 | 68 | 285 | 74,750 |
| Michael Allen | 72 | 71 | 74 | 69 | 286 | 48,012.50 |
| Craig Barlow | 76 | 67 | 71 | 72 | 286 | 48,012.50 |
| Sergio Garcia | 72 | 71 | 73 | 70 | 286 | 48,012.50 |
| Lucas Glover | 70 | 73 | 72 | 71 | 286 | 48,012.50 |
| Paul Gow | 70 | 74 | 70 | 72 | 286 | 48,012.50 |
| Michael Long | 72 | 71 | 71 | 72 | 286 | 48,012.50 |
| Greg Owen | 72 | 73 | 71 | 70 | 286 | 48,012.50 |

|  | SCORES | | | | TOTAL | MONEY |
|---|---|---|---|---|---|---|
| Pat Perez | 70 | 71 | 68 | 77 | 286 | 48,012.50 |
| Kevin Sutherland | 70 | 68 | 74 | 74 | 286 | 48,012.50 |
| Hidemichi Tanaka | 68 | 68 | 75 | 75 | 286 | 48,012.50 |
| Woody Austin | 72 | 73 | 70 | 72 | 287 | 30,475 |
| Tom Byrum | 70 | 71 | 75 | 71 | 287 | 30,475 |
| Fred Funk | 69 | 73 | 74 | 71 | 287 | 30,475 |
| Lee Janzen | 73 | 72 | 71 | 71 | 287 | 30,475 |
| Neal Lancaster | 72 | 71 | 70 | 74 | 287 | 30,475 |
| Stephen Leaney | 72 | 73 | 68 | 74 | 287 | 30,475 |
| Ian Leggatt | 68 | 73 | 71 | 75 | 287 | 30,475 |
| Graeme McDowell | 73 | 71 | 67 | 76 | 287 | 30,475 |
| Briny Baird | 74 | 70 | 70 | 74 | 288 | 21,850 |
| Matt Gogel | 71 | 74 | 70 | 73 | 288 | 21,850 |
| Mathias Gronberg | 70 | 70 | 71 | 77 | 288 | 21,850 |
| Joe Ogilvie | 69 | 71 | 75 | 73 | 288 | 21,850 |
| Corey Pavin | 77 | 64 | 74 | 73 | 288 | 21,850 |
| Joey Snyder | 74 | 71 | 73 | 70 | 288 | 21,850 |
| Danny Briggs | 72 | 72 | 72 | 73 | 289 | 15,939 |
| Bill Glasson | 70 | 71 | 78 | 70 | 289 | 15,939 |
| J.L. Lewis | 69 | 73 | 72 | 75 | 289 | 15,939 |
| Hunter Mahan | 75 | 67 | 73 | 74 | 289 | 15,939 |
| Sean O'Hair | 72 | 69 | 72 | 76 | 289 | 15,939 |
| Alex Cejka | 72 | 72 | 76 | 70 | 290 | 13,531.67 |
| Robert Damron | 76 | 69 | 73 | 72 | 290 | 13,531.67 |
| Ryan Moore | 71 | 74 | 73 | 72 | 290 | 13,531.67 |
| Heath Slocum | 74 | 71 | 72 | 73 | 290 | 13,531.67 |
| Todd Fischer | 74 | 70 | 68 | 78 | 290 | 13,531.66 |
| Larry Mize | 70 | 73 | 70 | 77 | 290 | 13,531.66 |
| Brian Bateman | 68 | 77 | 70 | 76 | 291 | 12,822.50 |
| Steve Elkington | 74 | 71 | 74 | 72 | 291 | 12,822.50 |
| Tjaart van der Walt | 73 | 72 | 74 | 72 | 291 | 12,822.50 |
| Charlie Wi | 72 | 69 | 75 | 75 | 291 | 12,822.50 |
| Fredrik Jacobson | 72 | 71 | 72 | 77 | 292 | 12,477.50 |
| Justin Rose | 74 | 68 | 76 | 74 | 292 | 12,477.50 |
| Gavin Coles | 72 | 73 | 70 | 78 | 293 | 12,190 |
| John Rollins | 68 | 74 | 72 | 79 | 293 | 12,190 |
| Patrick Sheehan | 69 | 75 | 75 | 74 | 293 | 12,190 |
| Brendan Jones | 72 | 71 | 72 | 79 | 294 | 11,845 |
| Rocco Mediate | 77 | 67 | 77 | 73 | 294 | 11,845 |
| Jeff Sluman | 71 | 74 | 74 | 75 | 294 | 11,845 |
| Mark Calcavecchia | 76 | 69 | 77 | 74 | 296 | 11,615 |
| Billy Andrade | 72 | 73 | 73 | 80 | 298 | 11,500 |
| Steve Allan | 71 | 74 | 77 | 77 | 299 | 11,385 |
| Tom Gillis | 71 | 71 | 77 | 84 | 303 | 11,270 |

## Cialis Western Open

*Cog Hill Golf & Country Club, Dubsdread Course,*
Lemont, Illinois
Par 35-36–71; 7,326 yards

June 30-July 3
purse, $5,000,000

|  | SCORES | | | | TOTAL | MONEY |
|---|---|---|---|---|---|---|
| Jim Furyk | 64 | 70 | 67 | 69 | 270 | $900,000 |
| Tiger Woods | 73 | 66 | 67 | 66 | 272 | 540,000 |
| Ben Curtis | 64 | 71 | 66 | 74 | 275 | 340,000 |
| Billy Mayfair | 72 | 69 | 67 | 68 | 276 | 240,000 |
| Pat Perez | 74 | 66 | 67 | 70 | 277 | 190,000 |

| | SCORES | | | | TOTAL | MONEY |
|---|---|---|---|---|---|---|
| Brett Quigley | 69 | 69 | 69 | 70 | 277 | 190,000 |
| Charles Warren | 71 | 69 | 70 | 68 | 278 | 155,833.34 |
| Shaun Micheel | 71 | 67 | 68 | 72 | 278 | 155,833.33 |
| Heath Slocum | 72 | 70 | 67 | 69 | 278 | 155,833.33 |
| Tim Herron | 68 | 66 | 70 | 75 | 279 | 125,000 |
| Fredrik Jacobson | 73 | 68 | 70 | 68 | 279 | 125,000 |
| Bob Tway | 74 | 68 | 68 | 69 | 279 | 125,000 |
| Chris Couch | 66 | 67 | 74 | 73 | 280 | 96,666.67 |
| Craig Perks | 67 | 71 | 70 | 72 | 280 | 96,666.67 |
| Vijay Singh | 72 | 70 | 65 | 73 | 280 | 96,666.66 |
| Robert Allenby | 66 | 75 | 72 | 68 | 281 | 75,000 |
| Marco Dawson | 73 | 68 | 70 | 70 | 281 | 75,000 |
| Todd Fischer | 64 | 72 | 75 | 70 | 281 | 75,000 |
| Mark Hensby | 75 | 65 | 69 | 72 | 281 | 75,000 |
| D.J. Trahan | 71 | 69 | 69 | 72 | 281 | 75,000 |
| James Driscoll | 68 | 74 | 70 | 70 | 282 | 48,357.15 |
| Hunter Mahan | 70 | 71 | 71 | 70 | 282 | 48,357.15 |
| Alex Cejka | 71 | 70 | 70 | 71 | 282 | 48,357.14 |
| Steve Flesch | 69 | 67 | 73 | 73 | 282 | 48,357.14 |
| Brian Gay | 68 | 70 | 70 | 74 | 282 | 48,357.14 |
| Jerry Kelly | 70 | 70 | 69 | 73 | 282 | 48,357.14 |
| Duffy Waldorf | 69 | 65 | 74 | 74 | 282 | 48,357.14 |
| Stuart Appleby | 67 | 71 | 72 | 73 | 283 | 33,250 |
| Luke Donald | 70 | 72 | 73 | 68 | 283 | 33,250 |
| David Hearn | 71 | 70 | 69 | 73 | 283 | 33,250 |
| D.A. Points | 70 | 70 | 71 | 72 | 283 | 33,250 |
| Joey Sindelar | 68 | 72 | 73 | 70 | 283 | 33,250 |
| Chris Smith | 69 | 71 | 70 | 73 | 283 | 33,250 |
| Stephen Ames | 70 | 71 | 73 | 70 | 284 | 25,250 |
| Robert Damron | 71 | 71 | 72 | 70 | 284 | 25,250 |
| Bernhard Langer | 73 | 68 | 71 | 72 | 284 | 25,250 |
| Sean O'Hair | 70 | 71 | 75 | 68 | 284 | 25,250 |
| Geoff Ogilvy | 72 | 70 | 72 | 70 | 284 | 25,250 |
| Scott Verplank | 69 | 70 | 71 | 74 | 284 | 25,250 |
| Jonathan Byrd | 71 | 67 | 71 | 76 | 285 | 16,300 |
| Chad Campbell | 66 | 71 | 72 | 76 | 285 | 16,300 |
| Bob Estes | 69 | 72 | 73 | 71 | 285 | 16,300 |
| Robert Gamez | 68 | 71 | 72 | 74 | 285 | 16,300 |
| Neal Lancaster | 70 | 70 | 69 | 76 | 285 | 16,300 |
| Frank Lickliter | 72 | 67 | 75 | 71 | 285 | 16,300 |
| Scott McCarron | 70 | 67 | 72 | 76 | 285 | 16,300 |
| Scott Piercy | 72 | 69 | 72 | 72 | 285 | 16,300 |
| Ted Purdy | 72 | 66 | 75 | 72 | 285 | 16,300 |
| John Senden | 73 | 69 | 72 | 71 | 285 | 16,300 |
| Camilo Villegas | 73 | 68 | 71 | 73 | 285 | 16,300 |
| Brett Wetterich | 69 | 71 | 74 | 71 | 285 | 16,300 |
| Joe Durant | 72 | 67 | 73 | 74 | 286 | 11,900 |
| Roland Thatcher | 70 | 70 | 69 | 77 | 286 | 11,900 |
| Mark Calcavecchia | 70 | 72 | 70 | 75 | 287 | 11,550 |
| Todd Hamilton | 70 | 71 | 68 | 78 | 287 | 11,550 |
| K.J. Choi | 71 | 69 | 75 | 73 | 288 | 11,250 |
| Harrison Frazar | 66 | 74 | 73 | 75 | 288 | 11,250 |
| J.J. Henry | 70 | 72 | 75 | 71 | 288 | 11,250 |
| Joey Snyder | 69 | 72 | 71 | 76 | 288 | 11,250 |
| Woody Austin | 70 | 69 | 75 | 75 | 289 | 10,900 |
| Kent Jones | 68 | 73 | 72 | 76 | 289 | 10,900 |
| Franklin Langham | 71 | 71 | 74 | 73 | 289 | 10,900 |
| Chris Anderson | 72 | 67 | 77 | 74 | 290 | 10,650 |
| Brandt Jobe | 71 | 71 | 70 | 78 | 290 | 10,650 |
| John Cook | 73 | 68 | 78 | 73 | 292 | 10,500 |

| | SCORES | | | | TOTAL | MONEY |
|---|---|---|---|---|---|---|
| Jim Carter | 71 | 70 | 76 | 76 | 293 | 10,400 |
| Michael Long | 71 | 69 | 75 | 80 | 295 | 10,250 |
| Ryan Palmer | 70 | 71 | 74 | 80 | 295 | 10,250 |
| John Huston | 69 | 73 | 78 | 77 | 297 | 10,100 |
| Mike Small | 69 | 73 | 78 | 80 | 300 | 10,000 |

## John Deere Classic

*TPC at Deere Run,* Silvis, Illinois  
Par 35-36–71; 7,193 yards

July 7-10  
purse, $4,000,000

| | SCORES | | | | TOTAL | MONEY |
|---|---|---|---|---|---|---|
| Sean O'Hair | 66 | 69 | 68 | 65 | 268 | $720,000 |
| Robert Damron | 65 | 68 | 69 | 67 | 269 | 352,000 |
| Hank Kuehne | 68 | 66 | 67 | 68 | 269 | 352,000 |
| Mark Hensby | 70 | 66 | 70 | 64 | 270 | 165,333.34 |
| J.L. Lewis | 64 | 65 | 69 | 72 | 270 | 165,333.33 |
| Wes Short, Jr. | 66 | 67 | 71 | 66 | 270 | 165,333.33 |
| Hunter Mahan | 63 | 68 | 74 | 66 | 271 | 124,666.67 |
| Shigeki Maruyama | 68 | 63 | 72 | 68 | 271 | 124,666.67 |
| Richard Johnson | 65 | 68 | 68 | 70 | 271 | 124,666.66 |
| Jeff Brehaut | 66 | 70 | 66 | 70 | 272 | 100,000 |
| Kevin Stadler | 72 | 63 | 69 | 68 | 272 | 100,000 |
| D.J. Trahan | 68 | 69 | 67 | 68 | 272 | 100,000 |
| Jonathan Byrd | 70 | 69 | 70 | 64 | 273 | 68,571.43 |
| Carlos Franco | 68 | 68 | 67 | 70 | 273 | 68,571.43 |
| Todd Hamilton | 68 | 67 | 70 | 68 | 273 | 68,571.43 |
| Matt Kuchar | 71 | 67 | 67 | 68 | 273 | 68,571.43 |
| Heath Slocum | 68 | 69 | 67 | 69 | 273 | 68,571.43 |
| Esteban Toledo | 70 | 67 | 69 | 67 | 273 | 68,571.43 |
| Craig Bowden | 65 | 68 | 68 | 72 | 273 | 68,571.42 |
| Justin Bolli | 69 | 66 | 73 | 66 | 274 | 39,155.56 |
| Robert Gamez | 74 | 65 | 67 | 68 | 274 | 39,155.56 |
| Ryan Palmer | 66 | 68 | 74 | 66 | 274 | 39,155.56 |
| Joey Sindelar | 70 | 69 | 69 | 66 | 274 | 39,155.56 |
| Garrett Willis | 66 | 72 | 68 | 68 | 274 | 39,155.56 |
| Woody Austin | 72 | 65 | 68 | 69 | 274 | 39,155.55 |
| Brandt Jobe | 66 | 66 | 72 | 70 | 274 | 39,155.55 |
| Brendan Jones | 66 | 73 | 66 | 69 | 274 | 39,155.55 |
| Phillip Price | 69 | 69 | 67 | 69 | 274 | 39,155.55 |
| Billy Mayfair | 68 | 69 | 70 | 68 | 275 | 24,885.72 |
| John Senden | 69 | 67 | 69 | 70 | 275 | 24,885.72 |
| Brett Wetterich | 68 | 68 | 70 | 69 | 275 | 24,885.72 |
| Stewart Cink | 68 | 70 | 67 | 70 | 275 | 24,885.71 |
| Steve Lowery | 66 | 73 | 70 | 66 | 275 | 24,885.71 |
| Joey Snyder | 67 | 66 | 70 | 72 | 275 | 24,885.71 |
| Omar Uresti | 72 | 66 | 73 | 64 | 275 | 24,885.71 |
| Matt Gogel | 70 | 69 | 69 | 68 | 276 | 19,250 |
| Glen Hnatiuk | 65 | 71 | 69 | 71 | 276 | 19,250 |
| Zach Johnson | 68 | 69 | 66 | 73 | 276 | 19,250 |
| Kevin Sutherland | 70 | 69 | 68 | 69 | 276 | 19,250 |
| Tom Gillis | 68 | 69 | 70 | 70 | 277 | 15,200 |
| John Huston | 67 | 71 | 72 | 67 | 277 | 15,200 |
| Michael Long | 73 | 66 | 69 | 69 | 277 | 15,200 |
| Roland Thatcher | 71 | 68 | 69 | 69 | 277 | 15,200 |
| David Toms | 67 | 72 | 69 | 69 | 277 | 15,200 |
| Duffy Waldorf | 66 | 71 | 69 | 71 | 277 | 15,200 |

| | SCORES | | | TOTAL | MONEY |
|---|---|---|---|---|---|
| Guy Boros | 68 | 69 69 | 72 | 278 | 10,080 |
| Paul Claxton | 66 | 72 70 | 70 | 278 | 10,080 |
| Matt Davidson | 71 | 67 71 | 69 | 278 | 10,080 |
| Scott Gutschewski | 71 | 66 70 | 71 | 278 | 10,080 |
| Dudley Hart | 69 | 70 70 | 69 | 278 | 10,080 |
| David Hearn | 68 | 70 69 | 71 | 278 | 10,080 |
| Steve Jones | 68 | 71 71 | 68 | 278 | 10,080 |
| Will MacKenzie | 67 | 67 74 | 70 | 278 | 10,080 |
| John Maginnes | 70 | 67 68 | 73 | 278 | 10,080 |
| Blaine McCallister | 68 | 67 72 | 71 | 278 | 10,080 |
| Patrick Sheehan | 69 | 68 72 | 69 | 278 | 10,080 |
| Steve Stricker | 71 | 66 71 | 70 | 278 | 10,080 |
| Arjun Atwal | 70 | 68 69 | 72 | 279 | 8,920 |
| Jason Knutzon | 69 | 70 70 | 70 | 279 | 8,920 |
| Bob Heintz | 69 | 68 70 | 73 | 280 | 8,720 |
| Stephen Leaney | 70 | 68 69 | 73 | 280 | 8,720 |
| Darron Stiles | 68 | 68 71 | 73 | 280 | 8,720 |
| Paul Goydos | 69 | 68 75 | 69 | 281 | 8,480 |
| Kent Jones | 70 | 69 71 | 71 | 281 | 8,480 |
| Brenden Pappas | 67 | 71 72 | 71 | 281 | 8,480 |
| Michael Bradley | 69 | 70 72 | 71 | 282 | 8,240 |
| Glen Day | 66 | 70 76 | 70 | 282 | 8,240 |
| Jeff Sluman | 67 | 66 77 | 72 | 282 | 8,240 |
| Jeff Maggert | 71 | 67 73 | 72 | 283 | 8,080 |
| Dean Wilson | 67 | 69 74 | 74 | 284 | 8,000 |
| Mario Tiziani | 71 | 68 71 | 75 | 285 | 7,920 |
| Mike Springer | 68 | 71 73 | 74 | 286 | 7,840 |
| Olin Browne | 69 | 70 74 | 74 | 287 | 7,680 |
| Arron Oberholser | 68 | 71 74 | 74 | 287 | 7,680 |
| Grant Waite | 68 | 70 78 | 71 | 287 | 7,680 |
| Ted Purdy | 69 | 68 75 | 78 | 290 | 7,520 |

## The Open Championship

See European Tours chapter.

## B.C. Open

*En-Joie Golf Club*, Endicott, New York
Par 37-35–72; 6,974 yards

July 14-17
purse, $3,000,000

| | SCORES | | | TOTAL | MONEY |
|---|---|---|---|---|---|
| Jason Bohn | 64 | 68 66 | 66 | 264 | $540,000 |
| J.P. Hayes | 67 | 68 64 | 66 | 265 | 198,000 |
| Brendan Jones | 67 | 64 66 | 68 | 265 | 198,000 |
| Ryan Palmer | 67 | 64 67 | 67 | 265 | 198,000 |
| John Rollins | 67 | 68 64 | 66 | 265 | 198,000 |
| Michael Allen | 72 | 67 63 | 64 | 266 | 100,500 |
| Ben Crane | 64 | 69 69 | 64 | 266 | 100,500 |
| Mathias Gronberg | 65 | 67 68 | 66 | 266 | 100,500 |
| Arjun Atwal | 65 | 68 65 | 70 | 268 | 78,000 |
| Jay Delsing | 70 | 64 68 | 66 | 268 | 78,000 |
| Harrison Frazar | 66 | 73 67 | 62 | 268 | 78,000 |
| Joey Sindelar | 69 | 67 66 | 66 | 268 | 78,000 |
| Neal Lancaster | 73 | 66 66 | 64 | 269 | 51,428.58 |
| Glen Day | 63 | 71 69 | 66 | 269 | 51,428.57 |

| | SCORES | | | | TOTAL | MONEY |
|---|---|---|---|---|---|---|
| David Hearn | 68 | 67 | 64 | 70 | 269 | 51,428.57 |
| Matt Hendrix | 63 | 67 | 69 | 70 | 269 | 51,428.57 |
| D.A. Points | 71 | 68 | 64 | 66 | 269 | 51,428.57 |
| Chris Smith | 65 | 69 | 67 | 68 | 269 | 51,428.57 |
| Mike Springer | 64 | 69 | 69 | 67 | 269 | 51,428.57 |
| Doug Barron | 71 | 66 | 66 | 67 | 270 | 32,500 |
| David Edwards | 66 | 63 | 70 | 71 | 270 | 32,500 |
| John Huston | 68 | 69 | 66 | 67 | 270 | 32,500 |
| Hunter Mahan | 70 | 66 | 67 | 67 | 270 | 32,500 |
| Brenden Pappas | 64 | 73 | 68 | 65 | 270 | 32,500 |
| Roland Thatcher | 68 | 66 | 70 | 66 | 270 | 32,500 |
| Dan Forsman | 68 | 67 | 70 | 66 | 271 | 22,200 |
| Paul Gow | 72 | 65 | 68 | 66 | 271 | 22,200 |
| Scott Piercy | 67 | 72 | 67 | 65 | 271 | 22,200 |
| Brett Quigley | 67 | 70 | 66 | 68 | 271 | 22,200 |
| Mario Tiziani | 69 | 66 | 69 | 67 | 271 | 22,200 |
| Patrick Sheehan | 69 | 67 | 69 | 67 | 272 | 17,014.29 |
| Hideto Tanihara | 71 | 68 | 68 | 65 | 272 | 17,014.29 |
| Omar Uresti | 65 | 71 | 68 | 68 | 272 | 17,014.29 |
| Grant Waite | 71 | 67 | 69 | 65 | 272 | 17,014.29 |
| Michael Bradley | 70 | 66 | 64 | 72 | 272 | 17,014.28 |
| Arron Oberholser | 72 | 67 | 65 | 68 | 272 | 17,014.28 |
| Steve Stricker | 70 | 67 | 67 | 68 | 272 | 17,014.28 |
| Carlos Franco | 69 | 67 | 66 | 71 | 273 | 12,900 |
| Bradley Hughes | 67 | 67 | 69 | 70 | 273 | 12,900 |
| Steve Lowery | 68 | 69 | 68 | 68 | 273 | 12,900 |
| Carl Paulson | 70 | 66 | 69 | 68 | 273 | 12,900 |
| David Peoples | 68 | 70 | 68 | 67 | 273 | 12,900 |
| Guy Boros | 70 | 68 | 67 | 69 | 274 | 10,200 |
| Jeff Brehaut | 72 | 68 | 66 | 68 | 274 | 10,200 |
| Jeff Hart | 69 | 66 | 71 | 68 | 274 | 10,200 |
| Spencer Levin | 68 | 69 | 67 | 70 | 274 | 10,200 |
| Gavin Flint | 69 | 68 | 70 | 68 | 275 | 7,932 |
| Hank Kuehne | 66 | 72 | 68 | 69 | 275 | 7,932 |
| Frank Lickliter | 70 | 70 | 68 | 67 | 275 | 7,932 |
| Jim McGovern | 68 | 68 | 64 | 75 | 275 | 7,932 |
| Mark Wilson | 65 | 69 | 70 | 71 | 275 | 7,932 |
| Justin Bolli | 70 | 69 | 70 | 67 | 276 | 6,925.72 |
| Matt Davidson | 71 | 68 | 71 | 66 | 276 | 6,925.72 |
| Brad Fabel | 68 | 71 | 69 | 68 | 276 | 6,925.72 |
| Todd Fischer | 68 | 69 | 67 | 72 | 276 | 6,925.71 |
| Wayne Levi | 69 | 67 | 70 | 70 | 276 | 6,925.71 |
| Kevin Stadler | 71 | 68 | 65 | 72 | 276 | 6,925.71 |
| Hidemichi Tanaka | 67 | 72 | 68 | 69 | 276 | 6,925.71 |
| Paul Claxton | 71 | 69 | 70 | 67 | 277 | 6,540 |
| Marco Dawson | 70 | 70 | 65 | 72 | 277 | 6,540 |
| P.H. Horgan | 68 | 65 | 73 | 71 | 277 | 6,540 |
| Richard Johnson | 70 | 69 | 70 | 68 | 277 | 6,540 |
| John Senden | 67 | 69 | 72 | 69 | 277 | 6,540 |
| Mike Heinen | 69 | 70 | 69 | 70 | 278 | 6,300 |
| Jonathan Kaye | 71 | 69 | 68 | 70 | 278 | 6,300 |
| Spike McRoy | 70 | 68 | 71 | 69 | 278 | 6,300 |
| Wes Short, Jr. | 72 | 65 | 71 | 71 | 279 | 6,150 |
| Vaughn Taylor | 70 | 70 | 70 | 69 | 279 | 6,150 |
| Chris Anderson | 67 | 68 | 73 | 72 | 280 | 6,030 |
| Mike Hulbert | 68 | 70 | 74 | 68 | 280 | 6,030 |
| Steve Allan | 71 | 68 | 67 | 75 | 281 | 5,820 |
| Mark Brooks | 68 | 71 | 69 | 73 | 281 | 5,820 |
| Trevor Dodds | 67 | 71 | 71 | 72 | 281 | 5,820 |
| Matt Kuchar | 72 | 68 | 68 | 73 | 281 | 5,820 |

| | SCORES | | | | TOTAL | MONEY |
|---|---|---|---|---|---|---|
| Larry Mize | 73 | 67 | 71 | 70 | 281 | 5,820 |
| Dave Rummells | 67 | 69 | 70 | 76 | 282 | 5,640 |
| Tjaart van der Walt | 71 | 69 | 74 | 69 | 283 | 5,580 |

## U.S. Bank Championship in Milwaukee

*Brown Deer Park Golf Course*, Milwaukee, Wisconsin
Par 34-36–70; 6,759 yards

July 21-24
purse, $3,800,000

| | SCORES | | | | TOTAL | MONEY |
|---|---|---|---|---|---|---|
| Ben Crane | 62 | 65 | 64 | 69 | 260 | $684,000 |
| Scott Verplank | 64 | 65 | 64 | 71 | 264 | 410,400 |
| Chad Campbell | 66 | 68 | 66 | 65 | 265 | 258,400 |
| Jeff Sluman | 64 | 64 | 70 | 68 | 266 | 182,400 |
| Steve Elkington | 65 | 70 | 64 | 68 | 267 | 144,400 |
| Chris Smith | 64 | 67 | 65 | 71 | 267 | 144,400 |
| Mark Calcavecchia | 69 | 65 | 65 | 69 | 268 | 122,550 |
| Lee Janzen | 69 | 66 | 68 | 65 | 268 | 122,550 |
| Glen Day | 67 | 70 | 66 | 66 | 269 | 95,000 |
| Brad Faxon | 67 | 64 | 70 | 68 | 269 | 95,000 |
| John Huston | 68 | 67 | 65 | 69 | 269 | 95,000 |
| Kenny Perry | 63 | 69 | 64 | 73 | 269 | 95,000 |
| Dean Wilson | 66 | 69 | 66 | 68 | 269 | 95,000 |
| Briny Baird | 66 | 69 | 65 | 70 | 270 | 55,328 |
| Jason Bohn | 67 | 68 | 70 | 65 | 270 | 55,328 |
| Matt Davidson | 67 | 68 | 64 | 71 | 270 | 55,328 |
| Fred Funk | 69 | 67 | 64 | 70 | 270 | 55,328 |
| Richard Johnson | 68 | 70 | 65 | 67 | 270 | 55,328 |
| Jerry Kelly | 64 | 68 | 69 | 69 | 270 | 55,328 |
| Stephen Leaney | 65 | 69 | 68 | 68 | 270 | 55,328 |
| J.L. Lewis | 68 | 67 | 66 | 69 | 270 | 55,328 |
| Rocco Mediate | 69 | 68 | 66 | 67 | 270 | 55,328 |
| Bo Van Pelt | 70 | 65 | 64 | 71 | 270 | 55,328 |
| Tommy Armour | 66 | 65 | 68 | 72 | 271 | 34,960 |
| Olin Browne | 71 | 66 | 65 | 69 | 271 | 34,960 |
| Arjun Atwal | 69 | 67 | 65 | 71 | 272 | 29,260 |
| Bob Estes | 67 | 69 | 71 | 65 | 272 | 29,260 |
| Matt Kuchar | 68 | 68 | 66 | 70 | 272 | 29,260 |
| Brian Bateman | 65 | 70 | 69 | 69 | 273 | 21,694.55 |
| Brian Gay | 68 | 67 | 69 | 69 | 273 | 21,694.55 |
| Mathias Gronberg | 67 | 70 | 67 | 69 | 273 | 21,694.55 |
| Bradley Hughes | 69 | 67 | 68 | 69 | 273 | 21,694.55 |
| Kent Jones | 69 | 64 | 70 | 70 | 273 | 21,694.55 |
| Will MacKenzie | 69 | 68 | 70 | 66 | 273 | 21,694.55 |
| Steve Allan | 70 | 67 | 65 | 71 | 273 | 21,694.54 |
| Daniel Chopra | 66 | 68 | 65 | 74 | 273 | 21,694.54 |
| Kevin Streelman | 65 | 70 | 67 | 71 | 273 | 21,694.54 |
| Roland Thatcher | 65 | 69 | 65 | 74 | 273 | 21,694.54 |
| Brett Wetterich | 69 | 65 | 68 | 71 | 273 | 21,694.54 |
| Cameron Beckman | 65 | 70 | 71 | 68 | 274 | 12,973.20 |
| Alex Cejka | 68 | 68 | 69 | 69 | 274 | 12,973.20 |
| Jay Delsing | 66 | 71 | 67 | 70 | 274 | 12,973.20 |
| Steve Flesch | 69 | 68 | 65 | 72 | 274 | 12,973.20 |
| Dan Forsman | 67 | 71 | 67 | 69 | 274 | 12,973.20 |
| Robert Gamez | 67 | 69 | 70 | 68 | 274 | 12,973.20 |
| J.P. Hayes | 69 | 68 | 69 | 68 | 274 | 12,973.20 |
| Glen Hnatiuk | 70 | 66 | 67 | 71 | 274 | 12,973.20 |

|  | | SCORES | | | TOTAL | MONEY |
|---|---|---|---|---|---|---|
| Michael Long | 66 | 69 | 68 | 71 | 274 | 12,973.20 |
| D.A. Points | 70 | 68 | 67 | 69 | 274 | 12,973.20 |
| John Elliott | 68 | 68 | 69 | 70 | 275 | 8,925.78 |
| Nick Gilliam | 69 | 68 | 69 | 69 | 275 | 8,925.78 |
| Tim Herron | 66 | 70 | 72 | 67 | 275 | 8,925.78 |
| Hunter Mahan | 67 | 67 | 71 | 70 | 275 | 8,925.78 |
| Carl Pettersson | 68 | 68 | 67 | 72 | 275 | 8,925.78 |
| Phillip Price | 66 | 72 | 70 | 67 | 275 | 8,925.78 |
| Heath Slocum | 68 | 69 | 67 | 71 | 275 | 8,925.78 |
| James Driscoll | 69 | 65 | 68 | 73 | 275 | 8,925.77 |
| Harrison Frazar | 67 | 68 | 67 | 73 | 275 | 8,925.77 |
| Marco Dawson | 66 | 67 | 70 | 73 | 276 | 8,284 |
| David Edwards | 70 | 68 | 70 | 68 | 276 | 8,284 |
| J.J. Henry | 71 | 66 | 70 | 69 | 276 | 8,284 |
| Brett Quigley | 70 | 67 | 68 | 71 | 276 | 8,284 |
| Mario Tiziani | 71 | 67 | 67 | 71 | 276 | 8,284 |
| Frank Lickliter | 71 | 67 | 71 | 68 | 277 | 8,018 |
| Arron Oberholser | 69 | 69 | 69 | 70 | 277 | 8,018 |
| Carlos Franco | 70 | 67 | 69 | 72 | 278 | 7,828 |
| Jeff Hart | 71 | 66 | 67 | 74 | 278 | 7,828 |
| Kevin Stadler | 72 | 66 | 68 | 72 | 278 | 7,828 |
| Joey Sindelar | 69 | 69 | 69 | 72 | 279 | 7,676 |
| Hideto Tanihara | 66 | 68 | 72 | 74 | 280 | 7,600 |
| Tripp Isenhour | 68 | 68 | 75 | 70 | 281 | 7,448 |
| Blaine McCallister | 68 | 70 | 72 | 71 | 281 | 7,448 |
| Ryan Moore | 71 | 66 | 72 | 72 | 281 | 7,448 |
| David Hearn | 66 | 72 | 71 | 73 | 282 | 7,296 |
| Justin Bolli | 68 | 68 | 73 | 74 | 283 | 7,220 |
| Gene Sauers | 71 | 67 | 73 | 76 | 287 | 7,144 |

## Buick Open

*Warwick Hills Golf & Country Club*,
Grand Blanc, Michigan
Par 36-36–72; 7,127 yards

July 28-31
purse, $4,600,000

|  | | SCORES | | | TOTAL | MONEY |
|---|---|---|---|---|---|---|
| Vijay Singh | 65 | 66 | 63 | 70 | 264 | $828,000 |
| Zach Johnson | 68 | 66 | 65 | 69 | 268 | 404,800 |
| Tiger Woods | 71 | 61 | 70 | 66 | 268 | 404,800 |
| Robert Allenby | 70 | 65 | 70 | 65 | 270 | 220,800 |
| Dudley Hart | 68 | 66 | 71 | 66 | 271 | 184,000 |
| Jeff Brehaut | 68 | 67 | 69 | 68 | 272 | 159,850 |
| Jim Furyk | 66 | 71 | 67 | 68 | 272 | 159,850 |
| Craig Barlow | 66 | 67 | 71 | 69 | 273 | 128,800 |
| Richard Johnson | 69 | 69 | 67 | 68 | 273 | 128,800 |
| Sean O'Hair | 70 | 66 | 66 | 71 | 273 | 128,800 |
| Heath Slocum | 70 | 68 | 68 | 67 | 273 | 128,800 |
| Daniel Chopra | 71 | 66 | 68 | 69 | 274 | 87,400 |
| Chris DiMarco | 70 | 65 | 66 | 73 | 274 | 87,400 |
| Fred Funk | 68 | 66 | 70 | 70 | 274 | 87,400 |
| Stephen Leaney | 71 | 68 | 67 | 68 | 274 | 87,400 |
| Steve Lowery | 69 | 66 | 68 | 71 | 274 | 87,400 |
| Geoff Ogilvy | 66 | 71 | 65 | 72 | 274 | 87,400 |
| Briny Baird | 69 | 69 | 66 | 71 | 275 | 62,100 |
| Olin Browne | 66 | 73 | 64 | 72 | 275 | 62,100 |
| John Cook | 69 | 68 | 70 | 68 | 275 | 62,100 |

| | SCORES | | | | TOTAL | MONEY |
|---|---|---|---|---|---|---|
| Larry Mize | 69 | 68 | 67 | 71 | 275 | 62,100 |
| Chris Anderson | 72 | 68 | 68 | 68 | 276 | 38,410 |
| Jason Bohn | 65 | 69 | 69 | 73 | 276 | 38,410 |
| Paul Claxton | 71 | 69 | 65 | 71 | 276 | 38,410 |
| Hunter Haas | 72 | 66 | 68 | 70 | 276 | 38,410 |
| Glen Hnatiuk | 67 | 69 | 73 | 67 | 276 | 38,410 |
| Rocco Mediate | 71 | 66 | 72 | 67 | 276 | 38,410 |
| Justin Rose | 68 | 72 | 69 | 67 | 276 | 38,410 |
| John Senden | 70 | 70 | 69 | 67 | 276 | 38,410 |
| Steve Stricker | 68 | 66 | 73 | 69 | 276 | 38,410 |
| Roland Thatcher | 67 | 70 | 71 | 68 | 276 | 38,410 |
| Paul Goydos | 67 | 71 | 70 | 69 | 277 | 24,905.72 |
| Omar Uresti | 68 | 72 | 67 | 70 | 277 | 24,905.72 |
| Charles Warren | 72 | 68 | 68 | 69 | 277 | 24,905.72 |
| Steve Elkington | 69 | 68 | 68 | 72 | 277 | 24,905.71 |
| Mathias Gronberg | 69 | 71 | 67 | 70 | 277 | 24,905.71 |
| Franklin Langham | 73 | 66 | 67 | 71 | 277 | 24,905.71 |
| Hidemichi Tanaka | 69 | 69 | 68 | 71 | 277 | 24,905.71 |
| J.J. Henry | 68 | 71 | 70 | 69 | 278 | 18,400 |
| Brendan Jones | 70 | 68 | 68 | 72 | 278 | 18,400 |
| Ryan Palmer | 69 | 70 | 69 | 70 | 278 | 18,400 |
| Bob Tway | 70 | 70 | 68 | 70 | 278 | 18,400 |
| Scott Verplank | 73 | 66 | 72 | 67 | 278 | 18,400 |
| Nick Watney | 64 | 71 | 72 | 71 | 278 | 18,400 |
| Jeff Hart | 71 | 68 | 73 | 67 | 279 | 13,468.80 |
| Billy Mayfair | 71 | 66 | 70 | 72 | 279 | 13,468.80 |
| Ted Purdy | 70 | 68 | 69 | 72 | 279 | 13,468.80 |
| Wes Short, Jr. | 69 | 70 | 70 | 70 | 279 | 13,468.80 |
| Darron Stiles | 71 | 68 | 68 | 72 | 279 | 13,468.80 |
| Colby Beckstrom | 69 | 70 | 70 | 71 | 280 | 11,095.20 |
| J.P. Hayes | 69 | 69 | 69 | 73 | 280 | 11,095.20 |
| Will MacKenzie | 71 | 67 | 71 | 71 | 280 | 11,095.20 |
| Mario Tiziani | 70 | 66 | 72 | 72 | 280 | 11,095.20 |
| Tjaart van der Walt | 72 | 67 | 73 | 68 | 280 | 11,095.20 |
| Tommy Armour | 67 | 73 | 69 | 72 | 281 | 10,488 |
| Ian Leggatt | 71 | 69 | 67 | 74 | 281 | 10,488 |
| Tag Ridings | 73 | 67 | 70 | 71 | 281 | 10,488 |
| D.J. Brigman | 70 | 70 | 71 | 71 | 282 | 9,982 |
| Tom Byrum | 69 | 69 | 72 | 72 | 282 | 9,982 |
| Bob Estes | 71 | 69 | 70 | 72 | 282 | 9,982 |
| Lee Janzen | 70 | 68 | 70 | 74 | 282 | 9,982 |
| Neal Lancaster | 66 | 70 | 77 | 69 | 282 | 9,982 |
| Scott McCarron | 68 | 69 | 72 | 73 | 282 | 9,982 |
| John Rollins | 68 | 71 | 69 | 74 | 282 | 9,982 |
| Joey Sindelar | 70 | 69 | 76 | 67 | 282 | 9,982 |
| John Daly | 70 | 70 | 67 | 76 | 283 | 9,430 |
| Michael Harris | 73 | 67 | 73 | 70 | 283 | 9,430 |
| Bob Heintz | 68 | 70 | 71 | 74 | 283 | 9,430 |
| Rod Pampling | 67 | 73 | 68 | 75 | 283 | 9,430 |
| Paul Gow | 69 | 69 | 71 | 75 | 284 | 9,154 |
| Mark O'Meara | 72 | 67 | 73 | 72 | 284 | 9,154 |
| Frank Lickliter | 67 | 67 | 77 | 74 | 285 | 9,016 |
| Doug Barron | 69 | 71 | 70 | 76 | 286 | 8,878 |
| Mark Brooks | 66 | 71 | 72 | 77 | 286 | 8,878 |
| Andrew Magee | 70 | 70 | 75 | 73 | 288 | 8,740 |
| Matt Davidson | 71 | 69 | 74 | 75 | 289 | 8,602 |
| Joey Snyder | 68 | 72 | 74 | 75 | 289 | 8,602 |
| Steve Allan | 75 | 65 | 75 | 77 | 292 | 8,464 |
| *Ryan Brehm | 71 | 69 | 77 | 77 | 294 | |

## The International

*Castle Pines Golf Club*, Castle Rock, Colorado
Par 36-36–72; 7,619 yards

August 4-7
purse, $5,000,000

| | POINTS | | | | TOTAL | MONEY |
|---|---|---|---|---|---|---|
| Retief Goosen | 7 | 10 | 8 | 7 | 32 | $900,000 |
| Brandt Jobe | 13 | 9 | 12 | (-3) | 31 | 540,000 |
| Jeff Brehaut | 7 | 6 | 6 | 10 | 29 | 340,000 |
| Hank Kuehne | 3 | 8 | 6 | 10 | 27 | 240,000 |
| Charles Howell | 12 | 10 | (-4) | 8 | 26 | 200,000 |
| Joey Snyder | (-1) | 13 | 8 | 4 | 24 | 161,875 |
| Rod Pampling | 5 | 7 | 3 | 9 | 24 | 161,875 |
| Tim Clark | 6 | 6 | 6 | 8 | 24 | 161,875 |
| Tim Petrovic | 11 | 4 | 8 | 1 | 24 | 161,875 |
| Scott McCarron | 5 | 5 | 13 | 0 | 23 | 130,000 |
| Phil Mickelson | 3 | 14 | (-3) | 9 | 23 | 130,000 |
| Paul Gow | 6 | 4 | 7 | 5 | 22 | 105,000 |
| Steve Flesch | 1 | 8 | 12 | 1 | 22 | 105,000 |
| Stewart Cink | 9 | 8 | 3 | 2 | 22 | 105,000 |
| Carl Pettersson | 6 | 4 | 9 | 2 | 21 | 72,625 |
| Jonathan Byrd | 10 | 2 | 5 | 4 | 21 | 72,625 |
| Craig Barlow | 6 | 4 | 12 | (-1) | 21 | 72,625 |
| Mike Weir | 7 | 6 | 2 | 6 | 21 | 72,625 |
| Ryan Palmer | 5 | 3 | 8 | 5 | 21 | 72,625 |
| Daniel Chopra | 10 | 6 | 4 | 1 | 21 | 72,625 |
| Olin Browne | 4 | 3 | 8 | 6 | 21 | 72,625 |
| Billy Mayfair | 15 | 7 | 0 | (-1) | 21 | 72,625 |
| Justin Rose | 6 | 6 | 2 | 6 | 20 | 44,500 |
| D.J. Brigman | 3 | 10 | 11 | (-4) | 20 | 44,500 |
| Hunter Haas | 5 | 9 | 8 | (-2) | 20 | 44,500 |
| Brian Bateman | 5 | 3 | 0 | 12 | 20 | 44,500 |
| Chris Anderson | 10 | 8 | 2 | 0 | 20 | 44,500 |
| Phillip Price | 7 | 5 | 6 | 1 | 19 | 34,750 |
| John Huston | 6 | 4 | 5 | 4 | 19 | 34,750 |
| David Toms | 6 | 12 | 3 | (-2) | 19 | 34,750 |
| Cameron Beckman | 10 | 13 | 0 | (-4) | 19 | 34,750 |
| Sean O'Hair | 1 | 13 | 1 | 3 | 18 | 28,937.50 |
| Kevin Stadler | 5 | 10 | 10 | (-7) | 18 | 28,937.50 |
| Joe Ogilvie | 9 | 0 | 5 | 4 | 18 | 28,937.50 |
| Brad Faxon | 8 | (-1) | 4 | 7 | 18 | 28,937.50 |
| Hidemichi Tanaka | 7 | 7 | 7 | (-4) | 17 | 24,062.50 |
| Brett Quigley | 3 | 6 | 8 | 0 | 17 | 24,062.50 |
| Ben Crane | 9 | 7 | (-2) | 3 | 17 | 24,062.50 |
| Duffy Waldorf | 3 | 4 | 8 | 2 | 17 | 24,062.50 |
| Luke Donald | 7 | 3 | 8 | (-2) | 16 | 21,500 |
| Jeff Maggert | 6 | 5 | 7 | (-3) | 15 | 19,000 |
| Harrison Frazar | 4 | 8 | (-2) | 5 | 15 | 19,000 |
| D.A. Points | 12 | 2 | 1 | 0 | 15 | 19,000 |
| Larry Mize | 5 | 2 | 10 | (-2) | 15 | 19,000 |
| Rich Beem | 0 | 11 | 4 | (-1) | 14 | 15,050 |
| Glen Hnatiuk | (-1) | 12 | 6 | (-3) | 14 | 15,050 |
| D.J. Trahan | 3 | 10 | 7 | (-6) | 14 | 15,050 |
| Mark Wilson | 4 | 5 | 3 | 2 | 14 | 15,050 |
| Heath Slocum | 7 | 11 | (-4) | (-1) | 13 | 12,800 |
| Scott Gutschewski | 4 | 3 | (-1) | 7 | 13 | 12,800 |
| Bob Tway | 4 | 6 | 2 | (-1) | 11 | 11,925 |
| Greg Owen | 5 | 5 | (-2) | 3 | 11 | 11,925 |
| Geoff Ogilvy | 11 | (-2) | 4 | (-2) | 11 | 11,925 |
| Steve Allan | 8 | 6 | 0 | (-3) | 11 | 11,925 |

| | POINTS | | | TOTAL | MONEY |
|---|---|---|---|---|---|
| Steve Lowery | 5 | 6 (-1) | 0 | 10 | 11,450 |
| Corey Pavin | 10 (-3) | 2 | 1 | 10 | 11,450 |
| Frank Lickliter | 8 | 2 | 1 (-3) | 8 | 11,200 |
| Andrew Magee | 4 | 3 | 1 | 0 | 8 | 11,200 |
| Wil Collins | 2 | 5 (-1) | 2 | 8 | 11,200 |
| Patrick Sheehan | 3 | 4 | 4 (-5) | 6 | 11,000 |
| Franklin Langham | 5 | 6 (-3) | (-3) | 5 | 10,900 |
| K.J. Choi | 4 | 5 | 1 (-6) | 4 | 10,800 |
| Tom Pernice, Jr. | 7 | 3 (-3) | (-5) | 2 | 10,700 |

## PGA Championship

*Baltusrol Golf Club, Lower Course*, Springfield, New Jersey
Par 34-36–70; 7,392 yards
(Event completed on Monday—lightning delay.)

August 11-15
purse, $6,500,000

| | SCORES | | | | TOTAL | MONEY |
|---|---|---|---|---|---|---|
| Phil Mickelson | 67 | 65 | 72 | 72 | 276 | $1,170,000 |
| Steve Elkington | 68 | 70 | 68 | 71 | 277 | 572,000 |
| Thomas Bjorn | 71 | 71 | 63 | 72 | 277 | 572,000 |
| Tiger Woods | 75 | 69 | 66 | 68 | 278 | 286,000 |
| Davis Love | 68 | 68 | 68 | 74 | 278 | 286,000 |
| Geoff Ogilvy | 69 | 69 | 72 | 69 | 279 | 201,500 |
| Michael Campbell | 73 | 68 | 69 | 69 | 279 | 201,500 |
| Retief Goosen | 68 | 70 | 69 | 72 | 279 | 201,500 |
| Pat Perez | 68 | 71 | 67 | 73 | 279 | 201,500 |
| Ted Purdy | 69 | 75 | 70 | 66 | 280 | 131,800 |
| David Toms | 71 | 72 | 69 | 68 | 280 | 131,800 |
| Steve Flesch | 70 | 71 | 69 | 70 | 280 | 131,800 |
| Dudley Hart | 70 | 73 | 66 | 71 | 280 | 131,800 |
| Vijay Singh | 70 | 67 | 69 | 74 | 280 | 131,800 |
| Charles Howell | 70 | 71 | 68 | 72 | 281 | 102,500 |
| Stuart Appleby | 67 | 70 | 69 | 75 | 281 | 102,500 |
| Tim Clark | 71 | 73 | 70 | 68 | 282 | 82,500 |
| Zach Johnson | 70 | 70 | 73 | 69 | 282 | 82,500 |
| Trevor Immelman | 67 | 72 | 72 | 71 | 282 | 82,500 |
| Joe Ogilvie | 74 | 68 | 69 | 71 | 282 | 82,500 |
| Bo Van Pelt | 70 | 70 | 68 | 74 | 282 | 82,500 |
| Lee Westwood | 68 | 68 | 71 | 75 | 282 | 82,500 |
| Paul McGinley | 72 | 70 | 72 | 69 | 283 | 56,400 |
| Sergio Garcia | 72 | 70 | 71 | 70 | 283 | 56,400 |
| Shingo Katayama | 71 | 66 | 74 | 72 | 283 | 56,400 |
| Tom Pernice Jr. | 69 | 73 | 69 | 72 | 283 | 56,400 |
| Kenny Perry | 69 | 70 | 70 | 74 | 283 | 56,400 |
| Bob Estes | 71 | 72 | 73 | 68 | 284 | 41,500 |
| Vaughn Taylor | 75 | 69 | 71 | 69 | 284 | 41,500 |
| Chad Campbell | 71 | 71 | 70 | 72 | 284 | 41,500 |
| Arron Oberholser | 74 | 68 | 69 | 73 | 284 | 41,500 |
| Jesper Parnevik | 68 | 69 | 72 | 75 | 284 | 41,500 |
| Stewart Cink | 71 | 72 | 66 | 75 | 284 | 41,500 |
| Fredrik Jacobson | 72 | 69 | 73 | 71 | 285 | 31,916.67 |
| Scott Verplank | 71 | 72 | 71 | 71 | 285 | 31,916.67 |
| Jim Furyk | 72 | 71 | 69 | 73 | 285 | 31,916.67 |
| Jerry Kelly | 70 | 65 | 74 | 76 | 285 | 31,916.67 |
| Jason Bohn | 71 | 68 | 68 | 78 | 285 | 31,916.67 |
| Ben Curtis | 67 | 73 | 67 | 78 | 285 | 31,916.67 |
| Ben Crane | 68 | 76 | 72 | 70 | 286 | 22,300 |

| | SCORES | | | | TOTAL | MONEY |
|---|---|---|---|---|---|---|
| Steve Schneiter | 72 | 72 | 72 | 70 | 286 | 22,300 |
| Adam Scott | 74 | 69 | 72 | 71 | 286 | 22,300 |
| Patrick Sheehan | 73 | 71 | 71 | 71 | 286 | 22,300 |
| K.J. Choi | 71 | 70 | 73 | 72 | 286 | 22,300 |
| Miguel Angel Jimenez | 72 | 72 | 69 | 73 | 286 | 22,300 |
| John Rollins | 68 | 71 | 73 | 74 | 286 | 22,300 |
| Henrik Stenson | 74 | 67 | 75 | 71 | 287 | 15,370.84 |
| Heath Slocum | 68 | 75 | 73 | 71 | 287 | 15,370.84 |
| Ryan Palmer | 73 | 70 | 73 | 71 | 287 | 15,370.84 |
| Jose Maria Olazabal | 76 | 67 | 72 | 72 | 287 | 15,370.84 |
| Mike Weir | 72 | 72 | 71 | 72 | 287 | 15,370.84 |
| Y.E. Yang | 71 | 67 | 76 | 73 | 287 | 15,370.84 |
| J.L. Lewis | 72 | 72 | 70 | 73 | 287 | 15,370.84 |
| Todd Hamilton | 73 | 70 | 70 | 74 | 287 | 15,370.84 |
| Bernhard Langer | 68 | 72 | 72 | 75 | 287 | 15,370.84 |
| Ian Poulter | 69 | 74 | 69 | 75 | 287 | 15,370.84 |
| Fred Funk | 69 | 75 | 67 | 76 | 287 | 15,370.84 |
| Greg Owen | 68 | 69 | 70 | 80 | 287 | 15,370.84 |
| Scott McCarron | 72 | 72 | 74 | 70 | 288 | 13,342.86 |
| Sean O'Hair | 71 | 71 | 76 | 70 | 288 | 13,342.86 |
| Steve Webster | 72 | 70 | 75 | 71 | 288 | 13,342.86 |
| Carlos Franco | 70 | 70 | 76 | 72 | 288 | 13,342.86 |
| Paul Casey | 70 | 74 | 72 | 72 | 288 | 13,342.86 |
| Peter Hanson | 73 | 71 | 72 | 72 | 288 | 13,342.86 |
| Mark Hensby | 69 | 70 | 75 | 74 | 288 | 13,342.86 |
| Ron Philo Jr. | 71 | 73 | 73 | 72 | 289 | 12,750 |
| Luke Donald | 69 | 73 | 73 | 74 | 289 | 12,750 |
| Chris Riley | 72 | 68 | 72 | 77 | 289 | 12,750 |
| Woody Austin | 72 | 71 | 68 | 78 | 289 | 12,750 |
| Mark Calcavecchia | 70 | 69 | 77 | 74 | 290 | 12,450 |
| Fred Couples | 72 | 72 | 70 | 76 | 290 | 12,450 |
| Joe Durant | 73 | 71 | 73 | 74 | 291 | 12,250 |
| Stephen Ames | 67 | 72 | 74 | 78 | 291 | 12,250 |
| John Daly | 71 | 69 | 78 | 74 | 292 | 12,050 |
| Rory Sabbatini | 67 | 69 | 76 | 80 | 292 | 12,050 |
| Mike Small | 74 | 68 | 80 | 73 | 295 | 11,900 |
| Kevin Sutherland | 74 | 70 | 75 | 77 | 296 | 11,800 |
| Darrell Kestner | 72 | 70 | 78 | 79 | 299 | 11,700 |
| Hal Sutton | 69 | 73 | 80 | 78 | 300 | 11,600 |

**Out of Final 36 Holes**

| | | | | |
|---|---|---|---|---|
| Hunter Mahan | 72 | 73 | | 145 |
| Alex Cejka | 70 | 75 | | 145 |
| Tim Petrovic | 75 | 70 | | 145 |
| Lee Janzen | 71 | 74 | | 145 |
| Jeff Yurkiewicz | 72 | 73 | | 145 |
| Stephen Dodd | 74 | 71 | | 145 |
| Loren Roberts | 71 | 74 | | 145 |
| Nick Dougherty | 73 | 72 | | 145 |
| Justin Leonard | 69 | 76 | | 145 |
| Shaun Micheel | 72 | 73 | | 145 |
| Paul Azinger | 72 | 73 | | 145 |
| Chip Johnson | 72 | 74 | | 146 |
| Kevin Na | 70 | 76 | | 146 |
| Stephen Leaney | 74 | 72 | | 146 |
| Brett Quigley | 74 | 72 | | 146 |
| Jay Haas | 77 | 69 | | 146 |
| Rob Moss | 74 | 72 | | 146 |
| Chris DiMarco | 75 | 71 | | 146 |
| Niclas Fasth | 73 | 74 | | 147 |

|  | SCORES | | TOTAL |
|---|---|---|---|
| Bob Tway | 71 | 76 | 147 |
| Richard Green | 79 | 68 | 147 |
| Brett Melton | 72 | 75 | 147 |
| Travis Long | 76 | 71 | 147 |
| Bart Bryant | 75 | 72 | 147 |
| Brad Faxon | 73 | 74 | 147 |
| Billy Andrade | 76 | 71 | 147 |
| Thomas Levet | 79 | 68 | 147 |
| Richard Johnson | 73 | 74 | 147 |
| Peter Lonard | 71 | 76 | 147 |
| Tim Fleming | 74 | 74 | 148 |
| Billy Mayfair | 73 | 75 | 148 |
| Graeme McDowell | 72 | 76 | 148 |
| Brian Davis | 74 | 74 | 148 |
| David Howell | 78 | 70 | 148 |
| Jean-Francois Remesy | 71 | 77 | 148 |
| Jeff Coston | 74 | 74 | 148 |
| Colin Montgomerie | 77 | 71 | 148 |
| Maarten Lafeber | 77 | 71 | 148 |
| Mark Brooks | 78 | 71 | 149 |
| Nick O'Hern | 76 | 73 | 149 |
| Dave Tentis | 77 | 72 | 149 |
| Craig Parry | 76 | 74 | 150 |
| Bob Ford | 75 | 75 | 150 |
| Tim Thelen | 77 | 73 | 150 |
| Jonathan Kaye | 73 | 77 | 150 |
| Mark Mielke | 77 | 73 | 150 |
| Thongchai Jaidee | 76 | 74 | 150 |
| Rod Pampling | 73 | 77 | 150 |
| Shigeki Maruyama | 73 | 77 | 150 |
| Darren Clarke | 73 | 77 | 150 |
| Robert Allenby | 76 | 74 | 150 |
| Lucas Glover | 74 | 76 | 150 |
| Tom Lehman | 72 | 79 | 151 |
| Tim Herron | 78 | 73 | 151 |
| Arjun Atwal | 74 | 77 | 151 |
| Alan Morin | 76 | 75 | 151 |
| Chris Wiemers | 74 | 77 | 151 |
| David Duval | 77 | 74 | 151 |
| Brent Geiberger | 76 | 76 | 152 |
| Toru Taniguchi | 76 | 76 | 152 |
| Chris Starkjohann | 78 | 75 | 153 |
| Padraig Harrington | 76 | 77 | 153 |
| S.K. Ho | 76 | 77 | 153 |
| Michael Allen | 77 | 76 | 153 |
| Stephen Gallacher | 79 | 74 | 153 |
| Scott Spence | 79 | 74 | 153 |
| Jeff Sluman | 77 | 76 | 153 |
| Jeff Maggert | 73 | 81 | 154 |
| Don Berry | 76 | 78 | 154 |
| Wayne Grady | 78 | 78 | 156 |
| Rich Beem | 79 | 78 | 157 |
| Mike Reid | 78 | 79 | 157 |
| Kelly Mitchum | 78 | 80 | 158 |
| Rich Steinmetz | 81 | 77 | 158 |
| Jeff Martin | 80 | 78 | 158 |
| Craig Thomas | 80 | 79 | 159 |
| Tim Weinhart | 78 | 81 | 159 |

(Professionals who did not complete 72 holes received $2,000.)

# WGC - NEC Invitational

*Firestone Country Club, South Course,* Akron, Ohio
Par 35-35–70; 7,283 yards

August 18-21
purse, $7,500,000

| | SCORES | | | | TOTAL | MONEY |
|---|---|---|---|---|---|---|
| Tiger Woods | 66 | 70 | 67 | 71 | 274 | $1,300,000 |
| Chris DiMarco | 67 | 70 | 70 | 68 | 275 | 750,000 |
| Vijay Singh | 66 | 71 | 72 | 67 | 276 | 353,666.67 |
| Paul McGinley | 71 | 66 | 67 | 72 | 276 | 353,666.66 |
| Ryan Palmer | 72 | 68 | 67 | 69 | 276 | 353,666.66 |
| Luke Donald | 69 | 67 | 74 | 67 | 277 | 200,000 |
| David Howell | 70 | 68 | 70 | 69 | 277 | 200,000 |
| Kenny Perry | 70 | 69 | 64 | 74 | 277 | 200,000 |
| Zach Johnson | 70 | 70 | 69 | 69 | 278 | 135,000 |
| Colin Montgomerie | 70 | 72 | 68 | 68 | 278 | 135,000 |
| Jose Maria Olazabal | 72 | 68 | 66 | 72 | 278 | 135,000 |
| David Toms | 71 | 67 | 69 | 71 | 278 | 135,000 |
| Stuart Appleby | 68 | 70 | 67 | 74 | 279 | 94,400 |
| Sergio Garcia | 68 | 70 | 67 | 74 | 279 | 94,400 |
| Davis Love | 67 | 73 | 69 | 70 | 279 | 94,400 |
| Rod Pampling | 71 | 70 | 71 | 67 | 279 | 94,400 |
| Henrik Stenson | 66 | 71 | 72 | 70 | 279 | 94,400 |
| Thomas Bjorn | 70 | 67 | 72 | 71 | 280 | 83,000 |
| Paul Casey | 75 | 68 | 67 | 71 | 281 | 77,000 |
| Kenneth Ferrie | 71 | 70 | 73 | 67 | 281 | 77,000 |
| Jay Haas | 76 | 69 | 67 | 69 | 281 | 77,000 |
| Trevor Immelman | 73 | 71 | 71 | 66 | 281 | 77,000 |
| Justin Leonard | 72 | 66 | 71 | 72 | 281 | 77,000 |
| Jim Furyk | 72 | 73 | 68 | 69 | 282 | 69,000 |
| Padraig Harrington | 75 | 68 | 69 | 70 | 282 | 69,000 |
| Lee Westwood | 73 | 72 | 63 | 74 | 282 | 69,000 |
| John Daly | 71 | 69 | 69 | 74 | 283 | 65,000 |
| Bart Bryant | 74 | 73 | 67 | 70 | 284 | 60,200 |
| Darren Clarke | 76 | 68 | 72 | 68 | 284 | 60,200 |
| Fred Couples | 71 | 74 | 70 | 69 | 284 | 60,200 |
| Nick O'Hern | 68 | 73 | 72 | 71 | 284 | 60,200 |
| Rory Sabbatini | 73 | 69 | 67 | 75 | 284 | 60,200 |
| Chad Campbell | 72 | 72 | 69 | 72 | 285 | 56,000 |
| Niclas Fasth | 72 | 72 | 70 | 71 | 285 | 56,000 |
| Ian Poulter | 73 | 69 | 69 | 74 | 285 | 56,000 |
| Stephen Ames | 74 | 71 | 68 | 73 | 286 | 52,000 |
| Woody Austin | 73 | 68 | 77 | 68 | 286 | 52,000 |
| Peter Lonard | 74 | 71 | 68 | 73 | 286 | 52,000 |
| Adam Scott | 70 | 76 | 67 | 73 | 286 | 52,000 |
| Mike Weir | 71 | 69 | 70 | 76 | 286 | 52,000 |
| Angel Cabrera | 75 | 74 | 67 | 71 | 287 | 47,000 |
| Stewart Cink | 72 | 72 | 73 | 70 | 287 | 47,000 |
| Fred Funk | 74 | 71 | 69 | 73 | 287 | 47,000 |
| Tom Lehman | 73 | 71 | 75 | 68 | 287 | 47,000 |
| Geoff Ogilvy | 74 | 74 | 70 | 69 | 287 | 47,000 |
| Brent Geiberger | 70 | 76 | 69 | 73 | 288 | 43,500 |
| Thomas Levet | 72 | 71 | 72 | 73 | 288 | 43,500 |
| Shigeki Maruyama | 75 | 70 | 71 | 72 | 288 | 43,500 |
| Marc Cayeux | 71 | 75 | 71 | 72 | 289 | 42,250 |
| Steve Elkington | 72 | 76 | 75 | 66 | 289 | 42,250 |
| K.J. Choi | 71 | 76 | 69 | 74 | 290 | 40,250 |
| Tim Clark | 71 | 75 | 72 | 72 | 290 | 40,250 |
| Nick Dougherty | 67 | 81 | 70 | 72 | 290 | 40,250 |
| Phil Mickelson | 69 | 72 | 75 | 74 | 290 | 40,250 |

| | SCORES | | | | TOTAL | MONEY |
|---|---|---|---|---|---|---|
| Sean O'Hair | 70 | 74 | 73 | 73 | 290 | 40,250 |
| Scott Verplank | 73 | 73 | 67 | 77 | 290 | 40,250 |
| Miguel Angel Jimenez | 76 | 75 | 73 | 67 | 291 | 38,500 |
| Ben Crane | 74 | 75 | 71 | 73 | 293 | 36,500 |
| Stephen Gallacher | 74 | 74 | 75 | 70 | 293 | 36,500 |
| Retief Goosen | 77 | 73 | 73 | 70 | 293 | 36,500 |
| Mark Hensby | 70 | 76 | 71 | 76 | 293 | 36,500 |
| Thongchai Jaidee | 73 | 76 | 72 | 72 | 293 | 36,500 |
| Craig Parry | 79 | 71 | 73 | 70 | 293 | 36,500 |
| Chris Riley | 69 | 81 | 74 | 69 | 293 | 36,500 |
| Kazuhiko Hosokawa | 70 | 78 | 71 | 75 | 294 | 34,500 |
| Tim Petrovic | 80 | 73 | 69 | 73 | 295 | 34,000 |
| Richard Green | 76 | 78 | 69 | 73 | 296 | 33,500 |
| Michael Campbell | 72 | 74 | 78 | 74 | 298 | 33,000 |
| Stephen Dodd | 74 | 78 | 77 | 73 | 302 | 32,500 |
| Jyoti Randhawa | 79 | 77 | 75 | 73 | 304 | 32,000 |

## Reno-Tahoe Open

*Montreux Golf & Country Club,* Reno, Nevada
Par 36-36–72; 7,577 yards

August 18-21
purse, $3,000,000

| | SCORES | | | | TOTAL | MONEY |
|---|---|---|---|---|---|---|
| Vaughn Taylor | 64 | 67 | 64 | 72 | 267 | $540,000 |
| Jonathan Kaye | 69 | 66 | 68 | 67 | 270 | 324,000 |
| Todd Fischer | 65 | 67 | 69 | 70 | 271 | 204,000 |
| Aaron Baddeley | 67 | 70 | 66 | 70 | 273 | 124,000 |
| J.P. Hayes | 71 | 66 | 67 | 69 | 273 | 124,000 |
| J.J. Henry | 70 | 67 | 70 | 66 | 273 | 124,000 |
| Tag Ridings | 69 | 69 | 69 | 67 | 274 | 100,500 |
| Fredrik Jacobson | 65 | 70 | 68 | 72 | 275 | 93,000 |
| Steve Allan | 70 | 67 | 70 | 69 | 276 | 78,000 |
| Spike McRoy | 69 | 69 | 70 | 68 | 276 | 78,000 |
| Jesper Parnevik | 67 | 68 | 67 | 74 | 276 | 78,000 |
| Dean Wilson | 71 | 69 | 66 | 70 | 276 | 78,000 |
| Doug Barron | 73 | 70 | 69 | 65 | 277 | 60,000 |
| Duffy Waldorf | 67 | 70 | 70 | 70 | 277 | 60,000 |
| Craig Barlow | 68 | 68 | 71 | 71 | 278 | 51,000 |
| Justin Rose | 72 | 70 | 65 | 71 | 278 | 51,000 |
| Darron Stiles | 72 | 68 | 70 | 68 | 278 | 51,000 |
| Rich Beem | 74 | 65 | 72 | 68 | 279 | 39,120 |
| D.J. Brigman | 76 | 67 | 71 | 65 | 279 | 39,120 |
| Harrison Frazar | 74 | 66 | 67 | 72 | 279 | 39,120 |
| Bill Glasson | 72 | 62 | 73 | 72 | 279 | 39,120 |
| Kevin Na | 69 | 70 | 71 | 69 | 279 | 39,120 |
| Joe Ogilvie | 69 | 70 | 71 | 70 | 280 | 27,600 |
| David Peoples | 71 | 70 | 72 | 67 | 280 | 27,600 |
| Carl Pettersson | 70 | 72 | 70 | 68 | 280 | 27,600 |
| Kevin Sutherland | 70 | 69 | 71 | 70 | 280 | 27,600 |
| Michael Allen | 70 | 71 | 71 | 69 | 281 | 19,550 |
| Olin Browne | 71 | 71 | 71 | 68 | 281 | 19,550 |
| Jose Coceres | 71 | 70 | 71 | 69 | 281 | 19,550 |
| Mathias Gronberg | 71 | 67 | 69 | 74 | 281 | 19,550 |
| Tim Herron | 71 | 72 | 73 | 65 | 281 | 19,550 |
| Per-Ulrik Johansson | 75 | 67 | 70 | 69 | 281 | 19,550 |
| Neal Lancaster | 72 | 66 | 70 | 73 | 281 | 19,550 |
| Spencer Levin | 70 | 71 | 72 | 68 | 281 | 19,550 |

| | SCORES | | | | TOTAL | MONEY |
|---|---|---|---|---|---|---|
| D.A. Points | 79 | 63 | 69 | 70 | 281 | 19,550 |
| Hunter Haas | 73 | 68 | 67 | 74 | 282 | 14,130 |
| John Huston | 70 | 69 | 69 | 74 | 282 | 14,130 |
| Kent Jones | 72 | 69 | 67 | 74 | 282 | 14,130 |
| Matt Kuchar | 69 | 70 | 71 | 72 | 282 | 14,130 |
| Nick Watney | 74 | 70 | 67 | 71 | 282 | 14,130 |
| Briny Baird | 74 | 68 | 71 | 70 | 283 | 10,215 |
| John Cook | 72 | 70 | 71 | 70 | 283 | 10,215 |
| Brian Gay | 70 | 73 | 67 | 73 | 283 | 10,215 |
| Scott McCarron | 72 | 71 | 68 | 72 | 283 | 10,215 |
| Mark O'Meara | 74 | 69 | 70 | 70 | 283 | 10,215 |
| Patrick Sheehan | 76 | 67 | 71 | 69 | 283 | 10,215 |
| Kevin Stadler | 76 | 67 | 73 | 67 | 283 | 10,215 |
| Mario Tiziani | 71 | 70 | 72 | 70 | 283 | 10,215 |
| Guy Boros | 66 | 72 | 72 | 74 | 284 | 7,485 |
| Ben Curtis | 69 | 71 | 70 | 74 | 284 | 7,485 |
| Brenden Pappas | 69 | 71 | 71 | 73 | 284 | 7,485 |
| Y.E. Yang | 73 | 69 | 66 | 76 | 284 | 7,485 |
| Rich Barcelo | 75 | 65 | 73 | 72 | 285 | 6,945 |
| Roland Thatcher | 72 | 71 | 70 | 72 | 285 | 6,945 |
| Tjaart van der Walt | 74 | 68 | 74 | 69 | 285 | 6,945 |
| Garrett Willis | 71 | 71 | 69 | 74 | 285 | 6,945 |
| Danny Briggs | 69 | 72 | 74 | 71 | 286 | 6,750 |
| Todd Hamilton | 68 | 73 | 71 | 74 | 286 | 6,750 |
| Chris Anderson | 71 | 70 | 73 | 73 | 287 | 6,510 |
| Tommy Armour | 72 | 71 | 70 | 74 | 287 | 6,510 |
| Arjun Atwal | 74 | 70 | 69 | 74 | 287 | 6,510 |
| Danny Ellis | 74 | 67 | 80 | 66 | 287 | 6,510 |
| Rocco Mediate | 75 | 68 | 71 | 73 | 287 | 6,510 |
| Hidemichi Tanaka | 69 | 71 | 77 | 70 | 287 | 6,510 |
| Michael Long | 73 | 71 | 71 | 73 | 288 | 6,270 |
| Blaine McCallister | 73 | 69 | 74 | 72 | 288 | 6,270 |
| Glen Day | 74 | 70 | 70 | 75 | 289 | 6,150 |
| Scott Gutschewski | 71 | 71 | 73 | 74 | 289 | 6,150 |
| Charlie Wi | 74 | 70 | 71 | 75 | 290 | 6,060 |
| Bob Burns | 72 | 72 | 69 | 78 | 291 | 6,000 |
| Hank Kuehne | 74 | 68 | 76 | 75 | 293 | 5,940 |
| Hideto Tanihara | 73 | 70 | 77 | 76 | 296 | 5,880 |

## Buick Championship

*TPC at River Highlands*, Cromwell, Connecticut
Par 35-35–70; 6,820 yards

August 25-28
purse, $4,300,000

| | SCORES | | | | TOTAL | MONEY |
|---|---|---|---|---|---|---|
| Brad Faxon | 69 | 71 | 65 | 61 | 266 | $774,000 |
| Tjaart van der Walt | 68 | 66 | 68 | 64 | 266 | 464,400 |
| (Faxon defeated van der Walt on first playoff hole.) | | | | | | |
| Justin Rose | 65 | 63 | 70 | 69 | 267 | 292,400 |
| Michael Putnam | 65 | 69 | 71 | 63 | 268 | 177,733.34 |
| Ben Curtis | 64 | 68 | 67 | 69 | 268 | 177,733.33 |
| Jerry Kelly | 68 | 67 | 67 | 66 | 268 | 177,733.33 |
| Kenny Perry | 70 | 69 | 67 | 63 | 269 | 144,050 |
| Corey Pavin | 66 | 69 | 67 | 68 | 270 | 133,300 |
| Woody Austin | 69 | 68 | 65 | 69 | 271 | 116,100 |
| Darron Stiles | 71 | 69 | 63 | 68 | 271 | 116,100 |
| Nick Watney | 69 | 66 | 70 | 66 | 271 | 116,100 |

| | SCORES | | | | TOTAL | MONEY |
|---|---|---|---|---|---|---|
| Jeff Brehaut | 68 | 68 | 72 | 64 | 272 | 87,075 |
| Glen Day | 68 | 67 | 71 | 66 | 272 | 87,075 |
| Tom Gillis | 67 | 68 | 71 | 66 | 272 | 87,075 |
| Vaughn Taylor | 65 | 70 | 71 | 66 | 272 | 87,075 |
| Steve Allan | 70 | 68 | 68 | 67 | 273 | 66,650 |
| Robert Allenby | 68 | 66 | 72 | 67 | 273 | 66,650 |
| Jeff Maggert | 70 | 68 | 69 | 66 | 273 | 66,650 |
| Kevin Sutherland | 65 | 67 | 72 | 69 | 273 | 66,650 |
| Bart Bryant | 70 | 69 | 70 | 65 | 274 | 48,332 |
| Spencer Levin | 68 | 68 | 69 | 69 | 274 | 48,332 |
| Frank Lickliter | 68 | 70 | 68 | 68 | 274 | 48,332 |
| Pat Perez | 70 | 66 | 70 | 68 | 274 | 48,332 |
| Joey Sindelar | 75 | 62 | 72 | 65 | 274 | 48,332 |
| Hidemichi Tanaka | 66 | 70 | 74 | 65 | 275 | 32,823.34 |
| Bo Van Pelt | 67 | 71 | 71 | 66 | 275 | 32,823.34 |
| Jeff Hart | 71 | 67 | 68 | 69 | 275 | 32,823.33 |
| Peter Lonard | 68 | 71 | 68 | 68 | 275 | 32,823.33 |
| John Rollins | 74 | 66 | 69 | 66 | 275 | 32,823.33 |
| D.J. Trahan | 71 | 68 | 67 | 69 | 275 | 32,823.33 |
| Darren Clarke | 70 | 65 | 70 | 71 | 276 | 25,499 |
| Joe Durant | 66 | 73 | 69 | 68 | 276 | 25,499 |
| J.J. Henry | 67 | 67 | 73 | 69 | 276 | 25,499 |
| Spike McRoy | 68 | 71 | 66 | 71 | 276 | 25,499 |
| Tim Petrovic | 67 | 67 | 70 | 72 | 276 | 25,499 |
| Tom Byrum | 67 | 71 | 73 | 66 | 277 | 19,815.84 |
| Dudley Hart | 67 | 73 | 69 | 68 | 277 | 19,815.84 |
| Paul Azinger | 73 | 65 | 69 | 70 | 277 | 19,815.83 |
| Paul Gow | 69 | 70 | 69 | 69 | 277 | 19,815.83 |
| Matt Kuchar | 70 | 67 | 70 | 70 | 277 | 19,815.83 |
| Chris Smith | 66 | 67 | 75 | 69 | 277 | 19,815.83 |
| Doug Barron | 71 | 66 | 71 | 70 | 278 | 13,502 |
| Cameron Beckman | 68 | 69 | 72 | 69 | 278 | 13,502 |
| Jason Bohn | 67 | 70 | 71 | 70 | 278 | 13,502 |
| Mark Calcavecchia | 70 | 69 | 72 | 67 | 278 | 13,502 |
| Marco Dawson | 68 | 71 | 70 | 69 | 278 | 13,502 |
| Hunter Haas | 73 | 65 | 71 | 69 | 278 | 13,502 |
| Zach Johnson | 72 | 63 | 72 | 71 | 278 | 13,502 |
| Will MacKenzie | 70 | 66 | 71 | 71 | 278 | 13,502 |
| Patrick Sheehan | 72 | 65 | 71 | 70 | 278 | 13,502 |
| Michael Long | 71 | 68 | 68 | 72 | 279 | 10,348.67 |
| Lee Westwood | 69 | 69 | 70 | 71 | 279 | 10,348.67 |
| Dean Wilson | 67 | 66 | 73 | 73 | 279 | 10,348.66 |
| Brian Davis | 71 | 67 | 73 | 69 | 280 | 9,718 |
| Tim Herron | 70 | 67 | 73 | 70 | 280 | 9,718 |
| J.L. Lewis | 64 | 74 | 73 | 69 | 280 | 9,718 |
| Hunter Mahan | 69 | 71 | 72 | 68 | 280 | 9,718 |
| Kevin Na | 70 | 70 | 75 | 65 | 280 | 9,718 |
| Brenden Pappas | 69 | 69 | 71 | 71 | 280 | 9,718 |
| Omar Uresti | 69 | 70 | 71 | 70 | 280 | 9,718 |
| Paul Claxton | 68 | 71 | 72 | 70 | 281 | 9,331 |
| Mario Tiziani | 67 | 71 | 71 | 72 | 281 | 9,331 |
| Brian Gay | 71 | 66 | 73 | 72 | 282 | 9,116 |
| Matt Gogel | 73 | 66 | 73 | 70 | 282 | 9,116 |
| Jeff Sluman | 71 | 67 | 76 | 68 | 282 | 9,116 |
| Neal Lancaster | 71 | 69 | 70 | 73 | 283 | 8,858 |
| Franklin Langham | 65 | 70 | 75 | 73 | 283 | 8,858 |
| Len Mattiace | 71 | 68 | 71 | 73 | 283 | 8,858 |
| Robert Gamez | 69 | 70 | 71 | 74 | 284 | 8,643 |
| John Huston | 67 | 70 | 76 | 71 | 284 | 8,643 |
| D.A. Points | 67 | 72 | 73 | 73 | 285 | 8,471 |

| | SCORES | | | | TOTAL | MONEY |
|---|---|---|---|---|---|---|
| Joey Snyder | 69 | 71 | 69 | 76 | 285 | 8,471 |
| Steven Bowditch | 68 | 68 | 74 | 77 | 287 | 8,299 |
| Jason Gore | 74 | 65 | 76 | 72 | 287 | 8,299 |
| Brian Watts | 69 | 71 | 76 | 72 | 288 | 8,170 |
| D.J. Brigman | 73 | 67 | 78 | 74 | 292 | 8,041 |
| Dennis Paulson | 68 | 69 | 74 | 81 | 292 | 8,041 |

## Deutsche Bank Championship

*TPC of Boston,* Norton, Massachusetts
Par 36-35–71; 7,415 yards

September 2-5
purse, $5,500,000

| | SCORES | | | | TOTAL | MONEY |
|---|---|---|---|---|---|---|
| Olin Browne | 68 | 65 | 70 | 67 | 270 | $990,000 |
| Jason Bohn | 68 | 68 | 67 | 68 | 271 | 594,000 |
| Vaughn Taylor | 72 | 67 | 67 | 68 | 274 | 374,000 |
| Jeff Brehaut | 67 | 66 | 72 | 70 | 275 | 216,562.50 |
| Charles Howell | 72 | 67 | 69 | 67 | 275 | 216,562.50 |
| Carl Pettersson | 68 | 67 | 68 | 72 | 275 | 216,562.50 |
| Joey Sindelar | 67 | 68 | 69 | 71 | 275 | 216,562.50 |
| Fred Couples | 70 | 67 | 70 | 69 | 276 | 165,000 |
| Brandt Jobe | 71 | 67 | 69 | 69 | 276 | 165,000 |
| Marco Dawson | 69 | 66 | 71 | 71 | 277 | 126,500 |
| Kent Jones | 70 | 71 | 63 | 73 | 277 | 126,500 |
| Bo Van Pelt | 71 | 69 | 65 | 72 | 277 | 126,500 |
| Brett Wetterich | 68 | 68 | 69 | 72 | 277 | 126,500 |
| Mark Wilson | 67 | 70 | 71 | 69 | 277 | 126,500 |
| Robert Allenby | 69 | 65 | 71 | 73 | 278 | 70,125 |
| Billy Andrade | 66 | 68 | 69 | 75 | 278 | 70,125 |
| Brad Faxon | 74 | 67 | 66 | 71 | 278 | 70,125 |
| Scott Gutschewski | 67 | 71 | 70 | 70 | 278 | 70,125 |
| Tim Herron | 70 | 70 | 73 | 65 | 278 | 70,125 |
| Justin Leonard | 71 | 68 | 70 | 69 | 278 | 70,125 |
| Frank Lickliter | 69 | 67 | 74 | 68 | 278 | 70,125 |
| Rocco Mediate | 72 | 67 | 70 | 69 | 278 | 70,125 |
| Sean O'Hair | 68 | 71 | 70 | 69 | 278 | 70,125 |
| Brenden Pappas | 71 | 68 | 70 | 69 | 278 | 70,125 |
| Tim Petrovic | 68 | 66 | 74 | 70 | 278 | 70,125 |
| John Rollins | 72 | 68 | 63 | 75 | 278 | 70,125 |
| Jim Carter | 70 | 70 | 66 | 73 | 279 | 39,050 |
| Matt Kuchar | 71 | 67 | 70 | 71 | 279 | 39,050 |
| David Peoples | 71 | 70 | 69 | 69 | 279 | 39,050 |
| Justin Rose | 72 | 66 | 68 | 73 | 279 | 39,050 |
| Darron Stiles | 69 | 69 | 69 | 72 | 279 | 39,050 |
| Tommy Armour | 69 | 70 | 68 | 73 | 280 | 29,150 |
| Briny Baird | 66 | 69 | 72 | 73 | 280 | 29,150 |
| Doug Barron | 68 | 70 | 70 | 72 | 280 | 29,150 |
| D.J. Brigman | 72 | 68 | 69 | 71 | 280 | 29,150 |
| Dan Forsman | 68 | 69 | 72 | 71 | 280 | 29,150 |
| Brendan Jones | 70 | 70 | 70 | 70 | 280 | 29,150 |
| Jesper Parnevik | 68 | 68 | 75 | 69 | 280 | 29,150 |
| Marcel Siem | 74 | 62 | 72 | 72 | 280 | 29,150 |
| Craig Bowden | 70 | 68 | 73 | 70 | 281 | 20,350 |
| Glen Day | 72 | 68 | 71 | 70 | 281 | 20,350 |
| Lucas Glover | 69 | 70 | 72 | 70 | 281 | 20,350 |
| Franklin Langham | 71 | 66 | 71 | 73 | 281 | 20,350 |
| Billy Mayfair | 72 | 64 | 73 | 72 | 281 | 20,350 |

| | SCORES | | | | TOTAL | MONEY |
|---|---|---|---|---|---|---|
| Chris Smith | 71 | 69 | 68 | 73 | 281 | 20,350 |
| Tiger Woods | 65 | 73 | 72 | 71 | 281 | 20,350 |
| Cameron Beckman | 71 | 67 | 72 | 72 | 282 | 14,542 |
| Carlos Franco | 66 | 71 | 73 | 72 | 282 | 14,542 |
| Lee Janzen | 71 | 69 | 71 | 71 | 282 | 14,542 |
| Stephen Marino | 69 | 70 | 71 | 72 | 282 | 14,542 |
| Greg Owen | 69 | 71 | 71 | 71 | 282 | 14,542 |
| Tom Byrum | 68 | 72 | 72 | 71 | 283 | 12,636.25 |
| Todd Fischer | 71 | 70 | 73 | 69 | 283 | 12,636.25 |
| Harrison Frazar | 69 | 68 | 75 | 71 | 283 | 12,636.25 |
| Bradley Hughes | 71 | 68 | 71 | 73 | 283 | 12,636.25 |
| Trevor Immelman | 71 | 67 | 72 | 73 | 283 | 12,636.25 |
| Jonathan Kaye | 69 | 72 | 70 | 72 | 283 | 12,636.25 |
| Steve Lowery | 66 | 69 | 74 | 74 | 283 | 12,636.25 |
| Charlie Wi | 69 | 72 | 70 | 72 | 283 | 12,636.25 |
| Jonathan Byrd | 67 | 70 | 76 | 71 | 284 | 11,825 |
| Jason Gore | 69 | 67 | 73 | 75 | 284 | 11,825 |
| Bob Heintz | 71 | 69 | 71 | 73 | 284 | 11,825 |
| Neal Lancaster | 69 | 71 | 73 | 71 | 284 | 11,825 |
| Tom Pernice, Jr. | 73 | 66 | 71 | 74 | 284 | 11,825 |
| Ted Purdy | 71 | 66 | 76 | 71 | 284 | 11,825 |
| Arjun Atwal | 70 | 69 | 73 | 73 | 285 | 11,275 |
| Danny Ellis | 68 | 70 | 71 | 76 | 285 | 11,275 |
| Stephen Leaney | 67 | 71 | 76 | 71 | 285 | 11,275 |
| Dennis Paulson | 72 | 69 | 73 | 71 | 285 | 11,275 |
| Will MacKenzie | 67 | 68 | 77 | 74 | 286 | 10,945 |
| Joey Snyder | 73 | 65 | 77 | 71 | 286 | 10,945 |
| Paul Goydos | 70 | 69 | 73 | 75 | 287 | 10,725 |
| Tjaart van der Walt | 70 | 70 | 72 | 75 | 287 | 10,725 |
| Mathias Gronberg | 69 | 70 | 72 | 77 | 288 | 10,505 |
| John Senden | 75 | 66 | 73 | 74 | 288 | 10,505 |
| Robert Damron | 69 | 68 | 75 | 77 | 289 | 10,340 |
| Steve Flesch | 67 | 72 | 75 | 76 | 290 | 10,230 |

## Bell Canadian Open

*Shaughnessy Golf & Country Club,* Vancouver, British Columbia, Canada
Par 35-35–70; 6,946 yards

September 8-11
purse, $5,000,000

| | SCORES | | | | TOTAL | MONEY |
|---|---|---|---|---|---|---|
| Mark Calcavecchia | 65 | 67 | 72 | 71 | 275 | $900,000 |
| Ben Crane | 74 | 66 | 70 | 66 | 276 | 440,000 |
| Ryan Moore | 69 | 70 | 67 | 70 | 276 | 440,000 |
| Jesper Parnevik | 66 | 72 | 67 | 72 | 277 | 240,000 |
| Jerry Kelly | 72 | 66 | 69 | 71 | 278 | 190,000 |
| Joey Sindelar | 70 | 71 | 69 | 68 | 278 | 190,000 |
| Trevor Immelman | 71 | 68 | 70 | 70 | 279 | 155,833.34 |
| Stephen Ames | 73 | 70 | 64 | 72 | 279 | 155,833.33 |
| Vijay Singh | 73 | 66 | 68 | 72 | 279 | 155,833.33 |
| Arjun Atwal | 72 | 67 | 73 | 68 | 280 | 135,000 |
| Mathias Gronberg | 68 | 70 | 74 | 69 | 281 | 115,000 |
| Bob Heintz | 68 | 70 | 70 | 73 | 281 | 115,000 |
| John Huston | 69 | 72 | 70 | 70 | 281 | 115,000 |
| Briny Baird | 70 | 72 | 68 | 72 | 282 | 80,000 |
| Craig Barlow | 70 | 70 | 65 | 77 | 282 | 80,000 |
| Brian Davis | 70 | 71 | 66 | 75 | 282 | 80,000 |

| | SCORES | | | | TOTAL | MONEY |
|---|---|---|---|---|---|---|
| Carlos Franco | 68 | 70 | 70 | 74 | 282 | 80,000 |
| Matt Kuchar | 72 | 67 | 72 | 71 | 282 | 80,000 |
| Tom Pernice, Jr. | 68 | 72 | 71 | 71 | 282 | 80,000 |
| Ted Purdy | 67 | 72 | 72 | 71 | 282 | 80,000 |
| Michael Allen | 68 | 73 | 76 | 66 | 283 | 56,000 |
| Michael Harris | 72 | 70 | 67 | 74 | 283 | 56,000 |
| Rory Sabbatini | 73 | 68 | 69 | 73 | 283 | 56,000 |
| Billy Andrade | 70 | 73 | 68 | 73 | 284 | 42,625 |
| Scott Dunlap | 67 | 77 | 70 | 70 | 284 | 42,625 |
| Hunter Mahan | 71 | 70 | 72 | 71 | 284 | 42,625 |
| Peter Tomasulo | 73 | 70 | 70 | 71 | 284 | 42,625 |
| Harrison Frazar | 74 | 68 | 74 | 69 | 285 | 32,535.72 |
| Lucas Glover | 65 | 72 | 74 | 74 | 285 | 32,535.72 |
| Darron Stiles | 71 | 71 | 71 | 72 | 285 | 32,535.72 |
| Tommy Armour | 70 | 71 | 70 | 74 | 285 | 32,535.71 |
| Chris DiMarco | 70 | 73 | 68 | 74 | 285 | 32,535.71 |
| Franklin Langham | 72 | 70 | 69 | 74 | 285 | 32,535.71 |
| Joey Snyder | 71 | 69 | 71 | 74 | 285 | 32,535.71 |
| Craig Bowden | 76 | 68 | 73 | 69 | 286 | 24,650 |
| Jonathan Byrd | 68 | 76 | 71 | 71 | 286 | 24,650 |
| Jeff Hart | 69 | 72 | 71 | 74 | 286 | 24,650 |
| Kent Jones | 72 | 69 | 75 | 70 | 286 | 24,650 |
| Kevin Na | 70 | 72 | 67 | 77 | 286 | 24,650 |
| Jay Delsing | 70 | 72 | 74 | 71 | 287 | 18,000 |
| Bob Estes | 73 | 70 | 71 | 73 | 287 | 18,000 |
| Brent Geiberger | 68 | 71 | 75 | 73 | 287 | 18,000 |
| Scott Gutschewski | 70 | 74 | 70 | 73 | 287 | 18,000 |
| James McLean | 71 | 72 | 69 | 75 | 287 | 18,000 |
| Larry Mize | 70 | 71 | 74 | 72 | 287 | 18,000 |
| Loren Roberts | 70 | 70 | 75 | 72 | 287 | 18,000 |
| Mario Tiziani | 73 | 69 | 70 | 75 | 287 | 18,000 |
| Brandt Jobe | 67 | 73 | 75 | 73 | 288 | 12,720 |
| Neal Lancaster | 73 | 70 | 74 | 71 | 288 | 12,720 |
| John Rollins | 68 | 75 | 72 | 73 | 288 | 12,720 |
| Justin Rose | 74 | 66 | 74 | 74 | 288 | 12,720 |
| Craig Stadler | 70 | 72 | 71 | 75 | 288 | 12,720 |
| Aaron Baddeley | 69 | 71 | 73 | 76 | 289 | 11,633.34 |
| Brian Bateman | 71 | 72 | 71 | 75 | 289 | 11,633.33 |
| Scott McCarron | 68 | 72 | 71 | 78 | 289 | 11,633.33 |
| Notah Begay | 71 | 73 | 71 | 75 | 290 | 11,250 |
| Steve Collins | 73 | 69 | 70 | 78 | 290 | 11,250 |
| Robert Gamez | 73 | 71 | 71 | 75 | 290 | 11,250 |
| Michael Long | 74 | 69 | 75 | 72 | 290 | 11,250 |
| Steve Allan | 73 | 68 | 78 | 72 | 291 | 10,800 |
| Alex Cejka | 74 | 69 | 74 | 74 | 291 | 10,800 |
| Glen Day | 75 | 69 | 76 | 71 | 291 | 10,800 |
| Andrew Magee | 73 | 71 | 74 | 73 | 291 | 10,800 |
| Rod Pampling | 71 | 73 | 69 | 78 | 291 | 10,800 |
| Chris Anderson | 74 | 69 | 75 | 74 | 292 | 10,350 |
| Fred Funk | 72 | 72 | 73 | 75 | 292 | 10,350 |
| Scott Hend | 69 | 74 | 74 | 75 | 292 | 10,350 |
| Pat Perez | 71 | 73 | 73 | 75 | 292 | 10,350 |
| Paul Gow | 70 | 71 | 77 | 76 | 294 | 10,100 |
| Greg Owen | 73 | 71 | 77 | 75 | 296 | 10,000 |
| Mark O'Meara | 75 | 69 | 79 | 74 | 297 | 9,900 |
| Jim Carter | 69 | 74 | 75 | 80 | 298 | 9,800 |
| J.P. Hayes | 68 | 72 | 78 | 82 | 300 | 9,700 |

# 84 Lumber Classic

*Nemacolin Woodlands Resort & Spa, Mystic Rock Course,*
Farmington, Pennsylvania
Par 36-36–72; 7,516 yards

September 15-18
purse, $4,400,000

| | | SCORES | | | TOTAL | MONEY |
|---|---|---|---|---|---|---|
| Jason Gore | 65 | 72 | 67 | 70 | 274 | $792,000 |
| Carlos Franco | 69 | 69 | 68 | 69 | 275 | 475,200 |
| Ben Crane | 67 | 70 | 73 | 67 | 277 | 299,200 |
| Tim Herron | 70 | 68 | 70 | 70 | 278 | 211,200 |
| Cameron Beckman | 69 | 65 | 73 | 72 | 279 | 154,550 |
| Jonathan Byrd | 69 | 68 | 72 | 70 | 279 | 154,550 |
| Chris DiMarco | 70 | 70 | 67 | 72 | 279 | 154,550 |
| John Huston | 70 | 73 | 67 | 69 | 279 | 154,550 |
| Stuart Appleby | 67 | 66 | 75 | 72 | 280 | 114,400 |
| Justin Leonard | 73 | 64 | 70 | 73 | 280 | 114,400 |
| Rod Pampling | 70 | 67 | 69 | 74 | 280 | 114,400 |
| Tag Ridings | 68 | 71 | 67 | 74 | 280 | 114,400 |
| Craig Barlow | 70 | 66 | 70 | 75 | 281 | 82,500 |
| Steve Flesch | 72 | 70 | 68 | 71 | 281 | 82,500 |
| Phillip Price | 73 | 71 | 66 | 71 | 281 | 82,500 |
| Vijay Singh | 72 | 68 | 73 | 68 | 281 | 82,500 |
| Robert Allenby | 72 | 71 | 70 | 69 | 282 | 51,920 |
| Todd Fischer | 70 | 73 | 69 | 70 | 282 | 51,920 |
| Harrison Frazar | 73 | 71 | 74 | 64 | 282 | 51,920 |
| Dudley Hart | 69 | 72 | 75 | 66 | 282 | 51,920 |
| Zach Johnson | 67 | 73 | 68 | 74 | 282 | 51,920 |
| Will MacKenzie | 73 | 68 | 70 | 71 | 282 | 51,920 |
| Ryan Moore | 68 | 75 | 70 | 69 | 282 | 51,920 |
| Carl Pettersson | 66 | 70 | 70 | 76 | 282 | 51,920 |
| Joey Sindelar | 68 | 68 | 72 | 74 | 282 | 51,920 |
| Chris Smith | 68 | 66 | 74 | 74 | 282 | 51,920 |
| Steve Lowery | 74 | 70 | 68 | 71 | 283 | 33,880 |
| Paul Claxton | 69 | 72 | 70 | 73 | 284 | 30,580 |
| Shigeki Maruyama | 70 | 74 | 71 | 69 | 284 | 30,580 |
| Rocco Mediate | 72 | 71 | 72 | 69 | 284 | 30,580 |
| Phil Mickelson | 73 | 71 | 67 | 73 | 284 | 30,580 |
| D.A. Points | 72 | 71 | 73 | 69 | 285 | 24,904 |
| Rory Sabbatini | 70 | 74 | 70 | 71 | 285 | 24,904 |
| Vaughn Taylor | 71 | 71 | 70 | 73 | 285 | 24,904 |
| Charlie Wi | 65 | 73 | 75 | 72 | 285 | 24,904 |
| Dean Wilson | 71 | 69 | 72 | 73 | 285 | 24,904 |
| Stewart Cink | 70 | 70 | 71 | 75 | 286 | 19,800 |
| David Hearn | 73 | 69 | 72 | 72 | 286 | 19,800 |
| Peter Lonard | 72 | 70 | 74 | 70 | 286 | 19,800 |
| Jesper Parnevik | 70 | 72 | 69 | 75 | 286 | 19,800 |
| Michael Putnam | 71 | 73 | 70 | 72 | 286 | 19,800 |
| Brian Bateman | 72 | 71 | 71 | 73 | 287 | 13,816 |
| Glen Day | 71 | 73 | 74 | 69 | 287 | 13,816 |
| Frank Lickliter | 71 | 73 | 71 | 72 | 287 | 13,816 |
| Shaun Micheel | 65 | 74 | 74 | 74 | 287 | 13,816 |
| Mark O'Meara | 65 | 74 | 71 | 77 | 287 | 13,816 |
| Ted Purdy | 72 | 70 | 74 | 71 | 287 | 13,816 |
| John Senden | 75 | 65 | 72 | 75 | 287 | 13,816 |
| Joey Snyder | 74 | 68 | 70 | 75 | 287 | 13,816 |
| Roland Thatcher | 72 | 71 | 70 | 74 | 287 | 13,816 |
| Matt Gogel | 72 | 72 | 72 | 72 | 288 | 10,188.45 |
| Todd Hamilton | 73 | 71 | 75 | 69 | 288 | 10,188.45 |
| Brenden Pappas | 68 | 74 | 73 | 73 | 288 | 10,188.45 |

| | SCORES | | | | TOTAL | MONEY |
|---|---|---|---|---|---|---|
| Patrick Sheehan | 73 | 70 | 74 | 71 | 288 | 10,188.45 |
| Brian Gay | 73 | 70 | 68 | 77 | 288 | 10,188.44 |
| Hunter Haas | 71 | 69 | 71 | 77 | 288 | 10,188.44 |
| Scott Hend | 72 | 70 | 69 | 77 | 288 | 10,188.44 |
| Kent Jones | 73 | 68 | 72 | 75 | 288 | 10,188.44 |
| Heath Slocum | 71 | 71 | 72 | 74 | 288 | 10,188.44 |
| Woody Austin | 70 | 70 | 72 | 77 | 289 | 9,636 |
| Bob Burns | 67 | 70 | 76 | 76 | 289 | 9,636 |
| Steve Allan | 73 | 70 | 72 | 75 | 290 | 9,416 |
| Tom Pernice, Jr. | 71 | 72 | 73 | 74 | 290 | 9,416 |
| Kevin Stadler | 69 | 75 | 77 | 69 | 290 | 9,416 |
| Bradley Hughes | 73 | 71 | 77 | 70 | 291 | 9,196 |
| Lee Janzen | 70 | 73 | 73 | 75 | 291 | 9,196 |
| Alex Cejka | 71 | 72 | 74 | 76 | 293 | 9,064 |
| Pat Perez | 68 | 73 | 74 | 79 | 294 | 8,976 |
| Andrew Magee | 73 | 71 | 77 | 74 | 295 | 8,888 |
| Skip Kendall | 72 | 72 | 78 | 74 | 296 | 8,756 |
| Bo Van Pelt | 69 | 74 | 79 | 74 | 296 | 8,756 |
| Marco Dawson | 74 | 70 | 78 | 75 | 297 | 8,624 |
| Jeff Maggert | 72 | 71 | 83 | 73 | 299 | 8,536 |

## The Presidents Cup

See Special Events section.

## Valero Texas Open

*LaCantera Golf Club, Resort Course,* San Antonio, Texas
Par 35-35–70; 6,881 yards

September 22-25
purse, $3,500,000

| | SCORES | | | | TOTAL | MONEY |
|---|---|---|---|---|---|---|
| Robert Gamez | 62 | 68 | 68 | 64 | 262 | $630,000 |
| Olin Browne | 65 | 65 | 71 | 64 | 265 | 378,000 |
| Woody Austin | 63 | 67 | 67 | 69 | 266 | 203,000 |
| Mark Wilson | 65 | 67 | 66 | 68 | 266 | 203,000 |
| Bob Heintz | 65 | 65 | 69 | 68 | 267 | 133,000 |
| J.J. Henry | 66 | 67 | 66 | 68 | 267 | 133,000 |
| Dean Wilson | 66 | 62 | 70 | 70 | 268 | 117,250 |
| Jay Delsing | 67 | 71 | 68 | 63 | 269 | 94,500 |
| Harrison Frazar | 65 | 69 | 69 | 66 | 269 | 94,500 |
| Steve Lowery | 69 | 66 | 66 | 68 | 269 | 94,500 |
| Jeff Maggert | 63 | 66 | 70 | 70 | 269 | 94,500 |
| John Senden | 63 | 66 | 70 | 70 | 269 | 94,500 |
| Bart Bryant | 65 | 69 | 70 | 66 | 270 | 70,000 |
| Heath Slocum | 73 | 64 | 68 | 65 | 270 | 70,000 |
| Paul Claxton | 67 | 69 | 66 | 69 | 271 | 57,750 |
| Marco Dawson | 68 | 67 | 69 | 67 | 271 | 57,750 |
| Bob Estes | 71 | 66 | 68 | 66 | 271 | 57,750 |
| Joe Ogilvie | 69 | 66 | 68 | 68 | 271 | 57,750 |
| Chad Campbell | 74 | 65 | 65 | 68 | 272 | 42,420 |
| Alex Cejka | 66 | 67 | 68 | 71 | 272 | 42,420 |
| Brian Gay | 70 | 66 | 69 | 67 | 272 | 42,420 |
| Scott Gutschewski | 70 | 68 | 66 | 68 | 272 | 42,420 |
| Bob Tway | 69 | 68 | 69 | 66 | 272 | 42,420 |
| David Hearn | 64 | 69 | 72 | 68 | 273 | 32,200 |

| | SCORES | | | | TOTAL | MONEY |
|---|---|---|---|---|---|---|
| Michael Putnam | 71 | 67 | 68 | 67 | 273 | 32,200 |
| Tommy Armour | 72 | 65 | 71 | 66 | 274 | 24,850 |
| Aaron Baddeley | 65 | 72 | 70 | 67 | 274 | 24,850 |
| Jason Bohn | 66 | 72 | 68 | 68 | 274 | 24,850 |
| J.L. Lewis | 70 | 69 | 66 | 69 | 274 | 24,850 |
| Shigeki Maruyama | 68 | 71 | 68 | 67 | 274 | 24,850 |
| Rod Pampling | 65 | 70 | 69 | 70 | 274 | 24,850 |
| Hidemichi Tanaka | 69 | 70 | 70 | 65 | 274 | 24,850 |
| Gavin Coles | 66 | 70 | 70 | 69 | 275 | 18,491.67 |
| Rocco Mediate | 68 | 69 | 69 | 69 | 275 | 18,491.67 |
| Rory Sabbatini | 72 | 67 | 65 | 71 | 275 | 18,491.67 |
| Darron Stiles | 68 | 71 | 65 | 71 | 275 | 18,491.67 |
| Jose Coceres | 66 | 70 | 68 | 71 | 275 | 18,491.66 |
| Brad Lardon | 65 | 71 | 68 | 71 | 275 | 18,491.66 |
| Larry Mize | 65 | 74 | 71 | 66 | 276 | 14,700 |
| John Morgan | 65 | 69 | 72 | 70 | 276 | 14,700 |
| Vaughn Taylor | 69 | 69 | 71 | 67 | 276 | 14,700 |
| Omar Uresti | 67 | 72 | 71 | 66 | 276 | 14,700 |
| Cameron Beckman | 67 | 72 | 70 | 68 | 277 | 11,550 |
| Dan Forsman | 70 | 66 | 72 | 69 | 277 | 11,550 |
| Charles Howell | 68 | 71 | 68 | 70 | 277 | 11,550 |
| Corey Pavin | 71 | 68 | 70 | 68 | 277 | 11,550 |
| Tag Ridings | 66 | 68 | 76 | 67 | 277 | 11,550 |
| Briny Baird | 67 | 70 | 74 | 67 | 278 | 8,904 |
| Rich Beem | 68 | 66 | 72 | 72 | 278 | 8,904 |
| Carl Pettersson | 69 | 69 | 68 | 72 | 278 | 8,904 |
| Ted Purdy | 64 | 69 | 71 | 74 | 278 | 8,904 |
| Mike Standly | 67 | 72 | 72 | 67 | 278 | 8,904 |
| Arjun Atwal | 66 | 70 | 74 | 69 | 279 | 8,102.50 |
| Tom Byrum | 69 | 69 | 70 | 71 | 279 | 8,102.50 |
| Mathias Gronberg | 66 | 73 | 71 | 69 | 279 | 8,102.50 |
| Ryan Moore | 72 | 67 | 72 | 68 | 279 | 8,102.50 |
| Lee Janzen | 68 | 70 | 73 | 69 | 280 | 7,840 |
| Phillip Price | 64 | 72 | 73 | 71 | 280 | 7,840 |
| Nick Watney | 64 | 70 | 80 | 66 | 280 | 7,840 |
| Matt Davidson | 70 | 68 | 71 | 72 | 281 | 7,630 |
| David Duval | 69 | 68 | 70 | 74 | 281 | 7,630 |
| Richard Johnson | 70 | 69 | 73 | 69 | 281 | 7,630 |
| Notah Begay | 68 | 71 | 71 | 72 | 282 | 7,315 |
| Jeff Brehaut | 69 | 69 | 72 | 72 | 282 | 7,315 |
| John Elliott | 70 | 68 | 75 | 69 | 282 | 7,315 |
| Chris Riley | 69 | 69 | 74 | 70 | 282 | 7,315 |
| Akio Sadakata | 70 | 68 | 74 | 70 | 282 | 7,315 |
| Bo Van Pelt | 68 | 70 | 72 | 72 | 282 | 7,315 |
| Tripp Isenhour | 71 | 68 | 73 | 71 | 283 | 7,000 |
| David Lundstrom | 67 | 72 | 69 | 75 | 283 | 7,000 |
| Wes Short, Jr. | 69 | 70 | 75 | 69 | 283 | 7,000 |
| Brendan Jones | 65 | 74 | 73 | 72 | 284 | 6,860 |
| Will MacKenzie | 69 | 69 | 74 | 74 | 286 | 6,790 |
| Hal Sutton | 71 | 68 | 82 | 66 | 287 | 6,720 |

# Chrysler Classic of Greensboro

*Forest Oaks Country Club,* Greensboro, North Carolina
Par 36-36–72; 7,311 yards

September 29-October 2
purse, $5,000,000

| | SCORES | | | | TOTAL | MONEY |
|---|---|---|---|---|---|---|
| K.J. Choi | 64 | 69 | 67 | 66 | 266 | $900,000 |
| Shigeki Maruyama | 70 | 65 | 66 | 67 | 268 | 540,000 |
| Jason Bohn | 71 | 65 | 65 | 70 | 271 | 260,000 |
| Brandt Jobe | 72 | 65 | 67 | 67 | 271 | 260,000 |
| Charles Warren | 62 | 74 | 70 | 65 | 271 | 260,000 |
| Tim Clark | 66 | 69 | 70 | 68 | 273 | 156,500 |
| Tim Herron | 70 | 66 | 67 | 70 | 273 | 156,500 |
| Jerry Kelly | 70 | 68 | 67 | 68 | 273 | 156,500 |
| J.L. Lewis | 72 | 68 | 67 | 66 | 273 | 156,500 |
| Justin Rose | 69 | 65 | 68 | 71 | 273 | 156,500 |
| Kent Jones | 70 | 71 | 67 | 66 | 274 | 120,000 |
| Carl Pettersson | 69 | 67 | 69 | 69 | 274 | 120,000 |
| Sergio Garcia | 69 | 69 | 66 | 71 | 275 | 93,750 |
| Scott Gutschewski | 67 | 74 | 66 | 68 | 275 | 93,750 |
| Wes Short, Jr. | 68 | 70 | 69 | 68 | 275 | 93,750 |
| D.J. Trahan | 65 | 69 | 66 | 75 | 275 | 93,750 |
| Olin Browne | 68 | 72 | 65 | 71 | 276 | 72,500 |
| Dudley Hart | 70 | 67 | 70 | 69 | 276 | 72,500 |
| John Huston | 66 | 66 | 74 | 70 | 276 | 72,500 |
| Darron Stiles | 69 | 69 | 68 | 70 | 276 | 72,500 |
| Lucas Glover | 70 | 71 | 70 | 66 | 277 | 48,357.15 |
| J.J. Henry | 66 | 72 | 72 | 67 | 277 | 48,357.15 |
| Brian Bateman | 70 | 71 | 67 | 69 | 277 | 48,357.14 |
| Cameron Beckman | 70 | 69 | 70 | 68 | 277 | 48,357.14 |
| D.A. Points | 72 | 66 | 70 | 69 | 277 | 48,357.14 |
| Chris Smith | 72 | 65 | 72 | 68 | 277 | 48,357.14 |
| Duffy Waldorf | 69 | 71 | 67 | 70 | 277 | 48,357.14 |
| Jonathan Byrd | 67 | 73 | 70 | 68 | 278 | 33,250 |
| Steve Elkington | 70 | 70 | 69 | 69 | 278 | 33,250 |
| Robert Gamez | 72 | 69 | 63 | 74 | 278 | 33,250 |
| Hank Kuehne | 71 | 67 | 71 | 69 | 278 | 33,250 |
| Tim Petrovic | 70 | 69 | 70 | 69 | 278 | 33,250 |
| John Rollins | 67 | 68 | 71 | 72 | 278 | 33,250 |
| Marco Dawson | 72 | 68 | 68 | 71 | 279 | 24,714.29 |
| Brian Gay | 69 | 66 | 73 | 71 | 279 | 24,714.29 |
| Charles Howell | 69 | 71 | 68 | 71 | 279 | 24,714.29 |
| Ryan Moore | 72 | 69 | 70 | 68 | 279 | 24,714.29 |
| Paul Azinger | 69 | 71 | 66 | 73 | 279 | 24,714.28 |
| Daniel Chopra | 67 | 69 | 71 | 72 | 279 | 24,714.28 |
| Neal Lancaster | 71 | 70 | 67 | 71 | 279 | 24,714.28 |
| Steve Allan | 72 | 68 | 68 | 72 | 280 | 19,000 |
| Gavin Coles | 68 | 70 | 73 | 69 | 280 | 19,000 |
| Steve Lowery | 74 | 67 | 68 | 71 | 280 | 19,000 |
| Jeff Maggert | 69 | 71 | 70 | 70 | 280 | 19,000 |
| Tom Byrum | 71 | 67 | 72 | 71 | 281 | 14,300 |
| Chad Campbell | 69 | 72 | 69 | 71 | 281 | 14,300 |
| James Driscoll | 67 | 71 | 72 | 71 | 281 | 14,300 |
| Shaun Micheel | 75 | 66 | 69 | 71 | 281 | 14,300 |
| Tag Ridings | 71 | 68 | 75 | 67 | 281 | 14,300 |
| Mark Wilson | 72 | 67 | 66 | 76 | 281 | 14,300 |
| Justin Bolli | 69 | 72 | 69 | 72 | 282 | 11,840 |
| Robert Damron | 74 | 67 | 74 | 67 | 282 | 11,840 |
| Jonathan Kaye | 70 | 68 | 70 | 74 | 282 | 11,840 |
| Phillip Price | 69 | 71 | 71 | 71 | 282 | 11,840 |

| | SCORES | | | | TOTAL | MONEY |
|---|---|---|---|---|---|---|
| Charlie Wi | 70 | 71 | 70 | 71 | 282 | 11,840 |
| Tommy Armour | 71 | 70 | 72 | 70 | 283 | 11,200 |
| Joe Durant | 67 | 71 | 70 | 75 | 283 | 11,200 |
| Hunter Haas | 70 | 68 | 73 | 72 | 283 | 11,200 |
| Thomas Levet | 74 | 67 | 72 | 70 | 283 | 11,200 |
| Heath Slocum | 71 | 69 | 72 | 71 | 283 | 11,200 |
| Matt Gogel | 67 | 74 | 69 | 74 | 284 | 10,800 |
| Michael Long | 70 | 71 | 74 | 69 | 284 | 10,800 |
| Hidemichi Tanaka | 66 | 74 | 72 | 72 | 284 | 10,800 |
| Tom Lehman | 69 | 70 | 72 | 74 | 285 | 10,450 |
| Geoff Ogilvy | 68 | 73 | 72 | 72 | 285 | 10,450 |
| Adam Scott | 73 | 68 | 70 | 74 | 285 | 10,450 |
| Tjaart van der Walt | 73 | 68 | 70 | 74 | 285 | 10,450 |
| Jay Delsing | 71 | 68 | 73 | 74 | 286 | 10,000 |
| Peter Lonard | 71 | 70 | 72 | 73 | 286 | 10,000 |
| Billy Mayfair | 69 | 71 | 70 | 76 | 286 | 10,000 |
| Tom Pernice, Jr. | 72 | 69 | 71 | 74 | 286 | 10,000 |
| Patrick Sheehan | 71 | 68 | 76 | 71 | 286 | 10,000 |
| Hunter Mahan | 75 | 66 | 72 | 74 | 287 | 9,700 |
| Billy Andrade | 69 | 72 | 73 | 74 | 288 | 9,550 |
| Corey Pavin | 72 | 69 | 75 | 72 | 288 | 9,550 |
| Ben Curtis | 69 | 69 | 79 | 73 | 290 | 9,350 |
| Tom Gillis | 70 | 68 | 73 | 79 | 290 | 9,350 |

## WGC - American Express Championship

*Harding Park Golf Course,* San Francisco, California,
Par 35-35–70; 7,086 yards

October 6-9
purse, $7,500,000

| | SCORES | | | | TOTAL | MONEY |
|---|---|---|---|---|---|---|
| Tiger Woods | 67 | 68 | 68 | 67 | 270 | $1,300,000 |
| John Daly | 67 | 67 | 67 | 69 | 270 | 750,000 |
| (Woods defeated Daly on second playoff hole.) | | | | | | |
| Henrik Stenson | 70 | 67 | 67 | 68 | 272 | 353,666.67 |
| Sergio Garcia | 67 | 69 | 67 | 69 | 272 | 353,666.66 |
| Colin Montgomerie | 64 | 69 | 69 | 70 | 272 | 353,666.66 |
| David Howell | 67 | 67 | 74 | 67 | 275 | 187,500 |
| Graeme McDowell | 69 | 70 | 68 | 68 | 275 | 187,500 |
| Vijay Singh | 67 | 70 | 69 | 69 | 275 | 187,500 |
| David Toms | 68 | 68 | 70 | 69 | 275 | 187,500 |
| Stephen Ames | 72 | 64 | 71 | 69 | 276 | 140,000 |
| Stuart Appleby | 71 | 65 | 69 | 72 | 277 | 115,000 |
| Luke Donald | 70 | 71 | 68 | 68 | 277 | 115,000 |
| Davis Love | 71 | 68 | 71 | 67 | 277 | 115,000 |
| Shigeki Maruyama | 74 | 69 | 67 | 67 | 277 | 115,000 |
| Fred Couples | 74 | 69 | 66 | 69 | 278 | 87,333.34 |
| Chad Campbell | 67 | 70 | 70 | 71 | 278 | 87,333.33 |
| Jim Furyk | 68 | 67 | 71 | 72 | 278 | 87,333.33 |
| Angel Cabrera | 69 | 66 | 72 | 72 | 279 | 77,000 |
| Tim Clark | 69 | 69 | 72 | 69 | 279 | 77,000 |
| Stephen Dodd | 70 | 68 | 70 | 71 | 279 | 77,000 |
| Bradley Dredge | 69 | 69 | 72 | 69 | 279 | 77,000 |
| Ian Poulter | 67 | 70 | 72 | 70 | 279 | 77,000 |
| Charl Schwartzel | 72 | 66 | 74 | 67 | 279 | 77,000 |
| Mike Weir | 73 | 67 | 70 | 69 | 279 | 77,000 |
| Mark Calcavecchia | 67 | 68 | 74 | 71 | 280 | 66,000 |
| Yasuharu Imano | 69 | 68 | 72 | 71 | 280 | 66,000 |

| | SCORES | | | | TOTAL | MONEY |
|---|---|---|---|---|---|---|
| Brandt Jobe | 68 | 71 | 71 | 70 | 280 | 66,000 |
| Billy Mayfair | 69 | 67 | 73 | 71 | 280 | 66,000 |
| Fred Funk | 67 | 68 | 75 | 71 | 281 | 60,000 |
| Phil Mickelson | 71 | 69 | 73 | 68 | 281 | 60,000 |
| Adam Scott | 68 | 70 | 69 | 74 | 281 | 60,000 |
| Jason Bohn | 70 | 68 | 70 | 74 | 282 | 57,000 |
| Kenny Perry | 76 | 69 | 69 | 68 | 282 | 57,000 |
| Vaughn Taylor | 71 | 72 | 66 | 73 | 282 | 57,000 |
| Paul McGinley | 73 | 65 | 72 | 73 | 283 | 54,500 |
| Sean O'Hair | 68 | 67 | 71 | 77 | 283 | 54,500 |
| Olin Browne | 67 | 74 | 73 | 70 | 284 | 51,500 |
| Ben Crane | 70 | 68 | 76 | 70 | 284 | 51,500 |
| Niclas Fasth | 70 | 70 | 73 | 71 | 284 | 51,500 |
| Peter Lonard | 73 | 71 | 69 | 71 | 284 | 51,500 |
| Miguel Angel Jimenez | 69 | 70 | 73 | 73 | 285 | 48,500 |
| Rod Pampling | 67 | 71 | 76 | 71 | 285 | 48,500 |
| K.J. Choi | 70 | 71 | 72 | 73 | 286 | 46,000 |
| Zach Johnson | 68 | 69 | 74 | 75 | 286 | 46,000 |
| Simon Yates | 73 | 68 | 70 | 75 | 286 | 46,000 |
| Michael Campbell | 71 | 68 | 72 | 76 | 287 | 43,250 |
| Stewart Cink | 70 | 72 | 75 | 70 | 287 | 43,250 |
| Kenneth Ferrie | 74 | 67 | 71 | 75 | 287 | 43,250 |
| Justin Leonard | 75 | 72 | 71 | 69 | 287 | 43,250 |
| Joe Ogilvie | 71 | 74 | 68 | 75 | 288 | 42,000 |
| Nick Dougherty | 71 | 74 | 72 | 72 | 289 | 40,500 |
| Richard Green | 69 | 74 | 76 | 70 | 289 | 40,500 |
| Jose Maria Olazabal | 72 | 72 | 76 | 69 | 289 | 40,500 |
| Jyoti Randhawa | 70 | 70 | 74 | 75 | 289 | 40,500 |
| Lee Westwood | 71 | 75 | 75 | 68 | 289 | 40,500 |
| Bart Bryant | 71 | 76 | 71 | 72 | 290 | 38,500 |
| Mark Hensby | 72 | 74 | 71 | 73 | 290 | 38,500 |
| Nick O'Hern | 75 | 69 | 71 | 75 | 290 | 38,500 |
| Gavin Coles | 71 | 74 | 75 | 71 | 291 | 37,500 |
| Thongchai Jaidee | 73 | 72 | 73 | 74 | 292 | 37,000 |
| Tom Lehman | 73 | 74 | 72 | 74 | 293 | 36,500 |
| Scott Verplank | 72 | 69 | 76 | 77 | 294 | 35,750 |
| Euan Walters | 74 | 72 | 75 | 73 | 294 | 35,750 |
| Chris DiMarco | 71 | 75 | 73 | 76 | 295 | 34,750 |
| S.K. Ho | 72 | 77 | 71 | 75 | 295 | 34,750 |
| Ted Purdy | 71 | 75 | 75 | 76 | 297 | 34,000 |
| Padraig Harrington | 74 | 72 | 80 | 73 | 299 | 33,500 |
| Neil Cheetham | 77 | 78 | 72 | 76 | 303 | 33,000 |
| Warren Abery | 80 | 77 | 75 | 74 | 306 | 32,500 |
| Thomas Bjorn | 71 | 67 | 74 | WD | | |
| Steve Elkington | WD | | | | | |

# Michelin Championship at Las Vegas

*TPC at Summerlin:* Par 36-36–72; 7,243 yards
*TPC at The Canyons:* Par 36-35–71; 7,193 yards
Las Vegas, Nevada

October 13-16
purse, $4,000,000

| | SCORES | | | | TOTAL | MONEY |
|---|---|---|---|---|---|---|
| Wes Short, Jr. | 67 | 67 | 66 | 66 | 266 | $720,000 |
| Jim Furyk | 66 | 66 | 69 | 65 | 266 | 432,000 |
| (Short defeated Furyk on second playoff hole.) | | | | | | |
| Harrison Frazar | 68 | 63 | 68 | 69 | 268 | 232,000 |

| | SCORES | | | | TOTAL | MONEY |
|---|---|---|---|---|---|---|
| Ted Purdy | 67 | 65 | 65 | 71 | 268 | 232,000 |
| Charles Howell | 63 | 69 | 67 | 70 | 269 | 160,000 |
| Shigeki Maruyama | 65 | 65 | 72 | 68 | 270 | 139,000 |
| Nick Watney | 67 | 67 | 70 | 66 | 270 | 139,000 |
| Briny Baird | 62 | 66 | 78 | 65 | 271 | 112,000 |
| Steve Lowery | 67 | 68 | 64 | 72 | 271 | 112,000 |
| Will MacKenzie | 65 | 69 | 70 | 67 | 271 | 112,000 |
| Hidemichi Tanaka | 66 | 68 | 68 | 69 | 271 | 112,000 |
| Daniel Chopra | 70 | 67 | 70 | 65 | 272 | 81,000 |
| Stephen Leaney | 67 | 67 | 69 | 69 | 272 | 81,000 |
| Davis Love | 68 | 67 | 71 | 66 | 272 | 81,000 |
| Ryan Palmer | 62 | 72 | 68 | 70 | 272 | 81,000 |
| John Daly | 68 | 67 | 70 | 68 | 273 | 52,533.34 |
| Ryan Moore | 67 | 63 | 74 | 69 | 273 | 52,533.34 |
| Rod Pampling | 67 | 64 | 74 | 68 | 273 | 52,533.34 |
| Bart Bryant | 64 | 66 | 73 | 70 | 273 | 52,533.33 |
| Ben Crane | 67 | 65 | 72 | 69 | 273 | 52,533.33 |
| Scott Gutschewski | 64 | 71 | 67 | 71 | 273 | 52,533.33 |
| Geoff Ogilvy | 65 | 69 | 67 | 72 | 273 | 52,533.33 |
| Tom Pernice, Jr. | 65 | 68 | 70 | 70 | 273 | 52,533.33 |
| Bo Van Pelt | 70 | 66 | 67 | 70 | 273 | 52,533.33 |
| Lee Janzen | 66 | 69 | 70 | 69 | 274 | 31,900 |
| John Senden | 66 | 66 | 73 | 69 | 274 | 31,900 |
| Kevin Sutherland | 67 | 67 | 70 | 70 | 274 | 31,900 |
| Scott Verplank | 70 | 66 | 69 | 69 | 274 | 31,900 |
| Fred Funk | 67 | 68 | 70 | 70 | 275 | 25,433.34 |
| Jason Gore | 65 | 70 | 71 | 69 | 275 | 25,433.34 |
| Olin Browne | 67 | 65 | 75 | 68 | 275 | 25,433.33 |
| Joe Durant | 66 | 70 | 71 | 68 | 275 | 25,433.33 |
| Phillip Price | 68 | 66 | 68 | 73 | 275 | 25,433.33 |
| Jeff Sluman | 67 | 69 | 66 | 73 | 275 | 25,433.33 |
| Michael Allen | 64 | 68 | 73 | 71 | 276 | 20,150 |
| Fred Couples | 69 | 67 | 71 | 69 | 276 | 20,150 |
| Donnie Hammond | 68 | 68 | 69 | 71 | 276 | 20,150 |
| Charles Warren | 69 | 66 | 71 | 70 | 276 | 20,150 |
| Robert Allenby | 68 | 68 | 70 | 71 | 277 | 15,200 |
| Billy Andrade | 65 | 68 | 72 | 72 | 277 | 15,200 |
| Paul Azinger | 71 | 66 | 67 | 73 | 277 | 15,200 |
| Marco Dawson | 68 | 67 | 73 | 69 | 277 | 15,200 |
| Padraig Harrington | 69 | 67 | 72 | 69 | 277 | 15,200 |
| Ryuji Imada | 64 | 70 | 70 | 73 | 277 | 15,200 |
| Omar Uresti | 68 | 68 | 70 | 71 | 277 | 15,200 |
| Tjaart van der Walt | 64 | 71 | 68 | 74 | 277 | 15,200 |
| Frank Lickliter | 67 | 69 | 69 | 73 | 278 | 9,869.10 |
| Tommy Armour | 69 | 66 | 75 | 68 | 278 | 9,869.09 |
| Paul Claxton | 69 | 67 | 69 | 73 | 278 | 9,869.09 |
| James Driscoll | 69 | 68 | 70 | 71 | 278 | 9,869.09 |
| Brian Gay | 72 | 65 | 72 | 69 | 278 | 9,869.09 |
| Bill Glasson | 68 | 68 | 71 | 71 | 278 | 9,869.09 |
| Paul Goydos | 65 | 65 | 73 | 75 | 278 | 9,869.09 |
| Jerry Kelly | 67 | 69 | 67 | 75 | 278 | 9,869.09 |
| Carl Pettersson | 68 | 69 | 70 | 71 | 278 | 9,869.09 |
| Rory Sabbatini | 67 | 67 | 76 | 68 | 278 | 9,869.09 |
| Dean Wilson | 69 | 66 | 72 | 71 | 278 | 9,869.09 |
| Stuart Appleby | 67 | 70 | 71 | 71 | 279 | 8,640 |
| Robert Gamez | 67 | 70 | 69 | 73 | 279 | 8,640 |
| Lucas Glover | 66 | 66 | 73 | 74 | 279 | 8,640 |
| Hunter Haas | 65 | 69 | 73 | 72 | 279 | 8,640 |
| Bob Heintz | 68 | 69 | 72 | 70 | 279 | 8,640 |
| Billy Mayfair | 68 | 69 | 76 | 66 | 279 | 8,640 |

| | SCORES | | | | TOTAL | MONEY |
|---|---|---|---|---|---|---|
| Corey Pavin | 68 | 68 | 72 | 71 | 279 | 8,640 |
| Scott Piercy | 72 | 65 | 69 | 73 | 279 | 8,640 |
| Duffy Waldorf | 67 | 70 | 73 | 69 | 279 | 8,640 |
| Chad Campbell | 71 | 65 | 74 | 70 | 280 | 8,200 |
| J.J. Henry | 66 | 70 | 70 | 74 | 280 | 8,200 |
| Aaron Baddeley | 72 | 63 | 74 | 72 | 281 | 8,040 |
| Justin Leonard | 63 | 70 | 71 | 77 | 281 | 8,040 |
| Brent Geiberger | 66 | 71 | 75 | 70 | 282 | 7,880 |
| D.A. Points | 67 | 70 | 72 | 73 | 282 | 7,880 |
| Gavin Coles | 68 | 69 | 72 | 74 | 283 | 7,720 |
| John Huston | 70 | 65 | 72 | 76 | 283 | 7,720 |
| Joe Ogilvie | 67 | 68 | 70 | 80 | 285 | 7,600 |
| Todd Fischer | 70 | 66 | 78 | 72 | 286 | 7,480 |
| John Rollins | 67 | 69 | 76 | 74 | 286 | 7,480 |
| Jonathan Byrd | 67 | 69 | 70 | 81 | 287 | 7,360 |
| Mark Hensby | 69 | 67 | 75 | 79 | 290 | 7,280 |
| Gary Hallberg | 69 | 67 | 75 | 80 | 291 | 7,160 |
| Tom Lehman | 69 | 68 | 79 | 75 | 291 | 7,160 |
| Scott Hend | 68 | 69 | 76 | 83 | 296 | 7,040 |

## Funai Classic at the Walt Disney World Resort

*Walt Disney World Resort*, Lake Buena Vista, Florida
*Magnolia Course:* Par 36-36–72; 7,516 yards
*Palm Course:* Par 36-36–72; 6,957 yards

October 20-23
purse, $4,400,000

| | SCORES | | | | TOTAL | MONEY |
|---|---|---|---|---|---|---|
| Lucas Glover | 68 | 66 | 66 | 65 | 265 | $792,000 |
| Tom Pernice, Jr. | 67 | 62 | 68 | 69 | 266 | 475,200 |
| Rich Beem | 65 | 69 | 63 | 70 | 267 | 198,440 |
| Harrison Frazar | 67 | 66 | 66 | 68 | 267 | 198,440 |
| Geoff Ogilvy | 64 | 66 | 68 | 69 | 267 | 198,440 |
| Ryan Palmer | 67 | 70 | 66 | 64 | 267 | 198,440 |
| Justin Rose | 67 | 68 | 64 | 68 | 267 | 198,440 |
| Mark Calcavecchia | 64 | 69 | 65 | 70 | 268 | 132,000 |
| Brandt Jobe | 69 | 62 | 70 | 67 | 268 | 132,000 |
| Tim Clark | 66 | 65 | 66 | 72 | 269 | 110,000 |
| Tom Lehman | 65 | 70 | 69 | 65 | 269 | 110,000 |
| Mark Wilson | 67 | 68 | 63 | 71 | 269 | 110,000 |
| Ryan Moore | 64 | 71 | 67 | 68 | 270 | 88,000 |
| Heath Slocum | 67 | 69 | 69 | 65 | 270 | 88,000 |
| Robert Damron | 65 | 69 | 68 | 69 | 271 | 68,200 |
| Charles Howell | 65 | 68 | 72 | 66 | 271 | 68,200 |
| Greg Owen | 69 | 66 | 66 | 70 | 271 | 68,200 |
| Pat Perez | 64 | 70 | 69 | 68 | 271 | 68,200 |
| Carl Pettersson | 66 | 61 | 71 | 73 | 271 | 68,200 |
| Jeff Sluman | 69 | 66 | 68 | 68 | 271 | 68,200 |
| Craig Barlow | 71 | 64 | 68 | 69 | 272 | 38,200 |
| Bart Bryant | 67 | 67 | 68 | 70 | 272 | 38,200 |
| Daniel Chopra | 66 | 71 | 68 | 67 | 272 | 38,200 |
| Dudley Hart | 68 | 65 | 68 | 71 | 272 | 38,200 |
| Kent Jones | 66 | 64 | 70 | 72 | 272 | 38,200 |
| Steve Lowery | 64 | 67 | 70 | 71 | 272 | 38,200 |
| Rocco Mediate | 68 | 67 | 69 | 68 | 272 | 38,200 |
| John Rollins | 70 | 68 | 68 | 66 | 272 | 38,200 |
| Joey Snyder | 68 | 68 | 68 | 68 | 272 | 38,200 |
| Scott Verplank | 70 | 65 | 68 | 69 | 272 | 38,200 |

| | SCORES | | | | TOTAL | MONEY |
|---|---|---|---|---|---|---|
| Dean Wilson | 69 | 68 | 64 | 71 | 272 | 38,200 |
| Robert Gamez | 67 | 68 | 70 | 68 | 273 | 22,831.12 |
| Stuart Appleby | 69 | 68 | 68 | 68 | 273 | 22,831.11 |
| Stewart Cink | 69 | 69 | 68 | 67 | 273 | 22,831.11 |
| Brian Davis | 72 | 65 | 69 | 67 | 273 | 22,831.11 |
| Joe Durant | 71 | 66 | 70 | 66 | 273 | 22,831.11 |
| Bob Heintz | 67 | 71 | 67 | 68 | 273 | 22,831.11 |
| J.J. Henry | 64 | 70 | 70 | 69 | 273 | 22,831.11 |
| Stephen Leaney | 68 | 64 | 69 | 72 | 273 | 22,831.11 |
| Tag Ridings | 70 | 67 | 69 | 67 | 273 | 22,831.11 |
| Marco Dawson | 67 | 71 | 70 | 66 | 274 | 17,160 |
| Brendan Jones | 67 | 66 | 70 | 71 | 274 | 17,160 |
| D.A. Points | 66 | 72 | 68 | 68 | 274 | 17,160 |
| Bob Estes | 69 | 69 | 69 | 68 | 275 | 13,302.67 |
| Jason Gore | 65 | 67 | 71 | 72 | 275 | 13,302.67 |
| Ryuji Imada | 71 | 65 | 70 | 69 | 275 | 13,302.67 |
| J.L. Lewis | 74 | 63 | 66 | 72 | 275 | 13,302.67 |
| Chris Smith | 73 | 65 | 69 | 68 | 275 | 13,302.66 |
| Duffy Waldorf | 68 | 70 | 69 | 68 | 275 | 13,302.66 |
| Cameron Beckman | 74 | 64 | 67 | 71 | 276 | 10,395 |
| Todd Fischer | 68 | 70 | 67 | 71 | 276 | 10,395 |
| Carlos Franco | 70 | 67 | 70 | 69 | 276 | 10,395 |
| Tim Herron | 69 | 68 | 69 | 70 | 276 | 10,395 |
| Sean O'Hair | 67 | 70 | 68 | 71 | 276 | 10,395 |
| Vaughn Taylor | 70 | 66 | 68 | 72 | 276 | 10,395 |
| Bo Van Pelt | 66 | 70 | 70 | 70 | 276 | 10,395 |
| Brett Wetterich | 67 | 68 | 71 | 70 | 276 | 10,395 |
| Notah Begay | 65 | 70 | 70 | 72 | 277 | 9,680 |
| Retief Goosen | 71 | 65 | 73 | 68 | 277 | 9,680 |
| Hunter Haas | 63 | 71 | 71 | 72 | 277 | 9,680 |
| Neal Lancaster | 70 | 66 | 71 | 70 | 277 | 9,680 |
| Scott McCarron | 68 | 69 | 71 | 69 | 277 | 9,680 |
| Dennis Paulson | 68 | 70 | 69 | 71 | 278 | 9,372 |
| Nick Price | 65 | 68 | 72 | 73 | 278 | 9,372 |
| John Senden | 69 | 67 | 70 | 74 | 280 | 9,152 |
| Bob Sowards | 70 | 68 | 72 | 70 | 280 | 9,152 |
| Hidemichi Tanaka | 68 | 69 | 71 | 72 | 280 | 9,152 |
| Gavin Coles | 70 | 66 | 70 | 75 | 281 | 8,932 |
| Len Mattiace | 67 | 70 | 69 | 75 | 281 | 8,932 |
| Peter Lonard | 70 | 65 | 74 | 73 | 282 | 8,756 |
| Joey Sindelar | 73 | 65 | 71 | 73 | 282 | 8,756 |
| J.P. Hayes | 68 | 69 | 71 | 75 | 283 | 8,624 |
| Hank Kuehne | 73 | 65 | 75 | 75 | 288 | 8,536 |

# Chrysler Championship

*Westin Innisbrook Resort, Copperhead Course*,
Palm Harbor, Florida
Par 36-35–71; 7,230 yards

October 27-30
purse, $5,300,000

| | SCORES | | | | TOTAL | MONEY |
|---|---|---|---|---|---|---|
| Carl Pettersson | 69 | 68 | 67 | 71 | 275 | $954,000 |
| Chad Campbell | 70 | 70 | 69 | 67 | 276 | 572,400 |
| Stewart Cink | 71 | 70 | 71 | 67 | 279 | 216,164.29 |
| Tim Herron | 71 | 67 | 71 | 70 | 279 | 216,164.29 |
| Tag Ridings | 70 | 72 | 70 | 67 | 279 | 216,164.29 |
| Hidemichi Tanaka | 73 | 67 | 72 | 67 | 279 | 216,164.29 |

| | SCORES | | | | TOTAL | MONEY |
|---|---|---|---|---|---|---|
| Steve Lowery | 68 | 66 | 70 | 75 | 279 | 216,164.28 |
| Tom Pernice, Jr. | 71 | 66 | 70 | 72 | 279 | 216,164.28 |
| Bo Van Pelt | 71 | 65 | 73 | 70 | 279 | 216,164.28 |
| Jeff Brehaut | 65 | 74 | 69 | 72 | 280 | 132,500 |
| Daniel Chopra | 71 | 68 | 68 | 73 | 280 | 132,500 |
| Sean O'Hair | 73 | 69 | 69 | 69 | 280 | 132,500 |
| Bernhard Langer | 68 | 69 | 74 | 70 | 281 | 111,300 |
| Billy Mayfair | 68 | 75 | 70 | 69 | 282 | 98,050 |
| Patrick Sheehan | 76 | 67 | 69 | 70 | 282 | 98,050 |
| Tommy Armour | 72 | 70 | 70 | 71 | 283 | 82,150 |
| Bart Bryant | 73 | 69 | 69 | 72 | 283 | 82,150 |
| Charles Howell | 67 | 71 | 74 | 71 | 283 | 82,150 |
| Davis Love | 68 | 69 | 70 | 76 | 283 | 82,150 |
| Alex Cejka | 70 | 73 | 69 | 72 | 284 | 55,271.43 |
| Dan Forsman | 74 | 67 | 69 | 74 | 284 | 55,271.43 |
| John Huston | 71 | 68 | 72 | 73 | 284 | 55,271.43 |
| Rocco Mediate | 68 | 71 | 73 | 72 | 284 | 55,271.43 |
| Justin Rose | 70 | 68 | 76 | 70 | 284 | 55,271.43 |
| Dean Wilson | 67 | 72 | 72 | 73 | 284 | 55,271.43 |
| Vaughn Taylor | 73 | 71 | 72 | 68 | 284 | 55,271.42 |
| Bob Estes | 71 | 72 | 72 | 70 | 285 | 35,278.13 |
| Brandt Jobe | 70 | 72 | 72 | 71 | 285 | 35,278.13 |
| Jerry Kelly | 74 | 68 | 71 | 72 | 285 | 35,278.13 |
| Shigeki Maruyama | 71 | 73 | 71 | 70 | 285 | 35,278.13 |
| Stephen Ames | 70 | 72 | 74 | 69 | 285 | 35,278.12 |
| Stuart Appleby | 72 | 72 | 66 | 75 | 285 | 35,278.12 |
| Olin Browne | 70 | 72 | 74 | 69 | 285 | 35,278.12 |
| Robert Gamez | 70 | 70 | 70 | 75 | 285 | 35,278.12 |
| Fred Funk | 74 | 68 | 71 | 73 | 286 | 23,938.34 |
| Tom Lehman | 67 | 71 | 75 | 73 | 286 | 23,938.34 |
| J.L. Lewis | 72 | 69 | 72 | 73 | 286 | 23,938.34 |
| Woody Austin | 71 | 71 | 70 | 74 | 286 | 23,938.33 |
| Lucas Glover | 68 | 72 | 72 | 74 | 286 | 23,938.33 |
| Peter Lonard | 68 | 72 | 74 | 72 | 286 | 23,938.33 |
| Adam Scott | 69 | 72 | 74 | 71 | 286 | 23,938.33 |
| Wes Short, Jr. | 71 | 71 | 70 | 74 | 286 | 23,938.33 |
| Joey Sindelar | 72 | 71 | 69 | 74 | 286 | 23,938.33 |
| Brian Bateman | 73 | 69 | 72 | 73 | 287 | 15,317 |
| Jonathan Byrd | 71 | 73 | 69 | 74 | 287 | 15,317 |
| Brian Davis | 73 | 71 | 70 | 73 | 287 | 15,317 |
| Retief Goosen | 67 | 71 | 76 | 73 | 287 | 15,317 |
| Nick Price | 72 | 72 | 74 | 69 | 287 | 15,317 |
| John Senden | 71 | 70 | 73 | 73 | 287 | 15,317 |
| Heath Slocum | 71 | 69 | 74 | 73 | 287 | 15,317 |
| Bob Tway | 72 | 72 | 73 | 70 | 287 | 15,317 |
| Jason Allred | 72 | 72 | 70 | 74 | 288 | 12,359.60 |
| Len Mattiace | 73 | 70 | 71 | 74 | 288 | 12,359.60 |
| Jesper Parnevik | 68 | 76 | 69 | 75 | 288 | 12,359.60 |
| Charles Warren | 69 | 74 | 73 | 72 | 288 | 12,359.60 |
| Mark Wilson | 69 | 75 | 73 | 71 | 288 | 12,359.60 |
| Marco Dawson | 69 | 72 | 75 | 73 | 289 | 11,819 |
| Brent Geiberger | 74 | 68 | 76 | 71 | 289 | 11,819 |
| Kevin Na | 72 | 71 | 73 | 73 | 289 | 11,819 |
| Chris Riley | 69 | 71 | 73 | 76 | 289 | 11,819 |
| Steve Allan | 68 | 73 | 74 | 75 | 290 | 11,501 |
| Stephen Leaney | 73 | 70 | 70 | 77 | 290 | 11,501 |
| Ben Crane | 67 | 74 | 74 | 76 | 291 | 11,289 |
| Hunter Mahan | 73 | 71 | 71 | 76 | 291 | 11,289 |
| Cameron Beckman | 71 | 71 | 71 | 79 | 292 | 11,024 |
| Shaun Micheel | 72 | 72 | 76 | 72 | 292 | 11,024 |

| | SCORES | | | | TOTAL | MONEY |
|---|---|---|---|---|---|---|
| Joe Ogilvie | 72 | 72 | 75 | 73 | 292 | 11,024 |
| Jason Bohn | 75 | 68 | 75 | 75 | 293 | 10,759 |
| Mark Brooks | 73 | 68 | 74 | 78 | 293 | 10,759 |
| Greg Owen | 73 | 71 | 74 | 78 | 296 | 10,547 |
| Chris Smith | 73 | 71 | 77 | 75 | 296 | 10,547 |

## The Tour Championship

*East Lake Golf Club*, Atlanta, Georgia
Par 35-35–70; 6,980 yards

November 3-6
purse, $6,500,000

| | SCORES | | | | TOTAL | MONEY |
|---|---|---|---|---|---|---|
| Bart Bryant | 62 | 68 | 66 | 67 | 263 | $1,170,000 |
| Tiger Woods | 66 | 67 | 67 | 69 | 269 | 715,000 |
| Scott Verplank | 67 | 66 | 69 | 69 | 271 | 461,500 |
| Vijay Singh | 69 | 69 | 68 | 67 | 273 | 283,833.34 |
| Retief Goosen | 64 | 66 | 69 | 74 | 273 | 283,833.33 |
| Davis Love | 68 | 71 | 65 | 69 | 273 | 283,833.33 |
| Stuart Appleby | 70 | 65 | 71 | 68 | 274 | 209,625 |
| Ben Crane | 68 | 65 | 72 | 69 | 274 | 209,625 |
| Padraig Harrington | 71 | 66 | 68 | 69 | 274 | 209,625 |
| Adam Scott | 73 | 69 | 65 | 67 | 274 | 209,625 |
| Mark Calcavecchia | 72 | 69 | 68 | 66 | 275 | 176,800 |
| Sean O'Hair | 73 | 73 | 64 | 66 | 276 | 167,700 |
| Jim Furyk | 70 | 70 | 67 | 70 | 277 | 158,600 |
| Olin Browne | 70 | 67 | 71 | 70 | 278 | 143,866.67 |
| Tim Herron | 73 | 68 | 71 | 66 | 278 | 143,866.67 |
| Luke Donald | 70 | 67 | 70 | 71 | 278 | 143,866.66 |
| Chad Campbell | 72 | 68 | 70 | 69 | 279 | 130,000 |
| Chris DiMarco | 69 | 72 | 67 | 71 | 279 | 130,000 |
| Ted Purdy | 71 | 69 | 69 | 70 | 279 | 130,000 |
| Sergio Garcia | 66 | 72 | 71 | 72 | 281 | 123,500 |
| Kenny Perry | 65 | 73 | 71 | 72 | 281 | 123,500 |
| Tim Clark | 67 | 67 | 72 | 76 | 282 | 118,300 |
| David Toms | 72 | 72 | 68 | 70 | 282 | 118,300 |
| Fred Funk | 71 | 72 | 70 | 70 | 283 | 111,800 |
| Charles Howell | 67 | 68 | 70 | 78 | 283 | 111,800 |
| Billy Mayfair | 72 | 69 | 71 | 71 | 283 | 111,800 |
| Brandt Jobe | 73 | 71 | 70 | 70 | 284 | 107,900 |
| Justin Leonard | 70 | 74 | 71 | 72 | 287 | 106,600 |
| Lucas Glover | 72 | 70 | 73 | 74 | 289 | 105,300 |

## Southern Farm Bureau Classic

*Annandale Golf Club,* Madison, Mississippi
Par 36-36–72; 7,199 yards

November 3-6
purse, $3,000,000

| | SCORES | | | | TOTAL | MONEY |
|---|---|---|---|---|---|---|
| Heath Slocum | 69 | 68 | 64 | 66 | 267 | $540,000 |
| Carl Pettersson | 68 | 69 | 65 | 67 | 269 | 264,000 |
| Loren Roberts | 68 | 67 | 66 | 68 | 269 | 264,000 |
| Joey Snyder | 67 | 68 | 65 | 70 | 270 | 144,000 |
| Bo Van Pelt | 66 | 69 | 71 | 65 | 271 | 94,928.58 |
| Woody Austin | 69 | 69 | 67 | 66 | 271 | 94,928.57 |

| | SCORES | | | | TOTAL | MONEY |
|---|---|---|---|---|---|---|
| John Cook | 69 | 65 | 71 | 66 | 271 | 94,928.57 |
| Shaun Micheel | 68 | 69 | 68 | 66 | 271 | 94,928.57 |
| Tag Ridings | 68 | 66 | 68 | 69 | 271 | 94,928.57 |
| Bob Tway | 64 | 70 | 71 | 66 | 271 | 94,928.57 |
| Charlie Wi | 68 | 68 | 69 | 66 | 271 | 94,928.57 |
| Rocco Mediate | 70 | 66 | 71 | 66 | 273 | 58,800 |
| Tom Pernice, Jr. | 66 | 68 | 71 | 68 | 273 | 58,800 |
| Mario Tiziani | 69 | 68 | 69 | 67 | 273 | 58,800 |
| D.J. Trahan | 69 | 69 | 70 | 65 | 273 | 58,800 |
| Brett Wetterich | 68 | 67 | 70 | 68 | 273 | 58,800 |
| Aaron Baddeley | 73 | 67 | 67 | 67 | 274 | 31,500 |
| Cameron Beckman | 70 | 69 | 67 | 68 | 274 | 31,500 |
| Justin Bolli | 70 | 69 | 68 | 67 | 274 | 31,500 |
| Jonathan Byrd | 65 | 69 | 72 | 68 | 274 | 31,500 |
| Tom Byrum | 66 | 70 | 68 | 70 | 274 | 31,500 |
| Marco Dawson | 68 | 69 | 68 | 69 | 274 | 31,500 |
| Glen Day | 68 | 70 | 69 | 67 | 274 | 31,500 |
| Paul Gow | 67 | 70 | 67 | 70 | 274 | 31,500 |
| Scott Gutschewski | 71 | 67 | 68 | 68 | 274 | 31,500 |
| Bob Heintz | 69 | 70 | 67 | 68 | 274 | 31,500 |
| Steve Lowery | 69 | 69 | 70 | 66 | 274 | 31,500 |
| Kevin Na | 66 | 68 | 74 | 66 | 274 | 31,500 |
| Steve Stricker | 69 | 68 | 69 | 68 | 274 | 31,500 |
| Omar Uresti | 70 | 67 | 72 | 65 | 274 | 31,500 |
| Jeff Brehaut | 71 | 70 | 64 | 70 | 275 | 18,187.50 |
| Frank Lickliter | 70 | 65 | 70 | 70 | 275 | 18,187.50 |
| Kevin Stadler | 71 | 65 | 66 | 73 | 275 | 18,187.50 |
| Kirk Triplett | 67 | 70 | 69 | 69 | 275 | 18,187.50 |
| Craig Bowden | 71 | 67 | 67 | 71 | 276 | 14,790 |
| Brian Davis | 68 | 69 | 70 | 69 | 276 | 14,790 |
| Dan Forsman | 70 | 70 | 67 | 69 | 276 | 14,790 |
| Franklin Langham | 71 | 69 | 68 | 68 | 276 | 14,790 |
| Shigeki Maruyama | 70 | 68 | 69 | 69 | 276 | 14,790 |
| Steve Allan | 70 | 71 | 67 | 69 | 277 | 12,000 |
| Billy Andrade | 70 | 69 | 71 | 67 | 277 | 12,000 |
| Bob Estes | 69 | 70 | 69 | 69 | 277 | 12,000 |
| Tim Petrovic | 72 | 69 | 70 | 66 | 277 | 12,000 |
| Hunter Haas | 70 | 68 | 70 | 70 | 278 | 9,070 |
| J.J. Henry | 69 | 71 | 69 | 69 | 278 | 9,070 |
| Brett Quigley | 70 | 68 | 70 | 70 | 278 | 9,070 |
| Rob Rashell | 70 | 70 | 69 | 69 | 278 | 9,070 |
| Chris Smith | 71 | 66 | 74 | 67 | 278 | 9,070 |
| Hidemichi Tanaka | 69 | 68 | 70 | 71 | 278 | 9,070 |
| Danny Ellis | 70 | 69 | 72 | 68 | 279 | 7,236 |
| Bill Glasson | 70 | 69 | 71 | 69 | 279 | 7,236 |
| Brian Henninger | 67 | 73 | 71 | 68 | 279 | 7,236 |
| Joey Sindelar | 70 | 71 | 70 | 68 | 279 | 7,236 |
| Mark Wilson | 72 | 69 | 70 | 68 | 279 | 7,236 |
| Tommy Armour | 68 | 72 | 72 | 68 | 280 | 6,840 |
| Brad Lardon | 68 | 69 | 72 | 71 | 280 | 6,840 |
| Tjaart van der Walt | 71 | 70 | 71 | 68 | 280 | 6,840 |
| Briny Baird | 72 | 69 | 70 | 70 | 281 | 6,570 |
| Brian Bateman | 71 | 70 | 75 | 65 | 281 | 6,570 |
| Gavin Coles | 71 | 68 | 67 | 75 | 281 | 6,570 |
| Jeff Sluman | 69 | 72 | 72 | 68 | 281 | 6,570 |
| Darron Stiles | 72 | 69 | 67 | 73 | 281 | 6,570 |
| Casey Wittenberg | 72 | 67 | 74 | 68 | 281 | 6,570 |
| John Morgan | 71 | 70 | 72 | 69 | 282 | 6,330 |
| Charles Warren | 69 | 70 | 71 | 72 | 282 | 6,330 |
| Jose Coceres | 69 | 71 | 68 | 75 | 283 | 6,120 |

| | SCORES | | | | TOTAL | MONEY |
|---|---|---|---|---|---|---|
| Jay Delsing | 72 | 68 | 69 | 74 | 283 | 6,120 |
| Neal Lancaster | 71 | 69 | 70 | 73 | 283 | 6,120 |
| Will MacKenzie | 69 | 67 | 72 | 75 | 283 | 6,120 |
| Brenden Pappas | 71 | 68 | 76 | 68 | 283 | 6,120 |
| Roland Thatcher | 71 | 70 | 72 | 71 | 284 | 5,940 |
| Chris Anderson | 68 | 73 | 76 | 68 | 285 | 5,850 |
| Jeff Hart | 69 | 71 | 73 | 72 | 285 | 5,850 |
| Ben Curtis | 71 | 69 | 72 | 74 | 286 | 5,760 |
| Mark Brooks | 69 | 69 | 76 | 75 | 289 | 5,700 |

# Special Events

## Tavistock Cup

*Isleworth Country Club,* Windemere, Florida      March 29
Par 36-36–72; 7,544 yards      purse, $1,400,000
(Event shortened to one-day event due to
the extension of The Players Championship.)

### SINGLES
(Singles versus both players on other team; 1 point for win, ½ point for tie.)

Scott Hoch 73 (Isleworth) versus Mark McNulty 77 (Lake Nona)
Robert Allenby 71 and Craig Parry 74 (Isle.) versus Trevor Immelman 71 and Justin Rose 68 (LN)
Stuart Appleby 73 and John Cook 76 (Isle.) versus Retief Goosen 67 and Nick Faldo 75 (LN)
Charles Howell 72 and Lee Janzen 70 (Isle.) versus Ian Poulter 74 and Annika Sorenstam 73 (LN)
Tiger Woods 66 and Mark O'Meara 77 (Isle.) versus Ernie Els 68 and Sergio Garcia 73 (LN)

**TOTAL: Isleworth 8½ (Hoch 1, Allenby ½, Parry 0, Appleby 1, Cook 0, Howell 2, Janzen 2, Woods 2, O'Meara 0); Lake Nona 8½ (McNulty 0, Immelman 1½, Rose 2, Goosen 2, Faldo 1, Poulter 0, Sorenstam 0, Els 1, Garcia 1)**

(Following three playoff holes halved, the event was declared a tie and each member of both teams received $77,778. Tiger Woods received a $100,000 bonus and Retief Goosen received $50,000 for the lowest individual scores.)

## CVS Charity Classic

*Rhode Island Country Club,* Barrington, Rhode Island      July 27-28
Par 36-35–71; 6,694 yards      purse $1,300,000

| | SCORES | | TOTAL | MONEY (Team) |
|---|---|---|---|---|
| Fred Funk/Chris DiMarco | 61 | 62 | 123 | $250,000 |
| Dana Quigley/Brett Quigley | 64 | 61 | 125 | 157,500 |
| Brad Faxon/Sergio Garcia | 61 | 64 | 125 | 157,500 |

|  | SCORES | | TOTAL | MONEY (Team) |
|---|---|---|---|---|
| Davis Love/Lucas Glover | 64 | 62 | 126 | 120,000 |
| Scott McCarron/Tim Herron | 64 | 63 | 127 | 115,000 |
| Jay Haas/Bill Haas | 64 | 64 | 128 | 110,000 |
| Jeff Sluman/Paul Azinger | 66 | 63 | 129 | 105,000 |
| Peter Jacobsen/Patrick Sheehan | 65 | 66 | 131 | 97,500 |
| Kevin Stadler/Craig Stadler | 64 | 67 | 131 | 97,500 |
| Billy Andrade/Arnold Palmer. | 67 | 67 | 134 | 90,000 |

# The Presidents Cup

*Robert Trent Jones Golf Club,* Prince William County, Virginia          September 22-25
Par 35-37–72; 7,245 yards

## FIRST DAY
### Foursomes

Adam Scott and Retief Goosen (Int'l) defeated Tiger Woods and Fred Couples, 4 and 3.
Fred Funk and Jim Furyk (US) halved with Vijay Singh and Mark Hensby.
Phil Mickelson and Chris DiMarco (US) defeated Nick O'Hern and Tim Clark, 1 up.
Justin Leonard and Scott Verplank (US) defeated Peter Lonard and Stuart Appleby, 4 and 2.
Michael Campbell and Angel Cabrera (Int'l) defeated Davis Love and Kenny Perry, 2 and 1.
Trevor Immelman and Mike Weir (Int'l) defeated David Toms and Stewart Cink, 6 and 5.

**POINTS: United States Team 2½, International Team 3½**

## SECOND DAY
### Fourball

Mickelson and DiMarco (US) halved with Cabrera and Campbell.
Scott and Goosen (Int'l) defeated Couples and Toms, 3 and 1.
Leonard and Verplank (US) defeated Immelman and Weir, 2 and 1.
Funk and Cink (US) halved with Singh and Clark.
Lonard and O'Hern (Int'l) defeated Love and Perry, 3 and 2.
Woods and Furyk (US) defeated Appleby and Hensby, 3 and 2.

**POINTS: United States Team 5½, International Team 6½**

## THIRD DAY
### Foursomes

Leonard and Verplank (US) halved with Goosen and Scott.
Mickelson and DiMarco (US) defeated Cabrera and Campbell, 5 and 3.
Woods and Furyk (US) halved with Singh and Appleby.
Clark and O'Hern (Int'l) defeated Funk and Toms, 2 and 1.
Love and Cink (US) defeated Immelman and Weir, 1 up.

### Fourball

Goosen and Scott (Int'l) defeated Verplank and Leonard, 5 and 4.
Mickelson and DiMarco (US) defeated Lonard and O'Hern, 6 and 5.
Love and Couples (US) halved with Campbell and Cabrera.
Hensby and Clark (Int'l) defeated Perry and Cink, 5 and 3.
Woods and Furyk (US) defeated Singh and Appleby, 2 up.

**POINTS: United States Team 11, International Team 11**

**FOURTH DAY**
**Singles**

Leonard (US) defeated Clark, 4 and 3.
Toms (US) defeated Immelman, 2 and 1.
Goosen (Int'l) defeated Woods, 2 and 1.
Perry (US) defeated Hensby, 4 and 3.
Couples (US) defeated Singh, 1 up.
Weir (Int'l) defeated Verplank, 3 and 2.
Furyk (US) defeated Scott, 3 and 2.
Lonard (Int'l) defeated Cink, 3 and 2.
Campbell (Int'l) defeated Funk, 3 and 2.
Love (US) defeated O'Hern, 4 and 3.
Mickelson (US) halved with Cabrera.
DiMarco (US) defeated Appleby, 1 up.

**TOTAL POINTS: United States Team 18½, International Team 15½**

## Franklin Templeton Shootout

*Tiburon Golf Course,* Naples, Florida
Par 36-36–72; 7,288 yards

November 11-13
purse, $2,600,000

| | SCORES | | | TOTAL | MONEY (Each) |
|---|---|---|---|---|---|
| John Huston/Kenny Perry | 64 | 63 | 59 | 186 | $315,000 |
| Fred Couples/Adam Scott | 64 | 61 | 62 | 187 | 200,000 |
| Mark O'Meara/Nick Price | 64 | 65 | 60 | 189 | 115,000 |
| Greg Norman/Steve Elkington | 69 | 66 | 55 | 190 | 95,000 |
| John Daly/Tim Herron | 68 | 65 | 60 | 193 | 81,250 |
| Fred Funk/Jason Gore | 63 | 65 | 65 | 193 | 81,250 |
| Ryan Moore/Jesper Parnevik | 65 | 65 | 64 | 194 | 75,000 |
| Paul Azinger/Olin Browne | 66 | 68 | 61 | 195 | 71,250 |
| Mark Calcavecchia/Loren Roberts | 70 | 63 | 62 | 195 | 71,250 |
| Hank Kuehne/Jeff Sluman | 66 | 67 | 64 | 197 | 66,250 |
| Kirk Triplett/Jay Haas | 67 | 65 | 65 | 197 | 66,250 |
| Peter Jacobsen/Scott McCarron | 68 | 69 | 63 | 200 | 62,500 |

## PGA Grand Slam of Golf

*Poipu Golf Club,* Kauai, Hawaii
Par 36-36–72; 7,081 yards

November 22-23
purse, $1,000,000

| | SCORES | | TOTAL | MONEY |
|---|---|---|---|---|
| Tiger Woods | 67 | 64 | 131 | $400,000 |
| Phil Mickelson | 70 | 68 | 138 | 250,000 |
| Michael Campbell | 73 | 70 | 143 | 200,000 |
| Vijay Singh | 75 | 69 | 144 | 150,000 |

## MBNA WorldPoints Father-Son Challenge

*Champions Gate Golf Resort,* Orlando, Florida

*Par 37-35–72; 7,067 yards*

December 3-4

purse, $1,085,000

| | SCORES | | TOTAL | MONEY (Won by professional) |
|---|---|---|---|---|
| Bernhard/Stefan Langer | 59 | 61 | 120 | $200,000 |
| Raymond/Robert Floyd | 60 | 61 | 121 | 105,000 |
| Mark/Shaun O'Meara | 61 | 64 | 122 | 60,700 |
| Johnny/John Miller | 63 | 62 | 122 | 60,700 |
| Jerry/Wesley Pate | 63 | 62 | 122 | 60,700 |
| Vijay/Qass Singh | 64 | 61 | 122 | 60,700 |
| Hale/Steve Irwin | 66 | 59 | 122 | 60,700 |
| Larry/Josh Nelson | 65 | 61 | 126 | 48,000 |
| Jack/Jackie Nicklaus | 64 | 63 | 127 | 44,833 |
| Curtis/Tom Strange | 62 | 65 | 127 | 44,833 |
| Davis/Dru Love | 62 | 65 | 127 | 44,833 |
| Tom/David Kite | 66 | 62 | 128 | 43,250 |
| Lanny/Travis Wadkins | 63 | 65 | 128 | 43,250 |
| Arnold Palmer/Sam Saunders | 67 | 65 | 132 | 42,250 |
| Craig/Chris Stadler | 67 | 65 | 132 | 42,250 |
| Bob/David Charles | 65 | 68 | 133 | 41,500 |
| Lee/Tony Trevino | 68 | 68 | 136 | 41,000 |
| Fuzzy/Gretchen Zoeller | 71 | 66 | 137 | 40,500 |

## Target World Challenge

*Sherwood Country Club,* Thousand Oaks, California

*Par 36-36–72; 7,053 yards*

December 8-11

purse, $5,500,000

| | SCORES | | | | TOTAL | MONEY |
|---|---|---|---|---|---|---|
| Luke Donald | 72 | 68 | 68 | 64 | 272 | $1,300,000 |
| Darren Clarke | 65 | 73 | 64 | 72 | 274 | 800,000 |
| Michael Campbell | 63 | 72 | 68 | 73 | 276 | 475,000 |
| Padraig Harrington | 68 | 70 | 65 | 73 | 276 | 475,000 |
| Kenny Perry | 69 | 70 | 66 | 72 | 277 | 300,000 |
| David Toms | 73 | 70 | 70 | 66 | 279 | 240,000 |
| Tim Clark | 71 | 70 | 69 | 69 | 279 | 240,000 |
| Thomas Bjorn | 70 | 71 | 70 | 69 | 280 | 220,000 |
| Jim Furyk | 73 | 68 | 73 | 68 | 282 | 205,000 |
| Fred Couples | 71 | 68 | 70 | 73 | 282 | 205,000 |
| David Howell | 72 | 68 | 73 | 70 | 283 | 185,000 |
| Chris DiMarco | 72 | 68 | 70 | 73 | 283 | 185,000 |
| Fred Funk | 72 | 73 | 69 | 70 | 284 | 175,000 |
| Colin Montgomerie | 76 | 70 | 69 | 71 | 286 | 167,500 |
| Tiger Woods | 72 | 72 | 69 | 73 | 286 | 167,500 |
| Davis Love | 76 | 67 | 73 | 74 | 290 | 160,000 |

# Nationwide Tour

## BellSouth Panama Championship

*Panama Golf Club*, Panama City, Panama
Par 35-35–70; 6,818 yards

January 27-30
purse, $525,000

| | SCORES | | | | TOTAL | MONEY |
|---|---|---|---|---|---|---|
| Vance Veazey | 65 | 71 | 66 | 70 | 272 | $94,500 |
| Shane Bertsch | 70 | 65 | 68 | 70 | 273 | 34,650 |
| Jim McGovern | 69 | 72 | 64 | 68 | 273 | 34,650 |
| Jon Mills | 68 | 67 | 68 | 70 | 273 | 34,650 |
| Camilo Villegas | 67 | 66 | 71 | 69 | 273 | 34,650 |
| Scott Sterling | 69 | 67 | 72 | 67 | 275 | 18,900 |
| Jason Schultz | 70 | 70 | 67 | 69 | 276 | 15,815.63 |
| Chris Tidland | 69 | 69 | 69 | 69 | 276 | 15,815.63 |
| Steven Alker | 67 | 67 | 69 | 73 | 276 | 15,815.62 |
| Ricky Barnes | 68 | 69 | 68 | 71 | 276 | 15,815.62 |
| David Branshaw | 73 | 68 | 69 | 67 | 277 | 11,130 |
| Robin Freeman | 69 | 70 | 68 | 70 | 277 | 11,130 |
| Richard Johnson | 72 | 69 | 68 | 68 | 277 | 11,130 |
| Deane Pappas | 69 | 70 | 71 | 67 | 277 | 11,130 |
| Garrett Willis | 70 | 71 | 70 | 66 | 277 | 11,130 |
| Guy Boros | 72 | 69 | 71 | 67 | 279 | 6,895 |
| Chris Couch | 70 | 68 | 69 | 72 | 279 | 6,895 |
| Bubba Dickerson | 72 | 68 | 67 | 72 | 279 | 6,895 |
| Rick Fehr | 69 | 73 | 67 | 70 | 279 | 6,895 |
| Ryan Hietala | 64 | 71 | 70 | 74 | 279 | 6,895 |
| Jim Rutledge | 69 | 71 | 69 | 70 | 279 | 6,895 |
| Roger Tambellini | 70 | 70 | 73 | 66 | 279 | 6,895 |
| Johnson Wagner | 69 | 69 | 72 | 69 | 279 | 6,895 |
| Tyler Williamson | 69 | 69 | 71 | 70 | 279 | 6,895 |
| Nick Cassini | 69 | 73 | 70 | 68 | 280 | 4,305 |
| Bryce Molder | 70 | 72 | 65 | 73 | 280 | 4,305 |
| John Morse | 71 | 70 | 71 | 68 | 280 | 4,305 |
| Andres Romero | 71 | 70 | 71 | 68 | 280 | 4,305 |
| Kris Cox | 70 | 67 | 73 | 71 | 281 | 3,543.75 |
| Brian Smock | 70 | 71 | 70 | 70 | 281 | 3,543.75 |
| David Sutherland | 68 | 70 | 72 | 71 | 281 | 3,543.75 |
| Matt Weibring | 68 | 71 | 71 | 71 | 281 | 3,543.75 |

## Jacob's Creek Open

See Australasian Tour chapter.

## ING New Zealand PGA Championship

See Australasian Tour chapter.

## Chitimacha Louisiana Open

*Le Triomphe Country Club,* Broussard, Louisiana
Par 36-36–72; 7,204 yards

March 24-27
purse, $500,000

| | SCORES | | | | TOTAL | MONEY |
|---|---|---|---|---|---|---|
| Ryan Hietala | 66 | 71 | 65 | 68 | 270 | $90,000 |
| Sean O'Hair | 71 | 68 | 67 | 65 | 271 | 54,000 |
| Danny Ellis | 70 | 70 | 68 | 67 | 275 | 29,000 |
| Vance Veazey | 69 | 67 | 68 | 71 | 275 | 29,000 |
| Richard Johnson | 70 | 67 | 66 | 73 | 276 | 20,000 |
| Ken Duke | 71 | 69 | 70 | 67 | 277 | 18,000 |
| Kris Cox | 65 | 72 | 67 | 74 | 278 | 16,125 |
| Brandt Snedeker | 68 | 69 | 68 | 73 | 278 | 16,125 |
| Charley Hoffman | 71 | 68 | 69 | 71 | 279 | 13,500 |
| Troy Matteson | 73 | 66 | 70 | 70 | 279 | 13,500 |
| Brett Wetterich | 68 | 68 | 72 | 71 | 279 | 13,500 |
| David Branshaw | 70 | 70 | 69 | 71 | 280 | 10,125 |
| Mathias Gronberg | 70 | 70 | 72 | 68 | 280 | 10,125 |
| Steve Pleis | 72 | 66 | 67 | 75 | 280 | 10,125 |
| Dicky Pride | 71 | 69 | 66 | 74 | 280 | 10,125 |
| Kevin Durkin | 69 | 70 | 70 | 72 | 281 | 7,750 |
| Mike Heinen | 70 | 70 | 70 | 71 | 281 | 7,750 |
| Bubba Watson | 65 | 72 | 73 | 71 | 281 | 7,750 |
| Boo Weekley | 73 | 68 | 70 | 70 | 281 | 7,750 |
| Chris Anderson | 70 | 70 | 72 | 70 | 282 | 5,825 |
| Chad Collins | 71 | 69 | 68 | 74 | 282 | 5,825 |
| Wes Short, Jr. | 70 | 71 | 66 | 75 | 282 | 5,825 |
| Garrett Willis | 72 | 70 | 69 | 71 | 282 | 5,825 |
| Ricky Barnes | 69 | 69 | 69 | 76 | 283 | 3,937.50 |
| Jeff Brehaut | 69 | 66 | 70 | 78 | 283 | 3,937.50 |
| Hunter Haas | 72 | 68 | 73 | 70 | 283 | 3,937.50 |
| Anders Hultman | 70 | 70 | 68 | 75 | 283 | 3,937.50 |
| Bill Lunde | 68 | 68 | 74 | 73 | 283 | 3,937.50 |
| Jon Mills | 71 | 72 | 68 | 72 | 283 | 3,937.50 |
| Camilo Villegas | 73 | 69 | 70 | 71 | 283 | 3,937.50 |
| Scott Weatherly | 70 | 70 | 70 | 73 | 283 | 3,937.50 |

## Virginia Beach Open

*TPC of Virginia Beach,* Virginia Beach, Virginia
Par 36-36–72; 7,432 yards

April 21-24
purse, $450,000

| | SCORES | | | | TOTAL | MONEY |
|---|---|---|---|---|---|---|
| Troy Matteson | 69 | 65 | 73 | 68 | 275 | $81,000 |
| Chris Couch | 70 | 67 | 70 | 70 | 277 | 48,600 |
| David Branshaw | 70 | 71 | 68 | 69 | 278 | 26,100 |
| Chris Tidland | 70 | 67 | 71 | 70 | 278 | 26,100 |
| Bubba Watson | 72 | 67 | 67 | 73 | 279 | 18,000 |
| Chad Collins | 70 | 67 | 74 | 70 | 281 | 15,637.50 |
| Danny Ellis | 69 | 70 | 72 | 70 | 281 | 15,637.50 |
| Kevin Durkin | 75 | 66 | 73 | 68 | 282 | 12,150 |
| Robert Garrigus | 71 | 70 | 70 | 71 | 282 | 12,150 |
| Jeff Gove | 71 | 71 | 70 | 70 | 282 | 12,150 |
| Jerry Smith | 73 | 65 | 67 | 77 | 282 | 12,150 |
| Grant Waite | 70 | 70 | 72 | 70 | 282 | 12,150 |
| Steven Alker | 73 | 69 | 69 | 72 | 283 | 8,190 |

|  | SCORES |  |  |  | TOTAL | MONEY |
|---|---|---|---|---|---|---|
| Kris Cox | 71 | 72 | 70 | 70 | 283 | 8,190 |
| Steve Larick | 71 | 67 | 71 | 74 | 283 | 8,190 |
| Jim McGovern | 72 | 70 | 68 | 73 | 283 | 8,190 |
| Matt Weibring | 70 | 71 | 70 | 72 | 283 | 8,190 |
| Brad Fabel | 72 | 70 | 74 | 68 | 284 | 6,075 |
| Greg Kraft | 70 | 70 | 73 | 71 | 284 | 6,075 |
| Brandt Snedeker | 69 | 70 | 69 | 76 | 284 | 6,075 |
| Mike Sposa | 68 | 72 | 73 | 71 | 284 | 6,075 |
| Ryan Armour | 68 | 71 | 75 | 71 | 285 | 4,500 |
| Jason Enloe | 70 | 72 | 70 | 73 | 285 | 4,500 |
| Dan Olsen | 71 | 71 | 72 | 71 | 285 | 4,500 |
| Sean Pacetti | 70 | 69 | 69 | 77 | 285 | 4,500 |
| Chris Nallen | 68 | 69 | 73 | 76 | 286 | 3,345 |
| Tim O'Neal | 69 | 70 | 75 | 72 | 286 | 3,345 |
| Deane Pappas | 69 | 73 | 74 | 70 | 286 | 3,345 |
| Fran Quinn | 75 | 67 | 70 | 74 | 286 | 3,345 |
| Jason Schultz | 70 | 70 | 73 | 73 | 286 | 3,345 |
| Chip Sullivan | 72 | 70 | 75 | 69 | 286 | 3,345 |

## BMW Charity Pro-Am at The Cliffs

*The Cliffs Golf & Country Club,* Greenville, South Carolina
*Cliffs Valley:* Par 36-36–72; 7,023 yards
*Keowee Vineyards:* Par 36-35–71; 7,006 yards
*Cliffs at Walnut Grove:* Par 36-35–71; 7,000 yards
(Shortened to 54 holes—rain.)

April 28-May 1
purse, $625,000

|  | SCORES |  |  | TOTAL | MONEY |
|---|---|---|---|---|---|
| Shane Bertsch | 69 | 68 | 65 | 202 | $112,500 |
| Charley Hoffman | 64 | 71 | 68 | 203 | 55,000 |
| Bubba Watson | 68 | 64 | 71 | 203 | 55,000 |
| Robert Garrigus | 73 | 62 | 69 | 204 | 30,000 |
| Tim O'Neal | 68 | 68 | 69 | 205 | 22,812.50 |
| Roger Tambellini | 71 | 66 | 68 | 205 | 22,812.50 |
| Kyle Thompson | 68 | 67 | 70 | 205 | 22,812.50 |
| Jeff Klauk | 73 | 66 | 67 | 206 | 19,375 |
| Mathew Goggin | 66 | 65 | 76 | 207 | 15,625 |
| Jim McGovern | 69 | 67 | 71 | 207 | 15,625 |
| Matt Weibring | 67 | 68 | 72 | 207 | 15,625 |
| Tim Wilkinson | 70 | 69 | 68 | 207 | 15,625 |
| Chris Wollmann | 66 | 71 | 70 | 207 | 15,625 |
| Joseph Alfieri | 67 | 68 | 73 | 208 | 10,000 |
| Nick Cassini | 68 | 69 | 71 | 208 | 10,000 |
| Kevin Gessino-Kraft | 72 | 70 | 66 | 208 | 10,000 |
| Nathan Green | 71 | 69 | 68 | 208 | 10,000 |
| Dan Olsen | 69 | 68 | 71 | 208 | 10,000 |
| Tom Scherrer | 69 | 70 | 69 | 208 | 10,000 |
| Garrett Willis | 70 | 71 | 67 | 208 | 10,000 |
| Aaron Barber | 67 | 70 | 72 | 209 | 5,937.50 |
| Scott Dunlap | 67 | 71 | 71 | 209 | 5,937.50 |
| Keith Huber | 76 | 69 | 64 | 209 | 5,937.50 |
| Andrew Johnson | 67 | 67 | 75 | 209 | 5,937.50 |
| Troy Matteson | 71 | 68 | 70 | 209 | 5,937.50 |
| Vance Veazey | 72 | 67 | 70 | 209 | 5,937.50 |
| Scott Weatherly | 71 | 64 | 74 | 209 | 5,937.50 |
| Tyler Williamson | 71 | 68 | 70 | 209 | 5,937.50 |
| Ricky Barnes | 70 | 67 | 73 | 210 | 3,825 |

| | SCORES | | | TOTAL | MONEY |
|---|---|---|---|---|---|
| Chad Collins | 68 | 70 | 72 | 210 | 3,825 |
| Jason Enloe | 68 | 70 | 72 | 210 | 3,825 |
| Bill Haas | 71 | 73 | 66 | 210 | 3,825 |
| Chris Nallen | 69 | 74 | 67 | 210 | 3,825 |
| Jim Rutledge | 69 | 72 | 69 | 210 | 3,825 |
| Andy Sanders | 72 | 66 | 72 | 210 | 3,825 |
| Jerry Smith | 67 | 72 | 71 | 210 | 3,825 |
| Chris Tidland | 74 | 69 | 67 | 210 | 3,825 |
| Johnson Wagner | 67 | 72 | 71 | 210 | 3,825 |

## The Rex Hospital Open

*TPC at Wakefield Plantation,* Raleigh, North Carolina
Par 35-36–71; 7,257 yards

May 5-8
purse, $450,000

| | SCORES | | | | TOTAL | MONEY |
|---|---|---|---|---|---|---|
| Eric Axley | 69 | 67 | 67 | 67 | 270 | $81,000 |
| Troy Matteson | 68 | 65 | 70 | 69 | 272 | 48,600 |
| Ryan Armour | 68 | 68 | 70 | 67 | 273 | 30,600 |
| Matt Weibring | 72 | 71 | 65 | 67 | 275 | 21,600 |
| Craig Bowden | 63 | 69 | 75 | 69 | 276 | 17,100 |
| David McKenzie | 72 | 69 | 67 | 68 | 276 | 17,100 |
| Tjaart van der Walt | 68 | 70 | 67 | 72 | 277 | 15,075 |
| Donnie Hammond | 70 | 69 | 71 | 68 | 278 | 12,600 |
| Charley Hoffman | 69 | 69 | 65 | 75 | 278 | 12,600 |
| Cliff Kresge | 68 | 73 | 69 | 68 | 278 | 12,600 |
| Scott Petersen | 71 | 67 | 69 | 71 | 278 | 12,600 |
| Brendon de Jonge | 72 | 68 | 68 | 71 | 279 | 10,350 |
| Jason Caron | 67 | 72 | 68 | 73 | 280 | 9,000 |
| Roger Tambellini | 68 | 71 | 70 | 71 | 280 | 9,000 |
| Guy Boros | 75 | 69 | 68 | 69 | 281 | 7,875 |
| Bradley Heaven | 71 | 69 | 71 | 70 | 281 | 7,875 |
| Aaron Barber | 75 | 68 | 71 | 68 | 282 | 6,090 |
| Chad Collins | 68 | 73 | 71 | 70 | 282 | 6,090 |
| Tripp Isenhour | 73 | 69 | 70 | 70 | 282 | 6,090 |
| Tim O'Neal | 70 | 69 | 76 | 67 | 282 | 6,090 |
| Tim Simpson | 75 | 69 | 72 | 66 | 282 | 6,090 |
| Chris Tidland | 70 | 70 | 72 | 70 | 282 | 6,090 |
| Jeff Gove | 70 | 70 | 71 | 72 | 283 | 4,068 |
| Gabriel Hjertstedt | 71 | 73 | 68 | 71 | 283 | 4,068 |
| Brian Kortan | 71 | 69 | 71 | 72 | 283 | 4,068 |
| Tom Scherrer | 73 | 66 | 70 | 74 | 283 | 4,068 |
| Boo Weekley | 72 | 70 | 70 | 71 | 283 | 4,068 |
| Shane Bertsch | 69 | 71 | 68 | 76 | 284 | 3,114 |
| Craig Lile | 69 | 72 | 71 | 72 | 284 | 3,114 |
| Brad Ott | 73 | 66 | 73 | 72 | 284 | 3,114 |
| Brandt Snedeker | 69 | 73 | 69 | 73 | 284 | 3,114 |
| Bubba Watson | 70 | 69 | 74 | 71 | 284 | 3,114 |

# Rheem Classic

*Hardscrabble Country Club,* Fort Smith, Arkansas

*Par 35-35–70; 6,783 yards*

May 12-15

purse, $475,000

| | SCORES | | | | TOTAL | MONEY |
|---|---|---|---|---|---|---|
| Chris Couch | 69 | 66 | 70 | 60 | 265 | $85,500 |
| Troy Matteson | 65 | 71 | 67 | 67 | 270 | 51,300 |
| Aaron Barber | 65 | 71 | 66 | 69 | 271 | 22,800 |
| Danny Ellis | 69 | 72 | 64 | 66 | 271 | 22,800 |
| David Hearn | 67 | 72 | 67 | 65 | 271 | 22,800 |
| Camilo Villegas | 66 | 64 | 70 | 71 | 271 | 22,800 |
| Jason Schultz | 69 | 66 | 66 | 71 | 272 | 15,912.50 |
| Jeff Gove | 69 | 70 | 70 | 65 | 274 | 12,825 |
| Fran Quinn | 71 | 68 | 63 | 72 | 274 | 12,825 |
| Mike Springer | 70 | 70 | 67 | 67 | 274 | 12,825 |
| Kyle Thompson | 73 | 65 | 65 | 71 | 274 | 12,825 |
| Tjaart van der Walt | 71 | 68 | 67 | 68 | 274 | 12,825 |
| Brendon de Jonge | 71 | 66 | 71 | 67 | 275 | 9,183.34 |
| Mathew Goggin | 70 | 67 | 71 | 67 | 275 | 9,183.33 |
| Spike McRoy | 70 | 67 | 68 | 70 | 275 | 9,183.33 |
| Brian Kortan | 68 | 67 | 69 | 72 | 276 | 7,837.50 |
| Zoran Zorkic | 70 | 67 | 70 | 69 | 276 | 7,837.50 |
| David Branshaw | 67 | 73 | 68 | 69 | 277 | 5,985 |
| Nick Cassini | 70 | 67 | 67 | 73 | 277 | 5,985 |
| Jason Gore | 68 | 72 | 68 | 69 | 277 | 5,985 |
| Greg Kraft | 69 | 69 | 68 | 71 | 277 | 5,985 |
| Cameron Percy | 70 | 71 | 67 | 69 | 277 | 5,985 |
| Scott Weatherly | 68 | 68 | 71 | 70 | 277 | 5,985 |
| Bill Haas | 69 | 70 | 68 | 71 | 278 | 3,926.67 |
| Blaine McCallister | 68 | 72 | 69 | 69 | 278 | 3,926.67 |
| Jim Rutledge | 69 | 70 | 70 | 69 | 278 | 3,926.67 |
| Garrett Willis | 73 | 67 | 69 | 69 | 278 | 3,926.67 |
| Jerry Smith | 72 | 68 | 67 | 71 | 278 | 3,926.66 |
| Vance Veazey | 67 | 72 | 68 | 71 | 278 | 3,926.66 |
| Ben Bates | 64 | 71 | 73 | 71 | 279 | 2,945 |
| Dave Christensen | 68 | 68 | 68 | 75 | 279 | 2,945 |
| Scott Gardiner | 70 | 69 | 67 | 73 | 279 | 2,945 |
| Steve Larick | 73 | 68 | 69 | 69 | 279 | 2,945 |
| David McKenzie | 70 | 71 | 66 | 72 | 279 | 2,945 |
| Anthony Painter | 69 | 64 | 74 | 72 | 279 | 2,945 |
| Tom Scherrer | 65 | 71 | 72 | 71 | 279 | 2,945 |

# Henrico County Open

*The Dominion Club,* Richmond, Virginia

*Par 36-36–72; 7,089 yards*

May 19-22

purse, $450,000

| | SCORES | | | | TOTAL | MONEY |
|---|---|---|---|---|---|---|
| Chad Collins | 65 | 69 | 66 | 67 | 267 | $81,000 |
| Tom Scherrer | 68 | 67 | 65 | 69 | 269 | 48,600 |
| Ken Duke | 65 | 71 | 68 | 66 | 270 | 21,600 |
| Bill Lunde | 65 | 72 | 64 | 69 | 270 | 21,600 |
| Jon Mills | 69 | 69 | 63 | 69 | 270 | 21,600 |
| Dicky Pride | 68 | 72 | 68 | 62 | 270 | 21,600 |
| Camilo Villegas | 65 | 66 | 69 | 71 | 271 | 15,075 |
| Matt Weibring | 67 | 71 | 66 | 68 | 272 | 13,950 |

| | SCORES | | | | TOTAL | MONEY |
|---|---|---|---|---|---|---|
| Ricky Barnes | 67 | 73 | 68 | 65 | 273 | 11,700 |
| Kris Cox | 66 | 70 | 70 | 67 | 273 | 11,700 |
| Fran Quinn | 66 | 73 | 68 | 66 | 273 | 11,700 |
| Chris Wollmann | 67 | 72 | 68 | 66 | 273 | 11,700 |
| Steven Bowditch | 69 | 71 | 67 | 67 | 274 | 8,190 |
| Robin Freeman | 68 | 68 | 68 | 70 | 274 | 8,190 |
| Richard Johnson | 69 | 68 | 68 | 69 | 274 | 8,190 |
| Troy Matteson | 71 | 69 | 67 | 67 | 274 | 8,190 |
| John Morgan | 64 | 69 | 69 | 72 | 274 | 8,190 |
| David Branshaw | 68 | 72 | 65 | 70 | 275 | 6,075 |
| Mathew Goggin | 65 | 73 | 72 | 65 | 275 | 6,075 |
| Will MacKenzie | 65 | 75 | 66 | 69 | 275 | 6,075 |
| Blaine McCallister | 66 | 69 | 68 | 72 | 275 | 6,075 |
| Jason Caron | 66 | 72 | 68 | 70 | 276 | 4,005 |
| Joe Daley | 66 | 69 | 69 | 72 | 276 | 4,005 |
| Brendon de Jonge | 68 | 68 | 71 | 69 | 276 | 4,005 |
| Kim Felton | 72 | 68 | 67 | 69 | 276 | 4,005 |
| Bill Haas | 68 | 68 | 71 | 69 | 276 | 4,005 |
| David Hearn | 69 | 69 | 69 | 69 | 276 | 4,005 |
| David Morland | 68 | 71 | 69 | 68 | 276 | 4,005 |
| Cameron Percy | 67 | 70 | 68 | 71 | 276 | 4,005 |
| Kevin Durkin | 64 | 71 | 71 | 71 | 277 | 2,835 |
| Danny Ellis | 67 | 70 | 68 | 72 | 277 | 2,835 |
| Kelly Gibson | 69 | 69 | 70 | 69 | 277 | 2,835 |
| Nathan Green | 65 | 69 | 72 | 71 | 277 | 2,835 |
| Wes Short, Jr. | 65 | 74 | 68 | 70 | 277 | 2,835 |
| Ted Tryba | 65 | 72 | 70 | 70 | 277 | 2,835 |

## Chattanooga Classic

*Black Creek Club*, Chattanooga, Tennessee
Par 36-36–72; 7,044 yards

June 2-5
purse, $450,000

| | SCORES | | | | TOTAL | MONEY |
|---|---|---|---|---|---|---|
| Jason Schultz | 68 | 65 | 66 | 67 | 266 | $81,000 |
| Joe Daley | 68 | 68 | 64 | 66 | 266 | 33,600 |
| Jerry Smith | 67 | 64 | 70 | 65 | 266 | 33,600 |
| Scott Weatherly | 69 | 67 | 66 | 64 | 266 | 33,600 |
| (Schultz defeated Smith and Weatherly on first and Daley on sixth playoff hole.) | | | | | | |
| Troy Matteson | 69 | 64 | 68 | 66 | 267 | 17,100 |
| Willie Wood | 67 | 66 | 68 | 66 | 267 | 17,100 |
| Grant Waite | 68 | 66 | 68 | 66 | 268 | 15,075 |
| David McKenzie | 68 | 69 | 66 | 67 | 270 | 13,050 |
| David Morland | 67 | 66 | 71 | 66 | 270 | 13,050 |
| Bubba Watson | 67 | 72 | 64 | 67 | 270 | 13,050 |
| David Branshaw | 66 | 67 | 71 | 67 | 271 | 9,540 |
| Jason Gore | 69 | 70 | 67 | 65 | 271 | 9,540 |
| James Nitties | 64 | 69 | 67 | 71 | 271 | 9,540 |
| Esteban Toledo | 67 | 67 | 69 | 68 | 271 | 9,540 |
| Johnson Wagner | 66 | 67 | 66 | 72 | 271 | 9,540 |
| Ben Bates | 66 | 70 | 66 | 70 | 272 | 7,425 |
| Jeff Freeman | 67 | 67 | 71 | 67 | 272 | 7,425 |
| Joseph Alfieri | 67 | 70 | 68 | 68 | 273 | 6,300 |
| Kevin Gessino-Kraft | 68 | 68 | 69 | 68 | 273 | 6,300 |
| Steve Larick | 68 | 69 | 68 | 68 | 273 | 6,300 |
| Rich Barcelo | 71 | 65 | 69 | 69 | 274 | 4,530 |
| Ricky Barnes | 67 | 72 | 70 | 65 | 274 | 4,530 |

| | SCORES | | | | TOTAL | MONEY |
|---|---|---|---|---|---|---|
| Greg Chalmers | 73 | 66 | 67 | 68 | 274 | 4,530 |
| Nathan Green | 67 | 71 | 64 | 72 | 274 | 4,530 |
| Scott Petersen | 68 | 69 | 65 | 72 | 274 | 4,530 |
| B.J. Staten | 68 | 71 | 69 | 66 | 274 | 4,530 |
| Craig Carmichael | 70 | 67 | 68 | 70 | 275 | 2,979 |
| Kim Felton | 68 | 69 | 69 | 69 | 275 | 2,979 |
| Mathew Goggin | 66 | 64 | 74 | 71 | 275 | 2,979 |
| Donnie Hammond | 69 | 68 | 70 | 68 | 275 | 2,979 |
| Bill Lunde | 68 | 71 | 68 | 68 | 275 | 2,979 |
| Bryce Molder | 70 | 68 | 67 | 70 | 275 | 2,979 |
| Brenden Pappas | 70 | 69 | 65 | 71 | 275 | 2,979 |
| Jim Rutledge | 68 | 71 | 69 | 67 | 275 | 2,979 |
| Brian Smock | 68 | 68 | 68 | 71 | 275 | 2,979 |
| Vance Veazey | 69 | 67 | 69 | 70 | 275 | 2,979 |

## LaSalle Bank Open

*The Glen Club,* Glenview, Illinois
Par 36-35–71; 7,149 yards

June 9-12
purse, $750,000

| | SCORES | | | | TOTAL | MONEY |
|---|---|---|---|---|---|---|
| Chris Couch | 66 | 67 | 69 | 67 | 269 | $135,000 |
| Kevin Durkin | 70 | 69 | 67 | 67 | 273 | 56,000 |
| Paul Gow | 70 | 68 | 67 | 68 | 273 | 56,000 |
| Mario Tiziani | 67 | 70 | 68 | 68 | 273 | 56,000 |
| Mathew Goggin | 67 | 69 | 70 | 68 | 274 | 28,500 |
| Camilo Villegas | 72 | 67 | 70 | 65 | 274 | 28,500 |
| Steve LeBrun | 68 | 70 | 67 | 70 | 275 | 24,187.50 |
| Dicky Pride | 72 | 68 | 69 | 66 | 275 | 24,187.50 |
| Brendon de Jonge | 68 | 67 | 70 | 71 | 276 | 19,500 |
| Mathias Gronberg | 68 | 70 | 69 | 69 | 276 | 19,500 |
| Jon Mills | 67 | 70 | 67 | 72 | 276 | 19,500 |
| Roger Tambellini | 69 | 68 | 72 | 67 | 276 | 19,500 |
| Joel Kribel | 67 | 70 | 70 | 70 | 277 | 14,062.50 |
| Deane Pappas | 67 | 68 | 69 | 73 | 277 | 14,062.50 |
| Jim Rutledge | 70 | 70 | 75 | 62 | 277 | 14,062.50 |
| Tom Scherrer | 71 | 69 | 70 | 67 | 277 | 14,062.50 |
| Ryan Armour | 70 | 70 | 72 | 66 | 278 | 10,150 |
| Steven Bowditch | 70 | 72 | 68 | 68 | 278 | 10,150 |
| Jason Gore | 68 | 69 | 72 | 69 | 278 | 10,150 |
| Charley Hoffman | 69 | 66 | 72 | 71 | 278 | 10,150 |
| Tripp Isenhour | 71 | 71 | 72 | 64 | 278 | 10,150 |
| Tim O'Neal | 70 | 69 | 71 | 68 | 278 | 10,150 |
| Jess Daley | 70 | 64 | 71 | 74 | 279 | 6,780 |
| David McKenzie | 70 | 70 | 66 | 73 | 279 | 6,780 |
| James McLean | 69 | 71 | 74 | 65 | 279 | 6,780 |
| Wes Short, Jr. | 69 | 69 | 72 | 69 | 279 | 6,780 |
| Tim Wilkinson | 69 | 73 | 68 | 69 | 279 | 6,780 |
| Rick Fehr | 70 | 71 | 71 | 68 | 280 | 5,014.29 |
| Hideto Tanihara | 69 | 71 | 72 | 68 | 280 | 5,014.29 |
| Chris Tidland | 67 | 71 | 72 | 70 | 280 | 5,014.29 |
| Bubba Watson | 70 | 71 | 68 | 71 | 280 | 5,014.29 |
| Eric Axley | 68 | 74 | 70 | 68 | 280 | 5,014.28 |
| Aaron Barber | 67 | 75 | 70 | 68 | 280 | 5,014.28 |
| Kyle Thompson | 70 | 66 | 69 | 75 | 280 | 5,014.28 |

# Knoxville Open

*Fox Den Country Club,* Knoxville, Tennessee
Par 36-36–72; 7,110 yards

June 16-19
purse, $475,000

| | SCORES | | | | TOTAL | MONEY |
|---|---|---|---|---|---|---|
| Kim Felton | 71 | 70 | 67 | 69 | 277 | $85,500 |
| David Peoples | 76 | 66 | 67 | 69 | 278 | 51,300 |
| Mathew Goggin | 70 | 71 | 71 | 67 | 279 | 27,550 |
| Dan Olsen | 72 | 74 | 68 | 65 | 279 | 27,550 |
| Dave Christensen | 71 | 70 | 71 | 68 | 280 | 18,050 |
| Scott Gardiner | 72 | 69 | 69 | 70 | 280 | 18,050 |
| Nathan Green | 75 | 67 | 69 | 70 | 281 | 15,318.75 |
| Wes Short, Jr. | 71 | 71 | 68 | 71 | 281 | 15,318.75 |
| Deane Pappas | 72 | 71 | 69 | 70 | 282 | 13,775 |
| Rich Barcelo | 75 | 68 | 70 | 70 | 283 | 10,925 |
| Shane Bertsch | 69 | 70 | 71 | 73 | 283 | 10,925 |
| Will MacKenzie | 74 | 69 | 68 | 72 | 283 | 10,925 |
| Troy Matteson | 70 | 72 | 66 | 75 | 283 | 10,925 |
| Boo Weekley | 73 | 69 | 69 | 72 | 283 | 10,925 |
| Steven Alker | 70 | 70 | 72 | 72 | 284 | 7,837.50 |
| Charley Hoffman | 71 | 70 | 72 | 71 | 284 | 7,837.50 |
| Cliff Kresge | 72 | 69 | 72 | 71 | 284 | 7,837.50 |
| David McKenzie | 72 | 74 | 70 | 68 | 284 | 7,837.50 |
| Greg Chalmers | 74 | 71 | 73 | 67 | 285 | 5,360.72 |
| Kevin Durkin | 74 | 69 | 73 | 69 | 285 | 5,360.72 |
| Fran Quinn | 70 | 72 | 74 | 69 | 285 | 5,360.72 |
| Thomas Aiken | 75 | 69 | 71 | 70 | 285 | 5,360.71 |
| Tom Carter | 70 | 70 | 73 | 72 | 285 | 5,360.71 |
| Matt Gallant | 74 | 70 | 70 | 71 | 285 | 5,360.71 |
| Bill Haas | 74 | 68 | 72 | 71 | 285 | 5,360.71 |
| Brad Adamonis | 73 | 71 | 72 | 70 | 286 | 3,530.84 |
| Bubba Watson | 74 | 70 | 73 | 69 | 286 | 3,530.84 |
| Bubba Dickerson | 75 | 69 | 66 | 76 | 286 | 3,530.83 |
| Jason Enloe | 72 | 73 | 69 | 72 | 286 | 3,530.83 |
| Jason Schultz | 68 | 75 | 71 | 72 | 286 | 3,530.83 |
| Tim Wilkinson | 74 | 71 | 71 | 70 | 286 | 3,530.83 |

# Northeast Pennsylvania Classic

*Glenmaura National Golf Club,* Scranton, Pennsylvania
Par 35-36–71; 6,933 yards

June 23-26
purse, $450,000

| | SCORES | | | | TOTAL | MONEY |
|---|---|---|---|---|---|---|
| Greg Kraft | 65 | 64 | 68 | 70 | 267 | $81,000 |
| Tim O'Neal | 67 | 71 | 66 | 65 | 269 | 48,600 |
| Bubba Watson | 66 | 71 | 67 | 66 | 270 | 30,600 |
| David Branshaw | 69 | 68 | 67 | 68 | 272 | 19,800 |
| Joe Daley | 71 | 69 | 66 | 66 | 272 | 19,800 |
| Rich Barcelo | 68 | 72 | 66 | 67 | 273 | 16,200 |
| Doug Garwood | 66 | 74 | 66 | 68 | 274 | 15,075 |
| Ryan Armour | 67 | 68 | 72 | 68 | 275 | 13,050 |
| Troy Matteson | 71 | 66 | 71 | 67 | 275 | 13,050 |
| Brandt Snedeker | 68 | 70 | 67 | 70 | 275 | 13,050 |
| Craig Bowden | 70 | 69 | 65 | 72 | 276 | 10,350 |
| Kim Felton | 70 | 68 | 69 | 69 | 276 | 10,350 |
| Scott Gump | 69 | 69 | 70 | 68 | 276 | 10,350 |

| | SCORES | | | | TOTAL | MONEY |
|---|---|---|---|---|---|---|
| Richard Johnson | 70 | 72 | 68 | 67 | 277 | 8,100 |
| David Morland | 65 | 73 | 69 | 70 | 277 | 8,100 |
| Chris Tidland | 68 | 70 | 70 | 69 | 277 | 8,100 |
| Roger Tambellini | 72 | 69 | 72 | 65 | 278 | 5,888.58 |
| Jeff Burns | 69 | 70 | 69 | 70 | 278 | 5,888.57 |
| Jess Daley | 71 | 66 | 68 | 73 | 278 | 5,888.57 |
| Bubba Dickerson | 68 | 71 | 73 | 66 | 278 | 5,888.57 |
| Scott Gardiner | 71 | 70 | 69 | 68 | 278 | 5,888.57 |
| Jeff Gove | 67 | 70 | 67 | 74 | 278 | 5,888.57 |
| Johnson Wagner | 66 | 71 | 71 | 70 | 278 | 5,888.57 |
| Jaxon Brigman | 71 | 71 | 68 | 69 | 279 | 3,915 |
| Brendon de Jonge | 69 | 69 | 74 | 67 | 279 | 3,915 |
| Bryce Molder | 68 | 69 | 71 | 71 | 279 | 3,915 |
| David Peoples | 70 | 69 | 69 | 71 | 279 | 3,915 |
| Michael Clark | 70 | 68 | 71 | 71 | 280 | 3,114 |
| Keoke Cotner | 73 | 68 | 64 | 75 | 280 | 3,114 |
| Nathan Green | 67 | 72 | 68 | 73 | 280 | 3,114 |
| Pete Jordan | 68 | 71 | 69 | 72 | 280 | 3,114 |
| Matt Weibring | 65 | 69 | 74 | 72 | 280 | 3,114 |

## Lake Erie Charity Classic

*Peek'n Peak Resort, Upper Course,*
Findley Lake, New York
Par 36-36–72; 6,888 yards

June 30-July 3
purse, $450,000

| | SCORES | | | | TOTAL | MONEY |
|---|---|---|---|---|---|---|
| Esteban Toledo | 71 | 67 | 65 | 71 | 274 | $81,000 |
| Jeff Gove | 70 | 70 | 66 | 70 | 276 | 48,600 |
| Jamie Broce | 68 | 70 | 70 | 69 | 277 | 30,600 |
| David McKenzie | 72 | 68 | 70 | 68 | 278 | 21,600 |
| Jon Mills | 73 | 70 | 71 | 65 | 279 | 17,100 |
| Scott Parel | 70 | 71 | 65 | 73 | 279 | 17,100 |
| Craig Lile | 69 | 72 | 71 | 68 | 280 | 14,025 |
| David Morland | 69 | 72 | 69 | 70 | 280 | 14,025 |
| Matt Weibring | 70 | 71 | 69 | 70 | 280 | 14,025 |
| Jason Gore | 68 | 73 | 68 | 72 | 281 | 11,700 |
| Steve Larick | 67 | 74 | 70 | 70 | 281 | 11,700 |
| Bubba Dickerson | 67 | 68 | 74 | 73 | 282 | 8,820 |
| Richard Johnson | 69 | 71 | 70 | 72 | 282 | 8,820 |
| Tom Johnson | 71 | 67 | 75 | 69 | 282 | 8,820 |
| Jim McGovern | 72 | 70 | 69 | 71 | 282 | 8,820 |
| Roger Tambellini | 75 | 67 | 69 | 71 | 282 | 8,820 |
| Jason Dufner | 71 | 71 | 67 | 74 | 283 | 6,525 |
| Scott Petersen | 74 | 69 | 72 | 68 | 283 | 6,525 |
| Jerry Smith | 72 | 68 | 72 | 71 | 283 | 6,525 |
| Boo Weekley | 71 | 66 | 74 | 72 | 283 | 6,525 |
| Mathew Goggin | 71 | 70 | 71 | 72 | 284 | 5,040 |
| Deane Pappas | 70 | 70 | 72 | 72 | 284 | 5,040 |
| Tom Scherrer | 72 | 70 | 70 | 72 | 284 | 5,040 |
| Eric Axley | 71 | 70 | 70 | 74 | 285 | 3,816 |
| Rick Fehr | 68 | 71 | 71 | 75 | 285 | 3,816 |
| Cliff Kresge | 71 | 70 | 72 | 72 | 285 | 3,816 |
| Steve Pate | 74 | 65 | 72 | 74 | 285 | 3,816 |
| Kyle Thompson | 69 | 72 | 72 | 72 | 285 | 3,816 |
| Jay Don Blake | 71 | 72 | 66 | 77 | 286 | 2,988 |
| Craig Carmichael | 70 | 73 | 71 | 72 | 286 | 2,988 |

| | SCORES | | | | TOTAL | MONEY |
|---|---|---|---|---|---|---|
| Greg Chalmers | 70 | 73 | 71 | 72 | 286 | 2,988 |
| Bill Haas | 72 | 70 | 73 | 71 | 286 | 2,988 |
| Bubba Watson | 76 | 66 | 70 | 74 | 286 | 2,988 |

## National Mining Association Pete Dye Classic

*Pete Dye Golf Club,* Bridgeport, West Virginia                           July 7-10
Par 36-36–72; 7,248 yards                                       purse, $600,000

| | SCORES | | | | TOTAL | MONEY |
|---|---|---|---|---|---|---|
| Jason Gore | 69 | 66 | 68 | 68 | 271 | $108,000 |
| Doug LaBelle | 69 | 70 | 67 | 66 | 272 | 64,800 |
| Bubba Dickerson | 69 | 68 | 67 | 69 | 273 | 40,800 |
| Chris Couch | 68 | 70 | 67 | 69 | 274 | 28,800 |
| Kevin Gessino-Kraft | 68 | 69 | 68 | 70 | 275 | 21,075 |
| Nathan Green | 72 | 69 | 67 | 67 | 275 | 21,075 |
| Cliff Kresge | 70 | 65 | 73 | 67 | 275 | 21,075 |
| Bubba Watson | 69 | 70 | 67 | 69 | 275 | 21,075 |
| Kris Cox | 65 | 71 | 72 | 68 | 276 | 16,200 |
| Dan Olsen | 66 | 69 | 67 | 74 | 276 | 16,200 |
| Tom Scherrer | 70 | 70 | 67 | 69 | 276 | 16,200 |
| David Branshaw | 68 | 73 | 69 | 67 | 277 | 11,760 |
| Erik Compton | 71 | 68 | 70 | 68 | 277 | 11,760 |
| Kim Felton | 68 | 70 | 65 | 74 | 277 | 11,760 |
| Troy Matteson | 67 | 69 | 70 | 71 | 277 | 11,760 |
| Jim McGovern | 69 | 69 | 69 | 70 | 277 | 11,760 |
| Aaron Barber | 64 | 72 | 70 | 72 | 278 | 8,700 |
| Nick Cassini | 69 | 72 | 68 | 69 | 278 | 8,700 |
| Jeff Gove | 68 | 72 | 71 | 67 | 278 | 8,700 |
| Dicky Pride | 68 | 71 | 70 | 69 | 278 | 8,700 |
| Kris Blanks | 70 | 72 | 67 | 70 | 279 | 6,240 |
| David McKenzie | 68 | 72 | 73 | 66 | 279 | 6,240 |
| Todd Pinneo | 72 | 70 | 71 | 66 | 279 | 6,240 |
| Fran Quinn | 68 | 74 | 67 | 70 | 279 | 6,240 |
| Scott Weatherly | 67 | 74 | 67 | 71 | 279 | 6,240 |
| Jason Dufner | 69 | 69 | 71 | 71 | 280 | 4,371.43 |
| Jeff Freeman | 69 | 72 | 70 | 69 | 280 | 4,371.43 |
| Brian Henninger | 70 | 72 | 69 | 69 | 280 | 4,371.43 |
| Rick Price | 71 | 68 | 71 | 70 | 280 | 4,371.43 |
| Jim Rutledge | 69 | 72 | 69 | 70 | 280 | 4,371.43 |
| Chris Tidland | 68 | 71 | 71 | 70 | 280 | 4,371.43 |
| Brad Fabel | 70 | 70 | 69 | 71 | 280 | 4,371.42 |

## Scholarship America Showdown

*Troy Burne Golf Club,* Hudson, Wisconsin                           July 14-17
Par 36-34–70; 7,003 yards                                       purse, $525,000

| | SCORES | | | | TOTAL | MONEY |
|---|---|---|---|---|---|---|
| Jason Gore | 67 | 68 | 64 | 67 | 266 | $94,500 |
| Bill Haas | 71 | 65 | 67 | 67 | 270 | 56,700 |
| Matt Bettencourt | 70 | 69 | 66 | 69 | 274 | 27,300 |
| Jason Dufner | 65 | 69 | 66 | 74 | 274 | 27,300 |
| Jon Mills | 65 | 68 | 70 | 71 | 274 | 27,300 |

|  | SCORES | | | | TOTAL | MONEY |
|---|---|---|---|---|---|---|
| Eric Axley | 66 | 71 | 73 | 65 | 275 | 17,587.50 |
| Steve LeBrun | 65 | 61 | 75 | 74 | 275 | 17,587.50 |
| Chris Tidland | 71 | 67 | 69 | 68 | 275 | 17,587.50 |
| Steven Bowditch | 65 | 65 | 74 | 72 | 276 | 13,650 |
| Charley Hoffman | 64 | 70 | 75 | 67 | 276 | 13,650 |
| Andy Morse | 72 | 64 | 68 | 72 | 276 | 13,650 |
| Dicky Pride | 70 | 68 | 68 | 70 | 276 | 13,650 |
| Shane Bertsch | 70 | 68 | 68 | 71 | 277 | 9,555 |
| Anthony Painter | 65 | 68 | 71 | 73 | 277 | 9,555 |
| Brandt Snedeker | 63 | 71 | 70 | 73 | 277 | 9,555 |
| Peter Tomasulo | 67 | 68 | 69 | 73 | 277 | 9,555 |
| Chad Wilfong | 67 | 63 | 73 | 74 | 277 | 9,555 |
| Deane Pappas | 69 | 69 | 70 | 70 | 278 | 7,350 |
| Scott Petersen | 69 | 72 | 71 | 66 | 278 | 7,350 |
| Vance Veazey | 72 | 67 | 70 | 69 | 278 | 7,350 |
| Steven Alker | 69 | 70 | 66 | 74 | 279 | 5,460 |
| Kevin Durkin | 69 | 70 | 68 | 72 | 279 | 5,460 |
| Bryce Molder | 69 | 68 | 72 | 70 | 279 | 5,460 |
| Jerry Smith | 64 | 69 | 70 | 76 | 279 | 5,460 |
| Camilo Villegas | 69 | 69 | 67 | 74 | 279 | 5,460 |
| Jeff Burns | 74 | 67 | 68 | 71 | 280 | 3,990 |
| Greg Kraft | 67 | 70 | 69 | 74 | 280 | 3,990 |
| Joel Kribel | 72 | 68 | 72 | 68 | 280 | 3,990 |
| Scott Weatherly | 70 | 69 | 73 | 68 | 280 | 3,990 |
| Zoran Zorkic | 70 | 69 | 75 | 66 | 280 | 3,990 |

## Canadian PGA Championship

*Whistle Bear Golf Club*, Cambridge, Ontario, Canada
Par 36-36–72; 7,702 yards

July 21-24
purse, $450,000

|  | SCORES | | | | TOTAL | MONEY |
|---|---|---|---|---|---|---|
| Jon Mills | 68 | 67 | 63 | 71 | 269 | $81,000 |
| Ken Duke | 69 | 67 | 68 | 68 | 272 | 48,600 |
| Nick Cassini | 72 | 68 | 67 | 67 | 274 | 26,100 |
| Erik Compton | 71 | 66 | 69 | 68 | 274 | 26,100 |
| Kevin Johnson | 67 | 65 | 70 | 74 | 276 | 18,000 |
| Doug LaBelle | 65 | 74 | 67 | 71 | 277 | 15,637.50 |
| Jerry Smith | 67 | 71 | 72 | 67 | 277 | 15,637.50 |
| Carl Desjardins | 68 | 72 | 69 | 69 | 278 | 13,050 |
| Tom Scherrer | 70 | 71 | 67 | 70 | 278 | 13,050 |
| Kenneth Staton | 68 | 72 | 71 | 67 | 278 | 13,050 |
| Greg Chalmers | 70 | 72 | 69 | 68 | 279 | 9,900 |
| Kevin Durkin | 72 | 69 | 67 | 71 | 279 | 9,900 |
| John Mallinger | 74 | 68 | 67 | 70 | 279 | 9,900 |
| Rick Price | 66 | 69 | 73 | 71 | 279 | 9,900 |
| Eric Axley | 68 | 72 | 71 | 69 | 280 | 6,129 |
| Jason Buha | 65 | 71 | 71 | 73 | 280 | 6,129 |
| Dave Christensen | 70 | 70 | 67 | 73 | 280 | 6,129 |
| Todd Demsey | 68 | 71 | 69 | 72 | 280 | 6,129 |
| Bill Haas | 72 | 70 | 68 | 70 | 280 | 6,129 |
| Tom Johnson | 67 | 66 | 74 | 73 | 280 | 6,129 |
| Cliff Kresge | 70 | 70 | 67 | 73 | 280 | 6,129 |
| Han Lee | 70 | 71 | 72 | 67 | 280 | 6,129 |
| Jim McGovern | 68 | 70 | 72 | 70 | 280 | 6,129 |
| Bryce Molder | 66 | 70 | 71 | 73 | 280 | 6,129 |
| P.H. Horgan | 70 | 70 | 71 | 70 | 281 | 3,870 |

| | SCORES | | | | TOTAL | MONEY |
|---|---|---|---|---|---|---|
| Jon Rusk | 67 | 71 | 71 | 72 | 281 | 3,870 |
| Ricky Barnes | 73 | 67 | 71 | 71 | 282 | 3,195 |
| Kris Blanks | 72 | 69 | 70 | 71 | 282 | 3,195 |
| Jaime Gomez | 71 | 71 | 69 | 71 | 282 | 3,195 |
| Chris Kamin | 69 | 73 | 69 | 71 | 282 | 3,195 |
| Joel Kribel | 68 | 72 | 70 | 72 | 282 | 3,195 |
| Bubba Watson | 69 | 72 | 70 | 71 | 282 | 3,195 |

## Preferred Health Systems Wichita Open

*Crestview Country Club*, Wichita, Kansas
Par 35-36–71; 6,886 yards

July 28-31
purse, $475,000

| | SCORES | | | | TOTAL | MONEY |
|---|---|---|---|---|---|---|
| Joe Daley | 71 | 67 | 65 | 65 | 268 | $85,500 |
| Shane Bertsch | 65 | 71 | 67 | 65 | 268 | 51,300 |
| (Daley defeated Bertsch on first playoff hole.) | | | | | | |
| Mathew Goggin | 68 | 68 | 68 | 65 | 269 | 32,300 |
| Charley Hoffman | 65 | 68 | 67 | 70 | 270 | 20,900 |
| Jason Schultz | 66 | 67 | 70 | 67 | 270 | 20,900 |
| Chris Couch | 67 | 67 | 66 | 71 | 271 | 16,506.25 |
| Steve LeBrun | 67 | 69 | 66 | 69 | 271 | 16,506.25 |
| Erik Compton | 68 | 65 | 74 | 65 | 272 | 14,725 |
| Steven Bowditch | 68 | 71 | 66 | 68 | 273 | 10,291.67 |
| Justin Hicks | 69 | 68 | 69 | 67 | 273 | 10,291.67 |
| Joel Kribel | 67 | 68 | 69 | 69 | 273 | 10,291.67 |
| Tom Scherrer | 64 | 69 | 72 | 68 | 273 | 10,291.67 |
| Matt Weibring | 66 | 73 | 67 | 67 | 273 | 10,291.67 |
| Chad Wilfong | 69 | 67 | 71 | 66 | 273 | 10,291.67 |
| John Mallinger | 69 | 67 | 65 | 72 | 273 | 10,291.66 |
| Deane Pappas | 62 | 71 | 70 | 70 | 273 | 10,291.66 |
| Tim Wilkinson | 68 | 70 | 66 | 69 | 273 | 10,291.66 |
| Jay Don Blake | 71 | 68 | 68 | 67 | 274 | 6,412.50 |
| Dave Christensen | 68 | 69 | 68 | 69 | 274 | 6,412.50 |
| Martin Laird | 67 | 72 | 66 | 69 | 274 | 6,412.50 |
| Chris Wollmann | 69 | 70 | 66 | 69 | 274 | 6,412.50 |
| Ben Bates | 68 | 71 | 67 | 69 | 275 | 4,116.67 |
| Jamie Broce | 66 | 69 | 72 | 68 | 275 | 4,116.67 |
| Brendon de Jonge | 68 | 69 | 70 | 68 | 275 | 4,116.67 |
| Nathan Green | 73 | 66 | 69 | 67 | 275 | 4,116.67 |
| Tim Turpen | 69 | 67 | 73 | 66 | 275 | 4,116.67 |
| Bubba Watson | 69 | 69 | 68 | 69 | 275 | 4,116.67 |
| Jeremy Anderson | 68 | 65 | 71 | 71 | 275 | 4,116.66 |
| Jeff Gove | 67 | 71 | 67 | 70 | 275 | 4,116.66 |
| Fran Quinn | 68 | 69 | 64 | 74 | 275 | 4,116.66 |

## Cox Classic

*Champions Run*, Omaha, Nebraska
Par 36-36–72; 7,097 yards

August 4-7
purse, $625,000

| | SCORES | | | | TOTAL | MONEY |
|---|---|---|---|---|---|---|
| Jason Gore | 71 | 59 | 68 | 63 | 261 | $112,500 |
| Roger Tambellini | 66 | 63 | 68 | 64 | 261 | 67,500 |
| (Gore defeated Tambellini on second playoff hole.) | | | | | | |

| | SCORES | | | | TOTAL | MONEY |
|---|---|---|---|---|---|---|
| John Mallinger | 71 | 63 | 66 | 65 | 265 | 32,500 |
| Jon Mills | 67 | 60 | 71 | 67 | 265 | 32,500 |
| Scott Petersen | 66 | 65 | 63 | 71 | 265 | 32,500 |
| Steve LeBrun | 67 | 66 | 63 | 70 | 266 | 22,500 |
| Bill Haas | 69 | 66 | 66 | 66 | 267 | 20,937.50 |
| Greg Chalmers | 68 | 65 | 70 | 65 | 268 | 18,750 |
| Greg Kraft | 67 | 68 | 64 | 69 | 268 | 18,750 |
| Jeremy Anderson | 67 | 66 | 68 | 68 | 269 | 16,250 |
| Troy Matteson | 67 | 69 | 66 | 67 | 269 | 16,250 |
| Dicky Pride | 68 | 68 | 71 | 63 | 270 | 14,375 |
| Mathew Goggin | 67 | 70 | 67 | 67 | 271 | 12,083.34 |
| Joseph Alfieri | 69 | 66 | 67 | 69 | 271 | 12,083.33 |
| Joel Kribel | 70 | 67 | 66 | 68 | 271 | 12,083.33 |
| Tom Johnson | 67 | 69 | 67 | 69 | 272 | 9,375 |
| Steve Larick | 65 | 67 | 72 | 68 | 272 | 9,375 |
| Cameron Percy | 71 | 67 | 66 | 68 | 272 | 9,375 |
| Garrett Willis | 68 | 70 | 65 | 69 | 272 | 9,375 |
| Willie Wood | 68 | 67 | 67 | 70 | 272 | 9,375 |
| Rich Barcelo | 69 | 68 | 65 | 71 | 273 | 6,500 |
| Bubba Dickerson | 66 | 68 | 65 | 74 | 273 | 6,500 |
| Michael Letzig | 69 | 65 | 69 | 70 | 273 | 6,500 |
| Brent Schwarzrock | 70 | 68 | 67 | 68 | 273 | 6,500 |
| Camilo Villegas | 69 | 65 | 67 | 72 | 273 | 6,500 |
| Scott Gardiner | 67 | 69 | 67 | 71 | 274 | 5,000 |
| Donnie Hammond | 69 | 69 | 65 | 71 | 274 | 5,000 |
| Scott Weatherly | 66 | 72 | 72 | 64 | 274 | 5,000 |
| Dave Christensen | 69 | 69 | 68 | 69 | 275 | 4,150 |
| Chad Collins | 63 | 71 | 72 | 69 | 275 | 4,150 |
| Todd Demsey | 67 | 69 | 68 | 71 | 275 | 4,150 |
| Tom Scherrer | 70 | 67 | 71 | 67 | 275 | 4,150 |
| Johnson Wagner | 68 | 70 | 67 | 70 | 275 | 4,150 |

## Price Cutter Charity Championship

*Highland Springs Country Club*, Springfield, Missouri
Par 36-36–72; 7,060 yards

August 11-14
purse, $556,000

| | SCORES | | | | TOTAL | MONEY |
|---|---|---|---|---|---|---|
| Roger Tambellini | 65 | 70 | 67 | 65 | 267 | $100,080 |
| Steven Bowditch | 67 | 69 | 68 | 64 | 268 | 36,696 |
| Troy Matteson | 65 | 63 | 71 | 69 | 268 | 36,696 |
| David Peoples | 67 | 68 | 71 | 62 | 268 | 36,696 |
| Vance Veazey | 69 | 65 | 67 | 67 | 268 | 36,696 |
| Jason Dufner | 65 | 71 | 66 | 67 | 269 | 19,321 |
| Bill Haas | 64 | 69 | 70 | 66 | 269 | 19,321 |
| Pat Bates | 67 | 67 | 71 | 65 | 270 | 14,456 |
| Gabriel Hjertstedt | 67 | 67 | 67 | 69 | 270 | 14,456 |
| Kevin Johnson | 65 | 69 | 68 | 68 | 270 | 14,456 |
| Jerry Smith | 66 | 72 | 66 | 66 | 270 | 14,456 |
| Johnson Wagner | 68 | 67 | 70 | 65 | 270 | 14,456 |
| Scott Weatherly | 64 | 69 | 69 | 68 | 270 | 14,456 |
| Eric Axley | 66 | 70 | 69 | 66 | 271 | 10,008 |
| Kim Felton | 66 | 67 | 72 | 66 | 271 | 10,008 |
| Craig Lile | 68 | 67 | 68 | 68 | 271 | 10,008 |
| Rich Morris | 66 | 69 | 69 | 68 | 272 | 8,896 |
| Jeremy Anderson | 67 | 70 | 67 | 69 | 273 | 7,784 |
| Kevin Durkin | 71 | 65 | 70 | 67 | 273 | 7,784 |

|  | SCORES | | | | TOTAL | MONEY |
|---|---|---|---|---|---|---|
| Esteban Toledo | 68 | 71 | 68 | 66 | 273 | 7,784 |
| Kris Cox | 71 | 67 | 65 | 71 | 274 | 5,004 |
| Doug Garwood | 68 | 71 | 66 | 69 | 274 | 5,004 |
| Brian Guetz | 68 | 69 | 68 | 69 | 274 | 5,004 |
| Tripp Isenhour | 68 | 66 | 71 | 69 | 274 | 5,004 |
| Bryce Molder | 67 | 71 | 67 | 69 | 274 | 5,004 |
| David Morland | 72 | 67 | 67 | 68 | 274 | 5,004 |
| Andy Morse | 69 | 70 | 71 | 64 | 274 | 5,004 |
| Steve Pleis | 70 | 65 | 68 | 71 | 274 | 5,004 |
| Jason Schultz | 72 | 67 | 67 | 68 | 274 | 5,004 |
| Chad Wilfong | 67 | 72 | 66 | 69 | 274 | 5,004 |

## Xerox Classic

*Irondequoit Country Club*, Rochester, New York
Par 35-35–70; 6,720 yards

August 18-21
purse, $550,000

|  | SCORES | | | | TOTAL | MONEY |
|---|---|---|---|---|---|---|
| Rick Price | 67 | 63 | 68 | 71 | 269 | $99,000 |
| Andrew Pratt | 66 | 67 | 66 | 71 | 270 | 59,400 |
| Scott Gardiner | 70 | 63 | 67 | 71 | 271 | 28,600 |
| David McKenzie | 74 | 65 | 64 | 68 | 271 | 28,600 |
| Jeff Quinney | 68 | 68 | 65 | 70 | 271 | 28,600 |
| Ahmad Bateman | 71 | 67 | 69 | 65 | 272 | 19,800 |
| Eric Axley | 66 | 68 | 66 | 73 | 273 | 16,568.75 |
| Kim Felton | 65 | 67 | 70 | 71 | 273 | 16,568.75 |
| Todd Pinneo | 68 | 62 | 68 | 75 | 273 | 16,568.75 |
| Brent Schwarzrock | 65 | 70 | 67 | 71 | 273 | 16,568.75 |
| Bubba Dickerson | 64 | 70 | 68 | 72 | 274 | 12,100 |
| Bill Haas | 67 | 67 | 70 | 70 | 274 | 12,100 |
| Greg Kraft | 69 | 70 | 69 | 66 | 274 | 12,100 |
| Steve LeBrun | 66 | 69 | 68 | 71 | 274 | 12,100 |
| Barry Cheesman | 70 | 66 | 69 | 70 | 275 | 9,075 |
| Troy Matteson | 67 | 71 | 67 | 70 | 275 | 9,075 |
| Jim McGovern | 67 | 66 | 71 | 71 | 275 | 9,075 |
| Fran Quinn | 71 | 66 | 69 | 69 | 275 | 9,075 |
| Dave Christensen | 73 | 66 | 72 | 65 | 276 | 6,207.15 |
| Chris Tidland | 70 | 68 | 70 | 68 | 276 | 6,207.15 |
| Shane Bertsch | 68 | 68 | 71 | 69 | 276 | 6,207.14 |
| Kevin Gessino-Kraft | 66 | 72 | 68 | 70 | 276 | 6,207.14 |
| Brian Henninger | 70 | 66 | 65 | 75 | 276 | 6,207.14 |
| Jeff Klauk | 68 | 67 | 71 | 70 | 276 | 6,207.14 |
| Tim Wilkinson | 67 | 67 | 71 | 71 | 276 | 6,207.14 |
| Steven Alker | 70 | 69 | 70 | 68 | 277 | 4,290 |
| Jamie Broce | 70 | 69 | 69 | 69 | 277 | 4,290 |
| Nathan Green | 66 | 69 | 71 | 71 | 277 | 4,290 |
| Jon Mills | 67 | 70 | 68 | 72 | 277 | 4,290 |
| Aaron Barber | 71 | 64 | 71 | 72 | 278 | 3,300 |
| Craig Carmichael | 75 | 64 | 67 | 72 | 278 | 3,300 |
| Greg Chalmers | 67 | 68 | 70 | 73 | 278 | 3,300 |
| Kris Cox | 68 | 69 | 73 | 68 | 278 | 3,300 |
| Joe Daley | 67 | 65 | 73 | 73 | 278 | 3,300 |
| Carl Desjardins | 68 | 69 | 71 | 70 | 278 | 3,300 |
| Kevin Hall | 70 | 69 | 68 | 71 | 278 | 3,300 |
| Deane Pappas | 66 | 71 | 68 | 73 | 278 | 3,300 |
| Vance Veazey | 70 | 68 | 68 | 72 | 278 | 3,300 |

# Cleveland Open

*StoneWater Golf Club*, Highland Heights, Ohio
Par 35-36–71; 7,045 yards

August 25-28
purse, $450,000

| | SCORES | | | | TOTAL | MONEY |
|---|---|---|---|---|---|---|
| Andrew Johnson | 73 | 68 | 62 | 67 | 270 | $81,000 |
| Keoke Cotner | 71 | 69 | 68 | 65 | 273 | 48,600 |
| Dicky Pride | 67 | 66 | 71 | 70 | 274 | 26,100 |
| Tom Scherrer | 69 | 69 | 67 | 69 | 274 | 26,100 |
| David Morland | 71 | 72 | 64 | 68 | 275 | 18,000 |
| Ben Bates | 68 | 71 | 69 | 68 | 276 | 15,075 |
| Matthew Jones | 70 | 65 | 68 | 73 | 276 | 15,075 |
| Rick Price | 71 | 71 | 66 | 68 | 276 | 15,075 |
| Camilo Villegas | 68 | 72 | 67 | 70 | 277 | 12,600 |
| Tyler Williamson | 69 | 71 | 69 | 68 | 277 | 12,600 |
| Ahmad Bateman | 70 | 66 | 73 | 69 | 278 | 9,225 |
| Richie Coughlan | 76 | 66 | 68 | 68 | 278 | 9,225 |
| Jason Dufner | 67 | 73 | 69 | 69 | 278 | 9,225 |
| Kevin Gessino-Kraft | 70 | 70 | 69 | 69 | 278 | 9,225 |
| Justin Hicks | 76 | 67 | 69 | 66 | 278 | 9,225 |
| Garrett Willis | 69 | 67 | 73 | 69 | 278 | 9,225 |
| Eric Axley | 72 | 69 | 71 | 67 | 279 | 6,975 |
| Matt Weibring | 71 | 69 | 65 | 74 | 279 | 6,975 |
| Jeff Burns | 71 | 67 | 70 | 72 | 280 | 5,454 |
| Bubba Dickerson | 69 | 71 | 70 | 70 | 280 | 5,454 |
| Matt Gallant | 73 | 69 | 66 | 72 | 280 | 5,454 |
| David McKenzie | 68 | 70 | 74 | 68 | 280 | 5,454 |
| Scott Parel | 68 | 71 | 66 | 75 | 280 | 5,454 |
| Tom Carter | 68 | 72 | 70 | 71 | 281 | 3,720 |
| Dave Christensen | 68 | 72 | 70 | 71 | 281 | 3,720 |
| Todd Demsey | 72 | 65 | 72 | 72 | 281 | 3,720 |
| Doug Garwood | 71 | 72 | 66 | 72 | 281 | 3,720 |
| Keith Nolan | 68 | 74 | 69 | 70 | 281 | 3,720 |
| Scott Weatherly | 70 | 71 | 72 | 68 | 281 | 3,720 |
| Brendon de Jonge | 71 | 72 | 69 | 70 | 282 | 2,745 |
| Jeff Freeman | 73 | 69 | 71 | 69 | 282 | 2,745 |
| Donnie Hammond | 73 | 68 | 70 | 71 | 282 | 2,745 |
| P.H. Horgan | 68 | 73 | 70 | 71 | 282 | 2,745 |
| Tim O'Neal | 69 | 74 | 71 | 68 | 282 | 2,745 |
| Chris Tidland | 70 | 70 | 74 | 68 | 282 | 2,745 |
| Johnson Wagner | 69 | 70 | 71 | 72 | 282 | 2,745 |
| Boo Weekley | 71 | 72 | 72 | 67 | 282 | 2,745 |

# Alberta Classic

*Redwood Meadows Golf & Country Club*, Calgary,
Alberta, Canada
Par 35-36–71; 7,019 yards

September 1-4
purse, $450,000

| | SCORES | | | | TOTAL | MONEY |
|---|---|---|---|---|---|---|
| Peter Tomasulo | 73 | 61 | 72 | 69 | 275 | $81,000 |
| Aaron Barber | 72 | 70 | 64 | 71 | 277 | 48,600 |
| Nathan Green | 70 | 70 | 68 | 70 | 278 | 26,100 |
| David McKenzie | 65 | 71 | 69 | 73 | 278 | 26,100 |
| Stephen Gangluff | 70 | 69 | 70 | 70 | 279 | 17,100 |
| Cameron Percy | 70 | 72 | 67 | 70 | 279 | 17,100 |

| | SCORES | | | | TOTAL | MONEY |
|---|---|---|---|---|---|---|
| Alan McLean | 70 | 69 | 70 | 71 | 280 | 14,025 |
| Keith Nolan | 68 | 68 | 73 | 71 | 280 | 14,025 |
| Jason Schultz | 67 | 70 | 71 | 72 | 280 | 14,025 |
| Tom Carter | 70 | 71 | 71 | 69 | 281 | 11,700 |
| Michael Harris | 75 | 68 | 71 | 67 | 281 | 11,700 |
| Jay Delsing | 71 | 69 | 71 | 71 | 282 | 9,900 |
| Kevin Johnson | 67 | 67 | 74 | 74 | 282 | 9,900 |
| Chris Baryla | 67 | 73 | 70 | 73 | 283 | 7,875 |
| Erik Compton | 69 | 68 | 69 | 77 | 283 | 7,875 |
| Ken Duke | 71 | 70 | 70 | 72 | 283 | 7,875 |
| John Morse | 73 | 70 | 68 | 72 | 283 | 7,875 |
| Joseph Alfieri | 68 | 70 | 72 | 74 | 284 | 5,670 |
| David Branshaw | 67 | 67 | 70 | 80 | 284 | 5,670 |
| Todd Demsey | 70 | 72 | 68 | 74 | 284 | 5,670 |
| Blaine McCallister | 71 | 71 | 70 | 72 | 284 | 5,670 |
| Jim Rutledge | 71 | 71 | 72 | 70 | 284 | 5,670 |
| Brandt Snedeker | 70 | 71 | 69 | 74 | 284 | 5,670 |
| Chris Botsford | 71 | 69 | 71 | 74 | 285 | 3,720 |
| Per-Ulrik Johansson | 68 | 73 | 73 | 71 | 285 | 3,720 |
| Brian Kortan | 71 | 69 | 73 | 72 | 285 | 3,720 |
| Jim McGovern | 70 | 72 | 70 | 73 | 285 | 3,720 |
| Matt McQuillan | 72 | 70 | 69 | 74 | 285 | 3,720 |
| Jim Seki | 70 | 72 | 72 | 71 | 285 | 3,720 |
| Ben Bates | 72 | 70 | 72 | 72 | 286 | 2,745 |
| Matt Bettencourt | 66 | 71 | 76 | 73 | 286 | 2,745 |
| Jason Buha | 70 | 71 | 71 | 74 | 286 | 2,745 |
| Chad Collins | 66 | 73 | 69 | 78 | 286 | 2,745 |
| Eduardo Herrera | 69 | 72 | 71 | 74 | 286 | 2,745 |
| Jon Mills | 72 | 68 | 74 | 72 | 286 | 2,745 |
| Sam Randolph | 73 | 70 | 69 | 74 | 286 | 2,745 |
| Craig Taylor | 70 | 73 | 70 | 73 | 286 | 2,745 |

## Envirocare Utah Classic

*Willow Creek Country Club*, Sandy, Utah
Par 35-37–72; 7,104 yards

September 8-11
purse, $475,000

| | SCORES | | | | TOTAL | MONEY |
|---|---|---|---|---|---|---|
| Garrett Willis | 67 | 71 | 67 | 70 | 275 | $85,500 |
| Kris Cox | 71 | 68 | 69 | 68 | 276 | 35,466.67 |
| Brian Henninger | 71 | 68 | 68 | 69 | 276 | 35,466.67 |
| Mathew Goggin | 68 | 69 | 69 | 70 | 276 | 35,466.66 |
| Dave Christensen | 67 | 74 | 68 | 70 | 279 | 18,050 |
| Brendon de Jonge | 69 | 67 | 71 | 72 | 279 | 18,050 |
| Greg Chalmers | 72 | 69 | 67 | 72 | 280 | 14,804.17 |
| Deane Pappas | 71 | 71 | 71 | 67 | 280 | 14,804.17 |
| Tim Wilkinson | 69 | 70 | 69 | 72 | 280 | 14,804.16 |
| Bill Haas | 69 | 72 | 72 | 68 | 281 | 12,825 |
| Keoke Cotner | 72 | 71 | 71 | 68 | 282 | 10,925 |
| Ryan Hietala | 70 | 69 | 73 | 70 | 282 | 10,925 |
| Matthew Jones | 76 | 65 | 70 | 71 | 282 | 10,925 |
| Chris Couch | 68 | 71 | 72 | 72 | 283 | 8,075 |
| Jason Dufner | 75 | 68 | 71 | 69 | 283 | 8,075 |
| Nathan Green | 69 | 70 | 72 | 72 | 283 | 8,075 |
| Tom Scherrer | 71 | 68 | 73 | 71 | 283 | 8,075 |
| Chris Tidland | 76 | 66 | 70 | 71 | 283 | 8,075 |
| Chris Baryla | 72 | 68 | 77 | 67 | 284 | 6,175 |

|  | SCORES | | | | TOTAL | MONEY |
|---|---|---|---|---|---|---|
| Greg Kraft | 67 | 70 | 73 | 74 | 284 | 6,175 |
| Vance Veazey | 70 | 72 | 73 | 69 | 284 | 6,175 |
| Aaron Barber | 71 | 71 | 71 | 72 | 285 | 4,227.50 |
| Matt Bettencourt | 70 | 73 | 74 | 68 | 285 | 4,227.50 |
| David Branshaw | 68 | 74 | 72 | 71 | 285 | 4,227.50 |
| Michael Clark | 67 | 77 | 74 | 67 | 285 | 4,227.50 |
| Ken Duke | 69 | 71 | 72 | 73 | 285 | 4,227.50 |
| Jeff Freeman | 73 | 70 | 70 | 72 | 285 | 4,227.50 |
| Jerry Smith | 67 | 72 | 72 | 74 | 285 | 4,227.50 |
| Todd Tanner | 69 | 74 | 70 | 72 | 285 | 4,227.50 |
| Shane Bertsch | 70 | 71 | 76 | 69 | 286 | 3,087.50 |
| Robert Garrigus | 71 | 73 | 67 | 75 | 286 | 3,087.50 |
| Charley Hoffman | 66 | 77 | 70 | 73 | 286 | 3,087.50 |
| Rick Price | 72 | 71 | 74 | 69 | 286 | 3,087.50 |

## Mark Christopher Charity Classic

*Empire Lakes Golf Club*, Rancho Cucamonga, California
Par 35-36–71; 7,017 yards

September 15-18
purse, $475,000

|  | SCORES | | | | TOTAL | MONEY |
|---|---|---|---|---|---|---|
| Troy Matteson | 67 | 70 | 67 | 67 | 271 | $85,500 |
| Mathew Goggin | 71 | 63 | 71 | 68 | 273 | 35,466.67 |
| Johnson Wagner | 69 | 69 | 68 | 67 | 273 | 35,466.67 |
| Spike McRoy | 74 | 63 | 65 | 71 | 273 | 35,466.66 |
| Kevin Gessino-Kraft | 71 | 69 | 69 | 65 | 274 | 19,000 |
| David Branshaw | 69 | 69 | 66 | 71 | 275 | 15,912.50 |
| Danny Ellis | 70 | 70 | 68 | 67 | 275 | 15,912.50 |
| John Mallinger | 68 | 68 | 69 | 70 | 275 | 15,912.50 |
| Robin Byrd | 69 | 66 | 71 | 70 | 276 | 10,992.86 |
| Keith Huber | 68 | 68 | 71 | 69 | 276 | 10,992.86 |
| Tom Johnson | 71 | 70 | 66 | 69 | 276 | 10,992.86 |
| Jeff Klauk | 70 | 68 | 65 | 73 | 276 | 10,992.86 |
| Tom Scherrer | 65 | 69 | 73 | 69 | 276 | 10,992.86 |
| Jason Caron | 68 | 67 | 67 | 74 | 276 | 10,992.85 |
| Tom Carter | 67 | 70 | 66 | 73 | 276 | 10,992.85 |
| Michael Clark | 68 | 69 | 68 | 72 | 277 | 7,362.50 |
| Joe Daley | 70 | 71 | 65 | 71 | 277 | 7,362.50 |
| Scott Petersen | 70 | 70 | 66 | 71 | 277 | 7,362.50 |
| Jerry Smith | 68 | 71 | 68 | 70 | 277 | 7,362.50 |
| Kris Cox | 73 | 69 | 67 | 69 | 278 | 5,533.75 |
| Scott Dunlap | 73 | 68 | 70 | 67 | 278 | 5,533.75 |
| Camilo Villegas | 64 | 72 | 73 | 69 | 278 | 5,533.75 |
| Boo Weekley | 74 | 64 | 72 | 68 | 278 | 5,533.75 |
| Jaxon Brigman | 69 | 67 | 68 | 75 | 279 | 4,028 |
| Steve Collins | 73 | 69 | 67 | 70 | 279 | 4,028 |
| James McLean | 72 | 70 | 70 | 67 | 279 | 4,028 |
| James Oh | 71 | 67 | 72 | 69 | 279 | 4,028 |
| Garrett Willis | 68 | 68 | 70 | 73 | 279 | 4,028 |
| Esteban Toledo | 70 | 69 | 73 | 68 | 280 | 3,053.58 |
| Keoke Cotner | 72 | 70 | 69 | 69 | 280 | 3,053.57 |
| Jason Dufner | 71 | 64 | 73 | 72 | 280 | 3,053.57 |
| Jason Enloe | 71 | 71 | 68 | 70 | 280 | 3,053.57 |
| Bill Haas | 70 | 71 | 66 | 73 | 280 | 3,053.57 |
| Andrew Pratt | 65 | 74 | 68 | 73 | 280 | 3,053.57 |
| Steve Runge | 68 | 74 | 69 | 69 | 280 | 3,053.57 |

## Albertsons Boise Open

*Hillcrest Country Club*, Boise, Idaho
Par 36-35–71; 6,698 yards

September 22-25
purse, $650,000

| | SCORES | | | | TOTAL | MONEY |
|---|---|---|---|---|---|---|
| Greg Chalmers | 66 | 65 | 69 | 69 | 269 | $117,000 |
| Danny Ellis | 65 | 69 | 69 | 66 | 269 | 70,200 |
| (Chalmers defeated Ellis on first playoff hole.) | | | | | | |
| Nathan Green | 68 | 66 | 67 | 69 | 270 | 37,700 |
| Troy Matteson | 66 | 68 | 69 | 67 | 270 | 37,700 |
| Brian Henninger | 65 | 71 | 67 | 70 | 273 | 24,700 |
| Camilo Villegas | 68 | 65 | 72 | 68 | 273 | 24,700 |
| Cliff Kresge | 70 | 69 | 66 | 69 | 274 | 20,962.50 |
| Jason Schultz | 68 | 67 | 69 | 70 | 274 | 20,962.50 |
| Matt Hendrix | 67 | 69 | 71 | 68 | 275 | 18,200 |
| Keith Huber | 68 | 66 | 68 | 73 | 275 | 18,200 |
| Steven Bowditch | 70 | 68 | 72 | 66 | 276 | 14,300 |
| Robert Garrigus | 67 | 69 | 70 | 70 | 276 | 14,300 |
| Charley Hoffman | 67 | 67 | 71 | 71 | 276 | 14,300 |
| Bubba Watson | 66 | 70 | 70 | 70 | 276 | 14,300 |
| Jeff Freeman | 67 | 72 | 72 | 66 | 277 | 9,441.25 |
| Kevin Gessino-Kraft | 68 | 71 | 70 | 68 | 277 | 9,441.25 |
| Bill Haas | 70 | 68 | 71 | 68 | 277 | 9,441.25 |
| Matthew Jones | 68 | 70 | 74 | 65 | 277 | 9,441.25 |
| Brian Smock | 71 | 68 | 72 | 66 | 277 | 9,441.25 |
| Peter Tomasulo | 70 | 69 | 71 | 67 | 277 | 9,441.25 |
| Jimmy Walker | 67 | 70 | 72 | 68 | 277 | 9,441.25 |
| Matt Weibring | 67 | 69 | 72 | 69 | 277 | 9,441.25 |
| David Branshaw | 68 | 71 | 71 | 68 | 278 | 5,876 |
| Joe Daley | 65 | 72 | 69 | 72 | 278 | 5,876 |
| Tom Scherrer | 69 | 71 | 68 | 70 | 278 | 5,876 |
| Brent Schwarzrock | 67 | 69 | 70 | 72 | 278 | 5,876 |
| Vance Veazey | 68 | 69 | 73 | 68 | 278 | 5,876 |
| Eric Axley | 67 | 69 | 70 | 73 | 279 | 4,582.50 |
| John Engler | 69 | 69 | 70 | 71 | 279 | 4,582.50 |
| Matt Hansen | 67 | 69 | 74 | 69 | 279 | 4,582.50 |
| Jerry Smith | 68 | 69 | 74 | 68 | 279 | 4,582.50 |

## Oregon Classic

*Shadow Hills Country Club*, Junction City, Oregon
Par 36-36–72; 7,007 yards
(Fourth round cancelled—rain.)

September 29-October 2
purse, $450,000

| | SCORES | | | TOTAL | MONEY |
|---|---|---|---|---|---|
| Jeff Gove | 66 | 68 | 67 | 201 | $81,000 |
| Jamie Broce | 72 | 65 | 67 | 204 | 29,700 |
| Kris Cox | 66 | 69 | 69 | 204 | 29,700 |
| Esteban Toledo | 68 | 66 | 70 | 204 | 29,700 |
| Tim Wilkinson | 65 | 69 | 70 | 204 | 29,700 |
| Bill Haas | 74 | 66 | 66 | 206 | 15,637.50 |
| David Morland | 65 | 73 | 68 | 206 | 15,637.50 |
| Jeff Freeman | 67 | 73 | 67 | 207 | 13,950 |
| Jeremy Anderson | 72 | 65 | 71 | 208 | 11,250 |
| Greg Chalmers | 73 | 67 | 68 | 208 | 11,250 |
| Charley Hoffman | 67 | 70 | 71 | 208 | 11,250 |

| | SCORES | | | TOTAL | MONEY |
|---|---|---|---|---|---|
| Jon Mills | 66 | 69 | 73 | 208 | 11,250 |
| Tom Scherrer | 69 | 73 | 66 | 208 | 11,250 |
| Ryan Armour | 72 | 67 | 70 | 209 | 8,100 |
| Scott Dunlap | 69 | 70 | 70 | 209 | 8,100 |
| Kevin Gessino-Kraft | 69 | 74 | 66 | 209 | 8,100 |
| Barry Cheesman | 69 | 72 | 69 | 210 | 6,300 |
| Jason Enloe | 71 | 72 | 67 | 210 | 6,300 |
| Robert Garrigus | 68 | 71 | 71 | 210 | 6,300 |
| Spike McRoy | 73 | 70 | 67 | 210 | 6,300 |
| Bubba Watson | 73 | 66 | 71 | 210 | 6,300 |
| Joe Daley | 72 | 72 | 67 | 211 | 4,114.29 |
| Doug Garwood | 73 | 70 | 68 | 211 | 4,114.29 |
| Jeff Quinney | 71 | 73 | 67 | 211 | 4,114.29 |
| Johnson Wagner | 73 | 69 | 69 | 211 | 4,114.29 |
| Greg Kraft | 68 | 72 | 71 | 211 | 4,114.28 |
| Camilo Villegas | 70 | 67 | 74 | 211 | 4,114.28 |
| Grant Waite | 70 | 71 | 70 | 211 | 4,114.28 |
| Brendon de Jonge | 71 | 70 | 71 | 212 | 2,846.25 |
| Brian Henninger | 75 | 69 | 68 | 212 | 2,846.25 |
| Scott Petersen | 71 | 71 | 70 | 212 | 2,846.25 |
| Chez Reavie | 70 | 74 | 68 | 212 | 2,846.25 |
| Boyd Summerhays | 71 | 71 | 70 | 212 | 2,846.25 |
| Peter Tomasulo | 72 | 69 | 71 | 212 | 2,846.25 |
| Matt Weibring | 70 | 73 | 69 | 212 | 2,846.25 |
| Chad Wilfong | 75 | 67 | 70 | 212 | 2,846.25 |

## Gila River Golf Classic

*Whirlwind Golf Club, Cattail Course*, Chandler, Arizona
Par 36-36–72; 7,017 yards

October 6-9
purse, $450,000

| | SCORES | | | | TOTAL | MONEY |
|---|---|---|---|---|---|---|
| David McKenzie | 64 | 67 | 67 | 70 | 268 | $81,000 |
| Jon Mills | 71 | 66 | 63 | 69 | 269 | 48,600 |
| Jerry Smith | 66 | 66 | 73 | 66 | 271 | 30,600 |
| Cameron Percy | 68 | 67 | 69 | 69 | 273 | 19,800 |
| Camilo Villegas | 68 | 66 | 72 | 67 | 273 | 19,800 |
| Charley Hoffman | 68 | 64 | 74 | 68 | 274 | 16,200 |
| Craig Bowden | 67 | 70 | 66 | 72 | 275 | 14,512.50 |
| Craig Carmichael | 70 | 70 | 70 | 65 | 275 | 14,512.50 |
| Bubba Dickerson | 70 | 66 | 69 | 71 | 276 | 12,150 |
| Chez Reavie | 67 | 68 | 74 | 67 | 276 | 12,150 |
| Chris Wollmann | 69 | 70 | 71 | 66 | 276 | 12,150 |
| David Branshaw | 67 | 70 | 72 | 68 | 277 | 8,292.86 |
| Paul Gow | 70 | 67 | 69 | 71 | 277 | 8,292.86 |
| Ryan Hietala | 71 | 68 | 69 | 69 | 277 | 8,292.86 |
| Matt Weibring | 69 | 67 | 73 | 68 | 277 | 8,292.86 |
| Chad Wilfong | 69 | 69 | 70 | 69 | 277 | 8,292.86 |
| Nick Cassini | 65 | 66 | 72 | 74 | 277 | 8,292.85 |
| Jeff Klauk | 71 | 64 | 69 | 73 | 277 | 8,292.85 |
| Rich Barcelo | 70 | 66 | 71 | 71 | 278 | 4,770 |
| Jason Enloe | 68 | 71 | 71 | 68 | 278 | 4,770 |
| Kim Felton | 68 | 72 | 68 | 70 | 278 | 4,770 |
| Steve Friesen | 72 | 65 | 71 | 70 | 278 | 4,770 |
| Mathew Goggin | 68 | 68 | 71 | 71 | 278 | 4,770 |
| Greg Kraft | 69 | 70 | 69 | 70 | 278 | 4,770 |
| Jeff Overton | 70 | 69 | 72 | 67 | 278 | 4,770 |

| | SCORES | | | | TOTAL | MONEY |
|---|---|---|---|---|---|---|
| Jason Schultz | 70 | 68 | 72 | 68 | 278 | 4,770 |
| Esteban Toledo | 74 | 64 | 70 | 70 | 278 | 4,770 |
| Jaxon Brigman | 72 | 68 | 70 | 69 | 279 | 2,862 |
| Scott Gardiner | 68 | 72 | 67 | 72 | 279 | 2,862 |
| Robert Garrigus | 68 | 66 | 74 | 71 | 279 | 2,862 |
| Jeff Gove | 65 | 71 | 68 | 75 | 279 | 2,862 |
| Bill Haas | 69 | 68 | 72 | 70 | 279 | 2,862 |
| Joel Kribel | 70 | 68 | 71 | 70 | 279 | 2,862 |
| Spike McRoy | 68 | 70 | 73 | 68 | 279 | 2,862 |
| Dicky Pride | 66 | 70 | 73 | 70 | 279 | 2,862 |
| Fran Quinn | 67 | 67 | 70 | 75 | 279 | 2,862 |
| Bubba Watson | 66 | 70 | 70 | 73 | 279 | 2,862 |

# Permian Basin Charity Golf Classic

*Midland Country Club*, Midland, Texas
Par 36-36–72; 7,354 yards

October 13-16
purse, $475,000

| | SCORES | | | | TOTAL | MONEY |
|---|---|---|---|---|---|---|
| Kris Cox | 69 | 65 | 68 | 68 | 270 | $85,500 |
| Craig Bowden | 66 | 68 | 69 | 69 | 272 | 35,466.67 |
| Jerry Smith | 72 | 68 | 66 | 66 | 272 | 35,466.67 |
| Chris Tidland | 69 | 69 | 66 | 68 | 272 | 35,466.66 |
| Jeff Freeman | 71 | 66 | 69 | 67 | 273 | 19,000 |
| Rick Price | 67 | 68 | 72 | 67 | 274 | 15,378.13 |
| Scott Weatherly | 68 | 70 | 68 | 68 | 274 | 15,378.13 |
| Keoke Cotner | 70 | 68 | 67 | 69 | 274 | 15,378.12 |
| Camilo Villegas | 67 | 65 | 68 | 74 | 274 | 15,378.12 |
| Shane Bertsch | 73 | 67 | 65 | 70 | 275 | 11,875 |
| Joe Daley | 70 | 68 | 70 | 67 | 275 | 11,875 |
| Scott Gump | 68 | 68 | 67 | 72 | 275 | 11,875 |
| Jason Caron | 74 | 64 | 69 | 69 | 276 | 8,142.86 |
| Brendon de Jonge | 72 | 67 | 70 | 67 | 276 | 8,142.86 |
| Doug LaBelle | 71 | 69 | 70 | 66 | 276 | 8,142.86 |
| Craig Lile | 68 | 71 | 67 | 70 | 276 | 8,142.86 |
| Deane Pappas | 70 | 69 | 69 | 68 | 276 | 8,142.86 |
| Tim Wilkinson | 70 | 70 | 65 | 71 | 276 | 8,142.85 |
| Garrett Willis | 66 | 69 | 67 | 74 | 276 | 8,142.85 |
| Anthony Estorga | 71 | 69 | 70 | 67 | 277 | 4,697.23 |
| Esteban Toledo | 72 | 69 | 72 | 64 | 277 | 4,697.23 |
| Pat Bates | 72 | 66 | 69 | 70 | 277 | 4,697.22 |
| Craig Carmichael | 69 | 69 | 69 | 70 | 277 | 4,697.22 |
| Mathew Goggin | 70 | 67 | 69 | 71 | 277 | 4,697.22 |
| Kevin Johnson | 69 | 70 | 69 | 69 | 277 | 4,697.22 |
| Bryce Molder | 70 | 69 | 66 | 72 | 277 | 4,697.22 |
| David Morland | 70 | 70 | 68 | 69 | 277 | 4,697.22 |
| Jason Schultz | 70 | 67 | 68 | 72 | 277 | 4,697.22 |
| Greg Chalmers | 70 | 67 | 71 | 70 | 278 | 3,103.34 |
| David McKenzie | 66 | 74 | 70 | 68 | 278 | 3,103.34 |
| Steven Alker | 72 | 66 | 69 | 71 | 278 | 3,103.33 |
| Tripp Isenhour | 67 | 71 | 69 | 71 | 278 | 3,103.33 |
| Kyle Thompson | 70 | 69 | 68 | 71 | 278 | 3,103.33 |
| Peter Tomasulo | 73 | 67 | 68 | 70 | 278 | 3,103.33 |

# Nationwide Tour Championship

*Robert Trent Jones Golf Trail at Capitol Hill,*
*Senator Course*, Prattville, Alabama
Par 36-36–72; 7,661 yards

October 27-30
purse, $650,000

| | SCORES | | | | TOTAL | MONEY |
|---|---|---|---|---|---|---|
| David Branshaw | 71 | 65 | 69 | 71 | 276 | $117,000 |
| Eric Axley | 77 | 66 | 66 | 69 | 278 | 70,200 |
| Jerry Smith | 73 | 72 | 66 | 69 | 280 | 44,200 |
| Peter Tomasulo | 74 | 69 | 68 | 70 | 281 | 31,200 |
| Steven Bowditch | 71 | 68 | 70 | 73 | 282 | 26,000 |
| Mathew Goggin | 71 | 70 | 73 | 69 | 283 | 23,400 |
| Charley Hoffman | 73 | 74 | 69 | 70 | 286 | 20,258.34 |
| Ryan Armour | 69 | 70 | 73 | 74 | 286 | 20,258.33 |
| Bubba Dickerson | 72 | 72 | 69 | 73 | 286 | 20,258.33 |
| Chad Collins | 75 | 69 | 72 | 71 | 287 | 16,900 |
| Steve LeBrun | 72 | 71 | 70 | 74 | 287 | 16,900 |
| Tim O'Neal | 74 | 74 | 72 | 68 | 288 | 11,978.58 |
| Kim Felton | 72 | 73 | 72 | 71 | 288 | 11,978.57 |
| Ryan Hietala | 72 | 75 | 69 | 72 | 288 | 11,978.57 |
| Cliff Kresge | 68 | 73 | 74 | 73 | 288 | 11,978.57 |
| Troy Matteson | 75 | 69 | 72 | 72 | 288 | 11,978.57 |
| Jim McGovern | 68 | 72 | 71 | 77 | 288 | 11,978.57 |
| David McKenzie | 70 | 75 | 69 | 74 | 288 | 11,978.57 |
| Kris Cox | 73 | 72 | 73 | 71 | 289 | 7,878 |
| Brendon de Jonge | 73 | 73 | 70 | 73 | 289 | 7,878 |
| Jason Schultz | 70 | 72 | 76 | 71 | 289 | 7,878 |
| Brandt Snedeker | 72 | 74 | 71 | 72 | 289 | 7,878 |
| Tim Wilkinson | 72 | 74 | 69 | 74 | 289 | 7,878 |
| Bill Haas | 70 | 71 | 74 | 75 | 290 | 5,703.75 |
| Jon Mills | 67 | 70 | 73 | 80 | 290 | 5,703.75 |
| Rick Price | 68 | 73 | 74 | 75 | 290 | 5,703.75 |
| Tom Scherrer | 70 | 77 | 74 | 69 | 290 | 5,703.75 |
| David Morland | 67 | 73 | 75 | 76 | 291 | 4,875 |
| Scott Weatherly | 77 | 72 | 72 | 70 | 291 | 4,875 |
| Joe Daley | 71 | 72 | 76 | 73 | 292 | 4,231.50 |
| Ken Duke | 72 | 71 | 74 | 75 | 292 | 4,231.50 |
| Deane Pappas | 75 | 75 | 74 | 68 | 292 | 4,231.50 |
| David Peoples | 73 | 73 | 74 | 72 | 292 | 4,231.50 |
| Johnson Wagner | 73 | 76 | 72 | 71 | 292 | 4,231.50 |

# Canadian Tour

## Barton Creek Austin Pro-Am Classic

*Barton Creek,* Austin, Texas
*Fazio Canyons Course:* Par 36-36–72; 7,161 yards
*Crenshaw Cliffside Course:* Par 35-36–71; 6,553 yards

March 12-15
purse, US$100,000

| | SCORES | | | | TOTAL | MONEY |
|---|---|---|---|---|---|---|
| Scott Gibson | 70 | 70 | 68 | 70 | 278 | US$16,000 |
| Erik Compton | 72 | 69 | 70 | 76 | 287 | 6,800 |
| Brian Guetz | 71 | 76 | 71 | 69 | 287 | 6,800 |
| Blaine McCallister | 78 | 69 | 73 | 67 | 287 | 6,800 |
| John Mallinger | 70 | 78 | 73 | 67 | 288 | 4,000 |
| Brad Fritsch | 72 | 74 | 74 | 69 | 289 | 3,333 |
| Peter Tomasulo | 75 | 73 | 74 | 67 | 289 | 3,333 |
| Matt Weibring | 78 | 68 | 75 | 68 | 289 | 3,333 |
| Jaime Gomez | 70 | 75 | 74 | 71 | 290 | 2,500 |
| Michael Harris | 74 | 69 | 74 | 73 | 290 | 2,500 |
| Alan McLean | 80 | 66 | 70 | 74 | 290 | 2,500 |
| Jim Rutledge | 72 | 71 | 75 | 72 | 290 | 2,500 |
| Steve Schneiter | 69 | 73 | 77 | 71 | 290 | 2,500 |
| Chris Cureton | 78 | 72 | 75 | 66 | 291 | 1,850 |
| Chris Parra | 75 | 75 | 69 | 72 | 291 | 1,850 |
| Stephen Gangluff | 78 | 71 | 73 | 70 | 292 | 1,600 |
| Wes Short | 79 | 67 | 70 | 76 | 292 | 1,600 |
| Lee Williamson | 71 | 75 | 78 | 68 | 292 | 1,600 |
| Brock Mackenzie | 75 | 73 | 73 | 72 | 293 | 1,288 |
| David Mathis | 71 | 73 | 74 | 75 | 293 | 1,288 |
| Matt McQuillan | 74 | 75 | 70 | 74 | 293 | 1,288 |
| Ben Pettitt | 75 | 68 | 76 | 74 | 293 | 1,288 |
| David Faught | 75 | 75 | 71 | 73 | 294 | 1,100 |
| Robert Hamilton | 73 | 71 | 75 | 75 | 294 | 1,100 |
| Marcus Jones | 76 | 67 | 80 | 71 | 294 | 1,100 |
| Tim Balmer | 78 | 70 | 74 | 73 | 295 | 910 |
| Ben Bunny | 69 | 80 | 73 | 73 | 295 | 910 |
| Jason Hartwick | 81 | 66 | 76 | 72 | 295 | 910 |
| Wes Heffernan | 72 | 77 | 71 | 75 | 295 | 910 |
| Alex Rocha | 71 | 78 | 73 | 73 | 295 | 910 |
| Tele Wightman | 72 | 74 | 73 | 76 | 295 | 910 |

## Barton Creek Austin Challenge

*Barton Creek, Crenshaw Cliffside Course,* Austin, Texas
Par 35-36–71; 6,553 yards

March 17-20
purse, US$100,000

| | SCORES | | | | TOTAL | MONEY |
|---|---|---|---|---|---|---|
| Omar Uresti | 63 | 73 | 63 | 65 | 264 | US$16,000 |
| Derek Gillespie | 60 | 70 | 73 | 66 | 269 | 7,800 |
| Rob McMillan | 66 | 66 | 71 | 66 | 269 | 7,800 |
| Ben Bunny | 65 | 69 | 68 | 68 | 270 | 4,133 |
| Brian Guetz | 65 | 68 | 69 | 68 | 270 | 4,133 |

|  | SCORES | | | TOTAL | MONEY |
|---|---|---|---|---|---|
| Craig Matthew | 69 | 70 | 65 | 66 | 270 | 4,133 |
| Stuart Anderson | 70 | 67 | 65 | 69 | 271 | 3,100 |
| Michael Harris | 69 | 70 | 66 | 66 | 271 | 3,100 |
| Tom Johnson | 74 | 67 | 69 | 61 | 271 | 3,100 |
| Chris Carnahan | 67 | 74 | 67 | 64 | 272 | 2,300 |
| David Hearn | 69 | 69 | 63 | 71 | 272 | 2,300 |
| John Mallinger | 68 | 69 | 64 | 71 | 272 | 2,300 |
| Blaine McCallister | 68 | 73 | 69 | 62 | 272 | 2,300 |
| Alan McLean | 68 | 66 | 73 | 65 | 272 | 2,300 |
| Paul Danielson | 66 | 71 | 66 | 70 | 273 | 1,600 |
| Stephen Gangluff | 67 | 67 | 67 | 72 | 273 | 1,600 |
| Robert Hamilton | 66 | 71 | 69 | 67 | 273 | 1,600 |
| Iain Steel | 70 | 69 | 66 | 68 | 273 | 1,600 |
| Dong Yi | 67 | 72 | 69 | 65 | 273 | 1,600 |
| Matt Bettencourt | 64 | 72 | 70 | 68 | 274 | 1,250 |
| Brian Flugstad | 69 | 68 | 67 | 70 | 274 | 1,250 |
| Chris Parra | 68 | 71 | 69 | 66 | 274 | 1,250 |
| Doug LaBelle | 69 | 68 | 66 | 72 | 275 | 1,030 |
| Kyle Monfort | 71 | 69 | 68 | 67 | 275 | 1,030 |
| Alex Rocha | 67 | 74 | 67 | 67 | 275 | 1,030 |
| Jim Rutledge | 68 | 72 | 69 | 66 | 275 | 1,030 |
| Jason Schultz | 66 | 71 | 66 | 72 | 275 | 1,030 |
| Matt Weibring | 70 | 70 | 68 | 67 | 275 | 1,030 |
| Erik Compton | 67 | 72 | 69 | 68 | 276 | 804 |
| Jaime Gomez | 70 | 70 | 68 | 68 | 276 | 804 |
| Mike Grob | 74 | 68 | 66 | 68 | 276 | 804 |
| Matt McQuillan | 69 | 72 | 68 | 67 | 276 | 804 |
| Gordy Scutt | 69 | 68 | 71 | 68 | 276 | 804 |
| Brennan Webb | 69 | 72 | 67 | 68 | 276 | 804 |
| Stephen Woodard | 70 | 72 | 70 | 64 | 276 | 804 |

## Northern California Classic

*Brookside Golf & Country Club,* Stockton, California
Par 36-36–72; 6,720 yards

April 14-17
purse, US$100,000

|  | SCORES | | | TOTAL | MONEY |
|---|---|---|---|---|---|
| Jim Seki | 73 | 68 | 64 | 68 | 273 | US$16,000 |
| Rob Johnson | 68 | 69 | 66 | 72 | 275 | 9,600 |
| Peter Tomasulo | 76 | 65 | 69 | 66 | 276 | 6,000 |
| Blaine McCallister | 72 | 69 | 66 | 70 | 277 | 4,800 |
| Michael Harris | 69 | 70 | 69 | 70 | 278 | 4,000 |
| Scott Gibson | 71 | 68 | 68 | 72 | 279 | 3,225 |
| Tom Johnson | 70 | 69 | 69 | 71 | 279 | 3,225 |
| Chris Parra | 75 | 68 | 66 | 70 | 279 | 3,225 |
| Brennan Webb | 70 | 69 | 67 | 73 | 279 | 3,225 |
| Alex Rocha | 74 | 68 | 69 | 69 | 280 | 2,700 |
| Scott Ford | 75 | 71 | 64 | 71 | 281 | 2,200 |
| Stephen Gangluff | 75 | 70 | 65 | 71 | 281 | 2,200 |
| Bret Guetz | 75 | 66 | 69 | 71 | 281 | 2,200 |
| Jim Lemon | 72 | 70 | 70 | 69 | 281 | 2,200 |
| Ricky Barnes | 78 | 64 | 69 | 71 | 282 | 1,550 |
| Matt Bettencourt | 69 | 69 | 71 | 73 | 282 | 1,550 |
| Mike Grob | 75 | 71 | 69 | 67 | 282 | 1,550 |
| Jason Higton | 74 | 70 | 73 | 65 | 282 | 1,550 |
| Brian Nosler | 68 | 72 | 69 | 73 | 282 | 1,550 |
| Rob Oppenheim | 74 | 71 | 70 | 67 | 282 | 1,550 |

| | SCORES | | | | TOTAL | MONEY |
|---|---|---|---|---|---|---|
| Joe Acosta, Jr. | 74 | 65 | 74 | 70 | 283 | 1,079 |
| Brien Davis | 73 | 69 | 67 | 74 | 283 | 1,079 |
| Matt Hansen | 71 | 69 | 71 | 72 | 283 | 1,079 |
| Scott Hawley | 74 | 72 | 68 | 69 | 283 | 1,079 |
| John Humphries | 73 | 68 | 67 | 75 | 283 | 1,079 |
| Ryan Miller | 73 | 72 | 69 | 69 | 283 | 1,079 |
| Michael Walton | 73 | 70 | 68 | 72 | 283 | 1,079 |
| Stephen Woodard | 76 | 69 | 65 | 73 | 283 | 1,079 |
| Chris Carnahan | 69 | 70 | 72 | 73 | 284 | 875 |
| Scott Henderson | 75 | 69 | 70 | 70 | 284 | 875 |

## Foster Farms California Classic

*Del Rio Country Club,* Modesto, California  
Par 36-36–72; 6,837 yards

April 21-24  
purse, US$100,000

| | SCORES | | | | TOTAL | MONEY |
|---|---|---|---|---|---|---|
| Stuart Anderson | 66 | 70 | 69 | 66 | 271 | US$16,000 |
| Mike Grob | 67 | 68 | 70 | 68 | 273 | 9,600 |
| Brad Fritsch | 69 | 68 | 68 | 69 | 274 | 5,400 |
| Eugene Smith | 68 | 70 | 70 | 66 | 274 | 5,400 |
| Stephen Gangluff | 69 | 68 | 67 | 71 | 275 | 3,500 |
| John Mallinger | 69 | 71 | 70 | 65 | 275 | 3,500 |
| Iain Steel | 67 | 67 | 72 | 69 | 275 | 3,500 |
| Jon Turcott | 70 | 69 | 68 | 68 | 275 | 3,500 |
| Andrew Barnes | 69 | 66 | 71 | 70 | 276 | 2,600 |
| Brien Davis | 68 | 71 | 68 | 69 | 276 | 2,600 |
| Casey Martin | 71 | 66 | 70 | 69 | 276 | 2,600 |
| Steve Schneiter | 71 | 67 | 71 | 67 | 276 | 2,600 |
| Chris Baryla | 71 | 72 | 68 | 66 | 277 | 1,933 |
| Ryan Miller | 68 | 68 | 69 | 72 | 277 | 1,933 |
| Alex Rocha | 68 | 72 | 71 | 66 | 277 | 1,933 |
| Paul Danielson | 69 | 73 | 73 | 63 | 278 | 1,550 |
| Richard Gillot | 69 | 71 | 70 | 68 | 278 | 1,550 |
| Pat McDonald | 67 | 64 | 76 | 71 | 278 | 1,550 |
| Bryan Wright | 70 | 70 | 69 | 69 | 278 | 1,550 |
| Derek Gillespie | 71 | 66 | 72 | 70 | 279 | 1,275 |
| Matt Hansen | 71 | 67 | 69 | 72 | 279 | 1,275 |
| Michael Harris | 68 | 74 | 70 | 68 | 280 | 1,150 |
| Scott Hawley | 70 | 73 | 69 | 68 | 280 | 1,150 |
| Ron Won | 72 | 69 | 70 | 69 | 280 | 1,150 |
| Tom Johnson | 71 | 69 | 73 | 68 | 281 | 1,003 |
| Rob Labritz | 69 | 74 | 69 | 69 | 281 | 1,003 |
| Dan Swanson | 71 | 67 | 73 | 70 | 281 | 1,003 |
| George Bradford | 69 | 72 | 69 | 72 | 282 | 875 |
| Matt Seppanen | 71 | 65 | 75 | 71 | 282 | 875 |
| Adam Short | 71 | 71 | 72 | 68 | 282 | 875 |
| Brian Unk | 71 | 71 | 73 | 67 | 282 | 875 |

# Corona Mazatlan Classic

*El Cid Golf & Country Club,* Mazatlan, Mexico
Par 36-36–72; 6,623 yards

May 5-8
purse, US$125,000

| | SCORES | | | | TOTAL | MONEY |
|---|---|---|---|---|---|---|
| Jaime Gomez | 67 | 68 | 66 | 69 | 270 | US$20,000 |
| Brien Davis | 67 | 66 | 68 | 72 | 273 | 12,000 |
| Michael Harris | 64 | 73 | 71 | 66 | 274 | 7,500 |
| Robert Hamilton | 72 | 65 | 72 | 66 | 275 | 6,000 |
| George Bradford | 69 | 67 | 72 | 69 | 277 | 4,750 |
| Craig Taylor | 66 | 71 | 72 | 68 | 277 | 4,750 |
| Brad Fritsch | 70 | 65 | 70 | 73 | 278 | 3,875 |
| Derek Gillespie | 71 | 68 | 66 | 73 | 278 | 3,875 |
| David Mathis | 69 | 70 | 70 | 69 | 278 | 3,875 |
| Dong Yi | 70 | 72 | 69 | 68 | 279 | 3,375 |
| Stuart Anderson | 74 | 68 | 71 | 68 | 281 | 2,875 |
| Stephen Gangluff | 73 | 70 | 71 | 67 | 281 | 2,875 |
| Scott Hawley | 72 | 72 | 69 | 68 | 281 | 2,875 |
| Manuel Inman | 69 | 74 | 70 | 69 | 282 | 2,000 |
| Marcus Jones | 69 | 73 | 72 | 68 | 282 | 2,000 |
| Jim Lemon | 71 | 72 | 72 | 67 | 282 | 2,000 |
| Andy Matthews | 70 | 72 | 70 | 70 | 282 | 2,000 |
| Rob McMillan | 75 | 69 | 69 | 69 | 282 | 2,000 |
| Antonio Serna | 70 | 69 | 71 | 72 | 282 | 2,000 |
| Esteban Toledo | 74 | 69 | 68 | 71 | 282 | 2,000 |
| Scott Gibson | 67 | 70 | 71 | 75 | 283 | 1,500 |
| Matt Hansen | 74 | 71 | 73 | 65 | 283 | 1,500 |
| Michael Walton | 69 | 72 | 76 | 66 | 283 | 1,500 |
| Lindsay Bernakevitch | 70 | 72 | 75 | 67 | 284 | 1,258 |
| Mike Grob | 73 | 73 | 69 | 69 | 284 | 1,258 |
| Bret Guetz | 73 | 65 | 75 | 71 | 284 | 1,258 |
| Dan Swanson | 72 | 70 | 71 | 71 | 284 | 1,258 |
| Chris Wall | 68 | 78 | 72 | 66 | 284 | 1,258 |
| Glenn Collins | 69 | 74 | 72 | 70 | 285 | 1,094 |
| Juan Salazar | 73 | 69 | 74 | 69 | 285 | 1,094 |

# Michelin Morelia Classic

*Tres Marias Residential Golf Club,* Morelia, Mexico
Par 36-36–72; 7,553 yards

May 11-14
purse, US$125,000

| | SCORES | | | | TOTAL | MONEY |
|---|---|---|---|---|---|---|
| David Mathis | 71 | 67 | 69 | 64 | 271 | US$30,000 |
| Chris Baryla | 68 | 67 | 70 | 67 | 272 | 14,625 |
| Michael Walton | 67 | 65 | 68 | 72 | 272 | 14,625 |
| Peter Tomasulo | 72 | 70 | 69 | 62 | 273 | 9,000 |
| Stephen Gangluff | 70 | 71 | 67 | 66 | 274 | 6,812 |
| Ryan Miller | 69 | 69 | 67 | 69 | 274 | 6,812 |
| Russell Surber | 69 | 69 | 68 | 68 | 274 | 6,812 |
| Brad Fritsch | 74 | 66 | 66 | 70 | 276 | 5,438 |
| Robert Hamilton | 72 | 63 | 71 | 70 | 276 | 5,438 |
| Jose Trauwitz | 71 | 68 | 70 | 67 | 276 | 5,438 |
| Clint Jensen | 72 | 72 | 64 | 69 | 277 | 4,688 |
| Octavio Gonzalez | 70 | 71 | 70 | 67 | 278 | 4,125 |
| Manuel Inman | 71 | 72 | 67 | 68 | 278 | 4,125 |
| Antonio Maldonado | 73 | 71 | 69 | 66 | 279 | 3,562 |

| | SCORES | | | | TOTAL | MONEY |
|---|---|---|---|---|---|---|
| Brett Bingham | 70 | 71 | 74 | 65 | 280 | 3,281 |
| Oscar Serna | 71 | 68 | 71 | 70 | 280 | 3,281 |
| Paul Danielson | 73 | 70 | 70 | 68 | 281 | 2,719 |
| Trevar Matheson | 74 | 70 | 68 | 69 | 281 | 2,719 |
| Rob McMillan | 71 | 68 | 67 | 75 | 281 | 2,719 |
| Jesse Smith | 74 | 70 | 68 | 69 | 281 | 2,719 |
| Derek Gillespie | 70 | 68 | 72 | 72 | 282 | 2,250 |
| Bret Guetz | 69 | 72 | 74 | 67 | 282 | 2,250 |
| Scott Hawley | 70 | 70 | 73 | 69 | 282 | 2,250 |
| Stuart Anderson | 70 | 66 | 71 | 76 | 283 | 1,927 |
| Antonio Serna | 71 | 72 | 69 | 71 | 283 | 1,927 |
| Dan Swanson | 70 | 71 | 76 | 66 | 283 | 1,927 |
| Will Yanagisawa | 71 | 72 | 71 | 69 | 283 | 1,927 |
| Jaime Gomez | 70 | 73 | 71 | 70 | 284 | 1,697 |
| Michael Harris | 73 | 71 | 66 | 74 | 284 | 1,697 |
| Lee Curry | 69 | 74 | 71 | 71 | 285 | 1,584 |
| Dong Yi | 71 | 70 | 70 | 74 | 285 | 1,584 |

## Times Colonist Open

*Uplands Golf Club,* Victoria, British Columbia
Par 35-35–70; 6,420 yards

June 16-19
purse, C$150,000

| | SCORES | | | | TOTAL | MONEY |
|---|---|---|---|---|---|---|
| Craig Taylor | 68 | 66 | 66 | 62 | 262 | C$24,000 |
| Jaime Gomez | 69 | 67 | 64 | 68 | 268 | 14,400 |
| Derek Gillespie | 69 | 70 | 64 | 66 | 269 | 8,100 |
| Wes Heffernan | 65 | 72 | 66 | 66 | 269 | 8,100 |
| Peter Tomasulo | 69 | 68 | 67 | 66 | 270 | 5,700 |
| Will Yanagisawa | 70 | 67 | 65 | 68 | 270 | 5,700 |
| *Craig Doell | 69 | 66 | 68 | 68 | 271 | |
| Gordy Scutt | 71 | 68 | 67 | 66 | 272 | 4,950 |
| Luke Hickmott | 67 | 66 | 68 | 72 | 273 | 4,350 |
| Alex Rocha | 68 | 69 | 69 | 67 | 273 | 4,350 |
| Brian Unk | 67 | 71 | 69 | 66 | 273 | 4,350 |
| Marcus Jones | 69 | 69 | 69 | 67 | 274 | 3,600 |
| Jim Lemon | 67 | 70 | 68 | 69 | 274 | 3,600 |
| Lucas Bates | 70 | 71 | 68 | 66 | 275 | 2,571 |
| Paul Danielson | 69 | 73 | 67 | 66 | 275 | 2,571 |
| Stephen Gangluff | 69 | 69 | 72 | 65 | 275 | 2,571 |
| Mike Mezei | 66 | 73 | 68 | 68 | 275 | 2,571 |
| Ray Stewart | 66 | 72 | 67 | 70 | 275 | 2,571 |
| Dan Swanson | 68 | 71 | 68 | 68 | 275 | 2,571 |
| Peter Wilson | 68 | 69 | 69 | 69 | 275 | 2,571 |
| Ben Bunny | 69 | 72 | 68 | 67 | 276 | 1,838 |
| Scott Hawley | 67 | 69 | 68 | 72 | 276 | 1,838 |
| Anders Hultman | 69 | 71 | 63 | 73 | 276 | 1,838 |
| Jon Turcott | 69 | 69 | 69 | 69 | 276 | 1,838 |
| Chris Cureton | 69 | 72 | 69 | 67 | 277 | 1,541 |
| Craig Matthew | 67 | 66 | 73 | 71 | 277 | 1,541 |
| Jim Seki | 67 | 71 | 71 | 68 | 277 | 1,541 |
| Rick Todd | 71 | 68 | 70 | 68 | 277 | 1,541 |
| Brett Carman | 72 | 70 | 66 | 70 | 278 | 1,208 |
| Lee Curry | 72 | 70 | 65 | 71 | 278 | 1,208 |
| Scott Ford | 72 | 67 | 71 | 68 | 278 | 1,208 |
| Brian Guetz | 68 | 69 | 65 | 76 | 278 | 1,208 |
| Robert Hamilton | 66 | 75 | 70 | 67 | 278 | 1,208 |

|  | SCORES |  |  |  | TOTAL | MONEY |
|---|---|---|---|---|---|---|
| Craig Kanada | 66 | 71 | 69 | 72 | 278 | 1,208 |
| Trevar Matheson | 70 | 67 | 68 | 73 | 278 | 1,208 |
| Rob McMillan | 69 | 68 | 70 | 71 | 278 | 1,208 |
| Lee Williamson | 70 | 69 | 73 | 66 | 278 | 1,208 |

## Telus Edmonton Open

*Edmonton Country Club,* Edmonton, Alberta
Par 35-36–71; 6,816 yards

June 30-July 3
purse, C$150,000

|  | SCORES |  |  |  | TOTAL | MONEY |
|---|---|---|---|---|---|---|
| Matt McQuillan | 67 | 68 | 66 | 66 | 267 | C$24,000 |
| *Graham Delaet | 68 | 71 | 69 | 65 | 273 |  |
| Chris Cureton | 66 | 75 | 66 | 67 | 274 | 11,700 |
| Paul Danielson | 69 | 72 | 64 | 69 | 274 | 11,700 |
| Mike Belbin | 65 | 73 | 70 | 67 | 275 | 4,867 |
| Ben Bunny | 68 | 71 | 68 | 68 | 275 | 4,867 |
| Jaime Gomez | 67 | 71 | 69 | 68 | 275 | 4,867 |
| Brian Guetz | 67 | 69 | 69 | 70 | 275 | 4,867 |
| Jim Lemon | 69 | 67 | 71 | 68 | 275 | 4,867 |
| Brock Mackenzie | 68 | 70 | 68 | 69 | 275 | 4,867 |
| Peter Tomasulo | 67 | 66 | 70 | 72 | 275 | 4,867 |
| Jon Turcott | 69 | 65 | 68 | 73 | 275 | 4,867 |
| Brian Unk | 67 | 72 | 67 | 69 | 275 | 4,867 |
| Anders Hultman | 72 | 68 | 69 | 67 | 276 | 2,900 |
| Bobby Kalinowski | 71 | 65 | 68 | 72 | 276 | 2,900 |
| Todd Tanner | 68 | 68 | 69 | 71 | 276 | 2,900 |
| Matt Hansen | 64 | 66 | 74 | 73 | 277 | 2,400 |
| Scott Hawley | 66 | 71 | 69 | 71 | 277 | 2,400 |
| Rob McMillan | 73 | 66 | 68 | 70 | 277 | 2,400 |
| Stuart Anderson | 71 | 70 | 67 | 70 | 278 | 1,890 |
| John Ellis | 66 | 74 | 67 | 71 | 278 | 1,890 |
| Kent Fukushima | 68 | 73 | 69 | 68 | 278 | 1,890 |
| Eddie Heinen | 70 | 70 | 68 | 70 | 278 | 1,890 |
| Eugene Smith | 70 | 68 | 70 | 70 | 278 | 1,890 |
| Nick Davey | 74 | 67 | 70 | 68 | 279 | 1,453 |
| Wes Heffernan | 68 | 67 | 74 | 70 | 279 | 1,453 |
| Luke Hickmott | 66 | 70 | 69 | 74 | 279 | 1,453 |
| Clint Jensen | 70 | 69 | 68 | 72 | 279 | 1,453 |
| Brian Payne | 69 | 68 | 68 | 74 | 279 | 1,453 |
| Ben Pettitt | 69 | 69 | 68 | 73 | 279 | 1,453 |
| Dan Roberts | 68 | 68 | 70 | 73 | 279 | 1,453 |

## MTS Classic

*Pine Ridge Golf Club,* Winnipeg, Manitoba
Par 36-35–71; 6,522 yards

July 7-10
purse, C$150,000

|  | SCORES |  |  |  | TOTAL | MONEY |
|---|---|---|---|---|---|---|
| Lee Williamson | 69 | 68 | 67 | 72 | 276 | C$24,000 |
| Jaime Gomez | 70 | 72 | 68 | 67 | 277 | 14,400 |
| Daniel DeLeon | 70 | 67 | 68 | 73 | 278 | 9,000 |
| Anders Hultman | 76 | 66 | 72 | 66 | 280 | 7,200 |
| Marcus Jones | 73 | 70 | 68 | 71 | 282 | 6,000 |

| | SCORES | | | | TOTAL | MONEY |
|---|---|---|---|---|---|---|
| Derek Gillespie | 74 | 67 | 76 | 66 | 283 | 5,400 |
| Brien Davis | 72 | 69 | 71 | 72 | 284 | 4,200 |
| Ryan Ellis | 73 | 72 | 67 | 72 | 284 | 4,200 |
| Mike Grob | 69 | 68 | 75 | 72 | 284 | 4,200 |
| Bobby Kalinowski | 72 | 72 | 69 | 71 | 284 | 4,200 |
| David Mathis | 74 | 68 | 71 | 71 | 284 | 4,200 |
| Rob McMillan | 73 | 71 | 69 | 71 | 284 | 4,200 |
| Ben Pettitt | 75 | 71 | 69 | 70 | 285 | 3,000 |
| Michael Walton | 73 | 70 | 72 | 70 | 285 | 3,000 |
| Stuart Anderson | 75 | 71 | 67 | 73 | 286 | 2,150 |
| Brian Guetz | 72 | 73 | 72 | 69 | 286 | 2,150 |
| Michael Harris | 72 | 70 | 76 | 68 | 286 | 2,150 |
| Stuart Hendley | 77 | 66 | 72 | 71 | 286 | 2,150 |
| Luke Hickmott | 72 | 74 | 66 | 74 | 286 | 2,150 |
| Jason Higton | 73 | 70 | 70 | 73 | 286 | 2,150 |
| Dustin Risdon | 71 | 72 | 69 | 74 | 286 | 2,150 |
| Todd Tanner | 74 | 67 | 75 | 70 | 286 | 2,150 |
| Brian Unk | 71 | 71 | 73 | 71 | 286 | 2,150 |
| Chris Cureton | 72 | 70 | 74 | 71 | 287 | 1,509 |
| Josh Habig | 73 | 71 | 74 | 69 | 287 | 1,509 |
| Bryan Novoa | 73 | 71 | 73 | 70 | 287 | 1,509 |
| Justin Snelling | 71 | 73 | 70 | 73 | 287 | 1,509 |
| Brennan Webb | 78 | 67 | 70 | 72 | 287 | 1,509 |
| Nick Davey | 73 | 69 | 76 | 70 | 288 | 1,268 |
| Jim Lemon | 76 | 69 | 72 | 71 | 288 | 1,268 |
| Eugene Smith | 73 | 72 | 72 | 71 | 288 | 1,268 |
| Will Yanagisawa | 75 | 67 | 74 | 72 | 288 | 1,268 |

# Canadian PGA Championship

See Nationwide Tour section.

# Montreal Open

*Club de Golf de I'lle de Montreal,* Montreal, Quebec
Par 35-35–70; 7,255 yards

August 4-7
purse, C$150,000

| | SCORES | | | | TOTAL | MONEY |
|---|---|---|---|---|---|---|
| Peter Tomasulo | 68 | 67 | 68 | 71 | 274 | C$24,000 |
| Michael Harris | 67 | 71 | 65 | 74 | 277 | 14,400 |
| Stephen Gangluff | 67 | 71 | 69 | 72 | 279 | 8,100 |
| Rob Oppenheim | 67 | 72 | 72 | 68 | 279 | 8,100 |
| Chris Greenwood | 72 | 74 | 66 | 70 | 282 | 5,700 |
| Anders Hultman | 69 | 70 | 70 | 73 | 282 | 5,700 |
| Wes Heffernan | 71 | 68 | 73 | 71 | 283 | 4,800 |
| Kevin Senecal | 74 | 69 | 67 | 73 | 283 | 4,800 |
| Brad Fritsch | 73 | 67 | 75 | 69 | 284 | 4,200 |
| Jaime Gomez | 74 | 68 | 69 | 73 | 284 | 4,200 |
| Ben Bunny | 65 | 78 | 71 | 71 | 285 | 3,300 |
| David Mathis | 71 | 75 | 69 | 70 | 285 | 3,300 |
| Matt Seppanen | 74 | 73 | 70 | 68 | 285 | 3,300 |
| Jon Turcott | 70 | 72 | 69 | 74 | 285 | 3,300 |
| John Ellis | 70 | 69 | 76 | 71 | 286 | 2,700 |
| Matt Hansen | 70 | 69 | 70 | 78 | 287 | 2,325 |
| Berry Henson | 70 | 72 | 74 | 71 | 287 | 2,325 |
| Alejandro Quiroz | 72 | 74 | 67 | 74 | 287 | 2,325 |

| | SCORES | | | | TOTAL | MONEY |
|---|---|---|---|---|---|---|
| Chris Wisler | 73 | 71 | 74 | 69 | 287 | 2,325 |
| Scott Gibson | 76 | 71 | 69 | 72 | 288 | 1,800 |
| Clint Jensen | 76 | 70 | 72 | 70 | 288 | 1,800 |
| Craig Matthew | 76 | 70 | 72 | 70 | 288 | 1,800 |
| Justin Snelling | 76 | 69 | 70 | 73 | 288 | 1,800 |
| Peter Wilson | 66 | 71 | 75 | 76 | 288 | 1,800 |
| Stuart Anderson | 73 | 71 | 71 | 74 | 289 | 1,420 |
| Mike Grob | 73 | 74 | 71 | 71 | 289 | 1,420 |
| Josh Habig | 71 | 72 | 73 | 73 | 289 | 1,420 |
| Andy Matthews | 73 | 74 | 74 | 68 | 289 | 1,420 |
| Chris Parra | 73 | 72 | 68 | 76 | 289 | 1,420 |
| Will Yanagisawa | 71 | 73 | 75 | 70 | 289 | 1,420 |

## Bay Mills Open Players Championship

*Wild Bluff Golf Club*, Brimley, Michigan  
Par 36-36–72; 6,988 yards

August 25-28  
purse, US$200,000

| | SCORES | | | | TOTAL | MONEY |
|---|---|---|---|---|---|---|
| Michael Harris | 70 | 70 | 69 | 66 | 275 | US$32,000 |
| Anders Hultman | 67 | 68 | 73 | 67 | 275 | 19,200 |
| (Harris defeated Hultman on first playoff hole.) | | | | | | |
| Peter Tomasulo | 73 | 68 | 71 | 67 | 279 | 12,000 |
| Rob Oppenheim | 69 | 70 | 73 | 69 | 281 | 8,800 |
| Jon Turcott | 70 | 72 | 70 | 69 | 281 | 8,800 |
| Stephen Woodard | 72 | 75 | 69 | 66 | 282 | 7,200 |
| Ryan Ellis | 72 | 70 | 71 | 70 | 283 | 6,400 |
| Mike Grob | 68 | 68 | 75 | 72 | 283 | 6,400 |
| Stuart Anderson | 75 | 68 | 71 | 70 | 284 | 5,400 |
| Chris Baryla | 76 | 68 | 72 | 68 | 284 | 5,400 |
| Matt McQuillan | 71 | 68 | 73 | 72 | 284 | 5,400 |
| Paul Danielson | 69 | 71 | 70 | 75 | 285 | 4,200 |
| Robert Hamilton | 73 | 73 | 69 | 70 | 285 | 4,200 |
| Brian Unk | 73 | 71 | 71 | 70 | 285 | 4,200 |
| Luke Hickmott | 72 | 72 | 73 | 69 | 286 | 3,400 |
| Mike Mezei | 73 | 71 | 71 | 71 | 286 | 3,400 |
| Brennan Webb | 69 | 73 | 75 | 69 | 286 | 3,400 |
| Scott Gibson | 67 | 74 | 73 | 73 | 287 | 2,725 |
| Dave Levesque | 70 | 71 | 78 | 68 | 287 | 2,725 |
| Rob McMillan | 71 | 75 | 71 | 70 | 287 | 2,725 |
| Alex Rocha | 66 | 76 | 75 | 70 | 287 | 2,725 |
| Gordy Scutt | 76 | 70 | 69 | 73 | 288 | 2,300 |
| Tele Wightman | 71 | 70 | 74 | 73 | 288 | 2,300 |
| Will Yanagisawa | 75 | 70 | 67 | 76 | 288 | 2,300 |
| Lee Curry | 77 | 70 | 72 | 70 | 289 | 1,893 |
| John Ellis | 71 | 72 | 76 | 70 | 289 | 1,893 |
| Scott Ford | 73 | 74 | 68 | 74 | 289 | 1,893 |
| Jason Higton | 71 | 74 | 70 | 74 | 289 | 1,893 |
| Jim Lemon | 71 | 74 | 73 | 71 | 289 | 1,893 |
| Danny Paniccia | 72 | 71 | 74 | 72 | 289 | 1,893 |

## Alberta Classic

See Nationwide Tour section.

## Bell Canadian Open

See U.S. PGA Tour section.

## Niagara Fallsview Casino Resort Pro-Am Classic

*Thundering Waters Golf Club*, Niagara Falls, Ontario
Par 36-36–72; 7,322 yards

September 15-18
purse, C$100,000

| | SCORES | | | | TOTAL | MONEY |
|---|---|---|---|---|---|---|
| Michael Harris | 63 | 71 | 75 | 69 | 278 | C$18,000 |
| Brian Guetz | 71 | 69 | 72 | 68 | 280 | 7,467 |
| David Mathis | 68 | 68 | 68 | 76 | 280 | 7,467 |
| Jon Turcott | 72 | 72 | 68 | 68 | 280 | 7,467 |
| Ken Duke | 67 | 72 | 72 | 70 | 281 | 4,800 |
| Wes Heffernan | 69 | 75 | 70 | 68 | 282 | 4,000 |
| Jaime Gomez | 72 | 75 | 69 | 67 | 283 | 3,600 |
| Bryan Novoa | 69 | 74 | 72 | 70 | 285 | 3,100 |
| Brian Unk | 75 | 69 | 69 | 72 | 285 | 3,100 |
| Stephen Woodard | 70 | 73 | 72 | 70 | 285 | 3,100 |
| Josh Habig | 71 | 65 | 73 | 77 | 286 | 2,600 |
| Brock Mackenzie | 72 | 69 | 71 | 74 | 286 | 2,600 |
| Scott Gibson | 73 | 70 | 73 | 71 | 287 | 2,200 |
| Robert Hamilton | 76 | 71 | 70 | 70 | 287 | 2,200 |
| Lindsay Bernakevitch | 71 | 73 | 76 | 68 | 288 | 1,700 |
| Scott Ford | 68 | 76 | 73 | 71 | 288 | 1,700 |
| Chris Greenwood | 72 | 73 | 72 | 71 | 288 | 1,700 |
| Mike Grob | 73 | 72 | 73 | 70 | 288 | 1,700 |
| Craig Matthew | 71 | 70 | 76 | 71 | 288 | 1,700 |
| Scott Hawley | 75 | 70 | 72 | 72 | 289 | 1,350 |
| Eugene Smith | 75 | 71 | 67 | 76 | 289 | 1,350 |
| Chris Wall | 72 | 70 | 76 | 72 | 290 | 1,250 |
| Dirk Ayers | 70 | 73 | 71 | 78 | 292 | 1,125 |
| Chris Cureton | 72 | 71 | 71 | 78 | 292 | 1,125 |
| Kyle Kovacs | 72 | 74 | 70 | 76 | 292 | 1,125 |
| Alex Rocha | 73 | 73 | 72 | 74 | 292 | 1,125 |
| Bret Guetz | 71 | 75 | 78 | 69 | 293 | 942 |
| Matt McQuillan | 75 | 70 | 71 | 77 | 293 | 942 |
| Kyle Monfort | 75 | 70 | 75 | 73 | 293 | 942 |
| Jesse Smith | 73 | 71 | 77 | 72 | 293 | 942 |

# Tour de las Americas (South America)

## Costa Rica Open

*Cariari Country Club*, San Jose, Costa Rica
Par 35-36–71; 6,577 yards

February 10-13
purse, US$125,000

| | | SCORES | | | TOTAL | MONEY |
|---|---|---|---|---|---|---|
| Kyle Dobbs | 67 | 73 | 73 | 67 | 280 | US$20,000 |
| Sebastian Fernandez | 72 | 74 | 66 | 68 | 280 | 13,750 |
| (Dobbs defeated Fernandez on first playoff hole.) | | | | | | |
| Rodolfo Gonzalez | 70 | 73 | 71 | 69 | 283 | 8,125 |
| Miguel Carballo | 73 | 72 | 69 | 69 | 283 | 8,125 |
| Mark Pilkington | 73 | 73 | 70 | 70 | 286 | 5,625 |
| Michael Hoey | 70 | 70 | 72 | 74 | 286 | 5,625 |
| Paul Streeter | 70 | 76 | 75 | 66 | 287 | 3,312.50 |
| Iain Pyman | 74 | 74 | 71 | 68 | 287 | 3,312.50 |
| Roberto Coceres | 75 | 70 | 70 | 72 | 287 | 3,312.50 |
| Matthew Abbott | 72 | 72 | 70 | 73 | 287 | 3,312.50 |
| Oliver Whiteley | 71 | 72 | 76 | 69 | 288 | 2,375 |
| Carl Suneson | 73 | 73 | 72 | 70 | 288 | 2,375 |
| Rafael Gomez | 69 | 73 | 75 | 71 | 288 | 2,375 |
| Rafael Echenique | 73 | 72 | 77 | 67 | 289 | 1,812.50 |
| James Hepworth | 76 | 72 | 73 | 68 | 289 | 1,812.50 |
| Colm Moriarty | 72 | 69 | 78 | 70 | 289 | 1,812.50 |
| Marco Ruiz | 73 | 71 | 75 | 70 | 289 | 1,812.50 |
| Richard Terga | 74 | 73 | 71 | 71 | 289 | 1,812.50 |
| Gustavo Acosta | 73 | 69 | 73 | 74 | 289 | 1,812.50 |
| Ryan Grant | 74 | 72 | 74 | 70 | 290 | 1,239.58 |
| Angel Franco | 75 | 68 | 76 | 71 | 290 | 1,239.58 |
| Gareth Davies | 73 | 73 | 73 | 71 | 290 | 1,239.58 |
| Sergio Acevedo | 70 | 71 | 77 | 72 | 290 | 1,239.58 |
| Jamie Little | 74 | 69 | 75 | 72 | 290 | 1,239.58 |
| Jean-Baptiste Gonnet | 69 | 74 | 71 | 76 | 290 | 1,239.58 |
| Kariem Baraka | 73 | 76 | 72 | 70 | 291 | 1,087.50 |
| Juan Salazar | 70 | 73 | 76 | 72 | 291 | 1,087.50 |
| Christian Reimbold | 71 | 74 | 74 | 72 | 291 | 1,087.50 |
| Erol Simsek | 74 | 68 | 74 | 75 | 291 | 1,087.50 |
| Lee James | 74 | 74 | 72 | 72 | 292 | 1,000 |
| Juan Abbate | 67 | 77 | 75 | 73 | 292 | 1,000 |
| Manuel Inman | 73 | 73 | 73 | 73 | 292 | 1,000 |

## Panama Masters

*Summit Golf & Resort*, Panama City, Panama
Par 35-36–71; 6,676 yards

February 17-20
purse, US$125,000

| | | SCORES | | | TOTAL | MONEY |
|---|---|---|---|---|---|---|
| Kevin Haefner | 68 | 66 | 70 | 72 | 276 | US$20,000 |
| James Hepworth | 70 | 69 | 71 | 68 | 278 | 13,750 |
| Sebastian Fernandez | 70 | 72 | 70 | 68 | 280 | 7,500 |
| David Orr | 70 | 70 | 70 | 70 | 280 | 7,500 |
| Rafael Gomez | 69 | 72 | 67 | 72 | 280 | 7,500 |

| | SCORES | | | | TOTAL | MONEY |
|---|---|---|---|---|---|---|
| Marcus Higley | 70 | 70 | 70 | 71 | 281 | 4,500 |
| Erol Simsek | 70 | 69 | 69 | 73 | 281 | 4,500 |
| Kyle Dobbs | 72 | 70 | 72 | 68 | 282 | 2,937.50 |
| Benn Barham | 69 | 71 | 71 | 71 | 282 | 2,937.50 |
| Juan Salazar | 68 | 74 | 69 | 71 | 282 | 2,937.50 |
| Raphael Eyraud | 69 | 73 | 68 | 72 | 282 | 2,937.50 |
| Sean Whiffin | 67 | 71 | 75 | 70 | 283 | 2,312.50 |
| Miguel Guzman | 71 | 68 | 72 | 72 | 283 | 2,312.50 |
| Cesar Monasterio | 68 | 71 | 75 | 70 | 284 | 2,000 |
| Carlos De Corral | 70 | 69 | 72 | 73 | 284 | 2,000 |
| Kyron Sullivan | 69 | 73 | 67 | 75 | 284 | 2,000 |
| Jesus Amaya | 72 | 70 | 72 | 71 | 285 | 1,578.12 |
| Jorge Benedetti | 71 | 70 | 72 | 72 | 285 | 1,578.12 |
| Fabian Gomez | 72 | 69 | 71 | 73 | 285 | 1,578.12 |
| Steven Jeppesen | 69 | 72 | 70 | 74 | 285 | 1,578.12 |
| David Dixon | 69 | 70 | 74 | 73 | 286 | 1,212.50 |
| Iain Steel | 68 | 71 | 75 | 72 | 286 | 1,212.50 |
| Brad Sutterfield | 70 | 70 | 70 | 76 | 286 | 1,212.50 |
| Angel Franco | 72 | 70 | 67 | 77 | 286 | 1,212.50 |
| Paul Nilbrink | 69 | 72 | 73 | 73 | 287 | 1,112.50 |
| Matthew Abbott | 69 | 72 | 72 | 74 | 287 | 1,112.50 |
| Michael Hoey | 72 | 70 | 76 | 69 | 287 | 1,112.50 |
| Richard McEvoy | 70 | 72 | 69 | 76 | 287 | 1,112.50 |
| Iain Pyman | 67 | 74 | 73 | 74 | 288 | 1,037.50 |
| Jean-Baptiste Gonnet | 71 | 70 | 72 | 75 | 288 | 1,037.50 |

## Telefonica de Guatemala

*Hacienda Neuva Country Club*, Guatemala City, Guatemala
Par 36-36–72; 7,043 yards

February 24-27
purse, US$125,000

| | SCORES | | | | TOTAL | MONEY |
|---|---|---|---|---|---|---|
| Cesar Monasterio | 67 | 67 | 67 | 68 | 269 | US$20,000 |
| David Higgins | 68 | 67 | 69 | 65 | 269 | 13,750 |
| (Monasterio defeated Higgins on first playoff hole.) | | | | | | |
| Daniel Vancsik | 71 | 63 | 69 | 67 | 270 | 8,750 |
| Richard McEvoy | 71 | 68 | 66 | 66 | 271 | 7,500 |
| Pablo Del Grosso | 68 | 68 | 70 | 66 | 272 | 5,083.33 |
| James Hepworth | 64 | 67 | 71 | 70 | 272 | 5,083.33 |
| Miguel Rodriguez | 69 | 65 | 67 | 71 | 272 | 5,083.33 |
| Jesus Amaya | 71 | 68 | 69 | 65 | 273 | 3,250 |
| Jose Trauwitz | 66 | 69 | 69 | 69 | 273 | 3,250 |
| Ross Fisher | 66 | 70 | 73 | 65 | 274 | 2,625 |
| Roope Kakko | 68 | 72 | 65 | 69 | 274 | 2,625 |
| Marcus Higley | 69 | 66 | 71 | 69 | 275 | 2,250 |
| Denny Lucas | 70 | 67 | 69 | 69 | 275 | 2,250 |
| Andres Romero | 74 | 63 | 64 | 74 | 275 | 2,250 |
| Raphael Eyraud | 72 | 66 | 69 | 69 | 276 | 1,875 |
| Juan Abbate | 70 | 66 | 70 | 70 | 276 | 1,875 |
| Colm Moriarty | 71 | 67 | 68 | 70 | 276 | 1,875 |
| Rodolfo Gonzalez | 68 | 70 | 70 | 69 | 277 | 1,298.61 |
| Rafael Ponce | 72 | 69 | 68 | 68 | 277 | 1,298.61 |
| Martin Erlandsson | 68 | 68 | 71 | 70 | 277 | 1,298.61 |
| Brad Sutterfield | 67 | 73 | 70 | 67 | 277 | 1,298.61 |
| Marco Soffietti | 67 | 71 | 69 | 70 | 277 | 1,298.61 |
| Jean-Baptiste Gonnet | 72 | 68 | 70 | 67 | 277 | 1,298.61 |
| Paul Nilbrink | 70 | 63 | 73 | 71 | 277 | 1,298.61 |

| | SCORES | | | | TOTAL | MONEY |
|---|---|---|---|---|---|---|
| Marc Warren | 73 | 65 | 66 | 73 | 277 | 1,298.61 |
| David Dixon | 69 | 68 | 66 | 74 | 277 | 1,298.61 |
| Ivo Giner | 68 | 73 | 68 | 69 | 278 | 1,037.50 |
| Christian Reimbold | 69 | 68 | 72 | 69 | 278 | 1,037.50 |
| Erol Simsek | 68 | 70 | 69 | 71 | 278 | 1,037.50 |
| Julien Van Hauwe | 70 | 68 | 69 | 71 | 278 | 1,037.50 |
| Toni Karjalainen | 72 | 67 | 71 | 68 | 278 | 1,037.50 |
| Jamie Little | 69 | 70 | 71 | 68 | 278 | 1,037.50 |

## Siemens Venezuela Open

*Lagunita Country Club,* Caracas, Venezuela
Par 35-35–70; 6,909 yards

May 5-8
purse, US$60,000

| | SCORES | | | | TOTAL | MONEY |
|---|---|---|---|---|---|---|
| Miguel Rodriguez | 63 | 64 | 71 | 71 | 269 | US$10,800 |
| Jesus Amaya | 69 | 68 | 66 | 68 | 271 | 6,840 |
| Manuel Bermudez | 68 | 70 | 68 | 69 | 275 | 4,800 |
| Angel Franco | 69 | 69 | 67 | 72 | 277 | 3,840 |
| Jorge Benedetti | 69 | 71 | 68 | 70 | 278 | 3,120 |
| Pedro Martinez | 71 | 67 | 71 | 70 | 279 | 2,520 |
| Miguel Guzman | 74 | 71 | 67 | 68 | 280 | 1,723.20 |
| Diego Perez | 68 | 70 | 72 | 70 | 280 | 1,723.20 |
| Carlos Cardeza | 70 | 70 | 70 | 70 | 280 | 1,723.20 |
| Gustavo Acosta | 70 | 71 | 69 | 70 | 280 | 1,723.20 |
| Eduardo Argiro | 67 | 74 | 68 | 71 | 280 | 1,723.20 |
| Fabrizio Zanotti | 71 | 69 | 67 | 74 | 281 | 1,344 |
| Mauricio Molina | 66 | 73 | 72 | 71 | 282 | 1,254 |
| Pablo Del Grosso | 70 | 70 | 69 | 73 | 282 | 1,254 |
| Carlos Larrain | 69 | 75 | 72 | 67 | 283 | 1,074 |
| Alfredo Adrian | 73 | 68 | 74 | 68 | 283 | 1,074 |
| Troy Martin | 74 | 71 | 70 | 68 | 283 | 1,074 |
| Carlos Castro | 70 | 70 | 69 | 74 | 283 | 1,074 |
| Manuel Merizalde | 73 | 69 | 72 | 70 | 284 | 837 |
| Miguel Martinez | 73 | 69 | 72 | 70 | 284 | 837 |
| Cipriano Castro | 72 | 69 | 72 | 71 | 284 | 837 |
| Alejandro Villavicencio | 75 | 68 | 69 | 72 | 284 | 837 |
| Carlos Maestre | 71 | 70 | 74 | 70 | 285 | 704 |
| Otto Solis | 74 | 70 | 70 | 71 | 285 | 704 |
| Mark Monroe | 71 | 71 | 70 | 73 | 285 | 704 |
| Nicolas Sedler | 71 | 74 | 72 | 69 | 286 | 648 |
| Henrique Lavie | 70 | 72 | 74 | 70 | 286 | 648 |
| Fabian Gomez | 70 | 72 | 78 | 68 | 288 | 606 |
| Robert Twine | 74 | 70 | 70 | 74 | 288 | 606 |
| Alejandro Larrazabal | 71 | 73 | 68 | 77 | 289 | 588 |

## American Express Puerto Rico Open

*Costa Caribe Resort,* Ponce, Puerto Rico
Par 37-35–72; 7,227 yards

May 12-15
purse, US$125,000

| | SCORES | | | | TOTAL | MONEY |
|---|---|---|---|---|---|---|
| Daniel Barbetti | 66 | 67 | 70 | 65 | 268 | US$22,500 |
| Eduardo Argiro | 67 | 70 | 66 | 65 | 268 | 14,250 |

(Barbetti defeated Argiro on first playoff hole.)

| | | SCORES | | | TOTAL | MONEY |
|---|---|---|---|---|---|---|
| Geoffrey Sisk | 67 | 68 | 69 | 65 | 269 | 10,000 |
| Carlos Larrain | 68 | 69 | 65 | 69 | 271 | 8,000 |
| Richard Terga | 64 | 72 | 70 | 66 | 272 | 5,333.33 |
| Adam Spring | 70 | 65 | 68 | 69 | 272 | 5,333.33 |
| Jesus Amaya | 67 | 68 | 68 | 69 | 272 | 5,333.33 |
| Julio Zapata | 68 | 70 | 69 | 66 | 273 | 3,375 |
| Philippe Gasnier | 67 | 69 | 68 | 69 | 273 | 3,375 |
| Miguel Fernandez | 69 | 70 | 70 | 66 | 275 | 2,875 |
| Angel Franco | 65 | 73 | 67 | 70 | 275 | 2,875 |
| Gustavo Acosta | 67 | 70 | 72 | 67 | 276 | 2,437.50 |
| Tim Conley | 73 | 66 | 68 | 69 | 276 | 2,437.50 |
| Manuel Merizalde | 65 | 71 | 74 | 68 | 278 | 2,000 |
| Kyle Dobbs | 69 | 71 | 70 | 68 | 278 | 2,000 |
| Alejandro Larrazabal | 70 | 69 | 70 | 69 | 278 | 2,000 |
| Diego Vanegas | 72 | 69 | 68 | 69 | 278 | 2,000 |
| Fabrizio Zanotti | 69 | 69 | 70 | 70 | 278 | 2,000 |
| Noa Zelnik | 72 | 67 | 73 | 67 | 279 | 1,443.75 |
| Fabian Gomez | 69 | 66 | 74 | 70 | 279 | 1,443.75 |
| Jeff Yeckes | 72 | 70 | 66 | 71 | 279 | 1,443.75 |
| Miguel Rodriguez | 72 | 68 | 66 | 73 | 279 | 1,443.75 |
| Jorge Benedetti | 71 | 71 | 72 | 66 | 280 | 1,175 |
| Matthew Abbott | 68 | 75 | 68 | 69 | 280 | 1,175 |
| *Rafael Campos | 70 | 69 | 71 | 70 | 280 | |
| Mauricio Molina | 73 | 69 | 72 | 67 | 281 | 987.50 |
| Pedro Martinez | 71 | 72 | 68 | 70 | 281 | 987.50 |
| Wilfredo Morales | 74 | 71 | 66 | 70 | 281 | 987.50 |
| Ralf Geilenberg | 69 | 72 | 69 | 71 | 281 | 987.50 |
| Pablo Del Grosso | 73 | 71 | 65 | 72 | 281 | 987.50 |
| Robert Twine | 69 | 69 | 69 | 74 | 281 | 987.50 |

## Players Championship Acafest

*The Pierre Marques Acapulco,* Acapulco, Mexico
Par 36-36–72; 6,860 yards

May 20-22
purse, US$50,000

| | | SCORES | | TOTAL | MONEY |
|---|---|---|---|---|---|
| Antonio Serna | 69 | 71 | 65 | 205 | US$9,000 |
| Miguel Rodriguez | 72 | 70 | 64 | 206 | 5,700 |
| Jaime Gomez | 69 | 67 | 71 | 207 | 4,000 |
| Daniel Barbetti | 71 | 69 | 68 | 208 | 3,200 |
| Antonio Maldonado | 68 | 73 | 68 | 209 | 2,133.33 |
| Octavio Gonzalez | 68 | 73 | 68 | 209 | 2,133.33 |
| Julio Zapata | 68 | 71 | 70 | 209 | 2,133.33 |
| Jorge Benedetti | 72 | 68 | 70 | 210 | 1,470 |
| Oscar Serna | 71 | 67 | 72 | 210 | 1,470 |
| Gustavo Acosta | 71 | 69 | 71 | 211 | 1,320 |
| Raul Fretes | 72 | 69 | 71 | 212 | 1,107.50 |
| Clodomiro Carranza | 76 | 65 | 71 | 212 | 1,107.50 |
| Eracleo Bermudez | 71 | 67 | 74 | 212 | 1,107.50 |
| Rodolfo Gonzalez | 70 | 68 | 74 | 212 | 1,107.50 |
| Eduardo Gardino | 72 | 72 | 69 | 213 | 920 |
| Fabian Gomez | 73 | 73 | 67 | 213 | 920 |
| Mauricio Molina | 70 | 71 | 72 | 213 | 920 |
| Jeff Yeckes | 72 | 72 | 70 | 214 | 770 |
| Guadalupe Rodriguez | 76 | 68 | 70 | 214 | 770 |
| Robert Twine | 73 | 69 | 72 | 214 | 770 |
| Miguel Fernandez | 73 | 72 | 70 | 215 | 650 |

|  | SCORES | | | TOTAL | MONEY |
|---|---|---|---|---|---|
| Kyle Dobbs | 71 | 75 | 69 | 215 | 650 |
| Juan Salazar | 70 | 72 | 74 | 216 | 600 |
| Fabrizio Zanotti | 75 | 70 | 72 | 217 | 550 |
| Eduardo Argiro | 76 | 69 | 72 | 217 | 550 |
| Juan Pablo Jaramillo | 70 | 72 | 75 | 217 | 550 |
| John Bloomfield | 71 | 75 | 71 | 217 | 550 |
| Nicolas Sedler | 76 | 71 | 70 | 217 | 550 |
| Miguel Guzman | 74 | 70 | 74 | 218 | 490 |
| Tim Conley | 70 | 72 | 76 | 218 | 490 |
| Julian Nicolosi | 72 | 75 | 71 | 218 | 490 |

## American Express Brazil Classic

*San Fernando Golf Club,* Brazil
Par 35-36–71; 6,733 yards

June 2-5
purse, US$70,000

|  | SCORES | | | | TOTAL | MONEY |
|---|---|---|---|---|---|---|
| Miguel Fernandez | 70 | 67 | 67 | 71 | 275 | US$12,600 |
| Alex Rocha | 67 | 71 | 70 | 67 | 275 | 7,980 |
| (Fernandez defeated Rocha on first playoff hole.) | | | | | | |
| Philippe Gasnier | 69 | 69 | 69 | 71 | 278 | 5,600 |
| Rafael Navarro | 72 | 71 | 70 | 67 | 280 | 4,480 |
| Miguel Rodriguez | 72 | 73 | 69 | 67 | 281 | 2,986.66 |
| Raul Fretes | 69 | 72 | 71 | 69 | 281 | 2,986.66 |
| Carlos Dluhosch | 69 | 72 | 69 | 71 | 281 | 2,986.66 |
| Jose Trauwitz | 68 | 73 | 71 | 70 | 282 | 1,820 |
| Julio Zapata | 73 | 70 | 68 | 71 | 282 | 1,820 |
| Rodolfo Gonzalez | 65 | 73 | 70 | 74 | 282 | 1,820 |
| Clodomiro Carranza | 75 | 70 | 71 | 67 | 283 | 1,344 |
| Rafael Barcellos | 68 | 73 | 71 | 71 | 283 | 1,344 |
| Andres Moncayo | 72 | 70 | 70 | 71 | 283 | 1,344 |
| Joao Corteiz | 75 | 70 | 67 | 71 | 283 | 1,344 |
| Fabian Montovia | 65 | 74 | 72 | 72 | 283 | 1,344 |
| Cesar Costilla | 71 | 73 | 74 | 66 | 284 | 1,126 |
| Miguel Carballo | 71 | 73 | 69 | 71 | 284 | 1,126 |
| Miguel Guzman | 71 | 74 | 71 | 69 | 285 | 1,030 |
| Erik Andersson | 69 | 71 | 71 | 74 | 285 | 1,030 |
| Eduardo Vasconcellos | 70 | 72 | 74 | 70 | 286 | 861.50 |
| Fabrizio Zanotti | 76 | 68 | 71 | 71 | 286 | 861.50 |
| Manuel Bermudez | 74 | 71 | 70 | 71 | 286 | 861.50 |
| Mauricio Molina | 75 | 68 | 71 | 72 | 286 | 861.50 |
| Rafael Gonzalez | 75 | 70 | 73 | 69 | 287 | 732 |
| Jose Campra | 75 | 70 | 73 | 69 | 287 | 732 |
| Rafael Echenique | 71 | 72 | 72 | 72 | 287 | 732 |
| Ruberlei Felizardo | 72 | 69 | 71 | 75 | 287 | 732 |
| Jorge Benedetti | 70 | 71 | 78 | 69 | 288 | 662 |
| Diego Perez | 71 | 73 | 74 | 71 | 289 | 634 |
| Carlos Ferreira | 70 | 71 | 74 | 74 | 289 | 634 |
| Gustavo Acosta | 72 | 73 | 68 | 76 | 289 | 634 |

# MasterCard Brazil Open

*Costa de Sahuipe Golf Links*, Sahuipe, Brazil
Par 37-35–72; 6,933 yards

October 25-28
purse, US$100,000

| | SCORES | | | | TOTAL | MONEY |
|---|---|---|---|---|---|---|
| Miguel Guzman | 68 | 67 | 71 | 69 | 275 | US$17,000 |
| Eduardo Argiro | 75 | 71 | 69 | 67 | 282 | 11,300 |
| Mauricio Molina | 75 | 71 | 65 | 71 | 282 | 11,300 |
| Miguel Rodriguez | 70 | 69 | 74 | 70 | 283 | 5,082.50 |
| Nicolas Sedler | 70 | 71 | 71 | 71 | 283 | 5,082.50 |
| Philippe Gasnier | 71 | 68 | 72 | 72 | 283 | 5,082.50 |
| Fabrizio Zanotti | 74 | 66 | 70 | 73 | 283 | 5,082.50 |
| Alex Rodger | 72 | 72 | 70 | 71 | 285 | 2,850 |
| Walter Miranda | 69 | 67 | 77 | 73 | 286 | 2,650 |
| Cesar Costilla | 70 | 70 | 72 | 75 | 287 | 2,450 |
| Ronaldo Francisco | 74 | 69 | 74 | 71 | 288 | 2,150 |
| Ramon Franco | 73 | 69 | 72 | 74 | 288 | 2,150 |
| Angel Monguzzi | 73 | 72 | 74 | 70 | 289 | 1,850 |
| Pablo Del Grosso | 69 | 71 | 74 | 75 | 289 | 1,850 |
| Carlos Ferreira | 72 | 69 | 73 | 75 | 289 | 1,850 |
| Joao Corteiz | 75 | 73 | 72 | 70 | 290 | 1,550 |
| Carlos Cardeza | 72 | 73 | 72 | 73 | 290 | 1,550 |
| Erik Andersson | 71 | 71 | 74 | 74 | 290 | 1,550 |
| Joey Lamielle | 74 | 70 | 71 | 76 | 291 | 1,350 |
| Eduardo Vasconcellos | 74 | 74 | 72 | 72 | 292 | 1,150 |
| Patricio Vilaclara | 68 | 75 | 74 | 75 | 292 | 1,150 |
| Rafael Gonzalez | 71 | 72 | 74 | 75 | 292 | 1,150 |
| Gustavo Acosta | 72 | 74 | 76 | 71 | 293 | 975 |
| Raul Fretes | 74 | 75 | 72 | 72 | 293 | 975 |
| Christoph Guenther | 72 | 74 | 77 | 71 | 294 | 850 |
| Rafael Barcellos | 76 | 73 | 73 | 72 | 294 | 850 |
| Daniel Nunez | 78 | 72 | 69 | 75 | 294 | 850 |
| Acacio Pedro | 76 | 73 | 77 | 69 | 295 | 730 |
| Caim Vanderlei | 78 | 69 | 75 | 73 | 295 | 730 |
| Fabiano Dos Santos | 75 | 69 | 76 | 75 | 295 | 730 |
| Carlos Dluhosch | 68 | 78 | 73 | 76 | 295 | 730 |

# Torneo de Maestros Copa Personal

*Olivos Golf Club*, Buenos Aires, Argentina
Par 36-35–71; 6,740 yards

November 3-6
purse, US$70,000

| | SCORES | | | | TOTAL | MONEY |
|---|---|---|---|---|---|---|
| Angel Cabrera | 66 | 74 | 70 | 68 | 278 | US$13,500 |
| Julio Zapata | 72 | 66 | 73 | 70 | 281 | 8,250 |
| Andres Romero | 68 | 73 | 71 | 71 | 283 | 6,000 |
| Philippe Gasnier | 70 | 74 | 68 | 72 | 284 | 4,837.50 |
| *Emilio Dominguez | 69 | 74 | 69 | 74 | 286 | |
| Ricardo Gonzalez | 72 | 73 | 66 | 75 | 286 | 3,870 |
| Rodolfo Gonzalez | 73 | 71 | 71 | 72 | 287 | 2,790 |
| Jorge Berendt | 67 | 73 | 72 | 75 | 287 | 2,790 |
| Cesar Monasterio | 73 | 73 | 70 | 72 | 288 | 1,835.62 |
| Eduardo Argiro | 71 | 74 | 70 | 73 | 288 | 1,835.62 |
| Daniel Vancsik | 71 | 75 | 69 | 73 | 288 | 1,835.62 |
| Miguel Rodriguez | 72 | 69 | 70 | 77 | 288 | 1,835.62 |
| Cesar Costilla | 75 | 72 | 71 | 72 | 290 | 1,432.50 |

| | SCORES | | | | TOTAL | MONEY |
|---|---|---|---|---|---|---|
| Antonio Ortiz | 70 | 71 | 75 | 74 | 290 | 1,432.50 |
| Clodomiro Carranza | 68 | 73 | 81 | 69 | 291 | 1,282.50 |
| Gustavo Acosta | 73 | 74 | 71 | 73 | 291 | 1,282.50 |
| Nestor Bondarenco | 71 | 75 | 77 | 69 | 292 | 1,102.50 |
| Victor Leoni | 72 | 74 | 74 | 72 | 292 | 1,102.50 |
| Miguel Guzman | 73 | 74 | 72 | 73 | 292 | 1,102.50 |
| Walter Mendoza | 71 | 73 | 74 | 75 | 293 | 952.50 |
| Pablo Benzadon | 75 | 75 | 74 | 70 | 294 | 786 |
| Ricardo Ferrin | 71 | 76 | 76 | 71 | 294 | 786 |
| Angel Franco | 72 | 76 | 75 | 71 | 294 | 786 |
| Rafael Gomez | 72 | 73 | 75 | 74 | 294 | 786 |
| Pedro Martinez | 72 | 73 | 75 | 74 | 294 | 786 |
| Sebastian Villaverde | 76 | 72 | 76 | 71 | 295 | 656.25 |
| Raul Fretes | 76 | 72 | 74 | 73 | 295 | 656.25 |
| Omar Solis | 73 | 74 | 74 | 74 | 295 | 656.25 |
| Rafael Barcellos | 73 | 76 | 71 | 75 | 295 | 656.25 |
| Nicolas Sedler | 75 | 74 | 73 | 74 | 296 | 587.50 |
| Paulo Pinto | 75 | 74 | 71 | 76 | 296 | 587.50 |
| Ramiro Goti | 73 | 74 | 69 | 80 | 296 | 587.50 |

## Roberto de Vicenzo Classic

*San Eliseo Golf & Country Club*, Buenos Aires, Argentina
Par 36-36–72; 6,886 yards

November 11-13
purse, US$70,000

| | SCORES | | | TOTAL | MONEY |
|---|---|---|---|---|---|
| Andres Romero | 69 | 70 | 66 | 205 | US$12,000 |
| Hernan Rey | 67 | 74 | 68 | 209 | 7,500 |
| Mauricio Molina | 71 | 72 | 67 | 210 | 4,600 |
| Rodolfo Gonzalez | 72 | 67 | 71 | 210 | 4,600 |
| Walter Miranda | 70 | 68 | 72 | 210 | 4,600 |
| Ramiro Goti | 73 | 69 | 69 | 211 | 2,800 |
| Juan Abbate | 71 | 72 | 69 | 212 | 2,012.50 |
| Pablo Benzadon | 70 | 72 | 70 | 212 | 2,012.50 |
| Sebastian Fernandez | 74 | 68 | 70 | 212 | 2,012.50 |
| Clodomiro Carranza | 70 | 69 | 73 | 212 | 2,012.50 |
| Omar Reino | 71 | 75 | 67 | 213 | 1,383.33 |
| Cesar Costilla | 73 | 70 | 70 | 213 | 1,383.33 |
| Rafael Gomez | 63 | 76 | 74 | 213 | 1,383.33 |
| Miguel Fernandez | 72 | 69 | 73 | 214 | 1,150 |
| Esteban Isasi | 75 | 69 | 71 | 215 | 1,050 |
| Carlos Cardeza | 71 | 75 | 70 | 216 | 950 |
| Claudio Machado | 75 | 68 | 73 | 216 | 950 |
| Daniel Nunez | 72 | 71 | 73 | 216 | 950 |
| Nicolas Sedler | 72 | 70 | 74 | 216 | 950 |
| Marcos Figueroa | 75 | 72 | 70 | 217 | 890 |
| Eduardo Argiro | 72 | 71 | 74 | 217 | 890 |
| Angel Monguzzi | 71 | 69 | 77 | 217 | 890 |
| Francisco Ojeda | 74 | 73 | 71 | 218 | 860 |
| Gustavo Acosta | 74 | 72 | 72 | 218 | 860 |
| Rafael Echenique | 72 | 72 | 74 | 218 | 860 |
| Armando Saavedra | 73 | 74 | 72 | 219 | 835 |
| Daniel Vancsik | 75 | 70 | 74 | 219 | 835 |
| Omar Peralta | 76 | 71 | 73 | 220 | 800 |
| Alejandro Villavicencio | 76 | 71 | 73 | 220 | 800 |
| Raul Perez | 73 | 73 | 74 | 220 | 800 |
| Carlos Alvarez | 76 | 70 | 74 | 220 | 800 |
| Martin Velazquez | 75 | 71 | 74 | 220 | 800 |

## Abierto Mexicano Corona

*Club de Golf La Hacienda,* Mexico City, Mexico
Par 35-36–71; 7,306 yards

December 1-4
purse, US$305,000

| | SCORES | | | | TOTAL | MONEY |
|---|---|---|---|---|---|---|
| Antonio Maldonado | 69 | 69 | 70 | 67 | 275 | US$48,800 |
| Rafael Gomez | 68 | 72 | 67 | 69 | 276 | 27,450 |
| Mickael Dieu | 71 | 67 | 67 | 71 | 276 | 27,450 |
| Octavio Gonzalez | 72 | 70 | 63 | 72 | 277 | 18,300 |
| Daniel Barbetti | 69 | 74 | 65 | 70 | 278 | 15,250 |
| Marcus Higley | 76 | 68 | 71 | 65 | 280 | 9,455 |
| Hernan Rey | 68 | 73 | 71 | 68 | 280 | 9,455 |
| Peter Jespersen | 71 | 73 | 68 | 68 | 280 | 9,455 |
| Oskar Bergman | 69 | 67 | 71 | 73 | 280 | 9,455 |
| Brad Sutterfield | 73 | 70 | 72 | 66 | 281 | 6,201.66 |
| Alexander Noren | 71 | 71 | 69 | 70 | 281 | 6,201.66 |
| Cesar Monasterio | 71 | 68 | 70 | 72 | 281 | 6,201.66 |
| Johan Axgren | 72 | 72 | 69 | 69 | 282 | 5,337.50 |
| Anthony Grenier | 69 | 73 | 70 | 70 | 282 | 5,337.50 |
| Rafael Alarcon | 72 | 73 | 71 | 67 | 283 | 4,270 |
| Rodolfo Gonzalez | 71 | 70 | 73 | 69 | 283 | 4,270 |
| Miguel Carballo | 69 | 72 | 72 | 70 | 283 | 4,270 |
| Iain Steel | 73 | 69 | 70 | 71 | 283 | 4,270 |
| James Hepworth | 66 | 72 | 72 | 73 | 283 | 4,270 |
| Miguel Fernandez | 70 | 73 | 71 | 70 | 284 | 2,984.64 |
| David Patrick | 70 | 74 | 70 | 70 | 284 | 2,984.64 |
| Jean-Baptiste Gonnet | 71 | 69 | 73 | 71 | 284 | 2,984.64 |
| Rafael Cabrera Bello | 70 | 71 | 72 | 71 | 284 | 2,984.64 |
| Antonio Serna | 71 | 69 | 72 | 72 | 284 | 2,984.64 |
| James Heath | 68 | 70 | 72 | 74 | 284 | 2,984.64 |
| Sebastian Fernandez | 71 | 72 | 66 | 75 | 284 | 2,984.64 |
| Raul Fretes | 71 | 70 | 74 | 70 | 285 | 2,501 |
| Angel Franco | 73 | 72 | 70 | 70 | 285 | 2,501 |
| Rafael Echenique | 70 | 71 | 73 | 71 | 285 | 2,501 |
| Kariem Baraka | 69 | 72 | 72 | 72 | 285 | 2,501 |
| Horacio Morales | 72 | 73 | 68 | 72 | 285 | 2,501 |
| Alejandro Villavicencio | 68 | 73 | 71 | 73 | 285 | 2,501 |
| Alessio Bruschi | 73 | 70 | 69 | 73 | 285 | 2,501 |

## Abierto de Barranquilla

*Country Club de Barranquilla,* Colombia
Par 36-36–72

December 1-4
purse, US$65,000

| | SCORES | | | | TOTAL | MONEY |
|---|---|---|---|---|---|---|
| Oswaldo Villada | 70 | 71 | 70 | 75 | 286 | US$15,326.09 |
| Bernardo Gonzalez | 71 | 69 | 73 | 74 | 287 | 9,130.43 |
| Alvaro Pinedo | 75 | 70 | 72 | 73 | 290 | 3,668.48 |
| Mario Hurtado | 75 | 73 | 70 | 72 | 290 | 3,668.48 |
| Marcelo Soria | 69 | 72 | 74 | 75 | 290 | 3,668.48 |
| Gustavo Mendoza | 71 | 69 | 74 | 76 | 290 | 3,668.48 |
| Walter Miranda | 72 | 70 | 74 | 75 | 291 | 2,217.39 |
| Jesus Osmar | 73 | 73 | 72 | 74 | 292 | 1,760.87 |
| Jesus Rivas | 74 | 67 | 75 | 76 | 292 | 1,760.87 |
| Luis Zapata | 73 | 71 | 73 | 75 | 292 | 1,760.87 |
| Ralf Geilenberg | 71 | 71 | 74 | 76 | 292 | 1,760.87 |

| | SCORES | | | | TOTAL | MONEY |
|---|---|---|---|---|---|---|
| Angel Romero | 73 | 72 | 72 | 76 | 293 | 1,500 |
| Diego Vanegas | 73 | 71 | 76 | 74 | 294 | 1,385.87 |
| Manuel Merizalde | 71 | 72 | 75 | 76 | 294 | 1,385.87 |
| Diego Serna | 73 | 75 | 74 | 73 | 295 | 1,304.35 |
| Rafael Romero | 71 | 73 | 76 | 76 | 296 | 1,271.74 |
| Rodrigo Castaneda | 71 | 74 | 78 | 74 | 297 | 1,222.82 |
| Carlos Maestre | 73 | 72 | 78 | 74 | 297 | 1,222.82 |
| Cesar Serna | 73 | 72 | 79 | 74 | 298 | 1,125 |
| Jesus Amaya | 72 | 76 | 77 | 73 | 298 | 1,125 |
| Robert Herrera | 73 | 74 | 74 | 77 | 298 | 1,125 |
| Efren Cubillos | 76 | 72 | 70 | 80 | 298 | 1,125 |
| Jose Campra | 78 | 73 | 73 | 76 | 300 | 1,043.48 |
| Julio Hurtado | 75 | 76 | 74 | 76 | 301 | 1,010.87 |
| Ivan Rengifo | 73 | 75 | 77 | 77 | 302 | 978.26 |

# Visa Argentine Open

*Jockey Club,* Buenos Aires, Argentina
Par 34-36–70; 6,855 yards

December 8-11
purse, US$250,000

| | SCORES | | | | TOTAL | MONEY |
|---|---|---|---|---|---|---|
| Kevin Stadler | 69 | 66 | 67 | 72 | 274 | US$42,000 |
| Angel Cabrera | 66 | 71 | 68 | 71 | 276 | 27,500 |
| Andrew McArthur | 71 | 72 | 70 | 67 | 280 | 14,000 |
| Hernan Rey | 67 | 70 | 70 | 73 | 280 | 14,000 |
| Julio Zapata | 69 | 72 | 69 | 71 | 281 | 10,500 |
| Ricardo Gonzalez | 72 | 73 | 67 | 70 | 282 | 8,700 |
| Kasper Jorgensen | 68 | 70 | 74 | 71 | 283 | 6,900 |
| Roberto Coceres | 69 | 70 | 69 | 75 | 283 | 6,900 |
| Andres Romero | 72 | 75 | 71 | 66 | 284 | 5,600 |
| Johan Axgren | 70 | 70 | 74 | 71 | 285 | 4,633.33 |
| Cesar Monasterio | 72 | 69 | 73 | 71 | 285 | 4,633.33 |
| Miguel Fernandez | 71 | 69 | 72 | 73 | 285 | 4,633.33 |
| *Tomas Argonz | 70 | 71 | 69 | 75 | 285 | |
| Vicente Fernandez | 75 | 71 | 72 | 68 | 286 | 3,787.50 |
| Rodolfo Gonzalez | 70 | 74 | 70 | 72 | 286 | 3,787.50 |
| Fabian Gomez | 72 | 73 | 69 | 72 | 286 | 3,787.50 |
| Gustavo Rojas | 70 | 67 | 74 | 75 | 286 | 3,787.50 |
| Raul Fretes | 72 | 73 | 74 | 68 | 287 | 3,187.50 |
| Sebastian Fernandez | 73 | 69 | 75 | 70 | 287 | 3,187.50 |
| Craig Stadler | 72 | 72 | 71 | 72 | 287 | 3,187.50 |
| Alexander Noren | 72 | 72 | 65 | 78 | 287 | 3,187.50 |
| Carlos Franco | 72 | 73 | 72 | 71 | 288 | 2,887.50 |
| Cesar Costilla | 70 | 73 | 72 | 73 | 288 | 2,887.50 |
| Claudio Machado | 70 | 74 | 76 | 69 | 289 | 2,625 |
| Pablo Benzadon | 74 | 71 | 75 | 69 | 289 | 2,625 |
| Alfredo Garcia | 73 | 70 | 73 | 73 | 289 | 2,625 |
| *Luciano Giometti | 68 | 69 | 75 | 77 | 289 | |
| Eduardo Romero | 69 | 70 | 73 | 77 | 289 | 2,625 |
| Iain Steel | 74 | 70 | 68 | 77 | 289 | 2,625 |
| Peter Whiteford | 73 | 69 | 74 | 74 | 290 | 2,362.50 |
| Juan Abbate | 70 | 73 | 72 | 75 | 290 | 2,362.50 |
| *Alan Wagner | 72 | 69 | 73 | 76 | 290 | |

# European Tours

## South African Airways Open
See African Tours chapter.

## Caltex Masters
See Asia/Japan Tours chapter.

## Heineken Classic
See Australasian Tour chapter.

## Holden New Zealand Open
See Australasian Tour chapter.

## Carlsberg Malaysian Open
See Asia/Japan Tours chapter.

## Dubai Desert Classic

*Emirates Golf Club,* Dubai, United Arab Emirates
Par 35-37–72; 7,264 yards

March 3-6
purse, €1,692,170

| | SCORES | | | | TOTAL | MONEY |
|---|---|---|---|---|---|---|
| Ernie Els | 66 | 68 | 67 | 68 | 269 | €277,877.70 |
| Miguel Angel Jimenez | 67 | 65 | 68 | 70 | 270 | 144,812.30 |
| Stephen Dodd | 70 | 65 | 69 | 66 | 270 | 144,812.30 |
| Colin Montgomerie | 70 | 67 | 66 | 69 | 272 | 83,364.83 |
| Gregory Havret | 70 | 68 | 69 | 68 | 275 | 70,693.38 |
| Robert Karlsson | 69 | 70 | 68 | 69 | 276 | 50,018.90 |
| Lee Westwood | 70 | 68 | 67 | 71 | 276 | 50,018.90 |
| Nick Dougherty | 69 | 70 | 69 | 68 | 276 | 50,018.90 |
| David Howell | 67 | 71 | 69 | 70 | 277 | 35,346.69 |
| Soren Kjeldsen | 70 | 70 | 68 | 69 | 277 | 35,346.69 |
| Steve Webster | 72 | 69 | 72 | 65 | 278 | 27,243.63 |
| Jyoti Randhawa | 72 | 68 | 71 | 67 | 278 | 27,243.63 |
| Paul McGinley | 70 | 71 | 69 | 68 | 278 | 27,243.63 |
| Ian Garbutt | 72 | 67 | 72 | 67 | 278 | 27,243.63 |
| Jamie Donaldson | 70 | 68 | 69 | 71 | 278 | 27,243.63 |
| Marten Olander | 70 | 70 | 70 | 69 | 279 | 21,258.03 |
| David McKenzie | 70 | 72 | 70 | 67 | 279 | 21,258.03 |
| Peter Hedblom | 69 | 72 | 69 | 69 | 279 | 21,258.03 |
| James Kingston | 69 | 68 | 69 | 73 | 279 | 21,258.03 |
| Stephen Scahill | 70 | 71 | 66 | 72 | 279 | 21,258.03 |
| Bradley Dredge | 70 | 68 | 68 | 73 | 279 | 21,258.03 |
| Raphael Jacquelin | 71 | 72 | 69 | 68 | 280 | 17,339.88 |
| Richard Green | 71 | 70 | 72 | 67 | 280 | 17,339.88 |
| Anthony Wall | 70 | 71 | 69 | 70 | 280 | 17,339.88 |
| Henrik Stenson | 69 | 73 | 71 | 67 | 280 | 17,339.88 |
| Thomas Bjorn | 69 | 68 | 73 | 70 | 280 | 17,339.88 |
| Niclas Fasth | 72 | 66 | 73 | 69 | 280 | 17,339.88 |
| Jarrod Lyle | 68 | 70 | 68 | 74 | 280 | 17,339.88 |

| | SCORES | | | | TOTAL | MONEY |
|---|---|---|---|---|---|---|
| Peter Fowler | 69 | 69 | 69 | 74 | 281 | 13,065.54 |
| Jose Manuel Lara | 74 | 70 | 67 | 70 | 281 | 13,065.54 |
| Mattias Eliasson | 72 | 71 | 70 | 68 | 281 | 13,065.54 |
| Anders Hansen | 70 | 71 | 70 | 70 | 281 | 13,065.54 |
| Maarten Lafeber | 70 | 70 | 69 | 72 | 281 | 13,065.54 |
| Darren Fichardt | 70 | 70 | 72 | 69 | 281 | 13,065.54 |
| Gary Emerson | 72 | 69 | 70 | 70 | 281 | 13,065.54 |
| Toru Taniguchi | 70 | 68 | 71 | 72 | 281 | 13,065.54 |
| Joakim Haeggman | 70 | 70 | 70 | 71 | 281 | 13,065.54 |
| Steven O'Hara | 70 | 72 | 68 | 71 | 281 | 13,065.54 |
| Sam Osborne | 68 | 71 | 72 | 70 | 281 | 13,065.54 |
| Ian Woosnam | 74 | 69 | 70 | 69 | 282 | 9,837.05 |
| Zhang Lian-wei | 74 | 67 | 70 | 71 | 282 | 9,837.05 |
| Barry Lane | 73 | 71 | 66 | 72 | 282 | 9,837.05 |
| Phillip Archer | 72 | 66 | 71 | 73 | 282 | 9,837.05 |
| Soren Hansen | 71 | 69 | 70 | 72 | 282 | 9,837.05 |
| Gary Evans | 74 | 68 | 71 | 69 | 282 | 9,837.05 |
| Paul Sheehan | 70 | 68 | 70 | 74 | 282 | 9,837.05 |
| Francesco Molinari | 71 | 70 | 73 | 69 | 283 | 8,003.02 |
| Graeme Storm | 72 | 70 | 69 | 72 | 283 | 8,003.02 |
| Charl Schwartzel | 69 | 70 | 72 | 72 | 283 | 8,003.02 |
| Wade Ormsby | 73 | 71 | 69 | 70 | 283 | 8,003.02 |
| Andrew Marshall | 69 | 71 | 75 | 69 | 284 | 6,023.11 |
| Marc Cayeux | 72 | 70 | 68 | 74 | 284 | 6,023.11 |
| Stephen Gallacher | 72 | 71 | 71 | 70 | 284 | 6,023.11 |
| Alastair Forsyth | 70 | 71 | 72 | 71 | 284 | 6,023.11 |
| Simon Dyson | 71 | 70 | 71 | 72 | 284 | 6,023.11 |
| Louis Oosthuizen | 73 | 69 | 72 | 70 | 284 | 6,023.11 |
| Marcus Fraser | 74 | 69 | 69 | 72 | 284 | 6,023.11 |
| Ben Curtis | 70 | 71 | 70 | 73 | 284 | 6,023.11 |
| Sandy Lyle | 71 | 70 | 71 | 73 | 285 | 4,585.06 |
| Santiago Luna | 74 | 70 | 72 | 69 | 285 | 4,585.06 |
| David Carter | 72 | 70 | 71 | 72 | 285 | 4,585.06 |
| Matthew Kent | 74 | 69 | 72 | 70 | 285 | 4,585.06 |
| Robert-Jan Derksen | 74 | 70 | 71 | 71 | 286 | 3,834.78 |
| Peter Hanson | 70 | 74 | 71 | 71 | 286 | 3,834.78 |
| Pierre Fulke | 69 | 73 | 71 | 73 | 286 | 3,834.78 |
| Peter Gustafsson | 72 | 70 | 74 | 70 | 286 | 3,834.78 |
| Richard Sterne | 72 | 70 | 72 | 72 | 286 | 3,834.78 |
| Gordon Brand, Jr. | 74 | 70 | 70 | 73 | 287 | 3,012.52 |
| Mikko Ilonen | 71 | 73 | 70 | 73 | 287 | 3,012.52 |
| Lee Slattery | 73 | 71 | 69 | 74 | 287 | 3,012.52 |
| Martin Maritz | 71 | 73 | 67 | 76 | 287 | 3,012.52 |
| Damien McGrane | 71 | 69 | 73 | 75 | 288 | 2,490.50 |
| Fredrik Henge | 72 | 72 | 70 | 74 | 288 | 2,490.50 |
| Paul Broadhurst | 73 | 71 | 66 | 78 | 288 | 2,490.50 |
| David Park | 71 | 72 | 73 | 72 | 288 | 2,490.50 |
| Raymond Russell | 72 | 70 | 74 | 72 | 288 | 2,490.50 |
| Thongchai Jaidee | 72 | 71 | 76 | 69 | 288 | 2,490.50 |
| Patrik Sjoland | 70 | 72 | 73 | 74 | 289 | 2,480 |
| Jonathan Lomas | 73 | 70 | 69 | 78 | 290 | 2,475.50 |
| Francois Delamontagne | 75 | 69 | 73 | 73 | 290 | 2,475.50 |

# Qatar Masters

*Doha Golf Club,* Doha, Qatar
Par 36-36–72; 7,311 yards

March 10-13
purse, €1,141,050

| | SCORES | | | | TOTAL | MONEY |
|---|---|---|---|---|---|---|
| Ernie Els | 73 | 69 | 69 | 65 | 276 | €188,764.80 |
| Henrik Stenson | 67 | 73 | 66 | 71 | 277 | 125,838.10 |
| Richard Green | 67 | 68 | 73 | 71 | 279 | 63,764.73 |
| Pierre Fulke | 66 | 70 | 73 | 70 | 279 | 63,764.73 |
| Barry Lane | 71 | 69 | 69 | 71 | 280 | 40,546.67 |
| Robert Karlsson | 69 | 67 | 74 | 70 | 280 | 40,546.67 |
| James Kingston | 70 | 72 | 69 | 69 | 280 | 40,546.67 |
| Raphael Jacquelin | 70 | 68 | 73 | 70 | 281 | 25,445.49 |
| Gregory Havret | 71 | 67 | 72 | 71 | 281 | 25,445.49 |
| Louis Oosthuizen | 72 | 71 | 70 | 68 | 281 | 25,445.49 |
| Steve Webster | 73 | 69 | 69 | 71 | 282 | 20,839.63 |
| Jyoti Randhawa | 73 | 70 | 71 | 69 | 283 | 17,923.21 |
| David Park | 68 | 70 | 74 | 71 | 283 | 17,923.21 |
| Graeme Storm | 71 | 71 | 72 | 69 | 283 | 17,923.21 |
| Marcus Fraser | 69 | 71 | 70 | 73 | 283 | 17,923.21 |
| Ricardo Gonzalez | 69 | 70 | 74 | 71 | 284 | 14,978.48 |
| Thaworn Wiratchant | 69 | 68 | 75 | 72 | 284 | 14,978.48 |
| Niclas Fasth | 68 | 71 | 69 | 76 | 284 | 14,978.48 |
| Charl Schwartzel | 70 | 75 | 70 | 69 | 284 | 14,978.48 |
| Miguel Angel Martin | 70 | 71 | 74 | 70 | 285 | 12,474.65 |
| Arjun Atwal | 70 | 69 | 71 | 75 | 285 | 12,474.65 |
| Simon Yates | 71 | 73 | 71 | 70 | 285 | 12,474.65 |
| Bradley Dredge | 70 | 74 | 70 | 71 | 285 | 12,474.65 |
| David Lynn | 72 | 71 | 72 | 70 | 285 | 12,474.65 |
| Nick Dougherty | 73 | 68 | 71 | 73 | 285 | 12,474.65 |
| Steven O'Hara | 70 | 74 | 71 | 70 | 285 | 12,474.65 |
| Jeev Milkha Singh | 71 | 73 | 73 | 69 | 286 | 10,419.81 |
| Anders Hansen | 71 | 71 | 71 | 73 | 286 | 10,419.81 |
| Clay Devers | 70 | 71 | 72 | 73 | 286 | 10,419.81 |
| David Drysdale | 70 | 73 | 71 | 72 | 286 | 10,419.81 |
| Richard Sterne | 72 | 71 | 73 | 70 | 286 | 10,419.81 |
| Andrew Pitts | 69 | 74 | 73 | 71 | 287 | 8,542.95 |
| Darren Fichardt | 69 | 75 | 70 | 73 | 287 | 8,542.95 |
| Soren Hansen | 70 | 72 | 74 | 71 | 287 | 8,542.95 |
| Peter Hedblom | 70 | 73 | 74 | 70 | 287 | 8,542.95 |
| Stephen Dodd | 71 | 74 | 70 | 72 | 287 | 8,542.95 |
| Christopher Hanell | 71 | 70 | 75 | 71 | 287 | 8,542.95 |
| Terry Pilkadaris | 72 | 72 | 72 | 71 | 287 | 8,542.95 |
| Jose Manuel Lara | 70 | 73 | 71 | 74 | 288 | 6,569.01 |
| Soren Kjeldsen | 69 | 75 | 72 | 72 | 288 | 6,569.01 |
| Garry Houston | 67 | 76 | 76 | 69 | 288 | 6,569.01 |
| Scott Drummond | 74 | 71 | 71 | 72 | 288 | 6,569.01 |
| Nobuhito Sato | 69 | 72 | 73 | 74 | 288 | 6,569.01 |
| Miles Tunnicliff | 73 | 68 | 71 | 76 | 288 | 6,569.01 |
| Robert Coles | 71 | 70 | 74 | 73 | 288 | 6,569.01 |
| Prayad Marksaeng | 71 | 72 | 73 | 72 | 288 | 6,569.01 |
| Mads Vibe-Hastrup | 72 | 73 | 74 | 69 | 288 | 6,569.01 |
| Thongchai Jaidee | 71 | 71 | 73 | 73 | 288 | 6,569.01 |
| Robert-Jan Derksen | 74 | 71 | 70 | 74 | 289 | 4,756.87 |
| Paul Broadhurst | 73 | 68 | 74 | 74 | 289 | 4,756.87 |
| Gary Emerson | 72 | 72 | 74 | 71 | 289 | 4,756.87 |
| Anthony Kang | 68 | 72 | 77 | 72 | 289 | 4,756.87 |
| Christian Cevaer | 73 | 70 | 74 | 72 | 289 | 4,756.87 |
| Lee Sung-man | 73 | 70 | 75 | 71 | 289 | 4,756.87 |

| | SCORES | | | | TOTAL | MONEY |
|---|---|---|---|---|---|---|
| Mark Roe | 74 | 70 | 73 | 73 | 290 | 3,578.98 |
| Marten Olander | 71 | 72 | 71 | 76 | 290 | 3,578.98 |
| Anthony Wall | 70 | 73 | 74 | 73 | 290 | 3,578.98 |
| Martin Maritz | 75 | 70 | 74 | 71 | 290 | 3,578.98 |
| Matthew Kent | 74 | 71 | 72 | 73 | 290 | 3,578.98 |
| Peter Hanson | 70 | 74 | 71 | 76 | 291 | 2,888.10 |
| Carlos Rodiles | 70 | 75 | 74 | 72 | 291 | 2,888.10 |
| Philip Golding | 74 | 70 | 76 | 71 | 291 | 2,888.10 |
| Rolf Muntz | 71 | 73 | 74 | 73 | 291 | 2,888.10 |
| Jose-Filipe Lima | 75 | 68 | 76 | 72 | 291 | 2,888.10 |
| Adam Groom | 69 | 75 | 73 | 74 | 291 | 2,888.10 |
| Johan Axgren | 74 | 69 | 74 | 75 | 292 | 2,378.44 |
| Maarten Lafeber | 69 | 71 | 77 | 75 | 292 | 2,378.44 |
| Adam Fraser | 71 | 74 | 71 | 76 | 292 | 2,378.44 |
| Kenneth Ferrie | 74 | 70 | 73 | 76 | 293 | 2,110.39 |
| Paul Lawrie | 70 | 74 | 78 | 71 | 293 | 2,110.39 |
| Zhang Lian-wei | 71 | 74 | 74 | 75 | 294 | 1,696 |
| Paul McGinley | 71 | 71 | 76 | 76 | 294 | 1,696 |
| Gary Rusnak | 70 | 74 | 78 | 72 | 294 | 1,696 |
| Ian Woosnam | 72 | 72 | 76 | 76 | 296 | 1,690 |
| Fredrik Andersson Hed | 69 | 75 | 88 | 72 | 304 | 1,687 |

## TCL Classic
See Asia/Japan Tours chapter.

## Enjoy Jakarta Standard Chartered Indonesia Open
See Asia/Japan Tours chapter.

## Estoril Open de Portugal Caixa Geral de Depositos

*Oitavos Golf,* Quinta da Marinha, Portugal
Par 36-35–71; 6,893 yards

March 31-April 3
purse, €1,250,000

| | SCORES | | | | TOTAL | MONEY |
|---|---|---|---|---|---|---|
| Paul Broadhurst | 68 | 66 | 70 | 67 | 271 | €208,330 |
| Paul Lawrie | 69 | 67 | 66 | 70 | 272 | 138,880 |
| Jose-Filipe Lima | 69 | 65 | 69 | 70 | 273 | 78,250 |
| Richard Sterne | 71 | 67 | 70 | 66 | 274 | 62,500 |
| Barry Lane | 68 | 67 | 68 | 72 | 275 | 53,000 |
| Stephen Dodd | 68 | 69 | 70 | 69 | 276 | 43,750 |
| Gary Emerson | 73 | 71 | 66 | 67 | 277 | 37,500 |
| Ian Garbutt | 70 | 66 | 73 | 70 | 279 | 24,812.50 |
| Ignacio Garrido | 71 | 66 | 71 | 71 | 279 | 24,812.50 |
| Stephen Scahill | 67 | 70 | 72 | 70 | 279 | 24,812.50 |
| Niclas Fasth | 70 | 71 | 68 | 70 | 279 | 24,812.50 |
| Jamie Donaldson | 75 | 68 | 72 | 64 | 279 | 24,812.50 |
| Charl Schwartzel | 72 | 65 | 74 | 68 | 279 | 24,812.50 |
| Gonzalo Fernandez-Castano | 71 | 68 | 72 | 69 | 28,0 | 19125 |
| Peter Baker | 70 | 71 | 71 | 69 | 281 | 17,250 |
| Neil Cheetham | 67 | 71 | 71 | 72 | 281 | 17,250 |
| Jonathan Lomas | 68 | 71 | 69 | 73 | 281 | 17,250 |
| Simon Hurd | 71 | 69 | 71 | 70 | 281 | 17,250 |
| Steve Webster | 71 | 71 | 75 | 65 | 282 | 14,575 |
| Stuart Little | 69 | 67 | 75 | 71 | 282 | 14,575 |
| Marcel Siem | 72 | 67 | 72 | 71 | 282 | 14,575 |

| | SCORES | | | | TOTAL | MONEY |
|---|---|---|---|---|---|---|
| David Park | 73 | 66 | 75 | 68 | 282 | 14,575 |
| Alastair Forsyth | 69 | 69 | 69 | 75 | 282 | 14,575 |
| Roger Chapman | 71 | 67 | 73 | 72 | 283 | 12,812.50 |
| Jean-Francois Remesy | 70 | 70 | 73 | 70 | 283 | 12,812.50 |
| Fredrik Andersson Hed | 69 | 72 | 70 | 72 | 283 | 12,812.50 |
| Leif Westerberg | 69 | 70 | 71 | 73 | 283 | 12,812.50 |
| Cesar Monasterio | 69 | 67 | 74 | 74 | 284 | 10,937.50 |
| Titch Moore | 67 | 70 | 76 | 71 | 284 | 10,937.50 |
| Carlos Rodiles | 71 | 69 | 73 | 71 | 284 | 10,937.50 |
| Patrik Sjoland | 71 | 70 | 73 | 70 | 284 | 10,937.50 |
| Nick Dougherty | 72 | 67 | 74 | 71 | 284 | 10,937.50 |
| Stuart Manley | 72 | 71 | 68 | 73 | 284 | 10,937.50 |
| Klas Eriksson | 70 | 71 | 71 | 73 | 285 | 8,875 |
| Gary Murphy | 69 | 68 | 73 | 75 | 285 | 8,875 |
| David Gilford | 71 | 67 | 74 | 73 | 285 | 8,875 |
| Kenneth Ferrie | 71 | 71 | 74 | 69 | 285 | 8,875 |
| Jean-Francois Lucquin | 72 | 71 | 76 | 66 | 285 | 8,875 |
| Henrik Nystrom | 70 | 68 | 73 | 74 | 285 | 8,875 |
| Simon Dyson | 71 | 64 | 78 | 72 | 285 | 8,875 |
| Mark Foster | 73 | 70 | 76 | 67 | 286 | 7,500 |
| Damien McGrane | 70 | 70 | 78 | 68 | 286 | 7,500 |
| Jan-Are Larsen | 74 | 69 | 76 | 67 | 286 | 7,500 |
| Raymond Russell | 70 | 70 | 76 | 70 | 286 | 7,500 |
| Phillip Archer | 73 | 71 | 70 | 73 | 287 | 6,250 |
| Peter Hanson | 74 | 70 | 76 | 67 | 287 | 6,250 |
| Sam Little | 72 | 68 | 74 | 73 | 287 | 6,250 |
| Mads Vibe-Hastrup | 67 | 70 | 76 | 74 | 287 | 6,250 |
| David Griffiths | 74 | 69 | 76 | 68 | 287 | 6,250 |
| Hernan Rey | 77 | 66 | 75 | 69 | 287 | 6,250 |
| Jose Manuel Lara | 74 | 70 | 72 | 72 | 288 | 4,625 |
| Johan Axgren | 72 | 70 | 73 | 73 | 288 | 4,625 |
| Soren Kjeldsen | 73 | 68 | 76 | 71 | 288 | 4,625 |
| Garry Houston | 72 | 72 | 75 | 69 | 288 | 4,625 |
| Philip Golding | 73 | 69 | 73 | 73 | 288 | 4,625 |
| Van Phillips | 73 | 69 | 74 | 72 | 288 | 4,625 |
| John Bickerton | 71 | 72 | 73 | 72 | 288 | 4,625 |
| Peter Lawrie | 72 | 70 | 77 | 70 | 289 | 3,562.50 |
| Richard Bland | 72 | 71 | 77 | 69 | 289 | 3,562.50 |
| Simon Wakefield | 72 | 69 | 76 | 72 | 289 | 3,562.50 |
| Martin Maritz | 76 | 66 | 74 | 73 | 289 | 3,562.50 |
| Bradley Dredge | 73 | 69 | 76 | 72 | 290 | 3,250 |
| Sam Torrance | 73 | 71 | 74 | 73 | 291 | 2,875 |
| Matthew Blackey | 73 | 71 | 76 | 71 | 291 | 2,875 |
| David Carter | 72 | 71 | 75 | 73 | 291 | 2,875 |
| Ben Mason | 69 | 74 | 77 | 71 | 291 | 2,875 |
| Gabriel Canizares | 75 | 68 | 74 | 74 | 291 | 2,875 |
| Niki Zitny | 74 | 70 | 77 | 71 | 292 | 2,260 |
| Sven Struver | 72 | 72 | 77 | 71 | 292 | 2,260 |
| Johan Skold | 75 | 68 | 79 | 70 | 292 | 2,260 |
| Stephen Gallacher | 70 | 68 | 80 | 74 | 292 | 2,260 |
| Fredrik Henge | 72 | 72 | 76 | 73 | 293 | 1,870.50 |
| Markus Brier | 65 | 79 | 77 | 72 | 293 | 1,870.50 |
| Andre Cruse | 73 | 71 | 77 | 75 | 296 | 1,866 |
| Sergio Ribeiro | 74 | 70 | 81 | 75 | 300 | 1,863 |

# Madeira Island Open Caixa Geral de Depositos

*Santo da Serra Golf Club,* Madeira, Portugal
Par 36-36–72; 6,826 yards

April 7-10
purse, €600,000

| | SCORES | | | | TOTAL | MONEY |
|---|---|---|---|---|---|---|
| Robert-Jan Derksen | 67 | 70 | 71 | 67 | 275 | €100,000 |
| Andrew McLardy | 67 | 71 | 69 | 70 | 277 | 52,110 |
| Gary Orr | 69 | 70 | 69 | 69 | 277 | 52,110 |
| David Higgins | 69 | 66 | 74 | 69 | 278 | 30,000 |
| Tom Whitehouse | 71 | 69 | 71 | 69 | 280 | 25,440 |
| John Bickerton | 66 | 69 | 74 | 72 | 281 | 21,000 |
| Simon Wakefield | 68 | 71 | 73 | 70 | 282 | 14,610 |
| Andrew Coltart | 68 | 71 | 72 | 71 | 282 | 14,610 |
| Mikko Ilonen | 67 | 74 | 69 | 72 | 282 | 14,610 |
| Kyron Sullivan | 64 | 70 | 73 | 75 | 282 | 14,610 |
| Knud Storgaard | 69 | 74 | 71 | 69 | 283 | 10,680 |
| David Drysdale | 70 | 73 | 70 | 70 | 283 | 10,680 |
| Rolf Muntz | 70 | 67 | 73 | 74 | 284 | 8,844 |
| Jarmo Sandelin | 71 | 72 | 74 | 67 | 284 | 8,844 |
| Michael Kirk | 68 | 76 | 71 | 69 | 284 | 8,844 |
| Richard McEvoy | 65 | 74 | 73 | 72 | 284 | 8,844 |
| Stuart Manley | 70 | 70 | 72 | 72 | 284 | 8,844 |
| Van Phillips | 70 | 69 | 70 | 76 | 285 | 7,335 |
| Stephen Scahill | 64 | 73 | 72 | 76 | 285 | 7,335 |
| Graeme Storm | 74 | 69 | 74 | 68 | 285 | 7,335 |
| Matthew Morris | 65 | 74 | 76 | 70 | 285 | 7,335 |
| Roger Chapman | 69 | 75 | 73 | 69 | 286 | 5,970 |
| Mark Foster | 70 | 69 | 76 | 71 | 286 | 5,970 |
| Sven Struver | 70 | 72 | 72 | 72 | 286 | 5,970 |
| Jean Van de Velde | 68 | 72 | 72 | 74 | 286 | 5,970 |
| Francesco Molinari | 69 | 71 | 74 | 72 | 286 | 5,970 |
| Nicolas Colsaerts | 67 | 74 | 73 | 72 | 286 | 5,970 |
| Henrik Nystrom | 72 | 72 | 71 | 71 | 286 | 5,970 |
| Erol Simsek | 70 | 74 | 69 | 73 | 286 | 5,970 |
| Kariem Baraka | 68 | 72 | 73 | 73 | 286 | 5,970 |
| Richard Finch | 72 | 70 | 72 | 72 | 286 | 5,970 |
| Magnus P. Atlevi | 69 | 68 | 79 | 71 | 287 | 4,525.71 |
| Fredrik Henge | 70 | 72 | 74 | 71 | 287 | 4,525.71 |
| Robert Karlsson | 70 | 69 | 79 | 69 | 287 | 4,525.71 |
| Ian Garbutt | 73 | 71 | 71 | 72 | 287 | 4,525.71 |
| Markus Brier | 66 | 76 | 68 | 77 | 287 | 4,525.71 |
| Mads Vibe-Hastrup | 69 | 71 | 75 | 72 | 287 | 4,525.71 |
| Gregory Bourdy | 66 | 77 | 75 | 69 | 287 | 4,525.71 |
| Gordon Brand, Jr. | 72 | 72 | 70 | 74 | 288 | 3,780 |
| Gary Emerson | 66 | 77 | 70 | 75 | 288 | 3,780 |
| Peter Baker | 70 | 74 | 75 | 69 | 288 | 3,780 |
| Simon Hurd | 71 | 73 | 70 | 74 | 288 | 3,780 |
| Benn Barham | 67 | 74 | 76 | 71 | 288 | 3,780 |
| Santiago Luna | 69 | 71 | 72 | 77 | 289 | 3,000 |
| Gary Murphy | 68 | 71 | 78 | 72 | 289 | 3,000 |
| Martin Erlandsson | 72 | 72 | 74 | 71 | 289 | 3,000 |
| Shaun Webster | 68 | 72 | 75 | 74 | 289 | 3,000 |
| Joakim Backstrom | 72 | 69 | 73 | 75 | 289 | 3,000 |
| Marc Cayeux | 69 | 72 | 73 | 75 | 289 | 3,000 |
| Lee James | 68 | 70 | 75 | 76 | 289 | 3,000 |
| Roope Kakko | 70 | 72 | 75 | 72 | 289 | 3,000 |
| Paul Dwyer | 71 | 71 | 77 | 71 | 290 | 2,400 |
| Gary Clark | 73 | 68 | 78 | 71 | 290 | 2,400 |
| Miguel Angel Martin | 67 | 72 | 71 | 81 | 291 | 2,100 |

| | SCORES | | | | TOTAL | MONEY |
|---|---|---|---|---|---|---|
| Jesus Maria Arruti | 72 | 70 | 71 | 78 | 291 | 2,100 |
| Marco Ruiz | 67 | 75 | 71 | 78 | 291 | 2,100 |
| Garry Houston | 67 | 73 | 79 | 73 | 292 | 1,800 |
| Peter Lawrie | 69 | 75 | 76 | 72 | 292 | 1,800 |
| Matthew Blackey | 72 | 72 | 74 | 74 | 292 | 1,800 |
| Johan Axgren | 70 | 71 | 79 | 73 | 293 | 1,530 |
| Andrew Marshall | 74 | 70 | 75 | 74 | 293 | 1,530 |
| Sam Little | 70 | 71 | 74 | 78 | 293 | 1,530 |
| Massimo Florioli | 69 | 71 | 75 | 78 | 293 | 1,530 |
| Sam Walker | 75 | 69 | 77 | 72 | 293 | 1,530 |
| Gareth Paddison | 68 | 75 | 76 | 74 | 293 | 1,530 |
| Nuno Campino | 74 | 69 | 75 | 76 | 294 | 1,290 |
| Andre Cruse | 69 | 73 | 75 | 77 | 294 | 1,290 |
| Kalle Brink | 75 | 69 | 77 | 74 | 295 | 1,085 |
| Titch Moore | 70 | 72 | 77 | 76 | 295 | 1,085 |
| Stuart Little | 68 | 71 | 76 | 80 | 295 | 1,085 |
| Robert Coles | 70 | 73 | 76 | 76 | 295 | 1,085 |
| Raul Ballesteros | 71 | 73 | 73 | 79 | 296 | 897 |
| Fernando Roca | 72 | 71 | 78 | 76 | 297 | 894 |
| Antonio Sobrinho | 72 | 71 | 78 | 77 | 298 | 891 |
| Andrea Maestroni | 68 | 71 | 79 | 81 | 299 | 888 |
| Alvaro Salto | 72 | 69 | 79 | 80 | 300 | 885 |
| Raymond Russell | 70 | 73 | 81 | 77 | 301 | 880.50 |
| Robert Rock | 75 | 69 | 73 | 84 | 301 | 880.50 |
| Julien Clement | 71 | 68 | 77 | 86 | 302 | 876 |
| Duarte Freitas | 73 | 71 | 81 | 82 | 307 | 873 |

## Jazztel Open de Espana en Andalucia

*San Roque Club,* Cadiz, Spain
Par 36-36–72; 7,103 yards

April 14-17
purse, €1,650,000

| | SCORES | | | | TOTAL | MONEY |
|---|---|---|---|---|---|---|
| Peter Hanson | 70 | 68 | 71 | 71 | 280 | €275,000 |
| Peter Gustafsson | 70 | 69 | 75 | 66 | 280 | 183,330 |
| (Hanson defeated Gustafsson on first playoff hole.) | | | | | | |
| Peter Lawrie | 71 | 70 | 73 | 69 | 283 | 92,895 |
| Hennie Otto | 71 | 71 | 69 | 72 | 283 | 92,895 |
| Robert Karlsson | 72 | 71 | 71 | 71 | 285 | 63,855 |
| Stephen Dodd | 74 | 73 | 72 | 66 | 285 | 63,855 |
| Miguel Angel Martin | 71 | 72 | 72 | 71 | 286 | 49,500 |
| Raphael Jacquelin | 73 | 71 | 74 | 69 | 287 | 35,392.50 |
| Paul McGinley | 76 | 70 | 72 | 69 | 287 | 35,392.50 |
| Simon Khan | 73 | 73 | 72 | 69 | 287 | 35,392.50 |
| Steven O'Hara | 70 | 75 | 74 | 68 | 287 | 35,392.50 |
| Jose Manuel Lara | 73 | 72 | 68 | 75 | 288 | 25,542 |
| David Gilford | 75 | 71 | 70 | 72 | 288 | 25,542 |
| Sam Little | 74 | 70 | 74 | 70 | 288 | 25,542 |
| Ian Garbutt | 72 | 74 | 73 | 69 | 288 | 25,542 |
| Paul Lawrie | 72 | 72 | 69 | 75 | 288 | 25,542 |
| Damien McGrane | 73 | 74 | 69 | 73 | 289 | 20,955 |
| Stuart Little | 72 | 74 | 74 | 69 | 289 | 20,955 |
| Francois Delamontagne | 73 | 72 | 75 | 69 | 289 | 20,955 |
| Sebastian Fernandez | 73 | 72 | 70 | 74 | 289 | 20,955 |
| Jean-Francois Remesy | 75 | 73 | 71 | 71 | 290 | 16,912.50 |
| Soren Kjeldsen | 72 | 76 | 68 | 74 | 290 | 16,912.50 |
| Andrew Marshall | 72 | 71 | 75 | 72 | 290 | 16,912.50 |

| | SCORES | | | | TOTAL | MONEY |
|---|---|---|---|---|---|---|
| Nicolas Colsaerts | 77 | 69 | 73 | 71 | 290 | 16,912.50 |
| David Park | 72 | 72 | 73 | 73 | 290 | 16,912.50 |
| Jarmo Sandelin | 72 | 72 | 78 | 68 | 290 | 16,912.50 |
| Stephen Gallacher | 73 | 75 | 75 | 67 | 290 | 16,912.50 |
| David Griffiths | 77 | 68 | 73 | 72 | 290 | 16,912.50 |
| Jamie Donaldson | 74 | 68 | 74 | 74 | 290 | 16,912.50 |
| Martin Maritz | 72 | 73 | 74 | 71 | 290 | 16,912.50 |
| Mark Foster | 72 | 72 | 74 | 73 | 291 | 13,035 |
| Johan Axgren | 72 | 74 | 73 | 72 | 291 | 13,035 |
| Jonathan Lomas | 73 | 74 | 71 | 73 | 291 | 13,035 |
| Adam Mednick | 72 | 74 | 71 | 74 | 291 | 13,035 |
| Carlos De Corral | 74 | 73 | 72 | 72 | 291 | 13,035 |
| Oliver Wilson | 75 | 72 | 74 | 70 | 291 | 13,035 |
| Carl Suneson | 76 | 72 | 74 | 70 | 292 | 11,220 |
| Diego Borrego | 70 | 73 | 77 | 72 | 292 | 11,220 |
| David Lynn | 74 | 71 | 76 | 71 | 292 | 11,220 |
| Jose-Filipe Lima | 73 | 71 | 73 | 75 | 292 | 11,220 |
| Jose Manuel Carriles | 72 | 75 | 74 | 72 | 293 | 9,570 |
| Steve Webster | 79 | 69 | 75 | 70 | 293 | 9,570 |
| Andrea Maestroni | 72 | 76 | 73 | 72 | 293 | 9,570 |
| David Drysdale | 74 | 73 | 74 | 72 | 293 | 9,570 |
| Graeme Storm | 73 | 70 | 77 | 73 | 293 | 9,570 |
| Alfredo Garcia | 75 | 72 | 71 | 75 | 293 | 9,570 |
| Titch Moore | 75 | 73 | 71 | 75 | 294 | 7,920 |
| Marcel Siem | 73 | 75 | 70 | 76 | 294 | 7,920 |
| Fernando Roca | 72 | 75 | 75 | 72 | 294 | 7,920 |
| Ben Mason | 72 | 75 | 75 | 72 | 294 | 7,920 |
| Darren Fichardt | 75 | 72 | 71 | 77 | 295 | 6,435 |
| Jean Van de Velde | 73 | 71 | 77 | 74 | 295 | 6,435 |
| Mikko Ilonen | 73 | 70 | 75 | 77 | 295 | 6,435 |
| Robert Rock | 73 | 75 | 77 | 70 | 295 | 6,435 |
| Gregory Bourdy | 73 | 68 | 74 | 80 | 295 | 6,435 |
| Roger Chapman | 75 | 72 | 75 | 74 | 296 | 4,983 |
| Gary Murphy | 73 | 74 | 77 | 72 | 296 | 4,983 |
| Emanuele Canonica | 70 | 77 | 78 | 71 | 296 | 4,983 |
| Johan Skold | 75 | 73 | 71 | 77 | 296 | 4,983 |
| Leif Westerberg | 73 | 73 | 79 | 71 | 296 | 4,983 |
| Jose Rivero | 70 | 72 | 76 | 79 | 297 | 4,290 |
| Andrew Coltart | 73 | 75 | 75 | 74 | 297 | 4,290 |
| John Bickerton | 73 | 75 | 76 | 73 | 297 | 4,290 |
| Malcolm Mackenzie | 72 | 74 | 78 | 74 | 298 | 3,877.50 |
| Oskar Bergman | 71 | 74 | 76 | 77 | 298 | 3,877.50 |
| David Carter | 74 | 74 | 74 | 78 | 300 | 3,630 |
| Ricardo Gonzalez | 74 | 74 | 79 | 74 | 301 | 3,382.50 |
| Niclas Fasth | 74 | 71 | 78 | 78 | 301 | 3,382.50 |
| Fredrik Henge | 75 | 71 | 79 | 77 | 302 | 3,135 |
| Raul Ballesteros | 75 | 72 | 82 | 78 | 307 | 3,010 |
| Santiago Luna | 70 | 77 | 82 | 79 | 308 | 2,475 |

## Johnnie Walker Classic
See Asia/Japan Tours chapter.

## BMW Asian Open
See Asia/Japan Tours chapter.

## Telecom Italia Open

*Castello di Tolcinasco Golf & Country Club*, Milan, Italy
Par 36-36–72; 7,224 yards

May 5-8
purse, €1,300,000

| | SCORES | | | | TOTAL | MONEY |
|---|---|---|---|---|---|---|
| Steve Webster | 68 | 68 | 66 | 68 | 270 | €216,660 |
| Anders Hansen | 72 | 68 | 67 | 66 | 273 | 96,940 |
| Bradley Dredge | 67 | 66 | 71 | 69 | 273 | 96,940 |
| Richard Finch | 69 | 63 | 71 | 70 | 273 | 96,940 |
| Emanuele Canonica | 68 | 68 | 71 | 67 | 274 | 55,120 |
| Andrew McLardy | 72 | 69 | 68 | 69 | 278 | 36,530 |
| Jamie Spence | 69 | 71 | 65 | 73 | 278 | 36,530 |
| Simon Khan | 67 | 69 | 68 | 74 | 278 | 36,530 |
| Gonzalo Fernandez-Castano | 66 | 73 | 69 | 70 | 278 | 36,530 |
| Stuart Little | 72 | 64 | 69 | 74 | 279 | 23,302.50 |
| Marcel Siem | 68 | 68 | 71 | 72 | 279 | 23,302.50 |
| Gary Orr | 70 | 71 | 67 | 71 | 279 | 23,302.50 |
| Adam Groom | 69 | 68 | 72 | 70 | 279 | 23,302.50 |
| Soren Kjeldsen | 73 | 68 | 67 | 72 | 280 | 19,110 |
| David Drysdale | 69 | 70 | 66 | 75 | 280 | 19,110 |
| Gareth Paddison | 69 | 72 | 68 | 71 | 280 | 19,110 |
| Maarten Lafeber | 72 | 69 | 66 | 74 | 281 | 16,510 |
| Francesco Molinari | 69 | 70 | 69 | 73 | 281 | 16,510 |
| Joakim Haeggman | 73 | 68 | 68 | 72 | 281 | 16,510 |
| Jonathan Lomas | 70 | 71 | 67 | 73 | 281 | 16,510 |
| Gregory Havret | 70 | 65 | 77 | 70 | 282 | 14,495 |
| Angel Cabrera | 72 | 70 | 68 | 72 | 282 | 14,495 |
| David Lynn | 70 | 68 | 72 | 72 | 282 | 14,495 |
| Andres Romero | 69 | 70 | 71 | 72 | 282 | 14,495 |
| Gary Murphy | 67 | 72 | 66 | 78 | 283 | 12,350 |
| David Gilford | 67 | 73 | 73 | 70 | 283 | 12,350 |
| Sven Struver | 73 | 67 | 70 | 73 | 283 | 12,350 |
| Paul Broadhurst | 70 | 65 | 75 | 73 | 283 | 12,350 |
| Gary Emerson | 71 | 70 | 70 | 72 | 283 | 12,350 |
| Michael Hoey | 72 | 71 | 72 | 68 | 283 | 12,350 |
| Leif Westerberg | 72 | 69 | 69 | 73 | 283 | 12,350 |
| Johan Axgren | 73 | 68 | 71 | 72 | 284 | 10,088 |
| Jean-Francois Lucquin | 68 | 72 | 71 | 73 | 284 | 10,088 |
| Nicolas Colsaerts | 74 | 68 | 71 | 71 | 284 | 10,088 |
| Ivo Giner | 68 | 72 | 73 | 71 | 284 | 10,088 |
| Francois Delamontagne | 66 | 77 | 70 | 71 | 284 | 10,088 |
| Miguel Angel Martin | 69 | 70 | 71 | 75 | 285 | 8,710 |
| Sam Torrance | 69 | 73 | 68 | 75 | 285 | 8,710 |
| Robert Coles | 70 | 72 | 69 | 74 | 285 | 8,710 |
| Andrew Coltart | 73 | 70 | 69 | 73 | 285 | 8,710 |
| Robert Rock | 72 | 67 | 71 | 75 | 285 | 8,710 |
| Andrew Marshall | 71 | 70 | 74 | 71 | 286 | 7,670 |
| Michele Reale | 70 | 73 | 71 | 72 | 286 | 7,670 |
| Ian Garbutt | 69 | 73 | 70 | 74 | 286 | 7,670 |
| Roger Chapman | 73 | 70 | 69 | 75 | 287 | 6,890 |
| Klas Eriksson | 73 | 70 | 71 | 73 | 287 | 6,890 |
| Niki Zitny | 69 | 74 | 73 | 71 | 287 | 6,890 |
| Fredrik Henge | 69 | 73 | 70 | 76 | 288 | 5,850 |
| Sam Little | 70 | 73 | 71 | 74 | 288 | 5,850 |
| Gary Evans | 71 | 69 | 73 | 75 | 288 | 5,850 |
| David Carter | 72 | 70 | 77 | 69 | 288 | 5,850 |
| Carlos De Corral | 69 | 72 | 75 | 72 | 288 | 5,850 |
| Gordon Brand, Jr. | 75 | 68 | 68 | 78 | 289 | 4,345.71 |
| Costantino Rocca | 70 | 71 | 72 | 76 | 289 | 4,345.71 |

| | SCORES | | | | TOTAL | MONEY |
|---|---|---|---|---|---|---|
| Ian Woosnam | 73 | 67 | 75 | 74 | 289 | 4,345.71 |
| Jose Manuel Carriles | 71 | 67 | 74 | 77 | 289 | 4,345.71 |
| Joakim Backstrom | 69 | 70 | 75 | 75 | 289 | 4,345.71 |
| Julien Van Hauwe | 71 | 71 | 74 | 73 | 289 | 4,345.71 |
| Mikko Ilonen | 72 | 70 | 74 | 73 | 289 | 4,345.71 |
| Mark Roe | 70 | 70 | 72 | 78 | 290 | 3,380 |
| Johan Edfors | 73 | 70 | 72 | 75 | 290 | 3,380 |
| Rolf Muntz | 72 | 69 | 76 | 73 | 290 | 3,380 |
| Markus Brier | 72 | 69 | 74 | 75 | 290 | 3,380 |
| Gregory Bourdy | 74 | 68 | 70 | 78 | 290 | 3,380 |
| Garry Houston | 70 | 70 | 75 | 76 | 291 | 2,990 |
| Darren Fichardt | 76 | 67 | 70 | 80 | 293 | 2,795 |
| Sebastian Fernandez | 67 | 73 | 76 | 77 | 293 | 2,795 |
| Benoit Teilleria | 70 | 72 | 72 | 83 | 297 | 2,600 |
| Dean Robertson | 68 | 73 | 76 | 83 | 300 | 2,470 |
| Van Phillips | 74 | 69 | 80 | 78 | 301 | 2,165 |
| Stephen Gallacher | 71 | 71 | 77 | 82 | 301 | 2,165 |

## Daily Telegraph Dunlop Masters

*Marriott Forest of Arden,* Warwickshire, England
Par 36-36–72; 7,213 yards

May 12-15
purse, €2,532,800

| | SCORES | | | | TOTAL | MONEY |
|---|---|---|---|---|---|---|
| Thomas Bjorn | 73 | 68 | 73 | 68 | 282 | €417,753.10 |
| David Howell | 69 | 72 | 72 | 69 | 282 | 217,701.10 |
| Brian Davis | 69 | 71 | 73 | 69 | 282 | 217,701.10 |
| (Bjorn defeated Davis on first and Howell on second playoff hole.) | | | | | | |
| Michael Campbell | 73 | 70 | 67 | 73 | 283 | 125,327.40 |
| Steve Webster | 72 | 71 | 70 | 71 | 284 | 89,734.41 |
| Soren Hansen | 70 | 71 | 76 | 67 | 284 | 89,734.41 |
| Simon Khan | 71 | 77 | 69 | 67 | 284 | 89,734.41 |
| Robert-Jan Derksen | 71 | 75 | 70 | 69 | 285 | 56,313.78 |
| Maarten Lafeber | 73 | 73 | 70 | 69 | 285 | 56,313.78 |
| Darren Clarke | 74 | 72 | 72 | 67 | 285 | 56,313.78 |
| Gary Murphy | 75 | 73 | 68 | 71 | 287 | 40,956.99 |
| Barry Lane | 70 | 76 | 73 | 68 | 287 | 40,956.99 |
| Robert Karlsson | 74 | 73 | 73 | 67 | 287 | 40,956.99 |
| Stephen Dodd | 70 | 77 | 75 | 65 | 287 | 40,956.99 |
| Johan Skold | 74 | 74 | 72 | 67 | 287 | 40,956.99 |
| Roger Chapman | 73 | 73 | 76 | 66 | 288 | 32,534.99 |
| Mark Roe | 75 | 73 | 71 | 69 | 288 | 32,534.99 |
| Ian Poulter | 75 | 76 | 73 | 64 | 288 | 32,534.99 |
| David Drysdale | 72 | 74 | 72 | 70 | 288 | 32,534.99 |
| Graeme McDowell | 74 | 75 | 73 | 66 | 288 | 32,534.99 |
| Ian Woosnam | 74 | 71 | 75 | 69 | 289 | 28,323.99 |
| Brett Rumford | 72 | 74 | 74 | 69 | 289 | 28,323.99 |
| Marcus Fraser | 73 | 72 | 76 | 68 | 289 | 28,323.99 |
| Damien McGrane | 72 | 77 | 70 | 71 | 290 | 24,564.17 |
| Andrew McLardy | 70 | 76 | 73 | 71 | 290 | 24,564.17 |
| Colin Montgomerie | 72 | 75 | 74 | 69 | 290 | 24,564.17 |
| Bradley Dredge | 74 | 73 | 72 | 71 | 290 | 24,564.17 |
| Markus Brier | 74 | 73 | 72 | 71 | 290 | 24,564.17 |
| Patrik Sjoland | 71 | 74 | 74 | 71 | 290 | 24,564.17 |
| Oliver Wilson | 72 | 73 | 71 | 74 | 290 | 24,564.17 |
| Henrik Stenson | 77 | 71 | 74 | 69 | 291 | 20,102.52 |
| Paul Broadhurst | 73 | 73 | 70 | 75 | 291 | 20,102.52 |

| | SCORES | | | | TOTAL | MONEY |
|---|---|---|---|---|---|---|
| Joakim Haeggman | 73 | 73 | 75 | 70 | 291 | 20,102.52 |
| Angel Cabrera | 70 | 75 | 74 | 72 | 291 | 20,102.52 |
| Richard Sterne | 73 | 74 | 75 | 69 | 291 | 20,102.52 |
| Richard Green | 72 | 73 | 74 | 73 | 292 | 17,545.84 |
| Jean-Francois Lucquin | 74 | 73 | 72 | 73 | 292 | 17,545.84 |
| Paul McGinley | 72 | 79 | 73 | 68 | 292 | 17,545.84 |
| David Lynn | 69 | 77 | 76 | 70 | 292 | 17,545.84 |
| Alessandro Tadini | 72 | 74 | 72 | 75 | 293 | 15,540.60 |
| Christian Cevaer | 72 | 74 | 73 | 74 | 293 | 15,540.60 |
| Fredrik Andersson Hed | 74 | 73 | 73 | 73 | 293 | 15,540.60 |
| Mikko Ilonen | 73 | 73 | 73 | 74 | 293 | 15,540.60 |
| Gonzalo Fernandez-Castano | 75 | 74 | 72 | 73 | 294 | 14,287.32 |
| Scott Drummond | 70 | 75 | 75 | 75 | 295 | 12,783.39 |
| Nick O'Hern | 74 | 76 | 72 | 73 | 295 | 12,783.39 |
| Philip Golding | 73 | 74 | 80 | 68 | 295 | 12,783.39 |
| Robert Coles | 74 | 76 | 71 | 74 | 295 | 12,783.39 |
| Stephen Gallacher | 71 | 78 | 75 | 71 | 295 | 12,783.39 |
| Jean-Francois Remesy | 75 | 73 | 77 | 71 | 296 | 9,775.54 |
| Soren Kjeldsen | 75 | 75 | 76 | 70 | 296 | 9,775.54 |
| Andrew Marshall | 72 | 77 | 74 | 73 | 296 | 9,775.54 |
| Ignacio Garrido | 78 | 73 | 74 | 71 | 296 | 9,775.54 |
| Gary Orr | 76 | 74 | 76 | 70 | 296 | 9,775.54 |
| Lee Westwood | 76 | 75 | 74 | 71 | 296 | 9,775.54 |
| Simon Dyson | 71 | 73 | 76 | 76 | 296 | 9,775.54 |
| Peter Baker | 71 | 73 | 76 | 77 | 297 | 7,770.30 |
| Sam Torrance | 76 | 74 | 74 | 74 | 298 | 6,767.68 |
| Marten Olander | 74 | 77 | 78 | 69 | 298 | 6,767.68 |
| Ian Garbutt | 74 | 77 | 74 | 73 | 298 | 6,767.68 |
| Pierre Fulke | 70 | 77 | 76 | 75 | 298 | 6,767.68 |
| Terry Price | 72 | 79 | 74 | 73 | 298 | 6,767.68 |
| Gregory Bourdy | 75 | 75 | 75 | 73 | 298 | 6,767.68 |
| Stuart Manley | 79 | 71 | 73 | 75 | 298 | 6,767.68 |
| Klas Eriksson | 73 | 74 | 76 | 76 | 299 | 5,150.71 |
| Phillip Archer | 75 | 75 | 75 | 74 | 299 | 5,150.71 |
| Jamie Spence | 75 | 75 | 72 | 77 | 299 | 5,150.71 |
| Stuart Little | 72 | 78 | 74 | 75 | 299 | 5,150.71 |
| Richard Finch | 70 | 75 | 74 | 80 | 299 | 5,150.71 |
| Martin Maritz | 74 | 77 | 75 | 73 | 299 | 5,150.71 |
| Leif Westerberg | 72 | 77 | 74 | 77 | 300 | 3,760 |
| Emanuele Canonica | 74 | 74 | 84 | 69 | 301 | 3,757 |
| Mark Foster | 76 | 74 | 79 | 73 | 302 | 3,751 |
| Andrew Coltart | 74 | 77 | 79 | 72 | 302 | 3,751 |
| Robert Rock | 72 | 76 | 77 | 77 | 302 | 3,751 |
| Francesco Molinari | 73 | 78 | 78 | 75 | 304 | 3,743.50 |
| Benoit Teilleria | 74 | 77 | 78 | 75 | 304 | 3,743.50 |

## Nissan Irish Open

*Carton House Golf Club,* Maynooth Co., Kildare, Ireland
Par 36-36–72; 7,301 yards

May 19-22
purse, €2,000,000

| | SCORES | | | | TOTAL | MONEY |
|---|---|---|---|---|---|---|
| Stephen Dodd | 69 | 70 | 72 | 68 | 279 | €333,330 |
| David Howell | 70 | 70 | 69 | 70 | 279 | 222,220 |
| (Dodd defeated Howell on first playoff hole.) | | | | | | |
| Angel Cabrera | 71 | 73 | 69 | 68 | 281 | 112,600 |
| Nick Dougherty | 68 | 72 | 67 | 74 | 281 | 112,600 |

| | SCORES | | | | TOTAL | MONEY |
|---|---|---|---|---|---|---|
| Padraig Harrington | 73 | 72 | 68 | 69 | 282 | 71,600 |
| Nick O'Hern | 73 | 73 | 70 | 66 | 282 | 71,600 |
| Lee Westwood | 70 | 74 | 70 | 68 | 282 | 71,600 |
| Francois Delamontagne | 72 | 74 | 68 | 69 | 283 | 50,000 |
| Philip Golding | 72 | 69 | 72 | 71 | 284 | 39,000 |
| Richard Sterne | 72 | 73 | 69 | 70 | 284 | 39,000 |
| Steven O'Hara | 74 | 73 | 70 | 67 | 284 | 39,000 |
| Oliver Wilson | 72 | 71 | 66 | 75 | 284 | 39,000 |
| David Carter | 74 | 73 | 67 | 71 | 285 | 30,100 |
| Simon Dyson | 71 | 72 | 71 | 71 | 285 | 30,100 |
| Jose-Filipe Lima | 71 | 71 | 69 | 74 | 285 | 30,100 |
| Colm Moriarty | 69 | 74 | 72 | 70 | 285 | 30,100 |
| Darren Clarke | 70 | 75 | 69 | 72 | 286 | 27,000 |
| Jose Maria Olazabal | 74 | 71 | 68 | 74 | 287 | 24,450 |
| Garry Houston | 77 | 71 | 70 | 69 | 287 | 24,450 |
| Bradley Dredge | 72 | 68 | 75 | 72 | 287 | 24,450 |
| Graeme Storm | 71 | 75 | 73 | 68 | 287 | 24,450 |
| Maarten Lafeber | 72 | 73 | 75 | 68 | 288 | 21,100 |
| Andrew McLardy | 72 | 71 | 68 | 77 | 288 | 21,100 |
| Joakim Haeggman | 73 | 70 | 73 | 72 | 288 | 21,100 |
| Terry Price | 75 | 71 | 73 | 69 | 288 | 21,100 |
| Richard Finch | 71 | 75 | 72 | 70 | 288 | 21,100 |
| Charl Schwartzel | 74 | 72 | 73 | 69 | 288 | 21,100 |
| Sandy Lyle | 73 | 72 | 73 | 71 | 289 | 16,181.82 |
| Richard Green | 73 | 74 | 68 | 74 | 289 | 16,181.82 |
| Peter Hanson | 72 | 73 | 71 | 73 | 289 | 16,181.82 |
| Pelle Edberg | 72 | 68 | 73 | 76 | 289 | 16,181.82 |
| Titch Moore | 73 | 74 | 66 | 76 | 289 | 16,181.82 |
| Carlos Rodiles | 73 | 73 | 70 | 73 | 289 | 16,181.82 |
| Joakim Backstrom | 74 | 74 | 73 | 68 | 289 | 16,181.82 |
| Colin Montgomerie | 71 | 73 | 75 | 70 | 289 | 16,181.82 |
| Paul McGinley | 72 | 69 | 74 | 74 | 289 | 16,181.82 |
| Christian Cevaer | 73 | 73 | 68 | 75 | 289 | 16,181.82 |
| Stuart Manley | 72 | 74 | 69 | 74 | 289 | 16,181.82 |
| Mark Foster | 71 | 73 | 71 | 75 | 290 | 12,800 |
| Scott Drummond | 71 | 77 | 72 | 70 | 290 | 12,800 |
| Peter Lawrie | 74 | 71 | 74 | 71 | 290 | 12,800 |
| Paul Broadhurst | 72 | 75 | 72 | 71 | 290 | 12,800 |
| Henrik Stenson | 74 | 69 | 72 | 76 | 291 | 10,800 |
| Francesco Molinari | 74 | 72 | 73 | 72 | 291 | 10,800 |
| Jonathan Lomas | 73 | 73 | 72 | 73 | 291 | 10,800 |
| Peter O'Malley | 69 | 78 | 72 | 72 | 291 | 10,800 |
| David Higgins | 73 | 75 | 70 | 73 | 291 | 10,800 |
| Peter Gustafsson | 72 | 73 | 74 | 72 | 291 | 10,800 |
| Eduardo Romero | 72 | 74 | 72 | 74 | 292 | 8,000 |
| Ian Woosnam | 73 | 72 | 75 | 72 | 292 | 8,000 |
| Robert-Jan Derksen | 72 | 73 | 73 | 74 | 292 | 8,000 |
| Miguel Angel Jimenez | 71 | 72 | 77 | 72 | 292 | 8,000 |
| Simon Khan | 70 | 76 | 72 | 74 | 292 | 8,000 |
| Simon Wakefield | 71 | 75 | 75 | 71 | 292 | 8,000 |
| Lee Slattery | 72 | 72 | 73 | 75 | 292 | 8,000 |
| Brett Rumford | 73 | 73 | 75 | 71 | 292 | 8,000 |
| Gordon Brand, Jr. | 72 | 73 | 72 | 76 | 293 | 5,600 |
| Miguel Angel Martin | 72 | 76 | 73 | 72 | 293 | 5,600 |
| Jean-Francois Remesy | 71 | 72 | 73 | 77 | 293 | 5,600 |
| Trevor Immelman | 74 | 74 | 74 | 71 | 293 | 5,600 |
| Soren Hansen | 76 | 71 | 73 | 73 | 293 | 5,600 |
| Marc Cayeux | 71 | 73 | 74 | 75 | 293 | 5,600 |
| Ian Garbutt | 72 | 74 | 73 | 74 | 293 | 5,600 |
| Klas Eriksson | 68 | 76 | 73 | 77 | 294 | 4,300 |

| | SCORES | | | | TOTAL | MONEY |
|---|---|---|---|---|---|---|
| Gary Murphy | 73 | 72 | 73 | 76 | 294 | 4,300 |
| Gary Emerson | 76 | 71 | 74 | 73 | 294 | 4,300 |
| Rolf Muntz | 70 | 73 | 76 | 75 | 294 | 4,300 |
| Johan Skold | 72 | 76 | 74 | 72 | 294 | 4,300 |
| Jimmy Bolger | 73 | 73 | 71 | 77 | 294 | 4,300 |
| Raphael Jacquelin | 76 | 72 | 70 | 77 | 295 | 3,650 |
| Robert Karlsson | 72 | 75 | 75 | 74 | 296 | 3,000 |
| Mattias Eliasson | 69 | 75 | 73 | 80 | 297 | 2,995.50 |
| John Bickerton | 73 | 73 | 73 | 78 | 297 | 2,995.50 |
| Niki Zitny | 77 | 71 | 75 | 75 | 298 | 2,991 |

## BMW Championship

*Wentworth Club,* Surrey, England
Par 35-37–72; 7,072 yards

May 26-29
purse, €4,000,000

| | SCORES | | | | TOTAL | MONEY |
|---|---|---|---|---|---|---|
| Angel Cabrera | 70 | 70 | 66 | 67 | 273 | €666,660 |
| Paul McGinley | 72 | 64 | 72 | 67 | 275 | 444,440 |
| Nick O'Hern | 68 | 69 | 76 | 64 | 277 | 250,400 |
| David Howell | 70 | 72 | 66 | 71 | 279 | 200,000 |
| Marten Olander | 68 | 72 | 70 | 70 | 280 | 143,200 |
| Peter Hanson | 69 | 69 | 72 | 70 | 280 | 143,200 |
| Peter Hedblom | 68 | 65 | 73 | 74 | 280 | 143,200 |
| Michael Campbell | 71 | 68 | 71 | 71 | 281 | 94,800 |
| Jamie Donaldson | 73 | 71 | 69 | 68 | 281 | 94,800 |
| Bradley Dredge | 75 | 68 | 69 | 70 | 282 | 80,000 |
| Padraig Harrington | 70 | 68 | 74 | 71 | 283 | 62,457.14 |
| Gary Murphy | 74 | 68 | 70 | 71 | 283 | 62,457.14 |
| Steve Webster | 71 | 72 | 71 | 69 | 283 | 62,457.14 |
| Scott Drummond | 71 | 71 | 73 | 68 | 283 | 62,457.14 |
| Colin Montgomerie | 71 | 73 | 73 | 66 | 283 | 62,457.14 |
| Retief Goosen | 70 | 70 | 72 | 71 | 283 | 62,457.14 |
| Thongchai Jaidee | 72 | 67 | 71 | 73 | 283 | 62,457.14 |
| Peter Fowler | 68 | 76 | 74 | 66 | 284 | 48,900 |
| Damien McGrane | 69 | 71 | 72 | 72 | 284 | 48,900 |
| Paul Broadhurst | 70 | 70 | 74 | 70 | 284 | 48,900 |
| Luke Donald | 71 | 72 | 74 | 67 | 284 | 48,900 |
| Ian Woosnam | 75 | 69 | 71 | 70 | 285 | 42,800 |
| Jose Maria Olazabal | 72 | 69 | 71 | 73 | 285 | 42,800 |
| Thomas Bjorn | 71 | 71 | 75 | 68 | 285 | 42,800 |
| Peter Lonard | 69 | 70 | 75 | 71 | 285 | 42,800 |
| Richard Sterne | 73 | 71 | 72 | 69 | 285 | 42,800 |
| Soren Kjeldsen | 75 | 68 | 72 | 71 | 286 | 36,200 |
| Andrew Marshall | 72 | 72 | 70 | 72 | 286 | 36,200 |
| Jonathan Lomas | 72 | 68 | 78 | 68 | 286 | 36,200 |
| Niclas Fasth | 71 | 73 | 74 | 68 | 286 | 36,200 |
| Lee Westwood | 72 | 71 | 73 | 70 | 286 | 36,200 |
| Graeme McDowell | 67 | 76 | 75 | 68 | 286 | 36,200 |
| Nick Faldo | 70 | 71 | 77 | 69 | 287 | 29,666.67 |
| Richard Green | 71 | 70 | 77 | 69 | 287 | 29,666.67 |
| Trevor Immelman | 72 | 71 | 74 | 70 | 287 | 29,666.67 |
| Ian Poulter | 71 | 69 | 73 | 74 | 287 | 29,666.67 |
| Paul Lawrie | 73 | 70 | 70 | 74 | 287 | 29,666.67 |
| Ben Curtis | 68 | 71 | 76 | 72 | 287 | 29,666.67 |
| Robert-Jan Derksen | 71 | 69 | 76 | 72 | 288 | 23,200 |
| Peter Lawrie | 67 | 75 | 75 | 71 | 288 | 23,200 |

|                      | SCORES |    |    |    | TOTAL | MONEY  |
| -------------------- | -- | -- | -- | -- | ----- | ------ |
| Thomas Levet         | 72 | 72 | 73 | 71 | 288   | 23,200 |
| Philip Golding       | 71 | 73 | 74 | 70 | 288   | 23,200 |
| Stephen Dodd         | 69 | 74 | 74 | 71 | 288   | 23,200 |
| Ernie Els            | 73 | 69 | 75 | 71 | 288   | 23,200 |
| Robert Coles         | 69 | 71 | 76 | 72 | 288   | 23,200 |
| David Lynn           | 71 | 73 | 74 | 70 | 288   | 23,200 |
| Alastair Forsyth     | 69 | 72 | 75 | 72 | 288   | 23,200 |
| Steven O'Hara        | 69 | 72 | 73 | 74 | 288   | 23,200 |
| Raphael Jacquelin    | 70 | 73 | 76 | 70 | 289   | 16,400 |
| Henrik Stenson       | 70 | 74 | 71 | 74 | 289   | 16,400 |
| Marcel Siem          | 70 | 74 | 71 | 74 | 289   | 16,400 |
| Stephen Scahill      | 71 | 73 | 73 | 72 | 289   | 16,400 |
| David Carter         | 75 | 69 | 72 | 73 | 289   | 16,400 |
| Jose-Filipe Lima     | 67 | 73 | 78 | 71 | 289   | 16,400 |
| Marcus Fraser        | 68 | 72 | 78 | 71 | 289   | 16,400 |
| Kenneth Ferrie       | 72 | 69 | 76 | 73 | 290   | 12,300 |
| Miguel Angel Jimenez | 70 | 73 | 76 | 71 | 290   | 12,300 |
| Pierre Fulke         | 74 | 69 | 73 | 74 | 290   | 12,300 |
| Lee Slattery         | 70 | 69 | 84 | 67 | 290   | 12,300 |
| Soren Hansen         | 70 | 71 | 78 | 72 | 291   | 11,200 |
| Andrew Coltart       | 70 | 73 | 80 | 69 | 292   | 10,800 |
| Tony Johnstone       | 72 | 72 | 76 | 73 | 293   | 10,000 |
| Rolf Muntz           | 74 | 69 | 77 | 73 | 293   | 10,000 |
| Phil Edwards         | 71 | 72 | 75 | 75 | 293   | 10,000 |
| Patrik Sjoland       | 72 | 70 | 75 | 79 | 296   | 8,800  |
| Graeme Storm         | 73 | 71 | 82 | 70 | 296   | 8,800  |
| Simon Dyson          | 70 | 73 | 76 | 77 | 296   | 8,800  |
| Alessandro Tadini    | 73 | 70 | 76 | 78 | 297   | 7,800  |
| Scott Henderson      | 72 | 72 | 78 | 75 | 297   | 7,800  |
| Matthew King         | 72 | 71 | 82 | 77 | 302   | 7,300  |
| Miles Tunnicliff     | 72 | 72 | 81 | 79 | 304   | 6,000  |

## Celtic Manor Wales Open

*Celtic Manor Resort,* Newport, South Wales
Par 35-34–69; 6,743 yards

June 2-5
purse, €2,207,900

|                      | SCORES |    |    |    | TOTAL | MONEY        |
| -------------------- | -- | -- | -- | -- | ----- | ------------ |
| Miguel Angel Jimenez | 63 | 67 | 70 | 62 | 262   | €362,567.50  |
| Jose Manuel Lara     | 68 | 65 | 67 | 66 | 266   | 188,941.20   |
| Martin Erlandsson    | 69 | 65 | 69 | 63 | 266   | 188,941.20   |
| Jean-Francois Lucquin| 65 | 66 | 69 | 67 | 267   | 108,770.30   |
| Ian Woosnam          | 64 | 68 | 68 | 68 | 268   | 77,879.50    |
| Alessandro Tadini    | 65 | 62 | 72 | 69 | 268   | 77,879.50    |
| Joakim Haeggman      | 68 | 66 | 68 | 66 | 268   | 77,879.50    |
| David Lynn           | 63 | 66 | 72 | 69 | 270   | 46,662.44    |
| Jose-Filipe Lima     | 65 | 70 | 67 | 68 | 270   | 46,662.44    |
| Wade Ormsby          | 67 | 68 | 70 | 65 | 270   | 46,662.44    |
| Oliver Wilson        | 67 | 67 | 69 | 67 | 270   | 46,662.44    |
| Anthony Wall         | 70 | 68 | 66 | 67 | 271   | 35,241.56    |
| Gary Orr             | 66 | 70 | 67 | 68 | 271   | 35,241.56    |
| Nick Dougherty       | 65 | 72 | 65 | 69 | 271   | 35,241.56    |
| Steve Webster        | 68 | 71 | 68 | 65 | 272   | 31,325.83    |
| Michael Campbell     | 65 | 72 | 70 | 65 | 272   | 31,325.83    |
| Peter Senior         | 63 | 72 | 72 | 66 | 273   | 26,322.40    |
| Raphael Jacquelin    | 67 | 66 | 70 | 70 | 273   | 26,322.40    |
| Soren Kjeldsen       | 69 | 69 | 68 | 67 | 273   | 26,322.40    |
| Paul Broadhurst      | 70 | 68 | 70 | 65 | 273   | 26,322.40    |

| | SCORES | | | | TOTAL | MONEY |
|---|---|---|---|---|---|---|
| Richard Bland | 66 | 70 | 69 | 68 | 273 | 26,322.40 |
| Jan-Are Larsen | 67 | 68 | 69 | 69 | 273 | 26,322.40 |
| Paul Lawrie | 67 | 68 | 69 | 69 | 273 | 26,322.40 |
| Stuart Little | 64 | 69 | 72 | 69 | 274 | 21,645.28 |
| Robert Coles | 68 | 69 | 72 | 65 | 274 | 21,645.28 |
| Fredrik Andersson Hed | 67 | 70 | 69 | 68 | 274 | 21,645.28 |
| Terry Price | 70 | 67 | 65 | 72 | 274 | 21,645.28 |
| Francois Delamontagne | 66 | 66 | 71 | 71 | 274 | 21,645.28 |
| Richard Sterne | 67 | 72 | 70 | 65 | 274 | 21,645.28 |
| Gary Murphy | 68 | 71 | 69 | 67 | 275 | 17,765.81 |
| Jean-Francois Remesy | 69 | 68 | 74 | 64 | 275 | 17,765.81 |
| Soren Hansen | 67 | 70 | 70 | 68 | 275 | 17,765.81 |
| Christian Cevaer | 67 | 65 | 75 | 68 | 275 | 17,765.81 |
| Andrew Coltart | 65 | 74 | 66 | 70 | 275 | 17,765.81 |
| Richard Finch | 67 | 65 | 75 | 68 | 275 | 17,765.81 |
| David Howell | 71 | 67 | 72 | 66 | 276 | 14,357.67 |
| Kenneth Ferrie | 65 | 68 | 73 | 70 | 276 | 14,357.67 |
| Henrik Stenson | 67 | 69 | 71 | 69 | 276 | 14,357.67 |
| Ignacio Garrido | 66 | 71 | 70 | 69 | 276 | 14,357.67 |
| Bradley Dredge | 69 | 68 | 67 | 72 | 276 | 14,357.67 |
| Jarmo Sandelin | 68 | 67 | 69 | 72 | 276 | 14,357.67 |
| Leif Westerberg | 66 | 69 | 72 | 69 | 276 | 14,357.67 |
| Ben Mason | 67 | 67 | 70 | 72 | 276 | 14,357.67 |
| Sandy Lyle | 68 | 70 | 74 | 65 | 277 | 10,441.94 |
| David Gilford | 69 | 70 | 71 | 67 | 277 | 10,441.94 |
| Anders Hansen | 67 | 69 | 70 | 71 | 277 | 10,441.94 |
| Peter Lawrie | 68 | 71 | 69 | 69 | 277 | 10,441.94 |
| Nicolas Colsaerts | 70 | 68 | 71 | 68 | 277 | 10,441.94 |
| Paul McGinley | 68 | 70 | 71 | 68 | 277 | 10,441.94 |
| Simon Wakefield | 69 | 68 | 70 | 70 | 277 | 10,441.94 |
| Niclas Fasth | 68 | 69 | 67 | 73 | 277 | 10,441.94 |
| John Bickerton | 69 | 70 | 70 | 68 | 277 | 10,441.94 |
| James Heath | 63 | 69 | 70 | 75 | 277 | 10,441.94 |
| Gordon Brand, Jr. | 71 | 68 | 72 | 67 | 278 | 7,070.07 |
| Carlos Rodiles | 68 | 68 | 71 | 71 | 278 | 7,070.07 |
| Emanuele Canonica | 67 | 68 | 76 | 67 | 278 | 7,070.07 |
| Benoit Teilleria | 63 | 69 | 74 | 72 | 278 | 7,070.07 |
| Jamie Donaldson | 67 | 68 | 69 | 74 | 278 | 7,070.07 |
| Ross Fisher | 70 | 68 | 76 | 64 | 278 | 7,070.07 |
| Roger Chapman | 68 | 70 | 75 | 66 | 279 | 5,329.74 |
| Miguel Angel Martin | 69 | 66 | 73 | 71 | 279 | 5,329.74 |
| Marten Olander | 67 | 67 | 72 | 73 | 279 | 5,329.74 |
| Neil Cheetham | 65 | 72 | 71 | 71 | 279 | 5,329.74 |
| David Park | 68 | 67 | 75 | 69 | 279 | 5,329.74 |
| Stephen Gallacher | 66 | 68 | 76 | 69 | 279 | 5,329.74 |
| Graeme Storm | 68 | 68 | 72 | 71 | 279 | 5,329.74 |
| Marcus Fraser | 71 | 68 | 69 | 71 | 279 | 5,329.74 |
| Gary Emerson | 63 | 71 | 73 | 73 | 280 | 4,152.61 |
| Peter Hedblom | 66 | 71 | 73 | 70 | 280 | 4,152.61 |
| Brad Kennedy | 69 | 67 | 75 | 69 | 280 | 4,152.61 |
| Darren Fichardt | 69 | 69 | 72 | 71 | 281 | 3,261.50 |
| Hernan Rey | 70 | 68 | 72 | 71 | 281 | 3,261.50 |
| Simon Khan | 67 | 72 | 69 | 74 | 282 | 3,254 |
| David Drysdale | 69 | 68 | 73 | 72 | 282 | 3,254 |
| Adam Groom | 69 | 70 | 75 | 68 | 282 | 3,254 |
| Andrew Oldcorn | 66 | 73 | 72 | 72 | 283 | 3,245 |
| Andre Cruse | 67 | 72 | 78 | 66 | 283 | 3,245 |
| Marco Bernardini | 74 | 65 | 75 | 69 | 283 | 3,245 |
| Pelle Edberg | 72 | 66 | 78 | 72 | 288 | 3,239 |
| Fernando Roca | 70 | 69 | 77 | 77 | 293 | 3,236 |

# KLM Open

*Hilversumsche Golf Club,* Hilversum, Netherlands
Par 35-35–70; 6,660 yards

June 9-12
purse, €1,500,000

| | SCORES | | | | TOTAL | MONEY |
|---|---|---|---|---|---|---|
| Gonzalo Fernandez-Castano | 66 | 70 | 66 | 67 | 269 | €250,000 |
| Gary Emerson | 69 | 63 | 69 | 70 | 271 | 166,660 |
| Paul Broadhurst | 66 | 67 | 69 | 70 | 272 | 93,900 |
| Maarten Lafeber | 68 | 67 | 70 | 68 | 273 | 69,300 |
| Markus Brier | 67 | 68 | 69 | 69 | 273 | 69,300 |
| Robert Coles | 71 | 67 | 70 | 66 | 274 | 52,500 |
| Peter Senior | 70 | 67 | 68 | 70 | 275 | 41,250 |
| John Bickerton | 74 | 67 | 69 | 65 | 275 | 41,250 |
| Andrew Oldcorn | 69 | 67 | 70 | 71 | 277 | 26,592.86 |
| Damien McGrane | 68 | 70 | 71 | 68 | 277 | 26,592.86 |
| Alessandro Tadini | 70 | 64 | 71 | 72 | 277 | 26,592.86 |
| Pierre Fulke | 67 | 73 | 69 | 68 | 277 | 26,592.86 |
| David Lynn | 70 | 67 | 70 | 70 | 277 | 26,592.86 |
| Johan Skold | 68 | 70 | 72 | 67 | 277 | 26,592.86 |
| Steven O'Hara | 70 | 65 | 72 | 70 | 277 | 26,592.86 |
| Jamie Spence | 73 | 69 | 71 | 65 | 278 | 19,470 |
| Carlos Rodiles | 73 | 68 | 67 | 70 | 278 | 19,470 |
| Philip Golding | 74 | 67 | 69 | 68 | 278 | 19,470 |
| Andrew Marshall | 72 | 69 | 68 | 69 | 278 | 19,470 |
| Rolf Muntz | 69 | 69 | 72 | 68 | 278 | 19,470 |
| Miguel Angel Martin | 69 | 67 | 70 | 73 | 279 | 16,725 |
| Guido van der Valk | 66 | 70 | 72 | 71 | 279 | 16,725 |
| Alastair Forsyth | 72 | 65 | 73 | 69 | 279 | 16,725 |
| Martin Maritz | 69 | 70 | 71 | 69 | 279 | 16,725 |
| Santiago Luna | 69 | 73 | 71 | 67 | 280 | 14,250 |
| Francesco Molinari | 71 | 73 | 69 | 67 | 280 | 14,250 |
| Bradley Dredge | 73 | 70 | 68 | 69 | 280 | 14,250 |
| David Park | 73 | 69 | 73 | 65 | 280 | 14,250 |
| Ivo Giner | 69 | 73 | 68 | 70 | 280 | 14,250 |
| Gregory Bourdy | 71 | 69 | 68 | 72 | 280 | 14,250 |
| Marcus Fraser | 68 | 69 | 71 | 72 | 280 | 14,250 |
| Mark Roe | 68 | 73 | 70 | 70 | 281 | 11,156.25 |
| Robert-Jan Derksen | 68 | 72 | 71 | 70 | 281 | 11,156.25 |
| Jose Manuel Carriles | 70 | 71 | 71 | 69 | 281 | 11,156.25 |
| Anthony Wall | 69 | 71 | 68 | 73 | 281 | 11,156.25 |
| Stuart Little | 70 | 71 | 73 | 67 | 281 | 11,156.25 |
| Michael Jonzon | 71 | 70 | 73 | 67 | 281 | 11,156.25 |
| Christopher Hanell | 69 | 74 | 70 | 68 | 281 | 11,156.25 |
| Louis Oosthuizen | 72 | 70 | 69 | 70 | 281 | 11,156.25 |
| Gordon Brand, Jr. | 74 | 67 | 69 | 72 | 282 | 9,000 |
| Jose Manuel Lara | 70 | 72 | 68 | 72 | 282 | 9,000 |
| Darren Fichardt | 70 | 72 | 69 | 71 | 282 | 9,000 |
| Peter Baker | 69 | 71 | 73 | 69 | 282 | 9,000 |
| Richard Bland | 71 | 64 | 74 | 73 | 282 | 9,000 |
| Graeme Storm | 71 | 71 | 70 | 70 | 282 | 9,000 |
| Anders Hansen | 71 | 73 | 69 | 70 | 283 | 7,950 |
| Peter Fowler | 73 | 70 | 67 | 74 | 284 | 6,600 |
| Peter Lawrie | 70 | 70 | 74 | 70 | 284 | 6,600 |
| Ian Garbutt | 71 | 72 | 71 | 70 | 284 | 6,600 |
| Gary Orr | 72 | 70 | 75 | 67 | 284 | 6,600 |
| Simon Wakefield | 69 | 74 | 73 | 68 | 284 | 6,600 |
| Raymond Russell | 67 | 70 | 73 | 74 | 284 | 6,600 |
| David Carter | 71 | 73 | 70 | 70 | 284 | 6,600 |
| Sebastian Fernandez | 72 | 69 | 75 | 68 | 284 | 6,600 |

| | SCORES | | | | TOTAL | MONEY |
|---|---|---|---|---|---|---|
| Roger Chapman | 70 | 70 | 75 | 70 | 285 | 4,650 |
| Fredrik Henge | 68 | 71 | 73 | 73 | 285 | 4,650 |
| Paul Eales | 74 | 70 | 75 | 66 | 285 | 4,650 |
| Henrik Nystrom | 66 | 72 | 71 | 76 | 285 | 4,650 |
| Stuart Manley | 72 | 72 | 72 | 69 | 285 | 4,650 |
| Adam Groom | 66 | 71 | 78 | 70 | 285 | 4,650 |
| Phillip Archer | 70 | 74 | 69 | 73 | 286 | 3,825 |
| Leif Westerberg | 73 | 68 | 75 | 70 | 286 | 3,825 |
| Robert Rock | 71 | 70 | 72 | 73 | 286 | 3,825 |
| Ben Mason | 68 | 76 | 68 | 74 | 286 | 3,825 |
| Fredrik Andersson Hed | 75 | 67 | 75 | 70 | 287 | 3,225 |
| Benoit Teilleria | 68 | 76 | 66 | 77 | 287 | 3,225 |
| Brad Kennedy | 71 | 70 | 75 | 71 | 287 | 3,225 |
| Oliver Wilson | 72 | 72 | 69 | 74 | 287 | 3,225 |
| Mark Foster | 71 | 70 | 75 | 72 | 288 | 2,521.75 |
| Neil Cheetham | 69 | 71 | 73 | 75 | 288 | 2,521.75 |
| Patrik Sjoland | 73 | 68 | 75 | 72 | 288 | 2,521.75 |
| Kyron Sullivan | 68 | 70 | 75 | 75 | 288 | 2,521.75 |
| Cesar Monasterio | 71 | 73 | 70 | 75 | 289 | 2,242.50 |
| Francois Delamontagne | 72 | 72 | 74 | 71 | 289 | 2,242.50 |
| Pelle Edberg | 69 | 74 | 75 | 72 | 290 | 2,232 |
| Andrew McLardy | 73 | 69 | 76 | 72 | 290 | 2,232 |
| Sam Little | 72 | 72 | 71 | 75 | 290 | 2,232 |
| Jean-Francois Lucquin | 69 | 73 | 77 | 71 | 290 | 2,232 |
| Wade Ormsby | 71 | 73 | 75 | 71 | 290 | 2,232 |
| Rafael Gomez | 72 | 72 | 76 | 73 | 293 | 2,223 |
| Jan-Are Larsen | 71 | 72 | 78 | 73 | 294 | 2,220 |
| Tobias Dier | 70 | 74 | 73 | 80 | 297 | 2,217 |

## Aa St. Omer Open

*Aa St. Omer Golf Club,* Lumbres, France                                    June 16-19
Par 36-35–71; 6,880 yards                                    purse, €400,000

| | SCORES | | | | TOTAL | MONEY |
|---|---|---|---|---|---|---|
| Joakim Backstrom | 72 | 70 | 68 | 70 | 280 | €66,660 |
| Paul Dwyer | 73 | 68 | 71 | 68 | 280 | 44,440 |
| (Backstrom defeated Dwyer on first playoff hole.) | | | | | | |
| Michael Jonzon | 69 | 73 | 71 | 68 | 281 | 20,666.67 |
| Steven Jeppesen | 73 | 70 | 70 | 68 | 281 | 20,666.67 |
| James Heath | 70 | 66 | 73 | 72 | 281 | 20,666.67 |
| Alvaro Salto | 74 | 69 | 69 | 70 | 282 | 10,592 |
| Carl Suneson | 74 | 69 | 65 | 74 | 282 | 10,592 |
| James Hepworth | 69 | 71 | 69 | 73 | 282 | 10,592 |
| Ben Mason | 71 | 74 | 70 | 67 | 282 | 10,592 |
| Ross Fisher | 70 | 70 | 68 | 74 | 282 | 10,592 |
| Martin Erlandsson | 68 | 77 | 69 | 69 | 283 | 6,386.67 |
| Denny Lucas | 70 | 73 | 71 | 69 | 283 | 6,386.67 |
| Gary Orr | 71 | 71 | 68 | 73 | 283 | 6,386.67 |
| David Dixon | 76 | 69 | 70 | 68 | 283 | 6,386.67 |
| Roope Kakko | 72 | 71 | 73 | 67 | 283 | 6,386.67 |
| Miguel Carballo | 72 | 69 | 71 | 71 | 283 | 6,386.67 |
| Sion Bebb | 70 | 72 | 68 | 74 | 284 | 4,913.33 |
| Gary Clark | 74 | 67 | 73 | 70 | 284 | 4,913.33 |
| Iain Pyman | 72 | 71 | 66 | 75 | 284 | 4,913.33 |
| Stephen Browne | 71 | 70 | 71 | 72 | 284 | 4,913.33 |
| Matthew Morris | 70 | 72 | 72 | 70 | 284 | 4,913.33 |

| | SCORES | | | | TOTAL | MONEY |
|---|---|---|---|---|---|---|
| Adam Groom | 71 | 70 | 68 | 75 | 284 | 4,913.33 |
| Mark Mouland | 73 | 71 | 72 | 69 | 285 | 4,040 |
| Sven Struver | 73 | 72 | 72 | 68 | 285 | 4,040 |
| Jan-Are Larsen | 70 | 73 | 73 | 69 | 285 | 4,040 |
| Neil Cheetham | 68 | 76 | 70 | 71 | 285 | 4,040 |
| Tomas Jesus Munoz | 73 | 70 | 71 | 71 | 285 | 4,040 |
| Raphael De Sousa | 73 | 70 | 66 | 76 | 285 | 4,040 |
| Andres Romero | 71 | 71 | 72 | 71 | 285 | 4,040 |
| Cesar Monasterio | 74 | 69 | 72 | 71 | 286 | 3,217.14 |
| Hennie Otto | 68 | 73 | 75 | 70 | 286 | 3,217.14 |
| Sebastien Delagrange | 70 | 71 | 71 | 74 | 286 | 3,217.14 |
| David Higgins | 75 | 69 | 71 | 71 | 286 | 3,217.14 |
| David Orr | 72 | 73 | 68 | 73 | 286 | 3,217.14 |
| Kyron Sullivan | 76 | 66 | 69 | 75 | 286 | 3,217.14 |
| Thomas Nielsen | 72 | 72 | 72 | 70 | 286 | 3,217.14 |
| Raphael Eyraud | 68 | 75 | 73 | 71 | 287 | 2,400 |
| Phillip Archer | 69 | 73 | 72 | 73 | 287 | 2,400 |
| Jamie Little | 69 | 74 | 73 | 71 | 287 | 2,400 |
| Jesus Maria Arruti | 72 | 71 | 72 | 72 | 287 | 2,400 |
| David Dupart | 71 | 70 | 73 | 73 | 287 | 2,400 |
| Oskar Bergman | 72 | 73 | 70 | 72 | 287 | 2,400 |
| David Griffiths | 70 | 74 | 70 | 73 | 287 | 2,400 |
| Tom Whitehouse | 70 | 71 | 74 | 72 | 287 | 2,400 |
| Sebastian Fernandez | 74 | 71 | 67 | 75 | 287 | 2,400 |
| Craig Williams | 69 | 75 | 71 | 72 | 287 | 2,400 |
| Gareth Davies | 73 | 72 | 71 | 71 | 287 | 2,400 |
| Ariel Canete | 72 | 72 | 72 | 71 | 287 | 2,400 |
| Shaun Webster | 71 | 68 | 75 | 74 | 288 | 1,720 |
| Jean Van de Velde | 71 | 71 | 73 | 73 | 288 | 1,720 |
| Birgir Hafthorsson | 68 | 74 | 69 | 77 | 288 | 1,720 |
| Ivo Giner | 69 | 72 | 73 | 74 | 288 | 1,720 |
| Julien Quesne | 75 | 69 | 71 | 73 | 288 | 1,720 |
| Knud Storgaard | 72 | 69 | 75 | 73 | 289 | 1,328 |
| Paul Nilbrink | 73 | 69 | 72 | 75 | 289 | 1,328 |
| Per G. Nyman | 68 | 74 | 73 | 74 | 289 | 1,328 |
| Rafael Gomez | 72 | 69 | 72 | 76 | 289 | 1,328 |
| Jeppe Huldahl | 72 | 70 | 75 | 72 | 289 | 1,328 |
| Massimo Scarpa | 71 | 73 | 74 | 72 | 290 | 1,080 |
| Matthew Blackey | 73 | 71 | 76 | 70 | 290 | 1,080 |
| Jean-Nicolas Billot | 75 | 70 | 73 | 72 | 290 | 1,080 |
| Gabriel Canizares | 71 | 72 | 75 | 72 | 290 | 1,080 |
| Oliver Whiteley | 71 | 72 | 75 | 72 | 290 | 1,080 |
| Marcus Higley | 73 | 72 | 69 | 77 | 291 | 900 |
| Garry Houston | 72 | 69 | 74 | 76 | 291 | 900 |
| Pelle Edberg | 70 | 69 | 78 | 74 | 291 | 900 |
| Carlos De Corral | 74 | 71 | 70 | 76 | 291 | 900 |
| Lionel Alexandre | 74 | 71 | 69 | 78 | 292 | 725 |
| Benoit Teilleria | 72 | 72 | 75 | 73 | 292 | 725 |
| Edward Rush | 72 | 73 | 72 | 75 | 292 | 725 |
| Martin LeMesurier | 74 | 71 | 80 | 67 | 292 | 725 |
| Mattias Nilsson | 70 | 75 | 76 | 72 | 293 | 595.50 |
| Mark Sanders | 71 | 74 | 72 | 76 | 293 | 595.50 |
| Jeff Hall | 74 | 71 | 76 | 73 | 294 | 589.50 |
| Jamie Elson | 69 | 73 | 73 | 79 | 294 | 589.50 |
| Michael Kirk | 74 | 68 | 76 | 78 | 296 | 585 |
| Gustavo Rojas | 74 | 71 | 77 | 76 | 298 | 582 |

# Open de France

*Le Golf National,* Paris, France                                          June 23-26
Par 36-35–71; 7,214 yards                                          purse, €3,500,000

| | SCORES | | | | TOTAL | MONEY |
|---|---|---|---|---|---|---|
| Jean-Francois Remesy | 68 | 69 | 67 | 69 | 273 | €583,330 |
| Jean Van de Velde | 64 | 70 | 70 | 69 | 273 | 388,880 |
| (Remesy defeated Van de Velde on first playoff hole.) | | | | | | |
| Soren Hansen | 65 | 69 | 71 | 71 | 276 | 219,100 |
| Gregory Havret | 70 | 70 | 67 | 72 | 279 | 137,725 |
| Peter O'Malley | 69 | 68 | 70 | 72 | 279 | 137,725 |
| Francois Delamontagne | 67 | 68 | 71 | 73 | 279 | 137,725 |
| Richard Finch | 73 | 70 | 69 | 67 | 279 | 137,725 |
| Eduardo Romero | 70 | 62 | 72 | 76 | 280 | 72,100 |
| Jose Maria Olazabal | 69 | 70 | 70 | 71 | 280 | 72,100 |
| Anders Hansen | 67 | 71 | 70 | 72 | 280 | 72,100 |
| Jonathan Lomas | 65 | 69 | 71 | 75 | 280 | 72,100 |
| Bradley Dredge | 67 | 73 | 72 | 68 | 280 | 72,100 |
| Philip Golding | 69 | 69 | 68 | 75 | 281 | 52,675 |
| Stuart Little | 71 | 71 | 68 | 71 | 281 | 52,675 |
| Nick Dougherty | 72 | 68 | 69 | 72 | 281 | 52,675 |
| Richard Sterne | 67 | 75 | 70 | 69 | 281 | 52,675 |
| Martin Erlandsson | 68 | 67 | 75 | 72 | 282 | 44,450 |
| Colin Montgomerie | 69 | 72 | 70 | 71 | 282 | 44,450 |
| Ignacio Garrido | 72 | 66 | 75 | 69 | 282 | 44,450 |
| David Lynn | 73 | 68 | 70 | 71 | 282 | 44,450 |
| Robert-Jan Derksen | 71 | 69 | 69 | 74 | 283 | 38,500 |
| Marcel Siem | 69 | 68 | 72 | 74 | 283 | 38,500 |
| Jarmo Sandelin | 68 | 72 | 72 | 71 | 283 | 38,500 |
| Niclas Fasth | 69 | 68 | 75 | 71 | 283 | 38,500 |
| Wade Ormsby | 72 | 72 | 69 | 70 | 283 | 38,500 |
| Miguel Angel Martin | 72 | 70 | 71 | 71 | 284 | 33,250 |
| Jose Manuel Lara | 72 | 71 | 71 | 70 | 284 | 33,250 |
| Soren Kjeldsen | 72 | 72 | 66 | 74 | 284 | 33,250 |
| Francesco Molinari | 68 | 72 | 69 | 75 | 284 | 33,250 |
| Marc Cayeux | 68 | 72 | 71 | 73 | 284 | 33,250 |
| Klas Eriksson | 72 | 68 | 71 | 74 | 285 | 26,862.50 |
| Alessandro Tadini | 70 | 73 | 69 | 73 | 285 | 26,862.50 |
| Phillip Archer | 70 | 73 | 69 | 73 | 285 | 26,862.50 |
| Andrew McLardy | 67 | 71 | 75 | 72 | 285 | 26,862.50 |
| Stephen Dodd | 73 | 70 | 69 | 73 | 285 | 26,862.50 |
| Markus Brier | 74 | 70 | 69 | 72 | 285 | 26,862.50 |
| Stephen Gallacher | 71 | 70 | 71 | 73 | 285 | 26,862.50 |
| Ben Mason | 73 | 69 | 73 | 70 | 285 | 26,862.50 |
| Garry Houston | 67 | 73 | 71 | 75 | 286 | 22,050 |
| Paul Broadhurst | 71 | 72 | 69 | 74 | 286 | 22,050 |
| Miles Tunnicliff | 71 | 69 | 72 | 74 | 286 | 22,050 |
| Paul Lawrie | 71 | 70 | 69 | 76 | 286 | 22,050 |
| John Bickerton | 69 | 71 | 73 | 73 | 286 | 22,050 |
| Mark Roe | 69 | 75 | 69 | 74 | 287 | 18,200 |
| Brian Davis | 71 | 69 | 72 | 75 | 287 | 18,200 |
| Ricardo Gonzalez | 68 | 73 | 73 | 73 | 287 | 18,200 |
| Mads Vibe-Hastrup | 70 | 74 | 69 | 74 | 287 | 18,200 |
| Steven O'Hara | 74 | 70 | 75 | 68 | 287 | 18,200 |
| Stephen Browne | 68 | 76 | 69 | 74 | 287 | 18,200 |
| Sven Struver | 72 | 72 | 72 | 72 | 288 | 14,350 |
| Mattias Eliasson | 69 | 73 | 72 | 74 | 288 | 14,350 |
| Simon Wakefield | 71 | 73 | 72 | 72 | 288 | 14,350 |
| Alastair Forsyth | 71 | 70 | 72 | 75 | 288 | 14,350 |

| | SCORES | | | | TOTAL | MONEY |
|---|---|---|---|---|---|---|
| Brad Kennedy | 72 | 71 | 74 | 71 | 288 | 14,350 |
| Peter Hanson | 70 | 72 | 71 | 76 | 289 | 10,266.67 |
| Henrik Stenson | 70 | 71 | 71 | 77 | 289 | 10,266.67 |
| Miguel Angel Jimenez | 67 | 74 | 77 | 71 | 289 | 10,266.67 |
| Paul McGinley | 70 | 71 | 73 | 75 | 289 | 10,266.67 |
| Ian Garbutt | 72 | 71 | 68 | 78 | 289 | 10,266.67 |
| Pierre Fulke | 72 | 72 | 74 | 71 | 289 | 10,266.67 |
| Raymond Russell | 65 | 77 | 73 | 74 | 289 | 10,266.67 |
| David Carter | 70 | 74 | 69 | 76 | 289 | 10,266.67 |
| Gonzalo Fernandez-Castano | 71 | 73 | 74 | 71 | 289 | 10,266.67 |
| James Kingston | 72 | 71 | 73 | 74 | 290 | 8,400 |
| Anthony Wall | 71 | 71 | 71 | 78 | 291 | 7,700 |
| Andrew Marshall | 68 | 74 | 73 | 76 | 291 | 7,700 |
| Charl Schwartzel | 66 | 73 | 71 | 81 | 291 | 7,700 |
| Mark Foster | 70 | 70 | 74 | 78 | 292 | 6,107.40 |
| Scott Drummond | 69 | 72 | 74 | 77 | 292 | 6,107.40 |
| Peter Lawrie | 70 | 72 | 73 | 77 | 292 | 6,107.40 |
| Pelle Edberg | 69 | 74 | 71 | 78 | 292 | 6,107.40 |
| Thomas Levet | 72 | 72 | 72 | 76 | 292 | 6,107.40 |
| Costantino Rocca | 72 | 71 | 74 | 76 | 293 | 5,241 |
| Gary Murphy | 75 | 68 | 77 | 73 | 293 | 5,241 |
| Jarrod Moseley | 71 | 72 | 76 | 74 | 293 | 5,241 |
| Kenneth Ferrie | 70 | 73 | 75 | 76 | 294 | 5,235 |
| Terry Price | 70 | 71 | 76 | 78 | 295 | 5,232 |
| Richard Bland | 70 | 74 | 79 | 73 | 296 | 5,227.50 |
| Eric Moreul | 70 | 74 | 71 | 81 | 296 | 5,227.50 |
| Johan Axgren | 69 | 73 | 75 | 80 | 297 | 5,223 |
| Jan-Are Larsen | 73 | 71 | 74 | 80 | 298 | 5,218.50 |
| Brett Rumford | 69 | 75 | 76 | 78 | 298 | 5,218.50 |
| Gordon Brand, Jr. | 72 | 71 | 73 | 83 | 299 | 5,214 |
| Niki Zitny | 67 | 77 | 80 | 76 | 300 | 5,211 |
| David Drysdale | 72 | 70 | 80 | 79 | 301 | 5,208 |

## Smurfit European Open

*The K Club,* Straffan, Co. Kildare, Ireland
Par 35-37–72; 7,350 yards

June 30-July 3
purse, €3,482,520

| | SCORES | | | | TOTAL | MONEY |
|---|---|---|---|---|---|---|
| Kenneth Ferrie | 75 | 70 | 70 | 70 | 285 | €577,816.30 |
| Colin Montgomerie | 73 | 75 | 70 | 69 | 287 | 301,117.80 |
| Graeme Storm | 69 | 71 | 74 | 73 | 287 | 301,117.80 |
| Peter Hanson | 74 | 72 | 69 | 73 | 288 | 160,172.10 |
| Darren Clarke | 69 | 71 | 75 | 73 | 288 | 160,172.10 |
| Gary Murphy | 68 | 76 | 73 | 72 | 289 | 83,206.27 |
| Jose Manuel Lara | 70 | 76 | 70 | 73 | 289 | 83,206.27 |
| Brian Davis | 70 | 73 | 75 | 71 | 289 | 83,206.27 |
| Damien McGrane | 70 | 71 | 74 | 74 | 289 | 83,206.27 |
| Trevor Immelman | 66 | 76 | 74 | 73 | 289 | 83,206.27 |
| Jamie Spence | 76 | 67 | 73 | 73 | 289 | 83,206.27 |
| Andrew Coltart | 75 | 68 | 71 | 75 | 289 | 83,206.27 |
| Richard Green | 72 | 73 | 70 | 75 | 290 | 50,039.33 |
| Nick O'Hern | 69 | 74 | 72 | 75 | 290 | 50,039.33 |
| Lee Westwood | 73 | 74 | 72 | 71 | 290 | 50,039.33 |
| Retief Goosen | 67 | 74 | 77 | 72 | 290 | 50,039.33 |
| Nick Dougherty | 74 | 70 | 79 | 67 | 290 | 50,039.33 |
| Graeme McDowell | 72 | 75 | 70 | 73 | 290 | 50,039.33 |

| | SCORES | | | | TOTAL | MONEY |
|---|---|---|---|---|---|---|
| Raphael Jacquelin | 72 | 70 | 70 | 79 | 291 | 39,869.67 |
| Peter Hedblom | 73 | 70 | 75 | 73 | 291 | 39,869.67 |
| Jonathan Lomas | 68 | 72 | 72 | 79 | 291 | 39,869.67 |
| Brett Rumford | 69 | 71 | 75 | 76 | 291 | 39,869.67 |
| Jamie Donaldson | 69 | 70 | 82 | 70 | 291 | 39,869.67 |
| Gregory Bourdy | 73 | 73 | 74 | 71 | 291 | 39,869.67 |
| Steve Webster | 73 | 73 | 72 | 74 | 292 | 33,975.89 |
| Anthony Wall | 73 | 72 | 76 | 71 | 292 | 33,975.89 |
| Soren Hansen | 75 | 73 | 75 | 69 | 292 | 33,975.89 |
| Niclas Fasth | 70 | 74 | 72 | 76 | 292 | 33,975.89 |
| Michael Campbell | 74 | 72 | 71 | 75 | 292 | 33,975.89 |
| Santiago Luna | 72 | 73 | 75 | 73 | 293 | 29,815.58 |
| Maarten Lafeber | 71 | 76 | 75 | 71 | 293 | 29,815.58 |
| Greg Owen | 72 | 72 | 76 | 73 | 293 | 29,815.58 |
| Peter Fowler | 74 | 72 | 76 | 72 | 294 | 25,713.05 |
| Marten Olander | 73 | 71 | 75 | 75 | 294 | 25,713.05 |
| Phillip Archer | 74 | 72 | 71 | 77 | 294 | 25,713.05 |
| Fredrik Henge | 75 | 72 | 78 | 69 | 294 | 25,713.05 |
| Thomas Bjorn | 70 | 69 | 69 | 86 | 294 | 25,713.05 |
| Wade Ormsby | 74 | 70 | 74 | 76 | 294 | 25,713.05 |
| Bradley Dredge | 75 | 72 | 75 | 73 | 295 | 22,188.34 |
| Markus Brier | 71 | 70 | 80 | 74 | 295 | 22,188.34 |
| Terry Price | 73 | 75 | 74 | 73 | 295 | 22,188.34 |
| Mikko Ilonen | 72 | 72 | 75 | 76 | 295 | 22,188.34 |
| Rolf Muntz | 73 | 68 | 75 | 80 | 296 | 19,761.49 |
| Angel Cabrera | 71 | 77 | 69 | 79 | 296 | 19,761.49 |
| Charl Schwartzel | 73 | 68 | 79 | 76 | 296 | 19,761.49 |
| Marcel Siem | 70 | 75 | 77 | 75 | 297 | 17,334.64 |
| Gary Orr | 73 | 73 | 74 | 77 | 297 | 17,334.64 |
| Henrik Nystrom | 75 | 72 | 73 | 77 | 297 | 17,334.64 |
| Marcus Fraser | 77 | 70 | 72 | 78 | 297 | 17,334.64 |
| Roger Chapman | 69 | 74 | 78 | 77 | 298 | 14,561.10 |
| Paul Eales | 73 | 71 | 76 | 78 | 298 | 14,561.10 |
| Stephen Dodd | 74 | 70 | 76 | 78 | 298 | 14,561.10 |
| Ricardo Gonzalez | 74 | 71 | 76 | 77 | 298 | 14,561.10 |
| Anders Hansen | 70 | 70 | 80 | 79 | 299 | 12,480.94 |
| David Carter | 75 | 67 | 78 | 79 | 299 | 12,480.94 |
| Sven Struver | 71 | 74 | 75 | 80 | 300 | 10,863.04 |
| Johan Skold | 76 | 69 | 78 | 77 | 300 | 10,863.04 |
| Mads Vibe-Hastrup | 75 | 69 | 77 | 79 | 300 | 10,863.04 |
| Soren Kjeldsen | 72 | 76 | 77 | 76 | 301 | 9,360.70 |
| Paul Lawrie | 71 | 77 | 79 | 74 | 301 | 9,360.70 |
| Stephen Gallacher | 76 | 71 | 74 | 80 | 301 | 9,360.70 |
| Alastair Forsyth | 76 | 69 | 77 | 79 | 301 | 9,360.70 |
| David Griffiths | 73 | 75 | 76 | 77 | 301 | 9,360.70 |
| Jean Van de Velde | 74 | 72 | 74 | 82 | 302 | 8,147.28 |
| David Park | 75 | 70 | 80 | 77 | 302 | 8,147.28 |
| Mark Foster | 70 | 77 | 78 | 78 | 303 | 7,107.20 |
| Gregory Havret | 69 | 73 | 76 | 85 | 303 | 7,107.20 |
| Francois Delamontagne | 67 | 74 | 81 | 81 | 303 | 7,107.20 |
| Oliver Wilson | 73 | 72 | 78 | 80 | 303 | 7,107.20 |
| Leif Westerberg | 75 | 71 | 78 | 82 | 306 | 6,330.91 |
| Philip Golding | 72 | 74 | 79 | 83 | 308 | 5,200 |
| Tom Lehman | 75 | 71 | 79 | 84 | 309 | 5,197 |
| Fernando Roca | 72 | 74 | 84 | 80 | 310 | 5,194 |
| Costantino Rocca | 74 | 74 | 76 | | DQ | |

# JP McManus Pro-Am

*Adare Manor Hotel & Golf Resort,* Co. Limerick, Ireland
Par 36-36–72; 7,138 yards

July 4-5
purse, €500,000

| | SCORES | | TOTAL | MONEY |
|---|---|---|---|---|
| Padraig Harrington | 67 | 63 | 130 | €100,000 |
| Tim Clark | 69 | 67 | 136 | 50,000 |
| Luke Donald | 67 | 70 | 137 | 27,500 |
| Paul Casey | 68 | 69 | 137 | 27,500 |
| Richard Green | 69 | 69 | 138 | 20,000 |
| Ernie Els | 72 | 69 | 141 | 15,857.14 |
| David Higgins | 69 | 72 | 141 | 15,857.14 |
| Scott McCarron | 70 | 71 | 141 | 15,857.14 |
| Michael Campbell | 70 | 71 | 141 | 15,857.14 |
| Jesper Parnevik | 70 | 71 | 141 | 15,857.14 |
| Tiger Woods | 67 | 74 | 141 | 15,857.14 |
| Angel Cabrera | 72 | 69 | 141 | 15,857.14 |
| Trevor Immelman | 64 | 78 | 142 | 9,125 |
| Paul McGinley | 70 | 72 | 142 | 9,125 |
| Tom Lehman | 73 | 69 | 142 | 9,125 |
| Eduardo Romero | 69 | 73 | 142 | 9,125 |
| Graeme McDowell | 69 | 74 | 143 | 4,500 |
| Nick O'Hern | 73 | 70 | 143 | 4,500 |
| Sam Torrance | 72 | 71 | 143 | 4,500 |
| Peter Baker | 70 | 73 | 143 | 4,500 |
| Jarmo Sandelin | 70 | 73 | 143 | 4,500 |
| Darren Clarke | 73 | 71 | 144 | 3,000 |
| John Cook | 74 | 70 | 144 | 3,000 |
| Malcolm Mackenzie | 72 | 73 | 145 | 3,000 |
| Justin Rose | 74 | 71 | 145 | 3,000 |
| Andrew Coltart | 68 | 77 | 145 | 3,000 |
| Peter Lawrie | 71 | 74 | 145 | 3,000 |
| Ian Woosnam | 72 | 73 | 145 | 3,000 |
| Jose Maria Olazabal | 71 | 74 | 145 | 3,000 |
| Davis Love | 72 | 73 | 145 | 3,000 |
| Fred Funk | 73 | 72 | 145 | 3,000 |
| Stuart Appleby | 71 | 74 | 145 | 3,000 |
| Jerry Kelly | 75 | 70 | 145 | 3,000 |
| Thomas Bjorn | 79 | 67 | 146 | 3,000 |
| Roger Chapman | 75 | 71 | 146 | 3,000 |
| Lee Janzen | 74 | 72 | 146 | 3,000 |
| Ben Curtis | 72 | 74 | 146 | 3,000 |
| Colin Montgomerie | 73 | 73 | 146 | 3,000 |
| Fred Couples | 74 | 73 | 147 | 3,000 |
| Ian Poulter | 72 | 75 | 147 | 3,000 |
| Sandy Lyle | 72 | 75 | 147 | 3,000 |
| Lee Westwood | 70 | 77 | 147 | 3,000 |
| Jean Van de Velde | 73 | 74 | 147 | 3,000 |
| Philip Walton | 74 | 73 | 147 | 3,000 |
| Robert Allenby | 72 | 75 | 147 | 3,000 |
| Miguel Angel Jimenez | 75 | 74 | 149 | 3,000 |
| Mark O'Meara | 76 | 74 | 150 | 3,000 |
| Eamonn Darcy | 73 | 79 | 152 | 3,000 |
| Paul Broadhurst | 75 | 77 | 152 | 3,000 |
| Steve Webster | 73 | 79 | 152 | 3,000 |
| Greg Owen | 79 | 74 | 153 | 3,000 |
| Laura Davies | 77 | 76 | 153 | 3,000 |
| Christy O'Connor, Jr. | 76 | 80 | 156 | 3,000 |
| Rich Beem | 78 | 78 | 156 | 3,000 |

| | SCORES | | | TOTAL | MONEY |
|---|---|---|---|---|---|
| Gary Murphy | 82 | 78 | | 160 | 3,000 |
| Richard Boxall | | | | WD | 3,000 |

## Barclays Scottish Open

*Loch Lomond Golf Club,* Glasgow, Scotland
Par 36-35–71; 7,113 yards

July 7-10
purse, €3,564,990

| | SCORES | | | | TOTAL | MONEY |
|---|---|---|---|---|---|---|
| Tim Clark | 67 | 66 | 65 | 67 | 265 | €592,388 |
| Maarten Lafeber | 67 | 63 | 68 | 69 | 267 | 308,708.20 |
| Darren Clarke | 67 | 65 | 69 | 66 | 267 | 308,708.20 |
| Ian Poulter | 69 | 67 | 67 | 65 | 268 | 177,716.40 |
| Angel Cabrera | 64 | 67 | 68 | 70 | 269 | 127,244.94 |
| Luke Donald | 68 | 67 | 67 | 67 | 269 | 127,244.94 |
| Nick Dougherty | 66 | 69 | 67 | 67 | 269 | 127,244.94 |
| Miguel Angel Jimenez | 67 | 69 | 66 | 68 | 270 | 79,853.90 |
| Peter Hedblom | 67 | 68 | 68 | 67 | 270 | 79,853.90 |
| Alastair Forsyth | 68 | 64 | 67 | 71 | 270 | 79,853.90 |
| Ernie Els | 70 | 66 | 67 | 68 | 271 | 65,399.64 |
| Gary Orr | 68 | 65 | 71 | 68 | 272 | 59,179.56 |
| Adam Scott | 70 | 67 | 64 | 71 | 272 | 59,179.56 |
| Trevor Immelman | 74 | 66 | 65 | 68 | 273 | 51,182.32 |
| Henrik Stenson | 66 | 70 | 67 | 70 | 273 | 51,182.32 |
| Francesco Molinari | 70 | 66 | 68 | 69 | 273 | 51,182.32 |
| Fredrik Jacobson | 71 | 67 | 69 | 66 | 273 | 51,182.32 |
| Anthony Wall | 69 | 66 | 71 | 68 | 274 | 43,451.66 |
| Colin Montgomerie | 68 | 69 | 66 | 71 | 274 | 43,451.66 |
| David Lynn | 69 | 68 | 67 | 70 | 274 | 43,451.66 |
| Simon Dyson | 71 | 64 | 70 | 69 | 274 | 43,451.66 |
| Simon Khan | 67 | 67 | 70 | 71 | 275 | 39,097.61 |
| Greg Owen | 67 | 66 | 72 | 70 | 275 | 39,097.61 |
| Richard Finch | 68 | 71 | 68 | 68 | 275 | 39,097.61 |
| Jose Maria Olazabal | 68 | 69 | 69 | 70 | 276 | 34,832.41 |
| Paul Broadhurst | 73 | 65 | 65 | 73 | 276 | 34,832.41 |
| Richard Bland | 69 | 70 | 68 | 69 | 276 | 34,832.41 |
| David Drysdale | 67 | 69 | 70 | 70 | 276 | 34,832.41 |
| Lee Westwood | 65 | 69 | 72 | 70 | 276 | 34,832.41 |
| Mark Roe | 68 | 71 | 70 | 68 | 277 | 27,763.25 |
| Robert-Jan Derksen | 69 | 67 | 67 | 74 | 277 | 27,763.25 |
| Phillip Archer | 70 | 67 | 72 | 68 | 277 | 27,763.25 |
| Jonathan Lomas | 67 | 65 | 72 | 73 | 277 | 27,763.25 |
| Niclas Fasth | 69 | 70 | 69 | 69 | 277 | 27,763.25 |
| Tom Lehman | 66 | 69 | 71 | 71 | 277 | 27,763.25 |
| Terry Price | 69 | 68 | 67 | 73 | 277 | 27,763.25 |
| Thongchai Jaidee | 66 | 69 | 66 | 76 | 277 | 27,763.25 |
| Richard Sterne | 65 | 68 | 74 | 70 | 277 | 27,763.25 |
| Klas Eriksson | 68 | 70 | 68 | 72 | 278 | 22,392.27 |
| Andrew McLardy | 71 | 69 | 69 | 69 | 278 | 22,392.27 |
| John Bickerton | 71 | 69 | 72 | 66 | 278 | 22,392.27 |
| Christopher Hanell | 69 | 69 | 69 | 71 | 278 | 22,392.27 |
| Ben Mason | 72 | 65 | 68 | 73 | 278 | 22,392.27 |
| Eduardo Romero | 70 | 67 | 71 | 71 | 279 | 18,482.51 |
| Scott Henderson | 72 | 68 | 70 | 69 | 279 | 18,482.51 |
| Robert Allenby | 68 | 67 | 75 | 69 | 279 | 18,482.51 |
| Phil Mickelson | 67 | 72 | 71 | 69 | 279 | 18,482.51 |
| Retief Goosen | 71 | 67 | 71 | 70 | 279 | 18,482.51 |

|  | SCORES | | | TOTAL | MONEY |
|---|---|---|---|---|---|
| Marcus Fraser | 69 | 69 69 | 72 | 279 | 18,482.51 |
| Garry Houston | 70 | 69 69 | 72 | 280 | 14,572.75 |
| Thomas Levet | 71 | 68 71 | 70 | 280 | 14,572.75 |
| Philip Golding | 70 | 66 72 | 72 | 280 | 14,572.75 |
| Christian Cevaer | 71 | 69 72 | 68 | 280 | 14,572.75 |
| Gregory Bourdy | 66 | 72 71 | 71 | 280 | 14,572.75 |
| Ricardo Gonzalez | 68 | 70 72 | 71 | 281 | 12,084.72 |
| Stephen Gallacher | 68 | 70 74 | 69 | 281 | 12,084.72 |
| Simon Wakefield | 70 | 68 67 | 77 | 282 | 11,018.42 |
| Miguel Angel Martin | 66 | 73 71 | 73 | 283 | 9,774.40 |
| Scott Drummond | 72 | 67 71 | 73 | 283 | 9,774.40 |
| Paul Lawrie | 65 | 71 71 | 76 | 283 | 9,774.40 |
| David Griffiths | 69 | 69 73 | 72 | 283 | 9,774.40 |
| Jamie Donaldson | 71 | 65 75 | 72 | 283 | 9,774.40 |
| Gonzalo Fernandez-Castano | 73 | 67 71 | 72 | 283 | 9,774.40 |
| Oliver Wilson | 69 | 69 72 | 74 | 284 | 8,530.39 |
| Peter Gustafsson | 69 | 70 72 | 74 | 285 | 8,174.95 |
| Jamie Spence | 73 | 67 74 | 72 | 286 | 7,641.81 |
| Stuart Little | 64 | 73 73 | 76 | 286 | 7,641.81 |
| Raphael Jacquelin | 72 | 68 69 | 78 | 287 | 6,782.84 |
| Rolf Muntz | 69 | 69 73 | 76 | 287 | 6,782.84 |
| Louis Oosthuizen | 70 | 70 73 | 74 | 287 | 6,782.84 |
| Kenneth Ferrie | 67 | 71 79 | 71 | 288 | 5,331 |
| David Carter | 68 | 68 79 | 74 | 289 | 5,328 |

## The Open Championship

*The Old Course*, St. Andrews, Scotland
Par 36-36–72; 7,279 yards

July 14-17
purse, €5,607,600

|  | SCORES | | | TOTAL | MONEY |
|---|---|---|---|---|---|
| Tiger Woods | 66 | 67 71 | 70 | 274 | €1,047,362 |
| Colin Montgomerie | 71 | 66 70 | 72 | 279 | 625,508.10 |
| Jose Maria Olazabal | 68 | 70 68 | 74 | 280 | 352,757.50 |
| Fred Couples | 68 | 71 73 | 68 | 280 | 352,757.50 |
| Bernhard Langer | 71 | 69 70 | 71 | 281 | 177,712.20 |
| Sergio Garcia | 70 | 69 69 | 73 | 281 | 177,712.20 |
| Geoff Ogilvy | 71 | 74 67 | 69 | 281 | 177,712.20 |
| Vijay Singh | 69 | 69 71 | 72 | 281 | 177,712.20 |
| Retief Goosen | 68 | 73 66 | 74 | 281 | 177,712.20 |
| Michael Campbell | 69 | 72 68 | 72 | 281 | 177,712.20 |
| Nick Faldo | 74 | 69 70 | 69 | 282 | 97,099.22 |
| Ian Poulter | 70 | 72 71 | 69 | 282 | 97,099.22 |
| Kenny Perry | 71 | 71 68 | 72 | 282 | 97,099.22 |
| Graeme McDowell | 69 | 72 74 | 67 | 282 | 97,099.22 |
| David Frost | 77 | 65 72 | 69 | 283 | 67,330.44 |
| Nick O'Hern | 73 | 69 71 | 70 | 283 | 67,330.44 |
| Trevor Immelman | 68 | 70 73 | 72 | 283 | 67,330.44 |
| Darren Clarke | 73 | 70 67 | 73 | 283 | 67,330.44 |
| John Daly | 71 | 69 70 | 73 | 283 | 67,330.44 |
| Mark Hensby | 67 | 77 69 | 70 | 283 | 67,330.44 |
| *Lloyd Saltman | 73 | 71 68 | 71 | 283 | |
| Sean O'Hair | 73 | 67 70 | 73 | 283 | 67,330.44 |
| Brad Faxon | 72 | 66 70 | 76 | 284 | 47,276.77 |
| Scott Drummond | 74 | 71 69 | 70 | 284 | 47,276.77 |
| Scott Verplank | 68 | 70 72 | 74 | 284 | 47,276.77 |
| Tom Lehman | 75 | 69 70 | 70 | 284 | 47,276.77 |

| | SCORES | | | | TOTAL | MONEY |
|---|---|---|---|---|---|---|
| Tim Clark | 71 | 69 | 70 | 74 | 284 | 47,276.77 |
| *Eric Ramsay | 68 | 74 | 74 | 68 | 284 | |
| Nick Flanagan | 73 | 71 | 69 | 71 | 284 | 47,276.77 |
| Bart Bryant | 69 | 70 | 71 | 74 | 284 | 47,276.77 |
| Tadahiro Takayama | 72 | 72 | 70 | 70 | 284 | 47,276.77 |
| Sandy Lyle | 74 | 67 | 69 | 75 | 285 | 38,548.75 |
| Richard Green | 72 | 68 | 72 | 73 | 285 | 38,548.75 |
| Peter Hanson | 72 | 72 | 71 | 71 | 286 | 32,002.74 |
| Henrik Stenson | 74 | 67 | 73 | 72 | 286 | 32,002.74 |
| Thomas Levet | 69 | 71 | 75 | 71 | 286 | 32,002.74 |
| Ernie Els | 74 | 67 | 75 | 70 | 286 | 32,002.74 |
| Simon Dyson | 70 | 71 | 72 | 73 | 286 | 32,002.74 |
| Adam Scott | 70 | 71 | 70 | 75 | 286 | 32,002.74 |
| Joe Ogilvie | 74 | 70 | 73 | 69 | 286 | 32,002.74 |
| Tom Watson | 75 | 70 | 70 | 72 | 287 | 21,786.99 |
| Maarten Lafeber | 73 | 70 | 67 | 77 | 287 | 21,786.99 |
| Steve Webster | 71 | 72 | 71 | 73 | 287 | 21,786.99 |
| Tim Herron | 73 | 72 | 68 | 74 | 287 | 21,786.99 |
| Stuart Appleby | 72 | 68 | 72 | 75 | 287 | 21,786.99 |
| K.J. Choi | 75 | 68 | 71 | 73 | 287 | 21,786.99 |
| Bob Tway | 69 | 71 | 72 | 75 | 287 | 21,786.99 |
| Soren Hansen | 72 | 72 | 66 | 77 | 287 | 21,786.99 |
| Paul McGinley | 70 | 75 | 73 | 69 | 287 | 21,786.99 |
| Simon Khan | 69 | 70 | 78 | 70 | 287 | 21,786.99 |
| Hiroyuki Fujita | 72 | 68 | 74 | 73 | 287 | 21,786.99 |
| Justin Leonard | 73 | 71 | 75 | 69 | 288 | 15,901.36 |
| Miguel Angel Jimenez | 69 | 72 | 76 | 71 | 288 | 15,901.36 |
| Paul Lawrie | 72 | 71 | 75 | 70 | 288 | 15,901.36 |
| Fredrik Jacobson | 71 | 70 | 72 | 75 | 288 | 15,901.36 |
| Robert Allenby | 70 | 68 | 79 | 71 | 288 | 15,901.36 |
| Luke Donald | 68 | 73 | 77 | 70 | 288 | 15,901.36 |
| Bo Van Pelt | 72 | 67 | 73 | 76 | 288 | 15,901.36 |
| Thongchai Jaidee | 73 | 68 | 75 | 72 | 288 | 15,901.36 |
| Greg Norman | 72 | 71 | 70 | 76 | 289 | 14,546.70 |
| Mark Calcavecchia | 70 | 73 | 73 | 73 | 289 | 14,546.70 |
| Phil Mickelson | 74 | 67 | 72 | 76 | 289 | 14,546.70 |
| John Bickerton | 75 | 70 | 71 | 73 | 289 | 14,546.70 |
| *Edoardo Molinari | 70 | 70 | 74 | 75 | 289 | |
| Tino Schuster | 68 | 74 | 74 | 73 | 289 | 14,546.70 |
| Peter Lonard | 68 | 70 | 77 | 75 | 290 | 14,110.30 |
| David Smail | 73 | 72 | 69 | 77 | 291 | 13,601.16 |
| Duffy Waldorf | 74 | 68 | 81 | 68 | 291 | 13,601.16 |
| Chris Riley | 68 | 73 | 75 | 75 | 291 | 13,601.16 |
| Robert Rock | 73 | 71 | 75 | 72 | 291 | 13,601.16 |
| Chris DiMarco | 75 | 69 | 71 | 76 | 291 | 13,601.16 |
| Pat Perez | 72 | 70 | 72 | 77 | 291 | 13,601.16 |
| Patrik Sjoland | 74 | 71 | 76 | 71 | 292 | 13,092.03 |
| Ted Purdy | 72 | 72 | 77 | 72 | 293 | 12,801.10 |
| S.K. Ho | 73 | 71 | 72 | 77 | 293 | 12,801.10 |
| Scott Gutschewski | 76 | 69 | 75 | 73 | 293 | 12,801.10 |
| Steve Flesch | 74 | 70 | 72 | 78 | 294 | 12,510.16 |
| Rodney Pampling | 74 | 71 | 71 | 80 | 296 | 12,291.96 |
| Graeme Storm | 75 | 70 | 80 | 71 | 296 | 12,291.96 |
| *Matthew Richardson | 75 | 69 | 77 | 76 | 297 | |

**Out of Final 36 Holes**

| | | | | | | |
|---|---|---|---|---|---|---|
| Peter Fowler | 74 | 72 | | | 146 | 4,364.01 |
| Mark O'Meara | 71 | 75 | | | 146 | 4,364.01 |
| Peter Baker | 70 | 76 | | | 146 | 4,364.01 |

# Women's Tours

Annika Sorenstam posted 11 worldwide victories including two major championships.

Birdie Kim won the U.S. Women's Open.

Morgan Pressel challenged in the Open.

Paula Creamer won four tournaments.

Lorena Ochoa took the Rochester title.

Robert Laberge/Getty Images

Michelle Wie, age 16, became a professional.

Scott Halleran/Getty Images

Cristie Kerr was the Michelob champion.

Warren Little/Getty Images

Jeong Jang won the Weetabix British title.

Koichi Kamoshida/Getty Images

Ai Miyazato led the Japan LPGA Tour.

Natalie Gulbis was sixth on the money list.

Marisa Baena won the HSBC Match Play.

Meena Lee won the Canadian Women's Open.

Yuri Fudoh won six times in Japan.

Gloria Park finished ninth on the LPGA money list.

Hee-Won Han took the Office Depot title.

Catriona Matthew was 10th on the money list.

Candie Kung had seven top-10 finishes.

# Senior Tours

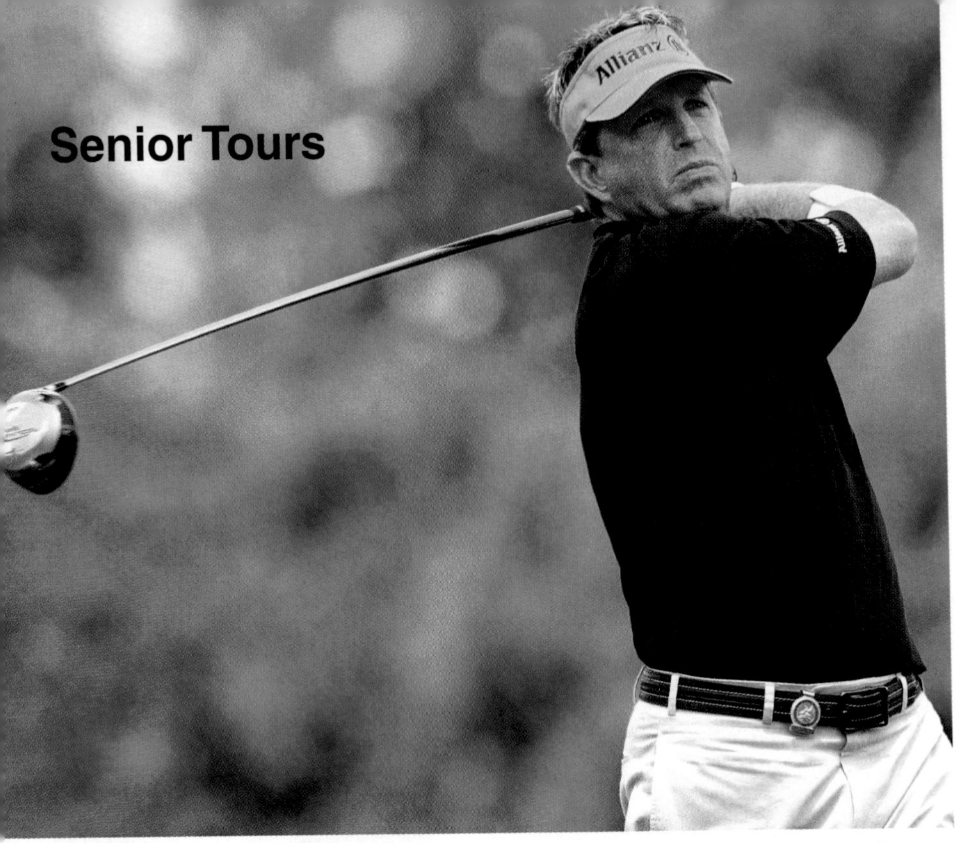


Andy Lyons/Getty Images

Dana Quigley led the U.S. Champions Tour, earning $2.1 million, along with two victories.

Scott Halleran/Getty Images

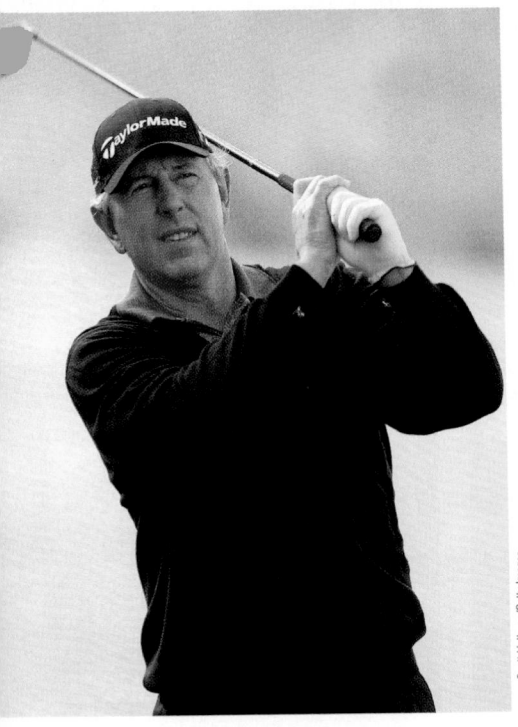

Hale Irwin won four times.

Lisa Blumenfeld/Getty Images

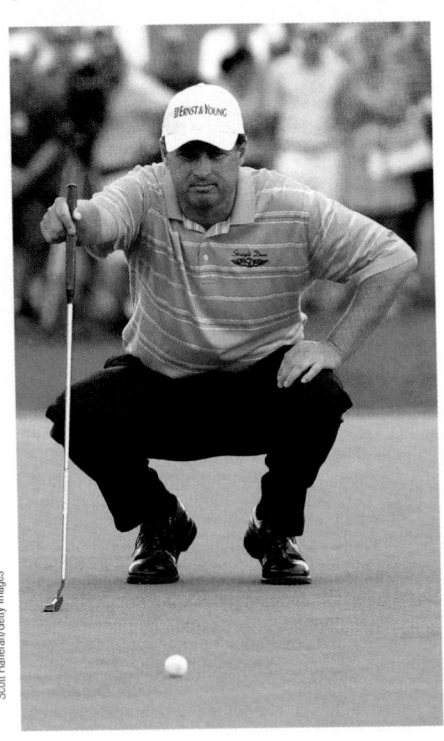

Loren Roberts was champion at the Tradition.

Craig Stadler didn't win but took second twice.

Mark McNulty was third in the money.

Jay Haas claimed two senior victories.

Mike Reid was Senior PGA champion.

Allen Doyle won the U.S. Senior Open.

Peter Jacobsen took the Ford Senior Players.

Tom Watson was the Senior British winner.

D.A. Weibring placed fourth on the money list.

| | SCORES | | TOTAL | MONEY |
|---|---|---|---|---|
| Joe Durant | 79 | 67 | 146 | 4,364.01 |
| Alex Cejka | 74 | 72 | 146 | 4,364.01 |
| Stephen Dodd | 75 | 71 | 146 | 4,364.01 |
| Thomas Bjorn | 72 | 74 | 146 | 4,364.01 |
| Lee Westwood | 76 | 70 | 146 | 4,364.01 |
| Daniel Chopra | 76 | 70 | 146 | 4,364.01 |
| Euan Walters | 72 | 74 | 146 | 4,364.01 |
| Charles Howell | 71 | 75 | 146 | 4,364.01 |
| Jack Nicklaus | 75 | 72 | 147 | 3,636.68 |
| Jean-Francois Remesy | 73 | 74 | 147 | 3,636.68 |
| Mardan Mamat | 75 | 72 | 147 | 3,636.68 |
| Jerry Kelly | 74 | 73 | 147 | 3,636.68 |
| Danny Chia | 74 | 73 | 147 | 3,636.68 |
| Alastair Forsyth | 77 | 70 | 147 | 3,636.68 |
| Y.E. Yang | 76 | 71 | 147 | 3,636.68 |
| Zach Johnson | 77 | 70 | 147 | 3,636.68 |
| Andrew Oldcorn | 76 | 72 | 148 | 3,636.68 |
| Ian Woosnam | 73 | 75 | 148 | 3,636.68 |
| Nick Price | 76 | 72 | 148 | 3,636.68 |
| Brian Davis | 77 | 71 | 148 | 3,636.68 |
| Fred Funk | 77 | 71 | 148 | 3,636.68 |
| Jim Furyk | 78 | 70 | 148 | 3,636.68 |
| Joakim Haeggman | 75 | 73 | 148 | 3,636.68 |
| Ignacio Garrido | 71 | 77 | 148 | 3,636.68 |
| Todd Hamilton | 74 | 74 | 148 | 3,636.68 |
| Shaun Micheel | 75 | 73 | 148 | 3,636.68 |
| Tom Byrum | 79 | 69 | 148 | 3,636.68 |
| Charl Schwartzel | 76 | 72 | 148 | 3,636.68 |
| Ben Curtis | 78 | 70 | 148 | 3,636.68 |
| Jason Allred | 74 | 74 | 148 | 3,636.68 |
| Stewart Cink | 76 | 73 | 149 | 3,273.01 |
| Kenneth Ferrie | 74 | 75 | 149 | 3,273.01 |
| Shigeki Maruyama | 77 | 72 | 149 | 3,273.01 |
| Davis Love | 75 | 74 | 149 | 3,273.01 |
| Lars Brovold | 75 | 74 | 149 | 3,273.01 |
| Angel Cabrera | 75 | 74 | 149 | 3,273.01 |
| Scott Hend | 73 | 76 | 149 | 3,273.01 |
| Martin Doyle | 73 | 76 | 149 | 3,273.01 |
| David Diaz | 74 | 75 | 149 | 3,273.01 |
| Jean Van de Velde | 77 | 73 | 150 | 3,273.01 |
| Robert Coles | 76 | 74 | 150 | 3,273.01 |
| Stephen Ames | 76 | 74 | 150 | 3,273.01 |
| Doug McGuigan | 74 | 76 | 150 | 3,273.01 |
| Paul Casey | 75 | 75 | 150 | 3,273.01 |
| Mike Weir | 76 | 75 | 151 | 3,273.01 |
| Andre Bossert | 74 | 77 | 151 | 3,273.01 |
| Murray Urquhart | 73 | 78 | 151 | 3,273.01 |
| Chad Campbell | 78 | 73 | 151 | 3,273.01 |
| Rory Sabbatini | 72 | 79 | 151 | 3,273.01 |
| *Oscar Floren | 73 | 78 | 151 | |
| Rich Barcelo | 80 | 71 | 151 | 3,273.01 |
| Peter Lawrie | 74 | 78 | 152 | 2,909.34 |
| Craig Parry | 78 | 74 | 152 | 2,909.34 |
| Wilhelm Schauman | 81 | 71 | 152 | 2,909.34 |
| Tim Petrovic | 77 | 75 | 152 | 2,909.34 |
| Toru Taniguchi | 75 | 78 | 153 | 2,909.34 |
| Andrew Butterfield | 77 | 76 | 153 | 2,909.34 |
| Stephen Gallacher | 75 | 78 | 153 | 2,909.34 |
| Rich Beem | 74 | 79 | 153 | 2,909.34 |
| Sean McDonagh | 77 | 76 | 153 | 2,909.34 |

| | SCORES | | TOTAL | MONEY |
|---|---|---|---|---|
| Marcus Fraser | 78 | 75 | 153 | 2,909.34 |
| *Robert Steele | 78 | 75 | 153 | |
| *Brian McElhinney | 78 | 75 | 153 | |
| Tony Jacklin | 79 | 76 | 155 | 2,909.34 |
| Chris Campbell | 81 | 74 | 155 | 2,909.34 |
| David Duval | 80 | 77 | 157 | 2,909.34 |
| Tom Pernice | 78 | 79 | 157 | 2,909.34 |
| John Wade | 76 | 82 | 158 | 2,909.34 |
| Andrew Marshall | 84 | 74 | 158 | 2,909.34 |
| Richard Moir | 83 | 75 | 158 | 2,909.34 |
| Pete Oakley | 81 | 78 | 159 | 2,909.34 |
| Thammanoon Srirot | 84 | 77 | 161 | 2,909.34 |
| David Toms | | | DQ | 2,909.34 |

## Deutsche Bank Players' Championship of Europe

*Gut Kaden*, Hamburg, Germany                                    July 21-24
Par 36-36–72; 7,290 yards                              purse, €3,300,000

| | SCORES | | | | TOTAL | MONEY |
|---|---|---|---|---|---|---|
| Niclas Fasth | 68 | 66 | 72 | 68 | 274 | €550,000 |
| Angel Cabrera | 69 | 70 | 68 | 67 | 274 | 366,660 |
| (Fasth defeated Cabrera on third playoff hole.) | | | | | | |
| John Daly | 74 | 64 | 73 | 65 | 276 | 185,790 |
| Stephen Gallacher | 68 | 71 | 68 | 69 | 276 | 185,790 |
| Bernhard Langer | 72 | 68 | 69 | 68 | 277 | 109,230 |
| Peter Lawrie | 71 | 65 | 70 | 71 | 277 | 109,230 |
| Bradley Dredge | 66 | 69 | 69 | 73 | 277 | 109,230 |
| Graeme Storm | 70 | 71 | 69 | 67 | 277 | 109,230 |
| K.J. Choi | 67 | 71 | 69 | 71 | 278 | 66,880 |
| Henrik Stenson | 65 | 72 | 69 | 72 | 278 | 66,880 |
| Richard Sterne | 70 | 70 | 67 | 71 | 278 | 66,880 |
| Nick Dougherty | 69 | 70 | 68 | 73 | 280 | 54,945 |
| Steven O'Hara | 68 | 70 | 69 | 73 | 280 | 54,945 |
| Anthony Wall | 71 | 71 | 68 | 71 | 281 | 45,595 |
| Thomas Levet | 68 | 74 | 73 | 66 | 281 | 45,595 |
| Emanuele Canonica | 70 | 69 | 69 | 73 | 281 | 45,595 |
| Pierre Fulke | 67 | 73 | 74 | 67 | 281 | 45,595 |
| Michael Campbell | 65 | 71 | 71 | 74 | 281 | 45,595 |
| Wade Ormsby | 66 | 73 | 69 | 73 | 281 | 45,595 |
| Marcel Siem | 67 | 71 | 72 | 72 | 282 | 39,600 |
| Mark Roe | 68 | 69 | 74 | 72 | 283 | 35,805 |
| Fredrik Henge | 68 | 74 | 71 | 70 | 283 | 35,805 |
| Joakim Backstrom | 67 | 73 | 69 | 74 | 283 | 35,805 |
| David Lynn | 70 | 72 | 72 | 69 | 283 | 35,805 |
| Andrew Coltart | 69 | 73 | 72 | 69 | 283 | 35,805 |
| Alastair Forsyth | 68 | 74 | 69 | 72 | 283 | 35,805 |
| Peter Hanson | 71 | 69 | 74 | 70 | 284 | 29,370 |
| Ian Poulter | 69 | 73 | 74 | 68 | 284 | 29,370 |
| Richard Bland | 70 | 70 | 74 | 70 | 284 | 29,370 |
| Robert Coles | 71 | 71 | 73 | 69 | 284 | 29,370 |
| David Park | 72 | 68 | 68 | 76 | 284 | 29,370 |
| Graeme McDowell | 69 | 72 | 70 | 73 | 284 | 29,370 |
| Louis Oosthuizen | 69 | 73 | 74 | 68 | 284 | 29,370 |
| Zhang Lian-wei | 69 | 72 | 72 | 72 | 285 | 23,760 |
| Brian Davis | 71 | 67 | 72 | 75 | 285 | 23,760 |
| Sam Little | 75 | 67 | 70 | 73 | 285 | 23,760 |

|  | SCORES | | | TOTAL | MONEY |
|---|---|---|---|---|---|
| Marc Cayeux | 69 | 72 | 74 | 70 | 285 | 23,760 |
| David Carter | 73 | 69 | 69 | 74 | 285 | 23,760 |
| Francois Delamontagne | 71 | 71 | 73 | 70 | 285 | 23,760 |
| Padraig Harrington | 70 | 71 | 76 | 69 | 286 | 20,790 |
| Jose Manuel Lara | 72 | 70 | 72 | 72 | 286 | 20,790 |
| Joakim Haeggman | 71 | 70 | 71 | 74 | 286 | 20,790 |
| Anders Hansen | 69 | 69 | 75 | 74 | 287 | 18,480 |
| Maarten Lafeber | 70 | 71 | 76 | 70 | 287 | 18,480 |
| Alessandro Tadini | 66 | 72 | 79 | 70 | 287 | 18,480 |
| Ian Garbutt | 72 | 69 | 73 | 73 | 287 | 18,480 |
| Paul McGinley | 70 | 72 | 72 | 74 | 288 | 16,170 |
| David Drysdale | 69 | 72 | 74 | 73 | 288 | 16,170 |
| David Griffiths | 70 | 71 | 74 | 73 | 288 | 16,170 |
| Mark Foster | 73 | 69 | 69 | 79 | 290 | 14,850 |
| Peter Fowler | 69 | 73 | 73 | 76 | 291 | 14,190 |
| Jean-Francois Remesy | 74 | 67 | 75 | 76 | 292 | 13,200 |
| Damien McGrane | 71 | 71 | 74 | 76 | 292 | 13,200 |
| Stuart Manley | 73 | 69 | 70 | 81 | 293 | 12,210 |

## Scandinavian Masters

*Kungsangen Golf Club*, Stockholm, Sweden
Par 36-35–71; 6,876 yards

July 28-31
purse, €1,600,000

|  | SCORES | | | TOTAL | MONEY |
|---|---|---|---|---|---|
| Mark Hensby | 65 | 68 | 64 | 65 | 262 | €266,660 |
| Henrik Stenson | 67 | 66 | 64 | 65 | 262 | 177,770 |
| (Hensby defeated Stenson on second playoff hole.) | | | | | | |
| Marc Cayeux | 63 | 69 | 68 | 65 | 265 | 90,080 |
| Bradley Dredge | 66 | 63 | 66 | 70 | 265 | 90,080 |
| Pierre Fulke | 67 | 63 | 70 | 68 | 268 | 61,920 |
| Adam Scott | 70 | 65 | 65 | 68 | 268 | 61,920 |
| Barry Lane | 64 | 66 | 65 | 74 | 269 | 38,960 |
| Martin Erlandsson | 69 | 65 | 69 | 66 | 269 | 38,960 |
| Gary Emerson | 69 | 67 | 66 | 67 | 269 | 38,960 |
| Henrik Nystrom | 66 | 65 | 69 | 69 | 269 | 38,960 |
| Zhang Lian-wei | 66 | 69 | 68 | 67 | 270 | 25,546.67 |
| Jean-Francois Remesy | 66 | 65 | 69 | 70 | 270 | 25,546.67 |
| Damien McGrane | 68 | 66 | 64 | 72 | 270 | 25,546.67 |
| Paul Broadhurst | 67 | 68 | 67 | 68 | 270 | 25,546.67 |
| Richard Finch | 71 | 64 | 65 | 70 | 270 | 25,546.67 |
| Wilhelm Schauman | 70 | 68 | 66 | 66 | 270 | 25,546.67 |
| Jamie Donaldson | 68 | 69 | 67 | 67 | 271 | 21,600 |
| Andrew McLardy | 66 | 71 | 65 | 70 | 272 | 18,986.67 |
| Henrik Bjornstad | 67 | 65 | 70 | 70 | 272 | 18,986.67 |
| Jarrod Moseley | 67 | 68 | 67 | 70 | 272 | 18,986.67 |
| Joakim Haeggman | 67 | 71 | 65 | 69 | 272 | 18,986.67 |
| Peter O'Malley | 66 | 68 | 67 | 71 | 272 | 18,986.67 |
| Johan Skold | 67 | 70 | 70 | 65 | 272 | 18,986.67 |
| *Alexander Noren | 69 | 66 | 69 | 68 | 272 | |
| Marten Olander | 68 | 70 | 69 | 66 | 273 | 15,920 |
| Peter Lawrie | 67 | 70 | 69 | 67 | 273 | 15,920 |
| Stuart Little | 69 | 66 | 68 | 70 | 273 | 15,920 |
| Johan Edfors | 67 | 67 | 69 | 70 | 273 | 15,920 |
| Simon Wakefield | 71 | 65 | 68 | 69 | 273 | 15,920 |
| Raymond Russell | 68 | 67 | 72 | 66 | 273 | 15,920 |
| Mark Roe | 70 | 65 | 67 | 72 | 274 | 12,680 |

| | SCORES | | | | TOTAL | MONEY |
|---|---|---|---|---|---|---|
| Mattias Eliasson | 67 | 69 | 70 | 68 | 274 | 12,680 |
| Andrew Marshall | 66 | 70 | 71 | 67 | 274 | 12,680 |
| Sam Little | 71 | 67 | 68 | 68 | 274 | 12,680 |
| Robert Karlsson | 65 | 69 | 71 | 69 | 274 | 12,680 |
| David Lynn | 70 | 65 | 71 | 68 | 274 | 12,680 |
| Fredrik Widmark | 68 | 70 | 69 | 67 | 274 | 12,680 |
| Peter Gustafsson | 71 | 64 | 71 | 68 | 274 | 12,680 |
| *David Palm | 70 | 65 | 72 | 67 | 274 | |
| Gordon Brand, Jr. | 69 | 66 | 71 | 69 | 275 | 10,240 |
| Johan Axgren | 70 | 66 | 71 | 68 | 275 | 10,240 |
| Ignacio Garrido | 74 | 62 | 68 | 71 | 275 | 10,240 |
| Stephen Scahill | 71 | 67 | 65 | 72 | 275 | 10,240 |
| Sam Walker | 67 | 70 | 71 | 67 | 275 | 10,240 |
| Hernan Rey | 69 | 69 | 71 | 66 | 275 | 10,240 |
| Robert-Jan Derksen | 72 | 66 | 69 | 69 | 276 | 8,160 |
| Scott Drummond | 71 | 66 | 71 | 68 | 276 | 8,160 |
| Joakim Backstrom | 68 | 69 | 70 | 69 | 276 | 8,160 |
| Peter Hedblom | 68 | 68 | 70 | 70 | 276 | 8,160 |
| Benoit Teilleria | 70 | 67 | 70 | 69 | 276 | 8,160 |
| Terry Price | 72 | 65 | 68 | 71 | 276 | 8,160 |
| Steven O'Hara | 67 | 70 | 68 | 71 | 276 | 8,160 |
| Ian Garbutt | 66 | 70 | 69 | 72 | 277 | 6,560 |
| Leif Westerberg | 69 | 67 | 69 | 72 | 277 | 6,560 |
| Martin Maritz | 73 | 65 | 67 | 72 | 277 | 6,560 |
| Jesper Parnevik | 71 | 66 | 67 | 74 | 278 | 5,097.14 |
| Fredrik Henge | 67 | 70 | 71 | 70 | 278 | 5,097.14 |
| Rolf Muntz | 71 | 67 | 68 | 72 | 278 | 5,097.14 |
| Gary Orr | 68 | 69 | 69 | 72 | 278 | 5,097.14 |
| Markus Brier | 70 | 66 | 71 | 71 | 278 | 5,097.14 |
| Ben Mason | 69 | 69 | 72 | 68 | 278 | 5,097.14 |
| Jose-Filipe Lima | 68 | 67 | 71 | 72 | 278 | 5,097.14 |
| Andrew Oldcorn | 66 | 68 | 75 | 70 | 279 | 4,080 |
| Richard Bland | 66 | 70 | 70 | 73 | 279 | 4,080 |
| Per-Ulrik Johansson | 66 | 70 | 76 | 67 | 279 | 4,080 |
| Oliver Wilson | 68 | 69 | 73 | 69 | 279 | 4,080 |
| Peter Fowler | 67 | 70 | 72 | 71 | 280 | 3,520 |
| Darren Fichardt | 72 | 66 | 68 | 74 | 280 | 3,520 |
| Andrew Coltart | 69 | 67 | 76 | 68 | 280 | 3,520 |
| Pelle Edberg | 66 | 70 | 78 | 67 | 281 | 3,120 |
| Stuart Manley | 68 | 70 | 73 | 70 | 281 | 3,120 |
| Peter Hanson | 69 | 68 | 69 | 76 | 282 | 2,575.67 |
| Arjun Atwal | 71 | 66 | 71 | 74 | 282 | 2,575.67 |
| Oskar Bergman | 72 | 66 | 70 | 74 | 282 | 2,575.67 |
| Simon Hurd | 69 | 68 | 72 | 74 | 283 | 2,394 |
| Gary Murphy | 68 | 70 | 77 | 72 | 287 | 2,389.50 |
| Phillip Archer | 68 | 70 | 77 | 72 | 287 | 2,389.50 |

## Johnnie Walker Championship at Gleneagles

*Gleneagles Hotel,* Perthshire, Scotland
Par 36-36–72; 7,136 yards

August 4-7
purse, €2,076,061

| | SCORES | | | | TOTAL | MONEY |
|---|---|---|---|---|---|---|
| Emanuele Canonica | 70 | 71 | 69 | 71 | 281 | €338,442.83 |
| Barry Lane | 73 | 74 | 66 | 70 | 283 | 135,095.01 |
| Nicolas Colsaerts | 70 | 71 | 67 | 75 | 283 | 135,095.01 |
| Bradley Dredge | 70 | 72 | 69 | 72 | 283 | 135,095.01 |

| | | SCORES | | | TOTAL | MONEY |
|---|---|---|---|---|---|---|
| David Lynn | 70 | 71 | 73 | 69 | 283 | 135,095.01 |
| Francesco Molinari | 75 | 69 | 71 | 69 | 284 | 65,997.29 |
| Wade Ormsby | 73 | 73 | 66 | 72 | 284 | 65,997.29 |
| Raphael Jacquelin | 75 | 66 | 76 | 68 | 285 | 41,832.13 |
| Steve Webster | 71 | 67 | 74 | 73 | 285 | 41,832.13 |
| Richard Bland | 71 | 71 | 68 | 75 | 285 | 41,832.13 |
| Sam Little | 71 | 68 | 75 | 71 | 285 | 41,832.13 |
| Gary Orr | 77 | 71 | 69 | 68 | 285 | 41,832.13 |
| Santiago Luna | 75 | 68 | 71 | 72 | 286 | 30,561.82 |
| Paul Broadhurst | 71 | 73 | 69 | 73 | 286 | 30,561.82 |
| Jonathan Lomas | 70 | 71 | 73 | 72 | 286 | 30,561.82 |
| Robert Coles | 74 | 72 | 69 | 71 | 286 | 30,561.82 |
| Robert-Jan Derksen | 73 | 71 | 73 | 70 | 287 | 24,943.59 |
| Damien McGrane | 70 | 72 | 69 | 76 | 287 | 24,943.59 |
| Ian Garbutt | 71 | 69 | 72 | 75 | 287 | 24,943.59 |
| Jose-Filipe Lima | 75 | 70 | 76 | 66 | 287 | 24,943.59 |
| Gregory Bourdy | 70 | 69 | 74 | 74 | 287 | 24,943.59 |
| Oliver Wilson | 76 | 71 | 70 | 70 | 287 | 24,943.59 |
| Jamie Spence | 71 | 73 | 70 | 74 | 288 | 21,728.34 |
| Carlos Rodiles | 74 | 72 | 70 | 72 | 288 | 21,728.34 |
| Paul Casey | 71 | 73 | 70 | 74 | 288 | 21,728.34 |
| Sandy Lyle | 73 | 72 | 70 | 74 | 289 | 18,682.31 |
| Andrew McLardy | 76 | 70 | 72 | 71 | 289 | 18,682.31 |
| Fredrik Henge | 72 | 76 | 71 | 70 | 289 | 18,682.31 |
| Robert Karlsson | 70 | 71 | 74 | 74 | 289 | 18,682.31 |
| Paul Lawrie | 74 | 68 | 75 | 72 | 289 | 18,682.31 |
| Raymond Russell | 75 | 71 | 71 | 72 | 289 | 18,682.31 |
| Ben Mason | 71 | 73 | 75 | 70 | 289 | 18,682.31 |
| Mark Foster | 68 | 70 | 77 | 75 | 290 | 15,483.98 |
| David Gilford | 75 | 70 | 73 | 72 | 290 | 15,483.98 |
| Mattias Eliasson | 71 | 72 | 77 | 70 | 290 | 15,483.98 |
| Christopher Doak | 72 | 74 | 69 | 75 | 290 | 15,483.98 |
| Peter Fowler | 76 | 71 | 70 | 74 | 291 | 12,793.32 |
| Gary Murphy | 71 | 76 | 72 | 72 | 291 | 12,793.32 |
| Johan Axgren | 75 | 72 | 70 | 74 | 291 | 12,793.32 |
| Peter Baker | 74 | 74 | 73 | 70 | 291 | 12,793.32 |
| Philip Golding | 73 | 73 | 72 | 73 | 291 | 12,793.32 |
| Miles Tunnicliff | 75 | 69 | 75 | 72 | 291 | 12,793.32 |
| Johan Skold | 71 | 74 | 68 | 78 | 291 | 12,793.32 |
| Richard Finch | 74 | 73 | 74 | 70 | 291 | 12,793.32 |
| Sebastian Fernandez | 73 | 73 | 75 | 70 | 291 | 12,793.32 |
| Malcolm Mackenzie | 73 | 72 | 73 | 74 | 292 | 9,341.16 |
| Anders Hansen | 73 | 74 | 68 | 77 | 292 | 9,341.16 |
| Kenneth Ferrie | 76 | 70 | 73 | 73 | 292 | 9,341.16 |
| Stuart Little | 74 | 74 | 73 | 71 | 292 | 9,341.16 |
| Jarrod Moseley | 75 | 72 | 70 | 75 | 292 | 9,341.16 |
| Simon Wakefield | 71 | 72 | 75 | 74 | 292 | 9,341.16 |
| Andrew Coltart | 74 | 69 | 74 | 75 | 292 | 9,341.16 |
| Terry Price | 76 | 72 | 72 | 72 | 292 | 9,341.16 |
| Mark Roe | 70 | 74 | 78 | 71 | 293 | 6,345.89 |
| Philip Walton | 74 | 73 | 70 | 76 | 293 | 6,345.89 |
| Gary Emerson | 72 | 71 | 73 | 77 | 293 | 6,345.89 |
| Andrew Marshall | 74 | 72 | 72 | 75 | 293 | 6,345.89 |
| Gregory Havret | 75 | 73 | 70 | 75 | 293 | 6,345.89 |
| Paul Eales | 74 | 71 | 75 | 73 | 293 | 6,345.89 |
| Graeme Storm | 72 | 73 | 72 | 76 | 293 | 6,345.89 |
| Alastair Forsyth | 74 | 74 | 69 | 76 | 293 | 6,345.89 |
| Roger Chapman | 71 | 73 | 79 | 71 | 294 | 4,473.96 |
| Andrew Oldcorn | 74 | 73 | 73 | 74 | 294 | 4,473.96 |
| Richard Green | 77 | 71 | 70 | 76 | 294 | 4,473.96 |

| | SCORES | | | | TOTAL | MONEY |
|---|---|---|---|---|---|---|
| Darren Fichardt | 70 | 76 | 73 | 75 | 294 | 4,473.96 |
| Martin Erlandsson | 72 | 70 | 74 | 78 | 294 | 4,473.96 |
| David Drysdale | 79 | 69 | 73 | 73 | 294 | 4,473.96 |
| Mark Sanders | 75 | 73 | 72 | 74 | 294 | 4,473.96 |
| Matthew Morris | 73 | 73 | 73 | 75 | 294 | 4,473.96 |
| Stuart Manley | 76 | 71 | 73 | 74 | 294 | 4,473.96 |
| Christian Cevaer | 73 | 72 | 72 | 78 | 295 | 3,044.50 |
| David Griffiths | 76 | 71 | 69 | 79 | 295 | 3,044.50 |
| Jose Manuel Lara | 74 | 72 | 76 | 74 | 296 | 3,031 |
| Fernando Roca | 72 | 75 | 73 | 76 | 296 | 3,031 |
| Simon Hurd | 73 | 75 | 75 | 73 | 296 | 3,031 |
| Leif Westerberg | 77 | 68 | 74 | 77 | 296 | 3,031 |
| Simon Dyson | 79 | 69 | 76 | 72 | 296 | 3,031 |
| Peter Gustafsson | 74 | 71 | 75 | 76 | 296 | 3,031 |
| Michael Kirk | 70 | 77 | 75 | 74 | 296 | 3,031 |
| Jarmo Sandelin | 75 | 71 | 71 | 80 | 297 | 3,019 |
| Peter Lawrie | 72 | 76 | 71 | 79 | 298 | 3,016 |
| Jose Manuel Carriles | 73 | 75 | 78 | 73 | 299 | 3,011.50 |
| Rolf Muntz | 72 | 76 | 78 | 73 | 299 | 3,011.50 |
| Ignacio Garrido | 72 | 76 | 73 | 79 | 300 | 3,007 |
| Stephen Browne | 75 | 73 | 79 | 74 | 301 | 3,004 |

## Cadillac Russian Open

*Le Meridien Moscow Country Club*, Moscow, Russia  
Par 36-36–72; 7,154 yards

August 11-14  
purse, €405,615

| | SCORES | | | | TOTAL | MONEY |
|---|---|---|---|---|---|---|
| Mikael Lundberg | 67 | 68 | 69 | 69 | 273 | €67,599.75 |
| Andrew Butterfield | 70 | 68 | 69 | 66 | 273 | 45,063.80 |
| (Lundberg defeated Butterfield on fourth playoff hole.) | | | | | | |
| David Drysdale | 67 | 72 | 70 | 67 | 276 | 22,836.11 |
| Jarrod Moseley | 70 | 70 | 68 | 68 | 276 | 22,836.11 |
| Fredrik Widmark | 67 | 67 | 71 | 72 | 277 | 17,198.06 |
| Benn Barham | 73 | 69 | 68 | 68 | 278 | 10,740.68 |
| Sebastien Delagrange | 72 | 67 | 66 | 73 | 278 | 10,740.68 |
| Jesus Maria Arruti | 67 | 70 | 70 | 71 | 278 | 10,740.68 |
| Michele Reale | 71 | 70 | 71 | 66 | 278 | 10,740.68 |
| Shaun Webster | 68 | 68 | 73 | 69 | 278 | 10,740.68 |
| Johan Edfors | 72 | 67 | 70 | 70 | 279 | 7,219.94 |
| Ben Mason | 68 | 68 | 71 | 72 | 279 | 7,219.94 |
| Roger Chapman | 70 | 72 | 69 | 69 | 280 | 5,978.76 |
| Toni Karjalainen | 72 | 72 | 67 | 69 | 280 | 5,978.76 |
| Martin Wiegele | 70 | 69 | 72 | 69 | 280 | 5,978.76 |
| Oliver Whiteley | 71 | 70 | 70 | 69 | 280 | 5,978.76 |
| Jamie Spence | 70 | 74 | 66 | 70 | 280 | 5,978.76 |
| Cesar Monasterio | 72 | 69 | 68 | 72 | 281 | 4,883.60 |
| Peter Whiteford | 70 | 69 | 67 | 75 | 281 | 4,883.60 |
| Michael Jonzon | 72 | 68 | 70 | 71 | 281 | 4,883.60 |
| Tom Whitehouse | 66 | 75 | 69 | 71 | 281 | 4,883.60 |
| Kyron Sullivan | 70 | 70 | 70 | 71 | 281 | 4,883.60 |
| Leif Westerberg | 74 | 68 | 71 | 69 | 282 | 4,218.39 |
| Mark Pilkington | 71 | 70 | 68 | 73 | 282 | 4,218.39 |
| Bertrand Cornut | 69 | 72 | 67 | 74 | 282 | 4,218.39 |
| Andrew Coltart | 72 | 72 | 71 | 67 | 282 | 4,218.39 |
| Michael Hoey | 71 | 73 | 68 | 70 | 282 | 4,218.39 |
| Denny Lucas | 71 | 67 | 73 | 72 | 283 | 3,609.97 |

| | SCORES | | | | TOTAL | MONEY |
|---|---|---|---|---|---|---|
| Anders S. Hansen | 72 | 71 | 69 | 71 | 283 | 3,609.97 |
| Stuart Manley | 75 | 67 | 69 | 72 | 283 | 3,609.97 |
| David Orr | 71 | 69 | 73 | 70 | 283 | 3,609.97 |
| Marc Warren | 74 | 64 | 76 | 69 | 283 | 3,609.97 |
| Carlos De Corral | 73 | 70 | 70 | 71 | 284 | 2,925.50 |
| Benoit Teilleria | 70 | 72 | 69 | 73 | 284 | 2,925.50 |
| Ivo Giner | 70 | 71 | 71 | 72 | 284 | 2,925.50 |
| Hernan Rey | 69 | 70 | 76 | 69 | 284 | 2,925.50 |
| Edward Rush | 71 | 69 | 74 | 70 | 284 | 2,925.50 |
| Ariel Canete | 75 | 69 | 70 | 70 | 284 | 2,925.50 |
| Tomas Jesus Munoz | 72 | 70 | 74 | 68 | 284 | 2,925.50 |
| Iain Pyman | 67 | 72 | 72 | 73 | 284 | 2,925.50 |
| Johan Axgren | 71 | 71 | 72 | 71 | 285 | 2,393.13 |
| Roope Kakko | 72 | 69 | 73 | 71 | 285 | 2,393.13 |
| Steven Jeppesen | 73 | 66 | 71 | 75 | 285 | 2,393.13 |
| Van Phillips | 70 | 70 | 72 | 73 | 285 | 2,393.13 |
| Terry Pilkadaris | 72 | 71 | 67 | 75 | 285 | 2,393.13 |
| Rafael Gomez | 73 | 71 | 71 | 71 | 286 | 1,987.51 |
| Sven Struver | 71 | 71 | 71 | 73 | 286 | 1,987.51 |
| Marcus Higley | 71 | 72 | 70 | 73 | 286 | 1,987.51 |
| Martin Lemesurier | 75 | 68 | 72 | 71 | 286 | 1,987.51 |
| Stephen Browne | 69 | 73 | 71 | 73 | 286 | 1,987.51 |
| Mark Mouland | 75 | 66 | 71 | 75 | 287 | 1,541.34 |
| Jose Manuel Carriles | 68 | 75 | 72 | 72 | 287 | 1,541.34 |
| Jan-Are Larsen | 70 | 73 | 68 | 76 | 287 | 1,541.34 |
| Craig Williams | 68 | 70 | 77 | 72 | 287 | 1,541.34 |
| David Dixon | 69 | 71 | 71 | 76 | 287 | 1,541.34 |
| Titch Moore | 70 | 73 | 71 | 73 | 287 | 1,541.34 |
| Diego Borrego | 73 | 71 | 71 | 73 | 288 | 1,176.28 |
| Andres Romero | 74 | 69 | 70 | 75 | 288 | 1,176.28 |
| Paul Eales | 75 | 69 | 73 | 71 | 288 | 1,176.28 |
| Peter Kaensche | 72 | 72 | 77 | 67 | 288 | 1,176.28 |
| Gareth Davies | 74 | 70 | 69 | 75 | 288 | 1,176.28 |
| Sam Little | 73 | 68 | 74 | 74 | 289 | 1,034.32 |
| Jeppe Huldahl | 69 | 74 | 74 | 72 | 289 | 1,034.32 |
| Julien Van Hauwe | 72 | 68 | 83 | 67 | 290 | 953.19 |
| Paul Dwyer | 74 | 69 | 73 | 74 | 290 | 953.19 |
| Mads Vibe-Hastrup | 73 | 71 | 73 | 74 | 291 | 872.07 |
| Daniel Vancsik | 71 | 73 | 78 | 69 | 291 | 872.07 |
| Niels Kraaij | 72 | 71 | 71 | 78 | 292 | 811.23 |
| Massimo Florioli | 70 | 73 | 81 | 74 | 298 | 770.67 |
| Matt Zapol | 71 | 71 | 79 | | WD | 746.33 |

## BMW International Open

*Golfclub Munchen Nord-Eichenreid*, Munich, Germany
Par 36-36–72; 6,963 yards

August 25-28
purse, €2,000,000

| | SCORES | | | | TOTAL | MONEY |
|---|---|---|---|---|---|---|
| David Howell | 66 | 68 | 66 | 65 | 265 | €333,330 |
| Brett Rumford | 65 | 67 | 69 | 65 | 266 | 173,710 |
| John Daly | 68 | 69 | 65 | 64 | 266 | 173,710 |
| Niclas Fasth | 71 | 68 | 64 | 64 | 267 | 92,400 |
| Soren Kjeldsen | 67 | 69 | 65 | 66 | 267 | 92,400 |
| Paul McGinley | 68 | 69 | 66 | 65 | 268 | 70,000 |
| Simon Dyson | 69 | 68 | 70 | 62 | 269 | 60,000 |
| Simon Khan | 68 | 65 | 68 | 69 | 270 | 50,000 |

| | SCORES | | | | TOTAL | MONEY |
|---|---|---|---|---|---|---|
| Bradley Dredge | 67 | 67 | 69 | 68 | 271 | 42,400 |
| Raphael Jacquelin | 72 | 68 | 64 | 67 | 271 | 42,400 |
| Angel Cabrera | 65 | 68 | 70 | 69 | 272 | 32,680 |
| Peter Lawrie | 70 | 70 | 68 | 64 | 272 | 32,680 |
| K.J. Choi | 70 | 68 | 68 | 66 | 272 | 32,680 |
| Luke Donald | 67 | 65 | 67 | 73 | 272 | 32,680 |
| Ricardo Gonzalez | 67 | 67 | 68 | 70 | 272 | 32,680 |
| Padraig Harrington | 69 | 67 | 70 | 67 | 273 | 27,000 |
| Peter Fowler | 68 | 69 | 69 | 67 | 273 | 27,000 |
| Martin Erlandsson | 68 | 67 | 69 | 69 | 273 | 27,000 |
| Phillip Archer | 66 | 70 | 71 | 67 | 274 | 24,000 |
| Robert Coles | 73 | 67 | 66 | 68 | 274 | 24,000 |
| Peter O'Malley | 67 | 70 | 66 | 71 | 274 | 24,000 |
| Thomas Bjorn | 66 | 71 | 68 | 70 | 275 | 22,300 |
| Miguel Angel Jimenez | 74 | 66 | 67 | 68 | 275 | 22,300 |
| Maarten Lafeber | 66 | 73 | 69 | 68 | 276 | 19,900 |
| Steven O'Hara | 71 | 68 | 69 | 68 | 276 | 19,900 |
| Garry Houston | 68 | 70 | 69 | 69 | 276 | 19,900 |
| Marcel Siem | 67 | 69 | 73 | 67 | 276 | 19,900 |
| David Lynn | 70 | 70 | 66 | 70 | 276 | 19,900 |
| Robert-Jan Derksen | 65 | 69 | 70 | 72 | 276 | 19,900 |
| Emanuele Canonica | 68 | 69 | 75 | 65 | 277 | 16,333.33 |
| Peter Hedblom | 66 | 74 | 65 | 72 | 277 | 16,333.33 |
| Graeme Storm | 66 | 73 | 69 | 69 | 277 | 16,333.33 |
| Nick Dougherty | 72 | 68 | 67 | 70 | 277 | 16,333.33 |
| Jamie Spence | 68 | 70 | 70 | 69 | 277 | 16,333.33 |
| Joakim Backstrom | 70 | 66 | 71 | 70 | 277 | 16,333.33 |
| Mark Foster | 70 | 66 | 69 | 73 | 278 | 14,200 |
| Soren Hansen | 70 | 69 | 73 | 66 | 278 | 14,200 |
| Thongchai Jaidee | 70 | 68 | 71 | 69 | 278 | 14,200 |
| Francois Delamontagne | 69 | 69 | 72 | 69 | 279 | 12,000 |
| Christian Cevaer | 69 | 69 | 70 | 71 | 279 | 12,000 |
| Stephen Gallacher | 69 | 66 | 73 | 71 | 279 | 12,000 |
| Leif Westerberg | 73 | 67 | 70 | 69 | 279 | 12,000 |
| Stuart Little | 67 | 70 | 69 | 73 | 279 | 12,000 |
| Ian Poulter | 66 | 69 | 72 | 72 | 279 | 12,000 |
| Mattias Eliasson | 70 | 68 | 71 | 70 | 279 | 12,000 |
| Nicolas Colsaerts | 70 | 70 | 67 | 72 | 279 | 12,000 |
| David Carter | 70 | 65 | 74 | 71 | 280 | 8,800 |
| David Griffiths | 66 | 71 | 70 | 73 | 280 | 8,800 |
| Paul Broadhurst | 73 | 66 | 73 | 68 | 280 | 8,800 |
| Bernhard Langer | 71 | 69 | 71 | 69 | 280 | 8,800 |
| Joakim Haeggman | 71 | 68 | 68 | 73 | 280 | 8,800 |
| Robert Karlsson | 70 | 67 | 71 | 72 | 280 | 8,800 |
| Jean-Francois Lucquin | 66 | 71 | 72 | 71 | 280 | 8,800 |
| Richard Finch | 71 | 67 | 71 | 71 | 280 | 8,800 |
| Tino Schuster | 70 | 70 | 73 | 68 | 281 | 6,600 |
| Miles Tunnicliff | 72 | 67 | 68 | 74 | 281 | 6,600 |
| Jonathan Lomas | 69 | 66 | 70 | 76 | 281 | 6,600 |
| Gonzalo Fernandez-Castano | 68 | 69 | 72 | 73 | 282 | 5,800 |
| Carlos Rodiles | 74 | 66 | 70 | 72 | 282 | 5,800 |
| Steve Webster | 74 | 66 | 70 | 72 | 282 | 5,800 |
| Mark Roe | 69 | 71 | 69 | 74 | 283 | 5,200 |
| Klas Eriksson | 70 | 70 | 74 | 69 | 283 | 5,200 |
| Gary Murphy | 69 | 71 | 68 | 75 | 283 | 5,200 |
| Jose Manuel Lara | 69 | 67 | 75 | 73 | 284 | 4,700 |
| Wade Ormsby | 72 | 67 | 75 | 70 | 284 | 4,700 |
| Scott Drummond | 68 | 72 | 70 | 75 | 285 | 4,400 |
| Ian Garbutt | 72 | 67 | 73 | 74 | 286 | 4,200 |
| Andrew Oldcorn | 70 | 70 | 75 | 72 | 287 | 4,000 |

| | SCORES | | | | TOTAL | MONEY |
|---|---|---|---|---|---|---|
| Alastair Forsyth | 70 | 67 | 75 | 77 | 289 | 3,725 |
| Jarmo Sandelin | 74 | 66 | 77 | 72 | 289 | 3,725 |

## Omega European Masters

*Crans-sur-Sierre Golf Club*, Crans Montana, Switzerland
Par 36-35–71; 6,857 yards

September 1-4
purse, €1,700,000

| | SCORES | | | | TOTAL | MONEY |
|---|---|---|---|---|---|---|
| Sergio Garcia | 66 | 65 | 71 | 68 | 270 | €283,330 |
| Peter Gustafsson | 69 | 70 | 68 | 64 | 271 | 188,880 |
| Paul Casey | 67 | 72 | 67 | 66 | 272 | 106,420 |
| Luke Donald | 66 | 72 | 66 | 69 | 273 | 78,540 |
| Garry Houston | 65 | 69 | 69 | 70 | 273 | 78,540 |
| Pierre Fulke | 69 | 67 | 70 | 68 | 274 | 59,500 |
| Philip Golding | 68 | 73 | 66 | 68 | 275 | 46,750 |
| Stuart Little | 69 | 70 | 69 | 67 | 275 | 46,750 |
| Jamie Spence | 71 | 70 | 70 | 65 | 276 | 33,150 |
| Paul Broadhurst | 67 | 69 | 71 | 69 | 276 | 33,150 |
| Steven O'Hara | 70 | 69 | 70 | 67 | 276 | 33,150 |
| Emanuele Canonica | 71 | 68 | 69 | 68 | 276 | 33,150 |
| Miguel Angel Jimenez | 71 | 69 | 67 | 70 | 277 | 26,690 |
| Henrik Stenson | 70 | 68 | 69 | 70 | 277 | 26,690 |
| Damien McGrane | 68 | 71 | 74 | 65 | 278 | 24,480 |
| Bradley Dredge | 72 | 68 | 67 | 71 | 278 | 24,480 |
| Francesco Molinari | 73 | 66 | 69 | 71 | 279 | 20,881.67 |
| Robert Karlsson | 70 | 68 | 71 | 70 | 279 | 20,881.67 |
| Jarmo Sandelin | 65 | 73 | 71 | 70 | 279 | 20,881.67 |
| Christian Cevaer | 67 | 71 | 70 | 71 | 279 | 20,881.67 |
| Maarten Lafeber | 69 | 74 | 65 | 71 | 279 | 20,881.67 |
| Andrew McLardy | 69 | 73 | 68 | 69 | 279 | 20,881.67 |
| Ricardo Gonzalez | 74 | 67 | 70 | 69 | 280 | 17,170 |
| Peter Lawrie | 68 | 69 | 75 | 68 | 280 | 17,170 |
| Mattias Eliasson | 72 | 68 | 71 | 69 | 280 | 17,170 |
| Oliver Wilson | 67 | 72 | 67 | 74 | 280 | 17,170 |
| Marc Cayeux | 75 | 68 | 71 | 66 | 280 | 17,170 |
| Ian Garbutt | 73 | 68 | 70 | 69 | 280 | 17,170 |
| Simon Khan | 70 | 72 | 66 | 72 | 280 | 17,170 |
| Tino Schuster | 70 | 70 | 72 | 69 | 281 | 14,365 |
| Johan Axgren | 68 | 74 | 69 | 70 | 281 | 14,365 |
| Anders Hansen | 67 | 70 | 67 | 77 | 281 | 14,365 |
| Darren Fichardt | 68 | 70 | 68 | 75 | 281 | 14,365 |
| Anthony Wall | 72 | 71 | 71 | 68 | 282 | 12,240 |
| Jose Manuel Lara | 73 | 68 | 72 | 69 | 282 | 12,240 |
| Miles Tunnicliff | 72 | 69 | 69 | 72 | 282 | 12,240 |
| Peter O'Malley | 68 | 71 | 71 | 72 | 282 | 12,240 |
| Leif Westerberg | 67 | 70 | 69 | 76 | 282 | 12,240 |
| Jean Van de Velde | 70 | 65 | 75 | 72 | 282 | 12,240 |
| Gary Emerson | 70 | 70 | 69 | 74 | 283 | 9,860 |
| Johan Skold | 72 | 71 | 71 | 69 | 283 | 9,860 |
| Peter Hedblom | 66 | 76 | 70 | 71 | 283 | 9,860 |
| Jan-Are Larsen | 68 | 72 | 70 | 73 | 283 | 9,860 |
| Stuart Manley | 70 | 72 | 67 | 74 | 283 | 9,860 |
| Peter Hanson | 72 | 69 | 71 | 71 | 283 | 9,860 |
| Raymond Russell | 71 | 72 | 73 | 67 | 283 | 9,860 |
| Ian Woosnam | 72 | 67 | 73 | 71 | 283 | 9,860 |
| Peter Senior | 68 | 73 | 71 | 72 | 284 | 7,140 |

|  | SCORES | | | | TOTAL | MONEY |
|---|---|---|---|---|---|---|
| Andrea Maestroni | 68 | 75 | 68 | 73 | 284 | 7,140 |
| Wade Ormsby | 70 | 73 | 76 | 65 | 284 | 7,140 |
| Graeme Storm | 71 | 65 | 74 | 74 | 284 | 7,140 |
| Stephen Scahill | 69 | 71 | 73 | 71 | 284 | 7,140 |
| Roger Chapman | 72 | 70 | 70 | 72 | 284 | 7,140 |
| Charl Schwartzel | 74 | 68 | 68 | 74 | 284 | 7,140 |
| Joakim Backstrom | 73 | 70 | 69 | 72 | 284 | 7,140 |
| Jose-Filipe Lima | 76 | 65 | 71 | 73 | 285 | 4,954.29 |
| *Edoardo Molinari | 72 | 71 | 67 | 75 | 285 | |
| Robert Rock | 69 | 71 | 73 | 72 | 285 | 4,954.29 |
| Lee Slattery | 71 | 72 | 72 | 70 | 285 | 4,954.29 |
| Andre Bossert | 69 | 70 | 74 | 72 | 285 | 4,954.29 |
| David Carter | 65 | 72 | 76 | 72 | 285 | 4,954.29 |
| Martin Erlandsson | 72 | 64 | 70 | 79 | 285 | 4,954.29 |
| Santiago Luna | 69 | 72 | 72 | 72 | 285 | 4,954.29 |
| Marten Olander | 72 | 71 | 75 | 68 | 286 | 4,080 |
| Gordon Brand, Jr. | 70 | 71 | 70 | 75 | 286 | 4,080 |
| Michael Jonzon | 67 | 73 | 72 | 74 | 286 | 4,080 |
| Fredrik Andersson Hed | 72 | 69 | 74 | 72 | 287 | 3,740 |
| Richard Bland | 67 | 76 | 73 | 73 | 289 | 3,570 |
| Simon Dyson | 74 | 68 | 70 | 78 | 290 | 3,315 |
| Brett Rumford | 75 | 68 | 73 | 74 | 290 | 3,315 |
| Mark Foster | 71 | 72 | 73 | 75 | 291 | 3,110 |
| Tobias Dier | 71 | 72 | 74 | 75 | 292 | 2,548.50 |
| Barry Lane | 72 | 70 | 75 | 75 | 292 | 2,548.50 |
| Patrik Sjoland | 68 | 75 | 73 | 78 | 294 | 2,544 |
| Mads Vibe-Hastrup | 71 | 72 | 75 | 77 | 295 | 2,541 |
| Phillip Archer | 73 | 69 | 83 | 73 | 298 | 2,538 |
| Marcus Knight | 70 | 72 | 77 | 81 | 300 | 2,535 |
| Nicolas Colsaerts | 71 | 72 | 76 | 82 | 301 | 2,532 |

# Linde German Masters

*Gut Larchenhof*, Cologne, Germany
Par 36-36–72; 7,289 yards

September 8-11
purse, €3,000,000

|  | SCORES | | | | TOTAL | MONEY |
|---|---|---|---|---|---|---|
| Retief Goosen | 67 | 68 | 66 | 67 | 268 | €500,000 |
| David Lynn | 68 | 67 | 67 | 67 | 269 | 199,582.50 |
| Jose Maria Olazabal | 68 | 65 | 70 | 66 | 269 | 199,582.50 |
| Nick Dougherty | 71 | 64 | 66 | 68 | 269 | 199,582.50 |
| Henrik Stenson | 71 | 66 | 64 | 68 | 269 | 199,582.50 |
| David Howell | 72 | 66 | 66 | 66 | 270 | 105,000 |
| Anthony Wall | 71 | 62 | 68 | 70 | 271 | 82,500 |
| Paul Casey | 67 | 67 | 71 | 66 | 271 | 82,500 |
| Angel Cabrera | 70 | 68 | 67 | 67 | 272 | 67,200 |
| Kenneth Ferrie | 68 | 72 | 66 | 67 | 273 | 57,600 |
| Ricardo Gonzalez | 67 | 71 | 71 | 64 | 273 | 57,600 |
| Niclas Fasth | 69 | 71 | 65 | 70 | 275 | 46,440 |
| Marc Cayeux | 66 | 69 | 72 | 68 | 275 | 46,440 |
| Pierre Fulke | 68 | 69 | 69 | 69 | 275 | 46,440 |
| Scott Drummond | 68 | 68 | 68 | 71 | 275 | 46,440 |
| Bernhard Langer | 67 | 69 | 71 | 68 | 275 | 46,440 |
| Philip Golding | 71 | 66 | 68 | 71 | 276 | 36,850 |
| Thomas Bjorn | 71 | 70 | 69 | 66 | 276 | 36,850 |
| Stephen Dodd | 69 | 70 | 70 | 67 | 276 | 36,850 |
| Simon Khan | 69 | 69 | 69 | 69 | 276 | 36,850 |

| | SCORES | | | | TOTAL | MONEY |
|---|---|---|---|---|---|---|
| Simon Dyson | 72 | 68 | 67 | 69 | 276 | 36,850 |
| Thomas Levet | 71 | 66 | 67 | 72 | 276 | 36,850 |
| Jose-Filipe Lima | 71 | 69 | 65 | 72 | 277 | 32,100 |
| Fredrik Andersson Hed | 69 | 70 | 66 | 72 | 277 | 32,100 |
| Andrew Coltart | 73 | 68 | 67 | 69 | 277 | 32,100 |
| Graeme Storm | 69 | 69 | 70 | 70 | 278 | 28,500 |
| Richard Green | 70 | 70 | 66 | 72 | 278 | 28,500 |
| Charl Schwartzel | 67 | 72 | 72 | 67 | 278 | 28,500 |
| Lee Slattery | 72 | 66 | 71 | 69 | 278 | 28,500 |
| Christian Cevaer | 71 | 71 | 70 | 66 | 278 | 28,500 |
| Marten Olander | 71 | 68 | 72 | 68 | 279 | 24,060 |
| Jonathan Lomas | 73 | 65 | 71 | 70 | 279 | 24,060 |
| Bradley Dredge | 66 | 75 | 68 | 70 | 279 | 24,060 |
| Paul Broadhurst | 69 | 68 | 73 | 69 | 279 | 24,060 |
| Jose Manuel Lara | 67 | 74 | 66 | 72 | 279 | 24,060 |
| Barry Lane | 66 | 72 | 70 | 72 | 280 | 21,000 |
| Peter Senior | 66 | 72 | 72 | 70 | 280 | 21,000 |
| Michael Campbell | 71 | 69 | 73 | 67 | 280 | 21,000 |
| Soren Hansen | 71 | 71 | 70 | 68 | 280 | 21,000 |
| Ian Woosnam | 75 | 67 | 68 | 71 | 281 | 19,200 |
| Graeme McDowell | 71 | 70 | 70 | 70 | 281 | 19,200 |
| John Bickerton | 72 | 70 | 71 | 69 | 282 | 17,100 |
| Damien McGrane | 71 | 70 | 70 | 71 | 282 | 17,100 |
| Steve Webster | 69 | 72 | 68 | 73 | 282 | 17,100 |
| Andrew Marshall | 66 | 71 | 74 | 71 | 282 | 17,100 |
| Mark Hensby | 71 | 71 | 68 | 72 | 282 | 17,100 |
| Gonzalo Fernandez-Castano | 71 | 67 | 73 | 72 | 283 | 13,200 |
| Mikael Lundberg | 71 | 71 | 72 | 69 | 283 | 13,200 |
| Robert Karlsson | 68 | 73 | 71 | 71 | 283 | 13,200 |
| Miles Tunnicliff | 74 | 68 | 73 | 68 | 283 | 13,200 |
| Carlos Rodiles | 72 | 67 | 74 | 70 | 283 | 13,200 |
| Stuart Little | 69 | 71 | 70 | 73 | 283 | 13,200 |
| Peter Hanson | 69 | 73 | 70 | 71 | 283 | 13,200 |
| Raymond Russell | 72 | 70 | 70 | 71 | 283 | 13,200 |
| Ignacio Garrido | 73 | 67 | 71 | 73 | 284 | 9,300 |
| Markus Brier | 66 | 73 | 72 | 73 | 284 | 9,300 |
| Alastair Forsyth | 69 | 71 | 74 | 70 | 284 | 9,300 |
| Louis Oosthuizen | 70 | 70 | 74 | 70 | 284 | 9,300 |
| Robert-Jan Derksen | 75 | 65 | 72 | 72 | 284 | 9,300 |
| Niki Zitny | 67 | 72 | 76 | 69 | 284 | 9,300 |
| Joakim Backstrom | 71 | 66 | 72 | 76 | 285 | 7,650 |
| Brett Rumford | 70 | 72 | 69 | 74 | 285 | 7,650 |
| Joakim Haeggman | 70 | 71 | 71 | 73 | 285 | 7,650 |
| Sven Struver | 70 | 68 | 73 | 74 | 285 | 7,650 |
| Ian Poulter | 72 | 70 | 74 | 70 | 286 | 6,900 |
| Andrew Oldcorn | 68 | 73 | 74 | 72 | 287 | 6,300 |
| Peter O'Malley | 71 | 71 | 72 | 73 | 287 | 6,300 |
| Andre Bossert | 72 | 69 | 73 | 73 | 287 | 6,300 |
| David Carter | 71 | 71 | 74 | 72 | 288 | 5,700 |
| Marcel Siem | 71 | 70 | 75 | 74 | 290 | 4,985 |
| Jean-Francois Remesy | 74 | 68 | 71 | 77 | 290 | 4,985 |
| Raphael Jacquelin | 71 | 71 | 74 | 75 | 291 | 4,497 |

# HSBC World Match Play

*Wentworth Club, West Course,* Surrey, England
Par 434 534 444–35; 345 434 455–37–72; 7,072 yards

September 15-18
purse, £2,440,000

## FIRST ROUND

Retief Goosen defeated Kenneth Ferrie, 8 and 7

| | | | | | | | | | | | | | | | | | | |
|---|---|---|---|---|---|---|---|---|---|---|---|---|---|---|---|---|---|---|
| Goosen | 5 | 2 | 3 | 5 | 3 | 3 | 4 | 3 | 4 | 2 | 4 | 4 | 4 | 2 | 5 | 3 | 5 | 5 |
| Ferrie | 4 | 3 | 4 | 3 | 3 | 4 | 4 | 4 | 4 | 3 | 4 | 5 | 4 | 3 | 4 | 5 | 4 | 5 |

Goosen leads, 4 up

| | | | | | | | | | | | |
|---|---|---|---|---|---|---|---|---|---|---|---|
| Goosen | 3 | 3 | 4 | 5 | 3 | 4 | 4 | 4 | 4 | 2 | 3 |
| Ferrie | 4 | 3 | 4 | 5 | 4 | 4 | 4 | 5 | 3 | 3 | 4 |

Mark Hensby defeated Colin Montgomerie, 2 and 1

| | | | | | | | | | | | | | | | | | | |
|---|---|---|---|---|---|---|---|---|---|---|---|---|---|---|---|---|---|---|
| Montgomerie | 4 | 2 | 4 | 4 | 3 | 4 | 4 | 4 | 4 | 3 | 4 | 4 | 4 | 4 | 5 | 4 | 3 | 4 |
| Hensby | 5 | 3 | 4 | 4 | 2 | 5 | 5 | 4 | 4 | 3 | 4 | 4 | 5 | 3 | 4 | 3 | C | 5 |

Montgomerie leads, 3 up

| | | | | | | | | | | | | | | | | | |
|---|---|---|---|---|---|---|---|---|---|---|---|---|---|---|---|---|---|
| Montgomerie | 5 | 3 | 5 | 4 | 4 | 4 | 4 | 4 | 5 | 3 | 4 | 4 | 4 | 3 | 4 | 4 | 4 |
| Hensby | 4 | 3 | 4 | 4 | 3 | 4 | 4 | 4 | 5 | 2 | 4 | 4 | 4 | 3 | 4 | 3 | 4 |

Steve Elkington defeated Tim Clark, 6 and 5

| | | | | | | | | | | | | | | | | | | |
|---|---|---|---|---|---|---|---|---|---|---|---|---|---|---|---|---|---|---|
| Clark | 4 | 3 | 5 | 4 | 4 | 4 | 4 | 4 | 4 | 4 | 4 | 5 | 4 | 3 | 4 | 4 | 4 | 5 |
| Elkington | 4 | 3 | 4 | 4 | 4 | 4 | 5 | 5 | 4 | 3 | 3 | 4 | 4 | 2 | 6 | 4 | 5 | 4 |

Elkington leads, 2 up

| | | | | | | | | | | | | |
|---|---|---|---|---|---|---|---|---|---|---|---|---|
| Clark | 4 | 3 | 5 | 4 | 4 | 4 | 4 | 4 | 3 | 4 | 5 | 4 |
| Elkington | 4 | 3 | 4 | 3 | 3 | 4 | 5 | 3 | 4 | 3 | 4 | 4 |

Michael Campbell defeated Geoff Ogilvy, 1 up

| | | | | | | | | | | | | | | | | | | |
|---|---|---|---|---|---|---|---|---|---|---|---|---|---|---|---|---|---|---|
| Campbell | 4 | 3 | 7 | 4 | 3 | 5 | 4 | 4 | 4 | 2 | 4 | 4 | 4 | 2 | 4 | 5 | 4 | 4 |
| Ogilvy | 5 | 3 | 5 | 4 | 2 | 5 | 4 | 4 | 5 | 2 | 4 | 6 | 4 | 3 | 4 | 3 | 5 | 5 |

Campbell leads, 3 up

| | | | | | | | | | | | | | | | | | | |
|---|---|---|---|---|---|---|---|---|---|---|---|---|---|---|---|---|---|---|
| Campbell | 3 | 3 | 4 | 4 | 2 | 4 | 6 | 4 | 4 | 3 | 4 | 5 | 3 | 3 | 5 | 4 | 5 | 4 |
| Ogilvy | 4 | 3 | 5 | 4 | 3 | 3 | 5 | 3 | 4 | 2 | 3 | 4 | 6 | 3 | 4 | 5 | 5 | 4 |

Luke Donald defeated Bernhard Langer, 7 and 6

| | | | | | | | | | | | | | | | | | | |
|---|---|---|---|---|---|---|---|---|---|---|---|---|---|---|---|---|---|---|
| Donald | 4 | 3 | 4 | 4 | 3 | 4 | 4 | 4 | 4 | 3 | 3 | 5 | 4 | 2 | 4 | 5 | 4 | 5 |
| Langer | 5 | 3 | 5 | 5 | 3 | 5 | 4 | 4 | 4 | 3 | 4 | 4 | 4 | 2 | 4 | 4 | 4 | 5 |

Donald leads, 3 up

| | | | | | | | | | | | | |
|---|---|---|---|---|---|---|---|---|---|---|---|---|
| Donald | 4 | 3 | 4 | 4 | 3 | 4 | 3 | 4 | 4 | 2 | 4 | 5 |
| Langer | 5 | 4 | 4 | 4 | 3 | 4 | 5 | 4 | 4 | 3 | 4 | 5 |

Paul McGinley defeated Thomas Bjorn, 6 and 5

| | | | | | | | | | | | | | | | | | | |
|---|---|---|---|---|---|---|---|---|---|---|---|---|---|---|---|---|---|---|
| Bjorn | 5 | 3 | 4 | 4 | 3 | 4 | 4 | 4 | 5 | 3 | 4 | 5 | 3 | 2 | 4 | 4 | 6 | 4 |
| McGinley | 5 | 2 | 4 | 4 | 4 | 4 | 4 | 4 | 4 | 3 | 5 | 4 | 4 | 4 | 4 | 5 | 5 | 4 |

Bjorn leads, 1 up

| | | | | | | | | | | | | | |
|---|---|---|---|---|---|---|---|---|---|---|---|---|---|
| Bjorn | 4 | 3 | 4 | 4 | 5 | 4 | 5 | 4 | 5 | 4 | 3 | 5 | 4 |
| McGinley | 4 | 3 | 4 | 4 | 3 | 3 | 4 | 3 | 5 | 3 | 2 | 4 | 4 |

Jose Maria Olazabal defeated David Howell, 1 up

| | | | | | | | | | | | | | | | | | | |
|---|---|---|---|---|---|---|---|---|---|---|---|---|---|---|---|---|---|---|
| Howell | 4 | 3 | 5 | 4 | 3 | 4 | 4 | 4 | 4 | 3 | 4 | 5 | 3 | 3 | 4 | 4 | 6 | 3 |
| Olazabal | 4 | 2 | 5 | 4 | 3 | 3 | 4 | 3 | 4 | 3 | 4 | 5 | 4 | 3 | 4 | 4 | 5 | 4 |

Olazabal leads, 2 up

| | | | | | | | | | | | | | | | | | | |
|---|---|---|---|---|---|---|---|---|---|---|---|---|---|---|---|---|---|---|
| Howell | 3 | 3 | 3 | 4 | 3 | 3 | 5 | 4 | 4 | 3 | 4 | 4 | 4 | 3 | 4 | 3 | 4 | 4 |
| Olazabal | 5 | 4 | 5 | 4 | 3 | 3 | 4 | 4 | 4 | 3 | 3 | 5 | 4 | 2 | 4 | 4 | 4 | 3 |

Angel Cabrera defeated Trevor Immelman, 2 and 1

| | | | | | | | | | | | | | | | | | | |
|---|---|---|---|---|---|---|---|---|---|---|---|---|---|---|---|---|---|---|
| Cabrera | 4 | 2 | 4 | 6 | 3 | 4 | 4 | 3 | 4 | 3 | 4 | 5 | 4 | 3 | 4 | 4 | 6 | 4 |
| Immelman | 4 | 3 | 5 | 3 | 3 | 3 | 5 | 5 | 3 | 3 | 5 | 5 | 4 | 3 | 5 | 4 | 4 | 5 |

Cabrera leads, 3 up

| | | | | | | | | | | | | | | | | | |
|---|---|---|---|---|---|---|---|---|---|---|---|---|---|---|---|---|---|
| Cabrera | 4 | 4 | 3 | 4 | 3 | 4 | 4 | 4 | 3 | 3 | 4 | 4 | 4 | 3 | 4 | 4 | 4 |
| Immelman | 5 | 3 | 4 | 4 | 5 | 4 | 3 | 4 | 6 | 2 | 3 | 3 | 4 | 3 | 4 | 4 | 4 |

# QUARTER-FINALS

**Retief Goosen defeated Mark Hensby, 12 and 11**

```
Goosen    4 3 4 4 2 4 3 4 4 3 4 4 3 3 4 4 4 5
Hensby    5 3 5 5 4 4 4 4 5 4 5 4 5 3 4 5 4 4
Goosen leads, 9 up
Goosen    4 3 4 4 3 3 4
Hensby    4 3 4 5 4 4 4
```

**Michael Campbell defeated Steve Elkington, 37th hole**

```
Elkington 4 3 3 5 3 4 4 4 4 2 4 4 6 2 4 4 5 5
Campbell  4 2 3 3 3 4 5 5 4 3 4 5 4 3 5 5 6 4
Elkington leads, 4 up
Elkington 4 3 5 5 4 4 4 3 4 3 5 5 5 4 4 5 6 4
Campbell  4 3 4 4 4 4 5 4 3 3 4 5 4 3 5 5 5 4
Match all-square
Elkington 5
Campbell  4
```

**Paul McGinley defeated Luke Donald, 9 and 8**

```
Donald    4 4 4 4 3 4 3 5 4 3 4 3 4 2 6 5 5 5
McGinley  4 3 3 4 2 3 4 4 4 3 4 4 3 3 5 4 5 4
McGinley leads, 6 up
Donald    4 3 5 4 3 3 5 5 4 3
McGinley  4 3 4 4 2 4 4 4 4 3
```

**Angel Cabrera defeated Jose Maria Olazabal, 4 and 3**

```
Olazabal  4 3 4 4 3 4 5 4 4 2 4 4 4 3 4 5 5 4
Cabrera   4 3 3 4 3 4 3 4 4 3 4 4 4 2 5 4 5 4
Cabrera leads, 2 up
Olazabal  4 3 5 5 3 4 5 4 4 2 4 4 6 3 4
Cabrera   4 3 5 3 2 4 5 4 5 3 4 4 4 2 4
```

# SEMI-FINALS

**Michael Campbell defeated Retief Goosen, 7 and 6**

```
Goosen    4 3 4 5 3 4 4 5 4 3 5 4 4 2 5 4 4 5
Campbell  4 3 4 3 2 3 3 5 4 3 3 4 4 3 3 4 5 4
Campbell leads, 5 up
Goosen    4 3 6 4 3 4 4 4 4 2 3 5
Campbell  4 3 5 4 3 3 4 3 4 2 4 5
```

**Paul McGinley defeated Angel Cabrera, 4 and 3**

```
McGinley  4 2 5 4 3 4 4 4 3 2 3 4 5 3 4 5 4 3
Cabrera   4 4 4 4 2 4 4 4 4 3 4 6 4 3 4 4 5 4
McGinley leads, 3 up
McGinley  4 2 5 4 2 4 3 4 4 3 4 4 4 4 4
Cabrera   4 2 4 4 3 4 3 4 5 4 3 4 4 3 5
```

# FINAL

**Michael Campbell defeated Paul McGinley, 2 and 1**

```
Campbell  5 3 4 4 3 3 4 5 3 2 4 4 4 3 4 5 5 4
McGinley  4 3 4 4 3 4 4 4 5 3 4 4 4 3 4 3 5 5
Campbell leads, 1 up
Campbell  3 3 4 4 3 4 5 4 5 4 4 4 5 3 4 4 4
McGinley  4 3 6 4 3 3 3 4 4 4 4 5 4 3 5 5 4
```

PRIZE MONEY: Campbell £1,000,000; McGinley £400,000; Cabrera, Goosen £120,000 each; Donald, Elkington, Hensby, Olazabal £80,000 each; Bjorn, Clark, Ferrie, Howell, Immelman, Langer, Montgomerie, Ogilvy £60,000 each.

LEGEND: C—conceded hole to opponent; W—won hole by concession without holing out; X—no total score.

# Seve Trophy

*The Wynyard Golf Club*, Billington, England
Par 35-36–71; 7,097 yards

September 22-25
purse, €2,000,000

## FIRST DAY
### Fourball

Thomas Bjorn and Henrik Stenson (Cont.) defeated Ian Poulter and Nick Dougherty, 2 up.
Colin Montgomerie and Graeme McDowell (GB&I) defeated Maarten Lafeber and Emanuele Canonica, 4 and 2.
Miguel Angel Jimenez and Jose Maria Olazabal (Cont.) defeated Stephen Dodd and Bradley Dredge, 4 and 2.
Niclas Fasth and Peter Hanson (Cont.) defeated David Howell and Paul Casey, 3 and 2.
Jean-Francois Remesy and Thomas Levet (Cont.) defeated Paul McGinley and Padraig Harrington, 1 up.

**POINTS: Great Britain & Ireland 1, Continental Europe 4**

## SECOND DAY
### Fourball

McGinley and Harrington (GB&I) defeated Fasth and Hanson, 3 and 1.
Howell and Casey (GB&I) defeated Jimenez and Olazabal, 5 and 4.
Bjorn and Stenson (Cont.) defeated Montgomerie and McDowell, 3 and 2.
Lafeber and Canonica (Cont.) defeated Dodd and Dredge, 2 up.
Poulter and Dougherty (GB&I) defeated Remesy and Levet, 5 and 4.

**POINTS: Great Britain & Ireland 4, Continental Europe 6**

## THIRD DAY
### Greensomes

McGinley and Harrington (GB&I) defeated Levet and Olazabal, 3 and 2.
Howell and Casey (GB&I) defeated Fasth and Hanson, 2 up.
Dodd and McDowell (GB&I) halved with Jimenez and Canonica.
Poulter and Dougherty (GB&I) halved with Bjorn and Stenson.

**POINTS: Great Britain & Ireland 7, Continental Europe 7**

### Foursomes

Harrington and McGinley (GB&I) halved with Levet and Remesy.
Casey and Howell (GB&I) defeated Jimenez and Canonica, 2 and 1.
Fasth and Stenson (Cont.) defeated Dredge and Poulter, 1 up.
Dougherty and Montgomerie (GB&I) defeated Bjorn and Lafeber, 1 up.

**POINTS: Great Britain & Ireland 9½, Continental Europe 8½**

## FOURTH DAY
### Singles

Olazabal (Cont.) defeated Montgomerie, 2 and 1.
Casey (GB&I) defeated Fasth, 4 and 3.
Poulter (GB&I) halved with Hanson.
Howell (GB&I) defeated Bjorn, 6 and 5.
Dodd (GB&I) defeated Remesy, 2 and 1.
Dredge (GB&I) defeated Levet, 2 and 1.
McDowell (GB&I) defeated Lafeber, 5 and 4.
McGinley (GB&I) defeated Jimenez, 1 up.

Canonica (Cont.) defeated Harrington, 2 and 1.
Dougherty (GB&I) halved with Stenson.

**TOTAL POINTS: Great Britain & Ireland 16½, Continental Europe 11½**

(Each member of the Great Britain & Ireland team received €125,000; each member of
the Continental Europe team received €75,000.)

# Dunhill Links Championship

*St. Andrews Old Course:* Par 36-36–72; 7,279 yards
*Carnoustie Championship Course:* Par 36-36–72; 7,112 yards
*Kingsbarns Golf Links:* Par 36-36–72; 7,099 yards
St. Andrews, Scotland

September 29-October 2
purse, €3,974,490

| | SCORES | | | | TOTAL | MONEY |
|---|---|---|---|---|---|---|
| Colin Montgomerie | 70 | 65 | 73 | 71 | 279 | €662,415.10 |
| Kenneth Ferrie | 68 | 68 | 67 | 77 | 280 | 441,607.30 |
| Henrik Stenson | 69 | 74 | 65 | 73 | 281 | 188,788.30 |
| Padraig Harrington | 70 | 70 | 71 | 70 | 281 | 188,788.30 |
| Anders Hansen | 69 | 71 | 72 | 69 | 281 | 188,788.30 |
| Robert Karlsson | 70 | 74 | 69 | 68 | 281 | 188,788.30 |
| Pierre Fulke | 71 | 66 | 72 | 73 | 282 | 88,101.21 |
| Darren Clarke | 68 | 75 | 69 | 70 | 282 | 88,101.21 |
| Stephen Gallacher | 74 | 73 | 67 | 68 | 282 | 88,101.21 |
| Lee Westwood | 71 | 71 | 69 | 71 | 282 | 88,101.21 |
| Titch Moore | 72 | 68 | 73 | 69 | 282 | 88,101.21 |
| Ricardo Gonzalez | 69 | 68 | 71 | 74 | 282 | 88,101.21 |
| Soren Kjeldsen | 70 | 72 | 69 | 72 | 283 | 61,074.67 |
| Maarten Lafeber | 72 | 70 | 73 | 68 | 283 | 61,074.67 |
| Miles Tunnicliff | 71 | 71 | 72 | 69 | 283 | 61,074.67 |
| Simon Khan | 69 | 72 | 74 | 69 | 284 | 53,655.63 |
| Paul Broadhurst | 70 | 71 | 73 | 70 | 284 | 53,655.63 |
| Raymond Russell | 73 | 70 | 72 | 69 | 284 | 53,655.63 |
| David Carter | 72 | 71 | 71 | 71 | 285 | 46,998.35 |
| Gary Orr | 72 | 71 | 70 | 72 | 285 | 46,998.35 |
| Carlos Rodiles | 70 | 73 | 69 | 73 | 285 | 46,998.35 |
| Nick O'Hern | 68 | 75 | 70 | 72 | 285 | 46,998.35 |
| Peter Gustafsson | 73 | 68 | 71 | 74 | 286 | 41,334.70 |
| Bradley Dredge | 68 | 73 | 73 | 72 | 286 | 41,334.70 |
| Paul Casey | 68 | 70 | 72 | 76 | 286 | 41,334.70 |
| Johan Axgren | 73 | 70 | 72 | 71 | 286 | 41,334.70 |
| Peter Hanson | 73 | 71 | 71 | 71 | 286 | 41,334.70 |
| Scott Drummond | 71 | 72 | 69 | 75 | 287 | 33,120.75 |
| Brian Davis | 68 | 71 | 77 | 71 | 287 | 33,120.75 |
| Martin Doyle | 73 | 72 | 66 | 76 | 287 | 33,120.75 |
| Rich Beem | 67 | 73 | 75 | 72 | 287 | 33,120.75 |
| Mark Foster | 70 | 70 | 73 | 74 | 287 | 33,120.75 |
| Andrew Marshall | 70 | 70 | 74 | 73 | 287 | 33,120.75 |
| Sam Little | 73 | 71 | 71 | 72 | 287 | 33,120.75 |
| Peter Hedblom | 70 | 69 | 76 | 72 | 287 | 33,120.75 |
| Jean Van de Velde | 72 | 74 | 70 | 71 | 287 | 33,120.75 |
| Christian Cevaer | 69 | 74 | 72 | 73 | 288 | 27,026.54 |
| Brett Rumford | 68 | 70 | 78 | 72 | 288 | 27,026.54 |
| Anthony Wall | 69 | 72 | 73 | 74 | 288 | 27,026.54 |
| David Howell | 67 | 74 | 76 | 71 | 288 | 27,026.54 |
| Alessandro Tadini | 67 | 72 | 73 | 77 | 289 | 22,257.15 |
| Mark Murless | 71 | 76 | 69 | 73 | 289 | 22,257.15 |

| | SCORES | | | | TOTAL | MONEY |
|---|---|---|---|---|---|---|
| Barry Lane | 72 | 70 | 74 | 73 | 289 | 22,257.15 |
| Richard Sterne | 74 | 71 | 71 | 73 | 289 | 22,257.15 |
| Niclas Fasth | 70 | 72 | 75 | 72 | 289 | 22,257.15 |
| Roger Chapman | 71 | 72 | 71 | 75 | 289 | 22,257.15 |
| Paul McGinley | 74 | 71 | 72 | 72 | 289 | 22,257.15 |
| Warren Abery | 69 | 71 | 75 | 74 | 289 | 22,257.15 |
| Darren Fichardt | 71 | 73 | 72 | 74 | 290 | 17,885.21 |
| Nick Dougherty | 68 | 74 | 73 | 75 | 290 | 17,885.21 |
| Simon Dyson | 69 | 73 | 73 | 75 | 290 | 17,885.21 |
| Phillip Archer | 70 | 73 | 71 | 77 | 291 | 13,380.79 |
| Richard Green | 70 | 71 | 70 | 80 | 291 | 13,380.79 |
| Ian Poulter | 71 | 73 | 72 | 75 | 291 | 13,380.79 |
| Andrew Coltart | 70 | 76 | 71 | 74 | 291 | 13,380.79 |
| Mark Roe | 70 | 74 | 72 | 75 | 291 | 13,380.79 |
| Ignacio Garrido | 74 | 66 | 75 | 76 | 291 | 13,380.79 |
| David Park | 70 | 72 | 74 | 75 | 291 | 13,380.79 |
| Terry Pilkadaris | 74 | 65 | 76 | 76 | 291 | 13,380.79 |
| Alastair Forsyth | 73 | 74 | 68 | 76 | 291 | 13,380.79 |
| Markus Brier | 72 | 70 | 75 | 76 | 293 | 10,532.40 |
| Joakim Backstrom | 70 | 75 | 71 | 77 | 293 | 10,532.40 |
| James Kingston | 70 | 75 | 70 | 79 | 294 | 9,737.50 |
| Jose Manuel Lara | 70 | 70 | 77 | 77 | 294 | 9,737.50 |
| Eduardo Romero | 69 | 74 | 74 | 83 | 300 | 9,141.33 |

## Abama Open de Canarias

*Abama Golf Club*, Canary Islands, Spain
Par 35-36–71; 6,857 yards

October 6-9
purse, €450,000

| | SCORES | | | | TOTAL | MONEY |
|---|---|---|---|---|---|---|
| John Bickerton | 69 | 68 | 69 | 68 | 274 | €75,000 |
| Michael Kirk | 69 | 66 | 75 | 69 | 279 | 39,085 |
| Stuart Little | 68 | 67 | 72 | 72 | 279 | 39,085 |
| Mark Roe | 69 | 68 | 71 | 72 | 280 | 19,110 |
| Johan Axgren | 72 | 67 | 71 | 70 | 280 | 19,110 |
| Marc Warren | 68 | 71 | 72 | 69 | 280 | 19,110 |
| Lee Slattery | 69 | 72 | 71 | 69 | 281 | 12,375 |
| Fredrik Widmark | 70 | 73 | 67 | 71 | 281 | 12,375 |
| Jose Manuel Carriles | 72 | 70 | 66 | 74 | 282 | 9,540 |
| Stephen Scahill | 70 | 66 | 73 | 73 | 282 | 9,540 |
| Jamie Spence | 69 | 69 | 72 | 73 | 283 | 7,026.43 |
| Martin Maritz | 74 | 71 | 72 | 66 | 283 | 7,026.43 |
| Gareth Davies | 74 | 71 | 73 | 65 | 283 | 7,026.43 |
| David Carter | 74 | 71 | 70 | 68 | 283 | 7,026.43 |
| Gareth Paddison | 74 | 68 | 68 | 73 | 283 | 7,026.43 |
| Gregory Bourdy | 69 | 71 | 72 | 71 | 283 | 7,026.43 |
| Peter Baker | 69 | 68 | 72 | 74 | 283 | 7,026.43 |
| Roger Chapman | 69 | 72 | 71 | 72 | 284 | 5,265 |
| Benoit Teilleria | 72 | 72 | 69 | 71 | 284 | 5,265 |
| Ivo Giner | 72 | 72 | 72 | 68 | 284 | 5,265 |
| Hernan Rey | 72 | 69 | 73 | 70 | 284 | 5,265 |
| Phillip Archer | 70 | 72 | 71 | 71 | 284 | 5,265 |
| Patrik Sjoland | 69 | 76 | 72 | 67 | 284 | 5,265 |
| Ignacio Garrido | 70 | 70 | 73 | 71 | 284 | 5,265 |
| Simon Hurd | 69 | 72 | 67 | 77 | 285 | 4,140 |
| Jesus Maria Arruti | 70 | 74 | 70 | 71 | 285 | 4,140 |
| Marcus Fraser | 71 | 72 | 74 | 68 | 285 | 4,140 |

| | SCORES | | | | TOTAL | MONEY |
|---|---|---|---|---|---|---|
| Manuel Quiros | 73 | 68 | 75 | 69 | 285 | 4,140 |
| Kariem Baraka | 71 | 68 | 70 | 76 | 285 | 4,140 |
| Mikko Ilonen | 72 | 69 | 68 | 76 | 285 | 4,140 |
| Daniel Vancsik | 72 | 67 | 70 | 76 | 285 | 4,140 |
| Sam Walker | 80 | 65 | 69 | 71 | 285 | 4,140 |
| Gordon Brand, Jr. | 70 | 74 | 68 | 73 | 285 | 4,140 |
| Michael Jonzon | 74 | 68 | 73 | 71 | 286 | 3,240 |
| Santiago Luna | 70 | 72 | 71 | 73 | 286 | 3,240 |
| Carl Suneson | 71 | 71 | 71 | 73 | 286 | 3,240 |
| Andrew Marshall | 72 | 73 | 73 | 68 | 286 | 3,240 |
| Paul Dwyer | 76 | 67 | 72 | 71 | 286 | 3,240 |
| Sion Bebb | 72 | 72 | 69 | 73 | 286 | 3,240 |
| Denny Lucas | 72 | 70 | 76 | 69 | 287 | 2,790 |
| Michael Hoey | 70 | 74 | 72 | 71 | 287 | 2,790 |
| Lars Brovold | 73 | 70 | 74 | 70 | 287 | 2,790 |
| Carlos Garcia | 73 | 70 | 72 | 72 | 287 | 2,790 |
| Niki Zitny | 76 | 68 | 74 | 70 | 288 | 2,295 |
| Mark Foster | 72 | 70 | 72 | 74 | 288 | 2,295 |
| Titch Moore | 68 | 68 | 76 | 76 | 288 | 2,295 |
| Alvaro Velasco | 71 | 73 | 70 | 74 | 288 | 2,295 |
| Garry Houston | 73 | 65 | 77 | 73 | 288 | 2,295 |
| Miguel Angel Martin | 71 | 71 | 76 | 70 | 288 | 2,295 |
| Ilya Goroneskoul | 71 | 72 | 73 | 72 | 288 | 2,295 |
| Carlos Rodiles | 74 | 69 | 72 | 74 | 289 | 1,710 |
| Jarrod Moseley | 73 | 67 | 73 | 76 | 289 | 1,710 |
| Magnus P. Atlevi | 74 | 71 | 72 | 72 | 289 | 1,710 |
| Ben Mason | 71 | 70 | 73 | 75 | 289 | 1,710 |
| David Dixon | 71 | 70 | 73 | 75 | 289 | 1,710 |
| Leif Westerberg | 71 | 72 | 73 | 73 | 289 | 1,710 |
| Johan Skold | 66 | 76 | 76 | 72 | 290 | 1,350 |
| Stephen Browne | 74 | 68 | 73 | 75 | 290 | 1,350 |
| Ariel Canete | 72 | 73 | 73 | 72 | 290 | 1,350 |
| Ricardo Gonzalez | 69 | 74 | 73 | 75 | 291 | 1,260 |
| Miguel Carballo | 71 | 72 | 74 | 75 | 292 | 1,147.50 |
| David Higgins | 77 | 68 | 81 | 66 | 292 | 1,147.50 |
| Pedro Linhart | 74 | 70 | 78 | 70 | 292 | 1,147.50 |
| Gary Clark | 73 | 72 | 71 | 76 | 292 | 1,147.50 |
| Alvaro Salto | 71 | 73 | 72 | 77 | 293 | 1,012.50 |
| Richard McEvoy | 71 | 73 | 77 | 72 | 293 | 1,012.50 |
| Rafael Gomez | 71 | 69 | 77 | 77 | 294 | 900 |
| Andres Romero | 66 | 72 | 73 | 83 | 294 | 900 |
| Edward Rush | 71 | 69 | 81 | 73 | 294 | 900 |
| Robert Rock | 71 | 73 | 82 | 71 | 297 | 820 |
| Matthew Morris | 76 | 69 | 72 | 91 | 308 | 675 |

# Open de Madrid

*Club de Campo*, Madrid, Spain
Par 36-35–71; 6,947 yards

October 13-16
purse, €1,000,000

| | SCORES | | | | TOTAL | MONEY |
|---|---|---|---|---|---|---|
| Raphael Jacquelin | 64 | 64 | 64 | 69 | 261 | €166,660 |
| Paul Lawrie | 68 | 66 | 66 | 64 | 264 | 111,110 |
| Anders Hansen | 67 | 69 | 66 | 64 | 266 | 56,300 |
| Darren Clarke | 64 | 67 | 68 | 67 | 266 | 56,300 |
| Ian Woosnam | 69 | 65 | 68 | 65 | 267 | 42,400 |
| Jose Manuel Lara | 67 | 69 | 68 | 64 | 268 | 32,500 |

| | SCORES | | | | TOTAL | MONEY |
|---|---|---|---|---|---|---|
| Jose-Filipe Lima | 66 | 66 | 67 | 69 | 268 | 32,500 |
| Colin Montgomerie | 72 | 66 | 65 | 66 | 269 | 22,466.67 |
| David Lynn | 69 | 69 | 65 | 66 | 269 | 22,466.67 |
| Gregory Bourdy | 69 | 68 | 67 | 65 | 269 | 22,466.67 |
| Miguel Angel Jimenez | 72 | 64 | 66 | 68 | 270 | 18,400 |
| Robert-Jan Derksen | 67 | 69 | 66 | 69 | 271 | 14,828.57 |
| Jose Maria Olazabal | 67 | 69 | 70 | 65 | 271 | 14,828.57 |
| Andrew Marshall | 70 | 68 | 65 | 68 | 271 | 14,828.57 |
| Stuart Little | 67 | 66 | 68 | 70 | 271 | 14,828.57 |
| James Kingston | 71 | 66 | 68 | 66 | 271 | 14,828.57 |
| David Park | 68 | 67 | 67 | 69 | 271 | 14,828.57 |
| Wade Ormsby | 70 | 70 | 65 | 66 | 271 | 14,828.57 |
| Mark Roe | 63 | 72 | 69 | 68 | 272 | 11,825 |
| Garry Houston | 68 | 71 | 68 | 65 | 272 | 11,825 |
| Ricardo Gonzalez | 72 | 67 | 64 | 69 | 272 | 11,825 |
| Alastair Forsyth | 66 | 71 | 67 | 68 | 272 | 11,825 |
| Mark Foster | 69 | 69 | 68 | 67 | 273 | 10,100 |
| Robert Karlsson | 63 | 76 | 65 | 69 | 273 | 10,100 |
| Fernando Roca | 69 | 68 | 70 | 66 | 273 | 10,100 |
| Ignacio Garrido | 74 | 65 | 66 | 68 | 273 | 10,100 |
| Gonzalo Fernandez-Castano | 67 | 71 | 65 | 70 | 273 | 10,100 |
| Brad Kennedy | 68 | 72 | 66 | 67 | 273 | 10,100 |
| Oliver Wilson | 69 | 68 | 70 | 66 | 273 | 10,100 |
| Gary Emerson | 67 | 64 | 73 | 71 | 275 | 8,450 |
| Gregory Havret | 69 | 68 | 70 | 68 | 275 | 8,450 |
| Christopher Hanell | 69 | 68 | 70 | 68 | 275 | 8,450 |
| Francois Delamontagne | 67 | 69 | 72 | 67 | 275 | 8,450 |
| Damien McGrane | 68 | 66 | 71 | 71 | 276 | 6,900 |
| Steve Webster | 72 | 68 | 69 | 67 | 276 | 6,900 |
| Phillip Archer | 70 | 67 | 66 | 73 | 276 | 6,900 |
| Ian Garbutt | 69 | 64 | 74 | 69 | 276 | 6,900 |
| Johan Skold | 69 | 68 | 68 | 71 | 276 | 6,900 |
| Simon Wakefield | 73 | 67 | 69 | 67 | 276 | 6,900 |
| Ivo Giner | 75 | 60 | 68 | 73 | 276 | 6,900 |
| Stuart Manley | 68 | 70 | 68 | 70 | 276 | 6,900 |
| Carlos De Corral | 71 | 66 | 68 | 71 | 276 | 6,900 |
| Marcel Siem | 70 | 66 | 70 | 71 | 277 | 5,900 |
| Miguel Angel Martin | 69 | 67 | 72 | 70 | 278 | 5,000 |
| Maarten Lafeber | 67 | 70 | 70 | 71 | 278 | 5,000 |
| Martin Erlandsson | 67 | 69 | 69 | 73 | 278 | 5,000 |
| Scott Drummond | 70 | 67 | 74 | 67 | 278 | 5,000 |
| Francesco Molinari | 72 | 67 | 68 | 71 | 278 | 5,000 |
| Markus Brier | 69 | 69 | 71 | 69 | 278 | 5,000 |
| Stephen Gallacher | 69 | 67 | 71 | 71 | 278 | 5,000 |
| Brett Rumford | 66 | 71 | 67 | 74 | 278 | 5,000 |
| Gary Murphy | 70 | 69 | 68 | 72 | 279 | 3,437.50 |
| Anthony Wall | 68 | 69 | 70 | 72 | 279 | 3,437.50 |
| Philip Golding | 74 | 65 | 70 | 70 | 279 | 3,437.50 |
| Richard Bland | 73 | 66 | 71 | 69 | 279 | 3,437.50 |
| Simon Khan | 68 | 69 | 72 | 70 | 279 | 3,437.50 |
| David Drysdale | 72 | 67 | 70 | 70 | 279 | 3,437.50 |
| Fredrik Andersson Hed | 69 | 71 | 68 | 71 | 279 | 3,437.50 |
| Graeme Storm | 66 | 68 | 73 | 72 | 279 | 3,437.50 |
| Alvaro Salto | 69 | 71 | 71 | 69 | 280 | 2,700 |
| Mattias Eliasson | 70 | 67 | 71 | 72 | 280 | 2,700 |
| Alessandro Tadini | 69 | 70 | 73 | 68 | 280 | 2,700 |
| Santiago Luna | 69 | 69 | 68 | 75 | 281 | 2,400 |
| Johan Axgren | 70 | 70 | 70 | 71 | 281 | 2,400 |
| Emanuele Canonica | 69 | 68 | 75 | 69 | 281 | 2,400 |
| Peter Hedblom | 68 | 70 | 70 | 74 | 282 | 2,006 |

| | SCORES | | | TOTAL | MONEY |
|---|---|---|---|---|---|
| Miles Tunnicliff | 71 | 69 | 73 | 69 | 282 | 2,006 |
| Neil Cheetham | 70 | 67 | 70 | 75 | 282 | 2,006 |
| Christian Cevaer | 66 | 70 | 74 | 72 | 282 | 2,006 |
| David Carter | 70 | 70 | 70 | 72 | 282 | 2,006 |
| *Jorge Mazario | 69 | 71 | 72 | 70 | 282 | |
| Soren Kjeldsen | 72 | 68 | 70 | 74 | 284 | 1,500 |
| Costantino Rocca | 71 | 69 | 74 | 71 | 285 | 1,495.50 |
| Jose Manuel Carriles | 70 | 69 | 75 | 71 | 285 | 1,495.50 |
| Rolf Muntz | 72 | 67 | 72 | 75 | 286 | 1,491 |

## Mallorca Classic

*Pula Golf Club*, Majorca, Spain
Par 35-35–70; 6,676 yards

October 20-23
purse, €1,500,000

| | SCORES | | | TOTAL | MONEY |
|---|---|---|---|---|---|
| Jose Maria Olazabal | 69 | 65 | 70 | 66 | 270 | €250,000 |
| Sergio Garcia | 69 | 69 | 71 | 66 | 275 | 111,853.30 |
| Jose Manuel Lara | 68 | 69 | 70 | 68 | 275 | 111,853.30 |
| Paul Broadhurst | 67 | 66 | 72 | 70 | 275 | 111,853.30 |
| Miles Tunnicliff | 69 | 68 | 70 | 69 | 276 | 53,700 |
| Bradley Dredge | 72 | 67 | 67 | 70 | 276 | 53,700 |
| Simon Wakefield | 69 | 71 | 67 | 69 | 276 | 53,700 |
| Mattias Eliasson | 68 | 68 | 70 | 71 | 277 | 33,700 |
| Jean Van de Velde | 70 | 71 | 66 | 70 | 277 | 33,700 |
| Miguel Angel Jimenez | 67 | 71 | 72 | 67 | 277 | 33,700 |
| Robert-Jan Derksen | 70 | 68 | 71 | 69 | 278 | 23,950 |
| David Park | 68 | 70 | 72 | 68 | 278 | 23,950 |
| Fredrik Andersson Hed | 70 | 71 | 69 | 68 | 278 | 23,950 |
| Andrew Coltart | 71 | 73 | 71 | 63 | 278 | 23,950 |
| John Bickerton | 67 | 71 | 70 | 70 | 278 | 23,950 |
| Graeme Storm | 70 | 71 | 69 | 68 | 278 | 23,950 |
| Soren Hansen | 70 | 69 | 66 | 74 | 279 | 19,050 |
| Robert Coles | 70 | 70 | 74 | 65 | 279 | 19,050 |
| Christopher Hanell | 73 | 69 | 69 | 68 | 279 | 19,050 |
| Wade Ormsby | 70 | 66 | 70 | 73 | 279 | 19,050 |
| Sam Little | 67 | 73 | 68 | 72 | 280 | 16,275 |
| Paul Lawrie | 70 | 71 | 71 | 68 | 280 | 16,275 |
| Stephen Scahill | 70 | 69 | 69 | 72 | 280 | 16,275 |
| Simon Khan | 67 | 69 | 72 | 72 | 280 | 16,275 |
| Markus Brier | 71 | 73 | 68 | 68 | 280 | 16,275 |
| Marcus Fraser | 71 | 70 | 71 | 68 | 280 | 16,275 |
| Miguel Angel Martin | 69 | 71 | 73 | 68 | 281 | 14,025 |
| Gregory Havret | 69 | 66 | 73 | 73 | 281 | 14,025 |
| Christian Cevaer | 72 | 68 | 71 | 70 | 281 | 14,025 |
| David Lynn | 70 | 68 | 72 | 71 | 281 | 14,025 |
| Santiago Luna | 69 | 69 | 71 | 73 | 282 | 11,190 |
| Andrew Oldcorn | 71 | 71 | 69 | 71 | 282 | 11,190 |
| Klas Eriksson | 68 | 72 | 69 | 73 | 282 | 11,190 |
| Robert Karlsson | 72 | 69 | 69 | 72 | 282 | 11,190 |
| Jonathan Lomas | 65 | 74 | 72 | 71 | 282 | 11,190 |
| Ricardo Gonzalez | 71 | 71 | 74 | 66 | 282 | 11,190 |
| Benoit Teilleria | 69 | 69 | 77 | 67 | 282 | 11,190 |
| Francois Delamontagne | 73 | 71 | 72 | 66 | 282 | 11,190 |
| Alastair Forsyth | 69 | 70 | 76 | 67 | 282 | 11,190 |
| Gonzalo Fernandez-Castano | 68 | 72 | 70 | 72 | 282 | 11,190 |
| Mark Roe | 69 | 72 | 72 | 70 | 283 | 8,550 |

| | SCORES | | | | TOTAL | MONEY |
|---|---|---|---|---|---|---|
| Jean-Francois Remesy | 69 | 70 | 74 | 70 | 283 | 8,550 |
| Peter Hanson | 69 | 73 | 70 | 71 | 283 | 8,550 |
| Jamie Spence | 72 | 70 | 72 | 69 | 283 | 8,550 |
| Jean-Francois Lucquin | 71 | 69 | 71 | 72 | 283 | 8,550 |
| Jarmo Sandelin | 71 | 73 | 69 | 70 | 283 | 8,550 |
| Carlos Del Moral | 69 | 70 | 76 | 68 | 283 | 8,550 |
| Mark Foster | 66 | 72 | 75 | 71 | 284 | 6,600 |
| Damien McGrane | 72 | 71 | 68 | 73 | 284 | 6,600 |
| Maarten Lafeber | 70 | 73 | 71 | 70 | 284 | 6,600 |
| Scott Drummond | 69 | 69 | 75 | 71 | 284 | 6,600 |
| Jesus Maria Arruti | 68 | 70 | 69 | 77 | 284 | 6,600 |
| Brad Kennedy | 69 | 70 | 72 | 73 | 284 | 6,600 |
| Alessandro Tadini | 70 | 71 | 68 | 76 | 285 | 5,100 |
| Ian Garbutt | 73 | 71 | 73 | 68 | 285 | 5,100 |
| Johan Skold | 71 | 73 | 69 | 72 | 285 | 5,100 |
| Robert Rock | 70 | 70 | 72 | 73 | 285 | 5,100 |
| Soren Kjeldsen | 69 | 75 | 70 | 72 | 286 | 4,200 |
| Garry Houston | 71 | 73 | 73 | 69 | 286 | 4,200 |
| Marcel Siem | 71 | 72 | 77 | 66 | 286 | 4,200 |
| Peter Hedblom | 70 | 73 | 69 | 74 | 286 | 4,200 |
| Raymond Russell | 74 | 70 | 72 | 70 | 286 | 4,200 |
| Niki Zitny | 70 | 72 | 75 | 70 | 287 | 3,375 |
| Jose Manuel Carriles | 69 | 74 | 74 | 70 | 287 | 3,375 |
| Matthew Blackey | 72 | 71 | 73 | 71 | 287 | 3,375 |
| Stephen Gallacher | 73 | 71 | 71 | 72 | 287 | 3,375 |
| Jose-Filipe Lima | 68 | 68 | 75 | 76 | 287 | 3,375 |
| Alfredo Garcia | 75 | 69 | 73 | 70 | 287 | 3,375 |
| Pelle Edberg | 70 | 71 | 72 | 75 | 288 | 2,613.33 |
| Nick Dougherty | 71 | 73 | 76 | 68 | 288 | 2,613.33 |
| Jamie Donaldson | 73 | 70 | 71 | 74 | 288 | 2,613.33 |
| Marten Olander | 68 | 71 | 80 | 70 | 289 | 2,247 |
| Phillip Archer | 71 | 73 | 75 | 71 | 290 | 2,241 |
| Andrea Maestroni | 73 | 68 | 71 | 78 | 290 | 2,241 |
| Fredrik Henge | 68 | 74 | 72 | 76 | 290 | 2,241 |
| Simon Hurd | 69 | 74 | 75 | 73 | 291 | 2,232 |
| Ivo Giner | 70 | 73 | 78 | 70 | 291 | 2,232 |
| Simon Dyson | 77 | 65 | 78 | 71 | 291 | 2,232 |
| Emanuele Canonica | 70 | 69 | 74 | 79 | 292 | 2,226 |
| Gary Murphy | 66 | 74 | 78 | 76 | 294 | 2,223 |

## Volvo Masters

*Club de Golf Valderrama*, Sotegrande, Spain      October 27-30
Par 35-36–71; 6,952 yards      purse, €3,928,500

| | SCORES | | | | TOTAL | MONEY |
|---|---|---|---|---|---|---|
| Paul McGinley | 74 | 68 | 65 | 67 | 274 | €666,660 |
| Sergio Garcia | 68 | 67 | 68 | 73 | 276 | 444,440 |
| Jose Maria Olazabal | 68 | 72 | 68 | 69 | 277 | 206,666.70 |
| Colin Montgomerie | 67 | 66 | 70 | 74 | 277 | 206,666.70 |
| Luke Donald | 68 | 73 | 72 | 64 | 277 | 206,666.70 |
| Paul Broadhurst | 71 | 69 | 67 | 71 | 278 | 140,000 |
| Simon Khan | 75 | 68 | 67 | 69 | 279 | 103,200 |
| Niclas Fasth | 70 | 70 | 71 | 68 | 279 | 103,200 |
| Lee Westwood | 71 | 69 | 67 | 72 | 279 | 103,200 |
| Padraig Harrington | 72 | 74 | 67 | 67 | 280 | 72,100 |
| Kenneth Ferrie | 72 | 72 | 70 | 66 | 280 | 72,100 |

| | SCORES | | | TOTAL | MONEY |
|---|---|---|---|---|---|
| Ian Poulter | 67 | 68 | 72 | 73 | 280 | 72,100 |
| Stephen Dodd | 71 | 72 | 70 | 67 | 280 | 72,100 |
| Michael Campbell | 72 | 69 | 68 | 72 | 281 | 62,200 |
| Bradley Dredge | 70 | 68 | 73 | 71 | 282 | 56,550 |
| Nick Dougherty | 71 | 70 | 76 | 65 | 282 | 56,550 |
| Paul Casey | 70 | 72 | 71 | 69 | 282 | 56,550 |
| Charl Schwartzel | 72 | 71 | 70 | 69 | 282 | 56,550 |
| Barry Lane | 76 | 70 | 69 | 68 | 283 | 50,000 |
| Henrik Stenson | 70 | 69 | 73 | 71 | 283 | 50,000 |
| Gregory Havret | 70 | 75 | 70 | 68 | 283 | 50,000 |
| Soren Kjeldsen | 71 | 74 | 73 | 66 | 284 | 43,585.71 |
| Steve Webster | 69 | 73 | 74 | 68 | 284 | 43,585.71 |
| Peter Hanson | 71 | 75 | 71 | 67 | 284 | 43,585.71 |
| Pierre Fulke | 76 | 73 | 67 | 68 | 284 | 43,585.71 |
| David Lynn | 73 | 73 | 68 | 70 | 284 | 43,585.71 |
| Thongchai Jaidee | 72 | 72 | 70 | 70 | 284 | 43,585.71 |
| Graeme McDowell | 72 | 71 | 69 | 72 | 284 | 43,585.71 |
| Raphael Jacquelin | 70 | 74 | 74 | 67 | 285 | 36,480 |
| Nick O'Hern | 72 | 67 | 70 | 76 | 285 | 36,480 |
| Miguel Angel Jimenez | 73 | 72 | 70 | 70 | 285 | 36,480 |
| Robert Karlsson | 69 | 73 | 70 | 73 | 285 | 36,480 |
| Stephen Gallacher | 73 | 69 | 73 | 70 | 285 | 36,480 |
| Maarten Lafeber | 70 | 75 | 72 | 70 | 287 | 32,250 |
| Soren Hansen | 72 | 75 | 68 | 72 | 287 | 32,250 |
| Angel Cabrera | 73 | 72 | 71 | 71 | 287 | 32,250 |
| Gonzalo Fernandez-Castano | 73 | 71 | 73 | 70 | 287 | 32,250 |
| David Howell | 71 | 72 | 71 | 74 | 288 | 29,100 |
| Robert-Jan Derksen | 73 | 71 | 71 | 73 | 288 | 29,100 |
| Jean-Francois Remesy | 74 | 76 | 69 | 69 | 288 | 29,100 |
| Anders Hansen | 73 | 74 | 71 | 72 | 290 | 25,950 |
| Richard Green | 71 | 75 | 72 | 72 | 290 | 25,950 |
| Peter Lawrie | 76 | 73 | 71 | 70 | 290 | 25,950 |
| Richard Sterne | 74 | 72 | 74 | 70 | 290 | 25,950 |
| Jose Manuel Lara | 75 | 73 | 69 | 74 | 291 | 22,800 |
| Damien McGrane | 75 | 73 | 71 | 72 | 291 | 22,800 |
| Graeme Storm | 76 | 75 | 67 | 73 | 291 | 22,800 |
| Jean Van de Velde | 78 | 73 | 73 | 68 | 292 | 21,000 |
| Paul Lawrie | 72 | 76 | 71 | 74 | 293 | 19,200 |
| Simon Dyson | 72 | 78 | 72 | 71 | 293 | 19,200 |
| Richard Finch | 79 | 74 | 68 | 72 | 293 | 19,200 |
| Peter Gustafsson | 78 | 74 | 72 | 70 | 294 | 17,500 |
| Peter Hedblom | 76 | 73 | 75 | 74 | 298 | 16,800 |
| Emanuele Canonica | 82 | 79 | 73 | 78 | 312 | 16,300 |
| Darren Clarke | 76 | 75 | | | WD | 15,800 |

# HSBC Champions Tournament

See Asia/Japan Tours chapter.

# WGC - Algarve World Cup in Portugal

*Victoria Clube de Golf,* Vilamoura, Portugal
Par 36-36–72; 7,198 yards
(Fourth round cancelled—rain.)

November 17-20
purse, US$4,000,000

| | INDIVIDUAL SCORES | | | TOTAL |
|---|---|---|---|---|
| **WALES—$1,400,000**<br>Stephen Dodd/Bradley Dredge | 61 | 67 | 61 | 189 |
| **ENGLAND—$550,000**<br>Luke DonaldDavid Howell | 59 | 69 | 63 | 191 |
| **SWEDEN—$550,000**<br>Niclas Fasth/Henrik Stenson | 61 | 67 | 63 | 191 |
| **FRANCE—$200,000**<br>Raphael Jacquelin/Thomas Levet | 63 | 70 | 61 | 194 |
| **DENMARK—$145,000**<br>Anders Hansen/Soren Hansen | 64 | 68 | 63 | 195 |
| **ARGENTINA—$117,500**<br>Angel Cabrera/Ricardo Gonzalez | 68 | 61 | 67 | 196 |
| **NETHERLANDS—$117,500**<br>Robert-Jan Derksen/Maarten Lafeber | 63 | 67 | 66 | 196 |
| **GERMANY—$95,000**<br>Alex Cejka/Christian Reimbold | 65 | 68 | 64 | 197 |
| **INDIA—$80,000**<br>Arjun Atwal/Jyoti Randhawa | 60 | 73 | 65 | 198 |
| **SPAIN—$67,500**<br>Sergio Garcia/Miguel Angel Jimenez | 62 | 72 | 65 | 199 |
| **CHINESE TAIPEI—$67,500**<br>Wang Ter-chang/Chang Tse-peng | 62 | 71 | 66 | 199 |
| **SOUTH KOREA—$55,000**<br>K.J. Choi/Chang Ik-je | 67 | 71 | 62 | 200 |
| **SOUTH AFRICA—$55,000**<br>Tim Clark/Trevor Immelman | 68 | 67 | 65 | 200 |
| **IRELAND—$55,000**<br>Padraig Harrington/Paul McGinley | 67 | 69 | 64 | 200 |
| **PARAGUAY—$48,500**<br>Carlos Franco/Marco Ruiz | 63 | 73 | 65 | 201 |
| **JAPAN—$48,500**<br>Yasuharu Imano/Takuya Taniguchi | 63 | 70 | 68 | 201 |
| **UNITED STATES—$46,000**<br>Stewart Cink/Zach Johnson | 65 | 70 | 67 | 202 |
| **MEXICO—$46,000**<br>Pablo Del Olmo/Alejandro Quiroz | 67 | 71 | 64 | 202 |

| | INDIVIDUAL SCORES | | | TOTAL |
|---|---|---|---|---|
| **AUSTRALIA—$46,000** | | | | |
| Mark Hensby/Peter Lonard | 60 | 73 | 69 | 202 |
| **SCOTLAND—$43,000** | | | | |
| Scott Drummond/Stephen Gallacher | 65 | 74 | 64 | 203 |
| **SINGAPORE—$43,000** | | | | |
| Lam Chih-bing /Mardan Mamat | 67 | 70 | 66 | 203 |
| **PORTUGAL—$43,000** | | | | |
| Jose-Filipe Lima/Antonio Sobrinho | 68 | 72 | 63 | 203 |
| **COLOMBIA—$41,000** | | | | |
| Eduardo Herrera/Diego Vanegas | 66 | 74 | 69 | 209 |
| **VENEZUELA—$40,000** | | | | |
| Manuel Bermudez/Carlos Larrain | 66 | 75 | 69 | 210 |

## Volvo China Open
See Asia/Japan Tours chaper.

## UBS Hong Kong Open
See Asia/Japan Tours chaper.

## Dunhill Championship
See African Tours chaper.

## South African Airways Open
See African Tours chaper.

# Challenge Tour

## Costa Rica Open
See American Tours chapter.

## Panama Masters
See American Tours chapter.

## Telefonica de Guatemala
See American Tours chapter.

## Tusker Kenya Open

*Karen Golf Club,* Nairobi, Kenya
Par 35-35–70; 6,918 yards

March 10-13
purse, €160,000

| | SCORES | | | | TOTAL | MONEY |
|---|---|---|---|---|---|---|
| Daniel Vancsik | 66 | 68 | 75 | 63 | 272 | €25,600 |
| Michael Kirk | 68 | 72 | 67 | 68 | 275 | 17,600 |
| Sam Walker | 70 | 70 | 68 | 68 | 276 | 11,200 |
| Paul Dwyer | 70 | 68 | 71 | 68 | 277 | 8,000 |
| Mikael Lundberg | 67 | 72 | 73 | 65 | 277 | 8,000 |
| Richard McEvoy | 69 | 71 | 68 | 69 | 277 | 8,000 |
| Carl Suneson | 70 | 67 | 69 | 73 | 279 | 4,480 |
| David Dixon | 73 | 67 | 71 | 68 | 279 | 4,480 |
| Ariel Canete | 71 | 69 | 69 | 70 | 279 | 4,480 |
| Raphael Eyraud | 70 | 73 | 68 | 69 | 280 | 2,902.86 |
| Chris Gane | 71 | 71 | 72 | 66 | 280 | 2,902.86 |
| Carlos Quevedo | 72 | 68 | 66 | 74 | 280 | 2,902.86 |
| David Higgins | 72 | 69 | 66 | 73 | 280 | 2,902.86 |
| Thomas Nielsen | 71 | 72 | 68 | 69 | 280 | 2,902.86 |
| James Kamte | 66 | 72 | 72 | 70 | 280 | 2,902.86 |
| Kyle Dobbs | 75 | 68 | 72 | 65 | 280 | 2,902.86 |
| Johan Edfors | 68 | 77 | 71 | 65 | 281 | 2,080 |
| Ajay Shah | 74 | 70 | 67 | 70 | 281 | 2,080 |
| Ross Wellington | 73 | 72 | 69 | 67 | 281 | 2,080 |
| Marcus Higley | 71 | 70 | 70 | 71 | 282 | 1,546 |
| Van Phillips | 71 | 72 | 70 | 69 | 282 | 1,546 |
| Tim Milford | 70 | 73 | 71 | 68 | 282 | 1,546 |
| Alan Michel | 70 | 73 | 70 | 69 | 282 | 1,546 |
| Christian Reimbold | 75 | 68 | 71 | 68 | 282 | 1,546 |
| David Patrick | 71 | 73 | 70 | 68 | 282 | 1,546 |
| Miguel Rodriguez | 67 | 71 | 71 | 73 | 282 | 1,546 |
| Miguel Carballo | 72 | 69 | 68 | 73 | 282 | 1,546 |
| Jamie Little | 71 | 71 | 69 | 72 | 283 | 1,280 |
| Mattias Nilsson | 72 | 70 | 71 | 70 | 283 | 1,280 |
| Kariem Baraka | 73 | 72 | 71 | 67 | 283 | 1,280 |
| David Orr | 72 | 69 | 72 | 70 | 283 | 1,280 |
| Rodolfo Gonzalez | 72 | 73 | 65 | 73 | 283 | 1,280 |
| Jamie Elson | 72 | 69 | 69 | 73 | 283 | 1,280 |
| Gareth Davies | 74 | 67 | 72 | 70 | 283 | 1,280 |

# Madeira Island Open Caixa Geral de Depositos

See PGA European Tour section.

# Peugeot Challenge R.C.G. El Prat

*Real Club de Golf El Prat,* Barcelona, Spain
Par 36-36–72; 6,465 yards

April 28-May 1
purse, €115,000

| | SCORES | | | | TOTAL | MONEY |
|---|---|---|---|---|---|---|
| Tomas Jesus Munoz | 72 | 74 | 73 | 68 | 287 | €18,400 |
| Marco Ruiz | 71 | 70 | 71 | 76 | 288 | 12,650 |
| Lee James | 69 | 69 | 76 | 75 | 289 | 7,475 |
| Michael Kirk | 73 | 73 | 77 | 66 | 289 | 7,475 |
| Carl Suneson | 73 | 76 | 68 | 73 | 290 | 5,175 |
| Vicente Blazquez | 74 | 73 | 75 | 68 | 290 | 5,175 |
| Gianluca Baruffaldi | 71 | 77 | 73 | 70 | 291 | 3,220 |
| David Higgins | 72 | 74 | 75 | 70 | 291 | 3,220 |
| Roope Kakko | 74 | 73 | 75 | 69 | 291 | 3,220 |
| Luis Claverie | 77 | 74 | 73 | 68 | 292 | 2,338.33 |
| Francisco Cea | 69 | 73 | 73 | 77 | 292 | 2,338.33 |
| Ivo Giner | 75 | 65 | 74 | 78 | 292 | 2,338.33 |
| Shaun Webster | 73 | 72 | 75 | 73 | 293 | 1,840 |
| Pedro Linhart | 72 | 71 | 74 | 76 | 293 | 1,840 |
| Mikael Lundberg | 74 | 76 | 73 | 70 | 293 | 1,840 |
| David Orr | 73 | 75 | 70 | 75 | 293 | 1,840 |
| Gary Birch, Jr. | 73 | 78 | 69 | 73 | 293 | 1,840 |
| Oskar Bergman | 76 | 73 | 70 | 75 | 294 | 1,437.50 |
| Kariem Baraka | 73 | 70 | 74 | 77 | 294 | 1,437.50 |
| Jose Manuel Carriles | 75 | 76 | 73 | 71 | 295 | 1,156.90 |
| Denny Lucas | 71 | 71 | 81 | 72 | 295 | 1,156.90 |
| Michael Hoey | 70 | 73 | 74 | 78 | 295 | 1,156.90 |
| Ignacio Feliu | 73 | 76 | 72 | 74 | 295 | 1,156.90 |
| Paul Dwyer | 74 | 77 | 73 | 71 | 295 | 1,156.90 |
| Chris Gane | 74 | 73 | 75 | 74 | 296 | 1,046.50 |
| Sam Walker | 73 | 70 | 79 | 74 | 296 | 1,046.50 |
| Massimo Scarpa | 75 | 74 | 72 | 76 | 297 | 954.50 |
| Benn Barham | 68 | 74 | 82 | 73 | 297 | 954.50 |
| Birgir Hafthorsson | 75 | 71 | 76 | 75 | 297 | 954.50 |
| Martin Wiegele | 74 | 73 | 75 | 75 | 297 | 954.50 |
| Carlos Aguilar | 76 | 72 | 76 | 73 | 297 | 954.50 |
| Jean-Baptiste Gonnet | 75 | 70 | 74 | 78 | 297 | 954.50 |

# FirstPlus Wales Challenge

*Vale Hotel Golf & Spa Resort,* Wales
Par 37-36–73; 7,413 yards

May 5-8
purse, €125,000

| | SCORES | | | | TOTAL | MONEY |
|---|---|---|---|---|---|---|
| Olivier David | 74 | 75 | 73 | 70 | 292 | €20,000 |
| Iain Pyman | 73 | 71 | 71 | 77 | 292 | 13,750 |
| (David defeated Pyman on second playoff hole.) | | | | | | |
| John Wade | 74 | 76 | 73 | 70 | 293 | 8,750 |
| Benn Barham | 72 | 75 | 75 | 72 | 294 | 7,500 |
| Richard Porter | 73 | 77 | 74 | 72 | 296 | 5,625 |

| | SCORES | | | | TOTAL | MONEY |
|---|---|---|---|---|---|---|
| Toni Karjalainen | 76 | 75 | 76 | 69 | 296 | 5,625 |
| Sion Bebb | 73 | 77 | 73 | 74 | 297 | 3,020.83 |
| Andrew Butterfield | 77 | 75 | 73 | 72 | 297 | 3,020.83 |
| David Higgins | 77 | 73 | 74 | 73 | 297 | 3,020.83 |
| Kyron Sullivan | 70 | 79 | 75 | 73 | 297 | 3,020.83 |
| David Patrick | 72 | 75 | 75 | 75 | 297 | 3,020.83 |
| Stuart Davis | 76 | 71 | 78 | 72 | 297 | 3,020.83 |
| Kalle Brink | 75 | 75 | 75 | 73 | 298 | 1,820.31 |
| Shaun Webster | 77 | 75 | 71 | 75 | 298 | 1,820.31 |
| John Davies | 73 | 72 | 81 | 72 | 298 | 1,820.31 |
| Carl Suneson | 72 | 69 | 75 | 82 | 298 | 1,820.31 |
| Paul Streeter | 69 | 77 | 76 | 76 | 298 | 1,820.31 |
| Murray Urquhart | 74 | 73 | 80 | 71 | 298 | 1,820.31 |
| Thomas Nielsen | 72 | 76 | 74 | 76 | 298 | 1,820.31 |
| Graham Gordon | 75 | 74 | 73 | 76 | 298 | 1,820.31 |
| James Lee | 77 | 73 | 74 | 75 | 299 | 1,237.50 |
| Stephen Dodd | 76 | 74 | 79 | 70 | 299 | 1,237.50 |
| Erol Simsek | 74 | 76 | 75 | 75 | 300 | 1,187.50 |
| Soren Juul Hansen | 74 | 74 | 73 | 79 | 300 | 1,187.50 |
| Mark Davis | 76 | 76 | 74 | 75 | 301 | 1,087.50 |
| Denny Lucas | 77 | 75 | 75 | 74 | 301 | 1,087.50 |
| Inaki Alustiza | 77 | 75 | 71 | 78 | 301 | 1,087.50 |
| Mikael Lundberg | 73 | 77 | 77 | 74 | 301 | 1,087.50 |
| Fredrik Widmark | 76 | 73 | 79 | 73 | 301 | 1,087.50 |
| Jorge Bartolome | 76 | 73 | 74 | 78 | 301 | 1,087.50 |

## XX Tessali-Metaponto Open di Puglia e Basilicata

*Riva dei Tessali:* Par 35-36–71; 6,503 yards
*Metaponto GC:* Par 36-36–72; 6,972 yards
Castellaneta, Italy

May 12-15
purse, €120,000

| | SCORES | | | | TOTAL | MONEY |
|---|---|---|---|---|---|---|
| Rafael Gomez | 71 | 67 | 66 | 63 | 267 | €19,200 |
| Johan Edfors | 67 | 66 | 67 | 68 | 268 | 13,200 |
| Sam Walker | 71 | 68 | 67 | 65 | 271 | 7,800 |
| Raphael Pellicioli | 67 | 69 | 65 | 70 | 271 | 7,800 |
| Andrew Butterfield | 65 | 76 | 64 | 67 | 272 | 5,400 |
| Steven Jeppesen | 69 | 64 | 69 | 70 | 272 | 5,400 |
| Michael Kirk | 68 | 65 | 72 | 68 | 273 | 3,840 |
| Jan-Are Larsen | 64 | 70 | 68 | 72 | 274 | 2,820 |
| Kariem Baraka | 69 | 69 | 68 | 68 | 274 | 2,820 |
| Sebastian Fernandez | 69 | 69 | 69 | 67 | 274 | 2,820 |
| Richard McEvoy | 65 | 72 | 69 | 68 | 274 | 2,820 |
| Bertrand Cornut | 70 | 70 | 66 | 69 | 275 | 2,160 |
| Jamie Elson | 68 | 69 | 70 | 68 | 275 | 2,160 |
| Peter Whiteford | 70 | 69 | 68 | 68 | 275 | 2,160 |
| Shaun Webster | 70 | 69 | 68 | 69 | 276 | 1,630 |
| Michael Hoey | 70 | 71 | 68 | 67 | 276 | 1,630 |
| Julien Van Hauwe | 74 | 66 | 67 | 69 | 276 | 1,630 |
| Carlos Quevedo | 69 | 68 | 68 | 71 | 276 | 1,630 |
| Soren Juul Hansen | 68 | 69 | 70 | 69 | 276 | 1,630 |
| Ross Fisher | 67 | 68 | 70 | 71 | 276 | 1,630 |
| Alberto Binaghi | 71 | 70 | 65 | 71 | 277 | 1,176 |
| Mattias Nilsson | 68 | 72 | 70 | 67 | 277 | 1,176 |
| Inder Van Weerelt | 69 | 72 | 64 | 72 | 277 | 1,176 |
| Peter Jespersen | 71 | 68 | 68 | 71 | 278 | 1,068 |

| | SCORES | | | | TOTAL | MONEY |
|---|---|---|---|---|---|---|
| Paul Dwyer | 71 | 68 | 69 | 70 | 278 | 1,068 |
| James Hepworth | 69 | 67 | 72 | 70 | 278 | 1,068 |
| Sebastien Delagrange | 70 | 69 | 69 | 70 | 278 | 1,068 |
| Marc Warren | 70 | 70 | 67 | 71 | 278 | 1,068 |
| Ben Welch | 71 | 67 | 70 | 70 | 278 | 1,068 |
| Cesar Monasterio | 72 | 68 | 67 | 72 | 279 | 912 |
| Marco Soffietti | 75 | 63 | 69 | 72 | 279 | 912 |
| Denny Lucas | 71 | 67 | 74 | 67 | 279 | 912 |
| Gabriel Canizares | 67 | 69 | 72 | 71 | 279 | 912 |
| Gareth Paddison | 70 | 70 | 70 | 69 | 279 | 912 |
| James Heath | 70 | 71 | 70 | 68 | 279 | 912 |
| Matthew Kent | 70 | 69 | 68 | 72 | 279 | 912 |

## Riu Tikida Hotels Moroccan Classic

*Golf du Soleil,* Agadir, Morocco
Par 36-35–71; 6,590 yards

May 26-29
purse, €130,000

| | SCORES | | | | TOTAL | MONEY |
|---|---|---|---|---|---|---|
| Fredrik Widmark | 66 | 70 | 63 | 70 | 269 | €20,800 |
| Gary Clark | 68 | 66 | 68 | 67 | 269 | 11,700 |
| Oliver Whiteley | 68 | 69 | 64 | 68 | 269 | 11,700 |
| (Widmark defeated Clark and Whiteley on first playoff hole.) | | | | | | |
| Ross Fisher | 67 | 71 | 66 | 67 | 271 | 7,800 |
| Michele Reale | 68 | 69 | 66 | 69 | 272 | 5,286.67 |
| Peter Whiteford | 72 | 69 | 67 | 64 | 272 | 5,286.67 |
| Gabriel Canizares | 70 | 67 | 66 | 69 | 272 | 5,286.67 |
| Marcus Higley | 67 | 65 | 72 | 69 | 273 | 2,938 |
| Carl Suneson | 69 | 68 | 66 | 70 | 273 | 2,938 |
| Birgir Hafthorsson | 73 | 66 | 68 | 66 | 273 | 2,938 |
| Bertrand Cornut | 70 | 68 | 67 | 68 | 273 | 2,938 |
| Colm Moriarty | 69 | 71 | 65 | 68 | 273 | 2,938 |
| Andre Bossert | 66 | 68 | 71 | 69 | 274 | 2,210 |
| Nicolas Joakimides | 67 | 70 | 69 | 68 | 274 | 2,210 |
| Mikael Lundberg | 72 | 65 | 67 | 70 | 274 | 2,210 |
| Shaun Webster | 72 | 67 | 70 | 66 | 275 | 1,703 |
| Paul Dwyer | 68 | 73 | 66 | 68 | 275 | 1,703 |
| Sion Bebb | 69 | 68 | 69 | 69 | 275 | 1,703 |
| Ivo Giner | 71 | 66 | 68 | 70 | 275 | 1,703 |
| Stuart Davis | 70 | 67 | 70 | 68 | 275 | 1,703 |
| James Hepworth | 71 | 65 | 69 | 71 | 276 | 1,287 |
| Jean-Nicolas Billot | 66 | 66 | 71 | 73 | 276 | 1,287 |
| Greig Hutcheon | 68 | 71 | 72 | 66 | 277 | 1,144 |
| Andrea Maestroni | 67 | 73 | 69 | 68 | 277 | 1,144 |
| Nicolas Vanhootegem | 67 | 68 | 73 | 69 | 277 | 1,144 |
| Sarel Son-Houi | 72 | 66 | 69 | 70 | 277 | 1,144 |
| Tino Schuster | 71 | 70 | 64 | 72 | 277 | 1,144 |
| Tom Whitehouse | 70 | 66 | 71 | 70 | 277 | 1,144 |
| Raphael Pellicioli | 68 | 69 | 72 | 68 | 277 | 1,144 |
| Jean-Baptiste Gonnet | 70 | 71 | 66 | 70 | 277 | 1,144 |
| Jerome Theunis | 73 | 64 | 70 | 70 | 277 | 1,144 |

# Thomas Bjorn Open

*Esbjerg Golfklub,* Esbjerg, Denmark
Par 35-36–71; 6,944 yards

June 9-12
purse, €115,000

| | SCORES | | | | TOTAL | MONEY |
|---|---|---|---|---|---|---|
| Toni Karjalainen | 66 | 73 | 74 | 75 | 288 | €18,400 |
| Oskar Bergman | 74 | 76 | 71 | 68 | 289 | 12,650 |
| Ariel Canete | 70 | 72 | 75 | 73 | 290 | 8,050 |
| Mikael Lundberg | 72 | 76 | 73 | 70 | 291 | 6,325 |
| Matthew Morris | 70 | 73 | 76 | 72 | 291 | 6,325 |
| Peter Jespersen | 73 | 78 | 69 | 72 | 292 | 3,565 |
| Edward Rush | 72 | 76 | 74 | 70 | 292 | 3,565 |
| Tuomas Tuovinen | 71 | 76 | 73 | 72 | 292 | 3,565 |
| Jamie Elson | 71 | 74 | 71 | 76 | 292 | 3,565 |
| Benn Barham | 70 | 78 | 71 | 74 | 293 | 2,415 |
| Lewis Atkinson | 76 | 72 | 71 | 74 | 293 | 2,415 |
| Kalle Brink | 72 | 78 | 72 | 72 | 294 | 1,840 |
| Sion Bebb | 70 | 77 | 77 | 70 | 294 | 1,840 |
| Mark Pilkington | 75 | 74 | 76 | 69 | 294 | 1,840 |
| Fredrik Widmark | 69 | 76 | 77 | 72 | 294 | 1,840 |
| Daniel Vancsik | 70 | 73 | 74 | 77 | 294 | 1,840 |
| Gareth Paddison | 72 | 74 | 80 | 68 | 294 | 1,840 |
| Jeppe Huldahl | 69 | 76 | 74 | 75 | 294 | 1,840 |
| Didier De Vooght | 76 | 72 | 74 | 73 | 295 | 1,244.88 |
| Matthew Cort | 71 | 77 | 76 | 71 | 295 | 1,244.88 |
| Kariem Baraka | 72 | 76 | 76 | 71 | 295 | 1,244.88 |
| Oskar Henningsson | 69 | 80 | 74 | 72 | 295 | 1,244.88 |
| Knud Storgaard | 72 | 76 | 75 | 73 | 296 | 1,069.50 |
| Paul Nilbrink | 69 | 75 | 77 | 75 | 296 | 1,069.50 |
| Peter Kaensche | 70 | 77 | 76 | 73 | 296 | 1,069.50 |
| Oyvind Rojahn | 70 | 76 | 76 | 74 | 296 | 1,069.50 |
| Tom Whitehouse | 69 | 78 | 76 | 74 | 297 | 977.50 |
| Soren Juul Hansen | 74 | 73 | 73 | 77 | 297 | 977.50 |
| Marc Warren | 71 | 77 | 75 | 74 | 297 | 977.50 |
| Peter Ankerso | 72 | 77 | 77 | 71 | 297 | 977.50 |

# Aa St. Omer Open

See PGA European Tour section.

# Galeria Kaufhof Pokal Challenge

*Rittergut Birkhof Golf Club,* Dusseldorf, Germany
Par 36-36–72; 6,807 yards

June 23-26
purse, €115,000

| | SCORES | | | | TOTAL | MONEY |
|---|---|---|---|---|---|---|
| Gareth Davies | 68 | 68 | 66 | 67 | 269 | €18,400 |
| Anders S. Hansen | 63 | 65 | 69 | 72 | 269 | 12,650 |
| (Davies defeated Hansen on first playoff hole.) | | | | | | |
| Ariel Canete | 70 | 63 | 69 | 68 | 270 | 8,050 |
| Iain Steel | 67 | 73 | 64 | 67 | 271 | 6,325 |
| David Dixon | 71 | 69 | 66 | 65 | 271 | 6,325 |
| Miguel Rodriguez | 67 | 66 | 71 | 68 | 272 | 4,140 |
| Daniel Wardrop | 67 | 70 | 70 | 65 | 272 | 4,140 |

| | SCORES | | | | TOTAL | MONEY |
|---|---|---|---|---|---|---|
| Mark Mouland | 66 | 67 | 69 | 71 | 273 | 2,702.50 |
| Paolo Terreni | 68 | 67 | 72 | 66 | 273 | 2,702.50 |
| Shaun Webster | 69 | 64 | 70 | 70 | 273 | 2,702.50 |
| Michele Reale | 66 | 72 | 68 | 67 | 273 | 2,702.50 |
| Thomas Nielsen | 69 | 63 | 72 | 70 | 274 | 2,185 |
| *Stephan Gross | 75 | 67 | 68 | 64 | 274 | |
| Jamie Little | 69 | 67 | 69 | 70 | 275 | 1,955 |
| Kariem Baraka | 68 | 66 | 69 | 72 | 275 | 1,955 |
| Oliver Whiteley | 68 | 68 | 70 | 69 | 275 | 1,955 |
| Chris Gane | 67 | 68 | 71 | 70 | 276 | 1,552.50 |
| Juan Abbate | 69 | 70 | 68 | 69 | 276 | 1,552.50 |
| Simon Lilly | 70 | 69 | 65 | 72 | 276 | 1,552.50 |
| Miguel Carballo | 66 | 71 | 68 | 71 | 276 | 1,552.50 |
| Benn Barham | 72 | 65 | 71 | 69 | 277 | 1,199.83 |
| Oskar Bergman | 67 | 72 | 70 | 68 | 277 | 1,199.83 |
| Roope Kakko | 72 | 70 | 67 | 68 | 277 | 1,199.83 |
| Euan Little | 71 | 71 | 68 | 68 | 278 | 1,035 |
| Didier De Vooght | 66 | 69 | 71 | 72 | 278 | 1,035 |
| Martin LeMesurier | 69 | 71 | 66 | 72 | 278 | 1,035 |
| Christian Reimbold | 71 | 67 | 70 | 70 | 278 | 1,035 |
| Ross Fisher | 70 | 67 | 70 | 71 | 278 | 1,035 |
| Marco Crespi | 70 | 68 | 71 | 69 | 278 | 1,035 |
| Gregory Molteni | 71 | 67 | 67 | 73 | 278 | 1,035 |

## Open Mahou de Madrid

*Club de Golf La Herreria,* Madrid, Spain
Par 35-36–71; 6,660 yards

June 30-July 3
purse, €120,000

| | SCORES | | | | TOTAL | MONEY |
|---|---|---|---|---|---|---|
| Benn Barham | 63 | 67 | 66 | 67 | 263 | €19,200 |
| Fredrik Widmark | 67 | 71 | 65 | 64 | 267 | 13,200 |
| Tomas Jesus Munoz | 66 | 70 | 65 | 67 | 268 | 7,800 |
| Andres Romero | 69 | 70 | 65 | 64 | 268 | 7,800 |
| Andrew Butterfield | 71 | 68 | 71 | 60 | 270 | 4,500 |
| Francisco Cea | 70 | 71 | 66 | 63 | 270 | 4,500 |
| Marco Ruiz | 70 | 68 | 68 | 64 | 270 | 4,500 |
| Johan Kok | 71 | 68 | 65 | 66 | 270 | 4,500 |
| Carl Suneson | 68 | 69 | 68 | 66 | 271 | 2,760 |
| Jean-Baptiste Gonnet | 67 | 68 | 71 | 65 | 271 | 2,760 |
| Johan Edfors | 66 | 69 | 69 | 68 | 272 | 2,400 |
| Iain Steel | 66 | 70 | 67 | 70 | 273 | 1,920 |
| Jesus Maria Arruti | 69 | 66 | 68 | 70 | 273 | 1,920 |
| Victor Casado | 67 | 70 | 71 | 65 | 273 | 1,920 |
| Marc Warren | 67 | 68 | 69 | 69 | 273 | 1,920 |
| Juan Parron | 69 | 68 | 64 | 72 | 273 | 1,920 |
| Miguel Carballo | 68 | 68 | 68 | 69 | 273 | 1,920 |
| Brad Sutterfield | 70 | 71 | 66 | 66 | 273 | 1,920 |
| Michele Reale | 68 | 68 | 67 | 71 | 274 | 1,410 |
| Jose Lorca | 68 | 68 | 68 | 70 | 274 | 1,410 |
| Marco Soffietti | 67 | 71 | 66 | 71 | 275 | 1,176 |
| Paul Dwyer | 69 | 67 | 70 | 69 | 275 | 1,176 |
| Matthew Kent | 69 | 70 | 64 | 72 | 275 | 1,176 |
| James Hepworth | 69 | 70 | 67 | 70 | 276 | 1,092 |
| Arnaud Langenaeken | 66 | 72 | 71 | 67 | 276 | 1,092 |
| Stuart Davis | 72 | 67 | 69 | 68 | 276 | 1,092 |
| Carlos Del Moral | 71 | 64 | 71 | 70 | 276 | 1,092 |

| | SCORES | | | | TOTAL | MONEY |
|---|---|---|---|---|---|---|
| Shaun Webster | 72 | 69 | 66 | 70 | 277 | 996 |
| Liam Bond | 71 | 69 | 68 | 69 | 277 | 996 |
| Iain Pyman | 72 | 67 | 69 | 69 | 277 | 996 |
| Dok Noh | 69 | 73 | 69 | 66 | 277 | 996 |

## Open des Volcans Challenge de France

*Golf des Volcans,* Clermont Ferrand, France
Par 36-35–71; 7,054 yards

July 7-10
purse, €120,000

| | SCORES | | | | TOTAL | MONEY |
|---|---|---|---|---|---|---|
| Ilya Goroneskoul | 73 | 67 | 64 | 67 | 271 | €19,200 |
| Nicolas Joakimides | 69 | 65 | 68 | 71 | 273 | 9,600 |
| Andrew Butterfield | 68 | 65 | 71 | 69 | 273 | 9,600 |
| Ariel Canete | 68 | 69 | 69 | 67 | 273 | 9,600 |
| Birgir Hafthorsson | 66 | 73 | 69 | 69 | 277 | 4,176 |
| Iain Pyman | 70 | 68 | 71 | 68 | 277 | 4,176 |
| Anders S. Hansen | 72 | 67 | 71 | 67 | 277 | 4,176 |
| Ross Fisher | 70 | 68 | 72 | 67 | 277 | 4,176 |
| Julien Xanthopoulos | 69 | 68 | 69 | 71 | 277 | 4,176 |
| Benoit Teilleria | 75 | 63 | 72 | 68 | 278 | 2,520 |
| Miguel Carballo | 67 | 69 | 72 | 70 | 278 | 2,520 |
| Gustavo Rojas | 69 | 71 | 70 | 69 | 279 | 2,280 |
| Shaun Webster | 74 | 68 | 71 | 67 | 280 | 2,100 |
| Andres Romero | 72 | 67 | 73 | 68 | 280 | 2,100 |
| Olivier David | 70 | 68 | 72 | 71 | 281 | 1,630 |
| Sion Bebb | 68 | 68 | 73 | 72 | 281 | 1,630 |
| Van Phillips | 72 | 67 | 72 | 70 | 281 | 1,630 |
| Lee James | 71 | 72 | 68 | 70 | 281 | 1,630 |
| Magnus Carlsson | 70 | 70 | 69 | 72 | 281 | 1,630 |
| Tom Whitehouse | 73 | 71 | 69 | 68 | 281 | 1,630 |
| Marcus Higley | 70 | 67 | 71 | 74 | 282 | 1,128 |
| Renaud Guillard | 69 | 66 | 76 | 71 | 282 | 1,128 |
| Mattias Nilsson | 68 | 73 | 69 | 72 | 282 | 1,128 |
| Thomas Nielsen | 70 | 71 | 69 | 72 | 282 | 1,128 |
| Marco Ruiz | 75 | 69 | 69 | 69 | 282 | 1,128 |
| Miguel Rodriguez | 74 | 68 | 70 | 70 | 282 | 1,128 |
| Oskar Henningsson | 73 | 69 | 70 | 70 | 282 | 1,128 |
| Alessandro Napoleoni | 73 | 69 | 72 | 69 | 283 | 1,008 |
| Michael Hoey | 73 | 69 | 70 | 71 | 283 | 1,008 |
| Ivo Giner | 72 | 70 | 70 | 71 | 283 | 1,008 |
| *Julien Guerrier | 69 | 75 | 66 | 73 | 283 | |

## Texbond Open

*Garda Golf Country Club*, Garda, Italy
Par 36-36–72; 7,112 yards

July 13-16
purse, €115,000

| | SCORES | | | | TOTAL | MONEY |
|---|---|---|---|---|---|---|
| Fredrik Widmark | 65 | 70 | 68 | 66 | 269 | €18,400 |
| Michael Hoey | 68 | 67 | 65 | 71 | 271 | 10,350 |
| Marc Warren | 69 | 68 | 66 | 68 | 271 | 10,350 |
| Lee James | 70 | 68 | 67 | 67 | 272 | 6,900 |
| Ross Fisher | 69 | 71 | 67 | 66 | 273 | 5,750 |

|  | SCORES | | | | TOTAL | MONEY |
|---|---|---|---|---|---|---|
| Julien Van Hauwe | 68 | 70 | 70 | 67 | 275 | 4,600 |
| Benn Barham | 67 | 67 | 70 | 72 | 276 | 3,220 |
| Anders S. Hansen | 70 | 68 | 68 | 70 | 276 | 3,220 |
| Richard McEvoy | 70 | 72 | 68 | 66 | 276 | 3,220 |
| Alberto Binaghi | 70 | 72 | 68 | 67 | 277 | 2,271.25 |
| Denny Lucas | 69 | 69 | 70 | 69 | 277 | 2,271.25 |
| Marco Ruiz | 74 | 69 | 66 | 68 | 277 | 2,271.25 |
| James Heath | 72 | 67 | 70 | 68 | 277 | 2,271.25 |
| Rafael Gomez | 70 | 72 | 67 | 69 | 278 | 1,897.50 |
| Andres Romero | 71 | 72 | 68 | 67 | 278 | 1,897.50 |
| Thomas Gogele | 67 | 73 | 68 | 71 | 279 | 1,552.50 |
| Massimo Florioli | 69 | 71 | 70 | 69 | 279 | 1,552.50 |
| Mark Pilkington | 70 | 70 | 68 | 71 | 279 | 1,552.50 |
| David Orr | 72 | 71 | 67 | 69 | 279 | 1,552.50 |
| Carl Suneson | 68 | 72 | 67 | 73 | 280 | 1,199.83 |
| Toni Karjalainen | 69 | 66 | 70 | 75 | 280 | 1,199.83 |
| Alfredo Garcia | 67 | 69 | 70 | 74 | 280 | 1,199.83 |
| Julien Clement | 72 | 66 | 74 | 69 | 281 | 1,023.50 |
| Ryan Reid | 73 | 68 | 72 | 68 | 281 | 1,023.50 |
| Rodolfo Gonzalez | 71 | 72 | 70 | 68 | 281 | 1,023.50 |
| Matthew Woods | 69 | 70 | 72 | 70 | 281 | 1,023.50 |
| Colm Moriarty | 67 | 74 | 69 | 71 | 281 | 1,023.50 |
| Marco Crespi | 69 | 70 | 69 | 73 | 281 | 1,023.50 |
| Julien Quesne | 71 | 71 | 70 | 69 | 281 | 1,023.50 |
| Andrea Zani | 69 | 68 | 69 | 75 | 281 | 1,023.50 |

# Ireland Ryder Cup Challenge

*Killarney Golf & Fishing Club*, Ireland
Par 36-36–72; 7,010 yards

July 28-31
purse, €130,000

|  | SCORES | | | | TOTAL | MONEY |
|---|---|---|---|---|---|---|
| Marc Warren | 67 | 67 | 72 | 66 | 272 | €20,800 |
| Peter Whiteford | 65 | 67 | 69 | 71 | 272 | 14,300 |
| (Warren defeated Whiteford on third playoff hole.) | | | | | | |
| Denny Lucas | 67 | 67 | 74 | 67 | 275 | 9,100 |
| Chris Gane | 71 | 67 | 71 | 70 | 279 | 6,500 |
| Martin Wiegele | 70 | 68 | 68 | 73 | 279 | 6,500 |
| Simon Lilly | 70 | 71 | 67 | 71 | 279 | 6,500 |
| Roope Kakko | 63 | 72 | 73 | 72 | 280 | 4,160 |
| Peter Kaensche | 65 | 72 | 81 | 63 | 281 | 2,748.57 |
| Massimo Scarpa | 71 | 70 | 70 | 70 | 281 | 2,748.57 |
| Didier De Vooght | 69 | 69 | 71 | 72 | 281 | 2,748.57 |
| Iain Pyman | 69 | 70 | 73 | 69 | 281 | 2,748.57 |
| Toni Karjalainen | 68 | 71 | 73 | 69 | 281 | 2,748.57 |
| Ross Fisher | 71 | 72 | 70 | 68 | 281 | 2,748.57 |
| Simon Thornton | 69 | 73 | 70 | 69 | 281 | 2,748.57 |
| Greig Hutcheon | 68 | 68 | 74 | 72 | 282 | 1,885 |
| Shaun Webster | 69 | 67 | 73 | 73 | 282 | 1,885 |
| Sion Bebb | 69 | 70 | 72 | 71 | 282 | 1,885 |
| Oskar Henningsson | 67 | 73 | 72 | 70 | 282 | 1,885 |
| Magnus P. Atlevi | 71 | 67 | 73 | 72 | 283 | 1,349.83 |
| Julien Van Hauwe | 73 | 69 | 72 | 69 | 283 | 1,349.83 |
| Matthew Woods | 68 | 68 | 74 | 73 | 283 | 1,349.83 |
| Raphael Pellicioli | 71 | 69 | 72 | 71 | 283 | 1,349.83 |
| Daniel Wardrop | 70 | 70 | 72 | 71 | 283 | 1,349.83 |
| Andrew Willey | 72 | 70 | 68 | 73 | 283 | 1,349.83 |

| | SCORES | | | | TOTAL | MONEY |
|---|---|---|---|---|---|---|
| Alberto Binaghi | 75 | 65 | 70 | 74 | 284 | 1,144 |
| Leslie Walker | 70 | 73 | 71 | 70 | 284 | 1,144 |
| Lee James | 69 | 72 | 69 | 74 | 284 | 1,144 |
| Christian Reimbold | 70 | 70 | 73 | 71 | 284 | 1,144 |
| Oliver Whiteley | 72 | 69 | 73 | 70 | 284 | 1,144 |
| Alessandro Napoleoni | 70 | 69 | 75 | 71 | 285 | 975 |
| John Wade | 66 | 73 | 74 | 72 | 285 | 975 |
| Paul Nilbrink | 70 | 70 | 73 | 72 | 285 | 975 |
| John Davies | 71 | 71 | 73 | 70 | 285 | 975 |
| Stefano Reale | 67 | 74 | 70 | 74 | 285 | 975 |
| Julien Clement | 69 | 74 | 71 | 71 | 285 | 975 |
| Michele Reale | 74 | 68 | 74 | 69 | 285 | 975 |
| Magnus Carlsson | 72 | 69 | 74 | 70 | 285 | 975 |

## Cadillac Russian Open

See PGA European Tour section.

## Rolex Trophy

*Golf Club de Geneve,* Geneva, Switzerland
Par 36-36–72; 6,727 yards

August 18-21
purse, €200,000

| | SCORES | | | | TOTAL | MONEY |
|---|---|---|---|---|---|---|
| Marc Warren | 64 | 68 | 69 | 71 | 272 | €17,000 |
| Denny Lucas | 68 | 69 | 64 | 71 | 272 | 11,000 |
| (Warren defeated Lucas on first playoff hole.) | | | | | | |
| Benn Barham | 66 | 72 | 68 | 69 | 275 | 9,000 |
| Toni Karjalainen | 69 | 70 | 69 | 67 | 275 | 9,000 |
| Daniel Vancsik | 68 | 68 | 68 | 72 | 276 | 7,500 |
| Marco Ruiz | 68 | 71 | 65 | 73 | 277 | 6,500 |
| Ariel Canete | 67 | 72 | 65 | 73 | 277 | 6,500 |
| Ross Fisher | 69 | 71 | 69 | 68 | 277 | 6,500 |
| Andrew Butterfield | 67 | 71 | 68 | 72 | 278 | 5,600 |
| Kyron Sullivan | 69 | 66 | 71 | 72 | 278 | 5,600 |
| Miguel Carballo | 68 | 72 | 68 | 70 | 278 | 5,600 |
| Michael Kirk | 66 | 73 | 70 | 70 | 279 | 5,100 |
| Brad Sutterfield | 69 | 67 | 71 | 72 | 279 | 5,100 |
| Michael Hoey | 66 | 68 | 72 | 75 | 281 | 4,650 |
| Carl Suneson | 67 | 71 | 71 | 72 | 281 | 4,650 |
| Fredrik Widmark | 66 | 72 | 70 | 73 | 281 | 4,650 |
| Steven Jeppesen | 67 | 67 | 69 | 78 | 281 | 4,650 |
| Peter Whiteford | 73 | 67 | 69 | 75 | 284 | 4,400 |

## Skandia PGA Open

*Arlandastad Golf Club*, Stockholm, Sweden
Par 34-36–70; 6,805 yards

August 18-21
purse, €110,618

| | SCORES | | | | TOTAL | MONEY |
|---|---|---|---|---|---|---|
| David Patrick | 66 | 69 | 66 | 71 | 272 | €17,193.32 |
| Stuart Davis | 67 | 69 | 67 | 69 | 272 | 11,820.41 |
| (Patrick defeated Davis on third playoff hole.) | | | | | | |

| | SCORES | | | | TOTAL | MONEY |
|---|---|---|---|---|---|---|
| Iain Steel | 74 | 67 | 70 | 63 | 274 | 7,522.08 |
| *David Palm | 70 | 70 | 65 | 69 | 274 | |
| Edward Rush | 68 | 68 | 70 | 69 | 275 | 5,372.91 |
| Colm Moriarty | 66 | 66 | 69 | 74 | 275 | 5,372.91 |
| Jaakko Makitalo | 65 | 69 | 72 | 69 | 275 | 5,372.91 |
| Tuomas Tuovinen | 68 | 71 | 68 | 69 | 276 | 3,438.66 |
| Johan Bjerhag | 70 | 69 | 70 | 68 | 277 | 2,650.64 |
| Simon Lilly | 69 | 71 | 65 | 72 | 277 | 2,650.64 |
| Alexander Noren | 70 | 69 | 69 | 69 | 277 | 2,650.64 |
| *Nils Bjorling | 68 | 73 | 69 | 67 | 277 | |
| Peter Malmgren | 69 | 73 | 65 | 71 | 278 | 2,041.71 |
| Pehr Magnebrant | 71 | 68 | 70 | 69 | 278 | 2,041.71 |
| Murray Urquhart | 74 | 69 | 66 | 69 | 278 | 2,041.71 |
| Wilhelm Schauman | 71 | 70 | 68 | 70 | 279 | 1,665.60 |
| Thomas Nielsen | 70 | 72 | 66 | 71 | 279 | 1,665.60 |
| Anders S. Hansen | 68 | 70 | 71 | 70 | 279 | 1,665.60 |
| Stephen Browne | 69 | 70 | 70 | 70 | 279 | 1,665.60 |
| Marcus Higley | 67 | 71 | 69 | 73 | 280 | 1,180.25 |
| Peter Jespersen | 70 | 72 | 70 | 68 | 280 | 1,180.25 |
| Paul Nilbrink | 75 | 67 | 69 | 69 | 280 | 1,180.25 |
| Julien Clement | 72 | 68 | 71 | 69 | 280 | 1,180.25 |
| Nicolas Vanhootegem | 69 | 73 | 73 | 65 | 280 | 1,180.25 |
| Julien Quesne | 69 | 68 | 75 | 68 | 280 | 1,180.25 |
| Kalle Brink | 67 | 70 | 72 | 72 | 281 | 956.38 |
| Magnus Sunesson | 70 | 69 | 74 | 68 | 281 | 956.38 |
| Julien Van Hauwe | 70 | 68 | 71 | 72 | 281 | 956.38 |
| Joakim Kristiansson | 72 | 70 | 69 | 70 | 281 | 956.38 |
| Magnus Carlsson | 71 | 70 | 71 | 69 | 281 | 956.38 |
| Hampus Von Post | 70 | 68 | 72 | 71 | 281 | 956.38 |

## Morson International Pro-Am Challenge

*Marriott Worsley Park Hotel & Country Club,*
*Greater Manchester, England*
*Par 35-35–70; 6,797 yards*

August 24-27
purse, €150,000

| | SCORES | | | | TOTAL | MONEY |
|---|---|---|---|---|---|---|
| Andres Romero | 69 | 65 | 69 | 68 | 271 | €24,000 |
| Marco Soffietti | 70 | 68 | 65 | 69 | 272 | 12,000 |
| Sion Bebb | 68 | 68 | 70 | 66 | 272 | 12,000 |
| Richard McEvoy | 72 | 70 | 64 | 66 | 272 | 12,000 |
| Shaun Webster | 70 | 71 | 64 | 68 | 273 | 6,100 |
| Julien Clement | 70 | 69 | 66 | 68 | 273 | 6,100 |
| Ariel Canete | 71 | 69 | 67 | 66 | 273 | 6,100 |
| Michiel Bothma | 65 | 71 | 70 | 68 | 274 | 3,525 |
| Johan Kok | 72 | 70 | 67 | 65 | 274 | 3,525 |
| Julien Quesne | 69 | 70 | 66 | 69 | 274 | 3,525 |
| Inder Van Weerelt | 69 | 67 | 71 | 67 | 274 | 3,525 |
| Johan Edfors | 71 | 69 | 68 | 67 | 275 | 2,625 |
| Andrew Butterfield | 70 | 69 | 70 | 66 | 275 | 2,625 |
| Magnus Carlsson | 68 | 72 | 67 | 68 | 275 | 2,625 |
| David Dixon | 69 | 67 | 71 | 68 | 275 | 2,625 |
| John Wade | 68 | 69 | 71 | 68 | 276 | 1,779.38 |
| Marcus Higley | 70 | 69 | 70 | 67 | 276 | 1,779.38 |
| Jamie Little | 70 | 68 | 70 | 68 | 276 | 1,779.38 |
| Murray Urquhart | 69 | 70 | 69 | 68 | 276 | 1,779.38 |
| Robert Rock | 67 | 73 | 67 | 69 | 276 | 1,779.38 |

| | SCORES | | | | TOTAL | MONEY |
|---|---|---|---|---|---|---|
| David Orr | 72 | 67 | 66 | 71 | 276 | 1,779.38 |
| Kyron Sullivan | 69 | 69 | 69 | 69 | 276 | 1,779.38 |
| Steven Jeppesen | 70 | 68 | 70 | 68 | 276 | 1,779.38 |
| Euan Little | 72 | 69 | 72 | 64 | 277 | 1,305 |
| Greig Hutcheon | 70 | 66 | 72 | 69 | 277 | 1,305 |
| Denny Lucas | 75 | 66 | 72 | 64 | 277 | 1,305 |
| Benn Barham | 70 | 67 | 68 | 72 | 277 | 1,305 |
| Christian Reimbold | 67 | 72 | 71 | 67 | 277 | 1,305 |
| David Patrick | 73 | 69 | 68 | 67 | 277 | 1,305 |
| Manuel Quiros | 69 | 64 | 71 | 73 | 277 | 1,305 |
| Gareth Wright | 70 | 71 | 69 | 67 | 277 | 1,305 |

## BA-CA Golf Open

*Fontana Golf Club*, Vienna, Austria
Par 35-36–71; 6,976 yards

September 1-4
purse, €150,000

| | SCORES | | | | TOTAL | MONEY |
|---|---|---|---|---|---|---|
| Michael Hoey | 67 | 64 | 67 | 67 | 265 | €24,000 |
| Steven Jeppesen | 67 | 65 | 68 | 66 | 266 | 16,500 |
| Olivier David | 66 | 69 | 67 | 66 | 268 | 10,500 |
| Andrew Butterfield | 65 | 67 | 68 | 69 | 269 | 8,250 |
| Christian Reimbold | 70 | 67 | 69 | 63 | 269 | 8,250 |
| Martin Wiegele | 66 | 74 | 66 | 64 | 270 | 5,000 |
| Michiel Bothma | 69 | 65 | 67 | 69 | 270 | 5,000 |
| Daniel Vancsik | 71 | 68 | 67 | 64 | 270 | 5,000 |
| Marcus Higley | 65 | 69 | 67 | 70 | 271 | 3,300 |
| Clemens Prader | 67 | 64 | 70 | 70 | 271 | 3,300 |
| Miguel Carballo | 67 | 66 | 71 | 67 | 271 | 3,300 |
| Mark Mouland | 69 | 68 | 63 | 73 | 273 | 2,775 |
| Massimo Scarpa | 69 | 69 | 68 | 67 | 273 | 2,775 |
| Jesus Maria Arruti | 71 | 68 | 69 | 66 | 274 | 2,325 |
| Toni Karjalainen | 71 | 66 | 68 | 69 | 274 | 2,325 |
| Jamie Elson | 71 | 67 | 68 | 68 | 274 | 2,325 |
| Craig Williams | 69 | 67 | 70 | 68 | 274 | 2,325 |
| Jose Manuel Carriles | 69 | 70 | 67 | 69 | 275 | 1,584.38 |
| Chris Gane | 70 | 68 | 66 | 71 | 275 | 1,584.38 |
| Markus Brier | 66 | 69 | 71 | 69 | 275 | 1,584.38 |
| Kariem Baraka | 66 | 73 | 71 | 65 | 275 | 1,584.38 |
| David Orr | 71 | 69 | 69 | 66 | 275 | 1,584.38 |
| Kyron Sullivan | 70 | 70 | 68 | 67 | 275 | 1,584.38 |
| Anders S. Hansen | 67 | 67 | 75 | 66 | 275 | 1,584.38 |
| Brad Sutterfield | 67 | 66 | 71 | 71 | 275 | 1,584.38 |
| Thomas Feyrsinger | 65 | 73 | 73 | 65 | 276 | 1,305 |
| Marco Soffietti | 69 | 71 | 72 | 64 | 276 | 1,305 |
| Sam Walker | 68 | 67 | 74 | 67 | 276 | 1,305 |
| Roope Kakko | 67 | 71 | 68 | 70 | 276 | 1,305 |
| Mattias Nilsson | 69 | 71 | 69 | 68 | 277 | 1,140 |
| Carl Suneson | 74 | 62 | 72 | 69 | 277 | 1,140 |
| Michele Reale | 70 | 69 | 70 | 68 | 277 | 1,140 |
| Claude Grenier | 68 | 67 | 73 | 69 | 277 | 1,140 |
| Wilhelm Schauman | 67 | 68 | 69 | 73 | 277 | 1,140 |
| Thomas Nielsen | 71 | 67 | 68 | 71 | 277 | 1,140 |
| Ross Fisher | 65 | 72 | 68 | 72 | 277 | 1,140 |

# Telia Challenge Waxholm

*Waxholm Golf Club,* Stockholm, Sweden
Par 36-37–73; 7,317 yards

September 8-11
purse, €108,198

| | SCORES | | | | TOTAL | MONEY |
|---|---|---|---|---|---|---|
| Morten Hagen | 72 | 68 | 72 | 68 | 280 | €17,259.88 |
| Christian Nilsson | 66 | 67 | 72 | 75 | 280 | 11,866.17 |
| (Hagen defeated Nilsson on fourth playoff hole.) | | | | | | |
| Magnus P. Atlevi | 72 | 69 | 69 | 72 | 282 | 7,011.83 |
| Tuomas Tuovinen | 69 | 71 | 71 | 71 | 282 | 7,011.83 |
| John Wade | 68 | 72 | 70 | 73 | 283 | 4,386.89 |
| Jean-Baptiste Gonnet | 72 | 68 | 69 | 74 | 283 | 4,386.89 |
| Steven Jeppesen | 76 | 69 | 70 | 68 | 283 | 4,386.89 |
| Jan-Are Larsen | 75 | 67 | 70 | 72 | 284 | 3,020.48 |
| Gary Clark | 72 | 73 | 70 | 70 | 285 | 2,373.23 |
| Fredrick Mansson | 71 | 73 | 71 | 70 | 285 | 2,373.23 |
| Anders S. Hansen | 73 | 73 | 71 | 68 | 285 | 2,373.23 |
| James Heath | 70 | 71 | 71 | 74 | 286 | 2,049.61 |
| Mattias Eliasson | 75 | 67 | 75 | 70 | 287 | 1,833.86 |
| Joakim Rask | 70 | 73 | 72 | 72 | 287 | 1,833.86 |
| Leif Westerberg | 72 | 72 | 74 | 69 | 287 | 1,833.86 |
| Julien Van Hauwe | 67 | 71 | 76 | 74 | 288 | 1,510.24 |
| Tom Whitehouse | 74 | 69 | 75 | 70 | 288 | 1,510.24 |
| Gary Lockerbie | 72 | 70 | 73 | 73 | 288 | 1,510.24 |
| Peter Jespersen | 72 | 71 | 72 | 74 | 289 | 1,120.09 |
| Magnus Carlsson | 73 | 72 | 70 | 74 | 289 | 1,120.09 |
| Wilhelm Schauman | 72 | 71 | 70 | 76 | 289 | 1,120.09 |
| Jeppe Huldahl | 72 | 68 | 78 | 71 | 289 | 1,120.09 |
| Kalle Edberg | 69 | 74 | 73 | 73 | 289 | 1,120.09 |
| Robert Eriksson | 72 | 73 | 69 | 75 | 289 | 1,120.09 |
| Pelle Edberg | 70 | 76 | 71 | 73 | 290 | 949.29 |
| Johan Edfors | 74 | 71 | 74 | 71 | 290 | 949.29 |
| Craig Williams | 72 | 73 | 72 | 73 | 290 | 949.29 |
| Roope Kakko | 74 | 69 | 74 | 73 | 290 | 949.29 |
| Anders Sjostrand | 71 | 72 | 77 | 70 | 290 | 949.29 |
| Paul Nilbrink | 74 | 71 | 72 | 74 | 291 | 841.42 |
| Greig Hutcheon | 69 | 75 | 73 | 74 | 291 | 841.42 |
| Mattias Nilsson | 72 | 72 | 76 | 71 | 291 | 841.42 |
| Andreas Ljunggren | 73 | 73 | 74 | 71 | 291 | 841.42 |
| Niklas Bruzelius | 71 | 71 | 73 | 76 | 291 | 841.42 |

# Rotterdam International Open

*Golf Club Broekpolder,* Vlaardingen, Netherlands
Par 36-36–72; 7,009 yards

September 15-18
purse, €115,000

| | SCORES | | | | TOTAL | MONEY |
|---|---|---|---|---|---|---|
| Per G. Nyman | 65 | 71 | 66 | 73 | 275 | €18,400 |
| Kyron Sullivan | 68 | 70 | 69 | 69 | 276 | 10,350 |
| Craig Williams | 73 | 67 | 68 | 68 | 276 | 10,350 |
| James Heath | 71 | 71 | 68 | 68 | 278 | 6,900 |
| Marcus Higley | 73 | 69 | 67 | 72 | 281 | 5,175 |
| Toni Karjalainen | 73 | 67 | 69 | 72 | 281 | 5,175 |
| Marco Soffietti | 70 | 70 | 70 | 72 | 282 | 3,450 |
| Oskar Henningsson | 71 | 71 | 73 | 67 | 282 | 3,450 |
| Tom Whitehouse | 75 | 71 | 70 | 67 | 283 | 2,645 |

| | SCORES | | | | TOTAL | MONEY |
|---|---|---|---|---|---|---|
| Ross Fisher | 68 | 76 | 70 | 69 | 283 | 2,645 |
| Birgir Hafthorsson | 71 | 73 | 74 | 66 | 284 | 2,242.50 |
| Sam Walker | 73 | 72 | 71 | 68 | 284 | 2,242.50 |
| Massimo Scarpa | 73 | 74 | 70 | 68 | 285 | 2,070 |
| John Wade | 68 | 72 | 71 | 75 | 286 | 1,559.69 |
| Carl Suneson | 72 | 72 | 71 | 71 | 286 | 1,559.69 |
| Michiel Bothma | 72 | 71 | 72 | 71 | 286 | 1,559.69 |
| Marco Ruiz | 72 | 72 | 73 | 69 | 286 | 1,559.69 |
| Gary Birch, Jr. | 70 | 76 | 71 | 69 | 286 | 1,559.69 |
| Marc Warren | 71 | 73 | 74 | 68 | 286 | 1,559.69 |
| Hernan Rey | 71 | 72 | 72 | 71 | 286 | 1,559.69 |
| Gary Lockerbie | 71 | 72 | 71 | 72 | 286 | 1,559.69 |
| Nicolas Vanhootegem | 71 | 73 | 72 | 71 | 287 | 1,069.50 |
| Didier De Vooght | 72 | 74 | 70 | 71 | 287 | 1,069.50 |
| Andrew Butterfield | 70 | 74 | 71 | 72 | 287 | 1,069.50 |
| Anders S. Hansen | 72 | 72 | 73 | 70 | 287 | 1,069.50 |
| Richard McEvoy | 69 | 71 | 74 | 73 | 287 | 1,069.50 |
| Miguel Carballo | 74 | 68 | 74 | 71 | 287 | 1,069.50 |
| Shaun Webster | 68 | 72 | 72 | 76 | 288 | 943 |
| Massimo Florioli | 69 | 76 | 74 | 69 | 288 | 943 |
| Mark Sanders | 73 | 72 | 70 | 73 | 288 | 943 |
| Brian Akstrup | 73 | 73 | 69 | 73 | 288 | 943 |
| David Patrick | 77 | 69 | 70 | 72 | 288 | 943 |

## Kazakhstan Open

*Nurtau Golf Club,* Almaty, Kazakhstan
Par 36-36–72; 7,107 yards

September 22-25
purse, €250,000

| | SCORES | | | | TOTAL | MONEY |
|---|---|---|---|---|---|---|
| Stephen Browne | 66 | 69 | 69 | 69 | 273 | €40,000 |
| Carl Suneson | 67 | 69 | 68 | 70 | 274 | 16,500 |
| Lee James | 70 | 68 | 64 | 72 | 274 | 16,500 |
| Tom Whitehouse | 71 | 70 | 66 | 67 | 274 | 16,500 |
| Colm Moriarty | 68 | 70 | 67 | 69 | 274 | 16,500 |
| Steven Jeppesen | 66 | 70 | 69 | 69 | 274 | 16,500 |
| Ivo Giner | 71 | 65 | 68 | 73 | 277 | 7,500 |
| Andres Romero | 66 | 73 | 74 | 64 | 277 | 7,500 |
| Denny Lucas | 69 | 69 | 68 | 72 | 278 | 5,500 |
| Julien Clement | 67 | 65 | 72 | 74 | 278 | 5,500 |
| Sam Osborne | 64 | 69 | 75 | 70 | 278 | 5,500 |
| Peter Jespersen | 73 | 65 | 69 | 72 | 279 | 3,637.50 |
| Sion Bebb | 69 | 73 | 68 | 69 | 279 | 3,637.50 |
| David Higgins | 67 | 68 | 70 | 74 | 279 | 3,637.50 |
| Kariem Baraka | 68 | 72 | 71 | 68 | 279 | 3,637.50 |
| Sam Walker | 70 | 69 | 65 | 75 | 279 | 3,637.50 |
| Daniel Vancsik | 69 | 68 | 67 | 75 | 279 | 3,637.50 |
| David Patrick | 70 | 66 | 72 | 71 | 279 | 3,637.50 |
| Gareth Paddison | 71 | 72 | 67 | 69 | 279 | 3,637.50 |
| James Heath | 70 | 67 | 72 | 70 | 279 | 3,637.50 |
| Ross Fisher | 70 | 69 | 69 | 71 | 279 | 3,637.50 |
| Benn Barham | 70 | 70 | 68 | 72 | 280 | 2,400 |
| Michael Jonzon | 68 | 72 | 70 | 70 | 280 | 2,400 |
| David Orr | 67 | 71 | 70 | 72 | 280 | 2,400 |
| Michele Reale | 69 | 68 | 71 | 73 | 281 | 2,250 |
| Richard McEvoy | 72 | 69 | 73 | 67 | 281 | 2,250 |
| Miguel Carballo | 69 | 69 | 75 | 68 | 281 | 2,250 |

| | SCORES | | | TOTAL | MONEY |
|---|---|---|---|---|---|
| Marcus Higley | 72 | 71 | 70 | 69 | 282 | 2,025 |
| Iain Steel | 74 | 68 | 70 | 70 | 282 | 2,025 |
| Gary Clark | 73 | 70 | 70 | 69 | 282 | 2,025 |
| Kyron Sullivan | 69 | 69 | 71 | 73 | 282 | 2,025 |
| Sebastian Fernandez | 67 | 71 | 68 | 76 | 282 | 2,025 |
| Brad Sutterfield | 69 | 72 | 71 | 70 | 282 | 2,025 |

## Open de Toulouse

*Golf de Palmola,* Toulouse, France
Par 36-36–72; 6,801 yards

September 29-October 2
purse, €115,000

| | SCORES | | | | TOTAL | MONEY |
|---|---|---|---|---|---|---|
| Brad Sutterfield | 69 | 70 | 66 | 66 | 271 | €18,400 |
| Jan-Are Larsen | 67 | 73 | 66 | 67 | 273 | 8,337.50 |
| Andres Romero | 67 | 68 | 69 | 69 | 273 | 8,337.50 |
| David Dixon | 69 | 65 | 67 | 72 | 273 | 8,337.50 |
| Steven Jeppesen | 68 | 70 | 66 | 69 | 273 | 8,337.50 |
| Olivier David | 73 | 67 | 63 | 71 | 274 | 3,833.33 |
| Sam Walker | 69 | 70 | 68 | 67 | 274 | 3,833.33 |
| Ariel Canete | 70 | 71 | 66 | 67 | 274 | 3,833.33 |
| Marco Soffietti | 75 | 66 | 66 | 68 | 275 | 2,760 |
| Erol Simsek | 74 | 69 | 64 | 69 | 276 | 2,530 |
| Juan Abbate | 71 | 68 | 68 | 70 | 277 | 2,185 |
| David Patrick | 69 | 68 | 69 | 71 | 277 | 2,185 |
| Thomas Fournier | 70 | 68 | 66 | 73 | 277 | 2,185 |
| Jean Marc de Polo | 71 | 67 | 69 | 71 | 278 | 1,897.50 |
| Christian Reimbold | 70 | 71 | 64 | 73 | 278 | 1,897.50 |
| Denny Lucas | 65 | 69 | 73 | 72 | 279 | 1,610 |
| Raphael Pellicioli | 72 | 67 | 70 | 70 | 279 | 1,610 |
| Matthew Morris | 67 | 68 | 71 | 73 | 279 | 1,610 |
| Mark Mouland | 70 | 72 | 71 | 67 | 280 | 1,216.70 |
| Raphael Eyraud | 71 | 68 | 71 | 70 | 280 | 1,216.70 |
| Paul Nilbrink | 67 | 71 | 71 | 71 | 280 | 1,216.70 |
| Soren Juul Hansen | 70 | 71 | 66 | 73 | 280 | 1,216.70 |
| Cedric Menut | 75 | 66 | 65 | 74 | 280 | 1,216.70 |
| *Sebastien Clement | 68 | 69 | 72 | 71 | 280 | |
| Jean-Nicolas Billot | 74 | 67 | 69 | 71 | 281 | 1,058 |
| Gareth Davies | 70 | 68 | 76 | 67 | 281 | 1,058 |
| Julien Quesne | 73 | 69 | 68 | 71 | 281 | 1,058 |
| Marcus Higley | 73 | 70 | 67 | 72 | 282 | 977.50 |
| Marco Ruiz | 73 | 68 | 71 | 70 | 282 | 977.50 |
| Oliver Whiteley | 71 | 70 | 70 | 71 | 282 | 977.50 |
| Miguel Carballo | 71 | 69 | 70 | 72 | 282 | 977.50 |

## Abama Open de Canarias

See European Tour section.

# Apulia San Domenico Grand Final

*San Domenico Golf Club*, Puglia, Italy
Par 35-37–72; 7,006 yards

October 19-22
purse, €250,000

| | SCORES | | | | TOTAL | MONEY |
|---|---|---|---|---|---|---|
| Carl Suneson | 69 | 71 | 65 | 68 | 273 | €42,800 |
| Daniel Vancsik | 69 | 69 | 70 | 66 | 274 | 22,310 |
| Marc Warren | 67 | 69 | 71 | 67 | 274 | 22,310 |
| Benn Barham | 67 | 71 | 67 | 70 | 275 | 12,850 |
| Marco Ruiz | 68 | 67 | 68 | 73 | 276 | 10,912 |
| Stephen Browne | 75 | 65 | 68 | 69 | 277 | 10,000 |
| Lee James | 68 | 70 | 68 | 72 | 278 | 9,212 |
| Cesar Monasterio | 69 | 69 | 72 | 69 | 279 | 7,536.50 |
| James Hepworth | 67 | 70 | 70 | 72 | 279 | 7,536.50 |
| Fredrik Widmark | 69 | 68 | 73 | 69 | 279 | 7,536.50 |
| Ariel Canete | 71 | 68 | 69 | 71 | 279 | 7,536.50 |
| Toni Karjalainen | 70 | 71 | 70 | 69 | 280 | 5,276.50 |
| Kyron Sullivan | 72 | 66 | 74 | 68 | 280 | 5,276.50 |
| David Dixon | 74 | 68 | 72 | 66 | 280 | 5,276.50 |
| Steven Jeppesen | 71 | 71 | 69 | 69 | 280 | 5,276.50 |
| Michael Hoey | 69 | 72 | 72 | 68 | 281 | 3,650.33 |
| Richard McEvoy | 71 | 68 | 71 | 71 | 281 | 3,650.33 |
| Ross Fisher | 74 | 71 | 68 | 68 | 281 | 3,650.33 |
| Michael Jonzon | 71 | 66 | 73 | 72 | 282 | 3,187 |
| Gareth Davies | 69 | 71 | 71 | 72 | 283 | 2,913.33 |
| Miguel Carballo | 72 | 73 | 70 | 68 | 283 | 2,913.33 |
| Brad Sutterfield | 72 | 70 | 72 | 69 | 283 | 2,913.33 |
| Shaun Webster | 70 | 73 | 74 | 67 | 284 | 2,699 |
| Denny Lucas | 69 | 70 | 77 | 69 | 285 | 2,403.33 |
| Olivier David | 67 | 72 | 76 | 70 | 285 | 2,403.33 |
| Andrew Butterfield | 73 | 71 | 72 | 69 | 285 | 2,403.33 |
| David Higgins | 70 | 74 | 72 | 69 | 285 | 2,403.33 |
| Andres Romero | 70 | 71 | 72 | 72 | 285 | 2,403.33 |
| Sebastian Fernandez | 71 | 69 | 75 | 70 | 285 | 2,403.33 |
| Marcus Higley | 74 | 68 | 74 | 70 | 286 | 2,030.40 |
| Rafael Gomez | 69 | 69 | 75 | 73 | 286 | 2,030.40 |
| Tom Whitehouse | 72 | 70 | 70 | 74 | 286 | 2,030.40 |
| Colm Moriarty | 79 | 69 | 68 | 70 | 286 | 2,030.40 |
| James Heath | 77 | 71 | 69 | 69 | 286 | 2,030.40 |

# Asian Tour

## Caltex Masters

*Laguna National Golf & Country Club*, Singapore
Par 36-36–72; 7,207 yards

January 27-30
purse, US$1,000,000

| | SCORES | | | | TOTAL | MONEY |
|---|---|---|---|---|---|---|
| Nick Dougherty | 68 | 67 | 68 | 67 | 270 | US$166,660 |
| Maarten Lafeber | 69 | 70 | 67 | 69 | 275 | 86,855 |
| Colin Montgomerie | 65 | 71 | 69 | 70 | 275 | 86,855 |
| Thomas Bjorn | 72 | 66 | 67 | 72 | 277 | 50,000 |
| Peter Lawrie | 74 | 72 | 68 | 66 | 280 | 29,133.33 |
| Lee Westwood | 70 | 73 | 70 | 67 | 280 | 29,133.33 |
| Robert Coles | 72 | 69 | 71 | 68 | 280 | 29,133.33 |
| Marcus Fraser | 71 | 70 | 70 | 69 | 280 | 29,133.33 |
| Gregory Havret | 70 | 70 | 69 | 71 | 280 | 29,133.33 |
| Liang Wen-chong | 70 | 68 | 71 | 71 | 280 | 29,133.33 |
| Peter Hedblom | 71 | 69 | 66 | 75 | 281 | 18,400 |
| Peter Senior | 72 | 71 | 70 | 69 | 282 | 16,650 |
| Mo Joong-kyung | 72 | 72 | 68 | 70 | 282 | 16,650 |
| James Kingston | 73 | 73 | 68 | 69 | 283 | 14,400 |
| Paul Marantz | 73 | 68 | 71 | 71 | 283 | 14,400 |
| Kim Felton | 70 | 73 | 69 | 71 | 283 | 14,400 |
| Jamie Donaldson | 70 | 68 | 72 | 73 | 283 | 14,400 |
| Graeme McDowell | 74 | 69 | 69 | 72 | 284 | 12,433.33 |
| Angelo Que | 70 | 70 | 70 | 74 | 284 | 12,433.33 |
| Soren Hansen | 69 | 70 | 69 | 76 | 284 | 12,433.33 |
| Barry Lane | 73 | 73 | 71 | 68 | 285 | 10,850 |
| Anders Hansen | 72 | 73 | 70 | 70 | 285 | 10,850 |
| Jose-Filipe Lima | 76 | 68 | 70 | 71 | 285 | 10,850 |
| Zhang Lian-wei | 72 | 72 | 70 | 71 | 285 | 10,850 |
| Jean-Francois Lucquin | 69 | 74 | 69 | 73 | 285 | 10,850 |
| Jason Knutzon | 69 | 71 | 70 | 75 | 285 | 10,850 |
| Fredrik Andersson | 75 | 69 | 75 | 67 | 286 | 9,050 |
| Boonchu Ruangkit | 73 | 72 | 73 | 68 | 286 | 9,050 |
| Mardan Mamat | 74 | 72 | 71 | 69 | 286 | 9,050 |
| Philip Golding | 75 | 70 | 71 | 70 | 286 | 9,050 |
| Mads Vibe-Hastrup | 73 | 71 | 72 | 70 | 286 | 9,050 |
| Chen Yuan-chi | 72 | 72 | 71 | 71 | 286 | 9,050 |
| Simon Yates | 71 | 74 | 75 | 67 | 287 | 6,105.26 |
| Graeme Storm | 75 | 69 | 73 | 70 | 287 | 6,105.26 |
| Trevor Immelman | 76 | 70 | 71 | 70 | 287 | 6,105.26 |
| Greg Chalmers | 71 | 70 | 75 | 71 | 287 | 6,105.26 |
| Adam Groom | 69 | 72 | 75 | 71 | 287 | 6,105.26 |
| Mike Cunning | 72 | 74 | 71 | 70 | 287 | 6,105.26 |
| Jose Manuel Lara | 73 | 70 | 73 | 71 | 287 | 6,105.26 |
| Scott Drummond | 72 | 74 | 70 | 71 | 287 | 6,105.26 |
| Paul Lawrie | 72 | 73 | 71 | 71 | 287 | 6,105.26 |
| Soren Kjeldsen | 69 | 73 | 73 | 72 | 287 | 6,105.26 |
| Jyoti Randhawa | 73 | 68 | 74 | 72 | 287 | 6,105.26 |
| Klas Eriksson | 74 | 71 | 70 | 72 | 287 | 6,105.26 |
| Thaworn Wiratchant | 74 | 72 | 69 | 72 | 287 | 6,105.26 |
| David Bransdon | 72 | 74 | 69 | 72 | 287 | 6,105.26 |
| Danny Chia | 68 | 70 | 75 | 74 | 287 | 6,105.26 |
| Raymond Russell | 73 | 67 | 72 | 75 | 287 | 6,105.26 |

| | SCORES | | | | TOTAL | MONEY |
|---|---|---|---|---|---|---|
| Marcus Both | 75 | 69 | 69 | 74 | 287 | 6,105.26 |
| Brad Kennedy | 72 | 71 | 68 | 76 | 287 | 6,105.26 |
| Terry Pilkadaris | 73 | 71 | 67 | 76 | 287 | 6,105.26 |
| Lin Keng-chi | 74 | 72 | 73 | 69 | 288 | 3,900 |
| Steve Webster | 74 | 70 | 72 | 72 | 288 | 3,900 |
| Amandeep Johl | 74 | 72 | 70 | 72 | 288 | 3,900 |
| Edward Loar | 74 | 71 | 75 | 69 | 289 | 3,100 |
| Simon Khan | 72 | 72 | 72 | 73 | 289 | 3,100 |
| Simon Dyson | 72 | 70 | 73 | 74 | 289 | 3,100 |
| David Howell | 73 | 72 | 70 | 74 | 289 | 3,100 |
| Choi Gwang-soo | 72 | 74 | 69 | 74 | 289 | 3,100 |
| Corey Harris | 75 | 69 | 69 | 76 | 289 | 3,100 |
| Edward Michaels | 71 | 75 | 75 | 69 | 290 | 2,500 |
| Peter O'Malley | 74 | 71 | 72 | 73 | 290 | 2,500 |
| Peter Hanson | 76 | 68 | 72 | 74 | 290 | 2,500 |
| Prayad Marksaeng | 72 | 71 | 72 | 75 | 290 | 2,500 |
| Rick Gibson | 72 | 70 | 71 | 77 | 290 | 2,500 |
| Joakim Haeggman | 73 | 71 | 74 | 73 | 291 | 2,050 |
| Mark Foster | 68 | 76 | 71 | 76 | 291 | 2,050 |
| Chung Joon | 73 | 72 | 70 | 76 | 291 | 2,050 |
| Costantino Rocca | 72 | 73 | 67 | 79 | 291 | 2,050 |
| Harmeet Kahlon | 71 | 75 | 75 | 71 | 292 | 1,539.30 |
| Brett Rumford | 69 | 72 | 77 | 74 | 292 | 1,539.30 |
| Hendrik Buhrmann | 70 | 76 | 73 | 73 | 292 | 1,539.30 |
| Eiji Mizoguchi | 75 | 71 | 72 | 74 | 292 | 1,539.30 |
| Richard Bland | 72 | 72 | 74 | 74 | 292 | 1,539.30 |
| Gerry Norquist | 74 | 72 | 71 | 75 | 292 | 1,539.30 |
| Roger Chapman | 72 | 71 | 74 | 75 | 292 | 1,539.30 |
| Unho Park | 72 | 74 | 75 | 72 | 293 | 1,471.28 |
| Rahil Gangjee | 77 | 69 | 74 | 73 | 293 | 1,471.28 |
| Ted Oh | 73 | 71 | 74 | 75 | 293 | 1,471.28 |
| Markus Brier | 74 | 71 | 72 | 76 | 293 | 1,471.28 |
| Poh Eng Wah | 74 | 70 | 76 | 74 | 294 | 1,455.62 |
| Jamie Spence | 71 | 75 | 74 | 74 | 294 | 1,455.62 |
| Gaurav Ghei | 74 | 72 | 74 | 74 | 294 | 1,455.62 |
| Pablo Del Olmo | 74 | 70 | 74 | 76 | 294 | 1,455.62 |
| Carlos Rodiles | 73 | 73 | 74 | 75 | 295 | 1,445.83 |
| Jarmo Sandelin | 72 | 72 | 80 | 72 | 296 | 1,439.97 |
| Chawalit Plaphol | 74 | 69 | 84 | 69 | 296 | 1,439.97 |
| Ross Bain | 75 | 70 | 77 | 75 | 297 | 1,432.14 |
| Bill Fung | 75 | 68 | 76 | 78 | 297 | 1,432.14 |
| Sushi Ishigaki | 73 | 68 | 76 | 81 | 298 | 1,426.26 |

## Carlsberg Malaysian Open

*Saujana Golf & Country Club*, Kuala Lumpur, Malaysia
Par 36-36–72; 6,971 yards

February 17-20
purse, US$1,210,000

| | SCORES | | | | TOTAL | MONEY |
|---|---|---|---|---|---|---|
| Thongchai Jaidee | 64 | 66 | 67 | 70 | 267 | US$201,660 |
| Jyoti Randhawa | 70 | 68 | 65 | 67 | 270 | 134,440 |
| Henrik Stenson | 69 | 64 | 71 | 67 | 271 | 75,746 |
| Paul McGinley | 68 | 70 | 70 | 68 | 276 | 55,902 |
| Niclas Fasth | 67 | 70 | 71 | 68 | 276 | 55,902 |
| Miguel Angel Jimenez | 68 | 67 | 73 | 69 | 277 | 39,325 |
| Prom Meesawat | 68 | 65 | 71 | 73 | 277 | 39,325 |
| Gary Orr | 71 | 69 | 70 | 68 | 278 | 27,184.67 |

| | SCORES | | | TOTAL | MONEY |
|---|---|---|---|---|---|
| Liang Wen-chong | 70 | 70 | 69 | 69 | 278 | 27,184.67 |
| Padraig Harrington | 71 | 66 | 67 | 74 | 278 | 27,184.67 |
| Scott Barr | 73 | 71 | 67 | 68 | 279 | 20,852.33 |
| Thaworn Wiratchant | 69 | 70 | 71 | 69 | 279 | 20,852.33 |
| Simon Yates | 69 | 69 | 69 | 72 | 279 | 20,852.33 |
| Graeme Storm | 71 | 72 | 69 | 68 | 280 | 17,061 |
| Adam Blyth | 69 | 71 | 70 | 70 | 280 | 17,061 |
| Simon Dyson | 68 | 68 | 73 | 71 | 280 | 17,061 |
| Anders Hansen | 69 | 68 | 72 | 71 | 280 | 17,061 |
| Pelle Edberg | 67 | 69 | 71 | 73 | 280 | 17,061 |
| Greg Hanrahan | 71 | 73 | 69 | 68 | 281 | 13,915 |
| Francois Delamontagne | 69 | 70 | 71 | 71 | 281 | 13,915 |
| Terry Pilkadaris | 67 | 76 | 67 | 71 | 281 | 13,915 |
| Mattias Eliasson | 71 | 70 | 73 | 67 | 281 | 13,915 |
| Peter Gustafsson | 70 | 65 | 72 | 74 | 281 | 13,915 |
| Robert-Jan Derksen | 71 | 69 | 67 | 74 | 281 | 13,915 |
| Maarten Lafeber | 69 | 68 | 72 | 73 | 282 | 12,221 |
| Marcus Fraser | 73 | 71 | 70 | 68 | 282 | 12,221 |
| Thomas Bjorn | 68 | 64 | 73 | 77 | 282 | 12,221 |
| Danny Chia | 73 | 70 | 70 | 70 | 283 | 10,406 |
| Rick Gibson | 73 | 68 | 70 | 72 | 283 | 10,406 |
| Peter Lawrie | 71 | 70 | 70 | 72 | 283 | 10,406 |
| James Kingston | 75 | 69 | 70 | 69 | 283 | 10,406 |
| Simon Wakefield | 70 | 74 | 70 | 69 | 283 | 10,406 |
| Chawalit Plaphol | 73 | 70 | 74 | 66 | 283 | 10,406 |
| Stuart Manley | 70 | 71 | 66 | 76 | 283 | 10,406 |
| Francesco Molinari | 69 | 73 | 71 | 71 | 284 | 8,228 |
| Richard Moir | 69 | 73 | 71 | 71 | 284 | 8,228 |
| Brad Kennedy | 74 | 68 | 69 | 73 | 284 | 8,228 |
| Ian Garbutt | 73 | 70 | 70 | 71 | 284 | 8,228 |
| Wang Ter-chang | 71 | 70 | 74 | 69 | 284 | 8,228 |
| Thammanoon Srirot | 72 | 66 | 78 | 68 | 284 | 8,228 |
| Prayad Marksaeng | 70 | 71 | 76 | 67 | 284 | 8,228 |
| David Bransdon | 68 | 71 | 68 | 77 | 284 | 8,228 |
| Olle Nordberg | 71 | 71 | 71 | 72 | 285 | 6,171 |
| Richard Finch | 72 | 70 | 70 | 73 | 285 | 6,171 |
| Adam Groom | 68 | 72 | 72 | 73 | 285 | 6,171 |
| Emanuele Canonica | 67 | 70 | 74 | 74 | 285 | 6,171 |
| Johan Skold | 70 | 71 | 70 | 74 | 285 | 6,171 |
| Mardan Mamat | 70 | 71 | 73 | 71 | 285 | 6,171 |
| Henrik Nystrom | 75 | 67 | 72 | 71 | 285 | 6,171 |
| Angelo Que | 73 | 70 | 71 | 71 | 285 | 6,171 |
| Jarrod Moseley | 67 | 73 | 76 | 69 | 285 | 6,171 |
| Hendrik Buhrmann | 70 | 71 | 72 | 73 | 286 | 4,719 |
| Choi Gwang-soo | 74 | 70 | 67 | 75 | 286 | 4,719 |
| Gary Murphy | 71 | 66 | 71 | 78 | 286 | 4,719 |
| Leif Westerberg | 73 | 68 | 72 | 74 | 287 | 3,902.25 |
| Lin Keng-chi | 70 | 70 | 73 | 74 | 287 | 3,902.25 |
| Jeev Milkha Singh | 71 | 70 | 73 | 73 | 287 | 3,902.25 |
| Mikko Ilonen | 71 | 71 | 72 | 73 | 287 | 3,902.25 |
| Ross Bain | 72 | 69 | 73 | 74 | 288 | 3,267 |
| Jason Knutzon | 72 | 72 | 71 | 73 | 288 | 3,267 |
| Costantino Rocca | 74 | 70 | 73 | 71 | 288 | 3,267 |
| Amandeep Johl | 69 | 73 | 76 | 70 | 288 | 3,267 |
| Shaifubari Muda | 69 | 75 | 74 | 70 | 288 | 3,267 |
| Unho Park | 72 | 70 | 71 | 76 | 289 | 2,783 |
| Sushi Ishigaki | 70 | 73 | 73 | 73 | 289 | 2,783 |
| Jean-Francois Lucquin | 71 | 71 | 75 | 72 | 289 | 2,783 |
| Anthony Kang | 71 | 68 | 71 | 80 | 290 | 2,480.50 |
| Jan Are Larsen | 73 | 71 | 72 | 74 | 290 | 2,480.50 |

|  | SCORES |  |  |  | TOTAL | MONEY |
|---|---|---|---|---|---|---|
| Corey Harris | 69 | 74 | 70 | 78 | 291 | 2,257.50 |
| V.S. Moorrthy | 72 | 72 | 77 | 70 | 291 | 2,257.50 |
| David Drysdale | 69 | 72 | 74 | 77 | 292 | 1,809.32 |
| Raphal Jacquelin | 74 | 70 | 74 | 74 | 292 | 1,809.32 |
| Terry Price | 70 | 74 | 76 | 72 | 292 | 1,809.32 |
| Soren Hansen | 70 | 74 | 76 | 72 | 292 | 1,809.32 |
| Chen Tze-chung | 70 | 74 | 78 | 78 | 300 | 1,799.67 |

## Myanmar Open

*Yangon Golf Club*, Yangon, Myanmar
Par 36-36–72; 7,063 yards

February 24-27
purse, US$200,000

|  | SCORES |  |  |  | TOTAL | MONEY |
|---|---|---|---|---|---|---|
| Scott Strange | 69 | 72 | 69 | 67 | 277 | US$32,300 |
| Rick Gibson | 76 | 66 | 69 | 68 | 279 | 22,260 |
| Thongchai Jaidee | 67 | 70 | 69 | 74 | 280 | 11,200 |
| Ashok Kumar | 75 | 68 | 65 | 72 | 280 | 11,200 |
| Lu Wen-teh | 70 | 70 | 71 | 70 | 281 | 8,000 |
| Arjun Singh | 71 | 70 | 70 | 71 | 282 | 7,000 |
| Jason Dawes | 69 | 73 | 73 | 68 | 283 | 6,000 |
| Anthony Kang | 71 | 71 | 74 | 68 | 284 | 4,730 |
| Boonchu Ruangkit | 68 | 68 | 73 | 75 | 284 | 4,730 |
| Thaworn Wiratchant | 75 | 69 | 72 | 69 | 285 | 3,701.33 |
| Yeh Chang-ting | 68 | 76 | 72 | 69 | 285 | 3,701.33 |
| Ted Oh | 71 | 71 | 70 | 73 | 285 | 3,701.33 |
| Mardan Mamat | 71 | 75 | 72 | 68 | 286 | 3,072 |
| Mukesh Kumar | 70 | 71 | 74 | 71 | 286 | 3,072 |
| Prayad Marksaeng | 70 | 71 | 71 | 74 | 286 | 3,072 |
| Airil Rizman Zahari | 71 | 71 | 75 | 70 | 287 | 2,700 |
| Chen Tze-chung | 74 | 70 | 71 | 72 | 287 | 2,700 |
| Chawalit Plaphol | 73 | 67 | 73 | 74 | 287 | 2,700 |
| Matthew Cort | 67 | 76 | 74 | 71 | 288 | 2,252.50 |
| Gaurav Ghei | 73 | 71 | 74 | 70 | 288 | 2,252.50 |
| Sung Mao-chang | 68 | 77 | 74 | 69 | 288 | 2,252.50 |
| Gary Rusnak | 76 | 72 | 73 | 67 | 288 | 2,252.50 |
| Olle Nordberg | 68 | 73 | 75 | 72 | 288 | 2,252.50 |
| Satoshi Tomiyama | 74 | 71 | 71 | 72 | 288 | 2,252.50 |
| Adam Le Vesconte | 72 | 72 | 71 | 73 | 288 | 2,252.50 |
| Andrew Pitts | 69 | 70 | 72 | 77 | 288 | 2,252.50 |
| Mike Cunning | 71 | 69 | 77 | 72 | 289 | 1,830 |
| Lin Chie-hsiang | 72 | 75 | 73 | 69 | 289 | 1,830 |
| Jason Knutzon | 73 | 74 | 70 | 72 | 289 | 1,830 |
| Frankie Minoza | 73 | 73 | 71 | 72 | 289 | 1,830 |
| Richard Moir | 71 | 71 | 74 | 73 | 289 | 1,830 |
| Edward Loar | 72 | 70 | 72 | 75 | 289 | 1,830 |

# Thai Airways International Thailand Open

*Blue Canyon Country Club,* Phuket, Thailand
Par 36-36–72; 7,049 yards

March 3-6
purse, US$500,000

| | SCORES | | | | TOTAL | MONEY |
|---|---|---|---|---|---|---|
| Richard Lee | 70 | 70 | 69 | 70 | 279 | US$78,750 |
| Scott Barr | 65 | 68 | 74 | 72 | 279 | 54,000 |
| (Lee defeated Barr on first playoff hole.) | | | | | | |
| Bryan Saltus | 70 | 72 | 70 | 68 | 280 | 27,375 |
| Scott Strange | 68 | 67 | 73 | 72 | 280 | 27,375 |
| Harmeet Kahlon | 70 | 70 | 67 | 74 | 281 | 19,400 |
| Ross Bain | 72 | 73 | 71 | 69 | 285 | 13,912.50 |
| Larry Austin | 72 | 69 | 72 | 72 | 285 | 13,912.50 |
| Chris Rodgers | 70 | 70 | 73 | 72 | 285 | 13,912.50 |
| Prayad Marksaeng | 72 | 70 | 70 | 73 | 285 | 13,912.50 |
| Wang Ter-chang | 72 | 73 | 70 | 71 | 286 | 9,253.33 |
| Jeev Milkha Singh | 65 | 69 | 74 | 78 | 286 | 9,253.33 |
| Angelo Que | 71 | 70 | 67 | 78 | 286 | 9,253.33 |
| Andrew Buckle | 70 | 75 | 71 | 71 | 287 | 7,522.50 |
| Andrew Pitts | 71 | 75 | 70 | 71 | 287 | 7,522.50 |
| Koji Katoh | 73 | 69 | 72 | 73 | 287 | 7,522.50 |
| Greg Hanrahan | 68 | 74 | 72 | 73 | 287 | 7,522.50 |
| Lin Keng-chi | 69 | 73 | 76 | 70 | 288 | 6,250 |
| Rick Gibson | 74 | 69 | 72 | 73 | 288 | 6,250 |
| Kang Wook-soon | 73 | 71 | 71 | 73 | 288 | 6,250 |
| Noppajak Meesom | 67 | 75 | 72 | 74 | 288 | 6,250 |
| Gerry Norquist | 69 | 72 | 72 | 75 | 288 | 6,250 |
| Martin Doyle | 69 | 75 | 76 | 69 | 289 | 5,550 |
| Thaworn Wiratchant | 74 | 73 | 70 | 72 | 289 | 5,550 |
| Mike Capone | 71 | 69 | 70 | 79 | 289 | 5,550 |
| Lu Wen-teh | 71 | 75 | 74 | 70 | 290 | 4,875 |
| Adam Blyth | 72 | 69 | 76 | 73 | 290 | 4,875 |
| *Chinarat Phadungsil | 70 | 72 | 73 | 75 | 290 | |
| Ron Won | 69 | 73 | 73 | 75 | 290 | 4,875 |
| Jason Knutzon | 72 | 70 | 73 | 75 | 290 | 4,875 |
| Yoshinobu Tsukada | 66 | 76 | 72 | 76 | 290 | 4,875 |
| Craig Warren | 71 | 72 | 71 | 76 | 290 | 4,875 |

# Qatar Masters

See European Tours chapter.

# TCL Classic

*Yalong Bay Golf Club,* Sanya, Hainen Island, China
Par 36-36–72; 7,097 yards

March 17-20
purse, US$1,000,000

| | SCORES | | | | TOTAL | MONEY |
|---|---|---|---|---|---|---|
| Paul Casey | 64 | 68 | 68 | 66 | 266 | US$166,660 |
| Paul McGinley | 65 | 69 | 69 | 63 | 266 | 111,110 |
| (Casey defeated McGinley on second playoff hole.) | | | | | | |
| Thomas Bjorn | 66 | 67 | 68 | 66 | 267 | 51,666.67 |
| Kang Wook-soon | 68 | 69 | 65 | 65 | 267 | 51,666.67 |
| Chawalit Plaphol | 64 | 70 | 66 | 67 | 267 | 51,666.67 |

| | SCORES | | | | TOTAL | MONEY |
|---|---|---|---|---|---|---|
| Colin Montgomerie | 67 | 65 | 68 | 68 | 268 | 35,000 |
| Edward Loar | 69 | 65 | 69 | 66 | 269 | 25,800 |
| Lin Wen-tang | 70 | 64 | 69 | 66 | 269 | 25,800 |
| Ivo Giner | 67 | 66 | 69 | 67 | 269 | 25,800 |
| Lu Wen-teh | 69 | 64 | 72 | 66 | 271 | 19,200 |
| Alejandro Quiroz | 65 | 65 | 72 | 69 | 271 | 19,200 |
| Michael Campbell | 68 | 66 | 70 | 68 | 272 | 15,825 |
| David Bransdon | 70 | 65 | 68 | 69 | 272 | 15,825 |
| Keith Horne | 69 | 66 | 67 | 70 | 272 | 15,825 |
| Terry Pilkadaris | 66 | 67 | 68 | 71 | 272 | 15,825 |
| Ted Oh | 69 | 67 | 71 | 66 | 273 | 13,800 |
| Johan Edfors | 64 | 69 | 70 | 70 | 273 | 13,800 |
| Peter Fowler | 70 | 68 | 68 | 68 | 274 | 12,900 |
| Daniel Vancsik | 68 | 68 | 71 | 68 | 275 | 11,825 |
| Raphael Jacquelin | 67 | 68 | 70 | 70 | 275 | 11,825 |
| Steven Jeppesen | 68 | 66 | 70 | 71 | 275 | 11,825 |
| Thaworn Wiratchant | 68 | 67 | 69 | 71 | 275 | 11,825 |
| Adam Fraser | 69 | 69 | 71 | 67 | 276 | 10,250 |
| Lin Keng-chi | 66 | 67 | 75 | 68 | 276 | 10,250 |
| Scott Strange | 67 | 70 | 70 | 69 | 276 | 10,250 |
| Gregory Bourdy | 68 | 68 | 70 | 70 | 276 | 10,250 |
| Jeev Milkha Singh | 69 | 68 | 69 | 70 | 276 | 10,250 |
| Ariel Canete | 65 | 72 | 69 | 70 | 276 | 10,250 |
| Gonzalo Fernandez | 65 | 72 | 73 | 67 | 277 | 7,725 |
| Larry Austin | 71 | 67 | 71 | 68 | 277 | 7,725 |
| Dean Robertson | 66 | 72 | 71 | 68 | 277 | 7,725 |
| Marcus Both | 68 | 70 | 70 | 69 | 277 | 7,725 |
| Ian Garbutt | 68 | 70 | 70 | 69 | 277 | 7,725 |
| Stuart Little | 71 | 64 | 72 | 70 | 277 | 7,725 |
| James Kingston | 68 | 69 | 70 | 70 | 277 | 7,725 |
| Simon Yates | 68 | 67 | 71 | 71 | 277 | 7,725 |
| Frankie Minoza | 66 | 71 | 70 | 70 | 277 | 7,725 |
| Prayad Marksaeng | 69 | 68 | 69 | 71 | 277 | 7,725 |
| Mo Joong-kyung | 66 | 68 | 70 | 73 | 277 | 7,725 |
| Amandeep Johl | 67 | 68 | 68 | 74 | 277 | 7,725 |
| Michael Jonzon | 66 | 71 | 72 | 69 | 278 | 5,700 |
| Gary Evans | 68 | 70 | 71 | 69 | 278 | 5,700 |
| Zhang Lian-wei | 69 | 69 | 71 | 69 | 278 | 5,700 |
| Simon Hurd | 69 | 66 | 72 | 71 | 278 | 5,700 |
| Nicolas Colsaerts | 69 | 67 | 71 | 71 | 278 | 5,700 |
| Fredrik Henge | 68 | 68 | 71 | 71 | 278 | 5,700 |
| Hendrik Buhrmann | 68 | 68 | 68 | 74 | 278 | 5,700 |
| Martin Erlandsson | 67 | 70 | 73 | 69 | 279 | 4,100 |
| Emanuele Canonica | 67 | 67 | 74 | 71 | 279 | 4,100 |
| Chang Tse-peng | 68 | 67 | 73 | 71 | 279 | 4,100 |
| Pelle Edberg | 69 | 68 | 71 | 71 | 279 | 4,100 |
| Liang Wen-chong | 68 | 70 | 70 | 71 | 279 | 4,100 |
| David Griffiths | 67 | 71 | 70 | 71 | 279 | 4,100 |
| Pablo Del Olmo | 68 | 67 | 72 | 72 | 279 | 4,100 |
| Ross Bain | 65 | 69 | 71 | 74 | 279 | 4,100 |
| Choi Gwang-soo | 65 | 67 | 73 | 74 | 279 | 4,100 |
| Chung Joon | 68 | 69 | 74 | 69 | 280 | 3,000 |
| Johan Skold | 70 | 68 | 71 | 71 | 280 | 3,000 |
| Bryan Saltus | 66 | 71 | 71 | 72 | 280 | 3,000 |
| Robert-Jan Derksen | 69 | 69 | 73 | 70 | 281 | 2,700 |
| Paul Marantz | 67 | 71 | 72 | 71 | 281 | 2,700 |
| Zheng Wen-gen | 67 | 71 | 70 | 73 | 281 | 2,700 |
| Boonchu Ruangkit | 68 | 69 | 74 | 71 | 282 | 2,450 |
| Steven O'Hara | 65 | 70 | 71 | 76 | 282 | 2,450 |
| Harmeet Kahlon | 67 | 70 | 74 | 73 | 284 | 2,150 |

| | SCORES | | | TOTAL | MONEY |
|---|---|---|---|---|---|
| Darren Griff | 65 | 72 | 74 | 73 | 284 | 2,150 |
| Li Chao | 72 | 66 | 71 | 75 | 284 | 2,150 |
| Corey Harris | 65 | 71 | 72 | 76 | 284 | 2,150 |
| Robert Rock | 70 | 68 | 74 | 73 | 285 | 1,743.33 |
| John Mellor | 69 | 68 | 75 | 73 | 285 | 1,743.33 |
| Shang Lei | 69 | 69 | 72 | 75 | 285 | 1,743.33 |
| Miguel Angel Martin | 66 | 72 | 74 | 75 | 287 | 1,495.96 |

## Enjoy Jakarta Standard Chartered Indonesia Open

*Cengkareng Golf Club,* Jakarta, Indonesia                               March 24-27
Par 36-34–70; 6,851 yards                                           purse, US$1,000,000

| | SCORES | | | TOTAL | MONEY |
|---|---|---|---|---|---|
| Thaworn Wiratchant | 63 | 63 | 66 | 63 | 255 | US$166,660 |
| Raphael Jacquelin | 64 | 67 | 64 | 65 | 260 | 111,110 |
| Adam Fraser | 66 | 65 | 68 | 62 | 261 | 62,600 |
| Frankie Minoza | 67 | 67 | 62 | 66 | 262 | 46,200 |
| Colin Montgomerie | 67 | 69 | 66 | 60 | 262 | 46,200 |
| Eiji Mizoguchi | 64 | 69 | 64 | 66 | 263 | 35,000 |
| Gary Simpson | 67 | 67 | 64 | 67 | 265 | 24,350 |
| Marcus Both | 67 | 69 | 66 | 63 | 265 | 24,350 |
| Ariel Canete | 69 | 68 | 63 | 65 | 265 | 24,350 |
| Chris Williams | 63 | 68 | 66 | 68 | 265 | 24,350 |
| Richard Moir | 66 | 70 | 65 | 65 | 266 | 15,966.67 |
| Clay Devers | 67 | 67 | 68 | 64 | 266 | 15,966.67 |
| Hennie Otto | 67 | 66 | 67 | 66 | 266 | 15,966.67 |
| Thongchai Jaidee | 66 | 66 | 65 | 69 | 266 | 15,966.67 |
| Paul McGinley | 69 | 68 | 64 | 65 | 266 | 15,966.67 |
| Mardan Mamat | 65 | 65 | 66 | 70 | 266 | 15,966.67 |
| Mahal Pearce | 66 | 67 | 66 | 68 | 267 | 13,200 |
| Terry Pilkadaris | 67 | 64 | 67 | 69 | 267 | 13,200 |
| Boonchu Ruangkit | 65 | 70 | 66 | 67 | 268 | 11,342.86 |
| Gaurav Ghei | 64 | 70 | 68 | 66 | 268 | 11,342.86 |
| Thammanoon Srirot | 68 | 66 | 68 | 66 | 268 | 11,342.86 |
| Simon Hurd | 70 | 67 | 63 | 68 | 268 | 11,342.86 |
| Terry Price | 66 | 66 | 68 | 68 | 268 | 11,342.86 |
| Shiv Kapur | 65 | 66 | 71 | 66 | 268 | 11,342.86 |
| Arjun Atwal | 62 | 69 | 71 | 66 | 268 | 11,342.86 |
| Jochen Lupprian | 67 | 69 | 65 | 68 | 269 | 9,500 |
| Miguel Angel Martin | 68 | 67 | 71 | 63 | 269 | 9,500 |
| Ron Won | 64 | 71 | 68 | 66 | 269 | 9,500 |
| Zhang Lian-wei | 67 | 67 | 69 | 66 | 269 | 9,500 |
| Andrew Buckle | 64 | 69 | 67 | 69 | 269 | 9,500 |
| Brad Kennedy | 66 | 69 | 66 | 69 | 270 | 7,566.67 |
| Peter Gustafsson | 68 | 66 | 67 | 69 | 270 | 7,566.67 |
| Gonzalo Fernandez | 69 | 67 | 68 | 66 | 270 | 7,566.67 |
| Unho Park | 67 | 66 | 69 | 68 | 270 | 7,566.67 |
| Daniel Vancsik | 66 | 66 | 68 | 70 | 270 | 7,566.67 |
| Satoshi Tomiyama | 69 | 63 | 68 | 70 | 270 | 7,566.67 |
| Harmeet Kahlon | 70 | 67 | 65 | 68 | 270 | 7,566.67 |
| Michael Hoey | 62 | 68 | 69 | 71 | 270 | 7,566.67 |
| Ivo Giner | 71 | 66 | 65 | 68 | 270 | 7,566.67 |
| Matthew Blackey | 70 | 66 | 65 | 70 | 271 | 5,800 |
| Peter Fowler | 66 | 68 | 69 | 68 | 271 | 5,800 |
| Mike Cunning | 65 | 71 | 67 | 68 | 271 | 5,800 |
| Jarrod Lyle | 68 | 68 | 68 | 67 | 271 | 5,800 |

|  | SCORES |  |  |  | TOTAL | MONEY |
|---|---|---|---|---|---|---|
| Anthony Kang | 66 | 67 | 67 | 71 | 271 | 5,800 |
| Simon Yates | 69 | 68 | 67 | 67 | 271 | 5,800 |
| Wade Ormsby | 68 | 69 | 67 | 67 | 271 | 5,800 |
| Francesco Molinari | 67 | 70 | 67 | 67 | 271 | 5,800 |
| Alessandro Tadini | 66 | 70 | 68 | 68 | 272 | 4,400 |
| Ted Oh | 67 | 68 | 67 | 70 | 272 | 4,400 |
| Paul Marantz | 66 | 69 | 68 | 69 | 272 | 4,400 |
| Matthew Cort | 63 | 73 | 70 | 66 | 272 | 4,400 |
| Scott Barr | 64 | 69 | 69 | 70 | 272 | 4,400 |
| David Griffiths | 67 | 66 | 70 | 69 | 272 | 4,400 |
| Scott Strange | 69 | 67 | 67 | 70 | 273 | 3,125 |
| Johan Skold | 65 | 70 | 69 | 69 | 273 | 3,125 |
| Jeppe Huldahl | 69 | 67 | 70 | 67 | 273 | 3,125 |
| Mike Capone | 68 | 68 | 66 | 71 | 273 | 3,125 |
| Cesar Monasterio | 69 | 67 | 69 | 68 | 273 | 3,125 |
| Darren Griff | 70 | 62 | 73 | 68 | 273 | 3,125 |
| Wang Ter-chang | 67 | 70 | 67 | 69 | 273 | 3,125 |
| Nicolas Colsaerts | 65 | 62 | 71 | 75 | 273 | 3,125 |
| Stephen Browne | 67 | 66 | 70 | 71 | 274 | 2,600 |
| Gerry Norquist | 70 | 66 | 68 | 71 | 275 | 2,300 |
| Benoit Teilleria | 65 | 71 | 64 | 75 | 275 | 2,300 |
| David Orr | 65 | 71 | 68 | 71 | 275 | 2,300 |
| Amandeep Johl | 68 | 69 | 67 | 71 | 275 | 2,300 |
| Keith Horne | 68 | 69 | 67 | 71 | 275 | 2,300 |
| Lu Wen-teh | 70 | 66 | 70 | 70 | 276 | 1,910 |
| Pablo Del Olmo | 67 | 69 | 69 | 71 | 276 | 1,910 |
| Sam Walker | 65 | 71 | 72 | 68 | 276 | 1,910 |
| Edward Michaels | 68 | 69 | 69 | 71 | 277 | 1,498.15 |
| Prayad Marksaeng | 69 | 68 | 70 | 70 | 277 | 1,498.15 |
| Soren Kjeldsen | 67 | 70 | 71 | 70 | 278 | 1,490.16 |
| Sung Mao-chang | 71 | 66 | 68 | 73 | 278 | 1,490.16 |
| Kao Bo-song | 70 | 65 | 74 | 70 | 279 | 1,482.18 |
| Lee Sung-man | 68 | 69 | 67 | 75 | 279 | 1,482.18 |
| Philip Walton | 67 | 69 | 71 | 73 | 280 | 1,474.19 |
| Kariem Baraka | 67 | 70 | 75 | 68 | 280 | 1,474.19 |
| Corey Harris | 69 | 68 | 73 | 74 | 284 | 1,468.20 |

# Visa Dynasty Cup

*Mission Hills Golf Club, World Cup Course,* Shenzhen, China          April 15-17
Par 36-36–72; 7,102 yards

## FIRST DAY
### Foursomes

Zhang Lian-wei and Liang Wen-chong (Asia) defeated Shigeki Maruyama and Keiichiro Fukabori, 2 and 1.

Boonchu Ruangkit and Prayad Marksaeng (Asia) defeated Shingo Katayama and Takashi Kamiyama, 3 and 2.

Hideki Kase and Ryoken Kawagishi (Japan) defeated Thaworn Wiratchant and Thammanoon Srirot, 5 and 4.

Tomohiro Kondo and Takuya Taniguchi (Japan) defeated Thongchai Jaidee and Mardan Mamat, 5 and 3.

Mo Joong-kyung and Angelo Que (Asia) halved with Toru Suzuki and Tetsuji Hiratsuka.

Katsumasa Miyamoto and Hiroyuki Fujita (Japan) defeated Jyoti Randhawa and Amandeep Johl, 3 and 2.

**FIRST-DAY POINTS: Asia 2½, Japan 3½**

## SECOND DAY
### Fourballs

Kondo and Taniguchi (Japan) defeated Boonchu and Prayad, 6 and 5.
Thongchai and Mamat (Asia) defeated Suzuki and Hiratsuka, 3 and 1.
Zhang and Liang (Asia) defeated Kase and Kawagishi, 2 and 1.
Johl and Thammanoon (Asia) defeated Miyamoto and Fujita, 3 and 2.
Mo and Que (Asia) halved with Maruyama and Fukabori.
Randhawa and Thaworn (Asia) halved with Katayama and Kamiyama.

**SECOND-DAY POINTS: Asia 4, Japan 2**
**TOTAL POINTS: Asia 6½, Japan 5½**

## THIRD DAY
### Singles

Boonchu (Asia) defeated Taniguchi, 2 and 1.
Thaworn (Asia) halved with Kondo.
Johl (Asia) halved with Fujita.
Mo (Asia) halved with Kamiyama.
Que (Asia) defeated Kase, 1 up.
Thammanoon (Asia) defeated Kawagishi, 4 and 3.
Mamat (Asia) defeated Suzuki, 3 and 1.
Prayad (Asia) defeated Miyamoto, 4 and 2.
Thongchai (Asia) halved with Hiratsuka.
Fukabori (Japan) defeated Liang, 1 up.
Katayama (Japan) defeated Randhawa, 1 up.
Zhang (Asia) defeated Maruyama, 3 and 2.

**THIRD-DAY POINTS: Asia 8, Japan 4**
**TOTAL POINTS: Asia 14½, Japan 9½**

# Johnnie Walker Classic

*Pine Valley Golf Resort,* Beijing, China
Par 36-36–72; 7,056 yards

April 21-24
purse, US$2,350,000

| | SCORES | | | | TOTAL | MONEY |
|---|---|---|---|---|---|---|
| Adam Scott | 63 | 66 | 69 | 72 | 270 | US$398,785 |
| Retief Goosen | 68 | 67 | 68 | 70 | 273 | 265,844 |
| Michael Campbell | 70 | 65 | 68 | 72 | 275 | 123,625 |
| Henrik Stenson | 70 | 67 | 66 | 72 | 275 | 123,625 |
| Richard Sterne | 68 | 66 | 70 | 71 | 275 | 123,625 |
| Colin Montgomerie | 68 | 70 | 69 | 69 | 276 | 71,782 |
| Ernie Els | 71 | 67 | 69 | 69 | 276 | 71,782 |
| Brett Rumford | 71 | 71 | 65 | 69 | 276 | 71,782 |
| Luke Donald | 73 | 67 | 65 | 72 | 277 | 53,597 |
| Scott Drummond | 69 | 71 | 65 | 73 | 278 | 42,890 |
| Sergio Garcia | 67 | 71 | 67 | 73 | 278 | 42,890 |
| Santiago Luna | 70 | 70 | 66 | 72 | 278 | 42,890 |
| Steven O'Hara | 72 | 65 | 69 | 72 | 278 | 42,890 |
| Gary Rusnak | 68 | 65 | 71 | 75 | 279 | 35,891 |
| David Park | 70 | 68 | 67 | 74 | 279 | 35,891 |
| Thongchai Jaidee | 70 | 72 | 64 | 74 | 280 | 31,644 |
| Gregory Havret | 71 | 70 | 67 | 72 | 280 | 31,644 |
| Terry Price | 73 | 66 | 70 | 71 | 280 | 31,644 |
| Simon Dyson | 72 | 71 | 66 | 71 | 280 | 31,644 |
| Wade Ormsby | 71 | 67 | 68 | 75 | 281 | 27,835 |

|  | SCORES | | | | TOTAL | MONEY |
|---|---|---|---|---|---|---|
| Trevor Immelman | 71 | 70 | 66 | 74 | 281 | 27,835 |
| Unho Park | 70 | 71 | 69 | 71 | 281 | 27,835 |
| Prayad Marksaeng | 68 | 71 | 66 | 77 | 282 | 24,166 |
| Emanuele Canonica | 72 | 66 | 68 | 76 | 282 | 24,166 |
| K.J. Choi | 72 | 65 | 70 | 75 | 282 | 24,166 |
| Anthony Wall | 73 | 66 | 69 | 74 | 282 | 24,166 |
| Kenneth Ferrie | 74 | 67 | 68 | 73 | 282 | 24,166 |
| Terry Pilkadaris | 70 | 73 | 67 | 72 | 282 | 24,166 |
| Gareth Paddison | 71 | 68 | 72 | 71 | 282 | 24,166 |
| Peter Hanson | 70 | 65 | 73 | 75 | 283 | 18,962 |
| Paul Casey | 72 | 68 | 70 | 73 | 283 | 18,962 |
| David Bransdon | 69 | 70 | 71 | 73 | 283 | 18,962 |
| Soren Hansen | 70 | 69 | 71 | 73 | 283 | 18,962 |
| Thomas Bjorn | 72 | 70 | 68 | 73 | 283 | 18,962 |
| Maarten Lafeber | 73 | 68 | 70 | 72 | 283 | 18,962 |
| Martin Doyle | 74 | 68 | 69 | 72 | 283 | 18,962 |
| Steve Collins | 74 | 68 | 71 | 70 | 283 | 18,962 |
| Richard Moir | 73 | 65 | 70 | 76 | 284 | 14,346 |
| Miles Tunnicliff | 68 | 71 | 70 | 75 | 284 | 14,346 |
| Peter Lawrie | 69 | 71 | 69 | 75 | 284 | 14,346 |
| Simon Wakefield | 70 | 70 | 69 | 75 | 284 | 14,346 |
| Kim Felton | 71 | 70 | 69 | 74 | 284 | 14,346 |
| Scott Gardiner | 72 | 67 | 71 | 74 | 284 | 14,346 |
| Anders Hansen | 72 | 70 | 71 | 71 | 284 | 14,346 |
| Wang Ter-chang | 68 | 72 | 75 | 69 | 284 | 14,346 |
| Christian Cevaer | 74 | 69 | 72 | 69 | 284 | 14,346 |
| Peter Senior | 72 | 71 | 73 | 68 | 284 | 14,346 |
| Lin Wen-ko | 71 | 70 | 66 | 78 | 285 | 10,767 |
| Barry Lane | 69 | 72 | 69 | 75 | 285 | 10,767 |
| Jose Manuel Lara | 72 | 69 | 69 | 75 | 285 | 10,767 |
| James Nitties | 72 | 69 | 70 | 74 | 285 | 10,767 |
| Ricky Schmidt | 72 | 70 | 70 | 73 | 285 | 10,767 |
| Paul Lawrie | 70 | 69 | 72 | 75 | 286 | 8,613 |
| Simon Yates | 70 | 71 | 71 | 74 | 286 | 8,613 |
| Liang Wen-chong | 71 | 72 | 70 | 73 | 286 | 8,613 |
| Adam Groom | 70 | 71 | 74 | 71 | 286 | 8,613 |
| Marcus Fraser | 71 | 70 | 71 | 75 | 287 | 7,058 |
| Chen Yuan-chi | 67 | 71 | 74 | 75 | 287 | 7,058 |
| Peter O'Malley | 68 | 74 | 71 | 74 | 287 | 7,058 |
| Patrik Sjoland | 74 | 69 | 72 | 72 | 287 | 7,058 |
| Chawalit Plaphol | 66 | 71 | 72 | 79 | 288 | 6,340 |
| Peter Fowler | 71 | 71 | 73 | 73 | 288 | 6,340 |
| Zhang Lian-wei | 73 | 68 | 71 | 77 | 289 | 5,264 |
| Jean-Francois Lucquin | 71 | 71 | 70 | 77 | 289 | 5,264 |
| Edward Loar | 70 | 72 | 71 | 76 | 289 | 5,264 |
| Marcus Both | 73 | 69 | 71 | 76 | 289 | 5,264 |
| Wayne Perske | 74 | 68 | 72 | 75 | 289 | 5,264 |
| Anthony Kang | 71 | 72 | 71 | 75 | 289 | 5,264 |
| Chris Gray | 70 | 72 | 74 | 73 | 289 | 5,264 |
| Richard Lee | 71 | 70 | 70 | 79 | 290 | 3,784 |
| Miguel Angel Jimenez | 71 | 71 | 71 | 77 | 290 | 3,784 |
| Peter Hedblom | 73 | 69 | 72 | 76 | 290 | 3,784 |
| Kurt Barnes | 73 | 70 | 71 | 76 | 290 | 3,784 |
| Carlos Rodiles | 72 | 71 | 73 | 76 | 292 | 3,576 |
| Marcus Cain | 74 | 68 | 72 | 79 | 293 | 3,572 |
| Gary Simpson | 72 | 70 | 74 | 78 | 294 | 3,568 |

# BMW Asian Open

*Tomson Shanghai Pudong Golf Club,* Shanghai, China
Par 36-36–72; 7,300 yards

April 28-May 1
purse, US$1,500,000

| | SCORES | | | | TOTAL | MONEY |
|---|---|---|---|---|---|---|
| Ernie Els | 67 | 62 | 68 | 65 | 262 | US$250,000 |
| Simon Wakefield | 67 | 69 | 66 | 73 | 275 | 166,660 |
| Thomas Bjorn | 71 | 65 | 68 | 72 | 276 | 93,900 |
| Eddie Lee | 67 | 66 | 73 | 72 | 278 | 69,300 |
| Jean-Francois Lucquin | 70 | 66 | 69 | 73 | 278 | 69,300 |
| Stuart Little | 71 | 70 | 72 | 66 | 279 | 48,750 |
| Luke Donald | 70 | 69 | 68 | 72 | 279 | 48,750 |
| James Kingston | 70 | 71 | 69 | 70 | 280 | 35,550 |
| Soren Hansen | 69 | 70 | 68 | 73 | 280 | 35,550 |
| Peter Hedblom | 72 | 69 | 70 | 70 | 281 | 26,887 |
| David Park | 70 | 69 | 71 | 71 | 281 | 26,887 |
| Edward Michaels | 74 | 69 | 67 | 71 | 281 | 26,887 |
| Jeev Milkha Singh | 69 | 68 | 70 | 74 | 281 | 26,887 |
| Zhang Lian-wei | 70 | 71 | 69 | 72 | 282 | 22,500 |
| Simon Dyson | 70 | 74 | 66 | 72 | 282 | 22,500 |
| Mo Joong-kyung | 73 | 68 | 70 | 72 | 283 | 19,837 |
| Jyoti Randhawa | 70 | 74 | 67 | 72 | 283 | 19,837 |
| Patrik Sjoland | 70 | 68 | 72 | 73 | 283 | 19,837 |
| Raphael Jacquelin | 67 | 67 | 75 | 74 | 283 | 19,837 |
| Niki Zitny | 75 | 69 | 71 | 69 | 284 | 16,293 |
| Kenneth Ferrie | 72 | 68 | 74 | 70 | 284 | 16,293 |
| Jason Knutzon | 71 | 72 | 71 | 70 | 284 | 16,293 |
| Christian Cevaer | 70 | 69 | 73 | 72 | 284 | 16,293 |
| Anthony Wall | 71 | 69 | 72 | 72 | 284 | 16,293 |
| Mark Foster | 70 | 72 | 70 | 72 | 284 | 16,293 |
| Adam Groom | 72 | 71 | 69 | 72 | 284 | 16,293 |
| Wade Ormsby | 72 | 67 | 71 | 74 | 284 | 16,293 |
| Francois Delamontagne | 72 | 70 | 71 | 72 | 285 | 13,800 |
| Miguel Angel Jimenez | 70 | 73 | 69 | 73 | 285 | 13,800 |
| Jean Van de Velde | 67 | 69 | 72 | 77 | 285 | 13,800 |
| Christopher Hanell | 70 | 73 | 74 | 69 | 286 | 11,190 |
| Colin Montgomerie | 73 | 70 | 73 | 70 | 286 | 11,190 |
| Miles Tunnicliff | 72 | 70 | 73 | 71 | 286 | 11,190 |
| Terry Price | 74 | 70 | 69 | 73 | 286 | 11,190 |
| Jose Manuel Lara | 73 | 71 | 69 | 73 | 286 | 11,190 |
| Larry Austin | 67 | 72 | 73 | 74 | 286 | 11,190 |
| Peter Hanson | 73 | 69 | 70 | 74 | 286 | 11,190 |
| Greg Hanrahan | 72 | 72 | 67 | 75 | 286 | 11,190 |
| Richard Sterne | 69 | 69 | 71 | 77 | 286 | 11,190 |
| Peter Lawrie | 67 | 70 | 71 | 78 | 286 | 11,190 |
| Philip Golding | 74 | 70 | 71 | 72 | 287 | 8,850 |
| Jarrod Lyle | 72 | 70 | 71 | 74 | 287 | 8,850 |
| Peter Fowler | 71 | 70 | 71 | 75 | 287 | 8,850 |
| Marcus Both | 70 | 72 | 70 | 75 | 287 | 8,850 |
| David Bransdon | 71 | 70 | 70 | 76 | 287 | 8,850 |
| Alastair Forsyth | 72 | 70 | 75 | 71 | 288 | 7,200 |
| Oliver Wilson | 71 | 70 | 75 | 72 | 288 | 7,200 |
| Adam Blyth | 74 | 69 | 72 | 73 | 288 | 7,200 |
| Lin Wen-tang | 72 | 72 | 71 | 73 | 288 | 7,200 |
| Michael Campbell | 73 | 71 | 70 | 74 | 288 | 7,200 |
| Anders Hansen | 70 | 72 | 70 | 76 | 288 | 7,200 |
| Brad Kennedy | 71 | 71 | 75 | 72 | 289 | 5,550 |
| Thammanoon Srirot | 72 | 70 | 74 | 73 | 289 | 5,550 |
| Mardan Mamat | 73 | 71 | 71 | 74 | 289 | 5,550 |

| | SCORES | | | | TOTAL | MONEY |
|---|---|---|---|---|---|---|
| Ross Bain | 72 | 68 | 74 | 75 | 289 | 5,550 |
| Liang Wen-chong | 70 | 71 | 72 | 76 | 289 | 5,550 |
| Peter O'Malley | 70 | 74 | 73 | 73 | 290 | 4,125 |
| Kim Felton | 70 | 72 | 74 | 74 | 290 | 4,125 |
| Ted Oh | 71 | 73 | 71 | 75 | 290 | 4,125 |
| Edward Loar | 72 | 68 | 74 | 76 | 290 | 4,125 |
| Carlos Rodiles | 69 | 71 | 74 | 76 | 290 | 4,125 |
| Nick Dougherty | 71 | 72 | 70 | 77 | 290 | 4,125 |
| Charl Schwartzel | 71 | 71 | 70 | 78 | 290 | 4,125 |
| Thaworn Wiratchant | 74 | 69 | 68 | 79 | 290 | 4,125 |
| Rahil Gangjee | 75 | 69 | 73 | 74 | 291 | 3,300 |
| Costantino Rocca | 74 | 68 | 71 | 78 | 291 | 3,300 |
| Prom Meesawat | 71 | 72 | 70 | 78 | 291 | 3,300 |
| Jason Dawes | 73 | 71 | 74 | 74 | 292 | 3,000 |
| James Heath | 73 | 70 | 73 | 77 | 293 | 2,521 |
| Anthony Kang | 72 | 68 | 75 | 78 | 293 | 2,521 |
| Nick Faldo | 72 | 70 | 73 | 78 | 293 | 2,521 |
| Ben Mason | 76 | 67 | 72 | 78 | 293 | 2,521 |
| Bryan Saltus | 73 | 71 | 72 | 80 | 296 | 2,242 |
| Paul Casey | 73 | 71 | 78 | 76 | 298 | 2,238 |
| Lee Sung-man | 70 | 74 | 75 | 82 | 301 | 2,234 |

## SK Telecom Open

*Il Dong Lakes Golf Club,* Seoul, Korea
Par 36-36–72; 7,079 yards

May 5-8
purse, US$500,000

| | SCORES | | | | TOTAL | MONEY |
|---|---|---|---|---|---|---|
| K.J. Choi | 67 | 71 | 68 | 69 | 275 | US$100,000 |
| Fred Couples | 70 | 70 | 71 | 69 | 280 | 40,000 |
| Andrew Buckle | 68 | 68 | 70 | 74 | 280 | 40,000 |
| Thaworn Wiratchant | 70 | 72 | 67 | 72 | 281 | 24,000 |
| Park Boo-won | 70 | 69 | 70 | 73 | 282 | 20,000 |
| Edward Loar | 71 | 72 | 72 | 68 | 283 | 16,300 |
| Simon Yates | 70 | 75 | 69 | 69 | 283 | 16,300 |
| Clay Devers | 71 | 73 | 71 | 69 | 284 | 13,600 |
| Prom Meesawat | 72 | 72 | 73 | 68 | 285 | 11,200 |
| Kim Dae-sub | 69 | 77 | 70 | 69 | 285 | 11,200 |
| Gary Rusnak | 72 | 72 | 67 | 74 | 285 | 11,200 |
| Shiv Kapur | 69 | 70 | 76 | 71 | 286 | 8,000 |
| Keith Horne | 73 | 74 | 69 | 70 | 286 | 8,000 |
| Park Do-kyu | 71 | 73 | 71 | 71 | 286 | 8,000 |
| Richard Moir | 72 | 71 | 71 | 72 | 286 | 8,000 |
| Kang Kyung-nam | 68 | 71 | 75 | 72 | 286 | 8,000 |
| Kim Su-nam | 71 | 72 | 71 | 72 | 286 | 8,000 |
| Sushi Ishigaki | 70 | 72 | 74 | 71 | 287 | 6,000 |
| *Kim Kyung-tae | 72 | 71 | 75 | 69 | 287 | |
| *Kang Sung-hoon | 71 | 72 | 75 | 69 | 287 | |
| Rick Gibson | 70 | 73 | 71 | 73 | 287 | 6,000 |
| Jang Ik-jae | 72 | 72 | 70 | 73 | 287 | 6,000 |
| Ron Won | 73 | 69 | 74 | 72 | 288 | 5,000 |
| Mo Joong-kyung | 70 | 71 | 75 | 72 | 288 | 5,000 |
| Kim Seung-hyuk | 73 | 73 | 72 | 70 | 288 | 5,000 |
| Choi Sang-ho | 68 | 76 | 71 | 73 | 288 | 5,000 |
| Bryan Saltus | 73 | 69 | 71 | 75 | 288 | 5,000 |
| Larry Austin | 71 | 73 | 73 | 72 | 289 | 3,711 |
| David Bransdon | 71 | 74 | 73 | 71 | 289 | 3,711 |

| | SCORES | | | | TOTAL | MONEY |
|---|---|---|---|---|---|---|
| Choi Gwang-soo | 72 | 74 | 70 | 73 | 289 | 3,711 |
| Gary Simpson | 69 | 75 | 75 | 70 | 289 | 3,711 |
| Terry Pilkadaris | 67 | 71 | 81 | 70 | 289 | 3,711 |
| Alejandro Quiroz | 76 | 71 | 73 | 69 | 289 | 3,711 |
| Anthony Kang | 72 | 72 | 70 | 75 | 289 | 3,711 |
| Craig Warren | 69 | 75 | 70 | 75 | 289 | 3,711 |
| Koji Katoh | 67 | 71 | 72 | 79 | 289 | 3,711 |

## Macau Open

*Macau Golf & Country Club,* Macau
Par 35-36–71; 6,027 yards

May 12-15
purse, US$275,000

| | SCORES | | | | TOTAL | MONEY |
|---|---|---|---|---|---|---|
| Wang Ter-chang | 66 | 69 | 67 | 68 | 270 | US$43,312 |
| Marcus Both | 65 | 68 | 72 | 66 | 271 | 23,168 |
| Jarrod Lyle | 67 | 70 | 67 | 67 | 271 | 23,168 |
| Terry Pilkadaris | 67 | 68 | 71 | 68 | 274 | 11,183 |
| Jason Knutzon | 67 | 68 | 69 | 70 | 274 | 11,183 |
| Edward Loar | 71 | 66 | 66 | 71 | 274 | 11,183 |
| Anthony Kang | 70 | 68 | 71 | 67 | 276 | 8,085 |
| Zhang Lian-wei | 69 | 70 | 74 | 65 | 278 | 5,915 |
| Arjun Singh | 71 | 68 | 72 | 67 | 278 | 5,915 |
| Corey Harris | 68 | 71 | 68 | 71 | 278 | 5,915 |
| Suk Jong-yul | 67 | 68 | 70 | 73 | 278 | 5,915 |
| Fred Couples | 68 | 72 | 69 | 70 | 279 | 4,571 |
| Lin Chie-hsiang | 69 | 71 | 66 | 73 | 279 | 4,571 |
| Chen Tze-chung | 69 | 70 | 72 | 69 | 280 | 3,877 |
| Andrew Pitts | 69 | 70 | 70 | 71 | 280 | 3,877 |
| Lu Wen-teh | 69 | 70 | 70 | 71 | 280 | 3,877 |
| Kao Bo-song | 71 | 66 | 70 | 73 | 280 | 3,877 |
| Jason Dawes | 67 | 67 | 72 | 74 | 280 | 3,877 |
| Scott Strange | 72 | 70 | 69 | 70 | 281 | 3,410 |
| Craig Warren | 72 | 70 | 72 | 68 | 282 | 3,093 |
| Lu Wei-chih | 74 | 69 | 70 | 69 | 282 | 3,093 |
| Amandeep Johl | 70 | 71 | 71 | 70 | 282 | 3,093 |
| P. Gunasegaran | 73 | 69 | 70 | 70 | 282 | 3,093 |
| Frankie Minoza | 73 | 69 | 70 | 70 | 282 | 3,093 |
| Lu Wei-lan | 66 | 66 | 73 | 77 | 282 | 3,093 |
| Rahil Gangjee | 70 | 72 | 71 | 70 | 283 | 2,640 |
| Thaworn Wiratchant | 71 | 68 | 73 | 71 | 283 | 2,640 |
| Alejandro Quiroz | 70 | 68 | 74 | 71 | 283 | 2,640 |
| Harmeet Kahlon | 71 | 67 | 72 | 73 | 283 | 2,640 |
| Zheng Wen-gen | 65 | 70 | 72 | 76 | 283 | 2,640 |

## Philippine Open

*Mt. Malarayat Golf & Country Club,* Manila, Philippines
Par 71; 5,682 yards

May 19-22
purse, US$200,000

| | SCORES | | | | TOTAL | MONEY |
|---|---|---|---|---|---|---|
| Adam Le Vesconte | 71 | 70 | 67 | 64 | 272 | US$31,500 |
| Gerald Rosales | 69 | 73 | 67 | 67 | 276 | 21,600 |
| Jason Dawes | 72 | 72 | 62 | 72 | 278 | 12,100 |
| Ron Won | 69 | 71 | 72 | 70 | 282 | 8,780 |

|  | SCORES | | | | TOTAL | MONEY |
|---|---|---|---|---|---|---|
| Bryan Saltus | 68 | 74 | 68 | 72 | 282 | 8,780 |
| Danny Chia | 72 | 71 | 72 | 68 | 283 | 5,565 |
| Andrew Buckle | 66 | 73 | 73 | 71 | 283 | 5,565 |
| *Juvic Pagunsan | 68 | 72 | 69 | 74 | 283 | |
| Darren Griff | 69 | 72 | 68 | 74 | 283 | 5,565 |
| Boonchu Ruangkit | 70 | 68 | 69 | 76 | 283 | 5,565 |
| Gary Rusnak | 76 | 71 | 70 | 67 | 284 | 3,305 |
| Gilberto Morales | 71 | 70 | 72 | 71 | 284 | 3,305 |
| Keith Horne | 72 | 73 | 68 | 71 | 284 | 3,305 |
| Rey Pagunsan | 70 | 72 | 69 | 73 | 284 | 3,305 |
| R. Nachimuthu | 72 | 73 | 67 | 72 | 284 | 3,305 |
| Tony Lascuna | 72 | 71 | 68 | 73 | 284 | 3,305 |
| Shaaban Hussein | 73 | 70 | 67 | 74 | 284 | 3,305 |
| Sung Mao-chang | 69 | 78 | 70 | 68 | 285 | 2,500 |
| Felix Casas | 70 | 70 | 75 | 70 | 285 | 2,500 |
| Arjun Singh | 72 | 70 | 72 | 71 | 285 | 2,500 |
| Lee Seong-ki | 71 | 75 | 67 | 72 | 285 | 2,500 |
| Somkiat Srisanga | 67 | 75 | 67 | 76 | 285 | 2,500 |
| Atthaphon Prathummanee | 71 | 74 | 72 | 69 | 286 | 2,070 |
| Rick Gibson | 71 | 70 | 75 | 70 | 286 | 2,070 |
| Hisaki Takeuchi | 71 | 73 | 72 | 70 | 286 | 2,070 |
| Chris Gill | 72 | 69 | 74 | 71 | 286 | 2,070 |
| *Jay Bayron | 76 | 68 | 71 | 71 | 286 | |
| Robin Hodgetts | 75 | 70 | 69 | 72 | 286 | 2,070 |
| Airil Rizman Zahari | 70 | 72 | 72 | 72 | 286 | 2,070 |
| Richard Backwell | 71 | 75 | 68 | 72 | 286 | 2,070 |
| Jochen Lupprian | 71 | 70 | 72 | 73 | 286 | 2,070 |

## KT&G Maekyung Open

*Nam Seoul Country Club,* Seoul, Korea
Par 36-36–72; 6,796 yards

May 26-29
purse, US$500,000

|  | SCORES | | | | TOTAL | MONEY |
|---|---|---|---|---|---|---|
| Choi Sang-ho | 66 | 70 | 72 | 70 | 278 | US$98,039 |
| Thaworn Wiratchant | 71 | 71 | 69 | 70 | 281 | 61,274 |
| Sung Si-woo | 72 | 70 | 70 | 70 | 282 | 29,411 |
| *Kim Kyung-tae | 71 | 69 | 74 | 70 | 284 | |
| Kim Hyung-tae | 70 | 74 | 69 | 71 | 284 | 24,509 |
| Park No-seok | 72 | 74 | 71 | 68 | 285 | 14,460 |
| Bae Sang-moon | 72 | 74 | 70 | 69 | 285 | 14,460 |
| Marcus Both | 71 | 70 | 73 | 71 | 285 | 14,460 |
| Boonchu Ruangkit | 72 | 71 | 71 | 71 | 285 | 14,460 |
| Alistair Presnell | 73 | 76 | 70 | 67 | 286 | 8,888 |
| Moon Ji-wook | 72 | 74 | 72 | 68 | 286 | 8,888 |
| Kang Ji-man | 70 | 74 | 70 | 72 | 286 | 8,888 |
| Prom Meesawat | 75 | 71 | 73 | 68 | 287 | 7,156 |
| Chung Joon | 70 | 76 | 74 | 67 | 287 | 7,156 |
| Nam Young-woo | 72 | 76 | 71 | 69 | 288 | 6,568 |
| *Hur In-hoi | 74 | 69 | 71 | 74 | 288 | |
| Edward Loar | 73 | 70 | 69 | 76 | 288 | 6,568 |
| Amandeep Johl | 72 | 71 | 70 | 75 | 288 | 6,568 |
| Choi Ho-sung | 75 | 71 | 72 | 71 | 289 | 5,506 |
| Choi Gwang-soo | 71 | 74 | 73 | 71 | 289 | 5,506 |
| Kang Wook-soon | 73 | 74 | 70 | 72 | 289 | 5,506 |
| Simon Yates | 75 | 69 | 73 | 72 | 289 | 5,506 |
| Alejandro Quiroz | 70 | 72 | 73 | 74 | 289 | 5,506 |

| | SCORES | | | | TOTAL | MONEY |
|---|---|---|---|---|---|---|
| Larry Austin | 76 | 73 | 72 | 68 | 289 | 5,506 |
| Kong John-joon | 73 | 71 | 71 | 74 | 289 | 5,506 |
| David Oh | 71 | 71 | 73 | 74 | 289 | 5,506 |
| Park Do-kyu | 72 | 70 | 73 | 74 | 289 | 5,506 |
| Andrew Pitts | 72 | 74 | 72 | 72 | 290 | 4,607 |
| Yoo Jong-koo | 74 | 75 | 71 | 70 | 290 | 4,607 |
| Jun Tae-hyun | 76 | 72 | 73 | 69 | 290 | 4,607 |

## Brunei Open

*Empire Hotel & Country Club,* Bandar Seri Begawan, Brunei
Par 36-35–71; 7,029 yards

June 23-26
purse, US$300,000

| | SCORES | | | | TOTAL | MONEY |
|---|---|---|---|---|---|---|
| Terry Pilkadaris | 67 | 63 | 68 | 67 | 265 | US$47,250 |
| Jarrod Lyle | 67 | 63 | 69 | 71 | 270 | 32,400 |
| Rick Gibson | 69 | 67 | 69 | 66 | 271 | 16,425 |
| Matt Keegan | 71 | 66 | 67 | 67 | 271 | 16,425 |
| Danny Chia | 63 | 66 | 72 | 71 | 272 | 11,640 |
| Lin Wen-tang | 71 | 68 | 66 | 68 | 273 | 10,260 |
| Ahmad Bateman | 70 | 69 | 68 | 68 | 275 | 7,710 |
| Scott Barr | 73 | 68 | 66 | 68 | 275 | 7,710 |
| Amandeep Johl | 67 | 70 | 68 | 70 | 275 | 7,710 |
| Robin Hodgetts | 69 | 69 | 69 | 69 | 276 | 5,552 |
| Adam Le Vesconte | 68 | 68 | 70 | 70 | 276 | 5,552 |
| Lu Wen-teh | 68 | 69 | 68 | 71 | 276 | 5,552 |
| Anthony Kang | 69 | 71 | 69 | 68 | 277 | 4,608 |
| Andrew Pitts | 69 | 67 | 72 | 69 | 277 | 4,608 |
| Gary Simpson | 70 | 68 | 68 | 71 | 277 | 4,608 |
| Frankie Minoza | 67 | 74 | 72 | 65 | 278 | 3,967 |
| Ross Bain | 67 | 70 | 73 | 68 | 278 | 3,967 |
| Gaurav Ghei | 67 | 71 | 71 | 69 | 278 | 3,967 |
| Lin Chie-hsiang | 67 | 68 | 70 | 73 | 278 | 3,967 |
| Mahal Pearce | 70 | 69 | 71 | 69 | 279 | 3,420 |
| Jerome Delariarte | 70 | 69 | 71 | 69 | 279 | 3,420 |
| Prom Meesawat | 68 | 66 | 74 | 71 | 279 | 3,420 |
| Firoz Ali | 69 | 71 | 67 | 72 | 279 | 3,420 |
| Rashid Ismail | 70 | 65 | 70 | 74 | 279 | 3,420 |
| Atthaphon Prathummanee | 70 | 69 | 71 | 70 | 280 | 2,970 |
| Sung Mao-chang | 67 | 70 | 72 | 71 | 280 | 2,970 |
| Marcus Both | 71 | 70 | 68 | 71 | 280 | 2,970 |
| Somkiat Srisanga | 67 | 69 | 72 | 72 | 280 | 2,970 |
| Adam Fraser | 71 | 64 | 72 | 73 | 280 | 2,970 |
| Darren Griff | 71 | 65 | 75 | 70 | 281 | 2,655 |
| Jason Dawes | 66 | 73 | 68 | 74 | 281 | 2,655 |

## Volkswagon Masters China

*Jinghua Golf Club*, Beijing, China
Par 36-36–72; 7,211 yards

September 1-4
purse, US$300,000

| | SCORES | | | | TOTAL | MONEY |
|---|---|---|---|---|---|---|
| Retief Goosen | 64 | 67 | 71 | 64 | 266 | US$47,250 |
| Michael Campbell | 67 | 65 | 71 | 69 | 272 | 32,400 |

|  | SCORES | | | TOTAL | MONEY |
|---|---|---|---|---|---|
| Zhang Lian-wei | 69 68 70 70 | | | 277 | 18,150 |
| David Bransdon | 71 68 66 73 | | | 278 | 14,700 |
| Adam Blyth | 69 68 68 74 | | | 279 | 10,950 |
| Gary Simpson | 66 68 72 73 | | | 279 | 10,950 |
| Gary Rusnak | 67 71 71 71 | | | 280 | 8,220 |
| Lu Wen-teh | 68 72 68 72 | | | 280 | 8,220 |
| Li Chao | 68 75 70 68 | | | 281 | 5,634 |
| Thaworn Wiratchant | 72 69 71 69 | | | 281 | 5,634 |
| Hendrik Buhrmann | 72 68 72 69 | | | 281 | 5,634 |
| Andrew Buckle | 69 69 72 71 | | | 281 | 5,634 |
| Mardan Mamat | 71 70 67 73 | | | 281 | 5,634 |
| Prom Meesawat | 70 70 75 67 | | | 282 | 4,320 |
| Edward Michaels | 75 67 72 68 | | | 282 | 4,320 |
| Arjun Singh | 75 69 66 72 | | | 282 | 4,320 |
| Lin Wen-tang | 70 70 68 74 | | | 282 | 4,320 |
| Edward Loar | 71 71 73 68 | | | 283 | 3,795 |
| Kurt Barnes | 73 72 67 71 | | | 283 | 3,795 |
| Jarrod Lyle | 72 72 69 71 | | | 284 | 3,465 |
| Anura Rohana | 70 71 68 75 | | | 284 | 3,465 |
| Scott Barr | 70 69 70 75 | | | 284 | 3,465 |
| Ron Won | 69 69 69 77 | | | 284 | 3,465 |
| Digvijay Singh | 71 68 74 72 | | | 285 | 3,015 |
| Phillip Price | 73 70 70 72 | | | 285 | 3,015 |
| Gerald Rosales | 73 70 69 73 | | | 285 | 3,015 |
| Darren Griff | 66 76 70 73 | | | 285 | 3,015 |
| Shiv Kapur | 72 71 69 73 | | | 285 | 3,015 |
| Gaurav Ghei | 72 72 68 73 | | | 285 | 3,015 |
| Anthony Kang | 70 73 72 71 | | | 286 | 2,472 |
| Guido van der Valk | 70 76 69 71 | | | 286 | 2,472 |
| Keith Horne | 71 70 71 74 | | | 286 | 2,472 |
| Pat Giles | 74 69 69 74 | | | 286 | 2,472 |
| Mahal Pearce | 69 74 69 74 | | | 286 | 2,472 |
| Chen Tze-chung | 68 69 73 76 | | | 286 | 2,472 |
| Adam Groom | 72 69 69 76 | | | 286 | 2,472 |

## Singapore Open

*Sentosa Golf Club*, Singapore
Par 71; 6,943 yards

September 8-11
purse, US$2,000,000

|  | SCORES | | | TOTAL | MONEY |
|---|---|---|---|---|---|
| Adam Scott | 70 69 67 65 | | | 271 | US$315,000 |
| Lee Westwood | 71 71 68 68 | | | 278 | 216,000 |
| Andrew Buckle | 71 65 72 71 | | | 279 | 121,000 |
| Ted Oh | 69 70 72 70 | | | 281 | 98,000 |
| Thongchai Jaidee | 67 73 68 74 | | | 282 | 77,600 |
| Anthony Kang | 67 72 72 73 | | | 284 | 63,600 |
| Mahal Pearce | 68 70 71 75 | | | 284 | 63,600 |
| Prom Meesawat | 73 71 72 70 | | | 286 | 45,133 |
| Nick O'Hern | 71 68 73 74 | | | 286 | 45,133 |
| Edward Michaels | 69 67 71 79 | | | 286 | 45,133 |
| Chapchai Nirat | 67 74 74 72 | | | 287 | 35,520 |
| Lu Wen-teh | 71 73 71 72 | | | 287 | 35,520 |
| Liang Wen-chong | 70 73 72 73 | | | 288 | 32,160 |
| Terry Pilkadaris | 71 70 75 73 | | | 289 | 30,000 |
| Jyoti Randhawa | 74 69 72 74 | | | 289 | 30,000 |
| Lin Keng-chi | 72 71 75 72 | | | 290 | 25,960 |

| | SCORES | | | TOTAL | MONEY |
|---|---|---|---|---|---|
| Chawalit Plaphol | 71 | 71 | 75 | 73 | 290 | 25,960 |
| David Bransdon | 74 | 74 | 72 | 70 | 290 | 25,960 |
| Mardan Mamat | 73 | 74 | 70 | 73 | 290 | 25,960 |
| Alistair Presnell | 75 | 72 | 67 | 76 | 290 | 25,960 |
| Keith Horne | 71 | 77 | 73 | 71 | 292 | 23,100 |
| Gerry Norquist | 73 | 74 | 70 | 75 | 292 | 23,100 |
| Marcus Both | 69 | 72 | 77 | 75 | 293 | 21,000 |
| Angelo Que | 69 | 79 | 71 | 74 | 293 | 21,000 |
| Corey Harris | 73 | 74 | 72 | 74 | 293 | 21,000 |
| Sung Mao-chang | 72 | 70 | 76 | 75 | 293 | 21,000 |
| Frankie Minoza | 70 | 73 | 73 | 77 | 293 | 21,000 |
| Ashok Kumar | 72 | 76 | 72 | 74 | 294 | 17,250 |
| Lin Wen-tang | 73 | 68 | 77 | 76 | 294 | 17,250 |
| Rick Gibson | 76 | 70 | 72 | 76 | 294 | 17,250 |
| Kao Bo-song | 74 | 72 | 74 | 74 | 294 | 17,250 |
| Unho Park | 75 | 72 | 70 | 77 | 294 | 17,250 |
| Paul Marantz | 74 | 74 | 73 | 73 | 294 | 17,250 |
| Zhang Lian-wei | 74 | 72 | 75 | 73 | 294 | 17,250 |
| Mike Capone | 72 | 75 | 69 | 78 | 294 | 17,250 |

## Taiwan Open

*Chang Gung Golf Club*, Chinese Taipei
Par 36-36–72; 6,501 yards

September 15-18
purse, US$300,000

| | SCORES | | | TOTAL | MONEY |
|---|---|---|---|---|---|
| Thaworn Wiratchant | 73 | 65 | 68 | 64 | 270 | US$47,250 |
| Chapchai Nirat | 70 | 68 | 66 | 67 | 271 | 32,400 |
| Terry Pilkadaris | 70 | 65 | 70 | 68 | 273 | 14,830 |
| Lu Wei-lan | 70 | 69 | 67 | 67 | 273 | 14,830 |
| Scott Strange | 67 | 72 | 64 | 70 | 273 | 14,830 |
| Lu Wen-hsyong | 69 | 69 | 71 | 68 | 277 | 10,260 |
| Shiv Kapur | 73 | 66 | 72 | 67 | 278 | 7,282 |
| Wang Ter-chang | 75 | 64 | 71 | 68 | 278 | 7,282 |
| Kao Bo-song | 67 | 74 | 68 | 69 | 278 | 7,282 |
| Ted Oh | 71 | 70 | 68 | 69 | 278 | 7,282 |
| Yeh Chang-ting | 69 | 72 | 70 | 68 | 279 | 5,160 |
| Hsieh Chin-sheng | 71 | 70 | 68 | 70 | 279 | 5,160 |
| Adam Blyth | 65 | 72 | 68 | 74 | 279 | 5,160 |
| Jason Knutzon | 72 | 72 | 66 | 70 | 280 | 4,320 |
| Chen Tsang-te | 73 | 68 | 69 | 70 | 280 | 4,320 |
| Lin Chie-hsiang | 72 | 68 | 69 | 71 | 280 | 4,320 |
| Chang Tse-peng | 67 | 67 | 72 | 74 | 280 | 4,320 |
| Boonchu Ruangkit | 69 | 73 | 73 | 66 | 281 | 3,387 |
| Chen Chih-hong | 72 | 71 | 72 | 66 | 281 | 3,387 |
| Mardan Mamat | 71 | 73 | 70 | 67 | 281 | 3,387 |
| Chen Tze-ming | 72 | 68 | 73 | 68 | 281 | 3,387 |
| Gerald Rosales | 71 | 67 | 74 | 69 | 281 | 3,387 |
| Chung Chun-hsing | 73 | 70 | 69 | 69 | 281 | 3,387 |
| Prom Meesawat | 69 | 75 | 68 | 69 | 281 | 3,387 |
| Lin Wen-tang | 73 | 71 | 67 | 70 | 281 | 3,387 |
| Rick Gibson | 69 | 69 | 71 | 72 | 281 | 3,387 |
| Brad Kennedy | 66 | 71 | 71 | 73 | 281 | 3,387 |
| Chris Rodgers | 75 | 66 | 74 | 67 | 282 | 2,745 |
| Arjun Singh | 72 | 69 | 72 | 69 | 282 | 2,745 |
| Gary Rusnak | 72 | 72 | 69 | 69 | 282 | 2,745 |
| Pat Giles | 65 | 75 | 71 | 71 | 282 | 2,745 |

# Mercuries Taiwan Masters

*Taiwan Golf & Country Club*, Taiwan, Chinese Taipei
Par 36-36–72; 7,015 yards

September 22-25
purse, US$400,000

| | SCORES | | | | TOTAL | MONEY |
|---|---|---|---|---|---|---|
| Lu Wei-chih | 71 | 69 | 70 | 74 | 284 | US$79,112 |
| Lin Wen-tang | 70 | 69 | 73 | 74 | 286 | 47,467 |
| Kurt Barnes | 76 | 66 | 71 | 74 | 287 | 21,096 |
| Lu Wei-lan | 74 | 70 | 70 | 73 | 287 | 21,096 |
| Lu Wen-teh | 70 | 71 | 70 | 76 | 287 | 21,096 |
| Pat Giles | 73 | 70 | 74 | 71 | 288 | 13,844 |
| Chen Yuan-chi | 71 | 74 | 70 | 74 | 289 | 10,878 |
| Andrew Pitts | 72 | 74 | 70 | 73 | 289 | 10,878 |
| Angelo Que | 71 | 74 | 75 | 70 | 290 | 7,252 |
| Scott Barr | 71 | 77 | 72 | 70 | 290 | 7,252 |
| Matt Keegan | 74 | 72 | 72 | 72 | 290 | 7,252 |
| Gaurav Ghei | 75 | 73 | 72 | 71 | 291 | 6,131 |
| Ron Won | 73 | 73 | 66 | 79 | 291 | 6,131 |
| Atthaphon Prathummanee | 74 | 74 | 72 | 72 | 292 | 5,092 |
| Gary Simpson | 74 | 73 | 72 | 73 | 292 | 5,092 |
| Chapchai Nirat | 72 | 75 | 72 | 73 | 292 | 5,092 |
| Gary Rusnak | 72 | 72 | 73 | 75 | 292 | 5,092 |
| Rick Gibson | 74 | 72 | 74 | 73 | 293 | 4,351 |
| Shiv Kapur | 74 | 72 | 73 | 74 | 293 | 4,351 |
| Wang Ter-chang | 71 | 74 | 71 | 77 | 293 | 4,351 |
| Hsieh Min-nan | 72 | 75 | 74 | 73 | 294 | 3,935 |
| Uttam Singh Mundy | 76 | 72 | 72 | 74 | 294 | 3,935 |
| Olle Nordberg | 71 | 73 | 75 | 75 | 294 | 3,935 |
| Jason Dawes | 75 | 71 | 72 | 76 | 294 | 3,935 |
| Mardan Mamat | 71 | 75 | 76 | 73 | 295 | 3,599 |
| Pablo Del Olmo | 76 | 71 | 73 | 75 | 295 | 3,599 |
| Hsu Mong-nan | 68 | 78 | 73 | 76 | 295 | 3,599 |
| Gilberto Morales | 70 | 73 | 73 | 79 | 295 | 3,599 |
| Hendrik Buhrmann | 76 | 72 | 76 | 72 | 296 | 3,204 |
| Harmeet Kahlon | 71 | 75 | 78 | 72 | 296 | 3,204 |
| Kao Bo-song | 71 | 75 | 75 | 75 | 296 | 3,204 |
| Hsieh Tung-shu | 73 | 73 | 76 | 74 | 296 | 3,204 |
| Chris Rodgers | 73 | 72 | 73 | 78 | 296 | 3,204 |
| Ross Bain | 75 | 71 | 70 | 80 | 296 | 3,204 |

# Crowne Plaza Open

*Grand Epoch City Golf Club*, Beijing, China
Par 36-36–72; 6,458 yards

September 29-October 2
purse, US$200,000

| | SCORES | | | | TOTAL | MONEY |
|---|---|---|---|---|---|---|
| Prayad Marksaeng | 72 | 70 | 70 | 68 | 280 | US$31,500 |
| Marcus Both | 72 | 69 | 71 | 68 | 280 | 21,600 |
| (Prayad defeated Both on first playoff hole.) | | | | | | |
| Alistair Presnell | 74 | 69 | 70 | 68 | 281 | 9,886 |
| Digvijay Singh | 68 | 72 | 71 | 70 | 281 | 9,886 |
| Shiv Kapur | 74 | 70 | 68 | 69 | 281 | 9,886 |
| Liang Wen-chong | 74 | 71 | 71 | 70 | 286 | 5,933 |
| Mardan Mamat | 76 | 69 | 69 | 72 | 286 | 5,933 |
| Chen Yuan-chi | 77 | 70 | 66 | 73 | 286 | 5,933 |
| Guido van der Valk | 73 | 71 | 70 | 73 | 287 | 4,460 |

| | SCORES | | | | TOTAL | MONEY |
|---|---|---|---|---|---|---|
| Jason Dawes | 72 | 71 | 73 | 73 | 289 | 3,386 |
| Thaworn Wiratchant | 69 | 72 | 75 | 73 | 289 | 3,386 |
| Darren Griff | 74 | 73 | 68 | 74 | 289 | 3,386 |
| Andrew Buckle | 74 | 71 | 69 | 75 | 289 | 3,386 |
| Prom Meesawat | 71 | 71 | 71 | 76 | 289 | 3,386 |
| Lu Wen-teh | 74 | 71 | 66 | 78 | 289 | 3,386 |
| Boonchu Ruangkit | 74 | 72 | 74 | 70 | 290 | 2,645 |
| Hendrik Buhrmann | 76 | 68 | 75 | 71 | 290 | 2,645 |
| Eiji Mizoguchi | 76 | 70 | 71 | 73 | 290 | 2,645 |
| Ron Won | 74 | 72 | 70 | 74 | 290 | 2,645 |
| Yoshinobu Tsukada | 75 | 71 | 74 | 71 | 291 | 2,280 |
| Chapchai Nirat | 74 | 66 | 78 | 73 | 291 | 2,280 |
| Corey Harris | 76 | 72 | 70 | 73 | 291 | 2,280 |
| Pat Giles | 73 | 71 | 73 | 74 | 291 | 2,280 |
| Olle Nordberg | 75 | 70 | 71 | 75 | 291 | 2,280 |
| Li Chao | 70 | 76 | 72 | 74 | 292 | 2,070 |
| Zheng Wen-gen | 73 | 73 | 70 | 76 | 292 | 2,070 |
| Richard Moir | 74 | 71 | 75 | 73 | 293 | 1,920 |
| Lin Wen-hong | 78 | 71 | 71 | 73 | 293 | 1,920 |
| Aung Win | 73 | 75 | 72 | 73 | 293 | 1,920 |
| Kao Bo-song | 77 | 68 | 76 | 73 | 294 | 1,648 |
| Mike Capone | 72 | 75 | 73 | 74 | 294 | 1,648 |
| Rafael Ponce | 74 | 68 | 75 | 77 | 294 | 1,648 |
| Atthaphon Prathummanee | 73 | 74 | 71 | 76 | 294 | 1,648 |
| Rahil Gangjee | 76 | 68 | 73 | 77 | 294 | 1,648 |
| Sung Mao-chang | 79 | 69 | 69 | 77 | 294 | 1,648 |
| Chris Rodgers | 73 | 73 | 70 | 78 | 294 | 1,648 |

## Bangkok Airways Open

*Santiburi Samui Country Club*, Koh Samui, Thailand
Par 36-36–72; 6,881 yards

October 13-16
purse, US$200,000

| | SCORES | | | | TOTAL | MONEY |
|---|---|---|---|---|---|---|
| Lu Wen-teh | 69 | 69 | 67 | 72 | 277 | US$31,500 |
| Thammanoon Srirot | 67 | 65 | 74 | 71 | 277 | 21,600 |
| (Lu defeated Thammanoon on first playoff hole.) | | | | | | |
| Prayad Marksaeng | 69 | 71 | 71 | 67 | 278 | 12,100 |
| Shiv Kapur | 69 | 72 | 72 | 66 | 279 | 9,800 |
| Chen Yuan-chi | 69 | 73 | 70 | 69 | 281 | 7,300 |
| Thongchai Jaidee | 69 | 70 | 73 | 69 | 281 | 7,300 |
| Andrew Buckle | 72 | 73 | 71 | 66 | 282 | 4,855 |
| Unho Park | 70 | 70 | 75 | 67 | 282 | 4,855 |
| Chawalit Plaphol | 65 | 68 | 79 | 70 | 282 | 4,855 |
| Robin Hodgetts | 69 | 73 | 71 | 69 | 282 | 4,855 |
| Prom Meesawat | 71 | 71 | 69 | 72 | 283 | 3,552 |
| Frankie Minoza | 68 | 70 | 71 | 74 | 283 | 3,552 |
| Thaworn Wiratchant | 68 | 76 | 68 | 72 | 284 | 3,216 |
| *Chinarat Phandungsilp | 74 | 71 | 72 | 69 | 286 | |
| Matt Keegan | 69 | 72 | 74 | 72 | 287 | 2,940 |
| Kao Bo-song | 70 | 70 | 75 | 72 | 287 | 2,940 |
| Uttam Singh Mundy | 72 | 73 | 68 | 74 | 287 | 2,940 |
| Gaurav Ghei | 69 | 71 | 73 | 75 | 288 | 2,700 |
| Eiji Mizoguchi | 74 | 72 | 70 | 73 | 289 | 2,530 |
| Dean Alaban | 72 | 71 | 72 | 74 | 289 | 2,530 |
| *Kwanchai Tannin | 75 | 71 | 72 | 72 | 290 | |
| Lu Wei-lan | 68 | 72 | 77 | 73 | 290 | 2,340 |

|  | SCORES | | | | TOTAL | MONEY |
|---|---|---|---|---|---|---|
| Digvijay Singh | 76 | 71 | 70 | 73 | 290 | 2,340 |
| Yoshinobu Tsukada | 72 | 73 | 70 | 75 | 290 | 2,340 |
| Steven Tan | 71 | 73 | 74 | 73 | 291 | 2,070 |
| Darren Griff | 69 | 72 | 77 | 73 | 291 | 2,070 |
| Satoshi Shimouchi | 70 | 75 | 74 | 72 | 291 | 2,070 |
| Lin Wen-hong | 71 | 70 | 79 | 71 | 291 | 2,070 |
| Rafael Ponce | 77 | 72 | 72 | 70 | 291 | 2,070 |
| Olle Nordberg | 72 | 71 | 68 | 80 | 291 | 2,070 |

## Hero Honda Indian Open

*Delhi Golf Club*, New Delhi, India
Par 36-36–72; 6,831 yards

October 27-30
purse, US$300,000

|  | SCORES | | | | TOTAL | MONEY |
|---|---|---|---|---|---|---|
| Thaworn Wiratchant | 68 | 66 | 68 | 70 | 272 | US$47,250 |
| Gaurav Ghei | 67 | 72 | 69 | 66 | 274 | 32,400 |
| Hendrik Buhrmann | 66 | 70 | 69 | 70 | 275 | 16,425 |
| Prom Meesawat | 69 | 67 | 69 | 70 | 275 | 16,425 |
| Terry Pilkadaris | 67 | 70 | 70 | 71 | 278 | 11,640 |
| Mukesh Kumar | 71 | 69 | 71 | 68 | 279 | 9,540 |
| Jyoti Randhawa | 69 | 70 | 67 | 73 | 279 | 9,540 |
| Ashok Kumar | 69 | 71 | 72 | 68 | 280 | 6,770 |
| Rick Gibson | 73 | 65 | 73 | 69 | 280 | 6,770 |
| Shiv Kapur | 70 | 69 | 72 | 69 | 280 | 6,770 |
| Arjun Atwal | 70 | 68 | 73 | 70 | 281 | 5,017 |
| Shamim Khan | 71 | 68 | 71 | 71 | 281 | 5,017 |
| Scott Taylor | 71 | 67 | 72 | 71 | 281 | 5,017 |
| Jaiveer Virk | 68 | 71 | 68 | 74 | 281 | 5,017 |
| Jochen Lupprian | 70 | 72 | 71 | 69 | 282 | 3,980 |
| Gary Simpson | 68 | 69 | 73 | 72 | 282 | 3,980 |
| James Kingston | 76 | 66 | 68 | 72 | 282 | 3,980 |
| Bryan Saltus | 68 | 70 | 70 | 74 | 282 | 3,980 |
| Digvijay Singh | 66 | 70 | 72 | 74 | 282 | 3,980 |
| Harmeet Kahlon | 71 | 64 | 73 | 74 | 282 | 3,980 |
| Somkiat Srisanga | 71 | 68 | 73 | 71 | 283 | 3,465 |
| Alistair Presnell | 69 | 70 | 72 | 72 | 283 | 3,465 |
| C. Muniyappa | 70 | 69 | 75 | 70 | 284 | 2,882 |
| Atthaphon Prathummanee | 68 | 69 | 76 | 71 | 284 | 2,882 |
| P. Gunasegaran | 71 | 70 | 72 | 71 | 284 | 2,882 |
| Yeh Chang-ting | 67 | 75 | 71 | 71 | 284 | 2,882 |
| S.S.P. Chowrasia | 75 | 69 | 69 | 71 | 284 | 2,882 |
| Robin Hodgetts | 72 | 70 | 69 | 73 | 284 | 2,882 |
| Muhammed Munir | 68 | 72 | 69 | 75 | 284 | 2,882 |
| Yusuf Ali | 72 | 67 | 70 | 75 | 284 | 2,882 |
| Ross Bain | 69 | 73 | 68 | 74 | 284 | 2,882 |
| Marcus Both | 70 | 66 | 71 | 77 | 284 | 2,882 |
| Anura Rohana | 64 | 75 | 69 | 76 | 284 | 2,882 |

# Double A International Open

*St. Andrews Hill Golf Club*, Rayong, Thailand
Par 36-36–72; 7,619 yards

November 3-6
purse, US$300,000

| | SCORES | | | | TOTAL | MONEY |
|---|---|---|---|---|---|---|
| *Chinarat Phadungsil | 73 | 68 | 70 | 67 | 278 | |
| Shiv Kapur | 66 | 68 | 72 | 72 | 278 | US$47,250 |
| (Phadungsil defeated Kapur on second playoff hole.) | | | | | | |
| Thongchai Jaidee | 67 | 71 | 69 | 72 | 279 | 32,400 |
| Harmeet Kahlon | 71 | 69 | 71 | 69 | 280 | 14,830 |
| Jason Dawes | 68 | 71 | 71 | 70 | 280 | 14,830 |
| Thammanoon Srirot | 69 | 68 | 72 | 71 | 280 | 14,830 |
| Unho Park | 68 | 73 | 72 | 68 | 281 | 10,260 |
| Amandeep Johl | 73 | 71 | 68 | 70 | 282 | 8,820 |
| Larry Austin | 73 | 69 | 71 | 70 | 283 | 6,770 |
| Rahil Gangjee | 71 | 73 | 69 | 70 | 283 | 6,770 |
| Jochen Lupprian | 71 | 69 | 70 | 73 | 283 | 6,770 |
| Gaurav Ghei | 74 | 71 | 70 | 69 | 284 | 4,785 |
| Angelo Que | 69 | 70 | 75 | 70 | 284 | 4,785 |
| James Kingston | 71 | 73 | 71 | 69 | 284 | 4,785 |
| Chris Travers | 72 | 69 | 73 | 70 | 284 | 4,785 |
| Scott Strange | 70 | 72 | 70 | 72 | 284 | 4,785 |
| Kenny Walker | 66 | 73 | 71 | 74 | 284 | 4,785 |
| Wang Ter-chang | 68 | 73 | 74 | 70 | 285 | 3,695 |
| Digvijay Singh | 73 | 73 | 69 | 70 | 285 | 3,695 |
| Thaworn Wiratchant | 69 | 76 | 69 | 71 | 285 | 3,695 |
| Steven Tan | 70 | 70 | 72 | 73 | 285 | 3,695 |
| Pat Giles | 70 | 71 | 70 | 74 | 285 | 3,695 |
| Simon Yates | 70 | 68 | 71 | 76 | 285 | 3,695 |
| Olle Nordberg | 70 | 74 | 71 | 71 | 286 | 3,240 |
| Prom Meesawat | 72 | 71 | 71 | 72 | 286 | 3,240 |
| Gerald Rosales | 72 | 70 | 68 | 76 | 286 | 3,240 |
| Gary Simpson | 76 | 70 | 69 | 72 | 287 | 2,925 |
| Sung Mao-chang | 71 | 72 | 71 | 73 | 287 | 2,925 |
| Alistair Presnell | 73 | 67 | 73 | 74 | 287 | 2,925 |
| Prayad Marksaeng | 75 | 71 | 73 | 68 | 287 | 2,925 |

# HSBC Champions Tournament

*Sheshan International Golf Club*, Shanghai, China
Par 36-36–72; 7,143 yards

November 10-13
purse, US$5,000,000

| | SCORES | | | | TOTAL | MONEY |
|---|---|---|---|---|---|---|
| David Howell | 65 | 67 | 68 | 68 | 268 | US$833,300 |
| Tiger Woods | 65 | 69 | 67 | 70 | 271 | 555,550 |
| Nick Dougherty | 64 | 68 | 73 | 69 | 274 | 281,500 |
| Nick O'Hern | 67 | 67 | 67 | 73 | 274 | 281,500 |
| Vijay Singh | 67 | 69 | 70 | 69 | 275 | 194,000 |
| Thomas Bjorn | 67 | 69 | 69 | 70 | 275 | 194,000 |
| Paul Casey | 67 | 68 | 73 | 68 | 276 | 150,000 |
| Jean-Francois Remesy | 70 | 67 | 70 | 70 | 277 | 118,500 |
| Thaworn Wiratchant | 67 | 68 | 69 | 73 | 277 | 118,500 |
| Michael Campbell | 66 | 70 | 69 | 73 | 278 | 100,000 |
| Paul Lawrie | 64 | 75 | 70 | 70 | 279 | 92,200 |
| Lee Westwood | 70 | 69 | 74 | 67 | 280 | 81,533 |
| Arjun Atwal | 69 | 70 | 73 | 68 | 280 | 81,533 |
| K.J. Choi | 65 | 71 | 74 | 70 | 280 | 81,533 |

|  | SCORES | | | | TOTAL | MONEY |
|---|---|---|---|---|---|---|
| Steve Webster | 72 | 70 | 71 | 68 | 281 | 69,875 |
| Padraig Harrington | 69 | 72 | 72 | 68 | 281 | 69,875 |
| Thongchai Jaidee | 67 | 73 | 71 | 70 | 281 | 69,875 |
| Peter O'Malley | 64 | 72 | 73 | 72 | 281 | 69,875 |
| John Bickerton | 68 | 72 | 72 | 70 | 282 | 58,566 |
| Steven Bowditch | 71 | 69 | 71 | 71 | 282 | 58,566 |
| Robert-Jan Derksen | 65 | 70 | 74 | 73 | 282 | 58,566 |
| Peter Hanson | 69 | 70 | 70 | 73 | 282 | 58,566 |
| Ian Poulter | 67 | 69 | 73 | 73 | 282 | 58,566 |
| Paul Broadhurst | 76 | 69 | 69 | 68 | 282 | 58,566 |
| Niclas Fasth | 70 | 74 | 69 | 70 | 283 | 48,100 |
| Thomas Aiken | 72 | 72 | 69 | 70 | 283 | 48,100 |
| Prayad Marksaeng | 70 | 70 | 75 | 68 | 283 | 48,100 |
| Richard Sterne | 73 | 70 | 73 | 67 | 283 | 48,100 |
| Raphael Jacquelin | 74 | 71 | 67 | 71 | 283 | 48,100 |
| Kenneth Ferrie | 66 | 69 | 74 | 74 | 283 | 48,100 |
| Zhang Lian-wei | 67 | 68 | 73 | 75 | 283 | 48,100 |
| Gonzalo Fernandez-Castano | 70 | 70 | 74 | 70 | 284 | 39,850 |
| Charl Schwartzel | 68 | 70 | 76 | 70 | 284 | 39,850 |
| Henrik Stenson | 69 | 74 | 72 | 69 | 284 | 39,850 |
| Bradley Dredge | 77 | 68 | 73 | 66 | 284 | 39,850 |
| Titch Moore | 69 | 71 | 73 | 72 | 285 | 35,033 |
| Richard Green | 71 | 73 | 72 | 69 | 285 | 35,033 |
| Maarten Lafeber | 72 | 71 | 74 | 68 | 285 | 35,033 |
| Graeme McDowell | 70 | 67 | 75 | 74 | 286 | 33,000 |
| Craig Parry | 71 | 72 | 71 | 73 | 287 | 31,500 |
| Colin Montgomerie | 74 | 71 | 68 | 74 | 287 | 31,500 |
| Terry Pilkadaris | 69 | 72 | 76 | 71 | 288 | 29,000 |
| Simon Wakefield | 68 | 72 | 77 | 71 | 288 | 29,000 |
| Stephen Dodd | 73 | 75 | 71 | 69 | 288 | 29,000 |
| Wang Ter-chang | 71 | 70 | 72 | 76 | 289 | 25,500 |
| Barry Lane | 73 | 70 | 70 | 76 | 289 | 25,500 |
| Jyoti Randhawa | 73 | 69 | 75 | 72 | 289 | 25,500 |
| Emanuele Canonica | 70 | 75 | 77 | 67 | 289 | 25,500 |
| Thomas Levet | 70 | 73 | 73 | 74 | 290 | 21,500 |
| Liang Wen-chong | 72 | 70 | 71 | 77 | 290 | 21,500 |
| Euan Walters | 70 | 72 | 75 | 73 | 290 | 21,500 |
| Lu Wen-teh | 72 | 75 | 72 | 71 | 290 | 21,500 |
| Paul McGinley | 73 | 70 | 71 | 78 | 292 | 19,000 |
| Miguel Angel Jimenez | 70 | 72 | 76 | 76 | 294 | 17,000 |
| Scott Strange | 69 | 76 | 76 | 73 | 294 | 17,000 |
| Adam Le Vesconte | 72 | 70 | 80 | 72 | 294 | 17,000 |
| Chinarat Phadungsil | 72 | 75 | 74 | 74 | 295 | 14,500 |
| Neil Cheetham | 75 | 72 | 77 | 71 | 295 | 14,500 |
| Joakim Backstrom | 74 | 73 | 75 | 74 | 296 | 12,500 |
| Richard Lee | 68 | 77 | 78 | 73 | 296 | 12,500 |
| *Hu Mu | 78 | 70 | 81 | 68 | 297 | |
| Lu Wei-chih | 71 | 75 | 77 | 76 | 299 | 10,500 |
| Sandy Lyle | 73 | 76 | 76 | 74 | 299 | 10,500 |
| Marc Warren | 76 | 72 | 71 | 80 | 299 | 10,500 |
| Brett Rumford | 79 | 72 | 73 | 76 | 300 | 9,250 |
| Wu Wei-huang | 73 | 75 | 79 | 73 | 300 | 9,250 |
| Marc Cayeux | 74 | 74 | 74 | 79 | 301 | 8,250 |
| Huang Yong-huan | 77 | 76 | 76 | 72 | 301 | 8,250 |
| Shang Lei | 78 | 74 | 81 | 71 | 304 | 7,750 |
| Li Chao | 73 | 82 | 72 | 78 | 305 | 7,500 |
| Mikael Lundberg | 78 | 73 | 79 | 77 | 307 | 7,250 |
| Qiu Zhi-feng | 79 | 74 | 80 | 77 | 310 | 7,000 |
| Yuan Hao | 75 | 77 | 86 | 73 | 311 | 6,750 |
| Kim Felton | | | | | WD | 6,500 |

# Carlsberg Masters Vietnam

*Chi Linh Star Golf & Country Club,* Hanoi, Vietnam
Par 36-36–72

November 17-20
purse, US$200,000

| | SCORES | | | | TOTAL | MONEY |
|---|---|---|---|---|---|---|
| Thaworn Wiratchant | 72 | 66 | 72 | 71 | 281 | US$31,500 |
| Chris Rodgers | 67 | 74 | 69 | 73 | 283 | 21,600 |
| Frankie Minoza | 70 | 68 | 76 | 70 | 284 | 12,100 |
| Yoshinobu Tsukada | 69 | 71 | 73 | 73 | 286 | 8,133 |
| James Stewart | 70 | 71 | 73 | 72 | 286 | 8,133 |
| Danny Chia | 66 | 74 | 70 | 76 | 286 | 8,133 |
| Ron Won | 71 | 73 | 75 | 68 | 287 | 5,140 |
| Dean Alaban | 71 | 74 | 74 | 68 | 287 | 5,140 |
| Firoz Ali | 75 | 68 | 74 | 70 | 287 | 5,140 |
| Chris Travers | 72 | 73 | 75 | 68 | 288 | 3,835 |
| Suk Jong-ryul | 71 | 74 | 71 | 72 | 288 | 3,835 |
| Amandeep Johl | 75 | 70 | 73 | 71 | 289 | 3,325 |
| Richard Backwell | 71 | 75 | 72 | 71 | 289 | 3,325 |
| Mukesh Kumar | 72 | 73 | 72 | 73 | 290 | 3,060 |
| Gerald Rosales | 72 | 76 | 73 | 70 | 291 | 2,880 |
| Chapchai Nirat | 72 | 78 | 70 | 71 | 291 | 2,880 |
| Prom Meesawat | 73 | 75 | 73 | 71 | 292 | 2,463 |
| Corey Harris | 71 | 77 | 74 | 70 | 292 | 2,463 |
| Lin Chie-hsiang | 71 | 75 | 73 | 73 | 292 | 2,463 |
| Akinori Tani | 71 | 75 | 72 | 74 | 292 | 2,463 |
| Anthony Kang | 75 | 71 | 72 | 74 | 292 | 2,463 |
| Simon Yates | 71 | 74 | 72 | 75 | 292 | 2,463 |
| Hendrik Buhrmann | 73 | 73 | 78 | 69 | 293 | 2,190 |
| Richard Moir | 72 | 75 | 78 | 68 | 293 | 2,190 |
| Alistair Presnell | 69 | 80 | 75 | 70 | 294 | 1,920 |
| Larry Austin | 73 | 73 | 78 | 70 | 294 | 1,920 |
| Gurbaaz Mann | 76 | 75 | 74 | 69 | 294 | 1,920 |
| Adam Groom | 71 | 75 | 74 | 74 | 294 | 1,920 |
| Cookie Lao | 75 | 74 | 71 | 74 | 294 | 1,920 |
| Somkiet Srisanga | 71 | 70 | 77 | 76 | 294 | 1,920 |
| Vivek Bhandari | 78 | 71 | 69 | 76 | 294 | 1,920 |

# Volvo China Open

*Shenzhen Golf Club,* Shenzhen, China
Par 36-36–72; 7,127 yards

November 24-27
purse, US$1,300,000

| | SCORES | | | | TOTAL | MONEY |
|---|---|---|---|---|---|---|
| Paul Casey | 71 | 69 | 70 | 65 | 275 | US$216,660 |
| Oliver Wilson | 68 | 67 | 71 | 69 | 275 | 144,440 |
| (Casey defeated Wilson on first playoff hole.) | | | | | | |
| Barry Lane | 67 | 74 | 67 | 68 | 276 | 81,380 |
| Chawalit Plaphol | 65 | 67 | 74 | 71 | 277 | 60,060 |
| Ross Fisher | 69 | 68 | 68 | 72 | 277 | 60,060 |
| Peter Lawrie | 69 | 72 | 68 | 69 | 278 | 45,500 |
| Thongchai Jaidee | 72 | 70 | 70 | 67 | 279 | 31,655 |
| Jyoti Randhawa | 71 | 67 | 71 | 70 | 279 | 31,655 |
| Miles Tunnicliff | 68 | 70 | 70 | 71 | 279 | 31,655 |
| Zhang Lian-wei | 70 | 71 | 66 | 72 | 279 | 31,655 |
| Scott Strange | 73 | 67 | 70 | 70 | 280 | 23,920 |
| Simon Yates | 68 | 68 | 74 | 71 | 281 | 19,277 |

|  | SCORES | | | TOTAL | MONEY |
|---|---|---|---|---|---|
| Kenneth Ferrie | 70 | 70 | 70 | 71 | 281 | 19,277 |
| Keith Horne | 74 | 68 | 68 | 71 | 281 | 19,277 |
| Francois Delamontagne | 65 | 70 | 74 | 72 | 281 | 19,277 |
| Fredrik Widmark | 75 | 65 | 69 | 72 | 281 | 19,277 |
| Anders Hansen | 70 | 70 | 69 | 72 | 281 | 19,277 |
| Gaurav Ghei | 72 | 70 | 67 | 72 | 281 | 19,277 |
| Anthony Wall | 71 | 71 | 71 | 69 | 282 | 15,158 |
| Soren Hansen | 70 | 72 | 70 | 70 | 282 | 15,158 |
| Gregory Bourdy | 73 | 69 | 70 | 70 | 282 | 15,158 |
| Johan Skold | 68 | 75 | 69 | 70 | 282 | 15,158 |
| Soren Kjeldsen | 74 | 67 | 67 | 74 | 282 | 15,158 |
| David Park | 69 | 73 | 71 | 70 | 283 | 13,325 |
| Thaworn Wiratchant | 72 | 68 | 72 | 71 | 283 | 13,325 |
| Boonchu Ruangkit | 67 | 73 | 71 | 72 | 283 | 13,325 |
| Daniel Vancsik | 73 | 70 | 68 | 72 | 283 | 13,325 |
| Rahil Gangjee | 72 | 71 | 71 | 70 | 284 | 11,765 |
| Jose Manuel Lara | 69 | 75 | 70 | 70 | 284 | 11,765 |
| Joakim Haeggman | 74 | 69 | 70 | 71 | 284 | 11,765 |
| Jean Van de Velde | 73 | 70 | 69 | 72 | 284 | 11,765 |
| Nicolas Colsaerts | 73 | 69 | 74 | 69 | 285 | 10,088 |
| Terry Pilkadaris | 68 | 71 | 76 | 70 | 285 | 10,088 |
| Scott Drummond | 73 | 70 | 70 | 72 | 285 | 10,088 |
| Brad Kennedy | 72 | 70 | 70 | 73 | 285 | 10,088 |
| Shiv Kapur | 69 | 70 | 70 | 76 | 285 | 10,088 |
| Lu Wen-teh | 73 | 69 | 76 | 68 | 286 | 8,450 |
| Wang Ter-chang | 71 | 72 | 73 | 70 | 286 | 8,450 |
| Chapchai Nirat | 72 | 71 | 73 | 70 | 286 | 8,450 |
| Adam Blyth | 70 | 72 | 73 | 71 | 286 | 8,450 |
| Ariel Canete | 73 | 70 | 71 | 72 | 286 | 8,450 |
| Hendrik Buhrmann | 76 | 68 | 70 | 72 | 286 | 8,450 |
| Robert Karlsson | 73 | 71 | 69 | 73 | 286 | 8,450 |
| Peter Gustafsson | 72 | 72 | 74 | 69 | 287 | 6,760 |
| Leif Westerberg | 73 | 70 | 74 | 70 | 287 | 6,760 |
| Adam Groom | 70 | 71 | 74 | 72 | 287 | 6,760 |
| Ron Won | 74 | 68 | 71 | 74 | 287 | 6,760 |
| Clay Devers | 71 | 72 | 70 | 74 | 287 | 6,760 |
| Steven Jeppesen | 72 | 69 | 71 | 75 | 287 | 6,760 |
| Nick Dougherty | 73 | 70 | 76 | 69 | 288 | 5,330 |
| Lee Sung-man | 70 | 73 | 74 | 71 | 288 | 5,330 |
| Marc Warren | 71 | 73 | 71 | 73 | 288 | 5,330 |
| Gary Rusnak | 72 | 72 | 71 | 73 | 288 | 5,330 |
| Anthony Kang | 69 | 72 | 73 | 74 | 288 | 5,330 |
| Mo Joong-kyung | 71 | 73 | 74 | 71 | 289 | 4,290 |
| Stephen Dodd | 71 | 71 | 74 | 73 | 289 | 4,290 |
| Carl Suneson | 71 | 73 | 71 | 74 | 289 | 4,290 |
| Gary Murphy | 71 | 72 | 77 | 70 | 290 | 3,640 |
| Lu Wei-lan | 74 | 70 | 75 | 71 | 290 | 3,640 |
| Marten Olander | 72 | 72 | 73 | 73 | 290 | 3,640 |
| Chang Tse-peng | 69 | 73 | 74 | 74 | 290 | 3,640 |
| Andrew Butterfield | 68 | 72 | 75 | 75 | 290 | 3,640 |
| Gary Emerson | 74 | 70 | 75 | 72 | 291 | 3,120 |
| Alistair Presnell | 74 | 70 | 74 | 73 | 291 | 3,120 |
| Danny Chia | 70 | 72 | 72 | 77 | 291 | 3,120 |
| Lin Keng-chi | 70 | 74 | 71 | 77 | 292 | 2,860 |
| Joakim Backstrom | 69 | 73 | 74 | 77 | 293 | 2,730 |

# UBS Hong Kong Open

*Hong Kong Golf Club,* Hong Kong
Par 34-36–70; 6,722 yards

December 1-4
purse, US$1,200,000

| | SCORES | | | TOTAL | MONEY |
|---|---|---|---|---|---|
| Colin Montgomerie | 69 | 66 | 66 | 70 | 271 | US$200,000 |
| Thammanoon Srirot | 71 | 67 | 66 | 68 | 272 | 72,266 |
| Edward Loar | 68 | 64 | 71 | 69 | 272 | 72,266 |
| Lin Keng-chi | 68 | 69 | 66 | 69 | 272 | 72,266 |
| K.J. Choi | 67 | 72 | 64 | 69 | 272 | 72,266 |
| James Kingston | 68 | 69 | 64 | 71 | 272 | 72,266 |
| Thongchai Jaidee | 68 | 68 | 67 | 70 | 273 | 30,960 |
| Damien McGrane | 68 | 71 | 63 | 71 | 273 | 30,960 |
| Kang Wook-soon | 64 | 70 | 68 | 71 | 273 | 30,960 |
| Simon Yates | 69 | 69 | 61 | 75 | 274 | 24,000 |
| Peter Gustafsson | 69 | 69 | 67 | 70 | 275 | 20,680 |
| Rick Gibson | 65 | 66 | 71 | 73 | 275 | 20,680 |
| Martin Erlandsson | 65 | 68 | 68 | 74 | 275 | 20,680 |
| Ted Oh | 72 | 67 | 67 | 70 | 276 | 17,280 |
| Richard Bland | 70 | 68 | 67 | 71 | 276 | 17,280 |
| Andrew Butterfield | 69 | 65 | 69 | 73 | 276 | 17,280 |
| Maarten Lafeber | 72 | 68 | 63 | 73 | 276 | 17,280 |
| Jose Manuel Lara | 67 | 70 | 69 | 71 | 277 | 14,670 |
| Scott Barr | 67 | 72 | 67 | 71 | 277 | 14,670 |
| Soren Kjeldsen | 66 | 69 | 70 | 72 | 277 | 14,670 |
| Jeev Milkha Singh | 69 | 69 | 66 | 73 | 277 | 14,670 |
| Thomas Bjorn | 70 | 68 | 72 | 68 | 278 | 13,200 |
| Liang Wen-chong | 72 | 69 | 66 | 71 | 278 | 13,200 |
| Sam Little | 69 | 72 | 65 | 72 | 278 | 13,200 |
| Simon Dyson | 71 | 67 | 71 | 70 | 279 | 11,760 |
| Gaurav Ghei | 68 | 72 | 67 | 72 | 279 | 11,760 |
| Joakim Haeggman | 71 | 68 | 67 | 73 | 279 | 11,760 |
| Marc Cayeux | 68 | 68 | 68 | 75 | 279 | 11,760 |
| Oliver Wilson | 75 | 64 | 64 | 76 | 279 | 11,760 |
| Brad Kennedy | 70 | 69 | 70 | 71 | 280 | 9,510 |
| Gregory Havret | 71 | 70 | 68 | 71 | 280 | 9,510 |
| Anders Hansen | 73 | 67 | 69 | 71 | 280 | 9,510 |
| Gary Murphy | 68 | 73 | 67 | 72 | 280 | 9,510 |
| Chawalit Plaphol | 72 | 67 | 68 | 73 | 280 | 9,510 |
| Adam Le Vesconte | 68 | 70 | 69 | 73 | 280 | 9,510 |
| Shiv Kapur | 69 | 70 | 68 | 73 | 280 | 9,510 |
| Marcus Both | 67 | 68 | 71 | 74 | 280 | 9,510 |
| Prayad Marksaeng | 68 | 71 | 72 | 70 | 281 | 7,320 |
| Angelo Que | 74 | 65 | 70 | 72 | 281 | 7,320 |
| Jean Van de Velde | 70 | 70 | 69 | 72 | 281 | 7,320 |
| Pablo Del Olmo | 68 | 70 | 70 | 73 | 281 | 7,320 |
| Miguel Angel Jimenez | 69 | 67 | 71 | 74 | 281 | 7,320 |
| Francois Delamontagne | 66 | 69 | 72 | 74 | 281 | 7,320 |
| Robert-Jan Derksen | 69 | 69 | 68 | 75 | 281 | 7,320 |
| Wang Ter-chang | 72 | 68 | 66 | 75 | 281 | 7,320 |
| Miles Tunnicliff | 68 | 70 | 67 | 76 | 281 | 7,320 |
| Philip Golding | 70 | 70 | 65 | 77 | 282 | 6,120 |
| Adam Groom | 70 | 70 | 70 | 73 | 283 | 5,520 |
| Kenneth Ferrie | 68 | 72 | 69 | 74 | 283 | 5,520 |
| Jyoti Randhawa | 65 | 71 | 72 | 75 | 283 | 5,520 |
| Thaworn Wiratchant | 69 | 68 | 69 | 77 | 283 | 5,520 |
| Gary Emerson | 70 | 69 | 72 | 73 | 284 | 4,560 |
| Christian Cevaer | 72 | 68 | 70 | 74 | 284 | 4,560 |
| Scott Strange | 71 | 64 | 74 | 75 | 284 | 4,560 |
| Nick Dougherty | 71 | 70 | 69 | 74 | 284 | 4,560 |

| | SCORES | | | | TOTAL | MONEY |
|---|---|---|---|---|---|---|
| Ian Garbutt | 67 | 74 | 73 | 72 | 286 | 3,560 |
| Prom Meesawat | 71 | 69 | 72 | 74 | 286 | 3,560 |
| Gary Rusnak | 71 | 69 | 72 | 74 | 286 | 3,560 |
| Peter Lawrie | 72 | 69 | 71 | 74 | 286 | 3,560 |
| David Park | 72 | 68 | 71 | 75 | 286 | 3,560 |
| Nicolas Colsaerts | 69 | 69 | 71 | 77 | 286 | 3,560 |
| Chang Tse-peng | 67 | 73 | 72 | 75 | 287 | 3,000 |
| Amandeep Johl | 72 | 69 | 71 | 75 | 287 | 3,000 |
| Terry Pilkadaris | 69 | 68 | 73 | 77 | 287 | 3,000 |
| Mo Joong-kyung | 70 | 68 | 75 | 76 | 289 | 2,520 |
| Lee Sung-man | 73 | 68 | 71 | 77 | 289 | 2,520 |
| Barry Lane | 68 | 70 | 73 | 78 | 289 | 2,520 |
| Simon Wakefield | 73 | 68 | 70 | 78 | 289 | 2,520 |
| Richard McEvoy | 66 | 73 | 69 | 81 | 289 | 2,520 |

## Volvo Masters of Asia

*Thai Country Club*, Bangkok, Thailand
Par 36-36–72; 7,052 yards

December 8-11
purse, US$600,000

| | SCORES | | | | TOTAL | MONEY |
|---|---|---|---|---|---|---|
| Shiv Kapur | 66 | 67 | 68 | 67 | 268 | US$108,000 |
| Jyoti Randhawa | 70 | 64 | 67 | 69 | 270 | 69,000 |
| Marcus Both | 69 | 66 | 66 | 71 | 272 | 40,000 |
| Chawalit Plaphol | 69 | 70 | 67 | 69 | 275 | 29,350 |
| Frankie Minoza | 70 | 74 | 65 | 68 | 277 | 23,100 |
| Andrew Buckle | 66 | 71 | 70 | 71 | 278 | 20,000 |
| Kang Wook-soon | 71 | 73 | 70 | 66 | 280 | 16,350 |
| Chapchai Nirat | 71 | 68 | 68 | 73 | 280 | 16,350 |
| Ted Oh | 68 | 73 | 69 | 71 | 281 | 12,700 |
| Simon Yates | 71 | 69 | 69 | 72 | 281 | 12,700 |
| Wang Ter-chang | 71 | 71 | 69 | 71 | 282 | 10,600 |
| Prom Meesawat | 67 | 72 | 70 | 73 | 282 | 10,600 |
| Terry Pilkadaris | 69 | 71 | 70 | 73 | 283 | 9,600 |
| Lin Keng-chi | 73 | 72 | 72 | 67 | 284 | 7,857 |
| Mo Joong-kyung | 74 | 68 | 71 | 71 | 284 | 7,857 |
| Prayad Marksaeng | 72 | 72 | 68 | 72 | 284 | 7,857 |
| Thaworn Wiratchant | 71 | 73 | 67 | 73 | 284 | 7,857 |
| Lu Wen-teh | 71 | 67 | 71 | 75 | 284 | 7,857 |
| Adam Fraser | 68 | 69 | 72 | 75 | 284 | 7,857 |
| Zhang Lian-wei | 72 | 66 | 70 | 76 | 284 | 7,857 |
| Jason Knutzon | 70 | 70 | 73 | 72 | 285 | 6,517 |
| Scott Strange | 70 | 69 | 73 | 73 | 285 | 6,517 |
| Gary Simpson | 69 | 71 | 72 | 73 | 285 | 6,517 |
| Adam Blyth | 73 | 75 | 69 | 69 | 286 | 6,200 |
| Gaurav Ghei | 72 | 69 | 74 | 72 | 287 | 5,975 |
| Anthony Kang | 68 | 76 | 70 | 73 | 287 | 5,975 |
| Mahal Pearce | 70 | 73 | 74 | 71 | 288 | 5,600 |
| Liang Wen-chong | 74 | 75 | 68 | 71 | 288 | 5,600 |
| Thongchai Jaidee | 70 | 71 | 75 | 72 | 288 | 5,600 |
| Richard Lee | 73 | 71 | 73 | 72 | 289 | 5,150 |
| Boonchu Ruangkit | 70 | 72 | 72 | 75 | 289 | 5,150 |
| Gary Rusnak | 74 | 70 | 70 | 75 | 289 | 5,150 |

## Asia/Japan Okinawa Open

See Japan Tour section.

# Japan Tour

## Token Homemate Cup

*Token Tado Country Club,* Mie
Par 35-36–71; 7,083 yards
(Second round cancelled—snow.)

March 24-27
purse, ¥100,000,000

| | SCORES | | | TOTAL | MONEY |
|---|---|---|---|---|---|
| Tadahiro Takayama | 67 | 72 | 66 | 205 | ¥15,000,000 |
| Nozomi Kawahara | 70 | 67 | 68 | 205 | 7,500,000 |
| (Takayama defeated Kawahara on third playoff hole.) | | | | | |
| Steven Conran | 69 | 70 | 67 | 206 | 5,100,000 |
| Craig Jones | 69 | 69 | 69 | 207 | 3,600,000 |
| Y.E. Yang | 70 | 70 | 68 | 208 | 2,850,000 |
| Hiroyuki Fujita | 66 | 74 | 68 | 208 | 2,850,000 |
| Jeev Milkha Singh | 70 | 75 | 64 | 209 | 2,292,500 |
| Naoki Ohta | 69 | 72 | 68 | 209 | 2,292,500 |
| Toru Taniguchi | 68 | 69 | 72 | 209 | 2,292,500 |
| Takashi Kanemoto | 73 | 70 | 67 | 210 | 1,815,000 |
| Nobumitsu Yuhara | 70 | 70 | 70 | 210 | 1,815,000 |
| Hideto Tanihara | 67 | 70 | 73 | 210 | 1,815,000 |
| Nobuhiro Masuda | 73 | 73 | 65 | 211 | 1,305,000 |
| Tatsuhiko Takahashi | 66 | 75 | 70 | 211 | 1,305,000 |
| Mitsuo Harada | 71 | 69 | 71 | 211 | 1,305,000 |
| Kyoji Hirota | 72 | 68 | 71 | 211 | 1,305,000 |
| Shuji Ito | 67 | 73 | 71 | 211 | 1,305,000 |
| Tomohiro Kondo | 67 | 76 | 69 | 212 | 1,005,000 |
| Kaname Yokoo | 74 | 69 | 69 | 212 | 1,005,000 |
| Takashi Kamiyama | 70 | 69 | 73 | 212 | 1,005,000 |
| Yumihiko Hatone | 68 | 74 | 71 | 213 | 795,000 |
| Tetsuji Hiratsuka | 75 | 70 | 68 | 213 | 795,000 |
| Yutaka Horinouchi | 73 | 70 | 70 | 213 | 795,000 |
| Kiyoshi Murota | 71 | 72 | 70 | 213 | 795,000 |
| Naoya Sugiyama | 69 | 72 | 73 | 214 | 585,000 |
| Ryoken Kawagishi | 73 | 73 | 68 | 214 | 585,000 |
| Koki Idoki | 71 | 73 | 70 | 214 | 585,000 |
| Katsunori Kuwabara | 71 | 73 | 70 | 214 | 585,000 |
| Chris Campbell | 72 | 70 | 72 | 214 | 585,000 |
| Ryuichi Oda | 69 | 73 | 72 | 214 | 585,000 |
| Hidemasa Hoshino | 70 | 70 | 74 | 214 | 585,000 |

## Tsuruya Open

*Yamanohara Golf Club,* Kawanishi, Hyogo
Par 35-36–71; 6,778 yards

April 21-24
purse, ¥100,000,000

| | SCORES | | | | TOTAL | MONEY |
|---|---|---|---|---|---|---|
| Naomichi Ozaki | 67 | 69 | 67 | 68 | 271 | ¥20,000,000 |
| Ryoken Kawagishi | 70 | 74 | 64 | 66 | 274 | 8,400,000 |
| Paul Sheehan | 63 | 73 | 67 | 71 | 274 | 8,400,000 |
| Kiyoshi Murota | 68 | 73 | 67 | 68 | 276 | 4,400,000 |

|  | SCORES |  |  | TOTAL | MONEY |
|---|---|---|---|---|---|
| Takuya Taniguchi | 73 | 65 | 69 | 69 | 276 | 4,400,000 |
| S.K. Ho | 67 | 71 | 70 | 69 | 277 | 3,450,000 |
| Toyokazu Fujishima | 69 | 70 | 67 | 71 | 277 | 3,450,000 |
| Yumihiko Hatone | 69 | 72 | 71 | 66 | 278 | 2,935,000 |
| Y.E. Yang | 68 | 72 | 68 | 70 | 278 | 2,935,000 |
| Hiroyuki Fujita | 69 | 72 | 68 | 70 | 279 | 2,420,000 |
| Tomohiro Kondo | 70 | 72 | 65 | 72 | 279 | 2,420,000 |
| Craig Jones | 69 | 69 | 68 | 73 | 279 | 2,420,000 |
| Kenichi Kuboya | 69 | 74 | 70 | 67 | 280 | 1,686,666 |
| Daisuke Maruyama | 68 | 76 | 67 | 69 | 280 | 1,686,666 |
| Shigeru Nonaka | 69 | 71 | 70 | 70 | 280 | 1,686,666 |
| Steven Conran | 70 | 70 | 69 | 71 | 280 | 1,686,666 |
| Hideki Kase | 69 | 68 | 71 | 72 | 280 | 1,686,666 |
| Mitsuo Harada | 70 | 71 | 66 | 73 | 280 | 1,686,666 |
| Kim Jong-duck | 74 | 69 | 65 | 73 | 281 | 1,340,000 |
| Jun Kikuchi | 71 | 72 | 72 | 67 | 282 | 1,140,000 |
| Nobuhito Sato | 71 | 71 | 70 | 70 | 282 | 1,140,000 |
| Chang Ik-je | 67 | 73 | 71 | 71 | 282 | 1,140,000 |
| Yoshinobu Tsukada | 70 | 70 | 69 | 73 | 282 | 1,140,000 |
| Mo Joong-kyung | 68 | 77 | 70 | 68 | 283 | 820,000 |
| Chris Campbell | 70 | 74 | 70 | 69 | 283 | 820,000 |
| Taichiro Kiyota | 73 | 69 | 72 | 69 | 283 | 820,000 |
| Hidemasa Hoshino | 71 | 74 | 68 | 70 | 283 | 820,000 |
| Makoto Inoue | 66 | 77 | 69 | 71 | 283 | 820,000 |
| Yutaka Horinouchi | 71 | 74 | 67 | 71 | 283 | 820,000 |
| Yasuharu Imano | 72 | 69 | 71 | 71 | 283 | 820,000 |

## Chunichi Crowns

*Nagoya Golf Club, Wago Course*, Aichi
Par 35-35–70; 6,547 yards

April 28-May 1
purse, ¥120,000,000

|  | SCORES |  |  | TOTAL | MONEY |
|---|---|---|---|---|---|
| Naomichi Ozaki | 68 | 67 | 67 | 67 | 269 | ¥24,000,000 |
| Steven Conran | 71 | 64 | 68 | 66 | 269 | 12,000,000 |
| (Ozaki defeated Conran on second playoff hole.) |  |  |  |  |  |  |
| Y.E. Yang | 61 | 71 | 71 | 67 | 270 | 8,160,000 |
| Daisuke Maruyama | 69 | 64 | 68 | 70 | 271 | 5,280,000 |
| Trevor Immelman | 67 | 67 | 70 | 67 | 271 | 5,280,000 |
| Kiyoshi Murota | 66 | 71 | 69 | 66 | 272 | 4,140,000 |
| Katsumune Imai | 68 | 70 | 66 | 68 | 272 | 4,140,000 |
| Toru Taniguchi | 67 | 70 | 67 | 69 | 273 | 3,273,000 |
| Keiichiro Fukabori | 70 | 68 | 67 | 68 | 273 | 3,273,000 |
| Kaname Yokoo | 69 | 67 | 68 | 69 | 273 | 3,273,000 |
| Soushi Tajima | 73 | 67 | 66 | 67 | 273 | 3,273,000 |
| Tateo Ozaki | 69 | 64 | 70 | 71 | 274 | 2,544,000 |
| Katsuya Nakagawa | 68 | 65 | 74 | 67 | 274 | 2,544,000 |
| Hiroyuki Fujita | 69 | 70 | 68 | 68 | 275 | 2,184,000 |
| Kiyoshi Maita | 65 | 66 | 74 | 71 | 276 | 1,624,000 |
| Naoya Sugiyama | 65 | 70 | 73 | 68 | 276 | 1,624,000 |
| Yasuharu Imano | 68 | 71 | 68 | 69 | 276 | 1,624,000 |
| Gregory Meyer | 69 | 66 | 72 | 69 | 276 | 1,624,000 |
| Katsumasa Miyamoto | 70 | 67 | 68 | 71 | 276 | 1,624,000 |
| Tomohiro Kondo | 72 | 70 | 66 | 68 | 276 | 1,624,000 |
| Satoru Hirota | 70 | 71 | 70 | 65 | 276 | 1,624,000 |
| Masaya Tomita | 67 | 70 | 70 | 69 | 276 | 1,624,000 |
| Casey Wittenberg | 69 | 71 | 67 | 69 | 276 | 1,624,000 |

| | SCORES | | | | TOTAL | MONEY |
|---|---|---|---|---|---|---|
| Shingo Katayama | 67 | 71 | 72 | 67 | 277 | 1,080,000 |
| Yusaku Miyazato | 63 | 71 | 72 | 71 | 277 | 1,080,000 |
| S.K. Ho | 71 | 70 | 65 | 71 | 277 | 1,080,000 |
| Jun Kikuchi | 73 | 69 | 65 | 71 | 278 | 912,000 |
| Dinesh Chand | 69 | 73 | 69 | 67 | 278 | 912,000 |
| Hidemasa Hoshino | 71 | 70 | 66 | 71 | 278 | 912,000 |
| Takuya Taniguchi | 66 | 72 | 71 | 69 | 278 | 912,000 |

## Japan PGA Championship

*Tamana Country Club*, Kumamoto
Par 36-36–72; 7,018 yards

May 12-15
purse, ¥110,000,000

| | SCORES | | | | TOTAL | MONEY |
|---|---|---|---|---|---|---|
| S.K. Ho | 68 | 68 | 67 | 69 | 272 | ¥22,000,000 |
| Hideto Tanihara | 68 | 67 | 70 | 69 | 274 | 11,000,000 |
| Yasuharu Imano | 72 | 70 | 68 | 65 | 275 | 7,480,000 |
| Tetsuji Hiratsuka | 67 | 71 | 70 | 68 | 276 | 5,280,000 |
| Hiroyuki Fujita | 65 | 71 | 69 | 72 | 277 | 4,400,000 |
| Keiichiro Fukabori | 74 | 72 | 68 | 64 | 278 | 3,960,000 |
| Ryoken Kawagishi | 73 | 68 | 65 | 73 | 279 | 3,630,000 |
| Tomohiro Kondo | 72 | 68 | 68 | 72 | 280 | 2,888,600 |
| Shingo Katayama | 70 | 72 | 71 | 67 | 280 | 2,888,600 |
| Toru Taniguchi | 67 | 71 | 72 | 70 | 280 | 2,888,600 |
| Masashi Ozaki | 69 | 70 | 70 | 71 | 280 | 2,888,600 |
| David Smail | 67 | 71 | 70 | 72 | 280 | 2,888,600 |
| Naomichi Ozaki | 70 | 71 | 73 | 67 | 281 | 2,222,000 |
| Kazuhiko Hosokawa | 72 | 70 | 68 | 72 | 282 | 2,002,000 |
| Tsukasa Watanabe | 76 | 70 | 69 | 68 | 283 | 1,676,400 |
| Paul Sheehan | 70 | 73 | 70 | 70 | 283 | 1,676,400 |
| Daisuke Maruyama | 73 | 71 | 69 | 70 | 283 | 1,676,400 |
| Yusaku Miyazato | 68 | 72 | 71 | 72 | 283 | 1,676,400 |
| Yumihiko Hatone | 69 | 74 | 67 | 73 | 283 | 1,676,400 |
| Takao Shimada | 73 | 73 | 69 | 69 | 284 | 1,342,000 |
| Hideki Kase | 71 | 71 | 71 | 71 | 284 | 1,342,000 |
| Yutaka Horinouchi | 72 | 69 | 73 | 71 | 285 | 1,122,000 |
| Hidemasa Hoshino | 69 | 73 | 72 | 71 | 285 | 1,122,000 |
| Prayad Marksaeng | 72 | 73 | 66 | 74 | 285 | 1,122,000 |
| Steven Conran | 74 | 69 | 72 | 71 | 286 | 924,000 |
| Shinichi Yokota | 73 | 71 | 69 | 73 | 286 | 924,000 |
| Kaname Yokoo | 71 | 72 | 69 | 74 | 286 | 924,000 |
| Toshinori Muto | 67 | 78 | 67 | 74 | 286 | 924,000 |
| Norio Shinozaki | 73 | 73 | 67 | 74 | 287 | 770,000 |
| Komei Oda | 72 | 74 | 72 | 69 | 287 | 770,000 |
| Chawalit Plaphol | 73 | 70 | 70 | 74 | 287 | 770,000 |

## Munsingwear Open KSB Cup

*Tojigaoka Marine Hills Golf Club*, Okayama
Par 36-36–72; 7,017 yards

May 19-22
purse, ¥100,000,000

| | SCORES | | | | TOTAL | MONEY |
|---|---|---|---|---|---|---|
| Hiroyuki Fujita | 63 | 66 | 72 | 69 | 270 | ¥20,000,000 |
| Tadahiro Takayama | 73 | 66 | 64 | 70 | 273 | 8,400,000 |

| | SCORES | | | | TOTAL | MONEY |
|---|---|---|---|---|---|---|
| Steven Conran | 68 | 66 | 69 | 70 | 273 | 8,400,000 |
| Hideto Tanihara | 69 | 67 | 70 | 70 | 276 | 4,800,000 |
| Toru Taniguchi | 70 | 70 | 69 | 68 | 277 | 3,633,333 |
| Yasuharu Imano | 71 | 67 | 68 | 71 | 277 | 3,633,333 |
| Craig Jones | 66 | 74 | 66 | 71 | 277 | 3,633,333 |
| Christian Pena | 70 | 68 | 72 | 68 | 278 | 2,830,000 |
| Shinichi Yokota | 69 | 67 | 71 | 71 | 278 | 2,830,000 |
| Keiichiro Fukabori | 68 | 73 | 66 | 71 | 278 | 2,830,000 |
| Hidemasa Hoshino | 73 | 69 | 67 | 70 | 279 | 2,220,000 |
| Nobuhiro Masuda | 74 | 68 | 70 | 67 | 279 | 2,220,000 |
| Masaya Tomita | 69 | 69 | 68 | 73 | 279 | 2,220,000 |
| Naomichi Ozaki | 72 | 66 | 69 | 73 | 280 | 1,620,000 |
| Hideki Kase | 69 | 70 | 75 | 66 | 280 | 1,620,000 |
| Ryuichi Oda | 69 | 71 | 72 | 68 | 280 | 1,620,000 |
| Tomohiro Kondo | 71 | 66 | 73 | 70 | 280 | 1,620,000 |
| Daisuke Maruyama | 71 | 66 | 72 | 71 | 280 | 1,620,000 |
| Yumihiko Hatone | 69 | 72 | 73 | 67 | 281 | 1,140,000 |
| Yusaku Miyazato | 72 | 70 | 69 | 70 | 281 | 1,140,000 |
| Shingo Katayama | 71 | 70 | 69 | 71 | 281 | 1,140,000 |
| Jun Kikuchi | 67 | 70 | 72 | 72 | 281 | 1,140,000 |
| Mitsuhiro Tateyama | 70 | 71 | 67 | 73 | 281 | 1,140,000 |
| Taichi Teshima | 68 | 70 | 70 | 73 | 281 | 1,140,000 |
| Osamu Yamaguchi | 72 | 69 | 72 | 69 | 282 | 820,000 |
| Prayad Marksaeng | 68 | 71 | 73 | 70 | 282 | 820,000 |
| Masaki Sakurai | 76 | 63 | 72 | 71 | 282 | 820,000 |
| Hisayuki Sasaki | 69 | 72 | 69 | 72 | 282 | 820,000 |
| Toshimitsu Izawa | 71 | 67 | 66 | 78 | 282 | 820,000 |
| Satoru Hirota | 71 | 68 | 75 | 69 | 283 | 634,000 |
| Yutaka Horinouchi | 72 | 70 | 72 | 69 | 283 | 634,000 |
| Yoshinobu Tsukada | 70 | 67 | 74 | 72 | 283 | 634,000 |
| Kaname Yokoo | 69 | 70 | 72 | 72 | 283 | 634,000 |
| Gregory Meyer | 69 | 69 | 70 | 75 | 283 | 634,000 |

## Mitsubishi Diamond Cup

*Higashi Hirono Golf Club,* Ibaragi
Par 35-35–70; 7,002 yards

May 26-29
purse, ¥110,000,000

| | SCORES | | | | TOTAL | MONEY |
|---|---|---|---|---|---|---|
| Chang Ik-je | 74 | 69 | 64 | 68 | 275 | ¥22,000,000 |
| Ryoken Kawagishi | 70 | 70 | 71 | 67 | 278 | 9,240,000 |
| Shingo Katayama | 70 | 71 | 72 | 65 | 278 | 9,240,000 |
| Daisuke Maruyama | 71 | 69 | 72 | 67 | 279 | 5,280,000 |
| S.K. Ho | 73 | 71 | 68 | 68 | 280 | 4,180,000 |
| Tatsuhiko Takahashi | 72 | 69 | 71 | 68 | 280 | 4,180,000 |
| Paul Sheehan | 68 | 70 | 73 | 70 | 281 | 3,242,250 |
| Keiichiro Fukabori | 69 | 73 | 71 | 68 | 281 | 3,242,250 |
| Ryuichi Oda | 72 | 69 | 71 | 69 | 281 | 3,242,250 |
| Toshimitsu Izawa | 70 | 73 | 67 | 71 | 281 | 3,242,250 |
| Yasuharu Imano | 74 | 72 | 67 | 69 | 282 | 2,442,000 |
| Shinichi Akiba | 71 | 73 | 69 | 69 | 282 | 2,442,000 |
| Chawalit Plaphol | 70 | 71 | 72 | 69 | 282 | 2,442,000 |
| Nobuhiro Masuda | 75 | 68 | 70 | 70 | 283 | 1,892,000 |
| Shinichi Yokota | 74 | 72 | 69 | 68 | 283 | 1,892,000 |
| Ippei Sadanobu | 72 | 72 | 73 | 66 | 283 | 1,892,000 |
| Kim Jong-duck | 73 | 70 | 70 | 71 | 284 | 1,569,333 |
| Mitsuhiro Tateyama | 72 | 74 | 70 | 68 | 284 | 1,569,333 |

| | SCORES | | | | TOTAL | MONEY |
|---|---|---|---|---|---|---|
| Yudai Maeda | 74 | 70 | 70 | 70 | 284 | 1,569,333 |
| Tomohiro Kondo | 77 | 68 | 69 | 71 | 285 | 1,210,000 |
| Craig Jones | 72 | 74 | 70 | 69 | 285 | 1,210,000 |
| Nozomi Kawahara | 73 | 72 | 69 | 71 | 285 | 1,210,000 |
| Masaya Tomita | 69 | 73 | 70 | 73 | 285 | 1,210,000 |
| Jyoti Randhawa | 72 | 70 | 70 | 73 | 285 | 1,210,000 |
| Tadahiro Takayama | 75 | 73 | 68 | 70 | 286 | 946,000 |
| Kiyoshi Maita | 76 | 71 | 72 | 67 | 286 | 946,000 |
| Yoshiaki Kimura | 77 | 71 | 69 | 69 | 286 | 946,000 |
| Hiroyuki Fujita | 73 | 72 | 74 | 68 | 287 | 772,200 |
| Yumihiko Hatone | 72 | 74 | 67 | 74 | 287 | 772,200 |
| David Smail | 73 | 71 | 76 | 67 | 287 | 772,200 |
| Prayad Marksaeng | 72 | 72 | 72 | 71 | 287 | 772,200 |
| Yoshinobu Tsukada | 72 | 76 | 68 | 71 | 287 | 772,200 |

## JCB Classic Sendai

*Omotezao Kokusai Golf Club,* Shibata, Miyagi
Par 36-35–71; 6,625 yards

June 2-5
purse, ¥100,000,000

| | SCORES | | | | TOTAL | MONEY |
|---|---|---|---|---|---|---|
| S.K. Ho | 63 | 67 | 66 | 69 | 265 | ¥20,000,000 |
| Shinichi Yokota | 70 | 65 | 65 | 66 | 266 | 10,000,000 |
| Toshimitsu Izawa | 66 | 68 | 64 | 70 | 268 | 6,800,000 |
| Keiichiro Fukabori | 68 | 68 | 67 | 66 | 269 | 3,750,000 |
| Chris Campbell | 66 | 67 | 67 | 69 | 269 | 3,750,000 |
| Shingo Katayama | 67 | 69 | 67 | 66 | 269 | 3,750,000 |
| Takuya Taniguchi | 67 | 68 | 68 | 66 | 269 | 3,750,000 |
| Ryuichi Oda | 63 | 69 | 70 | 67 | 269 | 3,750,000 |
| Tetsuji Hiratsuka | 69 | 68 | 67 | 66 | 270 | 2,520,000 |
| Daisuke Maruyama | 68 | 67 | 69 | 66 | 270 | 2,520,000 |
| Tomohiro Kondo | 66 | 66 | 70 | 68 | 270 | 2,520,000 |
| Masaya Tomita | 68 | 66 | 67 | 69 | 270 | 2,520,000 |
| Seiki Okuda | 68 | 67 | 69 | 67 | 271 | 1,686,666 |
| Kazuhiko Hosokawa | 66 | 69 | 68 | 68 | 271 | 1,686,666 |
| Prayad Marksaeng | 70 | 68 | 69 | 64 | 271 | 1,686,666 |
| Katsumune Imai | 68 | 64 | 69 | 70 | 271 | 1,686,666 |
| Kiyoshi Miyazato | 68 | 68 | 68 | 67 | 271 | 1,686,666 |
| Yutaka Horinouchi | 67 | 68 | 67 | 69 | 271 | 1,686,666 |
| Kaname Yokoo | 68 | 66 | 70 | 68 | 272 | 1,340,000 |
| Kazuhiro Takami | 64 | 72 | 69 | 69 | 274 | 1,100,000 |
| Lin Keng-chi | 67 | 67 | 69 | 71 | 274 | 1,100,000 |
| Katsuya Nakagawa | 66 | 69 | 69 | 70 | 274 | 1,100,000 |
| Tadahiro Takayama | 65 | 71 | 71 | 67 | 274 | 1,100,000 |
| Yudai Maeda | 66 | 71 | 69 | 68 | 274 | 1,100,000 |
| Toru Suzuki | 68 | 69 | 68 | 70 | 275 | 880,000 |
| Nozomi Kawahara | 72 | 68 | 65 | 70 | 275 | 880,000 |
| Hiroyuki Fujita | 69 | 68 | 70 | 69 | 276 | 760,000 |
| Taichi Teshima | 67 | 73 | 68 | 68 | 276 | 760,000 |
| Gregory Meyer | 72 | 67 | 69 | 68 | 276 | 760,000 |
| Satoru Hirota | 71 | 70 | 66 | 69 | 276 | 760,000 |

## Mandom Lucido Yomiuri Open

*Yomiuri Country Club,* Nishinomiya, Hyogo  
Par 36-36–72; 7,161 yards

June 16-19  
purse, ¥100,000,000

| | SCORES | | | | TOTAL | MONEY |
|---|---|---|---|---|---|---|
| Satoru Hirota | 66 | 68 | 69 | 67 | 270 | ¥20,000,000 |
| Tetsuji Hiratsuka | 64 | 70 | 66 | 71 | 271 | 8,400,000 |
| Shinichi Akiba | 67 | 68 | 65 | 71 | 271 | 8,400,000 |
| Ryoken Kawagishi | 65 | 63 | 72 | 72 | 272 | 4,400,000 |
| Tadahiro Takayama | 67 | 68 | 67 | 70 | 272 | 4,400,000 |
| Hidemasa Hoshino | 68 | 66 | 70 | 70 | 274 | 3,600,000 |
| Kiyoshi Maita | 69 | 67 | 68 | 71 | 275 | 3,056,666 |
| Lin Keng-chi | 68 | 67 | 71 | 69 | 275 | 3,056,666 |
| Ryuichi Oda | 70 | 68 | 69 | 68 | 275 | 3,056,666 |
| Hiroyuki Fujita | 68 | 70 | 65 | 73 | 276 | 2,220,000 |
| Shinichi Yokota | 68 | 68 | 69 | 71 | 276 | 2,220,000 |
| Katsuya Nakagawa | 69 | 69 | 71 | 67 | 276 | 2,220,000 |
| Kaname Yokoo | 69 | 67 | 68 | 72 | 276 | 2,220,000 |
| S.K. Ho | 70 | 65 | 68 | 73 | 276 | 2,220,000 |
| Toru Suzuki | 71 | 66 | 71 | 69 | 277 | 1,570,000 |
| Nozomi Kawahara | 65 | 68 | 72 | 72 | 277 | 1,570,000 |
| Liang Wen-chong | 71 | 68 | 70 | 68 | 277 | 1,570,000 |
| Chang Ik-je | 70 | 69 | 68 | 70 | 277 | 1,570,000 |
| Shigeru Nonaka | 66 | 66 | 74 | 72 | 278 | 1,260,000 |
| Yasuharu Imano | 74 | 67 | 69 | 68 | 278 | 1,260,000 |
| Prayad Marksaeng | 69 | 71 | 73 | 65 | 278 | 1,260,000 |
| Hideki Kase | 72 | 70 | 68 | 69 | 279 | 852,000 |
| Kazuhiko Hosokawa | 67 | 70 | 70 | 72 | 279 | 852,000 |
| Chris Campbell | 69 | 68 | 71 | 71 | 279 | 852,000 |
| Katsumasa Miyamoto | 68 | 72 | 70 | 69 | 279 | 852,000 |
| Scott Laycock | 70 | 71 | 68 | 70 | 279 | 852,000 |
| Katsumune Imai | 68 | 69 | 74 | 68 | 279 | 852,000 |
| Nobuhiro Masuda | 71 | 69 | 71 | 68 | 279 | 852,000 |
| Sushi Ishigaki | 67 | 71 | 71 | 70 | 279 | 852,000 |
| Yutaka Horinouchi | 72 | 66 | 73 | 68 | 279 | 852,000 |
| Koichi Kashimura | 66 | 73 | 70 | 70 | 279 | 852,000 |

## Mizuno Open

*Setonaikai Golf Club,* Kasaoka, Okayama  
Par 36-36–72; 7,293 yards

June 23-26  
purse, ¥100,000,000

| | SCORES | | | | TOTAL | MONEY |
|---|---|---|---|---|---|---|
| Chris Campbell | 68 | 68 | 71 | 71 | 278 | ¥20,000,000 |
| David Smail | 71 | 70 | 67 | 70 | 278 | 8,400,000 |
| Tadahiro Takayama | 67 | 74 | 64 | 73 | 278 | 8,400,000 |
| (Campbell defeated Smail and Takayama on second playoff hole.) | | | | | | |
| Thammanoon Srirot | 72 | 70 | 71 | 66 | 279 | 4,400,000 |
| Hidemasa Hoshino | 68 | 73 | 69 | 69 | 279 | 4,400,000 |
| Nozomi Kawahara | 72 | 68 | 70 | 70 | 280 | 3,316,666 |
| Daisuke Maruyama | 71 | 68 | 70 | 71 | 280 | 3,316,666 |
| Y.E. Yang | 68 | 70 | 71 | 71 | 280 | 3,316,666 |
| Steven Conran | 70 | 74 | 68 | 69 | 281 | 2,320,000 |
| Prayad Marksaeng | 73 | 70 | 69 | 69 | 281 | 2,320,000 |
| Toshinori Muto | 66 | 76 | 70 | 69 | 281 | 2,320,000 |
| Takashi Kanemoto | 74 | 71 | 66 | 70 | 281 | 2,320,000 |

| | SCORES | | | | TOTAL | MONEY |
|---|---|---|---|---|---|---|
| Craig Jones | 68 | 69 | 74 | 70 | 281 | 2,320,000 |
| Shinichi Akiba | 70 | 69 | 70 | 72 | 281 | 2,320,000 |
| Hiroyuki Fujita | 67 | 71 | 70 | 74 | 282 | 1,670,000 |
| Shintaro Iizuka | 66 | 70 | 71 | 75 | 282 | 1,670,000 |
| Chang Ik-je | 76 | 69 | 70 | 68 | 283 | 1,262,857 |
| Naomichi Ozaki | 69 | 73 | 73 | 68 | 283 | 1,262,857 |
| Keiichiro Fukabori | 73 | 72 | 70 | 68 | 283 | 1,262,857 |
| Katsunori Kuwabara | 73 | 72 | 68 | 70 | 283 | 1,262,857 |
| Taichi Teshima | 73 | 67 | 73 | 70 | 283 | 1,262,857 |
| Tetsuji Hiratsuka | 71 | 69 | 72 | 71 | 283 | 1,262,857 |
| Tsukasa Watanabe | 69 | 67 | 72 | 75 | 283 | 1,262,857 |
| Azuma Yano | 76 | 69 | 69 | 70 | 284 | 900,000 |
| Gregory Meyer | 71 | 71 | 74 | 68 | 284 | 900,000 |
| Unho Park | 71 | 69 | 70 | 74 | 284 | 900,000 |
| Paul Sheehan | 68 | 72 | 75 | 70 | 285 | 760,000 |
| Toru Suzuki | 71 | 67 | 76 | 71 | 285 | 760,000 |
| David Ishii | 72 | 72 | 73 | 68 | 285 | 760,000 |
| Dinesh Chand | 73 | 69 | 76 | 67 | 285 | 760,000 |

## Japan Golf Tour Championship

*Shishido Hills Country Club,* Tomobe, Ibaragi
Par 35-35–70; 7,147 yards

June 30-July 3
purse, ¥120,000,000

| | SCORES | | | | TOTAL | MONEY |
|---|---|---|---|---|---|---|
| Kazuhiko Hosokawa | 70 | 67 | 67 | 69 | 273 | ¥24,000,000 |
| Yasuharu Imano | 68 | 68 | 69 | 68 | 273 | 10,080,000 |
| David Smail | 66 | 66 | 70 | 71 | 273 | 10,080,000 |
| (Hosokawa defeated Imano and Smail on second playoff hole.) | | | | | | |
| Hidemasa Hoshino | 72 | 69 | 67 | 67 | 275 | 5,760,000 |
| Katsumasa Miyamoto | 70 | 64 | 77 | 65 | 276 | 4,800,000 |
| Jun Kikuchi | 68 | 70 | 67 | 72 | 277 | 4,320,000 |
| Scott Laycock | 71 | 69 | 71 | 68 | 279 | 3,960,000 |
| Liang Wen-chong | 69 | 69 | 67 | 76 | 281 | 3,522,000 |
| Kiyoshi Miyazato | 71 | 69 | 68 | 73 | 281 | 3,522,000 |
| Taichi Teshima | 71 | 68 | 70 | 73 | 282 | 2,784,000 |
| Chawalit Plaphol | 71 | 70 | 70 | 71 | 282 | 2,784,000 |
| Paul Sheehan | 68 | 71 | 70 | 73 | 282 | 2,784,000 |
| Chang Ik-je | 68 | 72 | 72 | 70 | 282 | 2,784,000 |
| Tomohiro Kondo | 71 | 71 | 72 | 69 | 283 | 2,064,000 |
| S.K. Ho | 68 | 73 | 74 | 68 | 283 | 2,064,000 |
| Yoshikazu Haku | 73 | 69 | 70 | 71 | 283 | 2,064,000 |
| Toru Taniguchi | 72 | 68 | 69 | 75 | 284 | 1,662,000 |
| Mamoru Osanai | 71 | 70 | 71 | 72 | 284 | 1,662,000 |
| Prayad Marksaeng | 71 | 72 | 70 | 71 | 284 | 1,662,000 |
| Kaname Yokoo | 73 | 68 | 67 | 76 | 284 | 1,662,000 |
| Hiroyuki Fujita | 73 | 70 | 71 | 71 | 285 | 1,233,600 |
| Makoto Inoue | 74 | 69 | 72 | 70 | 285 | 1,233,600 |
| Yusaku Miyazato | 72 | 72 | 72 | 69 | 285 | 1,233,600 |
| Nozomi Kawahara | 68 | 74 | 72 | 71 | 285 | 1,233,600 |
| Nobuhiro Masuda | 70 | 73 | 69 | 73 | 285 | 1,233,600 |
| Hiroshi Goda | 71 | 69 | 72 | 74 | 286 | 960,000 |
| Daisuke Maruyama | 70 | 68 | 76 | 72 | 286 | 960,000 |
| Shingo Katayama | 70 | 71 | 69 | 76 | 286 | 960,000 |
| Christian Pena | 71 | 70 | 70 | 75 | 286 | 960,000 |
| Chris Campbell | 71 | 72 | 71 | 73 | 287 | 840,000 |

# Woodone Open Hiroshima

*Hiroshima Country Club,* Higashi, Hiroshima
Par 35-36–71; 6,932 yards

July 7-10
purse, ¥100,000,000

| | SCORES | | | | TOTAL | MONEY |
|---|---|---|---|---|---|---|
| Takao Nogami | 68 | 67 | 67 | 68 | 270 | ¥20,000,000 |
| Dinesh Chand | 69 | 71 | 68 | 63 | 271 | 10,000,000 |
| Nobuhito Sato | 69 | 68 | 67 | 70 | 274 | 6,800,000 |
| Katsumasa Miyamoto | 66 | 69 | 72 | 68 | 275 | 4,800,000 |
| Kazuhiko Hosokawa | 69 | 71 | 67 | 69 | 276 | 3,800,000 |
| Takashi Kanemoto | 69 | 70 | 71 | 66 | 276 | 3,800,000 |
| Yusaku Miyazato | 70 | 70 | 69 | 68 | 277 | 3,056,666 |
| Shingo Katayama | 69 | 68 | 70 | 70 | 277 | 3,056,666 |
| Katsuya Nakagawa | 70 | 70 | 65 | 72 | 277 | 3,056,666 |
| Katsumune Imai | 68 | 69 | 69 | 72 | 278 | 2,620,000 |
| Yeh Wei-tze | 75 | 67 | 68 | 69 | 279 | 2,420,000 |
| Tatsuhiko Takahashi | 69 | 70 | 70 | 71 | 280 | 2,120,000 |
| Tateo Ozaki | 69 | 69 | 69 | 73 | 280 | 2,120,000 |
| Tetsuji Hiratsuka | 71 | 67 | 69 | 74 | 281 | 1,770,000 |
| Hidemasa Hoshino | 70 | 68 | 68 | 75 | 281 | 1,770,000 |
| Taichi Teshima | 67 | 70 | 76 | 69 | 282 | 1,520,000 |
| Tomohiro Kondo | 70 | 72 | 70 | 70 | 282 | 1,520,000 |
| Kiyoshi Maita | 69 | 70 | 72 | 71 | 282 | 1,520,000 |
| Ryoken Kawagishi | 68 | 73 | 72 | 70 | 283 | 1,300,000 |
| Azuma Yano | 67 | 72 | 73 | 71 | 283 | 1,300,000 |
| Daisuke Maruyama | 67 | 74 | 73 | 70 | 284 | 974,285 |
| Chang Ik-je | 70 | 70 | 74 | 70 | 284 | 974,285 |
| Yasuharu Imano | 68 | 70 | 75 | 71 | 284 | 974,285 |
| Takashi Yasukawa | 73 | 69 | 71 | 71 | 284 | 974,285 |
| Yoshinori Ono | 75 | 67 | 70 | 72 | 284 | 974,285 |
| Satoshi Higashi | 67 | 70 | 74 | 73 | 284 | 974,285 |
| Shinichi Akiba | 69 | 71 | 71 | 73 | 284 | 974,285 |
| Soshi Tajima | 72 | 69 | 75 | 69 | 285 | 760,000 |
| Shigeru Nonaka | 70 | 73 | 71 | 71 | 285 | 760,000 |
| Kazuhiko Takami | 70 | 73 | 71 | 72 | 286 | 621,666 |
| Yasuaki Takashima | 70 | 71 | 75 | 70 | 286 | 621,666 |
| Ryuichi Oda | 67 | 74 | 73 | 72 | 286 | 621,666 |
| Osamu Yamaguchi | 71 | 71 | 72 | 72 | 286 | 621,666 |
| Yutaka Horinouchi | 68 | 67 | 78 | 73 | 286 | 621,666 |
| Takenori Hiraishi | 67 | 71 | 72 | 76 | 286 | 621,666 |

# Sega Sammy Cup

*North Country Golf Club,* Hokkaido
Par 36-36–72; 7,078 yards

July 21-24
purse, ¥120,000,000

| | SCORES | | | | TOTAL | MONEY |
|---|---|---|---|---|---|---|
| Lin Keng-chi | 69 | 69 | 69 | 68 | 275 | ¥24,000,000 |
| Kiyoshi Maita | 75 | 68 | 67 | 66 | 276 | 12,000,000 |
| Yoichi Shimizu | 69 | 73 | 69 | 66 | 277 | 8,160,000 |
| Shingo Katayama | 69 | 70 | 68 | 71 | 278 | 5,760,000 |
| Tetsuji Hiratsuka | 72 | 69 | 71 | 67 | 279 | 4,360,000 |
| Dinesh Chand | 69 | 69 | 71 | 70 | 279 | 4,360,000 |
| Scott Laycock | 66 | 70 | 73 | 70 | 279 | 4,360,000 |
| Ryoken Kawagishi | 70 | 69 | 71 | 70 | 280 | 3,030,000 |
| Jeev Milkha Singh | 70 | 69 | 68 | 73 | 280 | 3,030,000 |

| | SCORES | | | | TOTAL | MONEY |
|---|---|---|---|---|---|---|
| Prayad Marksaeng | 71 | 68 | 71 | 70 | 280 | 3,030,000 |
| Hidemasa Hoshino | 71 | 71 | 67 | 71 | 280 | 3,030,000 |
| Yoshinobu Tsukada | 73 | 71 | 68 | 68 | 280 | 3,030,000 |
| Chang Ik-je | 72 | 72 | 65 | 71 | 280 | 3,030,000 |
| Nobuhito Sato | 72 | 68 | 70 | 71 | 281 | 2,184,000 |
| Mamoru Osanai | 68 | 71 | 71 | 72 | 282 | 1,884,000 |
| Yoshiaki Mano | 72 | 71 | 70 | 69 | 282 | 1,884,000 |
| Kiyoshi Miyazato | 73 | 67 | 72 | 70 | 282 | 1,884,000 |
| Ryuichi Oda | 76 | 67 | 67 | 72 | 282 | 1,884,000 |
| Katsunari Takahashi | 69 | 73 | 71 | 70 | 283 | 1,608,000 |
| Masahiro Kuramoto | 75 | 68 | 74 | 67 | 284 | 1,280,000 |
| Hisayuki Sasaki | 72 | 70 | 68 | 74 | 284 | 1,280,000 |
| Naoya Sugiyama | 74 | 71 | 70 | 69 | 284 | 1,280,000 |
| Kazuhiko Hosokawa | 72 | 69 | 69 | 74 | 284 | 1,280,000 |
| Satoshi Tomiyama | 70 | 72 | 69 | 73 | 284 | 1,280,000 |
| Nobuhiro Masuda | 72 | 69 | 72 | 71 | 284 | 1,280,000 |
| Tsukasa Watanabe | 70 | 70 | 73 | 72 | 285 | 849,333 |
| Takashi Kanemoto | 66 | 75 | 71 | 73 | 285 | 849,333 |
| Kenichi Kuboya | 75 | 67 | 72 | 71 | 285 | 849,333 |
| Yusaku Miyazato | 69 | 70 | 71 | 75 | 285 | 849,333 |
| Satoru Hirota | 72 | 72 | 72 | 69 | 285 | 849,333 |
| Yudai Maeda | 67 | 76 | 71 | 71 | 285 | 849,333 |
| Tatsuhiko Takahashi | 74 | 70 | 75 | 66 | 285 | 849,333 |
| Hiromichi Kubo | 72 | 72 | 68 | 73 | 285 | 849,333 |
| Toshinori Muto | 76 | 67 | 69 | 73 | 285 | 849,333 |

## Aiful Cup

*Daisen Ark Country Club*, Tottori
Par 36-35–71; 7,031 yards

July 28-31
purse, ¥120,000,000

| | SCORES | | | | TOTAL | MONEY |
|---|---|---|---|---|---|---|
| Tatsuhiko Takahashi | 69 | 64 | 66 | 69 | 268 | ¥24,000,000 |
| Yasuaki Takashima | 68 | 68 | 67 | 66 | 269 | 12,000,000 |
| Liang Wen-chong | 69 | 67 | 69 | 65 | 270 | 5,400,000 |
| Paul Sheehan | 68 | 68 | 68 | 66 | 270 | 5,400,000 |
| Kaname Yokoo | 67 | 68 | 68 | 67 | 270 | 5,400,000 |
| Ryoken Kawagishi | 71 | 66 | 65 | 68 | 270 | 5,400,000 |
| Masayuki Kawamura | 69 | 64 | 69 | 68 | 270 | 5,400,000 |
| Jun Kikuchi | 66 | 66 | 71 | 68 | 271 | 3,522,000 |
| Toshimitsu Izawa | 71 | 65 | 66 | 69 | 271 | 3,522,000 |
| Katsumasa Miyamoto | 70 | 69 | 64 | 69 | 272 | 3,024,000 |
| Soshi Tajima | 68 | 67 | 66 | 71 | 272 | 3,024,000 |
| David Smail | 70 | 70 | 69 | 64 | 273 | 2,184,000 |
| S.K. Ho | 71 | 69 | 66 | 67 | 273 | 2,184,000 |
| Satoru Hirota | 71 | 68 | 67 | 67 | 273 | 2,184,000 |
| Takuya Taniguchi | 69 | 69 | 68 | 67 | 273 | 2,184,000 |
| Yasuharu Imano | 66 | 72 | 67 | 68 | 273 | 2,184,000 |
| Nobuhito Sato | 68 | 67 | 69 | 69 | 273 | 2,184,000 |
| Jeev Milkha Singh | 74 | 65 | 69 | 66 | 274 | 1,560,000 |
| Chawalit Plaphol | 72 | 67 | 68 | 67 | 274 | 1,560,000 |
| Yusaku Miyazato | 67 | 70 | 68 | 69 | 274 | 1,560,000 |
| Katsunari Takahashi | 69 | 65 | 67 | 73 | 274 | 1,560,000 |
| Y.E. Yang | 74 | 63 | 71 | 67 | 275 | 1,100,571 |
| Shinichi Yokota | 69 | 69 | 70 | 67 | 275 | 1,100,571 |
| Mamoru Osanai | 68 | 68 | 72 | 67 | 275 | 1,100,571 |
| Takashi Kanemoto | 73 | 66 | 70 | 66 | 275 | 1,100,571 |

| | SCORES | | | | TOTAL | MONEY |
|---|---|---|---|---|---|---|
| Yuji Igarashi | 71 | 68 | 67 | 69 | 275 | 1,100,571 |
| Makoto Inoue | 71 | 65 | 68 | 71 | 275 | 1,100,571 |
| Keiichiro Fukabori | 68 | 64 | 70 | 73 | 275 | 1,100,571 |
| David Ishii | 67 | 69 | 71 | 69 | 276 | 799,200 |
| *Ryota Ito | 71 | 67 | 70 | 68 | 276 | |
| Toyokazu Fujishima | 73 | 65 | 70 | 68 | 276 | 799,200 |
| Nobuyuki Okuwa | 70 | 69 | 67 | 70 | 276 | 799,200 |
| Toru Taniguchi | 71 | 68 | 71 | 66 | 276 | 799,200 |
| Tadahisa Inoue | 65 | 70 | 69 | 72 | 276 | 799,200 |

## Sun Chlorella Classic

*Otaru Country Club,* Hokkaido
Par 36-36–72; 7,342 yards

August 4-7
purse, ¥150,000,000

| | SCORES | | | | TOTAL | MONEY |
|---|---|---|---|---|---|---|
| Keiichiro Fukabori | 67 | 70 | 70 | 66 | 273 | ¥30,000,000 |
| Hidemasa Hoshino | 64 | 69 | 73 | 68 | 274 | 15,000,000 |
| Paul Sheehan | 72 | 68 | 66 | 70 | 276 | 10,200,000 |
| Tomohiro Kondo | 71 | 69 | 68 | 70 | 278 | 5,625,000 |
| Satoru Hirota | 67 | 71 | 71 | 69 | 278 | 5,625,000 |
| Yeh Wei-tze | 72 | 70 | 66 | 70 | 278 | 5,625,000 |
| Kiyoshi Miyazato | 69 | 70 | 68 | 71 | 278 | 5,625,000 |
| Yutaka Horinouchi | 72 | 69 | 70 | 67 | 278 | 5,625,000 |
| Toshimitsu Izawa | 68 | 69 | 72 | 71 | 280 | 3,780,000 |
| Dinesh Chand | 75 | 67 | 70 | 68 | 280 | 3,780,000 |
| Shingo Katayama | 70 | 66 | 75 | 69 | 280 | 3,780,000 |
| Toshinori Muto | 72 | 67 | 70 | 71 | 280 | 3,780,000 |
| Tetsuji Hiratsuka | 70 | 70 | 67 | 74 | 281 | 2,692,500 |
| Yasuharu Imano | 72 | 67 | 70 | 72 | 281 | 2,692,500 |
| Mitsuhiro Tateyama | 71 | 70 | 72 | 68 | 281 | 2,692,500 |
| Liang Wen-chong | 69 | 69 | 71 | 72 | 281 | 2,692,500 |
| Kiyoshi Murota | 70 | 68 | 71 | 73 | 282 | 2,280,000 |
| Satoshi Higashi | 72 | 67 | 73 | 71 | 283 | 2,010,000 |
| Takashi Kanemoto | 71 | 70 | 71 | 71 | 283 | 2,010,000 |
| Yoshikazu Haku | 75 | 68 | 70 | 70 | 283 | 2,010,000 |
| Tateo Ozaki | 70 | 72 | 71 | 72 | 285 | 1,650,000 |
| Kaname Yokoo | 67 | 73 | 74 | 71 | 285 | 1,650,000 |
| Tadahiro Takayama | 73 | 70 | 70 | 72 | 285 | 1,650,000 |
| Lin Keng-chi | 73 | 69 | 71 | 73 | 286 | 1,290,000 |
| Mamoru Osanai | 69 | 73 | 76 | 68 | 286 | 1,290,000 |
| Daisuke Maruyama | 72 | 68 | 75 | 71 | 286 | 1,290,000 |
| Jeev Milkha Singh | 73 | 72 | 69 | 72 | 286 | 1,290,000 |
| Sushi Ishigaki | 72 | 73 | 68 | 73 | 286 | 1,290,000 |
| Yusaku Miyazato | 71 | 72 | 72 | 72 | 287 | 1,080,000 |
| Thammanoon Srirot | 70 | 75 | 70 | 72 | 287 | 1,080,000 |

# Under Armour KBC Augusta

*Keya Golf Club*, Shima, Fukuoka
Par 35-36–71; 7,154 yards

August 25-28
purse, ¥100,000,000

| | SCORES | | | TOTAL | MONEY |
|---|---|---|---|---|---|
| Toshimitsu Izawa | 67 | 65 | 67 | 65 | 264 | ¥20,000,000 |
| Ryuichi Oda | 66 | 68 | 69 | 66 | 269 | 8,400,000 |
| Prayad Marksaeng | 69 | 68 | 67 | 65 | 269 | 8,400,000 |
| Tadahiro Takayama | 65 | 73 | 67 | 66 | 271 | 4,800,000 |
| S.K. Ho | 69 | 68 | 68 | 67 | 272 | 4,000,000 |
| Keiichiro Fukabori | 69 | 68 | 70 | 66 | 273 | 3,450,000 |
| *Ryota Ito | 67 | 69 | 69 | 68 | 273 | |
| Katsumasa Miyamoto | 69 | 71 | 63 | 70 | 273 | 3,450,000 |
| Tomohiro Kondo | 68 | 67 | 69 | 70 | 274 | 2,830,000 |
| Kazuhiko Hosokawa | 64 | 71 | 68 | 71 | 274 | 2,830,000 |
| Gregory Meyer | 68 | 68 | 67 | 71 | 274 | 2,830,000 |
| Tatsuya Mitsuhashi | 68 | 72 | 70 | 65 | 275 | 2,120,000 |
| Soshi Tajima | 69 | 70 | 70 | 66 | 275 | 2,120,000 |
| Go Higaki | 66 | 71 | 70 | 68 | 275 | 2,120,000 |
| Chris Campbell | 69 | 70 | 66 | 70 | 275 | 2,120,000 |
| Norio Shinozaki | 68 | 69 | 73 | 66 | 276 | 1,480,000 |
| Nobuyuki Okuwa | 69 | 73 | 68 | 66 | 276 | 1,480,000 |
| Thammanoon Srirot | 65 | 72 | 72 | 67 | 276 | 1,480,000 |
| Unho Park | 66 | 69 | 73 | 68 | 276 | 1,480,000 |
| Satoru Hirota | 66 | 69 | 72 | 69 | 276 | 1,480,000 |
| Hidemasa Hoshino | 70 | 66 | 68 | 72 | 276 | 1,480,000 |
| Yeh Wei-tze | 71 | 71 | 68 | 67 | 277 | 974,285 |
| Mamoru Osanai | 69 | 70 | 71 | 67 | 277 | 974,285 |
| Nobuhiro Masuda | 68 | 70 | 71 | 68 | 277 | 974,285 |
| Shinichi Yokota | 67 | 70 | 71 | 69 | 277 | 974,285 |
| Jun Kikuchi | 70 | 68 | 70 | 69 | 277 | 974,285 |
| Kaname Yokoo | 70 | 70 | 68 | 69 | 277 | 974,285 |
| Hidezumi Shirakata | 70 | 67 | 69 | 71 | 277 | 974,285 |
| Tateo Ozaki | 69 | 71 | 71 | 67 | 278 | 670,000 |
| Steven Conran | 72 | 68 | 70 | 68 | 278 | 670,000 |
| Yutaka Horinouchi | 67 | 69 | 73 | 69 | 278 | 670,000 |
| Lin Keng-chi | 70 | 72 | 67 | 69 | 278 | 670,000 |
| Kiyoshi Maita | 68 | 71 | 69 | 70 | 278 | 670,000 |
| Yasuharu Imano | 68 | 70 | 69 | 71 | 278 | 670,000 |
| Takuya Taniguchi | 68 | 71 | 66 | 73 | 278 | 670,000 |

# Fujisankei Classic

*Fujizakura Country Club*, Yamanashi
Par 71; 7,454 yards

September 1-4
purse, ¥150,000,000

| | SCORES | | | TOTAL | MONEY |
|---|---|---|---|---|---|
| Daisuke Maruyama | 67 | 68 | 65 | 71 | 271 | ¥30,000,000 |
| Shingo Katayama | 72 | 66 | 70 | 70 | 278 | 15,000,000 |
| Kim Jong-duck | 72 | 71 | 70 | 66 | 279 | 8,700,000 |
| Azuma Yano | 68 | 72 | 71 | 68 | 279 | 8,700,000 |
| Makoto Inoue | 71 | 70 | 73 | 67 | 281 | 5,231,250 |
| Prayad Marksaeng | 70 | 65 | 75 | 71 | 281 | 5,231,250 |
| Yusaku Miyazato | 67 | 70 | 72 | 72 | 281 | 5,231,250 |
| Craig Jones | 69 | 69 | 70 | 73 | 281 | 5,231,250 |
| Kazuhiko Hosokawa | 72 | 70 | 69 | 71 | 282 | 4,080,000 |

| | SCORES | | | | TOTAL | MONEY |
|---|---|---|---|---|---|---|
| Takuya Taniguchi | 70 | 66 | 72 | 74 | 282 | 4,080,000 |
| S.K. Ho | 70 | 70 | 75 | 68 | 283 | 3,060,000 |
| Ryuichi Oda | 70 | 68 | 76 | 69 | 283 | 3,060,000 |
| Hisayuki Sasaki | 72 | 66 | 75 | 70 | 283 | 3,060,000 |
| Paul Sheehan | 70 | 67 | 73 | 73 | 283 | 3,060,000 |
| Chang Ik-je | 70 | 64 | 73 | 76 | 283 | 3,060,000 |
| Nobuhiro Masuda | 73 | 71 | 69 | 71 | 284 | 2,355,000 |
| Thammanoon Srirot | 72 | 70 | 69 | 73 | 284 | 2,355,000 |
| Takashi Kamiyama | 74 | 71 | 71 | 69 | 285 | 1,890,000 |
| Kaname Yokoo | 71 | 73 | 71 | 70 | 285 | 1,890,000 |
| Takashi Kanemoto | 71 | 74 | 70 | 70 | 285 | 1,890,000 |
| Lin Keng-chi | 68 | 72 | 71 | 74 | 285 | 1,890,000 |
| Soushi Tajima | 71 | 68 | 71 | 75 | 285 | 1,890,000 |
| Jeev Milkha Singh | 71 | 72 | 75 | 68 | 286 | 1,395,000 |
| Yoshiaki Mano | 69 | 70 | 75 | 72 | 286 | 1,395,000 |
| Osamu Yamaguchi | 71 | 71 | 72 | 72 | 286 | 1,395,000 |
| Yasuharu Imano | 69 | 73 | 71 | 73 | 286 | 1,395,000 |
| Katsumune Imai | 72 | 71 | 73 | 71 | 287 | 1,110,000 |
| Shinichi Yokota | 74 | 71 | 70 | 72 | 287 | 1,110,000 |
| Sushi Ishigaki | 74 | 70 | 70 | 73 | 287 | 1,110,000 |
| Y.E. Yang | 71 | 69 | 72 | 75 | 287 | 1,110,000 |
| Chawalit Plaphol | 73 | 65 | 71 | 78 | 287 | 1,110,000 |

## Suntory Open

*Sobu Country Club*, Inzai, Chiba
Par 35-35–70; 7,123 yards

September 8-11
purse, ¥100,000,000

| | SCORES | | | | TOTAL | MONEY |
|---|---|---|---|---|---|---|
| Yasuharu Imano | 65 | 64 | 70 | 68 | 267 | ¥20,000,000 |
| Mamoru Osanai | 69 | 68 | 62 | 70 | 269 | 10,000,000 |
| Shingo Katayama | 68 | 67 | 67 | 69 | 271 | 6,800,000 |
| Tateo Izawa | 68 | 71 | 66 | 67 | 272 | 4,400,000 |
| Steven Conran | 68 | 68 | 65 | 71 | 272 | 4,400,000 |
| Koki Idoki | 68 | 70 | 66 | 69 | 273 | 3,316,666 |
| S.K. Ho | 67 | 69 | 67 | 70 | 273 | 3,316,666 |
| Takashi Kanemoto | 70 | 68 | 66 | 69 | 273 | 3,316,666 |
| Yeh Wei-tze | 74 | 68 | 67 | 65 | 274 | 2,620,000 |
| Ryoken Kawagishi | 68 | 69 | 70 | 67 | 274 | 2,620,000 |
| Takuya Taniguchi | 69 | 68 | 67 | 70 | 274 | 2,620,000 |
| Yoshinobu Tsukada | 67 | 68 | 73 | 67 | 275 | 2,120,000 |
| Tatsuya Mitsuhashi | 70 | 67 | 67 | 71 | 275 | 2,120,000 |
| Shinichi Yokota | 68 | 68 | 72 | 68 | 276 | 1,670,000 |
| Hiroshi Goda | 65 | 71 | 71 | 69 | 276 | 1,670,000 |
| David Smail | 72 | 67 | 68 | 69 | 276 | 1,670,000 |
| Takenori Hiraishi | 70 | 68 | 68 | 70 | 276 | 1,670,000 |
| Chang Ik-je | 70 | 67 | 69 | 71 | 277 | 1,300,000 |
| Yutaka Horinouchi | 74 | 68 | 64 | 71 | 277 | 1,300,000 |
| Hiroaki Iijima | 69 | 70 | 67 | 71 | 277 | 1,300,000 |
| Hidemasa Hoshino | 67 | 68 | 70 | 72 | 277 | 1,300,000 |
| Satoshi Higashi | 72 | 69 | 69 | 68 | 278 | 964,000 |
| Y.E. Yang | 67 | 70 | 71 | 70 | 278 | 964,000 |
| Kiyoshi Maita | 70 | 70 | 68 | 70 | 278 | 964,000 |
| Yudai Maeda | 66 | 75 | 65 | 72 | 278 | 964,000 |
| Keiichiro Fukabori | 68 | 68 | 68 | 74 | 278 | 964,000 |
| Shigeru Nonaka | 66 | 72 | 72 | 69 | 279 | 740,000 |
| Nozomi Kawahara | 73 | 69 | 67 | 70 | 279 | 740,000 |

| | SCORES | | | | TOTAL | MONEY |
|---|---|---|---|---|---|---|
| Katsunori Kuwabara | 75 | 66 | 69 | 69 | 279 | 740,000 |
| Gregory Meyer | 70 | 69 | 68 | 72 | 279 | 740,000 |
| Azuma Yano | 71 | 71 | 71 | 66 | 279 | 740,000 |

## ANA Open

*Sapporo Golf Club, Wattsu Course,*
Kitahiroshima, Hokkaido
Par 36-36–72; 7,063 yards

September 15-18
purse, ¥100,000,000

| | SCORES | | | | TOTAL | MONEY |
|---|---|---|---|---|---|---|
| Keiichiro Fukabori | 72 | 62 | 72 | 68 | 274 | ¥20,000,000 |
| Yasuharu Imano | 70 | 66 | 70 | 68 | 274 | 10,000,000 |
| (Fukabori defeated Imano on first playoff hole.) | | | | | | |
| Steven Conran | 68 | 69 | 72 | 66 | 275 | 5,200,000 |
| Hidemasa Hoshino | 66 | 71 | 70 | 68 | 275 | 5,200,000 |
| Chawalit Plaphol | 71 | 67 | 68 | 69 | 275 | 5,200,000 |
| Tomohiro Kondo | 68 | 69 | 70 | 69 | 276 | 3,600,000 |
| Sushi Ishigaki | 72 | 64 | 79 | 62 | 277 | 3,056,666 |
| Soushi Tajima | 71 | 68 | 70 | 68 | 277 | 3,056,666 |
| Shinichi Yokota | 68 | 71 | 70 | 68 | 277 | 3,056,666 |
| Makoto Inoue | 73 | 68 | 69 | 68 | 278 | 2,520,000 |
| Y.E. Yang | 72 | 67 | 68 | 71 | 278 | 2,520,000 |
| Takashi Kanemoto | 69 | 69 | 73 | 68 | 279 | 2,020,000 |
| Yeh Wei-tze | 72 | 69 | 70 | 68 | 279 | 2,020,000 |
| Shingo Katayama | 69 | 66 | 75 | 69 | 279 | 2,020,000 |
| *Ryota Ito | 70 | 70 | 70 | 69 | 279 | |
| Gregory Meyer | 68 | 71 | 71 | 70 | 280 | 1,620,000 |
| Paul Sheehan | 70 | 70 | 69 | 71 | 280 | 1,620,000 |
| Katsuyoshi Tomori | 70 | 69 | 69 | 72 | 280 | 1,620,000 |
| Katsumune Imai | 72 | 68 | 75 | 66 | 281 | 1,220,000 |
| Jun Kikuchi | 69 | 69 | 73 | 70 | 281 | 1,220,000 |
| Tetsuji Hiratsuka | 68 | 69 | 74 | 70 | 281 | 1,220,000 |
| Daisuke Maruyama | 70 | 67 | 73 | 71 | 281 | 1,220,000 |
| Tsuneyuki Nakajima | 69 | 70 | 71 | 71 | 281 | 1,220,000 |
| Jeev Milkha Singh | 67 | 70 | 70 | 74 | 281 | 1,220,000 |
| Yoshinobu Tsukada | 67 | 70 | 76 | 69 | 282 | 860,000 |
| Hisayuki Sasaki | 72 | 68 | 73 | 69 | 282 | 860,000 |
| Tadahiro Takayama | 69 | 71 | 73 | 69 | 282 | 860,000 |
| Hirofumi Miyase | 67 | 72 | 73 | 70 | 282 | 860,000 |
| S.K. Ho | 75 | 65 | 69 | 73 | 282 | 860,000 |
| Chris Campbell | 70 | 70 | 71 | 72 | 283 | 720,000 |
| Kiyoshi Murota | 70 | 65 | 74 | 74 | 283 | 720,000 |

## Acom International

*Ishioka Golf Club,* Ogawa, Ibaragi
Par 36-35–71; 7,046 yards

September 22-25
purse, ¥120,000,000

| | SCORES | | | | TOTAL | MONEY |
|---|---|---|---|---|---|---|
| David Smail | 64 | 65 | 69 | 73 | 271 | ¥24,000,000 |
| Taichi Teshima | 71 | 66 | 68 | 68 | 273 | 12,000,000 |
| Shingo Katayama | 70 | 64 | 65 | 75 | 274 | 8,160,000 |
| Paul Sheehan | 70 | 67 | 65 | 73 | 275 | 5,760,000 |

| | SCORES | | | | TOTAL | MONEY |
|---|---|---|---|---|---|---|
| Tatsuhiko Takahashi | 67 | 69 | 70 | 70 | 276 | 4,185,000 |
| Shigeru Nonaka | 66 | 66 | 74 | 70 | 276 | 4,185,000 |
| Yoshikazu Haku | 65 | 70 | 68 | 73 | 276 | 4,185,000 |
| Scott Laycock | 68 | 63 | 69 | 76 | 276 | 4,185,000 |
| Gregory Meyer | 70 | 69 | 70 | 68 | 277 | 3,144,000 |
| S.K. Ho | 66 | 66 | 76 | 69 | 277 | 3,144,000 |
| Yasuharu Imano | 69 | 68 | 69 | 71 | 277 | 3,144,000 |
| Shinichi Yokota | 68 | 66 | 74 | 70 | 278 | 2,424,000 |
| Tomohiro Kondo | 73 | 67 | 68 | 70 | 278 | 2,424,000 |
| Takuya Taniguchi | 67 | 64 | 72 | 75 | 278 | 2,424,000 |
| Steven Conran | 71 | 67 | 71 | 70 | 279 | 1,776,000 |
| Toshimitsu Izawa | 69 | 68 | 71 | 71 | 279 | 1,776,000 |
| Toru Taniguchi | 68 | 69 | 71 | 71 | 279 | 1,776,000 |
| Prayad Marksaeng | 71 | 68 | 67 | 73 | 279 | 1,776,000 |
| Lin Keng-chi | 66 | 68 | 69 | 76 | 279 | 1,776,000 |
| *Yui Ueda | 68 | 66 | 68 | 77 | 279 | |
| Shinichi Akiba | 74 | 67 | 68 | 71 | 280 | 1,320,000 |
| Toru Suzuki | 71 | 69 | 70 | 70 | 280 | 1,320,000 |
| Hisayuki Sasaki | 71 | 64 | 69 | 76 | 280 | 1,320,000 |
| Eiji Mizoguchi | 70 | 69 | 70 | 72 | 281 | 984,000 |
| Takao Nogami | 71 | 70 | 68 | 72 | 281 | 984,000 |
| Hidemasa Hoshino | 70 | 70 | 68 | 73 | 281 | 984,000 |
| Kaname Yokoo | 71 | 64 | 72 | 74 | 281 | 984,000 |
| Ippei Sadanobu | 69 | 66 | 71 | 75 | 281 | 984,000 |
| Soushi Tajima | 72 | 68 | 72 | 69 | 281 | 984,000 |
| Mitsuhiro Tateyama | 69 | 66 | 70 | 76 | 281 | 984,000 |

## Coca-Cola Tokai Classic

*Miyoshi Country Club, West Course,* Aichi
Par 36-36–72; 7,180 yards

October 6-9
purse, ¥120,000,000

| | SCORES | | | | TOTAL | MONEY |
|---|---|---|---|---|---|---|
| Y.E. Yang | 66 | 72 | 65 | 67 | 270 | ¥24,000,000 |
| Taichi Teshima | 69 | 71 | 66 | 68 | 274 | 12,000,000 |
| Kiyoshi Maita | 69 | 69 | 69 | 69 | 276 | 6,960,000 |
| Takuya Taniguchi | 66 | 71 | 68 | 71 | 276 | 6,960,000 |
| Dinesh Chand | 69 | 69 | 70 | 69 | 277 | 4,560,000 |
| Shingo Katayama | 67 | 73 | 68 | 69 | 277 | 4,560,000 |
| Jun Kikuchi | 71 | 69 | 67 | 71 | 278 | 3,960,000 |
| Toru Taniguchi | 66 | 72 | 73 | 68 | 279 | 3,396,000 |
| Daisuke Maruyama | 68 | 71 | 67 | 73 | 279 | 3,396,000 |
| Katsumasa Miyamoto | 67 | 72 | 67 | 73 | 279 | 3,396,000 |
| Takashi Kamiyama | 69 | 70 | 73 | 68 | 280 | 2,784,000 |
| Yoshinobu Tsukada | 69 | 70 | 72 | 69 | 280 | 2,784,000 |
| *Kim Kyung-tae | 71 | 69 | 71 | 69 | 280 | |
| Gregory Meyer | 67 | 74 | 72 | 68 | 281 | 1,908,000 |
| Mitsuhiro Tateyama | 74 | 68 | 70 | 69 | 281 | 1,908,000 |
| Tadahiro Takayama | 71 | 70 | 70 | 70 | 281 | 1,908,000 |
| Nobuyuki Okuwa | 74 | 67 | 69 | 71 | 281 | 1,908,000 |
| Jeev Milkha Singh | 65 | 71 | 74 | 71 | 281 | 1,908,000 |
| Hiroyuki Fujita | 73 | 69 | 68 | 71 | 281 | 1,908,000 |
| Kazuhiko Hosokawa | 71 | 68 | 69 | 73 | 281 | 1,908,000 |
| Yusaku Miyazato | 68 | 74 | 66 | 73 | 281 | 1,908,000 |
| Norio Shinozaki | 67 | 70 | 74 | 71 | 282 | 1,368,000 |
| Shinichi Akiba | 69 | 74 | 68 | 71 | 282 | 1,368,000 |
| Hiroshi Iwata | 71 | 72 | 70 | 70 | 283 | 1,176,000 |

| | SCORES | | | TOTAL | MONEY |
|---|---|---|---|---|---|
| Hideki Kase | 73 | 70 | 71 | 69 | 283 | 1,176,000 |
| Katsumune Imai | 73 | 70 | 71 | 70 | 284 | 984,000 |
| Yoshikazu Haku | 69 | 72 | 72 | 71 | 284 | 984,000 |
| Tsuyoshi Yoneyama | 72 | 71 | 72 | 69 | 284 | 984,000 |
| Kenichi Kuboya | 72 | 67 | 72 | 73 | 284 | 984,000 |
| Masashi Ozaki | 70 | 71 | 68 | 75 | 284 | 984,000 |

## Japan Open

*Hirono Golf Club*, Hyogo
Par 36-36–72; 7,015 yards

October 13-16
purse, ¥120,000,000

| | SCORES | | | | TOTAL | MONEY |
|---|---|---|---|---|---|---|
| Shingo Katayama | 71 | 73 | 70 | 68 | 282 | ¥24,000,000 |
| Craig Parry | 73 | 72 | 67 | 72 | 284 | 11,250,000 |
| Ryoken Kawagishi | 72 | 66 | 72 | 74 | 284 | 11,250,000 |
| Keiichiro Fukabori | 71 | 71 | 74 | 69 | 285 | 5,080,000 |
| Takuya Taniguchi | 71 | 74 | 70 | 70 | 285 | 5,080,000 |
| Toshimitsu Izawa | 73 | 70 | 67 | 75 | 285 | 5,080,000 |
| Dinesh Chand | 67 | 76 | 70 | 73 | 286 | 3,288,000 |
| Tadahiro Takayama | 70 | 70 | 72 | 74 | 286 | 3,288,000 |
| Akinori Tani | 73 | 70 | 76 | 68 | 287 | 2,535,000 |
| Hiroyuki Fujita | 72 | 70 | 70 | 75 | 287 | 2,535,000 |
| Taichi Teshima | 74 | 71 | 73 | 70 | 288 | 1,800,000 |
| Y.E. Yang | 73 | 71 | 72 | 72 | 288 | 1,800,000 |
| Steven Conran | 70 | 70 | 75 | 73 | 288 | 1,800,000 |
| *Lee Won-joon | 70 | 72 | 73 | 73 | 288 | |
| Hisayuki Sasaki | 73 | 69 | 70 | 76 | 288 | 1,800,000 |
| Paul Sheehan | 71 | 71 | 75 | 72 | 289 | 1,404,000 |
| David Smail | 71 | 69 | 75 | 74 | 289 | 1,404,000 |
| Tatsuhiko Ichihara | 73 | 72 | 70 | 74 | 289 | 1,404,000 |
| Hidemasa Hoshino | 72 | 73 | 75 | 70 | 290 | 1,254,000 |
| Tomohiro Kondo | 71 | 74 | 71 | 74 | 290 | 1,254,000 |
| *Ryouma Imai | 75 | 69 | 70 | 76 | 290 | |
| Tadahisa Inoue | 72 | 73 | 73 | 73 | 291 | 1,136,666 |
| Takashi Kamiyama | 74 | 72 | 71 | 74 | 291 | 1,136,666 |
| *Kim Kyung-tae | 73 | 74 | 70 | 74 | 291 | |
| Lin Keng-chi | 68 | 75 | 73 | 75 | 291 | 1,136,666 |
| Chang Ik-je | 71 | 76 | 74 | 71 | 292 | 1,040,000 |
| Toru Suzuki | 72 | 73 | 75 | 72 | 292 | 1,040,000 |
| Kiyoshi Maita | 74 | 72 | 74 | 72 | 292 | 1,040,000 |
| Kaname Yokoo | 73 | 75 | 72 | 72 | 292 | 1,040,000 |
| Yoshiaki Kimura | 70 | 71 | 73 | 78 | 292 | 1,040,000 |

## Bridgestone Open

*Sodegaura Country Club*, Chiba
Par 36-36–72; 7,138 yards

October 20-23
purse, ¥110,000,000

| | SCORES | | | | TOTAL | MONEY |
|---|---|---|---|---|---|---|
| David Smail | 66 | 72 | 67 | 67 | 272 | ¥22,000,000 |
| Toru Suzuki | 70 | 70 | 68 | 66 | 274 | 11,000,000 |
| Katsuyoshi Tomori | 66 | 72 | 69 | 69 | 276 | 7,480,000 |
| Keiichiro Fukabori | 67 | 72 | 71 | 67 | 277 | 4,317,500 |

| | SCORES | | | | TOTAL | MONEY |
|---|---|---|---|---|---|---|
| Tetsuji Hiratsuka | 69 | 71 | 68 | 69 | 277 | 4,317,500 |
| Kaname Yokoo | 69 | 66 | 72 | 70 | 277 | 4,317,500 |
| Makoto Inoue | 70 | 65 | 71 | 71 | 277 | 4,317,500 |
| Hiroyuki Fujita | 71 | 68 | 72 | 67 | 278 | 3,113,000 |
| Lin Keng-chi | 69 | 72 | 71 | 66 | 278 | 3,113,000 |
| Yusaku Miyazato | 69 | 68 | 68 | 73 | 278 | 3,113,000 |
| Steven Conran | 68 | 73 | 69 | 69 | 279 | 2,552,000 |
| Tadahiro Takayama | 71 | 68 | 68 | 72 | 279 | 2,552,000 |
| Ryoken Kawagishi | 72 | 71 | 68 | 69 | 280 | 1,698,888 |
| Chang Ik-je | 71 | 72 | 68 | 69 | 280 | 1,698,888 |
| Ryuichi Oda | 71 | 69 | 71 | 69 | 280 | 1,698,888 |
| Scott Laycock | 69 | 73 | 69 | 69 | 280 | 1,698,888 |
| Kim Jong-duck | 65 | 72 | 72 | 71 | 280 | 1,698,888 |
| Tatsuya Mitsuhashi | 70 | 73 | 66 | 71 | 280 | 1,698,888 |
| Takuya Taniguchi | 72 | 70 | 67 | 71 | 280 | 1,698,888 |
| Y.E. Yang | 70 | 71 | 68 | 71 | 280 | 1,698,888 |
| Gregory Meyer | 69 | 66 | 71 | 74 | 280 | 1,698,888 |
| Toru Taniguchi | 70 | 72 | 70 | 69 | 281 | 1,166,000 |
| Azuma Yano | 69 | 74 | 66 | 72 | 281 | 1,166,000 |
| Dinesh Chand | 71 | 66 | 74 | 71 | 282 | 880,000 |
| Craig Jones | 67 | 72 | 72 | 71 | 282 | 880,000 |
| Prayad Marksaeng | 70 | 72 | 71 | 69 | 282 | 880,000 |
| Yasuharu Imano | 71 | 72 | 70 | 69 | 282 | 880,000 |
| Jeev Milkha Singh | 70 | 72 | 72 | 68 | 282 | 880,000 |
| Tomohiro Kondo | 73 | 70 | 66 | 73 | 282 | 880,000 |
| Masashi Ozaki | 67 | 70 | 71 | 74 | 282 | 880,000 |
| Soushi Tajima | 72 | 67 | 69 | 74 | 282 | 880,000 |

## ABC Championship

*ABC Golf Club*, Tojo, Hyogo
Par 36-36–72; 7,217 yards

October 27-30
purse, ¥120,000,000

| | SCORES | | | | TOTAL | MONEY |
|---|---|---|---|---|---|---|
| Shingo Katayama | 70 | 65 | 70 | 69 | 274 | ¥24,000,000 |
| Dinesh Chand | 68 | 72 | 68 | 68 | 276 | 12,000,000 |
| Daisuke Maruyama | 72 | 68 | 70 | 67 | 277 | 5,760,000 |
| Chang Ik-je | 69 | 72 | 69 | 67 | 277 | 5,760,000 |
| Jun Kikuchi | 70 | 70 | 70 | 67 | 277 | 5,760,000 |
| Lin Keng-chi | 66 | 69 | 71 | 71 | 277 | 5,760,000 |
| Nobuhiro Masuda | 69 | 72 | 71 | 66 | 278 | 3,960,000 |
| Prayad Marksaeng | 69 | 73 | 69 | 68 | 279 | 3,522,000 |
| Tsuneyuki Nakajima | 71 | 69 | 70 | 69 | 279 | 3,522,000 |
| Azuma Yano | 73 | 66 | 72 | 69 | 280 | 2,664,000 |
| S.K. Ho | 68 | 72 | 70 | 70 | 280 | 2,664,000 |
| Takuya Taniguchi | 78 | 65 | 67 | 70 | 280 | 2,664,000 |
| Yusaku Miyazato | 69 | 67 | 72 | 72 | 280 | 2,664,000 |
| Toru Taniguchi | 69 | 70 | 67 | 74 | 280 | 2,664,000 |
| Keiichiro Fukabori | 67 | 72 | 72 | 70 | 281 | 1,828,800 |
| Kenichi Kuboya | 68 | 72 | 70 | 71 | 281 | 1,828,800 |
| Ryuichi Oda | 67 | 73 | 70 | 71 | 281 | 1,828,800 |
| Tadahiro Takayama | 70 | 72 | 68 | 71 | 281 | 1,828,800 |
| Shinichi Akiba | 70 | 68 | 70 | 73 | 281 | 1,828,800 |
| Hisayuki Sasaki | 71 | 72 | 70 | 69 | 282 | 1,464,000 |
| Taichi Teshima | 73 | 70 | 69 | 70 | 282 | 1,464,000 |
| Hirofumi Miyase | 70 | 74 | 70 | 69 | 283 | 1,188,000 |
| Tsuyoshi Yoneyama | 69 | 70 | 72 | 72 | 283 | 1,188,000 |

| | SCORES | | | | TOTAL | MONEY |
|---|---|---|---|---|---|---|
| Scott Laycock | 73 | 73 | 71 | 66 | 283 | 1,188,000 |
| Katsunori Kuwabara | 66 | 72 | 72 | 73 | 283 | 1,188,000 |
| Jeev Milkha Singh | 72 | 68 | 73 | 71 | 284 | 936,000 |
| Katsumune Imai | 74 | 72 | 68 | 70 | 284 | 936,000 |
| Takao Nogami | 70 | 74 | 68 | 72 | 284 | 936,000 |
| Kim Jong-duck | 75 | 71 | 69 | 69 | 284 | 936,000 |
| Yoshiaki Mano | 74 | 69 | 68 | 73 | 284 | 936,000 |

## Asahiryokuken Yomiuri Asoiizuka Memorial

*Asoiizuka Golf Club*, Fukuoka
Par 36-36–72; 7,106 yards

November 3-6
purse, ¥100,000,000

| | SCORES | | | | TOTAL | MONEY |
|---|---|---|---|---|---|---|
| Azuma Yano | 69 | 67 | 67 | 67 | 270 | ¥20,000,000 |
| Taichi Teshima | 68 | 68 | 68 | 67 | 271 | 7,200,000 |
| Dinesh Chand | 69 | 67 | 67 | 68 | 271 | 7,200,000 |
| Nozomi Kawahara | 69 | 66 | 67 | 69 | 271 | 7,200,000 |
| Shingo Katayama | 65 | 69 | 68 | 70 | 272 | 4,000,000 |
| Tetsuji Hiratsuka | 70 | 70 | 67 | 67 | 274 | 3,600,000 |
| Yoshinobu Tsukada | 66 | 73 | 71 | 65 | 275 | 2,842,000 |
| *Naoya Takemoto | 70 | 68 | 69 | 68 | 275 | |
| Lin Keng-chi | 70 | 68 | 69 | 68 | 275 | 2,842,000 |
| Shinichi Yokota | 69 | 68 | 69 | 69 | 275 | 2,842,000 |
| Satoru Hirota | 69 | 66 | 67 | 73 | 275 | 2,842,000 |
| Gregory Meyer | 72 | 69 | 68 | 67 | 276 | 1,820,000 |
| Kiyoshi Miyazato | 69 | 68 | 69 | 70 | 276 | 1,820,000 |
| Katsumasa Miyamoto | 67 | 73 | 67 | 69 | 276 | 1,820,000 |
| Mamoru Osanai | 69 | 73 | 63 | 71 | 276 | 1,820,000 |
| Taichiro Kiyota | 69 | 70 | 66 | 71 | 276 | 1,820,000 |
| Liang Wen-chong | 66 | 71 | 66 | 73 | 276 | 1,820,000 |
| Katsunori Kuwabara | 70 | 73 | 69 | 65 | 277 | 1,380,000 |
| Hideki Kase | 68 | 68 | 71 | 70 | 277 | 1,380,000 |
| Masaya Tomida | 69 | 70 | 71 | 68 | 278 | 1,100,000 |
| Norio Shinozaki | 77 | 66 | 68 | 67 | 278 | 1,100,000 |
| Takuya Taniguchi | 69 | 70 | 70 | 69 | 278 | 1,100,000 |
| Tsuyoshi Yoneyama | 69 | 70 | 70 | 69 | 278 | 1,100,000 |
| Yeh Wei-tze | 72 | 71 | 70 | 65 | 278 | 1,100,000 |
| *Hiroshi Kohno | 71 | 72 | 67 | 69 | 279 | |
| Ippei Sadanobu | 68 | 71 | 71 | 69 | 279 | 780,000 |
| Nobuhito Sato | 69 | 69 | 71 | 70 | 279 | 780,000 |
| Yasuharu Imano | 70 | 69 | 70 | 70 | 279 | 780,000 |
| S.K. Ho | 68 | 68 | 72 | 71 | 279 | 780,000 |
| Yusaku Miyazato | 69 | 74 | 65 | 71 | 279 | 780,000 |
| Satoshi Higashi | 69 | 69 | 70 | 71 | 279 | 780,000 |

## Mitsui Sumitomo Visa Taiheiyo Masters

*Taiheiyo Club, Gotemba Course,* Shizuoka
Par 36-36–72; 7,246 yards

November 10-13
purse, ¥150,000,000

| | SCORES | | | | TOTAL | MONEY |
|---|---|---|---|---|---|---|
| Darren Clarke | 66 | 71 | 65 | 68 | 270 | ¥30,000,000 |
| Mitsuhiro Tateyama | 72 | 67 | 66 | 67 | 272 | 15,000,000 |

| | SCORES | | | | TOTAL | MONEY |
|---|---|---|---|---|---|---|
| Hideki Kase | 66 | 66 | 70 | 72 | 274 | 10,200,000 |
| Katsumune Imai | 68 | 67 | 73 | 68 | 276 | 6,600,000 |
| Dinesh Chand | 68 | 71 | 68 | 69 | 276 | 6,600,000 |
| Y.E. Yang | 72 | 71 | 68 | 66 | 277 | 5,400,000 |
| Toru Suzuki | 71 | 70 | 69 | 68 | 278 | 4,585,000 |
| Daisuke Maruyama | 69 | 68 | 72 | 69 | 278 | 4,585,000 |
| Toshimitsu Izawa | 68 | 73 | 68 | 69 | 278 | 4,585,000 |
| Tatsuhiko Takahashi | 70 | 69 | 70 | 70 | 279 | 3,630,000 |
| S.K. Ho | 68 | 70 | 70 | 71 | 279 | 3,630,000 |
| Hisayuki Sasaki | 71 | 68 | 69 | 71 | 279 | 3,630,000 |
| Nozomi Kawahara | 71 | 71 | 73 | 65 | 280 | 2,692,500 |
| Toru Taniguchi | 73 | 69 | 70 | 68 | 280 | 2,692,500 |
| Katsumasa Miyamoto | 73 | 64 | 71 | 72 | 280 | 2,692,500 |
| Ryuichi Oda | 69 | 70 | 69 | 72 | 280 | 2,692,500 |
| Kazuhiko Hosokawa | 68 | 72 | 74 | 68 | 282 | 1,894,285 |
| Azuma Yano | 70 | 72 | 73 | 67 | 282 | 1,894,285 |
| Kim Jong-duck | 69 | 75 | 70 | 68 | 282 | 1,894,285 |
| Kiyoshi Miyazato | 71 | 71 | 70 | 70 | 282 | 1,894,285 |
| Scott Laycock | 70 | 72 | 69 | 71 | 282 | 1,894,285 |
| Yusaku Miyazato | 72 | 68 | 69 | 73 | 282 | 1,894,285 |
| Steven Conran | 71 | 67 | 69 | 75 | 282 | 1,894,285 |
| Hideto Tanihara | 73 | 70 | 72 | 68 | 283 | 1,290,000 |
| Shinichi Yokota | 70 | 72 | 71 | 70 | 283 | 1,290,000 |
| Katsuyoshi Tomori | 75 | 67 | 70 | 71 | 283 | 1,290,000 |
| Kaname Yokoo | 72 | 71 | 69 | 71 | 283 | 1,290,000 |
| Bubba Watson | 75 | 70 | 71 | 67 | 283 | 1,290,000 |
| Chris Campbell | 70 | 73 | 71 | 70 | 284 | 1,050,000 |
| Katsunori Kuwabara | 72 | 72 | 69 | 71 | 284 | 1,050,000 |
| Kenichi Kuboya | 70 | 69 | 73 | 72 | 284 | 1,050,000 |

## Dunlop Phoenix

*Phoenix Country Club,* Miyazaki
Par 35-35–70; 6,907 yards

November 17-20
purse, ¥200,000,000

| | SCORES | | | | TOTAL | MONEY |
|---|---|---|---|---|---|---|
| Tiger Woods | 65 | 67 | 68 | 72 | 272 | ¥40,000,000 |
| Kaname Yokoo | 68 | 67 | 68 | 69 | 272 | 20,000,000 |
| (Woods defeated Yokoo on fourth playoff hole.) | | | | | | |
| Jim Furyk | 67 | 64 | 70 | 73 | 274 | 13,600,000 |
| Katsumasa Miyamoto | 71 | 69 | 69 | 66 | 275 | 9,600,000 |
| Gonzalo Fernandez-Castano | 72 | 66 | 72 | 66 | 276 | 8,000,000 |
| Liang Wen-chong | 72 | 65 | 68 | 72 | 277 | 7,200,000 |
| Hideto Tanihara | 69 | 72 | 68 | 69 | 278 | 6,350,000 |
| David Duval | 64 | 68 | 71 | 75 | 278 | 6,350,000 |
| S.K. Ho | 70 | 67 | 73 | 69 | 279 | 5,240,000 |
| Shinichi Yokota | 67 | 72 | 71 | 69 | 279 | 5,240,000 |
| Tetsuji Hiratsuka | 68 | 67 | 72 | 72 | 279 | 5,240,000 |
| Nozomi Kawahara | 72 | 70 | 66 | 72 | 280 | 4,440,000 |
| Paul Sheehan | 70 | 72 | 73 | 66 | 281 | 3,274,285 |
| Kiyoshi Maita | 72 | 71 | 71 | 67 | 281 | 3,274,285 |
| Katsunori Kuwabara | 72 | 69 | 70 | 70 | 281 | 3,274,285 |
| Toru Suzuki | 71 | 67 | 73 | 70 | 281 | 3,274,285 |
| Tomohiro Kondo | 67 | 70 | 73 | 71 | 281 | 3,274,285 |
| Soushi Tajima | 73 | 68 | 70 | 70 | 281 | 3,274,285 |
| Michael Campbell | 72 | 66 | 70 | 73 | 281 | 3,274,285 |
| Tsuyoshi Yoneyama | 72 | 66 | 75 | 69 | 282 | 2,360,000 |

| | SCORES | | | TOTAL | MONEY |
|---|---|---|---|---|---|
| Ryuchi Oda | 70 | 71 | 71 | 70 | 282 | 2,360,000 |
| Daisuke Maruyama | 72 | 71 | 67 | 72 | 282 | 2,360,000 |
| Shigeru Nonaka | 72 | 71 | 72 | 68 | 283 | 1,860,000 |
| Katsumune Imai | 73 | 70 | 71 | 69 | 283 | 1,860,000 |
| Toru Taniguchi | 72 | 67 | 74 | 70 | 283 | 1,860,000 |
| Azuma Yano | 70 | 71 | 71 | 71 | 283 | 1,860,000 |
| Kiyoshi Miyazato | 72 | 70 | 74 | 68 | 284 | 1,600,000 |
| Kenichi Kuboya | 71 | 71 | 68 | 74 | 284 | 1,600,000 |
| Dinesh Chand | 74 | 66 | 73 | 72 | 285 | 1,365,000 |
| Hidemasa Hoshino | 72 | 67 | 74 | 72 | 285 | 1,365,000 |
| Masashi Ozaki | 72 | 71 | 69 | 73 | 285 | 1,365,000 |
| Prayad Marksaeng | 69 | 69 | 72 | 75 | 285 | 1,365,000 |

## Casio World Open

*Kochi Kuroshio Country Club,* Kochi
Par 36-36–72; 7,220 yards

November 24-27
purse, ¥140,000,000

| | SCORES | | | | TOTAL | MONEY |
|---|---|---|---|---|---|---|
| Toru Taniguchi | 70 | 70 | 68 | 69 | 277 | ¥28,000,000 |
| Kim Jong-duck | 73 | 68 | 68 | 70 | 279 | 14,000,000 |
| Yasuharu Imano | 75 | 68 | 69 | 68 | 280 | 9,520,000 |
| Yoshikazu Haku | 72 | 67 | 73 | 69 | 281 | 5,786,666 |
| Hidemasa Hoshino | 71 | 69 | 72 | 69 | 281 | 5,786,666 |
| Tsuyoshi Yoneyama | 69 | 73 | 69 | 70 | 281 | 5,786,666 |
| Nozomi Kawahara | 72 | 68 | 73 | 69 | 282 | 3,978,800 |
| Hiroyuki Fujita | 72 | 71 | 70 | 69 | 282 | 3,978,800 |
| Kazuhiko Hosokawa | 72 | 69 | 70 | 71 | 282 | 3,978,800 |
| Toru Suzuki | 70 | 68 | 72 | 72 | 282 | 3,978,800 |
| Hideto Tanihara | 72 | 68 | 70 | 72 | 282 | 3,978,800 |
| Satoshi Higashi | 73 | 70 | 72 | 68 | 283 | 2,632,000 |
| Ryuichi Oda | 72 | 69 | 72 | 70 | 283 | 2,632,000 |
| Taichi Teshima | 69 | 69 | 73 | 72 | 283 | 2,632,000 |
| Mamo Osanai | 71 | 67 | 73 | 72 | 283 | 2,632,000 |
| Yeh Wei-tze | 71 | 70 | 70 | 72 | 283 | 2,632,000 |
| Naoya Sugiyama | 72 | 73 | 71 | 68 | 284 | 1,997,333 |
| Prayad Marksaeng | 73 | 73 | 69 | 69 | 284 | 1,997,333 |
| Dinesh Chand | 71 | 72 | 70 | 71 | 284 | 1,997,333 |
| Nobuhito Sato | 71 | 73 | 73 | 68 | 285 | 1,452,000 |
| Jeev Milkha Singh | 71 | 71 | 73 | 70 | 285 | 1,452,000 |
| Gonzalo Fernandez-Castano | 73 | 72 | 69 | 71 | 285 | 1,452,000 |
| Hideki Kase | 71 | 70 | 72 | 72 | 285 | 1,452,000 |
| Taichiro Kiyota | 72 | 73 | 68 | 72 | 285 | 1,452,000 |
| Mitsuhiro Tateyama | 70 | 69 | 73 | 73 | 285 | 1,452,000 |
| Tetsuji Hiratsuka | 74 | 68 | 69 | 74 | 285 | 1,452,000 |
| Y.E. Yang | 72 | 68 | 74 | 72 | 286 | 1,092,000 |
| Shinichi Akiba | 72 | 74 | 68 | 72 | 286 | 1,092,000 |
| Tatsuya Mitsuhashi | 73 | 69 | 71 | 73 | 286 | 1,092,000 |
| Takuya Taniguchi | 72 | 73 | 71 | 71 | 287 | 887,600 |
| Christian Pena | 72 | 75 | 68 | 72 | 287 | 887,600 |
| Hisayuki Sasaki | 73 | 70 | 75 | 69 | 287 | 887,600 |
| Ryoken Kawagishi | 70 | 71 | 73 | 73 | 287 | 887,600 |
| Shinichi Yokota | 71 | 71 | 70 | 75 | 287 | 887,600 |

## Golf Nippon Series JT Cup

*Tokyo Yomiuri Country Club,* Tokyo
Par 35-35–70; 6,961 yards

December 1-4
purse, ¥100,000,000

| | SCORES | | | | TOTAL | MONEY |
|---|---|---|---|---|---|---|
| Yasuharu Imano | 72 | 67 | 63 | 67 | 269 | ¥30,000,000 |
| Shinichi Yokota | 67 | 68 | 68 | 68 | 271 | 13,500,000 |
| Taichi Teshima | 69 | 69 | 69 | 65 | 272 | 6,275,000 |
| Toru Taniguchi | 64 | 70 | 72 | 66 | 272 | 6,275,000 |
| Toshimitsu Izawa | 73 | 68 | 64 | 68 | 273 | 3,850,000 |
| Keiichiro Fukabori | 68 | 71 | 66 | 68 | 273 | 3,850,000 |
| Chris Campbell | 69 | 67 | 73 | 65 | 274 | 3,175,000 |
| Y.E. Yang | 71 | 68 | 67 | 68 | 274 | 3,175,000 |
| Naomichi Ozaki | 67 | 69 | 70 | 69 | 275 | 2,900,000 |
| Paul Sheehan | 71 | 67 | 70 | 68 | 276 | 2,550,000 |
| Chang Ik-je | 73 | 66 | 68 | 69 | 276 | 2,550,000 |
| Hiroyuki Fujita | 72 | 69 | 70 | 67 | 278 | 1,962,500 |
| Dinesh Chand | 74 | 66 | 69 | 69 | 278 | 1,962,500 |
| Satoru Hirota | 67 | 71 | 70 | 70 | 278 | 1,962,500 |
| Kiyoshi Miyazato | 68 | 68 | 67 | 75 | 278 | 1,962,500 |
| Steven Conran | 70 | 69 | 72 | 69 | 280 | 1,500,000 |
| Ryoken Kawagishi | 68 | 71 | 71 | 70 | 280 | 1,500,000 |
| Hidemasa Hoshino | 70 | 71 | 69 | 70 | 280 | 1,500,000 |
| Kaname Yokoo | 68 | 71 | 70 | 71 | 280 | 1,500,000 |
| Tetsuji Hiratsuka | 68 | 71 | 73 | 70 | 282 | 1,250,000 |
| Azuma Yano | 75 | 71 | 69 | 68 | 283 | 1,200,000 |
| David Smail | 71 | 68 | 71 | 74 | 284 | 1,100,000 |
| Takao Nogami | 71 | 72 | 71 | 71 | 285 | 933,333 |
| Kazuhiko Hosokawa | 76 | 66 | 72 | 71 | 285 | 933,333 |
| Tatsuhiko Takahashi | 74 | 68 | 69 | 74 | 285 | 933,333 |
| Tadahiro Takayama | 71 | 67 | 76 | 72 | 286 | 860,000 |

## Asia/Japan Okinawa Open

*Naha Golf Club,* Okinawa
Par 36-35–71, 6,801 yards

December 15-18
purse, ¥100,000,000

| | SCORES | | | | TOTAL | MONEY |
|---|---|---|---|---|---|---|
| Tadahiro Takayama | 70 | 68 | 68 | 70 | 276 | ¥20,000,000 |
| Kiyoshi Miyazato | 68 | 67 | 70 | 71 | 276 | 10,000,000 |
| (Takayama defeated Miyazato on second playoff hole.) | | | | | | |
| Kenichi Kuboya | 67 | 72 | 68 | 70 | 277 | 5,800,000 |
| Tetsuji Hiratsuka | 71 | 68 | 64 | 74 | 277 | 5,800,000 |
| Thaworn Wiratchant | 69 | 67 | 72 | 71 | 279 | 3,800,000 |
| Kaname Yokoo | 65 | 70 | 69 | 75 | 279 | 3,800,000 |
| Taichi Teshima | 72 | 70 | 71 | 68 | 281 | 3,056,666 |
| Y.E. Yang | 71 | 69 | 69 | 72 | 281 | 3,056,666 |
| Scott Strange | 70 | 69 | 69 | 73 | 281 | 3,056,666 |
| Chris Campbell | 68 | 68 | 74 | 72 | 282 | 2,420,000 |
| Eiji Mizoguchi | 72 | 68 | 68 | 74 | 282 | 2,420,000 |
| Toru Taniguchi | 71 | 67 | 67 | 77 | 282 | 2,420,000 |
| Marcus Both | 70 | 67 | 74 | 72 | 283 | 1,686,666 |
| Scott Laycock | 73 | 66 | 72 | 72 | 283 | 1,686,666 |
| Keiichiro Fukabori | 73 | 68 | 70 | 72 | 283 | 1,686,666 |
| Tommy Nakajima | 69 | 71 | 70 | 73 | 283 | 1,686,666 |
| Yasuharu Imano | 71 | 64 | 73 | 75 | 283 | 1,686,666 |

| | SCORES | | | TOTAL | MONEY |
|---|---|---|---|---|---|
| Shiv Kapur | 72 | 65 | 71 | 75 | 283 | 1,686,666 |
| Ron Won | 71 | 70 | 71 | 72 | 284 | 1,180,000 |
| Yeh Wei-tze | 71 | 73 | 68 | 72 | 284 | 1,180,000 |
| Dinesh Chand | 65 | 72 | 74 | 73 | 284 | 1,180,000 |
| Prayad Marksaeng | 70 | 69 | 75 | 70 | 284 | 1,180,000 |
| Ross Bain | 72 | 68 | 70 | 74 | 284 | 1,180,000 |
| Unho Park | 70 | 69 | 73 | 73 | 285 | 940,000 |
| Kazuhiko Hosokawa | 71 | 70 | 71 | 74 | 286 | 840,000 |
| Jarrod Lyle | 74 | 69 | 68 | 75 | 286 | 840,000 |
| Jason Knutzon | 68 | 71 | 72 | 75 | 286 | 840,000 |
| Hiroyuki Fujita | 66 | 71 | 72 | 77 | 286 | 840,000 |
| Nobuhito Sato | 73 | 70 | 70 | 74 | 287 | 651,666 |
| Jeev Milkha Singh | 71 | 67 | 74 | 75 | 287 | 651,666 |
| Shinichi Akiba | 70 | 70 | 74 | 73 | 287 | 651,666 |
| Ryuichi Oda | 69 | 67 | 74 | 77 | 287 | 651,666 |
| Tsuyoshi Yoneyama | 70 | 69 | 70 | 78 | 287 | 651,666 |
| Charlie Wi | 72 | 70 | 67 | 78 | 287 | 651,666 |

# Australasian Tour

## Heineken Classic

*Royal Melbourne Golf Club*, Melbourne, Victoria
Par 36-35–71; 6,954 yards

February 3-6
purse, A$2,000,000

| | SCORES | | | | TOTAL | MONEY |
|---|---|---|---|---|---|---|
| Craig Parry | 69 | 66 | 65 | 70 | 270 | €225,367.70 |
| Nick O'Hern | 69 | 67 | 63 | 71 | 270 | 127,708.40 |
| (Parry defeated O'Hern on fourth playoff hole.) | | | | | | |
| Simon Dyson | 68 | 70 | 65 | 68 | 271 | 72,305.47 |
| Jarrod Lyle | 68 | 66 | 66 | 71 | 271 | 72,305.47 |
| Ernie Els | 72 | 64 | 66 | 70 | 272 | 50,081.71 |
| Trevor Immelman | 65 | 69 | 70 | 69 | 273 | 42,569.45 |
| Henrik Stenson | 69 | 66 | 68 | 70 | 273 | 42,569.45 |
| Peter Lonard | 65 | 68 | 70 | 71 | 274 | 35,057.20 |
| Simon Khan | 69 | 71 | 68 | 66 | 274 | 35,057.20 |
| Camilo Villegas | 66 | 71 | 68 | 70 | 275 | 31,301.07 |
| Colin Montgomerie | 68 | 65 | 72 | 71 | 276 | 23,287.99 |
| Gregory Havret | 72 | 66 | 71 | 67 | 276 | 23,287.99 |
| Richard Bland | 70 | 67 | 71 | 68 | 276 | 23,287.99 |
| Christopher Hanell | 69 | 71 | 67 | 69 | 276 | 23,287.99 |
| Brett Rumford | 70 | 66 | 66 | 74 | 276 | 23,287.99 |
| Steve Webster | 65 | 72 | 66 | 74 | 277 | 17,152.98 |
| Nobuhito Sato | 72 | 70 | 69 | 66 | 277 | 17,152.98 |
| Mark Foster | 68 | 73 | 68 | 69 | 278 | 14,210.68 |
| David Smail | 69 | 67 | 75 | 67 | 278 | 14,210.68 |
| Stuart Appleby | 72 | 67 | 71 | 68 | 278 | 14,210.68 |
| Barry Lane | 73 | 67 | 66 | 73 | 279 | 11,268.38 |
| Maarten Lafeber | 70 | 70 | 67 | 72 | 279 | 11,268.38 |
| David McKenzie | 71 | 70 | 70 | 68 | 279 | 11,268.38 |
| Robert Karlsson | 72 | 65 | 71 | 71 | 279 | 11,268.38 |
| Brad Lamb | 66 | 72 | 70 | 71 | 279 | 11,268.38 |
| Graeme McDowell | 70 | 70 | 67 | 72 | 279 | 11,268.38 |
| Martin Doyle | 73 | 67 | 70 | 69 | 279 | 11,268.38 |
| Brad Kennedy | 70 | 68 | 70 | 71 | 279 | 11,268.38 |
| Richard Green | 70 | 69 | 70 | 71 | 280 | 8,013.07 |
| Matthew Ecob | 72 | 67 | 71 | 70 | 280 | 8,013.07 |
| Raymond Russell | 72 | 67 | 71 | 70 | 280 | 8,013.07 |
| Jamie Donaldson | 69 | 68 | 71 | 72 | 280 | 8,013.07 |
| Chris Campbell | 71 | 69 | 69 | 71 | 280 | 8,013.07 |
| James Nitties | 68 | 67 | 71 | 74 | 280 | 8,013.07 |
| Soren Kjeldsen | 69 | 68 | 72 | 72 | 281 | 6,635.83 |
| Peter O'Malley | 70 | 66 | 72 | 73 | 281 | 6,635.83 |
| Gary Simpson | 70 | 71 | 65 | 75 | 281 | 6,635.83 |
| Paul Sheehan | 70 | 70 | 71 | 70 | 281 | 6,635.83 |
| Peter Fowler | 73 | 67 | 73 | 69 | 282 | 5,383.78 |
| Garry Houston | 72 | 69 | 73 | 68 | 282 | 5,383.78 |
| Fredrik Henge | 70 | 69 | 70 | 73 | 282 | 5,383.78 |
| Stephen Scahill | 74 | 67 | 69 | 72 | 282 | 5,383.78 |
| Niclas Fasth | 71 | 70 | 72 | 69 | 282 | 5,383.78 |
| Lee Slattery | 69 | 71 | 71 | 71 | 282 | 5,383.78 |
| Klas Eriksson | 71 | 67 | 73 | 72 | 283 | 3,881.33 |
| Gavin Coles | 73 | 67 | 68 | 75 | 283 | 3,881.33 |
| Paul Lawrie | 71 | 70 | 72 | 70 | 283 | 3,881.33 |
| Markus Brier | 71 | 71 | 70 | 71 | 283 | 3,881.33 |

| | SCORES | | | | TOTAL | MONEY |
|---|---|---|---|---|---|---|
| Alastair Forsyth | 70 | 69 | 74 | 70 | 283 | 3,881.33 |
| Adam Scott | 72 | 68 | 75 | 68 | 283 | 3,881.33 |
| Greg Chalmers | 73 | 68 | 67 | 76 | 284 | 2,472.78 |
| Mathew Goggin | 73 | 69 | 72 | 70 | 284 | 2,472.78 |
| Simon Wakefield | 68 | 72 | 72 | 72 | 284 | 2,472.78 |
| John Bickerton | 66 | 72 | 72 | 74 | 284 | 2,472.78 |
| Stephen Gallacher | 69 | 73 | 71 | 71 | 284 | 2,472.78 |
| Adam Crawford | 68 | 72 | 69 | 75 | 284 | 2,472.78 |
| David Bransdon | 70 | 71 | 69 | 75 | 285 | 2,015.79 |
| Nick Dougherty | 68 | 69 | 71 | 77 | 285 | 2,015.79 |
| Andrew Buckle | 71 | 69 | 68 | 77 | 285 | 2,015.79 |
| Mat Hendrix | 68 | 74 | 72 | 71 | 285 | 2,015.79 |
| Danny Vera | 69 | 70 | 71 | 75 | 285 | 2,015.79 |
| Jose Manuel Lara | 70 | 72 | 73 | 71 | 286 | 1,903.11 |
| Sven Struver | 71 | 71 | 71 | 73 | 286 | 1,903.11 |
| Miles Tunnicliff | 69 | 72 | 73 | 72 | 286 | 1,903.11 |
| Terry Price | 70 | 67 | 71 | 78 | 286 | 1,903.11 |
| Steven Conran | 73 | 66 | 73 | 75 | 287 | 1,807.12 |
| Emanuele Canonica | 73 | 67 | 67 | 80 | 287 | 1,807.12 |
| Steven O'Hara | 73 | 69 | 73 | 72 | 287 | 1,807.12 |
| Peter Senior | 73 | 69 | 76 | 70 | 288 | 1,610.54 |
| Phillip Archer | 70 | 71 | 72 | 75 | 288 | 1,610.54 |
| Tony Christie | 70 | 68 | 73 | 77 | 288 | 1,610.54 |
| Martin Maritz | 70 | 71 | 72 | 75 | 288 | 1,610.54 |
| Steven Bowditch | 72 | 68 | 71 | 77 | 288 | 1,610.54 |
| Dean Alaban | 72 | 70 | 68 | 78 | 288 | 1,610.54 |
| Mads Vibe-Hastrup | 69 | 72 | 73 | 75 | 289 | 1,498.70 |
| Costantino Rocca | 73 | 69 | 76 | 72 | 290 | 1,415.44 |
| Scott Drummond | 73 | 68 | 73 | 76 | 290 | 1,415.44 |
| Philip Golding | 71 | 70 | 75 | 74 | 290 | 1,415.44 |
| Ignacio Garrido | 70 | 72 | 72 | 76 | 290 | 1,415.44 |
| Graeme Storm | 69 | 68 | 75 | 78 | 290 | 1,415.44 |
| Jose-Filipe Lima | 74 | 68 | 79 | 69 | 290 | 1,415.44 |
| Chris Downes | 71 | 71 | 78 | 71 | 291 | 1,332.17 |

# Holden New Zealand Open

*Gulf Harbour Country Club,* Auckland, New Zealand
Par 36-36–72; 6,978 yards

February 10-13
purse, NZ$1,500,000

| | SCORES | | | | TOTAL | MONEY |
|---|---|---|---|---|---|---|
| Niclas Fasth | 65 | 63 | 75 | 63 | 266 | €156,671.20 |
| Miles Tunnicliff | 67 | 63 | 70 | 66 | 266 | 88,780.35 |
| (Fasth defeated Tunnicliff on second playoff hole.) | | | | | | |
| Richard Green | 70 | 63 | 69 | 68 | 270 | 50,265.35 |
| Simon Nash | 65 | 67 | 71 | 67 | 270 | 50,265.35 |
| Robert Karlsson | 68 | 65 | 72 | 66 | 271 | 33,075.03 |
| Peter O'Malley | 68 | 70 | 66 | 67 | 271 | 33,075.03 |
| Jose Manuel Lara | 66 | 67 | 72 | 68 | 273 | 22,485.22 |
| Damien McGrane | 67 | 66 | 72 | 68 | 273 | 22,485.22 |
| Steven Alker | 69 | 65 | 72 | 67 | 273 | 22,485.22 |
| Jarrod Moseley | 66 | 66 | 73 | 68 | 273 | 22,485.22 |
| Rolf Muntz | 67 | 66 | 72 | 68 | 273 | 22,485.22 |
| Oliver Wilson | 66 | 65 | 68 | 74 | 273 | 22,485.22 |
| Ricky Schmidt | 68 | 69 | 73 | 64 | 274 | 14,230.97 |
| Peter Lawrie | 68 | 68 | 70 | 68 | 274 | 14,230.97 |
| Lee Slattery | 68 | 70 | 66 | 70 | 274 | 14,230.97 |

| | SCORES | | | | TOTAL | MONEY |
|---|---|---|---|---|---|---|
| Marcus Fraser | 68 | 67 | 68 | 71 | 274 | 14,230.97 |
| Greg Chalmers | 71 | 66 | 74 | 64 | 275 | 10,238.03 |
| Stephen Scahill | 69 | 71 | 70 | 65 | 275 | 10,238.03 |
| Alastair Forsyth | 65 | 71 | 71 | 68 | 275 | 10,238.03 |
| Andrew Buckle | 67 | 69 | 74 | 65 | 275 | 10,238.03 |
| Peter Senior | 68 | 71 | 71 | 66 | 276 | 8,529.88 |
| Anders Hansen | 69 | 69 | 72 | 66 | 276 | 8,529.88 |
| Simon Khan | 66 | 70 | 69 | 71 | 276 | 8,529.88 |
| Barry Cheesman | 69 | 69 | 69 | 69 | 276 | 8,529.88 |
| Peter Hedblom | 73 | 67 | 71 | 66 | 277 | 6,789.09 |
| Nick Dougherty | 70 | 69 | 71 | 67 | 277 | 6,789.09 |
| Brett Rumford | 67 | 69 | 69 | 72 | 277 | 6,789.09 |
| Andrew Tschudin | 68 | 72 | 66 | 71 | 277 | 6,789.09 |
| Paul Sheehan | 67 | 67 | 75 | 68 | 277 | 6,789.09 |
| James Nitties | 69 | 71 | 72 | 65 | 277 | 6,789.09 |
| David Bransdon | 68 | 70 | 71 | 69 | 278 | 5,135.33 |
| Garry Houston | 66 | 67 | 72 | 73 | 278 | 5,135.33 |
| Mathew Goggin | 69 | 69 | 70 | 70 | 278 | 5,135.33 |
| Fredrik Henge | 71 | 68 | 70 | 69 | 278 | 5,135.33 |
| Craig Parry | 68 | 68 | 69 | 73 | 278 | 5,135.33 |
| Joakim Haeggman | 65 | 70 | 73 | 70 | 278 | 5,135.33 |
| Jose-Filipe Lima | 68 | 66 | 75 | 70 | 279 | 4,439.02 |
| Steven Jeffress | 68 | 71 | 73 | 67 | 279 | 4,439.02 |
| Costantino Rocca | 71 | 68 | 73 | 68 | 280 | 4,090.86 |
| Peter Fowler | 69 | 71 | 71 | 69 | 280 | 4,090.86 |
| Steve Webster | 70 | 69 | 80 | 62 | 281 | 2,872.30 |
| Marcus Cain | 68 | 67 | 76 | 70 | 281 | 2,872.30 |
| Kenneth Ferrie | 72 | 65 | 74 | 70 | 281 | 2,872.30 |
| Matthew Ecob | 70 | 69 | 72 | 70 | 281 | 2,872.30 |
| Andrew Marshall | 69 | 70 | 71 | 71 | 281 | 2,872.30 |
| Christopher Hanell | 65 | 70 | 76 | 70 | 281 | 2,872.30 |
| Gary Simpson | 70 | 69 | 74 | 68 | 281 | 2,872.30 |
| Brad Lamb | 68 | 72 | 72 | 69 | 281 | 2,872.30 |
| Wayne Perske | 69 | 68 | 71 | 73 | 281 | 2,872.30 |
| Martin Maritz | 66 | 70 | 75 | 70 | 281 | 2,872.30 |
| Steven Bowditch | 64 | 69 | 79 | 69 | 281 | 2,872.30 |
| Adam Groom | 66 | 72 | 69 | 74 | 281 | 2,872.30 |
| Peter Hanson | 69 | 68 | 77 | 68 | 282 | 1,493.82 |
| Emanuele Canonica | 69 | 68 | 72 | 73 | 282 | 1,493.82 |
| Paul Lawrie | 71 | 69 | 71 | 71 | 282 | 1,493.82 |
| Terry Price | 69 | 69 | 74 | 70 | 282 | 1,493.82 |
| Kim Felton | 67 | 72 | 74 | 69 | 282 | 1,493.82 |
| Nathan Green | 70 | 67 | 73 | 72 | 282 | 1,493.82 |
| Martin Doyle | 70 | 68 | 74 | 70 | 282 | 1,493.82 |
| Dean Alaban | 70 | 68 | 74 | 70 | 282 | 1,493.82 |
| Mattias Eliasson | 70 | 69 | 74 | 70 | 283 | 1,323 |
| Christian Cevaer | 69 | 70 | 74 | 70 | 283 | 1,323 |
| John Bickerton | 69 | 71 | 72 | 71 | 283 | 1,323 |
| Graeme Storm | 71 | 69 | 72 | 71 | 283 | 1,323 |
| Scott Gardiner | 69 | 70 | 71 | 73 | 283 | 1,323 |
| Craig Carmichael | 70 | 69 | 73 | 71 | 283 | 1,323 |
| Mark Foster | 69 | 71 | 73 | 71 | 284 | 1,178.95 |
| Barry Lane | 69 | 69 | 76 | 70 | 284 | 1,178.95 |
| Marten Olander | 70 | 68 | 73 | 73 | 284 | 1,178.95 |
| Phillip Archer | 69 | 67 | 78 | 70 | 284 | 1,178.95 |
| Nobuhito Sato | 67 | 71 | 73 | 73 | 284 | 1,178.95 |
| Gareth Paddison | 70 | 70 | 75 | 69 | 284 | 1,178.95 |
| Craig Jones | 70 | 70 | 75 | 70 | 285 | 1,074.94 |
| Mikko Ilonen | 69 | 71 | 74 | 72 | 286 | 1,050.13 |
| Jamie Donaldson | 71 | 68 | 74 | 73 | 286 | 1,050.13 |

| | SCORES | | | | TOTAL | MONEY |
|---|---|---|---|---|---|---|
| Jason Dawes | 67 | 73 | 75 | 72 | 287 | 1,025.33 |
| Ben Burge | 69 | 71 | 74 | 74 | 288 | 1,008.79 |
| Alistair Presnell | 66 | 73 | 77 | 74 | 290 | 992.25 |
| Adam Crawford | 66 | 71 | 77 | 79 | 293 | 975.71 |

## Jacob's Creek Open

*Royal Adelaide Golf Club*, Adelaide, South Australia February 17-20
Par 37-36–73; 7,196 yards purse, A$1,000,000

| | SCORES | | | | TOTAL | MONEY |
|---|---|---|---|---|---|---|
| Steven Bowditch | 67 | 67 | 72 | 71 | 277 | A$180,000 |
| Ryan Armour | 69 | 75 | 69 | 69 | 282 | 84,750 |
| Nathan Green | 71 | 70 | 71 | 70 | 282 | 84,750 |
| Greg Chalmers | 68 | 71 | 73 | 71 | 283 | 44,000 |
| Craig Jones | 68 | 73 | 71 | 71 | 283 | 44,000 |
| Brandt Snedeker | 72 | 69 | 72 | 71 | 284 | 34,000 |
| Wayne Grady | 72 | 72 | 68 | 72 | 284 | 34,000 |
| Peter Fowler | 69 | 73 | 74 | 69 | 285 | 28,000 |
| Brent Schwarzrock | 70 | 69 | 70 | 76 | 285 | 28,000 |
| David Smail | 72 | 69 | 75 | 70 | 286 | 18,914.28 |
| Peter O'Malley | 74 | 71 | 71 | 70 | 286 | 18,914.28 |
| Cliff Kresge | 67 | 74 | 74 | 71 | 286 | 18,914.28 |
| Vance Veazey | 70 | 74 | 71 | 71 | 286 | 18,914.28 |
| James Nitties | 71 | 72 | 75 | 68 | 286 | 18,914.28 |
| Chris Tidland | 71 | 68 | 74 | 73 | 286 | 18,914.28 |
| Greg Kraft | 72 | 69 | 71 | 74 | 286 | 18,914.28 |
| Jon O'Sullivan | 73 | 72 | 71 | 71 | 287 | 11,490 |
| Jason Dufner | 70 | 71 | 75 | 71 | 287 | 11,490 |
| Anthony Painter | 71 | 71 | 73 | 72 | 287 | 11,490 |
| Paul Sheehan | 72 | 71 | 72 | 72 | 287 | 11,490 |
| Mathew Goggin | 74 | 71 | 69 | 73 | 287 | 11,490 |
| Grant Waite | 73 | 70 | 73 | 72 | 288 | 9,183.33 |
| Jeremy Anderson | 70 | 75 | 72 | 71 | 288 | 9,183.33 |
| Dan Olsen | 69 | 70 | 78 | 71 | 288 | 9,183.33 |
| David McKenzie | 74 | 71 | 69 | 74 | 288 | 9,183.33 |
| Shane Bertsch | 70 | 71 | 73 | 74 | 288 | 9,183.33 |
| Bill Haas | 71 | 70 | 73 | 74 | 288 | 9,183.33 |
| Wayne Perske | 76 | 69 | 71 | 73 | 289 | 6,542.85 |
| Keoke Cotner | 69 | 70 | 77 | 73 | 289 | 6,542.85 |
| Doug LaBelle | 72 | 68 | 75 | 74 | 289 | 6,542.85 |
| Bubba Watson | 71 | 72 | 74 | 72 | 289 | 6,542.85 |
| Jeff Gove | 69 | 72 | 74 | 74 | 289 | 6,542.85 |
| Jason Schultz | 74 | 68 | 72 | 75 | 289 | 6,542.85 |
| Dean Pappas | 72 | 68 | 71 | 78 | 289 | 6,542.85 |

## ING New Zealand PGA Championship

*Clearwater Resort*, Christchurch, New Zealand February 24-27
Par 36-36–72; 7,137 yards purse, A$762,000

| | SCORES | | | | TOTAL | MONEY |
|---|---|---|---|---|---|---|
| Peter O'Malley | 66 | 68 | 71 | 69 | 274 | A$138,357 |
| Steven Bowditch | 64 | 71 | 76 | 63 | 274 | 78,402.30 |

(O'Malley defeated Bowditch on fourth playoff hole.)

| | SCORES | | | | TOTAL | MONEY |
|---|---|---|---|---|---|---|
| Jerry Smith | 70 | 70 | 67 | 70 | 277 | 44,389.54 |
| Johnson Wagner | 68 | 69 | 68 | 72 | 277 | 44,389.54 |
| Steven Jeffress | 67 | 72 | 69 | 70 | 278 | 27,671.40 |
| Troy Matteson | 70 | 70 | 68 | 70 | 278 | 27,671.40 |
| Brandt Snedeker | 69 | 68 | 70 | 71 | 278 | 27,671.40 |
| Kris Cox | 68 | 72 | 72 | 67 | 279 | 18,908.79 |
| Craig Carmichael | 70 | 69 | 72 | 68 | 279 | 18,908.79 |
| Jaxon Brigman | 69 | 69 | 70 | 71 | 279 | 18,908.79 |
| Camilo Villegas | 69 | 67 | 71 | 72 | 279 | 18,908.79 |
| Kim Felton | 70 | 71 | 66 | 72 | 279 | 18,908.79 |
| Scott Weatherly | 70 | 69 | 76 | 65 | 280 | 11,580.99 |
| Joel Kribel | 74 | 68 | 71 | 67 | 280 | 11,580.99 |
| Greg Kraft | 69 | 71 | 72 | 68 | 280 | 11,580.99 |
| Jon Mills | 66 | 70 | 75 | 69 | 280 | 11,580.99 |
| Scott Sterling | 69 | 72 | 70 | 69 | 280 | 11,580.99 |
| Jeff Gove | 67 | 68 | 70 | 75 | 280 | 11,580.99 |
| Pat Bates | 70 | 70 | 74 | 67 | 281 | 8,314.23 |
| Ricky Barnes | 68 | 70 | 72 | 71 | 281 | 8,314.23 |
| Mahal Pearce | 73 | 68 | 67 | 73 | 281 | 8,314.23 |
| Dan Olsen | 71 | 69 | 73 | 69 | 282 | 7,635.25 |
| Andrew Tschudin | 69 | 72 | 71 | 70 | 282 | 7,635.25 |
| Jarrod Lyle | 67 | 67 | 72 | 76 | 282 | 7,635.25 |
| Tony Christie | 66 | 73 | 77 | 67 | 283 | 6,118.45 |
| Charles Hoffman | 73 | 69 | 74 | 67 | 283 | 6,118.45 |
| Jim Rutledge | 71 | 71 | 73 | 68 | 283 | 6,118.45 |
| Jason Schultz | 68 | 69 | 75 | 71 | 283 | 6,118.45 |
| Nathan Green | 70 | 71 | 71 | 71 | 283 | 6,118.45 |
| Mathew Goggin | 69 | 73 | 72 | 70 | 284 | 4,563.86 |
| Chris Campbell | 73 | 69 | 72 | 70 | 284 | 4,563.86 |
| Barry Cheesman | 71 | 71 | 71 | 71 | 284 | 4,563.86 |
| Ryan Haller | 73 | 69 | 71 | 71 | 284 | 4,563.86 |
| Chris Downes | 69 | 70 | 73 | 72 | 284 | 4,563.86 |
| David McKenzie | 71 | 69 | 71 | 73 | 284 | 4,563.86 |
| Matthew Ecob | 70 | 70 | 71 | 73 | 284 | 4,563.86 |
| Vance Veazey | 69 | 70 | 71 | 74 | 284 | 4,563.86 |

## Johnnie Walker Classic
See Asia/Japan chapter.

## HSBC Champions Tournament
See Asia/Japan chapter.

## MFS Australian Open

*Moonah Links,* Rye, Victoria
Par 36-36—72; 7,466 yards

November 24-27
purse, A$1,250,000

| | SCORES | | | | TOTAL | MONEY |
|---|---|---|---|---|---|---|
| Robert Allenby | 63 | 72 | 72 | 77 | 284 | A$225,000 |
| John Senden | 69 | 71 | 75 | 70 | 285 | 90,625 |
| Nick O'Hern | 67 | 75 | 71 | 72 | 285 | 90,625 |
| Paul Sheehan | 69 | 71 | 72 | 73 | 285 | 90,625 |
| Mathew Goggin | 76 | 71 | 69 | 70 | 286 | 47,500 |
| Aaron Baddeley | 70 | 70 | 73 | 73 | 286 | 47,500 |

| | SCORES | | | | TOTAL | MONEY |
|---|---|---|---|---|---|---|
| Martin Doyle | 71 | 71 | 72 | 73 | 287 | 40,000 |
| Stuart Appleby | 70 | 73 | 72 | 73 | 288 | 35,000 |
| Rod Pampling | 70 | 70 | 73 | 75 | 288 | 35,000 |
| Lucas Parsons | 69 | 75 | 75 | 70 | 289 | 26,562.50 |
| Chris Campbell | 68 | 73 | 77 | 71 | 289 | 26,562.50 |
| Matthew Ballard | 70 | 74 | 74 | 71 | 289 | 26,562.50 |
| Greg Chalmers | 72 | 72 | 72 | 73 | 289 | 26,562.50 |
| Adam Scott | 66 | 73 | 77 | 74 | 290 | 19,750 |
| Camilo Villegas | 71 | 72 | 73 | 74 | 290 | 19,750 |
| Bubba Watson | 71 | 74 | 71 | 74 | 290 | 19,750 |
| *Andrew Tampion | 76 | 71 | 71 | 73 | 291 | |
| Peter Senior | 69 | 72 | 76 | 74 | 291 | 15,104.16 |
| Steven Bowditch | 70 | 73 | 74 | 74 | 291 | 15,104.16 |
| Nathan Green | 70 | 70 | 76 | 75 | 291 | 15,104.16 |
| *David Lutterus | 72 | 73 | 75 | 72 | 292 | |
| Adam Crawford | 74 | 70 | 73 | 75 | 292 | 13,500 |
| Craig Jones | 69 | 76 | 76 | 72 | 293 | 12,750 |
| Daniel Chopra | 72 | 72 | 76 | 73 | 293 | 12,750 |
| Peter Lonard | 74 | 72 | 73 | 74 | 293 | 12,750 |
| *Ashley Hall | 70 | 73 | 76 | 75 | 294 | |
| Steve Alker | 72 | 73 | 78 | 72 | 295 | 11,291.66 |
| Mahal Pearce | 70 | 75 | 75 | 75 | 295 | 11,291.66 |
| Scott Laycock | 65 | 76 | 76 | 78 | 295 | 11,291.66 |
| Craig Parry | 74 | 74 | 77 | 71 | 296 | 9,291.66 |
| Spencer Levin | 64 | 77 | 79 | 76 | 296 | 9,291.66 |
| Geoff Ogilvy | 66 | 77 | 77 | 76 | 296 | 9,291.66 |

## Cadbury Schweppes Australian PGA Championship

*Hyatt Regency Coolum Resort,* Coolum Beach, Queensland  
Par 36-36–72; 6,852 yards

December 1-4  
purse, A$1,200,000

| | SCORES | | | | TOTAL | MONEY |
|---|---|---|---|---|---|---|
| Robert Allenby | 68 | 71 | 64 | 67 | 270 | A$216,000 |
| Mathew Goggin | 68 | 74 | 66 | 63 | 271 | 122,400 |
| Rod Pampling | 70 | 71 | 65 | 69 | 275 | 62,200 |
| Nick O'Hern | 74 | 67 | 65 | 69 | 275 | 62,200 |
| Nathan Green | 68 | 67 | 68 | 72 | 275 | 62,200 |
| John Senden | 72 | 70 | 67 | 67 | 276 | 40,800 |
| Wade Ormsby | 71 | 66 | 69 | 70 | 276 | 40,800 |
| Stuart Appleby | 72 | 71 | 67 | 69 | 279 | 34,800 |
| Marcus Fraser | 72 | 70 | 70 | 68 | 280 | 28,200 |
| Peter O'Malley | 71 | 71 | 70 | 68 | 280 | 28,200 |
| Richard Green | 71 | 71 | 69 | 69 | 280 | 28,200 |
| Steven Bowditch | 70 | 66 | 70 | 74 | 280 | 28,200 |
| Michael Campbell | 71 | 69 | 67 | 74 | 281 | 21,600 |
| Greg Chalmers | 69 | 74 | 69 | 70 | 282 | 18,960 |
| Shaun Micheel | 73 | 70 | 68 | 71 | 282 | 18,960 |
| Sam Torrance | 72 | 71 | 67 | 72 | 282 | 18,960 |
| Nigel Spence | 74 | 68 | 71 | 70 | 283 | 13,087.50 |
| Scott Laycock | 71 | 70 | 73 | 69 | 283 | 13,087.50 |
| Mahal Pearce | 73 | 67 | 72 | 71 | 283 | 13,087.50 |
| Pat Giles | 70 | 69 | 76 | 68 | 283 | 13,087.50 |
| Michael Wright | 72 | 71 | 69 | 71 | 283 | 13,087.50 |
| Craig Parry | 68 | 74 | 74 | 67 | 283 | 13,087.50 |
| Richard Swift | 67 | 71 | 73 | 72 | 283 | 13,087.50 |
| Adam Bland | 72 | 70 | 69 | 72 | 283 | 13,087.50 |

| | SCORES | | | | TOTAL | MONEY |
|---|---|---|---|---|---|---|
| Bradley Iles | 71 | 69 | 73 | 71 | 284 | 9,552 |
| Brad McIntosh | 71 | ·71 | 70 | 72 | 284 | 9,552 |
| Bubba Watson | 74 | 69 | 68 | 73 | 284 | 9,552 |
| Scott Gardiner | 72 | 71 | 68 | 73 | 284 | 9,552 |
| Ryan Haller | 70 | 73 | 65 | 76 | 284 | 9,552 |
| Peter Fowler | 74 | 69 | 71 | 71 | 285 | 7,512 |
| Camilo Villegas | 73 | 71 | 70 | 71 | 285 | 7,512 |
| Leigh McKechnie | 73 | 70 | 70 | 72 | 285 | 7,512 |
| Rowan Beste | 75 | 70 | 70 | 70 | 285 | 7,512 |
| David McKenzie | 74 | 68 | 67 | 76 | 285 | 7,512 |

## MasterCard Masters

*Huntingdale Golf Club,* Melbourne, Victoria  
Par 36-36–72; 7,040 yards

December 8-11  
purse, A$1,250,000

| | SCORES | | | | TOTAL | MONEY |
|---|---|---|---|---|---|---|
| Robert Allenby | 67 | 68 | 68 | 68 | 271 | A$225,000 |
| Bubba Watson | 70 | 65 | 69 | 67 | 271 | 127,500 |
| (Allenby defeated Watson on first playoff hole.) | | | | | | |
| Nick O'Hern | 64 | 66 | 70 | 73 | 273 | 84,375 |
| John Senden | 67 | 70 | 68 | 70 | 275 | 60,000 |
| Paul Casey | 70 | 70 | 68 | 70 | 278 | 50,000 |
| Bradley Iles | 68 | 69 | 74 | 68 | 279 | 42,500 |
| Peter Lonard | 72 | 68 | 70 | 69 | 279 | 42,500 |
| Stuart Appleby | 72 | 69 | 66 | 73 | 280 | 36,250 |
| Peter O'Malley | 68 | 72 | 73 | 68 | 281 | 29,375 |
| Jarrod Moseley | 72 | 66 | 73 | 70 | 281 | 29,375 |
| Gareth Paddison | 71 | 72 | 68 | 70 | 281 | 29,375 |
| Paul Sheehan | 69 | 72 | 68 | 72 | 281 | 29,375 |
| *Oliver Fisher | 70 | 72 | 74 | 66 | 282 | |
| Aron Price | 74 | 70 | 71 | 67 | 282 | 19,600 |
| Euan Walters | 73 | 72 | 70 | 67 | 282 | 19,600 |
| *Jason Day | 72 | 67 | 74 | 69 | 282 | |
| Brad McIntosh | 75 | 67 | 70 | 70 | 282 | 19,600 |
| Kim Felton | 70 | 71 | 70 | 71 | 282 | 19,600 |
| Steven Bowditch | 74 | 69 | 68 | 71 | 282 | 19,600 |
| Craig Parry | 73 | 68 | 74 | 68 | 283 | 13,890.62 |
| Paul Gow | 76 | 68 | 67 | 72 | 283 | 13,890.62 |
| Brad Lamb | 71 | 73 | 66 | 73 | 283 | 13,890.62 |
| Martin Doyle | 69 | 67 | 73 | 74 | 283 | 13,890.62 |
| Michael Wright | 72 | 72 | 72 | 68 | 284 | 11,479.16 |
| Mathew Goggin | 71 | 75 | 70 | 68 | 284 | 11,479.16 |
| Adrian Percey | 71 | 70 | 74 | 69 | 284 | 11,479.16 |
| Adam Scott | 76 | 70 | 68 | 70 | 284 | 11,479.16 |
| Steve Collins | 71 | 75 | 68 | 70 | 284 | 11,479.16 |
| Ryan Haller | 74 | 72 | 66 | 72 | 284 | 11,479.16 |
| Nick Flanagan | 71 | 70 | 75 | 69 | 285 | 8,875 |
| Dean Alaban | 69 | 70 | 76 | 70 | 285 | 8,875 |
| Rod Pampling | 75 | 68 | 71 | 71 | 285 | 8,875 |

# African Tours

## South African Airways Open

*Durban Country Club*, Durban, South Africa
Par 36-36–72; 6,747 yards

January 20-23
purse, £500,000

| | SCORES | | | | TOTAL | MONEY |
|---|---|---|---|---|---|---|
| Tim Clark | 68 | 71 | 68 | 66 | 273 | R894,635.50 |
| Charl Schwartzel | 68 | 72 | 71 | 68 | 279 | 521,776.34 |
| Gregory Havret | 69 | 69 | 72 | 69 | 279 | 521,776.34 |
| Nick Dougherty | 73 | 73 | 68 | 66 | 280 | 220,119.97 |
| James Kingston | 71 | 70 | 72 | 67 | 280 | 220,119.97 |
| Darren Clarke | 72 | 74 | 67 | 67 | 280 | 220,119.97 |
| Graeme Storm | 71 | 68 | 69 | 72 | 280 | 220,119.97 |
| Gregory Bourdy | 75 | 70 | 68 | 68 | 281 | 118,482.58 |
| David Howell | 73 | 70 | 67 | 71 | 281 | 118,482.58 |
| Titch Moore | 65 | 70 | 72 | 74 | 281 | 118,482.58 |
| Tjaart van der Walt | 66 | 71 | 70 | 74 | 281 | 118,482.58 |
| Des Terblanche | 68 | 72 | 73 | 69 | 282 | 86,773.98 |
| Paul Eales | 74 | 69 | 70 | 69 | 282 | 86,773.98 |
| Louis Oosthuizen | 69 | 69 | 73 | 71 | 282 | 86,773.98 |
| Hendrik Buhrmann | 70 | 67 | 70 | 75 | 282 | 86,773.98 |
| Marten Olander | 72 | 73 | 71 | 67 | 283 | 76,157.26 |
| Werner Geyer | 71 | 72 | 71 | 69 | 283 | 76,157.26 |
| Hennie Otto | 71 | 72 | 71 | 70 | 284 | 66,059.58 |
| Jaco Van Zyl | 70 | 70 | 72 | 72 | 284 | 66,059.58 |
| Lee Slattery | 73 | 68 | 71 | 72 | 284 | 66,059.58 |
| Bruce Vaughan | 65 | 73 | 73 | 73 | 284 | 66,059.58 |
| Neil Cheetham | 70 | 70 | 70 | 74 | 284 | 66,059.58 |
| Bobby Lincoln | 71 | 70 | 69 | 74 | 284 | 66,059.58 |
| Johan Edfors | 74 | 69 | 73 | 69 | 285 | 52,847.67 |
| Fulton Allem | 74 | 69 | 72 | 70 | 285 | 52,847.67 |
| Jonathan Lomas | 72 | 73 | 70 | 70 | 285 | 52,847.67 |
| Simon Hurd | 75 | 66 | 73 | 71 | 285 | 52,847.67 |
| Lars Brovold | 68 | 72 | 73 | 72 | 285 | 52,847.67 |
| Phillip Archer | 72 | 70 | 71 | 72 | 285 | 52,847.67 |
| Kenneth Ferrie | 72 | 72 | 69 | 72 | 285 | 52,847.67 |
| Ian Garbutt | 71 | 70 | 71 | 73 | 285 | 52,847.67 |
| Garry Houston | 74 | 68 | 70 | 73 | 285 | 52,847.67 |
| Richard Sterne | 74 | 71 | 73 | 68 | 286 | 42,466.88 |
| Leif Westerberg | 74 | 71 | 73 | 68 | 286 | 42,466.88 |
| Marcel Siem | 69 | 77 | 72 | 68 | 286 | 42,466.88 |
| Fredrik Henge | 71 | 69 | 76 | 70 | 286 | 42,466.88 |
| Stuart Manley | 76 | 67 | 72 | 71 | 286 | 42,466.88 |
| Darren Fichardt | 70 | 73 | 72 | 71 | 286 | 42,466.88 |
| Andrew McLardy | 69 | 69 | 75 | 73 | 286 | 42,466.88 |
| Scott Dunlap | 71 | 75 | 71 | 70 | 287 | 36,804.63 |
| Gavan Levenson | 74 | 70 | 71 | 72 | 287 | 36,804.63 |
| Trevor Immelman | 70 | 73 | 69 | 75 | 287 | 36,804.63 |
| Ross Wellington | 69 | 70 | 77 | 72 | 288 | 32,841.05 |
| Mokgeteng John Mashego | 71 | 72 | 73 | 72 | 288 | 32,841.05 |
| Jean Hugo | 74 | 67 | 73 | 74 | 288 | 32,841.05 |
| Francesco Molinari | 72 | 71 | 71 | 74 | 288 | 32,841.05 |
| Ashley Roestoff | 74 | 70 | 75 | 70 | 289 | 27,745.03 |
| David Griffiths | 74 | 72 | 73 | 70 | 289 | 27,745.03 |

| | SCORES | | | | TOTAL | MONEY |
|---|---|---|---|---|---|---|
| Warren Abery | 73 | 70 | 75 | 71 | 289 | 27,745.03 |
| Andrew Butterfield | 75 | 71 | 70 | 73 | 289 | 27,745.03 |
| Nicolas Colsaerts | 71 | 74 | 70 | 74 | 289 | 27,745.03 |
| Marc Cayeux | 72 | 69 | 80 | 69 | 290 | 21,516.55 |
| Malcolm Mackenzie | 68 | 76 | 77 | 69 | 290 | 21,516.55 |
| Soren Kjeldsen | 72 | 74 | 72 | 72 | 290 | 21,516.55 |
| Matthew Blackey | 72 | 72 | 71 | 75 | 290 | 21,516.55 |
| Ben Mason | 75 | 70 | 70 | 75 | 290 | 21,516.55 |
| Lindani Ndwandwe | 69 | 72 | 73 | 76 | 290 | 21,516.55 |
| Martin Maritz | 75 | 68 | 76 | 72 | 291 | 16,986.75 |
| Jason Kelly | 73 | 70 | 76 | 72 | 291 | 16,986.75 |
| Michiel Bothma | 70 | 73 | 75 | 73 | 291 | 16,986.75 |
| Niki Zitny | 75 | 69 | 74 | 73 | 291 | 16,986.75 |
| Martin Erlandsson | 75 | 71 | 70 | 75 | 291 | 16,986.75 |
| Thomas Aiken | 72 | 73 | 76 | 71 | 292 | 14,155.62 |
| Stephen Browne | 78 | 67 | 74 | 73 | 292 | 14,155.62 |
| Andrea Maestroni | 74 | 69 | 75 | 74 | 292 | 14,155.62 |
| Michael Kirk | 72 | 70 | 75 | 75 | 292 | 14,155.62 |
| Philip Golding | 69 | 76 | 70 | 77 | 292 | 14,155.62 |
| Oliver Wilson | 72 | 73 | 76 | 72 | 293 | 12,456.95 |
| Gary Murphy | 76 | 70 | 81 | 68 | 295 | 10,569.53 |
| David Frost | 72 | 72 | 77 | 74 | 295 | 10,569.53 |
| Chris Williams | 68 | 78 | 73 | 76 | 295 | 10,569.53 |
| Chris Davison | 72 | 73 | 77 | 74 | 296 | 8,469.59 |
| Joachim Backstrom | 73 | 70 | 78 | 76 | 297 | 8,445.70 |
| Alain Norris | 73 | 72 | 83 | 71 | 299 | 8,421.92 |
| *Jakobus Roos | 73 | 72 | 79 | 77 | 301 | |
| Tony Johnstone | 77 | 68 | 83 | 75 | 303 | 8,398.14 |
| Cody Freeman | 71 | 75 | 77 | 81 | 304 | 8,374.24 |

## Dimension Data Pro-Am

*Gary Player Country Club:* Par 36-36–72; 7,831 yards
*Lost City Golf Course:* Par 36-36–72; 6,983 yards
Sun City, South Africa

January 27-30
purse, R1,000,000

| | SCORES | | | | TOTAL | MONEY |
|---|---|---|---|---|---|---|
| Simon Wakefield | 72 | 70 | 68 | 69 | 279 | R158,500 |
| Nic Henning | 70 | 70 | 71 | 71 | 282 | 115,000 |
| Tjaart van der Walt | 69 | 74 | 72 | 71 | 286 | 69,100 |
| Louis Oosthuizen | 72 | 71 | 70 | 74 | 287 | 49,100 |
| Andrew Butterfield | 72 | 71 | 74 | 71 | 288 | 35,100 |
| Phillip Archer | 73 | 69 | 72 | 74 | 288 | 35,100 |
| Darren Fichardt | 70 | 72 | 70 | 76 | 288 | 35,100 |
| Charl Schwartzel | 73 | 76 | 66 | 75 | 290 | 24,100 |
| Nick Price | 70 | 73 | 76 | 72 | 291 | 18,000 |
| Malcolm Mackenzie | 75 | 73 | 70 | 73 | 291 | 18,000 |
| Chris Davison | 72 | 74 | 71 | 74 | 291 | 18,000 |
| Scott Dunlap | 71 | 75 | 69 | 76 | 291 | 18,000 |
| Ben Mason | 73 | 69 | 72 | 77 | 291 | 18,000 |
| Andrew McLardy | 73 | 75 | 75 | 69 | 292 | 13,114.28 |
| Stuart Little | 72 | 72 | 77 | 71 | 292 | 13,114.28 |
| Grant Muller | 74 | 73 | 73 | 72 | 292 | 13,114.28 |
| Mark Mouland | 77 | 72 | 69 | 74 | 292 | 13,114.28 |
| Anton Haig | 72 | 74 | 71 | 75 | 292 | 13,114.28 |
| Ulrich van den Berg | 73 | 73 | 70 | 76 | 292 | 13,114.28 |
| Callie Swart | 78 | 66 | 76 | 72 | 292 | 13,114.28 |

| | SCORES | | | | TOTAL | MONEY |
|---|---|---|---|---|---|---|
| Alan Michell | 75 | 72 | 78 | 68 | 293 | 10,250 |
| Marc Cayeux | 76 | 71 | 75 | 71 | 293 | 10,250 |
| Johan Edfors | 75 | 72 | 75 | 71 | 293 | 10,250 |
| Alan McLean | 71 | 77 | 74 | 71 | 293 | 10,250 |
| Jaco Van Zyl | 74 | 74 | 73 | 72 | 293 | 10,250 |
| Keith Horne | 73 | 68 | 76 | 76 | 293 | 10,250 |
| Justin Walters | 70 | 73 | 73 | 77 | 293 | 10,250 |
| Ryan Tipping | 76 | 70 | 73 | 74 | 293 | 10,250 |
| Richard Sterne | 72 | 75 | 76 | 71 | 294 | 8,316.66 |
| Sean Farrell | 78 | 71 | 73 | 72 | 294 | 8,316.66 |
| Roger Wessels | 75 | 74 | 73 | 72 | 294 | 8,316.66 |
| Patrick O'Brien | 76 | 66 | 77 | 75 | 294 | 8,316.66 |
| Bradford Vaughan | 71 | 71 | 75 | 77 | 294 | 8,316.66 |
| Francesco Molinari | 71 | 76 | 73 | 74 | 294 | 8,316.66 |

## Nashua Masters

*Wild Coast Sun Country Club*, Port Edward, Natal
Par 35-35–70; 6,351 yards

February 3-6
purse, R1,000,000

| | SCORES | | | | TOTAL | MONEY |
|---|---|---|---|---|---|---|
| Richard Sterne | 68 | 64 | 67 | 70 | 269 | R158,500 |
| Titch Moore | 65 | 71 | 68 | 66 | 270 | 92,050 |
| Grant Muller | 66 | 69 | 67 | 68 | 270 | 92,050 |
| James Kingston | 67 | 75 | 61 | 68 | 271 | 49,100 |
| Andrew McLardy | 68 | 70 | 67 | 69 | 274 | 32,350 |
| Henk Alberts | 71 | 65 | 68 | 70 | 274 | 32,350 |
| Mark Murless | 69 | 68 | 67 | 70 | 274 | 32,350 |
| Mike Lamb | 67 | 68 | 68 | 71 | 274 | 32,350 |
| Andrew Butterfield | 68 | 70 | 72 | 65 | 275 | 20,100 |
| Darren Fichardt | 68 | 73 | 65 | 69 | 275 | 20,100 |
| Cody Freeman | 72 | 69 | 68 | 67 | 276 | 16,600 |
| Thomas Aiken | 67 | 72 | 69 | 68 | 276 | 16,600 |
| Tjaart van der Walt | 68 | 69 | 70 | 69 | 276 | 16,600 |
| Bradley Davison | 69 | 72 | 70 | 66 | 277 | 13,850 |
| Michael Kirk | 69 | 73 | 69 | 66 | 277 | 13,850 |
| Lars Brovold | 67 | 76 | 67 | 67 | 277 | 13,850 |
| Nic Henning | 72 | 67 | 69 | 69 | 277 | 13,850 |
| Warren Abery | 72 | 66 | 73 | 67 | 278 | 11,400 |
| Andre Cruse | 69 | 71 | 71 | 67 | 278 | 11,400 |
| Bradford Vaughan | 68 | 71 | 71 | 68 | 278 | 11,400 |
| Adilson da Silva | 69 | 70 | 71 | 68 | 278 | 11,400 |
| Derek Crawford | 68 | 70 | 69 | 71 | 278 | 11,400 |
| Sammy Daniels | 69 | 71 | 67 | 71 | 278 | 11,400 |
| Anton Haig | 71 | 69 | 66 | 72 | 278 | 11,400 |
| Andre Bossert | 71 | 70 | 72 | 66 | 279 | 9,350 |
| Justin Walters | 72 | 69 | 69 | 69 | 279 | 9,350 |
| Nico van Rensburg | 72 | 71 | 67 | 69 | 279 | 9,350 |
| Jean Hugo | 70 | 68 | 71 | 70 | 279 | 9,350 |
| Hendrik Buhrmann | 68 | 68 | 70 | 73 | 279 | 9,350 |
| Jaco Van Zyl | 70 | 67 | 69 | 73 | 279 | 9,350 |

# Telkom PGA Championship

*Woodhill Country Club*, Pretoria, South Africa
Par 36-36–72; 7,382 yards

February 17-20
purse, R1,750,000

| | SCORES | | | | TOTAL | MONEY |
|---|---|---|---|---|---|---|
| Warren Abery | 68 | 68 | 68 | 69 | 273 | R277,375 |
| Charl Schwartzel | 66 | 69 | 72 | 67 | 274 | 161,087.50 |
| Jaco Van Zyl | 65 | 71 | 66 | 72 | 274 | 161,087.50 |
| Doug McGuigan | 71 | 67 | 68 | 70 | 276 | 78,925 |
| Alan McLean | 72 | 72 | 62 | 70 | 276 | 78,925 |
| Nic Henning | 70 | 68 | 70 | 69 | 277 | 61,425 |
| Titch Moore | 68 | 73 | 65 | 72 | 278 | 50,925 |
| Marc Cayeux | 69 | 73 | 69 | 68 | 279 | 39,550 |
| Louis Oosthuizen | 66 | 73 | 67 | 73 | 279 | 39,550 |
| Martin Maritz | 69 | 71 | 71 | 69 | 280 | 32,112.50 |
| Bobby Lincoln | 68 | 68 | 71 | 73 | 280 | 32,112.50 |
| Matthew Kent | 70 | 71 | 72 | 68 | 281 | 26,075 |
| Johan Kok | 69 | 72 | 69 | 71 | 281 | 26,075 |
| Jean Hugo | 67 | 71 | 71 | 72 | 281 | 26,075 |
| Darren Fichardt | 69 | 69 | 70 | 73 | 281 | 26,075 |
| Keith Horne | 71 | 67 | 69 | 74 | 281 | 26,075 |
| Adilson da Silva | 71 | 68 | 71 | 72 | 282 | 22,487.50 |
| Dion Fourie | 67 | 70 | 70 | 75 | 282 | 22,487.50 |
| Mark Murless | 71 | 73 | 70 | 69 | 283 | 20,475 |
| Werner Geyer | 72 | 71 | 69 | 71 | 283 | 20,475 |
| Andrew McLardy | 71 | 70 | 70 | 72 | 283 | 20,475 |
| Andrew Butterfield | 71 | 73 | 71 | 69 | 284 | 19,250 |
| Tyrone van Aswegen | 69 | 72 | 75 | 69 | 285 | 17,937.50 |
| Tjaart van der Walt | 69 | 72 | 70 | 74 | 285 | 17,937.50 |
| Des Terblanche | 75 | 68 | 68 | 74 | 285 | 17,937.50 |
| Vaughn Groenewald | 72 | 69 | 69 | 75 | 285 | 17,937.50 |
| Steve Basson | 73 | 69 | 76 | 68 | 286 | 15,200 |
| Jonas Wahlstedt | 71 | 69 | 76 | 70 | 286 | 15,200 |
| Sean Farrell | 70 | 71 | 75 | 70 | 286 | 15,200 |
| James Kamte | 71 | 70 | 73 | 72 | 286 | 15,200 |
| Andre Bossert | 74 | 67 | 72 | 73 | 286 | 15,200 |
| Ryan Dreyer | 71 | 72 | 69 | 74 | 286 | 15,200 |
| Gary Thain | 72 | 69 | 69 | 76 | 286 | 15,200 |

# Vodacom Tour Championship

*Country Club Johannesburg, Woodmead Course,*
Johannesburg, South Africa
Par 36-36–72; 7,413 yards

February 24-27
purse, R2,000,000

| | SCORES | | | | TOTAL | MONEY |
|---|---|---|---|---|---|---|
| Marc Cayeux | 70 | 70 | 67 | 61 | 268 | R317,000 |
| Keith Horne | 70 | 69 | 66 | 69 | 274 | 230,000 |
| Andrew McLardy | 71 | 68 | 70 | 67 | 276 | 118,200 |
| Nic Henning | 68 | 67 | 73 | 68 | 276 | 118,200 |
| Ulrich van den Berg | 73 | 69 | 67 | 68 | 277 | 64,700 |
| Justin Walters | 69 | 74 | 66 | 68 | 277 | 64,700 |
| Richard Sterne | 69 | 73 | 66 | 69 | 277 | 64,700 |
| Hendrik Buhrmann | 67 | 70 | 68 | 72 | 277 | 64,700 |
| Bobby Lincoln | 71 | 69 | 70 | 68 | 278 | 40,200 |
| Darren Fichardt | 69 | 72 | 67 | 70 | 278 | 40,200 |

|  | SCORES | | | TOTAL | MONEY |
|---|---|---|---|---|---|
| Bruce Vaughan | 69 | 69 | 75 | 66 | 279 | 31,400 |
| Ashley Roestoff | 72 | 73 | 65 | 69 | 279 | 31,400 |
| Henk Alberts | 68 | 73 | 68 | 70 | 279 | 31,400 |
| Desvonde Botes | 67 | 74 | 68 | 70 | 279 | 31,400 |
| Bradford Vaughan | 66 | 73 | 69 | 71 | 279 | 31,400 |
| Doug McGuigan | 73 | 68 | 71 | 68 | 280 | 25,700 |
| Grant Muller | 68 | 70 | 72 | 70 | 280 | 25,700 |
| Louis Oosthuizen | 67 | 71 | 71 | 71 | 280 | 25,700 |
| Steve Basson | 73 | 67 | 68 | 72 | 280 | 25,700 |
| Brett Liddle | 73 | 69 | 70 | 69 | 281 | 23,000 |
| Divan van den Heever | 69 | 72 | 69 | 71 | 281 | 23,000 |
| Mark Murless | 68 | 73 | 73 | 68 | 282 | 20,500 |
| Omar Sandys | 69 | 73 | 72 | 68 | 282 | 20,500 |
| Gary Thain | 65 | 69 | 79 | 69 | 282 | 20,500 |
| Michael Kirk | 71 | 71 | 70 | 70 | 282 | 20,500 |
| Lee Slattery | 69 | 73 | 69 | 71 | 282 | 20,500 |
| Paul Eales | 70 | 70 | 70 | 72 | 282 | 20,500 |
| Warren Abery | 73 | 71 | 71 | 68 | 283 | 17,320 |
| Hennie Otto | 70 | 74 | 71 | 68 | 283 | 17,320 |
| Martin Maritz | 71 | 71 | 71 | 70 | 283 | 17,320 |
| Steve van Vuuren | 70 | 72 | 68 | 73 | 283 | 17,320 |
| Anton Haig | 74 | 68 | 67 | 74 | 283 | 17,320 |

## Hassan II Trophy

*Dar-es-Salam Golf Club, Red Course,* Rabat, Morocco
Par 36-37–73; 7,307 yards

February 24-27
purse, US$621,000

|  | SCORES | | | TOTAL | MONEY |
|---|---|---|---|---|---|
| Erik Compton | 71 | 69 | 69 | 68 | 277 | US$200,000 |
| Jose-Filipe Lima | 72 | 70 | 69 | 71 | 282 | 100,000 |
| Santiago Luna | 71 | 67 | 76 | 71 | 285 | 35,000 |
| Gregory Bourdy | 68 | 73 | 72 | 72 | 285 | 35,000 |
| Gregory Havret | 74 | 66 | 68 | 77 | 285 | 35,000 |
| Andrew Coltart | 73 | 72 | 69 | 72 | 286 | 17,500 |
| Jean-Francois Remesy | 75 | 68 | 69 | 74 | 286 | 17,500 |
| Carl Suneson | 70 | 70 | 75 | 72 | 287 | 9,400 |
| Miguel Angel Martin | 70 | 71 | 73 | 73 | 287 | 9,400 |
| Youness El Hassani | 71 | 73 | 69 | 74 | 287 | 9,400 |
| David Lynn | 70 | 69 | 73 | 75 | 287 | 9,400 |
| Marcel Siem | 72 | 74 | 64 | 77 | 287 | 9,400 |
| David Gilford | 74 | 70 | 71 | 73 | 288 | 8,000 |
| Raphael Jacquelin | 71 | 71 | 72 | 74 | 288 | 8,000 |
| Richard Finch | 73 | 71 | 72 | 74 | 290 | 8,000 |
| Abdelhaq Sabi | 72 | 71 | 71 | 76 | 290 | 8,000 |
| Keith Clearwater | 74 | 72 | 71 | 75 | 292 | 8,000 |
| Ty Tryon | 78 | 72 | 73 | 70 | 294 | 8,000 |
| Mustapha El Kharraz | 70 | 74 | 75 | 75 | 294 | 8,000 |
| Ferdinand Roca | 73 | 70 | 77 | 75 | 295 | 7,000 |
| Philip Golding | 71 | 72 | 74 | 78 | 295 | 7,000 |
| Matthew Blackey | 72 | 72 | 75 | 77 | 296 | 7,000 |
| Patrick Damron | 73 | 76 | 77 | 75 | 301 | 7,000 |
| Seiji Ebihara | 75 | 78 | 72 | 78 | 303 | 7,000 |
| Derek Gillespie | 73 | 78 | 74 | 78 | 303 | 7,000 |
| Marc Farry | 77 | 74 | 73 | 78 | 303 | 7,000 |
| Faycal Serghini | 74 | 73 | 76 | 80 | 303 | 7,000 |
| Bobby Casper | 74 | 75 | 79 | 77 | 305 | 7,000 |

| | SCORES | | | | TOTAL | MONEY |
|---|---|---|---|---|---|---|
| Marwane Chemssedine | 81 | 78 | 82 | 85 | 327 | 7,000 |
| Nicolas Colsaerts | 73 | | | | DQ | 7,000 |

## FNB Botswana Open

*Phakalane Golf Club,* Gaborone, Botswana  
Par 36-36–72; 7,446 yards

March 17-19  
purse, R250,000

| | SCORES | | | TOTAL | MONEY |
|---|---|---|---|---|---|
| Nico van Rensburg | 68 | 66 | 67 | 201 | R39,250 |
| Warren Abery | 67 | 70 | 65 | 202 | 28,750 |
| Ross Wellington | 68 | 68 | 69 | 205 | 20,000 |
| Des Terblanche | 71 | 67 | 68 | 206 | 13,000 |
| Adilson da Silva | 67 | 68 | 71 | 206 | 13,000 |
| Andre Cruse | 71 | 69 | 67 | 207 | 8,750 |
| Joe Nawanga | 68 | 72 | 68 | 208 | 7,000 |
| Lindani Ndwandwe | 70 | 70 | 68 | 208 | 7,000 |
| Grant Muller | 69 | 71 | 69 | 209 | 5,308.33 |
| Wickus Myburgh | 68 | 71 | 70 | 209 | 5,308.33 |
| Ashley Roestoff | 70 | 67 | 72 | 209 | 5,308.33 |
| Chris Swanepoel, Jr. | 70 | 67 | 73 | 210 | 4,675 |
| Steve Basson | 74 | 68 | 69 | 211 | 3,735 |
| Desvonde Botes | 68 | 73 | 70 | 211 | 3,735 |
| Callie Swart | 69 | 72 | 70 | 211 | 3,735 |
| Leonard Loxton | 70 | 70 | 71 | 211 | 3,735 |
| Jean Hugo | 70 | 70 | 71 | 211 | 3,735 |
| Tyrol Auret | 69 | 70 | 72 | 211 | 3,735 |
| Nico Le Grange | 74 | 65 | 72 | 211 | 3,735 |
| Gary Thain | 67 | 72 | 72 | 211 | 3,735 |
| Mike Lamb | 67 | 71 | 73 | 211 | 3,735 |
| Mark Murless | 68 | 66 | 77 | 211 | 3,735 |
| Sean Farrell | 71 | 72 | 69 | 212 | 2,750 |
| Ian Hutchings | 70 | 71 | 71 | 212 | 2,750 |
| Doug McGuigan | 68 | 72 | 72 | 212 | 2,750 |
| Shaun Norris | 72 | 68 | 72 | 212 | 2,750 |
| Henk Alberts | 69 | 71 | 72 | 212 | 2,750 |
| Sammy Daniels | 70 | 69 | 73 | 212 | 2,750 |
| John Bele | 73 | 70 | 70 | 213 | 2,350 |
| Michael McGill | 71 | 70 | 72 | 213 | 2,350 |
| David Ryan | 68 | 72 | 73 | 213 | 2,350 |

## Parmalat Classic

*Paarl Golf Club,* Paarl, South Africa  
Par 36-36–72; 6,734 yards

April 7-9  
purse, R300,000

| | SCORES | | | TOTAL | MONEY |
|---|---|---|---|---|---|
| Ulrich van den Berg | 67 | 65 | 69 | 201 | R47,100 |
| Lindani Ndwandwe | 70 | 70 | 62 | 202 | 29,250 |
| Peter Karmis | 70 | 69 | 63 | 202 | 29,250 |
| Chris Williams | 64 | 70 | 69 | 203 | 17,700 |
| Michiel Bothma | 67 | 68 | 69 | 204 | 13,500 |
| Keith Horne | 67 | 69 | 69 | 205 | 9,100 |
| Sammy Daniels | 67 | 68 | 70 | 205 | 9,100 |

| | SCORES | | | TOTAL | MONEY |
|---|---|---|---|---|---|
| Bradford Vaughan | 64 | 67 | 74 | 205 | 9,100 |
| Bafana Hlophe | 70 | 67 | 69 | 206 | 6,370 |
| Jaco Van Zyl | 68 | 69 | 69 | 206 | 6,370 |
| Warren Abery | 68 | 68 | 70 | 206 | 6,370 |
| Ross Wellington | 67 | 72 | 68 | 207 | 5,475 |
| Ryan Dreyer | 70 | 67 | 70 | 207 | 5,475 |
| Jaco Rall | 74 | 68 | 66 | 208 | 4,807.50 |
| Mark Murless | 72 | 69 | 67 | 208 | 4,807.50 |
| Thabang Simon | 69 | 72 | 67 | 208 | 4,807.50 |
| Desvonde Botes | 70 | 68 | 70 | 208 | 4,807.50 |
| Thomas Aiken | 69 | 73 | 67 | 209 | 4,200 |
| Werner Geyer | 68 | 70 | 71 | 209 | 4,200 |
| Nico Le Grange | 64 | 74 | 71 | 209 | 4,200 |
| Adilson da Silva | 68 | 71 | 71 | 210 | 3,825 |
| Alan Michell | 70 | 68 | 72 | 210 | 3,825 |
| Paul Bradshaw | 70 | 73 | 68 | 211 | 3,300 |
| Ian Hutchings | 71 | 71 | 69 | 211 | 3,300 |
| Michael McGill | 68 | 73 | 70 | 211 | 3,300 |
| Nico van Rensburg | 70 | 70 | 71 | 211 | 3,300 |
| Omar Sandys | 68 | 71 | 72 | 211 | 3,300 |
| Tyrol Auret | 71 | 67 | 73 | 211 | 3,300 |
| Danny Poulter | 71 | 72 | 69 | 212 | 2,775 |
| John Bele | 70 | 71 | 71 | 212 | 2,775 |
| Mokgeteng John Mashego | 69 | 72 | 71 | 212 | 2,775 |
| James Buzzard | 67 | 71 | 74 | 212 | 2,775 |

# Capital Alliance Royal Swazi Sun Open

*Royal Swazi Sun Country Club,* Mbabane, Swaziland
Par 36-36–72; 5,983 yards

May 4-7
purse, R500,000

| | POINTS | | | | TOTAL | MONEY |
|---|---|---|---|---|---|---|
| Hendrik Buhrmann | 11 | 7 | 10 | 14 | 42 | R79,250 |
| Ross Wellington | 11 | 8 | 16 | 6 | 41 | 57,500 |
| Brett Liddle | 5 | 13 | 0 | 21 | 39 | 35,700 |
| Jaco Van Zyl | 9 | 9 | 13 | 7 | 38 | 25,250 |
| Ryan Dreyer | 12 | 11 | 6 | 6 | 35 | 19,675 |
| Warrick Druian | 12 | 7 | 11 | 5 | 35 | 19,675 |
| Thabang Simon | -4 | 12 | 10 | 15 | 33 | 15,100 |
| Adilson da Silva | 10 | 1 | 17 | 4 | 32 | 12,550 |
| Lindani Ndwandwe | 6 | 8 | 7 | 10 | 31 | 11,000 |
| David Ryan | 12 | 8 | 5 | 5 | 30 | 9,950 |
| Nico Le Grange | 2 | 8 | 4 | 15 | 29 | 8,237.50 |
| Thomas Aiken | 12 | 2 | 6 | 9 | 29 | 8,237.50 |
| Wallie Coetsee | 3 | 7 | 6 | 13 | 29 | 8,237.50 |
| Mark Murless | 12 | -1 | 12 | 6 | 29 | 8,237.50 |
| Sean Farrell | 0 | 7 | 6 | 15 | 28 | 6,950 |
| Tongoona Charamba | 6 | 5 | 4 | 13 | 28 | 6,950 |
| Sammy Daniels | 13 | -2 | 11 | 6 | 28 | 6,950 |
| Mike Lamb | 6 | 4 | 5 | 12 | 27 | 6,450 |
| Werner Geyer | 2 | 15 | 4 | 5 | 26 | 6,150 |
| Desvonde Botes | 6 | 9 | 1 | 10 | 26 | 6,150 |
| Ulrich van den Berg | 4 | 3 | 14 | 4 | 25 | 5,700 |
| Nicholas Lawrence | 9 | 3 | 11 | 2 | 25 | 5,700 |
| Ryan Reid | 4 | 4 | 16 | 1 | 25 | 5,700 |
| Jean Hugo | 3 | 7 | 4 | 9 | 23 | 5,175 |
| Albert Kruger | 3 | 15 | -1 | 6 | 23 | 5,175 |

| | POINTS | | | | TOTAL | MONEY |
|---|---|---|---|---|---|---|
| Des Terblanche | 3 | 11 | 9 | 0 | 23 | 5,175 |
| Michiel Bothma | 4 | 5 | 6 | 8 | 23 | 5,175 |
| Jaco Rall | 5 | 0 | 11 | 6 | 22 | 4,800 |
| Alex Baillie | 1 | 7 | 7 | 6 | 21 | 4,575 |
| Ian Hutchings | 2 | 5 | 9 | 5 | 21 | 4,575 |

## Vodacom Origins of Golf Tour at Pretoria

*Pretoria Country Club,* Pretoria, South Africa
Par 36-36–72; 7,063 yards

May 11-13
purse, R330,000

| | SCORES | | | TOTAL | MONEY |
|---|---|---|---|---|---|
| Desvonde Botes | 66 | 65 | 71 | 202 | R51,810 |
| Jean Hugo | 64 | 68 | 70 | 202 | 37,950 |
| (Botes defeated Hugo on first playoff hole.) | | | | | |
| Jaco Van Zyl | 67 | 73 | 68 | 208 | 22,935 |
| Vaughn Groenewald | 68 | 69 | 71 | 208 | 22,935 |
| Sammy Daniels | 71 | 69 | 69 | 209 | 13,200 |
| James Kamte | 68 | 69 | 72 | 209 | 13,200 |
| Steve van Vuuren | 71 | 70 | 69 | 210 | 9,240 |
| Henk Alberts | 68 | 69 | 73 | 210 | 9,240 |
| Thomas Aiken | 71 | 71 | 69 | 211 | 7,007 |
| Brett Liddle | 71 | 70 | 70 | 211 | 7,007 |
| Grant Veenstra | 68 | 72 | 71 | 211 | 7,007 |
| Dean Lambert | 76 | 66 | 70 | 212 | 6,171 |
| Chris Williams | 73 | 71 | 69 | 213 | 5,621 |
| Nico van Rensburg | 70 | 73 | 70 | 213 | 5,621 |
| Bafana Hlophe | 71 | 70 | 72 | 213 | 5,621 |
| Jaco Rall | 73 | 70 | 71 | 214 | 5,082 |
| Alan Michell | 68 | 73 | 73 | 214 | 5,082 |
| Sean Farrell | 74 | 71 | 70 | 215 | 4,537.50 |
| Doug McGuigan | 74 | 69 | 72 | 215 | 4,537.50 |
| Mark Murless | 71 | 70 | 74 | 215 | 4,537.50 |
| Steve Basson | 72 | 67 | 76 | 215 | 4,537.50 |
| Kevin Stone | 69 | 73 | 74 | 216 | 3,971 |
| Rich Fulford | 70 | 72 | 74 | 216 | 3,971 |
| Ashley Roestoff | 70 | 71 | 75 | 216 | 3,971 |
| Mokgeteng John Mashego | 72 | 74 | 71 | 217 | 3,498 |
| Adilson da Silva | 78 | 68 | 71 | 217 | 3,498 |
| Wallie Coetsee | 70 | 70 | 77 | 217 | 3,498 |
| Ross Wellington | 67 | 71 | 79 | 217 | 3,498 |
| Omar Sandys | 75 | 70 | 73 | 218 | 3,151.50 |
| Nico Le Grange | 71 | 74 | 73 | 218 | 3,151.50 |

## Vodacom Origins of Golf Tour at Pezula

*Pezula Championship Course,* Knysna, South Africa
Par 36-36–72; 7,006 yards

May 25-27
purse, R330,000

| | SCORES | | | TOTAL | MONEY |
|---|---|---|---|---|---|
| Desvonde Botes | 66 | 67 | 65 | 198 | R51,810 |
| Ian Hutchings | 67 | 68 | 69 | 204 | 37,950 |
| Nico van Rensburg | 70 | 68 | 68 | 206 | 26,400 |
| Adilson da Silva | 68 | 70 | 69 | 207 | 19,470 |

| | SCORES | | | TOTAL | MONEY |
|---|---|---|---|---|---|
| Doug McGuigan | 71 | 72 | 65 | 208 | 13,200 |
| Ashley Roestoff | 73 | 68 | 67 | 208 | 13,200 |
| Ulrich van den Berg | 73 | 70 | 66 | 209 | 9,900 |
| Alan Michell | 69 | 73 | 68 | 210 | 7,700 |
| Warren Abery | 72 | 69 | 69 | 210 | 7,700 |
| Paul Bradshaw | 71 | 69 | 70 | 210 | 7,700 |
| Thabang Simon | 67 | 74 | 70 | 211 | 6,182 |
| Chris Williams | 70 | 71 | 70 | 211 | 6,182 |
| Tyrol Auret | 71 | 68 | 72 | 211 | 6,182 |
| Ross Wellington | 70 | 74 | 68 | 212 | 5,187.60 |
| Ryan Tipping | 69 | 75 | 68 | 212 | 5,187.60 |
| Thomas Aiken | 72 | 73 | 67 | 212 | 5,187.60 |
| Jaco Van Zyl | 73 | 73 | 66 | 212 | 5,187.60 |
| Sammy Daniels | 76 | 71 | 65 | 212 | 5,187.60 |
| Mark Murless | 75 | 70 | 68 | 213 | 4,455 |
| Mike Lamb | 78 | 64 | 71 | 213 | 4,455 |
| Steve Basson | 75 | 66 | 72 | 213 | 4,455 |
| Mohamed Tayob | 73 | 71 | 70 | 214 | 3,971 |
| Lindani Ndwandwe | 72 | 70 | 72 | 214 | 3,971 |
| Brett Liddle | 67 | 74 | 73 | 214 | 3,971 |
| Steve van Vuuren | 73 | 71 | 71 | 215 | 3,498 |
| Peter Karmis | 72 | 71 | 72 | 215 | 3,498 |
| Jean Hugo | 69 | 77 | 69 | 215 | 3,498 |
| David Ryan | 73 | 75 | 67 | 215 | 3,498 |
| Omar Sandys | 75 | 69 | 72 | 216 | 3,052.50 |
| Andre Cruse | 71 | 72 | 73 | 216 | 3,052.50 |
| Teboho Sefatsa | 74 | 69 | 73 | 216 | 3,052.50 |
| Tongoona Charamba | 73 | 69 | 74 | 216 | 3,052.50 |

## Vodacom Origins of Golf Tour at Wild Coast Sun

*Wild Coast Sun Country Club,* Port Edward, South Africa                 June 29-July 1
Par 35-35–70; 6,351 yards                                                                     purse, R330,000

| | SCORES | | | TOTAL | MONEY |
|---|---|---|---|---|---|
| Dean Lambert | 70 | 68 | 67 | 205 | R51,810 |
| Lindani Ndwandwe | 66 | 72 | 68 | 206 | 32,175 |
| Grant Muller | 66 | 71 | 69 | 206 | 32,175 |
| Mark Murless | 71 | 69 | 67 | 207 | 13,942.50 |
| Dijon Tintinger | 70 | 70 | 67 | 207 | 13,942.50 |
| Jean Hugo | 66 | 70 | 71 | 207 | 13,942.50 |
| Alex Haindl | 63 | 71 | 73 | 207 | 13,942.50 |
| Mohamed Tayob | 69 | 73 | 66 | 208 | 8,085 |
| Chris Williams | 71 | 67 | 70 | 208 | 8,085 |
| Sammy Daniels | 70 | 70 | 69 | 209 | 6,369 |
| Bradley Davison | 67 | 70 | 72 | 209 | 6,369 |
| James Kamte | 69 | 68 | 72 | 209 | 6,369 |
| Vaughn Groenewald | 70 | 66 | 73 | 209 | 6,369 |
| Jaco Van Zyl | 72 | 68 | 70 | 210 | 5,288.25 |
| Nic Henning | 68 | 70 | 72 | 210 | 5,288.25 |
| Keith Horne | 71 | 72 | 67 | 210 | 5,288.25 |
| Warren Abery | 68 | 70 | 72 | 210 | 5,288.25 |
| Werner Geyer | 67 | 74 | 70 | 211 | 4,620 |
| Warrick Druian | 71 | 68 | 72 | 211 | 4,620 |
| Mike Lamb | 69 | 73 | 69 | 211 | 4,620 |
| Jeff Inglis | 76 | 64 | 72 | 212 | 4,207.50 |
| Sean Farrell | 68 | 74 | 70 | 212 | 4,207.50 |

| | SCORES | | | TOTAL | MONEY |
|---|---|---|---|---|---|
| Ross Wellington | 70 | 71 | 72 | 213 | 3,762 |
| Des Terblanche | 72 | 69 | 72 | 213 | 3,762 |
| Andrew Curlewis | 72 | 69 | 72 | 213 | 3,762 |
| Ryan Dreyer | 69 | 70 | 74 | 213 | 3,762 |
| Thomas Aiken | 66 | 75 | 73 | 214 | 3,258.75 |
| Hendrik Buhrmann | 67 | 72 | 75 | 214 | 3,258.75 |
| Patrick O'Brien | 68 | 71 | 75 | 214 | 3,258.75 |
| Nico Le Grange | 75 | 69 | 70 | 214 | 3,258.75 |

## Vodacom Origins of Golf Tour at Bloemfontein

*Bloemfontein Golf Club*, Bloemfontein, South Africa
Par 36-36–72; 7,269 yards

August 24-26
purse, R330,000

| | SCORES | | | TOTAL | MONEY |
|---|---|---|---|---|---|
| Nic Henning | 68 | 70 | 67 | 205 | R51,810 |
| Doug McGuigan | 66 | 69 | 71 | 206 | 37,950 |
| Henk Alberts | 70 | 72 | 67 | 209 | 22,935 |
| Alex Haindl | 71 | 65 | 73 | 209 | 22,935 |
| Desvonde Botes | 70 | 73 | 67 | 210 | 11,220 |
| Bradford Vaughan | 74 | 66 | 70 | 210 | 11,220 |
| Thomas Aiken | 68 | 72 | 70 | 210 | 11,220 |
| Warren Abery | 68 | 68 | 74 | 210 | 11,220 |
| Alan Michell | 74 | 69 | 68 | 211 | 7,260 |
| Fulton Allem | 71 | 70 | 70 | 211 | 7,260 |
| Mark Murless | 71 | 69 | 72 | 212 | 6,039 |
| Nico van Rensburg | 71 | 69 | 72 | 212 | 6,039 |
| Adilson da Silva | 69 | 76 | 67 | 212 | 6,039 |
| Steve Basson | 66 | 70 | 76 | 212 | 6,039 |
| Grant Muller | 73 | 70 | 70 | 213 | 5,082 |
| Warrick Druian | 69 | 73 | 71 | 213 | 5,082 |
| Nico Le Grange | 73 | 69 | 71 | 213 | 5,082 |
| Thabang Simon | 67 | 78 | 68 | 213 | 5,082 |
| Ross Wellington | 72 | 69 | 73 | 214 | 4,455 |
| Jean Hugo | 69 | 71 | 74 | 214 | 4,455 |
| Tongoona Charamba | 75 | 71 | 68 | 214 | 4,455 |
| Tyrol Auret | 70 | 73 | 72 | 215 | 3,767.50 |
| Divan van den Heever | 70 | 73 | 72 | 215 | 3,767.50 |
| Omar Sandys | 69 | 74 | 72 | 215 | 3,767.50 |
| Wickus Myburgh | 74 | 69 | 72 | 215 | 3,767.50 |
| Anton Haig | 69 | 72 | 74 | 215 | 3,767.50 |
| Paul Bradshaw | 71 | 69 | 75 | 215 | 3,767.50 |
| John Bele | 71 | 72 | 73 | 216 | 3,151.50 |
| Keith Horne | 72 | 72 | 72 | 216 | 3,151.50 |
| Hanno de Weerd | 76 | 64 | 76 | 216 | 3,151.50 |
| Eugen Marugi | 74 | 71 | 71 | 216 | 3,151.50 |

# Telkom PGA Pro-Am

*Centurion Country Club*, Pretoria, South Africa
Par 36-36–72; 7,328 yards

August 31-September 2
purse, R300,000

| | SCORES | | | TOTAL | MONEY |
|---|---|---|---|---|---|
| Thomas Aiken | 68 | 66 | 67 | 201 | R47,100 |
| Henk Alberts | 74 | 67 | 66 | 207 | 34,500 |
| Omar Sandys | 71 | 69 | 69 | 209 | 20,850 |
| Andre Cruse | 71 | 66 | 72 | 209 | 20,850 |
| Nico Le Grange | 75 | 70 | 66 | 211 | 10,200 |
| Ross Wellington | 72 | 71 | 68 | 211 | 10,200 |
| Hennie Otto | 71 | 70 | 70 | 211 | 10,200 |
| Mark Murless | 72 | 69 | 70 | 211 | 10,200 |
| Warren Abery | 72 | 72 | 68 | 212 | 5,860 |
| Doug McGuigan | 73 | 71 | 68 | 212 | 5,860 |
| Adilson da Silva | 73 | 70 | 69 | 212 | 5,860 |
| Ian Hutchings | 73 | 70 | 69 | 212 | 5,860 |
| Hennie Rootman | 71 | 71 | 70 | 212 | 5,860 |
| Steve Basson | 70 | 69 | 73 | 212 | 5,860 |
| Chris Swanepoel, Jr. | 71 | 69 | 73 | 213 | 4,620 |
| Thabang Simon | 69 | 71 | 73 | 213 | 4,620 |
| Tyrol Auret | 67 | 72 | 74 | 213 | 4,620 |
| Jaco Van Zyl | 68 | 70 | 75 | 213 | 4,620 |
| Jean Hugo | 68 | 74 | 72 | 214 | 4,125 |
| Leonard Loxton | 67 | 73 | 74 | 214 | 4,125 |
| Nic Henning | 74 | 70 | 71 | 215 | 3,555 |
| Steve van Vuuren | 72 | 72 | 71 | 215 | 3,555 |
| Ashley Roestoff | 69 | 75 | 71 | 215 | 3,555 |
| Bradford Vaughan | 71 | 72 | 72 | 215 | 3,555 |
| Alan Michell | 75 | 66 | 74 | 215 | 3,555 |
| Ulrich van den Berg | 69 | 69 | 77 | 215 | 3,555 |
| Grant Muller | 73 | 71 | 72 | 216 | 2,962.50 |
| Kevin Stone | 74 | 70 | 72 | 216 | 2,962.50 |
| Mike Lamb | 70 | 73 | 73 | 216 | 2,962.50 |
| Patrick O'Brien | 72 | 68 | 76 | 216 | 2,962.50 |

# Vodacom Origins of Golf Tour at Erinvale

*Erinvale Golf Club*, Somerset West, South Africa
Par 36-36–72; 7,090 yards

September 7-9
purse, R330,000

| | SCORES | | | TOTAL | MONEY |
|---|---|---|---|---|---|
| Hennie Otto | 71 | 63 | 68 | 202 | R51,810 |
| Thomas Aiken | 67 | 67 | 69 | 203 | 37,950 |
| Nico Le Grange | 69 | 68 | 68 | 205 | 22,935 |
| Jean Hugo | 67 | 66 | 72 | 205 | 22,935 |
| Eugen Marugi | 68 | 72 | 66 | 206 | 13,200 |
| Jaco Van Zyl | 69 | 67 | 70 | 206 | 13,200 |
| Tyrol Auret | 73 | 68 | 66 | 207 | 9,900 |
| Warren Abery | 68 | 74 | 66 | 208 | 8,580 |
| Titch Moore | 70 | 70 | 70 | 210 | 7,590 |
| Ian Hutchings | 74 | 70 | 68 | 212 | 6,715.50 |
| Steve van Vuuren | 69 | 72 | 71 | 212 | 6,715.50 |
| Bafana Hlophe | 70 | 73 | 70 | 213 | 5,643 |
| Patrick O'Brien | 75 | 68 | 70 | 213 | 5,643 |
| Bradford Vaughan | 68 | 74 | 71 | 213 | 5,643 |

| | SCORES | | | TOTAL | MONEY |
|---|---|---|---|---|---|
| Bradley Davison | 71 | 70 | 72 | 213 | 5,643 |
| Vaughn Groenewald | 73 | 68 | 72 | 213 | 5,643 |
| Dijon Tintinger | 71 | 73 | 70 | 214 | 4,796 |
| Dean Lambert | 73 | 69 | 72 | 214 | 4,796 |
| Ryan Tipping | 68 | 73 | 73 | 214 | 4,796 |
| Nic Henning | 70 | 75 | 70 | 215 | 4,207.50 |
| Ulrich van den Berg | 74 | 71 | 70 | 215 | 4,207.50 |
| Chris Swanepoel, Jr. | 75 | 68 | 72 | 215 | 4,207.50 |
| Steve Basson | 72 | 74 | 69 | 215 | 4,207.50 |
| Mike Michell | 71 | 72 | 73 | 216 | 3,630 |
| Grant Veenstra | 70 | 73 | 73 | 216 | 3,630 |
| Brett Liddle | 72 | 70 | 74 | 216 | 3,630 |
| Bobby Lincoln | 73 | 74 | 69 | 216 | 3,630 |
| Peter Karmis | 75 | 70 | 72 | 217 | 3,151.50 |
| Doug McGuigan | 70 | 72 | 75 | 217 | 3,151.50 |
| Grant Muller | 72 | 76 | 69 | 217 | 3,151.50 |
| Anton Haig | 75 | 74 | 68 | 217 | 3,151.50 |

## Seekers Travel Pro-Am

*Dainfern Country Club,* Johannesburg, South Africa
Par 36-36–72; 7,258 yards

September 29-October 1
purse, R300,000

| | SCORES | | | TOTAL | MONEY |
|---|---|---|---|---|---|
| Anton Haig | 70 | 66 | 68 | 204 | R47,100 |
| Nic Henning | 67 | 69 | 68 | 204 | 34,500 |
| (Haig defeated Henning on first playoff hole.) | | | | | |
| Ross Wellington | 66 | 72 | 68 | 206 | 20,850 |
| Kevin Stone | 67 | 67 | 72 | 206 | 20,850 |
| Doug McGuigan | 71 | 69 | 67 | 207 | 9,540 |
| Brett Liddle | 70 | 70 | 67 | 207 | 9,540 |
| Adilson da Silva | 72 | 65 | 70 | 207 | 9,540 |
| Ian Hutchings | 68 | 68 | 71 | 207 | 9,540 |
| Bradford Vaughan | 68 | 68 | 71 | 207 | 9,540 |
| Eugen Marugi | 72 | 66 | 70 | 208 | 6,105 |
| John Bele | 71 | 66 | 71 | 208 | 6,105 |
| Ulrich van den Berg | 68 | 68 | 73 | 209 | 5,610 |
| Nico van Rensburg | 69 | 72 | 69 | 210 | 4,820 |
| Sean Farrell | 74 | 67 | 69 | 210 | 4,820 |
| Wallie Coetsee | 68 | 72 | 70 | 210 | 4,820 |
| Divan van den Heever | 73 | 66 | 71 | 210 | 4,820 |
| Desvonde Botes | 66 | 72 | 72 | 210 | 4,820 |
| Werner Geyer | 72 | 66 | 72 | 210 | 4,820 |
| Grant Veenstra | 74 | 69 | 68 | 211 | 3,762.85 |
| Vaughn Groenewald | 70 | 72 | 69 | 211 | 3,762.85 |
| Andy Matthews | 70 | 72 | 69 | 211 | 3,762.85 |
| Lindani Ndwandwe | 69 | 71 | 71 | 211 | 3,762.85 |
| Patrick O'Brien | 71 | 69 | 71 | 211 | 3,762.85 |
| Bradley Davison | 68 | 72 | 71 | 211 | 3,762.85 |
| James Kamte | 68 | 70 | 73 | 211 | 3,762.85 |
| Dean Lambert | 74 | 69 | 69 | 212 | 3,180 |
| Callie Swart | 72 | 71 | 69 | 212 | 3,180 |
| Henk Alberts | 69 | 70 | 74 | 213 | 2,955 |
| Rich Fulford | 73 | 65 | 75 | 213 | 2,955 |
| Steve van Vuuren | 74 | 70 | 70 | 214 | 2,600 |
| Kenneth Dube | 71 | 72 | 71 | 214 | 2,600 |
| Bafana Hlophe | 72 | 70 | 72 | 214 | 2,600 |

|  | SCORES | TOTAL | MONEY |
|---|---|---|---|
| Chris Davison | 73 69 72 | 214 | 2,600 |
| Chris Swanepoel, Jr. | 74 67 73 | 214 | 2,600 |
| Dion Fourie | 69 69 76 | 214 | 2,600 |

## Bearingman Highveld Classic

*Witbank Golf Club*, Witbank, South Africa
Par 36-36–72; 6,702 yards

October 7-9
purse, R400,000

|  | SCORES | TOTAL | MONEY |
|---|---|---|---|
| Bradford Vaughan | 69 66 66 | 201 | R62,800 |
| Peter Karmis | 69 65 69 | 203 | 39,000 |
| Thomas Aiken | 67 67 69 | 203 | 39,000 |
| Andre Cruse | 69 72 64 | 205 | 20,800 |
| Doug McGuigan | 72 66 67 | 205 | 20,800 |
| Hendrik Buhrmann | 71 66 69 | 206 | 14,000 |
| Nic Henning | 74 65 68 | 207 | 10,533.33 |
| Desvonde Botes | 73 66 68 | 207 | 10,533.33 |
| Alan Michell | 66 70 71 | 207 | 10,533.33 |
| Steve van Vuuren | 71 69 68 | 208 | 8,140 |
| Bafana Hlophe | 70 68 70 | 208 | 8,140 |
| Grant Muller | 74 67 68 | 209 | 7,300 |
| Callie Swart | 73 67 69 | 209 | 7,300 |
| Barry Painting | 73 70 67 | 210 | 6,288 |
| Kevin Stone | 75 67 68 | 210 | 6,288 |
| Mark Murless | 71 70 69 | 210 | 6,288 |
| Nico van Rensburg | 76 65 69 | 210 | 6,288 |
| Hennie Otto | 71 70 69 | 210 | 6,288 |
| Omar Sandys | 74 70 67 | 211 | 4,930 |
| Chris Williams | 72 72 67 | 211 | 4,930 |
| Ulrich van den Berg | 74 70 67 | 211 | 4,930 |
| David Ryan | 73 71 67 | 211 | 4,930 |
| Michiel Bothma | 72 71 68 | 211 | 4,930 |
| Jean Hugo | 74 69 68 | 211 | 4,930 |
| Vaughn Groenewald | 72 70 69 | 211 | 4,930 |
| Mike Lamb | 68 72 71 | 211 | 4,930 |
| James Kamte | 69 74 69 | 212 | 3,950 |
| Chris Davison | 73 70 69 | 212 | 3,950 |
| Fulton Allem | 71 72 69 | 212 | 3,950 |
| Nico Le Grange | 69 69 74 | 212 | 3,950 |

## MTC Namibia PGA Championship

*Windhoek Country Club*, Namibia
Par 35-36–71; 7,106 yards

October 13-15
purse, R500,000

|  | SCORES | TOTAL | MONEY |
|---|---|---|---|
| Thomas Aiken | 64 67 67 | 198 | R79,250 |
| Keith Horne | 69 68 65 | 202 | 34,912.50 |
| Sean Farrell | 63 70 69 | 202 | 34,912.50 |
| Werner Geyer | 66 67 69 | 202 | 34,912.50 |
| Michiel Bothma | 66 64 72 | 202 | 34,912.50 |
| Andre Cruse | 69 68 66 | 203 | 16,625 |
| Peter Karmis | 67 65 71 | 203 | 16,625 |

| | SCORES | | | TOTAL | MONEY |
|---|---|---|---|---|---|
| Wallie Coetsee | 67 | 68 | 69 | 204 | 11,775 |
| Jean Hugo | 69 | 66 | 69 | 204 | 11,775 |
| Divan van den Heever | 70 | 68 | 67 | 205 | 9,950 |
| Adilson da Silva | 70 | 71 | 65 | 206 | 9,100 |
| Doug McGuigan | 70 | 69 | 68 | 207 | 7,762.50 |
| Leonard Loxton | 69 | 70 | 68 | 207 | 7,762.50 |
| Dijon Tintinger | 68 | 70 | 69 | 207 | 7,762.50 |
| Tongoona Charamba | 68 | 68 | 71 | 207 | 7,762.50 |
| Des Terblanche | 73 | 68 | 67 | 208 | 6,375 |
| Ian Hutchings | 71 | 70 | 67 | 208 | 6,375 |
| Langley Perrins | 68 | 70 | 70 | 208 | 6,375 |
| Warrick Druian | 72 | 66 | 70 | 208 | 6,375 |
| Brett Liddle | 68 | 70 | 70 | 208 | 6,375 |
| Nico van Rensburg | 71 | 66 | 71 | 208 | 6,375 |
| Bradford Vaughan | 68 | 74 | 67 | 209 | 5,250 |
| Bobby Lincoln | 69 | 71 | 69 | 209 | 5,250 |
| Ryan Tipping | 70 | 70 | 69 | 209 | 5,250 |
| Rudy Whitfield | 69 | 70 | 70 | 209 | 5,250 |
| Chris Swanepoel, Jr. | 70 | 68 | 71 | 209 | 5,250 |
| Trevor Dodds | 71 | 67 | 71 | 209 | 5,250 |
| Mike Lamb | 70 | 67 | 72 | 209 | 5,250 |
| Henk Alberts | 68 | 73 | 69 | 210 | 4,525 |
| Stefaan van den Heever | 72 | 68 | 70 | 210 | 4,525 |
| Steve Basson | 74 | 65 | 71 | 210 | 4,525 |

## Vodacom Origins of Golf Tour Championship

*The Links at Fancourt*, George, South Africa
Par 36-37–73; 7,566 yards

October 19-21
purse, R400,000

| | SCORES | | | TOTAL | MONEY |
|---|---|---|---|---|---|
| Steve Basson | 69 | 79 | 70 | 218 | R62,800 |
| Chris Williams | 75 | 77 | 70 | 222 | 46,000 |
| Adilson da Silva | 74 | 81 | 69 | 224 | 27,800 |
| Warren Abery | 71 | 82 | 71 | 224 | 27,800 |
| Ulrich van den Berg | 75 | 80 | 72 | 227 | 16,000 |
| Tyrol Auret | 73 | 79 | 75 | 227 | 16,000 |
| Chris Swanepoel, Jr. | 72 | 84 | 72 | 228 | 10,533.33 |
| Doug McGuigan | 75 | 79 | 74 | 228 | 10,533.33 |
| Steve van Vuuren | 68 | 83 | 77 | 228 | 10,533.33 |
| Michiel Bothma | 75 | 84 | 70 | 229 | 8,140 |
| Keith Horne | 74 | 81 | 74 | 229 | 8,140 |
| Alan Michell | 74 | 84 | 72 | 230 | 7,133.33 |
| Lindani Ndwandwe | 73 | 84 | 73 | 230 | 7,133.33 |
| Albert Kruger | 78 | 78 | 74 | 230 | 7,133.33 |
| Jean Hugo | 77 | 81 | 74 | 232 | 6,160 |
| Dijon Tintinger | 73 | 84 | 75 | 232 | 6,160 |
| Grant Muller | 79 | 76 | 77 | 232 | 6,160 |
| Thomas Aiken | 76 | 78 | 78 | 232 | 6,160 |
| Shaun Norris | 78 | 83 | 73 | 234 | 5,106.66 |
| Mike Michell | 77 | 84 | 73 | 234 | 5,106.66 |
| Sean Farrell | 77 | 82 | 75 | 234 | 5,106.66 |
| Chris Davison | 76 | 82 | 76 | 234 | 5,106.66 |
| Bradford Vaughan | 72 | 86 | 76 | 234 | 5,106.66 |
| Mike Lamb | 77 | 80 | 77 | 234 | 5,106.66 |
| Werner Geyer | 76 | 82 | 77 | 235 | 4,240 |
| Fulton Allem | 78 | 80 | 77 | 235 | 4,240 |

| | SCORES | | | TOTAL | MONEY |
|---|---|---|---|---|---|
| Vaughn Groenewald | 74 | 83 | 78 | 235 | 4,240 |
| Dion Fourie | 72 | 84 | 79 | 235 | 4,240 |
| Nico van Rensburg | 76 | 87 | 73 | 236 | 3,475 |
| Desvonde Botes | 79 | 82 | 75 | 236 | 3,475 |
| Ryan Tipping | 73 | 87 | 76 | 236 | 3,475 |
| Brett Liddle | 72 | 86 | 78 | 236 | 3,475 |
| Thabang Simon | 78 | 80 | 78 | 236 | 3,475 |
| Nico Le Grange | 77 | 80 | 79 | 236 | 3,475 |
| Hendrik Buhrmann | 75 | 81 | 80 | 236 | 3,475 |
| Mark Murless | 75 | 77 | 84 | 236 | 3,475 |

## Platinum Classic

*Mooi Nooi Golf Club*, Rustenburg, South Africa
Par 36-36–72; 6,916 yards

October 27-29
purse, R500,000

| | SCORES | | | TOTAL | MONEY |
|---|---|---|---|---|---|
| Jaco Van Zyl | 67 | 65 | 66 | 198 | R79,250 |
| Grant Muller | 68 | 63 | 67 | 198 | 57,500 |
| (Van Zyl defeated Muller on first playoff hole.) | | | | | |
| Wallie Coetsee | 66 | 66 | 68 | 200 | 30,475 |
| Warren Abery | 66 | 65 | 69 | 200 | 30,475 |
| Johan Kok | 66 | 69 | 68 | 203 | 18,150 |
| Bradford Vaughan | 69 | 65 | 69 | 203 | 18,150 |
| Bobby Lincoln | 69 | 64 | 70 | 203 | 18,150 |
| Mark Murless | 67 | 71 | 66 | 204 | 11,775 |
| Michiel Bothma | 69 | 66 | 69 | 204 | 11,775 |
| Darren Fichardt | 71 | 64 | 70 | 205 | 9,525 |
| Des Terblanche | 64 | 70 | 71 | 205 | 9,525 |
| Jean Hugo | 71 | 68 | 67 | 206 | 7,450 |
| Andy Matthews | 67 | 70 | 69 | 206 | 7,450 |
| Tyrone van Aswegen | 68 | 68 | 70 | 206 | 7,450 |
| Doug McGuigan | 69 | 66 | 71 | 206 | 7,450 |
| Nico Le Grange | 69 | 66 | 71 | 206 | 7,450 |
| Hennie Otto | 67 | 67 | 72 | 206 | 7,450 |
| Marc Cayeux | 71 | 67 | 69 | 207 | 6,150 |
| Grant Veenstra | 70 | 66 | 71 | 207 | 6,150 |
| Gary Thain | 67 | 69 | 71 | 207 | 6,150 |
| Nico van Rensburg | 69 | 65 | 73 | 207 | 6,150 |
| Omar Sandys | 70 | 70 | 68 | 208 | 5,475 |
| Alan Michell | 71 | 68 | 69 | 208 | 5,475 |
| Desvonde Botes | 71 | 68 | 69 | 208 | 5,475 |
| Andrew Curlewis | 68 | 69 | 71 | 208 | 5,475 |
| Mohamed Tayob | 68 | 71 | 70 | 209 | 5,025 |
| Titch Moore | 69 | 68 | 72 | 209 | 5,025 |
| Keith Horne | 70 | 71 | 69 | 210 | 4,800 |
| Ross Wellington | 73 | 71 | 67 | 211 | 4,325 |
| Jeff Inglis | 71 | 72 | 68 | 211 | 4,325 |
| Trevor Fisher, Jr. | 75 | 67 | 69 | 211 | 4,325 |
| Anil Shah | 70 | 70 | 71 | 211 | 4,325 |
| Adilson da Silva | 70 | 70 | 71 | 211 | 4,325 |
| Callie Swart | 72 | 68 | 71 | 211 | 4,325 |
| Sean Farrell | 70 | 69 | 72 | 211 | 4,325 |

## HSBC Champions Tournament

See Asia/Japan Tours chapter.

## Limpopo Classic

*Polokwane Golf Club,* Pietersburg, South Africa
Par 35-36–71; 7,101 yards

November 17-20
purse, R1,000,000

| | SCORES | | | | TOTAL | MONEY |
|---|---|---|---|---|---|---|
| Bradford Vaughan | 65 | 67 | 64 | 69 | 265 | R158,500 |
| Titch Moore | 64 | 71 | 67 | 66 | 268 | 115,000 |
| Richard Sterne | 66 | 66 | 71 | 66 | 269 | 53,100 |
| Darren Fichardt | 69 | 66 | 68 | 66 | 269 | 53,100 |
| Retief Goosen | 68 | 66 | 68 | 67 | 269 | 53,100 |
| Mark Murless | 68 | 70 | 66 | 66 | 270 | 29,433.33 |
| Tjaart van der Walt | 71 | 62 | 70 | 67 | 270 | 29,433.33 |
| Grant Veenstra | 66 | 70 | 65 | 69 | 270 | 29,433.33 |
| Chris Williams | 68 | 67 | 70 | 66 | 271 | 20,100 |
| Dion Fourie | 68 | 65 | 70 | 68 | 271 | 20,100 |
| Keith Horne | 71 | 65 | 71 | 65 | 272 | 16,100 |
| Ulrich van den Berg | 69 | 66 | 71 | 66 | 272 | 16,100 |
| James Kingston | 69 | 67 | 69 | 67 | 272 | 16,100 |
| Anton Haig | 66 | 70 | 68 | 68 | 272 | 16,100 |
| Jon Bethwaite | 67 | 67 | 73 | 66 | 273 | 13,850 |
| Nic Henning | 70 | 64 | 69 | 70 | 273 | 13,850 |
| Brett Liddle | 74 | 68 | 68 | 65 | 275 | 12,850 |
| Mohamed Tayob | 69 | 69 | 69 | 68 | 275 | 12,850 |
| Hennie Otto | 75 | 66 | 69 | 66 | 276 | 11,360 |
| Charl Schwartzel | 70 | 70 | 69 | 67 | 276 | 11,360 |
| Dean Lambert | 69 | 70 | 68 | 69 | 276 | 11,360 |
| Alan Michell | 76 | 64 | 67 | 69 | 276 | 11,360 |
| Werner Geyer | 71 | 69 | 66 | 70 | 276 | 11,360 |
| Tongoona Charamba | 72 | 68 | 70 | 67 | 277 | 10,100 |
| Johan Kok | 66 | 69 | 73 | 69 | 277 | 10,100 |
| Leonard Loxton | 69 | 70 | 69 | 69 | 277 | 10,100 |
| Michiel Bothma | 68 | 72 | 71 | 67 | 278 | 8,920 |
| Barry Painting | 71 | 71 | 69 | 67 | 278 | 8,920 |
| Doug McGuigan | 71 | 67 | 71 | 69 | 278 | 8,920 |
| Andre Cruse | 69 | 69 | 70 | 70 | 278 | 8,920 |
| Jeff Inglis | 72 | 66 | 70 | 70 | 278 | 8,920 |

## Nelson Mandela Invitational

*Arabella Country Club,* Hermanus, South Africa
Par 36-36–72; 6,976 yards

November 26-27
purse, R250,000

| | SCORES | | TOTAL | MONEY (Each) |
|---|---|---|---|---|
| Tim Clark/Vincent Tshabalala | 63 | 64 | 127 | R125,000 |
| Trevor Immelman/Gary Player | 65 | 66 | 131 | |
| John Bland/Retief Goosen | 66 | 67 | 133 | |
| Bobby Lincoln/Charl Schwartzel | 67 | 66 | 133 | |
| Mark McNulty/Omar Sandys | 69 | 65 | 134 | |
| Simon Hobday/Lee Westwood | 67 | 68 | 135 | |
| Hugh Baiocchi/Catrin Nilsmark | 71 | 71 | 142 | |
| Andrew Coltart/Solly Sepeng | 70 | 74 | 144 | |

# Nedbank Golf Challenge

*Gary Player Country Club,* Sun City, South Africa  
Par 36-36–72; 7,832 yards

December 1-4  
purse, US$4,060,000

| | SCORES | | | | TOTAL | MONEY |
|---|---|---|---|---|---|---|
| Jim Furyk | 68 | 70 | 72 | 72 | 282 | $1,200,000 |
| Darren Clarke | 67 | 70 | 76 | 69 | 282 | 433,000 |
| Retief Goosen | 70 | 69 | 71 | 72 | 282 | 433,000 |
| Adam Scott | 72 | 69 | 68 | 73 | 282 | 433,000 |
| (Furyk defeated Goosen on first and Clarke and Scott on second playoff hole.) | | | | | | |
| Luke Donald | 70 | 68 | 75 | 70 | 283 | 250,000 |
| Tim Clark | 70 | 72 | 67 | 75 | 284 | 225,000 |
| Chris DiMarco | 72 | 71 | 72 | 73 | 288 | 210,000 |
| Angel Cabrera | 71 | 64 | 74 | 80 | 289 | 195,000 |
| Ernie Els | 72 | 70 | 73 | 75 | 290 | 185,000 |
| Kenny Perry | 76 | 72 | 75 | 68 | 291 | 175,000 |
| Sergio Garcia | 74 | 70 | 74 | 74 | 292 | 165,000 |
| Stewart Cink | 73 | 76 | 78 | 71 | 298 | 155,000 |

# Dunhill Championship

*Leopard Creek Country Club,* Malelane, South Africa  
Par 35-37–72; 7,249 yards

December 8-11  
purse, €1,000,000

| | SCORES | | | | TOTAL | MONEY |
|---|---|---|---|---|---|---|
| Ernie Els | 71 | 67 | 68 | 68 | 274 | €158,579 |
| Louis Oosthuizen | 69 | 67 | 71 | 70 | 277 | 92,096 |
| Charl Schwartzel | 70 | 67 | 70 | 70 | 277 | 92,096 |
| Trevor Immelman | 69 | 69 | 74 | 68 | 280 | 38,619 |
| Bobby Lincoln | 72 | 70 | 73 | 65 | 280 | 38,619 |
| David Lynn | 73 | 68 | 71 | 68 | 280 | 38,619 |
| Ulrich van den Berg | 70 | 69 | 65 | 76 | 280 | 38,619 |
| Sean Farrell | 69 | 68 | 73 | 71 | 281 | 20,485 |
| Joakim Haeggman | 70 | 70 | 73 | 68 | 281 | 20,485 |
| Alan Michell | 70 | 68 | 71 | 72 | 281 | 20,485 |
| Jaco Van Zyl | 68 | 71 | 69 | 73 | 281 | 20,485 |
| Thomas Aiken | 69 | 71 | 73 | 69 | 282 | 15,608 |
| Phillip Archer | 66 | 70 | 74 | 72 | 282 | 15,608 |
| Titch Moore | 68 | 68 | 73 | 73 | 282 | 15,608 |
| Gregory Bourdy | 74 | 69 | 69 | 71 | 283 | 13,607 |
| Johan Edfors | 68 | 73 | 72 | 70 | 283 | 13,607 |
| Richard Finch | 73 | 68 | 71 | 71 | 283 | 13,607 |
| Ariel Canete | 72 | 69 | 71 | 72 | 284 | 11,572 |
| Pelle Edberg | 71 | 71 | 71 | 71 | 284 | 11,572 |
| Mattias Eliasson | 73 | 72 | 65 | 74 | 284 | 11,572 |
| Keith Horne | 73 | 71 | 65 | 75 | 284 | 11,572 |
| Doug McGuigan | 68 | 69 | 72 | 75 | 284 | 11,572 |
| Ross Wellington | 72 | 68 | 76 | 68 | 284 | 11,572 |
| Miguel Carballo | 70 | 75 | 69 | 71 | 285 | 10,105 |
| Gary Clark | 69 | 73 | 74 | 69 | 285 | 10,105 |
| Gary Murphy | 71 | 69 | 77 | 68 | 285 | 10,105 |
| Michiel Bothma | 64 | 71 | 78 | 73 | 286 | 8,471 |
| James Kingston | 70 | 67 | 73 | 76 | 286 | 8,471 |
| Jonathan Lomas | 72 | 67 | 72 | 75 | 286 | 8,471 |
| Martin Maritz | 71 | 73 | 69 | 73 | 286 | 8,471 |
| Damien McGrane | 70 | 70 | 76 | 70 | 286 | 8,471 |

| | SCORES | | | TOTAL | MONEY |
|---|---|---|---|---|---|
| Matthew Millar | 73 | 67 | 73 | 73 | 286 | 8,471 |
| Brandon Pieters | 70 | 74 | 73 | 69 | 286 | 8,471 |
| Jarmo Sandelin | 67 | 73 | 73 | 73 | 286 | 8,471 |
| Richard Sterne | 72 | 71 | 73 | 70 | 286 | 8,471 |
| David Carter | 69 | 73 | 74 | 71 | 287 | 6,603 |
| Michael Lamb | 73 | 72 | 67 | 75 | 287 | 6,603 |
| Jean-Francois Remesy | 71 | 71 | 74 | 71 | 287 | 6,603 |
| Stephen Scahill | 72 | 66 | 73 | 76 | 287 | 6,603 |
| Marcel Siem | 72 | 71 | 73 | 71 | 287 | 6,603 |
| Tjaart van der Walt | 72 | 70 | 73 | 72 | 287 | 6,603 |
| Steve van Vuuren | 72 | 72 | 73 | 70 | 287 | 6,603 |
| Grant Veenstra | 69 | 68 | 74 | 76 | 287 | 6,603 |
| Leif Westerberg | 70 | 73 | 71 | 73 | 287 | 6,603 |
| Felipe Aguilar | 71 | 70 | 71 | 76 | 288 | 5,103 |
| Nic Henning | 70 | 67 | 80 | 71 | 288 | 5,103 |
| Garry Houston | 74 | 69 | 70 | 75 | 288 | 5,103 |
| Francesco Molinari | 71 | 71 | 76 | 70 | 288 | 5,103 |
| Christian Nilsson | 68 | 71 | 70 | 79 | 288 | 5,103 |
| Tyrone Van Aswegen | 70 | 75 | 70 | 73 | 288 | 5,103 |
| Tuomas Tuovinen | 68 | 74 | 72 | 75 | 289 | 4,402 |
| Magnus P. Atlevi | 70 | 73 | 73 | 74 | 290 | 4,002 |
| Matthew Richardson | 74 | 68 | 75 | 73 | 290 | 4,002 |
| Oliver Whiteley | 73 | 69 | 71 | 77 | 290 | 4,002 |
| Ross Fisher | 68 | 72 | 71 | 80 | 291 | 3,502 |
| Patrick O'Brien | 70 | 70 | 75 | 76 | 291 | 3,502 |
| Gregory Havret | 71 | 70 | 70 | 81 | 292 | 3,102 |
| Sam Walker | 71 | 74 | 74 | 73 | 292 | 3,102 |
| Ben Willman | 71 | 71 | 74 | 76 | 292 | 3,102 |
| Andrew Butterfield | 72 | 73 | 73 | 76 | 294 | 2,651 |
| Jason Kelly | 73 | 70 | 79 | 72 | 294 | 2,651 |
| Brett Liddle | 78 | 67 | 73 | 76 | 294 | 2,651 |
| Mike Michell | 71 | 72 | 76 | 75 | 294 | 2,651 |
| Hennie Otto | 76 | 68 | 72 | 78 | 294 | 2,651 |
| Justin Walters | 71 | 69 | 75 | 79 | 294 | 2,651 |
| Adilson da Silva | 73 | 71 | 72 | 79 | 295 | 2,251 |
| Johan Kok | 69 | 74 | 73 | 79 | 295 | 2,251 |
| Jean Hugo | 67 | 74 | 74 | 81 | 296 | 1,901 |
| Toni Karjalainen | 69 | 72 | 81 | 74 | 296 | 1,901 |
| Thabang Simon | 71 | 72 | 75 | 78 | 296 | 1,901 |
| Anders Sjostrand | 75 | 67 | 73 | 81 | 296 | 1,901 |
| Nico van Rensburg | 72 | 72 | 76 | 76 | 296 | 1,901 |
| Darren Fichardt | 71 | 73 | 76 | 77 | 297 | 1,501 |
| Anton Haig | 79 | 66 | 80 | 72 | 297 | 1,501 |
| Francisco Valera | 72 | 71 | 76 | 78 | 297 | 1,501 |
| Phil Worthington | 73 | 71 | 77 | 81 | 302 | 1,398 |
| Neil Cheetham | 73 | 70 | 80 | 80 | 303 | 1,395 |

## South African Airways Open

*The Links,* Fancourt, South Africa
Par 36-37–73; 7,435 yards

December 15-18
purse, €1,000,000

| | SCORES | | | TOTAL | MONEY |
|---|---|---|---|---|---|
| Retief Goosen | 73 | 70 | 69 | 70 | 282 | €158,579.29 |
| Ernie Els | 76 | 70 | 69 | 68 | 283 | 115,057.53 |
| Gregory Bourdy | 75 | 75 | 70 | 70 | 290 | 59,129.57 |
| Darren Fichardt | 78 | 69 | 69 | 74 | 290 | 59,129.57 |

| | SCORES | | | TOTAL | MONEY |
|---|---|---|---|---|---|
| Gregory Havret | 72 | 74 | 74 | 72 | 292 | 35,117.56 |
| Keith Horne | 73 | 72 | 72 | 75 | 292 | 35,117.56 |
| Mattias Eliasson | 70 | 75 | 72 | 75 | 292 | 35,117.56 |
| Francesco Molinari | 71 | 75 | 72 | 75 | 293 | 24,112.06 |
| Tim Clark | 68 | 78 | 72 | 76 | 294 | 20,110.06 |
| Ross Fisher | 68 | 70 | 78 | 78 | 294 | 20,110.06 |
| James Kingston | 71 | 73 | 76 | 75 | 295 | 17,608.80 |
| Trevor Immelman | 77 | 74 | 73 | 72 | 296 | 15,607.80 |
| Hendrik Buhrmann | 80 | 73 | 69 | 74 | 296 | 15,607.80 |
| Charl Schwartzel | 70 | 74 | 75 | 77 | 296 | 15,607.80 |
| Bobby Lincoln | 77 | 73 | 75 | 72 | 297 | 13,606.80 |
| Tjaart van der Walt | 76 | 71 | 75 | 75 | 297 | 13,606.80 |
| Ian Hutchings | 74 | 74 | 72 | 77 | 297 | 13,606.80 |
| Andrew McLardy | 72 | 78 | 74 | 74 | 298 | 11,930.96 |
| Mike Lamb | 79 | 72 | 73 | 74 | 298 | 11,930.96 |
| Johan Edfors | 73 | 75 | 72 | 78 | 298 | 11,930.96 |
| Louis Oosthuizen | 76 | 72 | 69 | 81 | 298 | 11,930.96 |
| Jean-Francois Remesy | 75 | 72 | 76 | 76 | 299 | 10,705.35 |
| Miguel Carballo | 78 | 76 | 69 | 76 | 299 | 10,705.35 |
| Henrik Nystrom | 69 | 77 | 73 | 80 | 299 | 10,705.35 |
| Gary Clark | 77 | 76 | 72 | 75 | 300 | 9,354.68 |
| Ariel Canete | 79 | 75 | 71 | 75 | 300 | 9,354.68 |
| Leif Westerberg | 76 | 72 | 76 | 76 | 300 | 9,354.68 |
| David Lynn | 72 | 74 | 77 | 77 | 300 | 9,354.68 |
| Oliver Whiteley | 72 | 75 | 76 | 77 | 300 | 9,354.68 |
| Jean Hugo | 73 | 74 | 75 | 78 | 300 | 9,354.68 |
| Peter Karmis | 76 | 75 | 77 | 73 | 301 | 8,004 |
| Des Terblanche | 76 | 74 | 75 | 76 | 301 | 8,004 |
| David Dixon | 77 | 77 | 71 | 76 | 301 | 8,004 |
| Mark Murless | 75 | 75 | 74 | 77 | 301 | 8,004 |
| Justin Rose | 74 | 75 | 74 | 78 | 301 | 8,004 |
| John Bele | 72 | 73 | 83 | 74 | 302 | 6,703.35 |
| Phillip Archer | 74 | 73 | 80 | 75 | 302 | 6,703.35 |
| Steve van Vuuren | 75 | 77 | 74 | 76 | 302 | 6,703.35 |
| Jonathan Lomas | 76 | 73 | 76 | 77 | 302 | 6,703.35 |
| David Drysdale | 77 | 77 | 71 | 77 | 302 | 6,703.35 |
| Marc Cayeux | 75 | 75 | 73 | 79 | 302 | 6,703.35 |
| Leonard Loxton | 73 | 71 | 78 | 80 | 302 | 6,703.35 |
| Warren Abery | 75 | 74 | 73 | 80 | 302 | 6,703.35 |
| Ross Wellington | 78 | 76 | 78 | 71 | 303 | 5,602.80 |
| Lee Slattery | 76 | 75 | 76 | 76 | 303 | 5,602.80 |
| Richard Sterne | 75 | 73 | 78 | 77 | 303 | 5,602.80 |
| Michele Reale | 78 | 75 | 77 | 74 | 304 | 4,802.40 |
| Andrew Coltart | 75 | 76 | 78 | 75 | 304 | 4,802.40 |
| Omar Sandys | 79 | 74 | 76 | 75 | 304 | 4,802.40 |
| Martin Maritz | 78 | 76 | 73 | 77 | 304 | 4,802.40 |
| Scott Dunlap | 74 | 77 | 72 | 81 | 304 | 4,802.40 |
| Malcolm Mackenzie | 75 | 77 | 81 | 72 | 305 | 3,701.85 |
| Dean Lambert | 73 | 78 | 80 | 74 | 305 | 3,701.85 |
| Michiel Bothma | 82 | 71 | 77 | 75 | 305 | 3,701.85 |
| Alan Michell | 75 | 75 | 79 | 76 | 305 | 3,701.85 |
| Andrew Butterfield | 74 | 77 | 78 | 76 | 305 | 3,701.85 |
| Desvonde Botes | 73 | 80 | 75 | 77 | 305 | 3,701.85 |
| Patrick O'Brien | 78 | 74 | 87 | 67 | 306 | 2,801.40 |
| Adilson da Silva | 79 | 74 | 80 | 73 | 306 | 2,801.40 |
| Francisco Valera | 77 | 77 | 77 | 75 | 306 | 2,801.40 |
| Dijon Tintinger | 77 | 77 | 77 | 75 | 306 | 2,801.40 |
| Kevin Stone | 75 | 74 | 78 | 79 | 306 | 2,801.40 |
| Joakim Haeggman | 76 | 75 | 76 | 79 | 306 | 2,801.40 |
| David Griffiths | 73 | 77 | 75 | 81 | 306 | 2,801.40 |

| | SCORES | | | | TOTAL | MONEY |
|---|---|---|---|---|---|---|
| Chris Davison | 75 | 75 | 79 | 78 | 307 | 2,351.18 |
| Titch Moore | 74 | 76 | 79 | 78 | 307 | 2,351.18 |
| Brett Liddle | 79 | 75 | 79 | 75 | 308 | 2,001 |
| Doug McGuigan | 79 | 72 | 81 | 76 | 308 | 2,001 |
| Jaco Van Zyl | 71 | 82 | 78 | 77 | 308 | 2,001 |
| Anton Haig | 72 | 79 | 79 | 78 | 308 | 2,001 |
| Garry Houston | 82 | 72 | 76 | 78 | 308 | 2,001 |
| Trevor Fisher, Jr. | 77 | 75 | 82 | 75 | 309 | 1,700.85 |
| Bradford Vaughan | 77 | 76 | 78 | 79 | 310 | 1,600.80 |
| James Kamte | 77 | 75 | 80 | 79 | 311 | 1,450.73 |
| Warrick Druian | 72 | 78 | 80 | 81 | 311 | 1,450.73 |
| Ashley Roestoff | 80 | 73 | 83 | 76 | 312 | 1,397 |
| Shaun Norris | 75 | 79 | 84 | 75 | 313 | 1,391 |
| Steven Jeppesen | 80 | 72 | 83 | 78 | 313 | 1,391 |
| Felipe Aguilar | 77 | 77 | 81 | 78 | 313 | 1,391 |
| Neil Cheetham | 76 | 78 | 80 | 88 | 322 | 1,385 |

# Senior Tours

## MasterCard Championship

*Hualalai Golf Club*, Ka'upulehu-Kona, Hawaii
Par 36-36–72; 7,053 yards

January 21-23
purse, $1,600,000

| | SCORES | | | TOTAL | MONEY |
|---|---|---|---|---|---|
| Dana Quigley | 67 | 65 | 66 | 198 | $272,000 |
| Tom Watson | 64 | 64 | 70 | 198 | 163,000 |
| (Quigley defeated Watson on third playoff hole.) | | | | | |
| Hale Irwin | 69 | 65 | 65 | 199 | 110,000 |
| Gil Morgan | 68 | 64 | 67 | 199 | 110,000 |
| Wayne Levi | 66 | 65 | 71 | 202 | 77,500 |
| Mark McNulty | 69 | 66 | 67 | 202 | 77,500 |
| Rodger Davis | 68 | 69 | 66 | 203 | 60,500 |
| Craig Stadler | 67 | 67 | 69 | 203 | 60,500 |
| Tom Purtzer | 68 | 67 | 69 | 204 | 51,000 |
| Peter Jacobsen | 69 | 69 | 67 | 205 | 43,250 |
| Fuzzy Zoeller | 68 | 68 | 69 | 205 | 43,250 |
| David Eger | 70 | 69 | 67 | 206 | 35,500 |
| Bob Gilder | 68 | 67 | 71 | 206 | 35,500 |
| Morris Hatalsky | 67 | 70 | 69 | 206 | 35,500 |
| Bruce Fleisher | 69 | 69 | 69 | 207 | 30,000 |
| John Jacobs | 67 | 67 | 73 | 207 | 30,000 |
| Tom Jenkins | 69 | 67 | 72 | 208 | 26,250 |
| Don Pooley | 69 | 67 | 72 | 208 | 26,250 |
| Jim Ahern | 70 | 69 | 70 | 209 | 21,000 |
| Ed Fiori | 71 | 68 | 70 | 209 | 21,000 |
| Stewart Ginn | 69 | 71 | 69 | 209 | 21,000 |
| Mark James | 71 | 67 | 71 | 209 | 21,000 |
| Tom Kite | 70 | 67 | 72 | 209 | 21,000 |
| Larry Nelson | 69 | 69 | 71 | 209 | 21,000 |
| D.A. Weibring | 68 | 67 | 74 | 209 | 21,000 |
| Allen Doyle | 71 | 68 | 71 | 210 | 16,166.67 |
| Bruce Lietzke | 72 | 71 | 67 | 210 | 16,166.67 |
| Vicente Fernandez | 67 | 71 | 72 | 210 | 16,166.66 |
| Jim Thorpe | 70 | 70 | 71 | 211 | 15,000 |
| Bruce Summerhays | 69 | 69 | 74 | 212 | 14,500 |
| Doug Tewell | 74 | 65 | 74 | 213 | 13,750 |
| Lee Trevino | 72 | 69 | 72 | 213 | 13,750 |
| Dave Barr | 74 | 68 | 72 | 214 | 13,000 |
| Jay Sigel | 72 | 71 | 72 | 215 | 12,500 |
| Pete Oakley | 75 | 69 | 72 | 216 | 12,000 |
| Gary Player | 74 | 74 | 71 | 219 | 11,500 |
| Arnold Palmer | 80 | 81 | 81 | 242 | 11,000 |

## Turtle Bay Championship

*Turtle Bay Resort, Palmer Course*, Oahu, Hawaii
Par 36-36–72; 7,044 yards

January 28-30
purse, $1,500,000

| | SCORES | | | TOTAL | MONEY |
|---|---|---|---|---|---|
| Hale Irwin | 67 | 66 | 67 | 200 | $225,000 |
| Dana Quigley | 68 | 68 | 69 | 205 | 132,000 |

| | SCORES | | | TOTAL | MONEY |
|---|---|---|---|---|---|
| Allen Doyle | 67 | 68 | 71 | 206 | 99,000 |
| Tom Watson | 70 | 69 | 67 | 206 | 99,000 |
| Bruce Fleisher | 70 | 72 | 65 | 207 | 55,200 |
| Wayne Levi | 68 | 70 | 69 | 207 | 55,200 |
| Dick Mast | 69 | 69 | 69 | 207 | 55,200 |
| Don Pooley | 70 | 67 | 70 | 207 | 55,200 |
| Jay Sigel | 69 | 70 | 68 | 207 | 55,200 |
| Larry Nelson | 69 | 68 | 71 | 208 | 36,000 |
| Don Reese | 70 | 68 | 70 | 208 | 36,000 |
| Jim Thorpe | 68 | 71 | 69 | 208 | 36,000 |
| Tom McKnight | 70 | 68 | 71 | 209 | 29,250 |
| Mark McNulty | 70 | 71 | 68 | 209 | 29,250 |
| Keith Fergus | 67 | 69 | 74 | 210 | 24,030 |
| Joe Inman | 70 | 71 | 69 | 210 | 24,030 |
| Gary McCord | 68 | 73 | 69 | 210 | 24,030 |
| Gil Morgan | 67 | 69 | 74 | 210 | 24,030 |
| John Ross | 70 | 71 | 69 | 210 | 24,030 |
| Tom Herzan | 72 | 69 | 70 | 211 | 18,600 |
| Tom Jenkins | 71 | 69 | 71 | 211 | 18,600 |
| Bruce Lietzke | 69 | 70 | 72 | 211 | 18,600 |
| Brad Bryant | 70 | 70 | 72 | 212 | 15,375 |
| Walter Hall | 70 | 70 | 72 | 212 | 15,375 |
| Ron Streck | 73 | 70 | 69 | 212 | 15,375 |
| Bobby Wadkins | 69 | 71 | 72 | 212 | 15,375 |
| Jim Colbert | 73 | 72 | 68 | 213 | 11,914.29 |
| Bob Gilder | 68 | 72 | 73 | 213 | 11,914.29 |
| Mike Reid | 69 | 71 | 73 | 213 | 11,914.29 |
| D.A. Weibring | 70 | 69 | 74 | 213 | 11,914.29 |
| Jim Ahern | 71 | 68 | 74 | 213 | 11,914.28 |
| John Harris | 70 | 69 | 74 | 213 | 11,914.28 |
| John Jacobs | 70 | 69 | 74 | 213 | 11,914.28 |
| R.W. Eaks | 69 | 70 | 75 | 214 | 9,225 |
| Graham Marsh | 71 | 70 | 73 | 214 | 9,225 |
| Jerry Pate | 71 | 67 | 76 | 214 | 9,225 |
| Tom Purtzer | 70 | 71 | 73 | 214 | 9,225 |
| Hugh Baiocchi | 69 | 70 | 76 | 215 | 7,950 |
| Morris Hatalsky | 69 | 70 | 76 | 215 | 7,950 |
| Leonard Thompson | 73 | 70 | 72 | 215 | 7,950 |

## ACE Group Classic

*The Club at TwinEagles*, Naples, Florida
Par 36-36–72; 7,102 yards

February 18-20
purse, $1,600,000

| | SCORES | | | TOTAL | MONEY |
|---|---|---|---|---|---|
| Mark James | 69 | 68 | 66 | 203 | $240,000 |
| Hale Irwin | 67 | 70 | 68 | 205 | 128,000 |
| Tom Wargo | 70 | 69 | 66 | 205 | 128,000 |
| Mike Reid | 70 | 68 | 68 | 206 | 78,933.34 |
| Mike McCullough | 66 | 69 | 71 | 206 | 78,933.33 |
| Jerry Pate | 68 | 70 | 68 | 206 | 78,933.33 |
| Wayne Levi | 68 | 72 | 67 | 207 | 57,600 |
| Morris Hatalsky | 70 | 72 | 66 | 208 | 44,000 |
| Tom Jenkins | 72 | 70 | 66 | 208 | 44,000 |
| Bruce Lietzke | 71 | 69 | 68 | 208 | 44,000 |
| Des Smyth | 69 | 72 | 67 | 208 | 44,000 |
| Jim Albus | 72 | 67 | 70 | 209 | 31,600 |

| | SCORES | | | TOTAL | MONEY |
|---|---|---|---|---|---|
| Rodger Davis | 72 | 70 | 67 | 209 | 31,600 |
| Bruce Fleisher | 70 | 71 | 68 | 209 | 31,600 |
| Don Pooley | 69 | 70 | 70 | 209 | 31,600 |
| R.W. Eaks | 66 | 72 | 72 | 210 | 26,400 |
| D.A. Weibring | 70 | 69 | 71 | 210 | 26,400 |
| Don Reese | 72 | 69 | 70 | 211 | 24,000 |
| Tom Purtzer | 70 | 73 | 69 | 212 | 21,173.34 |
| Joe Inman | 71 | 72 | 69 | 212 | 21,173.33 |
| Dana Quigley | 72 | 70 | 70 | 212 | 21,173.33 |
| Mark Johnson | 72 | 75 | 66 | 213 | 16,453.34 |
| Leonard Thompson | 68 | 74 | 71 | 213 | 16,453.34 |
| Hajime Meshiai | 74 | 74 | 65 | 213 | 16,453.33 |
| Gil Morgan | 70 | 69 | 74 | 213 | 16,453.33 |
| J.C. Snead | 71 | 69 | 73 | 213 | 16,453.33 |
| Jim Thorpe | 68 | 73 | 72 | 213 | 16,453.33 |
| Brad Bryant | 75 | 69 | 70 | 214 | 12,960 |
| Walter Hall | 72 | 73 | 69 | 214 | 12,960 |
| Rick Rhoden | 73 | 73 | 68 | 214 | 12,960 |
| Ron Streck | 68 | 71 | 75 | 214 | 12,960 |
| David Eger | 78 | 72 | 65 | 215 | 10,800 |
| Gary Koch | 70 | 75 | 70 | 215 | 10,800 |
| Mike Sullivan | 77 | 72 | 66 | 215 | 10,800 |
| Bobby Wadkins | 70 | 73 | 72 | 215 | 10,800 |
| Jim Ahern | 70 | 75 | 71 | 216 | 8,832 |
| Raymond Floyd | 70 | 75 | 71 | 216 | 8,832 |
| Graham Marsh | 71 | 72 | 73 | 216 | 8,832 |
| Mark McNulty | 74 | 72 | 70 | 216 | 8,832 |
| Craig Stadler | 73 | 77 | 66 | 216 | 8,832 |

## Outback Steakhouse Pro-Am

*TPC of Tampa Bay,* Lutz, Florida
Par 35-36–71; 6,783 yards
(Event shortened to 36 holes and completed on Monday — rain.)

February 25-28
purse, $1,600,000

| | SCORES | | TOTAL | MONEY |
|---|---|---|---|---|
| Hale Irwin | 66 | 68 | 134 | $240,000 |
| Morris Hatalsky | 68 | 67 | 135 | 128,800 |
| Mark McNulty | 67 | 68 | 135 | 128,800 |
| Vicente Fernandez | 67 | 69 | 136 | 86,400 |
| Tom Wargo | 68 | 68 | 136 | 86,400 |
| Wayne Levi | 69 | 68 | 137 | 57,600 |
| Jerry Pate | 70 | 67 | 137 | 57,600 |
| Don Pooley | 69 | 68 | 137 | 57,600 |
| Tom Kite | 68 | 70 | 138 | 41,600 |
| Mark McCumber | 68 | 70 | 138 | 41,600 |
| D.A. Weibring | 69 | 69 | 138 | 41,600 |
| John Jacobs | 68 | 71 | 139 | 31,600 |
| Gary Koch | 69 | 70 | 139 | 31,600 |
| Graham Marsh | 68 | 71 | 139 | 31,600 |
| Tom Purtzer | 69 | 70 | 139 | 31,600 |
| John Harris | 65 | 75 | 140 | 23,386.67 |
| Tom McKnight | 69 | 71 | 140 | 23,386.67 |
| Craig Stadler | 72 | 68 | 140 | 23,386.67 |
| Fuzzy Zoeller | 72 | 68 | 140 | 23,386.67 |
| Brad Bryant | 67 | 73 | 140 | 23,386.66 |
| Pete Oakley | 70 | 70 | 140 | 23,386.66 |

|  | SCORES | | | TOTAL | MONEY |
|---|---|---|---|---|---|
| Ron Streck | 70 | 71 | | 141 | 17,653.34 |
| Andy Bean | 71 | 70 | | 141 | 17,653.33 |
| Rodger Davis | 71 | 70 | | 141 | 17,653.33 |
| John Bland | 71 | 71 | | 142 | 14,266.67 |
| Tom Jenkins | 67 | 75 | | 142 | 14,266.67 |
| Mark Johnson | 69 | 73 | | 142 | 14,266.67 |
| Jim Thorpe | 73 | 69 | | 142 | 14,266.67 |
| Jim Dent | 69 | 73 | | 142 | 14,266.66 |
| Bruce Fleisher | 68 | 74 | | 142 | 14,266.66 |
| Ben Crenshaw | 72 | 71 | | 143 | 10,560 |
| Bob Gilder | 71 | 72 | | 143 | 10,560 |
| Gil Morgan | 74 | 69 | | 143 | 10,560 |
| Don Reese | 69 | 74 | | 143 | 10,560 |
| Mike Reid | 70 | 73 | | 143 | 10,560 |
| Curtis Strange | 72 | 71 | | 143 | 10,560 |
| Bobby Wadkins | 69 | 74 | | 143 | 10,560 |
| Bob Eastwood | 74 | 70 | | 144 | 8,000 |
| David Eger | 72 | 72 | | 144 | 8,000 |
| Keith Fergus | 73 | 71 | | 144 | 8,000 |
| Ed Fiori | 70 | 74 | | 144 | 8,000 |
| Gary Player | 70 | 74 | | 144 | 8,000 |
| Des Smyth | 71 | 73 | | 144 | 8,000 |

## SBC Classic

*Valencia Country Club,* Valencia, California
Par 36-36–72; 6,905 yards

March 11-13
purse, $1,550,000

|  | SCORES | | | TOTAL | MONEY |
|---|---|---|---|---|---|
| Des Smyth | 71 | 72 | 68 | 211 | $232,500 |
| Mark McNulty | 72 | 66 | 74 | 212 | 124,000 |
| D.A. Weibring | 71 | 69 | 72 | 212 | 124,000 |
| Gary McCord | 74 | 66 | 73 | 213 | 83,700 |
| Craig Stadler | 72 | 72 | 69 | 213 | 83,700 |
| Keith Fergus | 72 | 65 | 77 | 214 | 58,900 |
| Mike Reid | 70 | 71 | 73 | 214 | 58,900 |
| Brad Bryant | 73 | 74 | 68 | 215 | 46,500 |
| Tom McKnight | 74 | 70 | 71 | 215 | 46,500 |
| Bruce Fleisher | 75 | 71 | 70 | 216 | 37,200 |
| Don Pooley | 72 | 71 | 73 | 216 | 37,200 |
| Don Reese | 72 | 73 | 71 | 216 | 37,200 |
| Lanny Wadkins | 73 | 70 | 74 | 217 | 31,000 |
| Hale Irwin | 73 | 73 | 72 | 218 | 25,600.84 |
| Bruce Summerhays | 78 | 71 | 69 | 218 | 25,600.84 |
| Isao Aoki | 69 | 73 | 76 | 218 | 25,600.83 |
| Wayne Levi | 76 | 68 | 74 | 218 | 25,600.83 |
| Tom Purtzer | 72 | 73 | 73 | 218 | 25,600.83 |
| Dana Quigley | 77 | 69 | 72 | 218 | 25,600.83 |
| Andy Bean | 76 | 70 | 73 | 219 | 18,677.50 |
| Hajime Meshiai | 76 | 70 | 73 | 219 | 18,677.50 |
| Mike Sullivan | 78 | 73 | 68 | 219 | 18,677.50 |
| Bobby Wadkins | 75 | 72 | 72 | 219 | 18,677.50 |
| David Eger | 73 | 73 | 74 | 220 | 15,887.50 |
| Jerry Pate | 72 | 74 | 74 | 220 | 15,887.50 |
| Rodger Davis | 77 | 75 | 69 | 221 | 12,348.34 |
| Ed Dougherty | 78 | 73 | 70 | 221 | 12,348.34 |
| Walter Hall | 74 | 76 | 71 | 221 | 12,348.34 |

| | SCORES | | | TOTAL | MONEY |
|---|---|---|---|---|---|
| Jim Colbert | 77 | 72 | 72 | 221 | 12,348.33 |
| R.W. Eaks | 75 | 73 | 73 | 221 | 12,348.33 |
| Bob Gilder | 71 | 72 | 78 | 221 | 12,348.33 |
| Morris Hatalsky | 73 | 71 | 77 | 221 | 12,348.33 |
| Tom Jenkins | 73 | 75 | 73 | 221 | 12,348.33 |
| Lonnie Nielsen | 74 | 72 | 75 | 221 | 12,348.33 |
| John Bland | 76 | 74 | 72 | 222 | 8,757.50 |
| Allen Doyle | 77 | 69 | 76 | 222 | 8,757.50 |
| Vicente Fernandez | 76 | 71 | 75 | 222 | 8,757.50 |
| Bruce Lietzke | 82 | 71 | 69 | 222 | 8,757.50 |
| Jim Thorpe | 74 | 73 | 75 | 222 | 8,757.50 |
| Tom Wargo | 75 | 73 | 74 | 222 | 8,757.50 |

## Toshiba Senior Classic

*Newport Beach Country Club,* Newport Beach, California  
Par 35-36–71; 6,571 yards

March 18-20  
purse, $1,650,000

| | SCORES | | | TOTAL | MONEY |
|---|---|---|---|---|---|
| Mark Johnson | 67 | 63 | 70 | 200 | $247,500 |
| Keith Fergus | 67 | 66 | 71 | 204 | 132,000 |
| Wayne Levi | 66 | 68 | 70 | 204 | 132,000 |
| John Bland | 70 | 66 | 69 | 205 | 81,400 |
| Gil Morgan | 65 | 70 | 70 | 205 | 81,400 |
| Don Pooley | 70 | 70 | 65 | 205 | 81,400 |
| Rodger Davis | 70 | 68 | 68 | 206 | 59,400 |
| Jim Albus | 71 | 67 | 69 | 207 | 40,307.15 |
| Bruce Lietzke | 67 | 70 | 70 | 207 | 40,307.15 |
| Allen Doyle | 67 | 70 | 70 | 207 | 40,307.14 |
| Morris Hatalsky | 67 | 70 | 70 | 207 | 40,307.14 |
| Tom Jenkins | 66 | 68 | 73 | 207 | 40,307.14 |
| Mark McNulty | 67 | 69 | 71 | 207 | 40,307.14 |
| Dave Stockton | 69 | 68 | 70 | 207 | 40,307.14 |
| Brad Bryant | 67 | 71 | 70 | 208 | 26,433 |
| Vicente Fernandez | 68 | 71 | 69 | 208 | 26,433 |
| Bruce Fleisher | 70 | 71 | 67 | 208 | 26,433 |
| Lonnie Nielsen | 67 | 69 | 72 | 208 | 26,433 |
| Tom Purtzer | 68 | 69 | 71 | 208 | 26,433 |
| Graham Marsh | 70 | 73 | 66 | 209 | 18,005.63 |
| Des Smyth | 68 | 73 | 68 | 209 | 18,005.63 |
| J.C. Snead | 67 | 73 | 69 | 209 | 18,005.63 |
| Tom Wargo | 72 | 69 | 68 | 209 | 18,005.63 |
| Walter Hall | 70 | 69 | 70 | 209 | 18,005.62 |
| Hale Irwin | 68 | 69 | 72 | 209 | 18,005.62 |
| Tom McKnight | 72 | 68 | 69 | 209 | 18,005.62 |
| Lanny Wadkins | 69 | 68 | 72 | 209 | 18,005.62 |
| Dave Eichelberger | 68 | 68 | 74 | 210 | 13,365 |
| Joe Inman | 72 | 70 | 68 | 210 | 13,365 |
| Hajime Meshiai | 71 | 70 | 69 | 210 | 13,365 |
| D.A. Weibring | 72 | 66 | 72 | 210 | 13,365 |
| John Harris | 70 | 72 | 69 | 211 | 11,632.50 |
| Bruce Summerhays | 68 | 77 | 66 | 211 | 11,632.50 |
| Jim Ahern | 68 | 74 | 70 | 212 | 8,151 |
| Ben Crenshaw | 68 | 67 | 77 | 212 | 8,151 |
| Terry Dill | 71 | 73 | 68 | 212 | 8,151 |
| Ed Dougherty | 70 | 71 | 71 | 212 | 8,151 |
| R.W. Eaks | 71 | 68 | 73 | 212 | 8,151 |

|  | SCORES | | | TOTAL | MONEY |
|---|---|---|---|---|---|
| Raymond Floyd | 71 | 72 | 69 | 212 | 8,151 |
| Hubert Green | 73 | 68 | 71 | 212 | 8,151 |
| Jerry Pate | 73 | 69 | 70 | 212 | 8,151 |
| Don Reese | 71 | 71 | 70 | 212 | 8,151 |
| Mike Reid | 70 | 65 | 77 | 212 | 8,151 |
| Jay Sigel | 69 | 69 | 74 | 212 | 8,151 |
| Doug Tewell | 71 | 72 | 69 | 212 | 8,151 |
| Leonard Thompson | 69 | 71 | 72 | 212 | 8,151 |
| Howard Twitty | 75 | 67 | 70 | 212 | 8,151 |
| Bobby Wadkins | 70 | 69 | 73 | 212 | 8,151 |

## Liberty Mutual Legends of Golf

*Westin Savannah Harbor Golf Resort & Spa,*      April 22-24
Savannah, Georgia      purse, $2,400,000
Par 36-36–72; 6,997 yards

|  | SCORES | | | TOTAL | MONEY |
|---|---|---|---|---|---|
| Des Smyth | 66 | 71 | 71 | 208 | $382,000 |
| Tom Jenkins | 70 | 67 | 73 | 210 | 228,000 |
| Wayne Levi | 67 | 68 | 76 | 211 | 165,500 |
| Tom Purtzer | 65 | 71 | 75 | 211 | 165,500 |
| Jim Thorpe | 69 | 70 | 73 | 212 | 123,000 |
| Andy Bean | 67 | 74 | 72 | 213 | 91,000 |
| Mark McNulty | 70 | 68 | 75 | 213 | 91,000 |
| D.A. Weibring | 69 | 71 | 73 | 213 | 91,000 |
| David Eger | 72 | 70 | 72 | 214 | 61,300 |
| Bob Gilder | 71 | 68 | 75 | 214 | 61,300 |
| Jay Haas | 67 | 73 | 74 | 214 | 61,300 |
| Morris Hatalsky | 67 | 74 | 73 | 214 | 61,300 |
| Craig Stadler | 68 | 71 | 75 | 214 | 61,300 |
| Ben Crenshaw | 69 | 73 | 73 | 215 | 42,750 |
| Mark James | 71 | 70 | 74 | 215 | 42,750 |
| Gil Morgan | 68 | 71 | 76 | 215 | 42,750 |
| Leonard Thompson | 69 | 69 | 77 | 215 | 42,750 |
| Bruce Fleisher | 70 | 70 | 76 | 216 | 33,000 |
| Mark Johnson | 69 | 75 | 72 | 216 | 33,000 |
| Gary Koch | 68 | 73 | 75 | 216 | 33,000 |
| Dana Quigley | 69 | 70 | 77 | 216 | 33,000 |
| Bruce Summerhays | 70 | 72 | 74 | 216 | 33,000 |
| Allen Doyle | 70 | 73 | 74 | 217 | 24,775 |
| Tom Kite | 69 | 74 | 74 | 217 | 24,775 |
| Don Pooley | 72 | 71 | 74 | 217 | 24,775 |
| J.C. Snead | 69 | 70 | 78 | 217 | 24,775 |
| Curtis Strange | 72 | 69 | 77 | 218 | 21,200 |
| Jim Dent | 68 | 72 | 79 | 219 | 18,800 |
| Dave Eichelberger | 72 | 71 | 76 | 219 | 18,800 |
| Bobby Wadkins | 71 | 71 | 77 | 219 | 18,800 |
| John Jacobs | 74 | 72 | 74 | 220 | 16,150 |
| Dave Stockton | 73 | 72 | 75 | 220 | 16,150 |
| Bob Murphy | 73 | 72 | 76 | 221 | 14,233.34 |
| Mark McCumber | 70 | 73 | 78 | 221 | 14,233.33 |
| Jerry Pate | 72 | 72 | 77 | 221 | 14,233.33 |
| Hale Irwin | 71 | 76 | 75 | 222 | 13,100 |
| Vicente Fernandez | 72 | 75 | 76 | 223 | 12,400 |
| Pete Oakley | 73 | 70 | 80 | 223 | 12,400 |

| | SCORES | | | TOTAL | MONEY |
|---|---|---|---|---|---|
| Larry Nelson | 68 | 75 | 81 | 224 | 11,600 |
| Jay Sigel | 76 | 71 | 77 | 224 | 11,600 |

## FedEx Kinko's Classic

*The Hills Country Club,* Austin, Texas
Par 36-36–72; 6,942 yards

April 29-May 1
purse, $1,650,000

| | SCORES | | | TOTAL | MONEY |
|---|---|---|---|---|---|
| Jim Thorpe | 69 | 69 | 68 | 206 | $247,500 |
| Dana Quigley | 70 | 70 | 70 | 210 | 145,200 |
| Mark Johnson | 68 | 73 | 70 | 211 | 108,900 |
| Wayne Levi | 71 | 67 | 73 | 211 | 108,900 |
| Brad Bryant | 68 | 72 | 72 | 212 | 68,200 |
| Bruce Fleisher | 69 | 70 | 73 | 212 | 68,200 |
| Curtis Strange | 67 | 74 | 71 | 212 | 68,200 |
| Mark James | 72 | 68 | 73 | 213 | 52,800 |
| Morris Hatalsky | 70 | 72 | 72 | 214 | 42,900 |
| Graham Marsh | 70 | 75 | 69 | 214 | 42,900 |
| Craig Stadler | 74 | 71 | 69 | 214 | 42,900 |
| Bob Gilder | 72 | 74 | 69 | 215 | 32,587.50 |
| Joe Inman | 69 | 74 | 72 | 215 | 32,587.50 |
| Tom Jenkins | 74 | 73 | 68 | 215 | 32,587.50 |
| Tom Kite | 76 | 70 | 69 | 215 | 32,587.50 |
| Hajime Meshiai | 72 | 70 | 74 | 216 | 27,225 |
| Mike Reid | 72 | 74 | 70 | 216 | 27,225 |
| Gibby Gilbert | 74 | 74 | 69 | 217 | 24,007.50 |
| D.A. Weibring | 71 | 75 | 71 | 217 | 24,007.50 |
| Ed Dougherty | 75 | 72 | 71 | 218 | 19,371 |
| Keith Fergus | 71 | 75 | 72 | 218 | 19,371 |
| Gil Morgan | 71 | 72 | 75 | 218 | 19,371 |
| Bob Murphy | 72 | 74 | 72 | 218 | 19,371 |
| Tom Purtzer | 71 | 74 | 73 | 218 | 19,371 |
| David Eger | 73 | 70 | 76 | 219 | 15,730 |
| Larry Nelson | 72 | 71 | 76 | 219 | 15,730 |
| Lonnie Nielsen | 72 | 74 | 73 | 219 | 15,730 |
| Vicente Fernandez | 72 | 73 | 75 | 220 | 13,068 |
| Hale Irwin | 73 | 75 | 72 | 220 | 13,068 |
| Dan Pohl | 75 | 71 | 74 | 220 | 13,068 |
| Don Pooley | 73 | 74 | 73 | 220 | 13,068 |
| Bruce Summerhays | 73 | 72 | 75 | 220 | 13,068 |
| Rodger Davis | 76 | 71 | 74 | 221 | 10,175 |
| R.W. Eaks | 71 | 76 | 74 | 221 | 10,175 |
| Mike Hill | 74 | 73 | 74 | 221 | 10,175 |
| Tom McKnight | 73 | 76 | 72 | 221 | 10,175 |
| Dave Stockton | 75 | 72 | 74 | 221 | 10,175 |
| Leonard Thompson | 70 | 77 | 74 | 221 | 10,175 |
| Jim Colbert | 74 | 76 | 72 | 222 | 8,250 |
| Hubert Green | 72 | 78 | 72 | 222 | 8,250 |
| Gary Koch | 73 | 73 | 76 | 222 | 8,250 |
| Mark McCumber | 76 | 73 | 73 | 222 | 8,250 |

# Blue Angels Classic

*The Moors Golf Club,* Milton, Florida
Par 35-35–70; 6,832 yards
(Playoff completed on Monday—darkness.)

May 13-16
purse, $1,500,000

|  | SCORES | | | TOTAL | MONEY |
|---|---|---|---|---|---|
| Jim Thorpe | 63 | 64 | 67 | 194 | $225,000 |
| Morris Hatalsky | 63 | 65 | 66 | 194 | 132,000 |
| (Thorpe defeated Hatalsky on third playoff hole.) | | | | | |
| Peter Jacobsen | 65 | 67 | 65 | 197 | 82,500 |
| Tom Jenkins | 66 | 65 | 66 | 197 | 82,500 |
| Don Pooley | 68 | 66 | 63 | 197 | 82,500 |
| Fuzzy Zoeller | 67 | 66 | 64 | 197 | 82,500 |
| Dave Barr | 65 | 70 | 63 | 198 | 51,000 |
| Dana Quigley | 66 | 65 | 67 | 198 | 51,000 |
| Allen Doyle | 69 | 64 | 66 | 199 | 34,750 |
| David Eger | 67 | 64 | 68 | 199 | 34,750 |
| Vicente Fernandez | 63 | 69 | 67 | 199 | 34,750 |
| Tom Purtzer | 67 | 67 | 65 | 199 | 34,750 |
| Craig Stadler | 69 | 60 | 70 | 199 | 34,750 |
| Mike Sullivan | 68 | 63 | 68 | 199 | 34,750 |
| Ben Crenshaw | 68 | 68 | 64 | 200 | 21,993.75 |
| Rodger Davis | 67 | 65 | 68 | 200 | 21,993.75 |
| Bruce Fleisher | 66 | 66 | 68 | 200 | 21,993.75 |
| John Harris | 65 | 67 | 68 | 200 | 21,993.75 |
| Gary Koch | 66 | 69 | 65 | 200 | 21,993.75 |
| Wayne Levi | 68 | 64 | 68 | 200 | 21,993.75 |
| Hajime Meshiai | 64 | 66 | 70 | 200 | 21,993.75 |
| Tom Wargo | 68 | 67 | 65 | 200 | 21,993.75 |
| Bruce Lietzke | 64 | 71 | 66 | 201 | 16,125 |
| Dick Mast | 64 | 67 | 70 | 201 | 16,125 |
| R.W. Eaks | 66 | 70 | 66 | 202 | 13,680 |
| Mike Hill | 67 | 70 | 65 | 202 | 13,680 |
| Norm Jarvis | 66 | 71 | 65 | 202 | 13,680 |
| Tom McKnight | 66 | 67 | 69 | 202 | 13,680 |
| Des Smyth | 73 | 63 | 66 | 202 | 13,680 |
| Hugh Baiocchi | 67 | 64 | 72 | 203 | 10,830 |
| John Bland | 68 | 69 | 66 | 203 | 10,830 |
| John Jacobs | 67 | 66 | 70 | 203 | 10,830 |
| Mark McNulty | 66 | 70 | 67 | 203 | 10,830 |
| Curtis Strange | 70 | 62 | 71 | 203 | 10,830 |
| Jim Ahern | 69 | 67 | 68 | 204 | 8,475 |
| Larry Nelson | 68 | 69 | 67 | 204 | 8,475 |
| Jerry Pate | 67 | 67 | 70 | 204 | 8,475 |
| Sammy Rachels | 68 | 69 | 67 | 204 | 8,475 |
| Leonard Thompson | 68 | 67 | 69 | 204 | 8,475 |
| Bobby Wadkins | 67 | 67 | 70 | 204 | 8,475 |

# Bruno's Memorial Classic

*Greystone Golf & Country Club,* Hoover, Alabama
Par 36-36–72; 7,092 yards

May 20-22
purse, $1,500,000

|  | SCORES | | | TOTAL | MONEY |
|---|---|---|---|---|---|
| D.A. Weibring | 67 | 65 | 69 | 201 | $225,000 |
| Tom Jenkins | 67 | 70 | 66 | 203 | 120,000 |

| | SCORES | | | TOTAL | MONEY |
|---|---|---|---|---|---|
| Tom Kite | 70 | 63 | 70 | 203 | 120,000 |
| Mark McNulty | 74 | 65 | 66 | 205 | 90,000 |
| Dana Quigley | 65 | 68 | 73 | 206 | 72,000 |
| Hale Irwin | 69 | 72 | 66 | 207 | 57,000 |
| Lonnie Nielsen | 72 | 64 | 71 | 207 | 57,000 |
| Brad Bryant | 75 | 64 | 69 | 208 | 39,600 |
| Bruce Fleisher | 68 | 70 | 70 | 208 | 39,600 |
| John Jacobs | 71 | 71 | 66 | 208 | 39,600 |
| Mark Johnson | 67 | 71 | 70 | 208 | 39,600 |
| Jay Sigel | 68 | 70 | 70 | 208 | 39,600 |
| Rodger Davis | 71 | 74 | 64 | 209 | 26,250 |
| Vicente Fernandez | 70 | 69 | 70 | 209 | 26,250 |
| Mark James | 68 | 69 | 72 | 209 | 26,250 |
| Jerry Pate | 70 | 71 | 68 | 209 | 26,250 |
| Des Smyth | 71 | 68 | 70 | 209 | 26,250 |
| Fuzzy Zoeller | 71 | 71 | 67 | 209 | 26,250 |
| Wayne Levi | 70 | 68 | 72 | 210 | 20,475 |
| Bobby Wadkins | 72 | 67 | 71 | 210 | 20,475 |
| Ben Crenshaw | 72 | 70 | 69 | 211 | 16,650 |
| Raymond Floyd | 68 | 71 | 72 | 211 | 16,650 |
| Bruce Lietzke | 70 | 72 | 69 | 211 | 16,650 |
| Curtis Strange | 67 | 70 | 74 | 211 | 16,650 |
| Leonard Thompson | 71 | 71 | 69 | 211 | 16,650 |
| Allen Doyle | 68 | 70 | 74 | 212 | 13,350 |
| Keith Fergus | 70 | 72 | 70 | 212 | 13,350 |
| Larry Nelson | 73 | 70 | 69 | 212 | 13,350 |
| Bruce Summerhays | 72 | 72 | 68 | 212 | 13,350 |
| Ed Dougherty | 72 | 73 | 68 | 213 | 11,550 |
| Dave Eichelberger | 71 | 72 | 70 | 213 | 11,550 |
| Isao Aoki | 70 | 72 | 72 | 214 | 10,350 |
| Bob Murphy | 73 | 73 | 68 | 214 | 10,350 |
| Tom Wargo | 66 | 74 | 74 | 214 | 10,350 |
| Bob Eastwood | 74 | 69 | 72 | 215 | 8,640 |
| Mike Hill | 69 | 72 | 74 | 215 | 8,640 |
| James Mason | 74 | 70 | 71 | 215 | 8,640 |
| Hajime Meshiai | 75 | 70 | 70 | 215 | 8,640 |
| Jim Thorpe | 70 | 77 | 68 | 215 | 8,640 |
| R.W. Eaks | 70 | 73 | 73 | 216 | 7,650 |

## Senior PGA Championship

*Laurel Valley Golf Club,* Ligonier, Pennsylvania　　　　　　May 26-29
Par 36-36–72; 7,107 yards　　　　　　　　　　　　purse, $2,000,000

| | SCORES | | | | TOTAL | MONEY |
|---|---|---|---|---|---|---|
| Mike Reid | 70 | 70 | 70 | 70 | 280 | $360,000 |
| Dana Quigley | 71 | 71 | 66 | 72 | 280 | 176,000 |
| Jerry Pate | 70 | 68 | 72 | 70 | 280 | 176,000 |
| (Reid defeated Quigley and Pate on first playoff hole.) | | | | | | |
| Morris Hatalsky | 74 | 70 | 70 | 70 | 284 | 96,000 |
| Tom Jenkins | 74 | 70 | 72 | 71 | 287 | 76,000 |
| Allen Doyle | 72 | 73 | 71 | 72 | 288 | 60,000 |
| Peter Jacobsen | 71 | 71 | 71 | 75 | 288 | 60,000 |
| Des Smyth | 74 | 76 | 70 | 68 | 288 | 60,000 |
| Mark McNulty | 74 | 66 | 76 | 72 | 288 | 60,000 |
| Tom Kite | 71 | 73 | 74 | 71 | 289 | 44,250 |
| Mark James | 73 | 71 | 75 | 70 | 289 | 44,250 |

| | SCORES | | | | TOTAL | MONEY |
|---|---|---|---|---|---|---|
| Dave Barr | 69 | 72 | 71 | 77 | 289 | 44,250 |
| R.W. Eaks | 69 | 70 | 73 | 77 | 289 | 44,250 |
| Bruce Summerhays | 77 | 70 | 71 | 72 | 290 | 32,000 |
| Luis Carbonetti | 71 | 73 | 72 | 74 | 290 | 32,000 |
| Raymond Floyd | 70 | 72 | 71 | 77 | 290 | 32,000 |
| Graham Marsh | 68 | 74 | 74 | 74 | 290 | 32,000 |
| Hajime Meshiai | 70 | 71 | 77 | 72 | 290 | 32,000 |
| Jim Thorpe | 73 | 74 | 72 | 72 | 291 | 23,000 |
| Lonnie Nielsen | 76 | 73 | 73 | 69 | 291 | 23,000 |
| Bruce Lietzke | 77 | 72 | 71 | 71 | 291 | 23,000 |
| Tom Purtzer | 77 | 67 | 76 | 71 | 291 | 23,000 |
| Rodger Davis | 80 | 67 | 72 | 73 | 292 | 16,500 |
| Jim Colbert | 73 | 75 | 73 | 71 | 292 | 16,500 |
| Gil Morgan | 71 | 75 | 73 | 73 | 292 | 16,500 |
| Larry Nelson | 72 | 71 | 73 | 76 | 292 | 16,500 |
| Don Reese | 71 | 76 | 72 | 74 | 293 | 13,250 |
| John Chillas | 71 | 75 | 73 | 74 | 293 | 13,250 |
| Tsuneyuki Nakajima | 73 | 73 | 71 | 76 | 293 | 13,250 |
| Tom Watson | 71 | 74 | 72 | 76 | 293 | 13,250 |
| D.A. Weibring | 75 | 72 | 75 | 72 | 294 | 11,000 |
| Darrell Kestner | 75 | 74 | 71 | 74 | 294 | 11,000 |
| Bruce Fleisher | 71 | 74 | 75 | 74 | 294 | 11,000 |
| Ben Crenshaw | 75 | 70 | 73 | 76 | 294 | 11,000 |
| Tom McKnight | 69 | 72 | 75 | 78 | 294 | 11,000 |
| Mark McCumber | 73 | 75 | 73 | 74 | 295 | 8,825 |
| Keith Fergus | 73 | 74 | 75 | 73 | 295 | 8,825 |
| Mark Lye | 74 | 74 | 74 | 73 | 295 | 8,825 |
| James Mason | 72 | 78 | 71 | 74 | 295 | 8,825 |
| Wayne Levi | 74 | 73 | 73 | 76 | 296 | 7,050 |
| Mike Sullivan | 76 | 72 | 76 | 72 | 296 | 7,050 |
| Butch Sheehan | 75 | 71 | 73 | 77 | 296 | 7,050 |
| Bob Ford | 74 | 74 | 74 | 74 | 296 | 7,050 |
| Mark Johnson | 72 | 77 | 72 | 75 | 296 | 7,050 |
| Jim Ahern | 72 | 78 | 74 | 72 | 296 | 7,050 |

## Allianz Championship

*Tournament Club of Iowa,* Polk City, Iowa  
Par 35-36–71; 6,756 yards

June 3-5  
purse, $1,500,000

| | SCORES | | | TOTAL | MONEY |
|---|---|---|---|---|---|
| Tom Jenkins | 65 | 72 | 67 | 204 | $225,000 |
| D.A. Weibring | 71 | 67 | 66 | 204 | 132,000 |
| (Jenkins defeated Weibring on second playoff hole.) | | | | | |
| Mike Reid | 69 | 66 | 71 | 206 | 108,000 |
| Dave Barr | 69 | 72 | 66 | 207 | 69,000 |
| Bob Gilder | 71 | 66 | 70 | 207 | 69,000 |
| Mike McCullough | 70 | 68 | 69 | 207 | 69,000 |
| Dana Quigley | 70 | 69 | 68 | 207 | 69,000 |
| Rodger Davis | 72 | 68 | 68 | 208 | 38,000 |
| Bruce Fleisher | 67 | 70 | 71 | 208 | 38,000 |
| Raymond Floyd | 70 | 70 | 68 | 208 | 38,000 |
| Mark James | 72 | 67 | 69 | 208 | 38,000 |
| James Mason | 69 | 69 | 70 | 208 | 38,000 |
| Pete Oakley | 74 | 65 | 69 | 208 | 38,000 |
| Ed Dougherty | 67 | 72 | 70 | 209 | 27,000 |
| Mark Lye | 70 | 70 | 69 | 209 | 27,000 |

|  | SCORES | | | TOTAL | MONEY |
|---|---|---|---|---|---|
| Mike Sullivan | 65 | 76 | 68 | 209 | 27,000 |
| Andy Bean | 70 | 72 | 68 | 210 | 20,575 |
| Morris Hatalsky | 70 | 67 | 73 | 210 | 20,575 |
| Mark Johnson | 70 | 72 | 68 | 210 | 20,575 |
| Gil Morgan | 71 | 67 | 72 | 210 | 20,575 |
| Dan Pohl | 72 | 68 | 70 | 210 | 20,575 |
| Leonard Thompson | 68 | 73 | 69 | 210 | 20,575 |
| Jim Ahern | 66 | 74 | 71 | 211 | 13,172.73 |
| John Bland | 68 | 72 | 71 | 211 | 13,172.73 |
| David Eger | 74 | 70 | 67 | 211 | 13,172.73 |
| Keith Fergus | 68 | 72 | 71 | 211 | 13,172.73 |
| Walter Hall | 72 | 70 | 69 | 211 | 13,172.73 |
| Norm Jarvis | 70 | 70 | 71 | 211 | 13,172.73 |
| Wayne Levi | 75 | 68 | 68 | 211 | 13,172.73 |
| Don Reese | 71 | 71 | 69 | 211 | 13,172.73 |
| Doug Johnson | 72 | 67 | 72 | 211 | 13,172.72 |
| Dick Mast | 67 | 72 | 72 | 211 | 13,172.72 |
| Jerry Pate | 73 | 67 | 71 | 211 | 13,172.72 |
| Lonnie Nielsen | 71 | 71 | 70 | 212 | 9,450 |
| Jay Sigel | 72 | 70 | 70 | 212 | 9,450 |
| Ron Streck | 66 | 75 | 71 | 212 | 9,450 |
| Brad Bryant | 72 | 74 | 67 | 213 | 7,500 |
| Jose Maria Canizares | 72 | 68 | 73 | 213 | 7,500 |
| John Harris | 72 | 73 | 68 | 213 | 7,500 |
| John Jacobs | 72 | 73 | 68 | 213 | 7,500 |
| Graham Marsh | 67 | 74 | 72 | 213 | 7,500 |
| Tom Purtzer | 72 | 69 | 72 | 213 | 7,500 |
| Bruce Summerhays | 69 | 72 | 72 | 213 | 7,500 |
| Bobby Wadkins | 73 | 71 | 69 | 213 | 7,500 |

## Bayer Advantage Classic

*Nicklaus Golf Club at LionsGate,* Overland Park, Kansas
Par 36-36–72; 7,000 yards
(Event shortened and completed on Monday—rain.)

June 10-13
purse, $1,650,000

|  | SCORES | | TOTAL | MONEY |
|---|---|---|---|---|
| Dana Quigley | 67 | 66 | 133 | $248,000 |
| Gil Morgan | 65 | 68 | 133 | 132,500 |
| Tom Watson | 67 | 66 | 133 | 132,500 |
| (Quigley defeated Morgan and Watson on first playoff hole.) | | | | |
| Jerry Pate | 69 | 65 | 134 | 99,100 |
| Dan Pohl | 67 | 68 | 135 | 79,200 |
| Jim Ahern | 66 | 70 | 136 | 53,460 |
| James Mason | 68 | 68 | 136 | 53,460 |
| Gary McCord | 67 | 69 | 136 | 53,460 |
| Jim Thorpe | 69 | 67 | 136 | 53,460 |
| D.A. Weibring | 68 | 68 | 136 | 53,460 |
| R.W. Eaks | 65 | 72 | 137 | 33,000 |
| Mark James | 71 | 66 | 137 | 33,000 |
| Dick Mast | 67 | 70 | 137 | 33,000 |
| Mike McCullough | 69 | 68 | 137 | 33,000 |
| Lonnie Nielsen | 67 | 70 | 137 | 33,000 |
| Mike Reid | 70 | 67 | 137 | 33,000 |
| Jim Colbert | 67 | 71 | 138 | 23,331 |
| Rodger Davis | 67 | 71 | 138 | 23,331 |
| Morris Hatalsky | 68 | 70 | 138 | 23,331 |

| | SCORES | | | TOTAL | MONEY |
|---|---|---|---|---|---|
| Tom Jenkins | 69 | 69 | | 138 | 23,331 |
| Jay Sigel | 71 | 67 | | 138 | 23,331 |
| Jim Albus | 71 | 68 | | 139 | 16,967.50 |
| Brad Bryant | 70 | 69 | | 139 | 16,967.50 |
| Ed Dougherty | 71 | 68 | | 139 | 16,967.50 |
| John Harris | 68 | 71 | | 139 | 16,967.50 |
| Mike Sullivan | 73 | 66 | | 139 | 16,967.50 |
| Howard Twitty | 70 | 69 | | 139 | 16,967.50 |
| Hugh Baiocchi | 70 | 70 | | 140 | 11,490 |
| Andy Bean | 69 | 71 | | 140 | 11,490 |
| Jim Dent | 68 | 72 | | 140 | 11,490 |
| Allen Doyle | 71 | 69 | | 140 | 11,490 |
| David Eger | 73 | 67 | | 140 | 11,490 |
| Bruce Fleisher | 71 | 69 | | 140 | 11,490 |
| Norm Jarvis | 69 | 71 | | 140 | 11,490 |
| Wayne Levi | 70 | 70 | | 140 | 11,490 |
| Mark McNulty | 67 | 73 | | 140 | 11,490 |
| Don Pooley | 69 | 71 | | 140 | 11,490 |
| John Ross | 72 | 68 | | 140 | 11,490 |
| John Bland | 71 | 70 | | 141 | 8,085 |
| Bob Eastwood | 71 | 70 | | 141 | 8,085 |
| Bob Ford | 70 | 71 | | 141 | 8,085 |
| Don Reese | 71 | 70 | | 141 | 8,085 |
| Bruce Summerhays | 72 | 69 | | 141 | 8,085 |

# Bank of America Championship

*Nashawtuc Country Club,* Concord, Massachusetts
Par 36-36–72; 6,729 yards

June 24-26
purse, $1,600,000

| | SCORES | | | TOTAL | MONEY |
|---|---|---|---|---|---|
| Mark McNulty | 67 | 69 | 68 | 204 | $240,000 |
| Don Pooley | 68 | 71 | 65 | 204 | 128,000 |
| Tom Purtzer | 71 | 64 | 69 | 204 | 128,000 |
| (McNulty defeated Pooley on first and Purtzer on second playoff hole.) | | | | | |
| D.A. Weibring | 69 | 69 | 69 | 207 | 78,933.34 |
| John Bland | 68 | 69 | 70 | 207 | 78,933.33 |
| Bruce Lietzke | 72 | 66 | 69 | 207 | 78,933.33 |
| David Eger | 68 | 71 | 69 | 208 | 46,720 |
| Hale Irwin | 70 | 68 | 70 | 208 | 46,720 |
| Jerry Pate | 68 | 69 | 71 | 208 | 46,720 |
| Des Smyth | 69 | 73 | 66 | 208 | 46,720 |
| Leonard Thompson | 66 | 71 | 71 | 208 | 46,720 |
| Ed Dougherty | 68 | 74 | 67 | 209 | 29,028.58 |
| Bob Eastwood | 71 | 69 | 69 | 209 | 29,028.57 |
| John Jacobs | 71 | 68 | 70 | 209 | 29,028.57 |
| Dana Quigley | 68 | 72 | 69 | 209 | 29,028.57 |
| Craig Stadler | 72 | 68 | 69 | 209 | 29,028.57 |
| Bruce Summerhays | 69 | 71 | 69 | 209 | 29,028.57 |
| Howard Twitty | 73 | 69 | 67 | 209 | 29,028.57 |
| Andy Bean | 71 | 67 | 72 | 210 | 21,840 |
| Morris Hatalsky | 72 | 71 | 67 | 210 | 21,840 |
| R.W. Eaks | 71 | 65 | 75 | 211 | 16,560 |
| John Harris | 67 | 71 | 73 | 211 | 16,560 |
| Tom Jenkins | 73 | 68 | 70 | 211 | 16,560 |
| Gary McCord | 70 | 72 | 69 | 211 | 16,560 |
| Dan Pohl | 71 | 68 | 72 | 211 | 16,560 |

| | SCORES | | | TOTAL | MONEY |
|---|---|---|---|---|---|
| Dave Stockton | 71 | 69 | 71 | 211 | 16,560 |
| Ron Streck | 72 | 69 | 70 | 211 | 16,560 |
| Jim Thorpe | 70 | 73 | 68 | 211 | 16,560 |
| Keith Fergus | 72 | 71 | 69 | 212 | 12,360 |
| Bob Gilder | 70 | 74 | 68 | 212 | 12,360 |
| Tom McKnight | 67 | 72 | 73 | 212 | 12,360 |
| Jay Sigel | 72 | 72 | 68 | 212 | 12,360 |
| Allen Doyle | 72 | 71 | 70 | 213 | 10,080 |
| Bruce Fleisher | 73 | 68 | 72 | 213 | 10,080 |
| Joe Inman | 72 | 72 | 69 | 213 | 10,080 |
| Mark Johnson | 75 | 68 | 70 | 213 | 10,080 |
| Tom Wargo | 71 | 71 | 71 | 213 | 10,080 |
| Jim Ahern | 68 | 75 | 71 | 214 | 8,000 |
| Jim Albus | 73 | 72 | 69 | 214 | 8,000 |
| Hajime Meshiai | 75 | 72 | 67 | 214 | 8,000 |
| Gil Morgan | 72 | 72 | 70 | 214 | 8,000 |
| Doug Tewell | 71 | 71 | 72 | 214 | 8,000 |
| Bobby Wadkins | 69 | 72 | 73 | 214 | 8,000 |

## Commerce Bank Championship

*Eisenhower Park, Red Course,* East Meadow, New York
Par 35-36–71; 6,904 yards

July 1-3
purse, $1,500,000

| | SCORES | | | TOTAL | MONEY |
|---|---|---|---|---|---|
| Ron Streck | 62 | 68 | 67 | 197 | $225,000 |
| Jim Ahern | 69 | 66 | 65 | 200 | 132,000 |
| Dan Pohl | 67 | 66 | 68 | 201 | 99,000 |
| Craig Stadler | 64 | 68 | 69 | 201 | 99,000 |
| Tom Jenkins | 69 | 63 | 70 | 202 | 72,000 |
| R.W. Eaks | 67 | 68 | 68 | 203 | 48,600 |
| Dave Eichelberger | 65 | 67 | 71 | 203 | 48,600 |
| Darrell Kestner | 65 | 68 | 70 | 203 | 48,600 |
| Gary McCord | 65 | 68 | 70 | 203 | 48,600 |
| D.A. Weibring | 66 | 67 | 70 | 203 | 48,600 |
| Morris Hatalsky | 68 | 67 | 69 | 204 | 30,900 |
| Mark James | 69 | 67 | 68 | 204 | 30,900 |
| Wayne Levi | 65 | 72 | 67 | 204 | 30,900 |
| Tom McKnight | 66 | 72 | 66 | 204 | 30,900 |
| Bobby Wadkins | 70 | 66 | 68 | 204 | 30,900 |
| Mark Johnson | 68 | 67 | 70 | 205 | 23,287.50 |
| James Mason | 69 | 68 | 68 | 205 | 23,287.50 |
| Lonnie Nielsen | 69 | 68 | 68 | 205 | 23,287.50 |
| Tom Purtzer | 70 | 65 | 70 | 205 | 23,287.50 |
| John Harris | 66 | 67 | 73 | 206 | 17,610 |
| John Jacobs | 72 | 66 | 68 | 206 | 17,610 |
| Hajime Meshiai | 68 | 70 | 68 | 206 | 17,610 |
| Gil Morgan | 67 | 67 | 72 | 206 | 17,610 |
| Jay Sigel | 68 | 68 | 70 | 206 | 17,610 |
| Ed Dougherty | 68 | 67 | 72 | 207 | 13,987.50 |
| Allen Doyle | 69 | 71 | 67 | 207 | 13,987.50 |
| Des Smyth | 68 | 67 | 72 | 207 | 13,987.50 |
| Jim Thorpe | 69 | 68 | 70 | 207 | 13,987.50 |
| Brad Bryant | 71 | 68 | 69 | 208 | 10,864.29 |
| Jerry Pate | 70 | 69 | 69 | 208 | 10,864.29 |
| Don Pooley | 68 | 72 | 68 | 208 | 10,864.29 |
| Dana Quigley | 67 | 72 | 69 | 208 | 10,864.29 |

|  | SCORES | | | TOTAL | MONEY |
|---|---|---|---|---|---|
| Rodger Davis | 69 | 69 | 70 | 208 | 10,864.28 |
| Vicente Fernandez | 66 | 71 | 71 | 208 | 10,864.28 |
| Leonard Thompson | 67 | 70 | 71 | 208 | 10,864.28 |
| Isao Aoki | 70 | 71 | 68 | 209 | 8,280 |
| Dave Barr | 68 | 70 | 71 | 209 | 8,280 |
| John Bland | 71 | 69 | 69 | 209 | 8,280 |
| Jim Colbert | 68 | 71 | 70 | 209 | 8,280 |
| Bruce Summerhays | 69 | 69 | 71 | 209 | 8,280 |

## Ford Senior Players Championship

*TPC of Michigan,* Dearborn, Michigan
Par 36-36–72; 7,069 yards

July 7-10
purse, $2,500,000

|  | SCORES | | | | TOTAL | MONEY |
|---|---|---|---|---|---|---|
| Peter Jacobsen | 70 | 66 | 71 | 66 | 273 | $375,000 |
| Hale Irwin | 68 | 68 | 68 | 70 | 274 | 220,000 |
| Tom McKnight | 68 | 67 | 70 | 71 | 276 | 165,000 |
| Tom Watson | 66 | 72 | 70 | 68 | 276 | 165,000 |
| Allen Doyle | 74 | 67 | 69 | 68 | 278 | 87,500 |
| Gary McCord | 68 | 71 | 69 | 70 | 278 | 87,500 |
| Gil Morgan | 72 | 66 | 67 | 73 | 278 | 87,500 |
| Larry Nelson | 68 | 74 | 67 | 69 | 278 | 87,500 |
| Dana Quigley | 67 | 66 | 72 | 73 | 278 | 87,500 |
| D.A. Weibring | 70 | 70 | 73 | 65 | 278 | 87,500 |
| David Eger | 71 | 71 | 65 | 72 | 279 | 51,500 |
| Morris Hatalsky | 68 | 70 | 70 | 71 | 279 | 51,500 |
| Gary Koch | 71 | 68 | 72 | 68 | 279 | 51,500 |
| Bruce Lietzke | 69 | 72 | 69 | 69 | 279 | 51,500 |
| Mark McNulty | 71 | 68 | 70 | 70 | 279 | 51,500 |
| Brad Bryant | 69 | 71 | 72 | 68 | 280 | 41,250 |
| Leonard Thompson | 70 | 72 | 70 | 68 | 280 | 41,250 |
| Jay Haas | 71 | 71 | 71 | 68 | 281 | 32,208.34 |
| John Harris | 69 | 69 | 77 | 66 | 281 | 32,208.34 |
| Isao Aoki | 66 | 69 | 73 | 73 | 281 | 32,208.33 |
| Dick Mast | 70 | 67 | 75 | 69 | 281 | 32,208.33 |
| Don Pooley | 70 | 71 | 65 | 75 | 281 | 32,208.33 |
| Doug Tewell | 72 | 70 | 65 | 74 | 281 | 32,208.33 |
| Jim Colbert | 69 | 74 | 69 | 70 | 282 | 25,000 |
| Graham Marsh | 64 | 76 | 72 | 70 | 282 | 25,000 |
| Ron Streck | 66 | 70 | 72 | 74 | 282 | 25,000 |
| Andy Bean | 68 | 72 | 73 | 70 | 283 | 21,750 |
| Bruce Fleisher | 68 | 69 | 72 | 74 | 283 | 21,750 |
| Lonnie Nielsen | 70 | 69 | 73 | 71 | 283 | 21,750 |
| Jose Maria Canizares | 74 | 73 | 71 | 66 | 284 | 17,285.72 |
| Mike McCullough | 72 | 75 | 68 | 69 | 284 | 17,285.72 |
| Craig Stadler | 73 | 69 | 72 | 70 | 284 | 17,285.72 |
| Ed Dougherty | 74 | 72 | 67 | 71 | 284 | 17,285.71 |
| Wayne Levi | 67 | 74 | 69 | 74 | 284 | 17,285.71 |
| Jerry Pate | 68 | 70 | 72 | 74 | 284 | 17,285.71 |
| Tom Wargo | 72 | 74 | 66 | 72 | 284 | 17,285.71 |

## Senior British Open

See European Seniors Tour section.

# U.S. Senior Open

*NCR Country Club, South Course,* Kettering, Ohio
Par 36-35–71; 7,000 yards

July 28-31
purse, $2,600,000

| | SCORES | | | | TOTAL | MONEY |
|---|---|---|---|---|---|---|
| Allen Doyle | 71 | 67 | 73 | 63 | 274 | $470,000 |
| D.A. Weibring | 70 | 67 | 68 | 70 | 275 | 227,457 |
| Loren Roberts | 66 | 67 | 69 | 73 | 275 | 227,457 |
| Greg Norman | 68 | 70 | 69 | 69 | 276 | 121,887 |
| Wayne Levi | 68 | 67 | 74 | 68 | 277 | 93,100 |
| Tom Watson | 68 | 65 | 73 | 71 | 277 | 93,100 |
| Mark McNulty | 70 | 67 | 74 | 67 | 278 | 75,720 |
| Craig Stadler | 64 | 69 | 69 | 76 | 278 | 75,720 |
| Dana Quigley | 73 | 71 | 66 | 69 | 279 | 61,846 |
| Rodger Davis | 69 | 72 | 67 | 71 | 279 | 61,846 |
| Des Smyth | 70 | 66 | 70 | 73 | 279 | 61,846 |
| Bruce Lietzke | 71 | 73 | 70 | 67 | 281 | 52,290 |
| Bob Gilder | 69 | 72 | 71 | 69 | 281 | 52,290 |
| Walter Hall | 72 | 70 | 71 | 69 | 282 | 44,089 |
| Tom Jenkins | 72 | 65 | 72 | 73 | 282 | 44,089 |
| Perry Arthur | 71 | 72 | 66 | 73 | 282 | 44,089 |
| Raymond Floyd | 69 | 67 | 69 | 77 | 282 | 44,089 |
| Larry Nelson | 74 | 70 | 71 | 68 | 283 | 35,192 |
| John Harris | 69 | 75 | 70 | 69 | 283 | 35,192 |
| Ron Streck | 69 | 70 | 73 | 71 | 283 | 35,192 |
| Gil Morgan | 70 | 70 | 72 | 71 | 283 | 35,192 |
| Jay Haas | 72 | 70 | 75 | 67 | 284 | 28,620 |
| Hajime Meshiai | 70 | 69 | 73 | 72 | 284 | 28,620 |
| Don Pooley | 72 | 67 | 71 | 74 | 284 | 28,620 |
| Hale Irwin | 71 | 69 | 74 | 71 | 285 | 25,230 |
| R.W. Eaks | 70 | 71 | 72 | 73 | 286 | 22,107 |
| Peter Jacobsen | 72 | 71 | 70 | 73 | 286 | 22,107 |
| Bruce Summerhays | 68 | 69 | 73 | 76 | 286 | 22,107 |
| Lonnie Nielsen | 71 | 72 | 74 | 70 | 287 | 18,604 |
| Dan Pohl | 69 | 74 | 71 | 73 | 287 | 18,604 |
| James Blair | 71 | 70 | 77 | 70 | 288 | 16,945 |
| Roy Vucinich | 74 | 70 | 74 | 70 | 288 | 16,945 |
| Doug Tewell | 75 | 70 | 73 | 70 | 288 | 16,945 |
| *George Zahringer | 72 | 70 | 74 | 72 | 288 | |
| *Greg Reynolds | 71 | 72 | 71 | 74 | 288 | |
| David Eger | 70 | 69 | 74 | 75 | 288 | 16,945 |
| Vance Heafner | 74 | 69 | 77 | 69 | 289 | 14,403 |
| Tom Kite | 74 | 71 | 73 | 71 | 289 | 14,403 |
| Morris Hatalsky | 69 | 76 | 72 | 72 | 289 | 14,403 |
| Vicente Fernandez | 72 | 71 | 73 | 73 | 289 | 14,403 |
| Dale Douglass | 73 | 70 | 73 | 73 | 289 | 14,403 |
| David Lundstrom | 70 | 72 | 71 | 76 | 289 | 14,403 |

# 3M Championship

*TPC of the Twin Cities,* Blaine, Minnesota
Par 36-36–72; 6,909 yards

August 5-7
purse, $1,750,000

| | SCORES | | | TOTAL | MONEY |
|---|---|---|---|---|---|
| Tom Purtzer | 63 | 69 | 69 | 201 | $262,500 |
| Lonnie Nielsen | 67 | 68 | 67 | 202 | 140,000 |

| | SCORES | | | TOTAL | MONEY |
|---|---|---|---|---|---|
| Craig Stadler | 68 | 67 | 67 | 202 | 140,000 |
| Graham Marsh | 67 | 71 | 65 | 203 | 105,000 |
| Mark McNulty | 67 | 72 | 66 | 205 | 72,333.34 |
| Tom Kite | 67 | 69 | 69 | 205 | 72,333.33 |
| Gil Morgan | 67 | 69 | 69 | 205 | 72,333.33 |
| Morris Hatalsky | 68 | 68 | 70 | 206 | 48,125 |
| Bruce Lietzke | 64 | 71 | 71 | 206 | 48,125 |
| Bruce Summerhays | 69 | 69 | 68 | 206 | 48,125 |
| D.A. Weibring | 71 | 65 | 70 | 206 | 48,125 |
| Andy Bean | 70 | 67 | 70 | 207 | 36,750 |
| Dana Quigley | 69 | 69 | 69 | 207 | 36,750 |
| Jose Maria Canizares | 68 | 71 | 69 | 208 | 32,375 |
| David Eger | 67 | 68 | 73 | 208 | 32,375 |
| Brad Bryant | 67 | 70 | 72 | 209 | 28,875 |
| Tom Jenkins | 69 | 69 | 71 | 209 | 28,875 |
| Don Pooley | 70 | 72 | 68 | 210 | 26,250 |
| Bob Gilder | 68 | 72 | 71 | 211 | 21,233.34 |
| Don Reese | 66 | 74 | 71 | 211 | 21,233.34 |
| Jim Ahern | 69 | 67 | 75 | 211 | 21,233.33 |
| Walter Hall | 70 | 69 | 72 | 211 | 21,233.33 |
| Mark Lye | 70 | 70 | 71 | 211 | 21,233.33 |
| Hajime Meshiai | 69 | 66 | 76 | 211 | 21,233.33 |
| R.W. Eaks | 70 | 71 | 71 | 212 | 14,000 |
| Dave Eichelberger | 73 | 69 | 70 | 212 | 14,000 |
| Keith Fergus | 70 | 69 | 73 | 212 | 14,000 |
| Bruce Fleisher | 70 | 73 | 69 | 212 | 14,000 |
| Hale Irwin | 72 | 69 | 71 | 212 | 14,000 |
| Wayne Levi | 69 | 72 | 71 | 212 | 14,000 |
| Mike McCullough | 71 | 69 | 72 | 212 | 14,000 |
| Mike Sullivan | 73 | 70 | 69 | 212 | 14,000 |
| Leonard Thompson | 68 | 71 | 73 | 212 | 14,000 |
| Jim Thorpe | 72 | 71 | 69 | 212 | 14,000 |
| Bobby Wadkins | 68 | 71 | 73 | 212 | 14,000 |
| Dave Barr | 69 | 71 | 73 | 213 | 8,767.50 |
| Danny Edwards | 74 | 69 | 70 | 213 | 8,767.50 |
| John Harris | 67 | 74 | 72 | 213 | 8,767.50 |
| Joe Inman | 68 | 72 | 73 | 213 | 8,767.50 |
| Dick Mast | 72 | 66 | 75 | 213 | 8,767.50 |
| Tom McKnight | 70 | 70 | 73 | 213 | 8,767.50 |
| John Ross | 67 | 72 | 74 | 213 | 8,767.50 |
| Curtis Strange | 69 | 72 | 72 | 213 | 8,767.50 |
| Ron Streck | 70 | 71 | 72 | 213 | 8,767.50 |
| Fuzzy Zoeller | 71 | 72 | 70 | 213 | 8,767.50 |

## Boeing Greater Seattle Classic

*TPC at Snoqualmie Ridge,* Snoqualmie, Washington
Par 36-36–72; 7,264 yards

August 19-21
purse, $1,600,000

| | SCORES | | | TOTAL | MONEY |
|---|---|---|---|---|---|
| David Eger | 68 | 64 | 67 | 199 | $240,000 |
| Tom Kite | 66 | 69 | 67 | 202 | 140,800 |
| Brad Bryant | 66 | 68 | 69 | 203 | 105,600 |
| John Harris | 67 | 67 | 69 | 203 | 105,600 |
| Morris Hatalsky | 66 | 66 | 72 | 204 | 76,800 |
| Craig Stadler | 67 | 65 | 73 | 205 | 64,000 |
| Hale Irwin | 67 | 69 | 70 | 206 | 54,400 |

| | SCORES | | | TOTAL | MONEY |
|---|---|---|---|---|---|
| Bruce Summerhays | 68 | 69 | 69 | 206 | 54,400 |
| Don Pooley | 71 | 64 | 73 | 208 | 40,000 |
| Dana Quigley | 69 | 69 | 70 | 208 | 40,000 |
| Mike Reid | 73 | 67 | 68 | 208 | 40,000 |
| Dave Stockton | 69 | 73 | 66 | 208 | 40,000 |
| Jim Ahern | 68 | 69 | 72 | 209 | 27,222.86 |
| R.W. Eaks | 70 | 70 | 69 | 209 | 27,222.86 |
| Bruce Fleisher | 70 | 70 | 69 | 209 | 27,222.86 |
| Walter Hall | 68 | 71 | 70 | 209 | 27,222.86 |
| Bobby Wadkins | 71 | 67 | 71 | 209 | 27,222.86 |
| James Mason | 67 | 67 | 75 | 209 | 27,222.85 |
| D.A. Weibring | 68 | 67 | 74 | 209 | 27,222.85 |
| Andy Bean | 67 | 70 | 73 | 210 | 16,688 |
| Keith Fergus | 71 | 71 | 68 | 210 | 16,688 |
| Peter Jacobsen | 67 | 71 | 72 | 210 | 16,688 |
| Norm Jarvis | 75 | 67 | 68 | 210 | 16,688 |
| Bruce Lietzke | 67 | 69 | 74 | 210 | 16,688 |
| Mark McNulty | 73 | 68 | 69 | 210 | 16,688 |
| Dan Pohl | 68 | 71 | 71 | 210 | 16,688 |
| John Ross | 71 | 69 | 70 | 210 | 16,688 |
| Ron Streck | 72 | 67 | 71 | 210 | 16,688 |
| Doug Tewell | 70 | 70 | 70 | 210 | 16,688 |
| Rick Rhoden | 72 | 70 | 69 | 211 | 12,053.34 |
| Bob Gilder | 71 | 68 | 72 | 211 | 12,053.33 |
| Jim Thorpe | 66 | 69 | 76 | 211 | 12,053.33 |
| Tom Jenkins | 70 | 72 | 70 | 212 | 10,560 |
| Graham Marsh | 70 | 70 | 72 | 212 | 10,560 |
| Tom McKnight | 70 | 70 | 72 | 212 | 10,560 |
| Mike McCullough | 72 | 72 | 69 | 213 | 9,173.34 |
| Allen Doyle | 70 | 73 | 70 | 213 | 9,173.33 |
| Tom Purtzer | 70 | 69 | 74 | 213 | 9,173.33 |
| John Bland | 69 | 69 | 76 | 214 | 7,200 |
| Ben Crenshaw | 74 | 68 | 72 | 214 | 7,200 |
| Ed Dougherty | 72 | 69 | 73 | 214 | 7,200 |
| Vicente Fernandez | 69 | 69 | 76 | 214 | 7,200 |
| Tom Herzan | 71 | 72 | 71 | 214 | 7,200 |
| John Jacobs | 70 | 72 | 72 | 214 | 7,200 |
| Doug Johnson | 70 | 73 | 71 | 214 | 7,200 |
| Gil Morgan | 75 | 69 | 70 | 214 | 7,200 |
| Lonnie Nielsen | 73 | 71 | 70 | 214 | 7,200 |

## JELD-WEN Tradition

*Reserve Vineyards & Golf Club,* Aloha, Oregon
Par 36-36–72; 6,998 yards

August 25-28
purse, $2,500,000

| | SCORES | | | | TOTAL | MONEY |
|---|---|---|---|---|---|---|
| Loren Roberts | 67 | 69 | 70 | 67 | 273 | $375,000 |
| Dana Quigley | 67 | 72 | 66 | 68 | 273 | 220,000 |
| (Roberts defeated Quigley on second playoff hole.) | | | | | | |
| Gil Morgan | 69 | 64 | 70 | 71 | 274 | 180,000 |
| Mark James | 71 | 66 | 70 | 68 | 275 | 150,000 |
| James Mason | 71 | 70 | 68 | 67 | 276 | 103,333.34 |
| Tom Jenkins | 69 | 66 | 69 | 72 | 276 | 103,333.33 |
| Doug Tewell | 70 | 67 | 66 | 73 | 276 | 103,333.33 |
| Mark McNulty | 71 | 65 | 70 | 71 | 277 | 80,000 |
| R.W. Eaks | 68 | 74 | 70 | 69 | 281 | 62,500 |

| | SCORES | | | TOTAL | MONEY |
|---|---|---|---|---|---|
| Mike Reid | 72 | 71 | 70 | 68 | 281 | 62,500 |
| Tom Watson | 74 | 71 | 70 | 66 | 281 | 62,500 |
| D.A. Weibring | 67 | 70 | 70 | 74 | 281 | 62,500 |
| Bob Gilder | 72 | 68 | 74 | 68 | 282 | 47,500 |
| John Harris | 67 | 71 | 71 | 73 | 282 | 47,500 |
| Jerry Pate | 71 | 68 | 68 | 75 | 282 | 47,500 |
| Brad Bryant | 71 | 66 | 73 | 73 | 283 | 37,650 |
| Walter Hall | 68 | 73 | 71 | 71 | 283 | 37,650 |
| Mark McCumber | 68 | 73 | 66 | 76 | 283 | 37,650 |
| Dan Pohl | 72 | 71 | 69 | 71 | 283 | 37,650 |
| Des Smyth | 73 | 71 | 70 | 69 | 283 | 37,650 |
| Dave Barr | 69 | 71 | 74 | 70 | 284 | 30,000 |
| Ed Dougherty | 75 | 70 | 69 | 70 | 284 | 30,000 |
| Vicente Fernandez | 75 | 71 | 70 | 69 | 285 | 25,625 |
| Jay Haas | 73 | 71 | 72 | 69 | 285 | 25,625 |
| Joe Inman | 71 | 71 | 71 | 72 | 285 | 25,625 |
| Craig Stadler | 72 | 68 | 72 | 73 | 285 | 25,625 |
| Jose Maria Canizares | 72 | 71 | 69 | 74 | 286 | 20,750 |
| Morris Hatalsky | 73 | 71 | 72 | 70 | 286 | 20,750 |
| Dick Mast | 73 | 69 | 70 | 74 | 286 | 20,750 |
| Tom Purtzer | 74 | 71 | 69 | 72 | 286 | 20,750 |
| Howard Twitty | 75 | 68 | 71 | 72 | 286 | 20,750 |
| Isao Aoki | 74 | 69 | 72 | 72 | 287 | 16,875 |
| John Bland | 73 | 72 | 71 | 71 | 287 | 16,875 |
| Mark Johnson | 68 | 72 | 74 | 73 | 287 | 16,875 |
| Dave Stockton | 70 | 69 | 75 | 73 | 287 | 16,875 |
| Bruce Fleisher | 72 | 73 | 74 | 69 | 288 | 13,541.67 |
| Tom Kite | 77 | 68 | 70 | 73 | 288 | 13,541.67 |
| Wayne Levi | 74 | 74 | 70 | 70 | 288 | 13,541.67 |
| Don Pooley | 70 | 71 | 73 | 74 | 288 | 13,541.67 |
| Allen Doyle | 68 | 73 | 71 | 76 | 288 | 13,541.66 |
| Pete Oakley | 71 | 70 | 71 | 76 | 288 | 13,541.66 |

## Wal-Mart First Tee Open at Pebble Beach

*Pebble Beach Golf Links,* Pebble Beach, California
Par 36-36–72; 6,822 yards
*Del Monte Golf Course,* Monterey, California
Par 36-36–72; 6,357 yards

September 2-4
purse, $2,000,000

| | SCORES | | | TOTAL | MONEY |
|---|---|---|---|---|---|
| Hale Irwin | 66 | 69 | 68 | 203 | $300,000 |
| Morris Hatalsky | 69 | 68 | 67 | 204 | 146,666.67 |
| Craig Stadler | 69 | 68 | 67 | 204 | 146,666.67 |
| Gil Morgan | 70 | 65 | 69 | 204 | 146,666.66 |
| Bruce Fleisher | 72 | 67 | 66 | 205 | 82,666.67 |
| Jim Thorpe | 69 | 70 | 66 | 205 | 82,666.67 |
| Don Pooley | 70 | 67 | 68 | 205 | 82,666.66 |
| Mark McNulty | 68 | 73 | 65 | 206 | 64,000 |
| Jay Haas | 69 | 70 | 69 | 208 | 54,000 |
| Lonnie Nielsen | 70 | 67 | 71 | 208 | 54,000 |
| Larry Nelson | 70 | 70 | 69 | 209 | 44,000 |
| Dana Quigley | 66 | 73 | 70 | 209 | 44,000 |
| Loren Roberts | 72 | 71 | 66 | 209 | 44,000 |
| David Eger | 72 | 67 | 71 | 210 | 35,000 |
| Walter Hall | 67 | 71 | 72 | 210 | 35,000 |
| Wayne Levi | 70 | 72 | 68 | 210 | 35,000 |

| | SCORES | | | TOTAL | MONEY |
|---|---|---|---|---|---|
| Gary McCord | 71 | 69 | 70 | 210 | 35,000 |
| Ben Crenshaw | 69 | 74 | 68 | 211 | 26,520 |
| Keith Fergus | 70 | 68 | 73 | 211 | 26,520 |
| Vicente Fernandez | 71 | 72 | 68 | 211 | 26,520 |
| Bob Gilder | 67 | 73 | 71 | 211 | 26,520 |
| Dan Pohl | 70 | 69 | 72 | 211 | 26,520 |
| John Bland | 69 | 70 | 73 | 212 | 19,171.43 |
| Mark Johnson | 70 | 72 | 70 | 212 | 19,171.43 |
| Dave Stockton | 71 | 71 | 70 | 212 | 19,171.43 |
| Curtis Strange | 68 | 73 | 71 | 212 | 19,171.43 |
| Bobby Wadkins | 72 | 70 | 70 | 212 | 19,171.43 |
| D.A. Weibring | 75 | 68 | 69 | 212 | 19,171.43 |
| Mark McCumber | 69 | 69 | 74 | 212 | 19,171.42 |
| Bruce Lietzke | 70 | 70 | 73 | 213 | 14,440 |
| Graham Marsh | 75 | 70 | 68 | 213 | 14,440 |
| Tom Purtzer | 70 | 73 | 70 | 213 | 14,440 |
| Jay Sigel | 72 | 69 | 72 | 213 | 14,440 |
| Fuzzy Zoeller | 73 | 74 | 66 | 213 | 14,440 |
| Ron Streck | 71 | 71 | 72 | 214 | 12,600 |
| Bob Eastwood | 71 | 70 | 74 | 215 | 11,250 |
| John Harris | 68 | 75 | 72 | 215 | 11,250 |
| Jerry Pate | 73 | 70 | 72 | 215 | 11,250 |
| Lanny Wadkins | 68 | 75 | 72 | 215 | 11,250 |
| Joe Inman | 73 | 70 | 73 | 216 | 9,000 |
| Tom Kite | 70 | 70 | 76 | 216 | 9,000 |
| Des Smyth | 69 | 71 | 76 | 216 | 9,000 |
| Bruce Summerhays | 68 | 72 | 76 | 216 | 9,000 |
| Doug Tewell | 67 | 73 | 76 | 216 | 9,000 |
| Jeff Thomsen | 72 | 72 | 72 | 216 | 9,000 |
| Tom Wargo | 73 | 71 | 72 | 216 | 9,000 |

## Constellation Energy Classic

*Hayfields Country Club*, Hunt Valley, Maryland
Par 36-36–72; 6,983 yards

September 16-18
purse, $1,700,000

| | SCORES | | | TOTAL | MONEY |
|---|---|---|---|---|---|
| Bob Gilder | 64 | 67 | 67 | 198 | $255,000 |
| Morris Hatalsky | 69 | 64 | 69 | 202 | 149,600 |
| Curtis Strange | 68 | 66 | 69 | 203 | 122,400 |
| D.A. Weibring | 67 | 66 | 71 | 204 | 102,000 |
| John Bland | 67 | 70 | 68 | 205 | 74,800 |
| Tom Watson | 66 | 68 | 71 | 205 | 74,800 |
| Gary McCord | 69 | 69 | 68 | 206 | 61,200 |
| Bruce Fleisher | 69 | 66 | 72 | 207 | 46,750 |
| Hajime Meshiai | 67 | 69 | 71 | 207 | 46,750 |
| Pete Oakley | 69 | 67 | 71 | 207 | 46,750 |
| Rick Rhoden | 68 | 68 | 71 | 207 | 46,750 |
| Jim Colbert | 68 | 72 | 68 | 208 | 33,575 |
| Joe Inman | 71 | 69 | 68 | 208 | 33,575 |
| James Mason | 70 | 69 | 69 | 208 | 33,575 |
| Don Pooley | 71 | 69 | 68 | 208 | 33,575 |
| John Jacobs | 67 | 71 | 71 | 209 | 26,392.50 |
| Dan Pohl | 66 | 70 | 73 | 209 | 26,392.50 |
| Dana Quigley | 71 | 70 | 68 | 209 | 26,392.50 |
| John Ross | 68 | 69 | 72 | 209 | 26,392.50 |
| Andy Bean | 68 | 72 | 70 | 210 | 18,991.43 |

|  | SCORES | | | TOTAL | MONEY |
|---|---|---|---|---|---|
| Keith Fergus | 69 | 70 | 71 | 210 | 18,991.43 |
| Tom Kite | 73 | 67 | 70 | 210 | 18,991.43 |
| Gary Koch | 72 | 67 | 71 | 210 | 18,991.43 |
| Wayne Levi | 71 | 70 | 69 | 210 | 18,991.43 |
| Graham Marsh | 71 | 72 | 67 | 210 | 18,991.43 |
| Larry Nelson | 67 | 71 | 72 | 210 | 18,991.42 |
| Brad Bryant | 71 | 67 | 73 | 211 | 15,470 |
| Mike Hill | 73 | 71 | 68 | 212 | 13,175 |
| Tom Jenkins | 69 | 73 | 70 | 212 | 13,175 |
| Tom McKnight | 72 | 70 | 70 | 212 | 13,175 |
| Jerry Pate | 73 | 68 | 71 | 212 | 13,175 |
| Mike Sullivan | 71 | 70 | 71 | 212 | 13,175 |
| Bruce Summerhays | 72 | 70 | 70 | 212 | 13,175 |
| Jim Albus | 71 | 72 | 70 | 213 | 10,234 |
| Ed Dougherty | 71 | 70 | 72 | 213 | 10,234 |
| R.W. Eaks | 75 | 68 | 70 | 213 | 10,234 |
| Mike McCullough | 71 | 69 | 73 | 213 | 10,234 |
| Rocky Thompson | 70 | 73 | 70 | 213 | 10,234 |
| Dave Barr | 70 | 71 | 73 | 214 | 7,480 |
| Raymond Floyd | 73 | 72 | 69 | 214 | 7,480 |
| Walter Hall | 71 | 74 | 69 | 214 | 7,480 |
| John Harris | 74 | 70 | 70 | 214 | 7,480 |
| Doug Johnson | 70 | 74 | 70 | 214 | 7,480 |
| Mark McCumber | 74 | 67 | 73 | 214 | 7,480 |
| Lonnie Nielsen | 73 | 71 | 70 | 214 | 7,480 |
| Jay Sigel | 71 | 72 | 71 | 214 | 7,480 |
| Des Smyth | 71 | 74 | 69 | 214 | 7,480 |
| Jim Thorpe | 73 | 71 | 70 | 214 | 7,480 |

## SAS Championship

*Prestonwood Country Club*, Cary, North Carolina
Par 36-36–72; 7,137 yards

September 30-October 2
purse, $1,900,000

|  | SCORES | | | TOTAL | MONEY |
|---|---|---|---|---|---|
| Hale Irwin | 69 | 68 | 66 | 203 | $285,000 |
| Bob Gilder | 68 | 66 | 71 | 205 | 152,000 |
| Tom Jenkins | 70 | 65 | 70 | 205 | 152,000 |
| Craig Stadler | 71 | 66 | 69 | 206 | 114,000 |
| Danny Edwards | 69 | 68 | 71 | 208 | 91,200 |
| Bruce Lietzke | 69 | 71 | 69 | 209 | 64,600 |
| Gary McCord | 70 | 67 | 72 | 209 | 64,600 |
| Lonnie Nielsen | 69 | 69 | 71 | 209 | 64,600 |
| Bobby Wadkins | 69 | 69 | 71 | 209 | 64,600 |
| R.W. Eaks | 67 | 66 | 77 | 210 | 47,500 |
| James Mason | 70 | 69 | 71 | 210 | 47,500 |
| Brad Bryant | 72 | 70 | 69 | 211 | 35,466.67 |
| Bruce Fleisher | 70 | 71 | 70 | 211 | 35,466.67 |
| Walter Hall | 70 | 71 | 70 | 211 | 35,466.67 |
| Wayne Levi | 72 | 71 | 68 | 211 | 35,466.67 |
| Rodger Davis | 70 | 66 | 75 | 211 | 35,466.66 |
| Tom Kite | 71 | 68 | 72 | 211 | 35,466.66 |
| Jim Ahern | 74 | 71 | 67 | 212 | 25,982.50 |
| Andy Bean | 71 | 71 | 70 | 212 | 25,982.50 |
| Don Pooley | 73 | 68 | 71 | 212 | 25,982.50 |
| Scott Simpson | 68 | 72 | 72 | 212 | 25,982.50 |
| David Eger | 71 | 72 | 70 | 213 | 22,040 |

| | SCORES | | | TOTAL | MONEY |
|---|---|---|---|---|---|
| Bruce Summerhays | 66 | 71 | 77 | 214 | 20,900 |
| Bob Eastwood | 71 | 73 | 71 | 215 | 18,164 |
| John Jacobs | 72 | 72 | 71 | 215 | 18,164 |
| Gil Morgan | 70 | 75 | 70 | 215 | 18,164 |
| Mike San Filippo | 72 | 70 | 73 | 215 | 18,164 |
| Curtis Strange | 74 | 69 | 72 | 215 | 18,164 |
| Joe Inman | 70 | 75 | 71 | 216 | 15,390 |
| Gary Koch | 71 | 74 | 71 | 216 | 15,390 |
| John Bland | 76 | 72 | 69 | 217 | 13,110 |
| Vicente Fernandez | 74 | 69 | 74 | 217 | 13,110 |
| Hajime Meshiai | 74 | 71 | 72 | 217 | 13,110 |
| Larry Nelson | 76 | 68 | 73 | 217 | 13,110 |
| Jim Thorpe | 73 | 68 | 76 | 217 | 13,110 |
| Tom McKnight | 72 | 74 | 72 | 218 | 10,687.50 |
| Rick Rhoden | 78 | 68 | 72 | 218 | 10,687.50 |
| Howard Twitty | 73 | 73 | 72 | 218 | 10,687.50 |
| Tom Wargo | 75 | 69 | 74 | 218 | 10,687.50 |
| Dave Barr | 71 | 71 | 77 | 219 | 8,930 |
| Mike Donald | 74 | 76 | 69 | 219 | 8,930 |
| Norm Jarvis | 75 | 71 | 73 | 219 | 8,930 |
| Jay Sigel | 72 | 70 | 77 | 219 | 8,930 |
| Mike Sullivan | 73 | 74 | 72 | 219 | 8,930 |

## Greater Hickory Classic at Rock Barn

*Rock Barn Golf & Spa, Jones Course*, Conover, North Carolina      October 7-9
Par 35-37–72; 7,087 yards      purse, $1,600,000

| | SCORES | | | TOTAL | MONEY |
|---|---|---|---|---|---|
| Jay Haas | 68 | 67 | 65 | 200 | $240,000 |
| Dana Quigley | 68 | 64 | 70 | 202 | 140,800 |
| Loren Roberts | 68 | 65 | 70 | 203 | 115,200 |
| John Harris | 69 | 70 | 66 | 205 | 61,714.29 |
| Jerry Pate | 73 | 65 | 67 | 205 | 61,714.29 |
| Don Pooley | 68 | 71 | 66 | 205 | 61,714.29 |
| Jim Thorpe | 71 | 67 | 67 | 205 | 61,714.29 |
| Tom McKnight | 67 | 68 | 70 | 205 | 61,714.28 |
| Craig Stadler | 70 | 67 | 68 | 205 | 61,714.28 |
| Tom Wargo | 71 | 66 | 68 | 205 | 61,714.28 |
| Brad Bryant | 69 | 67 | 70 | 206 | 35,200 |
| Gil Morgan | 68 | 70 | 68 | 206 | 35,200 |
| Lonnie Nielsen | 66 | 70 | 70 | 206 | 35,200 |
| Jim Ahern | 69 | 66 | 72 | 207 | 28,000 |
| John Bland | 69 | 68 | 70 | 207 | 28,000 |
| Bruce Lietzke | 70 | 70 | 67 | 207 | 28,000 |
| Mark McNulty | 70 | 69 | 68 | 207 | 28,000 |
| Vicente Fernandez | 68 | 71 | 69 | 208 | 22,560 |
| Bruce Fleisher | 72 | 66 | 70 | 208 | 22,560 |
| Graham Marsh | 67 | 72 | 69 | 208 | 22,560 |
| Keith Fergus | 66 | 72 | 71 | 209 | 17,760 |
| Morris Hatalsky | 74 | 68 | 67 | 209 | 17,760 |
| Wayne Levi | 65 | 72 | 72 | 209 | 17,760 |
| Dan Pohl | 69 | 71 | 69 | 209 | 17,760 |
| Mike Sullivan | 73 | 70 | 66 | 209 | 17,760 |
| Bob Gilder | 72 | 68 | 70 | 210 | 14,240 |
| Mike McCullough | 70 | 70 | 70 | 210 | 14,240 |
| Bob Murphy | 74 | 69 | 67 | 210 | 14,240 |

| | SCORES | | | TOTAL | MONEY |
|---|---|---|---|---|---|
| Des Smyth | 75 | 71 | 64 | 210 | 14,240 |
| Bob Eastwood | 69 | 70 | 72 | 211 | 11,800 |
| James Mason | 69 | 71 | 71 | 211 | 11,800 |
| Ron Streck | 68 | 74 | 69 | 211 | 11,800 |
| Bobby Wadkins | 73 | 68 | 70 | 211 | 11,800 |
| Jose Maria Canizares | 75 | 67 | 70 | 212 | 10,320 |
| John Ross | 70 | 70 | 72 | 212 | 10,320 |
| Jim Colbert | 76 | 68 | 69 | 213 | 9,000 |
| Danny Edwards | 70 | 72 | 71 | 213 | 9,000 |
| David Eger | 72 | 73 | 68 | 213 | 9,000 |
| Howard Twitty | 72 | 70 | 71 | 213 | 9,000 |
| Mark Johnson | 72 | 70 | 72 | 214 | 7,520 |
| Hajime Meshiai | 75 | 70 | 69 | 214 | 7,520 |
| Don Reese | 73 | 73 | 68 | 214 | 7,520 |
| Doug Tewell | 70 | 72 | 72 | 214 | 7,520 |
| Leonard Thompson | 75 | 70 | 69 | 214 | 7,520 |

## Administaff Small Business Classic

*Augusta Pines Golf Club*, Spring, Texas
Par 36-36–72; 7,006 yards

October 14-16
purse, $1,600,000

| | SCORES | | | TOTAL | MONEY |
|---|---|---|---|---|---|
| Mark McNulty | 66 | 68 | 66 | 200 | $240,000 |
| Gil Morgan | 67 | 67 | 67 | 201 | 140,800 |
| Hale Irwin | 66 | 68 | 68 | 202 | 115,200 |
| Brad Bryant | 66 | 66 | 71 | 203 | 96,000 |
| Jay Haas | 65 | 69 | 70 | 204 | 70,400 |
| Bruce Lietzke | 72 | 65 | 67 | 204 | 70,400 |
| John Bland | 68 | 68 | 69 | 205 | 51,200 |
| Don Pooley | 70 | 68 | 67 | 205 | 51,200 |
| Bobby Wadkins | 66 | 71 | 68 | 205 | 51,200 |
| Dave Barr | 67 | 67 | 72 | 206 | 40,000 |
| Bruce Fleisher | 69 | 68 | 69 | 206 | 40,000 |
| Jose Maria Canizares | 72 | 67 | 68 | 207 | 29,866.67 |
| John Mahaffey | 69 | 73 | 65 | 207 | 29,866.67 |
| James Mason | 71 | 70 | 66 | 207 | 29,866.67 |
| Ron Streck | 71 | 69 | 67 | 207 | 29,866.67 |
| R.W. Eaks | 68 | 71 | 68 | 207 | 29,866.66 |
| Tom Jenkins | 70 | 67 | 70 | 207 | 29,866.66 |
| Ben Crenshaw | 70 | 68 | 70 | 208 | 21,880 |
| Morris Hatalsky | 65 | 69 | 74 | 208 | 21,880 |
| Dan Pohl | 69 | 69 | 70 | 208 | 21,880 |
| Scott Simpson | 72 | 69 | 67 | 208 | 21,880 |
| Des Smyth | 65 | 74 | 70 | 209 | 17,653.34 |
| Tom Kite | 72 | 66 | 71 | 209 | 17,653.33 |
| Bob Murphy | 68 | 70 | 71 | 209 | 17,653.33 |
| Keith Fergus | 75 | 70 | 65 | 210 | 14,920 |
| Mark James | 71 | 72 | 67 | 210 | 14,920 |
| Mike Sullivan | 67 | 68 | 75 | 210 | 14,920 |
| Fuzzy Zoeller | 71 | 72 | 67 | 210 | 14,920 |
| David Eger | 70 | 70 | 71 | 211 | 12,640 |
| Walter Hall | 74 | 70 | 67 | 211 | 12,640 |
| Joe Inman | 73 | 71 | 67 | 211 | 12,640 |
| Hugh Baiocchi | 74 | 70 | 68 | 212 | 10,102.86 |
| Graham Marsh | 70 | 73 | 69 | 212 | 10,102.86 |
| Lonnie Nielsen | 72 | 72 | 68 | 212 | 10,102.86 |

| | SCORES | | | TOTAL | MONEY |
|---|---|---|---|---|---|
| Roy Vucinich | 70 | 72 | 70 | 212 | 10,102.86 |
| Lanny Wadkins | 72 | 71 | 69 | 212 | 10,102.86 |
| Mark Johnson | 72 | 70 | 70 | 212 | 10,102.85 |
| Dick Mast | 71 | 71 | 70 | 212 | 10,102.85 |
| Jim Ahern | 74 | 68 | 71 | 213 | 7,840 |
| Danny Edwards | 67 | 73 | 73 | 213 | 7,840 |
| Bob Gilder | 76 | 68 | 69 | 213 | 7,840 |
| Tom McKnight | 71 | 71 | 71 | 213 | 7,840 |
| D.A. Weibring | 69 | 73 | 71 | 213 | 7,840 |

## SBC Championship

*Oak Hills Country Club*, San Antonio, Texas
Par 35-36–71; 6,670 yards

October 21-23
purse, $1,550,000

| | SCORES | | | TOTAL | MONEY |
|---|---|---|---|---|---|
| Jay Haas | 67 | 66 | 66 | 199 | $232,500 |
| Tom Purtzer | 72 | 66 | 63 | 201 | 136,400 |
| Mark James | 66 | 66 | 70 | 202 | 111,600 |
| R.W. Eaks | 68 | 69 | 66 | 203 | 83,700 |
| Dana Quigley | 67 | 64 | 72 | 203 | 83,700 |
| Tom Kite | 72 | 65 | 67 | 204 | 55,800 |
| Jerry Pate | 65 | 71 | 68 | 204 | 55,800 |
| Gil Morgan | 64 | 71 | 69 | 204 | 55,800 |
| Bruce Fleisher | 68 | 66 | 71 | 205 | 41,850 |
| Dan Pohl | 65 | 69 | 71 | 205 | 41,850 |
| Fuzzy Zoeller | 70 | 69 | 67 | 206 | 34,100 |
| Mark McNulty | 65 | 72 | 69 | 206 | 34,100 |
| Morris Hatalsky | 66 | 69 | 71 | 206 | 34,100 |
| Dick Mast | 71 | 70 | 66 | 207 | 26,350 |
| D.A. Weibring | 69 | 70 | 68 | 207 | 26,350 |
| Don Pooley | 68 | 70 | 69 | 207 | 26,350 |
| Gary Koch | 72 | 66 | 69 | 207 | 26,350 |
| Andy Bean | 68 | 68 | 71 | 207 | 26,350 |
| John Bland | 70 | 70 | 68 | 208 | 19,878.75 |
| Hale Irwin | 70 | 69 | 69 | 208 | 19,878.75 |
| Scott Simpson | 72 | 63 | 73 | 208 | 19,878.75 |
| Lonnie Nielsen | 65 | 70 | 73 | 208 | 19,878.75 |
| Keith Fergus | 71 | 69 | 69 | 209 | 15,531 |
| Mike McCullough | 71 | 72 | 66 | 209 | 15,531 |
| Bobby Wadkins | 71 | 66 | 72 | 209 | 15,531 |
| Jim Thorpe | 71 | 65 | 73 | 209 | 15,531 |
| Tom Jenkins | 70 | 66 | 73 | 209 | 15,531 |
| Ed Dougherty | 67 | 73 | 70 | 210 | 11,020.50 |
| Larry Nelson | 70 | 71 | 69 | 210 | 11,020.50 |
| Tom McKnight | 70 | 70 | 70 | 210 | 11,020.50 |
| Vicente Fernandez | 70 | 70 | 70 | 210 | 11,020.50 |
| Bruce Summerhays | 69 | 72 | 69 | 210 | 11,020.50 |
| Craig Stadler | 67 | 72 | 71 | 210 | 11,020.50 |
| Bill Rogers | 72 | 67 | 71 | 210 | 11,020.50 |
| Bob Gilder | 72 | 67 | 71 | 210 | 11,020.50 |
| Rodger Davis | 75 | 67 | 68 | 210 | 11,020.50 |
| John Harris | 62 | 72 | 76 | 210 | 11,020.50 |
| Bruce Lietzke | 71 | 70 | 70 | 211 | 7,750 |
| Mike Sullivan | 71 | 70 | 70 | 211 | 7,750 |
| J.C. Snead | 74 | 67 | 70 | 211 | 7,750 |
| Hubert Green | 74 | 67 | 70 | 211 | 7,750 |

| | SCORES | | | TOTAL | MONEY |
|---|---|---|---|---|---|
| Tom Wargo | 70 | 72 | 69 | 211 | 7,750 |
| Ben Crenshaw | 70 | 73 | 68 | 211 | 7,750 |

## Charles Schwab Cup Championship

*Sonoma Golf Club*, Sonoma, California  
Par 36-36–72; 7,012 yards

October 27-30  
purse, $2,500,000

| | SCORES | | | | TOTAL | MONEY |
|---|---|---|---|---|---|---|
| Tom Watson | 69 | 70 | 69 | 64 | 272 | $440,000 |
| Jay Haas | 70 | 69 | 63 | 71 | 273 | 254,000 |
| Tom Kite | 72 | 68 | 68 | 67 | 275 | 213,000 |
| Mark McNulty | 72 | 72 | 65 | 68 | 277 | 176,000 |
| Dana Quigley | 69 | 71 | 68 | 70 | 278 | 128,500 |
| Loren Roberts | 69 | 69 | 70 | 70 | 278 | 128,500 |
| Tom Purtzer | 70 | 71 | 70 | 69 | 280 | 105,000 |
| Craig Stadler | 69 | 70 | 72 | 70 | 281 | 93,000 |
| Morris Hatalsky | 70 | 70 | 71 | 71 | 282 | 76,000 |
| Gil Morgan | 69 | 69 | 71 | 73 | 282 | 76,000 |
| Lonnie Nielsen | 66 | 72 | 70 | 74 | 282 | 76,000 |
| Mark James | 69 | 73 | 70 | 71 | 283 | 64,000 |
| Brad Bryant | 71 | 70 | 74 | 69 | 284 | 53,750 |
| Hale Irwin | 72 | 70 | 72 | 70 | 284 | 53,750 |
| Bruce Lietzke | 73 | 72 | 69 | 70 | 284 | 53,750 |
| Des Smyth | 69 | 70 | 74 | 71 | 284 | 53,750 |
| Jerry Pate | 67 | 72 | 77 | 69 | 285 | 39,583.34 |
| Jim Thorpe | 73 | 68 | 75 | 69 | 285 | 39,583.34 |
| Tom Jenkins | 69 | 73 | 73 | 70 | 285 | 39,583.33 |
| Don Pooley | 70 | 74 | 72 | 69 | 285 | 39,583.33 |
| Mike Reid | 72 | 72 | 71 | 70 | 285 | 39,583.33 |
| D.A. Weibring | 69 | 73 | 72 | 71 | 285 | 39,583.33 |
| Mark Johnson | 75 | 71 | 70 | 70 | 286 | 32,000 |
| Bob Gilder | 71 | 71 | 75 | 70 | 287 | 28,666.67 |
| Wayne Levi | 76 | 68 | 72 | 71 | 287 | 28,666.67 |
| Bruce Fleisher | 68 | 71 | 74 | 74 | 287 | 28,666.66 |
| Peter Jacobsen | 73 | 72 | 72 | 72 | 289 | 26,000 |
| David Eger | 76 | 72 | 77 | 73 | 298 | 25,000 |
| R.W. Eaks | 71 | 74 | | | WD | |
| Allen Doyle | 77 | | | | WD | |

# European Seniors Tour

## DGM Barbados Open

*Royal Westmoreland Golf Club,* St. James, Barbados
Par 36-36–72; 6,814 yards

March 2-4
purse, €189,465

| | SCORES | | | TOTAL | MONEY |
|---|---|---|---|---|---|
| Denis O'Sullivan | 68 | 68 | 70 | 206 | €29,752.76 |
| John Grace | 70 | 66 | 73 | 209 | 19,835.18 |
| Emilio Rodriguez Pareja | 71 | 68 | 71 | 210 | 13,884.62 |
| Carl Mason | 67 | 72 | 72 | 211 | 10,909.34 |
| Nick Job | 69 | 75 | 68 | 212 | 8,449.78 |
| Terry Gale | 73 | 70 | 69 | 212 | 8,449.78 |
| David J. Russell | 75 | 69 | 70 | 214 | 7,140.66 |
| John Morgan | 73 | 72 | 70 | 215 | 5,950.55 |
| Bruce Heuchan | 72 | 72 | 71 | 215 | 5,950.55 |
| Denis Durnian | 71 | 74 | 71 | 216 | 4,264.56 |
| Sam Torrance | 71 | 66 | 79 | 216 | 4,264.56 |
| Gery Watine | 70 | 73 | 73 | 216 | 4,264.56 |
| Luis Carbonetti | 77 | 68 | 71 | 216 | 4,264.56 |
| David Good | 72 | 71 | 73 | 216 | 4,264.56 |
| Pete Oakley | 71 | 70 | 75 | 216 | 4,264.56 |
| Giuseppe Cali | 71 | 73 | 73 | 217 | 3,272.80 |
| Horacio Carbonetti | 73 | 70 | 74 | 217 | 3,272.80 |
| Tony Charnley | 72 | 74 | 72 | 218 | 2,796.76 |
| Bob Cameron | 75 | 73 | 70 | 218 | 2,796.76 |
| Delroy Cambridge | 71 | 71 | 76 | 218 | 2,796.76 |
| Bill Longmuir | 72 | 74 | 73 | 219 | 2,314.10 |
| Manuel Pinero | 72 | 74 | 73 | 219 | 2,314.10 |
| Rex Caldwell | 77 | 70 | 72 | 219 | 2,314.10 |
| Adan Sowa | 74 | 75 | 71 | 220 | 2,033.11 |
| Jim Rhodes | 72 | 75 | 73 | 220 | 2,033.11 |
| Noel Ratcliffe | 74 | 71 | 76 | 221 | 1,844.67 |
| Hank Woodrome | 67 | 77 | 77 | 221 | 1,844.67 |
| Gavan Levenson | 70 | 78 | 74 | 222 | 1,606.65 |
| Martin Gray | 74 | 73 | 75 | 222 | 1,606.65 |
| Malcolm Gregson | 74 | 72 | 76 | 222 | 1,606.65 |
| Victor Garcia | 74 | 73 | 75 | 222 | 1,606.65 |

## Tobago Plantations Seniors Classic

*Tobago Plantations Beach & Golf Resort,* Tobago
Par 36-36–72; 6,752 yards

March 11-13
purse, €188,764

| | SCORES | | | TOTAL | MONEY |
|---|---|---|---|---|---|
| Luis Carbonetti | 69 | 71 | 68 | 208 | €28,314.71 |
| Bill Longmuir | 69 | 69 | 72 | 210 | 16,045 |
| Horacio Carbonetti | 71 | 69 | 70 | 210 | 16,045 |
| Carl Mason | 70 | 68 | 73 | 211 | 7,860.16 |
| Noel Ratcliffe | 68 | 72 | 71 | 211 | 7,860.16 |
| Gery Watine | 69 | 71 | 71 | 211 | 7,860.16 |

| | SCORES | | | TOTAL | MONEY |
|---|---|---|---|---|---|
| Chuck Milne | 70 | 71 | 70 | 211 | 7,860.16 |
| Tony Allen | 74 | 71 | 66 | 211 | 7,860.16 |
| Nick Job | 69 | 72 | 71 | 212 | 5,096.65 |
| Delroy Cambridge | 71 | 67 | 74 | 212 | 5,096.65 |
| Jim Rhodes | 71 | 73 | 69 | 213 | 4,011.25 |
| Bob Cameron | 65 | 74 | 74 | 213 | 4,011.25 |
| John Grace | 70 | 71 | 72 | 213 | 4,011.25 |
| Hank Woodrome | 69 | 75 | 69 | 213 | 4,011.25 |
| Eamonn Darcy | 66 | 74 | 74 | 214 | 3,397.77 |
| John Morgan | 73 | 72 | 71 | 216 | 3,209 |
| Tommy Horton | 72 | 75 | 70 | 217 | 3,020.24 |
| Maurice Bembridge | 70 | 77 | 71 | 218 | 2,307.65 |
| Emilio Rodriguez Pareja | 71 | 71 | 76 | 218 | 2,307.65 |
| David J. Russell | 71 | 73 | 74 | 218 | 2,307.65 |
| Jerry Bruner | 75 | 72 | 71 | 218 | 2,307.65 |
| Mike Ferguson | 74 | 72 | 72 | 218 | 2,307.65 |
| Neville Clarke | 73 | 71 | 74 | 218 | 2,307.65 |
| Bruce Heuchan | 71 | 73 | 74 | 218 | 2,307.65 |
| Lee Carter | 71 | 72 | 75 | 218 | 2,307.65 |
| Craig Maltman | 69 | 79 | 71 | 219 | 1,642.25 |
| Giuseppe Cali | 75 | 74 | 70 | 219 | 1,642.25 |
| Malcolm Gregson | 73 | 75 | 71 | 219 | 1,642.25 |
| Armando Saavedra | 72 | 73 | 74 | 219 | 1,642.25 |
| Jeff Van Wagenen | 69 | 74 | 76 | 219 | 1,642.25 |

## Jolie Ville Sharm El Sheikh Seniors Open

*Jolie Ville Golf Resort,* Sharm El Skeikh, Egypt

Par 35-35–70; 6,546 yards

April 21-23

purse, €197,245

| | SCORES | | | TOTAL | MONEY |
|---|---|---|---|---|---|
| Bob Lendzion | 65 | 67 | 66 | 198 | €29,586.87 |
| David J. Russell | 63 | 66 | 70 | 199 | 16,765.89 |
| Mokgeteng John Mashego | 69 | 66 | 64 | 199 | 16765.89 |
| John Benda | 64 | 68 | 68 | 200 | 10,848.52 |
| Gavan Levenson | 68 | 67 | 66 | 201 | 8,915.51 |
| Bob Cameron | 68 | 66 | 68 | 202 | 7,889.83 |
| Craig Maltman | 70 | 70 | 66 | 206 | 7,100.85 |
| Bruce Heuchan | 70 | 68 | 69 | 207 | 6,311.87 |
| Eamonn Darcy | 70 | 69 | 69 | 208 | 5,325.64 |
| Chuck Milne | 69 | 67 | 72 | 208 | 5,325.64 |
| Mike Miller | 71 | 67 | 71 | 209 | 4,063.26 |
| Gery Watine | 69 | 70 | 70 | 209 | 4,063.26 |
| Armando Saavedra | 69 | 69 | 71 | 209 | 4,063.26 |
| Luis Carbonetti | 69 | 70 | 70 | 209 | 4,063.26 |
| John Chillas | 72 | 70 | 67 | 209 | 4,063.26 |
| Malcolm Gregson | 71 | 69 | 70 | 210 | 3,155.93 |
| Gordon Townhill | 68 | 71 | 71 | 210 | 3,155.93 |
| Delroy Cambridge | 68 | 68 | 74 | 210 | 3,155.93 |
| Nick Job | 71 | 70 | 70 | 211 | 2,457.68 |
| Carl Mason | 70 | 72 | 69 | 211 | 2,457.68 |
| Jim Rhodes | 70 | 68 | 73 | 211 | 2,457.68 |
| Tony Allen | 69 | 66 | 76 | 211 | 2,457.68 |
| Paul Reed | 68 | 71 | 72 | 211 | 2,457.68 |
| Antonio Garrido | 70 | 74 | 68 | 212 | 2,021.77 |
| Jean Pierre Sallat | 71 | 71 | 70 | 212 | 2,021.77 |
| Denis Durnian | 74 | 70 | 69 | 213 | 1,794.94 |

|  | SCORES | | | TOTAL | MONEY |
|---|---|---|---|---|---|
| Kevin Spurgeon | 69 | 72 | 72 | 213 | 1,794.94 |
| Giuseppe Cali | 70 | 71 | 72 | 213 | 1,794.94 |
| Tony Charnley | 71 | 71 | 72 | 214 | 1,367.57 |
| Bill Longmuir | 72 | 71 | 71 | 214 | 1,367.57 |
| Denis O'Sullivan | 72 | 72 | 70 | 214 | 1,367.57 |
| Jeff Van Wagenen | 70 | 67 | 77 | 214 | 1,367.57 |
| Horacio Carbonetti | 73 | 72 | 69 | 214 | 1,367.57 |
| Stephen Chadwick | 70 | 71 | 73 | 214 | 1,367.57 |
| Hank Woodrome | 73 | 69 | 72 | 214 | 1,367.57 |
| Mike Ferguson | 74 | 70 | 70 | 214 | 1,367.57 |
| Lee Carter | 73 | 70 | 71 | 214 | 1,367.57 |

## Nokia 9300 Italian Seniors Open

*Circolo Golf Venezia,* Venice, Italy
Par 35-37–72; 6,757 yards

May 20-22
purse, €170,000

|  | SCORES | | | TOTAL | MONEY |
|---|---|---|---|---|---|
| Gery Watine | 67 | 70 | 68 | 205 | €25,500 |
| Eamonn Darcy | 69 | 69 | 67 | 205 | 17,000 |
| (Watine defeated Darcy on first playoff hole.) | | | | | |
| Gavan Levenson | 69 | 68 | 70 | 207 | 11,900 |
| Nick Job | 69 | 72 | 67 | 208 | 8,517 |
| Sam Torrance | 71 | 69 | 68 | 208 | 8,517 |
| Bruce Heuchan | 74 | 68 | 68 | 210 | 6,800 |
| Carl Mason | 70 | 72 | 69 | 211 | 5,440 |
| Emilio Rodriguez Pareja | 72 | 69 | 70 | 211 | 5,440 |
| Alan Tapie | 71 | 72 | 68 | 211 | 5,440 |
| Craig Maltman | 72 | 68 | 73 | 213 | 4,420 |
| Luis Carbonetti | 70 | 69 | 75 | 214 | 3,910 |
| Horacio Carbonetti | 71 | 72 | 71 | 214 | 3,910 |
| Tony Charnley | 71 | 72 | 72 | 215 | 3,400 |
| Adan Sowa | 68 | 72 | 76 | 216 | 3,145 |
| Jim Rhodes | 72 | 73 | 71 | 216 | 3,145 |
| Bob Byman | 73 | 73 | 71 | 217 | 2,720 |
| Donald Stirling | 74 | 68 | 75 | 217 | 2,720 |
| Lee Carter | 72 | 72 | 73 | 217 | 2,720 |
| Tommy Horton | 72 | 71 | 75 | 218 | 2,118.20 |
| Bill Longmuir | 75 | 73 | 70 | 218 | 2,118.20 |
| Denis O'Sullivan | 72 | 70 | 76 | 218 | 2,118.20 |
| Jean Pierre Sallat | 73 | 74 | 71 | 218 | 2,118.20 |
| Paul Reed | 73 | 71 | 74 | 218 | 2,118.20 |
| Martin Gray | 70 | 72 | 77 | 219 | 1,742.50 |
| Eddie Polland | 76 | 71 | 72 | 219 | 1,742.50 |
| Giuseppe Cali | 74 | 74 | 72 | 220 | 1,445 |
| Guillermo Encina | 74 | 71 | 75 | 220 | 1,445 |
| John Chillas | 74 | 72 | 74 | 220 | 1,445 |
| Brian Jones | 72 | 72 | 76 | 220 | 1,445 |
| Delroy Cambridge | 73 | 72 | 75 | 220 | 1,445 |
| Alan Mew | 76 | 70 | 74 | 220 | 1,445 |

## AIB Irish Seniors Open

*The Heritage at Killenard,* Ireland
Par 36-36–72; 6,839 yards

June 3-5
purse, €400,000

| | SCORES | | | TOTAL | MONEY |
|---|---|---|---|---|---|
| Noel Ratcliffe | 71 | 68 | 71 | 210 | €60,000 |
| Luis Carbonetti | 70 | 69 | 73 | 212 | 40,000 |
| John Chillas | 70 | 71 | 72 | 213 | 28,000 |
| Sam Torrance | 68 | 75 | 71 | 214 | 22,000 |
| Eamonn Darcy | 72 | 73 | 71 | 216 | 17,040 |
| Des Smyth | 73 | 71 | 72 | 216 | 17,040 |
| Craig Maltman | 73 | 72 | 72 | 217 | 12,200 |
| Martin Poxon | 71 | 75 | 71 | 217 | 12,200 |
| David J. Russell | 71 | 76 | 70 | 217 | 12,200 |
| Bruce Heuchan | 71 | 73 | 73 | 217 | 12,200 |
| Jim Rhodes | 67 | 77 | 74 | 218 | 9,200 |
| Alan Mew | 73 | 70 | 75 | 218 | 9,200 |
| Nick Job | 70 | 76 | 73 | 219 | 7,000 |
| Bob Shearer | 71 | 75 | 73 | 219 | 7,000 |
| Jerry Bruner | 74 | 75 | 70 | 219 | 7,000 |
| Bob Cameron | 76 | 73 | 70 | 219 | 7,000 |
| Seiji Ebihara | 71 | 70 | 78 | 219 | 7,000 |
| Rex Caldwell | 76 | 73 | 70 | 219 | 7,000 |
| Manuel Pinero | 76 | 72 | 72 | 220 | 4,984 |
| Emilio Rodriguez | 75 | 70 | 75 | 220 | 4,984 |
| Terry Gale | 74 | 75 | 71 | 220 | 4,984 |
| Alan Tapie | 72 | 79 | 69 | 220 | 4,984 |
| Horacio Carbonetti | 76 | 73 | 71 | 220 | 4,984 |
| Carl Mason | 75 | 75 | 71 | 221 | 3,657.14 |
| Mike Miller | 73 | 74 | 74 | 221 | 3,657.14 |
| Martin Gray | 75 | 75 | 71 | 221 | 3,657.14 |
| Kevin Spurgeon | 72 | 71 | 78 | 221 | 3,657.14 |
| David Oakley | 71 | 78 | 72 | 221 | 3,657.14 |
| Tony Allen | 72 | 78 | 71 | 221 | 3,657.14 |
| Lee Carter | 68 | 83 | 70 | 221 | 3,657.14 |

## Irvine Whitlock Seniors Classic

*La Moye Golf Club,* Jersey, Channel Isles
Par 36-36–72; 6,581 yards

June 10-12
purse, €177,826

| | SCORES | | | TOTAL | MONEY |
|---|---|---|---|---|---|
| Sam Torrance | 65 | 68 | 72 | 205 | €26,673.84 |
| David J. Russell | 67 | 69 | 73 | 209 | 17,782.56 |
| John Morgan | 72 | 72 | 67 | 211 | 9,344.74 |
| Jean Pierre Sallat | 66 | 73 | 72 | 211 | 9,344.74 |
| Mokgeteng John Mashego | 69 | 72 | 70 | 211 | 9,344.74 |
| Bruce Heuchan | 68 | 73 | 70 | 211 | 9,344.74 |
| Tommy Horton | 70 | 71 | 71 | 212 | 6,401.72 |
| Martin Poxon | 71 | 73 | 69 | 213 | 5,334.77 |
| Jim Rhodes | 69 | 71 | 73 | 213 | 5,334.77 |
| Tony Charnley | 75 | 70 | 69 | 214 | 4,623.47 |
| Bill Longmuir | 72 | 75 | 68 | 215 | 4,089.99 |
| Bobby Lincoln | 71 | 73 | 71 | 215 | 4,089.99 |
| Gery Watine | 72 | 71 | 73 | 216 | 3,378.69 |
| Kevin Spurgeon | 71 | 76 | 69 | 216 | 3,378.69 |

| | SCORES | | | TOTAL | MONEY |
|---|---|---|---|---|---|
| Bob Cameron | 77 | 68 | 71 | 216 | 3,378.69 |
| Maurice Bembridge | 72 | 73 | 72 | 217 | 2,599.22 |
| Giuseppe Cali | 72 | 73 | 72 | 217 | 2,599.22 |
| Terry Gale | 70 | 74 | 73 | 217 | 2,599.22 |
| Denis O'Sullivan | 72 | 73 | 72 | 217 | 2,599.22 |
| Jerry Bruner | 72 | 74 | 71 | 217 | 2,599.22 |
| David Good | 72 | 75 | 70 | 217 | 2,599.22 |
| Denis Durnian | 73 | 69 | 76 | 218 | 2,062.78 |
| Mike Miller | 74 | 74 | 71 | 219 | 1,781.81 |
| Simon Owen | 72 | 74 | 73 | 219 | 1,781.81 |
| Alan Tapie | 73 | 72 | 74 | 219 | 1,781.81 |
| Eddie Polland | 68 | 79 | 72 | 219 | 1,781.81 |
| Alan Mew | 75 | 73 | 71 | 219 | 1,781.81 |
| Noel Ratcliffe | 71 | 77 | 72 | 220 | 1,378.15 |
| Emilio Rodriguez | 74 | 78 | 68 | 220 | 1,378.15 |
| Bob Shearer | 75 | 75 | 70 | 220 | 1,378.15 |
| John Chillas | 76 | 73 | 71 | 220 | 1,378.15 |
| Gordon Townhill | 73 | 74 | 73 | 220 | 1,378.15 |
| Delroy Cambridge | 70 | 75 | 75 | 220 | 1,378.15 |

## The Mobile Cup

*Collingtree Park Golf Club,* Northampton, England
Par 36-36–72; 6,730 yards

June 17-19
purse, €186,856

| | SCORES | | | TOTAL | MONEY |
|---|---|---|---|---|---|
| Giuseppe Cali | 66 | 70 | 72 | 208 | €29,343.01 |
| Martin Gray | 67 | 72 | 70 | 209 | 19,562 |
| Alan Tapie | 68 | 69 | 73 | 210 | 13,693.39 |
| Gordon Townhill | 66 | 74 | 71 | 211 | 9,800.57 |
| Horacio Carbonetti | 73 | 69 | 69 | 211 | 9,800.57 |
| Delroy Cambridge | 74 | 71 | 67 | 212 | 7,824.81 |
| Bob Larratt | 73 | 67 | 73 | 213 | 7,042.33 |
| Eamonn Darcy | 74 | 67 | 73 | 214 | 5,607.77 |
| Kevin Spurgeon | 73 | 72 | 69 | 214 | 5,607.77 |
| Rex Caldwell | 71 | 69 | 74 | 214 | 5,607.77 |
| John Chillas | 71 | 73 | 71 | 215 | 4,499.26 |
| Bob Cameron | 69 | 73 | 73 | 215 | 4,499.26 |
| Tony Charnley | 70 | 74 | 72 | 216 | 3,814.59 |
| David Oakley | 74 | 72 | 70 | 216 | 3,814.59 |
| Jim Rhodes | 74 | 70 | 73 | 217 | 3,521.16 |
| Noel Ratcliffe | 71 | 73 | 74 | 218 | 3,037 |
| Gavan Levenson | 75 | 70 | 73 | 218 | 3,037 |
| Guillermo Encina | 72 | 73 | 73 | 218 | 3,037 |
| Bruce Heuchan | 73 | 73 | 72 | 218 | 3,037 |
| Maurice Bembridge | 73 | 73 | 73 | 219 | 2,296.58 |
| John Morgan | 73 | 71 | 75 | 219 | 2,296.58 |
| Manuel Pinero | 73 | 77 | 69 | 219 | 2,296.58 |
| Armando Saavedra | 78 | 72 | 69 | 219 | 2,296.58 |
| Luis Carbonetti | 76 | 72 | 71 | 219 | 2,296.58 |
| Bill Longmuir | 78 | 72 | 70 | 220 | 1,864.91 |
| Simon Owen | 71 | 72 | 77 | 220 | 1,864.91 |
| Seiji Ebihara | 78 | 71 | 71 | 220 | 1,864.91 |
| Martin Poxon | 73 | 74 | 74 | 221 | 1,623.64 |
| Keith Williams | 75 | 74 | 72 | 221 | 1,623.64 |
| Bobby Lincoln | 76 | 72 | 73 | 221 | 1,623.64 |

# De Vere Northumberland Seniors Classic

*De Vere Slaley Hall, Priestman Course,*
Hexham, England
Par 36-36–72; 6,838 yards

June 24-26
purse, €223,847

| | SCORES | | | TOTAL | MONEY |
|---|---|---|---|---|---|
| Carl Mason | 68 | 63 | 69 | 200 | €33,577.20 |
| Eamonn Darcy | 68 | 68 | 67 | 203 | 22,384.80 |
| Seiji Ebihara | 72 | 69 | 65 | 206 | 13,990.50 |
| Delroy Cambridge | 68 | 70 | 68 | 206 | 13,990.50 |
| Manuel Pinero | 70 | 66 | 71 | 207 | 10,117.93 |
| Mark James | 73 | 67 | 68 | 208 | 8,058.53 |
| David J. Russell | 68 | 70 | 70 | 208 | 8,058.53 |
| David Oakley | 68 | 70 | 70 | 208 | 8,058.53 |
| Noel Ratcliffe | 67 | 72 | 70 | 209 | 5,820.05 |
| Guillermo Encina | 69 | 72 | 68 | 209 | 5,820.05 |
| Bob Cameron | 71 | 70 | 68 | 209 | 5,820.05 |
| Nick Job | 70 | 72 | 68 | 210 | 4,297.88 |
| Sam Torrance | 68 | 74 | 68 | 210 | 4,297.88 |
| Gavan Levenson | 72 | 70 | 68 | 210 | 4,297.88 |
| Luis Carbonetti | 72 | 66 | 72 | 210 | 4,297.88 |
| Jim Rhodes | 68 | 73 | 69 | 210 | 4,297.88 |
| Denis Durnian | 74 | 68 | 69 | 211 | 2,983.57 |
| Ian Mosey | 73 | 74 | 64 | 211 | 2,983.57 |
| Kevin Spurgeon | 68 | 74 | 69 | 211 | 2,983.57 |
| Bob Shearer | 73 | 70 | 68 | 211 | 2,983.57 |
| John Chillas | 73 | 71 | 67 | 211 | 2,983.57 |
| Hank Woodrome | 73 | 69 | 69 | 211 | 2,983.57 |
| Mike Ferguson | 68 | 75 | 68 | 211 | 2,983.57 |
| Bob Lendzion | 71 | 68 | 73 | 212 | 2,238.48 |
| Martin Foster | 72 | 67 | 73 | 212 | 2,238.48 |
| David Good | 68 | 72 | 72 | 212 | 2,238.48 |
| Emilio Rodriguez | 74 | 68 | 71 | 213 | 1,947.48 |
| Horacio Carbonetti | 72 | 72 | 69 | 213 | 1,947.48 |
| John Curtis | 72 | 71 | 70 | 213 | 1,947.48 |
| John Morgan | 70 | 75 | 69 | 214 | 1,616.18 |
| Russell Weir | 71 | 72 | 71 | 214 | 1,616.18 |
| Adan Sowa | 74 | 72 | 68 | 214 | 1,616.18 |
| Dragon Taki | 72 | 71 | 71 | 214 | 1,616.18 |
| Bruce Heuchan | 73 | 70 | 71 | 214 | 1,616.18 |

# Ryder Cup Wales Seniors Open

*Royal St. David's Golf Club,* Harlech, Wales
Par 36-33–69; 6,565 yards

July 1-3
purse, €753,679

| | SCORES | | | TOTAL | MONEY |
|---|---|---|---|---|---|
| Carl Mason | 68 | 69 | 65 | 202 | €113,052 |
| Bob Charles | 68 | 69 | 70 | 207 | 64,062.80 |
| Denis O'Sullivan | 70 | 69 | 68 | 207 | 64,062.80 |
| Nick Job | 67 | 69 | 72 | 208 | 41,452.40 |
| Sam Torrance | 69 | 69 | 71 | 209 | 30,448.67 |
| John Chillas | 67 | 71 | 71 | 209 | 30,448.67 |
| Bob Cameron | 68 | 73 | 68 | 209 | 30,448.67 |
| Tommy Horton | 70 | 73 | 67 | 210 | 21,605.49 |
| Noel Ratcliffe | 72 | 71 | 67 | 210 | 21,605.49 |

|  | SCORES | | | TOTAL | MONEY |
|---|---|---|---|---|---|
| Delroy Cambridge | 72 | 70 | 68 | 210 | 21,605.49 |
| Bill Longmuir | 71 | 73 | 67 | 211 | 17,334.64 |
| Martin Gray | 71 | 70 | 70 | 211 | 17,334.64 |
| Terry Gale | 73 | 69 | 70 | 212 | 15,073.60 |
| Eamonn Darcy | 70 | 70 | 73 | 213 | 12,812.56 |
| Ian Mosey | 70 | 72 | 71 | 213 | 12,812.56 |
| Martin Poxon | 73 | 69 | 71 | 213 | 12,812.56 |
| Gery Watine | 71 | 70 | 72 | 213 | 12,812.56 |
| Gavan Levenson | 69 | 72 | 72 | 213 | 12,812.56 |
| Denis Durnian | 71 | 72 | 71 | 214 | 9,665.95 |
| Luis Carbonetti | 73 | 71 | 70 | 214 | 9,665.95 |
| Horacio Carbonetti | 69 | 71 | 74 | 214 | 9,665.95 |
| John Grace | 70 | 72 | 72 | 214 | 9,665.95 |
| Neil Coles | 70 | 73 | 72 | 215 | 7,386.06 |
| Manuel Pinero | 75 | 72 | 68 | 215 | 7,386.06 |
| Giuseppe Cali | 70 | 70 | 75 | 215 | 7,386.06 |
| Adan Sowa | 76 | 70 | 69 | 215 | 7,386.06 |
| David Creamer | 74 | 69 | 72 | 215 | 7,386.06 |
| Seiji Ebihara | 76 | 70 | 69 | 215 | 7,386.06 |
| Ray Carrasco | 75 | 71 | 70 | 216 | 6,104.81 |
| Martin Foster | 73 | 67 | 76 | 216 | 6,104.81 |

## Nigel Mansell Sunseeker International Classic

*Woodbury Park Hotel Golf & Country Club,* Devon, England
Par 37-35–72; 6,962 yards

July 8-10
purse, €222,118

|  | SCORES | | | TOTAL | MONEY |
|---|---|---|---|---|---|
| Jim Rhodes | 69 | 68 | 71 | 208 | €33,317.78 |
| Tony Charnley | 69 | 72 | 70 | 211 | 22,211.85 |
| Carl Mason | 75 | 66 | 71 | 212 | 13,882.41 |
| Delroy Cambridge | 70 | 71 | 71 | 212 | 13,882.41 |
| Gavan Levenson | 69 | 71 | 74 | 214 | 8,507.14 |
| Kevin Spurgeon | 76 | 71 | 67 | 214 | 8,507.14 |
| Giuseppe Cali | 71 | 68 | 75 | 214 | 8,507.14 |
| Luis Carbonetti | 75 | 68 | 71 | 214 | 8,507.14 |
| Emilio Rodriguez | 73 | 74 | 68 | 215 | 5,775.08 |
| John Chillas | 70 | 75 | 70 | 215 | 5,775.08 |
| Tony Allen | 71 | 70 | 74 | 215 | 5,775.08 |
| Bob Charles | 73 | 69 | 74 | 216 | 4,264.68 |
| Martin Poxon | 74 | 72 | 70 | 216 | 4,264.68 |
| David J. Russell | 74 | 67 | 75 | 216 | 4,264.68 |
| Martin Foster | 69 | 73 | 74 | 216 | 4,264.68 |
| Seiji Ebihara | 76 | 69 | 71 | 216 | 4,264.68 |
| Tommy Horton | 69 | 74 | 74 | 217 | 3,237.38 |
| Craig Maltman | 75 | 71 | 71 | 217 | 3,237.38 |
| Mike Miller | 72 | 72 | 73 | 217 | 3,237.38 |
| Ian Mosey | 70 | 74 | 73 | 217 | 3,237.38 |
| Nick Job | 75 | 73 | 70 | 218 | 2,406.28 |
| Russell Weir | 73 | 71 | 74 | 218 | 2,406.28 |
| Guillermo Encina | 74 | 72 | 72 | 218 | 2,406.28 |
| Jerry Bruner | 74 | 72 | 72 | 218 | 2,406.28 |
| David Good | 75 | 74 | 69 | 218 | 2,406.28 |
| Rex Caldwell | 71 | 73 | 74 | 218 | 2,406.28 |
| Eamonn Darcy | 73 | 72 | 74 | 219 | 1,843.58 |
| Bill Longmuir | 74 | 71 | 74 | 219 | 1,843.58 |
| John Morgan | 72 | 77 | 70 | 219 | 1,843.58 |

| | | SCORES | | | TOTAL | MONEY |
|---|---|---|---|---|---|---|
| Martin Gray | 78 | 69 | 72 | | 219 | 1,843.58 |
| Jean Pierre Sallat | 72 | 75 | 72 | | 219 | 1,843.58 |

## Senior British Open

*Royal Aberdeen Golf Club,* Aberdeen, Scotland       July 21-24
Par 36-35–71; 6,836 yards       purse, €1,457,507

| | | SCORES | | | TOTAL | MONEY |
|---|---|---|---|---|---|---|
| Tom Watson | 75 | 71 | 64 | 70 | 280 | €229,849.90 |
| Des Smyth | 73 | 72 | 68 | 67 | 280 | 153,306.10 |
| (Watson defeated Smyth on third playoff hole.) | | | | | | |
| Greg Norman | 76 | 67 | 70 | 68 | 281 | 86,302.96 |
| Craig Stadler | 73 | 68 | 70 | 72 | 283 | 68,969.54 |
| Loren Roberts | 72 | 74 | 71 | 67 | 284 | 58,438.39 |
| Derrick Cooper | 73 | 80 | 64 | 70 | 287 | 44,819.28 |
| David Eger | 80 | 70 | 72 | 65 | 287 | 44,819.28 |
| Mark McNulty | 76 | 72 | 72 | 68 | 288 | 34,448.36 |
| Eduardo Romero | 75 | 71 | 75 | 69 | 290 | 27,942.25 |
| Martin Gray | 77 | 73 | 71 | 69 | 290 | 27,942.25 |
| Ray Stewart | 73 | 77 | 75 | 65 | 290 | 27,942.25 |
| John Bland | 76 | 78 | 65 | 72 | 291 | 22,300.39 |
| Mark James | 74 | 75 | 70 | 72 | 291 | 22,300.39 |
| Noel Ratcliffe | 80 | 74 | 69 | 68 | 291 | 22,300.39 |
| Lonnie Nielsen | 81 | 74 | 70 | 67 | 292 | 20,275.73 |
| Carl Mason | 75 | 78 | 68 | 72 | 293 | 17,375.04 |
| Giuseppe Cali | 73 | 73 | 77 | 70 | 293 | 17,375.04 |
| John Chillas | 75 | 74 | 73 | 71 | 293 | 17,375.04 |
| Horacio Carbonetti | 75 | 73 | 72 | 73 | 293 | 17,375.04 |
| Seiji Ebihara | 77 | 70 | 72 | 74 | 293 | 17,375.04 |
| Bob Gilder | 76 | 74 | 72 | 71 | 293 | 17,375.04 |
| Frank Conner | 73 | 74 | 75 | 71 | 293 | 17,375.04 |
| Bill Longmuir | 80 | 71 | 72 | 71 | 294 | 15,090.27 |
| Katsuyoshi Tomori | 78 | 76 | 73 | 67 | 294 | 15,090.27 |
| Ian Mosey | 76 | 77 | 66 | 76 | 295 | 13,691.95 |
| Martin Poxon | 81 | 73 | 74 | 67 | 295 | 13,691.95 |
| Luis Carbonetti | 76 | 78 | 74 | 67 | 295 | 13,691.95 |
| David Oakley | 80 | 77 | 65 | 73 | 295 | 13,691.95 |
| Eamonn Darcy | 78 | 74 | 78 | 66 | 296 | 11,951.32 |
| Sam Torrance | 77 | 75 | 75 | 69 | 296 | 11,951.32 |
| Andy Bean | 76 | 75 | 74 | 71 | 296 | 11,951.32 |
| Tom McKnight | 82 | 75 | 66 | 73 | 296 | 11,951.32 |
| Alan Tapie | 74 | 75 | 77 | 71 | 297 | 10,667.09 |
| Bruce Heuchan | 77 | 78 | 71 | 71 | 297 | 10,667.09 |
| Don Reese | 77 | 76 | 72 | 72 | 297 | 10,667.09 |
| Maurice Bembridge | 77 | 75 | 75 | 71 | 298 | 9,370.73 |
| David J. Russell | 80 | 74 | 70 | 74 | 298 | 9,370.73 |
| Isao Aoki | 75 | 75 | 75 | 73 | 298 | 9,370.73 |
| Denis O'Sullivan | 76 | 77 | 72 | 73 | 298 | 9,370.73 |
| Bobby Lincoln | 77 | 72 | 75 | 74 | 298 | 9,370.73 |
| Mike Ferguson | 77 | 78 | 70 | 73 | 298 | 9,370.73 |

# De Vere PGA Seniors Championship

*De Vere Carden Park*, Cheshire, England
Par 36-36–72; 6,868 yards

August 4-7
purse, €290,098

| | SCORES | | | | TOTAL | MONEY |
|---|---|---|---|---|---|---|
| Sam Torrance | 66 | 70 | 66 | 69 | 271 | €48,344.83 |
| David J. Russell | 71 | 66 | 70 | 68 | 275 | 30,837.42 |
| Nick Job | 69 | 67 | 70 | 70 | 276 | 16,100.44 |
| Carl Mason | 66 | 70 | 70 | 70 | 276 | 16,100.44 |
| Ian Mosey | 73 | 69 | 66 | 69 | 277 | 11,894.02 |
| Bill Longmuir | 67 | 69 | 73 | 69 | 278 | 10,225.95 |
| Martin Gray | 67 | 72 | 71 | 68 | 278 | 10,225.95 |
| Giuseppe Cali | 70 | 70 | 71 | 69 | 280 | 9,138.09 |
| John Chillas | 67 | 71 | 72 | 71 | 281 | 8,050.22 |
| Bob Boyd | 73 | 71 | 69 | 68 | 281 | 8,050.22 |
| Bob Cameron | 67 | 73 | 72 | 70 | 282 | 6,962.35 |
| John Bland | 66 | 74 | 69 | 74 | 283 | 5,584.39 |
| John Morgan | 67 | 71 | 76 | 69 | 283 | 5,584.39 |
| John Benda | 73 | 69 | 68 | 73 | 283 | 5,584.39 |
| David Oakley | 70 | 74 | 70 | 70 | 284 | 4,170.16 |
| Denis O'Sullivan | 69 | 72 | 71 | 72 | 284 | 4,170.16 |
| Tony Charnley | 69 | 73 | 72 | 71 | 285 | 3,281.01 |
| Tommy Horton | 73 | 74 | 69 | 69 | 285 | 3,281.01 |
| Craig Maltman | 70 | 73 | 69 | 73 | 285 | 3,281.01 |
| Ray Stewart | 69 | 73 | 71 | 72 | 285 | 3,281.01 |
| Bruce Heuchan | 70 | 74 | 72 | 69 | 285 | 3,281.01 |
| Gery Watine | 70 | 72 | 73 | 71 | 286 | 2,959 |
| David Good | 68 | 72 | 74 | 73 | 287 | 2,886.47 |
| Eamonn Darcy | 69 | 72 | 72 | 75 | 288 | 2,632.64 |
| Terry Gale | 69 | 70 | 79 | 70 | 288 | 2,632.64 |
| Bobby Lincoln | 72 | 73 | 71 | 72 | 288 | 2,632.64 |
| Seiji Ebihara | 67 | 73 | 72 | 76 | 288 | 2,632.64 |
| Delroy Cambridge | 70 | 72 | 75 | 71 | 288 | 2,632.64 |
| Alan Mew | 68 | 77 | 71 | 72 | 288 | 2,632.64 |
| Martin Poxon | 70 | 74 | 73 | 72 | 289 | 2,378.80 |

# Bad Ragaz PGA Seniors Open

*Golf Club Bad Ragaz*, Zurich, Switzerland
Par 35-35–70; 6,130 yards

August 12-14
purse, €210,000

| | SCORES | | | TOTAL | MONEY |
|---|---|---|---|---|---|
| Terry Gale | 67 | 66 | 66 | 199 | €31,500 |
| Gery Watine | 65 | 71 | 65 | 201 | 17,850 |
| Luis Carbonetti | 66 | 67 | 68 | 201 | 17,850 |
| John Bland | 68 | 64 | 71 | 203 | 10,521 |
| David Oakley | 69 | 69 | 65 | 203 | 10,521 |
| Kevin Spurgeon | 68 | 71 | 65 | 204 | 7,140 |
| Giuseppe Cali | 67 | 68 | 69 | 204 | 7,140 |
| Jerry Bruner | 62 | 70 | 72 | 204 | 7,140 |
| Horacio Carbonetti | 67 | 67 | 70 | 204 | 7,140 |
| Gordon J. Brand | 67 | 68 | 70 | 205 | 5,250 |
| Mokgeteng John Mashego | 66 | 66 | 73 | 205 | 5,250 |
| Noel Ratcliffe | 66 | 66 | 74 | 206 | 3,920 |
| Martin Gray | 67 | 72 | 67 | 206 | 3,920 |
| Adan Sowa | 67 | 68 | 71 | 206 | 3,920 |

| | SCORES | | | TOTAL | MONEY |
|---|---|---|---|---|---|
| Denis O'Sullivan | 69 | 68 | 69 | 206 | 3,920 |
| John Benda | 68 | 69 | 69 | 206 | 3,920 |
| Delroy Cambridge | 67 | 67 | 72 | 206 | 3,920 |
| Bob Charles | 68 | 73 | 66 | 207 | 2,784.60 |
| Tony Charnley | 70 | 71 | 66 | 207 | 2,784.60 |
| Tommy Horton | 68 | 71 | 68 | 207 | 2,784.60 |
| Ian Mosey | 66 | 70 | 71 | 207 | 2,784.60 |
| Bob Shearer | 70 | 67 | 70 | 207 | 2,784.60 |
| John Chillas | 69 | 70 | 69 | 208 | 2,310 |
| Nick Job | 70 | 69 | 70 | 209 | 1,920 |
| Martin Poxon | 72 | 68 | 69 | 209 | 1,920 |
| Gavan Levenson | 70 | 70 | 69 | 209 | 1,920 |
| Peter Townsend | 68 | 70 | 71 | 209 | 1,920 |
| Alan Tapie | 68 | 72 | 69 | 209 | 1,920 |
| Steve Wild | 70 | 68 | 71 | 209 | 1,920 |
| Mike Ferguson | 70 | 72 | 67 | 209 | 1,920 |

## Travis Perkins Senior Masters

*Wentworth Club, Edinburgh Course,* Surrey, England
Par 36-36–72; 6,873 yards

August 19-21
purse, €328,556

| | SCORES | | | TOTAL | MONEY |
|---|---|---|---|---|---|
| Eduardo Romero | 70 | 67 | 68 | 205 | €49,283.44 |
| Nick Job | 76 | 67 | 70 | 213 | 27,927.28 |
| Luis Carbonetti | 72 | 73 | 68 | 213 | 27,927.28 |
| Terry Gale | 72 | 72 | 70 | 214 | 18,070.59 |
| Gordon J. Brand | 74 | 69 | 72 | 215 | 13,996.50 |
| Guillermo Encina | 78 | 71 | 66 | 215 | 13,996.50 |
| Bill Longmuir | 73 | 76 | 67 | 216 | 10,020.97 |
| David J. Russell | 78 | 66 | 72 | 216 | 10,020.97 |
| Gery Watine | 73 | 70 | 73 | 216 | 10,020.97 |
| Bobby Lincoln | 71 | 73 | 72 | 216 | 10,020.97 |
| John Morgan | 74 | 73 | 70 | 217 | 7,228.24 |
| Bob Boyd | 73 | 73 | 71 | 217 | 7,228.24 |
| Rex Caldwell | 77 | 67 | 73 | 217 | 7,228.24 |
| Emilio Rodriguez | 75 | 75 | 68 | 218 | 5,585.46 |
| Sam Torrance | 73 | 72 | 73 | 218 | 5,585.46 |
| David Oakley | 73 | 74 | 71 | 218 | 5,585.46 |
| Gordon Townhill | 76 | 70 | 72 | 218 | 5,585.46 |
| Bruce Heuchan | 76 | 73 | 69 | 218 | 5,585.46 |
| Rodger Davis | 72 | 73 | 74 | 219 | 3,986.48 |
| Jeff Hawkes | 68 | 76 | 75 | 219 | 3,986.48 |
| Malcolm Gregson | 74 | 75 | 70 | 219 | 3,986.48 |
| Bob Cameron | 73 | 70 | 76 | 219 | 3,986.48 |
| Mokgeteng John Mashego | 68 | 75 | 76 | 219 | 3,986.48 |
| Delroy Cambridge | 73 | 73 | 73 | 219 | 3,986.48 |
| Neil Coles | 76 | 76 | 68 | 220 | 3,063.79 |
| Kevin Spurgeon | 71 | 76 | 73 | 220 | 3,063.79 |
| Jerry Bruner | 72 | 75 | 73 | 220 | 3,063.79 |
| Horacio Carbonetti | 76 | 71 | 73 | 220 | 3,063.79 |
| Ian Mosey | 71 | 78 | 72 | 221 | 2,483.89 |
| Martin Poxon | 73 | 72 | 76 | 221 | 2,483.89 |
| Gavan Levenson | 75 | 73 | 73 | 221 | 2,483.89 |
| Bill Hardwick | 73 | 76 | 72 | 221 | 2,483.89 |
| Alan Mew | 74 | 74 | 73 | 221 | 2,483.89 |

# Charles Church Scottish Seniors Open

*The Roxburghe Hotel & Golf Course,* Kelso, Scotland
Par 36-36–72; 6,911 yards

August 26-28
purse, €221,660

| | SCORES | | | TOTAL | MONEY |
|---|---|---|---|---|---|
| Nick Job | 69 | 66 | 71 | 206 | €33,217.43 |
| Jean Pierre Sallat | 69 | 67 | 71 | 207 | 22,144.95 |
| Terry Gale | 76 | 67 | 70 | 213 | 15,501.47 |
| Tony Charnley | 71 | 70 | 73 | 214 | 12,179.72 |
| Brian Jones | 69 | 73 | 73 | 215 | 10,009.52 |
| Bobby Lincoln | 73 | 67 | 76 | 216 | 8,415.08 |
| Bruce Heuchan | 74 | 68 | 74 | 216 | 8,415.08 |
| Kevin Spurgeon | 69 | 73 | 75 | 217 | 7,086.38 |
| Giuseppe Cali | 70 | 71 | 77 | 218 | 5,757.69 |
| Denis O'Sullivan | 72 | 74 | 72 | 218 | 5,757.69 |
| Bob Boyd | 73 | 70 | 75 | 218 | 5,757.69 |
| Sam Torrance | 73 | 76 | 70 | 219 | 4,251.83 |
| Gavan Levenson | 74 | 68 | 77 | 219 | 4,251.83 |
| Bob Larratt | 70 | 76 | 73 | 219 | 4,251.83 |
| Simon Owen | 73 | 71 | 75 | 219 | 4,251.83 |
| Mokgeteng John Mashego | 68 | 72 | 79 | 219 | 4,251.83 |
| Gordon J. Brand | 72 | 75 | 73 | 220 | 3,227.63 |
| David J. Russell | 70 | 72 | 78 | 220 | 3,227.63 |
| Bob Lendzion | 75 | 75 | 70 | 220 | 3,227.63 |
| Bob Cameron | 69 | 73 | 78 | 220 | 3,227.63 |
| Craig Maltman | 74 | 74 | 73 | 221 | 2,518.99 |
| Robin Mann | 76 | 73 | 72 | 221 | 2,518.99 |
| Gary Wintz | 72 | 75 | 74 | 221 | 2,518.99 |
| Alan Mew | 76 | 72 | 73 | 221 | 2,518.99 |
| Bill Longmuir | 70 | 76 | 76 | 222 | 1,929.77 |
| Ian Mosey | 72 | 80 | 70 | 222 | 1,929.77 |
| Malcolm Gregson | 72 | 73 | 77 | 222 | 1,929.77 |
| David Oakley | 72 | 75 | 75 | 222 | 1,929.77 |
| Jim Rhodes | 72 | 75 | 75 | 222 | 1,929.77 |
| David Good | 75 | 74 | 73 | 222 | 1,929.77 |
| Steve Stull | 77 | 72 | 73 | 222 | 1,929.77 |

# Bovis Lend Lease European Senior Masters

*Woburn Golf Club, Dukes Course*, Milton Keynes, England
Par 35-37–72; 6,896 yards

September 2-4
purse, €329,832

| | SCORES | | | TOTAL | MONEY |
|---|---|---|---|---|---|
| Mark James | 70 | 71 | 66 | 207 | €49,474.80 |
| Sam Torrance | 68 | 72 | 67 | 207 | 32,983.20 |
| (James defeated Torrance on first playoff hole.) | | | | | |
| Kevin Spurgeon | 67 | 68 | 73 | 208 | 23,088.24 |
| Emilio Rodriguez | 71 | 69 | 70 | 210 | 18,140.76 |
| Martin Gray | 71 | 69 | 72 | 212 | 13,325.21 |
| Alan Tapie | 72 | 66 | 74 | 212 | 13,325.21 |
| Pete Oakley | 71 | 70 | 71 | 212 | 13,325.21 |
| Carl Mason | 70 | 76 | 67 | 213 | 9,894.96 |
| Giuseppe Cali | 69 | 75 | 69 | 213 | 9,894.96 |
| Gordon J. Brand | 71 | 69 | 74 | 214 | 8,575.63 |
| Guillermo Encina | 72 | 75 | 68 | 215 | 7,915.97 |
| Nick Job | 71 | 71 | 74 | 216 | 7,256.30 |

|  | SCORES | | | TOTAL | MONEY |
|---|---|---|---|---|---|
| Martin Foster | 76 | 70 | 71 | 217 | 6,266.81 |
| Bob Boyd | 67 | 75 | 75 | 217 | 6,266.81 |
| David Good | 71 | 75 | 71 | 217 | 6,266.81 |
| Terry Gale | 72 | 75 | 72 | 219 | 4,967.27 |
| Bob Cameron | 72 | 71 | 76 | 219 | 4,967.27 |
| Horacio Carbonetti | 70 | 75 | 74 | 219 | 4,967.27 |
| Mike Ferguson | 75 | 73 | 71 | 219 | 4,967.27 |
| Delroy Cambridge | 73 | 74 | 72 | 219 | 4,967.27 |
| Maurice Bembridge | 75 | 72 | 73 | 220 | 3,751.84 |
| Bill Longmuir | 75 | 75 | 70 | 220 | 3,751.84 |
| Luis Carbonetti | 71 | 75 | 74 | 220 | 3,751.84 |
| Bill Hardwick | 73 | 73 | 74 | 220 | 3,751.84 |
| Manuel Pinero | 71 | 75 | 75 | 221 | 3,215.86 |
| Jim Rhodes | 75 | 72 | 74 | 221 | 3,215.86 |
| Ian Mosey | 72 | 71 | 79 | 222 | 3,001.47 |
| Tony Charnley | 73 | 73 | 77 | 223 | 2,612.27 |
| Denis Durnian | 73 | 73 | 77 | 223 | 2,612.27 |
| Jeff Hawkes | 70 | 75 | 78 | 223 | 2,612.27 |
| Malcolm Gregson | 74 | 76 | 73 | 223 | 2,612.27 |
| Alan Mew | 72 | 76 | 75 | 223 | 2,612.27 |

## Scandinavian Senior Open

*Royal Copenhagen Golf Club,* Copenhagen, Denmark
Par 71; 6,342 yards

September 9-11
purse, €250,000

|  | SCORES | | | TOTAL | MONEY |
|---|---|---|---|---|---|
| Bill Longmuir | 66 | 66 | 64 | 196 | €39,893.62 |
| Giuseppe Cali | 68 | 65 | 67 | 200 | 26,595.74 |
| Bob Cameron | 69 | 69 | 63 | 201 | 18,617.02 |
| David J. Russell | 72 | 67 | 63 | 202 | 13,324.47 |
| Martin Gray | 69 | 69 | 64 | 202 | 13,324.47 |
| Guillermo Encina | 68 | 67 | 69 | 204 | 10,638.30 |
| Eamonn Darcy | 71 | 65 | 69 | 205 | 8,111.70 |
| Ian Mosey | 71 | 66 | 68 | 205 | 8,111.70 |
| Kevin Spurgeon | 68 | 68 | 69 | 205 | 8,111.70 |
| Horacio Carbonetti | 66 | 67 | 72 | 205 | 8,111.70 |
| Tommy Horton | 70 | 67 | 69 | 206 | 5,167.17 |
| Martin Poxon | 73 | 68 | 65 | 206 | 5,167.17 |
| Noel Ratcliffe | 69 | 70 | 67 | 206 | 5,167.17 |
| Gery Watine | 69 | 69 | 68 | 206 | 5,167.17 |
| Terry Gale | 68 | 67 | 71 | 206 | 5,167.17 |
| Denis O'Sullivan | 70 | 65 | 71 | 206 | 5,167.17 |
| Martin Foster | 69 | 69 | 68 | 206 | 5,167.17 |
| Alan Tapie | 69 | 73 | 66 | 208 | 3,636.97 |
| Luis Carbonetti | 68 | 71 | 69 | 208 | 3,636.97 |
| Jim Rhodes | 69 | 71 | 68 | 208 | 3,636.97 |
| David Good | 70 | 70 | 68 | 208 | 3,636.97 |
| Nick Job | 71 | 69 | 69 | 209 | 2,934.40 |
| David Oakley | 70 | 68 | 71 | 209 | 2,934.40 |
| Delroy Cambridge | 70 | 69 | 70 | 209 | 2,934.40 |
| Jerry Bruner | 73 | 71 | 66 | 210 | 2,659.57 |
| Mike Miller | 69 | 72 | 70 | 211 | 2,367.02 |
| Gavan Levenson | 65 | 68 | 78 | 211 | 2,367.02 |
| John Chillas | 74 | 67 | 70 | 211 | 2,367.02 |
| Pete Oakley | 70 | 71 | 70 | 211 | 2,367.02 |
| Bruce Heuchan | 70 | 71 | 71 | 212 | 2,101.06 |

# Bendinat London Seniors Masters

*London Golf Club,* Kent, England
Par 36-36–72; 6,968 yards

September 23-25
purse, €221,488

| | SCORES | | | TOTAL | MONEY |
|---|---|---|---|---|---|
| Sam Torrance | 64 | 67 | 70 | 201 | €33,223.28 |
| David J. Russell | 69 | 65 | 70 | 204 | 22,148.85 |
| Gordon J. Brand | 70 | 68 | 68 | 206 | 12,565.78 |
| Nick Job | 68 | 69 | 69 | 206 | 12,565.78 |
| Jose Rivero | 70 | 67 | 69 | 206 | 12,565.78 |
| Giuseppe Cali | 69 | 66 | 74 | 209 | 7,530.61 |
| Terry Gale | 69 | 70 | 70 | 209 | 7,530.61 |
| John Chillas | 72 | 69 | 68 | 209 | 7,530.61 |
| Jean Pierre Sallat | 70 | 73 | 66 | 209 | 7,530.61 |
| John Bland | 70 | 74 | 66 | 210 | 5,537.21 |
| Carl Mason | 69 | 71 | 70 | 210 | 5,537.21 |
| Denis O'Sullivan | 72 | 68 | 73 | 213 | 4,651.26 |
| John Benda | 72 | 74 | 67 | 213 | 4,651.26 |
| Bill Longmuir | 73 | 68 | 73 | 214 | 4,097.54 |
| Bob Boyd | 72 | 70 | 72 | 214 | 4,097.54 |
| Ian Mosey | 71 | 72 | 72 | 215 | 3,438.61 |
| Kevin Spurgeon | 76 | 70 | 69 | 215 | 3,438.61 |
| Jerry Bruner | 75 | 72 | 68 | 215 | 3,438.61 |
| Mike Ferguson | 72 | 72 | 71 | 215 | 3,438.61 |
| Neil Coles | 72 | 70 | 74 | 216 | 2,536.04 |
| Craig Maltman | 72 | 71 | 73 | 216 | 2,536.04 |
| Mike Miller | 76 | 68 | 72 | 216 | 2,536.04 |
| Guillermo Encina | 70 | 74 | 72 | 216 | 2,536.04 |
| Gordon Townhill | 73 | 70 | 73 | 216 | 2,536.04 |
| Hank Woodrome | 72 | 71 | 73 | 216 | 2,536.04 |
| David Oakley | 71 | 78 | 68 | 217 | 2,015.55 |
| Delroy Cambridge | 72 | 68 | 77 | 217 | 2,015.55 |
| Gary Wintz | 70 | 73 | 74 | 217 | 2,015.55 |
| Bob Cameron | 75 | 72 | 71 | 218 | 1,838.36 |
| Robin Mann | 72 | 73 | 74 | 219 | 1,749.76 |

# Castellon Costa Azahar Open de Espana

*Club de Campo del Mediterraneo,*
Castellon, Spain
Par 36-36–72; 6,706 yards

September 30-October 2
purse, €250,000

| | SCORES | | | TOTAL | MONEY |
|---|---|---|---|---|---|
| Bob Boyd | 68 | 66 | 71 | 205 | €37,500 |
| Jose Rivero | 67 | 68 | 71 | 206 | 21,250 |
| Jim Rhodes | 66 | 69 | 71 | 206 | 21,250 |
| Gery Watine | 70 | 70 | 67 | 207 | 13,750 |
| Gordon J. Brand | 70 | 70 | 68 | 208 | 11,300 |
| Giuseppe Cali | 66 | 72 | 71 | 209 | 9,000 |
| Luis Carbonetti | 71 | 71 | 67 | 209 | 9,000 |
| Mokgeteng John Mashego | 72 | 64 | 73 | 209 | 9,000 |
| Terry Gale | 66 | 73 | 71 | 210 | 6,750 |
| Guillermo Encina | 70 | 68 | 72 | 210 | 6,750 |
| Bob Lendzion | 70 | 72 | 69 | 211 | 5,750 |
| Jerry Bruner | 72 | 65 | 74 | 211 | 5,750 |
| Malcolm Gregson | 72 | 70 | 70 | 212 | 4,875 |

|  | SCORES | | | TOTAL | MONEY |
|---|---|---|---|---|---|
| Delroy Cambridge | 66 | 74 | 72 | 212 | 4,875 |
| Nick Job | 69 | 75 | 69 | 213 | 4,005 |
| Carl Mason | 68 | 73 | 72 | 213 | 4,005 |
| David J. Russell | 70 | 67 | 76 | 213 | 4,005 |
| Gavan Levenson | 69 | 70 | 74 | 213 | 4,005 |
| Bruce Heuchan | 68 | 71 | 74 | 213 | 4,005 |
| Eamonn Darcy | 75 | 67 | 72 | 214 | 3,012.50 |
| Armando Saavedra | 71 | 70 | 73 | 214 | 3,012.50 |
| Bob Cameron | 74 | 70 | 70 | 214 | 3,012.50 |
| David Good | 71 | 71 | 72 | 214 | 3,012.50 |
| Maurice Bembridge | 72 | 70 | 73 | 215 | 2,625 |
| Tommy Horton | 75 | 70 | 71 | 216 | 2,383.33 |
| Eddie Polland | 72 | 72 | 72 | 216 | 2,383.33 |
| Hank Woodrome | 74 | 68 | 74 | 216 | 2,383.33 |
| Bill Longmuir | 73 | 70 | 74 | 217 | 1,896.43 |
| Craig Maltman | 70 | 73 | 74 | 217 | 1,896.43 |
| Ian Mosey | 69 | 74 | 74 | 217 | 1,896.43 |
| Alan Tapie | 66 | 72 | 79 | 217 | 1,896.43 |
| John Chillas | 70 | 73 | 74 | 217 | 1,896.43 |
| Horacio Carbonetti | 73 | 71 | 73 | 217 | 1,896.43 |
| Tony Allen | 73 | 69 | 75 | 217 | 1,896.43 |

## Algarve Seniors Open of Portugal

*Quinta da Cima Golf*, Algarve, Portugal
Par 36-36–72; 6,815 yards

October 7-9
purse, €300,000

|  | SCORES | | | TOTAL | MONEY |
|---|---|---|---|---|---|
| Jerry Bruner | 66 | 68 | 71 | 205 | €45,000 |
| Jose Rivero | 68 | 70 | 68 | 206 | 22,500 |
| Sam Torrance | 68 | 66 | 72 | 206 | 22,500 |
| Eddie Polland | 67 | 69 | 70 | 206 | 22,500 |
| Guillermo Encina | 66 | 69 | 73 | 208 | 13,560 |
| Antonio Garrido | 72 | 67 | 70 | 209 | 9,720 |
| Carl Mason | 68 | 71 | 70 | 209 | 9,720 |
| Giuseppe Cali | 71 | 68 | 70 | 209 | 9,720 |
| John Chillas | 69 | 67 | 73 | 209 | 9,720 |
| Mike Ferguson | 68 | 70 | 71 | 209 | 9,720 |
| Bill Longmuir | 73 | 70 | 67 | 210 | 6,375 |
| Ian Mosey | 69 | 71 | 70 | 210 | 6,375 |
| Emilio Rodriguez | 70 | 70 | 70 | 210 | 6,375 |
| Bruce Heuchan | 72 | 66 | 72 | 210 | 6,375 |
| Brian Evans | 71 | 70 | 70 | 211 | 5,400 |
| Gavan Levenson | 69 | 71 | 72 | 212 | 5,100 |
| Gordon J. Brand | 72 | 68 | 73 | 213 | 4,510 |
| Bob Cameron | 69 | 72 | 72 | 213 | 4,510 |
| Horacio Carbonetti | 72 | 70 | 71 | 213 | 4,510 |
| Adan Sowa | 71 | 69 | 74 | 214 | 3,522 |
| David Oakley | 67 | 71 | 76 | 214 | 3,522 |
| David Good | 72 | 72 | 70 | 214 | 3,522 |
| Hank Woodrome | 70 | 70 | 74 | 214 | 3,522 |
| Rex Caldwell | 68 | 74 | 72 | 214 | 3,522 |
| Craig Maltman | 70 | 72 | 73 | 215 | 2,925 |
| John Benda | 66 | 75 | 74 | 215 | 2,925 |
| Mike Miller | 69 | 68 | 79 | 216 | 2,490 |
| Kevin Spurgeon | 72 | 70 | 74 | 216 | 2,490 |
| Terry Gale | 72 | 68 | 76 | 216 | 2,490 |

| | SCORES | TOTAL | MONEY |
|---|---|---|---|
| Denis O'Sullivan | 72  72  72 | 216 | 2,490 |
| Martin Foster | 71  73  72 | 216 | 2,490 |

## Arcapita Seniors Tour Championship

*Riffa Golf Club*, Bahrain  
Par 36-36–72; 6,808 yards

November 10-12  
purse, €380,454

| | SCORES | TOTAL | MONEY |
|---|---|---|---|
| Des Smyth | 68  68  70 | 206 | €59,168.63 |
| John Chillas | 73  68  67 | 208 | 39,445.75 |
| Gordon J. Brand | 70  71  68 | 209 | 22,378.89 |
| Sam Torrance | 75  68  66 | 209 | 22,378.89 |
| Giuseppe Cali | 73  70  66 | 209 | 22,378.89 |
| Jose Rivero | 72  74  66 | 212 | 14,200.47 |
| Luis Carbonetti | 72  69  71 | 212 | 14,200.47 |
| Horacio Carbonetti | 68  72  72 | 212 | 14,200.47 |
| David Good | 73  70  71 | 214 | 10,650.35 |
| Bruce Heuchan | 75  71  68 | 214 | 10,650.35 |
| Emilio Rodriguez | 71  73  71 | 215 | 9,466.98 |
| Manuel Pinero | 76  71  69 | 216 | 8,020.64 |
| Martin Gray | 72  73  71 | 216 | 8,020.64 |
| Kevin Spurgeon | 73  73  70 | 216 | 8,020.64 |
| Bob Cameron | 74  70  73 | 217 | 7,100.23 |
| Tommy Horton | 73  72  73 | 218 | 5,940.53 |
| Gavan Levenson | 72  70  76 | 218 | 5,940.53 |
| Alan Tapie | 73  74  71 | 218 | 5,940.53 |
| Denis O'Sullivan | 73  72  73 | 218 | 5,940.53 |
| Tony Allen | 71  68  79 | 218 | 5,940.53 |
| Ian Mosey | 76  71  72 | 219 | 4,602 |
| Mike Ferguson | 73  74  72 | 219 | 4,602 |
| Rex Caldwell | 69  73  77 | 219 | 4,602 |
| Noel Ratcliffe | 76  71  73 | 220 | 4,043.19 |
| David J. Russell | 73  73  74 | 220 | 4,043.19 |
| Craig Maltman | 72  77  72 | 221 | 3,747.35 |
| Bob Boyd | 79  70  73 | 222 | 3,589.56 |
| Terry Gale | 75  77  71 | 223 | 3,352.89 |
| Hank Woodrome | 75  73  75 | 223 | 3,352.89 |
| Tony Charnley | 79  70  75 | 224 | 2,847.98 |
| David Oakley | 77  72  75 | 224 | 2,847.98 |
| Jerry Bruner | 80  75  69 | 224 | 2,847.98 |
| Martin Foster | 76  70  78 | 224 | 2,847.98 |
| John Benda | 72  69  83 | 224 | 2,847.98 |

# Japan Senior Tour

## Oberst Senior Open

*Karasuyamajo County Club,* Hoi-gun, Aichi
Par 36-36–72; 6,845 yards

May 18-20
purse, ¥20,000,000

| | SCORES | | | TOTAL | MONEY |
|---|---|---|---|---|---|
| Takashi Miyoshi | 73 | 68 | 69 | 210 | ¥3,600,000 |
| Hideto Shigenobu | 70 | 68 | 73 | 211 | 1,800,000 |
| Yoshitaka Yamamoto | 69 | 74 | 70 | 213 | 1,200,000 |
| Yoshio Fumiyama | 71 | 74 | 70 | 215 | 800,000 |
| Seiji Ebihara | 70 | 71 | 74 | 215 | 800,000 |
| Shuichi Sano | 72 | 67 | 76 | 215 | 800,000 |
| Katsuyoshi Tomori | 77 | 71 | 68 | 216 | 550,000 |
| Tadami Ueno | 72 | 74 | 70 | 216 | 550,000 |
| Koichi Uehara | 76 | 71 | 70 | 217 | 440,000 |
| Choi Sang-ho | 75 | 71 | 71 | 217 | 440,000 |
| Kazunari Shinoda | 76 | 72 | 70 | 218 | 390,000 |
| Katsunari Takahashi | 71 | 74 | 73 | 218 | 390,000 |
| Takaaki Fukuzawa | 71 | 74 | 74 | 219 | 340,000 |
| Dragon Taki | 71 | 73 | 75 | 219 | 340,000 |
| Hisashi Nakase | 72 | 72 | 75 | 219 | 340,000 |
| Kimpachi Yoshimura | 74 | 74 | 72 | 220 | 290,000 |
| Takeshi Shibata | 73 | 73 | 74 | 220 | 290,000 |
| Mikio Ichikawa | 72 | 74 | 75 | 221 | 237,500 |
| Seiji Kusakabe | 77 | 75 | 69 | 221 | 237,500 |
| Toyotake Nakao | 73 | 73 | 75 | 221 | 237,500 |
| Hikaru Emoto | 73 | 72 | 76 | 221 | 237,500 |
| Minoru Hatsumi | 75 | 75 | 72 | 222 | 185,666 |
| Chen Tze-ming | 75 | 75 | 72 | 222 | 185,666 |
| Saburo Fujiki | 74 | 74 | 74 | 222 | 185,666 |
| Teruyasu Hayashi | 73 | 72 | 77 | 222 | 185,666 |
| Hideaki Yamashita | 71 | 72 | 79 | 222 | 185,666 |
| Norihiko Matsumoto | 71 | 73 | 78 | 222 | 185,666 |
| Yuichi Yokoshima | 76 | 74 | 73 | 223 | 145,714 |
| Tadao Furuichi | 76 | 73 | 74 | 223 | 145,714 |
| Seiji Ogawa | 74 | 76 | 73 | 223 | 145,714 |
| Katsuji Hasegawa | 74 | 77 | 72 | 223 | 145,714 |
| Kunio Yamashita | 76 | 75 | 72 | 223 | 145,714 |
| Kikuo Arai | 73 | 74 | 76 | 223 | 145,714 |
| Motomasa Aoki | 77 | 75 | 71 | 223 | 145,714 |

## Aderans Wellness Open

*Nakajo Golf Club,* Nakajo, Niigata
Par 36-36–72; 6,984 yards

June 10-12
purse, ¥60,000,000

| | SCORES | | | TOTAL | MONEY |
|---|---|---|---|---|---|
| Katsuyoshi Tomori | 69 | 67 | 67 | 203 | ¥12,000,000 |
| Minoru Hatsumi | 68 | 69 | 68 | 205 | 5,700,000 |
| Tateo Ozaki | 71 | 71 | 67 | 209 | 3,750,000 |

|  | SCORES | | | TOTAL | MONEY |
|---|---|---|---|---|---|
| Noboru Fujiike | 71 | 73 | 69 | 213 | 2,529,000 |
| Fumio Tanaka | 72 | 71 | 71 | 214 | 1,687,500 |
| Fujio Kobayashi | 71 | 71 | 72 | 214 | 1,687,500 |
| Katsunari Takahashi | 71 | 71 | 72 | 214 | 1,687,500 |
| Teruo Nakamura | 69 | 70 | 75 | 214 | 1,687,500 |
| Toyotake Nakao | 72 | 70 | 73 | 215 | 1,266,000 |
| Tadami Ueno | 73 | 74 | 69 | 216 | 1,200,000 |
| Toru Nakayama | 72 | 75 | 70 | 217 | 1,020,000 |
| Takaaki Fukuzawa | 75 | 72 | 70 | 217 | 1,020,000 |
| Renkyoku Sugiyama | 73 | 72 | 72 | 217 | 1,020,000 |
| Koji Okuno | 72 | 71 | 74 | 217 | 1,020,000 |
| Kenjiro Iwama | 69 | 72 | 76 | 217 | 1,020,000 |
| Hikaru Emoto | 76 | 73 | 69 | 218 | 1,020,000 |
| Yoshitaka Yamamoto | 73 | 74 | 71 | 218 | 1,020,000 |
| Takeshi Shibata | 72 | 74 | 72 | 218 | 1,020,000 |
| Kazuo Kanayama | 72 | 73 | 73 | 218 | 1,020,000 |
| Hideto Shigenobu | 72 | 72 | 74 | 218 | 1,020,000 |
| Toshihiko Kikuichi | 77 | 73 | 69 | 219 | 630,000 |
| Shuichi Sano | 78 | 68 | 73 | 219 | 630,000 |
| Yurio Akitomi | 73 | 71 | 75 | 219 | 630,000 |
| Koichi Uehara | 79 | 70 | 71 | 220 | 540,000 |
| Takashi Miyoshi | 70 | 77 | 73 | 220 | 540,000 |
| Tokio Kaneko | 72 | 67 | 81 | 220 | 540,000 |
| Chen Tze-ming | 74 | 75 | 72 | 221 | 465,000 |
| Hsieh Min-nan | 75 | 73 | 73 | 221 | 465,000 |
| Nichito Hashimoto | 75 | 72 | 75 | 222 | 420,000 |
| Yoshimi Niizeki | 73 | 74 | 75 | 222 | 420,000 |
| Yuichi Yokoshima | 72 | 74 | 76 | 222 | 420,000 |

## Fancl Senior Classic

*Susono Country Club*, Shizuoka
Par 36-36–72; 6,851 yards

August 19-21
purse, ¥60,000,000

|  | SCORES | | | TOTAL | MONEY |
|---|---|---|---|---|---|
| Takashi Miyoshi | 67 | 69 | 71 | 207 | ¥15,000,000 |
| Dragon Taki | 72 | 68 | 67 | 207 | 6,900,000 |
| (Miyoshi defeated Taki on fourth playoff hole.) | | | | | |
| David Ishii | 68 | 68 | 72 | 208 | 3,600,000 |
| Tsuneyuki Nakajima | 75 | 67 | 70 | 212 | 2,120,000 |
| Katsuji Hasegawa | 67 | 73 | 72 | 212 | 2,120,000 |
| Teruo Nakamura | 71 | 73 | 68 | 212 | 2,120,000 |
| Toyotake Nakao | 69 | 75 | 69 | 213 | 1,620,000 |
| Tateo Ozaki | 73 | 71 | 70 | 214 | 1,233,000 |
| Takaaki Fukuzawa | 69 | 72 | 73 | 214 | 1,233,000 |
| Katsuyoshi Tomori | 73 | 68 | 73 | 214 | 1,233,000 |
| Chen Tze-ming | 75 | 70 | 69 | 214 | 1,233,000 |
| Shuichi Sato | 72 | 70 | 73 | 215 | 938,000 |
| Fumio Tanaka | 73 | 68 | 74 | 215 | 938,000 |
| Takeru Shibata | 72 | 73 | 70 | 215 | 938,000 |
| Seiji Ebihara | 70 | 70 | 76 | 216 | 742,500 |
| Kiyoshi Murota | 77 | 69 | 70 | 216 | 742,500 |
| Hisao Inoue | 70 | 73 | 73 | 216 | 742,500 |
| Hideto Shigenobu | 69 | 73 | 74 | 216 | 742,500 |
| Yasuhiro Funatogawa | 70 | 75 | 72 | 217 | 654,000 |
| Minoru Hatsumi | 74 | 73 | 71 | 218 | 594,000 |
| Koji Okuno | 72 | 72 | 74 | 218 | 594,000 |

| | SCORES | | | TOTAL | MONEY |
|---|---|---|---|---|---|
| Noboru Fujiike | 69 | 72 | 77 | 218 | 594,000 |
| Kikuo Arai | 70 | 74 | 75 | 219 | 473,142 |
| Hsieh Min-nan | 72 | 72 | 75 | 219 | 473,142 |
| Katsunari Takahashi | 69 | 76 | 74 | 219 | 473,142 |
| Toru Nakayama | 76 | 72 | 71 | 219 | 473,142 |
| Yukio Noguchi | 76 | 73 | 70 | 219 | 473,142 |
| Yasuhiro Dato | 74 | 69 | 76 | 219 | 473,142 |
| Yasuhiro Miyamoto | 73 | 73 | 73 | 219 | 473,142 |
| Yoshikazu Yokoshima | 73 | 74 | 73 | 220 | 380,000 |
| Miyoshi Tomita | 76 | 71 | 73 | 220 | 380,000 |
| Yoshitaka Yamamoto | 73 | 75 | 72 | 220 | 380,000 |

## Arde Pro Cup

*Okanokoen Kiyosato Golf Club,* Yamanashi  
Par 36-36–72; 6,740 yards

August 26-28  
purse, ¥20,000,000

| | SCORES | | | TOTAL | MONEY |
|---|---|---|---|---|---|
| Takashi Miyoshi | 65 | 62 | 73 | 200 | ¥3,600,000 |
| Yoshimi Niizeki | 72 | 66 | 65 | 203 | 1,300,000 |
| Yoshitaka Yamamoto | 69 | 68 | 66 | 203 | 1,300,000 |
| Kimpachi Yoshimura | 71 | 67 | 65 | 203 | 1,300,000 |
| Takaaki Fukuzawa | 67 | 72 | 65 | 204 | 800,000 |
| Dragon Taki | 68 | 67 | 70 | 205 | 700,000 |
| Katsunari Takahashi | 71 | 67 | 68 | 206 | 520,000 |
| Saburo Fujiki | 69 | 69 | 68 | 206 | 520,000 |
| Tadami Ueno | 68 | 70 | 68 | 206 | 520,000 |
| Kenjiro Iwama | 69 | 69 | 69 | 207 | 415,000 |
| Takeru Shibata | 68 | 72 | 67 | 207 | 415,000 |
| Mikio Ichikawa | 71 | 68 | 69 | 208 | 332,500 |
| Koji Okuno | 66 | 70 | 72 | 208 | 332,500 |
| Toyotake Nakao | 70 | 66 | 72 | 208 | 332,500 |
| Hisashi Nakase | 70 | 67 | 71 | 208 | 332,500 |
| Yoshio Fumiyama | 71 | 66 | 72 | 209 | 260,000 |
| Teruo Nakamura | 67 | 75 | 67 | 209 | 260,000 |
| Kunio Yamashita | 70 | 71 | 68 | 209 | 260,000 |
| Yukio Noguchi | 70 | 72 | 68 | 210 | 202,666 |
| Minoru Hatsumi | 69 | 69 | 72 | 210 | 202,666 |
| Hideto Shigenobu | 71 | 69 | 70 | 210 | 202,666 |
| Seiji Ebihara | 72 | 71 | 68 | 211 | 163,600 |
| Hikaru Emoto | 71 | 71 | 69 | 211 | 163,600 |
| Shuichi Sano | 69 | 71 | 71 | 211 | 163,600 |
| Kazushige Shida | 72 | 69 | 70 | 211 | 163,600 |
| Fumio Tanaka | 69 | 68 | 74 | 211 | 163,600 |
| Motomasa Aoki | 70 | 70 | 72 | 212 | 144,000 |
| Koichi Uehara | 70 | 68 | 74 | 212 | 144,000 |
| Yukio Ishizawa | 73 | 68 | 71 | 212 | 144,000 |
| Toru Nakayama | 71 | 69 | 73 | 213 | 132,000 |
| Hiroshi Ishii | 71 | 72 | 70 | 213 | 132,000 |
| Kazuo Kanayama | 74 | 70 | 69 | 213 | 132,000 |

# PGA Philanthropy Rebornest Senior Open

*Big Risac Country Club,* Miyagi
Par 36-36–72; 6,917 yards

August 31-September 3
purse, ¥30,000,000

| | SCORES | | | | TOTAL | MONEY |
|---|---|---|---|---|---|---|
| Katsunari Takahashi | 72 | 70 | 65 | 68 | 275 | ¥5,400,000 |
| Hideaki Yamashita | 74 | 68 | 70 | 69 | 281 | 2,250,000 |
| Kimpachi Yoshimura | 68 | 73 | 65 | 75 | 281 | 2,250,000 |
| Yoshitaka Yamamoto | 73 | 71 | 69 | 69 | 282 | 1,350,000 |
| Takashi Miyoshi | 72 | 76 | 71 | 65 | 284 | 1,200,000 |
| Toru Nakayama | 76 | 70 | 68 | 72 | 286 | 975,000 |
| Hisao Inoue | 74 | 70 | 72 | 70 | 286 | 975,000 |
| Hikaru Emoto | 73 | 72 | 71 | 71 | 287 | 695,000 |
| Tadami Ueno | 72 | 73 | 72 | 70 | 287 | 695,000 |
| Koji Okuno | 73 | 69 | 72 | 73 | 287 | 695,000 |
| Akira Yabe | 72 | 70 | 70 | 76 | 288 | 577,500 |
| Noboru Fujiike | 73 | 73 | 72 | 70 | 288 | 577,500 |
| Yoshimi Niizeki | 71 | 74 | 75 | 69 | 289 | 465,000 |
| Kazuo Kanayama | 74 | 70 | 71 | 74 | 289 | 465,000 |
| Toyotake Nakao | 73 | 72 | 72 | 72 | 289 | 465,000 |
| Yukio Ishizawa | 74 | 71 | 70 | 74 | 289 | 465,000 |
| Seiji Ebihara | 73 | 76 | 74 | 67 | 290 | 360,000 |
| Teruo Nakamura | 72 | 72 | 75 | 71 | 290 | 360,000 |
| Chen Tze-ming | 68 | 75 | 78 | 69 | 290 | 360,000 |
| Motomasa Aoki | 74 | 71 | 73 | 73 | 291 | 269,400 |
| Toshihiko Otsuka | 73 | 75 | 69 | 74 | 291 | 269,400 |
| Dragon Taki | 72 | 76 | 70 | 73 | 291 | 269,400 |
| Minoru Hatsumi | 72 | 74 | 73 | 72 | 291 | 269,400 |
| Tatsuo Fujima | 76 | 70 | 73 | 72 | 291 | 269,400 |
| Masaru Amano | 74 | 74 | 70 | 74 | 292 | 222,000 |
| Kinya Aoyagi | 75 | 71 | 74 | 72 | 292 | 222,000 |
| Shiochi Sato | 75 | 72 | 73 | 72 | 292 | 222,000 |
| Kiyoshi Hinata | 73 | 73 | 74 | 72 | 292 | 222,000 |
| Hisashi Terada | 75 | 71 | 75 | 71 | 292 | 222,000 |
| Fujio Kobayashi | 71 | 73 | 75 | 74 | 293 | 190,500 |
| Shuichi Sano | 75 | 69 | 72 | 77 | 293 | 190,500 |
| Katsumi Nanjo | 75 | 75 | 72 | 71 | 293 | 190,500 |
| Yoshio Fumiyama | 74 | 72 | 71 | 76 | 293 | 190,500 |
| Nichito Hashimoto | 76 | 70 | 73 | 74 | 293 | 190,500 |
| Tadao Furuichi | 76 | 73 | 71 | 73 | 293 | 190,500 |

# Japan PGA Senior Championship

*Eniwa Country Club,* Hokkaido
Par 36-36–72; 6,920 yards

September 29-October 2
purse, ¥50,000,000

| | SCORES | | | | TOTAL | MONEY |
|---|---|---|---|---|---|---|
| Kiyoshi Murota | 65 | 71 | 69 | 70 | 275 | ¥10,000,000 |
| Tateo Ozaki | 66 | 70 | 69 | 76 | 281 | 3,875,000 |
| Masahiro Kuramoto | 69 | 74 | 68 | 70 | 281 | 3,875,000 |
| Tsuneyuki Nakajima | 67 | 72 | 70 | 73 | 282 | 2,050,000 |
| Kimpachi Yoshimura | 71 | 74 | 72 | 67 | 284 | 1,750,000 |
| Yoshimi Niizeki | 73 | 71 | 70 | 71 | 285 | 1,375,000 |
| Katsuyoshi Tomori | 70 | 75 | 68 | 72 | 285 | 1,375,000 |
| Isao Aoki | 71 | 72 | 73 | 70 | 286 | 1,077,500 |
| Hisashi Nakase | 72 | 70 | 74 | 70 | 286 | 1,077,500 |

| | SCORES | | | | TOTAL | MONEY |
|---|---|---|---|---|---|---|
| Seiji Ebihara | 72 | 73 | 73 | 71 | 289 | 975,000 |
| Takaaki Fukuzawa | 73 | 73 | 74 | 69 | 289 | 975,000 |
| Yoshio Fumiyama | 70 | 72 | 76 | 73 | 291 | 800,000 |
| Takeru Shibata | 70 | 76 | 72 | 73 | 291 | 800,000 |
| Toyotake Nakao | 70 | 72 | 74 | 75 | 291 | 800,000 |
| Noboru Fujiike | 75 | 70 | 72 | 74 | 291 | 800,000 |
| Nichito Hashimoto | 73 | 77 | 72 | 69 | 291 | 800,000 |
| Hisao Inoue | 72 | 75 | 75 | 70 | 292 | 650,000 |
| Kenjiro Iwama | 69 | 77 | 73 | 74 | 293 | 625,000 |
| Motomasa Aoki | 76 | 73 | 74 | 71 | 294 | 550,000 |
| Saburo Fujiki | 69 | 77 | 71 | 77 | 294 | 550,000 |
| Toshihiko Kikuichi | 75 | 71 | 75 | 73 | 294 | 550,000 |
| Hideto Shigenobu | 73 | 71 | 75 | 75 | 294 | 550,000 |
| Kazushige Oyo | 72 | 74 | 74 | 74 | 294 | 550,000 |
| David Ishii | 73 | 75 | 74 | 74 | 296 | 475,000 |
| Koichi Uehara | 76 | 75 | 71 | 75 | 297 | 425,000 |
| Hikaru Emoto | 74 | 75 | 71 | 77 | 297 | 425,000 |
| Shuichi Sano | 76 | 74 | 74 | 73 | 297 | 425,000 |
| Kinya Aoyagi | 74 | 72 | 74 | 78 | 298 | 356,250 |
| Yoshikazu Yokoshima | 70 | 75 | 76 | 77 | 298 | 356,250 |
| Tadami Ueno | 74 | 73 | 79 | 72 | 298 | 356,250 |
| Kazuo Kanayama | 70 | 78 | 77 | 73 | 298 | 356,250 |

## Japan Senior Open

*Ranzan Country Club*, Saitama
Par 36-36–72; 6,757 yards

November 3-6
purse, ¥50,000,000

| | SCORES | | | | TOTAL | MONEY |
|---|---|---|---|---|---|---|
| Tsuneyuki Nakajima | 74 | 68 | 70 | 70 | 282 | ¥10,000,000 |
| Toshiaki Sudo | 71 | 72 | 68 | 72 | 283 | 4,687,500 |
| Katsuyoshi Tomori | 71 | 70 | 68 | 74 | 283 | 4,687,500 |
| Chen Tze-ming | 71 | 73 | 67 | 73 | 284 | 2,550,000 |
| Terry Gale | 68 | 71 | 73 | 73 | 285 | 2,100,000 |
| Motomasa Aoki | 72 | 74 | 69 | 71 | 286 | 1,390,750 |
| Seiji Ebihara | 74 | 71 | 70 | 71 | 286 | 1,390,750 |
| Takaaki Fukuzawa | 73 | 71 | 72 | 70 | 286 | 1,390,750 |
| Kiyoshi Murota | 70 | 72 | 70 | 74 | 286 | 1,390,750 |
| Hajime Meshiai | 75 | 72 | 74 | 68 | 289 | 990,000 |
| Katsumi Nanjo | 74 | 71 | 74 | 71 | 290 | 815,000 |
| Yoshikazu Yokoshima | 73 | 73 | 71 | 73 | 290 | 815,000 |
| Masaru Amano | 73 | 76 | 70 | 72 | 291 | 685,000 |
| Kimpachi Yoshimura | 73 | 73 | 72 | 73 | 291 | 685,000 |
| Yoshitaka Yamamoto | 74 | 71 | 76 | 71 | 292 | 597,500 |
| Tsunemi Nakajima | 74 | 73 | 72 | 73 | 292 | 597,500 |
| Katsunari Takahashi | 72 | 75 | 72 | 74 | 293 | 522,500 |
| Yasuzo Hagewara | 73 | 75 | 70 | 75 | 293 | 522,500 |
| Saburo Fujiki | 73 | 73 | 73 | 74 | 293 | 522,500 |
| Hideto Shigenobu | 73 | 77 | 71 | 72 | 293 | 522,500 |
| Gohei Sato | 79 | 72 | 70 | 73 | 294 | 467,500 |
| Koji Okuno | 74 | 74 | 74 | 72 | 294 | 467,500 |
| Kikuo Arai | 72 | 74 | 72 | 78 | 296 | 438,000 |
| Eitchi Itai | 71 | 74 | 78 | 73 | 296 | 438,000 |
| Hisao Inoue | 75 | 74 | 73 | 74 | 296 | 438,000 |
| Noboru Fujiike | 75 | 73 | 74 | 74 | 296 | 438,000 |
| Yoshio Fumiyama | 77 | 74 | 74 | 72 | 297 | 410,000 |
| Toyotake Nakao | 74 | 75 | 75 | 73 | 297 | 410,000 |

| | SCORES | | | TOTAL | MONEY |
|---|---|---|---|---|---|
| Dragon Taki | 78 73 71 | | 76 | 298 | 375,000 |
| Yoshimi Niizeki | 77 71 77 | | 73 | 298 | 375,000 |
| Takeshi Kitadai | 77 74 74 | | 73 | 298 | 375,000 |
| Toshiharu Morimoto | 74 74 74 | | 76 | 298 | 375,000 |
| David Ishii | 75 75 73 | | 75 | 298 | 375,000 |

## Kinojyo Senior Open

*Kinojyo Golf Club,* Okayama
Par 36-36–72; 8,653 yards

November 25-27
purse, ¥20,000,000

| | SCORES | | | TOTAL | MONEY |
|---|---|---|---|---|---|
| Hajime Meshiai | 65 | 70 | 72 | 207 | ¥3,600,000 |
| Seiji Ebihara | 70 | 70 | 68 | 208 | 1,800,000 |
| Minoru Hatsumi | 72 | 67 | 70 | 209 | 1,200,000 |
| Masaru Amano | 68 | 70 | 72 | 210 | 900,000 |
| Toru Nakamura | 70 | 66 | 75 | 211 | 800,000 |
| Toru Nakayama | 71 | 73 | 69 | 213 | 565,000 |
| Tadami Ueno | 66 | 72 | 75 | 213 | 565,000 |
| Kimpachi Yoshimura | 68 | 76 | 69 | 213 | 565,000 |
| David Ishii | 68 | 74 | 71 | 213 | 565,000 |
| Hikaru Emoto | 72 | 72 | 70 | 214 | 390,000 |
| Fujio Kobayashi | 68 | 73 | 73 | 214 | 390,000 |
| Saburo Fujiki | 71 | 71 | 72 | 214 | 390,000 |
| Tsunemi Nakajima | 74 | 67 | 73 | 214 | 390,000 |
| Katsumi Nanjo | 71 | 67 | 77 | 215 | 300,000 |
| Takaaki Fukuzawa | 70 | 69 | 76 | 215 | 300,000 |
| Akira Yabe | 74 | 68 | 73 | 215 | 300,000 |
| Teruo Nakamura | 70 | 74 | 71 | 215 | 300,000 |
| Yoshitaka Yamamoto | 74 | 73 | 68 | 215 | 300,000 |
| Kazushige Shida | 71 | 71 | 74 | 216 | 220,000 |
| Takeru Shibata | 74 | 69 | 73 | 216 | 220,000 |
| Noboru Fujiike | 69 | 77 | 70 | 216 | 220,000 |
| Takashi Miyoshi | 73 | 73 | 70 | 216 | 220,000 |
| Nichito Hashimoto | 69 | 73 | 74 | 216 | 220,000 |
| Toyotake Nakao | 69 | 73 | 75 | 217 | 185,000 |
| Takayoshi Nishikawa | 74 | 71 | 72 | 217 | 185,000 |
| Dragon Taki | 74 | 71 | 73 | 218 | 161,000 |
| Hideto Shigenobu | 70 | 73 | 75 | 218 | 161,000 |
| Kunio Yamashita | 76 | 71 | 71 | 218 | 161,000 |
| Yukio Ishizawa | 71 | 75 | 72 | 218 | 161,000 |
| Isao Aoki | 70 | 73 | 76 | 219 | 142,000 |
| Motomasa Aoki | 74 | 73 | 72 | 219 | 142,000 |
| Yoshio Fumiyama | 74 | 71 | 74 | 219 | 142,000 |
| Koji Okuno | 69 | 75 | 75 | 219 | 142,000 |
| Tadao Furuichi | 75 | 72 | 72 | 219 | 142,000 |

# Women's Tours

## Women's World Cup of Golf

See South African Women's Tour section.

## SBS Open at Turtle Bay

*Turtle Bay Resort, Palmer Course*, Oahu, Hawaii
Par 36-36–72; 6,520 yards

February 24-26
purse, $1,000,000

| | SCORES | | | TOTAL | MONEY |
|---|---|---|---|---|---|
| Jennifer Rosales | 66 | 69 | 73 | 208 | $150,000 |
| *Michelle Wie | 70 | 70 | 70 | 210 | |
| Cristie Kerr | 70 | 68 | 72 | 210 | 91,544 |
| Reilley Rankin | 71 | 66 | 75 | 212 | 66,409 |
| Heather Bowie | 68 | 75 | 70 | 213 | 42,184 |
| Nicole Perrot | 72 | 69 | 72 | 213 | 42,184 |
| Hee-Won Han | 70 | 70 | 73 | 213 | 42,184 |
| Catriona Matthew | 75 | 69 | 70 | 214 | 22,905 |
| Gloria Park | 73 | 69 | 72 | 214 | 22,905 |
| Tina Barrett | 72 | 70 | 72 | 214 | 22,905 |
| Carin Koch | 70 | 72 | 72 | 214 | 22,905 |
| Rosie Jones | 70 | 69 | 75 | 214 | 22,905 |
| Sung Ah Yim | 68 | 75 | 72 | 215 | 17,542 |
| Dorothy Delasin | 71 | 75 | 70 | 216 | 14,635 |
| Leta Lindley | 72 | 72 | 72 | 216 | 14,635 |
| Pat Hurst | 70 | 73 | 73 | 216 | 14,635 |
| Angela Stanford | 68 | 74 | 74 | 216 | 14,635 |
| Lorena Ochoa | 68 | 72 | 76 | 216 | 14,635 |
| Beth Daniel | 71 | 76 | 70 | 217 | 10,945 |
| Candie Kung | 73 | 73 | 71 | 217 | 10,945 |
| Young Jo | 74 | 71 | 72 | 217 | 10,945 |
| Michele Redman | 76 | 68 | 73 | 217 | 10,945 |
| Tracy Hanson | 72 | 72 | 73 | 217 | 10,945 |
| Birdie Kim | 72 | 71 | 74 | 217 | 10,945 |
| Amy Hung | 71 | 72 | 74 | 217 | 10,945 |
| Michelle Estill | 72 | 70 | 75 | 217 | 10,945 |
| Hilary Lunke | 76 | 72 | 70 | 218 | 8,530 |
| Grace Park | 70 | 76 | 72 | 218 | 8,530 |
| Becky Morgan | 70 | 76 | 72 | 218 | 8,530 |
| Lorie Kane | 75 | 70 | 73 | 218 | 8,530 |
| Catherine Cartwright | 73 | 71 | 74 | 218 | 8,530 |

## MasterCard Classic

*Bosque Real Country Club,* Mexico City, Mexico
Par 36-36–72; 6,932 yards

March 4-6
purse, $1,200,000

| | SCORES | | | TOTAL | MONEY |
|---|---|---|---|---|---|
| Annika Sorenstam | 70 | 71 | 68 | 209 | $180,000 |
| Karrie Webb | 71 | 71 | 70 | 212 | 109,852 |

|  | SCORES | | | TOTAL | MONEY |
|---|---|---|---|---|---|
| Hee-Won Han | 66 | 76 | 71 | 213 | 70,669 |
| Cristie Kerr | 70 | 68 | 75 | 213 | 70,669 |
| Lorena Ochoa | 71 | 75 | 68 | 214 | 49,619 |
| Paula Creamer | 73 | 74 | 68 | 215 | 37,289 |
| Michele Redman | 73 | 70 | 72 | 215 | 37,289 |
| Helen Alfredsson | 73 | 73 | 70 | 216 | 28,268 |
| Kim Saiki | 71 | 74 | 71 | 216 | 28,268 |
| Janice Moodie | 73 | 73 | 71 | 217 | 21,243 |
| Leta Lindley | 71 | 75 | 71 | 217 | 21,243 |
| Riko Higashio | 75 | 69 | 73 | 217 | 21,243 |
| Soo Young Moon | 71 | 72 | 74 | 217 | 21,243 |
| Young Jo | 67 | 75 | 75 | 217 | 21,243 |
| Laura Diaz | 74 | 72 | 72 | 218 | 16,119 |
| Soo-Yun Kang | 73 | 73 | 72 | 218 | 16,119 |
| Vicki Goetze-Ackerman | 74 | 71 | 73 | 218 | 16,119 |
| Moira Dunn | 68 | 72 | 78 | 218 | 16,119 |
| Mi Hyun Kim | 72 | 74 | 73 | 219 | 12,653 |
| Beth Bauer | 71 | 74 | 74 | 219 | 12,653 |
| Liselotte Neumann | 73 | 71 | 75 | 219 | 12,653 |
| Grace Park | 72 | 72 | 75 | 219 | 12,653 |
| Carin Koch | 70 | 74 | 75 | 219 | 12,653 |
| Gloria Park | 69 | 75 | 75 | 219 | 12,653 |
| Dina Ammaccapane | 71 | 71 | 77 | 219 | 12,653 |
| Sae-Hee Son | 70 | 70 | 79 | 219 | 12,653 |
| Karen Stupples | 75 | 74 | 71 | 220 | 9,285 |
| Seol-An Jeon | 75 | 73 | 72 | 220 | 9,285 |
| Catriona Matthew | 76 | 71 | 73 | 220 | 9,285 |
| Wendy Ward | 73 | 73 | 74 | 220 | 9,285 |
| Joanne Morley | 72 | 73 | 75 | 220 | 9,285 |
| Natalie Gulbis | 74 | 69 | 77 | 220 | 9,285 |
| Laura Davies | 73 | 70 | 77 | 220 | 9,285 |
| Patricia Meunier-Lebouc | 69 | 74 | 77 | 220 | 9,285 |

## Safeway International

*Superstition Mountain Golf & Country Club,*
Superstition Mountain, Arizona
Par 36-36–72; 6,620 yards

March 17-20
purse, $1,400,000

|  | SCORES | | | | TOTAL | MONEY |
|---|---|---|---|---|---|---|
| Annika Sorenstam | 66 | 69 | 72 | 70 | 277 | $210,000 |
| Lorena Ochoa | 65 | 67 | 71 | 74 | 277 | 129,113 |
| (Sorenstam defeated Ochoa on first playoff hole.) | | | | | | |
| Juli Inkster | 66 | 73 | 69 | 72 | 280 | 83,060 |
| Soo-Yun Kang | 68 | 66 | 70 | 76 | 280 | 83,060 |
| Liselotte Neumann | 70 | 70 | 70 | 71 | 281 | 53,017 |
| Rosie Jones | 74 | 71 | 64 | 72 | 281 | 53,017 |
| Michele Redman | 75 | 72 | 68 | 67 | 282 | 39,939 |
| Natalie Gulbis | 69 | 76 | 70 | 68 | 283 | 30,396 |
| Laura Diaz | 73 | 67 | 74 | 69 | 283 | 30,396 |
| Gloria Park | 72 | 69 | 70 | 72 | 283 | 30,396 |
| Candie Kung | 69 | 70 | 72 | 72 | 283 | 30,396 |
| Jennifer Rosales | 72 | 73 | 69 | 70 | 284 | 23,964 |
| *Michelle Wie | 73 | 67 | 73 | 71 | 284 | |
| Siew-Ai Lim | 65 | 72 | 73 | 74 | 284 | 23,964 |
| Malinda Johnson | 72 | 75 | 70 | 68 | 285 | 20,547 |
| Silvia Cavalleri | 72 | 70 | 71 | 72 | 285 | 20,547 |

| | SCORES | | | TOTAL | MONEY |
|---|---|---|---|---|---|
| Karen Stupples | 67 | 71 | 74 73 | 285 | 20,547 |
| Maria Hjorth | 73 | 74 | 73 66 | 286 | 17,955 |
| Cristie Kerr | 72 | 73 | 70 71 | 286 | 17,955 |
| Moira Dunn | 68 | 74 | 76 69 | 287 | 15,410 |
| Young Kim | 74 | 72 | 71 70 | 287 | 15,410 |
| Christina Kim | 72 | 73 | 68 74 | 287 | 15,410 |
| Tina Barrett | 72 | 71 | 70 74 | 287 | 15,410 |
| Hee-Won Han | 72 | 69 | 72 74 | 287 | 15,410 |
| Brittany Lincicome | 71 | 71 | 66 79 | 287 | 15,410 |
| Meg Mallon | 71 | 74 | 74 69 | 288 | 12,276 |
| Wendy Doolan | 70 | 73 | 74 71 | 288 | 12,276 |
| Beth Daniel | 69 | 74 | 72 73 | 288 | 12,276 |
| Karrie Webb | 69 | 72 | 72 75 | 288 | 12,276 |
| Paula Creamer | 69 | 71 | 73 75 | 288 | 12,276 |
| Carin Koch | 73 | 68 | 71 76 | 288 | 12,276 |

# Kraft Nabisco Championship

*Mission Hills Country Club,* Rancho Mirage, California
Par 36-36–72; 6,535 yards

March 24-27
purse, $1,800,000

| | SCORES | | | TOTAL | MONEY |
|---|---|---|---|---|---|
| Annika Sorenstam | 70 | 69 | 66 68 | 273 | $270,000 |
| Rosie Jones | 69 | 70 | 71 71 | 281 | 166,003 |
| Laura Diaz | 75 | 69 | 71 68 | 283 | 106,791 |
| Cristie Kerr | 72 | 70 | 70 71 | 283 | 106,791 |
| Grace Park | 73 | 68 | 76 67 | 284 | 68,165 |
| Mi Hyun Kim | 69 | 71 | 72 72 | 284 | 68,165 |
| Juli Inkster | 70 | 74 | 72 69 | 285 | 51,350 |
| Lorie Kane | 71 | 76 | 69 70 | 286 | 44,988 |
| Candie Kung | 72 | 73 | 71 71 | 287 | 34,591 |
| Wendy Doolan | 74 | 69 | 73 71 | 287 | 34,591 |
| Dorothy Delasin | 71 | 72 | 73 71 | 287 | 34,591 |
| Beth Daniel | 74 | 72 | 69 72 | 287 | 34,591 |
| Reilley Rankin | 73 | 68 | 74 72 | 287 | 34,591 |
| *Michelle Wie | 70 | 74 | 73 71 | 288 | |
| Kim Saiki | 74 | 71 | 70 73 | 288 | 27,175 |
| Brandie Burton | 72 | 71 | 72 73 | 288 | 27,175 |
| Hee-Won Han | 76 | 71 | 69 73 | 289 | 24,267 |
| Natalie Gulbis | 73 | 71 | 72 73 | 289 | 24,267 |
| Shi Hyun Ahn | 77 | 76 | 71 66 | 290 | 21,692 |
| Paula Creamer | 74 | 72 | 72 72 | 290 | 21,692 |
| Young Kim | 76 | 70 | 70 74 | 290 | 21,692 |
| *Morgan Pressel | 70 | 73 | 72 75 | 290 | |
| Karen Stupples | 69 | 80 | 70 73 | 292 | 19,086 |
| Pat Hurst | 71 | 74 | 74 73 | 292 | 19,086 |
| Sherri Steinhauer | 71 | 72 | 75 74 | 292 | 19,086 |
| Laura Davies | 73 | 71 | 71 77 | 292 | 19,086 |
| Jeong Jang | 77 | 74 | 71 71 | 293 | 16,723 |
| Dawn Coe-Jones | 74 | 73 | 74 72 | 293 | 16,723 |
| Se Ri Pak | 77 | 70 | 70 76 | 293 | 16,723 |
| Stacy Prammanasudh | 75 | 74 | 74 71 | 294 | 14,565 |
| Jill McGill | 73 | 72 | 77 72 | 294 | 14,565 |
| Michelle Estill | 71 | 79 | 71 73 | 294 | 14,565 |
| Carin Koch | 70 | 73 | 75 76 | 294 | 14,565 |
| *Julieta Granada | 75 | 71 | 70 78 | 294 | |

# LPGA Takefuji Classic

*Las Vegas Country Club,* Las Vegas, Nevada
Par 36-36–72; 6,550 yards

April 14-16
purse, $1,100,000

| | SCORES | | | TOTAL | MONEY |
|---|---|---|---|---|---|
| Wendy Ward | 65 | 68 | 67 | 200 | $165,000 |
| Lorena Ochoa | 74 | 63 | 65 | 202 | 101,967 |
| Shi Hyun Ahn | 68 | 72 | 63 | 203 | 65,596 |
| Paula Creamer | 70 | 68 | 65 | 203 | 65,596 |
| *In-Bee Park | 66 | 71 | 67 | 204 | |
| Juli Inkster | 72 | 67 | 67 | 206 | 46,057 |
| Jeong Jang | 72 | 70 | 65 | 207 | 32,286 |
| Nicole Perrot | 66 | 71 | 70 | 207 | 32,286 |
| Moira Dunn | 69 | 67 | 71 | 207 | 32,286 |
| Young Kim | 70 | 71 | 67 | 208 | 20,572 |
| Hee-Won Han | 71 | 69 | 68 | 208 | 20,572 |
| Heather Bowie | 68 | 72 | 68 | 208 | 20,572 |
| Stacy Prammanasudh | 69 | 70 | 69 | 208 | 20,572 |
| Mikaela Parmlid | 67 | 72 | 69 | 208 | 20,572 |
| Wendy Doolan | 66 | 72 | 70 | 208 | 20,572 |
| Janice Moodie | 72 | 69 | 68 | 209 | 14,052 |
| Aree Song | 67 | 74 | 68 | 209 | 14,052 |
| Lorie Kane | 70 | 70 | 69 | 209 | 14,052 |
| Amy Hung | 68 | 72 | 69 | 209 | 14,052 |
| Michele Redman | 70 | 68 | 71 | 209 | 14,052 |
| Mi Hyun Kim | 66 | 71 | 72 | 209 | 14,052 |
| Karrie Webb | 65 | 71 | 73 | 209 | 14,052 |
| Marisa Baena | 68 | 73 | 69 | 210 | 10,489 |
| Stephanie Louden | 71 | 69 | 70 | 210 | 10,489 |
| Johanna Head | 71 | 69 | 70 | 210 | 10,489 |
| Seol-An Jeon | 70 | 70 | 70 | 210 | 10,489 |
| Patricia Meunier-Lebouc | 68 | 72 | 70 | 210 | 10,489 |
| Sophie Gustafson | 67 | 73 | 70 | 210 | 10,489 |
| Natalie Gulbis | 72 | 67 | 71 | 210 | 10,489 |
| Tina Barrett | 71 | 68 | 71 | 210 | 10,489 |

# Corona Morelia Championship

*Tres Marias Residential Golf Club,* Michoacan, Mexico
Par 36-36–72; 6,763 yards

April 21-24
purse, $1,000,000

| | SCORES | | | | TOTAL | MONEY |
|---|---|---|---|---|---|---|
| Carin Koch | 68 | 69 | 71 | 71 | 279 | $150,000 |
| Karine Icher | 73 | 72 | 70 | 70 | 285 | 90,899 |
| Catriona Matthew | 73 | 71 | 70 | 72 | 286 | 58,476 |
| Wendy Ward | 71 | 69 | 68 | 78 | 286 | 58,476 |
| Dorothy Delasin | 71 | 78 | 68 | 70 | 287 | 34,257 |
| Soo Young Moon | 72 | 73 | 72 | 70 | 287 | 34,257 |
| Natalie Gulbis | 66 | 75 | 72 | 74 | 287 | 34,257 |
| Gloria Park | 75 | 70 | 71 | 72 | 288 | 23,391 |
| Tina Barrett | 70 | 75 | 71 | 72 | 288 | 23,391 |
| Charlotta Sorenstam | 71 | 72 | 74 | 72 | 289 | 20,155 |
| Giulia Sergas | 69 | 74 | 75 | 73 | 291 | 17,468 |
| Audra Burks | 68 | 75 | 75 | 73 | 291 | 17,468 |
| Stacy Prammanasudh | 72 | 72 | 70 | 77 | 291 | 17,468 |
| Nancy Scranton | 69 | 76 | 77 | 70 | 292 | 14,880 |

|  | SCORES | | | | TOTAL | MONEY |
|---|---|---|---|---|---|---|
| Leta Lindley | 72 | 71 | 73 | 76 | 292 | 14,880 |
| Ji Yeon Lee | 76 | 72 | 76 | 69 | 293 | 11,986 |
| Aree Song | 76 | 72 | 76 | 69 | 293 | 11,986 |
| Jung Yeon Lee | 76 | 73 | 73 | 71 | 293 | 11,986 |
| Lorena Ochoa | 73 | 71 | 76 | 73 | 293 | 11,986 |
| Paula Creamer | 70 | 77 | 72 | 74 | 293 | 11,986 |
| Young Kim | 71 | 74 | 71 | 77 | 293 | 11,986 |
| Sung Ah Yim | 73 | 70 | 73 | 77 | 293 | 11,986 |
| Malinda Johnson | 81 | 70 | 71 | 72 | 294 | 9,692 |
| Tracy Hanson | 76 | 74 | 71 | 73 | 294 | 9,692 |
| Kris Tschetter | 74 | 70 | 76 | 74 | 294 | 9,692 |
| Maria Hjorth | 69 | 72 | 75 | 78 | 294 | 9,692 |
| Nicole Perrot | 74 | 76 | 73 | 72 | 295 | 8,299 |
| Joanne Morley | 76 | 69 | 77 | 73 | 295 | 8,299 |
| Young Jo | 70 | 75 | 76 | 74 | 295 | 8,299 |
| Yu Ping Lin | 77 | 67 | 74 | 77 | 295 | 8,299 |

## Franklin American Mortgage Championship

*Vanderbilt Legends Club, Ironhorse Course,*
Franklin, Tennessee
Par 36-36–72; 6,458 yards

April 28-May 1
purse, $1,000,000

|  | SCORES | | | | TOTAL | MONEY |
|---|---|---|---|---|---|---|
| Stacy Prammanasudh | 70 | 70 | 65 | 69 | 274 | $150,000 |
| Lorena Ochoa | 71 | 68 | 68 | 70 | 277 | 90,899 |
| Cristie Kerr | 70 | 69 | 72 | 68 | 279 | 52,670 |
| Christina Kim | 71 | 70 | 69 | 69 | 279 | 52,670 |
| Catriona Matthew | 72 | 71 | 65 | 71 | 279 | 52,670 |
| Rachel Hetherington | 71 | 74 | 72 | 67 | 284 | 28,782 |
| Karrie Webb | 76 | 65 | 72 | 71 | 284 | 28,782 |
| Heather Bowie | 74 | 66 | 72 | 72 | 284 | 28,782 |
| Jeong Jang | 74 | 67 | 70 | 74 | 285 | 22,147 |
| Grace Park | 70 | 71 | 70 | 75 | 286 | 20,155 |
| Jill McGill | 77 | 69 | 71 | 70 | 287 | 16,933 |
| Emilee Klein | 77 | 70 | 69 | 71 | 287 | 16,933 |
| Wendy Ward | 71 | 68 | 76 | 72 | 287 | 16,933 |
| Giulia Sergas | 77 | 65 | 70 | 75 | 287 | 16,933 |
| Karen Stupples | 73 | 75 | 70 | 70 | 288 | 13,669 |
| Liselotte Neumann | 72 | 67 | 76 | 73 | 288 | 13,669 |
| Sophie Gustafson | 71 | 72 | 71 | 74 | 288 | 13,669 |
| Pat Hurst | 72 | 71 | 76 | 70 | 289 | 11,466 |
| Natalie Gulbis | 76 | 71 | 70 | 72 | 289 | 11,466 |
| Laura Diaz | 74 | 71 | 70 | 74 | 289 | 11,466 |
| Hee-Won Han | 71 | 69 | 75 | 74 | 289 | 11,466 |
| Moira Dunn | 76 | 69 | 69 | 75 | 289 | 11,466 |
| Soo Young Moon | 79 | 69 | 73 | 69 | 290 | 9,516 |
| Patricia Baxter-Johnson | 77 | 73 | 70 | 70 | 290 | 9,516 |
| Young Jo | 72 | 72 | 76 | 70 | 290 | 9,516 |
| Joo Mi Kim | 75 | 72 | 70 | 73 | 290 | 9,516 |
| Young Kim | 74 | 70 | 71 | 75 | 290 | 9,516 |
| Denise Killeen | 77 | 72 | 73 | 69 | 291 | 7,522 |
| Laura Davies | 74 | 72 | 75 | 70 | 291 | 7,522 |
| Candy Hannemann | 75 | 71 | 73 | 72 | 291 | 7,522 |
| Mardi Lunn | 74 | 69 | 76 | 72 | 291 | 7,522 |
| Lorie Kane | 73 | 71 | 74 | 73 | 291 | 7,522 |
| Angela Jerman | 76 | 71 | 70 | 74 | 291 | 7,522 |
| Mhairi McKay | 77 | 67 | 71 | 76 | 291 | 7,522 |

# Michelob Ultra Open at Kingsmill

*Kingsmill Resort & Spa, River Course,*
Williamsburg, Virginia
Par 36-35–71; 6,306 yards

May 5-8
purse, $2,200,000

| | SCORES | | | | TOTAL | MONEY |
|---|---|---|---|---|---|---|
| Cristie Kerr | 68 | 68 | 68 | 72 | 276 | $330,000 |
| Jill McGill | 68 | 72 | 69 | 72 | 281 | 200,915 |
| Michele Redman | 69 | 69 | 74 | 70 | 282 | 116,417 |
| Catriona Matthew | 70 | 71 | 70 | 71 | 282 | 116,417 |
| Natalie Gulbis | 69 | 73 | 67 | 73 | 282 | 116,417 |
| Gloria Park | 71 | 71 | 72 | 69 | 283 | 68,200 |
| A.J. Eathorne | 69 | 69 | 75 | 70 | 283 | 68,200 |
| Rosie Jones | 71 | 70 | 75 | 69 | 285 | 47,300 |
| Juli Inkster | 69 | 75 | 70 | 71 | 285 | 47,300 |
| Mi Hyun Kim | 69 | 72 | 71 | 73 | 285 | 47,300 |
| Shi Hyun Ahn | 69 | 70 | 73 | 73 | 285 | 47,300 |
| Silvia Cavalleri | 67 | 74 | 73 | 72 | 286 | 36,153 |
| Grace Park | 69 | 73 | 71 | 73 | 286 | 36,153 |
| Annika Sorenstam | 76 | 67 | 69 | 74 | 286 | 36,153 |
| Stacy Prammanasudh | 72 | 74 | 70 | 71 | 287 | 29,480 |
| Marcy Hart | 72 | 73 | 70 | 72 | 287 | 29,480 |
| Beth Bader | 75 | 68 | 70 | 74 | 287 | 29,480 |
| Nicole Perrot | 70 | 69 | 74 | 74 | 287 | 29,480 |
| Rachel Hetherington | 73 | 73 | 74 | 68 | 288 | 23,556 |
| *Morgan Pressel | 73 | 70 | 76 | 69 | 288 | |
| Lorie Kane | 70 | 75 | 72 | 71 | 288 | 23,556 |
| Laura Davies | 71 | 75 | 70 | 72 | 288 | 23,556 |
| Jennifer Rosales | 70 | 72 | 74 | 72 | 288 | 23,556 |
| Jimin Kang | 69 | 72 | 75 | 72 | 288 | 23,556 |
| Beth Daniel | 70 | 71 | 74 | 73 | 288 | 23,556 |
| Lindsey Wright | 71 | 73 | 70 | 74 | 288 | 23,556 |
| Meg Mallon | 73 | 72 | 74 | 70 | 289 | 18,024 |
| Malinda Johnson | 72 | 70 | 76 | 71 | 289 | 18,024 |
| Kim Williams | 72 | 70 | 74 | 73 | 289 | 18,024 |
| Nancy Scranton | 73 | 71 | 71 | 74 | 289 | 18,024 |
| Laura Diaz | 68 | 75 | 72 | 74 | 289 | 18,024 |
| Jenna Daniels | 73 | 69 | 73 | 74 | 289 | 18,024 |
| Wendy Doolan | 69 | 71 | 74 | 75 | 289 | 18,024 |

# Chick-fil-A Charity Championship

*Eagle's Landing Country Club,* Stockbridge, Georgia
Par 36-36–72; 6,394 yards

May 12-15
purse, $1,600,000

| | SCORES | | | | TOTAL | MONEY |
|---|---|---|---|---|---|---|
| Annika Sorenstam | 67 | 64 | 67 | 67 | 265 | $240,000 |
| Candie Kung | 69 | 71 | 70 | 65 | 275 | 147,558 |
| Cristie Kerr | 68 | 73 | 70 | 65 | 276 | 107,043 |
| Silvia Cavalleri | 74 | 70 | 65 | 69 | 278 | 67,996 |
| Wendy Ward | 69 | 73 | 67 | 69 | 278 | 67,996 |
| Emilee Klein | 70 | 70 | 68 | 70 | 278 | 67,996 |
| Birdie Kim | 69 | 73 | 69 | 69 | 280 | 36,920 |
| Laura Davies | 66 | 76 | 69 | 69 | 280 | 36,920 |
| Candy Hannemann | 69 | 72 | 68 | 71 | 280 | 36,920 |
| Lorena Ochoa | 68 | 71 | 70 | 71 | 280 | 36,920 |

| | SCORES | | | | TOTAL | MONEY |
|---|---|---|---|---|---|---|
| Heather Bowie | 68 | 69 | 72 | 71 | 280 | 36,920 |
| Michelle Ellis | 72 | 72 | 70 | 67 | 281 | 25,771 |
| Young Kim | 70 | 76 | 67 | 68 | 281 | 25,771 |
| Moira Dunn | 79 | 66 | 67 | 69 | 281 | 25,771 |
| Leta Lindley | 71 | 72 | 69 | 69 | 281 | 25,771 |
| Kim Saiki | 74 | 72 | 70 | 66 | 282 | 20,601 |
| Reilley Rankin | 70 | 72 | 70 | 70 | 282 | 20,601 |
| Joo Mi Kim | 70 | 72 | 70 | 70 | 282 | 20,601 |
| Sung Ah Yim | 70 | 70 | 72 | 70 | 282 | 20,601 |
| Rachel Hetherington | 69 | 73 | 74 | 67 | 283 | 17,935 |
| Maria Hjorth | 74 | 69 | 71 | 69 | 283 | 17,935 |
| Beth Daniel | 70 | 70 | 70 | 73 | 283 | 17,935 |
| Catherine Cartwright | 69 | 74 | 72 | 69 | 284 | 14,876 |
| Pat Hurst | 75 | 68 | 71 | 70 | 284 | 14,876 |
| *Morgan Pressel | 71 | 72 | 71 | 70 | 284 | |
| Natalie Gulbis | 71 | 71 | 72 | 70 | 284 | 14,876 |
| Christina Kim | 74 | 71 | 68 | 71 | 284 | 14,876 |
| Carin Koch | 69 | 76 | 68 | 71 | 284 | 14,876 |
| Giulia Sergas | 67 | 75 | 71 | 71 | 284 | 14,876 |
| Jimin Kang | 72 | 72 | 68 | 72 | 284 | 14,876 |

## Sybase Classic

*Wykagyl Country Club,* New Rochelle, New York
Par 35-36–71; 6,161 yards

May 19-22
purse, $1,250,000

| | SCORES | | | | TOTAL | MONEY |
|---|---|---|---|---|---|---|
| Paula Creamer | 69 | 68 | 71 | 70 | 278 | $187,500 |
| Jeong Jang | 71 | 71 | 70 | 67 | 279 | 98,252 |
| Gloria Park | 67 | 70 | 71 | 71 | 279 | 98,252 |
| Christina Kim | 65 | 72 | 70 | 73 | 280 | 63,911 |
| Heather Bowie | 69 | 71 | 69 | 72 | 281 | 46,765 |
| Joo Mi Kim | 72 | 65 | 71 | 73 | 281 | 46,765 |
| Mi Hyun Kim | 69 | 72 | 69 | 72 | 282 | 35,229 |
| Tina Barrett | 71 | 75 | 72 | 65 | 283 | 27,954 |
| Soo-Yun Kang | 69 | 76 | 69 | 69 | 283 | 27,954 |
| Michele Redman | 72 | 67 | 71 | 73 | 283 | 27,954 |
| Hee-Won Han | 67 | 72 | 74 | 71 | 284 | 22,603 |
| Siew-Ai Lim | 66 | 73 | 70 | 75 | 284 | 22,603 |
| Jean Bartholomew | 71 | 76 | 70 | 68 | 285 | 19,829 |
| Grace Park | 77 | 67 | 68 | 73 | 285 | 19,829 |
| Young Kim | 74 | 71 | 70 | 71 | 286 | 17,584 |
| Candie Kung | 70 | 74 | 70 | 72 | 286 | 17,584 |
| Marcy Hart | 75 | 70 | 74 | 68 | 287 | 16,212 |
| Cristie Kerr | 72 | 72 | 75 | 69 | 288 | 15,152 |
| Sarah Lee | 70 | 74 | 73 | 71 | 288 | 15,152 |
| Meena Lee | 76 | 71 | 73 | 69 | 289 | 13,105 |
| Sherri Steinhauer | 74 | 72 | 73 | 70 | 289 | 13,105 |
| Jenna Daniels | 74 | 70 | 74 | 71 | 289 | 13,105 |
| Meg Mallon | 72 | 72 | 74 | 71 | 289 | 13,105 |
| Celeste Troche | 71 | 71 | 74 | 73 | 289 | 13,105 |
| Miriam Nagl | 67 | 72 | 77 | 73 | 289 | 13,105 |
| Marisa Baena | 73 | 76 | 71 | 70 | 290 | 11,255 |
| Dawn Coe-Jones | 77 | 72 | 70 | 71 | 290 | 11,255 |
| Jimin Kang | 74 | 75 | 71 | 71 | 291 | 9,802 |
| Rachel Hetherington | 74 | 74 | 72 | 71 | 291 | 9,802 |
| Janice Moodie | 73 | 74 | 73 | 71 | 291 | 9,802 |

| | SCORES | | | | TOTAL | MONEY |
|---|---|---|---|---|---|---|
| Emilee Klein | 73 | 72 | 74 | 72 | 291 | 9,802 |
| Karen Stupples | 73 | 70 | 74 | 74 | 291 | 9,802 |

## LPGA Corning Classic

*Corning Country Club,* Corning, New York
Par 36-36–72; 6,062 yards

May 26-29
purse, $1,100,000

| | SCORES | | | | TOTAL | MONEY |
|---|---|---|---|---|---|---|
| Jimin Kang | 69 | 70 | 68 | 66 | 273 | $165,000 |
| Meena Lee | 69 | 71 | 68 | 67 | 275 | 87,085 |
| Annika Sorenstam | 69 | 68 | 69 | 69 | 275 | 87,085 |
| Moira Dunn | 70 | 68 | 71 | 68 | 277 | 51,121 |
| Hee-Won Han | 74 | 69 | 62 | 72 | 277 | 51,121 |
| Liselotte Neumann | 72 | 69 | 69 | 68 | 278 | 31,962 |
| Sung Ah Yim | 70 | 69 | 70 | 69 | 278 | 31,962 |
| Karine Icher | 70 | 66 | 68 | 74 | 278 | 31,962 |
| Rosie Jones | 71 | 71 | 69 | 68 | 279 | 22,567 |
| Sophie Gustafson | 66 | 73 | 72 | 68 | 279 | 22,567 |
| Michelle Ellis | 71 | 72 | 67 | 69 | 279 | 22,567 |
| Natalie Gulbis | 72 | 69 | 71 | 68 | 280 | 18,164 |
| Sherri Turner | 66 | 71 | 74 | 69 | 280 | 18,164 |
| Dorothy Delasin | 71 | 71 | 67 | 71 | 280 | 18,164 |
| Nancy Harvey | 71 | 69 | 72 | 69 | 281 | 16,027 |
| *Brittany Lang | 71 | 71 | 69 | 70 | 281 | |
| Jill McGill | 74 | 70 | 68 | 71 | 283 | 15,143 |
| Dina Ammaccapane | 74 | 70 | 71 | 69 | 284 | 13,485 |
| Laurie Rinker | 69 | 75 | 71 | 69 | 284 | 13,485 |
| Kris Tamulis | 73 | 68 | 72 | 71 | 284 | 13,485 |
| Joo Mi Kim | 72 | 68 | 71 | 73 | 284 | 13,485 |
| Laura Diaz | 75 | 68 | 73 | 69 | 285 | 11,827 |
| Nanci Bowen | 74 | 69 | 72 | 70 | 285 | 11,827 |
| Carin Koch | 75 | 69 | 70 | 71 | 285 | 11,827 |
| Diana D'Alessio | 77 | 70 | 70 | 69 | 286 | 10,169 |
| Nancy Scranton | 73 | 72 | 71 | 70 | 286 | 10,169 |
| Patricia Baxter-Johnson | 72 | 71 | 71 | 72 | 286 | 10,169 |
| Miriam Nagl | 73 | 69 | 72 | 72 | 286 | 10,169 |
| Kim Williams | 73 | 70 | 69 | 74 | 286 | 10,169 |
| Marisa Baena | 73 | 74 | 72 | 68 | 287 | 8,021 |
| Joanne Morley | 74 | 72 | 71 | 70 | 287 | 8,021 |
| Emilee Klein | 75 | 70 | 72 | 70 | 287 | 8,021 |
| Helen Alfredsson | 74 | 71 | 72 | 70 | 287 | 8,021 |
| Becky Iverson | 72 | 73 | 71 | 71 | 287 | 8,021 |
| Beth Bauer | 73 | 71 | 71 | 72 | 287 | 8,021 |
| Tina Fischer | 73 | 71 | 70 | 73 | 287 | 8,021 |

## ShopRite LPGA Classic

*Marriott Seaview Resort & Spa, Bay Course,*
Galloway Twp., New Jersey
Par 36-35–71; 6,071 yards

June 3-5
purse, $1,400,000

| | SCORES | | | TOTAL | MONEY |
|---|---|---|---|---|---|
| Annika Sorenstam | 67 | 65 | 64 | 196 | $210,000 |
| Juli Inkster | 65 | 67 | 68 | 200 | 127,554 |
| Catriona Matthew | 71 | 66 | 64 | 201 | 82,057 |
| Laura Davies | 71 | 62 | 68 | 201 | 82,057 |
| Jeong Jang | 70 | 70 | 65 | 205 | 52,377 |
| Pat Hurst | 71 | 64 | 70 | 205 | 52,377 |
| Jimin Kang | 71 | 73 | 62 | 206 | 37,013 |
| Mi Hyun Kim | 69 | 71 | 66 | 206 | 37,013 |
| Joanne Morley | 73 | 67 | 68 | 208 | 29,680 |
| Natalie Gulbis | 71 | 67 | 70 | 208 | 29,680 |
| Stacy Prammanasudh | 75 | 67 | 67 | 209 | 25,315 |
| Cristie Kerr | 74 | 66 | 69 | 209 | 25,315 |
| Christina Kim | 74 | 70 | 66 | 210 | 20,392 |
| Janice Moodie | 73 | 70 | 67 | 210 | 20,392 |
| Karrie Webb | 75 | 67 | 68 | 210 | 20,392 |
| Karen Stupples | 73 | 67 | 70 | 210 | 20,392 |
| Carin Koch | 71 | 67 | 72 | 210 | 20,392 |
| Sarah Lee | 75 | 68 | 68 | 211 | 16,376 |
| Nanci Bowen | 73 | 70 | 68 | 211 | 16,376 |
| Brittany Lincicome | 76 | 66 | 69 | 211 | 16,376 |
| Shi Hyun Ahn | 71 | 70 | 70 | 211 | 16,376 |
| Beth Daniel | 77 | 68 | 67 | 212 | 13,869 |
| Marisa Baena | 76 | 67 | 69 | 212 | 13,869 |
| Jill McGill | 72 | 70 | 70 | 212 | 13,869 |
| Aree Song | 73 | 68 | 71 | 212 | 13,869 |
| Kris Tschetter | 71 | 70 | 71 | 212 | 13,869 |
| Karine Icher | 72 | 73 | 68 | 213 | 11,425 |
| Lorie Kane | 74 | 70 | 69 | 213 | 11,425 |
| Heather Daly-Donofrio | 74 | 69 | 70 | 213 | 11,425 |
| Liselotte Neumann | 74 | 69 | 70 | 213 | 11,425 |
| *Julieta Granada | 72 | 71 | 70 | 213 | |
| Heather Bowie | 71 | 71 | 71 | 213 | 11,425 |

## McDonald's LPGA Championship

*Bulle Rock Golf Course,* Havre de Grace, Maryland
Par 36-36–72; 6,486 yards

June 9-12
purse, $1,800,000

| | SCORES | | | | TOTAL | MONEY |
|---|---|---|---|---|---|---|
| Annika Sorenstam | 68 | 67 | 69 | 73 | 277 | $270,000 |
| *Michelle Wie | 69 | 71 | 71 | 69 | 280 | |
| Paula Creamer | 68 | 73 | 74 | 67 | 282 | 140,517 |
| Laura Davies | 67 | 70 | 74 | 71 | 282 | 140,517 |
| Lorena Ochoa | 72 | 72 | 68 | 72 | 284 | 82,486 |
| Natalie Gulbis | 67 | 71 | 73 | 73 | 284 | 82,486 |
| Mi Hyun Kim | 69 | 75 | 74 | 67 | 285 | 43,993 |
| Pat Hurst | 72 | 73 | 71 | 69 | 285 | 43,993 |
| Gloria Park | 71 | 71 | 72 | 71 | 285 | 43,993 |
| Carin Koch | 74 | 70 | 69 | 72 | 285 | 43,993 |
| Moira Dunn | 71 | 68 | 72 | 74 | 285 | 43,993 |

|  | SCORES | | | | TOTAL | MONEY |
|---|---|---|---|---|---|---|
| Young Kim | 73 | 68 | 68 | 76 | 285 | 43,993 |
| Candie Kung | 72 | 73 | 73 | 68 | 286 | 29,309 |
| Juli Inkster | 75 | 71 | 71 | 69 | 286 | 29,309 |
| Jeong Jang | 71 | 71 | 69 | 75 | 286 | 29,309 |
| Lindsey Wright | 71 | 72 | 72 | 72 | 287 | 23,899 |
| Angela Stanford | 69 | 73 | 73 | 72 | 287 | 23,899 |
| Jennifer Rosales | 71 | 73 | 69 | 74 | 287 | 23,899 |
| Marisa Baena | 70 | 69 | 73 | 75 | 287 | 23,899 |
| Karrie Webb | 74 | 75 | 72 | 67 | 288 | 19,797 |
| Beth Bader | 72 | 72 | 72 | 72 | 288 | 19,797 |
| Laura Diaz | 67 | 72 | 76 | 73 | 288 | 19,797 |
| Heather Bowie | 72 | 71 | 71 | 74 | 288 | 19,797 |
| Meena Lee | 70 | 71 | 72 | 75 | 288 | 19,797 |
| Shi Hyun Ahn | 78 | 71 | 72 | 68 | 289 | 16,096 |
| Hee-Won Han | 73 | 74 | 72 | 70 | 289 | 16,096 |
| Leta Lindley | 72 | 72 | 75 | 70 | 289 | 16,096 |
| Il Mi Chung | 71 | 68 | 79 | 71 | 289 | 16,096 |
| Kristi Albers | 70 | 72 | 73 | 74 | 289 | 16,096 |
| Karen Stupples | 72 | 71 | 71 | 75 | 289 | 16,096 |

## Wegmans Rochester LPGA

*Locust Hill Country Club,* Pittsford, New York — June 16-19
Par 35-37–72; 6,221 yards — purse, $1,500,000

|  | SCORES | | | | TOTAL | MONEY |
|---|---|---|---|---|---|---|
| Lorena Ochoa | 67 | 69 | 72 | 65 | 273 | $225,000 |
| Paula Creamer | 71 | 68 | 67 | 71 | 277 | 136,665 |
| Rosie Jones | 71 | 72 | 67 | 68 | 278 | 99,141 |
| Jeong Jang | 75 | 68 | 71 | 66 | 280 | 76,694 |
| Laurie Rinker | 75 | 72 | 68 | 66 | 281 | 56,118 |
| Gloria Park | 71 | 70 | 73 | 67 | 281 | 56,118 |
| Laura Diaz | 70 | 75 | 70 | 68 | 283 | 37,536 |
| Dorothy Delasin | 71 | 72 | 70 | 70 | 283 | 37,536 |
| Becky Morgan | 64 | 74 | 71 | 74 | 283 | 37,536 |
| Tina Barrett | 74 | 72 | 67 | 71 | 284 | 25,640 |
| Candie Kung | 73 | 70 | 70 | 71 | 284 | 25,640 |
| Patricia Baxter-Johnson | 72 | 71 | 70 | 71 | 284 | 25,640 |
| Mi Hyun Kim | 74 | 66 | 72 | 72 | 284 | 25,640 |
| Catriona Matthew | 74 | 70 | 67 | 73 | 284 | 25,640 |
| Maria Hjorth | 68 | 70 | 73 | 73 | 284 | 25,640 |
| Jennifer Rosales | 72 | 70 | 71 | 72 | 285 | 19,978 |
| Laura Davies | 71 | 71 | 71 | 72 | 285 | 19,978 |
| Sherri Steinhauer | 75 | 70 | 73 | 68 | 286 | 17,546 |
| Hee-Won Han | 75 | 72 | 70 | 69 | 286 | 17,546 |
| Karine Icher | 74 | 72 | 70 | 70 | 286 | 17,546 |
| Lee Ann Walker-Cooper | 74 | 71 | 70 | 71 | 286 | 17,546 |
| Marcy Hart | 74 | 74 | 70 | 69 | 287 | 14,591 |
| Christina Kim | 70 | 75 | 73 | 69 | 287 | 14,591 |
| Brittany Lincicome | 74 | 72 | 70 | 71 | 287 | 14,591 |
| Yu Ping Lin | 73 | 74 | 68 | 72 | 287 | 14,591 |
| Emilee Klein | 71 | 73 | 70 | 73 | 287 | 14,591 |
| Mikaela Parmlid | 76 | 71 | 66 | 74 | 287 | 14,591 |
| Angela Stanford | 76 | 71 | 73 | 68 | 288 | 11,990 |
| Leslie Spalding | 74 | 72 | 73 | 69 | 288 | 11,990 |
| Nancy Scranton | 72 | 71 | 74 | 71 | 288 | 11,990 |
| Meena Lee | 73 | 72 | 70 | 73 | 288 | 11,990 |

# U.S. Women's Open

*Cherry Hills Country Club,* Cherry Hills Village, Colorado
Par 36-35–71; 6,749 yards

June 23-26
purse, $3,100,000

|  | SCORES | | | | TOTAL | MONEY |
|---|---|---|---|---|---|---|
| Birdie Kim | 74 | 72 | 69 | 72 | 287 | $560,000 |
| *Brittany Lang | 69 | 77 | 72 | 71 | 289 | |
| *Morgan Pressel | 71 | 73 | 70 | 75 | 289 | |
| Lorie Kane | 74 | 71 | 76 | 69 | 290 | 272,723 |
| Natalie Gulbis | 70 | 75 | 74 | 71 | 290 | 272,723 |
| Lorena Ochoa | 74 | 68 | 77 | 72 | 291 | 116,310 |
| Karine Icher | 69 | 75 | 75 | 72 | 291 | 116,310 |
| Candie Kung | 73 | 73 | 71 | 74 | 291 | 116,310 |
| Young Jo | 74 | 71 | 70 | 76 | 291 | 116,310 |
| Cristie Kerr | 74 | 71 | 72 | 75 | 292 | 80,523 |
| Angela Stanford | 69 | 74 | 73 | 76 | 292 | 80,523 |
| Karen Stupples | 75 | 70 | 69 | 78 | 292 | 80,523 |
| Soo-Yun Kang | 74 | 74 | 74 | 71 | 293 | 61,402 |
| Meg Mallon | 71 | 74 | 75 | 73 | 293 | 61,402 |
| *Paige Mackenzie | 75 | 75 | 69 | 74 | 293 | |
| Heather Bowie | 77 | 73 | 69 | 74 | 293 | 61,402 |
| Tina Barrett | 73 | 74 | 71 | 75 | 293 | 61,402 |
| Jamie Hullett | 75 | 72 | 70 | 76 | 293 | 61,402 |
| Leta Lindley | 73 | 76 | 73 | 72 | 294 | 47,480 |
| Rosie Jones | 73 | 72 | 74 | 75 | 294 | 47,480 |
| Liselotte Neumann | 70 | 75 | 73 | 76 | 294 | 47,480 |
| Paula Creamer | 74 | 69 | 72 | 79 | 294 | 47,480 |
| Gloria Park | 74 | 75 | 74 | 73 | 296 | 34,556 |
| Sarah Huarte | 74 | 76 | 73 | 73 | 296 | 34,556 |
| Jennifer Rosales | 72 | 76 | 73 | 75 | 296 | 34,556 |
| Laura Diaz | 75 | 73 | 72 | 76 | 296 | 34,556 |
| Helen Alfredsson | 72 | 73 | 74 | 77 | 296 | 34,556 |
| Annika Sorenstam | 71 | 75 | 73 | 77 | 296 | 34,556 |
| Nicole Perrot | 70 | 70 | 78 | 78 | 296 | 34,556 |
| *Michelle Wie | 69 | 73 | 72 | 82 | 296 | |

# HSBC Women's World Match Play

*Hamilton Farm Golf Club,* Gladstone, New Jersey
Par 36-36–72; 6,523 yards

June 30-July 3
purse, $2,000,000

## FIRST ROUND

Annika Sorenstam defeated Joanne Morley, 2 and 1.
Tina Barrett defeated Young Kim, 5 and 3.
Mi Hyun Kim defeated Meg Mallon, 4 and 2.
Rachel Hetherington defeated Se Ri Pak, 1 up.
Candie Kung defeated Candy Hannemann, 2 and 1.
Leta Lindley defeated Stacy Prammanasudh, 2 and 1.
A.J. Eathorne defeated Catriona Matthew, 21 holes.
Dorothy Delasin defeated Heather Bowie, 3 and 2.
Paula Creamer defeated Maria Hjorth, 4 and 3.
Karrie Webb defeated Soo-Yun Kang, 3 and 2.
Jeong Jang defeated Reilley Rankin, 4 and 3.
*Shinobu Moromizato defeated Emilee Klein, 2 up.
Marisa Baena defeated Natalie Gulbis, 1 up.
Grace Park defeated Michele Redman, 2 and 1.
Beth Daniel defeated Lorie Kane, 5 and 4.

Jennifer Rosales defeated Angela Stanford, 1 up.
Cristie Kerr defeated Lindsey Wright, 2 and 1.
Liselotte Neumann defeated Moira Dunn, 4 and 3.
Kim Saiki defeated Laura Davies, 6 and 4.
Meena Lee defeated Hee-Won Han, 19 holes.
Wendy Doolan defeated Rosie Jones, 2 and 1.
Pat Hurst defeated Jimin Kang, 2 up.
Gloria Park defeated Janice Moodie, 2 and 1.
Nicole Perrot defeated Jill McGill, 5 and 3.
Laurie Rinker defeated Lorena Ochoa, 2 and 1.
Christina Kim defeated Karen Stupples, 3 and 2.
Wendy Ward defeated Joo Mi Kim, 3 and 1.
Silvia Cavalleri defeated Carin Koch, 20 holes.
Sophie Gustafson defeated Birdie Kim, 1 up.
Shi Hyun Ahn defeated Karine Icher, 2 and 1.
Juli Inkster defeated Sung Ah Yim, 3 and 1.
Ai Miyazato defeated Laura Diaz, 2 and 1.

(Each losing player received $5,000.)

## SECOND ROUND

Sorenstam defeated Barrett, 21 holes.
Hetherington defeated Mi Hyun Kim, 5 and 4.
Kung defeated Lindley, 19 holes.
Eathorne defeated Delasin, 2 up.
Webb defeated Creamer, 2 and 1.
Jang defeated *Moromizato, 1 up.
Baena defeated Grace Park, 19 holes.
Rosales defeated Daniel, 5 and 3.
Neumann defeated Kerr, 4 and 3.
Lee defeated Saiki, 4 and 2.
Hurst defeated Doolan, 1 up.
Perrot defeated Gloria Park, 4 and 3.
Christina Kim defeated Rinker, 5 and 3.
Ward defeated Cavalleri, 2 and 1.
Gustafson defeated Ahn, 19 holes.
Miyazato defeated Inkster, 1 up.

(Each losing player received $10,322.)

## THIRD ROUND

Sorenstam defeated Hetherington, 2 and 1.
Kung defeated Eathorne, 4 and 3.
Webb defeated Jang, 4 and 2.
Baena defeated Rosales, 20 holes.
Lee defeated Neumann, 3 and 2.
Hurst defeated Perrot, 22 holes.
Ward defeated Christina Kim, 1 up.
Gustafson defeated Miyazato, 1 up.

(Each losing player received $25,000.)

## QUARTER-FINALS

Kung defeated Sorenstam, 1 up.
Baena defeated Webb, 2 and 1.
Lee defeated Hurst, 1 up.
Ward defeated Gustafson, 2 and 1.

(Each losing player received $50,000.)

## SEMI-FINALS

Baena defeated Kung, 2 up.
Lee defeated Ward, 1 up.

### PLAYOFF FOR THIRD-FOURTH PLACE

Ward defeated Kung, 2 and 1.

(Ward earned $200,000; Kung earned $150,000.)

### FINAL

Baena defeated Lee, 1 up.

(Baena earned $500,000; Lee earned $300,000.)

# Jamie Farr Owens Corning Classic

*Highland Meadows Golf Club,* Sylvania, Ohio
Par 34-37–71; 6,408 yards

July 7-10
purse, $1,200,000

| | SCORES | | | | TOTAL | MONEY |
|---|---|---|---|---|---|---|
| Heather Bowie | 72 | 66 | 69 | 67 | 274 | $180,000 |
| Gloria Park | 67 | 70 | 71 | 66 | 274 | 109,852 |

(Bowie defeated Park on third playoff hole.)

| | | | | | | |
|---|---|---|---|---|---|---|
| Sung Ah Yim | 69 | 70 | 68 | 68 | 275 | 70,669 |
| Hee-Won Han | 69 | 67 | 66 | 73 | 275 | 70,669 |
| Paula Creamer | 72 | 68 | 72 | 64 | 276 | 45,108 |
| Jeong Jang | 68 | 69 | 67 | 72 | 276 | 45,108 |
| Pat Hurst | 71 | 70 | 67 | 69 | 277 | 30,172 |
| Leta Lindley | 69 | 69 | 68 | 71 | 277 | 30,172 |
| Meg Mallon | 68 | 69 | 68 | 72 | 277 | 30,172 |
| Marilyn Lovander | 69 | 68 | 68 | 73 | 278 | 24,358 |
| Candie Kung | 72 | 68 | 70 | 69 | 279 | 22,554 |
| Rachel Hetherington | 73 | 69 | 69 | 69 | 280 | 17,682 |
| Young Jo | 72 | 70 | 69 | 69 | 280 | 17,682 |
| Michele Redman | 71 | 69 | 71 | 69 | 280 | 17,682 |
| Marisa Baena | 69 | 72 | 69 | 70 | 280 | 17,682 |
| Mi Hyun Kim | 72 | 68 | 69 | 71 | 280 | 17,682 |
| Carri Wood | 69 | 71 | 69 | 71 | 280 | 17,682 |
| Beth Daniel | 70 | 65 | 73 | 72 | 280 | 17,682 |
| Angela Stanford | 67 | 77 | 67 | 70 | 281 | 13,593 |
| Natalie Gulbis | 71 | 72 | 67 | 71 | 281 | 13,593 |
| Laura Diaz | 72 | 70 | 68 | 71 | 281 | 13,593 |
| Young Kim | 68 | 72 | 70 | 71 | 281 | 13,593 |
| Joo Mi Kim | 73 | 70 | 71 | 68 | 282 | 11,499 |
| Suzann Pettersen | 72 | 72 | 68 | 70 | 282 | 11,499 |
| *Morgan Pressel | 70 | 73 | 69 | 70 | 282 | |
| Candy Hannemann | 69 | 73 | 70 | 70 | 282 | 11,499 |
| Janell Howland | 75 | 68 | 67 | 72 | 282 | 11,499 |
| Karen Weiss | 70 | 70 | 70 | 72 | 282 | 11,499 |
| Johanna Head | 69 | 73 | 72 | 69 | 283 | 9,090 |
| Young-A Yang | 70 | 69 | 74 | 70 | 283 | 9,090 |
| Emilee Klein | 71 | 72 | 69 | 71 | 283 | 9,090 |
| Sherri Turner | 73 | 70 | 68 | 72 | 283 | 9,090 |
| Soo-Yun Kang | 71 | 71 | 68 | 73 | 283 | 9,090 |
| Beth Bader | 70 | 70 | 68 | 75 | 283 | 9,090 |
| Birdie Kim | 65 | 71 | 71 | 76 | 283 | 9,090 |

# BMO Financial Group Canadian Women's Open

*Glen Arbour Golf Course*, Halifax, Nova Scotia, Canada
Par 36-36–72; 6,285 yards

July 14-17
purse, $1,300,000

| | SCORES | | | | TOTAL | MONEY |
|---|---|---|---|---|---|---|
| Meena Lee | 73 | 68 | 69 | 69 | 279 | $195,000 |
| Katherine Hull | 72 | 70 | 69 | 69 | 280 | 120,196 |
| Leta Lindley | 71 | 71 | 71 | 68 | 281 | 69,646 |
| Il Mi Chung | 69 | 68 | 72 | 72 | 281 | 69,646 |
| Angela Stanford | 69 | 69 | 70 | 73 | 281 | 69,646 |
| Brittany Lang | 69 | 73 | 72 | 68 | 282 | 35,865 |
| Johanna Head | 69 | 71 | 74 | 68 | 282 | 35,865 |
| Dorothy Delasin | 71 | 69 | 69 | 73 | 282 | 35,865 |
| Janice Moodie | 66 | 69 | 72 | 75 | 282 | 35,865 |
| Emily Bastel | 67 | 74 | 70 | 72 | 283 | 26,652 |
| Michelle Estill | 72 | 73 | 71 | 68 | 284 | 21,729 |
| Diana D'Alessio | 70 | 74 | 71 | 69 | 284 | 21,729 |
| Beth Bader | 70 | 72 | 72 | 70 | 284 | 21,729 |
| Nancy Scranton | 72 | 68 | 74 | 70 | 284 | 21,729 |
| Christina Kim | 70 | 69 | 73 | 72 | 284 | 21,729 |
| Meg Mallon | 70 | 72 | 74 | 69 | 285 | 16,452 |
| Emilee Klein | 72 | 73 | 70 | 70 | 285 | 16,452 |
| Patricia Baxter-Johnson | 72 | 72 | 71 | 70 | 285 | 16,452 |
| Lindsey Wright | 75 | 69 | 70 | 71 | 285 | 16,452 |
| Young-A Yang | 70 | 68 | 76 | 71 | 285 | 16,452 |
| Kris Tschetter | 72 | 71 | 74 | 69 | 286 | 14,609 |
| Danielle Ammaccapane | 73 | 74 | 71 | 69 | 287 | 13,556 |
| Young Jo | 72 | 73 | 71 | 71 | 287 | 13,556 |
| Brittany Lincicome | 71 | 74 | 70 | 72 | 287 | 13,556 |
| Mikaela Parmlid | 72 | 69 | 76 | 71 | 288 | 12,339 |
| Tina Fischer | 72 | 71 | 73 | 72 | 288 | 12,339 |
| Lorie Kane | 74 | 72 | 74 | 69 | 289 | 10,974 |
| Dawn Coe-Jones | 73 | 70 | 76 | 70 | 289 | 10,974 |
| Yu Ping Lin | 73 | 72 | 72 | 72 | 289 | 10,974 |
| Jamie Hullett | 73 | 72 | 70 | 74 | 289 | 10,974 |

# Evian Masters
See Ladies European Tour section.

# Weetabix Women's British Open
See Ladies European Tour section.

# Safeway Classic

*Columbia Edgewater Country Club*, Portland, Oregon
Par 36-36–72; 6,327 yards

August 19-21
purse, $1,400,000

| | SCORES | | | TOTAL | MONEY |
|---|---|---|---|---|---|
| Soo-Yun Kang | 64 | 68 | 69 | 201 | $210,000 |
| Jeong Jang | 67 | 68 | 70 | 205 | 127,855 |
| Gloria Park | 67 | 68 | 71 | 206 | 92,750 |
| Joo Mi Kim | 69 | 68 | 71 | 208 | 71,750 |
| Beth Daniel | 68 | 71 | 70 | 209 | 52,500 |

| | SCORES | | | TOTAL | MONEY |
|---|---|---|---|---|---|
| Sung Ah Yim | 64 | 73 | 72 | 209 | 52,500 |
| Pat Hurst | 67 | 72 | 71 | 210 | 35,117 |
| Amy Hung | 67 | 71 | 72 | 210 | 35,117 |
| Rosie Jones | 65 | 73 | 72 | 210 | 35,117 |
| Sherri Steinhauer | 72 | 70 | 69 | 211 | 22,663 |
| Jill McGill | 70 | 71 | 70 | 211 | 22,663 |
| Heather Daly-Donofrio | 70 | 70 | 71 | 211 | 22,663 |
| Johanna Head | 69 | 70 | 72 | 211 | 22,663 |
| Jean Bartholomew | 69 | 69 | 73 | 211 | 22,663 |
| Natalie Gulbis | 67 | 71 | 73 | 211 | 22,663 |
| Aree Song | 66 | 70 | 75 | 211 | 22,663 |
| Hee-Won Han | 65 | 71 | 75 | 211 | 22,663 |
| Grace Park | 73 | 72 | 67 | 212 | 15,843 |
| Kris Tschetter | 71 | 74 | 67 | 212 | 15,843 |
| Heather Bowie | 69 | 72 | 71 | 212 | 15,843 |
| Christina Kim | 70 | 70 | 72 | 212 | 15,843 |
| Sherri Turner | 70 | 68 | 74 | 212 | 15,843 |
| Karrie Webb | 70 | 67 | 75 | 212 | 15,843 |
| Kim Saiki | 73 | 70 | 70 | 213 | 13,125 |
| Michele Redman | 70 | 72 | 71 | 213 | 13,125 |
| Lorie Kane | 70 | 70 | 73 | 213 | 13,125 |
| Wendy Doolan | 66 | 72 | 75 | 213 | 13,125 |
| Becky Iverson | 71 | 72 | 71 | 214 | 11,004 |
| Sophie Gustafson | 73 | 69 | 72 | 214 | 11,004 |
| Allison Hanna | 71 | 71 | 72 | 214 | 11,004 |
| Candie Kung | 70 | 72 | 72 | 214 | 11,004 |
| Marcy Hart | 70 | 70 | 74 | 214 | 11,004 |

# Wendy's Championship for Children

*Tartan Fields Golf Club*, Dublin, Ohio
Par 36-36–72; 6,515 yards

August 25-28
purse, $1,100,000

| | SCORES | | | | TOTAL | MONEY |
|---|---|---|---|---|---|---|
| Cristie Kerr | 68 | 67 | 66 | 69 | 270 | $165,000 |
| Annika Sorenstam | 69 | 67 | 69 | 66 | 271 | 87,742 |
| Paula Creamer | 68 | 66 | 66 | 71 | 271 | 87,742 |
| Jeong Jang | 68 | 67 | 70 | 67 | 272 | 51,507 |
| Pat Hurst | 67 | 68 | 67 | 70 | 272 | 51,507 |
| Karrie Webb | 67 | 66 | 70 | 70 | 273 | 34,524 |
| Soo-Yun Kang | 66 | 66 | 69 | 72 | 273 | 34,524 |
| Michele Redman | 67 | 67 | 68 | 72 | 274 | 27,563 |
| Young Kim | 70 | 67 | 72 | 66 | 275 | 20,519 |
| Catriona Matthew | 66 | 66 | 77 | 66 | 275 | 20,519 |
| Rachel Hetherington | 67 | 69 | 71 | 68 | 275 | 20,519 |
| Nadina Taylor | 67 | 69 | 71 | 68 | 275 | 20,519 |
| Emily Bastel | 69 | 67 | 70 | 69 | 275 | 20,519 |
| Lorena Ochoa | 72 | 64 | 67 | 72 | 275 | 20,519 |
| Marisa Baena | 66 | 71 | 72 | 67 | 276 | 14,589 |
| Michelle Estill | 76 | 65 | 67 | 68 | 276 | 14,589 |
| Kim Saiki | 71 | 68 | 68 | 69 | 276 | 14,589 |
| Maria Hjorth | 70 | 68 | 67 | 71 | 276 | 14,589 |
| Amy Hung | 68 | 67 | 68 | 73 | 276 | 14,589 |
| Meg Mallon | 71 | 70 | 70 | 66 | 277 | 11,916 |
| Christina Kim | 71 | 69 | 71 | 66 | 277 | 11,916 |
| Candie Kung | 72 | 68 | 70 | 67 | 277 | 11,916 |
| Karen Stupples | 71 | 67 | 70 | 69 | 277 | 11,916 |

| | SCORES | | | | TOTAL | MONEY |
|---|---|---|---|---|---|---|
| Wendy Ward | 69 | 67 | 69 | 72 | 277 | 11,916 |
| Heather Daly-Donofrio | 66 | 74 | 72 | 66 | 278 | 9,856 |
| Kate Golden | 71 | 70 | 68 | 69 | 278 | 9,856 |
| Stacy Prammanasudh | 71 | 66 | 71 | 70 | 278 | 9,856 |
| *Morgan Pressel | 70 | 67 | 71 | 70 | 278 | |
| Helen Alfredsson | 67 | 72 | 67 | 72 | 278 | 9,856 |
| Sophie Gustafson | 69 | 71 | 64 | 74 | 278 | 9,856 |

## State Farm Classic

*Rail Golf Course*, Springfield, Illinois
Par 36-36–72; 6,649 yards

September 1-4
purse, $1,300,000

| | SCORES | | | | TOTAL | MONEY |
|---|---|---|---|---|---|---|
| Pat Hurst | 67 | 69 | 65 | 70 | 271 | $195,000 |
| Cristie Kerr | 68 | 70 | 67 | 69 | 274 | 117,373 |
| Natalie Gulbis | 66 | 71 | 70 | 68 | 275 | 75,507 |
| Heather Bowie | 65 | 71 | 71 | 68 | 275 | 75,507 |
| *Morgan Pressel | 72 | 70 | 68 | 66 | 276 | |
| Maria Hjorth | 69 | 67 | 71 | 69 | 276 | 53,015 |
| Hee-Won Han | 68 | 69 | 70 | 70 | 277 | 39,843 |
| Catriona Matthew | 69 | 69 | 67 | 72 | 277 | 39,843 |
| Sung Ah Yim | 71 | 70 | 69 | 68 | 278 | 25,683 |
| Karine Icher | 71 | 70 | 69 | 68 | 278 | 25,683 |
| Moira Dunn | 71 | 69 | 70 | 68 | 278 | 25,683 |
| Audra Burks | 71 | 68 | 71 | 68 | 278 | 25,683 |
| Aree Song | 69 | 73 | 66 | 70 | 278 | 25,683 |
| Kim Williams | 70 | 68 | 66 | 74 | 278 | 25,683 |
| Juli Inkster | 71 | 71 | 69 | 68 | 279 | 17,736 |
| Emily Bastel | 71 | 70 | 69 | 69 | 279 | 17,736 |
| Mi Hyun Kim | 70 | 70 | 69 | 70 | 279 | 17,736 |
| Dorothy Delasin | 71 | 67 | 71 | 70 | 279 | 17,736 |
| Diana D'Alessio | 70 | 72 | 66 | 71 | 279 | 17,736 |
| Suzann Pettersen | 76 | 67 | 69 | 68 | 280 | 14,266 |
| Mardi Lunn | 71 | 71 | 69 | 69 | 280 | 14,266 |
| Mikaela Parmlid | 71 | 70 | 70 | 69 | 280 | 14,266 |
| Michelle Ellis | 73 | 69 | 68 | 70 | 280 | 14,266 |
| Joanne Mills | 70 | 71 | 69 | 70 | 280 | 14,266 |
| Laura Diaz | 73 | 69 | 73 | 66 | 281 | 10,178 |
| Karen Weiss | 71 | 70 | 72 | 68 | 281 | 10,178 |
| A.J. Eathorne | 73 | 70 | 69 | 69 | 281 | 10,178 |
| Joo Mi Kim | 72 | 70 | 70 | 69 | 281 | 10,178 |
| Jill McGill | 71 | 71 | 70 | 69 | 281 | 10,178 |
| Shi Hyun Ahn | 72 | 66 | 73 | 70 | 281 | 10,178 |
| Sherri Turner | 66 | 69 | 76 | 70 | 281 | 10,178 |
| Christina Kim | 72 | 71 | 67 | 71 | 281 | 10,178 |
| Rachel Hetherington | 67 | 73 | 70 | 71 | 281 | 10,178 |
| Ashli Bunch | 72 | 66 | 72 | 71 | 281 | 10,178 |
| Gloria Park | 70 | 70 | 69 | 72 | 281 | 10,178 |
| Tina Barrett | 66 | 69 | 74 | 72 | 281 | 10,178 |
| Heather Daly-Donofrio | 71 | 67 | 70 | 73 | 281 | 10,178 |

# Solheim Cup

*Crooked Stick Golf Club,* Carmel, Indiana                    September 9-11
Par 36-36–72; 6,553 yards

## FIRST DAY
### Foursomes

Beth Daniel and Paula Creamer (USA) halved with Carin Koch and Catriona Matthew.
Laura Davies and Maria Hjorth (Europe) defeated Cristie Kerr and Natalie Gulbis,
2 and 1.
Christina Kim and Pat Hurst (USA) halved with Sophie Gustafson and Trish Johnson.
Annika Sorenstam and Suzann Pettersen (Europe) defeated Michele Redman and Laura
Diaz, 1 up.

**TOTAL: United States 1, Europe 3**

### Fourballs

Rosie Jones and Meg Mallon (USA) defeated Maria Hjorth and Iben Tinning, 3 and 2.
Cristie Kerr and Natalie Gulbis (USA) defeated Sophie Gustafson and Karen Stupples,
2 and 1.
Annika Sorenstam and Catriona Matthew (Europe) defeated Pat Hurst and Wendy
Ward, 2 and 1.
Laura Davies and Suzann Pettersen (Europe) defeated Paula Creamer and Juli Inkster,
4 and 3.

**TOTAL: United States 3, Europe 5**

## SECOND DAY
### Foursomes

Kim and Gulbis (USA) defeated Gwladys Nocera and Ludivine Kreutz, 4 and 2.
Creamer and Inkster (USA) defeated Davies and Hjorth, 3 and 2.
Gustafson and Koch (Europe) defeated Diaz and Ward, 5 and 3.
Redman and Hurst (USA) defeated Sorenstam and Matthew, 2 up.

**TOTAL: United States 6, Europe 6**

### Fourballs

Daniel and Inkster (USA) halved with Tinning and Johnson.
Jones and Mallon (USA) halved with Gustafson and Pettersen.
Kerr and Creamer (USA) defeated Koch and Matthew, 1 up.
Davies and Sorenstam (Europe) defeated Hurst and Kim, 4 and 2.

**TOTAL: United States 8, Europe 8**

## THIRD DAY
### Singles

Inkster (USA) defeated Gustafson, 2 and 1.
Creamer (USA) defeated Davies, 7 and 5.
Hurst (USA) defeated Johnson, 2 and 1.
Diaz (USA) defeated Tinning, 6 and 5.
Kim (USA) defeated Kreutz, 5 and 4.
Sorenstam (Europe) defeated Daniel, 4 and 3.
Gulbis (USA) defeated Hjorth, 2 and 1.
Matthew (Europe) defeated Ward, 3 and 2.
Koch (Europe) defeated Redman, 2 and 1.
Nocera (Europe) defeated Kerr, 2 and 1.

Mallon (USA) defeated Stupples, 3 and 1.
Jones (USA) halved with Pettersen.

**TOTAL: United States 15½, Europe 12½**

# John Q. Hammons Hotel Classic

*Cedar Ridge Country Club*, Tulsa, Oklahoma
Par 36-35–71; 6,571 yards

September 16-18
purse, $1,000,000

| | SCORES | | | TOTAL | MONEY |
|---|---|---|---|---|---|
| Annika Sorenstam | 68 | 67 | 73 | 208 | $150,000 |
| Paula Creamer | 69 | 71 | 69 | 209 | 90,899 |
| Diana D'Alessio | 68 | 74 | 69 | 211 | 58,476 |
| Maria Hjorth | 64 | 72 | 75 | 211 | 58,476 |
| Karine Icher | 67 | 70 | 75 | 212 | 41,058 |
| Miriam Nagl | 74 | 71 | 68 | 213 | 27,124 |
| Jeong Jang | 70 | 72 | 71 | 213 | 27,124 |
| Suzann Pettersen | 73 | 68 | 72 | 213 | 27,124 |
| Leta Lindley | 70 | 70 | 73 | 213 | 27,124 |
| Michele Redman | 72 | 71 | 71 | 214 | 18,746 |
| Mi Hyun Kim | 69 | 74 | 71 | 214 | 18,746 |
| Shi Hyun Ahn | 71 | 71 | 72 | 214 | 18,746 |
| Carin Koch | 74 | 73 | 68 | 215 | 14,532 |
| Moira Dunn | 73 | 71 | 71 | 215 | 14,532 |
| Michelle Estill | 74 | 69 | 72 | 215 | 14,532 |
| Rachel Hetherington | 68 | 73 | 74 | 215 | 14,532 |
| Michelle Ellis | 67 | 69 | 79 | 215 | 14,532 |
| Stephanie Louden | 72 | 73 | 71 | 216 | 11,877 |
| Catriona Matthew | 73 | 71 | 72 | 216 | 11,877 |
| Meena Lee | 73 | 70 | 73 | 216 | 11,877 |
| Aree Song | 75 | 73 | 69 | 217 | 10,262 |
| Silvia Cavalleri | 75 | 72 | 70 | 217 | 10,262 |
| Karen Stupples | 72 | 72 | 73 | 217 | 10,262 |
| Stacy Prammanasudh | 74 | 68 | 75 | 217 | 10,262 |
| Sherri Steinhauer | 71 | 70 | 76 | 217 | 10,262 |
| Young Jo | 79 | 69 | 70 | 218 | 8,311 |
| Nadina Taylor | 75 | 73 | 70 | 218 | 8,311 |
| Jennifer Rosales | 73 | 75 | 70 | 218 | 8,311 |
| Becky Iverson | 76 | 70 | 72 | 218 | 8,311 |
| Jackie Gallagher-Smith | 73 | 73 | 72 | 218 | 8,311 |
| Nicole Jeray | 71 | 71 | 76 | 218 | 8,311 |

# Office Depot Championship

*Trump National Golf Club*, Los Angeles, California
Par 37-34–71; 6,017 yards

September 30-October 2
purse, $1,300,000

| | SCORES | | | TOTAL | MONEY |
|---|---|---|---|---|---|
| Hee-Won Han | 65 | 68 | 68 | 201 | $195,000 |
| Soo-Yun Kang | 71 | 66 | 66 | 203 | 117,899 |
| Catriona Matthew | 69 | 68 | 68 | 205 | 85,527 |
| Natalie Gulbis | 66 | 69 | 71 | 206 | 59,708 |
| Karine Icher | 65 | 68 | 73 | 206 | 59,708 |
| Katherine Hull | 68 | 70 | 69 | 207 | 40,021 |
| Jeong Jang | 67 | 66 | 74 | 207 | 40,021 |

| | SCORES | | | TOTAL | MONEY |
|---|---|---|---|---|---|
| Marisa Baena | 68 | 69 | 71 | 208 | 31,952 |
| Kim Saiki | 69 | 71 | 69 | 209 | 25,416 |
| Annika Sorenstam | 69 | 70 | 70 | 209 | 25,416 |
| Young Jo | 71 | 67 | 71 | 209 | 25,416 |
| Mi Hyun Kim | 67 | 69 | 73 | 209 | 25,416 |
| Shi Hyun Ahn | 71 | 68 | 71 | 210 | 19,365 |
| Rosie Jones | 68 | 70 | 72 | 210 | 19,365 |
| Beth Daniel | 69 | 68 | 73 | 210 | 19,365 |
| Michele Redman | 68 | 68 | 74 | 210 | 19,365 |
| Moira Dunn | 71 | 71 | 69 | 211 | 15,191 |
| Il Mi Chung | 70 | 72 | 69 | 211 | 15,191 |
| Nadina Taylor | 69 | 73 | 69 | 211 | 15,191 |
| Liselotte Neumann | 72 | 66 | 73 | 211 | 15,191 |
| Jamie Hullett | 68 | 69 | 74 | 211 | 15,191 |
| Nicole Perrot | 65 | 72 | 74 | 211 | 15,191 |
| A.J. Eathorne | 69 | 76 | 67 | 212 | 12,114 |
| Aree Song | 71 | 72 | 69 | 212 | 12,114 |
| Meena Lee | 71 | 71 | 70 | 212 | 12,114 |
| Stephanie Louden | 69 | 73 | 70 | 212 | 12,114 |
| Eva Dahllof | 68 | 69 | 75 | 212 | 12,114 |
| Wendy Ward | 65 | 72 | 75 | 212 | 12,114 |
| Lorena Ochoa | 68 | 75 | 70 | 213 | 9,369 |
| Michelle Estill | 69 | 72 | 72 | 213 | 9,369 |
| Hana Kim | 71 | 68 | 74 | 213 | 9,369 |
| Juli Inkster | 70 | 68 | 75 | 213 | 9,369 |
| Gloria Park | 66 | 71 | 76 | 213 | 9,369 |
| Tina Barrett | 70 | 66 | 77 | 213 | 9,369 |
| Jennifer Rosales | 66 | 70 | 77 | 213 | 9,369 |

## Longs Drugs Challenge

*The Ridge Golf Club*, Auburn, California
Par 36-35–71; 6,204 yards

October 6-9
purse, $1,000,000

| | SCORES | | | | TOTAL | MONEY |
|---|---|---|---|---|---|---|
| Nicole Perrot | 69 | 66 | 64 | 71 | 270 | $150,000 |
| Hee-Won Han | 73 | 63 | 66 | 69 | 271 | 91,325 |
| Catriona Matthew | 70 | 69 | 67 | 68 | 274 | 58,750 |
| Liselotte Neumann | 68 | 70 | 64 | 72 | 274 | 58,750 |
| Shi Hyun Ahn | 69 | 68 | 71 | 67 | 275 | 37,500 |
| Lindsey Wright | 67 | 68 | 70 | 70 | 275 | 37,500 |
| Karrie Webb | 71 | 67 | 71 | 67 | 276 | 23,875 |
| Heather Bowie | 70 | 69 | 69 | 68 | 276 | 23,875 |
| Young Kim | 67 | 72 | 69 | 68 | 276 | 23,875 |
| Jean Bartholomew | 73 | 64 | 71 | 68 | 276 | 23,875 |
| Natalie Gulbis | 70 | 67 | 76 | 64 | 277 | 16,042 |
| Nadina Taylor | 68 | 72 | 69 | 68 | 277 | 16,042 |
| Helen Alfredsson | 71 | 68 | 70 | 68 | 277 | 16,042 |
| Juli Inkster | 72 | 66 | 67 | 72 | 277 | 16,042 |
| Jennifer Rosales | 71 | 66 | 67 | 73 | 277 | 16,042 |
| Sherri Steinhauer | 70 | 65 | 69 | 73 | 277 | 16,042 |
| Christina Kim | 68 | 68 | 74 | 68 | 278 | 12,700 |
| Dawn Coe-Jones | 67 | 66 | 72 | 73 | 278 | 12,700 |
| Pat Hurst | 68 | 72 | 71 | 68 | 279 | 11,500 |
| Wendy Ward | 69 | 73 | 67 | 70 | 279 | 11,500 |
| Beth Daniel | 66 | 69 | 70 | 74 | 279 | 11,500 |
| Candie Kung | 72 | 69 | 70 | 69 | 280 | 9,930 |

| | SCORES | | | | TOTAL | MONEY |
|---|---|---|---|---|---|---|
| Annika Sorenstam | 68 | 69 | 71 | 72 | 280 | 9,930 |
| Jimin Kang | 72 | 70 | 65 | 73 | 280 | 9,930 |
| Candy Hannemann | 68 | 69 | 70 | 73 | 280 | 9,930 |
| Sherri Turner | 69 | 69 | 66 | 76 | 280 | 9,930 |
| Michelle Ellis | 70 | 71 | 73 | 67 | 281 | 8,180 |
| Joanne Morley | 68 | 67 | 74 | 72 | 281 | 8,180 |
| Lee Ann Walker-Cooper | 71 | 67 | 70 | 73 | 281 | 8,180 |
| Heather Daly-Donofrio | 69 | 66 | 73 | 73 | 281 | 8,180 |
| Marilyn Lovander | 66 | 71 | 69 | 75 | 281 | 8,180 |

## Samsung World Championship

*Bighorn Golf Course, Canyons Course,* Palm Desert, California  October 13-16
Par 36-36–72; 6,634 yards  purse, $850,000

| | SCORES | | | | TOTAL | MONEY |
|---|---|---|---|---|---|---|
| Annika Sorenstam | 64 | 71 | 66 | 69 | 270 | $212,500 |
| Paula Creamer | 66 | 69 | 73 | 70 | 278 | 135,250 |
| Gloria Park | 65 | 72 | 68 | 74 | 279 | 91,000 |
| Natalie Gulbis | 67 | 72 | 71 | 71 | 281 | 43,167 |
| Meena Lee | 69 | 69 | 72 | 71 | 281 | 43,167 |
| Cristie Kerr | 65 | 71 | 71 | 74 | 281 | 43,167 |
| Rosie Jones | 68 | 69 | 72 | 73 | 282 | 24,667 |
| Pat Hurst | 70 | 70 | 68 | 74 | 282 | 24,667 |
| Catriona Matthew | 70 | 66 | 71 | 75 | 282 | 24,667 |
| Wendy Ward | 74 | 74 | 68 | 68 | 284 | 18,250 |
| Candie Kung | 70 | 68 | 72 | 74 | 284 | 18,250 |
| Sophie Gustafson | 70 | 68 | 70 | 76 | 284 | 18,250 |
| Marisa Baena | 68 | 70 | 70 | 76 | 284 | 18,250 |
| Lorena Ochoa | 70 | 76 | 70 | 69 | 285 | 14,500 |
| Jeong Jang | 69 | 68 | 74 | 74 | 285 | 14,500 |
| Grace Park | 67 | 66 | 76 | 76 | 285 | 14,500 |
| Lorie Kane | 66 | 72 | 76 | 72 | 286 | 12,500 |
| Heather Bowie | 72 | 72 | 73 | 70 | 287 | 11,750 |
| Birdie Kim | 72 | 69 | 73 | 73 | 287 | 11,750 |
| Michelle Wie | 70 | 65 | 71 | | DQ | |

## CJ Nine Bridges Classic

*Nine Bridges Golf Club*, Jeju Island, South Korea  October 28-30
Par 36-36–72; 6,274 yards  purse, $1,350,000

| | SCORES | | | TOTAL | MONEY |
|---|---|---|---|---|---|
| Jee Young Lee | 65 | 73 | 73 | 211 | $202,500 |
| Carin Koch | 67 | 76 | 71 | 214 | 108,248 |
| Mi Hyun Kim | 70 | 71 | 73 | 214 | 108,248 |
| Hee Young Park | 69 | 73 | 73 | 215 | 63,544 |
| Jeong Jang | 67 | 74 | 74 | 215 | 63,544 |
| Grace Park | 73 | 73 | 70 | 216 | 42,592 |
| Rachel Hetherington | 71 | 73 | 72 | 216 | 42,592 |
| Janice Moodie | 72 | 76 | 69 | 217 | 32,287 |
| Sophie Gustafson | 70 | 78 | 69 | 217 | 32,287 |
| Beth Bader | 76 | 72 | 70 | 218 | 25,040 |
| Il Mi Chung | 73 | 74 | 71 | 218 | 25,040 |

| | SCORES | | | TOTAL | MONEY |
|---|---|---|---|---|---|
| Shi Hyun Ahn | 73 | 73 | 72 | 218 | 25,040 |
| Hee-Won Han | 75 | 70 | 73 | 218 | 25,040 |
| Annika Sorenstam | 75 | 75 | 70 | 220 | 18,136 |
| Hyun Hee Moon | 71 | 79 | 70 | 220 | 18,136 |
| Na Yeon Choi | 73 | 76 | 71 | 220 | 18,136 |
| Soo-Yun Kang | 81 | 67 | 72 | 220 | 18,136 |
| Aree Song | 71 | 76 | 73 | 220 | 18,136 |
| Sun Hwa Lee | 70 | 77 | 73 | 220 | 18,136 |
| Christina Kim | 74 | 72 | 74 | 220 | 18,136 |
| Heather Bowie | 76 | 74 | 71 | 221 | 14,976 |
| Gloria Park | 73 | 73 | 75 | 221 | 14,976 |
| Jeong Eun Lee | 73 | 74 | 75 | 222 | 13,135 |
| Joo Mi Kim | 72 | 75 | 75 | 222 | 13,135 |
| Kim Saiki | 72 | 74 | 76 | 222 | 13,135 |
| Wendy Doolan | 73 | 72 | 77 | 222 | 13,135 |
| Paula Creamer | 73 | 70 | 79 | 222 | 13,135 |
| So Young Park | 76 | 75 | 73 | 224 | 10,799 |
| Lorie Kane | 74 | 75 | 75 | 224 | 10,799 |
| Silvia Cavalleri | 73 | 75 | 76 | 224 | 10,799 |
| Sherri Steinhauer | 70 | 77 | 77 | 224 | 10,799 |
| Ran Hong | 70 | 77 | 77 | 224 | 10,799 |

## Mizuno Classic

See Japan LPGA Tour section.

## The Mitchell Company Tournament of Champions

*Robert Trent Jones Golf Trail, Magnolia Grove,*
Mobile, Alabama
Par 36-36–72; 6,253 yards

November 10-13
purse, $850,000

| | SCORES | | | | TOTAL | MONEY |
|---|---|---|---|---|---|---|
| Christina Kim | 67 | 67 | 72 | 67 | 273 | $138,000 |
| Rachel Hetherington | 69 | 65 | 72 | 68 | 274 | 85,833 |
| Liselotte Neumann | 66 | 72 | 67 | 71 | 276 | 61,483 |
| Juli Inkster | 67 | 73 | 68 | 69 | 277 | 47,657 |
| Heather Daly-Donofrio | 68 | 70 | 68 | 72 | 278 | 38,307 |
| Sophie Gustafson | 71 | 73 | 69 | 66 | 279 | 30,940 |
| Pat Hurst | 71 | 69 | 73 | 67 | 280 | 24,055 |
| Carin Koch | 72 | 71 | 69 | 68 | 280 | 24,055 |
| Heather Bowie | 71 | 72 | 69 | 69 | 281 | 18,372 |
| Janice Moodie | 70 | 69 | 73 | 69 | 281 | 18,372 |
| Angela Stanford | 72 | 67 | 69 | 72 | 281 | 18,372 |
| Soo-Yun Kang | 71 | 70 | 71 | 70 | 282 | 14,808 |
| Marisa Baena | 71 | 71 | 69 | 71 | 282 | 14,808 |
| Paula Creamer | 70 | 70 | 71 | 71 | 282 | 14,808 |
| Kim Saiki | 72 | 68 | 74 | 69 | 283 | 12,844 |
| Gloria Park | 74 | 70 | 69 | 70 | 283 | 12,844 |
| Lorena Ochoa | 69 | 73 | 73 | 69 | 284 | 11,654 |
| Jeong Jang | 73 | 70 | 68 | 73 | 284 | 11,654 |
| Hee-Won Han | 69 | 69 | 73 | 73 | 284 | 11,654 |
| Mi Hyun Kim | 72 | 72 | 74 | 67 | 285 | 11,008 |
| Birdie Kim | 70 | 73 | 74 | 69 | 286 | 10,611 |
| Karen Stupples | 70 | 80 | 66 | 71 | 287 | 9,529 |
| Sherri Steinhauer | 76 | 72 | 68 | 71 | 287 | 9,529 |

|  | SCORES |  |  |  | TOTAL | MONEY |
|---|---|---|---|---|---|---|
| Rosie Jones | 71 | 73 | 72 | 71 | 287 | 9,529 |
| Meena Lee | 70 | 73 | 72 | 72 | 287 | 9,529 |
| Patricia Meunier-Lebouc | 68 | 73 | 72 | 74 | 287 | 9,529 |
| Catriona Matthew | 70 | 74 | 74 | 70 | 288 | 8,520 |
| Jennifer Rosales | 73 | 69 | 73 | 73 | 288 | 8,520 |
| Beth Daniel | 76 | 68 | 73 | 72 | 289 | 7,988 |
| Nicole Perrot | 71 | 71 | 73 | 74 | 289 | 7,988 |

## ADT Championship

*Trump International Golf Club,* West Palm Beach, Florida          November 17-20
Par 36-36–72; 6,514 yards                                         purse, $1,000,000

|  | SCORES |  |  |  | TOTAL | MONEY |
|---|---|---|---|---|---|---|
| Annika Sorenstam | 69 | 70 | 74 | 69 | 282 | $215,000 |
| Soo-Yun Kang | 69 | 77 | 70 | 68 | 284 | 86,000 |
| Michele Redman | 69 | 73 | 74 | 68 | 284 | 86,000 |
| Liselotte Neumann | 69 | 74 | 71 | 70 | 284 | 86,000 |
| Catriona Matthew | 70 | 75 | 70 | 71 | 286 | 50,000 |
| Lorie Kane | 72 | 74 | 71 | 71 | 288 | 36,333 |
| Paula Creamer | 68 | 75 | 74 | 71 | 288 | 36,333 |
| Hee-Won Han | 67 | 74 | 74 | 73 | 288 | 36,333 |
| Christina Kim | 72 | 74 | 76 | 67 | 289 | 22,750 |
| Natalie Gulbis | 75 | 72 | 72 | 70 | 289 | 22,750 |
| Jeong Jang | 75 | 70 | 74 | 70 | 289 | 22,750 |
| Meena Lee | 72 | 71 | 74 | 72 | 289 | 22,750 |
| Marisa Baena | 74 | 74 | 66 | 76 | 290 | 17,250 |
| Cristie Kerr | 76 | 66 | 76 | 73 | 291 | 16,250 |
| Mi Hyun Kim | 75 | 73 | 76 | 68 | 292 | 14,000 |
| Gloria Park | 73 | 75 | 73 | 71 | 292 | 14,000 |
| Jennifer Rosales | 77 | 71 | 71 | 73 | 292 | 14,000 |
| Heather Bowie | 71 | 74 | 71 | 76 | 292 | 14,000 |
| Sophie Gustafson | 75 | 72 | 73 | 74 | 294 | 11,875 |
| Wendy Ward | 73 | 72 | 73 | 76 | 294 | 11,875 |
| Pat Hurst | 73 | 77 | 71 | 74 | 295 | 11,250 |
| Juli Inkster | 80 | 68 | 77 | 71 | 296 | 10,488 |
| Karrie Webb | 72 | 77 | 74 | 73 | 296 | 10,488 |
| Carin Koch | 73 | 73 | 76 | 74 | 296 | 10,488 |
| Candie Kung | 71 | 73 | 78 | 74 | 296 | 10,488 |
| Lorena Ochoa | 77 | 72 | 75 | 74 | 298 | 9,700 |
| Karine Icher | 74 | 73 | 78 | 74 | 299 | 9,300 |
| Rosie Jones | 74 | 75 | 77 | 74 | 300 | 9,000 |
| Young Kim | 75 | 74 | 77 | 75 | 301 | 8,850 |
| Birdie Kim | 72 | 77 | 77 | 81 | 307 | 8,700 |

# Ladies European Tour

## Samsung Ladies Masters

*Laguna National Golf & Country Club,* Singapore
Par 36-36–72; 6,012 yards

February 3-5
purse, US$200,000

|  | SCORES | | | TOTAL | MONEY |
|---|---|---|---|---|---|
| Bo Bae Song | 65 | 66 | 75 | 206 | €30,000 |
| Charlotta Sorenstam | 72 | 64 | 71 | 207 | 20,300 |
| Laura Davies | 69 | 69 | 70 | 208 | 12,400 |
| Lynnette Brooky | 68 | 70 | 70 | 208 | 12,400 |
| Mi Ye Na | 68 | 69 | 75 | 212 | 8,480 |
| Libby Smith | 70 | 70 | 73 | 213 | 7,000 |
| Kyung Eun Bae | 74 | 69 | 71 | 214 | 5,500 |
| Elisa Serramia | 68 | 72 | 74 | 214 | 5,500 |
| Anne-Marie Knight | 74 | 73 | 68 | 215 | 4,053.33 |
| Eun Hee Ji | 72 | 74 | 69 | 215 | 4,053.33 |
| Jane Leary | 70 | 72 | 73 | 215 | 4,053.33 |
| Eun Jin Kim | 74 | 68 | 74 | 216 | 3,440 |
| Sun Wook Lim | 73 | 73 | 71 | 217 | 2,946.66 |
| Marine Monnet-Melocco | 68 | 77 | 72 | 217 | 2,946.66 |
| Cecilia Ekelundh | 71 | 73 | 73 | 217 | 2,946.66 |
| Asa Gottmo | 71 | 72 | 74 | 217 | 2,946.66 |
| Kirsty Taylor | 73 | 70 | 74 | 217 | 2,946.66 |
| Linda Wessberg | 70 | 70 | 77 | 217 | 2,946.66 |
| Chang Kyung Woo | 71 | 75 | 72 | 218 | 2,490 |
| Bo Mi Suh | 76 | 69 | 73 | 218 | 2,490 |
| Riikka Hakkarainen | 72 | 72 | 74 | 218 | 2,490 |
| Hee Young Park | 72 | 72 | 74 | 218 | 2,490 |
| Soo-Yun Kang | 71 | 72 | 75 | 218 | 2,490 |
| Hey Kyung Son | 69 | 74 | 75 | 218 | 2,490 |
| Lora Fairclough | 71 | 76 | 72 | 219 | 2,160 |
| Minea Blomqvist | 66 | 81 | 72 | 219 | 2,160 |
| Hyun Hee Moon | 75 | 72 | 72 | 219 | 2,160 |
| Ji Won Yoon | 74 | 71 | 74 | 219 | 2,160 |
| Joanne Mills | 70 | 75 | 74 | 219 | 2,160 |
| Rebecca Coakley | 69 | 78 | 73 | 220 | 1,950 |
| Maria Hjorth | 73 | 74 | 73 | 220 | 1,950 |

## Women's World Cup of Golf

See South African Women's Tour section.

## ANZ Ladies Masters

See Australian Women's Tour section.

# Princess Lalla Meriem Cup

*Dar-es-Salam Golf Club, Blue Course,* Rabat, Morocco
Par 36-37–73; 6,780 yards

February 25-27
purse, US$72,000

| | SCORES | | | TOTAL | MONEY |
|---|---|---|---|---|---|
| Ana B. Sanchez | 70 | 75 | 78 | 223 | US$16,500 |
| Rebecca Hudson | 71 | 73 | 79 | 223 | 10,500 |
| (Sanchez defeated Hudson in playoff.) | | | | | |
| Virginie Auffret | 74 | 75 | 78 | 227 | 7,500 |
| Laura Cabanillas Gomez | 71 | 78 | 81 | 230 | 5,250 |
| Monica Cosenza | 75 | 72 | 83 | 230 | 5,250 |
| Jehanne Jail | 78 | 72 | 82 | 232 | 3,000 |
| Peggy Frayss | 74 | 75 | 85 | 234 | 3,000 |
| Tullia Calzavara | 78 | 74 | 83 | 235 | 3,000 |
| Virginie Didelon-Requier | 75 | 80 | 83 | 238 | 3,000 |
| Regine Lautens | 77 | 73 | 88 | 238 | 3,000 |
| Elisabeth Quelhas | 81 | 77 | 82 | 240 | 3,000 |
| Mounya Amalou-Sayeh | 78 | 77 | 85 | 240 | 3,000 |
| Valerie Michaud | 83 | 77 | 82 | 242 | 3,000 |
| Xonia Wunsch | 76 | 81 | 88 | 245 | 3,000 |

# Thailand Ladies Open

*Alpine Golf & Sports Club,* Bangkok, Thailand
Par 36-36–72; 6,062 yards

March 31-April 3
purse, US$330,000

| | SCORES | | | | TOTAL | MONEY |
|---|---|---|---|---|---|---|
| Shani Waugh | 67 | 71 | 71 | 73 | 282 | €37,271.25 |
| Gwladys Nocera | 72 | 70 | 68 | 72 | 282 | 25,220.21 |
| (Waugh defeated Nocera on first playoff hole.) | | | | | | |
| Jeong Eun Lee | 73 | 69 | 71 | 70 | 283 | 13,782.08 |
| Ran Hong | 69 | 72 | 71 | 71 | 283 | 13,782.08 |
| *Shinobu Moromizato | 74 | 68 | 70 | 71 | 283 | |
| Hee Young Park | 70 | 75 | 67 | 71 | 283 | 13,782.08 |
| Asa Gottmo | 71 | 70 | 73 | 70 | 284 | 8,075.44 |
| Virada Nirapathpongporn | 71 | 68 | 73 | 72 | 284 | 8,075.44 |
| Charlotta Sorenstam | 71 | 74 | 70 | 70 | 285 | 5,888.86 |
| *Titiya Plucksataporn | 68 | 74 | 70 | 73 | 285 | |
| Yu Chuan Tai | 68 | 72 | 70 | 75 | 285 | 5,888.86 |
| Tullia Calzavara | 76 | 68 | 68 | 74 | 286 | 4,770.72 |
| Ludivine Kreutz | 70 | 71 | 69 | 76 | 286 | 4,770.72 |
| Karine Icher | 75 | 72 | 72 | 68 | 287 | 3,876.21 |
| Iben Tinning | 72 | 74 | 71 | 70 | 287 | 3,876.21 |
| Hong Mei Yang | 67 | 71 | 77 | 72 | 287 | 3,876.21 |
| Bo Bae Song | 71 | 72 | 72 | 72 | 287 | 3,876.21 |
| Marine Monnet-Melocco | 71 | 72 | 69 | 75 | 287 | 3,876.21 |
| Eun Hee Ji | 76 | 73 | 71 | 68 | 288 | 3,379.26 |
| Janell Howland | 72 | 75 | 72 | 69 | 288 | 3,379.26 |
| Yun Jye Wei | 70 | 70 | 77 | 71 | 288 | 3,379.26 |
| Linda Wessberg | 72 | 72 | 71 | 74 | 289 | 3,205.33 |
| Veronica Zorzi | 72 | 74 | 73 | 71 | 290 | 3,056.24 |
| Na Zhang | 72 | 75 | 71 | 72 | 290 | 3,056.24 |
| Rungthiwa Pangian | 70 | 70 | 73 | 77 | 290 | 3,056.24 |
| Maria Hjorth | 73 | 75 | 71 | 72 | 291 | 2,869.89 |
| Mikaela Parmlid | 77 | 69 | 70 | 75 | 291 | 2,869.89 |

| | SCORES | | | | TOTAL | MONEY |
|---|---|---|---|---|---|---|
| Cecilia Ekelundh | 72 | 73 | 74 | 73 | 292 | 2,683.53 |
| Lynnette Brooky | 71 | 77 | 70 | 74 | 292 | 2,683.53 |
| Sun Wook Lim | 70 | 71 | 71 | 80 | 292 | 2,683.53 |

## Tenerife Ladies Open

*Golf Costa Adeje,* Tenerife, Spain
Par 36-36–72; 6,080 yards

April 7-10
purse, €242,000

| | SCORES | | | | TOTAL | MONEY |
|---|---|---|---|---|---|---|
| Ludivine Kreutz | 69 | 69 | 69 | 70 | 277 | €36,300 |
| Miriam Nagl | 70 | 69 | 71 | 69 | 279 | 24,563 |
| Diana Luna | 73 | 71 | 68 | 69 | 281 | 15,004 |
| Eleanor Pilgrim | 69 | 68 | 73 | 71 | 281 | 15,004 |
| Rikke Rasmussen | 76 | 67 | 70 | 69 | 282 | 10,260.80 |
| Trish Johnson | 71 | 75 | 65 | 72 | 283 | 7,865 |
| Marta Prieto | 70 | 72 | 67 | 74 | 283 | 7,865 |
| Katie Bakken | 66 | 77 | 72 | 69 | 284 | 4,985.20 |
| Sara Beautell | 72 | 71 | 72 | 69 | 284 | 4,985.20 |
| Gwladys Nocera | 71 | 70 | 73 | 70 | 284 | 4,985.20 |
| Martina Eberl | 74 | 67 | 72 | 71 | 284 | 4,985.20 |
| Georgina Simpson | 70 | 69 | 71 | 74 | 284 | 4,985.20 |
| Karine Icher | 74 | 71 | 72 | 68 | 285 | 3,896.20 |
| Asa Gottmo | 75 | 70 | 70 | 71 | 286 | 3,605.80 |
| *Belen Mozo | 74 | 73 | 66 | 73 | 286 | |
| Sophie Giquel | 70 | 72 | 71 | 73 | 286 | 3,605.80 |
| Nienke Nijenhuis | 69 | 72 | 69 | 76 | 286 | 3,605.80 |
| Minea Blomqvist | 72 | 70 | 75 | 70 | 287 | 3,248.85 |
| Laura Cabanillas | 73 | 70 | 73 | 71 | 287 | 3,248.85 |
| Kirsty Taylor | 70 | 72 | 76 | 69 | 287 | 3,248.85 |
| Nora Angehrn | 73 | 71 | 71 | 72 | 287 | 3,248.85 |
| Lynn Kenny | 69 | 75 | 74 | 70 | 288 | 2,795.10 |
| Ana Larraneta | 69 | 74 | 74 | 71 | 288 | 2,795.10 |
| Rebecca Coakley | 70 | 72 | 73 | 73 | 288 | 2,795.10 |
| Becky Brewerton | 73 | 70 | 72 | 73 | 288 | 2,795.10 |
| Ana B. Sanchez | 72 | 72 | 75 | 69 | 288 | 2,795.10 |
| Judith Van Hagen | 73 | 75 | 71 | 69 | 288 | 2,795.10 |
| Sophie Sandolo | 72 | 67 | 74 | 75 | 288 | 2,795.10 |
| Tullia Calzavara | 76 | 69 | 67 | 76 | 288 | 2,795.10 |
| Elin Ohlsson | 73 | 68 | 75 | 73 | 289 | 2,395.80 |
| Sara Jelander | 71 | 71 | 76 | 71 | 289 | 2,395.80 |
| Rebecca Hudson | 68 | 74 | 71 | 76 | 289 | 2,395.80 |

## Open de Espana Feminino

*Panoramica Golf & Country Club,* Castellon, Spain
Par 36-36–72; 6,063 yards

May 12-15
purse, €275,000

| | SCORES | | | | TOTAL | MONEY |
|---|---|---|---|---|---|---|
| Iben Tinning | 70 | 63 | 70 | 70 | 273 | €41,250 |
| Linda Wessberg | 66 | 72 | 70 | 68 | 276 | 27,912.50 |
| Marine Monnet-Melocco | 70 | 66 | 69 | 72 | 277 | 19,250 |
| Lynnette Brooky | 69 | 70 | 72 | 67 | 278 | 13,255 |
| Martina Eberl | 67 | 69 | 70 | 72 | 278 | 13,255 |

| | SCORES | | | | TOTAL | MONEY |
|---|---|---|---|---|---|---|
| Sophie Sandolo | 67 | 68 | 73 | 71 | 279 | 9,625 |
| Rebecca Coakley | 69 | 73 | 69 | 69 | 280 | 6,696.25 |
| Asa Gottmo | 69 | 69 | 72 | 70 | 280 | 6,696.25 |
| Nicole Stillig-Gogele | 67 | 73 | 69 | 71 | 280 | 6,696.25 |
| Fany Schaeffer | 69 | 67 | 67 | 77 | 280 | 6,696.25 |
| Federica Piovano | 67 | 71 | 75 | 68 | 281 | 4,895 |
| Virginie Lagoutte | 73 | 69 | 69 | 70 | 281 | 4,895 |
| Eleanor Pilgrim | 70 | 69 | 77 | 66 | 282 | 4,051.66 |
| Minea Blomqvist | 72 | 71 | 71 | 68 | 282 | 4,051.66 |
| Marta Prieto | 66 | 74 | 71 | 71 | 282 | 4,051.66 |
| *Maria Hernandez | 73 | 68 | 70 | 71 | 282 | |
| Veronica Zorzi | 69 | 67 | 74 | 72 | 282 | 4,051.66 |
| Nina Karlsson | 70 | 71 | 69 | 72 | 282 | 4,051.66 |
| Laura Cabanillas | 71 | 68 | 68 | 75 | 282 | 4,051.66 |
| Gwladys Nocera | 74 | 70 | 72 | 67 | 283 | 3,382.50 |
| Ludivine Kreutz | 73 | 69 | 71 | 70 | 283 | 3,382.50 |
| Tullia Calzavara | 68 | 76 | 69 | 70 | 283 | 3,382.50 |
| Kirsty Taylor | 72 | 67 | 73 | 71 | 283 | 3,382.50 |
| Nienke Nijenhuis | 71 | 69 | 72 | 71 | 283 | 3,382.50 |
| Rebecca Hudson | 70 | 68 | 73 | 72 | 283 | 3,382.50 |
| Stefania Croce | 71 | 68 | 70 | 74 | 283 | 3,382.50 |
| Trish Johnson | 73 | 69 | 73 | 69 | 284 | 2,887.50 |
| Becky Brewerton | 71 | 73 | 71 | 69 | 284 | 2,887.50 |
| Miriam Nagl | 67 | 69 | 78 | 70 | 284 | 2,887.50 |
| Sophie Giquel | 71 | 70 | 73 | 70 | 284 | 2,887.50 |
| Maria Beautell | 68 | 70 | 74 | 72 | 284 | 2,887.50 |
| *Emma Cabrera | 67 | 73 | 72 | 72 | 284 | |

## Siemens Austrian Ladies Open

*Golfclub Fohrenwald-Wiener,* Neustadt, Austria
Par 37-35–72; 6,194 yards

May 26-29
purse, €250,000

| | SCORES | | | | TOTAL | MONEY |
|---|---|---|---|---|---|---|
| Federica Piovano | 70 | 62 | 72 | 68 | 272 | €37,500 |
| Gwladys Nocera | 70 | 65 | 68 | 70 | 273 | 25,375 |
| Laura Davies | 67 | 68 | 71 | 71 | 277 | 15,500 |
| Marta Prieto | 68 | 68 | 70 | 71 | 277 | 15,500 |
| Kris Lindstrom | 70 | 70 | 70 | 68 | 278 | 9,675 |
| Veronica Zorzi | 71 | 67 | 70 | 70 | 278 | 9,675 |
| Sophie Sandolo | 66 | 69 | 71 | 73 | 279 | 7,500 |
| Iben Tinning | 73 | 68 | 72 | 67 | 280 | 5,616.66 |
| Lynnette Brooky | 68 | 71 | 71 | 70 | 280 | 5,616.66 |
| Georgina Simpson | 66 | 73 | 70 | 71 | 280 | 5,616.66 |
| Karen Lunn | 72 | 68 | 75 | 66 | 281 | 4,193.75 |
| Amanda Moltke-Leth | 72 | 68 | 73 | 68 | 281 | 4,193.75 |
| Anja Monke | 73 | 64 | 75 | 69 | 281 | 4,193.75 |
| Laurette Maritz | 72 | 66 | 72 | 71 | 281 | 4,193.75 |
| Jane Leary | 74 | 69 | 73 | 66 | 282 | 3,725 |
| Anne-Marie Knight | 74 | 71 | 72 | 66 | 283 | 3,450 |
| Becky Brewerton | 70 | 71 | 73 | 69 | 283 | 3,450 |
| Nienke Nijenhuis | 71 | 69 | 73 | 70 | 283 | 3,450 |
| Ana Larraneta | 70 | 70 | 72 | 71 | 283 | 3,450 |
| Rebecca Stevenson | 71 | 73 | 74 | 66 | 284 | 3,075 |
| Rebecca Coakley | 73 | 70 | 72 | 69 | 284 | 3,075 |
| Julie Forbes | 73 | 71 | 71 | 69 | 284 | 3,075 |
| Rebecca Hudson | 69 | 72 | 72 | 71 | 284 | 3,075 |

|  | SCORES | | | | TOTAL | MONEY |
|---|---|---|---|---|---|---|
| Marine Monnet-Melocco | 66 | 72 | 72 | 74 | 284 | 3,075 |
| Katie Bakken | 73 | 70 | 72 | 70 | 285 | 2,775 |
| Virginie Lagoutte | 67 | 70 | 74 | 74 | 285 | 2,775 |
| Alison Munt | 68 | 72 | 69 | 76 | 285 | 2,775 |
| Linda Wessberg | 72 | 73 | 75 | 66 | 286 | 2,437.50 |
| Riikka Hakkarainen | 74 | 73 | 72 | 67 | 286 | 2,437.50 |
| Minea Blomqvist | 70 | 72 | 75 | 69 | 286 | 2,437.50 |
| Denise Simon | 69 | 70 | 77 | 70 | 286 | 2,437.50 |
| Sophie Hunter | 74 | 69 | 71 | 72 | 286 | 2,437.50 |
| Virginie Auffret | 70 | 69 | 74 | 73 | 286 | 2,437.50 |

## BMW Ladies Italian Open

*Sheraton Golf Parco de' Medici,* Rome, Italy
Par 35-37–72; 6,145 yards

June 2-5
purse, €300,000

|  | SCORES | | | | TOTAL | MONEY |
|---|---|---|---|---|---|---|
| Iben Tinning | 69 | 70 | 66 | 66 | 271 | €45,000 |
| Veronica Zorzi | 66 | 73 | 67 | 66 | 272 | 30,450 |
| Lynnette Brooky | 64 | 71 | 72 | 66 | 273 | 18,600 |
| Sophie Sandolo | 69 | 69 | 69 | 66 | 273 | 18,600 |
| Ludivine Kreutz | 65 | 72 | 70 | 68 | 275 | 11,610 |
| Asa Gottmo | 72 | 66 | 67 | 70 | 275 | 11,610 |
| Lara Tadiotto | 71 | 68 | 72 | 65 | 276 | 8,250 |
| Marta Prieto | 66 | 74 | 67 | 69 | 276 | 8,250 |
| Karen Margrethe Juul | 70 | 70 | 71 | 67 | 278 | 6,720 |
| Jehanne Jail | 72 | 71 | 71 | 65 | 279 | 5,377.50 |
| Virginie Auffret | 72 | 71 | 70 | 66 | 279 | 5,377.50 |
| Rebecca Coakley | 66 | 72 | 71 | 70 | 279 | 5,377.50 |
| Minea Blomqvist | 69 | 69 | 71 | 70 | 279 | 5,377.50 |
| Alison Munt | 71 | 71 | 68 | 70 | 280 | 4,402.50 |
| Elisa Serramia | 71 | 70 | 68 | 71 | 280 | 4,402.50 |
| Martina Eberl | 69 | 65 | 72 | 74 | 280 | 4,402.50 |
| Ana Larraneta | 71 | 69 | 66 | 74 | 280 | 4,402.50 |
| Linda Wessberg | 73 | 67 | 73 | 68 | 281 | 3,922.50 |
| Cherie Byrnes | 70 | 72 | 70 | 69 | 281 | 3,922.50 |
| Federica Piovano | 73 | 71 | 67 | 70 | 281 | 3,922.50 |
| Cecilia Ekelundh | 67 | 72 | 70 | 72 | 281 | 3,922.50 |
| Denise Simon | 74 | 68 | 72 | 68 | 282 | 3,555 |
| Lora Fairclough | 69 | 73 | 71 | 69 | 282 | 3,555 |
| Anja Monke | 71 | 71 | 70 | 70 | 282 | 3,555 |
| Karen Lunn | 72 | 69 | 70 | 71 | 282 | 3,555 |
| Trish Johnson | 67 | 72 | 72 | 72 | 283 | 3,195 |
| Marine Monnet-Melocco | 68 | 72 | 71 | 72 | 283 | 3,195 |
| Kris Lindstrom | 71 | 68 | 71 | 73 | 283 | 3,195 |
| Marianne Skarpnord | 71 | 68 | 71 | 73 | 283 | 3,195 |
| Miriam Nagl | 73 | 69 | 73 | 69 | 284 | 2,880 |
| Nicole Stillig-Gogele | 66 | 71 | 75 | 72 | 284 | 2,880 |
| Gwladys Nocera | 71 | 67 | 73 | 73 | 284 | 2,880 |

# Vediorbis Arras Open de France Dames

*Le Golf d'Arras,* Anzin St. Aubin, Arras, France
Par 36-36–72; 6,195 yards

June 9-12
purse, €300,000

| | | SCORES | | | TOTAL | MONEY |
|---|---|---|---|---|---|---|
| Veronica Zorzi | 73 | 70 | 65 | 68 | 276 | €45,000 |
| Trish Johnson | 70 | 69 | 69 | 69 | 277 | 30,450 |
| Lynnette Brooky | 71 | 68 | 74 | 67 | 280 | 21,000 |
| Gwladys Nocera | 73 | 67 | 71 | 70 | 281 | 13,140 |
| Ludivine Kreutz | 71 | 69 | 68 | 73 | 281 | 13,140 |
| Judith Van Hagen | 69 | 73 | 66 | 73 | 281 | 13,140 |
| Helena Alterby | 71 | 72 | 68 | 71 | 282 | 9,000 |
| Marine Monnet-Melocco | 73 | 71 | 71 | 68 | 283 | 6,435 |
| Anja Monke | 72 | 67 | 74 | 70 | 283 | 6,435 |
| Cecilia Ekelundh | 71 | 74 | 66 | 72 | 283 | 6,435 |
| Suzanne Dickens | 70 | 70 | 70 | 73 | 283 | 6,435 |
| Julie Forbes | 69 | 74 | 70 | 71 | 284 | 4,995 |
| Sophie Giquel | 73 | 71 | 68 | 72 | 284 | 4,995 |
| Laura Cabanillas | 69 | 75 | 74 | 68 | 286 | 4,275 |
| Iben Tinning | 72 | 72 | 72 | 70 | 286 | 4,275 |
| Sophie Sandolo | 68 | 73 | 72 | 73 | 286 | 4,275 |
| Nicole Stillig-Gogele | 66 | 76 | 71 | 73 | 286 | 4,275 |
| Karen Lunn | 69 | 67 | 74 | 76 | 286 | 4,275 |
| Diana Luna | 72 | 67 | 70 | 77 | 286 | 4,275 |
| Kirsty Taylor | 70 | 72 | 76 | 69 | 287 | 3,735 |
| Linda Wessberg | 71 | 73 | 72 | 71 | 287 | 3,735 |
| Laurette Maritz | 69 | 73 | 71 | 74 | 287 | 3,735 |
| Ana Larraneta | 71 | 72 | 69 | 75 | 287 | 3,735 |
| Rebecca Stevenson | 68 | 72 | 75 | 73 | 288 | 3,420 |
| Carina Vagner | 68 | 74 | 73 | 73 | 288 | 3,420 |
| Lara Tadiotto | 66 | 77 | 72 | 73 | 288 | 3,420 |
| Marina Arruti | 70 | 75 | 73 | 71 | 289 | 3,150 |
| Georgina Simpson | 69 | 74 | 72 | 74 | 289 | 3,150 |
| Ana B. Sanchez | 75 | 71 | 69 | 74 | 289 | 3,150 |
| Eleanor Pilgrim | 69 | 74 | 75 | 72 | 290 | 2,970 |

# Algarve Ladies Open of Portugal

*Gramacho Pestana Golf Resort,* Carvoeiro, Algarve, Portugal
Par 36-36–72; 5,918 yards

June 24-26
purse, €300,000

| | | SCORES | | TOTAL | MONEY |
|---|---|---|---|---|---|
| Cecilia Ekelundh | 77 | 66 | 67 | 210 | €45,000 |
| Ludivine Kreutz | 69 | 74 | 70 | 213 | 30,450 |
| Cherie Byrnes | 69 | 72 | 73 | 214 | 18,600 |
| Gwladys Nocera | 67 | 73 | 74 | 214 | 18,600 |
| Tullia Calzavara | 74 | 73 | 68 | 215 | 9,930 |
| Veronica Zorzi | 68 | 76 | 71 | 215 | 9,930 |
| Helena Alterby | 66 | 77 | 72 | 215 | 9,930 |
| Anja Monke | 70 | 71 | 74 | 215 | 9,930 |
| Georgina Simpson | 70 | 73 | 73 | 216 | 6,080 |
| Karen Lunn | 71 | 71 | 74 | 216 | 6,080 |
| Nina Reis | 74 | 66 | 76 | 216 | 6,080 |
| Lora Fairclough | 74 | 75 | 68 | 217 | 4,390 |
| Ursula Wikstrom | 76 | 72 | 69 | 217 | 4,390 |
| Minea Blomqvist | 73 | 74 | 70 | 217 | 4,390 |

| | SCORES | | | TOTAL | MONEY |
|---|---|---|---|---|---|
| Laura Cabanillas | 66 | 80 | 71 | 217 | 4,390 |
| Karin Borjeskog | 69 | 76 | 72 | 217 | 4,390 |
| Sophie Sandolo | 70 | 74 | 73 | 217 | 4,390 |
| Riikka Hakkarainen | 73 | 71 | 73 | 217 | 4,390 |
| Ana Larraneta | 71 | 72 | 74 | 217 | 4,390 |
| Lynn Kenny | 70 | 72 | 75 | 217 | 4,390 |
| Vicky Uwland | 78 | 70 | 70 | 218 | 3,555 |
| Marta Prieto | 76 | 72 | 70 | 218 | 3,555 |
| Julie Forbes | 72 | 74 | 72 | 218 | 3,555 |
| Mikaela Parmlid | 70 | 74 | 74 | 218 | 3,555 |
| Sarah Heath | 72 | 71 | 75 | 218 | 3,555 |
| Marine Monnet-Melocco | 73 | 68 | 77 | 218 | 3,555 |
| Amanda Moltke-Leth | 72 | 77 | 70 | 219 | 3,015 |
| Suzanne Dickens | 74 | 74 | 71 | 219 | 3,015 |
| Carmen Alonso Fuentes | 71 | 76 | 72 | 219 | 3,015 |
| Kris Lindstrom | 71 | 76 | 72 | 219 | 3,015 |
| Sara Beautell | 74 | 71 | 74 | 219 | 3,015 |
| Maria Boden | 75 | 70 | 74 | 219 | 3,015 |

## Ladies English Open

*Chart Hills Golf Club,* Kent, England
Par 36-36–72; 6,158 yards

July 8-10
purse, €165,000

| | SCORES | | | TOTAL | MONEY |
|---|---|---|---|---|---|
| Maria Hjorth | 68 | 69 | 67 | 204 | €24,750 |
| Minea Blomqvist | 67 | 69 | 69 | 205 | 16,747.50 |
| Laura Davies | 67 | 69 | 70 | 206 | 10,230 |
| Becky Brewerton | 68 | 68 | 70 | 206 | 10,230 |
| Karen Stupples | 70 | 71 | 66 | 207 | 6,996 |
| Linda Wessberg | 70 | 70 | 68 | 208 | 5,362.50 |
| Janice Moodie | 69 | 69 | 70 | 208 | 5,362.50 |
| Lynnette Brooky | 70 | 69 | 70 | 209 | 3,910.50 |
| Karen Margrethe Juul | 69 | 68 | 72 | 209 | 3,910.50 |
| Cecilia Ekelundh | 73 | 70 | 67 | 210 | 2,874.30 |
| Patricia Meunier-Lebouc | 74 | 67 | 69 | 210 | 2,874.30 |
| Iben Tinning | 71 | 69 | 70 | 210 | 2,874.30 |
| Trish Johnson | 68 | 71 | 71 | 210 | 2,874.30 |
| Ana Larraneta | 71 | 68 | 71 | 210 | 2,874.30 |
| Diana Luna | 70 | 71 | 70 | 211 | 2,347.12 |
| Lora Fairclough | 74 | 66 | 71 | 211 | 2,347.12 |
| Catriona Matthew | 70 | 69 | 72 | 211 | 2,347.12 |
| Lynn Kenny | 69 | 69 | 73 | 211 | 2,347.12 |
| Sophie Giquel | 71 | 69 | 72 | 212 | 2,128.50 |
| Amanda Moltke-Leth | 68 | 71 | 73 | 212 | 2,128.50 |
| Gwladys Nocera | 70 | 67 | 75 | 212 | 2,128.50 |
| Kirsty Taylor | 73 | 72 | 68 | 213 | 1,930.50 |
| Lara Tadiotto | 74 | 70 | 69 | 213 | 1,930.50 |
| Karen Lunn | 71 | 71 | 71 | 213 | 1,930.50 |
| Denise Simon | 73 | 69 | 71 | 213 | 1,930.50 |
| Stefania Croce | 69 | 69 | 75 | 213 | 1,930.50 |
| Lisa Holm Sorensen | 70 | 75 | 69 | 214 | 1,584 |
| Federica Piovano | 73 | 71 | 70 | 214 | 1,584 |
| Anja Monke | 71 | 72 | 71 | 214 | 1,584 |
| Sophie Sandolo | 70 | 73 | 71 | 214 | 1,584 |
| Carlie Butler | 73 | 69 | 72 | 214 | 1,584 |
| Eleanor Pilgrim | 71 | 68 | 75 | 214 | 1,584 |

|  | SCORES |  |  | TOTAL | MONEY |
|---|---|---|---|---|---|
| Veronica Zorzi | 69 | 70 | 75 | 214 | 1,584 |
| Kirsty Taylor | 69 | 69 | 76 | 214 | 1,584 |
| Rebecca Coakley | 68 | 68 | 78 | 214 | 1,584 |

## OTP Bank Ladies Central European Open

*Old Lake Golf & Country Club*, Tata, Budapest, Hungary
Par 35-36–71; 6,037 yards

July 14-16
purse, €166,000

|  | SCORES |  |  | TOTAL | MONEY |
|---|---|---|---|---|---|
| Ludivine Kreutz | 69 | 64 | 66 | 199 | €24,750 |
| Lora Fairclough | 68 | 68 | 67 | 203 | 12,402.50 |
| Minea Blomqvist | 72 | 64 | 67 | 203 | 12,402.50 |
| Samantha Head | 66 | 65 | 72 | 203 | 12,402.50 |
| Marta Prieto | 69 | 71 | 64 | 204 | 5,907 |
| Becky Brewerton | 70 | 68 | 66 | 204 | 5,907 |
| Nina Reis | 69 | 66 | 69 | 204 | 5,907 |
| Rebecca Hudson | 72 | 72 | 62 | 206 | 3,910.50 |
| Marine Monnet-Melocco | 70 | 67 | 69 | 206 | 3,910.50 |
| Barbara Paruscio | 68 | 68 | 71 | 207 | 3,300 |
| Nina Karlsson | 71 | 73 | 64 | 208 | 2,767.87 |
| Joanne Oliver | 74 | 66 | 68 | 208 | 2,767.87 |
| Karen Lunn | 70 | 69 | 69 | 208 | 2,767.87 |
| Joanne Mills | 72 | 67 | 69 | 208 | 2,767.87 |
| Karen Margrethe Juul | 69 | 74 | 66 | 209 | 2,282.50 |
| Kirsty Taylor | 75 | 66 | 68 | 209 | 2,282.50 |
| Gwladys Nocera | 71 | 68 | 70 | 209 | 2,282.50 |
| Maria Boden | 69 | 68 | 72 | 209 | 2,282.50 |
| Tullia Calzavara | 67 | 68 | 74 | 209 | 2,282.50 |
| Riikka Hakkarainen | 69 | 65 | 75 | 209 | 2,282.50 |
| Carlie Butler | 69 | 73 | 68 | 210 | 2,079 |
| Federica Piovano | 75 | 69 | 67 | 211 | 1,930.50 |
| Marianne Skarpnord | 68 | 74 | 69 | 211 | 1,930.50 |
| Laura Cabanillas | 72 | 69 | 70 | 211 | 1,930.50 |
| Hazel Kavanagh | 71 | 70 | 70 | 211 | 1,930.50 |
| Lotta Wahlin | 69 | 67 | 75 | 211 | 1,930.50 |
| Margherita Rigon | 72 | 71 | 69 | 212 | 1,707.75 |
| Nora Angehrn | 73 | 70 | 69 | 212 | 1,707.75 |
| Natalie Claire Booth | 73 | 69 | 70 | 212 | 1,707.75 |
| *Katharina Werdinig | 69 | 72 | 71 | 212 |  |
| Karin Borjeskog | 71 | 69 | 72 | 212 | 1,707.75 |

## Evian Masters

*Evian Masters Golf Club*, Evians-les-Bains, France
Par 36-36–72; 6,254 yards

July 20-23
purse, US$2,500,000

|  | SCORES |  |  |  | TOTAL | MONEY |
|---|---|---|---|---|---|---|
| Paula Creamer | 68 | 68 | 66 | 71 | 273 | €301,985.21 |
| *Michelle Wie | 75 | 70 | 68 | 68 | 281 |  |
| Lorena Ochoa | 71 | 69 | 72 | 69 | 281 | 183,001.48 |
| Lorie Kane | 71 | 74 | 66 | 71 | 282 | 132,755.15 |
| Helen Alfredsson | 74 | 72 | 72 | 65 | 283 | 67,296.01 |
| Maria Hjorth | 69 | 72 | 74 | 68 | 283 | 67,296.01 |

|  | SCORES | | | TOTAL | MONEY |
|---|---|---|---|---|---|
| Carin Koch | 66 | 73 | 74 | 70 | 283 | 67,296.01 |
| Meena Lee | 71 | 74 | 68 | 70 | 283 | 67,296.01 |
| Christina Kim | 68 | 68 | 75 | 72 | 283 | 67,296.01 |
| Karine Icher | 71 | 70 | 68 | 74 | 283 | 67,296.01 |
| Liselotte Neumann | 74 | 71 | 71 | 68 | 284 | 40,577.97 |
| Annika Sorenstam | 72 | 66 | 72 | 75 | 285 | 37,572.61 |
| Karrie Webb | 70 | 70 | 71 | 75 | 286 | 35,067.34 |
| Candie Kung | 70 | 75 | 74 | 68 | 287 | 30,058 |
| Gloria Park | 72 | 73 | 72 | 70 | 287 | 30,058 |
| Marisa Baena | 66 | 75 | 73 | 73 | 287 | 30,058 |
| Laura Davies | 69 | 70 | 70 | 78 | 287 | 30,058 |
| Iben Tinning | 72 | 72 | 74 | 70 | 288 | 25,448.90 |
| Michele Redman | 72 | 73 | 70 | 73 | 288 | 25,448.90 |
| Sophie Gustafson | 70 | 74 | 76 | 69 | 289 | 22,643.46 |
| Hee-Won Han | 71 | 73 | 72 | 73 | 289 | 22,643.46 |
| Kirsty Taylor | 69 | 75 | 71 | 74 | 289 | 22,643.46 |
| Shani Waugh | 72 | 72 | 70 | 75 | 289 | 22,643.46 |
| Jennifer Rosales | 77 | 70 | 71 | 72 | 290 | 19,871.70 |
| Sherri Steinhauer | 71 | 72 | 74 | 73 | 290 | 19,871.70 |
| Paula Marti | 74 | 69 | 71 | 76 | 290 | 19,871.70 |
| Grace Park | 73 | 75 | 74 | 69 | 291 | 17,052.91 |
| Rosie Jones | 74 | 76 | 70 | 71 | 291 | 17,052.91 |
| Veronica Zorzi | 75 | 70 | 74 | 72 | 291 | 17,052.91 |
| Becky Morgan | 74 | 75 | 68 | 74 | 291 | 17,052.91 |
| Bo Bae Song | 72 | 75 | 69 | 75 | 291 | 17,052.91 |

## Weetabix Women's British Open

*Royal Birkdale Golf Club,* Southport, England
Par 35-37–72; 6,463 yards

July 28-31
purse, £1,050,000

|  | SCORES | | | TOTAL | MONEY |
|---|---|---|---|---|---|
| Jeong Jang | 68 | 66 | 69 | 69 | 272 | €233,440 |
| Sophie Gustafson | 69 | 73 | 67 | 67 | 276 | 145,900 |
| Young Kim | 74 | 68 | 67 | 69 | 278 | 102,130 |
| *Michelle Wie | 75 | 67 | 67 | 69 | 278 | |
| Liselotte Neumann | 71 | 70 | 68 | 70 | 279 | 67,600.33 |
| Cristie Kerr | 73 | 66 | 69 | 71 | 279 | 67,600.33 |
| Annika Sorenstam | 73 | 69 | 66 | 71 | 279 | 67,600.33 |
| Natalie Gulbis | 76 | 70 | 68 | 66 | 280 | 48,876.50 |
| Grace Park | 77 | 68 | 67 | 68 | 280 | 48,876.50 |
| *Louise Stahle | 73 | 65 | 73 | 69 | 280 | |
| Ai Miyazato | 72 | 73 | 69 | 67 | 281 | 36,839.75 |
| Michele Redman | 75 | 71 | 67 | 68 | 281 | 36,839.75 |
| Karrie Webb | 75 | 66 | 69 | 71 | 281 | 36,839.75 |
| Karen Stupples | 74 | 71 | 65 | 71 | 281 | 36,839.75 |
| Yuri Fudo | 75 | 69 | 68 | 70 | 282 | 25,240.70 |
| Becky Morgan | 79 | 66 | 67 | 70 | 282 | 25,240.70 |
| Juli Inkster | 74 | 68 | 68 | 72 | 282 | 25,240.70 |
| Carin Koch | 76 | 68 | 66 | 72 | 282 | 25,240.70 |
| Paula Creamer | 75 | 69 | 65 | 73 | 282 | 25,240.70 |
| Pat Hurst | 75 | 65 | 70 | 73 | 283 | 20,790.75 |
| Catriona Matthew | 73 | 72 | 72 | 67 | 284 | 19,696.50 |
| Brandie Burton | 74 | 75 | 71 | 65 | 285 | 17,167.56 |
| Sophie Sandolo | 71 | 73 | 73 | 68 | 285 | 17,167.56 |
| Cecilia Ekelundh | 77 | 69 | 71 | 68 | 285 | 17,167.56 |
| Linda Wessberg | 72 | 71 | 73 | 69 | 285 | 17,167.56 |

| | SCORES | | | | TOTAL | MONEY |
|---|---|---|---|---|---|---|
| Candie Kung | 76 | 71 | 67 | 71 | 285 | 17,167.56 |
| Nicole Perrot | 70 | 72 | 69 | 74 | 285 | 17,167.56 |
| Christina Kim | 79 | 70 | 71 | 66 | 286 | 13,544.38 |
| Miriam Nagl | 74 | 75 | 69 | 68 | 286 | 13,544.38 |
| Anja Monke | 73 | 73 | 70 | 70 | 286 | 13,544.38 |
| Shi Hyun Ahn | 78 | 68 | 67 | 73 | 286 | 13,544.38 |
| Laura Davies | 76 | 70 | 66 | 74 | 286 | 13,544.38 |
| Becky Brewerton | 75 | 71 | 65 | 75 | 286 | 13,544.38 |

## Scandinavian TPC Hosted by Annika

*Barseback Golf & Country Club*, Malmo, Sweden
Par 36-36–72; 6,518 yards

August 4-7
purse, €500,000

| | SCORES | | | | TOTAL | MONEY |
|---|---|---|---|---|---|---|
| Annika Sorenstam | 70 | 75 | 67 | 72 | 284 | €75,000 |
| Natalie Gulbis | 74 | 72 | 69 | 70 | 285 | 50,750 |
| Carin Koch | 70 | 74 | 73 | 71 | 288 | 27,733.33 |
| Patricia Meunier-Lebouc | 72 | 74 | 71 | 71 | 288 | 27,733.33 |
| Gwladys Nocera | 74 | 69 | 71 | 74 | 288 | 27,733.33 |
| Suzann Pettersen | 72 | 72 | 69 | 76 | 289 | 17,500 |
| Helen Alfredsson | 71 | 74 | 73 | 73 | 291 | 13,750 |
| Maria Hjorth | 72 | 74 | 71 | 74 | 291 | 13,750 |
| Catriona Matthew | 75 | 73 | 73 | 72 | 293 | 10,600 |
| Liselotte Neumann | 68 | 74 | 76 | 75 | 293 | 10,600 |
| Minea Blomqvist | 72 | 72 | 83 | 68 | 295 | 9,200 |
| Ana B. Sanchez | 74 | 72 | 78 | 72 | 296 | 8,600 |
| Trish Johnson | 73 | 74 | 75 | 75 | 297 | 7,875 |
| Karine Icher | 74 | 74 | 72 | 77 | 297 | 7,875 |
| Louise Stahle | 79 | 72 | 74 | 73 | 298 | 7,325 |
| Bo Bae Song | 73 | 73 | 75 | 77 | 298 | 7,325 |
| Riikka Hakkarainen | 77 | 75 | 73 | 74 | 299 | 7,000 |
| Iben Tinning | 75 | 77 | 76 | 72 | 300 | 6,460 |
| Reilley Rankin | 74 | 74 | 78 | 74 | 300 | 6,460 |
| Diana Luna | 75 | 75 | 76 | 74 | 300 | 6,460 |
| Amanda Moltke-Leth | 71 | 77 | 75 | 77 | 300 | 6,460 |
| Joanne Mills | 73 | 75 | 74 | 78 | 300 | 6,460 |
| Rebecca Stevenson | 76 | 74 | 75 | 76 | 301 | 5,925 |
| Karin Sjodin | 79 | 72 | 74 | 76 | 301 | 5,925 |
| Charlotta Sorenstam | 74 | 75 | 77 | 76 | 302 | 5,475 |
| Carmen Alonso Fuentes | 74 | 76 | 76 | 76 | 302 | 5,475 |
| Judith Van Hagen | 76 | 76 | 74 | 76 | 302 | 5,475 |
| Cecilia Ekelundh | 74 | 74 | 75 | 79 | 302 | 5,475 |
| Marta Prieto | 72 | 78 | 77 | 76 | 303 | 4,875 |
| Rebecca Hudson | 79 | 73 | 75 | 76 | 303 | 4,875 |
| Becky Morgan | 72 | 78 | 75 | 78 | 303 | 4,875 |
| Elizabeth McKinnon | 79 | 73 | 71 | 80 | 303 | 4,875 |

# Wales Ladies Championship of Europe

*Machynys Peninsula Golf Club,* Llanelli, Wales
Par 36-36–72; 6,126 yards

August 11-14
purse, £350,000

| | SCORES | | | | TOTAL | MONEY |
|---|---|---|---|---|---|---|
| Kirsty Taylor | 61 | 68 | 70 | 75 | 274 | €76,597.50 |
| Laura Davies | 68 | 67 | 72 | 70 | 277 | 43,788.24 |
| Trish Johnson | 65 | 70 | 68 | 74 | 277 | 43,788.24 |
| Karen Margrethe Juul | 67 | 70 | 71 | 71 | 279 | 27,575.10 |
| Rebecca Coakley | 67 | 68 | 71 | 74 | 280 | 21,651.56 |
| Maria Hjorth | 72 | 68 | 72 | 69 | 281 | 16,596.12 |
| Becky Morgan | 69 | 67 | 73 | 72 | 281 | 16,596.12 |
| Iben Tinning | 68 | 73 | 71 | 70 | 282 | 12,102.40 |
| Lora Fairclough | 69 | 71 | 68 | 74 | 282 | 12,102.40 |
| Nienke Nijenhuis | 71 | 71 | 74 | 67 | 283 | 9,153.40 |
| Liza Walters | 71 | 70 | 74 | 68 | 283 | 9,153.40 |
| Ana Larraneta | 74 | 69 | 67 | 73 | 283 | 9,153.40 |
| Anja Monke | 68 | 68 | 73 | 74 | 283 | 9,153.40 |
| Gwladys Nocera | 68 | 71 | 74 | 71 | 284 | 7,736.35 |
| Johanna Head | 72 | 67 | 72 | 73 | 284 | 7,736.35 |
| Marlene Hedblom | 74 | 68 | 74 | 70 | 286 | 7,149.10 |
| Susan Parry | 66 | 72 | 75 | 73 | 286 | 7,149.10 |
| Riikka Hakkarainen | 72 | 68 | 73 | 73 | 286 | 7,149.10 |
| Marine Monnet-Melocco | 71 | 72 | 72 | 72 | 287 | 6,663.98 |
| Cecilia Ekelundh | 68 | 74 | 71 | 74 | 287 | 6,663.98 |
| Sophie Sandolo | 72 | 73 | 76 | 67 | 288 | 6,357.59 |
| Elisa Serramia | 71 | 74 | 73 | 70 | 288 | 6,357.59 |
| Tullia Calzavara | 72 | 72 | 75 | 70 | 289 | 5,974.60 |
| Pia Koivuranta | 69 | 76 | 73 | 71 | 289 | 5,974.60 |
| Nadina Taylor | 63 | 77 | 74 | 75 | 289 | 5,974.60 |
| Janice Moodie | 72 | 73 | 74 | 71 | 290 | 5,361.82 |
| Carina Vagner | 70 | 74 | 74 | 72 | 290 | 5,361.82 |
| Ludivine Kreutz | 67 | 73 | 77 | 73 | 290 | 5,361.82 |
| Minea Blomqvist | 71 | 71 | 75 | 73 | 290 | 5,361.82 |
| Sophie Giquel | 72 | 68 | 74 | 76 | 290 | 5,361.82 |

# Ladies Finnish Masters

*Helsinki Golf Club*, Helsinki, Finland
Par 34-37–71; 5,916 yards
(Event shortened to 36 holes—rain and wind.)

August 26-28
purse, €200,000

| | SCORES | | TOTAL | MONEY |
|---|---|---|---|---|
| Lisa Holm Sorensen | 70 | 70 | 140 | €30,000 |
| *Caroline Westrup | 70 | 71 | 141 | |
| Suzann Pettersen | 69 | 72 | 141 | 15,033.33 |
| Ursula Wikstrom | 70 | 71 | 141 | 15,033.33 |
| Cecilia Ekelundh | 68 | 73 | 141 | 15,033.33 |
| Becky Brewerton | 68 | 75 | 143 | 7,160 |
| Virginie Lagoutte | 71 | 72 | 143 | 7,160 |
| Natascha Fink | 72 | 71 | 143 | 7,160 |
| Jenni Kuosa | 69 | 75 | 144 | 4,740 |
| Johanna Waldh | 75 | 69 | 144 | 4,740 |
| *Kaisa Ruuttila | 69 | 75 | 144 | |
| Marta Prieto | 72 | 73 | 145 | 3,585 |
| Lora Fairclough | 73 | 72 | 145 | 3,585 |

| | SCORES | | | TOTAL | MONEY |
|---|---|---|---|---|---|
| Pia Koivuranta | 69 | 76 | | 145 | 3,585 |
| Susan Parry | 69 | 76 | | 145 | 3,585 |
| Trish Johnson | 74 | 72 | | 146 | 2,850 |
| Iben Tinning | 74 | 72 | | 146 | 2,850 |
| Gwladys Nocera | 72 | 74 | | 146 | 2,850 |
| Laura Cabanillas | 73 | 73 | | 146 | 2,850 |
| Laurette Maritz | 74 | 72 | | 146 | 2,850 |
| Rebecca Hudson | 71 | 75 | | 146 | 2,850 |
| Lynnette Brooky | 76 | 71 | | 147 | 2,460 |
| Ludivine Kreutz | 77 | 70 | | 147 | 2,460 |
| Federica Piovano | 72 | 75 | | 147 | 2,460 |
| Nina Karlsson | 74 | 73 | | 147 | 2,460 |
| Marina Arruti | 72 | 75 | | 147 | 2,460 |
| Minea Blomqvist | 74 | 74 | | 148 | 2,070 |
| Ana B. Sanchez | 76 | 72 | | 148 | 2,070 |
| Rebecca Coakley | 71 | 77 | | 148 | 2,070 |
| Nina Reis | 75 | 73 | | 148 | 2,070 |
| Asa Gottmo | 76 | 72 | | 148 | 2,070 |
| Emma Zackrisson | 75 | 73 | | 148 | 2,070 |
| Helena Alterby | 71 | 77 | | 148 | 2,070 |
| Virginie Auffret | 79 | 69 | | 148 | 2,070 |

## Nykredit Masters

*Kokkedal Golfklub*, Copenhagen, Denmark
Par 36-36–72; 6,189 yards

September 1-4
purse, €200,000

| | SCORES | | | | TOTAL | MONEY |
|---|---|---|---|---|---|---|
| Iben Tinning | 70 | 68 | 70 | 65 | 273 | €30,000 |
| Lora Fairclough | 65 | 69 | 75 | 66 | 275 | 20,300 |
| Cecilia Ekelundh | 67 | 70 | 69 | 70 | 276 | 14,000 |
| Minea Blomqvist | 70 | 70 | 70 | 67 | 277 | 10,800 |
| Johanna Waldh | 70 | 68 | 71 | 69 | 278 | 8,480 |
| Maria Blomqvist | 71 | 68 | 72 | 68 | 279 | 6,500 |
| Amanda Moltke-Leth | 72 | 66 | 71 | 70 | 279 | 6,500 |
| Sophie Sandolo | 70 | 70 | 73 | 67 | 280 | 5,000 |
| Sophie Giquel | 69 | 77 | 68 | 67 | 281 | 4,053.33 |
| Rebecca Coakley | 73 | 68 | 71 | 69 | 281 | 4,053.33 |
| Marine Monnet-Melocco | 74 | 70 | 68 | 69 | 281 | 4,053.33 |
| Becky Brewerton | 70 | 69 | 75 | 68 | 282 | 3,330 |
| Virginie Auffret | 74 | 69 | 71 | 68 | 282 | 3,330 |
| Asa Gottmo | 71 | 70 | 74 | 68 | 283 | 3,080 |
| Gwladys Nocera | 77 | 70 | 67 | 70 | 284 | 2,980 |
| Vicky Uwland | 74 | 68 | 75 | 68 | 285 | 2,880 |
| Julie Forbes | 74 | 70 | 72 | 70 | 286 | 2,652 |
| Riikka Hakkarainen | 72 | 72 | 72 | 70 | 286 | 2,652 |
| Kirsty Taylor | 70 | 72 | 74 | 70 | 286 | 2,652 |
| Linda Wessberg | 73 | 71 | 69 | 73 | 286 | 2,652 |
| Ana B. Sanchez | 71 | 70 | 75 | 70 | 286 | 2,652 |
| Laurette Maritz | 74 | 70 | 72 | 71 | 287 | 2,370 |
| Tullia Calzavara | 72 | 74 | 73 | 68 | 287 | 2,370 |
| Federica Piovano | 72 | 72 | 69 | 74 | 287 | 2,370 |
| Marta Prieto | 74 | 71 | 68 | 74 | 287 | 2,370 |
| Ursula Wikstrom | 73 | 72 | 71 | 72 | 288 | 2,100 |
| Julie Tvede | 75 | 66 | 73 | 74 | 288 | 2,100 |
| Nicola Moult | 72 | 74 | 73 | 69 | 288 | 2,100 |
| Nienke Nijenhuis | 72 | 70 | 76 | 70 | 288 | 2,100 |
| Anja Monke | 76 | 71 | 70 | 71 | 288 | 2,100 |

## Solheim Cup

See LPGA Tour section.

## KLM Ladies Open

*Kennemer Golf & Country Club*, Zandvoort, Netherlands
Par 36-36–72; 6,007 yards

September 16-18
purse, €165,000

| | SCORES | | | TOTAL | MONEY |
|---|---|---|---|---|---|
| Virginie Lagoutte | 73 | 75 | 67 | 215 | €24,750 |
| Eleanor Pilgrim | 74 | 70 | 71 | 215 | 16,747.50 |
| (Lagoutte defeated Pilgrim on second playoff hole.) | | | | | |
| Sara Jelander | 76 | 75 | 66 | 217 | 8,307.75 |
| Marine Monnet-Melocco | 76 | 73 | 68 | 217 | 8,307.75 |
| Amanda Moltke-Leth | 74 | 74 | 69 | 217 | 8,307.75 |
| Lora Fairclough | 79 | 66 | 72 | 217 | 8,307.75 |
| Sophie Giquel | 77 | 70 | 71 | 218 | 4,950 |
| Tullia Calzavara | 79 | 70 | 70 | 219 | 3,707 |
| Alison Munt | 76 | 73 | 70 | 219 | 3,707 |
| Riikka Hakkarainen | 74 | 74 | 71 | 219 | 3,707 |
| Kirsty Taylor | 75 | 77 | 68 | 220 | 2,843.50 |
| Trish Johnson | 76 | 72 | 72 | 220 | 2,843.50 |
| Elisa Serramia | 78 | 68 | 74 | 220 | 2,843.50 |
| Ursula Wikstrom | 76 | 74 | 71 | 221 | 2,385.90 |
| Ana Larraneta | 75 | 75 | 71 | 221 | 2,385.90 |
| Asa Gottmo | 76 | 73 | 72 | 221 | 2,385.90 |
| Sandra Carlborg | 76 | 72 | 73 | 221 | 2,385.90 |
| Susan Parry | 76 | 69 | 76 | 221 | 2,385.90 |
| Linda Wessberg | 79 | 73 | 70 | 222 | 2,079 |
| Denise Simon | 75 | 75 | 72 | 222 | 2,079 |
| Georgina Simpson | 77 | 73 | 72 | 222 | 2,079 |
| Elizabeth McKinnon | 72 | 76 | 74 | 222 | 2,079 |
| Wendy Dicks | 74 | 72 | 76 | 222 | 2,079 |
| Nienke Nijenhuis | 74 | 72 | 77 | 223 | 1,930.50 |
| Valerie Michaud | 76 | 78 | 70 | 224 | 1,782 |
| Elin Ohlsson | 74 | 76 | 74 | 224 | 1,782 |
| Karen Lunn | 75 | 75 | 74 | 224 | 1,782 |
| Carina Vagner | 75 | 74 | 75 | 224 | 1,782 |
| Kirsty Fisher | 75 | 73 | 76 | 224 | 1,782 |
| Lynn Kenny | 83 | 71 | 71 | 225 | 1,534.50 |
| Cherie Byrnes | 78 | 76 | 71 | 225 | 1,534.50 |
| Julie Forbes | 77 | 74 | 74 | 225 | 1,534.50 |
| Anja Monke | 78 | 73 | 74 | 225 | 1,534.50 |
| Laurette Maritz | 75 | 75 | 75 | 225 | 1,534.50 |

## Catalonia Ladies Masters

*Golf Platja de Pals,* Girona, Costa Brava, Spain
Par 36-37–73; 6,254 yards

September 22-24
purse, €190,000

| | SCORES | | | TOTAL | MONEY |
|---|---|---|---|---|---|
| Karine Icher | 70 | 69 | 68 | 207 | €34,000 |
| Gwladys Nocera | 68 | 71 | 69 | 208 | 10,750 |
| Paula Marti | 68 | 70 | 70 | 208 | 10,750 |

| | SCORES | | | TOTAL | MONEY |
|---|---|---|---|---|---|
| Sophie Sandolo | 69 | 68 | 71 | 208 | 10,750 |
| Lynnette Brooky | 71 | 70 | 68 | 209 | 6,000 |
| Anja Monke | 69 | 72 | 69 | 210 | 4,900 |
| Miriam Nagl | 72 | 68 | 70 | 210 | 4,900 |
| Iben Tinning | 69 | 70 | 71 | 210 | 4,900 |
| Tullia Calzavara | 70 | 73 | 68 | 211 | 4,400 |
| Asa Gottmo | 73 | 70 | 68 | 211 | 4,400 |
| *Carlota Ciganda | 74 | 73 | 65 | 212 | |
| Stephanie Arricau | 71 | 71 | 70 | 212 | 4,225 |
| Trish Johnson | 72 | 69 | 71 | 212 | 4,225 |
| Lora Fairclough | 73 | 69 | 71 | 213 | 4,125 |
| Marine Monnet-Melocco | 69 | 72 | 72 | 213 | 4,125 |
| Georgina Simpson | 72 | 70 | 72 | 214 | 4,025 |
| Amanda Moltke-Leth | 74 | 68 | 72 | 214 | 4,025 |
| Ana B. Sanchez | 76 | 71 | 68 | 215 | 3,925 |
| Karen Margrethe Juul | 72 | 70 | 73 | 215 | 3,925 |
| Riikka Hakkarainen | 73 | 72 | 71 | 216 | 3,825 |
| Sara Jelander | 72 | 71 | 73 | 216 | 3,825 |
| Cecilia Ekelundh | 69 | 75 | 73 | 217 | 3,725 |
| Diana Luna | 70 | 72 | 75 | 217 | 3,725 |
| Elisa Serramia | 69 | 77 | 72 | 218 | 3,625 |
| Johanna Waldh | 73 | 73 | 72 | 218 | 3,625 |
| Nadina Taylor | 76 | 72 | 71 | 219 | 3,525 |
| Marta Prieto | 71 | 72 | 76 | 219 | 3,525 |
| Ana Larraneta | 76 | 72 | 72 | 220 | 3,450 |
| Cherie Byrnes | 75 | 77 | 71 | 223 | 3,350 |
| Kirsty Taylor | 76 | 74 | 73 | 223 | 3,350 |
| Ludivine Kreutz | 77 | 70 | 76 | 223 | 3,350 |

# Japan LPGA Tour

## Daikin Orchid Ladies

*Ryukyu Golf Club,* Okinawa
Par 36-36–72; 6,393 yards

March 4-6
purse, ¥80,000,000

| | SCORES | | | TOTAL | MONEY |
|---|---|---|---|---|---|
| Orie Fujino | 69 | 76 | 72 | 217 | ¥14,400,000 |
| Michiko Hattori | 71 | 73 | 74 | 218 | 7,200,000 |
| Miho Koga | 76 | 73 | 71 | 220 | 5,600,000 |
| Midori Yoneyama | 78 | 72 | 71 | 221 | 4,000,000 |
| Michie Ohba | 75 | 70 | 76 | 221 | 4,000,000 |
| Shin Hyun Ju | 78 | 75 | 68 | 221 | 4,000,000 |
| Masaki Maeda | 72 | 74 | 76 | 222 | 2,065,600 |
| Yuri Fudoh | 72 | 75 | 75 | 222 | 2,065,600 |
| Chieko Amanuma | 74 | 72 | 76 | 222 | 2,065,600 |
| Yun-Jye Wei | 75 | 75 | 72 | 222 | 2,065,600 |
| Mihoko Takahashi | 74 | 75 | 73 | 222 | 2,065,600 |
| Toshimi Kimura | 78 | 75 | 70 | 223 | 1,328,000 |
| Yuka Shiroto | 75 | 77 | 71 | 223 | 1,328,000 |
| Julie Lu | 74 | 74 | 75 | 223 | 1,328,000 |
| Tamie Durdin | 73 | 75 | 75 | 223 | 1,328,000 |
| Ae-Sook Kim | 76 | 75 | 73 | 224 | 1,008,000 |
| Ikuyo Shiotani | 73 | 77 | 74 | 224 | 1,008,000 |
| Kasumi Fujii | 75 | 73 | 76 | 224 | 1,008,000 |
| Junko Omote | 79 | 72 | 73 | 224 | 1,008,000 |
| *Shinobu Miromizato | 72 | 77 | 75 | 224 | |
| *Mika Miyazato | 76 | 74 | 74 | 224 | |
| Fuki Kido | 74 | 75 | 76 | 225 | 776,000 |
| Hsiu-Feng Tseng | 74 | 80 | 71 | 225 | 776,000 |
| Kaori Harada | 79 | 75 | 71 | 225 | 776,000 |
| Yuriko Ohtsuka | 72 | 77 | 76 | 225 | 776,000 |
| Sakura Yokomine | 75 | 77 | 73 | 225 | 776,000 |
| Ai Miyazato | 75 | 75 | 76 | 226 | 704,000 |
| Jeong-Eun Lee | 77 | 73 | 76 | 226 | 704,000 |
| Jeon Mi Jung | 73 | 81 | 72 | 226 | 704,000 |
| Lu Ya Huei | 75 | 75 | 76 | 226 | 704,000 |

## Studio-Alice Women's Open

*Hanayashiki Golf Club, Yokawa Course,* Hyogo
Par 36-36–72; 6,456 yards

April 8-10
purse, ¥50,000,000

| | SCORES | | | TOTAL | MONEY |
|---|---|---|---|---|---|
| Michiko Hattori | 72 | 69 | 74 | 215 | ¥9,000,000 |
| Ai Miyazato | 70 | 73 | 75 | 218 | 4,400,000 |
| Namika Omata | 73 | 73 | 74 | 220 | 2,550,000 |
| Lu Ya Huei | 76 | 76 | 68 | 220 | 2,550,000 |
| Jeong Yun-Joo | 75 | 73 | 72 | 220 | 2,550,000 |
| Nikki Campbell | 73 | 72 | 75 | 220 | 2,550,000 |
| Sakura Yokomine | 69 | 72 | 79 | 220 | 2,550,000 |

|  | SCORES | | | TOTAL | MONEY |
|---|---|---|---|---|---|
| Chiaki Takahashi | 77 | 72 | 72 | 221 | 1,167,500 |
| Midori Yoneyama | 74 | 73 | 74 | 221 | 1,167,500 |
| Shin Hyun Ju | 74 | 73 | 74 | 221 | 1,167,500 |
| Toshimi Kimura | 72 | 71 | 78 | 221 | 1,167,500 |
| Itsumi Okada | 77 | 72 | 73 | 222 | 820,000 |
| Miho Koga | 72 | 75 | 75 | 222 | 820,000 |
| Shiho Ohyama | 75 | 70 | 77 | 222 | 820,000 |
| Akiko Fukushima | 77 | 73 | 73 | 223 | 535,000 |
| Yuka Shiroto | 76 | 75 | 72 | 223 | 535,000 |
| Tamie Durdin | 75 | 76 | 72 | 223 | 535,000 |
| Junko Omote | 80 | 71 | 72 | 223 | 535,000 |
| Naoko Takasaki | 75 | 75 | 73 | 223 | 535,000 |
| Yuri Fudoh | 72 | 78 | 73 | 223 | 535,000 |
| Yuka Irie | 73 | 76 | 74 | 223 | 535,000 |
| Michiko Mitsui | 72 | 76 | 75 | 223 | 535,000 |
| Kuniko Maeda | 73 | 75 | 75 | 223 | 535,000 |
| Aiko Yoshida | 71 | 74 | 78 | 223 | 535,000 |
| Keiko Sasaki | 75 | 73 | 76 | 224 | 405,000 |
| Yuriko Ohtsuka | 78 | 71 | 75 | 224 | 405,000 |
| Ji-Hee Lee | 73 | 76 | 75 | 224 | 405,000 |
| Julie Lu | 72 | 75 | 77 | 224 | 405,000 |
| Chieko Nishida | 78 | 73 | 74 | 224 | 405,000 |
| Hiroko Yamaguchi | 78 | 71 | 76 | 224 | 405,000 |
| Akane Iijima | 76 | 73 | 76 | 224 | 405,000 |

## Life Card Ladies

*Kumamoto Airport Country Club,* Kikuyo, Kumamoto
Par 36-36–72; 6,423 yards

April 15-17
purse, ¥60,000,000

|  | SCORES | | | TOTAL | MONEY |
|---|---|---|---|---|---|
| Sakura Yokomine | 73 | 71 | 71 | 215 | ¥10,800,000 |
| Julie Lu | 75 | 72 | 69 | 216 | 5,280,000 |
| Junko Omote | 72 | 77 | 68 | 217 | 3,600,000 |
| Jeong Yun-Joo | 72 | 74 | 71 | 217 | 3,600,000 |
| Lee Eun Hye | 75 | 71 | 71 | 217 | 3,600,000 |
| Ok-Hee Ku | 72 | 72 | 74 | 218 | 2,250,000 |
| Michiko Hattori | 72 | 73 | 73 | 218 | 2,250,000 |
| Noriko Aso | 74 | 73 | 72 | 219 | 1,410,000 |
| Ai Miyazato | 75 | 71 | 73 | 219 | 1,410,000 |
| Fuki Kido | 76 | 70 | 73 | 219 | 1,410,000 |
| Kaori Higo | 72 | 73 | 74 | 219 | 1,410,000 |
| Midori Yoneyama | 71 | 75 | 74 | 220 | 1,080,000 |
| Yuko Saitoh | 75 | 76 | 70 | 221 | 960,000 |
| Kaori Suzuki | 74 | 76 | 71 | 221 | 960,000 |
| *Shinobu Moromizato | 71 | 74 | 76 | 221 | |
| Ji-Hee Lee | 74 | 71 | 76 | 221 | 960,000 |
| Mikako Kanamori | 75 | 73 | 74 | 222 | 750,000 |
| Samantha Head | 74 | 74 | 74 | 222 | 750,000 |
| Chihiro Nakajima | 72 | 74 | 76 | 222 | 750,000 |
| Shin Hyun Ju | 73 | 73 | 76 | 222 | 750,000 |
| *Kumiko Kaneda | 74 | 72 | 76 | 222 | |
| Mitsuko Kawasaki | 77 | 75 | 72 | 224 | 552,000 |
| Toshimi Kimura | 78 | 74 | 72 | 224 | 552,000 |
| Saori Ishikawa | 76 | 75 | 73 | 224 | 552,000 |
| Akane Iijima | 75 | 76 | 73 | 224 | 552,000 |
| Yuka Irie | 73 | 76 | 75 | 224 | 552,000 |

| | SCORES | | | TOTAL | MONEY |
|---|---|---|---|---|---|
| Tamie Durdin | 77 | 72 | 75 | 224 | 552,000 |
| Mayumi Murai | 72 | 76 | 76 | 224 | 552,000 |
| Chieko Amanuma | 74 | 74 | 76 | 224 | 552,000 |
| Yuri Fudoh | 72 | 75 | 77 | 224 | 552,000 |

## Fujisankei Ladies Classic

*Kawana Hotel Golf Club, Fuji Course,* Shizuoka
Par 36-36–72; 6,456 yards

April 22-24
purse, ¥70,000,000

| | SCORES | | | TOTAL | MONEY |
|---|---|---|---|---|---|
| Kasumi Fujii | 71 | 72 | 70 | 213 | ¥12,600,000 |
| Akiko Fukushima | 70 | 68 | 75 | 213 | 6,160,000 |
| (Fujii defeated Fukushima on first playoff hole.) | | | | | |
| Kaori Higo | 73 | 66 | 75 | 214 | 4,900,000 |
| Yuri Fudoh | 70 | 71 | 74 | 215 | 3,850,000 |
| Noriko Aso | 71 | 71 | 73 | 215 | 3,850,000 |
| Hiromi Mogi | 72 | 73 | 71 | 216 | 2,625,000 |
| Yukari Baba | 72 | 71 | 73 | 216 | 2,625,000 |
| Miho Koga | 72 | 69 | 76 | 217 | 2,100,000 |
| Lu Ya Huei | 71 | 71 | 76 | 218 | 1,750,000 |
| Misato Nishikawa | 77 | 70 | 73 | 220 | 1,306,666 |
| Yun-Jye Wei | 75 | 72 | 73 | 220 | 1,306,666 |
| Hiroko Fujishima | 74 | 74 | 72 | 220 | 1,306,666 |
| Chihiro Nakajima | 73 | 73 | 75 | 221 | 1,120,000 |
| Jeong Yun-Joo | 77 | 71 | 73 | 221 | 1,120,000 |
| Michiko Hattori | 77 | 75 | 70 | 222 | 910,000 |
| Rie Fujiwara | 73 | 73 | 76 | 222 | 910,000 |
| Junko Omote | 72 | 73 | 77 | 222 | 910,000 |
| Tamie Durdin | 78 | 74 | 70 | 222 | 910,000 |
| Nichiko Kawasaki | 71 | 77 | 75 | 223 | 645,000 |
| Kaori Suzuki | 77 | 72 | 74 | 223 | 645,000 |
| Ayako Uehara | 78 | 71 | 74 | 223 | 645,000 |
| Yasuko Satoh | 76 | 74 | 73 | 223 | 645,000 |
| *Shinobu Moromizato | 77 | 75 | 71 | 223 | |
| Sakura Yokomine | 73 | 75 | 75 | 223 | 645,000 |
| Yuki Takeda | 75 | 73 | 75 | 223 | 645,000 |
| Lee Eun Hye | 74 | 73 | 76 | 223 | 645,000 |
| Mayumi Murai | 76 | 73 | 75 | 224 | 581,000 |
| Masaki Maeda | 79 | 73 | 73 | 225 | 553,000 |
| Chieko Amanuma | 76 | 72 | 77 | 225 | 553,000 |
| Yuriko Ohtsuka | 76 | 76 | 73 | 225 | 553,000 |

## Katokichi Queens

*Yashima Country Club,* Mure, Kagawa
Par 36-36–72; 6,265 yards

April 29-May 1
purse, ¥60,000,000

| | SCORES | | | TOTAL | MONEY |
|---|---|---|---|---|---|
| Midori Yoneyama | 70 | 68 | 68 | 206 | ¥10,800,000 |
| Ayako Uehara | 71 | 68 | 67 | 206 | 5,280,000 |
| (Yoneyama defeated Uehara on second playoff hole.) | | | | | |
| Michiko Hattori | 70 | 67 | 70 | 207 | 4,200,000 |
| Tamie Durdin | 75 | 67 | 66 | 208 | 3,600,000 |

| | SCORES | | | TOTAL | MONEY |
|---|---|---|---|---|---|
| Mihoko Takahashi | 69 | 70 | 70 | 209 | 2,700,000 |
| Miho Koga | 69 | 67 | 73 | 209 | 2,700,000 |
| Keiko Sasaki | 72 | 68 | 70 | 210 | 1,800,000 |
| Yukari Baba | 69 | 70 | 71 | 210 | 1,800,000 |
| Sakura Yokomine | 75 | 67 | 68 | 210 | 1,800,000 |
| Nikki Campbell | 68 | 70 | 73 | 211 | 1,200,000 |
| Mineko Nasu | 74 | 69 | 69 | 212 | 1,026,000 |
| Junko Omote | 72 | 69 | 71 | 212 | 1,026,000 |
| Julie Lu | 71 | 69 | 72 | 212 | 1,026,000 |
| Shin Hyun Ju | 74 | 70 | 68 | 212 | 1,026,000 |
| Yasuko Satoh | 75 | 71 | 67 | 213 | 756,000 |
| Shiho Ohyama | 73 | 69 | 71 | 213 | 756,000 |
| Miki Nakata | 73 | 71 | 69 | 213 | 756,000 |
| Chiaki Nagano | 73 | 71 | 69 | 213 | 756,000 |
| Lee Eun Hye | 75 | 70 | 68 | 213 | 756,000 |
| *Shinobu Moromizato | 75 | 67 | 71 | 213 | |
| Michie Ohba | 71 | 71 | 72 | 214 | 564,000 |
| Kasumi Fujii | 74 | 72 | 68 | 214 | 564,000 |
| Jeong-Eun Lee | 73 | 71 | 70 | 214 | 564,000 |
| Mikako Kanamori | 75 | 71 | 69 | 215 | 510,000 |
| Seiko Watanabe | 75 | 69 | 71 | 215 | 510,000 |
| Mikiyo Nishizuka | 75 | 68 | 72 | 215 | 510,000 |
| Hiroko Yamaguchi | 76 | 68 | 71 | 215 | 510,000 |
| Ku Yun Hee | 75 | 70 | 70 | 215 | 510,000 |
| Jeon Mi Jung | 72 | 71 | 72 | 215 | 510,000 |
| Aki Nakano | 70 | 75 | 71 | 216 | 450,000 |
| Kaori Harada | 75 | 70 | 71 | 216 | 450,000 |
| Akane Iijima | 75 | 70 | 71 | 216 | 450,000 |
| Gina Scott | 71 | 72 | 73 | 216 | 450,000 |

## Salonpas World Ladies

*Yomiuri Country Club,* Tokyo
Par 36-36–72; 6,471 yards

May 5-8
purse, ¥60,000,000

| | SCORES | | | | TOTAL | MONEY |
|---|---|---|---|---|---|---|
| Yuri Fudoh | 71 | 71 | 64 | 70 | 276 | ¥10,800,000 |
| Shiho Ohyama | 67 | 68 | 71 | 70 | 276 | 5,280,000 |
| (Fudoh defeated Ohyama on first playoff hole.) | | | | | | |
| Junko Omote | 72 | 69 | 68 | 69 | 278 | 4,200,000 |
| Ai Miyazato | 72 | 69 | 70 | 68 | 279 | 3,600,000 |
| Nikki Campbell | 75 | 70 | 69 | 67 | 281 | 3,000,000 |
| Chieko Amanuma | 70 | 73 | 70 | 69 | 282 | 2,400,000 |
| Sakura Yokomine | 71 | 69 | 73 | 70 | 283 | 2,100,000 |
| Young-Me Lee | 71 | 69 | 74 | 70 | 284 | 1,650,000 |
| Ji-Hee Lee | 70 | 76 | 72 | 66 | 284 | 1,650,000 |
| Hiroko Yamaguchi | 73 | 73 | 69 | 70 | 285 | 1,200,000 |
| Yun-Jye Wei | 72 | 74 | 74 | 66 | 286 | 1,026,000 |
| Song Bo Bae | 74 | 69 | 72 | 71 | 286 | 1,026,000 |
| Ye-Suhn Suh | 70 | 71 | 75 | 70 | 286 | 1,026,000 |
| Fuki Kido | 72 | 71 | 74 | 70 | 287 | 816,000 |
| Woo-Soon Ko | 73 | 71 | 72 | 71 | 287 | 816,000 |
| Naoko Takasaki | 71 | 73 | 70 | 73 | 287 | 816,000 |
| Lu Ya Huei | 74 | 69 | 73 | 71 | 287 | 816,000 |
| Mineko Nasu | 71 | 75 | 73 | 69 | 288 | 636,000 |
| Jeong Yun-Joo | 73 | 73 | 69 | 73 | 288 | 636,000 |
| Karrie Webb | 69 | 77 | 74 | 69 | 289 | 540,000 |

| | SCORES | | | | TOTAL | MONEY |
|---|---|---|---|---|---|---|
| *Kumiko Kaneda | 71 | 73 | 77 | 68 | 289 | |
| Tamie Durdin | 76 | 73 | 69 | 71 | 289 | 540,000 |
| Mikako Kanamori | 70 | 75 | 75 | 70 | 290 | 516,000 |
| Chikako Matsuzawa | 70 | 76 | 71 | 73 | 290 | 516,000 |
| Nobuko Kizawa | 73 | 73 | 73 | 72 | 291 | 474,000 |
| Ikuyo Shiotani | 73 | 74 | 71 | 73 | 291 | 474,000 |
| Michie Ohba | 72 | 74 | 73 | 72 | 291 | 474,000 |
| Orie Fujino | 72 | 76 | 74 | 69 | 291 | 474,000 |
| Lee Eun Hye | 73 | 75 | 70 | 73 | 291 | 474,000 |
| Akiko Fukushima | 74 | 72 | 73 | 73 | 292 | 414,000 |
| Misato Nishikawa | 70 | 74 | 76 | 72 | 292 | 414,000 |
| Mistuko Kawasaki | 72 | 73 | 76 | 71 | 292 | 414,000 |
| Michiko Mitsui | 70 | 74 | 74 | 74 | 292 | 414,000 |
| Ku Yun Hee | 77 | 72 | 76 | 67 | 292 | 414,000 |

## Vernal Ladies

*Fukuoka Century Golf Club,* Amagi, Fukuoka
Par 36-36–72; 6,584 yards

May 13-15
purse, ¥120,000,000

| | SCORES | | | TOTAL | MONEY |
|---|---|---|---|---|---|
| Ai Miyazato | 69 | 64 | 70 | 203 | ¥21,600,000 |
| Akiko Fukushima | 74 | 68 | 69 | 211 | 10,560,000 |
| Lee Eun Hye | 74 | 70 | 69 | 213 | 8,400,000 |
| Tamie Durdin | 73 | 66 | 75 | 214 | 7,200,000 |
| Fuki Kido | 70 | 74 | 71 | 215 | 5,400,000 |
| Mikiyo Nishizuka | 74 | 65 | 76 | 215 | 5,400,000 |
| Midori Yoneyama | 74 | 74 | 68 | 216 | 3,300,000 |
| Yuri Fudoh | 75 | 70 | 71 | 216 | 3,300,000 |
| Junko Omote | 72 | 71 | 73 | 216 | 3,300,000 |
| Shin Hyun Ju | 74 | 67 | 75 | 216 | 3,300,000 |
| Hiroko Yamaguchi | 75 | 72 | 71 | 218 | 2,184,000 |
| Ji-Hee Lee | 68 | 74 | 76 | 218 | 2,184,000 |
| Yun-Jye Wei | 76 | 73 | 70 | 219 | 1,884,000 |
| Shiho Ohyama | 73 | 73 | 73 | 219 | 1,884,000 |
| Nikki Campbell | 77 | 68 | 74 | 219 | 1,884,000 |
| Yuriko Ohtsuka | 74 | 76 | 70 | 220 | 1,584,000 |
| Masaki Maeda | 75 | 70 | 75 | 220 | 1,584,000 |
| Mihoko Takahashi | 72 | 73 | 76 | 221 | 1,200,000 |
| Eriko Moriyama | 77 | 72 | 72 | 221 | 1,200,000 |
| Jeon Mi Jung | 74 | 75 | 72 | 221 | 1,200,000 |
| Miho Koga | 74 | 73 | 74 | 221 | 1,200,000 |
| Mitsuko Kawasaki | 74 | 73 | 74 | 221 | 1,200,000 |
| Michie Ohba | 70 | 76 | 75 | 221 | 1,200,000 |
| Yoko Yamagishi | 77 | 72 | 73 | 222 | 1,008,000 |
| Woo-Soon Ko | 75 | 74 | 73 | 222 | 1,008,000 |
| Hiromi Mogi | 72 | 76 | 74 | 222 | 1,008,000 |
| Keiko Sasaki | 74 | 73 | 75 | 222 | 1,008,000 |
| Mineko Nasu | 79 | 68 | 75 | 222 | 1,008,000 |
| Ayako Uehara | 75 | 72 | 75 | 222 | 1,008,000 |
| Miyuki Shimabukuro | 73 | 74 | 76 | 223 | 912,000 |
| Kaori Harada | 74 | 73 | 76 | 223 | 912,000 |

# Chukyo TV Bridgestone Ladies Open

*Chukyo Golf Club,* Toyota, Aichi
Par 36-36–72; 6,399 yards

May 20-22
purse, ¥50,000,000

| | SCORES | | | TOTAL | MONEY |
|---|---|---|---|---|---|
| Ai Miyazato | 65 | 74 | 70 | 209 | ¥9,000,000 |
| Nikki Campbell | 69 | 68 | 72 | 209 | 4,500,000 |
| (Miyazato defeated Campbell on first playoff hole.) | | | | | |
| Hiroko Yamaguchi | 73 | 67 | 70 | 210 | 3,500,000 |
| *Shinobu Moromizato | 63 | 73 | 74 | 210 | |
| Lee Eun Hye | 69 | 70 | 72 | 211 | 3,000,000 |
| Junko Omote | 73 | 70 | 69 | 212 | 2,250,000 |
| Kaori Higo | 74 | 68 | 70 | 212 | 2,250,000 |
| Akiko Fukushima | 69 | 71 | 73 | 213 | 1,750,000 |
| Akane Iijima | 69 | 77 | 68 | 214 | 1,176,250 |
| Shiho Ohyama | 74 | 70 | 70 | 214 | 1,176,250 |
| Yun-Jye Wei | 71 | 71 | 72 | 214 | 1,176,250 |
| Kasumi Fujii | 69 | 72 | 73 | 214 | 1,176,250 |
| Young-Me Lee | 76 | 70 | 69 | 215 | 830,000 |
| Nobuko Kizawa | 71 | 73 | 71 | 215 | 830,000 |
| Michiko Hattori | 71 | 73 | 71 | 215 | 830,000 |
| Yuka Shiroto | 69 | 73 | 73 | 215 | 830,000 |
| Shoko Asano | 73 | 73 | 70 | 216 | 630,000 |
| Kuniko Maeda | 69 | 75 | 72 | 216 | 630,000 |
| Toshimi Kimura | 72 | 71 | 73 | 216 | 630,000 |
| Mayumi Shimomura | 69 | 74 | 73 | 216 | 630,000 |
| Mayumi Hirase | 72 | 73 | 72 | 217 | 480,000 |
| Yasuko Satoh | 72 | 74 | 71 | 217 | 480,000 |
| Noriko Aso | 74 | 71 | 72 | 217 | 480,000 |
| Misato Nishikawa | 74 | 70 | 73 | 217 | 480,000 |
| Julie Lu | 70 | 73 | 74 | 217 | 480,000 |
| Miyuki Shimabukuro | 70 | 71 | 76 | 217 | 480,000 |
| Sakura Yokomine | 75 | 73 | 70 | 218 | 425,000 |
| Ok-Hee Ku | 71 | 76 | 71 | 218 | 425,000 |
| Jeong-Eun Lee | 74 | 72 | 72 | 218 | 425,000 |
| Nachiyo Ohtani | 72 | 72 | 74 | 218 | 425,000 |
| Michie Ohba | 72 | 72 | 74 | 218 | 425,000 |

# Kosaido Ladies Golf Cup

*Chiba Kosaido Country Club,* Ichihara, Chiba
Par 36-36–72; 6,317 yards

May 27-29
purse, ¥60,000,000

| | SCORES | | | TOTAL | MONEY |
|---|---|---|---|---|---|
| Midori Yoneyama | 69 | 67 | 71 | 207 | ¥10,800,000 |
| Junko Omote | 67 | 70 | 70 | 207 | 5,280,000 |
| (Yoneyama defeated Omote on first playoff hole.) | | | | | |
| Fuki Kido | 69 | 69 | 70 | 208 | 4,200,000 |
| Ji-Hee Lee | 71 | 72 | 66 | 209 | 3,300,000 |
| Mihoko Takahashi | 70 | 72 | 67 | 209 | 3,300,000 |
| Kaori Nakamichi | 71 | 67 | 72 | 210 | 2,400,000 |
| Noriko Aso | 69 | 70 | 72 | 211 | 2,100,000 |
| Lu Ya Huei | 70 | 72 | 70 | 212 | 1,344,000 |
| Keiko Sasaki | 69 | 72 | 71 | 212 | 1,344,000 |
| Hiroko Yamaguchi | 71 | 70 | 71 | 212 | 1,344,000 |
| Woo-Soon Ko | 71 | 69 | 72 | 212 | 1,344,000 |

| | SCORES | | | TOTAL | MONEY |
|---|---|---|---|---|---|
| Michiko Hattori | 68 | 70 | 74 | 212 | 1,344,000 |
| Kaori Higo | 72 | 68 | 73 | 213 | 990,000 |
| Mineko Nasu | 69 | 70 | 74 | 213 | 990,000 |
| Naoko Takasaki | 70 | 72 | 72 | 214 | 870,000 |
| Yuri Fudoh | 67 | 73 | 74 | 214 | 870,000 |
| Jeon Mi Jung | 72 | 71 | 72 | 215 | 720,000 |
| Jeong Yun-Joo | 72 | 71 | 72 | 215 | 720,000 |
| Michiko Mitsui | 70 | 71 | 74 | 215 | 720,000 |
| Young-Me Lee | 71 | 74 | 71 | 216 | 552,000 |
| Jeong-Eun Lee | 72 | 73 | 71 | 216 | 552,000 |
| Shin Sora | 74 | 71 | 71 | 216 | 552,000 |
| Yuko Moriguchi | 72 | 73 | 71 | 216 | 552,000 |
| Akane Iijima | 70 | 74 | 72 | 216 | 552,000 |
| Mitsuko Kawasaki | 70 | 73 | 73 | 216 | 552,000 |
| Atomi Shiota | 72 | 71 | 73 | 216 | 552,000 |
| Miho Koga | 73 | 69 | 74 | 216 | 552,000 |
| Rui Kitada | 71 | 70 | 75 | 216 | 552,000 |
| Nahoko Hirao | 70 | 75 | 72 | 217 | 468,000 |
| Azumi Katoh | 71 | 74 | 72 | 217 | 468,000 |
| Hiromi Mogi | 72 | 73 | 72 | 217 | 468,000 |
| Miki Nakata | 73 | 70 | 74 | 217 | 468,000 |
| Ae-Sook Kim | 69 | 73 | 75 | 217 | 468,000 |

## Resort Trust Ladies

*Grande Nasushirakawa Golf Club,* Fukushima
Par 36-36–72; 6,447 yards

June 3-5
purse, ¥60,000,000

| | SCORES | | | TOTAL | MONEY |
|---|---|---|---|---|---|
| Mitsuko Kawasaki | 68 | 65 | 75 | 208 | ¥10,800,000 |
| Akiko Fukushima | 68 | 70 | 72 | 210 | 5,280,000 |
| Yuri Fudoh | 68 | 75 | 68 | 211 | 3,060,000 |
| Shiho Ohyama | 68 | 71 | 72 | 211 | 3,060,000 |
| Sakura Yokomine | 66 | 71 | 74 | 211 | 3,060,000 |
| Jeon Mi Jung | 67 | 70 | 74 | 211 | 3,060,000 |
| Lee Eun Hye | 71 | 65 | 75 | 211 | 3,060,000 |
| Mikiyo Nishizuka | 72 | 71 | 70 | 213 | 1,298,400 |
| Ku Yun Hee | 73 | 69 | 71 | 213 | 1,298,400 |
| Ai Miyazato | 71 | 71 | 71 | 213 | 1,298,400 |
| Michie Ohba | 68 | 71 | 74 | 213 | 1,298,400 |
| Yuki Fujita | 67 | 71 | 75 | 213 | 1,298,400 |
| Samantha Head | 72 | 72 | 70 | 214 | 876,000 |
| Lu Ya Huei | 71 | 70 | 73 | 214 | 876,000 |
| Kuniko Maeda | 70 | 72 | 74 | 216 | 636,000 |
| Yukari Baba | 67 | 78 | 71 | 216 | 636,000 |
| Rie Fujiwara | 69 | 72 | 75 | 216 | 636,000 |
| Noriko Aso | 74 | 67 | 75 | 216 | 636,000 |
| Chieko Nishida | 75 | 71 | 70 | 216 | 636,000 |
| Yun-Jye Wei | 69 | 69 | 78 | 216 | 636,000 |
| Misato Nishikawa | 72 | 71 | 74 | 217 | 450,000 |
| Hiromi Mogi | 67 | 76 | 74 | 217 | 450,000 |
| Park So Hyun | 71 | 73 | 73 | 217 | 450,000 |
| Nobuko Kizawa | 74 | 68 | 75 | 217 | 450,000 |
| Yuko Saitoh | 71 | 70 | 76 | 217 | 450,000 |
| Ai Ogawa | 75 | 68 | 75 | 218 | 378,857 |
| Ayako Okamoto | 74 | 69 | 75 | 218 | 378,857 |
| Michiko Mitsui | 70 | 72 | 76 | 218 | 378,857 |

|  | SCORES | TOTAL | MONEY |
|---|---|---|---|
| Mineko Nasu | 72 73 73 | 218 | 378,857 |
| Mizuho Ozawa | 71 70 77 | 218 | 378,857 |
| Chieko Amanuma | 70 71 77 | 218 | 378,857 |
| Akane Iijima | 72 74 72 | 218 | 378,857 |

## We Love Kobe Suntory Ladies Open

*Japan Memorial Golf Club,* Yoshikawa, Hyogo

June 9-12

Par 36-36–72; 6,528 yards

purse, ¥60,000,000

|  | SCORES | TOTAL | MONEY |
|---|---|---|---|
| Yuri Fudoh | 72 69 67 64 | 272 | ¥10,800,000 |
| Michie Ohba | 69 67 69 69 | 274 | 5,280,000 |
| Hiroko Yamaguchi | 70 69 69 69 | 277 | 4,200,000 |
| Yuriko Ohtsuka | 71 66 67 74 | 278 | 3,300,000 |
| Saiki Fujita | 71 72 69 66 | 278 | 3,300,000 |
| Ji-Hee Lee | 68 69 70 72 | 279 | 2,400,000 |
| Jeong Yun-Joo | 72 67 73 69 | 281 | 2,100,000 |
| Shiho Ohyama | 72 69 73 68 | 282 | 1,500,000 |
| Junko Omote | 71 71 68 72 | 282 | 1,500,000 |
| Julie Lu | 70 70 70 72 | 282 | 1,500,000 |
| *Kim Song Hee | 69 69 70 74 | 282 | |
| Mikiyo Nishizuka | 73 71 72 67 | 283 | 1,032,000 |
| Ai Miyazato | 72 70 70 71 | 283 | 1,032,000 |
| Yukari Baba | 69 71 75 68 | 283 | 1,032,000 |
| Lee Eun Hye | 71 70 70 73 | 284 | 912,000 |
| Miho Koga | 79 67 70 69 | 285 | 822,000 |
| Chieko Amanuma | 72 67 72 74 | 285 | 822,000 |
| Yuka Shiroto | 71 70 71 74 | 286 | 672,000 |
| Namika Omata | 73 69 71 73 | 286 | 672,000 |
| Yuki Takeda | 76 71 71 68 | 286 | 672,000 |
| Seiko Watanabe | 72 70 73 72 | 287 | 528,000 |
| Yun-Jye Wei | 72 67 76 72 | 287 | 528,000 |
| Kuniko Maeda | 72 72 73 70 | 287 | 528,000 |
| Mari Katayama | 77 69 72 69 | 287 | 528,000 |
| Samantha Head | 78 69 73 67 | 287 | 528,000 |
| Eriko Moriyama | 71 72 71 74 | 288 | 480,000 |
| Yui Kawahara | 73 75 71 69 | 288 | 480,000 |
| Jeon Mi Jung | 73 70 71 74 | 288 | 480,000 |
| *Chie Arimura | 77 72 69 71 | 289 | |
| Akane Iijima | 73 69 71 76 | 289 | 444,000 |
| Mayumi Shimomura | 75 70 73 71 | 289 | 444,000 |
| Lu Ya Huei | 74 70 74 71 | 289 | 444,000 |

## Apita Circle K Sankus Ladies

*U Green Golf Club,* Natatugawa, Gifu

June 17-19

Par 36-36–72; 6,347 yards

purse, ¥50,000,000

|  | SCORES | TOTAL | MONEY |
|---|---|---|---|
| Ok-Hee Ku | 70 68 71 | 209 | ¥10,800,000 |
| Chieko Amanuma | 69 70 72 | 211 | 5,280,000 |
| Ji-Hee Lee | 72 72 69 | 213 | 3,600,000 |
| Miho Koga | 70 73 70 | 213 | 3,600,000 |

| | SCORES | | | TOTAL | MONEY |
|---|---|---|---|---|---|
| Lu Ya Huei | 69 | 70 | 74 | 213 | 3,600,000 |
| Ayako Uehara | 72 | 70 | 72 | 214 | 2,250,000 |
| *Erina Hara | 68 | 72 | 74 | 214 | |
| Touko Mitsu | 71 | 72 | 71 | 214 | 2,250,000 |
| Shin Hyun Ju | 67 | 75 | 73 | 215 | 1,407,000 |
| Mineko Nasu | 72 | 71 | 72 | 215 | 1,407,000 |
| Nikki Campbell | 72 | 73 | 70 | 215 | 1,407,000 |
| Eriko Moriyama | 74 | 69 | 72 | 215 | 1,407,000 |
| Yun-Jye Wei | 77 | 69 | 70 | 216 | 978,000 |
| Tamie Durdin | 73 | 67 | 76 | 216 | 978,000 |
| Michiko Hattori | 68 | 74 | 74 | 216 | 978,000 |
| Hiromi Mogi | 71 | 74 | 71 | 216 | 978,000 |
| Junko Omote | 72 | 71 | 74 | 217 | 708,000 |
| Toshimi Kimura | 72 | 72 | 73 | 217 | 708,000 |
| Yasuko Satoh | 72 | 72 | 73 | 217 | 708,000 |
| Mihoko Takahashi | 76 | 69 | 72 | 217 | 708,000 |
| Kaori Harada | 73 | 72 | 72 | 217 | 708,000 |
| Michie Ohba | 75 | 69 | 74 | 218 | 546,000 |
| Yui Kawahara | 73 | 71 | 74 | 218 | 546,000 |
| Ji-Yeon Han | 76 | 71 | 71 | 218 | 546,000 |
| Yoko Yamagishi | 75 | 71 | 72 | 218 | 546,000 |
| Sakura Yokomine | 71 | 76 | 71 | 218 | 546,000 |
| Midori Yoneyama | 73 | 71 | 74 | 218 | 546,000 |
| Ai Ogawa | 74 | 72 | 73 | 219 | 462,000 |
| Fuki Kido | 71 | 71 | 77 | 219 | 462,000 |
| Keiko Sasaki | 71 | 73 | 75 | 219 | 462,000 |
| Jeon Mi Jung | 71 | 73 | 75 | 219 | 462,000 |
| Ye-Suhn Suh | 71 | 75 | 73 | 219 | 462,000 |
| Kanna Takanashi | 75 | 70 | 74 | 219 | 462,000 |
| Yukari Horikoshi | 74 | 73 | 72 | 219 | 462,000 |
| Michiko Mitsui | 74 | 69 | 76 | 219 | 462,000 |

## Promise Ladies

*Water Hills Golf Club*, Hyogo
Par 36-36–72; 6,387 yards

June 24-26
purse, ¥60,000,000

| | SCORES | | | TOTAL | MONEY |
|---|---|---|---|---|---|
| Ku Yun Hee | 67 | 68 | 66 | 201 | ¥10,800,000 |
| Junko Omote | 70 | 67 | 65 | 202 | 5,280,000 |
| Keiko Sasaki | 68 | 69 | 67 | 204 | 3,900,000 |
| Midori Yoneyama | 65 | 70 | 69 | 204 | 3,900,000 |
| Yun-Jye Wei | 72 | 71 | 64 | 207 | 2,500,000 |
| Miho Koga | 68 | 72 | 67 | 207 | 2,500,000 |
| Ji-Hee Lee | 69 | 67 | 71 | 207 | 2,500,000 |
| Atomi Shiota | 69 | 72 | 67 | 208 | 1,650,000 |
| Toshimi Kimura | 71 | 70 | 67 | 208 | 1,650,000 |
| Nikki Campbell | 72 | 70 | 67 | 209 | 1,200,000 |
| Sakura Yokomine | 71 | 72 | 67 | 210 | 1,086,000 |
| Fuki Kido | 67 | 73 | 70 | 210 | 1,086,000 |
| Aki Nakano | 66 | 76 | 69 | 211 | 786,000 |
| Yukari Baba | 72 | 70 | 69 | 211 | 786,000 |
| Ok-Hee Ku | 68 | 73 | 70 | 211 | 786,000 |
| Kasumi Fujii | 74 | 67 | 70 | 211 | 786,000 |
| Chieko Nishida | 67 | 73 | 71 | 211 | 786,000 |
| Lee Eun Hye | 69 | 71 | 71 | 211 | 786,000 |
| Yuka Shiroto | 67 | 72 | 72 | 211 | 786,000 |

|  | SCORES | | | TOTAL | MONEY |
|---|---|---|---|---|---|
| Ji-Yeon Han | 68 | 68 | 75 | 211 | 786,000 |
| Mitsuko Kawasaki | 69 | 75 | 68 | 212 | 516,000 |
| Yuriko Ohtsuka | 70 | 74 | 68 | 212 | 516,000 |
| Noriko Aso | 69 | 74 | 69 | 212 | 516,000 |
| Yuko Moriguchi | 70 | 73 | 69 | 212 | 516,000 |
| Jeong-Eun Lee | 73 | 69 | 70 | 212 | 516,000 |
| Azumi Katoh | 70 | 71 | 71 | 212 | 516,000 |
| Michiko Mitsui | 72 | 69 | 71 | 212 | 516,000 |
| Kaori Nakamichi | 72 | 69 | 71 | 212 | 516,000 |
| Hiroko Yamaguchi | 68 | 72 | 72 | 212 | 516,000 |
| Shin Hyun Ju | 71 | 70 | 72 | 213 | 444,000 |
| Yasuko Satoh | 67 | 72 | 74 | 213 | 444,000 |
| Kuniko Maeda | 68 | 71 | 74 | 213 | 444,000 |

## Belluna Ladies Cup

*Obatago Golf Club,* Kanra, Gunma
Par 36-36–72; 6,381 yards

July 1-3
purse, ¥60,000,000

|  | SCORES | | | TOTAL | MONEY |
|---|---|---|---|---|---|
| Kasumi Fujii | 69 | 66 | 69 | 204 | ¥10,800,000 |
| Toshimi Kimura | 69 | 69 | 68 | 206 | 5,400,000 |
| Sakura Yokomine | 68 | 72 | 67 | 207 | 3,600,000 |
| Yukari Baba | 66 | 72 | 69 | 207 | 3,600,000 |
| Mayumi Murai | 68 | 69 | 70 | 207 | 3,600,000 |
| Kuniko Maeda | 70 | 71 | 67 | 208 | 2,100,000 |
| Yun-Jye Wei | 68 | 71 | 69 | 208 | 2,100,000 |
| Ai Ogawa | 71 | 65 | 72 | 208 | 2,100,000 |
| Akane Iijima | 74 | 69 | 66 | 209 | 1,233,000 |
| Jeon Mi Jung | 71 | 70 | 68 | 209 | 1,233,000 |
| Kayo Yamada | 71 | 69 | 69 | 209 | 1,233,000 |
| Woo-Soon Ko | 75 | 64 | 70 | 209 | 1,233,000 |
| *Mika Miyazato | 70 | 66 | 73 | 209 | |
| Yuka Irie | 68 | 74 | 68 | 210 | 936,000 |
| Mika Saitoh | 72 | 69 | 69 | 210 | 936,000 |
| Mitsuko Kawasaki | 74 | 66 | 70 | 210 | 936,000 |
| Yuka Shiroto | 71 | 68 | 71 | 210 | 936,000 |
| Shin Hyun Ju | 69 | 74 | 68 | 211 | 626,000 |
| Yui Kawahara | 73 | 70 | 68 | 211 | 626,000 |
| Junko Omote | 73 | 69 | 69 | 211 | 626,000 |
| Julie Lu | 71 | 70 | 70 | 211 | 626,000 |
| Naoko Takasaki | 72 | 68 | 71 | 211 | 626,000 |
| Hiromi Mogi | 72 | 68 | 71 | 211 | 626,000 |
| Nikki Campbell | 72 | 68 | 71 | 211 | 626,000 |
| Kaori Higo | 67 | 72 | 72 | 211 | 626,000 |
| Ayako Uehara | 69 | 69 | 73 | 211 | 626,000 |
| Shiho Ohyama | 71 | 71 | 70 | 212 | 516,000 |
| Ae-Sook Kim | 72 | 70 | 70 | 212 | 516,000 |
| Yeo-Jin Kang | 71 | 68 | 73 | 212 | 516,000 |
| Nachiyo Ohtani | 68 | 70 | 74 | 212 | 516,000 |

# Chateaureze Queens Cup

*Chateaureze Country Club,* Sapporo, Hokkaido
Par 36-36–72; 6,464 yards

July 8-10
purse, ¥70,000,000

|  | SCORES | | | TOTAL | MONEY |
|---|---|---|---|---|---|
| Junko Omote | 69 | 75 | 70 | 214 | ¥12,600,000 |
| Michiko Hattori | 70 | 73 | 71 | 214 | 6,300,000 |
| (Omote defeated Hattori on second playoff hole.) | | | | | |
| Yeo-Jin Kang | 68 | 74 | 73 | 215 | 4,900,000 |
| Michie Ohba | 73 | 73 | 71 | 217 | 2,800,000 |
| Ji-Hee Lee | 74 | 72 | 71 | 217 | 2,800,000 |
| Midori Yoneyama | 73 | 72 | 72 | 217 | 2,800,000 |
| Jeon Mi Jung | 71 | 73 | 73 | 217 | 2,800,000 |
| Nobuko Kizawa | 71 | 72 | 74 | 217 | 2,800,000 |
| Ji-Yeon Han | 73 | 70 | 74 | 217 | 2,800,000 |
| Ai Ogawa | 72 | 74 | 72 | 218 | 1,196,000 |
| Kasumi Fujii | 75 | 71 | 72 | 218 | 1,196,000 |
| Mayumi Murai | 73 | 72 | 73 | 218 | 1,196,000 |
| Shiho Ohyama | 73 | 72 | 73 | 218 | 1,196,000 |
| Kaori Nakamichi | 71 | 73 | 74 | 218 | 1,196,000 |
| Kaori Higo | 71 | 73 | 74 | 218 | 1,196,000 |
| Sakura Yokomine | 72 | 71 | 75 | 218 | 1,196,000 |
| Hiromi Mogi | 77 | 73 | 69 | 219 | 788,200 |
| Yumiko Baba | 72 | 76 | 71 | 219 | 788,200 |
| Yui Kawahara | 72 | 75 | 72 | 219 | 788,200 |
| Kaori Harada | 73 | 72 | 74 | 219 | 788,200 |
| Orie Fujino | 70 | 74 | 75 | 219 | 788,200 |
| Hiroko Yamaguchi | 70 | 78 | 72 | 220 | 665,000 |
| Seiko Watanabe | 74 | 73 | 73 | 220 | 665,000 |
| Akiko Fukushima | 72 | 71 | 77 | 220 | 665,000 |
| Yun-Jye Wei | 73 | 77 | 71 | 221 | 616,000 |
| Tamie Durdin | 74 | 74 | 73 | 221 | 616,000 |
| Shin Hyun Ju | 74 | 72 | 75 | 221 | 616,000 |
| Toshimi Kimura | 65 | 80 | 76 | 221 | 616,000 |
| Mizuho Ozawa | 75 | 75 | 72 | 222 | 534,000 |
| Miki Nakata | 76 | 73 | 73 | 222 | 534,000 |
| Chihiro Nakajima | 71 | 77 | 74 | 222 | 534,000 |
| Yuriko Ohtsuka | 70 | 77 | 75 | 222 | 534,000 |
| Yuka Irie | 71 | 76 | 75 | 222 | 534,000 |
| Eriko Moriyama | 74 | 73 | 75 | 222 | 534,000 |
| Kuniko Maeda | 75 | 71 | 76 | 222 | 534,000 |

# Stanley Ladies

*Tomei Country Club*, Shizuoka
Par 36-36–72; 6,452 yards

July 15-17
purse, ¥60,000,000

|  | SCORES | | | TOTAL | MONEY |
|---|---|---|---|---|---|
| Junko Omote | 67 | 72 | 65 | 204 | ¥10,800,000 |
| Shin Hyun Ju | 71 | 70 | 64 | 205 | 5,280,000 |
| Kasumi Fujii | 67 | 71 | 69 | 207 | 4,200,000 |
| Miki Nakata | 68 | 70 | 70 | 208 | 3,600,000 |
| Michie Ohba | 71 | 72 | 66 | 209 | 3,000,000 |
| Mitsuko Kawasaki | 70 | 71 | 69 | 210 | 1,800,000 |
| Toshimi Kimura | 70 | 70 | 70 | 210 | 1,800,000 |
| Mikiyo Nishizuka | 70 | 71 | 69 | 210 | 1,800,000 |

| | SCORES | | | TOTAL | MONEY |
|---|---|---|---|---|---|
| Yukari Baba | 69 | 72 | 69 | 210 | 1,800,000 |
| Yuri Fudoh | 76 | 67 | 67 | 210 | 1,800,000 |
| Nikki Campbell | 72 | 69 | 70 | 211 | 1,140,000 |
| *Mika Miyazato | 70 | 70 | 71 | 211 | |
| Ku Yun Hee | 74 | 73 | 65 | 212 | 1,020,000 |
| Jeon Mi Jung | 70 | 72 | 70 | 212 | 1,020,000 |
| Sakura Yokomine | 70 | 70 | 72 | 212 | 1,020,000 |
| Yuka Irie | 71 | 74 | 68 | 213 | 726,857 |
| Rui Kitada | 73 | 71 | 69 | 213 | 726,857 |
| Chihiro Nakajima | 71 | 73 | 69 | 213 | 726,857 |
| Kaori Nakamichi | 73 | 72 | 68 | 213 | 726,857 |
| Michiko Hattori | 72 | 72 | 69 | 213 | 726,857 |
| Hiromi Mogi | 67 | 73 | 73 | 213 | 726,857 |
| Hiroko Yamaguchi | 75 | 70 | 68 | 213 | 726,857 |
| Mari Katayama | 69 | 75 | 70 | 214 | 576,000 |
| Ji-Hee Lee | 71 | 76 | 68 | 215 | 552,000 |
| Kyoko Ono | 73 | 74 | 68 | 215 | 552,000 |
| Yuki Takeda | 73 | 73 | 69 | 215 | 552,000 |
| Noriko Aso | 72 | 73 | 71 | 216 | 492,000 |
| Jae-Sook Won | 75 | 71 | 70 | 216 | 492,000 |
| Shiho Ohyama | 76 | 70 | 70 | 216 | 492,000 |
| Fuki Kido | 73 | 72 | 71 | 216 | 492,000 |
| Hikaru Kobayashi | 71 | 74 | 71 | 216 | 492,000 |
| Yuka Shiroto | 73 | 72 | 71 | 216 | 492,000 |
| Kaori Harada | 73 | 71 | 72 | 216 | 492,000 |
| *Yumiko Yoshida | 73 | 69 | 74 | 216 | |

## Crystal Geyser Ladies

*Keiyo Country Club*, Chiba
Par 36-36–72; 6,384 yards

August 5-7
purse, ¥60,000,000

| | SCORES | | | TOTAL | MONEY |
|---|---|---|---|---|---|
| Kasumi Fujii | 69 | 67 | 68 | 204 | ¥10,800,000 |
| Yuri Fudoh | 67 | 69 | 68 | 204 | 4,740,000 |
| Shiho Ohyama | 66 | 71 | 67 | 204 | 4,740,000 |
| (Fujii defeated Fudoh and Ohyama on first playoff hole.) | | | | | |
| Young-Me Lee | 69 | 68 | 70 | 207 | 3,300,000 |
| Lu Ya Huei | 70 | 66 | 71 | 207 | 3,300,000 |
| Shin Hyun Ju | 72 | 69 | 67 | 208 | 1,950,000 |
| Yukari Baba | 69 | 70 | 69 | 208 | 1,950,000 |
| Hiroko Yamaguchi | 70 | 69 | 69 | 208 | 1,950,000 |
| Mineko Nasu | 67 | 69 | 72 | 208 | 1,950,000 |
| Nato Nagai | 68 | 72 | 70 | 210 | 1,108,000 |
| Akane Iijima | 71 | 69 | 70 | 210 | 1,108,000 |
| Mayumi Shimomura | 68 | 71 | 71 | 210 | 1,108,000 |
| Ai Ogawa | 69 | 70 | 72 | 211 | 972,000 |
| Miho Koga | 73 | 70 | 69 | 212 | 792,000 |
| Ji-Hee Lee | 69 | 73 | 70 | 212 | 792,000 |
| Julie Lu | 71 | 71 | 70 | 212 | 792,000 |
| Sun Wook Lim | 73 | 68 | 71 | 212 | 792,000 |
| Grace Park | 70 | 69 | 73 | 212 | 792,000 |
| Yuko Saitoh | 69 | 72 | 72 | 213 | 612,000 |
| Atomi Shiota | 70 | 71 | 73 | 214 | 546,000 |
| Ye-Suhn Suh | 70 | 72 | 72 | 214 | 546,000 |
| Yuriko Ohtsuka | 71 | 74 | 70 | 215 | 498,000 |
| Yun-Hee Ku | 69 | 76 | 70 | 215 | 498,000 |

| | SCORES | | | TOTAL | MONEY |
|---|---|---|---|---|---|
| Yun-Jye Wei | 71 | 72 | 72 | 215 | 498,000 |
| Miki Nakata | 70 | 72 | 73 | 215 | 498,000 |
| Jeong-Eun Lee | 70 | 72 | 73 | 215 | 498,000 |
| Azumi Katoh | 68 | 69 | 78 | 215 | 498,000 |
| Hsiu-Feng Tseng | 74 | 72 | 70 | 216 | 402,000 |
| Nikki Campbell | 71 | 75 | 70 | 216 | 402,000 |
| Akiko Fukushima | 76 | 70 | 70 | 216 | 402,000 |
| Kayo Yamada | 74 | 70 | 72 | 216 | 402,000 |
| Hiromi Mogi | 72 | 72 | 72 | 216 | 402,000 |
| Orie Fujino | 71 | 73 | 72 | 216 | 402,000 |
| Mikiyo Nishizuka | 72 | 72 | 72 | 216 | 402,000 |
| Yoko Yamagishi | 67 | 76 | 73 | 216 | 402,000 |
| Yuki Takeda | 73 | 69 | 74 | 216 | 402,000 |
| Mayumi Murai | 72 | 69 | 75 | 216 | 402,000 |

## NEC Karuizawa 72

*Karuizawa 72 Golf Club*, Nagano
Par 36-36–72; 6,523 yards

August 12-14
purse, ¥60,000,000

| | SCORES | | | TOTAL | MONEY |
|---|---|---|---|---|---|
| Paula Creamer | 64 | 65 | 68 | 197 | ¥10,800,000 |
| Ai Miyazato | 67 | 64 | 69 | 200 | 5,280,000 |
| Shiho Ohyama | 66 | 66 | 69 | 201 | 4,200,000 |
| Yuri Fudoh | 68 | 65 | 69 | 202 | 3,600,000 |
| Akiko Fukushima | 69 | 67 | 67 | 203 | 3,000,000 |
| Michie Ohba | 70 | 65 | 70 | 205 | 2,250,000 |
| Yun-Jye Wei | 64 | 69 | 72 | 205 | 2,250,000 |
| Ku Yun Hee | 67 | 70 | 69 | 206 | 1,650,000 |
| Michiko Hattori | 69 | 66 | 71 | 206 | 1,650,000 |
| Keiko Sasaki | 70 | 65 | 72 | 207 | 1,132,000 |
| Rui Kitada | 64 | 71 | 72 | 207 | 1,132,000 |
| Nikki Campbell | 70 | 68 | 69 | 207 | 1,132,000 |
| Miho Koga | 68 | 69 | 71 | 208 | 948,000 |
| Yuka Shiroto | 68 | 71 | 69 | 208 | 948,000 |
| Julie Lu | 72 | 68 | 68 | 208 | 948,000 |
| *Mika Miyazato | 69 | 70 | 69 | 208 | |
| Namika Omata | 68 | 71 | 70 | 209 | 768,000 |
| Ji-Hee Lee | 69 | 68 | 72 | 209 | 768,000 |
| Akane Iijima | 70 | 70 | 69 | 209 | 768,000 |
| Kuniko Maeda | 72 | 67 | 71 | 210 | 618,000 |
| Yuka Irie | 69 | 67 | 74 | 210 | 618,000 |
| Kasumi Fujii | 76 | 66 | 69 | 211 | 558,000 |
| Shin Hyun Ju | 71 | 70 | 70 | 211 | 558,000 |
| Tamie Durdin | 69 | 73 | 69 | 211 | 558,000 |
| Sakura Yokomine | 72 | 71 | 68 | 211 | 558,000 |
| Hikaru Kobayashi | 71 | 71 | 70 | 212 | 510,000 |
| Hiromi Mogi | 69 | 71 | 72 | 212 | 510,000 |
| Mineko Nasu | 71 | 70 | 71 | 212 | 510,000 |
| Kaori Harada | 71 | 67 | 74 | 212 | 510,000 |
| Samantha Head | 68 | 72 | 73 | 213 | 450,000 |
| Hiroko Yamaguchi | 70 | 71 | 72 | 213 | 450,000 |
| Hisako Takeda | 73 | 69 | 71 | 213 | 450,000 |
| Kaori Nakamichi | 67 | 71 | 75 | 213 | 450,000 |
| Nobuko Kizawa | 72 | 69 | 72 | 213 | 450,000 |
| Yukari Horikoshi | 70 | 73 | 70 | 213 | 450,000 |

# New Caterpillar Mitsubishi Ladies

*Daihakone Country Club*, Hakone, Kanagawa
Par 36-37–73; 6,648 yards

August 19-21
purse, ¥60,000,000

|  | SCORES | | | TOTAL | MONEY |
|---|---|---|---|---|---|
| Ai Miyazato | 66 | 75 | 68 | 209 | ¥10,800,000 |
| Jeon Mi Jung | 71 | 71 | 70 | 212 | 4,740,000 |
| Hiromi Mogi | 69 | 72 | 71 | 212 | 4,740,000 |
| Shiho Ohyama | 73 | 68 | 72 | 213 | 3,600,000 |
| Noriko Aso | 71 | 75 | 68 | 214 | 2,700,000 |
| Akiko Fukushima | 67 | 75 | 72 | 214 | 2,700,000 |
| Shin Hyun Ju | 72 | 74 | 69 | 215 | 1,800,000 |
| Keiko Sasaki | 73 | 71 | 71 | 215 | 1,800,000 |
| Sakura Yokomine | 70 | 72 | 73 | 215 | 1,800,000 |
| Ku Yun Hee | 74 | 69 | 73 | 216 | 1,200,000 |
| Michie Ohba | 76 | 74 | 67 | 217 | 1,002,000 |
| Akane Iijima | 74 | 75 | 68 | 217 | 1,002,000 |
| Julie Lu | 73 | 74 | 70 | 217 | 1,002,000 |
| Hiroko Yamaguchi | 72 | 73 | 72 | 217 | 1,002,000 |
| Mitsuko Kawasaki | 72 | 72 | 73 | 217 | 1,002,000 |
| Kaori Harada | 74 | 73 | 71 | 218 | 822,000 |
| Kaori Nakamichi | 72 | 76 | 71 | 219 | 672,000 |
| Yui Kawahara | 74 | 74 | 71 | 219 | 672,000 |
| Junko Omote | 70 | 76 | 73 | 219 | 672,000 |
| Miho Koga | 74 | 71 | 74 | 219 | 672,000 |
| Kozue Azuma | 76 | 73 | 71 | 220 | 546,000 |
| Yuka Shiroto | 76 | 73 | 71 | 220 | 546,000 |
| Lee Eun Hye | 74 | 73 | 73 | 220 | 546,000 |
| Tamie Durdin | 72 | 74 | 74 | 220 | 546,000 |
| Yuriko Ohtsuka | 72 | 72 | 76 | 220 | 546,000 |
| Samantha Head | 74 | 75 | 72 | 221 | 492,000 |
| Young-Me Lee | 75 | 74 | 72 | 221 | 492,000 |
| Rui Kitada | 72 | 76 | 73 | 221 | 492,000 |
| Orie Fujiino | 74 | 72 | 75 | 221 | 492,000 |
| Woo-Soon Ko | 76 | 74 | 72 | 222 | 444,000 |
| Chiaki Nagano | 75 | 75 | 72 | 222 | 444,000 |
| Ai Ogawa | 76 | 73 | 73 | 222 | 444,000 |
| Jeong-Eun Lee | 73 | 73 | 76 | 222 | 444,000 |

# Yonex Ladies

*Yonex Country Club*, Teradomari, Niigata
Par 36-36–72; 6,316 yards

August 26-28
purse, ¥60,000,000

|  | SCORES | | | TOTAL | MONEY |
|---|---|---|---|---|---|
| Shin Hyun Ju | 71 | 68 | 70 | 209 | ¥10,800,000 |
| Yuko Saitoh | 71 | 71 | 68 | 210 | 4,740,000 |
| Midori Yoneyama | 71 | 67 | 72 | 210 | 4,740,000 |
| Yuri Fudoh | 72 | 69 | 70 | 211 | 3,000,000 |
| Atomi Shiota | 69 | 71 | 71 | 211 | 3,000,000 |
| Ai Miyazato | 72 | 68 | 71 | 211 | 3,000,000 |
| Miho Koga | 74 | 70 | 69 | 213 | 2,100,000 |
| Michie Ohba | 74 | 72 | 68 | 214 | 1,410,000 |
| Yukari Baba | 73 | 70 | 71 | 214 | 1,410,000 |
| Mihoko Takahashi | 74 | 68 | 72 | 214 | 1,410,000 |
| Mari Katayama | 69 | 72 | 73 | 214 | 1,410,000 |

| | SCORES | | | TOTAL | MONEY |
|---|---|---|---|---|---|
| Mineko Nasu | 73 | 71 | 71 | 215 | 930,000 |
| Nobuko Kizawa | 74 | 70 | 71 | 215 | 930,000 |
| Sakura Yokomine | 76 | 68 | 71 | 215 | 930,000 |
| Mitsuko Kawasaki | 73 | 70 | 72 | 215 | 930,000 |
| Lee Eun Hye | 74 | 69 | 72 | 215 | 930,000 |
| Hiromi Mogi | 73 | 69 | 73 | 215 | 930,000 |
| Ji-Hee Lee | 74 | 73 | 70 | 217 | 618,000 |
| Yoko Tsuchiya | 75 | 71 | 71 | 217 | 618,000 |
| Yun-Jye Wei | 74 | 71 | 72 | 217 | 618,000 |
| Misato Nishikawa | 73 | 71 | 73 | 217 | 618,000 |
| Kaori Harada | 75 | 69 | 73 | 217 | 618,000 |
| Mayumi Hirase | 71 | 69 | 77 | 217 | 618,000 |
| Yuriko Ohtsuka | 72 | 74 | 72 | 218 | 504,000 |
| Kuniko Maeda | 72 | 74 | 72 | 218 | 504,000 |
| Mikiyo Nishizuka | 74 | 72 | 72 | 218 | 504,000 |
| Yui Kawahara | 74 | 72 | 72 | 218 | 504,000 |
| *Maiko Wakabayashi | 73 | 74 | 71 | 218 | |
| Yoko Yamagishi | 75 | 73 | 70 | 218 | 504,000 |
| Shiho Ohyama | 76 | 72 | 70 | 218 | 504,000 |
| Junko Omote | 76 | 72 | 70 | 218 | 504,000 |
| Yuka Shiroto | 72 | 76 | 70 | 218 | 504,000 |
| Kasumi Fujii | 72 | 76 | 70 | 218 | 504,000 |

## Golf 5 Ladies

*Mizunami Country Club*, Gifu
Par 36-36–72; 6,469 yards

September 1-4
purse, ¥50,000,000

| | SCORES | | | TOTAL | MONEY |
|---|---|---|---|---|---|
| Yuri Fudoh | 72 | 69 | 64 | 205 | ¥9,000,000 |
| Yun-Jye Wei | 70 | 69 | 68 | 207 | 3,633,333 |
| Shin Hyun Ju | 71 | 68 | 68 | 207 | 3,633,333 |
| Akane Iijima | 67 | 69 | 71 | 207 | 3,633,333 |
| Fuki Kido | 73 | 69 | 67 | 209 | 1,937,500 |
| Noriko Aso | 70 | 70 | 69 | 209 | 1,937,500 |
| Sakura Yokomine | 70 | 70 | 69 | 209 | 1,937,500 |
| Ji-Hee Lee | 66 | 70 | 73 | 209 | 1,937,500 |
| Miho Koga | 71 | 72 | 67 | 210 | 1,060,000 |
| Hiroko Yamaguchi | 68 | 74 | 68 | 210 | 1,060,000 |
| Hikaru Kobayashi | 70 | 69 | 71 | 210 | 1,060,000 |
| Mayumi Murai | 73 | 71 | 67 | 211 | 830,000 |
| Yukari Baba | 66 | 74 | 71 | 211 | 830,000 |
| Ikuyo Shiotani | 69 | 70 | 72 | 211 | 830,000 |
| Ji-Yeon Han | 72 | 72 | 68 | 212 | 680,000 |
| Yun-Hee Ku | 70 | 72 | 70 | 212 | 680,000 |
| Jeon Mi Jung | 76 | 69 | 67 | 212 | 680,000 |
| Toshimi Kimura | 70 | 72 | 71 | 213 | 555,000 |
| Akiko Fukushima | 71 | 68 | 74 | 213 | 555,000 |
| Mikiyo Nishizuka | 73 | 72 | 69 | 214 | 465,000 |
| Namika Omata | 72 | 69 | 73 | 214 | 465,000 |
| Yui Kawahara | 73 | 68 | 73 | 214 | 465,000 |
| Chiaki Takahashi | 71 | 69 | 74 | 214 | 465,000 |
| Mari Katayama | 71 | 73 | 71 | 215 | 410,000 |
| Shiho Ohyama | 74 | 71 | 70 | 215 | 410,000 |
| Miyuki Shimabukuro | 69 | 73 | 73 | 215 | 410,000 |
| Ai Ogawa | 76 | 66 | 73 | 215 | 410,000 |
| Eriko Moriyama | 72 | 70 | 73 | 215 | 410,000 |

| | SCORES | | | TOTAL | MONEY |
|---|---|---|---|---|---|
| Kuniko Maeda | 72 | 69 | 74 | 215 | 410,000 |
| Kaori Higo | 71 | 75 | 69 | 215 | 410,000 |

## Japan LPGA Championship

*Meishin Yokaichi Country Club,* Shiga
Par 36-36–72; 6,509 yards

September 8-11
purse, ¥70,000,000

| | SCORES | | | | TOTAL | MONEY |
|---|---|---|---|---|---|---|
| Yuri Fudoh | 74 | 67 | 71 | 66 | 278 | ¥12,600,000 |
| Ai Miyazato | 71 | 69 | 71 | 69 | 280 | 6,160,000 |
| Sakura Yokomine | 71 | 70 | 70 | 71 | 282 | 4,550,000 |
| Shiho Ohyama | 67 | 76 | 67 | 72 | 282 | 4,550,000 |
| Kasumi Fujii | 70 | 74 | 71 | 68 | 283 | 3,500,000 |
| Shin Hyun Ju | 73 | 70 | 72 | 70 | 285 | 2,800,000 |
| Tomomi Hirose | 72 | 72 | 70 | 72 | 286 | 2,450,000 |
| Toshimi Kimura | 71 | 69 | 77 | 71 | 288 | 1,925,000 |
| Midori Yoneyama | 74 | 72 | 70 | 72 | 288 | 1,925,000 |
| Jeong Yun-Joo | 66 | 78 | 75 | 70 | 289 | 1,400,000 |
| Kaori Nakamichi | 73 | 77 | 76 | 64 | 290 | 1,190,000 |
| Jeon Mi Jung | 72 | 73 | 72 | 73 | 290 | 1,190,000 |
| Ji-Hee Lee | 72 | 74 | 70 | 74 | 290 | 1,190,000 |
| Kuniko Maeda | 73 | 74 | 74 | 70 | 291 | 1,015,000 |
| Yun-Hee Ku | 71 | 73 | 74 | 73 | 291 | 1,015,000 |
| Lee Eun Hye | 77 | 74 | 73 | 68 | 292 | 770,000 |
| Akiko Fukushima | 73 | 73 | 75 | 71 | 292 | 770,000 |
| Yun-Jye Wei | 70 | 73 | 77 | 72 | 292 | 770,000 |
| Mikiyo Nishizuka | 76 | 71 | 73 | 72 | 292 | 770,000 |
| Michiko Hattori | 73 | 71 | 75 | 73 | 292 | 770,000 |
| Saiki Fujita | 75 | 73 | 75 | 70 | 293 | 602,000 |
| Itsumi Okada | 76 | 71 | 73 | 73 | 293 | 602,000 |
| Michie Ohba | 76 | 74 | 69 | 74 | 293 | 602,000 |
| Yui Kawahara | 74 | 70 | 79 | 71 | 294 | 560,000 |
| Lim Sun Wok | 77 | 71 | 75 | 71 | 294 | 560,000 |
| Mihoko Takahashi | 74 | 74 | 73 | 73 | 294 | 560,000 |
| Rui Kitada | 72 | 76 | 73 | 74 | 295 | 532,000 |
| Junko Omote | 77 | 75 | 74 | 70 | 296 | 504,000 |
| Mineko Nasu | 73 | 76 | 77 | 70 | 296 | 504,000 |
| Kanna Takanashi | 72 | 75 | 78 | 71 | 296 | 504,000 |

## Munsingwear Ladies Tokai Classic

*Ryosen Golf Club,* Inabe, Mie
Par 36-36–72; 6,475 yards

September 16-18
purse, ¥60,000,000

| | SCORES | | | TOTAL | MONEY |
|---|---|---|---|---|---|
| Shiho Ohyama | 68 | 72 | 66 | 206 | ¥10,800,000 |
| Kaori Higo | 67 | 70 | 72 | 209 | 5,280,000 |
| Mikiyo Nishizuka | 73 | 68 | 70 | 211 | 3,900,000 |
| Midori Yoneyama | 74 | 69 | 68 | 211 | 3,900,000 |
| Akane Iijima | 69 | 74 | 69 | 212 | 2,500,000 |
| Michiko Mitsui | 71 | 70 | 71 | 212 | 2,500,000 |
| Yuko Saitoh | 71 | 73 | 68 | 212 | 2,500,000 |
| Miho Koga | 70 | 70 | 73 | 213 | 1,398,000 |

| | SCORES | | | TOTAL | MONEY |
|---|---|---|---|---|---|
| Rui Kitada | 75 | 70 | 68 | 213 | 1,398,000 |
| Mie Nakata | 70 | 72 | 71 | 213 | 1,398,000 |
| Hiromi Mogi | 69 | 71 | 73 | 213 | 1,398,000 |
| Yui Kawahara | 71 | 71 | 72 | 214 | 942,000 |
| Yoko Yamagishi | 71 | 72 | 71 | 214 | 942,000 |
| Yuka Shiroto | 70 | 72 | 72 | 214 | 942,000 |
| Michie Ohba | 71 | 70 | 73 | 214 | 942,000 |
| Fuki Kido | 73 | 69 | 73 | 215 | 650,000 |
| Chieko Amanuma | 75 | 69 | 71 | 215 | 650,000 |
| Yuriko Ohtsuka | 72 | 70 | 73 | 215 | 650,000 |
| Kaori Harada | 73 | 70 | 72 | 215 | 650,000 |
| Yuri Fudoh | 68 | 75 | 72 | 215 | 650,000 |
| Woo-Soon Ko | 76 | 68 | 71 | 215 | 650,000 |
| Jeon Mi Jung | 71 | 71 | 74 | 216 | 498,000 |
| Kuniko Maeda | 70 | 74 | 72 | 216 | 498,000 |
| Keiko Sasaki | 74 | 71 | 71 | 216 | 498,000 |
| Kasumi Fujii | 75 | 69 | 72 | 216 | 498,000 |
| Junko Omote | 73 | 73 | 70 | 216 | 498,000 |
| Aki Nakano | 73 | 67 | 76 | 216 | 498,000 |
| Yun-Hee Ku | 74 | 72 | 71 | 217 | 408,000 |
| Yukari Baba | 73 | 72 | 72 | 217 | 408,000 |
| Ae-Sook Kim | 74 | 71 | 72 | 217 | 408,000 |
| Shin Sora | 70 | 73 | 74 | 217 | 408,000 |
| Lu Ya Huei | 70 | 75 | 72 | 217 | 408,000 |
| Toshimi Kimura | 68 | 74 | 75 | 217 | 408,000 |
| Mihoko Takahashi | 72 | 71 | 74 | 217 | 408,000 |
| Junko Yasui | 71 | 71 | 75 | 217 | 408,000 |
| Noriko Aso | 74 | 71 | 72 | 217 | 408,000 |

## Miyagi TV Cup Dunlop Ladies Open

*Rifu Golf Club,* Miyagi
Par 36-36–72; 6,380 yards

September 22-25
purse, ¥60,000,000

| | SCORES | | | TOTAL | MONEY |
|---|---|---|---|---|---|
| Sakura Yokomine | 70 | 72 | 71 | 213 | ¥10,800,000 |
| Jeon Mi Jung | 69 | 71 | 73 | 213 | 5,280,000 |
| (Yokomine defeated Jung on second playoff hole.) | | | | | |
| Ji-Hee Lee | 72 | 72 | 71 | 215 | 4,200,000 |
| Nobuko Kizawa | 67 | 74 | 75 | 216 | 2,580,000 |
| Michiko Hattori | 69 | 73 | 74 | 216 | 2,580,000 |
| Kasumi Fujii | 73 | 71 | 72 | 216 | 2,580,000 |
| Shiho Ohyama | 72 | 71 | 73 | 216 | 2,580,000 |
| Yui Kawahara | 73 | 69 | 74 | 216 | 2,580,000 |
| Woo-Soon Ko | 70 | 74 | 73 | 217 | 1,221,000 |
| Kaori Harada | 70 | 71 | 76 | 217 | 1,221,000 |
| Eriko Moriyama | 77 | 67 | 73 | 217 | 1,221,000 |
| Akane Iijima | 71 | 74 | 72 | 217 | 1,221,000 |
| Hiroko Yamaguchi | 76 | 72 | 70 | 218 | 1,002,000 |
| Hikaru Kobayashi | 74 | 71 | 74 | 219 | 942,000 |
| *Kumiko Kaneda | 73 | 75 | 71 | 219 | |
| *Erika Kikuchi | 70 | 72 | 77 | 219 | |
| Ae-Sook Kim | 69 | 74 | 77 | 220 | 822,000 |
| Mikiyo Nishizuka | 74 | 71 | 75 | 220 | 822,000 |
| Kaori Nakamichi | 71 | 75 | 74 | 220 | 822,000 |
| Yuko Saitoh | 72 | 75 | 74 | 221 | 582,000 |
| Chihiro Nakajima | 74 | 72 | 75 | 221 | 582,000 |

| | SCORES | | | TOTAL | MONEY |
|---|---|---|---|---|---|
| Mie Nakata | 72 | 74 | 75 | 221 | 582,000 |
| Nikki Campbell | 72 | 73 | 76 | 221 | 582,000 |
| Junko Yasui | 73 | 73 | 75 | 221 | 582,000 |
| Junko Omote | 75 | 70 | 76 | 221 | 582,000 |
| Yuriko Ohtsuka | 73 | 71 | 77 | 221 | 582,000 |
| Masaki Maeda | 72 | 73 | 76 | 221 | 582,000 |

## Japan Women's Open

*Totsuka Country Club*, Kanagawa
Par 36-36–72; 6,453 yards

September 29-October 2
purse, ¥70,000,000

| | SCORES | | | | TOTAL | MONEY |
|---|---|---|---|---|---|---|
| Ai Miyazato | 69 | 69 | 72 | 73 | 283 | ¥14,000,000 |
| Akiko Fukushima | 73 | 70 | 73 | 72 | 288 | 7,700,000 |
| Kasumi Fujii | 69 | 73 | 77 | 71 | 290 | 4,497,500 |
| Yoko Inoue | 72 | 70 | 76 | 72 | 290 | 4,497,500 |
| Shinobu Moromizata | 72 | 72 | 75 | 72 | 291 | 2,940,000 |
| Midori Yoneyama | 76 | 72 | 74 | 72 | 294 | 2,340,000 |
| Yuko Saitoh | 74 | 76 | 78 | 67 | 295 | 1,759,000 |
| Nikki Campbell | 76 | 74 | 75 | 70 | 295 | 1,759,000 |
| Mitsuko Kawasaki | 73 | 76 | 74 | 72 | 295 | 1,759,000 |
| Mikiyo Nishizuka | 79 | 73 | 71 | 72 | 295 | 1,759,000 |
| Yui Kawahara | 77 | 74 | 72 | 73 | 296 | 1,021,500 |
| Hsiu-Feng Tseng | 74 | 72 | 76 | 74 | 296 | 1,021,500 |
| Yuriko Ohtsuka | 74 | 72 | 76 | 74 | 296 | 1,021,500 |
| Kaori Higo | 72 | 75 | 75 | 74 | 296 | 1,021,500 |
| Shiho Ohyama | 70 | 75 | 76 | 75 | 296 | 1,021,500 |
| Ji-Hee Lee | 71 | 75 | 73 | 77 | 296 | 1,021,500 |
| Yun-Jye Wei | 74 | 76 | 75 | 72 | 297 | 739,000 |
| Mizuho Ozawa | 77 | 74 | 73 | 73 | 297 | 739,000 |
| Miho Koga | 76 | 75 | 73 | 73 | 297 | 739,000 |
| *Kumiko Kaneda | 75 | 78 | 70 | 74 | 297 | |
| Yuri Fudoh | 78 | 71 | 72 | 77 | 298 | 669,000 |
| Keiko Sasaki | 76 | 75 | 74 | 74 | 299 | 609,000 |
| Kaori Nakamichi | 74 | 72 | 78 | 75 | 299 | 609,000 |
| Yun-Hee Ku | 72 | 74 | 76 | 77 | 299 | 609,000 |
| Hiroko Fujishima | 72 | 74 | 76 | 77 | 299 | 609,000 |
| Hiroko Yamaguchi | 74 | 72 | 75 | 78 | 299 | 609,000 |
| Michiko Mitsui | 78 | 74 | 76 | 72 | 300 | 550,000 |
| Lee Eun Hye | 76 | 74 | 77 | 73 | 300 | 550,000 |
| Mayumi Murai | 73 | 73 | 78 | 76 | 300 | 550,000 |
| Michie Ohba | 75 | 76 | 72 | 77 | 300 | 550,000 |

## Sankyo Ladies Open

*Akagi Country Club*, Niisato, Gunma
Par 36-36–72; 6,462 yards

October 7-9
purse, ¥60,000,000

| | SCORES | | | TOTAL | MONEY |
|---|---|---|---|---|---|
| Ji-Hee Lee | 67 | 68 | 73 | 208 | ¥10,800,000 |
| Sakura Yokomine | 71 | 70 | 68 | 209 | 4,740,000 |
| Yuri Fudoh | 63 | 73 | 73 | 209 | 4,740,000 |
| Tomishi Kimura | 69 | 68 | 73 | 210 | 3,300,000 |

| | SCORES | | | TOTAL | MONEY |
|---|---|---|---|---|---|
| Hikaru Kobayashi | 67 | 66 | 77 | 210 | 3,300,000 |
| Mikiyo Nishizuka | 70 | 70 | 71 | 211 | 2,400,000 |
| Kaori Higo | 73 | 69 | 70 | 212 | 1,800,000 |
| Kuniko Maeda | 70 | 70 | 72 | 212 | 1,800,000 |
| Hiromi Mogi | 68 | 69 | 75 | 212 | 1,800,000 |
| Akane Iijima | 75 | 68 | 70 | 213 | 1,140,000 |
| Miho Koga | 74 | 67 | 72 | 213 | 1,140,000 |
| Yuriko Ohtsuka | 70 | 71 | 72 | 213 | 1,140,000 |
| Hiroko Yamaguchi | 73 | 71 | 70 | 214 | 960,000 |
| Yukari Baba | 72 | 69 | 73 | 214 | 960,000 |
| Rui Kitada | 70 | 70 | 74 | 214 | 960,000 |
| Saya Manabe | 73 | 71 | 71 | 215 | 810,000 |
| Jeon Mi Jung | 71 | 71 | 73 | 215 | 810,000 |
| Hiromi Takesue | 72 | 72 | 72 | 216 | 642,000 |
| Shiho Ohyama | 72 | 71 | 73 | 216 | 642,000 |
| Mie Nakata | 71 | 71 | 74 | 216 | 642,000 |
| Yui Kawahara | 68 | 71 | 77 | 216 | 642,000 |
| Yoko Yamagishi | 72 | 74 | 71 | 217 | 564,000 |
| Fuki Kido | 71 | 72 | 74 | 217 | 564,000 |
| Akiko Fukushima | 76 | 66 | 75 | 217 | 564,000 |
| Mari Katayama | 73 | 72 | 73 | 218 | 522,000 |
| Samantha Head | 74 | 70 | 74 | 218 | 522,000 |
| Yun-Hee Ku | 69 | 71 | 78 | 218 | 522,000 |
| Mineko Nasu | 69 | 68 | 81 | 218 | 522,000 |
| Lim Sun Wok | 77 | 69 | 73 | 219 | 462,000 |
| Kaori Suzuki | 71 | 74 | 74 | 219 | 462,000 |
| Kaori Harada | 73 | 72 | 74 | 219 | 462,000 |
| Keiko Sasaki | 74 | 70 | 75 | 219 | 462,000 |
| Mizuho Ozawa | 71 | 72 | 76 | 219 | 462,000 |
| Yayoi Arasaki | 70 | 69 | 80 | 219 | 462,000 |

## Fujitsu Ladies

*Tokyu Seven Hundred Club*, Chiba
Par 36-36–72; 6,567 yards

October 14-16
purse, ¥60,000,000

| | SCORES | | | TOTAL | MONEY |
|---|---|---|---|---|---|
| Yuri Fudoh | 68 | 65 | 71 | 204 | ¥10,800,000 |
| Sakura Yokomine | 69 | 68 | 70 | 207 | 5,280,000 |
| Mikiyo Nishizuka | 76 | 64 | 70 | 210 | 4,200,000 |
| Michiko Hattori | 70 | 70 | 72 | 212 | 3,300,000 |
| Yayoi Arasaki | 76 | 66 | 70 | 212 | 3,300,000 |
| Yui Kawahara | 73 | 68 | 72 | 213 | 1,689,000 |
| Akane Iijima | 71 | 69 | 73 | 213 | 1,689,000 |
| Kasumi Fujii | 71 | 72 | 70 | 213 | 1,689,000 |
| Midori Yoneyama | 68 | 72 | 73 | 213 | 1,689,000 |
| Nobuko Kizawa | 72 | 71 | 70 | 213 | 1,689,000 |
| Shiho Ohyama | 73 | 68 | 72 | 213 | 1,689,000 |
| Orie Fujino | 70 | 72 | 72 | 214 | 1,014,000 |
| Ai Miyazato | 71 | 72 | 71 | 214 | 1,014,000 |
| Lim Sun Wok | 71 | 73 | 70 | 214 | 1,014,000 |
| Hiroko Yamaguchi | 75 | 67 | 73 | 215 | 864,000 |
| Jeon Mi Jung | 72 | 71 | 72 | 215 | 864,000 |
| Tamie Durdin | 72 | 73 | 71 | 216 | 714,000 |
| Atomi Shiota | 71 | 69 | 76 | 216 | 714,000 |
| Mizuho Ozawa | 70 | 73 | 73 | 216 | 714,000 |
| Ji-Yeon Han | 74 | 68 | 75 | 217 | 552,000 |

| | SCORES | | | TOTAL | MONEY |
|---|---|---|---|---|---|
| Young-Me Lee | 72 | 74 | 71 | 217 | 552,000 |
| Yuko Saitoh | 73 | 70 | 74 | 217 | 552,000 |
| Kang Yeo-Jin | 72 | 69 | 76 | 217 | 552,000 |
| Ok-Hee Ku | 73 | 71 | 73 | 217 | 552,000 |
| Kaori Nakamichi | 74 | 71 | 72 | 217 | 552,000 |
| Namika Omata | 71 | 74 | 72 | 217 | 552,000 |
| Yukari Baba | 72 | 72 | 73 | 217 | 552,000 |
| Samantha Head | 72 | 72 | 74 | 218 | 462,000 |
| Yuka Irie | 73 | 72 | 73 | 218 | 462,000 |
| Lee Eun Hye | 76 | 68 | 74 | 218 | 462,000 |
| Yuki Yamana | 75 | 70 | 73 | 218 | 462,000 |
| Yuki Takeda | 71 | 71 | 76 | 218 | 462,000 |
| Mihoko Takahashi | 72 | 72 | 74 | 218 | 462,000 |
| Jeong-Eun Lee | 75 | 71 | 72 | 218 | 462,000 |

## Masters Golf Club Ladies

*Masters Golf Club*, Hyogo
Par 36-36–72; 6,444 yards

October 21-23
purse, ¥120,000,000

| | SCORES | | | TOTAL | MONEY |
|---|---|---|---|---|---|
| Paula Creamer | 71 | 69 | 72 | 212 | ¥22,140,000 |
| Chieko Amanuma | 68 | 74 | 70 | 212 | 10,824,000 |
| (Creamer defeated Amanuma on first playoff hole.) | | | | | |
| Naoko Takasaki | 70 | 72 | 72 | 214 | 8,610,000 |
| Shinobu Moromizato | 70 | 74 | 71 | 215 | 4,920,000 |
| Julie Lu | 68 | 75 | 72 | 215 | 4,920,000 |
| Kyoko Kadokawa | 69 | 74 | 72 | 215 | 4,920,000 |
| Yuri Fudoh | 70 | 72 | 73 | 215 | 4,920,000 |
| Hiromi Mogi | 70 | 73 | 72 | 215 | 4,920,000 |
| Tamie Durdin | 66 | 76 | 73 | 215 | 4,920,000 |
| Jeon Mi Jung | 75 | 73 | 68 | 216 | 2,460,000 |
| Jeong Yun-Joo | 70 | 73 | 74 | 217 | 2,164,800 |
| Shiho Ohyama | 71 | 75 | 71 | 217 | 2,164,800 |
| Keiko Sasaki | 77 | 71 | 69 | 217 | 2,164,800 |
| Ai Miyazato | 73 | 71 | 74 | 218 | 1,734,300 |
| Hiroko Yamaguchi | 71 | 75 | 72 | 218 | 1,734,300 |
| Atomi Shiota | 72 | 72 | 74 | 218 | 1,734,300 |
| Toshimi Kimura | 71 | 72 | 75 | 218 | 1,734,300 |
| Yun-Jye Wei | 69 | 77 | 73 | 219 | 1,198,371 |
| Ayako Uehara | 70 | 72 | 77 | 219 | 1,198,371 |
| Yuko Saitoh | 70 | 76 | 73 | 219 | 1,198,371 |
| Midori Yoneyama | 73 | 72 | 74 | 219 | 1,198,371 |
| Hiromi Takesue | 74 | 73 | 72 | 219 | 1,198,371 |
| Hikaru Kobayashi | 72 | 74 | 73 | 219 | 1,198,371 |
| Mineko Nasu | 75 | 73 | 71 | 219 | 1,198,371 |
| Samantha Head | 75 | 69 | 76 | 220 | 996,300 |
| Masaki Maeda | 71 | 74 | 75 | 220 | 996,300 |
| Grace Park | 74 | 72 | 74 | 220 | 996,300 |
| Akiko Fukushima | 77 | 68 | 75 | 220 | 996,300 |
| Riko Higashio | 72 | 77 | 71 | 220 | 996,300 |
| Junko Omote | 73 | 75 | 72 | 220 | 996,300 |

## Hisako Higuchi IDC Otsukakagu Ladies

*Musashigoaka Golf Club*, Saitama
Par 36-36–72; 6,513 yards

October 28-30
purse, ¥70,000,000

| | SCORES | | | TOTAL | MONEY |
|---|---|---|---|---|---|
| Ai Miyazato | 67 | 68 | 67 | 202 | ¥12,600,000 |
| Julie Lu | 71 | 68 | 70 | 209 | 4,690,000 |
| Kaori Higo | 71 | 68 | 70 | 209 | 4,690,000 |
| Nikki Campbell | 72 | 70 | 67 | 209 | 4,690,000 |
| Shinobu Moromizato | 75 | 66 | 68 | 209 | 4,690,000 |
| Shiho Ohyama | 73 | 68 | 69 | 210 | 2,800,000 |
| Jeong-Eun Lee | 70 | 70 | 71 | 211 | 1,925,000 |
| Ji-Yeon Han | 73 | 69 | 69 | 211 | 1,925,000 |
| Yukari Baba | 71 | 70 | 70 | 211 | 1,925,000 |
| Keiko Sasaki | 68 | 72 | 71 | 211 | 1,925,000 |
| Yun-Jye Wei | 73 | 71 | 68 | 212 | 1,260,000 |
| Kuniko Maeda | 74 | 69 | 69 | 212 | 1,260,000 |
| Samantha Head | 72 | 69 | 72 | 213 | 945,000 |
| Miho Koga | 69 | 74 | 70 | 213 | 945,000 |
| Hiromi Mogi | 72 | 72 | 69 | 213 | 945,000 |
| Yuko Saitoh | 74 | 70 | 69 | 213 | 945,000 |
| Hikaru Kobayashi | 70 | 71 | 72 | 213 | 945,000 |
| Kaori Nakamichi | 70 | 73 | 70 | 213 | 945,000 |
| Misato Nishikawa | 71 | 69 | 73 | 213 | 945,000 |
| Yuka Irie | 71 | 73 | 70 | 214 | 644,000 |
| Woo-Soon Ko | 70 | 72 | 72 | 214 | 644,000 |
| Jeong Yun-Joo | 73 | 72 | 69 | 214 | 644,000 |
| Nobuko Kizawa | 73 | 69 | 72 | 214 | 644,000 |
| Junko Omote | 73 | 72 | 70 | 215 | 560,000 |
| Shin Hyun Ju | 72 | 70 | 73 | 215 | 560,000 |
| Mineko Nasu | 76 | 68 | 71 | 215 | 560,000 |
| Jeon Mi Jung | 71 | 73 | 71 | 215 | 560,000 |
| Yui Kawahara | 71 | 71 | 73 | 215 | 560,000 |
| Naoko Takasaki | 73 | 72 | 70 | 215 | 560,000 |
| Sakura Yokomine | 69 | 73 | 73 | 215 | 560,000 |
| Mie Nakata | 69 | 73 | 73 | 215 | 560,000 |

## Mizuno Classic

*Seta Golf Club, Kita Course*, Shiga
Par 36-36–72; 6,450 yards

November 4-6
purse, ¥110,000,000

| | SCORES | | | TOTAL | MONEY |
|---|---|---|---|---|---|
| Annika Sorenstam | 64 | 67 | 64 | 195 | ¥17,550,000 |
| Jennifer Rosales | 67 | 65 | 66 | 198 | 10,610,847 |
| Yuri Fudoh | 71 | 65 | 64 | 200 | 6,148,350 |
| Sophie Gustafson | 67 | 67 | 66 | 200 | 6,148,350 |
| Young Kim | 63 | 67 | 70 | 200 | 6,148,350 |
| Meena Lee | 67 | 69 | 66 | 202 | 3,359,889 |
| Karine Icher | 71 | 64 | 67 | 202 | 3,359,889 |
| Jeong Jang | 66 | 67 | 69 | 202 | 3,359,889 |
| Karrie Webb | 67 | 66 | 71 | 204 | 2,585,232 |
| Wendy Doolan | 70 | 71 | 64 | 205 | 2,051,829 |
| Ai Miyazato | 71 | 68 | 66 | 205 | 2,051,829 |
| Shi Hyun Ahn | 69 | 68 | 68 | 205 | 2,051,829 |
| Reilley Rankin | 69 | 67 | 69 | 205 | 2,051,829 |

| | SCORES | | | TOTAL | MONEY |
|---|---|---|---|---|---|
| Shiho Ohyama | 65 | 69 | 71 | 205 | 2,051,829 |
| Kasumi Fujii | 70 | 69 | 67 | 206 | 1,556,919 |
| Soo-Yun Kang | 67 | 70 | 69 | 206 | 1,556,919 |
| Silvia Cavalleri | 70 | 66 | 70 | 206 | 1,556,919 |
| Midori Yoneyama | 68 | 68 | 70 | 206 | 1,556,919 |
| Maria Hjorth | 70 | 69 | 68 | 207 | 1,382,589 |
| Mi Hyun Kim | 69 | 72 | 67 | 208 | 1,177,839 |
| Junko Omote | 69 | 70 | 69 | 208 | 1,177,839 |
| Miho Koga | 68 | 70 | 70 | 208 | 1,177,839 |
| Il Mi Chung | 66 | 72 | 70 | 208 | 1,177,839 |
| Candie Kung | 70 | 67 | 71 | 208 | 1,177,839 |
| Gloria Park | 68 | 69 | 71 | 208 | 1,177,839 |
| Sherri Steinhauer | 70 | 66 | 72 | 208 | 1,177,839 |
| Sakura Yokomine | 68 | 67 | 73 | 208 | 1,177,839 |
| Kaori Higo | 69 | 70 | 70 | 209 | 967,239 |
| Yun Hee Ku | 67 | 69 | 73 | 209 | 967,239 |
| Lorie Kane | 73 | 68 | 69 | 210 | 842,400 |
| A.J. Eathorne | 72 | 69 | 69 | 210 | 842,400 |
| Grace Park | 68 | 70 | 72 | 210 | 842,400 |
| Sung Ah Yim | 67 | 71 | 72 | 210 | 842,400 |
| Mikiyo Nishizuka | 68 | 69 | 73 | 210 | 842,400 |

## Itoen Ladies

*Great Island Club*, Chonan, Chiba
Par 36-36–72; 6,581 yards

November 11-13
purse, ¥70,000,000

| | SCORES | | | TOTAL | MONEY |
|---|---|---|---|---|---|
| Yuri Fudoh | 71 | 71 | 67 | 209 | ¥12,600,000 |
| Yuko Saitoh | 71 | 69 | 71 | 211 | 5,530,000 |
| Hiroko Yamaguchi | 72 | 72 | 67 | 211 | 5,530,000 |
| Shiho Ohyama | 71 | 75 | 67 | 213 | 4,200,000 |
| Noriko Aso | 73 | 69 | 72 | 214 | 3,150,000 |
| Hiromi Mogi | 69 | 74 | 71 | 214 | 3,150,000 |
| Shin Hyun Ju | 74 | 68 | 73 | 215 | 2,450,000 |
| Jeong Yun-Joo | 73 | 73 | 70 | 216 | 1,565,200 |
| Atomi Shiota | 71 | 71 | 74 | 216 | 1,565,200 |
| Mie Nakata | 72 | 73 | 71 | 216 | 1,565,200 |
| Jeong-Eun Lee | 74 | 68 | 74 | 216 | 1,565,200 |
| Yun-Hee Ku | 76 | 71 | 69 | 216 | 1,565,200 |
| Ji-Hee Lee | 71 | 70 | 76 | 217 | 1,148,000 |
| Ok-Hee Ku | 71 | 72 | 74 | 217 | 1,148,000 |
| Chihiro Nakajima | 72 | 74 | 72 | 218 | 868,000 |
| Toshimi Kimura | 74 | 72 | 72 | 218 | 868,000 |
| Mitsuko Kawasaki | 74 | 73 | 71 | 218 | 868,000 |
| Mikiyo Nishizuka | 73 | 71 | 74 | 218 | 868,000 |
| Seiko Watanabe | 74 | 75 | 69 | 218 | 868,000 |
| Michiko Hattori | 74 | 73 | 71 | 218 | 868,000 |
| Samantha Head | 72 | 73 | 74 | 219 | 637,000 |
| Nikki Campbell | 70 | 74 | 75 | 219 | 637,000 |
| Mineko Nasu | 70 | 76 | 73 | 219 | 637,000 |
| Akane Ohshiro | 72 | 74 | 73 | 219 | 637,000 |
| Tomoko Kusakabe | 77 | 72 | 70 | 219 | 637,000 |
| Akiko Fukushima | 76 | 73 | 70 | 219 | 637,000 |
| Tamie Durdin | 71 | 73 | 75 | 219 | 637,000 |
| Mari Katayama | 75 | 73 | 72 | 220 | 560,000 |
| Yui Kawahara | 72 | 73 | 75 | 220 | 560,000 |

| | SCORES | | | TOTAL | MONEY |
|---|---|---|---|---|---|
| Ae-Sook Kim | 74 | 73 | 73 | 220 | 560,000 |
| Yuriko Ohtsuka | 70 | 74 | 76 | 220 | 560,000 |

## Daioseishi Elleair Ladies Open

*Elleair Golf Club,* Ehime, Kagawa
Par 36-36–72; 6,460 yards

November 18-20
purse, ¥80,000,000

| | SCORES | | | TOTAL | MONEY |
|---|---|---|---|---|---|
| Ai Miyazato | 69 | 70 | 65 | 204 | ¥14,400,000 |
| Shiho Ohyama | 70 | 70 | 69 | 209 | 5,866,666 |
| Woo-Soon Ko | 69 | 69 | 71 | 209 | 5,866,666 |
| Kasumi Fujii | 69 | 70 | 70 | 209 | 5,866,666 |
| Ji-Hee Lee | 68 | 71 | 71 | 210 | 4,000,000 |
| Hiroko Yamaguchi | 69 | 72 | 72 | 213 | 2,600,000 |
| Nobuko Kizawa | 72 | 71 | 70 | 213 | 2,600,000 |
| Yukari Baba | 74 | 68 | 71 | 213 | 2,600,000 |
| Yuri Fudoh | 75 | 68 | 70 | 213 | 2,600,000 |
| Hiromi Mogi | 73 | 73 | 68 | 214 | 1,406,666 |
| Lee Eun Hye | 70 | 72 | 72 | 214 | 1,406,666 |
| Misato Nishikawa | 71 | 70 | 73 | 214 | 1,406,666 |
| Hsiu-Feng Tseng | 70 | 70 | 74 | 214 | 1,406,666 |
| Orie Fujino | 71 | 73 | 70 | 214 | 1,406,666 |
| Yun-Jye Wei | 71 | 71 | 72 | 214 | 1,406,666 |
| Yuka Irie | 70 | 67 | 78 | 215 | 1,008,000 |
| Rui Kitada | 69 | 74 | 72 | 215 | 1,008,000 |
| Shin Hyun Ju | 74 | 72 | 69 | 215 | 1,008,000 |
| Jeon Mi Jung | 77 | 65 | 73 | 215 | 1,008,000 |
| Michiko Hattori | 72 | 72 | 72 | 216 | 760,000 |
| Hiromi Takesue | 71 | 72 | 73 | 216 | 760,000 |
| Mayumi Shimomura | 73 | 69 | 74 | 216 | 760,000 |
| Miho Koga | 70 | 72 | 74 | 216 | 760,000 |
| Mineko Nasu | 70 | 75 | 71 | 216 | 760,000 |
| Kuniko Maeda | 71 | 72 | 73 | 216 | 760,000 |
| Chieko Amanuma | 72 | 70 | 74 | 216 | 760,000 |
| Mitsuko Kawasaki | 72 | 71 | 74 | 217 | 662,400 |
| Mie Nakata | 72 | 69 | 76 | 217 | 662,400 |
| Midori Yoneyama | 67 | 77 | 73 | 217 | 662,400 |
| Miyuki Shimabukuro | 74 | 72 | 71 | 217 | 662,400 |
| Toshimi Kimura | 70 | 75 | 72 | 217 | 662,400 |

## Japan LPGA Tour Championship

*Miyazaki Country Club,* Sadohara, Miyazaki
Par 36-36–72; 6,438 yards

November 24-27
purse, ¥60,000,000

| | SCORES | | | | TOTAL | MONEY |
|---|---|---|---|---|---|---|
| Shiho Ohyama | 70 | 67 | 75 | 71 | 283 | ¥15,000,000 |
| Yuri Fudoh | 73 | 70 | 72 | 72 | 287 | 8,700,000 |
| Sakura Yokomine | 75 | 73 | 72 | 69 | 289 | 6,000,000 |
| Jeon Mi Jung | 74 | 70 | 74 | 73 | 291 | 4,800,000 |
| Hiromi Mogi | 71 | 73 | 73 | 75 | 292 | 4,140,000 |
| Ji-Hee Lee | 76 | 75 | 72 | 70 | 293 | 2,952,000 |
| Junko Omote | 72 | 74 | 71 | 76 | 293 | 2,952,000 |

|  | SCORES |  |  | TOTAL | MONEY |
|---|---|---|---|---|---|
| Mitsuko Kawasaki | 69 | 73 76 75 | | 293 | 2,952,000 |
| Michiko Hattori | 72 | 73 74 75 | | 294 | 1,764,000 |
| Shin Hyun Ju | 74 | 73 74 74 | | 295 | 984,000 |
| Mikiyo Nishizuka | 75 | 73 71 76 | | 295 | 984,000 |
| Lee Eun Hye | 76 | 72 75 72 | | 295 | 984,000 |
| Ok-Hee Ku | 75 | 76 72 72 | | 295 | 984,000 |
| Akiko Fukushima | 73 | 74 73 77 | | 297 | 624,000 |
| Hiroko Yamaguchi | 77 | 72 72 76 | | 297 | 624,000 |
| Orie Fujino | 75 | 78 71 75 | | 299 | 474,000 |
| Nikki Campbell | 77 | 72 77 73 | | 299 | 474,000 |
| Chieko Amanuma | 76 | 76 70 78 | | 300 | 330,000 |
| Kasumi Fujii | 73 | 77 76 74 | | 300 | 330,000 |
| Miho Koga | 74 | 72 79 75 | | 300 | 330,000 |
| Midori Yoneyama | 75 | 74 72 79 | | 300 | 330,000 |
| Yun-Hee Ku | 73 | 78 76 75 | | 302 | 288,000 |

# Australian Women's Tour

## ABC Learning Centres & FADL Group Classic

*Lakelands Golf Club*, Gold Coast, Queensland
Par 36-36–72; 6,317 yards

February 11-13
purse, A$100,000

|  | SCORES |  |  | TOTAL | MONEY |
|---|---|---|---|---|---|
| Nikki Campbell | 70 | 64 | 70 | 204 | A$15,000 |
| Katherine Hull | 70 | 65 | 71 | 206 | 10,000 |
| Anne-Marie Knight | 70 | 67 | 71 | 208 | 6,000 |
| Karine Icher | 67 | 71 | 70 | 208 | 6,000 |
| Rebecca Coakley | 71 | 68 | 71 | 210 | 3,750 |
| Mardi Lunn | 69 | 70 | 71 | 210 | 3,750 |
| Amanda Moltke-Leth | 69 | 71 | 72 | 212 | 2,566.70 |
| Linda Wessberg | 68 | 69 | 75 | 212 | 2,566.70 |
| Gwladys Nocera | 72 | 69 | 71 | 212 | 2,566.70 |
| Karen Pearce | 68 | 71 | 74 | 213 | 2,000 |
| Loraine Lambert | 68 | 71 | 75 | 214 | 1,470 |
| Tamie Durdin | 72 | 67 | 75 | 214 | 1,470 |
| Maria Hjorth | 72 | 66 | 76 | 214 | 1,470 |
| Vicky Uwland | 70 | 70 | 74 | 214 | 1,470 |
| Rachel Bailey | 69 | 73 | 72 | 214 | 1,470 |
| Nancy Harvey | 73 | 69 | 73 | 215 | 1,203.30 |
| Fiona Pike | 74 | 68 | 73 | 215 | 1,203.30 |
| Iben Tinning | 74 | 69 | 72 | 215 | 1,203.30 |
| Marine Monnet-Melocco | 70 | 74 | 72 | 216 | 1,095 |
| Carina Vagner | 74 | 67 | 75 | 216 | 1,095 |
| Cecilia Ekelundh | 71 | 71 | 74 | 216 | 1,095 |
| Shani Waugh | 68 | 73 | 75 | 216 | 1,095 |

|  | SCORES | | | TOTAL | MONEY |
|---|---|---|---|---|---|
| Eleanor Pilgrim | 69 | 69 | 79 | 217 | 975 |
| Alison Munt | 71 | 71 | 75 | 217 | 975 |
| Sarah-Jane Kenyon | 72 | 70 | 75 | 217 | 975 |
| Asa Gottmo | 75 | 70 | 72 | 217 | 975 |
| Tamara Johns | 71 | 73 | 74 | 218 | 870 |
| Charlotta Sorenstam | 74 | 72 | 72 | 218 | 870 |
| Kathryn Marshall | 71 | 72 | 75 | 218 | 870 |
| Kylie Pratt | 73 | 70 | 76 | 219 | 780 |
| Cherie Byrnes | 72 | 73 | 74 | 219 | 780 |
| Bettina Hauert | 78 | 71 | 70 | 219 | 780 |

## Titanium Enterprises ALPG Players Championship

*Club Pelican*, Sunshine Coast, Queensland
Par 36-36–72; 6,276 yards

February 18-20
purse, A$200,000

|  | SCORES | | | TOTAL | MONEY |
|---|---|---|---|---|---|
| Katherine Hull | 69 | 69 | 70 | 208 | A$30,000 |
| Lynnette Brooky | 72 | 71 | 68 | 211 | 14,666.70 |
| Gwladys Nocera | 71 | 68 | 72 | 211 | 14,666.70 |
| Karine Icher | 70 | 71 | 70 | 211 | 14,666.70 |
| Sara Beautell | 70 | 75 | 67 | 212 | 6,400 |
| Iben Tinning | 72 | 71 | 69 | 212 | 6,400 |
| Cecilia Ekelundh | 71 | 69 | 72 | 212 | 6,400 |
| Lora Fairclough | 71 | 71 | 70 | 212 | 6,400 |
| Anne-Marie Knight | 68 | 69 | 76 | 213 | 3,800 |
| Kirsty Taylor | 70 | 73 | 70 | 213 | 3,800 |
| Sarah-Jane Kenyon | 73 | 71 | 69 | 213 | 3,800 |
| Nadina Taylor | 72 | 71 | 70 | 213 | 3,800 |
| Jane Leary | 75 | 67 | 72 | 214 | 2,560 |
| Rebecca Stevenson | 71 | 71 | 72 | 214 | 2,560 |
| Shani Waugh | 71 | 71 | 72 | 214 | 2,560 |
| Laura Davies | 72 | 71 | 71 | 214 | 2,560 |
| Georgina Simpson | 73 | 73 | 68 | 214 | 2,560 |
| Tamie Durdin | 72 | 71 | 71 | 214 | 2,560 |
| Hsiao-Chuan Lu | 74 | 70 | 71 | 215 | 2,172 |
| Fiona Pike | 70 | 68 | 77 | 215 | 2,172 |
| Becky Brewerton | 70 | 69 | 76 | 215 | 2,172 |
| Linda Wessberg | 71 | 69 | 75 | 215 | 2,172 |
| Marta Prieto | 72 | 73 | 70 | 215 | 2,172 |
| Alison Munt | 71 | 72 | 73 | 216 | 1,946.70 |
| Ludivine Kreutz | 77 | 69 | 70 | 216 | 1,946.70 |
| Veronica Zorzi | 72 | 75 | 69 | 216 | 1,946.70 |
| Nancy Harvey | 73 | 73 | 71 | 217 | 1,672 |
| Carlie Butler | 75 | 70 | 72 | 217 | 1,672 |
| Ursula Tuutti | 79 | 69 | 69 | 217 | 1,672 |
| Nikki Campbell | 74 | 71 | 72 | 217 | 1,672 |
| Helen Beatty | 69 | 73 | 75 | 217 | 1,672 |

# ANZ Ladies Masters

*Royal Pines Resort*, Gold Coast, Queensland
Par 37-35–72; 6,397 yards

February 24-27
purse, A$800,000

| | SCORES | | | | TOTAL | MONEY |
|---|---|---|---|---|---|---|
| Karrie Webb | 70 | 68 | 67 | 67 | 272 | A$120,000 |
| Ai Miyazato | 63 | 68 | 70 | 72 | 273 | 78,800 |
| Veronica Zorzi | 73 | 64 | 69 | 70 | 276 | 48,000 |
| Maria Hjorth | 71 | 65 | 71 | 69 | 276 | 48,000 |
| Nikki Campbell | 67 | 68 | 73 | 69 | 277 | 32,000 |
| Linda Wessberg | 67 | 70 | 71 | 70 | 278 | 26,800 |
| Hsiao-Chuan Lu | 71 | 72 | 69 | 67 | 279 | 18,500 |
| Iben Tinning | 69 | 71 | 70 | 69 | 279 | 18,500 |
| Shani Waugh | 69 | 69 | 72 | 69 | 279 | 18,500 |
| Cecilia Ekelundh | 68 | 69 | 67 | 75 | 279 | 18,500 |
| Tamie Durdin | 71 | 67 | 73 | 69 | 280 | 12,000 |
| Minea Blomqvist | 70 | 71 | 69 | 70 | 280 | 12,000 |
| Lora Fairclough | 68 | 71 | 73 | 69 | 281 | 10,180 |
| Kirsty Taylor | 67 | 71 | 69 | 74 | 281 | 10,180 |
| Becky Brewerton | 72 | 71 | 69 | 69 | 281 | 10,180 |
| *Tiffany Joh | 73 | 63 | 73 | 72 | 281 | |
| Rachel Hetherington | 69 | 68 | 70 | 74 | 281 | 10,180 |
| Karine Icher | 69 | 71 | 74 | 68 | 282 | 8,765.70 |
| Kathryn Marshall | 72 | 67 | 72 | 71 | 282 | 8,765.70 |
| Karen Stupples | 71 | 73 | 68 | 70 | 282 | 8,765.70 |
| Rebecca Stevenson | 70 | 69 | 72 | 71 | 282 | 8,765.70 |
| Nadina Taylor | 68 | 72 | 69 | 73 | 282 | 8,765.70 |
| Elisabeth Esterl | 68 | 69 | 73 | 72 | 282 | 8,765.70 |
| Marta Prieto | 70 | 69 | 74 | 69 | 282 | 8,765.70 |
| Fiona Pike | 70 | 74 | 71 | 68 | 283 | 7,720 |
| *Ya Ni Tseng | 70 | 69 | 73 | 71 | 283 | |
| Tina Fischer | 72 | 69 | 72 | 71 | 284 | 7,360 |
| Diana Luna | 70 | 70 | 72 | 73 | 285 | 6,546.70 |
| Katherine Hull | 66 | 74 | 72 | 73 | 285 | 6,546.70 |
| Eun A. Lim | 73 | 70 | 71 | 71 | 285 | 6,546.70 |
| Mardi Lunn | 72 | 70 | 71 | 72 | 285 | 6,546.70 |
| Tamara Johns | 72 | 70 | 70 | 73 | 285 | 6,546.70 |
| Amanda Moltke-Leth | 70 | 74 | 74 | 67 | 285 | 6,546.70 |

# South African Women's Tour

## Women's World Cup of Golf

*The Links, Fancourt Hotel & Country Club*, George
Par 36-37–73; 6,424 yards

February 11-13
purse, US$1,000,000

| | INDIVIDUAL SCORES | | | TOTAL |
|---|---|---|---|---|
| **JAPAN—$200,000** | | | | |
| Ai Miyazato/Rui Kitada | 68 | 72 | 149 | 287 |
| **PHILIPPINES—$123,000** | | | | |
| Jennifer Rosales/Dorothy Delasin | 68 | 77 | 146 | 291 |
| **KOREA—$123,000** | | | | |
| Jeong Jang/Bo Bae Song | 74 | 68 | 149 | 291 |
| **SCOTLAND—$75,000** | | | | |
| Catriona Matthew/Janice Moodie | 71 | 69 | 152 | 292 |
| **AUSTRALIA—$60,000** | | | | |
| Rachel Hetherington/Karrie Webb | 68 | 75 | 151 | 294 |
| **CANADA—$47,500** | | | | |
| Lorie Kane/Dawn Coe-Jones | 66 | 79 | 150 | 295 |
| **WALES—$47,500** | | | | |
| Becky Morgan/Becky Brewerton | 70 | 74 | 151 | 295 |
| **MEXICO—$40,000** | | | | |
| Lorena Ochoa/*Alejandra Martin Del Campo | 69 | 78 | 149 | 296 |
| **ENGLAND—$35,000** | | | | |
| Laura Davies/Karen Stupples | 69 | 74 | 154 | 297 |
| **SPAIN—$27,500** | | | | |
| Ana B. Sanchez/Paula Marti | 71 | 79 | 148 | 298 |
| **ITALY—$27,500** | | | | |
| Giulia Sergas/Diana Luna | 66 | 75 | 157 | 298 |
| **SOUTH AFRICA—$20,000** | | | | |
| Laurette Maritz/*Ashleigh Simon | 73 | 75 | 151 | 299 |
| **FINLAND—$18,000** | | | | |
| Riikka Hakkarainen/Minea Blomqvist | 71 | 77 | 152 | 300 |
| **UNITED STATES—$16,000** | | | | |
| Meg Mallon/Beth Daniel | 69 | 74 | 158 | 301 |
| **FRANCE—$15,000** | | | | |
| Patricia Meunier Lebouc/Stephanie Arricau | 73 | 77 | 154 | 304 |

| | INDIVIDUAL SCORES | | | TOTAL |
|---|---|---|---|---|
| **SWEDEN—$14,000**<br>Carin Koch/Sophie Gustafson | 68 | 79 | 158 | 305 |
| **MAYALSIA—$13,000**<br>Siew-Ai Lim/Cindy Lee | 74 | 79 | 157 | 310 |
| **NEW ZEALAND—$12,000**<br>Lynnette Brooky/Gina Scott | 72 | 78 | 164 | 314 |
| **GERMANY—$11,000**<br>Elisabeth Esterl/Martina Eberl | 72 | 88 | 161 | 321 |
| **AUSTRIA—$10,000**<br>Natascha Fink/Tina Schneeberger | 74 | 81 | 170 | 325 |

## Pam Golding Ladies International

*Mowbray Golf Club*, Cape Town
Par 36-36–72; 5,849 yards

February 22-24
purse, R300,000

| | SCORES | | | TOTAL | MONEY |
|---|---|---|---|---|---|
| *Ashleigh Simon | 73 | 76 | 67 | 216 | |
| Morgana Robbertze | 72 | 70 | 75 | 217 | R45,500 |
| *Gilly Tebbutt | 75 | 69 | 73 | 217 | |
| Vanessa Smith | 71 | 77 | 72 | 220 | 25,500 |
| Anna Tybring | 74 | 75 | 71 | 220 | 25,500 |
| Antonella Cvitan | 74 | 71 | 75 | 220 | 25,500 |
| Andrea Hirschhorn | 73 | 75 | 73 | 221 | 13,750 |
| Anna Becker | 72 | 77 | 72 | 221 | 13,750 |
| Kelly Hutcherson | 75 | 72 | 75 | 222 | 10,500 |
| Kirsty Fisher | 73 | 77 | 74 | 224 | 8,500 |
| Eva Steinberger | 74 | 73 | 77 | 224 | 8,500 |
| *Stacy Bregman | 73 | 73 | 78 | 224 | |
| Costanza Trussoni | 72 | 77 | 76 | 225 | 6,900 |
| Caryn Louw | 73 | 72 | 80 | 225 | 6,900 |
| Mandy Adamson | 75 | 76 | 74 | 225 | 6,900 |
| Francis Botha | 78 | 74 | 74 | 226 | 6,000 |
| Charlaine Coetzee-Hirst | 77 | 77 | 73 | 227 | 5,550 |
| Maria Beautell | 79 | 72 | 76 | 227 | 5,550 |
| Sophie Hunter | 76 | 77 | 75 | 228 | 5,100 |
| Sofia Johansson | 77 | 78 | 73 | 228 | 5,100 |
| Sandra Carlborg | 80 | 75 | 74 | 229 | 4,725 |
| Clare Lipscombe | 77 | 74 | 78 | 229 | 4,725 |
| *Lise Botha | 74 | 76 | 80 | 230 | |
| *Jacqui Rathfelder | 75 | 85 | 71 | 231 | |
| Laura Wright | 77 | 77 | 77 | 231 | 4,500 |
| Michelle de Vries | 73 | 82 | 77 | 232 | 4,275 |
| Louise Davis | 76 | 74 | 82 | 232 | 4,275 |
| *Ulrika van Niekerk | 76 | 79 | 77 | 232 | |
| Marie Allen | 78 | 78 | 77 | 233 | 3,975 |
| Letitia Moses | 77 | 80 | 76 | 233 | 3,975 |

# Acer Women's South African Open

*Royal Johannesburg & Kensington Golf Clubs,* Johannesburg
Par 37-35–72; 6,316 yards

March 2-4
purse, R300,000

| | SCORES | | | TOTAL | MONEY |
|---|---|---|---|---|---|
| Maria Boden | 70 | 65 | 69 | 204 | R45,500 |
| Mandy Adamson | 75 | 66 | 70 | 211 | 33,000 |
| Cecila Ekelundh | 71 | 70 | 71 | 212 | 24,000 |
| *Ashleigh Simon | 76 | 70 | 67 | 213 | |
| Laurette Maritz | 73 | 70 | 71 | 214 | 18,000 |
| Rebecca Hudson | 76 | 72 | 67 | 215 | 14,400 |
| Helena Svensson | 71 | 71 | 74 | 216 | 12,150 |
| *Iliska Verwey | 71 | 74 | 71 | 216 | |
| Lisa Jean | 73 | 68 | 76 | 217 | 10,350 |
| Johanna Waldh | 72 | 75 | 71 | 218 | 8,850 |
| Francis Botha | 74 | 71 | 74 | 219 | 7,200 |
| Andrea Hirschhorn | 71 | 76 | 72 | 219 | 7,200 |
| Anna Becker | 72 | 72 | 76 | 220 | 5,750 |
| Sandra Carlborg | 72 | 73 | 75 | 220 | 5,750 |
| Nora Angehrn | 71 | 74 | 75 | 220 | 5,750 |
| *Kelli Shean | 75 | 73 | 73 | 221 | |
| Sarah Heath | 73 | 75 | 73 | 221 | 4,970 |
| Caryn Louw | 75 | 74 | 72 | 221 | 4,970 |
| Carmen Alonso | 73 | 75 | 73 | 221 | 4,970 |
| Nina Reis | 76 | 74 | 72 | 222 | 4,500 |
| Eva Steinberger | 76 | 72 | 74 | 222 | 4,500 |
| Charlaine Coetzee-Hirst | 73 | 72 | 77 | 222 | 4,500 |
| Hanna-Sofia Svenningsson | 75 | 74 | 74 | 223 | 3,975 |
| Antonella Cvitan | 73 | 71 | 79 | 223 | 3,975 |
| Cherry Moulder | 75 | 73 | 75 | 223 | 3,975 |
| Josefine Skold | 75 | 73 | 75 | 223 | 3,975 |
| Emma Zackrisson | 76 | 74 | 74 | 224 | 3,225 |
| Vanessa Bell | 74 | 74 | 76 | 224 | 3,225 |
| Marie Allen | 74 | 78 | 72 | 224 | 3,225 |
| Sophie Hunter | 75 | 76 | 73 | 224 | 3,225 |
| Kirsty Fisher | 79 | 72 | 73 | 224 | 3,225 |
| Maria Beautell | 76 | 77 | 71 | 224 | 3,225 |

# Telkom Women's Classic

*Zwartkop Country Club,* Pretoria
Par 36-36–72; 6,215 yards

March 9-11
purse, R300,000

| | SCORES | | | TOTAL | MONEY |
|---|---|---|---|---|---|
| Laurette Maritz | 71 | 70 | 68 | 209 | R45,000 |
| Antonella Cvitan | 73 | 68 | 70 | 211 | 33,000 |
| Mandy Adamson | 74 | 70 | 68 | 212 | 21,000 |
| Carmen Alonso | 72 | 71 | 69 | 212 | 21,000 |
| Maria Boden | 69 | 75 | 69 | 213 | 11,437.50 |
| *Lumien Lausberg | 71 | 70 | 72 | 213 | |
| Anna Becker | 79 | 67 | 67 | 213 | 11,437.50 |
| Elin Ohlsson | 75 | 67 | 71 | 213 | 11,437.50 |
| Caryn Louw | 73 | 68 | 72 | 213 | 11,437.50 |
| Sara Jelander | 71 | 75 | 68 | 214 | 7,650 |
| Charlaine Coetzee-Hirst | 76 | 69 | 70 | 215 | 6,000 |
| Mette Buus | 77 | 71 | 67 | 215 | 6,000 |

|  | SCORES | | | TOTAL | MONEY |
|---|---|---|---|---|---|
| Louise Davis | 67 | 74 | 74 | 215 | 6,000 |
| Nora Angehrn | 68 | 78 | 69 | 215 | 6,000 |
| Marie Allen | 72 | 72 | 72 | 216 | 5,160 |
| *Lise Botha | 73 | 71 | 72 | 216 | |
| *Ashleigh Simon | 73 | 73 | 70 | 216 | |
| Nina Reis | 73 | 73 | 71 | 217 | 4,800 |
| Emelie Svenningsson | 70 | 76 | 71 | 217 | 4,800 |
| Lill Kristin Sather | 70 | 72 | 75 | 217 | 4,800 |
| Michelle de Vries | 70 | 74 | 74 | 218 | 4,275 |
| Emma Zackrisson | 70 | 74 | 74 | 218 | 4,275 |
| Peggy Fraysse | 76 | 74 | 68 | 218 | 4,275 |
| Lisa Jean | 75 | 74 | 69 | 218 | 4,275 |
| Maria Beautell | 73 | 73 | 73 | 219 | 3,525 |
| Josefine Skold | 70 | 76 | 73 | 219 | 3,525 |
| Andrea Hirschhorn | 73 | 74 | 72 | 219 | 3,525 |
| Cecilie Lundgreen | 77 | 72 | 70 | 219 | 3,525 |
| Anna Tybring | 68 | 79 | 72 | 219 | 3,525 |
| Hanna-Sofia Svenningsson | 66 | 77 | 76 | 219 | 3,525 |

## Nedbank Women's Masters

*Killarney Golf Club,* Johannesburg
Par 36-36–72; 6,195 yards

March 16-18
purse, R300,000

|  | SCORES | | | TOTAL | MONEY |
|---|---|---|---|---|---|
| Maria Beautell | 70 | 72 | 70 | 212 | R45,000 |
| Carmen Alonso | 69 | 69 | 74 | 212 | 33,000 |
| (Beautell defeated Alonso on first playoff hole.) | | | | | |
| *Ashleigh Simon | 69 | 74 | 70 | 213 | |
| Laurette Maritz | 71 | 73 | 70 | 214 | 24,000 |
| Vanessa Smith | 74 | 70 | 71 | 215 | 18,000 |
| Peggy Fraysse | 68 | 75 | 73 | 216 | 13,275 |
| Caryn Louw | 73 | 69 | 74 | 216 | 13,275 |
| Rebecca Hudson | 74 | 72 | 71 | 217 | 10,350 |
| Anna Tybring | 73 | 72 | 73 | 218 | 8,250 |
| Nora Angehrn | 71 | 74 | 73 | 218 | 8,250 |
| *Iliska Verwey | 72 | 72 | 75 | 219 | |
| Helena Svensson | 75 | 67 | 77 | 219 | 6,750 |
| Andrea Hirschhorn | 75 | 71 | 74 | 220 | 6,150 |
| Elin Ohlsson | 78 | 67 | 76 | 221 | 5,110 |
| Vanessa Bell | 70 | 75 | 76 | 221 | 5,110 |
| Emelie Svenningsson | 79 | 71 | 71 | 221 | 5,110 |
| Charlaine Coetzee-Hirst | 72 | 79 | 70 | 221 | 5,110 |
| Lill Kristin Sather | 73 | 75 | 73 | 221 | 5,110 |
| Morgana Robbertze | 75 | 73 | 73 | 221 | 5,110 |
| Lisa Jean | 72 | 76 | 74 | 222 | 4,425 |
| Mandy Adamson | 73 | 76 | 73 | 222 | 4,425 |
| Marie Allen | 75 | 73 | 75 | 223 | 4,125 |
| Lynn Kenny | 75 | 73 | 75 | 223 | 4,125 |
| Fany Schaeffer | 74 | 75 | 75 | 224 | 3,525 |
| Antonella Cvitan | 78 | 75 | 71 | 224 | 3,525 |
| Nina Reis | 77 | 78 | 69 | 224 | 3,525 |
| Sofia Johansson | 78 | 75 | 71 | 224 | 3,525 |
| Johanna Waldh | 79 | 74 | 71 | 224 | 3,525 |
| Cherry Moulder | 70 | 78 | 76 | 224 | 3,525 |
| *Stacy Bregman | 77 | 78 | 69 | 224 | |